HOLLYWOOD WAR FILMS, 1937–1945

HOLLYWOOD WAR FILMS, 1937–1945

An Exhaustive Filmography of American Feature-Length Motion Pictures Relating to World War II

by MICHAEL S. SHULL and
DAVID EDWARD WILT

McFarland & Company, Inc., Publishers
Jefferson, North Carolina, and London

British Library Cataloguing-in-Publication data are available

Library of Congress Cataloguing-in-Publication Data

Shull, Michael S., 1949–
    Hollywood war films, 1937–1945 : an exhaustive filmography of
American feature-length motion pictures relating to World War II /
[compiled] by Michael S. Shull and David Edward Wilt.
        p.   cm.
    Includes bibliographical references and indexes.   ∞
    ISBN 0-7864-0145-1 (lib. bdg. : 50# alk. paper)
    1. World War, 1939–1945—Motion pictures and the war.   2. World
War, 1939–1945—Film catalogs.   3. War films—United States.
I. Wilt, David E., 1955–   . II. Title.
D743.23.S55   1996
940.53—dc20   96-4799
                                                                          CIP

Manufactured in the United States of America

*McFarland & Company, Inc., Publishers
    Box 611, Jefferson, North Carolina 28640*

To all the "premature antifascists,"
the Boogie Woogie Bugle Boys,
the G.I. Joes and the
Riveters named Rosie...

Acknowledgments

The authors would like to acknowledge the assistance of a number of individuals and organizations. The Motion Picture section of the Library of Congress in Washington, D.C., not only contains a great deal of valuable research material (both films and paper material), but it also has a helpful and knowledgeable staff. Special thanks are extended to David Parker, Madeline Matz, and Rosemary Haines. The National Archives and the Libraries of the University of Maryland also served as important sources of information.

Other individuals—colleagues, friends, and family members—contributed in various ways to the completion of this project. While space prevents listing all of their names, we wish to express our thanks to everyone.

—MS & DW, November 1995

Table of Contents

Part Two: Waging War, 1942–1945

Filmography to Part Two

Filmographic Appendices

Introduction

Total war brings many changes. World War II altered the lives of every man, woman, and child in the United States.[1]*

At the time this book was compiled, the Second World War had been over for more than half a century. The majority of Americans alive in the mid–1990s were not even born when the Allies united to fight the Axis. Some may find it difficult even to name the principle Allied and Axis nations, so remote do the events seem.

It would be wrong, however, to assume a total ignorance of World War II on the part of today's Americans. Raised on a steady diet of television, many recognize Humphrey Bogart and Ingrid Bergman in *Casablanca*, have seen John Wayne battle the Japanese in *The Fighting Seabees*, *The Sands of Iwo Jima*, *Back to Bataan*, *The Flying Leathernecks* and *Operation Pacific*, are familiar with the ruthless Nazi officials of *Hitler's Madman* and *Invisible Agent*, and know about England's bravery from *Mrs. Miniver*. More Americans, of course, know the faces of Clark Gable and James Cagney than Charles de Gaulle and Chiang Kai-shek. For many, films have become history, and history has become that which is shown in films.

The authors of this study believe films are valuable historical documents, but do not feel motion pictures should be used as the sole source of information about attitudes and ideas of the past. There are many factors that must be taken into consideration when using films as documents, factors which in some ways make films useful and accurate, but which in other ways almost ensure that films present a distorted picture of the past.

On the one hand, films—at least commercially produced, fictional films—are certainly reflections of the society which produces them. As Siegfried Kracauer noted,

The films of a nation reflect its mentality in a more direct way than other artistic media for two reasons: First, films are never the product of an individual ... teamwork in this field tends to exclude arbitrary handling of screen material, suppressing individual peculiarities in favor of traits common to many people. Second, films address themselves, and appeal, to the anonymous multitude. Popular films ... can therefore be supposed to satisfy existing mass desires.[2]

But this is not to suggest that the contents of motion pictures should be accepted uncritically as historical fact. Blatant distortion of the facts is regularly practiced by filmmakers, sometimes rather innocently, sometimes with a deliberate goal in mind (propaganda), and sometimes unconsciously. Interpretation of film content is similarly imprecise, particularly when discussing films created outside one's own societal context.

In this study, feature-length fictional films produced in the United States between January 1, 1937, and September 30, 1945 (and see Appendix G concerning those films released in October through December of 1945), are analyzed as sociopolitical documents, both to learn about attitudes prevalent in U.S. society of the period and to point out the discrepancies between the reality of wartime America and its portrayal in Hollywood film.

It is difficult from a vantage point fifty years removed to understand the societal importance of motion pictures in pretelevision America. During 1942, 1943, and 1944, 85 million Americans attended the movies each week; this average rose to 90 million weekly in 1945 and stayed there until 1949, when the weekly attendance figures began to erode, both in the face of television's challenge, and the steady migration of America's population from the cities to the suburbs.[3]

World War II had turned the economy around, so money was not as tight in the war years as it had been during the Depression. Furthermore, going to the movies was inexpensive, many theaters changed their bill twice a week, and Americans in all but the smallest towns and isolated rural areas often had access to more than one movie house. All of these pragmatic factors combined to encourage frequent movie attendance.

But there were other, less tangible reasons why America loved the movies. They were entertainment, escapism, education, an experience which could be private, social, or communal. Although radio was a popular and pervasive medium (which shared many personalities with motion pictures), it was film stars who were the biggest celebrities of the day, film stars whose activities were featured in newspaper and magazine

All chapter notes begin on page 429.

1

stories. The motion picture companies —many of them vertically integrated from production through exhibition—were powerful, successful corporations, and the industry as a whole was enormously influential and respected.

Methodology

This book utilizes a methodology similar to that employed in the authors' earlier book *Doing Their Bit* (McFarland, 1987).[4] It is a methodology largely devised and refined by the authors, since existing methodologies in the field of film studies were not suitable for our purposes. We freely adapted strategies and methods from various disciplines, however, to arrive at our methodology, which combines qualitative content analysis with close readings of film texts.

Our method consists of two basic steps. The first is the collection of data. Films are, ideally, screened and references coded and recorded. In this particular study, we had a fairly complete list of coding terms compiled from our previous work on motion pictures and World War II. Some new terms were added, some were discarded, and others were combined into broader terms; some terms applicable only to 1937–1941 were dropped in the 1942–1945 section, and new terms were added. A definition of each of the coding terms used may be found in the brief section called "Abbreviations Used in the Filmography" which is attached to both the Part One filmography and that of Part Two.

Unlike some content analyses, however, our references often require interpretation of film content. For instance, when coding a reference to "bonds," we did not require a specific dialogue mention of War Bonds: the appearance of bonds posters, references to buying bonds or War Savings Stamps, and even references to Liberty Bonds (sold during World War I) were accepted as valid references to the concept of War Bonds. Similarly, the term "Nazi" did not signify only that precise word. Swastikas, references to or appearances by Nazi organizations (such as the Gestapo and the SS), and even slang references were interpreted and coded as references to the Nazi Party. On the other hand, an appearance of a German soldier was not automatically coded as "Nazi," since there was a clear distinction (in real life and in Hollywood films) between the Wehrmacht (the professional German Army) and the Nazi Party.

Many films in this study were screened by both authors; our coding terms were, however, defined clearly enough to allow either author to code an individual film with confidence. There are a number of references marked with a "?" in the filmographies. These references refer either to ambiguous coding (Does a character in blackface makeup count as a "black" character; is a particular character who speaks with a foreign accent and is played by Duncan Renaldo coded as a Latin American even if his nationality is not specified in the film),

or to films which were not screened but for which some information was obtained.

The authors were able to screen a large percentage of the films included in this study. For the others, we were forced to rely on other sources, including scripts, publicity material, contemporary reviews and articles, critical reviews and historical descriptions, and general reference works. The files of the Office of War Information were an invaluable source of information: from mid-1942 until late 1943, the OWI's film reviewers screened nearly every American feature film released and then filled out an evaluation form, describing the film and its contents in relation to the war. Some coding references were taken from these print sources, but where there was any doubt, the coding was given a "?" accordingly.[5]

The coding references, once assembled, were then collated and analyzed. The resulting statistics were employed in the thematic chapters as supporting evidence. These thematic chapters represent the second step of our methodology: each of the chapters deals with a particular topic covered in Hollywood's wartime films. The authors analyze what Hollywood had to say about, for instance, the Nazis, rationing, blacks, and women, and then compare this with "real life." Where there are differences—and there usually are—some attempt is made to discuss the reasons for Hollywood's divergence from reality. The reasons for the dichotomy are varied, ranging from direct U.S. government instructions about film content to what seem to be purely arbitrary decisions by filmmakers.

The analyses in these chapters required a great deal of extra-filmic research on World War II, American society, propaganda, the Hollywood film industry, and other topics that in one way or another affect film content, including "the ideological position of the creator of the movie, the particular structure of the entire motion picture industry, and even the audience's predispositions [which] all contribute to the 'meaning' of the film on the screen."[6]

Part One: The Crisis Abroad, 1937–1941

This portion of the book analyzes the content of feature films during the five years prior to America's formal entry into the war. Although Japan invaded China in 1931, and Hitler came to power in Germany in 1933, the actions of these two powers did not begin to engender worldwide apprehension until the latter part of the decade. It is at this point that our research into the extent of Hollywood's preoccupation with the major international issues of the day begins in earnest.

A casual observer might assume, given the isolationist attitudes of many Americans in the two decades following World War I, that popular films would tend to ignore world events. It is true that Hollywood motion pictures with unequivocal political positions were rare prior to 1939; beginning in late 1938, however, a substantial percentage of American-made films directly and indirectly alluded to current international events. This percentage increased significantly in the following three years. Furthermore, a number of these films began exhibiting an unmistakably antitotalitarian bias, and by 1941 there was little pretense of neutrality in Hollywood. This gradual change, and the way in which it appeared on screen, are the subjects of Part One.

Part Two: Waging War, 1942–1945

With the entry of the United States into the war after the Japanese attack on Pearl Harbor (December 7, 1941), the question was no longer whether films would address the war, but in what way. The majority of all Hollywood films of this period contain some allusion to World War II, a clear reflection of the extent to which the war affected everyday life in the United States.

The manner in which every facet of the war—the home front, the armed forces, our Allies, the enemy—was portrayed is instructive, since filmmakers were constantly juggling their patriotic urges, their need to make money, their desire to please the U.S. government, and their hopes of pleasing film audiences. What was said, how it was said, and what was left unsaid are all important.

It is hoped that this study will serve as an introduction to the uses of films as societal documents; that it will encourage other researchers to examine the sociopolitical context of motion pictures; and that it will shed light on the motion picture industry and American society during the Second World War.

The Filmographies and Analyses of Statistical Material

Filmographies in books dealing with film history and criticism (as opposed to larger cinematic reference works without subject specificity, such as the AFI catalogues) are traditionally comprised of lists of titles, essential production data and perhaps brief plot descriptions. They are usually limited to a narrow topic and include only those films consulted by the author of the book. It is not surprising, therefore, that filmographies are often considered rather dull reading and are consulted only for clues as to where one might pursue a topic of interest or for the refreshment of one's memory about the particulars of a specific film.

The filmographies for *Hollywood War Films* are intended not only to fulfill these purposes, but in addition to provide an overview of the scope and depth of war-related content appearing in Hollywood films of the 1937–1945 period. Each serially numbered film entry includes the title, the releasing company, the month of release, the name of the credited di-

rector, the genre, the general location of the film's action, the subject coding, and the film's predominant biases (1937–1941) or a numerical rating of the film's topical relevancy (1942–1945). In the text section of the filmographies, our primary goal is to give a description of the war-relevant material, and a brief plot summary (sometimes as brief as one sentence, for peripheral films). Historical information is included where it was felt that this would contribute to the reader's appreciation of the film. Although detailed analyses ("close readings") of some individual films may be found in the various subject chapters, one can, by simply reading the filmographies, get a good idea of the type of topical material present.

The filmographies represent a determined effort on the part of the authors to identify *all* American feature films released between January 1, 1937, and September 30, 1945, that in any way make reference to the world events which led up to American entry into World War II (i.e., the period 1937–1941) and to the direct American experience of the war itself (1942–1945). It is our belief that in order to discuss Hollywood's artistic efforts during the war, one must first identify the universe of motion pictures reflecting the realities of wartime America.

The methodology we chose involved examining print materials for those films which were found to be simply not available for viewing, despite diligent searching over a period of years.[7] It is probable that a certain number of films released during this period that are relevant to the war have not been identified by the authors. Scripts were consulted for many of the films that could not be seen, but nevertheless it is impossible to pinpoint every topical reference in dialogue, or appearance of a war bonds poster, ration sticker, or uniformed extra walking down the street, in a film that has not been seen.

We can say with some assurance, however, that any films we may have missed will almost certainly contain only passing topical references (or, using our 1942–1945 scale of war-relevance, films with 1 or 1.5 ratings as opposed to 2 and 3 ratings). If print materials (including scripts, pressbooks, secondary sources, contemporary reviews, and the like) did not give any indication that the film contains topical material, the chance that such material—should it appear in the film—is *significant* is very small.

Because of the vagaries of the film and video industries, there are certain classes of films which have proved extremely difficult to arrange to see. Columbia, Universal, and Monogram "B" musicals have very little commercial value today, so they are not shown on television and are not "officially" released on video.[8] Even nonmusical B pictures from these studios—as well as from PRC, Paramount, and some United Artists products—are hard to find, with the exception of horror films (which have retained some saleability). A number of these films—with contemporary settings and thus a possibility of some topical dialogue (even if the plot is not war-relevant)—could very well contain some war references.

Conversely, the authors were able to see nearly every RKO

Radio release from the period, as well as most of MGM and Warner Bros.' wartime productions. "A" films from Columbia, Twentieth Century–Fox, Paramount, Universal, and United Artists are generally available on television, videotape, or in film archives, with some surprising exceptions.[9]

About the Filmographies

Scope: The filmographies include commercial, feature-length, fictional films produced in the United States, which were released between January 1, 1937, and September 30, 1945. The following types of films, if included in the filmographies (for informational reasons—for example, foreign films with added U.S. footage) are marked with an asterisk (*):

- documentaries or semi-documentaries
- films made for a specific ethnic, regional, or otherwise limited audience (i.e., black films, religious films, foreign-language films even if produced in the United States)
- serials and feature versions of serials
- re-releases of prewar films
- foreign films

Company: Most of the films listed were released by one of the following companies:

Col—Columbia Pictures
TCF—20th Century–Fox
Univ—Universal Pictures
WB—Warner Bros.
MGM—Metro-Goldwyn-Mayer
RKO—RKO Radio Pictures
Mono—Monogram Pictures
Rep—Republic Pictures
UA—United Artists
PRC—Producers' Releasing Corporation
Para—Paramount Pictures
GN—Grand National Pictures
PDC—Producers' Distributing Corporation

There are a few films listed which were released on the states'-rights market (coded IND).

Date: National release date (where available). This information was taken from the *Motion Picture Herald* for sake of consistency. Where more than one month was listed (example, Mar-May), the earlier date is used. For films with no exact month of release (Paramount and RKO Radio both released films in "blocks"), a consensus of the *Variety*, *MPH*, *Film Daily* and *New York Times* review dates was used. Consensus or estimated release dates are identified with "*" after the month.

Director: Director as credited on film (uncredited directors are indicated in synopsis/comments).

Genre: Predominant genre of the film; films which combine elements of more than one genre (such as Spy Comedy) are indicated as such. Familiar genres used include:

Musical	Western
Romance	Fantasy
Horror	Spy
Crime or Mystery	Drama
Adventure	Historical drama
Comedy	

A few genre designations were created especially for this study:

Combat—film dealing with armed forces in combat.
Training—film which concentrates on the training of armed forces.
Resist—film which deals significantly with the actions of resistance groups in occupied countries.
War drama—dramatic film with significant plot emphasis on the war and its effects.

Location: The authors have attempted to indicate where any *significant* action in the film occurs.

Coding: Coding terms are explained more fully in the section "Abbreviations Used in the Filmography" which is attached to both Part One and Part Two filmographies.

Discernible Bias (1937–41 only): A code indicating the general political slant or bias imparted to the viewer by the film's content.

Relevance (1942–45 only): Films are rated according to the degree of war relevance.

1—minor relevance; war references could be removed without significantly changing the film; for example, a ration sticker on a car, a bonds poster in the background, or a brief dialogue reference.
2—moderate relevance;
3—heavy relevance; omission of war references would require major revisions to the film, or the film would not exist without war references.

Intermediate steps (1.5, 2.5) were included when the film's degree of war relevance seemed to fall between the major points.

Conclusions

The Second World War was perhaps *the* total war, one which touched nearly every nation on earth in some way. The

United States has certainly never been in a conflict which was felt on a wider scale. While Hollywood's contribution to the war effort is reasonably well known—as noted above, Hollywood war films still run constantly on television, regardless of the current political climate—the *breadth* of topical references in wartime films has never been examined in detail.

Realizing the extent and nature of Hollywood's war films is important, since motion pictures were a major component of American popular culture in this period. Films not only *reflected* wartime society, they *affected* wartime society. Consciously or unconsciously, with or without government encouragement and interference, filmmakers created documents which, even today, reveal a great deal about Americans during the war.

Part One

The Crisis Abroad, 1937–1941

1. Dim Clouds Behind the Glitter: American Feature Films Reflecting an Awareness of World Events, 1932-1936

The years 1932 and 1933 marked a major turning point in global events. The Depression had spread over virtually the entire world. Its ramifications were myriad as various nations and their leaders desperately groped for solutions. Adolf Hitler, appointed chancellor of Germany on January 30, 1933, prepared his people for a new order. Franklin Delano Roosevelt assumed the presidency of the United States and quickly launched the New Deal.

In the Soviet Union, Stalin had consolidated his political power and had forcibly imposed collectivization upon the' country's agrarian sector in order to accelerate the accumulation of capital necessary to fund massive industrialization. After completing its occupation of Manchuria (begun in 1931) and naming its new puppet state Manchukuo, Japan chose to abandon the League of Nations in 1933 when confronted with the world organization's report condemning Japanese aggression.

Meanwhile, in much of the remainder of China, a vicious civil war was raging between the ruling Nationalists and Mao Zedong's communist insurgents.

Over the next several years, Hitler would also remove Germany from the League and defiantly announce his nation's rearmament. In late 1935, Mussolini, in a bid to expand Italy's colonial empire, launched his invasion of Ethiopia. The Spanish Civil War erupted in the summer of 1936. Before the end of the year, German and Italian military units would join Franco's fascist rebels in Spain, and international brigades, composed mainly of individual volunteers from the left, would come to the assistance of the Spanish Republic.

America's Fear of Extremism

Indigenous fascist groups in the United States, such as the Silver Shirts, never attracted a significant national following. The potentially fascistic elements surrounding Huey Long and his "Share the Wealth" movement rapidly disintegrated following his assassination in 1935. Coinciding with the growing militancy of the fascist regimes and the blatant anti-Semitism of Nazi Germany, the extremist racism of the popular radio priest Charles E. Coughlin became an embarrassment and was increasingly muted after 1936.[1]

The Communist ideals of full equality and a controlled economy appealed to a number of Americans, particularly intellectuals, in the early years of the Depression. Support for the cause of antifascism via the Popular Front helped to sustain this during the latter half of the 1930s. But the American Communist Party's seemingly slavish obedience to the Comintern directives from Moscow ultimately alienated most of its American sympathizers. And the infamous ideological about-face following the Nazi-Soviet Pact of August 1939 irreparably discredited the Party.[2]

But alien "isms" of both the extreme right and left were essentially feared and distrusted by the citizens of the United States. Radical solutions to America's problems, though flirted with by a few, were therefore ultimately rejected.[3]

Pacifistic sentiments that manifested themselves in the early Thirties (reflected in such well-known films as *All Quiet on the Western Front*, a 1931 Universal production, and *Broken Lullaby*, a Paramount film released in 1932) peaked by the mid–1930s, after revelations of Communist Party involvement in the peace movement. In the latter half of the decade many of the remaining adherents of pacifism became emeshed with the isolationist cause.[4]

Between 1932 and 1934 several intriguing films were released in America that either directly or indirectly addressed the crucial world issues of the day. Some in Hollywood were even bold—or rash—enough to proffer extreme solutions of their own and to take direct stands with regard to the country's immediate domestic and international problems. Sometimes, rather exotic cinematic plots were concocted.[5]

An example of this trend would be the 1932 MGM release directed by Charles Brabin, *Washington Masquerade*, in which red-baiting is directly condemned on the floor of the Senate by an idealistic "man of the people" from a large midwestern state who declares, "There's nothing communistic about the statement [concerning the public's right to retain control over their natural resources]. It's plain American. …This land belongs to its millions of people!"

Later in the film the insidious effects of foreign influences upon lobbyists lead Senator Jefferson Keane (Lionel Barrymore) into accepting a bribe. Following his resignation, Keane confesses before a Senate investigation committee and dramatically condemns those with whom he became embroiled. That same year, in James Cruze's *Washington Merry-Go-Round* (Columbia), members of the Bonus Army (unemployed veterans demonstrating in Washington, D.C., for early payment of their benefits for service during World War I), led by a crusading freshman Congressman, take draconian measures against a politically corrupt and would-be American dictator.[6] Although these issues may seem somewhat innocuous today, at the time some temerity was required to address current controversies in a nonwartime atmosphere in what was considered to be a primarily entertainment medium. Incidentally, both of these films were released in the months immediately prior to the presidential election.

International Diplomacy

International diplomacy and its efforts at peace making were hilariously lampooned in two works of 1933. *Diplomaniacs*, an RKO release directed by William A. Seiter, was a vehicle for the popular comedy team of Wheeler and Woolsey. In an apparent indirect swipe at central European nationalism, the two zanies travel to the Geneva Peace Conference as representatives of the "Adoop" American Indian tribe. Wheeler and Woolsey are manipulated by a wise cracking agent provocateur (Hugh Herbert) in the employ of venal international munitions manufacturers into participating in a series of incidents leading to war. When they return home, the two are rewarded for their efforts by being drafted into the Army.

Several months later the Marx Brothers' *Duck Soup* (Paramount) was released. Although not well appreciated by American audiences at the time, its unremitting attack upon the hypocrisy of Western diplomacy probably reflected, in an admittedly distorted way, the traditional American distrust of so-called European entanglements.

The motion picture industry's increasingly erratic response to international uncertainties was probably best exemplified by yet another release from early 1933, the prophetic MGM film entitled *Men Must Fight*. Although his mother is a leading advocate of an antiwar movement, a son goes out to fight a war in "1940" America against a nebulously defined nation called "Eurasia." During a huge pacifist rally, newsreel footage of militaristic Japanese and Nazi parades is briefly superimposed. Later, aircraft carrier warfare is featured, the Panama Canal is captured and New York City is mercilessly bombed by enemy warplanes.

Perhaps reflecting the fears and doubts of the American people engendered by the world economic crisis and the blossoming of radical solutions proffered by the leaders in Italy, Germany, Japan and the Soviet Union, there were a relatively large number of American films released between 1932 and 1934 that engaged the topic of totalitarianism. In 1932 alone there were several motion pictures that directly attacked communism and the Soviet regime of Russia, including the big-budgeted *Rasputin and the Empress* (MGM) and *Forgotten Commandments* (Paramount).

Not surprisingly, paralleling the rise of Hitler's regime, a number of films were released between 1933 and 1934 that confronted fascism. Yet, with the exception of two independently produced films condemning the Nazi government, *The Wandering Jew* and *Are We Civilized?*, neither Hitler's nor Mussolini's right-wing totalitarianism regimes was directly attacked.[7] However, two films from 1933, both released by MGM, do make oblique pejorative references to Hitler, *Dancing Lady* and *The Nuisance*. For instance, in the latter film, the following response is made to a comment that all good doctors are German: "I understand all that has changed since Hitler was elected."

Domestic Concerns

Right-wing extremism at home was another matter. Released in April 1933, only a month after FDR entered office, the bizarre *Gabriel Over the White House* (MGM), directed by Gregory LaCava, portrayed the possible scenario of an authoritarian solution being taken by a president to cure the nation's ills.

Newly elected president Judson Hammond (Walter Huston) has a well-deserved reputation for a lack of political compassion and astuteness. For example, Hammond is puzzled by the passions he witnesses at a mass rally of the unemployed in

Baltimore. But after suffering near-fatal injuries in an automobile crash, the recuperating Hammond receives divine inspiration (through rustling bedroom curtains!) and thereupon embarks on a radical crusade to clean up America and eliminate international tensions exacerbated by the Depression. Assuming virtually dictatorial powers (without a serious constitutional challenge), the spiritually resurrected president fires his corrupt cabinet of party hacks, suspends Congress, creates an "Army of Construction" and declares "martial law" throughout the land (effecting a radical New Deal, of sorts).

When the leading gangster in the United States (an unspecified southern European, played by C. Henry Gordon) insultingly refuses the president's request that he emigrate to his native land, militarized Federal Police using armored cars capture the mobster and his cohorts, try them and then summarily execute them against a wall (the Statue of Liberty is framed in the background).

Turning his attention to the instability of international relations, Hammond invites the top representatives of the major powers to the presidential yacht (under false pretenses) and then proceeds to publicly harangue his captive audience during a radio address with regard to their countries' massive expenditures on armaments. He states that if they can afford billions on weapons, they should be able to pay their World War I debts owed to the United States. To make his point, Hammond crudely threatens the other leaders with a demonstration of America's military power, implying they must either agree to a disarmament pact or face an aggressively militaristic United States. The "Covenant of Washington" is concluded posthaste and signed by all. Having completed his divine mission, America's president then suffers a fatal heart attack, conveniently closing all the problems posed by the film.

The themes of pacifism and fascism were linked rather unusually in a release from late 1934. In William A. Wellman's *The President Vanishes* (Paramount) an American chief executive again takes extraordinary measures to deal with problems confronting the nation. In this case, President Stanley (Arthur Byron) arranges his own disappearance in order to deal with pro-war hysteria in the country. This war fever has been fanned by a cartel of industrialists in league with a newspaper magnate who controls a fascistic movement called the "Gray Shirts." In an unusual scene for an American film, a phalanx of these indigenous fascists brutally attacks an antiwar street rally of the Communist Party. Freed from constitutional restraints, the president and a small coterie of loyal servants (the "Secret Six") employ the extra-legal powers granted to them to facilitate the search for the "missing" Stanley. As a result, they succeed in exposing to the American people the dangerous machinations of the venal arms manufacturers and their fascist cat's-paws led by the fanatical Lincoln Lee. At the film's conclusion, the president makes a nationwide radio broadcast justifying his actions: "We must not declare war. ... So long

as I remain President not one American will be sent to a foreign land. ... The war mongers ask us to exchange a diet of peace for shot and shell. ... I have faith in the American people."

Over the next couple of years, as the economy picked up and fears of war and international upheaval temporarily abated, films that overtly expressed pacifistic sentiments practically disappeared from American movie screens.[8] The late 1934 Universal release, *The Man Who Reclaimed His Head*, in which a disillusioned French journalist (played by Claude Rains) decapitates the World War I era munitions maker who had cynically exploited him, is a major exception.

Pro-military and, more interestingly, antiespionage films, like those that had appeared between the late twenties and early thirties (*Lost at the Front*, 1st National, 1927; *The Flying Fleet*, MGM, 1929; *Dishonored*, Paramount, 1931), began to resurface in noticeable numbers in American theaters during 1935 and 1936. The former were mainly adventure films with a military motif, such as Warner Bros.'s *Devil Dogs of the Air* (1935) and Republic's *The Leathernecks Have Landed* (1936). The latter were largely mystery films with an espionage bent. Ironically, two of these films from 1935, *Death Flies East* (Columbia) and *Murder in the Fleet* (MGM), feature positive Asian and Japanese characters wrongly suspected of evil doing. Released in the winter of 1935, *Death Flies East* also includes a "European" named Pastoli among its suspects.[9]

Another phenomenon reveals itself in the films reflecting an awareness of international issues in 1935. Nearly half were anticommunist or anti-Soviet. Two of these films, *Chinatown Squad* (Universal)[10] and *Oil for the Lamps of China* (WB), deal directly with the Chinese Communists. Whereas the former film is politically vague, the latter specifically condemns the "communistic menace" and portrays Red Chinese soldiers as vicious anti-Western racists. It should be noted that 1935 was the year in which Mao's communist forces conducted their epic Long March to China's interior in order to survive a massive anticommunist campaign launched by the ruling Nationalist regime of Chiang Kai-shek.

The three other anticommunist anti-Soviet films were all released in the second half of the year and involved American youth. This is very logical considering the American student body by the mid–1930s had become very conscious of international events, was usually sympathetic to left-wing causes, and was largely opposed to war. At this time, the Comintern, the Soviet-dominated international communist organization, declared the Popular Front policy which was, in effect, a clarion call to all factions on the left to unite in a common cause against fascism. This apparently helped precipitate a rise in the influence of certain Communist-controlled youth organizations within the American antiwar movement. One such organization, the American League Against War and Fascism, was a leading participant in the nationwide student strike opposing war that was conducted during the spring of 1935. The

American public, though not totally unsympathetic to the students, negatively reacted to disclosures of communist involvement in the movement. As a result, by 1936, the pacifist movement was weakened, with the majority of its members having disassociated themselves from the American League. Furthermore, a minor Red Scare evolved, and some of its animus was directed against the intellectual/academic left.[11]

A motion picture that exploited this trend was Universal's *Fighting Youth*, in which the Communist-subverted "Student League of Freedom" launches a fall campaign on a midwestern college campus to disrupt the football team. In one of United Artists' major releases of 1935, *Red Salute*, starring Barbara Stanwyck and Robert Young, foreign-led communist agitation of American college students is directly attacked. Near the end of this film, the alien student "leader" of campus radicals addresses a May Day rally in Washington, D.C., during which he declares "militarism must be stamped out" and then disparages the uniform of the soldier hero. Following a brawl instigated by the patriotic soldier, played by Young, the roughed-up foreign communist is arrested by immigration authorities and informed that he will be deported on the first boat available.

The major international incident of late 1935 through mid-1936 was Mussolini's unprovoked invasion of Abyssinia (Ethiopia).[12] Yet not a single contemporary American feature film dealt with it, even as a subplot. Perhaps the thought of portraying heroic black soldiers fighting and killing white soldiers (even if they were fascist aggressors) was still considered politically and financially risky in the United States. One Paramount film released in the spring of 1936, *Big Brown Eyes*, did allude to the slow progress of the Italian Army in subduing the resistance of the African nation via a passing news reference (a radio broadcast in the back ground) during a scene. Metro-Goldwyn-Mayer's *These Three* contains an even more oblique reference to the Italo-Ethiopian War when the facetious comment is made about being able to easily purchase on the stock market "a million shares of Abyssinian preferred." *Anything Goes*, a popular film musical directed by Lewis Milestone for Paramount, was released before the conclusion of the war in Ethiopia. Based on a hit Broadway play with a musical score by Cole Porter that had opened in the fall of 1934, the motion picture version is noteworthy for what is not in it. The original lyrics to one of the major numbers from the musical, "You're the Top," play a rhyme off Mussolini's name. This benign reference to the Italian dictator has been pointedly removed from the lyrics in the film version of *Anything Goes*.[13]

Paradoxically, the comparatively obscure contemporaneous border war between Bolivia and Paraguay known as the Chaco War (1932–1935) was featured in the 1935 Universal release, *Storm Over the Andes*. In the film, Jack Holt plays an American soldier of fortune who flies combat missions for the Bolivian side. But, to quote the *Motion Picture Herald* review:

"Holt's attitude towards war, his superior officers and women is decidedly flippant."[14]

As an apparent result of a brief hiatus in international tensions, very few American feature motion pictures of 1936 even touched upon contemporary world issues. Only two films from major studios dealt directly with these problems. A romantic espionage thriller, starring Clark Gable as a foreign correspondent and Joan Crawford as an heiress, *Love on the Run* (MGM), concerns itself with the acquisition of English coastal defense plans by agents of an unspecified foreign power.

The General Died at Dawn (Paramount), with a screenplay by Clifford Odets, is more interesting, both politically and aesthetically. Outwardly, *The General Died at Dawn* can be interpreted as a prestige film released to highlight the talents of its romantically coupled screen stars, Gary Cooper and Madeleine Carroll. Yet interwoven throughout the plot are themes that are very germane to this study. Cooper, for instance, plays an idealistic American working for the people of a Chinese province oppressed by a despotic warlord. Cooper concludes an explanation of his motivations to Miss Carroll with the rhetorical query: "What's better work for an American than helping fight for democracy?" Later, the hero remains defiant after he is captured by warlord Yang, played by Akim Tamiroff. When the American calls him a "running dog," Yang's ruthlessly arrogant (unnamed) Prussian advisor (wearing a German style uniform) slaps Cooper. Yang then smugly states, "Very good man. Teach my men discipline and how to make war." There can be little doubt as to the advisor's nationality since earlier in the film he addresses Yang as "Herr General." In fact, both German and Italian military advisors were in China aiding the Nationists until 1938, when they were withdrawn at the request of the Japanese government.[15]

One in a Million, a 1936 release of Twentieth Century–Fox, whose subject matter would have easily lent itself to making a statement related to current international events, seems to have been deliberately depoliticized by producer Darryl F. Zanuck. Starring Norwegian Olympic skater Sonja Henie in her film debut and taking place during the XI Olympiad in Berlin, the motion picture's scenes in Germany contain absolutely no references to Hitler nor to the Nazi state. This is particularly interesting since Henie was courted by the Nazis throughout the Olympic events and even frequently appeared in Hitler's company. In fact, the only hint in the film to the growing militarism of the country hosting the Olympics is the rather large number of men in German style uniforms (sans Nazi iconography) that are seen in the stadium during the figure skating competition.

Finally, the independently produced feature, *I Was a Captive of Nazi Germany* (Malvina Pictures), was purportedly based on the experiences of an American journalist, Isobel Lillian Steele, imprisoned for several months in 1934 by the

I Was a Captive of Nazi Germany (1936): Independently produced and released, it provided an early look at the abuses of Hitler's regime.

Germans for alleged espionage activities. With Miss Steele playing the lead, supported by an anonymous cast, the film specifically attacks the policies of Hitler's police state, including Nazi anti–Semitism. Apparently, the motion picture was sponsored by the previously mentioned communist-affiliated League Against War and Fascism, thus leading to Miss Steele's being labeled a "communist agitator" in the *New York Times* review of her film.[16]

With over 500 feature films produced by the American motion picture industry during 1936, the 10 motion pictures identified in Appendix B as reflecting an awareness of international events during that year represent barely 3 percent of Hollywood's product. By the end of the following year, the growing world crisis would radically alter this percentage.

2. The Slide Towards Belligerency: An Overview, 1937–1941

By early 1937, following nearly two years of gradual economic recovery, the United States had plunged back into the Depression. Beyond America's borders, the world economy looked only somewhat brighter, and this was mainly due to industrial expansion resulting from increased militarization. Exploiting their growing military power, a few ideologically authoritarian states—particularly Germany, Italy, and Japan—were largely responsible for a dangerous crisis atmosphere that was rapidly enveloping and destabilizing international relations. The majority of Americans in 1937, although not totally unaware of this increasing tension, were mainly preoccupied with the more immediate demands of domestic survival. America had fought to make "the world safe for democracy" twenty years earlier, but many Americans now believed that the United States' participation in the First World War had been an aberration and that the international arms manufacturers had been the only winners. With millions unemployed and going hungry at home, it was difficult to become—let alone remain—militantly aroused over bombing victims in distant Shanghai and Guernica.

America's Reaction to World Events

There can be little doubt that 1937 represented a milestone in the history of this century. Mussolini, after brutally consolidating his occupation of Ethiopia, had then heavily committed his new Roman Empire to the aid of Franco's fascist rebels. Hitler and Stalin, backing opposing sides, also became deeply involved in Spain's civil war. The Third Reich's rearmament was accelerating unabated, and Hitler began to seriously push for annexation (*Anschluss*) of Austria. The great purge was inexorably consuming its victims in the Soviet Union. And, largely out of a mutual mistrust of Lenin's heirs, Japan and Germany had signed the anti–Comintern Pact in late 1936.[1] Finally, after years of Sino-Japanese hostilities, Japan launched a full-scale invasion of China in the summer of 1937. Relatively weak and consequently frightened, France and Great Britain had largely abdicated their international responsibilities as they began to rearm. The only other country with the potential to stem the catastrophic tide of events was the United States, which hid behind the physical barrier of two vast oceans and the diplomatic curtain of neutrality.

At the insistence of the majority of the American people, the response of the U.S. government to the Italian invasion of Abyssinia in October 1935 and the outbreak of the Spanish Civil War in the summer of 1936 was verbal admonishments and the imposition of arms embargoes through invocation of the 1935 Neutrality Act. This policy would more often benefit the aggressor rather than the victims of aggression. When President Roosevelt attempted to signal a more positive antitotalitarian American response, in his "quarantine the aggressor" speech of October 5, 1937, he was overwhelmingly opposed.[2]

During 1938, and until the German and Soviet invasions of Poland in September 1939, the public response of Americans to world events was predominantly reticent. Yet it should be noted that the generally positive attitude towards Germany—which had superseded the anti–German hysteria of the World War years—gradually dissipated after 1933, and was

considerably replaced by negative sentiments. The Nazi campaign against the institutions of the Christian churches, the regime's racial prejudice (particularly its anti–Semitism), and the militarization of German life offended the moral principles of many Americans.[3] Extensive media coverage of what was happening in Germany and the overt imitation of the Nazi Party by the German-American Bund probably intensified this growing distaste, and certainly clashed with the mid-thirties resurgence of pacifist sentiment in the United States. Similarly, a largely favorable disposition towards Mussolini and his Fascist regime dissolved following the invasion of Ethiopia and the Italian dictator's alliance with Hitler.

After the war began, most Americans, while now firmly convinced of German agression and sympathetic to the Western Allies, were still more concerned with the neutral rights of the United States than with the defeat of fascism. Hence, the so-called 200-mile "Neutrality Zone" was established less than a week after the outbreak of hostilities, in an attempt to keep the war away from the Western Hemisphere.[4]

In late October, FDR was able to ease the restrictions of the arms embargo, but only against heavy Congressional isolationist opposition. The Neutrality Act of 1939 allowed for the "cash and carry" purchase of goods by belligerents.[5] America's relative complacency drastically changed with the German Army's *Blitzkrieg* of the Lowlands and France in May 1940, Mussolini's attack on France's rear a few weeks later, and the aerial onslaught visited upon Britain by the *Luftwaffe* less than two months after the formal capitulation of France (25 June 1940).

As the war expanded and intensified, Americans could no longer ignore the violence taking place overseas. The sheer force of events resulted in the issue of the degree of U.S. involvement coming to the fore. But there was still a good deal of equivocation. In the 1940 presidential election, the Republican candidate, Wendell Wilkie, declared his support for "aid to Britain short of war," while somewhat paradoxically accusing Roosevelt of deliberately and secretly planning to actively involve the United States in the conflict.[6] Roosevelt responded by stating that he had no intention of ever sending American boys "into any foreign wars."[7] Meanwhile, he did consummate the Destroyer/Bases deal with Churchill in September, and openly supported the Selective Service Act (though preferring to call the draft euphemistically "the muster") which went into effect the following month.[8] Roosevelt was elected to an unprecedented third term, though by a far slimmer popular margin than in the previous two elections.[9]

This combination of an escalating world crisis and the election campaign triggered a nationwide debate between isolationists and those who would offer aid to the Allies but not go to war on their side (the so-called "aid short of war" supporters). The debate was not truly resolved until the Japanese assault on Pearl Harbor. Two diametrically opposed organizations arose at this time: the Committee to Defend American by Aiding the Allies, and the isolationist America First Committee. Both sides vociferously aired their respective beliefs to the public via print media ads, radio broadcasts, and mass meetings.[10]

Rather than choosing sides, most Americans apparently lingered uncomfortably in the middle of the debate while trying to go about their daily lives. But, like their elected representatives, who passed the Lend-Lease act in March 1941, they increasingly seemed to hope that support of the British short of direct American participation would lead to at least a halt in the advance of the Axis powers.[11] It would appear, in retrospect, that this very attitude could not help but lead inexorably to direct military involvement by the United States.

In the spring of 1941, Hitler's Wehrmacht swallowed up the Balkans, while his newly formed Afrika Korps, under Rommel, mauled the British forces in Italian Libya. In late June Hitler unleashed a multinational army of over three million men upon the U.S.S.R., and there seemed little chance of stopping the Nazi onslaught. Thus, despite the long-standing Western animosity towards the Communist regime—exacerbated by Stalin's short-lived August 1939 pact with Hitler and the ruthless Russian invasion of Finland in the winter of 1939–1949—both Britain and the United States quickly pledged aid to the Soviets.[12]

Meanwhile, the Japanese were emboldened by the fascist successes in Europe and Africa, and took advantage of the opportunities thus offered. In September 1940 the Tripartite Pact between Japan, Germany, and Italy was signed (completing the Axis); Japan then proceeded to occupy northern French Indochina. In July 1941, they seized southern Indochina from the Vichy-administered colonial government.

Although traditionally sympathetic to the Chinese, the U.S. government and the American people had, to a large extent, chosen to ignore or remain unaware of the possible consequences of Japanese in the Far East. Now, in rapid succession, FDR froze Japanese assets in America and then, when Japan's leaders refused to withdraw their troops from the Asian continent, imposed an oil embargo.[13] Because they were almost totally dependent upon oil from the United States and the Dutch East Indies (controlled by the Netherlands government-in-exile), the Japanese were left with limited options.

The American public, however, preoccupied by the events in Europe and the domestic controversy surrounding intervention or isolation, and deluded by a general attitude of racial superiority,[14] largely dismissed the Japanese as an immediate, serious threat. A little over five months later, planes launched from the flight decks of six Imperial Japanese Navy carriers shattered any remaining American complacency and conclusively ended the great debate over United States participation in the war.

A Banner Year for Hollywood

For the American motion picture industry, 1937 represented a peak year, both in product (number of films produced) and in overall profits since the economic collapse of 1929–1930. In fact, annual film output has yet to match 1937 levels, and it was not until 1942 that profits would reach the 1937 figures.[15]

The decline in the 1937–1941 period in these areas was due to the economic recession at home, and the deteriorating political situation overseas. The end result of assorted currency restrictions, censorship, war, and occupation governments was that fewer and fewer motion pictures produced in the United States were screened in traditional overseas markets, although a substantial number of foreign films (including German and Italian works) still managed to reach American theaters (foreign films, of course, never had the same impact in the United States as Hollywood films had in other countries). Expansion of the Latin American market provided certain limited possibilities. But only increased patronage in domestic theaters could have made up the difference; instead, the average weekly attendance in the United States actually declined during these years, from 88 million in 1937 to 85 million in 1941.[16]

In spite of the founding of the Hollywood Anti–Nazi League the previous year, films released in 1937 did not display an outstanding degree of international political prescience or any overt commitment to the cause of antifascism. Nonetheless, the number of films addressing the world crisis dramatically increased from the total of similar works produced in 1936. In real numbers, the total multiplied five-fold. Promilitary films represented the single largest category with a discernible bias; yet it should be noted that well over one third of the 1937 films reflecting an awareness of the world crisis were either totally noncommittal, or unabashedly pacifist in outlook.[17]

Hollywood Reacts to World Events

Largely in response to the outbreak of civil war in Spain in the summer of 1936, and in sympathy with the concept of the Popular Front, the Hollywood Anti–Nazi League was founded. At its zenith the organization would claim a membership of 5,000, and from its inception through 1939 the League raised over $90,000.[18] Among its major supporters were writer Dorothy Parker, director Fritz Lang (*Fury*, 1936; *Man Hunt*, 1941), actor Fredric March (*The Road to Glory*, 1936; *So Ends Our Night*, 1941), and composer Oscar Hammerstein.[19]

Despite the crystallization of antifascist sentiments associated with the Spanish Civil War, only a modest number of motion pictures were made which in any way related to the struggle. A single feature film from late 1936, *Great Guy* (Grand National), briefly alludes to it. During the two full years in which the armed conflict took place, 1937 and 1938, six films were released by the American film industry that directly referred to the Spanish Civil War (*Exiled from Shanghai, I Cover the War, Last Train from Madrid, Love Under Fire,* all 1937; *Blockade,* and *Gateway,* 1938).[20]

Whereas the American public never firmly committed itself to participation (as opposed to providing aid) in the war prior to December 7, 1941, several events occurred in late 1938 and early 1939 which appear to have had a decisive effect upon many in Hollywood. At home, the first major spy trials since World War I were conducted in New York. Then the Un-American Activities Committee (the Dies Committee) of the U.S. Congress was formed, and soon afterwards began to attack the Hollywood Anti–Nazi League.[21] Numerous individuals in the film community, especially those of European origin, were deeply disturbed by the declining fortunes of the Republican forces in Spain, and by the Anglo-French appeasement of Hitler at Munich. Finally, the Jewish members of the Hollywood establishment had every reason to be deeply offended by—and fearful of—the increasingly violent anti–Semitism which was officially sanctioned and promoted by the Nazi government of Germany (the first anti–Semitic laws were passed in September 1935).[22] Nazi brutality was highlighted by a nationwide pogrom on the night of November 8–9, 1938.[23]

Between 1938 and 1939 the percentage of the total output of Hollywood feature films reflecting an awareness of the world crisis increased from 14 to 17 percent. In modest, but significant numbers, American motion pictures increasingly reflected a new attitude of controlled belligerence. For instance, antifascist content is found in ten percent or more of those films demonstrating an interest in international affairs in both years. In addition, such films as United Artists' *Blockade* (1938) and MGM's *Three Comrades* (1938), though never attacking specific fascist regimes by name, delivered unequivocal statements against militarism and totalitarianism.

It would appear that 1939 was the turning point for American cinema with regard to its approach to the international situation. In that year, the number of films espousing pacifism or nonintervention peaked, while motion pictures attacking various forms of totalitarianism nearly tripled.[24]

In addition, the first overtly anti–Nazi films appeared in 1939 under such suggestive titles as *Beasts of Berlin* (PDC), *Confessions of a Nazi Spy* (WB), and *Everything Happens at Night* (TCF). As early as December 1938, the first qualified pro-intervention feature, *Thanks for Everything* (TCF), was released. Within a comedy framework, the film brings up the then-sensitive topic of conscription, and sanctions American participation in a European conflict, if it was determined that the security of the United States might be directly threatened.[25]

Reflecting the trend evident in the films they produced, many Hollywood personalities had taken an openly political stand by 1940. For instance, producer Walter Wanger, a Jew and a former admirer of Mussolini,[26] came out publicly for intervention. He became an active fund raiser, organizer, and speaker for the cause. Two relevant films he produced were Alfred Hitchcock's 1940 classic *Foreign Correspondent*, and *Sundown* (1941).

Also at this time, President Roosevelt and his family became visibly involved in the medium of motion pictures. In August, barely a month after FDR's nomination at the Democratic Convention, United Artists released the blatantly anti–Nazi British feature *Pastor Hall*. Roosevelt's son James, president of Globe Pictures, was directly responsible for financing this film's distribution in the United States. More importantly, Eleanor Roosevelt narrated a special foreword to the film, prepared by playwright Robert E. Sherwood. Two of Sherwood's plays had already been made into films reflecting an awareness of the world crisis: *Idiot's Delight* (1939), and *Abe Lincoln in Illinois* (1940). Though she names neither Hitler nor Germany, Mrs. Roosevelt clearly condemns aggression and the suppression of the freedom of worship.[27]

During the latter months of 1940, many more prominent film personages declared publicly for "aid short of war." One actor, Robert Montgomery (*Yellow Jack*, 1938; *The Earl of Chicago*, 1940) even became a volunteer ambulance driver in France with the American Field Service.[28]

However, some members of the film community actively defended isolationism. Robert Young and Lillian Gish, for instance, were prominent members of the America First committee.[29] As late as November 1941, Miss Gish wrote an apologia for her pro-war efforts during World War I (most notably *The Little American*, 1917) entitled "I Made War Propaganda."[30] However, one source states that Miss Gish privately complained of being blacklisted by Hollywood studios for her stand, and that she subsequently resigned from America First and refrained from participating in the public activities of the organization in an attempt to obtain work in films.[31]

Pro-interventionists, as distinguished from aid-short-of-war proponents, formally organized into the Fight for Freedom Committee in April 1941.[32] At this point, many Hollywood figures became actively involved. Douglas Fairbanks, Jr. (*Angels Over Broadway* and *Safari*, both 1940), Helen Hayes (*A Farewell to Arms*, reissued 1938), and Burgess Meredith (*Idiot's Delight*, 1939; *Tom, Dick and Harry*, 1941) were among its most prominent speakers and fund-raisers.[33] Samuel Goldwyn, who as early as 1933 organized a movement to employ individuals who lost their jobs in Germany following the Nazi takeover, was a heavy contributor.[34] So too were Darryl F. Zanuck, Walter Wanger, and the brothers Warner. Their influence was largely responsible for the success—both in funds and members—of the Fight for Freedom Committee of Southern California, as well as the accelerating flow of motion pictures with pro-intervention and antitotalitarian themes.

Top: *Blockade* (UA, 1938): In beseiged Castlemare, a city in the northern Basque section of Spain, the starving inhabitants queue up for food, touching the conscience of a spy, played by Madeleine Carroll. The film never clearly specified that it was set in the Spanish Civil War. Also seen: Reginald Denny. Bottom: *Beasts of Berlin* (PDC, 1939): An illegal printing press operated by members of the anti–Nazi German underground. A Blackshirt, who secretly belongs to the group, makes an unexpected visit. Alan Ladd, in an early role, is third from right. This film was originally released under the title *Hitler—Beast of Berlin*.

By the end of 1940, while the great debate over America's role in world events was belatedly arousing the public, pro-interventionist motion pictures released by Hollywood studios had nearly quadrupled the total for 1939 (an increase from 2 to 7).[35]

This growing partisanship led to a Senate investigation of "pro-war propaganda" produced by the industry. None other than Wendell Wilkie was retained to represent Hollywood at the hearings, in September 1941.[36] Twelve of the seventeen feature films cited by the Nye Committee were made in the United States. They included *Escape* (1940), *Mystery Sea Raider* (1940), *Sergeant York* (1941), and *That Hamilton Woman* (1941).[37]

The trend towards a more politically committed American cinema turned into an outspoken show of support for intervention in 1941. In just one year, the percentage of American feature films reflecting the awareness of the world crisis jumped from 19 percent to 29 percent. Pacifist and non-interventionist motion pictures virtually vanished from the screen. In fact, the only two pacifist films exhibited in 1941 were reissues. One, *Mata Hari* (MGM), does somewhat sympathetically portray the notorious World War I German spy's execution. The other, however, Universal's *All Quiet on the Western Front*, had its original pro–German slant altered by the addition of post–1930 newsreel footage accompanied by tendentious off-screen commentary relating Nazi excesses and aggression.

There was also a sustained increase in films promoting Americanism and democracy (fairly consistent at around 15 percent from 1939 through 1941). Finally, in direct response to the war's intensification and the introduction of the Selective Service Act, nearly a quarter of the films of 1941 with direct political content were concerned with the military or national preparedness.[38]

3. With Their Guard Down: The Nye Committee

We [Americans] can still laugh at ourselves. These poor boys [Nazis] over here have lost their sense of humor, if they ever had any—and any nation that doesn't know how to laugh is dangerous. The Man I Married *(TCF; August 1940).*

This place [Germany] isn't a country, but a Coney Island mad house! Escape *(MGM; November 1940).*

The Germany I loved doesn't exist any more. It was destroyed by men [Nazis] like you. They Dare Not Love *(Col.; April 1941).*

[when a weak-kneed rival repeatedly refuses to fight over another man's wife, the indignant husband sneers] I understand, you're an Isolationist. That Certain Feeling *(UA; April 1941).*

On September 9, 1941, the U.S. Senate, under the auspices of Senator D. Worth Clark of Idaho and Senator Gerald P. Nye of North Dakota, both leading advocates of the isolationist cause in America (a rubric that loosely embraced all those American citizens who ardently wished to prevent the country from becoming actively involved in World War II), began hearings to investigate "Moving-Picture Screen and Radio Propaganda" designed "to influence public sentiment in the direction of participation by the United States in the present European war."[1] Chaired by Senator D. Worth Clark, the subcommittee included isolationist senators Bennett Clark of Missouri and Burton Wheeler of Montana.

Were Nye and his fellow isolationists on the subcommittee crackpots, hysterical reactionaries and anti–Semites as many of their critics claimed, or was there, in fact, some substance to their charges?

In his opening statement, Senator Nye passionately proclaimed that the purpose of the hearings was to create a defense for the American people "against what I consider to be the most vicious propaganda that has ever been unleashed upon a civilized people." The senator further contended that the propaganda contained in many American films was a "one-sided ... appeal to our national hates or to hates that could be developed...."[2] The subcommittee would go on to single out 20 films that it considered to be egregiously propagandistic (refer to Appendix A). But only a dozen of these were actually American feature length fictional films, including *Escape*, *The Man I Married* and *They Dare Not Love*.

Hollywood Defends Itself

Wendell Wilkie, the 1940 Republican presidential candidate and outspoken internationalist, who had supported the FDR administration on peacetime conscription during the election campaign, was hired by the motion picture industry as the counsel to represent its case before the Senate subcommittee. In a letter addressed to Senator D. Worth Clark and read before the subcommittee's members on the first day of the hearings, Wilkie made clear the position of the American film industry:

We make no pretense of friendliness to Nazi Germany nor to the objectives and goals of this ruthless dictatorship. ... [The industry] looks with horror on the Nazi movement, and feels deep sorrow at the fate of the countries now under the domination of the Germans. ... Of the more than 1,000 feature pictures produced since the outbreak of the present war [in September 1939], only some fifty have had anything to do with the issues involved in the war or with the ideological beliefs of the participants. Some of these fifty, we are glad to admit, do portray nazi-ism (sic) for what it is—a cruel, lustful, ruthless, and cynical force. ... [But] The pictures portraying England and Germany do not purport to tell the American people what they should do about nazi-ism, save the knowledge of the true facts may, as it always has, influence the judgement of right-thinking men and women...

Backing off a bit, Wilkie asserted that Hollywood film producers were guided by nothing more subversive than the hope to satisfy the prevailing taste of the American people: "[The industry is an] instrument of entertainment, education, and information."[3] At this point, if one assumes Wilkie himself knew what was going on in the industry, he was being somewhat disingenuous.[4] In all of 1939 and 1940, nearly twenty percent of the fictional feature films released by Hollywood in neutral America contained references to the world crisis; a significant number of them were blatantly pro–Allies and pro-interventionist. By the end of 1941 almost a third (over 140 films) of all full-length American motion picture productions related in some way to the Second World War, virtually every one of which was directly or indirectly pro-interventionist.

At a subsequent convening of the hearings, Senator Nye awkwardly attempted to more clearly define his and the other isolationist members of the subcommittee's concerns about the ability of movies to politically influence the public:

The dangerous propaganda is that unloosed upon all the way from sixty to eighty million people [per week] who go into moving picture theatres of this country to be entertained. Getting there, Mr., or Mrs., or Miss America sits, with guard completely down, mind open, ready and eager to be entertained. ... If somewhere in that [film] is planted ... a narrative, a speech or a declaration, by a favorite actor or actress, which seems to pertain to causes which are obsessing so much of the world today, there is planted in the heart and in the mind a feeling, a sympathy, or a distress which is not easily eliminated....[5]

Resuming later that day, Nye further elaborated, in his rambling manner, upon his analysis of the propaganda threat posed to the American public by the film industry:

The truth is that there are only between 200 and 225 of what are called "quality" ["A," or high cost films; less than half the average yearly production during the Thirties] pictures produced by American producers annually. ... If out of 200 quality pictures 15 or 20 or more of these should be proven to be propaganda pictures, it could

hardly be said that the percentage was low. ... These alleged propaganda pictures, if they were conceived and produced for a purpose, would seem to have in mind a purpose growing out of the knowledge that you can't take the American people to war until you can make them hateful toward something. ... I have talked to many Americans. ... I have found them confessing an influence, for a moment at least, upon them by these propaganda pictures. And more and more every day I find Americans bitterly charging that the pictures seem to be in control of men entertaining vengeful spirits, born in the pain being visited upon their own people abroad.[6]

Charges that the subcommittee attacks upon the motion picture industry, and particularly Nye's accusations leveled at the leading movie producers (both before the subcommittee and outside the hearings in statements made to the public), were motivated by anti–Semitism, served to discredit the subcommittee.

Furthermore, throughout the course of the hearings, it became painfully clear that Nye and like-minded senators on the committee had personally viewed very few of the films they chose to single out as examples of the insidious propaganda that they feared and inveighed against. Senator Bennett Clark of Missouri, who, in a *Newsweek* magazine article, had melodramatically condemned the American film industry for "turning 17,000 theatres into 17,000 daily and nightly mass meetings for war," admitted that he had not seen any of the motion pictures named by the subcommittee and that he rarely attended the movies.[7] Barely two months later, following the Japanese attack upon Pearl Harbor, the issues raised by the subcommittee would be all but forgotten as the nation, as well as the film industry, made a commitment—for the duration—to winning the war.

In retrospect, though Nye and his fellow isolationists on the subcommittee had not screened all of the more obvious politically motivated films prior to the hearings, it appears they had become increasingly aware (or had been made aware by their constituents) of an expanding number of biased messages appearing in all sorts of films. Examples from this period would be the seemingly innocuous and easily forgettable western and horror films, such as *Buzzy and the Phantom Pinto* (Arthur Ziehm) and *King of the Zombies* (Monogram). Had the isolationist senators and their staffs (miniscule by today's standards) merely been unsophisticated in the mustering of evidence to support their suspicions and accusations? Nye's figure of 15 or 20 openly propagandistic motion pictures out of a total of 200 "quality" films released each year by Hollywood probably appeared to most people as a not particularly significant number. With hindsight and a great deal of research, it seems likely that the isolationist members of the subcommittee made the mistake of fixating on a few of the more blatant propagandistic films, e.g., *The Great Dictator* (UA, 1940) and *The Mortal Storm* (MGM, 1940), rather than documenting the large number of motion pictures containing less obvious, but nonetheless present, war-related messages (many of which are referred to as "Contraband Messages" in the filmographies and discussed in more detail in Chapter 4).

Top: *The Great Dictator* (UA, 1940): Two dictators, Il Digga Ditchi and Der Phooey (Jack Oakie and Charlie Chaplin, spoofing "Il Duce" Mussolini and "Der Fuehrer" Hitler) practice their fascist salutes. Bottom: *The Mortal Storm* (MGM, 1940): In 1933, a Stormtrooper patrol commanded by Robert Young prepares to intercept two lovers trying to ski across the German border to a still-independent Austria. German ski troops had been used in the April 1940 invasion of Norway. Also shown: Ward Bond.

In other words, Nye and his staff could not adequately focus on the forest of pro-interventionist messages contained in the films because of the conspicuous anti–Nazi foliage of some of the trees in the foreground. Though the hearings per se, to quote Bernard Dick, could best be described as a "monument to ignorance," it is equally myopic to dismiss the contention of the isolationists that the American film industry was stridently promoting interventionism in a significant number of its releases.[8]

Because, without a doubt, Hollywood initiated, via the content of its film productions, an undeclared war upon the militaristic totalitarian regimes even before Hitler's panzer columns pierced the heart of Poland in September of 1939.

4. Contraband Messages: References Within Films to World Events

The term "contraband message" (CM) has been borrowed from the book, *The Celluloid Weapon*. As stated by the coauthors, White and Averson: "The critical comment in the contraband message is incidental."[1] In our work such messages are defined as direct, veiled or allegorical references to current (1933–1945) international issues, superfluous to the main plot or theme of a given film. There can be multiple, totally unrelated, audio and visual communications of this type within a single motion picture. A substantial number of the films germane to this analysis have been classified in the 1937–41 Filmography under the general heading of contraband messages.

For a variety of reasons, such as the need to appear to be informed, to poke fun at established institutions, or to make an indirect political statement, some form of veiled communication has appeared in works of art since the beginning of recorded history. The inclusion of the likenesses of, or the allusion to, political personages and symbols or emblems connoting certain meanings or ideas in paintings, plays and literature has been and continues to be a common phenomenon.

The cinema, with its ability to reach a mass audience, is an ideal medium for both the overt and covert promotion of various ideas and causes. All the major belligerents during the first World War were quick to recognize and exploit this fact.

With the advent of sound, the potential for contraband messages within film was greatly expanded. The evolution of this kind of message within the texts of 1930s American films would appear to be largely the result of the industry not wishing to offend the Production Code, administered by the Hays Office or lose money by upsetting the fickle political or moral sensitivities of the American public. Thus, for most of the politically conscious in Hollywood, contraband messages became a relatively popular and safe means of masking "topical" references within film texts and for making a very brief political statement of conscience regarding the international situation, with a minimum of professional and financial risk.

Contraband messages within American motion pictures were delivered by various means. The most typical were fleeting utterances, one-liners, symbols, gestures or caricatures referring to or alluding to current events and personages. Sometimes the key words or phrases used were expressions whose meanings have changed or have been obscured with the passage of time, i.e., "fifth column," "Popular Front," "the corridor." Song lyrics provided another popular vehicle for the delivery of this type of message (for example, "The Last Time I Saw Paris" in MGM's 1941 release, *Lady Be Good*).[2]

By the mid–1930s numerous examples of contraband messages began to appear. In a scene from the 1934 comic classic, *Twentieth Century* (Columbia), John Barrymore's dictatorial stage director briefly fondles a megaphone liberally decorated with little swastikas while flirting with his protégée, played by Carole Lombard.

In RKO's *Roberta*, a 1935 Fred Astaire and Ginger Rogers vehicle, an American band from the midwest becomes stranded in France. Fortunately for them, their leader, played by Randolph Scott, has a worldly aunt who owns an exclusive Parisian designer dress shop. In one scene the aunt makes the following reference to the European proclivity for creating international tension: "If all the nobility settled down and got jobs maybe there wouldn't be as many wars." That single statement reflected American antimilitarism sentiment as well as a lingering Yankee distrust of European machinations, particularly those of the ruling elites.

The acceleration of events in Europe, in conjunction with increased isolationist sentiments at home, resulted in more frequent appearances of contraband messages in American films. Gary Cooper unwittingly becomes involved in "European entanglements" with an enigmatic aristocratic poseur played by Marlene Dietrich while motor touring in Spain in the early 1936 Paramount production *Desire*. Later that same year, Walter Huston, in the United Artists film version of the 1929 Sinclair Lewis novel, *Dodsworth*, expresses his disgust with his frivolous wife's affected continental snobbery as the two are traveling in Europe, by petulantly remarking, "No soldiers along the Canadian border comes closer to my idea of civilization."

Four out of the eleven contraband message films listed for 1937 refer to the Italo-Ethiopian War (1935–1936). In fact, all references to that war in American films between 1937 and 1941 are contraband messages. Were problems in Africa considered too remote to the concerns of Americans? If so, why did a comparatively high number of films referring to the Sino-Japanese War (three out of the nine coded films from 1937–1938, including *International Settlement*, released by TCF) have all or part of their activities take place in China during the conflict?

Five of the six motion pictures with references to the Italo-Ethiopian War in 1937 and 1938 were made by foreign correspondents who had previously been on assignments covering that war. All but one of these references are delivered in films categorized as containing contraband messages. The relevant scenes from two 1937 films are typical. In *I Cover the War* (Universal) a news rival of cameraman John Wayne reminds him that he is owed 20 dollars from when they were together in Addis Ababa. The following exchange takes place during a scene in China in *Too Hot to Handle* (MGM)[3] after it is suggested by a newsreel competitor that any recent combat footage of the Japanese sent back to the States would have had to be faked:

CHRIS HUNTER (CLARK GABLE): "Fake? Hey, that's an ugly four-letter word..."
BILL DENNIS (WALTER PIDGEON): "Well, how about that time in Ethiopia—those two generals coming out of Haile Selassie's palace after being decorated?"
HUNTER: "You just resented [being] ... scooped..."
DENNIS: "Sure, after I found out they were a couple of Greek waiters in bed sheets with shoe blacking all over their kissers!"

Contraband Messages Increase in Frequency

Contraband messages germane to this study began to appear in significant numbers in 1938 (15). The most common way of presenting the message was simply to make one or two brief references to the international crisis in the form of a signifying event, term, world leader's name or symbol. The average contraband message makes some reference to war in general or to specific current conflicts via certain key words or phrases, i.e., "convoy," "refugee," "draft," "good neighbor," "lend-lease," "sabotage," "fifth column." These references most frequently appear in films with a contemporary setting, and in the comedy, musical comedy and mystery/detective genres. In 1941 contraband messages represented the single largest general category of films reflecting an awareness of the world crisis (62 films out of the 146 identified as war-related).

Daughters Courageous is one of the more intriguing contraband message films. It was released by Warner Brothers in July 1939 as a follow-up to the studio's highly successful 1938 film, *Four Daughters*. Both motion pictures were directed by Michael Curtiz and starred John Garfield and the Lane Sisters. Because the former's character was killed off in *Four Daughters*, Warner Brothers could not make a direct sequel. *Daughters Courageous* was based on a play by Dorothy Bennett. The screenplay was written by brothers Julius J. and Philip G. Epstein, both well-known West Coast liberals and members of the Hollywood Anti–Nazi League.[4]

In this film, Garfield has been transformed from a brooding composer to a cocky Hispanic "proletarian scoundrel" named Gabriel, who thumbs his nose at bourgeoise morality. When not attempting to keep him out of trouble, or patronizing him, the daughters and their mother are engrossed in the petty travails of middle class parochial American existence, particularly centering around marriage, until the prodigal father, Jim Masters, played by Claude Rains, shows up at their doorstep. World-weary, Jim has roamed the globe for the past 20 years. Now he wishes to rest and and ponder on why there is "so much hate in one universe."

The four daughters quickly and collectively decide they are not going to allow their father to "warm his way" back into their lives. They agree to "freeze" him out of the house. One daughter declares, "He shall not pass ... in other words—Verdun."

The term "*Ils ne passeront pas!*" was coined by the French general Robert Nivelle in 1916 and almost immediately became the rallying cry for French resistance to the massive German offensive around the forts of Verdun.[5] More recently, in November 1936, during the fascist rebel siege of Madrid, the slogan "*no pasaran*" was constantly invoked in the press and during radio speeches by the defending Republican Madrilenos.[6] The Spanish Loyalists had only just surrendered to Franco's Nationalists in March 1939. The antifascist statement in the film is unequivocal.

Despite their announced intentions, wise, avuncular Jim rapidly melts the hearts of his long-abandoned daughters. After he gives some acting tips to Nora, the hardest, she confesses, "You might as well know—there's sort of a Popular Front against you." Soon afterwards her sisters, separately, also confide to their father about the now regretted former declaration of a "Popular Front" to keep Jim out of their affairs.

The concept of a "Popular Front" was well known throughout the latter half of the 1930s. From 1934 onward, the policy of the Comintern (the Communist International) was to establish a Popular Front, or alliance of all left-wing parties, to resist fascism and other right-wing parties that might assist fascism. The Popular Front was formally adopted at the 7th Congress of the Comintern in the summer of 1935 and lasted until the Nazi-Soviet Pact of August 1939.[7] It was a Popular Front coalition that governed Republican Spain during the Civil War, and the term became directly associated with the International Brigades fighting for the Loyalist regime against the rebel Nationalists.[8] Interestingly, John Garfield would later star in a 1943 film about an American survivor of one of the Brigades, *The Fallen Sparrow* (RKO).

At the conclusion of *Daughters Courageous*, Jim wisely elects to again leave the family that he cannot rightfully call his own. Gabriel, who had also disrupted the matriarchy by having an affair with the youngest daughter, Buff (Priscilla Lane), decides to join Jim in his travels. The well-meaning but

Too Hot to Handle (MGM, 1938) American newsreel cameraman Clark Gable records a Japanese bombing raid on a Chinese village. Note the Chinese troops at upper right. An elaborate "contraband message" in a film that was not particularly political.

myopic women and their small town friends are left to enjoy the short-lived tranquility of isolationism.

The following year, 1940, the year of Hitler's devastating spring victories in Western Europe, Hollywood was motivated to produce a significant number of motion pictures explicitly espousing causes relating to international events. Correspondingly, there was a dramatic increase in the number of contraband message films released that year (28, compared to 13 in 1939). Many of these contraband messages could best be described as generic references to the Second World War, e.g., *Cross Country Romance* (RKO) and *Love They Neighbor* (Paramount). Some are a little more specific by referring to the "war news": *Gold Rush Maisie* (MGM) and *Money and the Woman* (WB).

The hilarious script for *His Girl Friday* (Columbia) provides a superior example of a contraband message motion picture. It is a classic screwball comedy from 1940 directed by

Howard Hawks and starring Cary Grant and Rosaline Russell. It was a remake of the popular 1931 film, *Front Page* (UA), based on the eponymous Broadway hit written by Ben Hecht.

The original story centers around a group of journalists awaiting the imminent execution of a simple-minded anarchist for the murder of a "negro" police officer in a large city (unnamed, but obviously Chicago). The sheriff, running for re-election, latches onto the case and attempts to whip up anti-communist hysteria in order to win votes.

In the first motion picture version there are, not surprisingly, many references to the "Bolsheviks" and the "Red menace." In addition, reporter Hildy Johnson (Pat O'Brien), who plans to get married and abandon journalism, feels compelled to justify his actions. He thus makes a sarcastic comment to his compatriots regarding the absurdities of their profession, like "waking people up in the middle of the night asking them what they think of Mussolini."

It is particularly interesting to examine *His Girl Friday* because it can be clearly observed how the dialogue was deliberately changed to update the material and to slip in a political statement. For instance, in the 1940 film version many of the comments about communism have been dropped. But there is a reference to Stalin and the "Red Army" on the march (the invasion of Finland was in progress at the time of the film's release).

The altered scenes of the two motion pictures that parallel one another are even more revealing. When the 1940 Hildy, now a woman played by Rosalind Russell, makes her statement with regard to the callousness of her colleagues and her disgust with the profession, she states she has become tired of "calling people up in the middle of the night to ask whether Hitler is going to start another war."

During the central pressroom scene of both films, the "capture" and subsequent concealment of Earl Williams in a rolltop desk after his escape, there are again significant changes in dialogue. In 1931, Adolphe Menjou, as *Morning Post* editor Walter Burns, screams over the phone to his majordomo of the presses about the changing of the front page, "Junk the League of Nations!" In 1940, Cary Grant's hysterical Walter Burns shouts, "Never mind the European war, we've got something a whole lot more important than that. ... No, no, not the Polish corridor! ... Take Hitler and stick him on the funny page!"

Cary Grant's dialogue could be interpreted as a display of a growing disdain for Hitler and a tendency on the part of the American public to wish the war away. In fact, the general inactivity on the Western Front during the winter of 1940 led to it being called the "Phoney War" by the press. Later in *His Girl Friday*, there is barely concealed contempt for effeminate poetry-writing reporter Benzinger (Ernest Truex) when he requests to be sent to France as a "war correspondent." The war did not yet seem so threatening, since it appeared to be largely contained and far away from American shores. By the latter half of 1940, the whole picture would change. In 1941 contraband message films alone would nearly triple over the previous year (from 28 to 62). Military allusions, particularly to the draft, and pejorative references to the Axis powers and their leaders would predominate.

Negative Imaging

When it comes to political leaders, negative imaging was definitely preferred over positive imaging. Whereas Hitler was referred to—almost always pejoratively—in 38 films during 1940–1941, there were only seven references to Winston Churchill (all positive). A particularly quaint allusion is made to the British leader in the 1941 RKO release, *My Life With Caroline*, when the American star shakes the paw of an English bulldog, whom he has named Winston.

One of the earliest examples of a cinematic "pot-shot" being taken at Hitler is the gag in *His Girl Friday*, released in January 1940, about putting the Nazi leader in the "funny pages." By the spring of 1941 RKO could release *Tom, Dick and Harry*, in which two of the stars, on a movie date, hiss the newsreel presentation of a Hitler speech. In at least two other motion picture releases from 1941, characters respond to unbecoming actions by others with a contemptuous "Gestapo" crack, e.g., *Confessions of Boston Blackie* (Columbia) and *You Belong to Me* (Columbia).

Nearly a quarter of the forty-three references to the draft and draft avoidance occurring in 1941 Hollywood productions are also contraband messages. Most of these films contain relatively neutral messages. In at least two, however, *Charlie Chan in Rio* (TCF) and *The Great Mr. Nobody* (WB), a newly drafted individual is portrayed happily receiving his notice of conscription and then indulging in a bit of chauvinistic bravado.

At this point, the sheer volume and one-sidedness of contraband messages in American feature films, reinforcing the anti–Axis/pro–Allied/pro-preparedness bias contained in the more overtly politicized (propagandistic) fictional motion pictures, may very well have begun to have a cumulative effect upon the movie audience. Their ubiquitousness may even have contributed to the discomfort of America's leading isolationists with Hollywood's product, prompting the Nye subcommittee hearings in the U.S. Senate in the fall of 1941.

5. Films Against War and American Involvement in Conflict Overseas

The surge of pacifism which swept America in the mid–1930s, accelerated by the concomitant impact of the 1934 Nye Senate Committee on munitions and the beginnings of European rearmament, had tapered off somewhat by 1937. This was largely due to the rise of isolationism in the United States, as exemplified by the Congressional passage of the second Neutrality Act in 1937. Interestingly, the American peace movement unsuccessfully resisted this growing parochialistic nationalism. It wanted world peace, not an America insulated from the rest of the world.[1]

Pacifism in Hollywood Films

Three of the ten pacifist films produced by Hollywood in 1937 include attacks upon the munitions industry. They are *Espionage* (MGM), *Nancy Steele Is Missing* (TCF) and *They Gave Him a Gun* (MGM). Yet, the portrayal of the individual munitions makers in the first two films is ultimately sympathetic. The third motion picture, following an opening montage implicitly condemning the munitions industry, abandons its assault upon the industry and becomes a crime melodrama linked to an antiwar theme. Nevertheless, *They Gave Him a Gun* is one of the most hard-hitting pacifist films produced by Hollywood in the latter half of the 1930s.

They Gave Him a Gun is a morality play about the insidious effects of war on man, in which the motion picture's title literally bursts upon the screen from the barrel of a cannon. The credits follow, etched by machine gun fire. A revealing montage immediately follows, implicitly—along with the film title itself—indicting war and the munitions industry. Incorporating many Dutch tilts, there is a staccato series of camera shots (like the bursts of shells) of smoke-belching factories, and then of rifles, cannons and shells being manufactured. This provocative sequence climaxes with a barrage of fire from a row of field artillery pieces.

Among the draftees at a World War I training camp is a timid "hayseed" bookkeeper named Jim (Franchot Tone), who is made physically ill by the sadistic drill sergeant's (somewhat reminiscent of his German counterpart in the antiwar film classic, *All Quiet on the Western Front*) highly descriptive demonstration of the most effective use of a bayonet on a straw dummy. A near hysterical Jim tells his tentmate Fred (Spencer Tracy), a worldly carny, that he would rather desert than "go 3000 miles to butcher."

Particularly rare for American film at this time is a scene between the two comrades the following day, in which Fred cynically lectures Jim on the hypocrisy of patriotic slogans and concludes by informing him that only his army-issued rifle makes Jim "as good as anyone." The latter is transformed; Jim's gun becomes his god.

The scenes on the Western Front in *They Gave Him a Gun* relentlessly demythologize war. On the battlefields of France no glory is portrayed during an American assault upon the German lines. A Doughboy is blown up by a shell, and both his lifeless body and his rifle are shown soaring into the air. Another American soldier, his face torn apart by shrapnel, writhes in agony in the mud. Jim, wounded and half-crazed with fear, finds himself alone and clutching his rifle in a war-ravaged village. Beside a church across from a German heavy machine gun emplacement, the human killing machine reacts. Struggling to the top of the church's steeple, Jim gloats madly as he systematically shoots the enemy below, including the last surviving German soldier who pathetically begs to surrender before Jim heartlessly kills him.

Years later, Jim, the holder of the *Croix de Guerre* for valor in combat, is a professional gangland assassin commanding the "Veteran's Protective Association." His old war buddy, Fred, who now runs his own circus, arrives in town too late to save Jim from his inevitable fate. After Jim is gunned down by the police, led by his former drill sergeant, Fred bitterly queries, "Why don't you pin a medal on him now, Sergeant? He was your star pupil."

It is fascinating to compare *They Gave Him a Gun*, little known or discussed today, with the very popular and critically acclaimed 1941 Warner Brothers release, *Sergeant York*. The former film dehumanizes the war hero by stigmatizing him as a criminal psychopath and calls into question the state's formal recognition of a soldier successfully performing the function for which he is trained. The latter film glorifies and morally justifies a soldier's slaughter of the enemy in combat, first humanizing his persona (made easier by using real-life hero Alvin York) and then making an icon of his cinematic image (dressing up superstar Gary Cooper in the bemedaled regalia of an American Doughboy). Unlike Jim, the humane, Christian fundamentalist York spares the enemy who are willing to surrender.

In 1938, the year of the *Anschluss* and the Munich Crisis, 15 American motion pictures reflecting an awareness of the world crisis promoted either pacifism or noninterventionism. Ten advocated the former, the maximum number of pacifist films to be released in a given year during the 1937 to 1941 period. At least two of the pacifist motion pictures create and sustain exceptionally negative portrayals of arms dealers, e.g., *Four Men and a Prayer* (TCF) and *Sinners in Paradise* (Universal). Yet, in this year of growing world tension, the films classified as containing a noninterventionist bias are the most noteworthy.

In two Westerns, the ultimate genre employing the symbols of Americana, noninterventionism is advocated. Both films, *Border G-Men* (RKO) and *Pals of the Saddle* (Republic), address the issue of illegal arms exports and were released in the summer of 1938. *Pals of the Saddle* was the seventeenth edition of Republic studio's "Three Mesquiteers" series. In this typical horse opera of the period, the iconography of the Old West is incongruously attached to the present. And this time, instead of battling horse thieves, the three heroes are matched against murderous agents representing an unspecified foreign country attempting to smuggle "war materials" out of the United States in explicit violation of the Neutrality Act.

The Mesquiteers, one played by John Wayne, team up with U.S. Secret Service agents to prevent the surreptitious delivery of "monium," a chemical used in the manufacture of poison gas, to an outside power. Fear is directly expressed by a pretty female agent that if this should happen, serious "international complications could arise."

The motion picture's climax occurs as the foreign agents, led by a man named Harman (a Germanic surname), try to

Sergeant York (WB, 1941): An American icon in the flesh—Gary Cooper as the pacifist turned quintessential American war hero, Sgt. Alvin York, functioning as a filmic "I Want You" poster for the armed forces in 1941.

cross the "international border" (Mexico, though never specified) with enough monium "to kill a lot of people." They, along with their horse-drawn wagonloads of the chemical, are rounded up by the Mesquiteers and a cooperating troop of the U.S. Army cavalry.

This was not the first time the subject of poison gas had been broached in a feature film. In the futuristic British film *Things to Come* (UA) (based on H.G. Wells' novel, *The Shape of Things to Come*) released in America in the winter of 1936, a cataclysmic world struggle is portrayed erupting during the Christmas holidays. The initial battle sequences feature massive aerial bombings and gas attacks upon the civilian population.

The fear of poison gas was quite genuine at the time of the release of *Pals of the Saddle* in late August. This was the period of the Munich Crisis; Britain, for one, would issue over thirty million gas masks to its citizens before the war-threatening crisis was resolved at the end of September.

For many people, particularly in Europe, memories of the horrendous gas casualties on the battlefields of the First World

War were still quite fresh. More recently, in 1936, it had been revealed that the Italians employed an aerial-sprayed gas against the Ethiopians.[2] Through 1941 at least eight other American feature films would allude to gas warfare: *Mr. Wong, Detective* (Monogram, 1938); *Smashing the Spy Ring* (Columbia, 1938); *Charlie Chan in City in Darkness* (TCF, 1939); *Conspiracy* (RKO, 1939); *Espionage Agent* (WB, 1939); *The Great Dictator* (UA, 1940); *One Night in Lisbon* (Paramount, 1941); *Skylark* (Paramount, 1941).

Six American feature films released in 1939 have been classified as noninterventionist in the filmography for Part One. No further motion pictures so classified were produced by Hollywood after this year. Two of these films, *Espionage Agent* and *Homicide Bureau*, are of particular interest in this study. Released in January 1939, *Homicide Bureau* is the last American film to specifically condemn violations of the Neutrality Act and the only film to portray American citizens (as opposed to foreign agents) as the criminal perpetrators.

Released in October, only a month after the outbreak of World War II, the mixed messages contained within the text of *Espionage Agent* (WB) make it a rather peculiar motion picture. It virtually lectures the audience on the need to clamp down on foreign spy activities in this country in order to preserve our neutrality. The film opens with a montage of German acts of sabotage against the U.S. munitions industry in the period before we entered the First World War. It appears to imply that one way of helping to prevent America from becoming embroiled in the new European crisis would be to enact stringent antiespionage laws.

In a continuance of the extended opening montage sequence, the 17-year period between 1919 and 1936 is covered. The latter years are witness to new fighting, including the use of poison gas, and finally, the outbreak of the civil war in Spain (this war is specifically identified via a newspaper headline).

Without further explanation, the viewer is confronted with scenes of fighting in Morocco. The plight of a group of American tourists is graphically portrayed as they flee the war zone under aerial bombardment. In fact, the Spanish Civil War was initiated by an organized rebellion of troops in Spanish Morocco in July 1936. Although neither side is specifically identified, viewers are informed that the heroine has been interned by the "revolutionaries" (synonymous with Franco's fascist forces).[3] In addition, this incident highlights another major fear of the public at the time: the use of aircraft as a terror weapon against civilians.

With regard to the classification of this film as noninterventionist, a conversation that takes place between three young American consular officers in a bordering neutral country (presumably French Morocco) is most relevant. Two of the men are planning to return to America to attend the Foreign Service School. The third, who has just been assigned to Spain, makes the following critical statement: "When you get

In 1939, *Homicide Bureau* warned against selling armaments to foreign nations at war overseas.

back to the States try to convince them that isolationism is a political policy, not a brick wall around the country."

This is probably the first time during the 1937 to 1941 period that the politicized meaning of the term "isolationism" is used in an American film.[4] Though somewhat ambiguous, its usage in *Espionage Agent* would appear to support the policy of preventing the United States from directly intervening in European struggles, but not of total noninvolvement in world affairs, a seemingly fine, yet crucial, distinction at the time of the motion picture's release.

As if to emphasize this point, there are photos of former presidents Warren Harding and Herbert Hoover on the walls of the office, FDR's being conspicuously absent (distanced from the policy?). Harding was identified with "normalcy" (a term used in the film's opening montage) and Hoover with international humanitarianism (he had organized food relief to neutral civilians during the First World War). Later, while attending classes in Washington, D.C., the Foreign Service students are solemnly reminded by a lecturer, "You represent America and the American policy of maintaining peace."

Espionage Agent does not hesitate to condemn the "totalitarian" states. It specifically mentions Hitler, the Nazis, and the Russian spy trials. Through the vehicle of a lengthy lecture sequence at the Foreign Service School, the audience is also informed, in an "off-the-record" comment by the visiting secretary of state, "We are the richest storehouse of war material in the world ... [which] both sides want." This imparts a heavy-handed message that the United States must properly prepare and pass laws to foil increased spy and "alien" sabotage activities.

The remainder of *Espionage Agent* centers around one of the Foreign Service students, Barry Corvall (Joel McCrea), and his new wife (Brenda Marshall). He hastily resigns following his wife's disclosure of her past (unwilling) involvement with an international spy ring. The young couple decides to go to Europe and track down her erstwhile antagonists. Barry's motives include a desire to wake up the "Congressional ostriches" to the need for legislation against espionage, by proving the United States faces a genuine threat from foreign spies. Before he leaves, Barry is informed by friends in the Foreign Service that he will receive no official sanction, and is warned that if caught he could be beheaded (an allusion to the Nazi use of the guillotine).

While on the continent Barry and his wife hear the conclusion of a radio broadcast from Berlin of a speech by Hitler. An American foreign correspondent comments afterwards that war appears imminent and warns his listeners that a "lid tight censorship" will probably soon be instituted by the authorities. The newsman then rather histrionically states, "Let the hatreds of Europe remain in Europe. ... America should be neutral!"

The two lovers, after the usual perilous experiences, are able to break up the espionage ring which uses a phony peace organization in Switzerland as a front. Though purportedly a freelance outfit selling to the highest bidder, the spies are undoubtedly working for Germany. The opening chords of "Watch on the Rhine" are heard on the soundtrack whenever the spies appear on the screen and their leaders' surnames are Germanic (Strawn and Rader). And it is on a train in Germany (though the country remains unnamed) that the couple have their final confrontation with the spies. Yet, even at this point, the filmmakers steadfastly refuse to specifically identify the opposition as German. For instance, Blackshirts board the train at the border, but the, by then, ubiquitous swastika is conspicuously absent from their (blank) armbands.

The Corvalls escape and sail for America on "the last ship to leave [peacetime] England." A headline montage concludes with the announcement that 700 G-Men have been assigned to keep an eye on foreign agents.

Seventeen American motion pictures released between 1939 and 1941 have been classified in the Filmography as having a pacifist bias. But the message remains relatively pure in only some of the eleven pacifist films from 1939. Five of the six relevant 1940 releases are films with multiple biases, such as *Ski Patrol*, which is implicitly anti-Soviet as well as pacifistic. Two films listed coded as pacifist in 1940-41 are rereleases.

The strongest pacifist film produced by Hollywood in 1939 is *Idiot's Delight*.

Idiot's Delight is an MGM production released in the winter of 1939. It was based on the Pulitzer Prize-winning 1936 stage play by Robert E. Sherwood. The motion picture version is as revealing for how it altered the play as for its actual content. The play, for instance, was both strongly anti-war and unequivocally anti-fascist. The film only alludes to fascism and drops all direct references to particular regimes and their leaders. Furthermore, the communist Quillery in the play becomes a pacifist/idealist martyr in the film.[5]

Idiot's Delight takes place in 1939 at a hotel resort in the purposely ill-defined Alps region. Here, second-rate vaudeville hoofer Harry Van (Clark Gable), and his all-girl revue arrive to fill the entertainment bill (Gable actually performs a campy version of "Putting on the Ritz" with his Les Blondes). There is a European war scare occurring at the time (reminiscent of the Munich crisis). Although the Hotel Monte Gabriele is never identified as being in Italy, the staff intermittently speaks Italian and one waiter alludes in a conversation to the Alto Adige (a predominantly ethnic German province, formerly known as South Tyrol, annexed from Austria after the First World War).

Among the guests at the hotel is an old flame of Harry's, played by Norma Shearer (wearing a long blonde wig). She is posing as a White Russian "countess" accompanying her lover, a world famous munitions manufacturer named Achilles Weber (vaguely French, the character is played by Edward Arnold). Other guests include a naive English newlywed couple, an anti-war agitator named Quillery (Burgess Meredith), and a German professor who is experimenting on rats in search of a cure for cancer.

The mounting war crisis leads to a preemptive bomber raid by the host country upon its neighboring antagonist. Everyone at the hotel knows that this means a senseless general war. Yet most of the people stoically prepare to return to their respective countries and aid in the struggle. Some of the waiters at the hotel have already donned their (non-distinctive) reserve uniforms. Only the pacifist Quillery speaks out. He rants about war and "poison gas," and the insensitivity of the leaders of countries who murder thousands of each other's people in the name of nationalism. Quillery is led away by the local garrison troops to be summarily shot.

There are some subtle references inserted into the dialogue which identify the various protagonists. When the guests of the hotel gather around the radio to listen to the news, only wireless codes can be heard from Rome and Paris. The German channel monotonously plays the music of Richard Wagner, which by 1939 had become synonymous with Hitler and his Nazi regime.[6]

Perhaps most intriguing, though, is a pejorative casual reference to the Japanese invasion of China. The act's manager informs Harry that they may pass through the frontier the next day and that he plans to head straight back to peaceful California. Harry sardonically responds: "And run right into the Japs."

At the conclusion of *Idiot's Delight*, Harry and his former lover, now reconciled, bang away on a piano and dance in the hotel's observation room as exploding bombs rain down about them from unmarked attacking airplanes. The *New York Times* critic noted in his review that the British version of this

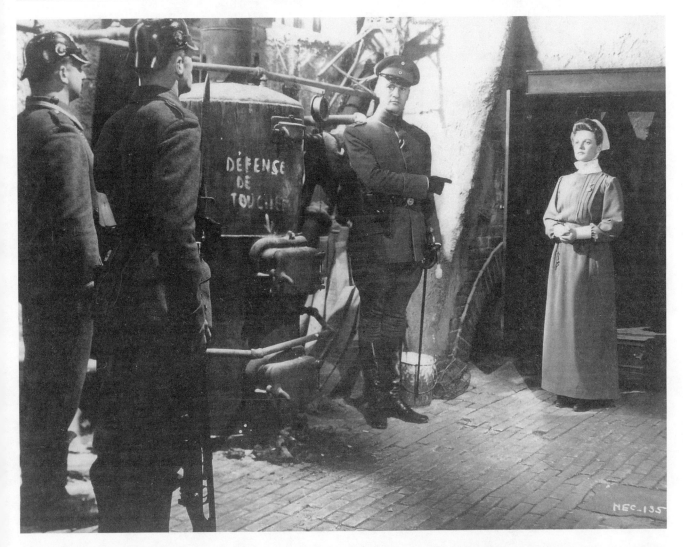

Nurse Edith Cavell (RKO, 1939): In occupied Belgium during WWI, the Germans suspect an English nurse (Anna Neagle) of harboring Allied soldiers in the basement of her Brussels hospital. The evil Prussian officer is played by George Sanders.

motion picture ends differently—with the two singing sentimental songs.[7]

Only a few more overtly pacifistic films would appear prior to the German invasion of Poland in September 1939. These include *Hidden Power* (Columbia), *Nurse Edith Cavell* (RKO) and *The Sun Never Sets* (Universal).

The Sun Never Sets, a shameless Hollywood promotion of the British empire released a couple of months before the onset of World War II, also contained a strident condemnation of militarism. Near the end of the film an off-screen radio announcer glumly deplores an impending international crisis brought on by the inflammatory propaganda of a would-be world dictator. As the audience is presented with a montage of stock footage depicting the mobilization of the world's armed forces the announcer prophetically concludes: "Democracies and dictators glare across the grim chessboard of life.... All humanity their pawns.... Chaos reins. Yesterday's dead for-

gotten, as we prepare a new pageant of modern bloodshed in which millions will die."

The outbreak of the war led to the hasty reissue of two additional pacifistic motion pictures: *All Quiet on the Western Front* (Universal, 1930) and *The Road to Glory* (TCF, 1936). Both films graphically portray the horrific results of combat during the 1914–1918 war. The former had newsreel film with an accompanying narrative inserted as a prologue and epilogue, edited to depict the events leading up to the first World War and the postwar era, through Hitler's consolidation of power and the remilitarization of Germany.

The first half of 1940 saw the release of two American films that combined anti-war appeals with attacks against the two major totalitarian regimes of Europe, the Soviet Union and Nazi Germany—*Ski Patrol* (Universal) and *Four Sons* (TCF).

Ski Patrol ironically juxtaposes near its beginning a 1936

Four Sons (TCF, 1940): This posed studio publicity portrait graphically depicts how Hitler's dismemberment of Czechoslovakia divided loyalties within a Czech family. The conflicting politics of brothers Chris (Don Ameche, second from left) and Karl (Alan Curtis, second from right) lead both to their deaths, as one joins the Nazis and the other remains loyal to Czechoslovakia.

Olympic awards dinner in which international brotherhood is glowingly espoused with a grim documentary montage of subsequent military events leading up to the invasion of Poland. It is also one of the earliest films to portray the collateral suffering of wartime civilians during a scene in which a young Finnish girl is killed by a Russian patrol bomber that strafes her village. The Finnish militia called-up to defend their country do not indulge in chauvinistic outbursts though and, in fact, are shown to very reluctantly take leave of their families. One young man, a recent Nobel Prize winner, only stoically complies under group pressure from his peers. Later, during an encounter between a Finnish patrol and a Soviet parachute attack group, that same man (upon his own initiative) fatally sacrifices himself (and his genius in the arts) to save his compatriots. However, during this engagement another young Finn refuses to fire his weapon at their Russian

enemies. The realistic portrayal of the Finnish ski troops in snow camouflage outfits fighting the Russians in standard field uniforms also visually emphasizes a white (virtuous; peaceful) versus black (evil; warlike) dichotomy.

Whereas the blatant pacifism of *Ski Patrol* masked a relatively subdued attack upon Soviet aggression (anti-communist rhetoric is never employed in the film), *Four Sons*, released in June, intermingled its anti-war stance with an unequivocal condemnation of Nazi Germany. Two scenes are particularly illustrative of this dual message. Frau Berni, the matriarch of a Sudeten German Czech family, loses her two eldest sons, who have chosen opposite sides, when the Nazis seize control of the Sudetenland after the infamous Munich accord. As she cradles the corpse of son Chris on the ground in front of her home, the camera pulls back to reveal Frau Berni entrapped within the frame between the Nazi slayers of Chris standing behind her in the background and the boots of the soldiers in the German army's victory parade marching past her in the foreground. The incorporation of the Sudetenland into the greater Reich means only enslavement to an ideology of death for this simple Czech peasant woman.

The second strongly pacifistic scene takes place near the end of *Four Sons*. The monocled leader of the same troop of local Nazis who had slain son Chris marches up to Frau Berni's house, gives her the fascist salute and then formally presents her with the Iron Cross. It is being posthumously awarded to her youngest son, Fritz, for his valor outside Warsaw during the German conquest of Poland. The benumbed woman, with the boxed medal held limply in her hands, stands silently in her courtyard as the ceremonial troop marches away. But her blank stare is almost immediately converted into an expression of utter horror as Frau Berni watches a local unit of armed Hitler Youth halt in front of her home and, upon command from their adult leader, mechanically obey his order to put on their gas masks. With renewed determination Frau Berni decides that her grandson will not be allowed to become a militaristic Nazi automaton. As "My Country Tis of Thee" swells on the soundtrack, *Four Sons* concludes with Frau Berni boarding the next train out of her village with the little boy on the first leg of their journey to a still peaceful America. After the defeat of France in June 1940 American films that in any way dealt with Nazi Germany dropped all pretense of pacifism and instead, directly glorified and/or advocated resistance to Hitler's Third Reich.

6. Hollywood's "Good Neighbor Policy" Toward Latin America

The achievements of the United States during the short period from 1938 ... until December 7, 1941, in developing a cultural policy with reference to Latin America were very slight. However, an essential part of the war-time foreign policy of this Government was firmly established during that period...[1]

Much the same could be said about Hollywood's treatment of Latin America during the 1937–1941 period. Certainly, after Pearl Harbor there was a concerted effort to promote hemispheric solidarity through motion pictures (which, after all, were being exported in large numbers to Latin America).

Government and industry organizations monitored appearances of Latin American performers, and promoted the inclusion of "Pan American" themes and motifs in Hollywood films. While there were no such official efforts made in the 1937–1941 period, a gradual attempt to foster a "Good Neighbor" feeling may be discerned.

The "Good Neighbor Policy"

The so-called "Good Neighbor Policy" of Franklin D. Roosevelt arose from a brief statement he made in his first inaugural address, on 4 March 1933: "In the field of world policy, I would dedicate this nation to the policy of the good neighbor..."[2]

From this point onward, Roosevelt and his advisors attempted to reverse the policy of intervention—both military and political—which had plagued U.S.-Latin American relations for most of the 20th century. Prior to FDR's presidency, it seemed the Marines were always being dispatched to Haiti, Nicaragua, or Mexico in an attempt to "protect American interests." During the Roosevelt administration, several clear opportunities for such intervention occurred, but—true to his word—Roosevelt chose not to intervene.

There was an altruistic aspect to the Good Neighbor Policy, but there were also practical reasons for a new attitude towards our hemispheric neighbors, most of which were attributable to the world situation. At the 1936 Buenos Aires convention of American republics, the United States delegation proposed promoting closer cultural relations between the countries of North and South America, "in an effort to develop a greater degree of solidarity within the Hemisphere, in view of Axis penetration in Latin America..."[3] In the furtherance of these aims, the State Department created a Division of Cultural Relations in 1938, and a multi-level Interdepartmental Committee on Cooperation with the American Republics was also formed.

Perhaps the most important step was taken in 1940, when Roosevelt appointed Nelson Rockefeller to head the Office for the Coordination of Commercial and Cultural Relations between the American Republics, an agency whose unwieldy name was later shortened to the Office of the Coordinator for Inter-American Affairs.[4]

Rockefeller's group was charged with improving relations with Latin America on nearly every level, although special attention was paid to promoting "democratic ideals" via the media.

Juarez (WB, 1939): Benito Juárez (Paul Muni), President of Mexico and an admirer of Abraham Lincoln (note portrait on the wall), organizes his people against their European oppressors and the local collaborators in this 19th-century period piece.

Hollywood Begins to Embrace the "Good Neighbor" Theme

What do the films of 1937–1941 show of these trends in inter-American politics? Frankly, very little until 1939. In the films included in our study released in 1937, for example, there are few references to "Latin America" (some of these merely refer to appearances of Latin American characters, who might appear in a totally different setting). The most notable film of the year in this regard is *Heroes of the Alamo* (Sunset Pictures, re-released through Columbia in 1938), which is distinctly *anti*-Latin American in tone.[5] In 1938, *Border G-Man* (RKO) dealt with smuggling arms to an unnamed Latin American nation in violation of the Neutrality Act; however, the action transpires in the United States, and the plot reinforces the popular image of Latin America as a place where revolutions break out with appalling frequency.

1939 saw the first signs of some attitude change in Hollywood. *Juarez* (Warner Bros.) was a biography of Benito Juárez (Paul Muni), embattled president of Mexico during the French Intervention and the reign of Maximilian which occurred in the 1860s. The film was a prestige production for the studio, but was not a great box office success.

Much of the film's footage was spent on the story of Maximilian (Brian Aherne) and his empress Carlota (Bette Davis), as well as the intrigues of Napoleon III (Claude Rains), but the basic themes of resistance to foreign intervention and invasion, and the "American" love of democracy were clearly delineated.

When Maximilian disembarks at Veracruz, the military band plays "Deutschland Uber Alles," the German national anthem, a direct linkage with Nazi aggression in the 1930s (ironically, Maximilian was Austrian, not German—of course, so was Hitler!). As he enters the city, the streets are full of soldiers, but the civilian population is noticeably absent, a scene which evokes the Nazi occupation of Czechoslovakia.[6]

In another sequence, Maximilian offers Juárez the position of Prime Minister in his government, since "only a word, democracy, stands between us." Juárez responds to this offer: "The right to rule ourselves *is* democracy ... the one thing Maximilian will not allow."

Maximilian signs the "Black Decree," which is used by the military to repress the Mexican people. A montage follows, depicting the suffering of the people, including mass executions. One shot in this sequence is a direct *homage* to Goya's painting "The Third of May," which portrayed the execution of citizens of Madrid by Napoleon I's occupation troops in 1808.

The United States Ambassador to France protests the use of French troops to prop up Maximilian's regime; later, Juárez's armies receive weapons from the United States to help them defeat Maximilian (ironically, at the time of this film's release, the Neutrality Acts were still in effect and the forces of Republican Spain were disintegrating for lack of arms). Bowing to American pressure, Napoleon III withdraws his support and Maximilian falls from power, dying stoically in front of a Mexican firing squad.

More typical of the period was *South of the Border* (Republic, 1939), one of cowboy star Gene Autry's most successful films. Westerns were one genre in which Latin Americans (usually Mexicans) had always appeared with some frequency, and a few of Autry's titles from the pre-war years indicate this: *Mexicali Rose* (1939), *Gaucho Serenade* (1940), *Rancho Grande* (1940), and *Down Mexico Way* (1941).

South of the Border (the title came from a popular song hit of the period) has a plot more reminiscent of spy-saboteur films of the 1937–1941 years than a routine Western: Gene and his sidekick Frog (Smiley Burnette) travel to the mythical nation of "Palermo," where they encounter revolutionaries in the pay of foreign agents. The agents have a clandestine short-wave radio station and submarine base, and intend to take over Palermo's oil concessions after their puppet government assumes power. This was obviously inspired by the Mexican expropriation of foreign oil properties in their country in 1938; when U.S. and British oil companies demanded a huge compensation for their losses, Mexico refused to pay and the United States and Britain placed Mexico under an oil embargo. Consequently, Mexico started selling oil to the Axis nations, a development which greatly disturbed the United States and British governments. *South of the Border* is not *specifically* set in Mexico, but the plot makes it sufficiently clear which real-life events were being referred to.

1940 and 1941 showed a definite progression in "Good Neighbor" themes, although films like *Marines Fly High* (RKO, 1940) were still being made. A disclaimer in this film says that revolutions are not taking place in the "stable democracies" of Latin America anymore, but the film depicts U.S. Marines directing the para-military police force of a Latin American nation against "revolutionaries" (a reference to Nicaragua, where the Marines set up the National Guard to combat the forces of Sandino).

There were even a few films which specifically addressed the topic of hemispheric defense and inter-American military cooperation. For example, *Wings of the Navy* (WB, 1939), which features a Brazilian pilot trainee at the Pensacola Naval Base. *Buck Privates* (Universal, 1941) portrays South American military observers watching Army maneuvers. And in *Skylark* (Paramount, 1941), Ray Milland departs at the film's end for an assignment involving "hemispheric defense" in South America.

More often, however, films like *Strike Up the Band* (MGM, 1940) were being made. This musical includes a major production number sequence in which "La Conga" is played. *Argentine Nights* (Universal, 1940) depicts a "goodwill tour" of the Andrews Sisters and the Ritz Brothers through South America, the "greatest publicity stunt since the Monroe Doctrine" (a reference to the 1823 declaration by the United States that the Western Hemisphere was "off limits" to European intervention).

These films illustrate how Latin American music could be used to advance (even if in a very peripheral way) the concept of Pan American solidarity. In the 1920s and 1930s, Latin music achieved some crossover popularity in the United States, but was still considered relatively narrow in appeal, or at the very least a "novelty." Xavier Cugat (a Spaniard) was the chief proponent of a kind of Americanized Latin music, but there were few other major bands or performers specializing in Latin music for the Anglo audience.

This began to change in the 1940s, and "an extremely important part was played by Hollywood ... musicals greatly advanced the spread of Latin rhythms and melodies into American culture...."[7] Latin artists such as Cugat, Carmen Miranda, Desi Arnaz, José Iturbide, Tito Guízar and others began to appear with greater frequency in Hollywood films, and there were numerous examples of Anglo artists performing Latin (or pseudo-Latin) musical numbers. Most of the music was modified Cuban or Brazilian "tropical" rhythms, although some regional styles—Mexican and Argentine—were showcased in a few films. But as always, Hollywood was not too worried about strict accuracy when it "borrowed" from other cultures. Nonetheless, the sudden flood of catchy Latin music was at least a step in the right direction towards recognition and appreciation of our hemispheric neighbors.

Argentina and Brazil were among the more popular locations for Hollywood films in the immediate pre-war period. During the war, Argentina was frowned upon as one of the only neutral nations in Latin America, but in 1940–1941 it was seen as picturesque, but sufficiently cosmopolitan and "civilized." *Down Argentine Way* (TCF, 1940), which introduced Brazilian singer Carmen Miranda to U.S. audiences, promoted a romance between America's Betty Grable and Argentine horse-breeder "Ricardo Quintana" (Don Ameche). A verbal reference is made in this film to "friendly neighbor relations."

That Night in Rio (TCF, 1941): Carmen Miranda was the most popular new star to emerge from Hollywood's Latin American phase.

Don Ameche was back in *That Night in Rio* (TCF, 1941), this time as an American who sings:

> My friends, I extend felicitations
> To our South American relations.
> May we never leave behind us
> All the common ties that bind us.

Similar sentiments were expressed in *They Met in Argentina* (RKO, 1941). In the opening musical number, two young women sing, "North America meet South America, there's only one America now." This theme was similar to that appearing in films linking the United States with Great Britain: emphasis was placed on "their" similarities and historical/cultural ties to "us." In the case of England, this concept had some validity for a large number of Americans; however, suddenly embracing Latin America as the "good neighbor"

of the United States could be seen as somewhat opportunistic, given the historical record prior to Roosevelt's presidency. Furthermore, most Latin American countries owed far greater cultural and historical allegiance to Spain, and their cultures were far closer to that country's than to the United States'.

But it cannot be denied that the Roosevelt policy of the Good Neighbor was effective in altering, at least in part, Latin American attitudes about the United States, and Axis penetration in Latin America was effectively stifled in virtually every American country.[8] As for Hollywood, it was not difficult to include a few Latin musical numbers or make some films with "local color," which was just about the extent of its efforts in the 1937–1941 period. But the groundwork was laid for stronger efforts once the United States entered the conflict in earnest.

7. Americanism: The Promotion of "American Ideals" Through Films with Historical Settings

In the years prior to the attack on Pearl Harbor, world events were viewed with detachment by most U.S. citizens:

...most Americans viewed the war as though part of an audience at an interesting motion picture. They readily identified the "cowboys" and the "Indians," and their emotions were aroused by the events on the screen. But the outcome, they [were] sure, would have no important impact upon their own lives and interests.[1]

Even though public opinion was largely on the side of the anti-fascist "underdogs"—China, Ethiopia, later France, Poland, Czechoslovakia, Great Britain[2]—this general anti-fascist feeling did not necessarily translate into a desire for active intervention in the conflict. There were in fact powerful and well-organized isolationist groups determined to keep the United States out of the war at all costs, and these groups dueled on a regular basis (often via the media) with the interventionists, who saw England as the last hope to stop Hitler before he reached the Western Hemisphere.

Hollywood films were similarly hesitant to "name names" or endorse active intervention in the 1937–1941 period, regardless of the personal opinion of filmmakers about the world situation. What did develop, however, was an increase in the promotion of "American ideals," which—by extrapolation—could be construed as a general anti-fascist trend in Hollywood film.

But these themes were presented in such a way that neither the isolationists nor the interventionists could complain too strongly: through historical films and the frequent use of "American icons," Hollywood used American history to promote democratic ideals and the superiority of the American way of life. If audiences inferred that this was a call for isolation or intervention, it was nonetheless "pro-American" and beyond open reproach.

Hollywood's Historical Films

Aside from Westerns, films with historical American settings had not been popular in the early 1930s. In 1930–1934 inclusive, for example, MGM produced only two films with settings or plots which could in any way be considered "historical American" or even "Americana." These were *A Lady's Morals* (1930), a biography of Jenny Lind, and the fictional *The Great Meadow* (1931), which dealt with pioneers in 1775. In contrast, MGM regularly turned out films with *foreign* historical settings such as *Rasputin and the Empress* (1932) and *Queen Cristina* (1933), along with a full slate of contemporary dramas, comedies, and musicals set either in the United States or various exotic and glamorous foreign locales. The other major studios produced much the same blend of material.

But as the decade drew to a close, the occasional historical American films such as *Daniel Boone* (RKO) and *The Last of the Mohicans* (UA, both 1936) gave way to an ever-growing number of films dealing with American history. As the statistics below show, films with an awareness of the current world situation and featuring historical American characters, themes, or references increased steadily from 1937 through 1941: 1937–7; 1938–9; 1939–16; 1940–16; 1941–32.

Some of these films were historical biographies or films dealing with actual historical figures: Abraham Lincoln (*Young Mister Lincoln*, TCF, and *Abe Lincoln in Illinois*, RKO, both 1939), Sam Houston (*Man of Conquest*, Republic, 1939), Benito Juárez (*Juarez*, WB, 1939—although this was a Mexican story, the film made numerous allusions to U.S. history and to current events)[3], Thomas Edison (*Young Tom Edison* and *Edison the Man*, both MGM, 1940), Brigham Young (*Brigham Young, Frontiersman*, TCF, 1940), Jean Lafitte (*The Buccaneer*, Paramount, 1938), and so on.

Other films were avowedly fictional or were highly fictionalized versions of real events, but still utilized historical figures: *Sante Fe Trail* (WB, 1940) featured actors portraying John Brown, Robert E. Lee, Jeb Stuart, George Custer, Phil Sheridan, and Jefferson Davis; *The Howards of Virginia* (Columbia, 1940) included George Washington; and *Northwest Passage* (MGM, 1940), which had nothing to do with the discovery of the Northwest Passage, focused on the exploits of Rogers' Rangers in the colonial period.

The Howards of Virginia, in addition to its overall message concerning the right to freedom for all men, touches on a number of themes of contemporary relevance. The film tells the story of America's struggle for independence through its portrayal of one Virginia family. One of the family members chooses to remain loyal to Great Britain, a "loyalist" in colonial period terms, but a "Quisling" to 1940 audiences. British troops land in Boston in 1769 to enforce the Declaratory Act, and march through the streets of the city. The reaction shots of American citizens watching the "invaders" are composed in a manner evoking the well-known newsreel footage of Parisians observing the German Army's victory parade down the Champs Elysées. "We have to create a free country for our children," one character says in this film, "so that this great land of ours will go on forever in peace and security." In a debate concerning the colonists' response to Britain's actions, one delegate says they must present a "united front," a contemporary term well known to audiences of the period.

There were other historical films which made no particular claims to historical verisimilitude. For instance, *Alleghany Uprising* (RKO, 1939), and *Drums Along the Mohawk* (TCF,

Drums Along the Mohawk (TCF, 1939): A determined colonial American, played by Henry Fonda, prepares to defend his homeland. His wife was played by Claudette Colbert, in this Technicolor affirmation of American values.

1939), set during the colonial period. At the conclusion of the Technicolor production *Drums Along the Mohawk*, the newly independent colonists gather to admire the new flag of their nation, and the heroine (Claudette Colbert) just happens to be wearing a red, white, and blue outfit as well.

Even some B Westerns tried to capture a little of the current vogue for historical themes, albeit indirectly, as in *The Return of Daniel Boone* and *Son of Davy Crockett* (both Columbia, 1941), which were routine Westerns about *descendants* of those famed historical figures.

What these films had in common was their depiction of the formation of America, celebrating real or fictional events from U.S. history, thereby glorifying American ideals and—at times—demonstrating their relevance to the current world situation. *Abe Lincoln in Illinois*, for example, draws some pointed allusions to the contemporary world situation, as Lincoln reluctantly leads the United States into war. He also refers to American ideals of freedom and democracy, saying they provide "hope to all the world."

Alleghany Uprising, while containing a relatively rare (for the 1937–1941 period) anti–British character, linked its story with contemporary events by depicting a traitor (i.e., a "fifth columnist" in the parlance of the day) in league with Indians against white settlers.

Thomas Edison, while a relatively contemporary figure, was enough of a legend to have his life dramatized in a two-film series by MGM. In *Edison, the Man*, "the freedom of the human mind" is celebrated, and it is clearly indicated that only in America could such a success story have taken place.[4]

Sergeant York (WB, 1941) again a biography of a recent "living legend," overstepped the bounds of strict neutrality somewhat, but managed to avoid a complete glorification of the military (unlike *The Fighting 69th*, released the previous year by the same company). It was made plain, however, that there were some things worth fighting for, even for conscientious objectors like Alvin York. Significantly, both *Sergeant York* and *The Fighting 69th* were World War I tales portraying the "Allies" (Britain, France, and the United States) facing the Germans, an alignment to be repeated in World War II.

All That Money Can Buy (RKO, 1941), while a fantasy, utilized the historical figure of Daniel Webster to extol America's greatest ideal, freedom: "It was for freedom we came to these shores ... you are Americans all, you can't be on the side of the oppressor."

Even completely fictional films promoted American ideals in a historical context. In *Kansas Terrors* (Republic, 1939), two cowboys deliver horses from the United States to a fictional Caribbean island (obviously meant to be Cuba), but stay to help the inhabitants rebel against the dictatorial military representative of a foreign ruler.

American Icons

Non-historical films also showed a heightened awareness of "Americanism" in this period. This was often accomplished by the display of "American icons." The following statistics show the significant increase in the appearance of such icons in topically relevant films of the period: 1937–15; 1938–12; 1939–28; 1940–23; 1941–44.

"American icons" include the American flag, portraits of George Washington or Abraham Lincoln, patriotic songs (the National Anthem, "Columbia, the Gem of the Ocean," "America, the Beautiful"), images of the Statue of Liberty or the Lincoln Memorial, quotes from the Declaration of Independence or the Gettysburg Address, and references to (or appearances of) historical and/or legendary American figures such as Davy Crockett, Daniel Boone, the "Spirit of '76" trio, and even more recent personages such as Teddy Roosevelt and General Pershing.

These references may seem innocuous, but they took on increased significance due to their placement and emphasis in the context of each film. In *Let Freedom Ring* (MGM, 1939), for instance, a post–Civil War tale of a railroad building in the West, Nelson Eddy caps the film with a stirring rendition of "The Star Spangled Banner." This reinforces the film's message about the freedoms—life, liberty, and the pursuit of happiness—which exist in the United States. In *Juarez*, the title character is framed in the same shot with a portrait of Abraham Lincoln, linking the Mexican leader—and his struggle to free his country from foreign domination—with the great U.S. president.

Musical numbers provided a good opportunity for visual display of icons, often reinforcing the lyrics of the songs. In *Playmates* (RKO, 1941), "Thank Your Lucky Stars and Stripes" is the opening number, and once again "American ideals" of freedom are glorified, with a flag motif: "...if you feel free ... and can say the things you choose ... you can thank your lucky stars and stripes." "You're a Lucky Fellow, Mr. Smith," from *Buck Privates* (Universal, 1941), is another no-

table example, as is the finale from *Strike Up the Band* (MGM, 1940), featuring Mickey Rooney in a Navy uniform and a superimposed American flag. Among the other films with iconographic musical numbers are *Cadet Girl* (TCF, 1941—"Uncle Sam gets Around"), *Nice Girl?* (Universal, 1941—"Thank You America"), *Sis Hopkins* (Republic, 1941—"That Ain't Hay, It's the USA").

Musical "quotes" also served as reinforcement for American themes: "Yankee Doodle" opens *Alleghany Uprising*; "Columbia, the Gem of the Ocean," is sung (by Gabby Hayes!) in *In Old Monterey* (Republic, 1939), to stir up patriotic feelings and encourage ranchers to cooperate with the U.S. army.

Other Means of Promoting Americanism

Other themes explored in the 1937–1941 period made linkages with Americanism. For instance, populist ideals and the concept that America is a "class-less" society (or at least, that one's class *at birth* was not necessarily the determinant of one's future) were discussed in films like *Meet John Doe* (WB, 1941), *You Can't Take It With You* (Columbia, 1938), *The Great Man Votes* (RKO, 1939), *Sorority House* (RKO, 1939), and even *The Grapes of Wrath* (TCF, 1940). None of these films attempted to portray the United States as Utopia, but anti-elitist sentiments were prominent, and the possibility of change for the better—both for individuals and for society as a whole—was always present. In the United States, the power to change was vested in "the people," not in a dictator or dictatorial elite, as films such as *Mr. Smith Goes to Washington* (Columbia, 1939) pointed out.

Films dealing with immigration to the United States constituted another trend of the period. Most of these films centered around *contemporary* immigrants or refugees, individuals either fleeing persecution (generally in Europe), or those choosing the United States, "the land of the free," over their former homes. Such films include *It Could Happen to You* (Republic, 1937), *Gateway* (TCF, 1938), *Exile Express* (Grand National, 1938), *Three Faces West* (Republic, 1940), and *Hold Back the Dawn* (Paramount, 1941). In many of these immigrant/refugee stories, the foreigners undergo considerable hardships but consider the end result—residency in the United States—worth the trouble.

In *Hold Back the Dawn*, Romanian gigolo Charles Boyer is forced to live in a shabby hotel just across the Mexican border, since the "quota" system for immigrants limits the number of entries from each foreign country. He takes a room recently vacated by "Herr Wexler," who hung himself in despair over his failure to get a visa. However, the other hopeful immigrants at the hotel celebrate the Fourth of July with a "patriotic" meal of "Boston baked beans and doughnuts," their faith in America undimmed.

A Viennese surgeon and his daughter arrive in the United

States in *Three Faces West* and are offered sanctuary in a Dust Bowl farming community. Despite the inhospitable environment, they eventually decide to "pioneer" in the United States, and the daughter rejects an offer of marriage from the man who helped them escape from Austria (he turns out to be a Nazi sympathizer anyway).

The American Legion was another repeated motif with "Americanism" overtones in the 1937–1941 period. Legion characters appear in *Confessions of a Nazi Spy* (WB, 1939), and *Public Deb Number One* (TCF, 1940). The Legion figures prominently in the plots of several other films, including *The Battle of Broadway* (TCF, 1938), *Sons of the Legion* (Paramount, 1938), and *Squadron of Honor* (Columbia, 1938). The Legion was depicted as an organization of patriots upholding American ideals.

Historical American themes, the display of American icons, and pro-American/pro-democracy themes, while on the surface harmless efforts to bolster pride in America and the nation's democratic ideals, were actually one additional step towards fostering a public attitude disposed towards intervention, in the same manner as pro-military and pro-British films of the period. However, isolationist forces—which *did* protest the "military glorification" and pro-British "propaganda" films[5]—were less likely to single out themes like these for criticism, since no one wanted to be accused of being "unpatriotic."

8. Service Pictures: In Peace and Preparing for War

The single greatest category of predominant discernible biases among American motion pictures exhibiting an awareness of world events is pro-military films. Eighty-two of the works listed in the Filmography have been placed under this heading. This chapter addresses all pro-military films except those released in 1941 promoting the draft, which are dealt with in Chapter 14.

Military films of a largely benign nature had appeared in modest numbers throughout the mid-1930s. Excluding the numerous service academy films, a sampling of these motion pictures would include *Come On, Marines* (Paramount, 1934), *Devil Dogs of the Air* (WB; 1935), *Born to Dance* (MGM, 1936) and *Devil's Squadron* (Columbia, 1936). Virtually all of these films, as well as their many successors, incorporate a romance into the plot. *Born to Dance* actually has a Navy lieutenant, played by Jimmy Stewart, singing (his real voice) "Easy To Love" to Eleanor Powell. In fact, girl chasing, particularly in a nightclub venue, remained a popular cinematic military pursuit throughout the period, from *Sweetheart of the Navy* (GN, 1937) to *Honolulu Lu* (Columbia, 1941).

Many of the soldiers, sailors and marines appear as adept at performing musical numbers as in carrying out their military duties. *Navy Spy* (GN; 1937), *The Singing Marine* (WB; 1937), *Submarine D-1* (WB; 1937), *Give Me a Sailor* (Paramount; 1938), *In Old Monterey* (Republic; 1939), *Cadet Girl* (TCF; 1941), *Keep 'Em Flying* (Universal; 1941), and *Navy Blues* (WB; 1941), all feature military personnel in musical production numbers. Dick Powell and his marine buddies conclude *The Singing Marine* with a hearty rendition of "The Song of the Marines." At the Rendezvous club in the Canal Zone, a boisterous group of submariners sing: "We're the Crazy Diving Boys." In *Cadet Girl* one of the featured musical numbers is "My Old Man Was an Army Man." And in *Navy Blues*, some sea-weary singing gobs aboard a warship are proud they answered Uncle Sam's call and helped the president's Good Neighbor policy by showing the flag in Latin America, but want to know: "When Are We Going to Land Abroad?"

The number of pro-military American films increased substantially during 1937. The U.S. Navy was the featured service in the majority of these motion pictures (12 out of 14). Three of these films involve members of the U.S. Navy combatting foreign spies—*The Holy Terror*; *Navy Blues*; *Navy Spy*. Two other Navy films, *Swing It Sailor* and *Wings Over Honolulu*, stress the combat readiness of the fleet. Strong isolationist sentiments had led to the passage of a revised Neutrality Act of 1937. Perhaps as a reflection of these views, the Navy was considered the paramount military service, not only to protect America's vast merchant fleet, but also as an armorplated buffer against foreign intrusions into the Western Hemisphere.

Of the eight pro-military films released between 1937 and 1941 that are also classified as anti-espionage in nature, all but two concern agents of foreign powers attempting to learn about secret military equipment. In *Holy Terror* (TCF; 1937), while a ten year old Jane Withers is performing a musical number with the gobs at a popular club, foreign spies stage a brawl. It seems the spies would like to have the building vacated so they can observe a new naval plane at the neighboring air base. Rival spy rings of unspecified national origin in *Trapped in the Sky* (Columbia; 1939), are so interested in an experimental electrically powered Army bomber plane, that they murder each others' gang members.

Parallel to the increasing numbers of pacifist and non-interventionist films released in 1938 and 1939 (See Chapter 5), pro-military films correspondingly reached their nadir in 1939 (total of 8). *Yellow Jack* (MGM), centering around the American military campaign in Cuba to conquer the deadly yellow fever, immediately following the Spanish-American

The Holy Terror (TCF, 1937): Mid-1930s service films often contained a musical production number. Jane Withers entertains Uncle Sam's sailors.

War, is particularly interesting. On two occasions during the film it is pointed out that American soldiers are working to help the world, not contribute to its destruction. The three featured soldiers volunteer for the medical experiments, which will finally prove that the mosquito is the carrier of the disease, are a Jewish Marxist named Busch (Sam Levene), a southern farmboy called "Jellybeans" (Buddy Ebsen) and a cocky Irish sergeant, played by Robert Montgomery. This is a classic example of the training/combat film ethnic mix formula that would be repeated time and again in American films featuring the military. For instance, Buddy Ebsen would appear in a similar role in the 1941 RKO release *Parachute Battalion*. Sam Levene would be the military unit's Jewish character in numerous films through 1945, including *Action in the North Atlantic* (WB; 1943), *Gung Ho!* (Universal; 1943), and *The Purple Heart* (TCF; 1944).

Reflecting a growing concern and fascination of the public with air power, over a quarter of the pro-military films in this period highlighted the air arms of the various services. *Test*

Pilot (1938), *Wings of the Navy* (1939), *Flight Command* and *I Wanted Wings* (1941) are examples of this trend.

Pro-Preparedness Films

Twenty Thousand Men a Year, a late 1939 release by 20th Century–Fox, categorized as Pro-Preparedness in the Filmography, involves the stepped-up training of civilian pilots, implicitly reflecting fears of potential military threats to this country. At least two 1940 films, *Arise, My Love* (Paramount; categorized as Pro-Intervention; Anti–Nazi) and *Flight Angels* (WB) refer to experienced civilian pilots who are needed as instructors for the military. In *Arise, My Love*, the American pilot has actually seen combat in Spain and with the RAF. By 1941, the continuing need to train thousands of new pilots would become so acute that civilian training schools would be placed under the Army Air Corps' supervision. Two motion pictures that take place at such air fields are *Flying Cadets*

I Wanted Wings (Paramount, 1941): With millions of young men in military training, accidents were bound to happen. But aviator Wayne Morris's mishap is lightened by the symbol of what we were fighting to protect: Mom (and her home cooking).

(Universal) and the Abbot and Costello military farce, *Keep 'Em Flying* (Universal).

    As early as the spring of 1938, with MGM's release of *Test Pilot*, the emphasis began to slowly shift away from chasing skirts to preparedness themes and/or the training and expansion of the U.S. military. The second half of *Test Pilot* features the testing of the prototype of the Army's new B-17 bomber. Two 1939 pro-military releases containing strong preparedness themes were *In Old Monterey* (Republic) and *The Real Glory* (UA). The former portrays Army sergeant Gene Autry conducting a July 4th meeting at the local town hall where, in order to convince some western ranchers that it is their patriotic duty to support a new Army Air Corps bombing range in their neighborhood, he shows newsreels of the warfare in China and Spain. Gene concludes:

What you saw there could happen right in this country. And will happen unless we have a fighting force so superior [Army planes are heard flying overhead] that no one will dare attack us. By that I don't

mean more men, more guns and more equipment than everyone else, but better men and better guns and better equipment...

    Wings of the Navy was released by Warner Brothers in early 1939. It was the first of a series of films dealing with the training of new pilots. To quote the *Variety* review: "a convincer to mould public opinion and support in favour of current government plans for wide expansion of American air defense."[1] Later films of this type include *I Wanted Wings* (1941). *Wings of the Navy* solemnly opens with the dedication of a monument at Arlington Cemetery to a (fictitious) Admiral Harrington. The speaker at the ceremonies notes that even in peacetime men still sacrifice their lives to protect America against war, and notes that one of the best ways to achieve security is through the creation of an "invincible air arm."[2]

    Wings of the Navy focuses on the youngest son of the late Admiral, Lt. Jerry Harrington (John Payne), who is inspired to leave the submarine service and head to Pensacola for flight training. His older brother, Cass (George Brent), involved in the designing of Navy planes, tries unsuccessfully to discourage Jerry.

On the train to Florida, Jerry meets some of his classmates. They include Scat Allen from Brooklyn (Frank McHugh) and Lt. Armando Costa, a "Brazilian Navy courtesy student."[3] The three go through flight training school together. The Navy's cooperation in this production is apparent from the large amount of actual footage used. From Pensacola, Jerry and his friends go to the San Diego Naval Air Station for final training in float biplanes. *Parachute Battalion* (RKO; 1941) is another training-oriented pro-military film which introduces the audience to the male leads on the train to camp.

While Jerry spends his off-duty hours making love to Cass' girl (played by Olivia De Havilland), Cass is working tirelessly to receive Navy Department approval for his plans for a new fighter plane, But, while he is instructing a nervous pilot trainee, Cass is crippled in a crackup.

Not long after Jerry receives his coveted wings, he helps Cass with the critical flight testing of the older brother's newly designed aircraft. The problem of blackouts during dives is a major concern, one that had cost the life of the first test pilot. Interestingly, in 1941, Warner Brothers would release *Dive Bomber*, dealing with the efforts of naval flight surgeons to find a method of preventing pilot blackouts.

During 1940 the number of pro-military films remained relatively low—four of the twelve dealt with the U.S. Navy and four with the military air arms. Several of the films occur in a non-contemporaneous setting or in a foreign locale and one, *The Fighting 69th*, takes place during the First World War. Although at first this low number may seem strange, with the Second World War in progress, there are probably two good explanations for the dearth of military related films in 1940.

First, much of the public dismissed the seriousness of the conflict, at least until after the fall of France in June. And second, somewhat paradoxically, with the daily news of military actions overseas, but with America remaining neutral, the old peacetime barracks stories probably seemed comparatively dull.

However, the growing feeling that America would eventually become involved in the "main event," reinforced by the introduction of peacetime conscription in late 1940, led Hollywood to release a plethora of pro-military films in 1941. In fact, the thirty-five 1941 pro-military films represent nearly a quarter of all films from that year reflecting an awareness of the world crisis. Over ten of these dealt exclusively with conscription (refer to Chapter 13), including such classics as *Buck Privates* and *Caught in the Draft*. Significantly, twenty of the 1941 pro-military films were comedy and musical comedy genre offerings.

Mock Combat Films

Although references to obvious future potential enemies were surprisingly low—and virtually non-existent in draft related films—surrogate combat was featured in many of these films, particularly in the form of maneuvers (7 in 1941; coded in the Filmography under Military Exercise). *Flight Command*, an early 1941 release from MGM, portrays the old-timers of the famous Hellcat naval fighter squadron grumbling when informed a recently deceased mate will be replaced by a new graduate from Pensacola. Implying that the accelerated training resulting from the National Defense program may have effected pilot quality, one officer adds: "We're getting tough assignments [now]—the closest to actual war conditions abroad."

Another motion picture release, from May of 1941, Paramount's *I Wanted Wings*, clearly indicates the growing militarization of America by framing its story with a simulated air raid upon Los Angeles. A reporter covering the mock night attack on the city comments: "We can be thankful the explosions ... [are] not real bombs ... America intends to be prepared."

Dive Bomber (WB), which, like *Flight Command*, features carrier pilots in the U.S. Pacific Fleet, is worth noting for its political ambiguity (possibly with racial implications). Although the Pacific Fleet had been built up with the threat of Japan specifically in mind, all the professional discussions of the pilots concerning contemporary events center around the war in Europe. One of the American pilots, grounded for medical reasons, joins the pilot ferry service transporting American-built bombers to Britain, with tragic results.

A definite indication of the more serious nature of the military training/surrogate combat of non-draftees is the number of deaths that occur. While not a single draftee is killed in a 1941 film, several regular military personnel are killed in training, testing of equipment, or maneuvers, e.g., *Dive Bomber*, *Flight Command*; *I Wanted Wings*.

Most pro-military motion pictures listed in the Filmography take place in a time frame contemporaneous to the period of the film's original release, but there were exceptions. One such exception, *The Fighting 69th*, like *Wings of the Navy* (both were released by Warner Brothers), begins with the training of military personnel. But *The Fighting 69th* deals with Army volunteers for the American Expeditionary Force being sent to France in 1917–1918. Furthermore, the second half of this World War I film centers on combat with the Germans. Although there are numerous films from 1940–1941 referring to WWI (total of 36), *The Fighting 69th* is one of only three films from those two years to actually portray combat taking place during that conflict. The other two are *All Quiet on the Western Front* (re-released from 1930, with added footage and commentary relating to the world crisis) and Howard Hawk's

Caught in the Draft (Paramount, 1941): Military marriages were a common occurrence in 1941. Andrew Tombes is the justice of the peace, Dorothy Lamour is the bride, and Bob Hope is the groom. Lynne Overman and Eddie Bracken serve as witnesses. Bob is wearing only his BVDs under his overcoat.

classic pro-draft work based on the life of one of America's heroes from the First World War, *Sergeant York*.

The First Pro-Draft Films

The Fighting 69th was released during the winter of 1940. Although it took place during World War I and featured volunteers, not draftees, it was a precursor of the pro-draft films that swamped American movie screens throughout the following year. The story itself centers around New York's predominantly Irish 69th Regiment, commanded by the soon to be famous "Wild Bill" Donovan. The much-decorated unit, originally formed during the Civil War, went on to greater glory in France in 1917–1918 as part of the Rainbow Division (so-called because it was composed of outfits from around the country). Lightened by some comic relief, a major theme conveyed by the film is the concept of a melting pot America rising above "sectional feuds" to become a force united to defeat its enemies.

The Fighting 69th uses the familiar character of the flawed hero, played by James Cagney, who redeems himself through making the ultimate sacrifice while fighting the "Heinies" in the no man's land of the Western Front. Service training films had repeatedly used this gambit before and numerous training films released during 1941 and into the first year of America's participation in the Second World War would likewise. The usual plot involves a rescue from a disaster at camp or on maneuvers, as in *The Dead End Kids on Dress Parade* (1939), *I Wanted Wings* (1941) and *To the Shores of Tripoli* (1942).

Most likely directed toward the racist policies of Nazi Germany, particularly anti–Semitism, well known to Americans by 1940, there is a Jewish hero with an Irish brogue in *The Fighting 69th*. At one point he is portrayed cheerfully offering to pump the organ during a Mass conducted near the

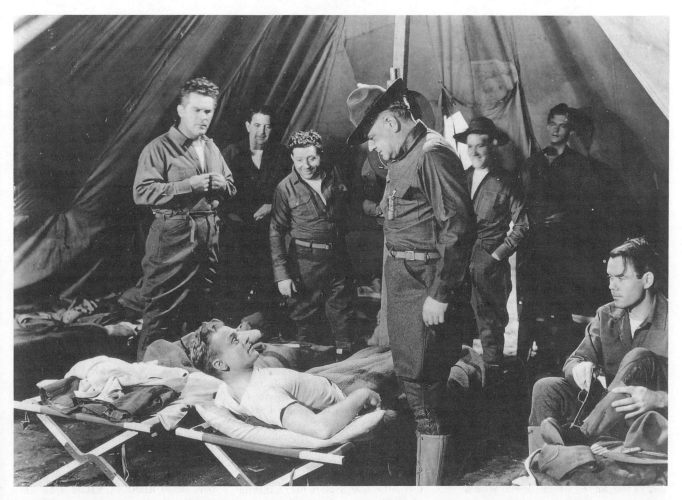

The Fighting 69th (WB, 1940): This film depicted average Americans in World War One, fighting against Germany, a situation that would soon be repeated in real life. James Cagney (reclining) is the center of attention as his sergeant (Alan Hale) and fellow soldiers (including Guinn Williams, Frank McHugh, and John Ridgeley) look on.

front by the beloved Father Duffy (Pat O'Brien). And when the Jew is mortally wounded in combat, it is a compassionate Father Duffy who stays by his side in a field hospital. Solemnly stating "God is one," Duffy administers to the soldier's final spiritual needs by reciting the "Hero of Israel" prayer—both in Hebrew and in English![4]

The Fighting 69th is unique among the pro-military films from before the war because there is *no* romantic interest. Between 1942 and 1945 there would be numerous examples of such films—*Wake Island* (Paramount; 1942), *Guadalcanal*

Diary (TCF; 1943), *Sahara* (Columbia; 1943), *Destination Tokyo* (WB), *Objective Burma!* (WB; 1945).

While the military had always been a popular topic of Hollywood films, during peace as well as war time, the pro-military films of the 1937–1941 period show a definite progression in theme and tone. From light-hearted adventure films, action comedies, and musicals, films dealing with America's armed forces eventually moved towards promoting preparedness, national defense, peacetime conscription, and even—albeit indirectly and with some trepidation—military intervention.

9. Espionage: The Fifth Column Lurks Behind the Screen

Arizona Gang Busters (PRC, 1940): "We've seen it [fifth column actions] happen in other countries and still we go on sleepwalking. We've got to wake up!"

Spy films have always been popular in Hollywood, just as spy novels and plays have long been popular forms of entertainment. Spy films in particular, however, seem to run in cycles: war inspires spy films, and other political events or trends also seem to trigger a new batch of such efforts.[1]

As can be seen from the Coding Statistics (Filmography), the incidence of "Spy-Saboteur" references in films referring to the growing world crisis increased steadily from 1937 through 1941. This illustrates an increased awareness of the world situation on the part of the American public, particularly since a number of these films deal with espionage *in* the United States. Even though the fighting was located in Europe, Asia and Africa, the United States could not be completely isolated, since foreign agents were, according to Hollywood, very active even here.

This is not to suggest that spy films had died out at the end of the First World War and did not reappear until 1937. Indeed, during the 1920s and into the 1930s Hollywood continued to make spy films of all types, if at a lesser pace than during wartime.

For example, in *The Silent Command* (1924), spies make plans to attack the Panama Canal and destroy the U.S. fleet. Double agents seek plans for the defense of Gibraltar during WWI in *Inside the Lines* (1930). *Secret Service* (1931) was a Richard Dix vehicle about Civil War spies. And in *Mystery Liner* (1934), spies try to obtain a secret device that allows ships to be directed by remote control.

These few examples illustrate some basic types of spy films: wartime spy films, peacetime spy films set in the United States, and peacetime spy films set in a foreign country. The first category includes not only films set during WWI and (later) WWII, but also period films dealing with conflicts ranging from the U.S. Civil War to the days of ancient Greece and Rome. For the most part, such films prior to WWII were usually *pro*-espionage in outlook, with the protagonist generally cast as a secret agent rather than a spy-catcher. During WWII and throughout the Cold War, the role of the counterspy came to the fore, with fewer films made about U.S. agents in foreign locales.

Peacetime spy films were rather different. Peacetime spy films set in other countries varied, depending upon the involvement of the protagonist. In *Happy Go Lucky* (1936), spies in Shanghai trying to obtain plans for a new military plane are depicted unfavorably; however, this setting could also allow for heroic, positively portrayed secret agents, particularly if the film was set in a country ruled by a repressive regime.

Films set *in* the United States, on the other hand, were almost always *anti*-espionage in tone, with foreign agents (or traitorous U.S. citizens) attempting to steal secret formulae, weapons, inventions, or plans.

Hollywood Spy Films, 1937–1941

The spy films of 1937–1941 followed much the same pattern as earlier years in terms of film types, although period spy films fell into some disfavor. However, to make up for this, the foreign intrigue films and films with domestic settings increased. The Bias Coding chart (Filmography) shows that the "Anti-Espionage" coding was the third most prevalent of the films in this study (after Pro-Military and Pro-American), reflecting fears on the part of Americans that foreign agents were at work in the United States, even though we were not yet entangled in the hostilities.

Oddly enough, spy films may have been one area where Hollywood was *not* sensationalizing reality. The evidence seems to indicate that, at least until the late 1930s, foreign agents had relatively little trouble operating in the United States, and yet very few people—in the government and out of it—knew of this or worried about it.

Although the U.S. was not at war, foreign powers were very interested in the latest industrial information, particularly those inventions with possible military applications. And America's relaxed attitude made such information fairly easy to obtain. German agents, for example, apparently made off with plans for planes, weapons and other technological advances, including the Norden bombsight, taking advantage of the absence of an organized counterspy operation.[2]

The FBI finally got wind of the German network of spies—through a combination of fortuitous circumstances—and the revelations that emerged led to a wave of anti–Nazi sentiment (although not enough to shake the beliefs of the non-interventionists). The fact-based *Confessions of a Nazi Spy* (1939) was one concrete result of the prewar spy scare. However, this film was relatively rare in that it "named names" and nationalities. Prior to this point (and for some time afterward), Hollywood was content to hint at the possible identities of those who would steal America's secrets.

In *Cipher Bureau* (Grand National, 1938), for instance, Major Waring (Leon Ames) of the Army's "Cipher Bureau" runs afoul of spies from an unspecified foreign country. The spies are led by "Herrick" and "Grood," played by Tenen Holtz and Gustav von Seyffertitz, while their female associate is named "Therese Brahm." Casting Germanic actors and giving them names which at least hinted at their national origins was one way of directing the audience's attention. This practice continued in Hollywood right up until the U.S. entered the war. Other examples of this indirect identification of spies include *Navy Secrets* (Monogram, 1939)—"Cronjer" (William von Brincken); *Arizona Gang Busters* (PRC, 1940)—"Karl Schmidt" (Arno Frey) and "Henry Hess" (Otto Reichow); and *The Deadly Game* (Monogram, 1941)—"Fritz" (Hans von Morhart) and "Brandt."

Sometimes Hollywood was a bit bolder. In the wake of *Confessions of a Nazi Spy*, *Espionage Agent* (Warner Brothers,

Arizona Gang Busters (PRC, 1940): Crack manhunter Trigger Tim (Tim McCoy) and his friend (Julian Rivero), an agent of the Mexican national police, combat Western Fifth Columnists posing as lawmen. McCoy was a Lt. Colonel in the Army Reserves who returned to active duty during World War Two.

1939), went a step further than most films. The film begins with footage of German sabotage in the United States in 1915, prior to the U.S. entry in WWI. As the film comes up to the present day, the Teutonic villainy is continued by "Rader" (James Stephenson), complete with a Luger pistol and the musical strains of "Watch on the Rhine." However, to hedge a bit, the film locates the headquarters of the spy ring in Geneva, Switzerland (the most neutral spot on earth!). *Espionage Agent* also weaves into its plot the passage of strong anti-espionage legislation in the United States (once again, probably inspired by the same revelations that gave rise to *Confessions of a Nazi Spy*).

Films set in foreign countries were somewhat freer to make implicit (and later, explicit) linkages between Germany (and to a lesser extent, Italy and Japan), and espionage. *Char-*

lie Chan at the Olympics (20th Century Fox, 1937), for instance, revolves around the theft of a remote-controlled airplane device from its testing ground in Hawaii. Although the thief is eventually revealed to be one of the developers of the plane (presumably a U.S. citizen), the bulk of the film is set in Nazi Germany at the 1936 Olympics, providing ample opportunity to link the Germans with espionage—and incidentally to criticize the Nazis on general principles (although the word "Nazi" is not spoken and no swastikas are shown, newsreel footage of Hitler does appear briefly).

For instance, Charlie Chan (Warner Oland) remarks that the Olympic Games will "provide an excellent opportunity for spies of all nations to carry on business." Exactly why he thinks this is not clear (a fascist police state is hardly the place for foreign spies to operate). Newsreel footage is integrated into the plot and this allows the filmmakers to make a few political points: the U.S. athletes do not give the traditional Olympic salute (it somewhat resembled the fascist salute), the U.S. flag is not lowered when the parade of athletes passes Hitler's spot on the reviewing stand, and a victorious Jesse Owens appears, refuting Hitler's well-known theories about "Aryan" supremacy (in added fictional footage, a black U.S. woman athlete is shown cheering Owens).

As time went on, Hollywood became bolder in its depiction of foreign agents. If there was still a lingering reluctance to openly identify Nazis as spies and saboteurs in the neutral U.S., it was open season on Nazis in foreign locales. *One Night in Lisbon* (Paramount, 1941) begins in London, where Dwight (Fred MacMurray), a Yank who ferries planes to England, meets English girl Leonora (Madeleine Carroll). She accompanies him to Lisbon, where he is to catch the Clipper back to America. However, Leonora also carries letters to the British ambassador in Lisbon, and Major Erich Strasser (possibly the brother of Major Heinrich Strasser of *Casablanca*) tries his best to obtain them.

International Lady (United Artists, 1941) was rather similar, with Nazi spy Carla (Ilona Massey) beginning her work in London, passing through Lisbon, and arriving in New York, pursued by an FBI man and a British secret agent. Carla turns her coat and joins the forces of democracy (prompted mostly by her attraction to the FBI man), and her Nazi comrades bite the dust.

As mentioned above, Germans bore the brunt of Hollywood's indirect vilification in the prewar years, in large part due to their WWI record of spying and sabotage in the U.S., and to the perception of Italians as generally "harmless."

There was almost no depiction of Japanese spies in the 1937–1941 period: in fact, the Japanese Mr. Moto (Peter Lorre) actually foils German spies in *Mr. Moto Takes a Chance*, and *Mr. Moto's Last Warning*, in 1938 and 1939, respectively! In the latter film, Moto becomes involved in a plot hatched by the German-accented Eric Norvel (George Sanders—wearing a monocle to reinforce his Prussian image) and the Italianate Fabian (Ricardo Cortez) to sink a French ship at the entrance to the Suez Canal, thereby blocking the canal and causing trouble between allies France and Britain. This film was an early example of the "Axis gang" motif which would later (particularly after 1941) become familiar, an explicit linkage of German, Italian, and Japanese spies in common cause.[3]

One film which did feature a gang of Asian spies was *Panama Patrol* (Grand National, 1939), a sequel to *Cipher Bureau*. In this entry, Major Waring (Leon Ames) uncovers an Asian spy posing as an Army interpreter (Abner Biberman—given the rather odd character name of "Artie Johnson"): target, the Panama Canal. The spies are not specifically identified as Japanese (in fact, some of the character names are *Chinese*), but there would have been little question in the minds of U.S.

audiences in 1939 about *which* Asian nation would be interested in the Panama Canal. Furthermore, the Sino-Japanese conflict had been given considerable publicity in the U.S. (including a number of film references in the 1937–1941 period), and public sympathy was virtually always with China.

One theme utilized in a number of films was that of U.S. citizens (often criminals) who aided foreign agents, generally for money, although there were a few examples of home-grown fascists and Bundists aiding the spies and saboteurs. *The Spy Ring* (Universal, 1938), for example, concerns the efforts of three spies to steal plans for a new machine gun, since they have been promised $2 million by a foreign government to obtain them. *Trapped in the Sky* (Columbia, 1939) not only features agents of another (unnamed) country, but also "freelance spies" who will sell to the highest bidder, and a traitorous inventor willing to sell his invention to a foreign nation. In some films the traitorous American is a dupe or is forced into aiding his country's enemies (*Down in San Diego*, 1941). In *Flying Wild* (Monogram, 1941), one character makes this clear: "the most vicious offenders are often born in America and just don't know what they're doing."

Exactly what were these cinematic spies after? For the most part, in spy films set in the United States, the agents are after plans for a fabulous new weapon of war: a new machine gun, a new poison gas, a "vapor fuel," a camouflage paint, a bombing device, an anti-aircraft gun, an air-raid detector, robot airplanes, other airplanes of all types (bombers and fighters—known as "pursuit planes"), new explosives, bombsights, and so on. Although the U.S. was not yet at war with anyone, a lot of inventions were being created just in case, and rather than buy them from U.S. companies like anybody else, the unnamed foreign countries decided to just steal them.

Since the United States was not directly involved in the hostilities, films in which secret plans, maps or drawings were sought by spies were often set in other countries. In *Man at Large* (TCF, 1941), Nazi spies are after information on convoys sailing from Canada to Britain; *Hawaii Calls* (RKO, 1938), a early and rare example where plans of *U.S.* fortifications (in Hawaii) are sought by foreign agents; in *A Trip to Paris* (TCF, 1938), it is plans for the Maginot Line in France.

Although in real life their functions were usually quite separate, in Hollywood (and thus in this study), spies and saboteurs were often one and the same. Spies tried to get information, but they were not above a little murder, kidnapping, and—at times—sabotage (or at least attempts at it). Once again, most early depictions of sabotage or planned sabotage occurred in films set in foreign countries. It was not until the "shooting war" started in 1939, along with the fairly open expressions of sympathy for the Allies exhibited by most Americans, that fears of sabotage began to manifest themselves in the content of Hollywood films.

In actuality, there was little or no Axis sabotage in the United States either before or after December 7, 1941. Prior to the official declaration of war, German and Japanese spymasters and diplomats wanted, at all costs, to avoid antagonizing the neutral United States. They wanted no repeat of the sometimes highly successful German campaign prior to the U.S. entry into WWI, in which a massive munitions dump in New Jersey was blown up, and numerous ships sailing to Great Britain were "seeded" with delayed-action bombs. It was not until the late 1930s that legal blame for all this was finally fixed on the German government, thus adding one more black mark against the Axis powers.[4]

In *Sabotage* (Republic, 1939), a mechanic at an aircraft factory is blamed for several mysterious crashes and is accused of being an enemy agent. The plant, which has a contract to supply planes for the military, has to close while the "accidents" are being investigated; the mechanic's father and his elderly friends expose the real culprits as agents of an unnamed foreign power. *Passport to Alcatraz* (Columbia, 1940) drew heavily on German activities in WWI for its plot: enemy agents are provided with fake passports (prior to America's entry into WWI, Germans resident in the U.S. who wanted to return to Germany to serve in the armed forces had to obtain false passports so they could leave the country) so that they can set up plans for massive sabotage of U.S. munitions plants (a reminder of the "Black Tom" explosion in New Jersey).

In a number of films, the enemy agents did a little of everything. *Flying Wild* (Monogram, 1941), starts off with sabotage of new airplanes at a factory, but then switches to a plot to steal plans for a new bombsight (this is actually cooked up by the film's protagonists—the East Side Kids—to trap the foreigners). Similarly, in *Emergency Landing* (PRC, 1941), spies first sabotage a remote-controlled plane, then steal another plane from the same factory. More saboteurs showed up in *Mister Dynamite* (Universal, 1941), and *Roar of the Press* (Monogram, 1941), to name just a few examples.

Part of the fear of spies and saboteurs which contributed to Hollywood's preoccupation with this subject in the 1937–1941 period (but especially in 1939–1941) was the news that the Axis was using a "fifth column" of spies and collaborators to pave the way for their invasions.[5] Military intelligence undoubtedly provided great assistance to the Germans and Japanese in their attacks on their European and Asian neighbors, but the near-panic that followed Germany's relatively easy conquests in the "*Blitzkreig*" period of 1939–1940 was largely unfounded, at least as far as the United States was concerned.

What then can we make of Hollywood's preoccupation with spies in the period prior to December 7, 1941? The spy

Passport to Alcatraz (Columbia, 1940): Jack Holt is assigned to break up a false passport ring which provides the phony documents to foreign agents conducting acts of sabotage against America's defense industry.

Sabotage (Republic, 1939): Workers at an aircraft plant witness the result of sabotage. A mechanic, played by Gordon Oliver (center right) is the prime suspect. Fears of sabotage became more pronounced in the U.S. with the outbreak of WWII in Europe. Also shown: Arleen Whelan.

films illustrate two things: first, they reflect America's desire to stay out of the war if possible, although for all but the most optimistic isolationists, it was clear that—sooner or later—America would enter the war. Hence we see the strong anti-espionage bias and a large number of films where sinister foreign agents practice their art in the United States. Second, the spy films illustrate the attitudes of Americans towards the belligerent parties, with Germans very early on being cast as villains. The U.S. was not at war, but our sympathies were fairly obvious.

10. Cinematic Vigilance Against the Totalitarian Regimes

Comrade X (MGM, 1940): "They're [the dictators] all hanging by their toes from chandeliers ... and throwing rocks at each other ... [N]obody's going to turn a machinegun on you if I can help it ... that's my politics."

Escape to Glory (Columbia, 1940): "I understand they've got it narrowed down to a point now where they hope to have babies born giving the fascist salute. Kind of tough on mothers, but it will be great for dictators."

The motion pictures included in the Filmography that are categorized as either Anti–Fascist, Anti–Totalitarian, Anti–German, Anti–Nazi, Anti–Japanese, or Anti–Soviet, when combined, number over ninety (or over a fifth) of all the films reflecting an awareness of the world crisis. They embrace a rather wide spectrum and therefore require more precise definitions. Three separate divisions within this area will be addressed in this chapter: anti–fascist films that confront indigenous fascism, those that oppose fascism abroad, and films that deal with the totalitarian regimes of the Soviet Union, Italy and Imperial Japan.

Four of the five anti–fascist films listed in the Filmography for 1937 take place in contemporary America. The fifth, *The Life of Emile Zola* (WB), takes place in France at the beginning of the century. Two of the motion pictures, *Black Legion* and *Nation Aflame* (Treasure Pictures), attack indigenous fascist organizations.

Fighting Fascism at Home

The screenplay for Warner Brothers' *Black Legion* was based on a story by Robert Lord, but the idea for the film was more than likely taken from the real life investigation of the murder of a young Roman Catholic WPA worker by members of the fascistic "Black Legion" of Detroit, founded in 1933 by a group of unemployed and semi-skilled working class men.[1]

Black Legion centers around Frank Taylor (Humphrey Bogart), a lathe operator in a factory, who becomes disenchanted when he is passed over for promotion to foreman by a young night-school educated East European named Dumbrowski. That evening, Frank listens to a hysterical diatribe on the radio: "America for Americans ... Join [our organization] before the Red, White and Blue is replaced by the flag of anarchy." Frank is impressed and favorably responds to an invitation the next day from a fellow worker (played by Joe Sawyer) to attend a meeting of friends who refuse to be "pushed around ... [by a] ...bunch of foreigners." In classic fascist style, economic frustrations are provided an outlet by targeting a foreign "other" as the cause of the problem.

Soon afterwards Frank decides to join the Black Legion that vows to "purge this land of these traitorous aliens ... [for] ... free, white, 100 percent Americans." At his firelit initiation ceremony (evoking images of Nazi rallies), the members all wear dark hoods (KKK linkage) with a skull and crossbones (a symbol used by both Mussolini's Blackshirts and Hitler's SS) inscribed upon the head pieces. On his knees, a pistol pointed at his head, Frank swears to promote the "extermination of anarchists and the Roman hierarchy." A few days later, the Dumbrowski poultry farm is torched at night and both the son and his elderly father are driven out of town as "undesirable aliens." At that time in Germany the achievement of racial purity through violence was advocated by the Nazi Party.

This doctrine of hate leads Frank down the path of irrational self-contradiction, a life of dissolution and eventually towards near madness. Although he initially gets the coveted foreman's position vacated by Dumbrowski, Frank's increasing drinking and belligerency eventually lead to his dismissal and to his wife leaving him. This moral descent finally culminates in Frank shooting his Irish-Catholic friend and neighbor (Dick Foran) when that man, kidnapped by the Legion, attempts to escape after he defiantly called the hooded bigots the "yellow legion."

At the sensational trial following his arrest for murder, a contrite Frank partially redeems himself by identifying the other members of the secret organization. The film's message is concisely summed up in a lecture the judge delivers to the nine convicted men at their sentencing:

[I]llegal and extra-legal organizations cannot be tolerated ... racial and religious prejudice must be suppressed.... The American people made their choice a long time ago.... Our democratic form of government must be guarded zealously.

Black Legion is a unique motion picture from the 1937 to 1941 period, since it specifically condemns not only racial and religious bigotry, but also anti-intellectualism. Although it never directly attacks any foreign governments or ideologies, *Black Legion* makes it clear that fascistic organizations are unacceptable to the American way of life.

It was one matter to condemn a pseudo-fascist group in middle America, quite another to specifically attack the Nazi government and its domestic adherents, the German-American Bund (established in 1936 under the leadership of Fritz Kuhn). Yet, that is exactly what Warner Brothers did in their 1939 motion picture, *Confessions of a Nazi Spy* (hereafter referred to as *Nazi Spy*). *Nazi Spy*'s screenplay was adapted from former FBI agent Leo G. Turrou's book, *The Nazi Conspiracy in America*, which rather sensationally related the true story of the arrest and subsequent conviction in December 1938 of four foreign agents—in the employ of Germany—for subversive activities in the United States.[2]

The film itself is given a semi-documentary gloss by its occasional use of an offscreen narrator (*March of Time* style), the insertion of newsreel footage and the then rather novel use of graphics.[3] After immediately establishing that international espionage directed against America is being carried out by Germany, the film audience is transported to a German-American Bund meeting in a Yorkville (the German section of New York City) beer hall. The crowd is listening to a seditious racial harangue from a Hitler-like gesticulating Dr. Kassel (Paul Lukas—whose wire-rim glasses create a physical resemblance to Himmler), standing in front of the side-by-side American and Nazi flags:

We are proud of our new Germany ... of its great Fuehrer, proud of our glorious blood and soil.... Germans must seize the power that is

Black Legion (WB, 1937): Humphrey Bogart portrays a disaffected blue collar worker who joins an indigenous fascistic organization called the "Black Legion." The "skull and cross-bones" motif was used both by Mussolini's Blackshirts and Hitler's SS.

rightfully theirs'…. Those who fight us must perish … Germans must save America from the chaos that breeds in democracy and racial equality … Seig Heil!

Nazi Spy actually centers around a German-American misfit (and unemployed Army deserter) named Kurt Schneider who, in hopes of making some fast money, communicates with German Naval Intelligence to volunteer his services. On board the German liner *S.S. Bismarck*, headed for America, the intelligence officer Schlager (George Sanders), accompanied by two thuggish Gestapo men, is ordered to make contact both with Dr. Kassel and Schneider. The ruthless nature of the Party is starkly asserted when Schlager cynically informs his Gestapo associates that the Naval officers who complained about a *S.S. Bismarck* crew replacement (for political reasons) conform because their families are "hostages of the Nazis."

Warner Brothers is relentless and innovative in its visual exploitation of Nazi icons to create and reinforce the sense of a direct threat to America. A newsreel of a Nazi Party rally in Germany shrilly concludes: "All Germans remain Germans— no matter where they are!" A swastika "iris in" opens up to a shot of Dr. Kassel (now in Nazi uniform) delivering another speech to his "racial comrades" insisting that in order to free America the United States Constitution must be destroyed. An American Legionnaire (wearing a member's cap; played by Ward Bond) stand up, reminds the Germans he fought them in the "last war," and proclaims: "We don't want any 'isms' in this country, except Americanism."[4] Following a brawl, the Legionnaire yells that the Nazis "are worse than gangsters," as he is forcibly removed from the hall.[5]

This Legionnaire's utterance creates a critical associative linkage, for over the next several years the cinematic portrayal of Nazis would greatly resemble that of the Hollywood gangster—with an accent. For instance, all the leading Nazi characters in *Nazi Spy* speak with heavy German accents. In numerous future films featuring American or British criminals (or former criminals), these denizens of the underworld will achieve redemption or be ennobled by fighting the Nazis, e.g., *Meet Boston Blackie* and *Scotland Yard*, q.v.

Once in the United States, Schlager orders Schneider to procure certain military secrets and graphically impresses upon Kassel, with the aid of this brutish Gestapo henchmen, that strict Party discipline must be maintained. A German-American Nazi who has expressed a dislike for Hitler is forcibly taken to the *S.S. Bismarck* to be sent back to Germany: "No one disagrees with the Party!"

Meanwhile, the FBI, having been tipped-off by British Intelligence (an early example of U.S.-British cooperation) to German machinations in the United States, places calm, but methodical, agent Ed Renard (Edward G. Robinson) in charge of eliminating the espionage activities of the "hysterical crackpots" who have gone "Hitler happy" in America.

In an interesting scene, Hitler's spectacular entrance in an open automobile through seemingly endless throngs of heiling admirers in the streets of Nuremberg—as portrayed in Leni Riefenstahl's classic 1934 propaganda film, *Triumph des Willens*—is imitated (including the use of Dutch tilts) in the portrayal of a uniformed Dr. Kassel entering the Horst Wessel Camp (named after the martyred street fighter for whom the Nazi Party song was named). Swastikas and SS runes abound. There is also a contingent of smiling Nazi maidens at this Hitler Youth camp in New Jersey. The cinematic message clearly being—It *is* happening here.

The FBI quickly runs down the amateur Schneider (played by Francis Lederer, who bears a striking resemblance to Deputy *Fuehrer* Rudolph Hess) and by appealing to his vanity induces the pathetically self-deluded man to reveal the activities of the other Nazis. Kassel is later visited by agent Renard. In a chilling sequence (considering the well-publicized anti–Semitism of the Nazi regime) the medical doctor proudly explains to an incredulous Renard that he is keeping detailed biographical files on important U.S. citizens, classifying them according to blood and race in order to "preserve Americanism." Kassel adds: "You must be aware of the insidious international conspiracy of subhumans [presumably meaning Jews]."

The remaining Nazi agents are rounded up following the cowardly Kassel's betrayal. When they learn of his treachery, Kassel's Nazi superiors have him kidnapped and brought to Germany. Meanwhile, Kassel's former cohorts in America are tried for treason. During the trial the conspiracy of the "*present* German Government ... [in a] ... world wide spy network" is documented. The name of Propaganda Minister Goebbels appears conspicuously on a detailed organizational chart of the network. At the spies' sentencing, in a scene reminiscent of Warner Brothers' concluding courtroom scene in *Black Legion*, the presiding judge states: "[You will] enjoy the

mercies of democracy.... In this country ... there is no sawdust spread upon the floor of our prison yards."

After this final court appearance, Ed Renard, in a typical American luncheon joint nearby, overhears a man at the counter tell a buddy he is glad the spies were convicted: "This ain't Europe. We'll show 'em!" Renard turns toward his companion and states (into the camera): "They're absolutely insane [the Nazis]. We'll fight if we're pushed too far." Perhaps a little prematurely, Warner Brothers had launched its undeclared war on the Nazis.

This was the first American feature film in the 1937–41 period, aside from the aforementioned brief shot of Hitler in *Charlie Chan at the Olympics*, to openly name and show images of Hitler and other members of the Nazi elite. According to one account of *Nazi Spy*, much was made of the fact that no actor could be found who was willing to impersonate Hitler.[6] However, the motion picture frequently makes verbal references to Hitler, or the *Fuehrer*, and shows various images of Hitler (portraits, busts, etc.). In addition, newsreel clips from at least one of Hitler's speeches and footage of him from *Triumph des Willens* are incorporated into *Nazi Spy*. The "Minister of Propaganda" is mouth-twitching never-named Goebbels look-alike, portrayed by Martin Kosleck. During a speech to Party members in which a world map behind him is bathed in the crooked shadow of the crooked cross flag (*hakenkreuz*/swastika) he proclaims: "Italy is with us, Japan is our ally ... Hungary is practically ours ... the success at Munich.... Now, we must concentrate on America."

Hollywood threw down the gauntlet with *Nazi Spy*. In the Warner Brothers Pressbook, the studio provided an editorial for exhibitors under the title, "Hitlerian Fungus," that among other things proudly declared it was the "first of the cinema films to withdraw operations from Germany when the Nazis came to power."[7] The Nazi government did not take this cinematic assault lightly and initiated a diplomatic counter-offensive that eventually led to the motion picture being banned in eighteen countries.[8]

One of the more unique anti-fascist films released in America is the seldom revived 1941 Paramount satire, *World Premiere*. In a bizarre opening, during which an Italian spy witnesses his predecessor's execution, and the RAF bombs German Intelligence headquarters, the leaders of the fascist secret services independently and separately decide to send agents to the United States to sabotage the release of an American "propaganda picture" that is deemed by them to be highly unflattering to the Axis. It is none too subtly suggested in the film that both agents chosen for the assignment are anxious to immediately leave their respective homelands. In fact, as the camera cuts away from the blasted shutters of the German headquarters there is a dissolve to a spinning globe revealing stitches over the geopolitical outline of Germany.

On the lot of "Bengal Studios" in Hollywood, USA, the shooting of a torrid concentration camp melodrama, "The

Earth's on Fire" (a joking reference to Paramount's 1939 anti-totalitarian documentary, *The World in Flames*), is not going well. The studio head, Duncan DeGrasse ("D.G."), played by John Barrymore, is a dictatorial paranoiac who is constantly giving people the "chop" (firing them). He commands that two "phony spies" be hired as extras for the film. Meanwhile, the two Axis partners, Scaletti (Luis Alberni) and Bushmaster (Sig Rumann), have arrived outside the studio lot in separate cabs, surreptitiously exchanging fascist salutes in the nearby bushes.

They sneak onto the Bengal lot and then wander around the set of "The Earth's on Fire" until they are mistaken for the spies from Central Casting: "No, we are from Central Powers."[9] Soon after the two fascist agents are signed on as eight-dollar-a-day extras, members of the cast begin receiving threatening notes and mysterious accidents start occurring on the film set.

Despite the protests of a nervous cast, D. G. manages to trick them all into taking a train to Washington, D.C., to attend the motion picture's world premiere.[10] The two foreign agents, joined by Field Marshall Muller disguised as a janitor (a face-slapping, shouting, Nazi fanatic stereotype played by Fritz Feld) are also on board. However, in an attempt to protect his oft-threatened motion picture, D. G. has placed the film cans in a tiger's cage (Bengal Film's elderly live quadrupedal trademark) in the baggage car. The two bungling fascist agents, attempting to steal the film, lock themselves in the beast's cage. Muller rescues them by tying the tiger's tail in a knot, slapping him and then ordering the animal back into the cage. "The Earth's on Fire" is unceremoniously chucked off the train and replaced with a motion picture Muller had made in Germany.

At the premiere, the audience is initially bewildered by the opening shots of a film ironically (considering Nazi conquests) entitled "The Land of Peace and Beauty," featuring happy beer-drinking Germanic peasants in a bucolic setting.

But then "The Earth's on Fire" appears on the screen and the odd prologue is accepted as just another inspiration by D. G. Meanwhile, a scuffle has occurred in the projection booth, where D. G.'s recovered film has been rushed in, ending with the crazed Muller locking his two cowardly partners in a side room with a radio bomb. When the explosive radio merely fizzles, the two nervous agents examine it: 'Made in Japan' (from the thirties to the fifties, this was a derogatory phrase in America denoting product inferiority).

World Premiere and *Nazi Spy* are the only two pre–1942 American feature films released that link the three Axis partners together.[11] Motion pictures suggesting incompetence and/or distrust between the various members of the Axis were not uncommon after America entered the war. Examples include: *The Devil with Hitler* (UA, 1942) and *Invisible Agent* (Universal, 1942).

Fighting Fascism Abroad

Of the thirteen anti-fascist motion pictures listed in the Filmography for 1937 and 1938, just one takes place in an actual contemporary foreign locale—*Blockade*. The film opens with a title indicating it is the spring of 1936 in Spain. And although the text of the film never specifies the political loyalties of its characters, it is strongly suggested that the hero fights for Republican Spain. That is, the hero and his compatriots wear the traditional Basque beret worn by many Loyalists, the aggression is initiated by the opposition (Franco's rebels full scale military activities against the Republic), and only the Nationalists and their foreign supporters (Italy and Germany) actually blockaded certain ports and achieved air superiority. Nevertheless, a film openly supporting the Republican regime would be viewed as particularly repugnant to conservative elements in America, since in their view, Soviet aid to the Loyalists inextricably linked that besieged government to communism. Therefore, the opposition forces in the film, presumably Franco's Nationalists, are coyly referred to throughout *Blockade* as either the "enemy" or "they."

Blockade, with a screenplay by the left-wing writer John Howard Lawson, features Henry Fonda as peasant farmer Marco, whose idyllic bliss in the Spanish countryside is shattered by the violence of the civil war. When the people of his area panic and begin to flee under the shelling of enemy invaders, he patriotically incites them to stay and fight (and to inspirationally sing at the barricades while defending "Our Valley"). Because of the initiative he displayed, Marco is commissioned as a political officer and given the responsibility of ferreting out spies at the blockaded port of Castlemare.[12]

Along the way, Marco falls in love with a beautiful blonde spy (a White Russian, implying an anti-communist motive against the Popular Front regime) working for the other side. Norma, played by Madeleine Carroll, is responsible for relaying information about the arrival of relief ships to a submarine waiting offshore. But while Norma is in Castlemare, she has a change of heart after witnessing the suffering of the people under aerial bombardment and starvation conditions.[13] In a particularly effective scene, Norma observes a peasant woman rocking her dead child in her arms on the steps of a bomb-wrecked church.

Thus, in addition to the implied anti-fascism, the theme of pacifism is also developed in *Blockade*. This is highlighted in a prophetic report prepared by an English journalist (Reginald Denny) for his newspaper:

The morale of the people is good in spite of the hunger and frequent air raids. I cannot help wondering what military advantage is gained by the suffering of non-combatants. As I sit here I see a nightmare vision of air raids sweeping over great cities ... London ... New York

When the blockade is finally broken it is portrayed as a triumph of the people over adversity; not as a military victory.

Interestingly, the montage sequence depicting the people of the city and the "peoples' soldiers" meeting and unloading the supply ship would appear to be a homage to Eisenstein.

The final impassioned speech delivered by Marco could be construed as a plea against the official non-interventionism of the U.S. government as mandated by the Neutrality Acts and possibly as a call for volunteers to aid the embattled Republican regime. With a redeemed Norma by his side, Marco turns to the camera and beseeches the audience:

Our country has been turned into a battlefield. There's no safety for old people or children ... churches, schools, hospitals ... are targets. It's not war. War is between soldiers. It's murder; murder of innocent people. There's no sense to it. The world can stop it! Where's the conscience of the world?

Anti–Italian Films

Apparently because the Italians were never considered a serious threat, no American films were discovered between 1937 and 1941 with an anti–Italian (or anti–Italian fascism) predominant discernible bias. For the years 1937 and 1938, only six films listed under various headings have been found that in any way acknowledge the existence of Mussolini's fascist state. All six make fleeting, non-biased references to the Italo-Ethiopian War. During 1939 three films name Mussolini: *Babes in Arms* (MGM), *Charlie Chan in City in Darkness* (TCF) and *The Roaring Twenties* (WB).

After Mussolini committed his empire to the global conflict in June 1940 the comments in American films were frequently pejorative, more often condescending. Between September 1940 and late 1941, at least nine American motion pictures were released containing references to Mussolini and his fascist regime. In *Arise, My Love* (Para, 1940), Italy's 1939 invasion of Albania is alluded to when an American newspaper editor in Paris bemoans having earlier missed the story when "King Zog lost Albania." In *One Night in Lisbon* (Para, 1941), when a Yankee bomber ferry pilot in London (Fred MacMurray) requests spaghetti from a Greek restaurant owner (the Italian army launched an ill-conceived and executed invasion of Greece on October 28, 1940), the American is politely informed he may have "liberty noodle strings." However, most references to Italians are derisive, as in *The Great Dictator* (1940), *Washington Melodrama* (1941), *Sundown* (1941) and *World Premiere* (1941). For instance, the outrageous caricatures of Mussolini ("Benzini Napoloni"; played by Jack Oakie), his wife and retinue in *The Great Dictator*. Some of these films question the martial prowess of the new Roman legions.[14] This is particularly evident in *Washington Melodrama* and *Sundown*. The former suggests the Italian army may be tiring of fighting alongside the Germans, and the latter sympathetically portrays an Italian officer who prefers to cook pasta for his British captors.

Sundown is unique in that it is the only pre–1942 American film to indicate that some Italians opposed Mussolini's fascist state. Pallini, the Italian POW played by Joseph Calleia, informs the other Europeans at a Kenyan outpost that he was a "political history teacher at Milano [who] ... taught too much" and was sent to Ethiopia: "[You] think I'm a coward.... Where there is power there must be one master, and I know what that means to my people." Pallini is later murdered by a Nazi posing as a Dutchman.[15]

Anti–Nazi Films

Twenty-seven films presenting a distinctly anti–Nazi bias were released by Hollywood between 1939 and 1941 (twelve in 1941 alone). Three films portray active German resistance to the Nazi regime—*Beasts of Berlin*, *The Great Dictator*, and *Underground*. In *Four Sons* an ethnic German who is a Czech citizen resists the Nazi absorption of the Sudetenland. Four films portray passive German resistance to the Nazis—*Escape*, *The Man I Married*, *The Mortal Storm*, and *So Ends Our Night*. A fifth film, *They Dare Not Love*, depicts an Austrian nobleman who opposes the Nazi takeover of his state. *Beasts of Berlin*, *The Great Dictator*, *The Man I Married* and *The Mortal Storm* directly confront the issue of anti–Semitism. *Escape* and *The Man I Married* feature Americans in Germany who are forced by events to oppose the Nazis.

None of the above films, representing most of the major anti–Nazi films produced by Hollywood prior to 1942, clearly define the ideological premises of National Socialism. Thus, the ideological threat remains murky. However, in true melodramatic fashion, all the films present the Third Reich as directly threatening or literally destroying the sanctity and unity of the family.

Mortal Storm, a prestigious MGM release based on a best-selling novel, portrays a "non–Aryan" professor of biology named Roth (Frank Morgan) who runs afoul of the new Nazi regime in 1933 when he disputes their ideologically based theories of racial purity and blood. His stepsons, who become Nazi Brownshirts the morning after Hitler is appointed the new Chancellor of Germany, denounce the professor and leave his home. The spurned lover of Roth's daughter, Fritz (Robert Young), an officer in the Brownshirts, leads an assault upon the elderly Roth that culminates in the professor being sent to a concentration camp.

The professor's daughter Freya (Margaret Sullivan) and her pacifist lover (James Stewart) try to coexist with the new regime, but are relentlessly hounded by the Nazis. In a not so subtle linkage of sexual frustration with the appeal of Nazism, Fritz commands the party of Brownshirts to shoot and kill Freya as she tries to ski across the border to Austria with her lover.

Underground was released by Warner Brothers in the summer of 1941. The *Motion Picture Herald* review states that *Underground* was based on "recent newspaper stories of Germany's illegal short wave radio system." However, it is doubtful whether the very small organized German resistance was actually involved with any radio transmissions.[16] *Underground* contains some of the most graphic portrayals of Nazi brutalities to appear on American movie screens prior to the entrance of the United States into the war.

Underground's plot focuses on a dedicated group of Germans opposed to Hitler's regime. They illegally print leaflets criticizing the government and make "Voice of Freedom" radio broadcasts over a clandestine radio transmitter. Naturally, the Gestapo is anxious to silence these traitors to the Fatherland.

The film is a classic example of Hollywood propaganda, full of direct and implied negative messages with regard to the Third Reich. For instance, immediately after a young German soldier named Kurt Francken (Jeffrey Lynn), who has returned from the front without a left arm, rhapsodizes about Nazi military victories and their benefits for the German people, his mother tells the maid to save the now valuable/scarce coffee grounds (due to the British naval blockade). The ironic juxtaposition is carried still further a few minutes later: a close family friend, whose son was killed when the battleship *Bismarck* was sunk by the Royal Navy in the North Atlantic (May 1941), arrives to visit. Later, one of the illegal radio broadcasts claims Rudolph Hess flew to England because it is "the only place where the Gestapo can't stop him from telling the truth."[17]

The Nazi regime is physically and symbolically omnipresent. In the opening scene of *Underground*, two resistance members are shown sharing a match in order to pass a message. But a swastika on the wall behind them intrudes, literally separating their heads in the shot. Even in the garage of one of the opposition leaders a swastika is present (as if watching). Images of Hitler are frequently displayed and people in Nazi Party uniforms and German military personnel constantly appear in scenes.

There are two scenes in *Underground* of whip-toting Blackshirts torturing political prisoners for information. The light effects and the slightly up-angle shots give the Nazis a deliberately devilish countenance. Following the first episode, the young heroine is released, but only after she agrees to sign a statement denying she was mistreated.

Most insidious of all is the way *Underground* shows the Nazis encouraging individuals to betray each other in the name of the state. The Gestapo chief, Heller (Martin Kosleck), positively gloats when he is led to believe that Kurt has deliberately informed on his resistance leader brother. But, in fact, as Eric Francken (Phillip Dorn) awaits the guillotine, he hears younger brother Kurt denounce Hitler's regime in a broadcast over a new secret radio: "The voice of free Germany ... [will continue] fighting oppression ... even in this period of medieval darkness."

Anti–Soviet Films

Between 1937 and 1941 nine American feature films were produced with a distinctly anti–Soviet bias. Seven were released during the period of the Nazi-Soviet Pact. Rather interestingly, six are also classified as belonging to the comedy genre—screwball comedies to be more accurate: to believe in communism implies a degree of insanity. Even in one of the non-comedic films, *Gateway* (TCF, 1938), the bitchy Soviet communist is portrayed as mad. One motion picture listed in the Filmography as anti-totalitarian should also be noted. Though taking place in a nineteenth century Ruritania, *The Son of Monte Cristo* (UA, 1940) attacks an alliance between a Germanic cabal in the country and Russia (read: the Nazi-Soviet Pact).

Ski Patrol, a war drama produced by Universal and released in May 1940, is unique, for it is the only fictional American film to portray the Russo-Finnish War (Nov. 1939–Mar. 1940). The film begins at the 1936 Berlin Olympics, depicting the competition for the ski marathon. Following the award ceremonies stressing international peace, a map montage traces the international events that culminated in the outbreak of the Second World War. Olympic skier Viktor Ryder (Phillip Dorn) is celebrating his sister's wedding at his home village when Soviet aircraft begin the invasion of Finland with a bombing raid. Viktor's sister is killed. Viktor and his fellow townsmen are mobilized and sent to the front. They are joined by two other former Olympic skiers, an American and a Pole. This is the earliest pre–1942 film to show an American volunteer participating in European combat.

Comrade X was released by MGM during the Christmas season of 1940, while the Soviet Union was still aligned with Nazi Germany. Although it bears some similarities to MGM's classic work from the previous year, *Ninotchka*, directed by Ernst Lubitsch, *Comrade X* is less sophisticated in its comic material and places a greater emphasis on current events (particularly Nazi-Soviet relations).

The tone of this political satire is immediately set by the opening scene at the International Press conference room in the Kremlin. The new head of the secret police (his predecessor was the "victim" of an untimely "traffic accident") has just announced that due to the "false stories and photos of forbidden places" that have recently been smuggled out of Russia by Comrade X, there will be further restrictions placed upon the foreign press corps. The pompous German correspondent, Emil von Hofer (Sig Rumann), boasts to his colleagues that he has no objections to the new policy. American newspaper woman Jane Wilson, played by Eve Arden, immediately retorts: "A German journalist is not in the position to complain about the absence of truth anywhere."

When McKinley B. Thompson (Clark Gable) returns to Moscow from an extended drinking bout (for information) with a Red Army officer, he discovers his hotel room has been expropriated by von Hofer. The German is rhapsodically dictating to a Russian secretary about the "gallant" Soviet Army. McKinley chases von Hofer out by shooting at imaginary rats in the room. Jane prances in a few seconds later and, when asked by McKinley about the news from the Kremlin, sarcastically states:

[it is] the same old rat trap full of stuffed shirts double crossing the masses.... Some day the people are going to get wise and take it apart brick by brick.

An indignant von Hofer returns with the hotel manager. McKinley retaliates by ad libbing a prophetic story over the phone about Nazi tank divisions smashing into the Ukraine, which inspires the patriotically aroused Russian manager to give the protesting von Hofer the bum's rush.

The remainder of the film addresses McKinley's efforts to get an idealistic communist woman streetcar operator named Theodore (all tram drivers are supposed to be male) out of Russia. Her father, a hotel janitor (played by Felix Brassart), is blackmailing the American because he knows McKinley is Comrade X. The janitor stoically explains that he fears for his daughter's life because true communists once were "very popular," but that now "the communists are being executed in order that communism shall succeed" (a classic one-liner capturing the double think rationales of the Communist Party justifying the Stalinist purges). Under the pretext of wanting her to help spread the word in benighted America, McKinley is able to woo and marry comely Theodore (Hedy Lamarr). But before they can leave the Soviet Union, her former mentor (played by Vladimir Sokoloff) becomes the latest head of the Secret Police (GPU) and decides that all of his disciples should be liquidated.

McKinley, his new bride and her father wind up in a crowded cell in the infamous Lubyanka prison. Some of Theodore's compatriots sing they are free just before being led away to be executed. Fortunately for Theodore, the brash Yank has a compromising photo of the new GPU chief. Hence, the three are able to get out of prison and make a break for freedom. Theodore bemoans the death of her soul. McKinley comforts her by remarking that although "it looks bad with a handful of high pressure guys peddling graveyards up and down every street of Europe," they will find peace in the United States.

After a wild car chase through the streets of Moscow (passing several large portraits of Stalin), the three refugees hop a military train passing through the freight yard. When it stops to unload tanks near the Romanian border, they are able to steal one of the vehicles and head for the Dniester River (Theodore received night school training in tank driving). Since it is the commander's tank, the rest of the armored unit dutifully follows orders over the radio. As the trio cross the border in the lead tank, the Romanians flee from what they believe to be an invasion.

This is not an idle cinematic joke, for early in the film the audience sees McKinley prepare a secret Comrade X report dated June 26, 1940. It is two days later that the crossing into Romania is made. And, in fact, on June 28, 1940, the Soviet Army had occupied the Romanian provinces of Bessarabia and Northern Bukovina in an attempt to strengthen Russia's western defensive position against a possible future clash with an expansionist Nazi Germany.[18]

Anti–Japanese Films

All nine of the motion pictures whose predominant discernible bias is listed in the Filmography as anti–Japanese relate to the Sino-Japanese War. Either all or part of the action of seven of these films takes place in China as well, i.e., *International Settlement* (1938), *Shadows Over Shanghai* (1938), *Too Hot to Handle* (1938), *Disputed Passage* (1939), *North of Shanghai* (1939), *Burma Convoy* (1941), *They Met in Bombay* (1941). Two of these films portray American volunteers actively aiding the cause of the Chinese—as medical volunteers in *Disputed Passage* and as truckers helping to supply China in *Burma Convoy*.

At least sixteen other films listed under other headings make direct references or allude to the Sino-Japanese War. Although none of these motion pictures specifically attack the totalitarian/militaristic regime of Japan or its leaders (unlike the numerous negative film references to Hitler and Mussolini after 1938), they do overtly or implicitly condemn the aggressive policies of the Imperial Japanese government as carried out against China. For instance, two of the films, *Men with Wings* (Paramount, 1938 and *Safari* (Paramount, 1940), refer to American volunteers in China engaging in combat with the Japanese.

They Met in Bombay was released by MGM in the summer of 1941, when relations between the United States and Japan had begun to rapidly deteriorate. The initial reels of this adventure film center around the competing efforts of two con artists, played by Clark Gable and Rosalind Russell, to steal a valuable necklace in Bombay. After double crossing each other they wind up together on the run. On a tramp steamer to Hong Kong they find romance. But, as they enter the harbor of the Crown Colony, the two lovers narrowly escape capture by the police. Unable as yet to unload the hot necklace, they quickly run out of cash. With the aid of obsequious Chinese tailors, Gable's character, Gerald, a former Canadian soldier, sartorially transforms himself into "Captain

Top: *Shadows Over Shanghai* (GN, 1938): A lecherous maverick Soviet agent (Robert Barrat) and his Chinese guerrilla band have captured the heroine (Linda Gray). Bottom: *North of Shanghai* (Columbia, 1939): Two American journalists and their Chinese associate film the Japanese bombing of Shanghai. Pictured: Keye Luke, James Craig, and Betty Furness.

They Met in Bombay (MGM, 1941): Clark Gable, cast as a Canadian impersonating a British officer, battles the Japanese invaders of China. At the time of this film's release, most U.S. troops were still wearing the "doughboy" style helmets.

Huston" of the King's Fusiliers.[19] He proceeds to exploit his military appearance in order to impound the monies of a Chinese firm he knows to be under investigation for swindling the British Army.

It is at this point that Captain Huston is waylaid by the military authorities and taken to the local commander's headquarters as a consequence of a "national emergency." The assembled officers are told: "[the] Japanese have landed on the peninsula ... [and that the British Army] must evacuate our citizens from Kwangtung Province."[20] Huston is assigned to take a detachment to Changlin to bring out "some important Chinese officials who have taken refuge there ... along with the white residents." With the Union Jack waving and the band playing "God Save the King" Gerald reluctantly departs for Changlin with his troops.

The British troops are cheered by the people as they enter the walled city in their lorries. But as they are preparing to leave with the evacuees, two armored cars and several truck-

loads of "Japs" (a rare prewar usage of this pejorative term in a film) pull up in the town square. The Japanese troops are wearing black, German style steel helmets.[21] Their vehicles are conspicuously emblazoned with the Rising Sun battle flag. An obnoxious Japanese officer, Colonel Shig Hashi, gets out of his staff car and tells Captain Huston that he claims the "occupation of this town by Japanese Imperial forces."[22] The colonel ominously adds that since many are spies, no Chinese will be allowed to depart. In response, Gerald orders his troops to form up in the town square and to march forward in front of their lorries. The Japanese troops react by setting up machine guns at the other end of the square. But as the stalwart Tommies advance, the Japanese are ordered to return to their trucks.

As the British drive down the narrow winding road towards Hong Kong, the agitated Japanese officer contacts his field commander by wireless and is given permission to intercept them. Japanese armored cars, supported by machine guns dug into the side of adjacent hills, attack Captain Huston's convoy. A full-fledged battle erupts in which the British are definitely being worsted. That is, until Gerald, with a satchel of grenades, single handedly knocks out four Japanese machine gun nests. This cinematic sequence is unique because it is the only pre–1942 American fictional motion picture to show regular troops of a Western power in direct combat with the Japanese. Within a year of the release of *They Met in Bombay*, American military personnel in Hollywood films would regularly be shown engaging in vicious combat with the Japanese.

11. Stop Hitler Now!
Isolationism Dies in Hollywood After the Fall of France

The Man I Married *(TCF; Aug. 1940):* "In the long run, of course, he won't win—but before he's through Schicky's [Hitler] going to spill an awful lot of blood."

Escape *(MGM; Nov. 1940):* "A World in ruins? Is that what your new savior [Hitler] can bring?"

Foreign Correspondent *(UA; Aug. 1940):* "These kind of people [fascists] are dangerous fanatics ... [They] combine a mad love of country with an equally mad indifference to life."

In a series of prestige films released by Hollywood between August and December of 1940 (after the fall of France, June 1940) a very clear and consistent message was projected before the American public—that complacency, indifference, ignorance to the realities of totalitarianism would no longer be acceptable—that in order to be able to uphold the ideals of American democracy amidst a widening world war, ordinary Americans, on their own initiative, must begin to actively resist or even directly combat the forces of the totalitarian regimes.

Complacent or naive Americans, some of whom even dismiss the dictatorships and their leaders as merely comical aberrations, are forced by world events and political realities directly affecting their lives to confront the inherent evil of the militaristic fascism. Four Hollywood "A" pictures with remarkably similar themes of formerly uncommitted Americans or discouraged premature resisters renewing their active anti-totalitarian stance were released by the major studios during the latter five months of 1940—*Arise, My Love, Escape, Foreign Correspondent*, and *The Man I Married*.

America's Cinematic Wake-Up Call

Each film features an American who is politically naive, cynically indifferent, or reluctant to become involved in world events. But through direct intrusions upon their personal lives they are compelled to confront the evils of the fascist regimes. And once they politically commit themselves, the Americans invariably take an equivocal anti-totalitarian stance—joining hands with future allies in two of the films. Although isolationism is never directly attacked, complacency with regards to the international situation is ultimately condemned (either directly or indirectly). In two of the films, *Arise, My Love* and *Foreign Correspondent*, the American audience is forthrightly addressed at the conclusion and exhorted to prepare to defend the United States against the omnipresent threat of the totalitarian states. In every one of the films Americans morally resist and condemn the totalitarian regimes. In each of the motion pictures Americans actively confront the military and the political police apparatus of the state. Explicit pejorative references to Hitler and/or Nazi Party appear in all four films. There are over ten references to Hitler in *The Man I Married*, at least half of which are negative. At one point in the film a cynical American journalist, played by Lloyd Nolan, calls Propaganda Minister Joseph Goebbels: "Gobble-gobbles."

None of the films contextually explore or analyze ideology. Yet, each film does contain at least one unequivocal condemnation of fascism and the Nazis. In *The Man I Married*, there is a virtual deluge of anti–Nazi vituperation. Released in August, it was the first American film since Warner Brothers' *Confessions of a Nazi Spy* to repeatedly attack the Nazis within its text.

Every one of the leading Americans involved are part of the working middle class. The two American stars in *Arise, My Love* are a female correspondent, who formerly wrote a fashion column, and an American volunteer flyer from Cleveland, who fought the fascists in Spain and who will later fight the Germans over Norway. In *Escape*, an American painter innocently enters 1936 Germany in search of his missing actress mother and winds up playing a cat-and-mouse game with the insidious representatives of the Nazi state in order to save his mother from execution in a concentration camp. A naive writer on interior design travels to 1938 Germany on vacation with her young son and her German-born husband in *The Man I Married*, and is plunged into the nightmare of Nazi fanaticism. *Foreign Correspondent* features a New York crime reporter who casually accepts a European assignment to get a fresh angle on Hitler and "those tough military boys of Europe," only to become involved with Nazi spies and the exposure of a phony world peace organization (a possible isolationist surrogate).

In all four films the American characters, always with the aid of sympathetic foreigners, are portrayed narrowly escaping death or imprisonment as a result of their encounters with the dictatorial regimes. In two of these Hollywood releases, the leading players are attacked by German military units as they attempt to flee Europe across the Atlantic. In both *Foreign Correspondent* and *Arise, My Love*, the characters decide to return to Europe and rededicate themselves to battling the evils of fascism.

By the latter half of 1940, in the increasingly politicized fictional world created by Hollywood, American movie audiences could no longer expect to remain immune from the realities of a world war initiated by aggressive totalitarian states. A closer reading of *Arise, My Love* and *The Man I Married* follows below.

Arise, My Love was released by Paramount in November 1940. It is a romantic adventure yarn that envelopes itself in the war crisis of 1939–1940. But it also is a marvelous reflection of Hollywood's perception of the changing attitudes of Americans towards the threat posed by the Nazi regime. For instance, it contains an oblique attack on the isolationists when the American ex-volunteer flyer for Republican Spain pointedly responds in the negative when asked if he ever met Lindbergh. The motion picture climaxes with an emotional pledge by the leading characters to themselves (and hence to the American movie audience of this box office hit) to help prepare our country to both morally and physically resist fascism.

Arise, My Love begins at a Spanish prison in the summer of 1939, several months after the conclusion of the civil war. The opening title states there are "only a few remaining soldiers ... who volunteered [to fight for the Republicans]."[1] There is an immediate cut to an overhead shot of a man being marched out to a wall, bound and then shot.[2] A brash American pilot named Tom Martin (Ray Milland), with a nervous monk keeping him company, is in a nearby cell awaiting his turn before the firing squad. When asked by the cleric if he has any regrets, Tom retorts he is annoyed that "I wasted my life on palooka preliminaries in Spain."

Tom is summoned to the governor's office and told he has been pardoned as a result of the entreaties of his wife and as a "gesture of friendship to your native land." Tom is somewhat perplexed, for he is a bachelor, but naturally he plays along. As he departs with his cloying "wife," story-hungry Augusta Nash of the Associated News, Tom asks the Spaniards

to take good care of Adolf. Noticing the blank stares he receives, Tom adds: "A rat. I taught him to hold his paw like that [he makes a quick fascist salute]." This is more than a simple anecdote. The mocking of the totalitarian regimes and their leaders was a common ploy in American films beginning in mid–1940 and lasting throughout the war years.

On the eve of the outbreak of the Second World War, after some romantic maneuvering in Paris, Augusta is assigned by her editor to go to Germany as "special Berlin Correspondent." It seems the publishers back home want "intimate personal stuff on Hitler and his gang" (gangster linkage). Tom joins Augusta on the train to Berlin. He plans to continue to Warsaw and fly with the Polish air force as a volunteer. She starts to read Hitler's *Mein Kampf* for homework, but in a classic cinematic slap at the Nazis, quickly begins to yawn and then angrily tosses the book out the window. The many expressions of insouciance towards the Nazis were an effective counterbalance to the harsh rhetoric and pretentious propaganda emanating from their totalitarian state. In the case of *Arise, My Love*, it also sets up the scenario for the portrayal of the lost innocence of the protagonists.

The two lovers get off the train in the forest of Compeigne and thus miss Hitler's invasion of Poland. They join other Americans (including some negative tourist stereotypes) fleeing the troubles of Europe, booking passage on the *S.S. Athenia*. Reunited on the Irish coast after the torpedoing of their ship (associations with the sinking of the *Lusitania* in 1915 and its impact on American intervention in WWI in 1917), Augusta tells Tom: "God knew better. He threw us right back after them."[3] They sadly part to confront the realities of war—Augusta to cover the fall of successive democratic states to invasion (documented in a series of sensational headlines with her byline) and Tom to fight in the war. They do not meet again until the French surrender ceremonies at Compeigne. Tom has received wounds over Norway that prevent him flying further combat missions for the RAF, but Augusta declares: "We're not crawling back [to the U.S.], we're marching back." As the two lovers embrace, she adds:

I want to write stories without somebody holding their hand over my mouth.... And you can still train new pilots.... Whose way of life shall it be—their's or ours?

The Man I Married was produced by 20th Century–Fox and released in August 1940. It features a politically naive native-born American who travels to the Third Reich with her little boy and her German-American husband. Carol Hoffman (Joan Bennett), who had "dreamed" of the old Germany of waltzes, becomes "a model of attitudinal transformation for American isolationists" after witnessing and being subjected to the brutal realities of the new Nazi Germany.[4]

But well before Carol is converted to anti–fascism, the movie audience is subjected to a series of connotative and denotative political messages simultaneously attacking the Nazi

Foreign Correspondent (UA, 1940): An American correspondent (Joel McCrea) broadcasts to the U.S. from a London studio as German bombers fly overhead: "Hang on to your lights, America. They're the only lights still on in the world." Laraine Day provides moral support at center left.

regime and creating a stark dichotomy between a free and peaceful America and a militaristic fascist Germany. For example, Carol is approached by her family doctor to take money to his brother, a famous philosopher, now in a concentration camp (anti–intellectualism; intolerance). After noting she is taking the *Bremen* at pier eighty-six, Carol remarks the British liner *Queen Mary* does not go to Germany. This is a brilliant little political set piece. Two widely publicized incidents had occurred concerning the *Bremen*. In 1935, communist demonstrators had boarded the ship in New York and ripped down the swastika (which had only just become the official flag of Nazi Germany). And in 1939, FDR had attempted to prevent the ship's departure from New York on the day of Hitler's invasion of Poland. "Eighty-six" is a popular term for trashing, or being trashed. And, of course, the implication of the *Queen Mary* is that the British refuse to deal with the Nazis. All of this in the first few minutes of a 1940 film, designated as taking place in the summer of 1938.

Furthermore, immediately after passing the stately and symbol-laden Statue of Liberty in New York harbor, a series of little swastika flags plot the ship's course to Bremershaven. The *Bremen*'s passengers are greeted at the dock by large swastika banners, Blackshirts in military formation, a band loudly playing the German national anthem and numerous "Heil Hitler" salutes.

Carol's values and self-esteem as a modern woman are almost immediately challenged upon setting foot on German soil by a humorless blonde female Nazi fanatic named Freda Heinkel, nee Sturm (Anna Sten). The two surnames connote militarism, violence and Nazi anti–Semitism. Heinkel was the name of one of the major manufacturers of German warplanes and "Sturm," which means storm in German, was also linked to the name of the Nazi Party's virulently anti–Semitic newspaper, *Der Sturmer*.

Carol, at first, is simply bored with the incessant Nazi rhetoric. During a Goebbels radio broadcast, which includes

The Man I Married (TCF, 1940): Joan Bennett, playing an American married to a German citizen, finds herself in trouble with the Gestapo after she attempts to hide an escaped political prisoner.

an anti-communist harangue (in German), Carol turns on a music box. During a display of military parachutists at a stadium, Carol compares their activities with a circus show. These are dangerous attitudes to display, even frivolously, around the ever-present Freda. Anyone who questions or disparages the Party line is immediately called a traitor by Freda (with ominous implications in a police state).

Although she is addressed as "Frau," the audience is never introduced to Freda's husband. Proclaiming that makeup does not befit the new German woman and wearing plain dresses, it is made to appear that Freda is married to the Nazi Party. And, in a form of ideological bigamy, she will later seduce Carol's husband into bed and into joining the Nazi Party. Carol responds to a growing awareness of the sexual/political challenge of Freda with the typical American antidote of humor, in the form of a ditty:

There once was a Nordic named Freda—Always quoting the words

of the leader—She wasn't born, people say, in the usual way—*Der Fuehrer* simply decreed her.

Carol is revolted after witnessing Nazis brutally forcing dispossessed Czechs to clean the streets of Berlin. Or to quote the sympathetic, but jaded, American journalist named Delane who opened her eyes to the Nazi abuses: "A Brownshirt *Blitzkrieg* against old people and kids." The journalist, who frequently disparages Hitler by calling him "Shicky," is amazed at Carol's (read isolationist's) political innocence: "My lady of the ivory tower.... Don't you read papers?" But she is only fully converted to anti–fascism after watching her husband at a Party rally performing like a "mechanical doll" for Hitler, the "master magician."

Carol swears she will crawl back, if necessary, to the United States with her son Ricky, when her husband demands the little boy be raised as a loyal Nazi in Germany. Ricky, however, would rather be the Lone Ranger than a future Party leader. But their escape from the Heiling Heel is only made possible when her father-in-law reveals his son is half–Jewish!

The audience is left to contemplate the fate of the half–Jew former Nazi as Carol and her son bid farewell to the journalist, promising to consume some hamburgers and chocolate sodas in his honor back in the good old USA. Delane will stay behind in Germany "for the duration," in order to keep his fellow Americans informed about the activities of "the little man with the moustache."

12. Cinematic Cheering for the Sentimental Favorites: Pro–French and Pro–English Films Come to the Front

International Squadron (WB, 1940): "There are more important things now, besides blondes and boogie woogie."

American motion pictures positively presenting the Western Allies—France and Britain—total fifty films between 1937 and 1941. Additionally, twenty-four Hollywood productions are classified in the Filmography as pro-interventionist—all of which favorably portray supplying or aiding the Allies (including China) against the Axis powers.

Pro–French Films

A mere seven Hollywood films were produced displaying a distinct pro–French bias. *The Road to Glory* (a 1939 re-release of a 1936 film by TCF) and *Pack Up Your Troubles* (TCF, 1939) were both released after the Nazi invasion of Poland, but take place during the First World War. The former is strongly pacifistic, while the latter stars the Ritz Brothers as crazy Doughboys who go behind German lines to rescue a French spy (the father of their favorite French girl).

Chasing Danger (TCF, 1939) and *Drums of the Desert* (Monogram, 1940) take place in France's North African colonies. The latter, released after France's defeat in 1940, uses the French Foreign Legion in an apparent attempt to avoid mentioning the collaborationist Vichy regime. In fact, the Vichy government is never specifically mentioned in a pre–1942 American film. However, there is a possible allusion to Vichy via a mysterious character named Henri Jerome, involved in espionage in the late 1940 Columbia release *Phantom Submarine* (classified Anti-Espionage in the Filmography).

The House Across the Bay (UA, 1940), a gangster film released before the Nazi spring offensive in the west, could be construed as making a pro–French gesture by showing Americans promoting warplane sales to French military officials.

Although the number of films specifically classified as Pro–French is limited, there are numerous references (70) to the French, the majority of which are positive, in American motion pictures from the period. These are listed under other headings (such as references to the French in a Pro-Intervention film—refer to Filmography). Two exceptions to this positive French portrayal would be the mixed messages presented in both *The Life of Emile Zola* (WB, 1937) and *A Trip to Paris* (TCF, 1938). For example, *The Life of Emile Zola* negatively portrays fascistic elements within the French Army. *In a Trip to Paris* the Jones family have their vacation in Paris rudely interrupted when they inadvertently become involved with "one of the most dangerous spy cliques in Europe," interested in France's massive defensive fortifications along her northern border with Germany, known as the Maginot Line.

Among the sixteen films referring to the French in 1939 are *Mr. Moto's Last Warning* (TCF) and *Disputed Passage* (Paramount). The former was released early in the year and focuses on the threat to international peace posed by foreign agents attempting to mine the Suez Canal on the eve of major joint maneuvers of the French and British fleets. The latter, released in the fall, includes scenes at a French-staffed hospital in China aiding victims of Japanese aggression.

Two American films contain scenes of French people preparing for possible war. *Charlie Chan in City in Darkness* (TCF, 1939) somewhat comically portrays a Frenchman's frenetic reactions to the diplomatic fluctuations surrounding the Munich Crisis. But, in *Arise, My Love* (Paramount, 1940), there is a poignant scene of a middle-aged French couple, who own an inn in the forest of Compeigne, reacting to the husband's mobilization after the Nazi invasion of Poland. Memories of the horrors associated with the First World War in which the husband was maimed are sadly evoked by the wife (Claudette Colbert) to a visiting American foreign correspondent. Later in the same film, the correspondent returns to the inn (now guarded by armed German soldiers) to cover the formal French surrender to Germany at Compeigne. When she asks the innkeeper's wife about her husband's fate, she learns that he was with the French Army defeated at Sedan.

Pack Up Your Troubles (TCF, 1939): The 3 Ritz Brothers double-talk some Germans into surrendering in this WWI-era comedy, made before the Nazi invasion of Poland (Sept. 1939) but released in October of that year, when it was becoming increasingly difficult to laugh at the German Army.

The fall of France was a traumatic event for many Americans, starkly revealing the potentially threatening implications of continued Nazi successes. Aside from the reference to France's defeat in *Arise, My Love*, at least seven other films, all released in 1941, make direct or indirect references to that event: *Affectionately Yours* (WB), *Flight Command* (MGM), *International Squadron* (WB), *Lady Be Good* (MGM), *Scotland Yard* (TCF), *Skylark* (Paramount), *A Yank in the RAF* (TCF). In the first film, an American correspondent, just back from Europe, bitterly comments that he was "in France that sad day they forgot to blow up the bridges." This not only refers to the Nazi destruction of the Allied armies in France, but implies that the activities of fifth columnists may have contributed to their defeat in the spring of 1940.

Three of these films specifically mention the evacuation of French and British troops from Dunkirk. And in *A Yank in the RAF*, an American flyer is actually shown battling the *Luftwaffe* over the skies of Dunkirk. *International Squadron* is the only pre–1942 American film release to allude to the Free French forces. One of the multinational squadron's pilots is French, and his girlfriend, whose school teacher father has been imprisoned by the Nazis in France, is a driver for the RAF's womens' auxiliary.

Pro–British Films

Unlike the relatively few overtly pro–French works from Hollywood, films about Britain and world events appeared in substantial numbers (45) from American studios throughout the 1937 to 1941 period. In fact, films promoting the glorious traditions of Britain and its empire had regularly been produced by American studios throughout the 1930s. A few of the more prominent examples before 1937 would include:

International Squadron (WB, 1941): Between combat missions, an American volunteer pilot for the RAF (Ronald Reagan) flirts with a French compatriot's girlfriend.

Clive of India (Fox, 1934), *Lives of a Bengal Lancer* (Paramount, 1935), *The Charge of the Light Brigade* (WB, 1936), *White Angel* (WB, 1936). Significant portions of the last two films deal with Britain's 19th century struggle with Russia in the Crimea. The cultural ties between the United States and Britain, along with the large number of British actors in Hollywood, made films containing pro–British messages quite popular.

Between 1937 and 1939 eighteen films containing a pro–British bias were released by Hollywood. Unlike many of the pre–1937 releases, a majority (11) of these motion pictures take place in a contemporary setting. In addition to those pro–British films that address espionage, at least two portray British citizens resisting fascism. In *Love Under Fire* (TCF, 1937) a British sea captain defies Spanish Nationalists (their political allegiance is implied, but not specifically identified) who stop and search his ship on the high seas. And in *The Sun Never Sets* (Universal, 1939), British colonial officers suppress

an arms dealer using a secret radio base in an African colony to broadcast inflammatory speeches threatening world peace.

Three films released from mid–1938 through mid–1939 (two classified Pro–British; one Pro–intervention) indicate that Britain is consciously preparing for a possible European war and that she looks to the U.S. for aid and moral support. In *Lord Jeff* (MGM, 1938), British merchant marine cadets are taught to bear in mind that their country can survive less than two months if her sea lines are cut. In *Thanks for Everything*, a bizarre 20th Century–Fox production released in December 1938 (classified Pro-Intervention), a couple of eccentric pollsters (played by Adolphe Menjou and Jack Oakie) are approached by the "Ambassador" of an unnamed country to determine whether, with regard to the recent war scare (read Munich Crisis), the average U.S. citizen would support his nation in a European conflict. When asked why this is important, the Ambassador states: "Our two countries are natural allies. Such information would be invaluable to us in our

A Yank in the RAF (TCF, 1941): Hollywood recreates the evacuation of Dunkirk and turns it into an icon of British resistance to the Nazis.

diplomatic relations with certain other countries." Finally, in a spring 1939 comedy release, entitled *I'm from Missouri* (Paramount), an American representing his state's mule breeders visits England in order to promote sales of the animals to the rapidly expanding British Army.

Eleven films displaying a pro–British bias were produced by American studios during 1940. About half of the films were released before and half after the defeat of France. Of the five films released through June of 1940 only one portrays actual combat between the British and Germans, *Women in War* (Republic). None of the five have American characters participating in the war effort. However, this began to radically change by August of 1940. And by the end of the year two pro–British films, *The Long Voyage Home* (UA) and *Escape to Glory* (Columbia), contained scenes in which Americans and Englishmen face death together while under attack by German armed forces. In *Escape to Glory*, American citizens actively contribute to the defense of a British freighter being

stalked by a U-Boat. One of the American passengers, a gangland murderer wanted by the authorities in the United States, morally redeems himself by leading a suicidal mission to destroy the German submarine.

Two additional motion pictures from 1940, classified as Pro-Intervention, should also be mentioned. Both *Arise, My Love* and *Foreign Correspondent* (UA) depict Americans covering the war in Europe. In the former, the male co-star (Ray Milland; born in Britain), is an American pilot who fought in Spain against the fascists and goes on to join the RAF in the struggle against Nazi Germany: "These English flyers know their stuff." The American pilot is later wounded while fighting the *Luftwaffe* over Norway. He pledges to return to the States and help train thousands of new pilots.

Surprisingly, one anti–British film (in fact, the only film with an anti–British bias released in America between 1937 and 1941), *Captain Caution*, appeared in the fall of 1940 (at the lowest point in British fortunes during the war). It takes

Women in War (Republic, 1940): On the streets of London, the war intrudes on a night on the town. Wendy Barrie (second from left) will soon trade her evening gown for a nurse's uniform. The German "pocket" battleship *Graf Spee* was scuttled off Uruguay in December 1939 after a sea battle with the British Royal Navy.

place during the Napoleonic era and condemns English violations of neutral American shipping. Britain, struggling alone against Nazi Germany in the latter months of 1940, had, on occasion in the past, infringed upon the neutral rights of non-belligerents.[1]

A veritable explosion of motion pictures was produced by Hollywood during 1941 supporting Britain's struggle against Nazi Germany. Thirty-five American films contain references to the British and to British military forces. Twenty-nine films have been classified as Pro–British and Pro–Intervention. Eight of these motion pictures are coded as promoting U.S.-British Cooperation. Two of these films, *International Lady* (UA) and *Man at Large* (TCF), portray English and American agents cooperating in the United States to overcome Axis spies and saboteurs attempting to disrupt American aid to Britain. Four other films (listed under both headings), *Confirm or Deny* (TCF), *International Squadron* (WB), *One Night in Lisbon* (Paramount) and *A Yank in the RAF* (TCF),

present Americans working alongside the English. In a war-related right of passage, all four American leads are shown experiencing the London Blitz.

By October 1941 the United States, as far as Hollywood was concerned, was fully behind the British war effort. Three American feature films released that month cinematically epitomize this commitment: *International Squadron*, *Sundown* (UA), *A Yank in the RAF*. The latter two best illustrate this assertion and will be discussed in more detail below.

A Yank in the RAF, along with *International Squadron*, was one of the first Hollywood productions to be released prior to 1942 portraying not only an American in an organized combat unit fighting regular German military forces, but also showing that the American feels morally justified in killing his Nazi enemies. The key point is that these American-made films glorify fellow citizens who are killing and being killed while engaged in combat with the military forces of countries that are *not* formally at war with the United States.

Confirm or Deny (TCF, 1941): Roddy McDowall plays a young Londoner who can take it during the Blitz. A traditional British cup of tea helps him cope with Hitler and the *Luftwaffe*'s depredations.

A Yank in the RAF was a vehemently pro-interventionist motion picture. It opens with an off screen narrator describing how the United States circumvented the provisions in its own Neutrality Act designed to prohibit direct delivery of planes to belligerents (the "Cash and Carry" provision). While the narrator is speaking, the film audience watches AT-6 military training planes being flown to the Canadian border and then taxied to the international line: "Democratic ingenuity and a stout rope did the rest [the planes are shown being towed across the border]." A brash Yank named Tim Baker (Tyrone Power), to the chagrin of a dour Canadian military official, flies his aircraft over the border and lands in Canada. The Canadian officer suggests that if Baker is so anxious to get nearer the action he can make good money ferrying bombers across the Atlantic to Britain. It is sarcastically added in a revealing aside: "Of course we wouldn't want you to go by the way of Berlin ... Although we expect you'll be 'over there' soon enough."

In wartime London Tim meets his old flame, Carol Brown, played by the soon-to-be number one G.I. pinup girl, Betty Grable. She performs at a popular nightclub, but during the day is a Volunteer Nurse's Aide. To convince Carol he is committed to the cause, Tim impetuously joins the RAF. But he is assigned to bomber command rather than to a fighter unit. Worse yet for Tim's pride, on his first mission over Germany the British drop leaflets instead of bombs. Observing German anti-aircraft shell bursts, Tim tells a British crew mate: "They're serious, even if we're not."

Soon after the Germans have launched their long-anticipated spring 1940 offensive, Baker's crew is sent against a target in Germany, and this time their American-built twin-engined Lockheed Hudson is loaded with bombs. An emphasis has been placed on the major ground action taking place in Belgium (an attempt to rekindle the sympathy generated for "little Belgium" in the First World War?). Amid heavy night action in the flak-filled skies over Germany, the RAF

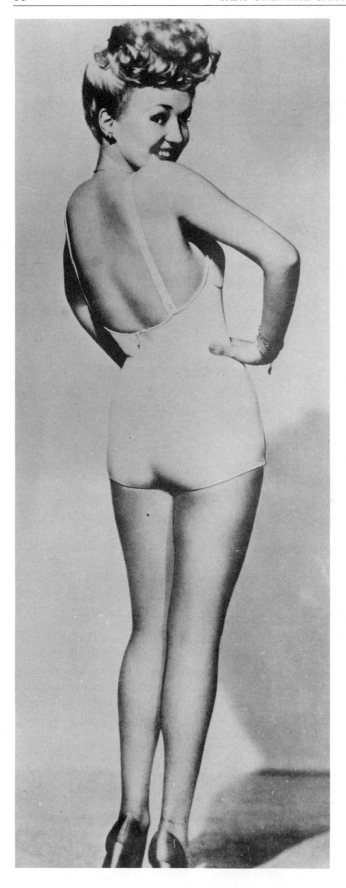

Betty Grable: one of the most famous pinup shots of the war. But even before this, she was a popular star in films like *A Yank in the RAF* (1941).

professionally carries out its duties. Tim's closest British friend, Roger (Reginald Gardiner), the pilot of another plane, suicidally dives his crippled craft into the targeted marshalling yards below. Tim and his crew are able to crash land their damaged bomber on the Dutch coast, which they believe is neutral territory (to further emphasize the Nazi disrespect of international law). However, as the crew enters a nearby farmhouse, they encounter a German Army patrol. One of Baker's crew is killed during the ensuing struggle. Corporal Harry Baker's sacrifice (the same surname is obviously used to underscore the ethnic links between Americans and the British) enables Tim and a fellow officer to make good their escape to England in a small boat.

With the Western armies collapsing in France, the British begin evacuating their surviving troops from Dunkirk (May 1940).[2] A desperate struggle for tactical air superiority rages and new fighter pilots are needed to make up for the high attrition rate. Tim is assigned to a fighter squadron as a replacement and is soon scrambling in one of the famous British Spitfires (an icon symbolizing Britain's ability and will to resist Hitler's Germany). It is at this point in *A Yank in the RAF* that a considerable amount of actual combat footage is inserted and used in rear screen shots. One may also briefly wonder when flying officer Baker received the training required to fly Britain's hottest fighter. In the plane-filled skies over Dunkirk, RAF pilot Baker almost maniacally pursues the enemy. Flaming German aircraft plunge towards the earth in prodigious numbers. Between deadly bursts of machine gun fire, Tim proclaims: "That's for Roger ... That's for the Corporal ... This one's just for me." As Tim makes his third and final kill, there is a cut to the opposing *Luftwaffe* pilot's incredulous stare, blood dripping from his lips. This relatively graphic depiction of violence was rare in American films at the time. It may therefore be interpreted as another example of the hardening of American attitudes against the Nazis.

The final combat scene of *International Squadron* is remarkably similar to the one described in *A Yank in the RAF*. However, in this film the cocky American pilot's selfishness has contributed to the death of a compatriot and he must therefore redeem himself. After boasting he will return with "Schicklegruber's mustache," Jimmy Grant (Ronald Reagan) makes a suicidal bombing run on a German munitions dump. As he methodically drops his bombs, Jimmy calmly states: "This one's for Frenchy ... This one's for you and me, Charlie ... Guess that one's just for me...."

Sundown (UA) is one of fifteen American films produced during 1941 whose predominant discernible bias was Pro-British. This is an engaging motion picture that manages to link British and Commonwealth administrators and military officers in cooperation, colonial black Askari troops, Arabs, a developed Italian character and an unspecified Nazi agent posing as a Dutch mineralogist. In addition, there is a beautiful half-breed native woman, whose presence raises touchy questions concerning racial prejudice.

Sundown takes place at a remote outpost named Manieka near the Ethiopian border in British East Africa (Kenya) following Britain's successful ouster of the Italian Army occupying Ethiopia during the spring of 1941.[3] But there are new fears of a native revolt inspired by the introduction of outside arms to the hostile Sensi tribe. A British military officer arrives by plane with troops and munitions to help secure his country's colonial presence.

The pith-helmeted stereotype, major Coombes (George Sanders) is amazed to find an Italian POW walking about freely at the station. Captain Pallini is equally indignant when challenged: "I do not believe in fighting ... I am an artist ... to cook is my pleasure." Pallini demands and receives a full military escort to the lockup.[4]

At this point Jon Kuypens, a "Hollander" who claims to have worked for the Italian government in Abyssinia, arrives. He is welcomed as a member of the Allies. Somewhat later, a supply caravan is fired upon and an Askari sergeant is killed. A captured rifle displays the markings of the Skoda arms plant of Czechoslovakia (a Nazi satellite). The British are disturbed by the implications. Pallini, a former political science teacher, enters the conversation by way of delivering a short "geopolitical" lecture:

If there is danger herre—crush it ... two-thirds of the world is water ... If you lose Africa, you lose the war ... They [the Nazis] came down from Norway ... along the coast ... By land they capture bases. Never by sea—they travel by land.

That evening a birthday party for Pallini is held that also touches on critical issues facing the defense of the British Empire during the war. Separate tables have been placed for the Europeans and for the non-whites, including the half-breed native woman, Zia (Gene Tierney). The local colonial officer, Crawford, a Canadian played by Bruce Cabot (an American surrogate), believes there should be no discrimination in the "bush." Crawford, whose father was killed at Verdun, adds: "The England that's going to win this war will do away with a lot of that nonsense." After a sniper incident, Pallini learns that Kuypens is plotting with the Sensi leader, Hamud. The Italian is found dead in a nearby sand dune the next morning (an Italian is also murdered by his German cohorts in TCF's *Man at Large*).

Kuypens sneaks away to help prepare the Arab revolt. He has a desert armory in a cave and is in radio contact with Germanic types in Yemen.[5] But the British arrive with the Union Jack flying, and with their brave Askari troops, proceed to defeat the presumably German-armed Arabs. Tear gas is used in the final assault on the rebel stronghold (the only known instance of a gas attack being conducted in an American-produced WWII combat scene between 1939 and 1945). Major Coombes kills Kuypens, but is mortally wounded himself. A dying Coombes tells Crawford that the church and the army are the bases of civilization: "The church holds it together; the Army defends it."

The final scene of *Sundown* takes place in a bomb-damaged London church. There are many wounded military personnel in the pews. Coombes' father, a bishop, presides at a memorial service for his son. Paraphrasing a final message from his son, the bishop patriotically concludes: "Fly high your flag upon the hill ... Keep bright your faith ... Until our England wins ... Who waits with faith, waits with victory."[6] For Hollywood, *only* a British victory would be acceptable.

13. Hollywood's Selectees on the March

> Buck Privates *(Universal): "[the Army is] excellently equipped to make a man out of a play-boy."*
>
> You're in the Army Now *(WB): "Only my feet know the sacrifices I'm makin' for my country."*

The single most important war-related event directly affecting a significant number of Americans prior to the United States becoming an active belligerent in World War II was the institution of peacetime conscription in October 1940. The Selective Service and Training Act authorizing a one year call-up of 900,000 men was enacted by the U.S. Congress on August 27, following a heated series of debates. Over sixteen million men had registered for the draft by the end of the year.

More than a million and a half men would actually be in the U.S. Army by December 7, 1941.[1]

Hollywood Films Addressing the Conscription

Over 125 feature films released by Hollywood between September 1939 and the end of 1941 refer to the various military services of the United States. Over thirty-five of these motion pictures, all released in 1941, are related in some way to the draft. Of these, the plots of ten center around men being drafted into the army or joining up and then attending training camp with draftees (most are identified under the "Training" genre heading in the Filmography).

One would think that the motion picture industry of a country preparing for war would clearly identify the potential enemy or military adversaries in its productions. However, in the American films dealing with the training of "Selectees" (as in Selective Service; being selected to serve your country) for military duty in the Uncle Sam's Army, this is decidedly not the case. With the single exception of the December Warners release, *You're in the Army Now*, where the Jimmy Durante character facetiously asks for a rifle to go after Hitler, the foes America's servicemen might encounter on future battlefields are never specified. For that matter, although several of the films conclude with maneuvers, or so-called "mock battles," the war in Europe is never discussed and the word "war" is seldom spoken. In addition, tactical and defensive operations are stressed in these Hollywood staged maneuvers as opposed to grand strategic and offensive operations (the implication being that our drafted boys are not being trained to be sent overseas to fight). A possible military encounter with Nazi Germany is indirectly addressed through the Warners biographical film, *Sergeant York*, portraying American soldiers in combat with the Germans during World War I. But in the draft-related films, there is never even an allusion to a possible threat emanating from either Italy or Japan.

In the training camps created by Hollywood, the men conscripted into military service in 1941 are less of a regional or ethnic cross-section than is generally expected in the casts of such films—particularly in light of the pre-existing formula for service training and combat films, i.e., *The Fighting 69th* (WB; 1940), *Parachute Battalion* (RKO; 1941) and *I Wanted Wings* (Paramount; 1941). The Jewish subway operator and the Tennessee farmboy in the World War I-era *Sergeant York* are a few of the rare exceptions depicted in 1941 draft-related feature films.

Hollywood's selectees of 1941 are overwhelmingly white urbanites from a non-specific ethnic background. American blacks do appear in a guardhouse musical scene (only) with Fred Astaire in Columbia's *You'll Never Get Rich*, but German-Americans and Italian-Americans are conspicuously absent from the ranks. Though Charlie Chan's son happily receives his draft notice at the end of series mystery *Charlie Chan in Rio* (TCF), the Chinese-American youth is not shown sharing a barracks with his white compatriots nor is he depicted in uniform. Perhaps as a reflection of the hard times of the Depression, several of the films do portray the leveling of members of the upper class through mixing with the working classes during basic training. This scenario is a major subplot in at least two draft films, *Great Guns* (TCF) and *Buck Pri-*

vates (Universal). Everyone has his place in America's non-elitest, democratic peoples' conscript army, even if it is to collect the garbage, like Laurel and Hardy wind up doing at the conclusion of *Great Guns*.

As in many of the military academy films and popular college campus films of the day, people from different socio-economic backgrounds are thrown together in several of the films topically related to peacetime conscription. *Great Guns* and *Buck Privates* both include boys from wealthy families who are democratized by their shared experiences in the ranks beside America's common men (frequently played by such well-known comedians as Abbott and Costello and Laurel and Hardy) and women. The middle class girlfriend of the rich guy (Lee Bowman) in *Buck Privates* admonishes his snobbery and proudly asserts that army life is a "great leveler." Making the grade, becoming part of the All-American team, is presented as a primary objective of military service for Uncle Sam.

The 1941 American draft films mimic their campus film counterparts in many ways.[2] The shared experience of a diverse group of young people in the camps is reminiscent of the college campus. Interestingly, although several campus films released in 1941 allude to military service, such as in the "It Makes No Difference When You're in the Army" song and dance finale from *Zis Boom Bah* (Monogram), only *Let's Go Collegiate* (Monogram) makes a direct reference to a man being drafted out of a university.

The atmosphere in the barracks (even when they are tents) resembles college dorms. The sergeants, appearing as rather thick-headed but good-natured house masters, attempt to impart the basics of military science/discipline. While the officers assume the roles of avuncular deans who arbitrate petty squabbles between the NCOs and the selectees and, when necessary, compassionately administer discipline to some of the more unruly boys. Many of the selectees' offenses are directly related to their attempts to win the girl. The daughter of the base commander is the primary romantic object in *Caught in the Draft*.

When the week of drills and classes is through, clean shaven college-like boys in well-pressed khaki head for the non-alcoholic recreation hall staffed by wholesome young coed hostesses (such as the Andrews Sisters in *Buck Privates*) or into town to meet the pretty local girls. The reality of tent encampments and of the hastily built wooden barracks with tarpaper roofs, often located in barren backwoods areas, has been largely ignored. The draft experience has become post–Depression graduate school for the New Deal masses.

The seamier side of America's rapid mobilization for "National Defense" is candidly addressed in only one low-budget independent film, *No Greater Sin* (University Film Prods.). Although this fall release does not specifically deal with the draft—its plot centers on a defense worker who contracts a social disease—it does address the problems the military faces with regard to criminal elements that establish themselves near military bases.

You're in the Army Now (WB, 1941): Sergeant Joe Sawyer cannot believe his new recruit, Jimmy Durante in drag, who sings "I'm Glad My Number Was Called." One of a number of comedy films about life in the Army for new soldiers (draftees and enlistees).

Although petty military rules are meant to be bent and humorless career sergeants are usually stereotyped as comic foils/straight men to the wise-cracking Joe American draftees, the U.S. Army and its officers, per se, are never attacked nor is their authority directly challenged in the motion pictures released by Hollywood. Instead, somewhat paradoxically, the power of the officer corps is deemphasized while its prestige is upheld. That is, officers do not in any way oppress the men or possess disproportionate privileges to those allowed their men. In *Sergeant York*, Tennessean Alvin York is gently turned from his pacifism, based on a literal interpretation of the Bible, and is *persuaded* by his commanding officer to see the patriotic light.

Deference, but not blind obeisance, is paid to rank. When the male leads in *Caught in the Draft* (Paramount) and *You'll Never Get Rich* are discovered impersonating officers to impress their girls, they are only mildly punished. And the draftee in *Tanks a Million* is actually congratulated by the base commander for delivering a highly praised speech in

his name that was broadcast nationwide to America's new enlisted men.

Some selectees, such as the playboy in *Buck Privates*, after proving their democratic worthiness, are even offered a chance to attend OCS (Officers' Candidate School).

The concept of serving one's country was glamorized on America's movie screens. In at least two motion pictures, *Buck Privates* and *You'll Never Get Rich*, the future soldiers engage in elaborate musical maneuvers on stage before they go into the field on military maneuvers. Our boys would rather be dancing than marching—or by extension, goosestepping. Both films feature the new inductees marching to the train station with musical accompaniment: the ubiquitous "You're in the Army Now" in the former and "I'm Shooting the Works for Uncle Sam" in the latter (sung by a phalanx of comely chorus girls). While traveling on the train to Camp Greely in *Buck Privates*, "Camp Hostess" girls, played by the Andrews Sisters, serenade the happy recruits with the patriotic "You're a Lucky Fellow Mr. Smith."

You'll Never Get Rich (Columbia, 1941): In the days before Pearl Harbor, the armed forces could be a pretty glamorous place to be. Private Fred Astaire dances his way to the altar with Rita Hayworth.

Having that Liberty gal carrying the torch for you ...
You can't know how much you rate—
thank all forty-eight ...
A family tree—
Washington, Jefferson and Lee ...
You've got the American way,
and that ain't hay...

You'll Never Get Rich concludes with Fred Astaire and Rita Hayworth dancing together atop a huge stage prop wedding-cake tank—a classic American cinematic antithesis to the Nazi icon of the Panzer spearheaded blitzkrieg. Reflecting the actual critical dearth of modern equipment available for the nation's new citizen soldiers, mechanized combat hardware is rarely displayed in the 1941 draft films (usually only in brief newsreel shots). Despite its title, no tanks are operated in the United Artists featurette, *Tanks a Million*. And the main use found for the tank Jimmy Durante commandeers in *You're in*

the *Army Now* is as a motorized prop in a hilarious scene involving the unscheduled relocation of the house of the colonel who commands the base.

Since most of these motion pictures dealing with conscription were presented in the comedy or musical comedy format, conflict/combat becomes sublimated into a series of games, and is largely personalized. It is a game to see whether or not one is drafted (*Caught in the Draft*); whether or not one can outsmart the dimwitted career sergeant (*Tanks a Million*); whether or not one can drill properly (*Buck Privates*). The experience of being a selectee is made to resemble a pleasant diversion, like a summer camping trip, with KP or guard duty as the most onerous possible assignment. But even KP was not as bad as it might appear to the audience of today. After a decade-long depression, the reality was that many drafted men were receiving, for the first time in their recent memory, three square meals a day.[3]

Great Guns (TCF, 1941): It's "another fine mess" for new recruits Laurel and Hardy, this time being read the riot act by their sergeant.

Unlike the American experience in the 1916–1917 period when a number of motion pictures were released portraying resistance to the draft (particularly by socialists)—such as the 1917 feature *Draft 258* (Metro)—there is not a single draft-related film released by Hollywood in 1941, which takes place in a contemporary setting, that attacks conscription or portrays individuals proselytizing others to actively resist the draft.[4] The eponymous World War I hero of *Sergeant York* does apply for "conscientious objector" status, but passively complies with the draft board's rejection of his petition, overcomes lingering doubts about the morality of war while in training camp, and later fights valiantly in France, killing and capturing scores of Germans in the process.

Mothers do encourage or acquiesce in their sons acquiring, or attempting to acquire, draft exemptions in at least two films, *Great Guns* and *Three Sons O' Guns* (WB). Interestingly, a Dr. Schickle (as in Schicklegruber—Hitler?) treats the young son of a rich lady for assorted supposed allergies in *Great Guns*. A significant portion of *Three Sons O' Guns* is devoted to a

mother's wayward brood attempting to obtain draft deferments. But when these machinations are exposed before the draft board by their patriotic aunt (Marjorie Rambeau), the three sons accept their obligation to serve. A year later they have become responsible citizen soldiers, all three electing to re-enlist.

All direct attempts at avoiding (as opposed to resisting) the draft are presented in a comedic format and ultimately fail. An acquaintance of the hero in *Tanks a Million* tells a girlfriend that the hero was a "sucker" for not keeping out of the draft and boasts that he fooled the doctor when he appeared for his army physical. Yet, without further explanation, this same man is shown in the next scene of *Tanks a Million* getting off the train at an army camp with the hero. A hilarious cinematic portrayal of someone trying to avoid military service occurs in *Caught in the Draft*, when the zany character played by Bob Hope tries to give himself flat feet (valid for a medical deferment) by repeatedly jumping off a baby grand piano without his shoes.

Three Sons O' Guns (WB, 1941): Uncle Sam's training camps have turned out responsible young men that their women can proudly march beside: Wayne Morris, William Orr, and Tom Brown (left to right) in the uniforms of the newly conscripted U.S. Army. Marjorie Rambeau, center.

An amusing anomaly related to draft avoidance takes place in a scene near the conclusion of *Swing It Soldier.* An obviously overweight man (played by radio personality Don Wilson) is falsely arrested by MPs, who are actually Army buddies of a romantic/business rival. He is accused of having allegedly ignored the notice to appear for his physical.

Since, in theory, the new draft was universal for all those men between the ages of twenty-one and thirty-one, conscription was presented as an inevitable experience for the nation's young men. One way to positively project this, as well as provide a rational explanation for why popular actors (especially comedians) who were obviously beyond the required registration age were being portrayed as soldier trainees, was to create comical situations whereby the men trick themselves into enlisting.

Hollywood actor Dan Bolton (Bob Hope), attempting to impress the Colonel's daughter (Dorothy Lamour) in *Caught in the Draft,* enlists by mistake with a real recruiting

officer instead of the phony whom he had earlier hired. In their flight from the police for illegally selling ties in the street, Abbot and Costello join a line into a movie theatre which is being used as an enlistment center. Having been told it costs nothing to enter the theatre and that they pay "$21 a month," Costello readily enters the building and signs up. And when the vacuum cleaner salesman played by Jimmy Durante in *You're in the Army Now* finishes his pitch to a friendly sergeant at an army recruiting office, the man congratulates the "Snozzola:" "I have a new vacuum cleaner and Uncle Sam has a new soldier."

The mere act of receiving one's draft notice in Hollywood films was frequently portrayed as an exhilarating experience or as a welcomed, as well as patriotic, means by which to escape domestic difficulties or some other personal problems. In *The Great Mr. Nobody,* a Warner Brothers release, lead actor Eddie Albert finally feels like somebody important when he opens his letter from the draft board. After excitedly telling his girl she will have to wait a little longer to get married, he runs over to an American flag and proudly salutes it. In *Charlie Chan in Rio*, with an insouciant air of confidence, the Asian sleuth's "number one" son informs his sage father that his presence in the U.S. Army means "the war's in the bag." "Dodo" Doubleday, a young man with a photographic memory who is about to enter military service in *Tanks a Million*, is so conscientious about being prepared that he reads an army training manual even while participating in a radio quiz show. For the young millionaire in *Great Guns*, his draft notice means a welcomed respite from an over-protective mother. And, for the professional dancer played by Fred Astaire in *You'll Never Get Rich*, his invitation to serve Uncle Sam provides him with an excuse to get away from problems with young ladies, exacerbated by his womanizing manager (played by Robert Benchley). Fred so much wants to join the army that he ingeniously overcomes a five pound underweight problem by placing weights in the lining of his hat.

Since the original conscription act mandated a one year enlistment term, subsequent congressional debates to extend the period of enlistment did arouse a considerable amount of public attention, including a degree of vocal resistance from many of the selectees and their families. In fact, the sardonic acronym "OHIO" ("Over the Hill in October") was frequently batted about at the training camps by first year selectees. It referred to their going AWOL when their original one year enlistment term expired in October of 1941. But when the period of enlistment was extended to thirty months in August, no viable opposition or active resistance materialized.[5] Not a single Hollywood film related to the draft explicitly addressed this sensitive topic. However, it would appear that at least one motion picture, *Swing It Soldier* (Universal), approached the topic indirectly. Released in early November, when the original selectees would have begun to be discharged, its story centers around the romantic complications created for a soldier when he is discharged from the army earlier than his tent mate.[6]

By presenting many of the draft-oriented American films in the comedy genre, the otherwise obvious potential lethality of military service in time of war is ameliorated. The comedy milieu also provides a means through which to subliminally deflate the stereotyped pomposity of the unnamed Nazi enemy. Perhaps the many funny routines used in the films to get around the inconveniences of military life by the recent former civilians were a method of displacement for a nation desperately attempting to get around the looming menace of the military might of Nazi Germany: maybe, if we go through the motions of preparing for war, the threat overseas will fade away. The forced entrance of the United States into the world conflict put an end to that chimera. And with America's men actually fighting and dying in the war, films that glamorized and trivialized military service all but disappeared.

14. Non–Feature Length Films Reflecting an Awareness of World Events, 1933–1941

Feature-length fictional films by no means had a monopoly on the theatre screens of 1930s and 1940s America. In fact, a plethora of newsreels, short documentaries, travelogues, studio promotional shorts, trailers, serials, animated cartoons, and fictional short subjects were shown along with the feature films, in virtually every cinema. As early as 1933, important short works revealing a budding awareness of events and people that would later play an important role in the war were beginning to appear on American movie screens.

The problem of current access to these films is even greater than that associated with full-length motion pictures of the period. Many of the short films are lost or inadequately cataloged. Only the perennially popular animated cartoons, particularly those from Warner Brothers, Paramount, and MGM, and the fictional shorts of the more successful comedy teams (such as Laurel and Hardy, and the Three Stooges), are readily available for screening. Recently, some of the *March of Time* newsreels, which regularly featured a blend of actual and "re-created" footage accompanied by blatantly tendentious narration, have become available on commercial videotape, but these are an exception to the rule.

Newsreels

There were a large number of newsreel services, usually issued in weekly, bi-weekly, or monthly "editions," averaging five to ten minutes in length. They were most often episodic and their commentary tended to veer from the incredibly naive or inane to the cynically sensational. Some of the competing companies in the late thirties included *Fox Movietone, International Newsreels, Paramount News* ("The Eyes and Ears of the World"), *Pathé*, and of course *The March of Time*.[1]

Until the last months of 1939, most newsreels spent more time on domestic issues than on foreign ones. An interesting exception to this was *Paramount News'* novel January 1939 summary entitled "1938—A Year of Contrasts." It "takes you into a typical American home and lets you hear Mr. Average

American give his concepts of the year's news." Preceded by the headline highlights of the past year, Mr. Average American tells his son about foreign oppression and European turmoil, contrasting them with American civil liberties as guaranteed by the Constitution and the Bill of Rights. The newsreel ends with footage of FDR reassuring a Canadian audience that the United States would not remain idle should Canada be invaded by a foreign power.[2]

Although all of the newsreels included material on foreign events, only *The March of Time* seems to have consistently emphasized international topics throughout the period. In one of its earliest "editions," *MOT* took a visibly sympathetic stand on the plight of Haile Selassie's efforts to save Ethiopia from a threatened invasion by Italy.[3] Until the fall of France in 1940, most of the other newsreel companies would more often present actual footage accompanied by a reasonably objective presentation of facts. For instance, the commentary of Lowell Thomas in *Fox Movietones*, although often containing witty asides, usually refrained from political editorializing.

Beginning in February 1935, the *March of Time* was issued approximately once a month, each "issue" averaging about 15 minutes in length. The "issues" contained actuality footage, so-called "reconstructions" (sometimes with the co-operation of the actual participants in the original events), and staged sequences; the accompanying commentary was delivered by the uniquely stentorian voice of Westbrook Van Voorhis.

The January 1938 *MOT*, "Nazi Germany—1938," won an Academy Award in 1939. A compilation of real and staged footage, it was pointedly unsympathetic to the Third Reich. The mere presentation of the topic was, furthermore, somewhat ahead of its time. For instance, the Warner Brothers theatre circuit refused to carry this issue of the *March of Time*: despite its obvious anti–Nazi slant, the chain still felt that the newsreel presented an image of the Fuehrer that some people might find admirable.[4] If anything, this controversy only reinforces the concept that the American public was still ambivalent about the world situation.

By 1939, the *March of Time* was appearing in 9,800 theatres and reaching an estimated 25 million people.[5] Between January 1937 and October 1941, nearly two-thirds of the "issues" touched in some way on world events. From mid–1940 onward, material on the war and U.S. national preparedness dominated the *March of Time*. A summer 1940 edition, "Gateway to Panama," emphasized the potential threat to the Canal Zone should the Nazis—who were winning victory after victory in Western Europe—gain control of French, Dutch, and British colonies in the Caribbean.

The titles of the last three issues of 1940 and the first three issues of 1941 illustrate this point further: "Mexico—Good Neighbor's Dilemma" (Vol. 7, No. 3, October 1940), "Arms and the Man—U.S.A." (Vol. 7, No. 4, November 1940),

"Labor and Defense" (Vol. 7, No. 5, December 1940), "Uncle Sam—the Non-belligerent" (Vol. 7, No. 6, January 1941), "Americans All" (Vol. 7, No. 7, February 1941), and "Australia at War" (Vol. 7, No. 8, March 1941).

Later in 1941, the *March of Time* released an issue with an unmistakable bias, in a format that resembled a fictional short rather than a newsreel. "Main Street U.S.A." dramatizes the hypothetical effects of a Nazi victory on the "Average American" in a small town setting.

Documentaries

The major studios and a myriad of independents produced a steady stream of non-fiction films: documentaries, semi-documentaries, travelogues, political films, and so on. The range of topics was virtually limitless; the quality was frequently abysmal. The length of these releases varied from one reel (ten minutes) to nearly two hours.

Although, like newsreels, "documentary" material is tangential to our study, it should be noted that these types of films were the major means of presenting the news *visually* to the public until the 1950s and the advent of television news. Therefore, a brief survey of non-fiction films germane to this study from the 1933–1941 period follows.

Partisan political gestures were more likely to appear in the studios' documentary films than their fictional features. Universal's *The Fighting President* (1933) is a 50-minute pictorial record of the life and achievements of America's new president, released a month after FDR entered office.[6] More startling when seen today is Columbia's feature-length March 1933 release, *Mussolini Speaks*. One of the opening titles of this heavily promoted film states that it is "described and interpreted by Lowell Thomas ... [and] dedicated to a man of the people whose deeds for his people will ever be an inspiration to mankind." After endorsing the "modern Caesar's" reconquest of Italy's Libyan colony and marveling over the aerial bombing of native insurgents, Thomas assures the movie audience that Mussolini "aims to make Italy one of the dominant nations of the world."[7] To quote the equally laudatory review in the *Film Daily*, the film is "an epic of a great modern nation in its fight to assume a leading place among the great powers."[8]

Beginning in the fall of 1934, the U.S. Senate's Nye Committee made headlines by claiming that unscrupulous businessmen had manipulated America's entry into WWI, and might try to do it again. Two independent semi-documentaries with suggestive titles, released late in the year, echo this thesis. *War is a Racket* (Eureka Productions) was based on a muckraking book written by Major General Smedley D. Butler, former commandant of the Marine Corps.[9] *Dealers in Death* (Topical Films), probably influenced by the spring 1934 publication of the book *Merchants of Death*, emphasizes the international collusion between arms manufacturers.[10] The film begins with a film clip of President Roosevelt speaking about the need to halt the arms race.[11] Another documentary from 1934 worth noting is *World in Revolt* (Mentone Productions). Over an hour in length, it concentrates on the dual threats of communism and fascism.[12]

A one-reel film in the Paramount *Varieties* series, "Famous People at Play" makes a prophetic observation. Following scenes of a polo-playing Will Rogers, a young King Peter of Yugoslavia, Germany's aged Kaiser Wilhelm in Dutch exile, and W. C. Fields amusing several young ladies with his acrobatics, the audience is shown Haile Selassie in full imperial regalia, as he inspects polo ponies imported to Ethiopia from Europe. The short was released in early summer 1935; narrator Justin Herman makes a prescient statement:

At the moment Haile Selassie seems to be having a bit of trouble with Mussolini. Those horses of his may end up in the Abyssinian cavalry.

Immediately after this segment, a robust Benito Mussolini is shown riding with his daughter, Eda. The accompanying commentary concludes: "Il Duce works hard and plays hard. He's a real man of iron."

Mussolini's army invaded Ethiopia on 3 October 1935. Later that month, Paramount released a "topical travelogue" entitled *Wings Over Ethiopia*. The *Motion Picture Herald* noted that the film avoided politics, but some of Selassie's best troops (probably the Imperial Guard) are shown.[13]

The resurgence of pacifism engendered by the intensifying world crisis in 1937 led to a number of non-fiction anti-war films. *I Hate War* (1937, released by the Communist-affiliated Kinotrade) took its title from a phrase in a 1936 speech by Franklin D. Roosevelt. It is a 24-minute compilation film containing newsreel footage accompanied by a highly biased narration tracing international upheavals from the First World War through the Spanish Civil War. The fascist dictators, militarism, and "concentration camps" are all specifically condemned. Mussolini, for instance, is stigmatized as a "modern Caesar" (compare this with Lowell Thomas' positive use of the same term in *Mussolini Speaks*) who, by giving his people weapons and teaching them the glories of war, has led them to neglect their own culture and to willfully "crush an ignorant and primitive race in Ethiopia." The film concludes with a paean to FDR's disarmament proposals, presented at the Pan American Conferences in December 1936.[14]

That same year, the classic work directed by Joris Ivens, *Spanish Earth* (Contemporary Historians), was released. Despite a somewhat ambiguous political commentary narrated by Ernest Hemingway—probably a reflection of the bitter ideological divisions within the forces fighting for Republican Spain—it is definitely anti–Franco.

The Dead March (Imperial Pictures) was another compilation film combining actual footage and staged scenes. Par-

ticularly gory footage from the battlefields of the First World War is incorporated in its narrative, which ranges from WWI to the Sino-Japanese conflict. Released in January 1938, this film is intentionally sardonic in its anti-war message. The unknown soldiers of five warring nations (Russia is not included) rise up from their graves and present their own nationalistic rationalizations in *favor* of the causes that led to their deaths in combat![15]

Five months later a pro-preparedness film, *The Fight for Peace* (Warwick Pictures), was released. Again, it was largely composed of newsreel footage; it concerns a country that is misled by pacifism into a false sense of national security, with tragic results.[16] This picture was re-released in 1941, when preparedness was even more topical.

Universal's 1939 two-reeler, *The March of Freedom*, waves the flag of American democracy as it attacks dangerous alien "isms." Obviously reflecting many Americans' fear of becoming entangled in a European conflagration, it concludes:

America must awaken to the danger! Dictatorship must never reach our shores! And the first step is preparedness! Rearmament ... to gird the country with a ring of steel! Gangster nations recognize no arguments but might! A moral rearmament of the Nation to steel our hearts and minds against insidious doctrines from abroad that undermine democracy ... It is the duty of every true American to combat the inroads of subversive doctrines![17]

One of the better-known documentaries of 1939 is *The Four Hundred Million* (History Today). Directed by Joris Ivens, the commentary was prepared by Hollywood screenwriter Dudley Nichols, and read by actor Fredric March. The film unequivocally condemns the Japanese invasion of China in July 1937, and glorifies the resistance of the Chinese peasants to the ongoing brutalities of the Japanese armed forces. In addition to scenes of military combat, gruesome footage of the effects of Japanese aerial bombing of civilian areas is shown, including scenes of dead and mangled children. The shipment of war material from America to Japan is criticized.

Through the first nine months of World War II, the few war-related American documentaries were usually little more than glorified newsreels which largely maintained a neutral stance. A qualified exception to this was one of the last non-fiction pacifist films produced before America entered the war, *Why This War?* (Jewell). Released in October 1939, it is a compilation film that is "a severe indictment of war in which those accused are war lords, profiteers and others." However, the film avoids taking sides and incorporates a neutrality speech delivered by President Roosevelt.[18]

American attitudes towards the war began to change rather drastically after the French surrender to Germany and Italy in June 1940. Released in late 1940 and suggestively subtitled "A Picture for Free People," Paramount's full-length documentary *World in Flames* is a powerful indictment of the totalitarian states. It begins with the leaders of the world solemnly renouncing war as a method of solving international disputes, at the signing of the Kellogg-Briand Pact in 1929. After detailing the aggressions of the totalitarian states throughout the thirties, the film concludes with the Destroyer/Bases deal between Britain and the United States, and scenes of an American nation vigorously rearming. *World in Flames* specifically condemns Nazi anti–Semitism and labels the Nazi-Soviet Pact as a deal between "fellow aggressors." In 1941, this film was cited by a Senate subcommittee investigating motion picture propaganda as a prime example of Hollywood's pro-intervention bias.[19]

By the beginning of 1941, the Second World War was intruding upon—if not dominating—the content of non-fiction films. In addition to American productions, a number of films made in Great Britain were released in the United States. For example, *This Is England* (Columbia),[20] and *A Letter from Home* (United Artists). The latter film was directed by Carol Reed and narrated by American war correspondent Edward R. Murrow; it was presented in the form of a letter from British parents to their children who had been evacuated to the United States.[21]

An MGM short entitled *Memories of Europe* was a compilation of prewar scenes in now-conquered European countries, which ended with a salute by the narrator to the citizens of those nations "who still remain defiant." This film may have been produced to accompany MGM's feature release, *Lady Be Good*, in which the nostalgic musical lament, "The Last Time I Saw Paris," is performed.

The majority of American-made non-fiction films of 1941 positively portray the military and promote national defense, while frequently making direct references to the Second World War. These films include *American Sea Power* (TCF), *Army Champions* (MGM),[22] and *Caribbean Sentinel* (TCF). This last film discusses the defense of the Panama Canal (a favorite location for espionage activities in fictional films of the era).[23]

In addition to the many films designed to glamorize the armed forces, films with practical educational purposes also began to appear. The American Society of Hygiene produced a short entitled *In Defense of the Nation*, which addressed the problem of social diseases, which had been exacerbated by the rapidly expanding military and the National Defense program.[24]

Some unusual borderline films were also released in 1941. In *Man, the Enigma*, a PRC-released short, a film showing various animals and insects battling with and devouring one another is turned into an analogy of democracy versus totalitarianism. According to a contemporary review, the "subject's introductory [sic] is a human background and it concludes on the same note to draw the contrast."[25]

Great white hunter Frank Buck compiled the most exciting scenes from earlier films documenting his adventures in the jungle capturing wild animals for American zoos, and made the feature-length *Jungle Cavalcade* (RKO). Buck introduces war-related commentary into the narration, referring to the combatants in a python-tiger battle as two "jungle dictators." He later describes an armor-plated Indian rhino as a "prehistoric Panzer Division."

Paramount's *Hands of Destiny* short subject features a renowned "expert" on "hand analysis," who delivers his interpretations of the readings of the hands of Hitler, Mussolini, Churchill, and Roosevelt to fellow travelers on a train.[26] *Hands of Destiny* was released in July 1941, the month following Hitler's massive invasion of the Soviet Union. To American audiences who were just beginning to grasp the almost unbelievably horrifying dimensions of the Second World War, this film's blend of fiction and non-fiction may not have seemed so strange, after all.

Serials

Throughout the 'teens and the twenties and into the sound era, movie serials were very popular, particularly with the younger members of the audience. By the mid–1930s, the average serial was 12 to 15 episodes long (the first episode was often three reels, and subsequent chapters were usually two reels).

Between 1937 and 1941, 58 serials were made in Hollywood. Of these, 15—or 26 percent—reflect an awareness of the world crisis (a significantly higher percentage than feature-length films from the same period). "Spies," "saboteurs," and "foreign agents," were frequently serial villains, yet in virtually none of these multi-part films were ideologies or nationalities specified.[27] Unlike feature films, actual world events were seldom referred to. Possibly the industry did not want to encourage national hatreds among the largely juvenile audience for serials; or, perhaps they simply felt viewers required an unconfusing, Manichean world so as not to distract them from the frenetic action on-screen.

Fighting Devil Dogs (Republic, 1938) is an exception. Most of the action takes place in some vague tropical protectorate, where the Marine heroes battle the villainous "Lightning." However, before the Marines are sent to this locale, they spend a little time in Shanghai, and witness some of the action of the Sino-Japanese War.

Buster Crabbe has the leading role in Universal's more typical serial, *Red Barry* (1938). Crabbe and his female reporter sidekick fight it out with mysterious, Slavic-named foreign agents who have stolen two million dollars from a "friendly Asian nation." The Soviet Union was actually giving aid to the Nationalist Chinese government at this time, and several pre-Pearl Harbor feature films also make vague allusions to money for China (sometimes specified, sometimes not).[28]

In the 1940 Universal serial *Junior G-Men*, the Dead End Kids (East Side Kids, whatever) team up with the FBI to foil the "Order of the Flaming Torch," that wishes to "overthrow the existing social order" and establish a (presumably) fascist-style government in its place. The theme of both this serial and *Red Barry* was unnamed "enemies" from "within," whose politics are never clearly delineated. In fact, these enemies of the American way of life are little more than shallow gangster stereotypes who have been vaguely politicized in an apparent attempt to appeal to the current interests and fears of less-sophisticated moviegoers.

Such obvious obscurantism was carried to its most absurd lengths in *King of the Royal Mounted* (Republic, 1940). A Canadian has invented "Compound X," which can cure infantile paralysis. But an unnamed country at war with Canada (guess who?) ascertains that "Compound X" has magnetic properties which could render British naval defenses useless against mines. Enemy agent Kettler (notice the Germanic surname) operates from a submarine, and he and his "fifth columnist" cohorts immediately create havoc and are challenged by the dedicated Mounties.[29]

Since Britain and her Commonwealth partner Canada were engaged in a desperate naval struggle in the North Atlantic with Germany at the time, there was little doubt as to the enemy country's identity, but Republic chose not to name names. The indirect linking of Germans with misuse of a compound intended to save the lives of children was an especially ingenious piece of anti-German propaganda.

The 1940 serials reflecting an awareness of the world crisis (23 percent of the serials released that year) chiefly dealt with foreign agents and saboteurs trying to disrupt America's defense industry. *King of the Texas Rangers* (Republic, 1940) is representative. The leader of the "fifth columnists," referred to as "His Excellency," travels around in a Zeppelin and is greeted in the name of "the cause" with the fascist salute by his German-accented minions. During 1941, *half* of all serials produced in Hollywood participated in this undeclared war.

Fictional Shorts

In addition to serials, fictional shorts were very popular throughout the thirties and forties. In contrast to the dramatic serials, the two-reel fictional shorts were primarily a comedy vehicle, particularly in earlier years. This may account for the relative scarcity of fictional shorts released during 1937 and 1938 which reflect an awareness of the coming war.

However, another genre of fictional shorts began to appear around this time. By the end of 1939, Warner Brothers, MGM, and the independent Academic Film Company had all initiated series dramatizing the lives of famous people and glorifying American institutions and values. The timing was hardly coincidental.

Warner Brothers produced a series of "Historical Featurettes" between 1936 and 1945 that paid homage to such American heroes and heroines as Patrick Henry, Andrew Jackson, Clara Barton, and Buffalo Bill. Most were shot in Technicolor and directed by studio regulars such as Michael Curtiz, Ray Enright, and Crane Wilbur. By early 1939, these fictional shorts were increasingly chauvinistic. According to a *New York Times* article:

Warners admits with some pride, unusual in Hollywood, that the short subjects have returned no profit, but they believe they are making an important contribution to the Americanism movement. At first there was resistance to the films from exhibitors, but this is being broken down ... Warners has offered the pictures to all schools and organizations without cost.[30]

Released in the spring of 1939, *Sons of Liberty* is particularly interesting. Directed by Michael Curtiz, the short deals with Haym Solomon (Claude Rains), the Polish-born American Jew who was responsible for raising large sums of money to support the American Revolution. A key scene in a synagogue emphasizes the lead character's religious heritage. And, at the cost of historical veracity, Solomon is erroneously depicted as having had direct contacts with George Washington.[31]

The MGM series entitled "John Nesbitt's Passing Parade," which began prior to 1939, spotlighted many of the world's great humanitarians such as Dr. George Washington Carver. Between 1939 and 1941, the series expanded and became more politicized. A young Fred Zinnemann began his American directorial career on several shorts in this series. Two of the 1939 entries focused on foreigners. A winter release, "The Story of Alfred Nobel" portrays the Swedish inventor of dynamite as a man "determined to do something for peace."[32] Produced after the outbreak of WWII, "The Giant of Norway" eulogizes the great explorer and humanitarian Fridtjof Nansen, who valiantly fought nationalistic prejudices in the 1920s as he directed League of Nations efforts to aid millions of refugees created by the geopolitical realignments of World War One.[33]

Part of the MGM series "Crime Does Not Pay," *While America Sleeps* appeared in theatres in the fall of 1939. It was probably the first fictional short to respond to the outbreak of war in Europe. At the end of the film, U.S. Attorney Arthur S. Sears admonishes the audience to beware of foreign espionage, because it threatens the country's security "in a world gone mad with oppression and conquest."[34]

The Academic Film series of "Patriotic Shorts" was launched in June 1940 with *Our Constitution*.[35] Eight shorts would be released before the end of 1941, including *Our Monroe Doctrine* (1940) and *Our Bill of Rights* (1941). The former film, released in November, is notable for one scene in which John Quincy Adams has an animated conversation with the Austrian emissary to the United States. This Germanic stereotype is "pointedly told of the U.S. determination to defend the liberty and freedom of action of the Pan-American nations."[36] Over a year earlier, President Roosevelt had reiterated America's determination to defend the Western Hemisphere from foreign interference.

By early 1940, a number of the comedy short subject series entries were containing topical material. For example, the Three Stooges (Columbia) took on Hitler and his cohorts in *You Nazty Spy!*. The film unfolds in "Moronika," and the opening title facetiously proclaims that any resemblance between the film's characters and any other persons is a "miracle."[37] Yet Hitler is specifically singled out for caricature by Moe Howard. The emblem of the Moronika state is depicted as two snakes entwined to form a swastika-like design. In one sense, *You Nazty Spy!* could even be viewed as a prescient comic allegory of the rise and fall of the Third Reich, since it portrays paperhanger Hailstone and his assistants Gallstone and Pebble (=Goering and Goebbels) seizing dictatorial power in their country, declaring war, and finally being overthrown and devoured by lions!

The Three Stooges would return to Moronika in the summer 1941 release *I'll Never Heil Again*. After goosestepping in tandem into their chambers, the three comedians caricaturing the Nazi elite (Curley is "Field Marshal Herring" and Larry is the "Minister of Propaganda") argue about why they have been unable to conquer "Great Mitten" (=Great Britain). Later, they confer with their "Axel" partners, including Mussolini-lookalike "Chiselini," a Japanese stereotype, and the enigmatic "Bey of Rum."[38] During a quarrel over possession of a globe, the Stooges toss it around in a football parody. In the melee that ensues, Moe is given a judo lesson and lands upside-down against a wall with his legs spread in the "V for Victory" configuration.

Out of Darkness, an MGM short released in the winter of 1941, dramatically glorifies the Belgian underground movements of the First and Second World Wars. The film concludes with a montage of Nazi conquests while an offscreen narrator proclaims: "We will never stop fighting you. Never, so long as a single invader remains on our soil."[39] This may be the only pre–1942 American fiction film of any length that makes a direct reference to non–German underground resistance to the Nazis.

A pro–Chinese message is quaintly delivered via a subtle attack on racial prejudice in the one-reel "Our Gang" short *Baby Blues* (MGM). Directed by Edward L. Cahn, the film was released in February 1941. The Gubitosi family is expecting their fourth "bambino." Mickey, the eldest son and a member of the Gang (played by a child actor who later changed his name to Robert Blake and had a long television career), picks up a magazine in a doctor's office and reads that every fourth child born in the world is Chinese. Fearful of an Asian sibling, he embarks on a panicky odyssey in an effort to clear the matter up. Spanky suggests that they make inquiries at the Lee Wong household. Over a traditional American meal of ham and eggs, the boys are disabused of any latent prejudices, and Mickey is reassured.

Most of the remaining relevant fictional shorts from 1941 deal with the draft (*The Blitz Kiss*, Columbia),[40] espionage (*Yankee Doodle Andy*, Columbia),[41] or preparedness (*Helping Hands*, MGM).[42] In spite of the varied themes, the majority of these shorts were comedic in tone.

Animated Cartoons

A considerable number of animated cartoons also reflected an awareness of world events. This should not be too surprising, since the majority of theatrical cartoons (those created prior to the late 1950s) were made to entertain all audiences, adults as well as children.[43]

As early as 1933, Warner Brothers released a "Merrie Melody" cartoon, *Wake Up the Gypsy in Me*, which referred to topical events. The lust for a cute little peasant girl of lascivious mad monk "Rice-Puddin'" (= Rasputin) leads to a "revolution" by hammer-and-sickle wielding Russians. During his attempted escape, the crazed monk is blown up by an anarchist's bomb and transformed into a Mahatma Gandhi-lookalike!

Throughout 1933, dictators Benito Mussolini and Adolf Hitler received animated attention. At the time, many people did not see these men as threatening, instead finding their wild gesticulations and bombastic speeches amusing. In contrast to the pejorative caricatures of the two fascist leaders during WWII, these early cartoons offer more neutral images of the men.

Mussolini makes at least three cartoon appearances in 1933, including *Scrappy's Party* (Columbia), and *I've Got to Sing a Torch Song* (Warner Brothers). In *I Like Mountain Music* (Warner Brothers), the fez-wearing Duce stands on a balcony, urging his Blackshirts to help apprehend a fleeing gangster. Mussolini made another cartoon appearance in April 1935, six months before the Italian invasion of Ethiopia: in *Buddy's Theatre* (Warner Brothers), a newsreel parody contains a visit with "Masoleum" in "Dome," Italy.

The early cartoon appearances of Germany's new chancellor, Nazi Party leader Adolf Hitler, are a bit more intriguing, since Hitler was not yet a well-known world figure. In *Cubby's World Flight* (Van Beuren), Cubby—a little bear—flies over Germany and observes Hitler and German president Paul von Hindenburg drinking beer together in a beer hall. In September 1933, Warner Brothers released *Bosko's Picture Show*. The "Out-of-Tone News" (a spoof of the *Fox Movietone* newsreel) contains a scene in which a toothy Hitler (dressed in lederhosen and wearing a swastika armband) chases Jimmy Durante with an axe! Hitler makes a brief appearance in another newsreel parody, part of *She Was an Acrobat's Daughter* (Warner Brothers, 1937), and then seems to have vanished from animated cartoons until the advent of WWII.

At the height of the peace movement in 1935, Columbia's animated *Peace Conference* was released. A quarrel breaks out at a gathering of world leaders (including "John Bull" for

England, and Mahatma Gandhi). Krazy Kat bursts into the conference in a tank, firing a shell from which a singing Bing Crosby emerges! However, Bing's crooning only briefly pacifies the delegates. When a giant from Mars crashes on Earth, it takes unified action from Uncle Sam, the other delegates, a "Rudy Vallee" shell, and a big band swing music shell to defeat the invader and restore peace to the world.

Over the next few years, cartoon references to the growing world crisis were generally oblique. For instance, Porky Pig passes a sign reading "It Can Happen Here" (a play on the title of *It Can't Happen Here*, the 1936 anti-fascist novel by Sinclair Lewis) as he enters "Wackyland" (*Porky Pig in Wacky-Land*, Warner Brothers, 1938).

The increasing gravity of events in the latter months of 1939 led to the production of several cartoons which abandoned their traditional comedy format. *Old Glory* (Warner Brothers), a color "Looney Tune," concerns Porky Pig's failed attempt to memorize the Pledge of Allegiance. He is sitting sadly under an American flag when a nearby statue of Uncle Sam comes to life and delivers an inspirational pep talk. Even more unusual was an MGM cartoon released during the 1939 Christmas season, *Peace on Earth*. A squirrel family celebrates the holidays in a battle-scarred world (they live in an overturned steel helmet, street lights are hung from bayonets)— the human race is now extinct, having destroyed itself in war many years earlier.

Most cartoons made through 1940 contain only peripheral topical references. For example, *Fightin' Pals* (Paramount), contains a brief scene in which Popeye sails to Africa to find his lost pal Bluto. As Popeye's boat nears Spain, a series of explosions (i.e., the Spanish Civil War, which had only recently concluded) drives him away. A reference to WWII is linked with the 1940 presidential election in *Swing Social* (MGM,

May 1940): a black-caricature baby fish named "FDR Jones" grasps a lollipop like a microphone and says "I'se hates war!"

In 1941, animated cartoons—like feature films—began to become more relevant (more than 15 percent of the cartoons released in this year had some topical content), and more aggressively anti-fascist. The "V for Victory" symbol of resistance to Nazi Germany was highlighted in the title of a Popeye cartoon: *The Might NaVy*. *The Home Guard* (TCF) features Gandy Goose and his farm militia versus heinous black vultures and their "Fifth Column," while Beethoven's Fifth Symphony is heard on the soundtrack. Columbia released two animated lectures attacking totalitarianism and promoting American intervention in the war: *Broken Treaties*[44] and *How War Came*.[45] The first cartoon makes a rare screen reference to the Nazi-Soviet Pact; both shorts negatively portray the fascist dictators. For instance, in *How War Came*, Hitler is caricatured as he says "Today we own only Germany, tomorrow the whole world."

The majority of topically relevant cartoons in 1941 concerned the armed forces, especially the draft (instituted in October 1940). While some of these cartoons contain only brief draft gags, a considerable number portray the travails of draftees and enlisted men in Army camps. Examples include *Boogie Woogie Bugle Boy of Company C* (Universal), *The Rookie Bear* (MGM), and *Rookie Revue* (Warner Brothers).

It is clear that from 1939 onwards, the American public was exposed to a significant number of cinematic references to the world situation. These references appeared not only in feature-length fictional films, but also in short subjects, cartoons, newsreels serials, and documentaries. In 1941, the final year of peace for America, U.S. film audiences saw a large number of films of all types containing almost exclusively pro-Allied, anti-fascist references to the conflict.

Filmography to Part One

This preliminary section contains the following material: Abbreviations used in the Filmography and statistical analyses of information found in the Filmography.

The filmographies for the prewar years (1937–1941) and the war years (1942–1945) are very similar in form and content, but there are some differences. The 1937–1941 filmography does not contain a numerical ranking of "war-relevance," chiefly because the oblique and tentative nature of topical references in the years prior to America's direct involvement in the war resulted in very few "highly" relevant films. Instead, a category called "Bias" was created, analyzing the primary topical theme of the film. These include "Pro-British," "Pacifist," "Pro-Military," and so forth. Such descriptors are obviously not necessary for wartime films, but it is important to see these for the *prewar* films, since some interesting trends can be discerned.

The coding terms differ slightly in the 1937–1941 and 1942–1945 filmographies: any term that appears in both filmographies is to be considered as used essentially identically, but there are terms which are unique to each era. Some of these are obvious: there are references to "Hitler" and "Mussolini" in both filmographies, since these were contemporary figures who lived throughout the period. However, references to rationing and shortages are not found in pre–1942 films, while topics such as the Italo-Ethiopian War are rarely mentioned in the 1942–1945 period.

Otherwise, the format of the filmographies is reasonably consistent. For more complete information see the Introduction.

Abbreviations Used in the Filmography

AF: Armed Forces/ appearance or explicit reference to national armies, navies, air forces, militia, etc. Sub-codes AF-A, AF-N refer to U.S. Army and Navy only; AF-W refers to women in uniformed services, including military nurses; armed forces of other nations are identified as AF-GER, AF-BRIT, AF-CHI, AF-JAP, etc.

Am Icons: American Icons/ visual and/or verbal evocations of patriotic symbols including the U.S. flag, Declaration of Independence, the Statue of Liberty.

Am Vols: American Volunteers/ depiction or explicit reference to U.S. citizens participating in foreign conflicts. Does not include those characters who are inadvertently drawn into wars, rebellions, etc. by virtue of being in the "wrong place at the wrong time."

Appeasement: Reference to prewar policy of the British government under Chamberlain (and Americans who endorsed the policy) which encouraged accommodation with Nazi Germany out of fear of another world war. After September 1939 was used pejoratively.

Arab: Arab/ depiction of Arab nationals.

Arms Control: Reference to international attempts to limit proliferation of war materials.

Arms Dealers: Arms Dealers/ depiction or explicit reference to individuals or organizations who sell and/or deliver munitions and arms to belligerent groups or nations.

Atroc: Atrocity/ depiction or explicit reference to war crimes and other actions which go beyond acceptable bounds of warfare, law enforcement, and political action. For example, massacres, execution without trial, torture.

Atroc-Conc: Atrocity-Concentration Camp/ depiction or explicit reference to concentration camps (not necessarily death camps, as in Nazi Germany, but these are included).

Austr: Austria/ depiction of Austrian national or reference to Austria, and *Anschluss*.

Belg: Belgium/ depiction of Belgian national or reference to Belgium.

Blk: Black/ appearance of any black character of any nationality.

Bonds: Bonds/ references to Defense, War, or Liberty (WWI) Bonds and Stamps.

Brit: British/ appearance of characters identified as being British nationals (including England, Scotland).

Can: Canada/ depiction of Canadian national or explicit reference to Canada.

Chamberlain: Chamberlain/ depiction or explicit reference to Neville Chamberlain, Prime Minister of Great Britain.

Chi: Chinese/ appearance of character of Chinese race.

Churchill: Churchill/ depiction or explicit reference to Winston Churchill, Prime Minister of Great Britain.

Collab: Collaborator/ appearance or explicit reference to a citizen of one nation who is in sympathy with or in the employ of a foreign enemy. Includes references to "traitors."

Comm: Communist/ explicit reference to Communism.

Czech: Czechoslovakia/ depiction of Czech national or reference to Czechoslovakia.

Den: Denmark/ explicit reference to Denmark or depiction of Danish national.

Dipl: Diplomat/ appearance of character in diplomatic corps.

Draft: Draft/ reference to conscription in the U.S.

Draft Avoid: Draft Avoidance/ reference to attempts to avoid military service, registering for draft, etc.

Dunkirk: Dunkirk/ May 1940 evacuation of remnants of British and French armies from France after defeat by Germans.

Fascism: Fascism/ explicit reference to "Fascism," but NOT including specific references to "Nazi" or other specific fascist organizations if otherwise coded.

FBI: Federal Bureau of Investigation/ depiction of FBI agent or explicit reference to operations of FBI.

FDR: Franklin D. Roosevelt/ explicit reference to the President of the United States during this period.

Fifth Col: Fifth Column/ explicit reference to "Fifth Column." Also includes foreign nationals resident in U.S. (i.e., German-American Bund) whose loyalties are suspect.

Fil: Filipino/ depiction of Philippine national or reference to Philippines.

Finn: Finland/ depiction of Finnish national or reference to Finland.

For Corr: Foreign Correspondent/ appearance of character identified as a journalist, news cameraman, newsreel photographer, radio reporter, etc., working overseas.

Fr: French/ appearance of character identified as French national.

Free Fr: Free French/ reference to French government-in-exile established after fall of France in 1940.

Ger: German/ appearance or explicit reference to German nationals or people of German descent.

Goebbels: Goebbels/ explicit reference to Franz Josef Goebbels, Nazi Minister of Propaganda.

Good Neighbor: Good Neighbor Policy/ reference to FDR's policy of fair and equitable relations with Latin America.

Goering: Goering/ explicit reference to Hermann Goering, head of German Luftwaffe.

Gre: Greek/ depiction of Greek national or person of Greek descent, or reference to Greece.

Hess: Hess/ explicit references to Rudolf Hess, deputy Fuehrer in Nazi Germany.

Hist Am: Historical American/ appearance or explicit reference to historical American figures such as former presidents (Lincoln, Washington), generals (Custer, Pershing), or statesmen.

Hitler: Adolf Hitler/ appearance or explicit reference to German leader of this period. Includes verbal references to "Schicklegruber." Note: A reference to "Hitler" or "Mussolini" is NOT double-coded as "German," or "Italian."

Home Def: Home Defense/ reference to civilian preparations for national defense, including air raid wardens, plane spotters, etc.

Ind Fasc Org: Indigenous Fascist Organization/ appearance or explicit reference to group of citizens (not foreign nationals) with fascist tendencies: example, the Ku Klux Klan.

Intell Serv: Intelligence Service/ reference to official intelligence organizations such as military intelligence, usually in counterspy or military espionage operations. FBI is not included in this coding.

Isolationist: Isolationist/ reference to U.S. attitudes opposing intervention in foreign wars.

Ital.: Italian/ appearance of character identified as Italian national or of Italian descent.

Italo-Eth: Italo-Ethiopian War/ reference to 1935-36 war in Ethiopia; also includes references to Ethiopian leader Haile Selassie when they refer to bravery, tenacity, etc.

Jap: Japanese/ appearance or explicit reference to Japanese nationals or actions of Japan as a nation.

Jew: Jew/ appearance of character identified as a Jew.

Latin Am: Latin American/ appearance of character of Hispanic background. Includes Mexicans, Brazilians, Argentines, Cubans, etc.

League Nat: League of Nations/ reference to League of Nations, international organization which was a forerunner to the United Nations.

Maginot Line: Maginot Line/ massive French fortifications on the German border.

Mil Exer: Military Exercises/ depiction or explicit reference to military maneuvers or training.

Mil School: Military School/ depiction of military school or academy.

Munich Crisis: Munich Crisis/ reference to the threat to world peace precipitated by Hitler's preparations for the invasion of Czechoslovakia in the spring of 1938, ostensibly to protect the Sudeten German minority. After a series of meeting in September 1938, an agreement was signed resolving the issue by ceding the Sudetenland to Germany.

Musso: Mussolini/ depiction or explicit reference to Italian leader of this period.

Natl Def: National Defense/ reference to plans or actions to build up U.S. military establishment prior to U.S. entry into WWII.

Nazi: Nazi/ explicit reference to Nazi party. Includes depiction of swastikas, references to the Gestapo, Blackshirts (SS), and Brownshirts (SA).

Neth: Netherlands/ depiction of Dutch national or reference to Netherlands or Dutch possessions.

Neutrality Act: Neutrality Act/ reference to a series of U.S. laws restricting relations with warring nations; also includes general references to "neutrality."

Nor: Norway/ reference to Norway or depiction of Norwegian national.

Pacifist: Pacifist/ reference to anti-war attitudes.

Peace Org: Peace Organization/ depiction or explicit reference to any group which opposes war.

Pol: Poland/ reference to Poland or depiction of Polish national or person of Polish descent.

Port: Portugal/ reference to Portugal or Portugese national.

Prod: Production/ depiction or explicit reference to industrial preparation for war.

Quotas: Immigration Quotas/ reference to U.S. laws restricting number of immigrants by country.

Ref: Refugee/ depiction or explicit reference to persons forced to flee their home countries due to war or political oppression.

Resist: Resistance/ depiction or explicit reference to forces fighting fascist or totalitarian governments, either in occupied nations or enemy countries themselves. Does not refer to national armed forces, except in the case where the country in question has surrendered and resistance forces continue to fight.

Rom: Romania/ also "Rumania." Reference to Romania or depiction of Romanian national.

Russ: Russian/ appearance of character identified as Russian national, or explicit reference to actions of Russian nation.

Russ-Finn War: Russo-Finnish War/ reference to war between Russia and Finland, 1939–1940.

Russ-Ger Co-op: Russian-German Cooperation/ reference to nonaggression pact signed by Stalin and Hitler; also includes depiction of Russian and German nationals acting as allies.

Secret Plans: Secret Plans/ reference to maps, plans, or documents of military or political value, usually as a target of spies.

Secret Weapon: Secret Weapon/ explicit reference or depiction of new weapon or invention intended for use in war.

Sino-Jap: Sino-Japanese War/ explicit reference to Japanese invasion of China and subsequent fighting there.

Spa: Spain/ depiction of Spanish national or reference to Spain, Franco.

Span Civ: Spanish Civil War/ explicit reference to war in Spain (1936–1939).

Spy-Sab: Spy-Saboteur/ appearance of character depicted as enemy national engaged in intelligence or sabotage operations in a friendly country (i.e., no FRIENDLY agents included).

Stalin: Josef Stalin/ reference to leader of USSR.

US-Brit Co-op: US-British Cooperation/ depiction or explicit reference to official or semi-official cooperation between governments of U.S. and Great Britain, or individuals acting on their behalf. Includes references to "Lend-lease."

USO: United Service Organization/ reference to organization providing recreational activities for servicemen. Also includes canteens, camp shows, etc. regardless of sponsoring organization.

V: "V"/ depiction of capital letter V when used to signify Allied Victory. Includes the "three dots and dash" Morse code, and opening notes of Beethoven's Fifth Symphony.

Vets: Veterans/ explicit reference or depiction of character identified as U.S. veteran of previous war (WWI, Spanish-American War, Civil War).

War Mats: War Materials/ explicit reference to munitions and other goods which are intended for use in a current armed conflict (including Spanish Civil War, WWII, Sino-Japanese War).

World Crisis: World Crisis/ explicit reference to unstable world situation, particularly prior to open hostilities in Europe.

WWI: World War One/ explicit reference to First World War; also referred to as "the last war," or "the Great War."

WWII: World War Two/ explicit reference to fighting in Europe which began in September 1939.

War Related American Films, 1937–1941

Company	1937	1938	1939	1940	1941	Total
Columbia	2/52	6/53	9/56	7/52	13/63	37/276
	4	11	16	13	19	13
MGM	5/51	7/46	9/51	16/44	23/47	60/239
	10	15	18	36	49	25
Paramount	3/61	11/50	6/58	7/48	17/45	44/262
	5	22	10	15	38	17
RKO	7/53	5/43	13/49	9/52	14/45	48/242
	13	12	27	17	31	20
TCF	9/61	11/56	12/59	14/49	15/57	61/282
	15	20	22	29	26	22
UA	0/25	3/16	2/18	6/21	10/25	21/105
	0	19	11	29	40	20
Univ	4/37	5/46	5/44	7/49	14/59	35/235
	11	11	11	14	24	15
WB	8/68	7/52	11/55	18/45	20/49	64/269
	12	13	18	40	41	24
Monogram	0/21	4/33	4/37	6/52	12/44	26/187
	0	12	11	12	27	14
Republic	3/56	5/24	7/45	3/50	7/54	25/229
	5	21	16	6	13	11
Grand Natl	4/36	2/21	2/6	—	—	8/63
	11	10	33			13
PDC/PRC	—	—	1/2	2/12	6/19	9/33
			50	17	32	27
TOTALS	45/521	66/440	81/480	95/474	151/507	438/2485
	9	15	17	20	30	18

NOTE: 11 films in the Filmography for Part One with company code IND (independent producing/releasing companies) are not included in the above statistics.

Discernible Biases Found in Films, 1937–1941

Type	1937	1938	1939	1940	1941
CM	11	16	13	33	64
Anti-Fascist	5	6	10	9	8
Anti-Totalitarian	0	1	1	4	8
Anti-German	1	1	4	6	2
Anti-Nazi	0	1	6	9	12
Anti-Japanese	0	3	4	0	2
Anti-Soviet	1	1	1	5	1
Anti-British	0	1	0	1	0
Pro-American	2	8	17	14	29
Pro-Democracy	1	1	3	2	2
Pro-British	5	8	5	11	15

Pro-French	0	1	3	2	1
Pro-Chinese	3	1	0	0	0
Pro-Military	14	15	8	12	38
Pro-Intervention	0	1	2	7	14
Preparedness	0	2	2	1	2
Anti-Espionage	5	8	17	16	17
Pacifist	10	11	11	6	1
Non-Intervention	1	5	6	0	0

Note: films were coded with up to three bias terms.

Frequency of Topical References in Films, 1937–1941

Coding Term	1937	1938	1939	1940	1941
American Icons	15	12	28	23	44
American Volunteers	1	4	2	6	9
Appeasement	0	1	0	0	3
Arab	2	1	2	2	2
AF-Air Corps	1	2	5	6	13
AF-Army	8	14	18	17	42
AF-Austrian	0	1	0	1	0
AF-British	3	6	11	17	16
AF-Chinese	3	2	4	1	1
AF-Coast Guard	1	2	1	0	0
AF-Czech	0	0	0	1	0
AF-Filipino	0	0	1	0	0
AF-Finnish	0	0	0	1	0
AF-French	3	3	10	4	4
AF-German	4	4	10	15	17
AF-Italian	0	3	0	0	2
AF-Japanese	1	3	2	1	1
AF-Marine Corps	5	6	1	6	9
AF-Merchant Marine	0	0	0	1	0
AF-Navy	15	14	10	19	26
AF-RAF	1	1	0	2	8
AF-Romanian	0	0	0	1	0
AF-Russian	0	0	0	3	1
AF-Women	1	5	5	4	2
Arms Control	0	2	0	0	0
Arms Dealers	2	6	10	3	1
Atrocities	6	2	9	7	7
Atroc-Conc Camp	1	0	5	8	6
Austria	0	0	1	7	5
Belgium	0	0	1	3	4
Black	9	19	17	36	55
Bonds	0	1	1	2	2
British	7	12	13	21	21
Canada	0	0	1	0	3
Chamberlain	0	0	1	4	1

China	11	10	13	8	17
Churchill	0	0	0	2	4
Collaborator	0	2	2	7	12
Communist	6	8	5	9	5
Czech	0	0	2	6	2
Denmark	0	0	0	1	1
Diplomat	10	8	15	7	7
Draft	2	2	2	2	35
Draft Avoidance	0	2	0	1	8
Dunkirk	0	0	0	0	3
Fascism	0	3	2	1	1
FBI	0	2	4	11	11
FDR	1	3	7	7	15
FDR-Eleanor	0	0	0	0	2
Fifth Column	0	0	0	7	12
Filipino	1	1	1	0	1
Finn	0	0	0	0	1
Foreign Correspondent	5	7	7	11	5
Free French	0	0	0	0	1
French	5	6	7	12	14
German	7	10	12	19	20
Goebbels	0	0	2	4	1
Goering	0	0	0	4	2
Good Neighbor	0	0	1	0	6
Greece	0	0	0	0	1
Hess	0	0	0	0	2
Historical American	8	10	19	18	36
Hitler	1	1	12	16	23
Home Defense	0	0	0	4	5
Indigenous Fascist Organization	2	0	2	1	1
Intelligence Services	5	8	5	7	5
Isolationist	0	0	2	0	4
Italian	7	7	10	14	17
Italo-Ethiopian War	4	2	0	2	3
Japan	1	5	4	5	4
Jew	2	4	9	11	8
Latin American	6	7	10	14	35
League of Nations	1	1	1	1	1
Maginot Line	0	1	1	0	0
Military Exercise	5	0	2	3	7
Military School	5	3	3	1	4
Munich Crisis	0	0	3	3	0
Mussolini	0	0	3	3	6
National Defense	0	0	3	0	12
Nazi	0	0	7	15	20
Netherlands	1	1	0	3	3
Neutrality Act	0	2	3	3	1
Norway	0	0	0	3	6
Pacifist	3	2	6	5	2
Peace Organization	1	1	1	2	0
Poland	1	1	3	8	5
Portugal	0	0	0	0	1
Production	0	0	2	6	9

Quotas	0	1	0	2	4
Refugee	1	2	2	6	17
Resistance	0	0	4	4	3
Romania	0	0	0	0	1
Russia	7	12	8	8	11
Russ-Finn War	0	0	0	5	0
Russ-Ger Co-op	0	0	0	5	1
Secret Plans	0	0	2	1	1
Secret Weapon	4	9	11	9	11
Sino-Jap War	1	8	8	4	5
Spain	0	2	0	0	1
Spanish Civil War	4	4	5	3	3
Spy-Saboteur	10	14	24	26	31
Stalin	0	0	1	6	0
US-British Co-op	0	1	4	4	8
USO	0	0	0	0	8
"V"	0	0	0	0	4
Veterans	2	3	7	3	4
War Materials	6	11	14	8	13
World War I	12	12	23	20	25
World War II	0	0	2	44	65
World Crisis	0	5	4	3	3

Filmographic Entries, 1937–1941

1937

1 ANGEL (Para, Oct) Ernst Lubitsch; *genre:* Comedy/Drama; *locations:* France, Great Britain; *Coding:* Dipl, Russ, League Nat, Brit, Fr, WWI; *biases:* Contraband Message, Pro-British

Marlene Dietrich plays the neglected wife of the British representative to the League of Nations. While he is traveling back and forth to Geneva in order to prevent wars, she has a brief extramarital fling in Paris. On the home front, the typically English butler thinks the two Soviet delegates who visited for dinner have possibilities, but worries that "they still dunk."

2 ANNAPOLIS SALUTE (RKO, Sept) Christy Cabanne; *genre:* Drama; *location:* United States; *coding:* Blk, Hist Am, Mil School, AF-N, Am Icons; *bias:* Pro-Military.

One of many service academy films released before and during the period, this is a reworking of RKO's 1933 production, *Midshipman Jack*. Additional predecessors include such films as *Flirtation Walk* (WB, 1934); *Annapolis Farewell* (Para., 1935); *Shipmates Forever* (WB, 1935). With varying degrees of emphasis, the plots would center around male camaraderie, girls, Americanism, and sports (particularly football). In this highly melodramatic work, Harry Carey, in what was to become a stereotyped role as the faithful old noncom (such as in *Air Force* [WB, 1943]), sees his son through romantic complications and confidently looks forward to a commission in the family.

3 BLACK LEGION (WB, Jan) Archie L. Mayo; *genre:* Drama; *location:* United States; *coding:* Pol, Ind Fasc Orge, Am Icons, Attroc, Hist Am; *biases:* Anti-Fascist, Pro-Democracy.

A young and struggling lathe operator, played by Humphrey Bogart, becomes entangled with a semi-fascist, hood-wearing group operating in the Midwest. He succumbs to their incendiary appeals to "100% Americans" to protect indigenous ideals and jobs from "traitorous aliens." A judge, upon sentencing several members of the Black Legion to life imprisonment for a hate inspired murder of an Irish-American, lectures the courtroom that "extra-legal organizations cannot be tolerated" in America today and that "our democratic form of government must be guarded zealously." Warner Bros. would create a similar scene two years later at the conclusion of *Confessions of a Nazi Spy,* q.v.

4 CALIFORNIA STRAIGHT AHEAD (Univ., May) Arthur Lubin; *genre:* Drama; *location:* United States; *coding:* Ital, War Mats, Chi; *biases:* Contraband Message.

John Wayne plays a small time truck driver who unsuccessfully struggles with rival independents. He later joins a major freight line based in Chicago. There he eventually becomes traffic supervisor. He accepts a rush load of airplane parts to be delivered to the West Coast for shipment to Japan. A race to Los Angeles ensues when his counterpart in a railroad views this as a business threat and accepts a duplicate order to deliver the war materials. A rare pre-war reference to U.S. sales of strategic materials to Japan.

5 CHARLIE CHAN AT THE OLYMPICS (TCF, May) H. Bruce Humberstone;

genre: Crime; *locations:* United States, Germany; *coding:* Spy-Sab, Chi, Arms Dealers, Secret Weapons, AF-A, AF-N, Am Icons, Ger, Hitler, Blk, Dip; *bias:* Anti-Espionage.

An airplane with an experimental robot pilot device being tested by the U.S. military is hijacked over Honolulu. In an aside, Charlie Chan states it would be "greatest blessing if all war fought with machines instead of human beings." He then proceeds to the 1936 Berlin Olympics in order to join son Lee, a member of the U.S. swimming team, and to catch up with suspected foreign agents. Newsreel footage is incorporated, including a fleeting long shot of Hitler receiving the fascist salute. German efficiency is lampooned via Charlie's sage advice to a feckless heel-clicking martinet of the Berlin police.

6 CHINA PASSAGE (RKO, Mar) Edward Killy; *genre:* Adventure; *locations:* China, United States; *coding:* AF-Chi, Am Vol, Chi, War Mats, AF-A, Brit; *bias:* Contraband Message.

A powerful general in northern China hires two American soldiers on leave to guard a valuable diamond that is to be exchanged for weapons. In the Chinese quarter of Shanghai, the transaction is about to be made when a battle erupts between two groups of soldiers, one faction using tear gas to immobilize their foes. When the smoke clears, the gem is gone. All foreigners in the area are rounded up, but the diamond is not retrieved. These same foreigners, including an American woman considered to be the prime suspect, board the *SS Asiatic* for San Francisco. After the murder of a couple of passengers, it is discovered that the culprit is an English jewel thief. The mysterious American woman turns out to be a U.S. customs agent.

7 CRACK-UP (TCF, Jan) Malcolm St. Clair; *genre:* Spy; *location:* United States; *coding:* AF-AC, Spy-Sab, Secret Weapons Dipl, Am Icons, AF-N, Intell Serv, Ger?, Ital?; *bias:* Anti-Espionage.

Peter Lorre plays the simple-minded, bugle-blowing Colonel Gimpy who, in reality, is Rudolf Maximilian Taggart, the spy of an unspecified country. He seeks the plans for a revolutionary designed aircraft, the "DOX," a giant passenger plane capable of flying from New York to Berlin. Gimpy's interest in the military potentials of the plane lead to bribery and murder. As a result, a traitorous American pilot seizes the aircraft's prototype on its maiden flight. The plane, its plans, and the foreign agents aboard are destroyed in mid-ocean by a fortuitous storm.

8 CRIMINAL LAWYER (RKO, Jan) Christy Cabanne; *genre:* Comedy; *location:* United States; *coding:* Chi, Ital, Italo-Eth, War, Ref; *bias:* Contraband Message.

This remake of RKO's *State's Attorney* (1932) features Lee Tracy as a cocky, hard-drinking lawyer with political ambitions. Character actor Erik Rhodes once again plays a fatuous Italian (Bandini this time; Tonetti in *Gay Divorcee* [RKO 1934]; Beddini in *Top Hat* [RKO 1935]). As the latest "crooner" sensation, Bandini invites Tracy's old flame to a benefit being held for an "Ethiopian war baby." The film was banned in Italy because the fascist regime found the ethnic stereotype offensive.

9 DEVIL'S PLAYGROUND (Col., Jan) Erle C. Kenton; *genre:* Drama; *locations:* United States, China; *coding:* Latin Am, Chi, AF-A, AF-N; *bias:* Pro-Military.

An updated version of Frank Capra's 1928 *Submarine* (Col.), this film gave the public a chance to see the Navy and some of its latest ships in action. It features a couple of Navy divers on the West Coast who have a falling-out over an amoral dancehall girl. When one diver is trapped on board a damaged submarine, the other—who has since discovered the woman's duplicity—comes to his friend's aid. At the film's conclusion, the two buddies are living it up in the Orient, while the woman is back hustling sailors in San Diego.

10 ESPIONAGE (MGM, Feb) Kurt Neumann; *genre:* Comedy/Drama; *locations:* France, Switzerland; *coding:* Comm, War Mats, For Corr, Atroc-Conc, Spy-Sab, Russ, Latin Am, Italo-Eth War, Dipl; *bias:* Pacifist.

An international munitions maker named Kronsky and his attractive female companion try to secretly board the "Trans-Continental Express" train in Paris. They are immediately pursued by a communist assassin and two rival American reporters. The distaff half of the correspondent duo is reminded by her compatriot that, due to her recent article—"Will Map of Europe Change Again"—that there are at least four countries through which the Express passes that would like to place her in a "concentration camp" (this is one of the earliest references to concentration camps in a feature film). Only after the train crosses the border into Switzerland is it revealed that the armaments couple was merely eloping, and that as a wedding present to his wife Kronsky plans to pursue less lethal business ventures in the future.

11 EXILED TO SHANGHAI (Rep, Dec) Nick Grinde; *genre:* Comedy/Drama; *locations:* United States, China; *coding:* AF-N?, AF-Jap, Span Civ, Sino-Jap War, For Corr, Chi; *biases:* Pro-China, Contraband Message.

News cameraman Ted Young returns from Spain after filming scenes of the Civil War. But at the New York Offices of *World Wide* he discovers that competitors had featured wired photos of his story a week earlier. Out of a job, he meets and falls in love with a girl involved with a company fraudulently promoting a long distance television scheme. When his major rival goes off to China, Ted tells the man, "That's war over there, whether they declare it or not." The film concludes with Ted and his girl watching a TV broadcast to the United States of the Japanese bombing of Shanghai.

12 FIRST LADY (WB, Dec) Stanley Logan; *genre:* Comedy/Drama; *location:* United States; *coding:* Peace Org, Am Icons, Blk, Dipl; *biases:* Pacifist, Contraband Message.

Based on the 1935 eponymous play by George S. Kaufman and Katherine Dayton, this film satirizes the behind-the-scenes political machinations that take place in Washington, D.C. Protagonist Lucy Chase Wayne (Kay Francis), the granddaughter of a former president, was purportedly based upon Theodore Roosevelt's real-life, acid-tongued daughter, Alice Roosevelt Longworth (1884–1980)—an outspoken pacifist and future leader of the isolationist America first Committee. Among the other characters appearing in the film is a sycophantish matron named Lavinia Mae Creevey. Mrs. Creevey, the self-proclaimed uniform-wearing leader of the xenophobic Women's Peace, Purity and Patriotism League, is hilariously performed by comedienne Louise Fazenda.

13 THE GOOD EARTH (MGM, Aug) Sidney Franklin; *genre:* Drama; *location:* China; *coding:* Chi, AF-Chi; *bias:* Pro-Chinese.

This is the cinematic version of Pearl Buck's 1931 Pulitzer Prize winning novel. It opens with a dedication to the "soul of a great nation...." Amidst impressive background shots, a Chinese family struggles against famine, revolution (1911) and its own devisive greed. It takes an invading horde of locusts (which sounds very much like massed aircraft) to reunite the family and renew their bonds with the people. It was a beautiful evocation of the ongoing plight of China and its people's need to band together against their common foes. Even more significant is the fact that this was one of the earliest examples of Chinese portrayed positively in an American feature film.

14 HELL DIVERS (1931 RE-RELEASE) (MGM, Jun) George Hill; *genre:* Adventure; *location:* Caribbean; *coding:* Latin Am, AF-N, Am Icons, Mil Exer; *bias:* Pro-Military.

In the tradition of Quirt and Flagg, as well as other earlier service films such as Wallace Beery's *We're in the Navy Now* (Par., 1926), Beery and a young co-starring Clark Gable engage in a friendly rivalry aboard the carrier *USS Saratoga*. During "sham war" exercises off the coast of Central America, the flying gobs wind up stranded on a deserted beach. Gunner Beery flies the wounded Gable back to their ship after the death of his pilot, but is himself mortally injured when he crash lands on the Saratoga's flight deck. Along with the *Flying Fleet* (MGM, 1929), this 1931 release was one of the earliest fiction films to feature America's naval carrier arm. Several other motion pictures produced by Hollywood between 1937 and 1941 would likewise feature it, e.g., *Swing It Sailor!* (Grand Nat., 1937); *Flight Command* (MGM, 1941); *Dive Bomber* (WB, 1941).

15 HEROES OF THE ALAMO (Ind, Aug) Harry Fraser; *genre:* Historical Drama; *location:* United States; *coding:* Hist Am, Am Icons, Latin Am, AF-A; *bias:* Pro-American.

A pantheon of early 19th–century American heroes triumps over Latin American despotism. This near-documentary styled feature is loosely based on the events leading up to and culminating in the Mexican seige of the Franciscan mission near San Antonio, during the 1836 Texas War for Independence. Columbia acquired this film and re-released it early in 1938.

16 HOLD 'EM NAVY! (Para, Nov) Kurt Neumann; *genre:* Drama; *location:* United States; *coding:* AF-A, AF-N, Am Icons, Mil School; *bias:* Pro-Military.

Another flag-waving Naval Academy film, but with the emphasis on football—the Army-Navy Game to be specific. Throughout most of the 1930s Hollywood released campus pigskin films during the fall.

17 THE HOLY TERROR (TCF, Feb) James Tinling; *genre:* Spy; *location:* United States; *coding:* Secret Weapons, AF-N, Spy-Sab, Am Icons, Mil Exer; *biases:* Anti-Espionage, Pro-Military.

Corky (Jane Withers), daughter of a Naval Air Service officer, is the pet of the base. She stages song and dance shows with the guys at the nearby Anchor Cafe. But spies of unspecified national origin have determined that the cafe affords a unique view of the hangar in which the Navy's newest pursuit plane is kept. Consequently, they rig a brawl in order to get the popular hangout closed. In her efforts to reopen the cafe and to clear her buddies, Corky discovers the spies secretly taking photos of the plane. She radios the squadron that just happens to be on maneuvers. In the final scene her dad reads a general citation from the acting Secretary of the Navy for "the apprehension of certain enemies of the U.S. Government."

18 I COVER THE WAR (Univ, Jul) Arthur Lubin; *genre:* Adventure; *locations:* Great Britain, Iraq, Spain; *coding:* For Corr, Span Civ, War Mats, AF-Brit, Arab, AF-RAF, Italo-Eth War, Dipl; *bias:* Pro-British.

After returning from assignment on the Spanish Civil War, Atlas Reel's ace cameraman, played by John Wayne, is sent by his London office to Mesopotamia. He arrives at the British outpost of "Samari," the scene of a desert rebellion against the government led by a bandit named El Kadar. Before Wayne gets the needed film footage, he makes a little love, tangles with international gun runners, deals with some spies and survives an encounter with bloodthirsty tribesmen. At the end, he and an American buddy help save a group of British Lancers from certain death. This film was presumably meant to take place during an actual revolt in Iraq that had occurred in 1935. It was suppressed by the Iraqi government with the aid of the British.

19 IT COULD HAPPEN TO YOU (Rep, Jun) Phil Rosen; *genre:* Drama; *location:* United States; *coding:* Ital, Ger, Spy-Sab, Am Icons, Russ; *biases:* Anti-Fascist, Pro-American.

The title of this muddled film was probably meant to suggest Sinclair Lewis's anti-fascist novel, *It Can't Happen Here* (1935). The story centers around Bob Ames, the weak-willed adopted son of a kindly immigrant. Bob repays the old man by robbing his candy store for the money needed to purchase a school that prepares foreigners for American citizenship. "Pa" is accidentally killed during the robbery. Bob is subsequently blackmailed by Professor Schwab, the Germanic director of the coveted Foreign American Institute, when he stupidly gives the man a bloodstained bill that has been identified in the papers as a vital piece of evidence in the crime. The so-called "professor" is an admirer of Nietzsche who is obsessed with the "will to power." He espouses a fascistic philosophy of "the weak shall inherit the earth and the unscrupulous shall take it from them." The two men force ignorant, illegal aliens to attend their classes by threatening them with deportation if they fail their citizenship exams. Bob is brought to trial, but is acquitted in a brilliant defense by Pa's lawyer son. Bob later confesses and exonerates his adoptive brother of complicity as an angry mob of immigrants threatens to kill the lawyer. Having reaffirmed the American system, Bob commits suicide.

20 LANCER SPY (TCF, Oct) Gregory Ratoff; *genre:* Spy; *locations:* Great Britain, Germany, Switzerland; *coding:* AF-Ger, Spy-Sab, AF-Brit, WWI, Dipl, Intell Serv, Hist Am; *biases:* Anti-German, Pro-British.

In his American screen debut, George Sanders plays a World War era British naval officer who assumes the identity of a captured German (look-alike) Imperial Guards officer. After surgically receiving a matching Heidelberg scar and learning to mimic his double's Prussian mannerisms (including wearing a monocle), he "escapes" to the Fatherland. Though the British spy is suspected of being an imposter by German intelligence, he wins the confidence of the elderly head of the Imperial Army, General von Meinhardi. With the decisive aid of a female enemy agent (played by Delores Del Rio), who has fallen in love with him, he is able to obtain the secret "Von Morhart Plan," outlining the Germans' 1917 offensive on the western front. The film's portrayal of German militarism swings awkwardly between parody and calumny—possibly intended as an oblique attack upon Hitler's regime. In one scene of particular relevance to the 1937 audience, General von Meinhardi, upon learning of the entry of the United States into the war, states to the British spy: "I wonder if militarism can breed anything but more militarism—if one war leads to anything but another."

21 THE LAST TRAIN FROM MADRID (Para, Jun) James Hogan; *genre:* War Drama; *location:* Spain; *coding:* Span Civ, AF-W, Pacifism, For Corr, Spy-Sab, Atroc; *bias:* Pacifist.

Though neither the Spanish Civil War, nor any of its participants are specifically identified, there can be no doubt as to when and where this film is supposed to be taking place. Aside from the title, a contemporary ad in a trade journal declares that it is "The first Picture of the Spanish Civil War!" The plot centers around a group of people, including foreign agents, a pacifist, and a jaded American reporter, who has written "too well" about the conflict, awaiting the final train scheduled to leave war-torn Madrid (under heavy seige between November 1936 and March 1937) for the Mediterranean seaport of Valencia (the actual Republican capital). There is an aerial bombing sequence that uses newsreel footage. Despite a prologue stressing its neutrality, the depiction of brutal (unnamed) Loyalists makes this film implicitly pro-Nationalist.

22 THE LIFE OF EMILE ZOLA (WB, Oct) William Dieterle; *genre:* Biography; *locations:* France, Great Britain, South America; *coding:* AF-Fr, Spy-Sab, Jew, Intell Ser, Ger, Fr; *biases:* Anti-Fascist, Pacifist.

Winner of the 1937 Academy Award for Best Picture, this film contains a strident and sincere plea against intolerance. In the latter two-thirds of the motion picture, the plot centers around the notorious turn-of-the-century Dreyfus Affair in France. The issue arose out of a case of espionage, but became a cause célèbre whose main issues were chauvinism and racial bigotry against Jews. Yet anti-semitism is only alluded to in the film. For instance, though the word "Jew" is never uttered, when the staff officers' roster is being examined for a possible suspect, a close-up shot is made of an accusatory finger pointing to the word "Jew" by Dreyfus' name. At another point a reactionary officer describes Dreyfus' alleged crime as a "stab in the back" of France. Ironically, the term was a well-known Nazi epithet at the time for the Social Democrats (some of whom were Jewish) who had signed the Versailles Treaty for Germany. Paul Muni stars in the title role as the famous French author who led the forces defending Dreyfus. Following the publication of Zola's famous "J'Accuse" letter to the President of the Republic, mobs incited by agents of the General Staff destroy pro-Dreyfus newspaper offices, burn books written by the author and even hang Zola in effigy. Eventually Dreyfus is released from years of imprisonment on Devil's Island and reinstated in the Army. But Zola, who was writing a new novel challenging the "militarists who would plunge us into a terrible war," dies on the eve of their triumph.

23 LOST HORIZON (Col, Sept) Frank Capra; *genre:* Adventure/Fantasy; *location:* Brit, China; *coding:* Brit, Ref, Chi, Dipl; *bias:* Pacifist.

Immediately following the credits of this Academy Award winning film the audience witnesses pandemonium at a Chinese airstrip which is under attack by "rebels." Foreign secretary Conway, England's "man of the east," played by Ronald Colman, oversees the evacuation of the foreign nationals. He, along with a few other occidentals, barely escape on the last plane out. But instead of heading for Shanghai, they discover their plane has been hijacked. They are subsequently forced down in the Himalayas, where they discover utopia in the land of "Shangri-La." There, Conway meets a fey "High Lama" who espouses a provocative philosophy questioning the integrity of the individual and his role in a civilization increasingly threatened by mass violence. Instilled with a new sense of mission, our formally jaded diplomat decides to return to the world in order to renew the struggle to save "civilization." In 1942 Columbia reissued a shortened version of the film under the title: *Lost Horizon of Shangri-La.* It had acquired a title following the credits that noted the upheavals in China, such as the revolution in Baskol, were exacerbated by the Japanese invasion of 1937.

24 LOVE UNDER FIRE (TCF, Jun) George Marshall; *genre:* Comedy/Drama; *location:* Fr, Spain; *coding:* Span Civ, Brit, WWI, Fr; *biases:* Pro-British, Non-Intervention.

In this adventure comedy, a cocky Scotland Yard detective (Don Ameche) arrives in Madrid to arrest an alleged jewel thief (Loretta Young). The unspecified Spanish Civil War, "revolution," provides a topical backdrop. Having fallen in love, naturally, the two leave Spain aboard a tramp British steamer. When a Spanish gunboat stops and searches the ship for a missing diamond necklace, the dipsomaniacal captain of the freighter solemnly informs the Spaniards that their actions could be viewed as "another Sarajevo." In an attempt to blockade the Republican port of Bilbao in the spring of 1937, the Nationalists illegally intercepted a number of foreign vessels in international waters.

25 NANCY STEELE IS MISSING (TCF, Mar) George Marshall; *genre:* Drama; *location:* United States; *coding:* Arms Dealers, Pacifism, Hist Am, Ital, FDR, Ger, WWI, Am Icons, War Mats, Blk, AF-MC, Brit; *bias:* Pacifist.

The opening shot of this film features a sign with Woodrow Wilson's portrait that states: "Re-Elect Woodrow Wilson and Keep Us Out of the War—Peace and Honor." But the main plot centers on the kidnapping of a munitions maker's infant daughter in 1917 as a means of personal revenge and as a protest against capitalist wars for profit. Significantly, the denouement does not occur until twenty years later. The influence of arms manufacturers upon America's entrance into the first World War was very much on the public's mind at the time. This film, which was released in the early months of 1937, followed closely upon the conclusion of the Senate Munitions Investigating Committee. This so-called "Nye Committee," had conducted hearings between 1934 and 1936.

26 NATION AFLAME (Ind, Oct) Victor Halperin; *genre:* Drama; *location:* United States; *coding:* Hist Am, Ind Fasc Org, WWI, Atroc; *bias:* Anti-Fascist.

Released in the fall of 1937, this film would appear to be an imitation of *Black Legion,* q.v. It depicts the formation of the fascistic "Avenging Angels" by a gang of racketeers headed by a demagogue and a weak politician. Their creed of 100% Americanism finds such popular support that its leaders achieve virtually unlimited political power. A romantically involved girl becomes convinced of the leader's viciousness. She then helps engineer the Angels' downfall.

27 NAVY BLUE AND GOLD (MGM, Nov) Sam Wood; *genre:* Military Training, Drama; *location:* United States; *coding:* AF-A, Hist Am, AF-N, Am Icons, WWI, Mil School; *bias:* Pro-Military.

Three American boys from different walks of life enter the Naval Academy. After swearing to "...defend the Constitution of the United States against all enemies, foreign and domestic...," they become hopelessly mired in romance and football. MGM reissued it in 1941.

28 NAVY BLUES (Rep, Apr) Ralph Staub; *genre:* Spy; *location:* United States; *coding:* AF-N, Spy-Sab, WWI, Intell Serv, AF-MC; *biases:* Anti-Espionage, Pro-Military.

When an American sailor on leave borrows a library book needed by a gang to solve codes he unwittingly becomes entangled in an attempt to assassinate a visiting prince. Naval intelligence becomes involved and eventually tracks down the "espionage ring" which has also been linked to sabotage. There is a reference to such an incident starting the "last war."

29 NAVY SPY (GN, Mar) Crane Wilbur, Joseph H. Lewis; *genre:* Spy; *location:* United States; *coding:* Ital?, Spy-Sab, AF-N, Atroc, Secret Weapons, Intell Serv, Am Icons; *biases:* Anti-Espionage, Pro-Military.

Unidentified foreign interests kidnap and torture musically inclined Lt. Carrington in an attempt to get him to sing about the new "vapor fuel" he has invented. A secret service agent and his girlfriend come to the rescue. A lot of stock footage of the U.S. Pacific fleet is incorporated in the film.

30 THE ROAD BACK (Univ, Aug) James Whale; *genre:* Drama; *location:* Germany; *coding:* Jew, Fr, AF-Ger, AF-A, WWI, Comm?; *bias:* Pacifist.

Adapted from the 1931 Remarque novel of the same title, this was billed as a sequel to *All Quiet on the Western Front.* It portrays the trials of the survivors of a German combat company when they return to a defeated homeland wracked by social and political upheaval. Despite a heavy dose of barracks humor, the film concludes on a somber note. The two leads, while pondering the negative effects of the war upon a comrade, see a goosestepping group of youths led by an evil-looking dwarf. As they comment on the futility of war, there is a montage of shots showing German rearmament. The armband-wearing soldiers are obviously meant to represent the anti-radical reactionary Free Corps movement in Germany of 1918–1923 and create associative linkages with the Nazi regime. On March 16, 1935, Hitler had proclaimed the revival of compulsory military service in Germany. Hitler's remilitarization of the Rhineland the following March confirmed German rearmament. There was a direct attempt by the Nazi government to stop production of this film. And in fact, as a result of continued German pressure, Universal made significant alterations in the film after it was completed.

31 SEA DEVILS (RKO, Feb) Ben Stoloff; *genre:* Adventure; *location:* United States; *coding:* Latin Am, AF-CG, WWI, Am Icons; *bias:* Pro-Military.

The valiant men of the neglected service, the Coast Guard, go on rescue missions and struggle with icebergs in the North Atlantic. A teenaged Ida Lupino plays the love interest.

32 SEVENTH HEAVEN (TCF, Mar) Henry King; *genre:* War Drama; *location:* France; *coding:* AF-Fr, WWI, AF-Ger, Comm?; *bias:* Pacifist.

This is a remake of a 1927 World War I era melodrama directed by Frank Borzage. It has a distinctly pacifistic slant. James Stewart and Simone Simon play a pair of lovers who struggle with poverty in a Left Bank Parisian slum known as "The Sock." When he, Chico, is called-up by the army in 1914, they decide to marry. Lacking the time to formally wed, they exchange personal vows. Though a professed atheist, Chico swears to God his undying love for Diane and that each day of their separation, at the same time (eleven) the couple will renew their vows. Over the next four years, while Chico fights on the western front and Diane works as a laundress at a military hospital, the two spiritually communicate with one another. But near the end of the war it appears that Chico's physical being succumbed to wounds received during a German gas attack. Nevertheless, his spirit remains with Diane in their seventh story garret, their "seventh heaven." On Armistice Day, November 11, 1918, at eleven, a blinded Chico is reunited with his faithful lover.

33 SHALL WE DANCE (RKO, May) Mark Sandrich; *genre:* Musical Comedy; *location:* United States; *coding:* Chi?, Blk, AF-MC?; *bias:* Contraband Message.

Peter Peters, alias "Petrov," (Fred Astaire) an American dancer turned famous continental ballet "artiste," is heading west across the Atlantic aboard an ocean liner. He is assiduously accosting a jaded homegrown "hoofer," played by Ginger Rogers. Looking for a change of pace, he joins the black crew in a chrome plated Art Deco engine room and begins to "jiggle" to the Gershwin tune, "Slap That Bass." The lyrics note the following: "The world is in a mess with politics and taxes/ And people grinding axes.../ Dictators would be better off/ If they zoom-zoomed now and then/ Today you can see that the happiest men...."

34 THE SINGING MARINE (WB, July) Ray Enright; *genre:* Musical; *locations:* United States, China; *coding:* AF-MC, Comm?, Chi; *bias:* Pro-Military.

A young Marine, played by Dick Powell, becomes a singing sensation, and it goes to his head. Eventually the Corps wins out over an entertainment career and he ships out to Shanghai. Action of a sort occurs when the Marine's agent falsely claims his client has

been kidnapped by Chinese "bandits" (frequently a euphemism for communists during this period). One of the big production numbers put together by Busby Berkeley, "Night Over Shanghai," would appear to exploit the continued interest in that troubled area that so fascinated Americans in the late 1930s.

35 SUBMARINE D-1 (WB, Nov) Lloyd Bacon; *genre:* Adventure; *locations:* United States, Panama; *coding:* Fil, Latin Am, AF-N, Mil Exer; *bias:* Pro-Military.

An armed forces film with the usual love story. A lot of documentary footage of submarines (even underwater shots) and of the Navy's other vessels is included. The main action centers around the use of a newly invented rescue air chamber after the D-1 is rammed and sunk by a cruiser while participating in joint maneuvers.

36 SWEETHEART OF THE NAVY (GN, Jun) Duncan Mansfield; *genre:* Romance; *location:* United States; *coding:* AF-N, Blk, Mil School, AF-MC; *bias:* Pro-Military.

Though short on action, this was another in a continuing line of patriotically romantic pro-service films. Some earlier examples include: *Hell Below* (MGM, 1933); *Come On, Marines* (Par., 1934); *Follow the Fleet* (RKO, 1936). The Fleet arrives in San Pedro (located south of Los Angeles, it was the home base of the Pacific Fleet until 1940) and the gobs descend upon the "Snug Harbor" cabaret run by a pretty singer. Unfortunately, their patronage is not enough to clear the debts incurred by her business partner's sudden desertion. By arranging a prize fight the boys eventually are able to help her out though. Meanwhile, she has fallen in love with one of the salts. But marriage will have to wait till after he completes his four years at the Naval Academy and becomes an officer.

37 SWING IT SAILOR! (GN, Nov) Raymond Cannon; *genre:* Comedy/Drama; *location:* United States; *coding:* Comm, AF-N, Russ, Mil Exer; *bias:* Pro-Military.

Following up on *Sweetheart of the Navy*, q.v., which was released earlier in the year, Grand National stuck to a recurrent Hollywood formula in military films—portraying the fact that the military, i.e., Uncle Sam must come before the pretty gal. It has the gobs stations aboard an aircraft carrier and features many shots of these vessels and their planes in action during Pacific Fleet maneuvers. A passing reference to a fleet visit to Vladivostok is made. Such a visit actually took place in the latter part of July in direct response to the full-scale Japanese invasion of China on July 5th.

38 THERE GOES MY GIRL (RKO, May) Ben Holmes; *genre:* Comedy; *location:* United States; *coding:* For Corr, Italo-Eth, War; *bias:* Contraband Message.

The managing editor of a big city newspaper tries to interfere with the marriage plans of his star reporter, played by Ann Sothern, to a rival newspaperman. After a staged murder interrupts the ceremonies the two lovers have a spat in a coffee shop. She tells the frustrated bridegroom he should be able to wait a couple of more days. He quips: "Yea, that's what you said a year ago when you went off to Ethiopia." There are definite similarities to the 1931 film, *The Front Page* (UA).

39 THEY GAVE HIM A GUN (MGM, May) W. S. Van Dyke; *genre:* Crime, Training/Combat; *locations:* United States, France; *coding:* AF-A, AF-Ger, AF-Fr, Blk, WWI, War Mats, Ger, Vets, Draft; *bias:* Pacifist.

A montage of arms manufacturing launches this film. Later sequences of fighting on the Western front and of writhing bodies in a military hospital emphasize the human suffering created by war. The premise of this otherwise typical gangster exercise is that the World War turned a timid bookkeeper (Franchot Tone) into a psychopath: "I got my diploma in France." Its pacifistic theme is unmistakable.

40 THEY WON'T FORGET (WB, Oct) Mervyn Leroy; *genre:* Drama; *location:* United States; *coding:* Hist Am, WWI, Vets, Blk, Am Icons, Atroc; *bias:* Anti-Fascist.

A prosecutor in a southern town turns a murder case into a political football. Hatred, bigotry and sectionalism are brought into the open. More than likely, this film was influenced by Lang's 1936 *Fury* (MGM). Although it does not deal as directly with the irrationality of the mob as did Lang's work, it is in fact climaxed by a senseless and ruthless lynching. This film was loosely based on a historical novel that had used the infamous Leo Frank case of 1913 as its source.

41 THINK FAST, MR. MOTO (TCF, Aug) Norman Foster; *genre:* Crime; *location:* China; *coding:* Jap, Russ, Ger; *bias:* Contraband Message.

Twentieth Century–Fox kicked off the Moto series with this film, starring Peter Lorre as the famous Japanese international police detective. It is a typical example of the thriller genre. What makes it relevant is that most of the action takes place in Shanghai. The story centers around the smuggling of diamonds and narcotics to the United States by "White Russians" (ousted from their homeland by the Soviets, forced out of Harbin by the Japanese during their 1931 invasion of Manchuria) who are manipulated by a ruthless and enigmatic Germanic type played by Sig Rumann.

42 TOVARICH (WB, Dec) Anatole Litvak; *genre:* Comedy; *location:* France; *coding:* Russ, Atroc, Comm, Brit, Fr, Dipl; *bias:* Anti-Soviet.

This comedy was based on a Jacques Deval play that had earlier been filmed in France (*Tovaritch*, 1935). It features an impoverished couple, former members of the Russian Royal Family, who opt for domestic service in Paris rather than use for themselves, give to a pretender to the throne, or surrender to the Soviets some forty billion francs entrusted to them by the late Tsar.

Only an appeal by a visiting "commissar" for financial aid to mother Russia in order to prevent the "enslavement" of her people to foreign business interests persuades the White comrades to relent. Anti-Soviet commentary is rather mild. There is a negative reference, by the commissar, to "British imperialism."

43 WALLABY JIM OF THE ISLANDS (GN, Oct) Charles Lamont; *genre:* Adventure; *location:* Pacific; *coding:* Neth, Brit; *bias:* Contraband Message.

Wallaby Jim, handsome singing captain of the brig *Kestral*, is a pearl trader in the South Pacific who is well known throughout the area and loved by the natives. His partner, Norman, becomes an unreliable drunkard after gambling away a considerable sum of money entrusted to him by Jim. A rival Dutch trader and his band of Germanic thugs take advantage of this to gain information from Norman about an unregistered claim of Wallaby's for a new pearl island.

This leads to a violent confrontation when Jim takes the *Kestral* to the island to intercept the thieves. The leader of the gang of cutthroats is named Adolph Richter (as in Adolf Hitler). The dictatorial Richter wears a monocle, speaks with a heavy German accent and enjoys physically abusing the natives, often contemptuously referring to them as "dummkopfs." Wallaby's chief mate just happens to be a Britisher named Limey.

44 WEE WILLIE WINKIE (TCF, Jul) John Ford; *genre:* Adventure; *locations:* Arab, India; *coding:* Dipl, AF-Brit; *bias:* Pro-British.

In this re-worked adaptation of a Kipling short story, an American widow traveling with her young daughter joins her British father-in-law on service in India. Priscilla, the daughter played by Shirley Temple, quickly softens grandfather's stiff upper lip. He then proceeds to paternalistically instruct her in Britain's Imperial mission: "Beyond that pass, thousands of savages are waiting to sweep down and ravage India. It's England's duty, it's my duty, to see that this doesn't happen...." The natives have the gall to break up the regimental dance while rescuing their imprisoned leader. Ingenuous Priscilla askes her Colonel grandfather why they are always fighting. He denies he wants war: "The Empire wants to be friends with everyone...." She then decides to go and explain this to the rebelling Khan, whom she had befriended while he was in captivity. The Colonel anxiously follows with troops and the Union Jack flying. But the little American emissary's sincerity aborts violence and re-established the bonds of Imperial friendship. This film was produced by Darryl F. Zanuck.

45 WEST OF SHANGHAI aka **WARLORD** (WB, Oct) John Farrow; *genre:* Adventure; *location:* China; *coding:* AF-Chi, Chi, Dipl, Atroc; *bias:* Pro-Chinese.

A group of American promoters and missionaries find themselves prisoners of a ruthless warlord. They are eventually rescued by Nationalist troops. It was the third filming of the Holbrook Blinn play, *The Bad Men*. Significantly, its original Mexican setting has been switched to China—presumably to cash in on the interest in the Sino-Japanese conflict.

46 WINGS OVER HONOLULU (Univ, May) H. C. Potter; *genre:* Drama; *location:* United States; *coding:* Blk, AF-N, Mil Exer, Mil School; *bias:* Pro-Military.

With "the cooperation of the United States Navy," we get to see all their planes and aircraft carriers stationed at Pearl Harbor while being entertained by a fluffy military romance. War games are depicted, featuring a flying boat squadron under the command of Ray Milland.

47 WISE GIRL (RKO, Dec) Leigh Jason; *genre:* Comedy; *location:* United States; *coding:* Russ?, Pacifism, Ital; *biases:* Contraband Message, Pacifist.

Miriam Hopkins plays the daughter of a millionaire who wants to attain custody of her deceased sister's two children from their guardian, a Greenwich Village artist. Miss Hopkins, Susan, goes to the Village incognito and wins the confidence of the artist, played by Ray Milland. The two young girls have been educated out of school by the free thinking, anti-capitalist Bohemian. Susan comes upon them playing a game in which the following interchange takes place:

SUSAN: ...What war are you playing today?
JOAN: We're not playing war, we're playing peace.
SUSAN: I thought I heard shooting.
JOAN: Oh, we were shooting the rats that get people into war. John [Milland] says they should be kicked in the pants and then shot.

The Juvenile Aid Society seizes the girls and a custody battle in court follows. The final solution is matrimony so that the four can live happily ever after.

1938

48 AIR DEVILS (Univ., May) John Rawlins; *genre:* Adventure; *location:* Pacific; *coding:* AF-N, AF-MC; *bias:* Pro-Military.

A couple of ex–Marines (Larry Blake and Dick Purcell) become flying policemen on a South Pacific island. When a shady character attempts to prevent the U.S. Navy from establishing an air base on the island, the patriotism of the two expatriates is aroused.

49 ARMY GIRL (Rep, Jul) George Nicholls, Jr.; *genre:* Romance; *location:* United States; *coding:* Latin Am, blk, AF-A; *bias:* Pro-Military.

A barracks love story. The new captain introduces the latest tank and meets the old commander's attractive young daughter. The high point of the film is a test race between the squat, turretless tank and the cavalry; a not so subtle plug for the mechanization of the army. This film contains a mildly pacifistic subtext by implying machines will take over fighting in any future war and thereby spare men's lives.

50 ARREST BULLDOG DRUMMOND (Para, Nov) James Hogan; *genre:* Crime; *locations:* Great Britain, Atlantic; *coding:* Spy-Sab, Blk, Pacifism, Secret Weapon; *biases:* Pro-British, Anti-Espionage.

Captain Drummond again interrupts his nuptials in order to neutralize some international spies. This time, the spies are slightly Germanic in nature. It appears their interest lies with an "atomic disintegrator" that has been invented by a disenchanted pacifist scientist who calls himself "The Earl of Destiny," and says "I can disarm the whole war-mad world!"

51 BATTLE OF BROADWAY (TCF, Apr) George Marshall; *genre:* Comedy/Drama; *location:* United States; *coding:* WWI, Vets, Blk; *biases:* Pro-American; Pro-Military.

In the year of the 75th anniversary of the Battle of Gettysburg, with memories of the Bonus Marchers fading, and with the international environment becoming increasingly dangerous, the premiere veteran's organization in the U.S., the American Legion, was having a revival. Between a comedic Quirt-Flagg combination, a love story and a couple of songs, the film works in a little flag-waving during the Legion's national convention.

52 BLOCKADE (UA, Jul) William Dieterle; *genre:* War Drama; *location:* Spain; *coding:* Span Civ, Spy-Sab, For Corr, Sp, Pacifism, AF-Ital, Collab, Brit, Atroc, Russ; *biases:* Anti-Fascist, Pacifist.

Although the country and date ("Spain,

1936") are given in the opening title, the various participants are never specifically identified in the Walter Wanger production. Nevertheless, the hero (Henry Fonda) and his compatriots wear the traditional Basque beret and a uniform which would sartorially link them with the Republican forces. If there is any overt political message in the film's text, it is more of a pacifistic one, particularly explicit in the concluding speech delivered by Fonda which is directly and impassionately addressed to the film audience.

53 BLUEBEARD'S EIGHTH WIFE (Para, Mar) Ernst Lubitsch; *genre:* Comedy; *location:* Europe; *coding:* Comm, Fr, World Crisis; *bias:* Contraband Message.

A young American millionaire's (Gary Cooper) attempt to purchase the top half only of a pair of pajamas elicits accusations of promoting communism from the management of a Riviera department store. He is told that there are already "enough troubles in Europe" without his making such revolutionary demands. The millionaire, who has had seven wives, encounters an impoverished French aristocrat (Claudette Colbert) at the same counter who wishes to purchase only the bottoms. The two marry soon afterwards and, symbolic of the current world turmoil, they spend their honeymoon quarreling across the map of Europe. They seem most antagonistic in Vienna and Prague (the capitals of the two countries Hitler chose to directly interfere with in that year). America's lack of understanding of the European situation would seem to be emphasized when the frustrated protagonist tries to cure a case of insomnia by spelling Czechoslovakia backwards. *Once Upon a Honeymoon* (RKO, 1942) may have been influenced by this work.

54 BORDER G-MAN (RKO, Jun) David Howard; *genre:* Western; *location:* United States; *coding:* Neutrality, Act, Latin Am, FBI, War Mats, Ger?, AF-CG; *bias:* Non-Intervention.

In this interesting combination of genres cowboy star George O'Brien plays Jim Galloway, a G-man incognito. He, his faithful sidekick, Smoky, and their musical group clash with a gang of smugglers attempting to deliver illegally trained men, horses, and guns to agents of an unnamed South American country. The violation of the Neutrality Act is specifically mentioned.

55 BROTHER RAT (WB, Oct) William Keighley; *genre:* Comedy; *location:* United States; *coding:* Hist Am, Mil School, Peace Organ, Am Icons; *bias:* Contraband Message.

Released a month after the Munich Crisis this film was based on the play written about VMI by a couple of its grads. It is a typical military academy farce of the period.

Material referring to contemporary world events is included. After being dressed down by an overzealous duty officer, Billy (Wayne Morris) petulantly remarks: "You know, it's guys like that that are responsible for peace movements getting started." Later, the same cadet while at a parlor petting session picks up a book from a table and produces nervous laughter when he shows the title: *It Can't Happen Here.* (A reference to the 1935 best seller written by Sinclair Lewis in which an American fascist movement takes over the country.)

56 THE BUCCANEER (Para, Feb) Cecil B. DeMille; *genre:* Biography; *location:* United States; *coding:* Dipl?, AF-A, AF-N, Fr, Ger, Blk, Hist Am, Am Icons, AF-Brit, Collab; *biases:* Pro-American, Anti-Brit.

The politics are superficial in this occasionally spectacular swashbuckler. It features the infamous pirate Lafitte (Fredric March) and his Bayou kingdom of "Baratarian" on the Louisiana coast. Most of the non-romantic action centers around the pirate's crucial decision to aid their American compatriots in repulsing the British attack on New Orleans in 1814. The motion picture is rabidly pro-American. A touch of Anglophobia is displayed in the encounters with British agents and traitorous American collaborationists, led by a U.S. senator.

57 BULLDOG DRUMMOND IN AFRICA (Para, Aug) Louis King; *genre:* Crime; *locations:* Great Britain, Africa; *coding:* Brit, Intell, Serv, Spy-Sab, WWI, Ger, Secret Weapons; *biases:* Pro-British, Anti-Espionage.

Some international spies kidnap the head of Scotland Yard, Col. Neilson, and carry him off to Spanish Morocco. He must either give up the secret of a radio-wave disintegrating device or be thrown to the lions. Again abandoning his wedding, Bulldog follows in hot pursuit and not long afterwards the lions are forced to settle for other fare.

58 BULLDOG DRUMMOND'S REVENGE (Para, Jan) Louis King; *genre:* Crime; *location:* Great Britain; *coding:* Spy-Sab, Jap?, Secret Weapon, War Mats, Brit, Intell Serv; *biases:* Pro-British, Anti-Espionage.

Adventure-seeking ex-British Army officer Hugh "Bulldog" Drummond first appeared in a 1920 novel. The character made his British film debut two years later, and in 1929 the first American film to feature the character appeared: *Bulldog Drummond* (UA). Most of the films about the character appeared in the late 1930s, with John Howard as Drummond. In this episode, after boarding the train ferry to Calais, his wedding is continually delayed by the annoyingly persistent attempts of a transvestite and a (presumably) Japanese spy, Sumio

Konda, to gain possession of the formula for a secret explosive called "hextonite."

59 CIPHER BUREAU (GN, Nov) Charles Lamont; *genre:* Spy; *location:* United States; *coding:* AF-A, AF-N, Spy-Sab, Secret Weapon, Am Icons, Ger; *biases:* Anti-Espionage, Anti-German.

A security leak of the plans for a new naval gun into the hands of enemy agents is discovered by the head of the decoding branch of the U.S. Army. Their country of origin is never named, but the spies' surnames are undoubtedly Teutonic. Eventually, suspicion falls on a beautiful pianist who is using radio performances to secretly transmit messages. Several devices used by America's secret agents to intercept and decipher coded messages are shown, including the goniometer to help locate hidden radio transmitters. The *New York Times* reviewer bemusedly noted that in several interior scenes at different locations in Washington, D.C., the same "reassuring facade of the National Capitol" appears through the venetian blinds. Three years later, *International Lady* (UA), q.v., would also feature musically coded messages delivered via radio.

60 COME ON, LEATHERNECKS (Rep, Aug) James Cruze; *genre:* Adventure; *locations:* United States, Philippines; *coding:* Fil, AF-MC, Arms Dealers, AF-N, Ger?, Mil School; *bias:* Pro-Military.

The hero wants to play football rather than be a good Marine. His colonel father thinks otherwise. He achieves the proper military élan while fighting gun runners led by "Otto Wagner," in the Philippines.

61 THE DAWN PATROL (WB, Dec) Edmund Goulding; *genre:* War Drama/Combat; *location:* France; *coding:* WWI, AF-Brit, AF-Ger; *biases:* Pacifist, Pro-British.

A timely and rather costly remake of Hawks' 1930 classic. In fact, the film incorporated much of the spectacular aerial footage shot for the original. The latter of two overt pacifistic comments refers to men dying in "future wars." The general tenor of the film places a greater emphasis than its predecessor on the bureaucratization and resulting dehumanization of war. It is also patently pro-British (the principal characters are all British expatriates).

62 THE DUKE OF WEST POINT (UA, Dec) Alfred E. Green; *genre:* Drama; *locations:* Great Britain, United States; *coding:* Mil School, AF-A, Am Icons, Brit, WWI?; *bias:* Pro-Military.

This is a notch above the buddy-boy, football-at-West Point routine which was featured earlier in the year in Paramount's *Touchdown Army*, q.v. It features a conceited army officer's son (Louis Hayward) who returns from Cambridge in order to become the fifth member of his family to attend the United States Military Academy at West Point. The highlight of the film is a hockey match between the Point and Canada's Royal Military College. The father of one of Hayward's roommates was "killed in action," presumably during the First World War.

63 EVERYBODY'S DOING IT (RKO, Jan) Christy Cabanne; *genre:* Comedy; *location:* United States; *coding:* World Crisis; *bias:* Contraband Message.

Bruce (Preston Foster) is a whiskey-swilling ad man cashing in on the picture puzzles craze that is sweeping America. He is kidnapped by a gang of crooks intent on getting the answers to a nationwide breakfast cereal contest that he has created. At one point early in the film, "Bubbles," the dumb blonde entertainer at Bruce's favorite watering hole, tells her girlfriend, "I'm going to steal Bruce right from under your eye, even if it starts a world war."

64 A FAREWELL TO ARMS (1932 Re-Release) (Para,) Frank Borzage; *genre:* War Drama; *locations:* Italy, Switzerland; *coding:* AF-Brit, AF-Austr, AF-W, WWI, AF-Ital, Am Vol; *bias:* Pacifist.

A reissue of the WWI era pacifistic film starring Gary Cooper and Helen Hayes that was based on the 1929 novel by Ernest Hemingway. Presumably reflecting the fears of the 1930s, there are air attacks on retreating troops and civilians in the film that were not in the book. Furthermore, the film has the heroine's death coincide with the Austrian acceptance of Italian armistice terms as dictated by Marshall Badoglio—the head of the Italian military under Mussolini and the commander of his legions in Ethiopia during 1936.

65 FLIGHT TO FAME (Col, Oct) C. C. Coleman, Jr.; *genre:* Crime; *location:* United States; *coding:* Secret Weapon, Latin Am, WWI, AF-A, Ger?; *bias:* Pro-Military.

An electronic death-ray mysteriously fails to work in a test before War Department officials. Meanwhile, a young army captain in love with the ray inventor's daughter has designed a new pursuit plane. But each time a model is test flown it is destroyed by a similar metal melting ray. Naturally, the inventor is suspected. But the culprit turns out to be a man who copied the ray's design in order to carry out a vendetta against pilots responsible for his disgrace during World War I. Interestingly, the killer's assistant is a Germanic type named Muller.

66 FOUR MEN AND A PRAYER (TCF, Apr) John Ford; *genre:* Drama; *locations:* Great Britain, India, United States, Latin America, Egypt; *coding:* Latin Am, AF-RAF, Atroc, Blk, AF-W, War Mats, Arms Dealers, AF-Brit, Dipl, Brit; *bias:* Pacifist.

A colonel cashiered from the British Indian Army returns home with papers proving that he was framed by an international armaments ring. He is murdered and the papers are stolen. His four sons, one of whom is the military attache at the British Embassy in Washington, join forces to clear his name. And with the aid of the daughter of the owner of "Atlas Arms" they are able to put an end to the gun running business. She has been appalled at witnessing the slaughter of an island kingdom rebel army, whose ranks included women and children. Her father's company had supplied arms to both sides. During a heated conversation, a revealing statement is made by the arms manufacturer to his daughter: "War is mass stupidity and collective insanity.... But, I'm not responsible if fools want to cut each others' throats." Darryl F. Zanuck was the producer of this anti-war statement.

67 GANGSTER'S BOY (Mono, Nov) William Nigh; *genre:* Drama; *location:* United States; *coding:* Hist Am, Mil School, FDR, Ital, AF-A; *bias:* Pro-American.

Andrew Jackson High's star pupil and athlete, who is preparing to go to West Point, is ostracized by his small town community when it is learned that his father is a "retired" racketeer. But Larry (Jackie Cooper) perseveres and delivers a patriotic graduation speech: "...[in this] world of confusion and bitterness, where certain forces have tried to destroy the foundations of our nation ... we [are] ... well armed ... [by] our forefathers.... We have what boys and girls in some other countries might not have ... [and] we will fight the good fight...." After being absolved of a false hit and run charge, Larry proudly prepares to enter the U.S. Military Academy.

68 GATEWAY (TCF, Aug) Alfred Werker; *genre:* Drama; *locations:* Atlantic, United States; *coding:* Ger, Brit, Ital, Russ, Pol, Comm, Ref, For Corr, Span Civ, Quotas, Jew, Am Icons, Chin, Hist Am; *biases:* Pro-American, Anti-Soviet, Anti-Nazi.

On board an ocean liner bound for New York, a war correspondent (Don Ameche) returning from Spain meets and courts an Irish girl named Catherine. In the process, he manages to compromise her which results in her detention at Ellis Island. Catherine's fellow detainees are a German-Jewish "political refugee" named Dr. Wielander who states that "in my country it's no longer popular to believe in democracy," a bitchy Russian communist and an Italian gangster. At a July 4th celebration the doctor proudly recites the opening passage from the Declaration of Independence. Upon approving Wielander's admission the immigration inspector tells the doctor, "... I suspect your country's loss to be our country's gain." Naturally, Dick, our correspondent, steps into the marital breach in order to rescue Catherine from deportation.

69 GIVE ME A SAILOR (Para, Aug) Eliot Nugent; *genre:* Comedy; *location:* United States; *coding:* AF-N; *bias:* Pro-Military.

Martha Raye received top-billing over Bob Hope in this comedy about two sailors in love with two girls (the other female lead was a young Betty Grable). The film opens with a montage of Navy ships and planes, and a chorus of sailors singing "The USA and You," including these lines: "Would I be sore, if a doggone war/ Ever came between us two./ I hope I stay in the USA,/ But if there comes a day/ When I must go away,/ I'll still be true, to the USA and you./ The film ends with documentary and re-created footage of the Navy Day celebrations (apparently in San Diego).

70 GOLD DIGGERS IN PARIS (WB, Jun) Ray Enright; *genre:* Musical Comedy; *locations:* United States, France; *coding:* Russ, Fr, AF-N, FDR; *biases:* Pro-Military, Pro-American.

The plot evolves around the Gold Diggers being mistakenly invited to enter in the Paris dancing exposition. Naturally, they win. What is interesting is that the singing leading man, played by Rudy Vallee, has a fondness for wearing American Naval officers' uniforms and impersonating FDR. In addition, as in many other films in which Busby Berkeley contributed, the final song and dance routine features a military motif. Probably the most notable earlier example being "The Forgotten Man" number from *The Gold Diggers of 1933* (WB). This time it is a full cast salute to a giant American Naval officer's cap. The Paris Exhibition lasted from May to November 1937. The most prominent pavilions were Nazi Germany's and the Soviet Union's. But New York City's Rockettes, on loan to the U.S. Pavilion, dazzled the Parisians with their precision dancing.

71 THE GOLDWYN FOLLIES (UA, Feb) George Marshal; *genre:* Musical Comedy; *location:* United States; *coding:* AF-N, Russ; *bias:* Contraband Message.

As its title implies, this Technicolor film is an episodic review whose weak Hollywood-discovery-of-new-talent plot is held together by a number of running gags and specialty acts, including three performed by the zany Ritz Brothers. During a scene in which a studio crew is shooting on location, a couple of local girls sit on a hill to observe the action. One of the young ladies notes that they better leave before they are accused of being international spies, "You know, like trying to get plans for the new navy or something." After much debate concerning potential threats to America's national security, a massive 10 year expansion program for the U.S. Navy, the New Deal administration's "New Navy," was approved in the summer of 1938.

72 HARD TO GET (WB, Nov) Ray Enright; *genre:* Comedy; *location:* United States; *coding:* Span Civ; *bias:* Contraband Message.

A rich heiress played by Olivia De Haviland takes a powder from visiting Newport with her domineering mother. While having her car filled with gas she turns on the radio. The station attendant alludes to the Spanish Civil War when he philosophically muses, "That's Spanish music, ain't it? I guess those poor people don't have much chance for dancin' anymore...."

73 HAWAII CALLS (RKO, Mar) Edward F. Cline; *genre:* Musical Comedy; *location:* United States; *coding:* AF-N, Spy-Sab, Jap?, Ger?; *biases:* Pro-Military, Anti-Espionage.

Juvenile crooner Bobby Breen plays a bootblack who stows away with a young Hawaiian newsboy on a ship bound for the Islands. He is caught, but his beautiful singing with the ship's band wins over the captain. Between songs, he and his sidekick help capture some international spies who have stolen the secret plans for a Hawaiian fortification from an American Naval officer. Among the spies are "Muller" and an Asian houseboy. The film concludes with the orphan's adoption by the officer.

74 HOLD THAT KISS (MGM, May) Edwin L. Marin; *genre:* Comedy; *location:* United States; *coding:* Chi, AF-N, Blk, Arms control; *bias:* Contraband Message.

He is a clerk at a travel agency and she is a model at a dress salon. Both believe the other is wealthy. During a special dinner for the "rich" beau at which her gambler brother impersonates a naval officer, a question is raised viz the 5:5:3 naval limitations ratio (At the Washington Naval Arms conference of 1921–1922 a warship tonnage ratio of 5:5:3 was established between the U.S., Britain and Japan. Following the 2nd London Naval conference of 1935–1936, Japan refused to go along with the modifications proposed by the British and Americans, subsequently leading to the largest peacetime naval appropriations in U.S. history). After the two comically show each other up at their respective jobs, the young couple seal their new relationship with a kiss.

75 HOLIDAY (Col, Jun) George Cukor; *genre:* Comedy; *location:* United States; *coding:* Fascism; *biases:* Anti-Fascist, Contraband Message.

A classic screwball comedy with a social message starring Katherine Hepburn and Cary Grant. During the crucial party sequence, the stereotypical bigoted, blue blood couple, the Crams, invade the protagonist's private "playroom," where they are facetiously greeted with a collective fascist salute by the liberated defenders of the spirit of the common man. Later, in the same scene, Mr. Cram states, "It wouldn't take that long [to make a lot of money] if we had the right kind of government." He is immediately and bitingly queried, "Like which country, Mr. Cram?" The screenplay was written by Donald Ogden Stewart, a member of the Hollywood Anti-Nazi League.

76 HOLLYWOOD HOTEL (WB, Jan) Busby Berkeley; *genre:* Musical Comedy; *location:* United States; *coding:* Russ, Blk, Sino-Jap War; *bias:* Contraband Message.

A singer/saxophonist in the Benny Goodman Band, Ronnie Bowers (Dick Powell), goes to Hollywood under contract. But no sooner does he arrive than he becomes entangled in assorted misadventures centering around an obnoxious starlett named Mona Marshall. The day after the premier of her latest film, which she refused to attend, her maid brings her the paper and suggests Mona read the gossip column. With the latest edition in her hands, Mona, pompously lectures her maid that there is far more important news than Hollywood gossip: "There happens to be a big war in China ... and they tell me Russia no longer has a Tsar...."

77 I AM THE LAW (Col, Sept) Alexander Hall; *genre:* Crime; *location:* United States; *coding:* Draft; *bias:* Contraband Message.

A college law professor cancels his planned overseas sabbatical after a newspaper friend informs him that rampant corruption has "sabotaged" the efforts of a governor's committee to combat organized crime in the city. The pipe smoking professor, played by Edward G. Robinson, later tells his wife that he has been "drafted" as a special prosecutor. When the professor's efforts are systematically thwarted by spies in his office, he establishes an independent crime committee at his home staffed by loyal former students whom he has enlisted "for the duration of the war." With the cooperation of the friendly newspaper editor and a select group of clean cops the professor eventually succeeds in rounding up the gangster "rodents." The martial rhetoric of this cinematic crime war is significant since the film was released during the height of the Munich crisis.

78 INTERNATIONAL SETTLEMENT (TCF, Feb) Eugene Forbe; *genre:* Adventure; *locations:* Pacific, China; *coding:* Ital, Ref, AF-Jap, Brit, Fr, Dipl?, For Corr, Arms Dealer, Italo-Eth War, Sino-Jap War, Chi, Am Vol, Latin Am; *biases:* Non-Intervention, Anti-Japanese.

This film opens with Lowell Thomas delivering a neutral commentary on the war in China. He concludes that, "Two proud and ancient nations [Japan is not specified] have declared there can be no diplomatic settlement of their differences. This is war without compromise. One that will end only in defeat or victory." This Darryl F. Zanuck production also incorporated several less objective newsreel shots of the Japanese bombing of Shanghai. The actual plot centers around a soldier of fortune, played by George Sanders, who has been hired as the "collector" of custom certificates needed to carry out a munitions deal that is to take place in Shanghai. In the process he becomes entangled in espionage and falls in love with a French singer played by Delores Del Rio. She saves his life during a Japanese aerial assault and later escapes with him aboard a ship full of refugees fleeing the war. Newsreel footage of the conflict in and around Shanghai, including grisly scenes of the Japanese bombing of the Chinese native quarter, had appeared in the September 10, 1937, "March of Time" release: "War in China." Since the second half of the 19th century an International Settlement with separate militarily armed national zones had evolved in Shanghai. In 1932 and again in July 1937 troops from Japan's sector invaded China. Eight months of bloody fighting followed the latter incident and precipitated a full-scale war; the Sino-Japanese War (1937– 1945).

79 INVISIBLE ENEMY (Rep, Apr) John H. Auer; *genre:* Adventure; *locations:* Great Britain, France; *coding:* Spy-Sab, Brit, Intell Serv, Russ, Latin Am; *bias:* Pacifist.

A down and out ex-intelligence officer from Britain breaks up an oil cartel, thus averting a world war. He also gets the girl.

80 THE INVISIBLE MENACE (WB, Jan) John Farrow; *genre:* Mystery; *locations:* United States, Haiti; *coding:* AF-A, Blk, AF-N, War Mats, Arms Dealers; *bias:* Pro-Military.

On a fog-bound army base with a munitions depot, Powder Island, located off shore from the U.S. mainland, a murder related to the activities of gunrunners is investigated. Among the suspects being scrutinized by a government agent is a civil engineer played by Boris Karloff. During an extended flashback, it is disclosed that the engineer's drinking problems had been responsible for a revolt of native laborers on a road construction project in Haiti during the U.S. military occupation of that troubled island nation (1915–1932). This film portrays positive benefits from U.S. military intervention in the Western Hemisphere, but obliquely attacks violations of the Neutrality Act. In 1943 it was remade as a war-related film entitled *Murder on the Waterfront*.

81 JUST AROUND THE CORNER (TCF, Nov) Irving Cummings; *genre:* Musical; *location:* United States; *coding:* World Crisis, Blk; *bias:* Contraband Message.

Shirley Temple helps her unemployed father—a previously high-paid New York architect—overcome Depression malaise and find a new backer for his prize project. Their former maid, worried about the impact on her boyfriend's job of shutdowns by a major financier, shows her man a relevant article in the morning newspaper. The headline reads: "Stocks Tumble as War Scare Spreads in Europe." This film was released on November 11, less than two months after the resolution of the Munich Crisis.

82 LITTLE ORPHAN ANNIE (Para, Dec) Ben Holmes; *genre:* Drama; *location:* United States; *coding:* Chi, Am Icons; *biases:* Pro-American, Anti-Fascist.

Having run away from her cruel guardian, Annie is taken in by the friendly immigrants of New York's East Side. Discovering that her new friends are exploited by a loan shark and his fascistic thugs, Annie decides to fight back. After reading a portion of the Declaration of Independence to the immigrants, she rallies them to organize resistance against the local bullies.

83 LITTLE TOUGH GUY (Univ, July) Harold Young; *genre:* Drama; *location:* United States; *coding:* Ital?, Sino-Jap War; *bias:* Contraband Message.

The family of a Dead End kid named Johnny is made destitute after the father is falsely accused and convicted of killing a policeman during a labor disturbance. To help support his family Johnny starts selling papers on an East Side street corner. One afternoon, he and some other newspaper boys discuss which headline to use while hawking the latest edition. One of the lead stories mentioned and then shown is "Japs Surround Chinese."

84 LORD JEFF (MGM, Jun) Sam Wood; *genre:* Drama/Training; *location:* Great Britain; *coding:* AF-Brit, US-Brit Coop, Brit; *biases:* Pro-British, Preparedness.

This was another entry in the surge of pro-British films produced by Hollywood in 1938. It features Britain's Russell-Cotes Nautical School that trains disadvantaged youth for entrance into the Royal Merchant Marine. The young trainees, starring Mickey Rooney and Freddie Bartholomew, are solemnly reminded that the United Kingdom can last only six weeks without supplies from overseas. Therefore, their country depends for survival upon the Merchant Navy under the protection of the Royal Fleet. Following the usual tribulations, the school's five best students head for NYC aboard the *Queen Mary* liner with the naval ensign waving and "Hail Britannia" playing on the sound track.

85 THE MARINES ARE HERE (Mono, Jun) Phil Rosen; *genre:* Adventure; *locations:* China, Philippines; *coding:* AF-MC, Chi, Comm?; *bias:* Pro-Military.

Jones and Hogan are two Marines stationed in China. When their sergeant is killed, Jones is sent to meet his relatives. In the Philippines, he falls in love with the sergeant's sister, but the romance causes him to neglect his duties, and he is sent back to China. Jones and Hogan distinguish themselves in action against "Chinese bandits," and all is forgiven and a marriage is in the offing. In August 1937, 1200 U.S. Marines were sent to Shanghai to safeguard American interests.

86 MEN WITH WINGS (Para, Oct) William A. Wellman; *genre:* Adventure; *locations:* United States, Great Britain, Morocco, China; *coding:* Corr, AF-W, Am Vol, AF-Ger, WWI, Sino-Jap War, AF-AC; *biases:* Preparedness, Pro-American.

In the final ten minutes of this Technicolor 'melo-history' of American aircraft, one of the heroes is killed while flying fighter missions for China against Japan, and the other successfully designs and builds a new bomber for the United States. At a military exposition an army observer states: "it makes all other planes of the all other countries ... obsolete." It was noted in the *New York Times'* review of October 27, 1938, that a pacifist ending was eliminated.

87 MISTER MOTO TAKES A CHANCE (TCF, Jun) Norman Foster; *genre:* Crime; *location:* Indo-China; *coding:* Intell Serv, Ger?, Jap, AF-Fr, For Corr, Brit, War Mats, AF-MC; *bias:* Pro-British.

In his fourth Moto film, Peter Lorre is joined by a pretty representative of British Intelligence and a couple of American newsreel men in French Indo-China to check up on a native uprising. The uprising has been secretly armed by weapons smuggled in by a Germanic trader named Zimmerman. Significantly, the insurrectionist leader envisions spearheading a movement that will ultimately force all foreigners out of Asia.

88 MISTER WONG, DETECTIVE (Mono, Oct) William Nigh; *genre:* Crime; *location:* United States; *coding:* Chi, Spy-Sab, Secret Weapon; *bias:* Anti-Espionage.

While investigating the murder of a client, Boris Karloff, in his film debut as the suave Chinese detective James Lee Wong, tangles with a gang of international spies. They want the formula of a poison gas for an unspecified foreign government. In an interesting twist, the agents are cleared of murder; the inventor of the gas is booked by the San Francisco Police Department.

89 MY BILL (WB, Jul) John Farrow; *genre:* Drama; *location:* United States; *coding:* World Crisis, Blk; *biases:* Pacifist, Contraband Message.

A loving widow (Kay Francis) living in a small town with her four children comes upon hard times. After glancing at the headlines while handing her eldest son the news section of the paper, she wearily states: "Wars, wars, it makes our troubles look insignificant."

90 NEXT TIME I MARRY (RKO, Dec) Garson Kanin; *genre:* Comedy; *location:* United States; *coding:* Pacifism, Jap, Ital, Blk, Comm?; *biases:* Pacifist, Contraband Message.

In order to be eligible for her inheritance, a spoiled young woman (Lucille Ball) must forsake her foreign "count" and find an American to marry. At a WPA work site she queries a handsome ditch digger if he is an American citizen. He positively responds: "...and I like penny candy, hate war and all good music except Ravel's Bolero. And my favorite color is red." Following the wedding the two rush off to Reno in a trailer to get a divorce. One night, by a campfire, he states he wrote poetry in college and then "wrote on war" after he graduated.

91 PALS OF THE SADDLE (Rep, Aug) George Sherman; *genre:* Western; *location:* United States; *coding:* Neutrality Act, War Mats, Spy-Sab, Secret Serv, AF-A; *bias:* Non-Intervention.

In 1936 Republic studios initiated a western series featuring the "Three Mesquiteers." In this, their seventeenth film, John Wayne debuted as the replacement for the character named Stoney Brooke. Like most of the other films of the series, *Pals of the Saddle* takes place in modern times. This film opens with a spinning globe followed by a montage of stock war scenes and newspaper headlines: "Congress Passes Neutrality Act"; "Foreign Agents Under Observation"; etc. The plot itself centers around our cowboy heroes foiling the attempt of some foreign agents to smuggle an explosive chemical used in poison gas, called "monium," across the border into Mexico for shipment to some unspecified country. The year before, the Mesquiteers had combatted local villains using fascist-like tactics to control an election in *Range Defenders*.

92 PORT OF MISSING GIRLS (Mono, Feb) Karl Brown; *genre:* Adventure; *locations:* China, United States; *coding:* AF-Chi, Blk, Latin Am, Russ, Dipl; *bias:* Pro-Chinese.

Della, a San Francisco nightclub singer, is wrongfully implicated in a gangland murder. She stows away aboard a steamer bound for Shanghai, "the port of missing girls." Chinese "General" Wong has arranged a secret arms shipment from the U.S. Wong states that he has permission from his government to deliver the concealed weapons upriver. While staying at a Shanghai boarding house, Della learns of a plot by criminals to seize the arms laden vessel. Having fallen in love with the ship's radio officer during the Pacific crossing, Della surrenders to the American consul so that the ship can be alerted to the impending attack.

93 ROOM SERVICE (RKO, Sept) William A Seiter; *genre:* Comedy; *location:* United States; *coding:* Russ, FDR, Hist Am; *biases:* Anti-Totalitarian, Contraband Message.

In this Marx brothers film, Leo Davis of "Oswego," middle America, writes a play featuring socially conscious miners called "Hail and Farewell." Groucho, of course, is the producer. There are a couple of jokes about Russians being shot and the "Hail and Farewell" salute looks all too much like a parody of the fascist salute. An extensive and bloody purge took place in the Soviet Union between 1936 and 1938.

94 SHADOWS OVER SHANGHAI (GN, Oct) Charles Lamont; *genre:* Spy. *location:* China; *coding:* Dipl, Chi, Spy-Sab, Russ, AF-Jap, For Corr, Sino-Jap War, War Mats, Chi, Comm, Intell Serv; *bias:* Anti-Japanese.

A pretty White Russian schoolteacher (Linda Gray) and an American newspaper photographer (James Dunn) must cope with a Japanese Army intelligence officer and an ex-Soviet agent, who controls a guerrilla army, in an attempt to transfer a valuable piece of jade to San Francisco. It means $5,000,000 for the war against Japan. Newsreel footage of the Japanese bombing of civilians has again been included. The Soviets were the Chinese government's main arms supplier during the first two years of the Sino-Japanese War.

95 SHARPSHOOTERS (TCF, Nov) James Tinling; *genre:* Drama/Adventure; *location:* Europe; *coding:* For Corr; *bias:* Anti-Fascist.

American newsreel men covering world events are once again featured. This time it is a twosome working for "Graphic Newsreel" in a present day mythical European kingdom. After filming a royal assassination they become entangled in palace intrigue. Eventually, though, with their aid, the country is rescued from a heel clicking cabal.

96 THE SHOPWORN ANGEL (MGM, July) H. C. Potter; *genre:* Drama; *locations:* United States, France; *coding:* AF-N, Am Icons, WWI, Hist Am, Draft Avoid, Bonds, Jew?, AF-A, Blk; *bias:* Pacifist.

April 6, 1917, the day the U.S. Congress declares war on the Kaiser's Germany, finds Daisy (Maureen Sullivan), a hungover Broadway actress, and Sam (Walter Pidgeon) her jaded long-time friend and confidant, gloomily discussing the impact of this event upon their lives. Daisy, while looking out her apartment window at the martial demonstrations below, comments on how the war has created "a terrifying hysteria ... [that] even makes the elevator boy want to join." Meanwhile, a wide-eyed new doughboy from the sticks, played by James Stewart (who else?) looks up at her high rise while marching past the cheering crowds lining the streets. It is not long before his and Daisy's lives romantically intersect. The doughboy then goes off to France to fight. While Daisy is entertaining the troops at a military camp, Sam brings the news of her lover's death. Actor Sam Levene appears in one of his earliest supporting roles as the tough-but-lovable urban Jewish sidekick. The original version of this pacifistic motion picture was released by Paramount in 1929. A passing remark complaining about the sugar shortages anticipates the myriad of such references made in wartime American films between 1942 and 1945.

97 SINNERS IN PARADISE (Univ, May) James Whale; *genre:* Drama; *locations:* United States, Pacific; *coding:* Sino-Jap War, Am Vol, Hitler, Arms Dealers, Chi; *bias:* Pacifist.

An airliner en route to China with an odd assortment of passengers—two rival arms dealers, a nurse, and a senator among them—crashes on an uncharted island inhabited by a mysterious man and his Chinese servant. When the man learns about the nature of the arms dealers' business, he calls them "murderers." At one point a radio report is heard which states: "All central Europe is tense, awaiting the next move of the dictator." Intrigue, murder and romance ensue as the survivors try to escape from the island and reach China. According to Cogley's *Report on Blacklisting: Movies*, the content of this film had been deliberately politicized by its screenwriters (including Lester Cole). For instance, the munitions dealers had originally been oil salesmen. Apropos of this, the *MPH* review is revealing: "The villains ... are the munitions salesmen, a circumstance in seeming consonance with the present attitude of Hollywood producers toward young men who sell cannon for a living."

98 SMASHING THE SPY RING (Col, Dec) Christy Cabanne; *genre:* Spy; *location:* United States; *coding:* FBI, Spy-Sab, Secret Weapon, Blk, Hist Am, AF-A, AF-N, War Mats; *bias:* Anti-Espionage.

After helping to capture a spy at a west coast aircraft factory, FBI man John Baxter (Ralph Bellamy) is called back to Washington. The boss wants him to track down the spy leader, who is known to be smuggling military information out of the country from the capital. Psychiatrist, Dr. Carter, heads the group of non-accented spies who collectively swear "allegiance to the homeland." The information they gather is concealed on surgical X-ray plates. Baxter falls in love with the sister of a G-man who is killed by the spies. John comforts her by stating: "He gave it [his life] for every father, mother and child in this country.... He was a soldier ... of peace, fighting the enemies of peace." Posing as the inventor of a new poison gas who suffers from amnesia, John is committed to Carter's sanitarium, a front for his espionage activities. With the needed proof obtained, Baxter's fellow agents close in on the spies.

99 SONS OF THE LEGION (Para, Sept) James Hogan; *genre:* Drama; *location:* United States; *coding:* Vets, Am Icons, WWI; *bias:* Pro-American.

A couple of young aspirants to juvenile legiondom (one of whom is played by Tim Holt), the "Junior American Legion," (the Legion instituted a Boys' State Program in 1935) help clear their father of a dishonorable discharge. The *New York Times* film review referred to the motion picture as "a fervid little homily on Americanism ... [that is] overburdened with patriotic cliches." The reviewer concluded: "Some parents might regard it as a clarion call to red-blooded, 100 percent American youths. Others of more cautious judgement might look upon it as a fatuous bit of jingoism—and not worth the time of intelligent children."

100 THE SPY RING (Univ, Jan) Joseph H. Lewis; *genre:* Spy; *location:* United States; *coding:* AF-A, Spy-Sab, Secret Weapon, Intell Serv; *biases:* Anti-Espionage, Pro-Military.

A California Army base becomes the center of attention for a murderous female espionage agent. The blonde vamp is after plans of a new device which converts most artillery into anti-aircraft weapons. There is a brief diversion in Washington, D.C., where she attracts the attention of an Army Intelligence officer. A polo match on the base is used to flush out and capture her gang of "free-lance" agents. The spy's political affiliations remain conspicuously noncommittal.

101 SQUADRON OF HONOR (Col, Jan) C. C. Coleman, Jr.; *genre:* Drama; *location:* United States; *coding:* Vets, Arms Control, WWI, Am Icons, Arms Dealers, Blk; *bias:* Non-Intervention.

Released very early in 1938, this film features the American Legion's national convention, promoting an arms control bill which would limit the sale of guns to all but private citizens. But before the plan can be passed, there is a violent confrontation with a murderous arms manufacturer who is desperately trying to change the decision. Between 1938 and 1940 the Legion took a pro-Neutrality stance, but never promoted arms control. Later, the American Legion would become associated with anti-Fascism as a result of its pronounced opposition to the German-American Bund. In fact, in *Confessions of a Nazi Spy* (1939, q.v.) there is a brawl between Legionnaires and Bundists.

102 STORM OVER BENGAL (Rep, Nov) Sidney Salkow: *genre:* Adventure; *location:* India; *coding:* Dipl, AF-Brit, Spy-Sab; *bias:* Pro-British.

A secret radio station established by outside forces spreads sedition in the Indian frontier state of "Llanapur." A young British officer (Richard Cromwell), who had earlier bungled a mission, gets the chance to redeem himself. He makes the supreme sacrifice in his airplane in order to uphold the Empire and save his regiment from imminent destruction.

103 SUBMARINE PATROL (TCF, Nov) John Ford; *genre:* War Drama/ Combat; *locations:* United States, Italy; *coding:* AF-N, AF-W, AF-Ger, AF-Ital, AF-MC, Ital, Am Icons, WWI; *bias:* Pacifist.

The reviewer for the *Motion Picture Herald* made direct linkages between this early November release and contemporary international events: "What with war on the front pages, in the ether and sprinkled widely over several sections of the globe, there would appear little reason for showmen to mask this blunt admission that the United States took part in a major conflict some 20 years ago.... Whatever box office poison there may have been in the term 'war picture' a while back probably is gone with the winds that blew across Munich." Based on a novel entitled *The Splinter Fleet*, this film deals with a wooden-hulled U.S. sub-chaser in the Adriatic (the Austro-Hungarian navy operated out of ports along the Dalmatian coast) during the First World War. However, it is more of a tale about a group of Americans struggling against the sea after being thrown together in wartime. The humane response to the fate of depth-charged German submariners gives the film a pronounced pacifist slant, a rare example of such attitudes in a film with a naval setting. Although Italy was an ally of the U.S. in WWI, in this Darryl F. Zanuck production Italian citizens are portrayed as harmless fools.

104 SUEZ (TCF, Oct) Allan Dwan; *genre:* Biography; *locations:* Great Britain, France, Egypt; *coding:* Brit, Fr, Ger, Blk, Arab, Dipl, AF-Fr, SP; *biases:* Pro-British, Pro-French.

This lavishly produced film starring Tyrone Power deals very loosely with the events leading up to de Lesseps' construction of the Suez Canal (the actual construction took place between 1852 and 1869). It is pro-French and blatantly pro-British Empire. In a parliamentary debate between the anti-imperialist Gladstone and his pro-imperialist opponent Disraeli, the latter is portrayed far more positively. But perhaps the passage most relevant to 1938 is the following pro-appeasement statement made by a political activist friend of de Lesseps: "I'm afraid there is little you or I, or anyone else, can do when Prussia rattles the saber."

105 TEST PILOT (MGM, Apr) Victor Fleming; *genre:* Drama; *location:* United States; *coding:* AF-AC, Secret Weapon; *bias:* Pro-Military.

A disclaimer about revealing any specific data about government aircraft appears in the opening titles of this aviation melodrama. Yet interestingly, it is America's newest bomber, the (unidentified in the film) YB-17 (the first production model of the famous "Flying Fortress") that is featured in the latter third of the film. Clark Gable gives up his career as a private test pilot to rejoin the Army Air Corps and instruct recruits in the operation of this bomber. The film concludes with the somewhat ambiguous image of his child's face superimposed on a skyful of military planes. Ironically, conventional thinking in the Army saw airpower only as close support for ground forces—those in the Air Corps who lobbied for "big bombers" often found themselves out in the cold. Frank Andrews, commander of the Army's air force, was transferred from Washington to San Antonio and reduced in rank from major general to colonel in 1939 for his outspoken advocacy of an independent air arm, which led him to vigorously promote the Air Corps (and air power in general) with both politicians and the general public.

106 THANKS FOR EVERYTHING (TCF, Dec) William A. Seiter; *genre:* Comedy; *location:* United States; *coding:* World Crisis, Appeasement, AF-A, Draft Avoid, Brit, Dipl, WWI, Draft, Blk, Am Icons, Russ, AF-MC; *bias:* Pro-Intervention.

This offbeat comedy centers around the exploitation of Henry Smith (Jack Haley) of Plainville, Mo., "the average man," by two partners in an advertising firm. The government of an unspecified country (presumably Great Britain) is so impressed by the firm's forecasts that they commission it to find out, in light of the world crisis "in the past few months" and the "natural" closeness of the two countries: "...how the average American feels about going to war. Would he enlist or would he have to be drafted? Would he fight at the drop of a few well-chosen slogans? Or does he want peace at any price?" The two operators subject Henry to a fake media barrage concerning a foreign war and assaults upon American honor. But rather than go to war, he would prefer to acquire "some exemptions." It is only when they convince him that the United States is brutally attacked that he demands to enlist. This was one of the first films to allude to the Czech crisis and the only one to mention an American draft until mid–1940. The film may have been inspired by a book written by a British officer, predicting that Americans would only allow themselves to enter another European war if they perceived that their national security would be imperiled by a German victory. The book was *England Expects Every American to Do His Duty*, by Quincy Howe (New York: Simon & Schuster, 1937).

107 THREE COMRADES (MGM, Jun) Frank Borzage; *genre:* Drama; *location:* Germany; *coding:* AF-Ger, WWI, Fascism, Jew, Comm, League Nat; *bias:* Anti-Fascist.

F. Scott Fitzgerald was the major contributor to the screenplay of this impassioned cinematic plea against bigotry adapted from a 1920s Remargue novel. Three former soldiers of the Kaiser and a loving consumptive lady friend (played by Margaret Sullivan) attempt to adjust to post-war Germany. Producer Joseph L. Mankiewicz insisted that the film contain no overt references to the Nazi regime. Nonetheless, there is a series of allusions to the origins of National Socialism. For instance, one of the three comrade veterans is killed as a result of his involvement in street battles between advocates of rival political ideologies (obviously meant to represent the fighting that actually took place during the latter years of the Wiemar Republic between paramilitary Reds and Nazi Brownshirts).

108 TOO HOT TO HANDLE (MGM, Sept) Jack Conway; *genre:* Adventure; *locations:* China, United States, Latin America; *coding:* AF-Jap, AF-Chi, Italo-Eth War, Chi, Sino-Jap War, For Corr, Span Civ, Blk, War Mats, AF-CG; *biases:* Anti-Japanese, CM.

News cameraman Chris Hunter, played by Clark Gable, is under pressure from his editor to send back from China "shots of bombings and assorted outrages." Desperate for combat footage, he yanks the lanyard of an unmanned anti-aircraft gun to lure some high-flying Japanese aircraft into camera range. So after he falls into a muddy bomb crater and ruins the film he just shot of one of the Japanese planes attacking, Chris improvises, using a model of a biplane on a string to stage a "bombing," (with firecrackers) of "innocent" Chinese civilians. Following his return to America, Chris persuades his aviatrix girlfriend (Myrna Loy) to fly low over a burning munitions ship. While Chris is shooting film from the plane's wing the "blockade runner full of TNT" blows up. The ship, which had refused to identify itself to authorities, was presumably headed for Spain. Further adventures include saving his girl's brother from voodoo-cultists in South America.

109 TOUCHDOWN, ARMY (Para, Oct) Jack Conway; *genre:* Adventure; *location:* United States; *coding:* AF-A, Am Icons, Hist Am, AF-N, Mil School; *bias:* Pro-Military.

Americanism and football at West Point are featured. The usual romantic rivalry ends in friendship during the annual Army-Navy football game.

110 A TRIP TO PARIS (TCF, May) Malcolm St. Clair; *genre:* Comedy/Drama; *locations:* United States, France; *coding:* Spy-Sab, AF-Fr, Intell Serv, Maginot Line?, Fr, Russ; *bias:* Non-Intervention.

Father and Mother Jones celebrate their 25th wedding anniversary by taking the whole family to Paris. Among assorted misadventures one son is mistaken for being a spy. Actually, he has been romantically used by a female spy who was attempting to smuggle the plans of a section of France's "border fortification" (the Maginot Line presumed) out of the country. After the real spies are apprehended by French counter-intelligence, the Jones family settles their hotel bill and hastily returns to the U.S.A. The Jones Family Series, starring Jed Prouty and Spring Byington, was released between 1936 and 1940.

111 YELLOW JACK (MGM, May) George B. Seitz; *genre:* Historical Drama; *location:* Cuba; *coding:* Comm, Hist Am, War Mats?, AF-A, AF-W, Jew, Latin Am; *biases:* Anti-Fascist, Pacifist, Pro-Military.

Although the story is ostensibly concerned with the turn-of-the-century research devoted to identifying the source of yellow fever, and in spite of the usual romantic interludes, there is incorporated into this film an unusually candid pitch against war and dictatorships. In addition, one of the lead characters is a heroically portrayed Jew and avowed Marxist who wants to return home in order to work for the "movement." Major Walter Reed remarks that the Army's call for volunteers for yellow fever experiments is one "...of the first times soldiers are being given a chance to do good instead of harm for the world." And, later, there is an unmistakable message for the 1938 audience in an impassioned monologue delivered by one of the doctors concerning the sacrifice of a medical colleague's life in the quest for the origin of the deadly fever: "...Will [the people of the world] ever hear of him? ...while they're on their knees to a bunch of prancing little murders with hot lead in their mouths who tell them how they are saving civilization...."

Although several contemporary reviews found distracting the romance between one of the volunteers (Robert Montgomery) and a nurse (Virginia Bruce), it does serve to indirectly point out that nurses served with the Army in Cuba (due to the severity of the yellow fever epidemic, the Army established an Auxiliary Nurse Corps in 1901; nearly 1500 nurses were hired).

112 YOU CAN'T TAKE IT WITH YOU (Col, Sept) Frank Capra; *genre:* Comedy/Drama; *location:* United States; *coding:* Hist Am, Russ, Blk, War Mats, Comm, Fascism; *bias:* Pro-Democracy.

Adapted from the Pulitzer Prize winning play, this film won an Academy Award for Best Picture of 1938. In this classic satire that features the members of an eccentric family, Capra presents his idealized vision of a democratic society in which free men should be able to do as they please. There are several direct references to communism, fascism and other "isms." One comment made by the old patriarch, "Grandpa" Vanderhoot, played by Lionel Barrymore, is particularly interesting: "Now days they say 'think the way I do or I'll bomb the living daylights out of you!'" A Wall Street banker (Edward Arnold) tries to force the family to sell their home so that he can build a munitions plant on the property.

113 YOUTH TAKES A FLING (Univ, Sept) Archie Mayo; *genre:* Comedy/Drama; *location:* United States; *coding:* Blk, Chi, Jap, Sino-Jap War; *bias:* Contraband Message.

Joe Meadows (Joel McCrea), a dreamer from Kansas, arrives in New York City with the intention of seeing the world while working on a freighter. The realities of Depression America quickly intrude after a visit to the Seaman's Hall. Joe then finds a job driving a truck for a large department store. Almost immediately, a girl working as a wedding gown model at the store targets Joe for matrimony. Later, when her roommate divulges that Joe is sneaking off on a boat for China, she quips, "I hope the Japs get him!" But Joe will never get near the Sino-Japanese War theatre—he becomes violently seasick on the tug transporting him to his ship.

1939

114 ALL QUIET ON THE WESTERN FRONT (Re-Released 1930) (Univ, Sept) Lewis Milestone; *genre:* War Drama/Comedy; *locations:* Germany, France; *coding:* WWI, AF-Ger, AF-Fr, Arms Dealers, WWII, Hitler, Nazi; *bias:* Pacifist.

Only a few weeks after the German invasion of Poland, Universal reissued this film adaptation of the classic Remarque anti-war novel. An ad in the *Motion Picture Herald* promoted the feature as "Uncensored." Actually, it had acquired a prologue and an epilogue containing stock historical shots of Germany accompanied by an off screen narrator making comparisons between the first World War and the horrors of the present conflict. The pacifistic slant of the trailer prepared for this version is unequivocable. The only dialogue sequence used is the one in which Katz suggests that whenever a war is about to start the country's leaders should be put in a ring to fight it out. And the most prominent visual scene is that in which a blinded soldier pitiably screams.

115 ALLEGHANY UPRISING (RKO, Nov) William A. Seiter; *genre:* Historical Drama; *location:* United States; *coding:* AF-A, AF-Brit, Arms Dealers, War Mats, Blk, Am Icons; *bias:* Pro-American.

This was another "historical" pro–American film, that possibly reflected the American public's confusion regarding the growing European tensions through its ambivalent treatment of the British. It opens with a rousing musical "Yankee Doodle" motif during the credits followed by a title describing the film as taking place "sixteen years before the revolution." The plot centers around colonists, led by John Wayne, defying a rigid British commander in order to attempt to stop the illegal supply of weapons to the Indians. As a precursor to World War II (1942–1945) era atrocity stories viz our enemies, it is of interest to note that the colonists are most incensed by the killing and scalping of some children at their school house by Indian raiders.

116 ANDY HARDY GETS SPRING FEVER (MGM, Jul) W.S. Van Dyke; *genre:* Comedy/Drama; *location:* United States; *coding:* AF-N, Natl Def; *biases:* Pro-American, Contraband Message.

In this seventh film of the Hardy family series, America's favorite celluloid son, played by Mickey Rooney, almost quits high school when he falls in love with an older college woman. But she is interested in a handsome Navy ensign stationed nearby at a newly established Naval Reserve Training Center. Small town Carvel is one of the first cinema burgs to get directly involved in America's incipient defense effort by reinforcing the highway that goes through the town, thus enabling it to handle heavy loads during a "national emergency."

117 BABES IN ARMS (MGM, Oct) Busby Berkeley; *genre:* Musical Comedy; *location:* United States; *coding:* Hist Am, Am Icons, Hitler, Musso, FDR, Good Neighbors, Blk; *biases:* Pro-American; Anti-Fascist.

Following an unsuccessful comeback attempt by a group of old-time vaudevillians, their children stage a popular musical comedy. As usual, Busby Berkeley inserts contemporary material. In the middle of one song-and-dance routine, Mickey Rooney no-so ambiguously stretches his eyelids into slits and declares: "Hi there, Chappie ... look over the seas and be happy." Throughout the typically elaborate patriotic finale, "In God's Country," there are lyrics such as "We got no *Duce*, no *Fuehrer* ... got no goosestep but Suzy-Q step."

118 BARRICADE (TCF, Dec) Gregory Ratoff; *genre:* Drama; *locations:* China, United States; *coding:* Hist Am, For Corr, Ger, Brit?, Dipl, Russ, Chi, AF-Chi, Sino-Jap War, FDR, Am Icons; *bias:* Pro-American.

An opening montage of China, accompanied by off-screen narration, culminates with urban bombing scenes: "Then, in August 1937, ... the helpless people became a human avalanche of escape...." Aboard a train heading to Shanghai from the interior a drunken unemployed correspondent, Hank Topping (Warner Baxter), encounters a phony White Russian played by Alice Faye. Due to the depredations of "Mongolian bandits," they become stranded at an isolated U.S. consulate run by a kindly old diplomat. A visiting Chinese Nationalist officer explains to the American consul that the bandits are relentless because they know "we are busy in the south," i.e., at war with the Japanese. The bandits later lay seige to the American compound and are about to massacre its inhabitants when nationalist troops come to the rescue. The Russian consul is the chess playing friend of his American counterpart. A rare positive portrayal of a Soviet representative during the era of the Nazi-Soviet Pact.

119 BEASTS OF BERLIN aka HITLER, BEAST OF BERLIN (PDC, Oct) Sherman Scott; *genre:* Resistance; *locations:* Germany, Switzerland; *coding:* Ger, AF-Ger, FDR, Hitler, Comm, Atroc-Conc, Atroc, Jew, Pol, Goebbels, Brit, AF-Brit, Fr, WWII, Nazi, WWI, Russ, Resist; *bias:* Anti-Nazi.

The original title of this film—*Hitler, Beast of Berlin* (reminiscent of the scurrilous 1917 film *The Kaiser, Beast of Berlin* [Renowned Pictures])—was censored. It was promoted in *the Motion Picture Herald* for several months prior to the film's release under the original title in a series of sensational ads which included: "Etched with the Heart's-Blood of a People Staggering Helplessly Under Ruthless Oppression!" and "The Mad Monster of Europe Is Loose!" Released in late 1939, the film was an adaptation of Shepard Traube's story *Goose Step*. The plot centers around a German opposition movement that, among other things, clandestinely prints leaflets attacking the "brutalities" of the Nazi regime. The resistance group is broken up by the Gestapo and most of its members are sent to a concentration camp. Anti-Semitism and anti-Christianity are specifically addressed. For instance, at the camp, an elderly "non-Aryan" (Jewish) scientist is forced by a sadistic guard to call himself a "swine" and a priest has his cassock stripped from his body. Eventually the hero escapes to Switzerland, rejoining his family, and ready to carry on the struggle. A newspaper montage accompanied by stock footage from old war films brings the story up to the outbreak of the second World War.

120 BLACKWELL'S ISLAND (WB, Mar) William McGann; *genre:* Crime; *location:* United States; *coding:* Fascism, Blk; *bias:* Anti-Fascist.

"Bull" Bransom, gangster, buffoon, and ally of crooked politicians heads the "Waterfront Protective Association." As portrayed by Stanley Fields, Bransom could be a Mussolini caricature. In fact, crusading reporter Tom Haydon (John Garfield) writes an article condemning Bull's racket as a "fascist scheme." When Bull is sent to prison, he makes himself leader of the "Prisoners' Mutual Protective Society," and proceeds to take over the institution. When in jail, Bull complains about Tom's unflattering newspaper descriptions of him. Tom sarcastically responds: "I was just referring to your overhanging brows and your piercing eyes ... you know, you're the kind of guy that becomes a dictator."

121 CALLING ALL MARINES (Rep, Sept) John H. Auer; *genre:* Crime/Spy; *location:* United States; *coding:* AF-MC, Secret Weapon, Spy-Sab, Am Icons, Collab, Chi; *biases:* Anti-Espionage, Pro-American.

A young hood named "Blackie" illegally enlists in the Corps in order to steal government plans of a secret radio-controlled aerial torpedo for a gangland connected politician. This politician just happens to be in alliance with agents of, to quote the *New York Times* film review, "some all-but-named" foreign power. At first Blackie is disliked by his cohorts, but then he saves one injured in a ship explosion (presumably the work of saboteurs). Their resulting change of heart and Blackie's loss of his heart to the pretty girl lead him to alter his evil ways. With a little timely help from his new friends, the "alien" spies' last ditch attempts to steal a prototype of the experimental torpedo are thwarted. A now enthusiastically patriotic Blackie is fully exonerated and wins the young lady.

122 CHARLIE CHAN IN CITY IN DARKNESS (TCF, Dec) Herbert I. Leeds; *genre:* Crime/Spy; *location:* France; *coding:* Intell Serv, War Mats, Chi, Dipl, Arms Dealers, WWI, Musso, Hitler, Chamberlain, Spy-Sab, Munich, AF-Fr, Maginot Line; *biases:* Anti-Espionage, Anti-Nazi.

The opening montage places us in Paris during the 1938 Munich crisis. It provides a timely backdrop for our peripatetic oriental sleuth. While attending an intelligence men's reunion, he solves some murders involving munitions dealings with unspecified foreign interests. Charlie appears to remain oblivious to the frequent blackouts until near the very end of the film when he delivers the following statement viz. Chamberlain's upcoming meeting with Hitler in Munich: "Wise man has said: Beware of spider who invites fly into parlor." The hysteria displayed by a Parisian police officer viz a possible gas attack had a basis in fact. During the recent war scare caused by the Munich Crisis nearly a third of the population of Paris had abandoned their city.

123 CHASING DANGER (TCF, May) Ricardo Cortez; *genre:* Adventure; *locations:* France, Africa; *coding:* For Corr, AF-Fr, Spy-Sab; *bias:* Pro-French.

An American newsreel man stationed in Paris becomes involved in foreign intrigue when he goes to French North Africa to cover an Arab revolt. It turns out that the Arabs have been incited and supplied with arms by an agent of an unspecified "European" nation whose precise aim is to undermine and then seize the French African Empire.

124 CHIP OF THE FLYING U (Univ, Nov) Ralph Staub; *genre:* Western; *location:* United States; *coding:* War Mats, Spy-Sab; *bias:* Anti-Espionage.

Johnny Mack Brown stars as Flying U foreman "Chip" Bennett in this musically accompanied prairie meller. The neighboring rival rancher, Duncan, just happens to be a foreign agent who has stashed contraband munitions in an abandoned shack on the Flying U. Duncan wants to buy out or force out the owners of the ranch so he and his compatriots can safely transfer the munitions to a boat. According to the *Variety* review, "their [the munitions runners'] chief is supposed to speak in stilted English, but only manages to appear awkward." In the climactic gun battle a few well placed shots by a pal of Chip's ignites the explosives and blows up the foreign agents.

125 COAST GUARD (Col, Aug) Edward Ludwig; *genre:* Adventure; *location:* United States; *coding:* AF-CG, AF-W?, Am Icons; *bias:* Pro-Military.

The Coast Guard is portrayed on life-saving missions, this time in the Arctic. There is also the requisite love story with a nurse.

126 CONFESSIONS OF A NAZI SPY (WB, May) Anatole Litvak; *genre:* spy; *locations:* United States, Germany, Great Britain; *coding:* Nazi, FBI, Vets, US-Brit Coop, Austr, Yugo, Pol, Span Civ, Fr, Ind Fasc Org, Hitler, Am Icons, Spy-Sab, AF-A, Czech, Comm, Atroc-Conc, Ital, Jap, Secret Weapon, Brit, WWI, AF-N, Latin Am, Munich, Goebbels, Austria, AF-AC, Intell Ser, Jew?; *biases:* Anti-Nazi, Anti-Esp.

Warner Bros. seemed to declare war on Nazi Germany and the German-American Bund in this cinematic example of "premature anti-fascism." Yet, although Hitler's name is invoked numerous times—and his image displayed as well—Germany's Fuehrer is never directly attacked nor disparaged. The story, loosely based upon the actual trial and conviction on charges of espionage of four Nazi agents in December 1938, is presented in a semi-documentary format. The film centers around the activities of a German medical doctor (played by Paul Lukas) who leads the American Nazi movement, and a down-and-out German-American (Francis Lederer) who offers his services to the Nazi military intelligence service in a pathetic attempt to acquire money and boost his self-esteem. This man's bungling spy activities bring him to the attention of the FBI. Through this one Nazi agent, American officials responsible for protecting the country from foreign espionage—led by an unflappable, pipe-smoking FBI agent (Edward G. Robinson)—are able to round up a German spy network subverting the American way of life. The film was re-released in 1940 with added documentary footage of Nazi aggression.

127 CONSPIRACY (RKO, Sept) Lew Landers; *genre:* Adventure/Resistance; *location:* ? *coding:* Resist, Am Vol, War Mats, Atroc-Conc, Am Icons; *bias:* Anti-Fascist.

An American radio operator (Allan Lane) jumps ship after discovering that his vessel is carrying a contraband cargo of chemicals used in the manufacture of poison gas. No sooner does he touch land than the secret police of the fascistic government of the nation (unnamed, apparently located in Central America but with various European and Mediterranean touches) are on his trail. With the aid of a local revolutionary woman (Linda Hayes) and an American expatriate he is able to make a dramatic escape. Despite a budding romance, the female freedom fighter decides to remain in her country to carry on the struggle. The *New York Times* critic commented on the deliberately muddled locale of this film: "The natives seemed to be Teutons, the atmosphere Central American, the language Esperanto and the street signs a blend of Russian and Polish, except that the word endings were either Spanish or Italian."

128 DAUGHTERS COURAGEOUS (WB, Jul) Michael Curtiz; *genre:* Drama; *location:* United States; *coding:* Span Civ; *biases:* Anti-Fascist, Contraband Message.

The romantic fluff of this Lane sisters melodrama is overwhelmed by pious reinforcements of the virtues of middle class morality. Somewhat paradoxically, the theme of anti-fascism has been inserted. When the three girls decide to "freeze out" their newly returned prodigal father they describe their collective decision on how to treat him as a "popular front." From 1934 onwards the policy of the Comintern was to create an alliance with all parties opposed to fascism. Under the banner of the popular front the Spanish Republic resisted Franco's Nationalist rebels.

129 THE DAY THE BOOKIES WEPT (RKO, Sept) Leslie Goodwins; *genre:* Comedy; *location:* United States; *coding:* Mil Exer; *bias:* Contraband Message.

Joe Penner plays a pigeon training cabbie in this farce that centers around the attempts of the goofy comedian and some buddies to make a killing at the tracks with a booze-swilling horse named Hiccup. Early in the film Joe looks up proudly from his rooftop coops at his massed pigeons flying in a complicated set of patterns (an animated sequence) and comments to his girl that the birds are performing "war maneuvers." The beginning of the *NYT* film review places the motion picture in its historical context: "Being a sucker for a long shot, nothing delights us more than seeing Germany and Russia shaking hands, Poland resisting the theoretically irresistible Nazi war machine, a Joe Penner comedy being rated in these columns as one of the funniest shows of the season."

130 THE DEAD END KIDS ON DRESS PARADE (WB, Nov) William Clemens; *genre:* Comedy/Drama; *location:* United States; *coding:* WWI, Mil School, AF-A, Mil Exer, Am Icons; *bias:* Pro-Military.

A retired army colonel promises to take care of a dying World War I buddy's son. The boy turns out to be a slum tough named Slip (Leo Gorcey). The colonel, head of a private military academy, tricks Slip into entering his school. The "Dead End Kid" proceeds to flout the institution's strict discipline and traditions. Slip has an altercation with the Cadet Major and brutally tosses him out a second story window. Despite ostracism, Slip repents and begins to take his studies seriously. He does well enough to be one of the few cadets selected to attend camp with the regular Army during summer maneuvers. When a fire breaks out in the munitions storeroom, Slip proves himself by saving the life of a schoolmate. As a reward for his heroism, the colonel presents the "model American" Slip with the Distinguished Service Cross his father had earned in the war. There is a noteworthy topical comment made in the penultimate paragraph of the *Variety* review: "The pacifistically-minded may also find objection as in other military school pictures, but more so now because of the war, to the glorious manner in which the soldier's life is painted. It looks like a partnership between WB and the recruiting service."

131 DISPUTED PASSAGE (Para, Oct) Frank Borzage; *genre:* Drama; *locations:* United States, China; *coding:* Chi, Sino-Jap War, Am Vol, Fr, AF-Jap, AF-W, Dipl, Atroc, AF-Chi, Hist Am; *bias:* Anti-Japanese.

A young doctor named Beaven becomes the assistant to a prominent neurological surgeon to whom science is god. Beaven meets Audrey Hilton (Dorothy Lamour) when he operates on her injured arm (apparently an old war wound). Audrey, who was brought up in China by native foster parents, has come to America to arrange a loan for her adopted country's struggle against the Japanese. After Audrey returns to China, a lovestruck Beaven abandons his position to find her. While traveling about the war-torn interior Beaven stops at a makeshift hospital run by a French doctor. Because the village is near a munitions dump it is regularly bombed by the "enemy." In a montage sequence Beaven is shown operating on women and children (no men of military age). An old woman asks (in Chinese) why the gods send some good men to help while sending others who want to hurt her. During another Japanese bomber attack Beaven is severely wounded while saving the little girl he had just operated on. A mercy flight from the U.S. by his surgeon mentor, Forster, is made to remove a piece of shrapnel from Beaven's brain. But Beaven has lost the will to live. Audrey is flown in from a Chinese military hospital by China's most famous real-life aviatrix, Lee Ya-ching. Forster is spiritually transformed when Beaven recovers from his coma.

132 DRUMS ALONG THE MOHAWK (TCF, Nov) John Ford; *genre:* Historical Drama; *location:* United States; *coding:* Hist Am, Am Icons, AF-A, AF-Brit, Pacifism, Blk, Collab; *bias:* Pro-American.

The executive producer of this Technicolor reaffirmation of American values and ideals was Darryl F. Zanuck. Family unity and, by extension, national unity are themes once again stressed by director John Ford. Following the Declaration of Independence, American colonists on the New York frontier must struggle with bloodthirsty Indians incited by pro-British Tories. Significantly, actual British involvement in the fight against the rebellious Americans is minimized. Released after the war in Europe had begun, the film reveals some latent isolationist tendencies. Perhaps this is most clearly indicated in a statement made by Mrs. Barnabus (Edna May Oliver): "I'll shoot the daylights out of anybody, British, Indian or Tory, that messes around in my business." Henry Fonda and Claudette Colbert were cast as a pioneer couple.

133 ESPIONAGE AGENT (WB, Oct) Lloyd Bacon; *genre:* Spy; *locations:* United States, Africa, Great Britain, Germany, Switzerland; *coding:* Span Civ, Dipl, Russ, Isolationism, Spy-Sab, WWI, FBI, Hitler, For Corr, FDR, Ger, Brit, Peace Org; *biases:* Non-Intervention, Anti-Espionage, Anti-German.

A young man (Joel McCrea) in the United States diplomatic service marries an attractive woman (Brenda Marshall) with a mysterious past. Soon after the marriage, she confesses that she was a spy. He reluctantly resigns and the two proceed to Europe to track down and expose her previous employers. Serious politics appear side by side with the melodramatic action. A specific plug for isolationism is made in a sequence about a State Department training session. In fact, the Department of State would be the most prominent advocate of appeasement within the government until the Pearl Harbor attack.

134 EVERYTHING HAPPENS AT NIGHT (TCF, Dec) Irving Cummings; *genre:* Drama; *locations:* Switzerland, Brit, France; *coding:* Ital, Pol, Jew, Ger, US-Brit Coop, For Corr, Nazi, Atroc-Conc, Pacifism, Ref, Brit, Am Icons; *biases:* Anti-Nazi, Pacifist?.

An English newspaperman (Ray Milland) and his American colleague (Robert Cummings) discover that an allegedly assassinated Nobel Prize-winning leader of a peace movement is alive and writing under an alias in Switzerland. They comically vie for the story and for his beautiful daughter, played by Sonja Henie. Although the country responsible for imprisoning the man in a "concentration camp" and desiring his death is never specifically identified, the movement's leader, his daughter, and the two reporters are chased from his mountain hideout by "Gestapo" agents (led by a sinister man wearing a monocle). Aboard a ship sailing for America the good doctor's daughter states: "The farther away from Brownshirts, purple shirts, pink shirts, green shirts ... the happier father will be." Cummings adds that the United States have become a "haven for

Europe's greatest minds—Toscanni, Einstein, Thomas Mann...."

135 EXILE EXPRESS (GN, May) Otis Garrett; *genre:* Drama; *location:* United States; *coding:* Spy-Sab, Am Icons, Blk, Russ, Secret Weapon; *biases:* Anti-Espionage, Pro-American.

The plot of this film centers around the plight of a girl alien (Anna Sten) in San Francisco, who is ordered deported when she is implicated in the murder of her employer. He was a chemist who had developed a compound which could kill off all plant life. Aided by a sympathetic newspaper reporter, the real culprit is exposed as Brandt (Germanic surname), an agent of a foreign government which is interested in the formula. At the end, as the reporter's new wife, Sten patriotically recites the oath of United States citizenship.

136 FIFTH AVENUE GIRL (RKO, Sept) Gregory Lacava; *genre:* Comedy/Drama; *location:* United States; *coding:* AF-N, Chi, Latin Am, Comm; *biases:* Anti-Fascist, Contraband Message.

This is a spoof on communist ideas taking place amid the chaos of a wealthy family in New York City. The dedicated communist chauffeur ultimately abandons his position and buys his own repair shop, and the unemployed heroine lands the humbled rich guy. About midway through the film there is a passing reference to the "United Front." By 1939, and until the signing of the Nazi-Soviet Pact in September of that year, the concept of a "United Front" had come to symbolize a Comintern policy promoting the unity of all leftist parties in the struggle against fascism.

137 GOLDEN BOY (Col, Sept) Rouben Mamoulian; *genre:* Drama; *location:* United States; *coding:* WWI, Blk, Jew, Fascism, World Crisis, Ital; *biases:* Anti-Fascist, Contraband Message.

A young Italian-American, played by William Holden, is a promising violinist. But he discovers he also has a talent for boxing. A classic spiritual struggle ensues. The cynical Jewish neighbor who plays chess with his father makes a direct reference to "fascism" and, a tantalizing comment linking the deteriorating situation overseas (the film was released only a couple of weeks before the invasion of Poland) and cinema attendance in America: "Every time I read in the papers what's happening in Europe I have to close the shop and go see a double feature." The screenplay was based upon the play written by Clifford Odets.

138 THE GREAT MAN VOTES (RKO, Jan) Garson Kanin; *genre:* Drama; *location:* United States; *coding:* Hist Am, Chi, Blk; *bias:* Pro-Democracy.

John Barrymore plays a former Harvard scholar who has lost all ambition and turned to the bottle following his wife's death. His two precocious children have a run-in at school with the local ward heeler's obnoxious son. With the assistance of their friendly new teacher, Barrymore's children inspire their father to regain his self-respect. He then resists the importunities of the ward heeler as to how he should cast the deciding vote in an upcoming mayoralty election. The newly restored citizen delivers a pro-democracy speech at the polls on election day: "[America is] a kindly land—where greatness is within a people, not a man. And where any man who calls himself great is only looking at his shadow from the shoulders of those who have lifted him up... My palace is the peoples' hall, the ballot box my throne ..., because being even the least in a land where strength is so generous is greatness in itself."

139 GUNGA DIN (RKO, Feb) George Stevens; *genre:* Adventure; *location:* India; *coding:* Atroc, AF-Brit; *bias:* Pro-British.

The screenplay for this high budget super adventure film was based on a Kipling poem. Three sergeant-comrades in service with Her Majesty's Indian Regiment do battle with fanatical ax-wielding tribesmen in the Punjab in the 19th century. A native water boy who dreams of being a bugler makes the ultimate sacrifice in order to save the brave soldiers and their Empire from the demonic cult of the "Thuggee." What is most interesting is that this is an American film that is gung ho for both the British colonial system and its military establishment. The British Government provided RKO with a "technical adviser." Even the girl is spurned in favor of duty to the Queen!

140 HEAVEN WITH A BARBED WIRE FENCE (TCF, Nov) Ricardo Cortez; *genre:* Drama; *location:* United States; *coding:* Span Civ, Russ, Ref; *bias:* Pro-American.

After spending six year's savings on a mail order purchase of an Arizona ranch, a New York department store clerk, played by a very young Glenn Ford, begins hitchhiking west. Along the way he teams up with a wayward "Professor," a tramp and a pretty Spanish Civil War refugee without papers. The quartet overcomes many hardships to make ends meet. The film concludes with a wedding in a town settled by White Russian immigrants.

141 HIDDEN POWER (Col, Sept) Lewis D. Collins; *genre:* Drama; *location:* United States; *coding:* Secret Weapon, Arms Dealers; *bias:* Pacifist.

The chemist hero stumbles upon a formula for the "deadliest explosive in the world" while attempting to develop a serum to cure bad burns. From then on he is continually harassed by amoral munitions makers and his venal wife. He perseveres with his research in spite of them. As a result, when his son is severely burned in a car accident, the drug is available to save the boy.

142 HOMICIDE BUREAU (Col, Jan) C. C. Coleman, Jr.; *genre:* Crime; *location:* United States; *coding:* War Mats, Neutrality Act, Arms Dealers, World Crisis; *bias:* Non-Intervention.

A group of racketeers pressure members of the local Junk Dealers Trade Association to sell the crooks their scrap metal. When the gangsters' main heavy asks their boss if the scrap iron is really worth that much "on the other side of the pond" he is told: "They've gotta have it to make munitions and it isn't easy for them to get on account of some neutrality laws...." While the mob goes about murdering uncooperative dealers, the police department's toughest homicide detective (Bruce Cabot) attempts to track them down. But he must overcome obstacles created by a "Citizen's League" that strongly objects to his bare knuckles method of interrogation. The film concludes with a gun battle between the gangsters and the police on the deck of a ship being loaded with scrap and contraband rifles packed in crates marked "Refrigerator." Columbia's press book for this motion picture suggested a promotional campaign that included a "Pledge" to be circulated among local scrap metal dealers in which they declare that they are "firmly opposed to the exportation of scrap metal to foreign warlords" and that they endorse *Homicide Bureau* "for bringing the international munitions racket to the attention of the public."

143 THE HUNCHBACK OF NOTRE DAME (RKO, Dec) William Dieterle; *genre:* Historical Drama; *location:* France; *coding:* Jew, AF-Fr, Atroc; *biases:* Anti-Fascist, Contraband Message.

Based on Victor Hugo's well-known novel, this film opens in Medieval France with a group of men gathered around a printing press. A poet waxes on the "freedom of thought," but is darkly admonished by the Grand Inquisitor, Bishop Frollo, that an uncontrolled press can "destroy a Kingdom." The latter goes on to inveigh against foreigners, particularly the gypsies, "a foreign race that is overrunning all of Europe." Meanwhile, a young gypsy girl played by Maureen O'Hara has entered Paris during the "Feast of Fools" hoping to gain an audience with the King in order to plead for tolerance for her oppressed people. While she is praying in church the lecherous Frollo rebukes her: "Praying cannot help you. You come from an evil race." The film's plea against bigotry is further emphasized in the scene where the gypsy girl is tortured to

make a false confession by Frollo's court. The script makes a deliberate parallel between the persecution of the gypsies in the Middle Ages and that of contemporary Jews. In fact, gypsies would also later become victims of the Nazi terror.

144 IDIOT'S DELIGHT (MGM, Jan) Clarence Brown; *genre:* Drama; *location:* Europe; *coding:* Arms Dealers, Pacifism, AF-Eur, Atroc, Russ, WWI, Brit, Ger, League Nat, Jap, Latin Am; *bias:* Pacifist.

A song and dance man played by Clark Gable, accompanied by the all girl sextet "Les Blondes," meets a counterfeit Russian countess (a former fellow vaudevillian) at an Alpine hotel near the Swiss border immediately before the outbreak of a world war. Burgess Meredith portrays a dedicated pacifist who is shot by the military police after he publicly denounces his host country for initiating a war. Serious barbs are directed at international munitions dealers and comic shots are made at the senselessness of war; shades of Paramount's *Duck Soup* (1933). The motion picture was a heavily censored adaptation of the blatantly anti-fascist play written by Robert E. Sherwood.

145 I'M FROM MISSOURI (Para, Apr) Theodore Reed; *genre:* Comedy; *locations:* United States, Great Britain; *coding:* War Mats, Am Icons, Dipl, AF-Brit, Arms Dealers, US-Brit Coop, Latin Am; *biases:* Pro-British, Pro-American.

As part of its response to world events the British Army announces plans to mechanize a number of its units and, as a consequence, do away with its mules. This arouses the concern of a Missouri banker and mule aficionado played by Bob Burns. Determined to save his business and that of his mule raising friends from possible bankruptcy, he travels to Britain with his social climbing wife and his prize mule, "Samson." Both British society and its military establishment are initially put off by the brash Yanks. But, by the end of the film, with the aid and advice of a friendly American machinery manufacturer, Burns is able to convince the British of the value of all forms of American aid to their growing defense needs. Due to the ongoing war crisis, the British announced peacetime conscription in April 1939, the month of this film's release.

146 IN OLD MONTEREY (Rep, Aug) Joseph Kane; *genre:* Western; *location:* United States; *coding:* Natl Def, AF-A, Span Civ, Hist Am, Sino-Jap War, Am Icons, War Mats; *biases:* Pro-Military, Preparedness.

The U.S. Army has been using an aerial bombing range that is contiguous to a ranching community. When the Army announces they will expropriate the rancher's property to expand the proving grounds, the ranch-

ers declare they will not leave. Sergeant Gene Autry, who is stationed at the nearby cavalry base, is sent to straighten things out. He and some buddies force the ranchers at a Town Hall meeting to watch newsreels of the fighting in Spain and the Japanese bombing of Shanghai. Autry points out that the government needs the land in order to test their latest equipment and that it will pay more than the fair price in compensation. The patriotically aroused ranchers, led by Gabby Hayes, break out in a chorus of "Columbia, The Gem of the Ocean." But, soon afterwards, a little boy is killed by an explosion which the ranchers blame on the Army. Actually, it is the result of the machinations of a greedy borax mine owner. When Gene proves this to the ranchers they turn on the mine owner and his compatriots. Autry and his pals assist with an ersatz tank.

147 JEEPERS CREEPERS (Rep, Oct) Frank McDonald; *genre:* Drama; *location:* United States; *coding:* AF-A, Draft, WWI, WWII, Chin, Latin Am, Sino-Jap, Vets; *biases:* Pro-American, Pacifist, Contraband Message.

The singing Weaver family in Pineville have their peaceful life disturbed when a greedy capitalist discovers that their land rests upon a rich coal vein. With an assist from Sheriff Roy Rogers and other locals, the depredations of strip mining are halted and peace is restored. At the beginning of the film, the villagers are gathered for their Sunday church meeting, Abner Weaver presiding as acting deacon. Admonishing those who have been missing services, Abner shows the congregation a newspaper as he reads the recent headlines to them: "Thousands killed in China Air Raid ... War Rages in Europe..." Abner adds that those troubles can be attributed to failure to attend church, that the Bible says "love thy neighbor," and that "we're gonna ask help for them folks out yonder." In production from 6 September through mid-month, and released in late October, this was probably the earliest feature-length film to acknowledge the outbreak of WWII.

148 JOE AND ETHEL TURP CALL ON THE PRESIDENT (MGM, Dec) Robert B. Sinclair; *genre:* Comedy/Drama; *location:* United States; *coding:* Ger, FDR, WWI, Hitler, Am Icons, Isolationist, Neutrality Act, World Crisis, Ital, Dipl, For Corr; *biases:* Pro-American, Anti-Nazi.

A Brooklyn couple, played by Ann Sothern and William Gargan, drive to Washington, D.C. to appeal to the President to reinstate their recently fired mailman. While an aide is explaining to the obstreperous Brooklynites that "The President" (Lewis Stone) has a very busy schedule, cheering and the voice of Hitler are heard coming from FDR's office next door. A heated discussion concerning "his ranting" follows between the president, a cabinet member and an isolationist senator. Seated at his desk, the frustrated chief executive wishes out loud that he "knew what the ordinary citizen was thinking." "Mr. and Mrs. Citizen" are ushered in by the aide, and between comments on the Dodgers and extended flashback sequences detailing the mailman's life, Joe Turp gives FDR the following advice on how to deal with "that big mouth": "It's like a guy calling you a so-and-so over the telephone. Best thing is to hang up and leave him worry about what you're going to do about it." In production immediately following the outbreak of WWII, the topical aspects of this December release appear to be directly based upon Hitler's infamous Kroll Opera House speech of April 28, 1939. In the speech, Hitler sarcastically responded to a personal message from FDR in which the American president had asked the German leader to publicly renounce further territorial ambitions.

149 JUAREZ (WB, Jun) William Dieterle; *genre:* Biography; *location:* Mexico; *coding:* Dipl, Latin Am, Hist Am, Ger, Resist, Atroc, AF-Fr; *bias:* Pro-Democracy.

One of the screenplay writers on this solid plug for democratic values was John Huston. The fight against foreign oppression and totalitarianism is depicted in this Warner Brothers' "biopic" of a sanitized Juárez (frequently framed next to a portrait of Lincoln) in a safe 19th century Mexican historical setting. In addition, the evils of racism (Juárez was of Indian parentage) are commented upon. Paul Muni stars in the title role. Later in the same year WB—1st Nat. released a more melodramatic version concentrating on the lives of Maximilian and his wife entitled *The Mad Empress* (directed and produced by Miguel C. Torres, the film was alternately titled *Juarez and Maximilian*).

150 KING OF CHINATOWN (Para, Mar) Nick Grinde; *genre:* Crime; *location:* United States; *coding:* Sino-Jap War, Am Icons, Chi; *bias:* Anti-Japanese.

A wounded gangster in San Francisco, played by Akim Tamiroff, is nursed back to health by Dr. Mary Ling (Anna May Wong). Later, when he is shot a second time, mortally, he gives her $50,000 in gratitude for her care to buy ambulances and medical equipment for China's struggle against Japanese aggression.

151 THE LADY AND THE MOB (Col, Apr) Ben Stoloff; *genre:* Comedy/ Drama; *location:* United States; *coding:* Ital, Am Icons, Hist Am, Blk; *biases:* Pro-American, Anti-Totalitarian.

Mrs. Hattie Leonard (Fay Bainter), the wealthy patriarch of a small New England town, becomes indignant when she learns her Italian cleaner (played by Henry Armetta) and other local businessmen are raising their fees in order to pay graft to a so-called "Protective Association." With the aid of some ex-thugs whom she has befriended and a specially armored limousine she calls her "tank," the tough old lady takes on the racketeers. In retaliation, the gang leader's gunmen are sent to terrorize the merchants. The businessmen go to Mrs. Leonard begging her to desist. Hattie responds with a patriotic speech, reminding them of the sacrifices of their forefathers at Valley Forge and Bull Run, and adding: "a real American has never tolerated, or never will tolerate, a dictator." Hattie concludes: "Give me liberty, or give me death!" The Italian cleaner, who has just received his citizenship papers, proudly informs the others that she has quoted Patrick Henry.

152 LET FREEDOM RING (MGM, Feb) Jack Conway; *genre:* Western; *location:* United States; *coding:* Jew, Russ, Ital, Spy-Sab, Am Icons; *biases:* Pro-American, Anti-Fascist.

A sepia-toned Nelson Eddy engages unpatriotically greedy types during the western expansion of the railroads in the post-Civil War era. The capitalistic tyrant from Wall Street, using fascistic tactics, combats the "artillery of freedom"—the printed word and patriotic songs. Foreign railroad workers are encouraged to fight, to "stand up and cheer" for the rights that exist only in America. The film concludes with a rousing rendition of "My Country, Tis of Thee."

153 THE LONE WOLF SPY HUNT (Col, Jan) Peter Godfrey; *genre:* Spy; *location:* United States; *coding:* Secret Weapon, Spy-Sab, FBI; *bias:* Anti-Espionage.

An espionage ring in Washington, D.C., led by an enigmatic Balkan millionaire, tries to steal secret anti-aircraft plans from the War Department. Between quips exchanged with a dizzy girlfriend and his sassy daughter, our special agent, former jewel thief Michael Lanyard (Warren William), flushes out the bad guys.

154 THE LOST PATROL (Re-Release '34) (RKO, Feb) John Ford; *genre:* Combat; *coding:* Pacifism, Arab, WWI, AF-Brit; *bias:* Pacifist.

This quintessential combat motion picture, featuring an isolated British army patrol fighting vicious Arabs in a barren World War I desert setting, grimly portrays the futility of war. Sans its pacifistic slant, this Ford directorial effort would provide the model for such classic World War II era combat films as *Bataan* (MGM, 1943) and *Sahara* (Col., 1943).

155 MAN ON CONQUEST (Rep, May) George Nicholls, Jr.; *genre:* Historical Drama; *location:* United States; *coding:* AF-A, Hist Am, Latin Am, Am Icons; *bias:* Pro-American.

Rabid jingoism marks Republic studio's "first real A" picture. Sam Houston (Richard Dix) and a cast of thousands defeat a dictatorial Santa Anna and soon thereafter annex Texas into the bosom of the benevolently democratic USA.

156 MIDNIGHT (Para, Mar) Mitchell Leisen; *genre:* Comedy; *location:* France; *coding:* World Crisis, Chi, Sin-Jap War; *bias:* Contraband Message.

Eve Peabody, an American showgirl, arrives in Paris after losing all her money at the wheel in Monte Carlo. Tiber Czerny, a cabbie, gives her a ride and a meal, but Eve takes a powder when the friendly proletarian offers her a room at his place. After palming off a pawn ticket as an invitation to a private music recital, Eve is rescued from detection by a wealthy guest who hires her to woo away his wife's lover. Posing as "Baroness Czerny," she embarks upon the conquest. Complications later arise when the tuxedo-attired Tiber Czerny arrives claiming to be Eve's husband. To maintain the ruse, a fake divorce from the cabbie is arranged. The judge is informed that their marriage papers were "bombed and destroyed" in Shanghai in 1937. The unsympathetic judge proceeds to lecture the couple: "I find it deplorable [that] ... in a time of vast world unrest two grown up people are unable to iron out their own childish ... squabbles."

157 MISTER MOTO'S LAST WARNING (TCF, Jan) Norman Foster; *genre:* Spy; *locations:* France, Egypt; *coding:* Munich, Spy-Sab, AF-Brit, AF-Fr, Dipl, Jap, Ger, Ital; *bias:* Anti-Espionage.

The Nipponese counterpart to Charlie Chan helps prevent foreign agents from creating a peace-threatening incident between France and Britain. The entrance channel to the Suez Canal is mined with the intent of destroying the flagship of a visiting French naval squadron. Eric Norvel (George Sanders) and a ventriloquist named Fabian (Ricardo Cortez) are the leaders of the foreign agents. Although the state, or states, they are meant to represent are never identified, their names suggest a German-Italian linkage. The successful Moto series was discontinued the following year, presumably due to increasing anti-Japanese sentiments in the United States.

158 MISTER SMITH GOES TO WASHINGTON (Col, Oct) Frank Capra; *genre:* Drama; *location:* United States; *coding:* Hist Am, Nazi, Ital, Blk, Jew, Am Icons, Dipl, Vets, Jap, Ind Fasc Org; *biases:* Pro-American, Anti-Fascist.

"Capracorn" is applied to Americanism and the struggle to maintain the democratic way in the face of political corruption and latent domestic fascism when a naive young midwesterner (played by James Stewart) is sent to the nation's capitol by a political machine to replace a Congressman who died in office. The granite inscriptions on the Lincoln Memorial are reverentially invoked. When the freshman Congressman resists the dictates of the machine, fascistic tactics are used to impugn him and force his removal from office. Congressman Smith embarks upon a one-man filibuster to buy the time to prove his innocence. Foreign observers in the Capitol's visitors gallery are shown paying close attention to democracy in action.

159 MISTER WONG IN CHINATOWN (Mono, Aug) William Nigh; *genre:* Crime; *location:* United States; *coding:* Chi, Sino-Jap War, AF-Chi, War Mats, Neutrality Act; *bias:* Anti-Japanese.

This was the third film in the Wong series, starring Boris Karloff. The first victim in a couple of poison dart murders just happens to be a Chinese princess secretly in America to purchase aircraft for her brother's army. Talk of plans to have the planes "smuggled out" of the country is obviously meant to be an indirect reference to U.S. neutrality laws.

160 MYSTERY PLANE (Mono, Mar) George Waggner; *genre:* Drama; *location:* United States; *coding:* AF-Fr, WWI, Af-AC, AF-N, Secret Weapon, Spy-Sab, Hist Am, Ger, Brit, Am Icons; *bias:* Anti-Espionage.

This film was the first in a series of "Tailspin Tommy" features based on the Hal Forrest newspaper cartoon, "Sky Pirate." The young hero and some friends have developed a radio-controlled bombing device. But criminals are interested in selling the device to foreign powers. Their leader observes that "the United States is notoriously slow to take advantage of improvements in armaments." His pilot, a washed-up first World War ace named Brandy, prefers not to get involved: "I don't mind smuggling in foreign aliens, ... [but] this thing can only be used for destruction.... Let Uncle Sam keep it. At least we know he won't use it to drop surprise packages on women and children." Tommy, his co-pilot and girlfriend are kidnapped by the criminals in order to force them to make drawings of the new weapon. After our heroes make an aerial escape, Brandy deliberately crashes the pursuing plane.

161 NAVY SECRETS (Mono, Feb) Howard Bretherton; *genre:* Spy; *location:* United States; *coding:* Ger, Secret Weapon, AF-N, Ital?, FBI, Intell Serv, Spy-Sab; *biases:* Anti-Espionage; Pro-Military.

The plot centers around an undercover naval intelligence agent attempting to sell plans of the Navy's new range finder to a group of foreign agents. One of the enemy agents is probably meant to be Italian and their "chief" wears a monocle and talks with a German accent. The review in the *Motion Picture Herald* is worth quoting: "Exhibitors alert to interests of the day have here a picture about which they can write ad copy fashioned directly after the headlines in the morning newspaper.... There is no whoopla or flag waving. The hero ... does his chores for the secret service in business-like fashion. The heroine ... serves her country without screaming about it. The place could be any seaport, the spies could be any nation's spies, and the time could be, doubtlessly is, now."

162 NICK CARTER, MASTER DETECTIVE (MGM, Dec) Jacques Tourneur; *genre:* Spy; *location:* United States; *coding:* Intell Serv, Ger, Spy-Sab, Prod, Secret Weapon, AF-CG?; *bias:* Anti-Espionage.

Nick Carter (Walter Pidgeon) is called to a California aircraft plant to investigate the disappearance of blueprints for the latest fighter plane. En route, he meets the inventor of a revolutionary "rocket plane." The new craft is later sabotaged on its test flight. Nick learns that the company doctor has been smuggling out secret plans inside bandages covering "injuries" faked by his Germanic cohorts. With the Coast Guard's aid, Nick rescues his kidnapped girlfriend and captures the fleeing spies. American cynicism about the state of the world at the time of the film's release is reflected in one character's statement: "Sometimes I think the world is past saving and we might as well get what we can."

163 NINOTCHKA (MGM, Nov) Ernst Lubitsch; *genre:* Romantic Comedy; *locations:* France, Russia, Turkey; *coding:* Fr, Atroc, Ger, Hitler, Stalin, Russ, Comm, WWII, AF-W, NAZI, Pol; *bias:* Anti-Soviet.

Comrade Ninotchka (Greta Garbo) succumbs to the lures of capitalism and romance when she is sent to Paris to negotiate the sale of Tsarist jewels. In Russia, Ninotchka, is shown stoically participating in the May Day parade: prominently displayed banners of Josef Stalin make this one of the few fictional films of the 1930s to graphically portray the Soviet dictator's personality cult. Ninotchka's revelation to her capitalist lover (Melvyn Douglas) that she had killed a Polish lancer (in the 1920-21 Russo Polish war) may have been a veiled allusion to Soviet participation in the invasion of Poland in September 1939.

164 NORTH OF SHANGHAI (Col, Feb) D. Ross Lederman; *genre:* War Drama; *locations:* Pacific, China; *coding:* AF-Chi, AF-Jap, Sino-Jap War, For Corr, Spy-Sab; *bias:* Anti-Japanese.

A one-page ad in the *Motion Picture Herald* declared: "Bursting Out of Today's Headlines!" An American female journalist (Betty Furness) and a newsreel cameraman (James Craig) are teamed up in Shanghai. They are joined by a Chinese cameraman named Jimmy Riley (Keye Luke), who helps them expose a spy network in the offices of Furness' newspaper. As a result, they also frustrate an attempt by the Japanese to bomb Shanghai's arsenal. Actual newsreel footage is integrated into the film, including scenes of ground combat and air raids.

165 NURSE EDITH CAVELL (RKO, Sept) Herbert Wilcox; *genre:* Biography/Resistance; *locations:* Belgium, Britain; *coding:* Jew, Resist, Belg, WWI, AF-Ger, AF-Brit, Dipl, Atroc, AF-Fr, Brit, Spy-Sab; *biases:* Pacifist, Anti-German.

This film, based upon a true incident in World War I, was produced in America under British supervision. The foreword bluntly states: "War is dedication to brutal force." A montage follows that shows an iron cross over the map of Belgium and actual footage of the German army's conquest of the country. A subsequent scene portrays the occupation troops in Brussels being billeted in civilian homes. Their commander is a hateful Prussian stereotype with a Heidelberg scar across his cheek. Edith Cavell (Anna Neagle), the British head nurse of a Brussels hospital, becomes the leader of a secret organization helping Allied servicemen caught behind the German lines. The Germans eventually penetrate the group and, after being tried by a military court, the noble nurse is executed by firing squad. Or, as a *Motion Picture Herald* ad put it, she was "Crushed by the Iron Fist of Germany's War Lords." The efforts of neutral American officials to intervene on her behalf are emphasized. Released right before the outbreak of WWII, the film's paradoxical conciliatory ending should also be noted. Cavell's image is superimposed upon Westminister Abbey, a choir singing in memorium for the nurse, as the following statement is made: "I realize patriotism is not enough. I must have no hatred nor bitterness towards anyone."

166 OUR LEADING CITIZEN (Para, Aug) Alfred Santell; *genre:* Drama; *location:* United States; *coding:* Pacifism, Comm, Hist Am, War Mats, Am Icons; *bias:* Pro-American.

Bob Burns is the senior partner in a law firm who espouses "Americanism." When a local industrialist lowers the wages at a mill by 10 percent, the workers strike. It is Burns' "middle of the road," democratic approach that squelches extremism of both the left and the right. Contemporary issues such as how to deal with communist agitation and the selling of goods to "belligerents" are specifically addressed. At the end, after several ultra patriotic speeches ("The only 'ism' we want here is patriotism"), Burns is nominated for the U.S. Senate.

167 PACK UP YOUR TROUBLES (TCF, Oct) H. Bruce Humberstone; *genre:* Comedy; *locations:* United States, France; *coding:* Spy-Sab, WWI, Hitler, AF-A, AF-Ger, AF-Fr, AF-Brit, Hist Am, FR; *biases:* Anti-German, Pro-French.

After America enters World War I, the three Ritz Brothers are informed by their agent that they might as well join up since "German acts" are definitely out. They wind up in France as mule attendants. There, they become involved with a French girl whose father is spying for the Entente. When he is in danger of being exposed, the comic trio seize an observation balloon and drop behind German lines. Doing their German double talk routine they convince the "Heinies" they are German soldiers who have escaped from a French P.O.W. camp. Eventually, they are even able to trick an enemy general into surrendering, thus enabling them to return to French lines and to save the spy who is a member of the General's staff. However, their act has been so convincing that the Ritz Brothers wind up in a French prison camp with the pompous General delivering harassing orders to them and other soldiers, including one named "Adolf."

168 PANAMA LADY (RKO, May) Jack Hively; *genre:* Drama; *locations:* United States, Latin America; *coding:* Latin Am, Chi, Arms Dealer, War Mats; *bias:* Non-Intervention.

Lucille Ball plays a cabaret entertainer who becomes stranded in Panama after being dumped by her commercial aviator boyfriend. When she learns that he is smuggling guns to South America to be shipped to other destinations: "There's a hungry war across the ocean that's got to be fed." There is a happy ending in New York.

169 PANAMA PATROL (GN, May) Charles Lamont; *genre:* Spy; *locations:* United States, Panama; *coding:* Spy-Sab, Chi, Dipl, AF-A, Secret Plans; *bias:* Anti-Espionage.

Leon Ames plays Major Philip Waring, head of the Army intelligence agency in Washington responsible for decoding intercepted messages between foreign governments. In the course of his duties he and a cohort stumble across an oriental spy ring plotting the takeover of the Panama Canal. The gang, identified as "Chinese," is quickly broken up. This film was made as a sequel to the 1938 release, *Cipher Bureau* q.v.

170 PRIDE OF THE NAVY (Rep, Jan) Charles Lamont; *genre:* Adventure; *location:* United States; *coding:* Secret Weapon, Mil School, AF-N; *bias:* Pro-Military.

Romance and action highlight this film featuring the design and testing of a high speed naval torpedo boat. A former officer turned speedboat driver (James Dunn), is enlisted to aid the Navy. Out of patriotism he re-designs the boat. At a surprise exhibition for a Congressional committee the boat is proven when it is used to explode a runaway live torpedo. In order to get the girl, he reluctantly accepts a reserve commission.

171 THE PRIVATE LIVES OF ELIZABETH AND ESSEX (WB, Nov) Michael Curtiz; *genre:* Historical Drama; *locations:* Great Britain, Ireland; *coding:* AF-Brit, Dipl, Brit; *biases:* Pro-British, Non-Intervention.

Queen Elizabeth (Bette Davis) and Essex (Errol Flynn) battle it out in this 17th-century Technicolor epic. Fearing Essex's popularity and power following his defeat of the Spanish at Cadiz, Elizabeth publicly snubs him. Later, Essex ignores Elizabeth's entreaties and allows himself to be goaded into commanding an army to quell a rebellion in Ireland. The stalwart queen states: "It takes more courage not to fight when one is surrounded by foolish hotheads urging wars in all directions." She reluctantly approves the mission. When Essex's expedition suffers setbacks, court intrigue obstructs the reinforcement of this army from England. In retaliation, Essex returns with part of his army and marches on London. Elizabeth is warned that Essex is threatening to "drag down your country and drown her in a sea of blood." Elizabeth regretfully agrees, and arranges for the vainglorious soldier to lose his head. Released only a couple of months after the outbreak of war in Europe, this film would appear to contain an isolationist message for the American audience.

172 THE REAL GLORY (UA, Sept) Henry Hathaway; *genre:* Adventure; *location:* Philippines; *coding:* Atroc, AF-A, AF-Fil; *biases:* Pro-Military, Preparedness.

In 1906, Yankee occupiers (including Gary Cooper and David Niven) must enlist and train Christian Filipinos to help convince their Muslim ("Moro") brothers on the island of Mindanao that they have been "liberated" from Spain. The probably unconscious patronizing of the Filipinos aside, there seems to be a genuine attempt to promote preparedness of the indigenous forces against outside (presumably Japanese) threats. For instance, the following comment is made: "From now on the little brothers will have to stand on their own feet." Interestingly, "several scenes of *The Real Glory* that hinted at the glorification of American militarism and of the military itself were deleted at the request of Philippine President Manuel Quezon." And because of the film's racial condescension, a 1942 reissue was cancelled as being too controversial. *Salute to the*

Marines (MGM, 1943) also dealt with Americans training Filipinos to defend themselves against Japanese aggression, but this time in a 1941 setting.

173 THE ROAD TO GLORY (Re-r '36) (TCF, Oct) Howard Hawks; *genre:* Combat; *location:* France; *coding:* WWI, AF-Fr, AF-Ger, Jew; *biases:* Pacifist, Pro-French.

In this reissued film (whose script was co-authored by William Faulkner), a battle hardened French officer discovers that his father is serving under him in the World War I trenches. Noble, though somewhat stoic, patriotism overcomes cynicism engendered by war weariness. Interestingly, some of the war footage from Fords' 1934 anti-war film *The World Moves On* (Fox), was incorporated into this motion picture.

174 THE ROARING TWENTIES (WB, Oct) Raoul Walsh; *genre:* Crime; *locations:* France, United States; *coding:* Czech, AF-Ger, Hist Am, WWI, AF-A, FDR, Musso, Vet, Hitler; *biases:* Pacifist, Contraband Message.

This classic Cagney/Bogart gangster film opens with an interesting montage superimposed within a spinning globe, incorporating documentary shots. A "March of Time" style off-screen narrator links FDR, "acquisitive power madmen" [Hitler, Mussolini], and the Nazi seizure of Czechoslovakia with Woodrow Wilson's signing of the peace treaty at Versailles and the bootleggers of the Twenties. Though not clearly stated, the film would appear to imply that the war made callous criminals of many American boys, and that the peace helped to create political gangsters overseas.

175 SABOTAGE (Rep, Oct) Harold Young; *genre:* Spy; *location:* United States; *coding:* FBI, Secret Weapon, Prod, AF-A, Vets, Spy-Sab, Hist Am, Am Icons; *bias:* Anti-Espionage.

The folks in a small town where a new bomber is being manufactured hastily condemn a young aviation mechanic as an enemy agent when several of the planes mysteriously crash. Things get even worse when the government, citing these incidents closes the "Midland" plant. His dad and some buddies from the old soldiers' home track down the real spies and obtain the necessary confessions leading to nationwide arrests of a sabotage ring. The irrationality of mob mentality and prejudices against older people are directly attacked. However, the foreign country involved is never specifically identified.

176 SHE GOES TO WAR (Re-r '29) (Ind, Nov) Mitchell Leichter; *genre:* War Drama; *locations:* United States, France; *coding:* WWI, AF-W, AF-A, AF-Ger, Fr; *bias:* Pacifist.

Mitchell Leichter edited the original 1929 WWI melodrama directed by Henry King and added sound and a musical score. A small town American society girl, Joan, who had volunteered as an ambulance driver in France, dons an officer's uniform, goes into battle and after capturing a German machine gun nest, becomes the idol of her regiment. According to the *MPH* review about twenty minutes were cut out of this version "removing most of the romance and emphasizing the battle sequences [including the use of tanks] and scenes that recall the horrors of war."

177 SKY PATROL (Mono, Sept) Howard Bretherton; *genre:* Adventure; *location:* United States; *coding:* AF-A, Arms Dealers, War Mats; *bias:* Non-Intervention.

This was the third film in the "Tailspin Tommy" series. The *Motion Picture Herald* review states: [It is a] beneficiary of contemporary events focusing public attention on the exportation of munitions from the United States to elsewhere. Dealt with here is the smuggling of guns and ammunition from a point in the Southwest, by means of hydroplane, to a ship twenty miles at sea. The smugglers are defeated and ultimately disposed of by the hero and other members of the United States Army sky patrol.

178 SLIGHTLY HONORABLE (UA, Dec) Tay Garnett; *genre:* Comedy; *location:* United States; *coding:* Spy-Sab; *biases:* Contraband Message, Anti-Espionage.

In this Walter Wanger production, Pat O'Brien is a wisecracking lawyer out to make a fast buck by exposing corruption on state highway contracts. A dizzy eighteen-year-old lady falls for him after an act of gallantry at a cocktail party. The next day she invades his offices, thereby evoking from the lawyer the despairing topical comment that there are already enough problems since the "...country [is now] teeming with international spies...."

179 SORORITY HOUSE (RKO, May) John Farrow; *genre:* Drama; *location:* United States; *coding:* Brit, Hist Am, Am Icons; *bias:* Pro-Democracy.

The screenplay of this film was written by left-wing writer Dalton Trumbo. Alice, a small town grocer's daughter, enters the local university and quickly becomes involved in sorority "rushing." In the process of winning a bid to the prestigious Gamma House, Alice begins to lose touch with her social origins. However, during a visit by her father, Alice becomes ashamed of her social affectations and tears up the cherished bid. At a small party in her boarding house Alice and her roomies pledge to be "strictly democratic" and to form their own "anti-sorority." "Her dad gently admonishes them for their snobbery and adds, "Strikes me that most of the grief in the world today is caused by people

... forming cliques and hating everybody else. Now call it what you will—sororities, ... or even nations, nobody has the right to go about tellin' the other fellow what he ought to do." In an earlier scene at the boarding house, a discussion about men leads one of the girls to remark that she prefers the "Anthony Eden type." The aristocratic Eden, Britain's Foreign Secretary during part of 1937–1938, had resigned over Prime Minister Chamberlain's appeasement policy. As a private citizen advocating British determination to resist further Axis aggression, the popular Eden made a highly publicized visit to America in December 1938.

180 SOUTH OF THE BORDER (Rep, Dec) George Sherman; *genre:* Western; *location:* Latin America; *coding:* Spy-Sab, War Mats, Latin Am, Dipl; *bias:* Non-Intervenon.

Having just completed an important mission south of the border, federal agent Gene Autry and his sidekick Frog (Smiley Burnette) are ordered by the American consul to investigate "a revolution sponsored by agents of a belligerent nation which hopes to gain control of Mexican oil concessions." The contested area is located on the Gulf Coast. The foreign agent, Saunders, poses as an entertainer and uses a secret short-wave radio set to contact submarines in order to obtain supplies and direct actions against the government. After singing his way into the people's confidence, Autry is able to prove Saunders' duplicity and alert the people to the threat of foreign intervention.

181 THE SPIRIT OF CULVER (Univ, Mar) Joseph Santley; *genre:* Drama; *location:* United States; *coding:* Mil School, Span Civ, WWI, AF-A; *biases:* Contraband Message, Anti-Fascist.

Two first-year plebes from differing social backgrounds (played by Freddie Bartholomew and Jackie Cooper) go through the usual trials at the Culver Military Academy. Cooper, the son of a shell-shocked WWI Medal of Honor winner, is attending the school on a scholarship. At one point, the upper-class boy mimics the famous lines from the July 1936 "No Pasaran" speech by "La Pasionara" (Spanish Communist Dolores Ibarron), which urged the people of the Spanish Republic to resist the fascists: "Sometimes it is better to die on your feet than live on your knees." Left-wing screenwriter Nathaniel West was responsible for the script.

182 STANLEY AND LIVINGSTONE (TCF, Aug) Henry King; *genre:* Biography; *locations:* Great Britain, Africa, United States; *coding:* Arab, Dipl, For Corr, US-Brit Coop, Blk, AF-A, Brit; *bias:* Pro-British.

This motion picture portrays the African expedition of the American reporter, Henry M. Stanley, to find the British explorer/mis-

sionary Dr. Livingstone. It is a subtle plug for Anglo-American cooperation and an epic evocation of the myth of the "white man's burden." It glosses over the very real prejudice and disdain of a supercilious British scientific establishment defending its vested interests and professional assumptions against an all too readily presumed American parvenu. Though racked with fever, Livingstone continues his civilizing mission and the charting of central Africa. He wants the "Dark Continent" opened up in order to end slavery and to spread the message of the brotherhood of man. Later, after receiving notification of Livingstone's death, Stanley (Spencer Tracy) returns to carry on the great man's work. The film concludes with a determined Stanley marching across a superimposed map of Africa to the strains of "Onward Christian Soldiers." This film was produced by Darryl F. Zanuck.

183 THE STORY OF VERNON AND IRENE CASTLE (RKO, Apr) H. C. Potter; *genre:* Biography; *locations:* United States, France; *coding:* WWI, AF-Brit, AF-W, AF-AC, AF-Ger, Fr, Bonds, Blk, Can; *bias:* Pro-Intervention.

With the situation heating up in Europe this Astaire–Rogers spring release was rather interesting. Based on the lives of the famous dancing couple, the latter half of the film centered on Vernon (an Englishman by birth) joining the Royal Flying Corps and fighting "over there." Its anti-isolationist stance was further emphasized by a direct reference to Irene's starring role in the 1917 pro-interventionist, notoriously anti-Japanese Hearst produced serial, *Patria* (Cosmopolitan Pictures). Ironically, Mrs. Irene Castle McLaughlin would become a prominent member of the America First movement.

184 THE SUN NEVER SETS (Univ, Jun) Rowland V. Lee; *genre:* Adventure; *locations:* Africa, Great Britain; *coding:* Brit, Dipl, Blk, Arms Dealers, Hist Am, War Mats, AF-Brit, Spy-Sab, Hitler, WWI, Draft; *biases:* Pro-British, Pacifist.

The Randolph family has faithfully served in Britain's colonial service for generations. It is also proudly pointed out that the American branch of the family included a governor of Virginia (a reference to Edmund Randolph, one of the delegates to the Constitutional Convention). Hugo Zuroff (Lionel Atwill), a scientist of unspecified national origin, has organized the accumulation of strategic metals mines, including molybdenum, and the broadcasting of incendiary propaganda from a secret base located in the interior of Britain's Gold Coast colony. He wants to precipitate an international war and become dictator of the world through his control of the metals required to produce war materials. Clive Randolph (Basil Rathbone) goes to Africa to discover the source of the "Mystery Radio" transmissions that are inciting incidents throughout the world, such as the sabotage of defense industries. During a conversation between Randolph and Zuroff, the latter confidently states: "Did it ever occur to you that it only takes one generation to make a dictator? It could be anyone—a paper hanger [an obvious allusion to Nazi Germany and Hitler], a fruit seller, a sign painter—perhaps, perhaps even a scientist." Later, as a smirking Zuroff listens to a European (BBC?) radio announcer bemoan the impending death of millions in the upcoming war—"We've raised a new crop of cannon fodder and the Grim Reaper impatiently sharpens his scythe"—a newsreel montage presents mobilization scenes. Zuroff and his cohorts are about to make a broadcast that will unleash a world war, when British bombers (with Randolph giving orders) destroy the bunker from which the radio transmissions are coming.

185 TELEVISION SPY (Para, Oct) Edward Dmytryk; *genre:* Spy; *location:* United States; *coding:* Blk, Spy-Sab, Secret Plans, AF-A, AF-N, Am Icons, Atroc-Con, Nat Def, Fr; *bias:* Anti-Espionage.

Agents with foreign-sounding names, but no accents, secretly make copies of the plans for a long distance television system at the lab of a wealthy entrepreneur where its young inventor is attempting to perfect the device. The spies then trick an old business rival into building an identical set from the plans. The wheelchair-bound entrepreneur is acutely aware of the military value of the invention: "Army and Navy men have told me that long distance television would give our nation the strongest hand ever held in an international poker game. So, we're going to deal them a royal flush.... From now on you'll [the inventor] still be on my payroll, but you'll be working for the old man with the whiskers [Uncle Sam]." The inventor eventually is able to foil the spy ring, operating on both coasts of the country, with the aid of his new devise. He also wins the heart of the pretty girl he has been ogling over the wide screen of his long distance television system.

186 THEY MADE HER A SPY (RKO, Apr) Jack Hively; *genre:* Spy; *location:* United States; *coding:* Spy-Sab, Blk, AF-A, Intell Ser, Am Icons; *bias:* Anti-Espionage.

Irene Eaton's (Sally Eilers) brother is killed during an Army test of a new mortar. Sabotage is suspected. When she appears at the War Department the sympathetic head of the Intelligence Bureau thinks she might be able to help the government break up a spy ring that is believed to be operating right in

Washington, D.C. Using a new "stratosphere" bomber for bait, with assistance from the ubiquitous newspaper man, Irene proves too much for the agents. And if things were not hot enough for the espionage leader, he is subjected to a lecture on the American legislative system by the elderly elevator operator at the Washington Monument immediately prior to his taking the final plunge.

187 THUNDER AFLOAT (MGM, Sept) George B. Seitz; *genre:* War Drama/Combat; *locations:* United States, Atlantic; *coding:* WWI, AF-N, Vets, Pacifism, AF-Ger, Am Icons; *biases:* Pro-Intervention, Anti-German.

When not bickering with an old antagonist who is now a fellow Naval Reservist, old salt Wallace Beery wreaks vengeance on the U-Boat and its nasty crew of "Heinies" that sank his beloved tug, the "Susan H." Released in the fall of 1939, the opening commentary about German "raiders" along America's Atlantic coastline in 1918 and the subsequent chorus of "Over There" had distinct interventionist overtones. *Thunder Afloat* was produced with the assistance of the Navy Department and the film's release date was advanced at the request of the government. Footage from this film was used in MGM's short *Ashcan Fleet*.

188 TRAPPED IN THE SKY (Col, Jun) Lewis D. Collins; *genre:* Spy; *location:* United States; *coding:* AF-AC, Spy-Sab, Secret Weapon, Blk, Am Icons, Ital?; *biases:* Anti-Espionage, Pro-Military.

The test model of a revolutionary electronic bombing plane that receives its energy from a huge power house on the ground mysteriously crashes on its maiden flight. Rival spy rings are interested, including one that is run by a Joseph Dure who uses the Borna News Alliance as a front. Although the country he represents is never named, Dure and his star agent, Baroness Irene del Trina (alias Carol Rayder), speak with Italian accents. Further sabotage, as well as the murders of Dure and his associate, ensue. It turns out that the inventor had sold out to Dure's key competitor. Major Rosten (Jack Holt) of the U.S. Army Air Corps eventually triumphs over the assorted enemies of the government. For his efforts, Rosten is rewarded with a promotion and command of the system of electric power houses required for the new bombers.

189 TWENTY THOUSAND (20,000) MEN A YEAR (TCF, Oct) Alfred E. Green; *genre:* Training; *location:* United States; *coding:* AF-AC, Chi, Jew; *bias:* Preparedness.

This film deals with the nationally sponsored college aviation training program that had been initiated earlier in 1939 by the Civil Aeronautics Authority. The opening

title proclaims that it provides "an education for the uses of peace—not war...." But the older sister of one of the students expresses her doubts about the "great future in a coming industry" that the program will allegedly provide by ominously stating that "it also prepares them for other things to come," e.g. war (there is also the obvious linkage with the apocalyptic world war British film of 1936). The pilot trainees make up the usual melting pot, this time including a Jew and a Chinese-American.

190 U-67 (Re-r '31) (Ind, ?) William Nigh; *genre:* Adventure; *location:* Atlantic; *coding:* AF-Ger, AF-N, WWI, Brit; *bias:* Anti-German.

This film, released by Astor in 1939 on the state's rights market, was a re-titled re-release of *The Sea Ghost*, a 1931 Peerless film. During WWI, a U-Boat sinks a passenger ship. Lt. Wilson (Alan Hale) halts his Navy sub-chaser in an attempt to rescue survivors, and the German sub escapes. In 1925, Wilson—now a merchant sailor—is reunited with the U-Boat captain to salvage the sunken ship. What was essentially a "sunken treasure" drama was billed as a war action film when re-released.

191 WINGS OF THE NAVY (WB, Feb) Lloyd Bacon; *genre:* Training; *location:* United States; *coding:* Hist Am, AF-N, Latin Am; *bias:* Pro-Military.

In this high budget production that incorporates extensive documentary footage, the older aviator brother gives up Olivia de Havilland to his younger aviator sibling. Between air training and romancing, a new plane is tested for the Navy, delivering a less than subtle message for the modernization of the U.S. naval air arm. The *Variety* review is explicit on this point when it states the film is "a convincer to mold public opinion and support in favor of current government plans for wide expansion of American air defense forces." In the prison warehouse movie theatre sequence of the Warner's gangster film released later in the year, *Each Dawn I Die*, the opening credits to *Wings of the Navy* are screened.

192 THE WOMEN (MGM, Sept) George Cukor; *genre:* Drama; *location:* United States; *coding:* Nazi; *bias:* Contraband Message.

This is the film adaptation of Clare Boothe Luce's satiric play. The somewhat talky script centers around the marital tribulations of a group of Fifth Avenue ladies. Near the end, Mary, who had gone to Reno and divorced her wayward spouse two years earlier, desires a reconciliation. In the course of a conversation her fatuous mother, Mrs. Morehead, makes the following comment: "Well, cheer up, Mary. Living alone has its compensations. Heaven knows, it's marvelous to be able to spread out in bed like a swastika."

193 YOU CAN'T CHEAT AN HONEST MAN (Univ, Feb) George Marshall; *genre:* Comedy; *location:* United States; *coding:* Hitler, Blk; *biases:* Anti-Nazi; Contraband Message.

W. C. Field's traveling show is beset by financial difficulties. At one point, while he is in the guise of "Buffalo Bella," two men make "her" an offer for the show. He identifies himself (with a lock of her wig over his lip) to them as "Gretta Shicklegruber ... one of the Shicklegruber sisters." This is one of the earliest fictional films to use this pejorative reference to Adolf Hitler.

194 YOUNG MR. LINCOLN (TCF, Jun) John Ford; *genre:* Biography; *location:* United States; *coding:* Hist Am, Blk, Am Icons, Vets; *bias:* Pro-American.

Prejudice and mob violence are attacked; Americanism is vigorously promoted. The executive producer for this timely film biography was Darryl F. Zanuck. Henry Fonda plays the young country lawyer named Abe Lincoln who prevents a lynching and then proves the innocence of the two brothers accused of murder. The Lincoln persona, a popular New Deal era American icon, had also featured prominently in MGM's moral fable of 1938, *Of Human Hearts.*

1940

195 ABE LINCOLN IN ILLINOIS (RKO, Apr) John Cromwell; *genre:* Biography; *location:* United States; *coding:* Blk, Hist Am, Am Icons, Jew; *bias:* Pro-American.

Raymond Massey repeated his stage role as Lincoln in this film version of the 1938 Robert E. Sherwood play. Sherwood, who would become a Roosevelt speech writer, had unabashedly linked the image of Lincoln with FDR. It is a reverent tribute to a great man and to the values considered most dear to America. The screenplay was laced with a message directly relevant to the 1940 audience. Though clearly established as a man of peace, Lincoln chooses, in the latter half of the film, to abandon appeasement of the pro-slavery elements knowing full well that his electoral victory will probably lead to a civil war. Contemporary allusions are most obvious as delivered through some of his speeches. In one, slavery is compared to the Biblical plight of the "Jews" and, in another, it is stated that the American dream provides "hope to all the world."

196 ANDY HARDY MEETS DEBU-TANTE (MGM, July) George B. Seitz; *genre:* Comedy; *location:* United States; *coding:* Am Icons, Blk, Hist Am, WWII; *biases:* Pro-American, Contraband Message.

Andy goes with his parents to New York City. The judge is there primarily to check up on the status of war defaulted European bonds that had been used as the endowment for Carvel's orphanage. Andy's personal mission is to try to arrange a meeting with a much publicized glamour girl. After Andy is humiliated at a smart club where he was unable to pay the bill, he tells his father that people from small towns have no class. The judge is incredulous. He takes Andy to the Hall of Fame and delivers a Churchillian homily on the blood and tears sacrifices of his American forefathers: "...They left you a heritage of freedom and equality. A heritage you should fight to keep. Instead of kicking it around and sniveling about class and money and social position." The *Variety* review notes that "His several dissertations on Americanism and the liberties enjoyed in this country hit the bull's eye in timeliness."

197 ANGELS OVER BROADWAY (Col, Sept) Ben Hecht, Lee Garmes; *genre:* Drama; *location:* United States; *coding:* WWII, Pol, Neth, Russo-Finn, War; *biases:* Contraband Message, Anti-Totalitarian.

On a rainy evening in New York City, the lives of three individuals on the financial-psychological edge come together. Somewhat at cross purposes, they make a stab at a killing in a high stakes poker game. When Bill (Douglas Fairbanks, Jr.) complains to his Russian exile girlfriend about how tough life is she suggests the "little guys" eventually make out. Bill cynically responds, "Yeh, what happened to the Poles, the Finns and the Dutch?"

198 ARGENTINE NIGHTS (Univ, Sept) Albert S. Rogell; *genre:* Musical Comedy; *locations:* United States, Argentina; *coding:* Hist Am, WWII, Latin Am; *biases:* Contraband Message, Pro-American.

In order to escape their creditors, a singing girl trio, the Andrews Sisters in their film debut, and their managers, played by the Ritz Brothers, embark upon a "goodwill tour" to South America. One of the zany brothers exaggeratedly states that it will be the "greatest publicity stunt since the Monroe Doctrine." While in Argentina another one of the brothers tells a pretty lady to "shoot the blitz to me princess."

199 ARISE, MY LOVE (Para, Nov) Mitchell Leisen; *genre:* War Drama; *locations:* Spain, France, Great Britain; *coding:* Russo-Finn, War, For Corr, Span Civ, WWI, WWII, Am Vol, Hitler, Nazi, AF-RAF, Belg, Pol, Nor, Fr, Chamberlain, Goebbels, AF-Ger, AF-Brit, Czech, AF-Fr, Ref, Ital; *biases:* Pro-Intervention, Anti-Nazi.

Miss Nash, an American correspondent played by Claudette Colbert, rescues a wise-cracking "volunteer" flyer (Ray Milland) from a Spanish firing squad in the summer of 1939. A romantic interlude in Paris ensues until she is reassigned to Berlin. It seems the other correspondent for "Associated News" had offended Herr Ribbentrop at a reception by "yelling for gefiltefish." After joining the Polish Air Force and later getting shot out of the skies over Norway while flying for the RAF, our globetrotting hero again meets up with Colbert during the French surrender ceremonies at Compiegne. Following a scene with an obnoxious German officer, a now somewhat exhausted but patriotically inspired Miss Nash declares they must return to America in order to urge the country to "arise ... and be strong."

200 ARIZONA GANG BUSTERS (PRC, Sept) Peter Stewart; *genre:* Western; *location:* United States; *coding:* Collab, Vets, Spy-Sab, Latin Am, Ital, Ger, FBI, Fifth Col; *biases:* Anti-German, Anti-Espionage.

A foreign agent (with the Germanic surname Schmidt) and his foreign-named cohorts (Mario and Hess) enlist a gang of American cutthroats for their nefarious activities. Operating near the Mexican border, the gang's aircraft, parachute, and surveying activities arouse the suspicion of local horse breeder Sue Lambert. When the sheriff refuses to investigate, Sue writes to the commander of the local American Legion Post. He tells her that five federal investigators have been murdered or have disappeared in the area, but dispatches a group of Legionnaires and "Trigger Tim" (Tim McCoy) to the scene. Soon afterwards, the Legionnaires are killed and the Lambert home is blown up by the "fifth columnists." Tim teams up with a mysterious Mexican, actually a captain in the Mexican federal police. They discover that wild horses are being used to smuggle vital defense information (suitable locations for a possible invasion of the United States) out of the country. The foreign agents and American traitors are relentlessly tracked down and captured. Concerns over so-called "Fifth Column" activities emanating from across the border became endemic in the Southwest U.S. in 1940.

201 BLACK DIAMONDS (Univ, Jul) Christy Cabanne; *genre:* Drama; *location:* United States; *coding:* WWII, War Corr; *bias:* Contraband Message.

Walter Norton (Richard Arlen) is a reporter who has received a coveted assignment to cover the war in Europe. En route, he visits his hometown in a coal mining region. Norton soon becomes sidetracked by troubles over the working conditions at the mines, where his father still works.

202 BRIGHAM YOUNG, FRONTIERSMAN (TCF, Sept) Henry Hathaway; *genre:* Biography; *location:* United States; *coding:* Atroc, AF-A, Jew, Hist Am; *bias:* Pro-American.

The blatant discrimination that was exercised against the Mormons in the 1840s is movingly portrayed in this film. In an early scene reminiscent of Nazi book burnings, the *Book of Mormon* is burned by an angry gentile mob. The Mormon's great trek that would eventually lead them to the land of the Salt Lake is chronicled and is deliberately suggestive of the Biblical flight of the Israelites from Egypt. Contemporary parallels to 1940 are inescapable. The heavy romance between Tyrone Power and Linda Darnell (an "outsider") aside, the American way is dramatically shown to triumph over religious bigotry and mob violence. This was a Darryl F. Zanuck production.

203 BRITISH INTELLIGENCE (WB, Jan) Terry Morse; *genre:* Spy; *locations:* Great Britain, France; *coding:* AF-Ger, WWI, Spy-Sab, Ger, AF-Brit, Hitler, Intell Serv; *biases:* Anti-German, Anti-Espionage.

This was the third film adaptation of the 1918 play written by Paul Kelly entitled *Three Faces East* (two earlier versions: Warners, 1926, Rupert Julian; WB, 1930, Roy Del Ruth). In this version, a pretty British double agent crosses swords with a German spy (Boris Karloff) working as the butler for a British cabinet member during WWI. In one interesting scene, a meek little German with a Chaplin mustache, named "Adolf," is humiliatingly dressed down by his superior officer. In addition, 'prophecies' about a future resurgence of Germany are thrown in at the end: "…We pray that each war will be the last. But always in the strange scheme of things some maniac with a lust for power arises and in one moment destroys the peace…. We hate war. We despise it. But when war comes, we must, and will, fight on…."

204 BROTHER ORCHID (WB, Jun) Lloyd Bacon; *genre:* Comedy; *location:* United States; *coding:* Blk, Ital, Brit, WWII; *bias:* Contraband Message.

Edward G. Robinson plays a good-natured gangster who takes refuge from the world in a monastery. When it looks like things on the outside are getting a little sticky he leaves his flowers in order to straighten up the rackets. He is assisted by several of his old pals, including one who just got back from one of those "foreign wars" where they were paying him for "piecework."

205 CALLING PHILO VANCE (WB, Feb) William Clemens; *genre:* Crime; *loca-* tions: Germany, United States, Italy; *coding:* Intell Serv, Spy-Sab, AF-A, Brit, Jap, Ger, Ital, Am Icons, Secret Weapon, Italo-Eth War, Nazi, Chi; *biases:* Anti-Espionage, Anti-Totalitarian.

This was a Hollywood remake of the 1933 Vance detective film, *The Kennel Murder Case* (WB). The altered plot centers around Vance's investigation of the mysterious death of the designer of a new bomber. In this updated version, the heavies have evolved into foreign agents—Italian, German and a Chinese maid working for the Japanese government (the earliest known film example of Axis collusion). Although the opening scenes take place in Vienna, the film avoids explicitly identifying the Nazi regime.

206 CAPTAIN CAUTION (UA, Aug) Richard Wallace; *genre:* Historical Drama; *locations:* United States, Atlantic; *coding:* Fr, AF-Mer, AF-Brit, Neutrality?; *bias:* Anti-British.

This was one of a very few films with a distinct anti-British flavor or, to quote one contemporary review (*MPH*), "There are no hands across-the-sea concessions." Released in mid–1940, it was probably the last of its ilk before America entered the war. The film begins shortly after the outbreak of the War of 1812. An American merchant ship, significantly named the "Olive Branch," its crew unaware of the war, is seized by a British warship. The plot, its *de rigeur* romance aside, again touches on what was probably the most sensitive recurrent issue between the two countries for over a century and a half: the doctrine of the freedom of the seas as applied to non-belligerents.

207 CHARLIE CHAN IN PANAMA (TCF, Mar) Norman Foster; *genre:* Crime/ Spy; *location:* Panama; *coding:* Ger, Intell Serv, AF-A, Chi, Brit, AF-N, Czech, Ref, Atroc-Conc, Spy-Sab, Atroc, Am Icons, Latin Am; *biases:* Anti-Espionage, Preparedness, Anti-German.

To be timed to a period of war crisis, foreign agents led by the mysterious Ryner (later revealed to be a woman) prepare to sabotage the Panama Canal and elements of the U.S. Fleet passing through it. On the plane to the Canal Zone Charlie Chan's fellow passengers include a young Czechoslovakian fleeing the "cruelty of the invaders." He comforts her: "On the soil of democracy you are safe from persecution." Detective Chan (played by Sidney Toler after the 1938 death of Warner Oland), reluctantly accepting assistance from his overzealous son, foils the plot only moments before disaster would have struck the strategic American facility. Charlie sagely states at the film's conclusion: "Intelligent defense of nation best guarantee of years of peace." A German spy ring had actually been uncovered in the Canal Zone in December 1938.

208 CHASING TROUBLE (Mono, Jan) Howard Bretherton; *genre:* Spy; *location:* United States; *coding:* Blk, Ger, FBI, Spy-Sab, AF-A, Secret Weapon, Hist Am; *bias:* Anti-Espionage.

With the aid of a correspondence course in handwriting analysis, and a sympathetic newspaper man, "Cupid" O'Brien, a florist's delivery boy played by Frankie Darro, breaks up a foreign sabotage ring (some of whom have Germanic names). The film's climax features the removal of a bomb in a floral arrangement sent to an aircraft plant about to begin the manufacture of a new bombsight. When his patriotism is questioned by the reporter, Cupid's black assistant responds: "How can I be a traitor to my country? … my grandpappy cooked for the U.S. Army." In Monogram's pre-release copyright synopsis one of the spy leaders was named Molotoff. Apparently the studio decided to back away from creating a negative linkage with Soviet Foreign Minister V. Molotov, for in the release print the character is named Retzloff.

209 CHRISTMAS IN JULY (Para, Oct) Preston Sturges; *genre:* Comedy; *location:* United States; *coding:* Blk, Jew, Ital, Hitler, Musso; *biases:* Anti-Fascist, Contraband Message.

A frustrated young man (Dick Powell) from New York's East Side enters a coffee slogan contest. As a practical joke some of his office co-workers send him an acceptance telegram, and he goes on a buying spree at a department store. When the hoax is discovered the indignant owner of the store goes to Dick's address only to discover a wild block party in progress. He demands that the local cop arrest all of them. The officer responds: "Who do you think you are, Hitler?" Later, when the outraged coffee company president arrives to retrieve his check, he too demands the arrest of all. This time the miffed officer quips: "Listen, Mussolini."

210 COMRADE X (MGM, Dec) King Vidor; *genre:* Comedy; *locations:* Russia, Romania, United States; *coding:* Comm, Nazi, Am Icons, For Corr, AF-W, Jap, AF-Rom, Stalin, Ger, Atroc, AF-Russ, WWII, Brit; *biases:* Anti-Soviet, Anti-Nazi.

American correspondent McKinley Thompson (Clark Gable), alias "Comrade X," has been smuggling derogatory stories about the Soviet government out of the Soviet Union. His identity is discovered by the porter, who immediately blackmails McKinley into smuggling the porter's daughter (Hedy Lamarr), out of Russia. Lamarr is a dedicated, idealistic Communist who operates a Moscow streetcar. Gable hops on for the ideological ride, and then proposes marriage. The secret police catch up with them outside the Kremlin walls. In an outrageous chase scene, the duo makes their escape to capitalist paradise aboard a commandeered Soviet tank. Early in the film, McKinley is asked by a colleague why the pompous Nazi journalist at their Moscow hotel is screaming in the hallway. The cocky American explains that he was "shooting at some rats and von Hoffer took it personally."

211 CONFESSIONS OF A NAZI SPY (WB, May) Anatole Litvak; *genre:* Spy; *locations:* United States, Germany, Great Britain; *coding:* Nazi, FBI, Vet, US-Brit Coop, Ind Fasc Org, Hitler, Am Icons, Spy-Sab, AF-A, AF-N, AF-AC, Czech, Austr, Comm, Fr, Span Civ, Yugo, FDR, Russo-Finn War, Pol, WWII, Atroc-Conc, Ital, Jap, Secret Weapon, Brit, WWI, Latin Am, Munich, Goebbels, AF-Ger, Intell Serv, Jew; *biases:* Anti-Nazi, Anti-Espionage.

See entry 126 (1939) for a more complete discussion of this seminal anti–Nazi film. This film was re-released in 1940 with added documentary footage of Nazi military aggression. In 1941, the U.S. Senate held hearings on "propaganda" in Hollywood films, and *Confessions of a Nazi Spy* was named as one of the chief offenders in this regard. Both Harry Warner and Anatole Litvak were subpoenaed to appear before the committee but the attack on Pearl Harbor in December of that year effectively put an end to the matter.

212 THE CROOKED ROAD (Rep, June) Phillip Rosen; *genre:* Crime; *location:* United States; *coding:* WWII, Blk, Brit; *bias:* Contraband Message.

Edmund Lowe plots to murder a man who is blackmailing him. He shoots the man in a confrontation, and frames Paul Fix for the crime. Fix is convicted of murder, but new evidence revealed by lawyer Henry Wilcoxon incriminates Lowe. However, it turns out Fix had actually poisoned the victim *before* Lowe shot him! At one point, Lowe's fiancee comments that the news coverage of the investigation has "pushed the war news right off the front page."

213 CROSS-COUNTRY ROMANCE (RKO, Jul) Frank Woodruff; *genre:* Comedy; *location:* United States; *coding:* Arms Dealer, WWII, Chi, AF-MC; *bias:* Contraband Message.

With obvious similarities to Capra's 1934 classic, *It Happened One Night* (Col.), a rich heiress takes a powder on her wedding day and hitches a ride west in a trailer with a young doctor planning to join a colleague in China. At the beginning of the film one of the wedding guests is spotted getting out of a car by a reporter in the crows: "There's Hildebrandt.... He's the biggest munitions manufacturer in the country.... Do you think

America will get into the war, Mr. Hildebrandt?" The heiress' mother threatens the police with a "blitzkrieg from the voters" if they fail to find her daughter. Meanwhile, romance blossoms on the road to San Francisco. Yet, during the frequent conversations the traveling couple have that refer to the doctor's intentions of participating in medical research in China, no mention is ever made of the Sino-Japanese War.

214 DANGER AHEAD (Mono, Jan) Ralph Staub; *genre:* Adventure; *location:* Canada; *coding:* Spy-Sab; *bias:* Contraband Message.

This was another entry in the "Renfrew of the Northwest Canadian Mounted Police" series. Based on the popular radio show featuring a singing Mountie, the first film version appeared in 1937: *Renfrew of the Royal Mounted* (Grand Nat.). The story centers around the theft of a gold shipment and the slaying of a driver of an armored truck. What is relevant is a conversation the Inspector has at the film's conclusion: "You say a foreign espionage agent has been flown into our country? Get me descriptions of the man and the pilot."

215 DEATH RIDES THE RANGE (Ind, Jan) Sam Newfield; *genre:* Western; *location:* United States; *coding:* Russ-Ger Coop?, Neutrality Act, Spy-Sab, FBI, Russ?, Ger?, Latin Am, Collab; *biases:* Anti-Espionage, Anti-Totalitarian.

Ken Maynard plays a federal agent posing as an unemployed cowboy. He investigates a range war precipitated by a traitor who heads up a "scientific expedition" that is actually a gang of foreign agents. A helium well has been discovered on land owned by a pretty cowgirl, and the gas is being secretly piped across the border to Mexico. (It is explained at one point that it is against the law to sell helium—used in airships—to any other country.) The spies include the Germanic "Baron Strakoff" and the (Russian?) Dr. Flothow. This film was released while the Russo-Finnish War was in progress (November 1939 to March 1940), and at a time when Germany and Russia were allies (August 1939 to June 1941). At the climax, Ken and some friends—including a Mexican—arrest the Baron and his gang on charges of espionage and murder.

216 A DISPATCH FROM REUTERS (WB, Oct) William Dieterle; *genre:* Biography; *locations:* Great Britain, Europe; *coding:* Brit, For Corr, Hist Am, Jew; *bias:* Pro-British.

In a 19th century setting anti-Semitism is alluded to in this Warner Bros. biopic of Paul Julius Reuter (Edward G. Robinson), founder of the famous international news agency. In an impassioned speech he delivers to Parliament near the film's end Reuter states: "A censored press is the tool of a corrupt minority.... A free press is the symbol of a free people. But to be worthy of freedom, the press must always tell the truth ... for truth is freedom and without truth there can only be slavery and degradation."

217 DOCTOR EHRLICH'S MAGIC BULLET (WB, Mar) William Dieterle; *genre:* Biography; *location:* Germany; *coding:* Ger, Jew; *bias:* Anti-Fascist.

One of the screenwriters for this film biography was John Huston. Edward G. Robinson portrays Dr. Paul Ehrlich, the *fin de siècle* German-Jewish scientist who discovered salvarsan, a remedy for syphilis. Although anti-Semitism is never specifically addressed, racism and prejudice are attacked. In one scene a jealous medical colleague, played by Sig Rumann, makes the comment: "I must confess a certain feeling about persons of his [Ehrlich's] faith in our profession...." And as a member of an investigating board visiting Ehrlich's research institute the same antagonist states: "[We are] surprised at the presence of an oriental doctor here ... when you could employ a doctor of pure German blood." Finally, there is the protagonist's deathbed statement: "There can be no final victory over diseases of the body unless diseases of the soul are overcome.... [We must never stop fighting] epidemics of ... greed, hate, ignorance...."

218 DOWN ARGENTINE WAY (TCF, Oct) Irving Cummings; *genre:* Musical Comedy; *location:* Argentina; *coding:* Latin Am, WWII?, Blk; *biases:* Contraband Message, Pro-American.

Betty Grable plays a fetching American heiress on a trip to Argentina looking for a good jumper. She meets and falls in love with a handsome local horse breeder. There is a topical reference in a club scene when a mixed drink that is composed of straight gin and an olive is called a "Blackout." But, more significantly, the whole film is built around poking fun at the premise of improving relations between North and South America. For instance, when Betty, in a garish red, white and blue outfit, spurns a comical gigolo played by Leonid Kinsky, it is referred to as an "international incident." The paid lothario peevishly declares: "I've had enough of these friendly neighbor relations." At the time, Hollywood was releasing a series of motion pictures about South America to bolster their foreign sales, having lost their European market to the Nazi conquests. And at the same time, the Roosevelt administration was assiduously cultivating its friendly neighbor policy in an attempt to promote western hemisphere solidarity against the possibility of future Nazi onslaught.

219 DRUMS OF THE DESERT (Mono, Sept) George Waggner; *genre:* Adventure; *locations:* France, Africa; *coding:* Am Vol, Arab, Blk, WWII, AF-Fr; *bias:* Pro-French.

Quoting the *Motion Picture Herald* review, this adventure film "strikes a topical note by introducing the use of parachute troops in the African desert on the part of the French Foreign Legion." The native black paratroopers' sergeant, played by Mantan Moreland, is an American from Harlem. The Legionnaires are deployed to suppress an Arab revolt. While inciting his people to take up arms the Arab leader states: "France soon will be struggling for its very existence on the continent. What better time to strike out here?"

220 THE EARL OF CHICAGO (MGM, Jan) Richard Thorpe; *genre:* Drama; *locations:* United States, Great Britain; *coding:* Churchill?, AF-Brit, WWII; *biases:* Pro-British, Contraband Message.

An American gangster in the post–Prohibition years is discovered to be the heir to a British title. Played by Robert Montgomery with an egregious accent, the gangster's past eventually leads to betrayal and murder. An accomplished heel all of his life, the trappings of British aristocracy afford him the grace of facing his execution with nobility. What makes this film relevant are the framing scenes of the castle taking place in the "present." The guide refers to the current Lord who is with his regiment in France, and to the closing of London museums in areas declared "unsafe." Many of the tourists are in uniform and all carry gas masks. This film was released in the winter of 1940 during the period often called "the phony war," when the French and British armies sat passively waiting a German initiative.

221 EARTHBOUND (TCF, June) Irving Pichel; *genre:* Fantasy/Drama; *locations:* France, Switzerland; *coding:* WWI, Fr, World Crisis, Brit; *biases:* Contraband Message, Pacifist.

While on a Swiss mountain climbing trip with his wife, Nick Desborough (Warner Baxter) receives an urgent telegram from his English friend Jeffrey (Henry Wilcoxin) to return to Paris. It is August 1939. On the train trip back the growing world crisis is brought home to Nick by a newspaper whose headline reads, "World Trembles on Verge of War," a mystical stranger who suggests the *Bible* has the answer to modern-day problems and by the comments of one Frenchman that he has a silver plate in his head from service in the "last war." Although the particulars of his research are never specified, Jeffrey requests and receives a large sum of money from Nick to complete a laboratory. As Nick writes the check, Jeffrey comments

that it "may make a difference to thousands of people—sick and wounded people." Nick is shot dead soon afterwards. The remainder of the film centers around Nick's ghost helping his widow discover his murderer.

222 EAST OF THE RIVER (WB, Nov) Alfred E. Green; *genre:* Crime; *location:* United States: *coding:* World Crisis; *bias:* Contraband Message.

A gangster, played by John Garfield, helps pay for his younger brother's college education. Problems arise when Garfield comes East for the graduation and falls for his brother's girl. The commencement speech included a timely admonition that outside of college the young people will have to confront "social and political passions that convulse the world."

223 EDISON, THE MAN (MGM, May) Clarence Brown; *genre:* Biography; *location:* United States; *coding:* Hist Am, Am Icons; *bias:* Pro-American.

This was yet another Hollywood panegyric to an American hero. At the very outset it established its relevance to contemporary events with a title quoting Emerson: "[The] true test of the civilization ... is the kind of men turned out." This is followed by an aged avuncular Edison, played by Spencer Tracy, being honored at a "Golden Jubilee of Light" banquet in 1929. The master of ceremonies states Edison had to overcome "prejudice" and that the most precious thing in life is "the freedom of the human mind." The body of the film then proceeds to recount Edison's career. In the last two minutes the wise old man of American technology imparts the following to his audience: "[The] confusion of the world today needs adjusting ... what man's mind can conceive, man's character can control."

224 ENEMY AGENT (Univ, Apr) Lew Landers; *genre:* Spy; *location:* United States: *coding:* Prod, FBI, Spy-Sab, Secret Weapon, Russ, Ger, Ital; *bias:* Anti-Espionage.

A young draftsman (Richard Cromwell) at an aircraft factory is framed for espionage by an enemy agent, Dr. Arnold (Philip Dorn). Due to a lack of evidence he is quickly released, but his career appears to be ruined. He investigates to determine who the real culprits are. He breaks into the apartment of the spy ring's leader, where he discovers photos of the blueprints for the factory's new bomber and its top-secret bombsight. Kidnapped by the spies, he is about to be tortured when his girlfriend and FBI agents posing as "drunken" college boys come to the rescue. Cromwell gets the girl, his job back, and a pat on the back from Uncle Sam. Universal used background music from *The Bride of Frankenstein* (1935), and incorporated stock footage from the 1937 serial

Radio Patrol to make this "B" picture seem more expensive than it was. Arnold's associates include Baronoff (Abner Biberman) and Calteroni (Luis Alberni).

225 ESCAPE (MGM, Nov) Mervyn Leroy; *genre:* Drama; *location:* Germany; *coding:* Jew?, Atroc-Conc, Hitler, AF-Ger, Nazi, Resist, Goering?; *bias:* Anti-Nazi.

The opening title coyly states that this motion picture takes place in 1936 near a town in the "Bavarian Alps." The American son of a famous foreign-born actress (played by Alla Nazimova) visits the swastika-littered Third Reich to find his missing mother. After many inquiries as to his mother's whereabouts, an evasive lawyer discloses that she was tried and convicted by the infamous "Peoples' Court" for harboring while living in the United States "renegade citizens" of the fascist regime. His mother was then sent to a concentration camp to await execution. Mark Preysing (Robert Taylor) embarks on a frantic campaign to obtain his mother's release and to get her out of the country he compares to a "Coney Island mad house." Eventually, by means of a coma-inducing drug injection administered by a sympathetic camp doctor, Mark is able to claim the body of his supposedly dead mother and remove her from the camp. Mark hides his revived mother in the home of an American-born countess, who is the lover of an Army staff officer. Overcoming her mixed feelings, the countess (Norma Shearer) helps the fugitives flee the fascist state. General Kurt von Kolb, played by Conrad Veidt, loyally serves the state while holding the Nazis, whom he always refers to as "they," in contempt.

226 ESCAPE TO GLORY aka SUBMARINE ZONE (Col, Nov) John Brahm; *genre:* War Drama; *locations:* Great Britain, Atlantic; *coding:* Spy-Sab, WWII, War Mats, AF-Ger, AF-Brit, Am Vol, Am Icons, WWI, Ger, For Corr, Pacifism, US-Brit Coop, Brit, Hitler?, Musso?; *biases:* Anti-Fascist, Pro-British.

Immediately following Hitler's September 1, 1939, invasion of Poland, a group of passengers board a British freighter bound for the United States. Some of them, including an obnoxious manufacturer, a cynical American soldier of fortune named Mike (Pat O'Brien) and a German doctor who espouses pacifistic sentiments, are gathered in the ship's lounge listening to radio reports on the crisis. The manufacturer dismisses the others' concerns: "They're just a couple of fake bad men [Hitler and Mussolini?] playing with shooting irons." But then it is announced that Britain is in a state of war (September 3rd) and the "enemy alien" doctor is told to remain in his cabin. Armed by a passing Royal Navy vessel that night, the following day the freighter is shelled by a surfaced U-Boat. After one of the freighter's two deck guns is destroyed, Mike takes command of the other gun and succeeds in forcing the U-Boat to submerge. While the ship's crew attempts to make repairs in a fog bank, the German doctor, a veteran of the first World War, uses a medical apparatus to make shortwave contact with the submarine. But he is exposed and a motor launch manned by an Anglo-American crew is loaded with bombs to destroy the U-Boat in a suicide mission.

227 THE FIGHTING 69TH (WB, Jan) William Keighley; *genre:* Training/Combat; *locations:* United States, France; *coding:* WWII, Hist Am, WWI, AF-N, Jew, AF-A, AF-Ger, Am Icons, AF-Fr, Brit; *biases:* Pro-Military, Pro-American.

A group of New York City Irish-Americans, including a Jew with a heavy brogue, join the Army in 1917. When a unit from Alabama teams up with them to form part of the famous Rainbow Division going overseas, some sectional animosities are aroused. The 69th's famous Major Donovan (George Brent) admonishes the troops and reminds them that they are now part of an "all American team." In France, the outfit's troublemaker, Jerry (James Cagney), is sentenced to a firing squad for an act of cowardice that led to the death of several of his mates. Jerry later flees his shell-wrecked cell, rejoins the 69th during an assault upon the German lines and achieves redemption by heroically sacrificing himself while blasting a hole through the "Heinie's" defenses. At the film's conclusion, the unit's chaplain, the beloved Father Duffy (Pat O'Brien), superimposed over the statue erected for him after his death in 1932, prays that for "evermore" America will remain "the citadel of peace."

228 FLIGHT ANGELS (WB, May) Lewis Seiler; *genre:* Drama; *location:* United States; *coding:* Blk, Sino-Jap War, AF-AC, Draft, FDR; *bias:* Pro-Military.

Federal Airline's top pilot, Chick Farber (Dennis Morgan), goes to pieces after learning his eyesight no longer meets flight requirements. He recklessly takes a prototype "stratosphere" plane the Army is interested in on a test flight and, as a consequence, loses his pilot's license. Despondent, he decides to join the Chinese Army Air Force. But fearing he may give away government secrets if he were captured, the U.S. Army forbids his leaving the country. In return, they offer him a commission as a flight instructor. Released during an ongoing Congressional debate over peacetime conscription, this film contains an early reference to it when Chick protests that he will only agree

to be drafted "in case of [a] national emergency."

229 FLORIAN (MGM, Mar) Robert Florey; *genre:* Historical Drama; *locations:* Austria, United States; *coding:* WWI, AF-Aust, Comm, Ger; *biases:* Pacifist, Anti-Soviet.

This is the story of the famous Austrian Lippinzan show horses that centers around the impact of WWI upon the prize steed Florian and his faithful keeper. There are several scenes in the film that would directly relate to 1940 audiences. At the beginning of *Florian* there are pro-democracy comments made during a discussion in a tavern. Later, there is a scene portraying Austria's revered Emperor in which it is implied Germany is forcing Austria into a world war. Finally, near the film's conclusion, the Imperial stud farm's doctor bemoans the destruction of the farm by Socialist revolutionaries following Austria's collapse in 1918: "Why is it that when men want to start a new order they start out by destroying everything of the old?"

230 FOREIGN CORRESPONDENT (UA, Aug) Alfred Hitchcock; *genre:* Adventure; *locations:* United States, Great Britain, Netherlands; *coding:* Peace Org, World Crisis, WWII, Nazi, Dipl, Brit, Neth, Ref, Atroc, AF-Ger, Pol, Den, Nor, For Corr, Hitler, Spy-Sab, Ger, FDR, Collab, WWII, Am Icons, US-Brit Coop, Belg; *bias:* Pro-Intervention.

Top crime reporter Johnny Jones (Joel McCrea) is assigned to pre-war Europe to cover the "crime happening on that bedeviled continent." Under the *nom de plume* "Huntley Haverstock," Johnny arrives in Britain and immediately suggests that an interview with Hitler might be useful. After meeting the lovely daughter of the leader of the Universal Peace Movement, Johnny attends an international peace conference in the Netherlands. There he becomes involved in the kidnapping of a leading diplomat by foreign agents (unnamed, but obviously German). Johnny and the lady eventually save the elderly diplomat. In the process they learn that her father is actually an enemy agent who has been using the peace movement as a front. On the day war is declared, the couple heads for the United States in a clipper only to be shot down by a German warship. At the end of this Walter Wanger production, the now experienced war correspondent makes an impassioned speech to his American compatriots over the BBC from London under aerial attack: "...This is a big story and you're part of it ... ring yourself around with steel America ... the lights have gone out in Europe! Hang on to your lights America—they're the only lights still

on in the world!" This film was released in late August, just as the London "Blitz" was beginning.

231 FOUR SONS (TCF, Jun) Archie Mayo; *genre:* Drama; *locations:* Czechoslovakia, United States; *coding:* Munich, WWI, WWII, Nazi, AF-Ger, AF-Czech, Hitler, Collab, Ref, Atroc-Conc, Pol, Austria, Spy-Sab, Russ; *biases:* Anti-Nazi, Pacifist.

This was a heavily revised remake of the 1928 anti-militarist World War I Fox melodrama directed by John Ford. The screenplay of this version was written by John Howard Lawson and the film was produced by Darryl F. Zanuck. A Czech family of German descent living in the Sudentenland is systematically dismembered by the encroachment of National Socialism. During the Munich Crisis of September-October 1938, the oldest son, Chris (Don Ameche) joins other loyal townsmen who mobilize to defend their country, while his Nazi-sympathizing brother Karl (Alan Curtis) deserts across the border to Germany. Following the political sellout of Czechoslovakia, Karl—now in the uniform of a Nazi stormtrooper—returns to his hometown with the occupying Germans. An attempt by Chris to warn townspeople that their names are on a Nazi "list" leads to the death of both brothers. The youngest brother, Fritz, is subsequently drafted into the Wehrmacht and is killed in the fall of 1939 while participating in the "liberation of Poland." Their sad but enobled mother (widowed in WWI) emigrates to America (where her only surviving son lives), taking her grandson with her to spare him the horror of war.

232 GHOST BREAKERS (Para, Jun) George Marshall; *genre:* Comedy; *locations:* United States, Caribbean; *coding:* Blk, Home Def; *bias:* Contraband Message.

Bob Hope plays a New York radio personality who accompanies Paulette Goddard to Cuba to help her claim a haunted castle. At the beginning, a thunderstorm knocks out the lights in Hope's Manhattan apartment. Startled by his black manservant, Bob delivers the following quip: "You look like a blackout in a blackout."

233 THE GHOST COMES HOME (MGM, Mar) William Thiele; *genre:* Comedy/Drama; *location:* United States; *coding:* Jew, Ital, Russ, Brit, WWII; *bias:* Contraband Message.

A meek and unsuccessful small-town businessman with some parasitic in-laws is contacted by an old friend who has become wealthy in Australia. The rich friend arranges for the middle-aged ingenue (Frank Morgan) to come to Australia to work out the details of an endowment he wishes to give his hometown. On the way to the docks to begin his journey, the simple man stops at a popular nightclub, becomes intoxicated, is clipped by a B-girl, participates in a brawl and, as a result, winds up being sent to jail for 60 days. The real fun begins when he returns home to discover his relatives have cashed in on his life insurance. A newspaper headline framed beneath his black draped photo on the mantel piece proclaims he perished at sea when his boat was sunk; a "Floating Mine Thought Cause." After half a year of international hostilities the sinking of a ship by a mine was an unpleasantly real possibility.

234 GO WEST (MGM, Dec) Edward Buzzell; *genre:* Comedy; *location:* United States; *coding:* Chi, Fifth Col; *bias:* Contraband Message.

As noted in the opening titles, the Marx Brothers are belatedly inspired by Horace Greeley's famous dictum. When Chico systematically, though unintentionally, reveals that the three zanies are attempting to retrieve a valuable deed from two showgirl rivals Groucho quips: "You're a one man fifth column." The topical comment is particularly interesting since the film takes place in a 19th century setting.

235 GOLD RUSH MAISIE (MGM, Jul) Edward L. Marin; *genre:* Comedy; *location:* United States; *coding:* WWII; *bias:* Contraband Message.

Maisie Doaks (Ann Sothern), wearing her series character's ubiquitous large and garish floppy hat has become stranded in a desert cafe after a job at a local girlie joint falls through. But suddenly things pick up when a nearby ghost town becomes a boom town following the discovery of gold. The owner of the cafe, with a paper announcing the "gold stampede" in his hands, comments that it has "even crowded the war news clear to the back page."

236 THE GRAPES OF WRATH (TCF, Mar) John Ford; *genre:* Drama; *location:* United States; *coding:* Comm; *biases:* Pro-Democracy, Pro-American.

This classic film was based on the 1939 novel written by John Steinbeck. The well-known Depression story centers around displaced "Okies" migrating to California in search of work and a new way of life. It graphically portrays the plight of domestic refugees; their struggle against hunger, exploitation, mob violence and the prejudice of people directed against so-called "outsiders," "foreigners" and "red agitators." The film also movingly stresses the importance of family unity and, implicitly, of American unity, in order for the nation and its democratic principals to survive. This is all underscored by the family matriarch, "Ma Joad" (Jane Darwell) in her concluding "we-the-people" speech. These were all themes that dealt with issues that went far beyond the borders of the USA in 1940.

237 THE GREAT DICTATOR (UA, Oct) Charles Chaplin; *genre:* Comedy/Drama; *locations:* Germany, Austria; *coding:* For Corr, Atroc-Conc, Goering, Goebbels, Hitler, Musso, Nazi, Jew, WWI, AF-Ger, Blk, Dipl, AF-Brit, Spy-Sab; *bias:* Anti-Fascist.

The release of this motion picture was delayed due to a fear of public reaction. It is a satiric rampage against a pair of Hitler and Mussolini caricatures that also directly addresses the official anti-semitism of the Nazi regime. The inimitable Chaplin plays both the megalomaniacal "Phooey" (as in Fuehrer) of Tomania, Adenoid Hynkel, and a passive Jewish war veteran suffering from amnesia who owns a barbershop in the ghetto. Jack Oakie plays the perfect buffoon in his role as Benzini Napoloni, "Il Digga Ditchi" (as in Il Duce) of Bacteria. In the last ten minutes of *The Great Dictator*, Chaplin makes an impassioned plea for tolerance and world peace directly to the film audience.

238 THE GREAT McGINTY (Para, Aug) Preston Sturges; *genre:* Comedy/Drama; *locations:* United States, Latin America; *coding:* AF-N, Hist Am, Blk; *bias:* Pro-Democracy.

Starring Brian Donlevy as an opportunistic rogue who rises to the governorship, this is a satiric parable that probes various aspects of local government corruption and the potential for demagoguery in the United States.

239 HE STAYED FOR BREAKFAST (Col, Aug) Alexander Hall; *genre:* Comedy; *location:* France; *coding:* Russ, Latin Am, Stalin, Fr, Comm, FDR, Hist Am, Fascism; *bias:* Anti-Soviet.

An inveterate communist agitator, Paul Beliot (Melvyn Douglas) is a waiter at a Parisian bistro. He takes a potshot at a banker when the man hooks his finger while drinking coffee. While being pursued by the police, Paul just happens to find refuge in the apartment of the banker's estranged American wife, played by Loretta Young. Paul explains to her that the "fat symbol of fascism ... insulted the workers' movement with his pretentious method of holding the cup at the 'Cafe Stalin.'" She asks Paul if he does not mean the Cafe Louis XV. The communist retorts: "When we take over, the Cafe Stalin." Over the next few days, Paul eats a lot of the lady's food, gives her a Marxist handbook and gets the maid drunk while attempting to convert the "victim of capitalist oppression." But when Paul's comrades try to force him to betray his capitalist protectress to the police, he contemptuously disavows the Party. Soon afterwards Paul leaves France with her to go to the U.S. According to Paul, "From now on I'm just gonna be a plain, ordinary middle class citizen. When I get to America I'm going to vote for Roosevelt." It is pointed out to Paul that he is not an American citizen, but he replies that FDR will still be running in five years. The film was, in fact, released during the height of the 1940 presidential election.

240 HELL'S ANGELS (Re-r '30) (Ind, Jan) Howard Hughes; *genre:* War, Drama/Combat; *locations:* Great Britain, France; *coding:* WWI, AF-Brit, AF-Ger; *bias:* Anti-German.

Independent distributor Astor distributed Howard Hughes' WWI blockbuster, first released in 1930. Spectacular aerial footage highlights the story of Ben Lyons and James Hall, two brothers who join the RAF and also fall in love with Jean Harlow. The Germans are portrayed as ruthless fanatics—in one scene, crew members on a Zeppelin leap to their deaths in an effort to lighten the load of the huge dirigible so it can complete its bombing mission over London!

241 HERE COMES THE NAVY (Re-r '34) (WB, Dec) Lloyd Bacon; *genre:* Training/Combat; *location:* United States; *coding:* Mil Exer, AF-N, Am Icons, Blk, FDR, AF-MC; *bias:* Pro-Military.

This was a timely re-release of a 1934 film featuring frequent action shots of naval vessels and aircraft engaged in fleet maneuvers. *The Motion Picture Herald* review noted: "What was originally intended as a comedy brawl between the star contestants [James Cagney and Pat O'Brien] as staged against a naval and aviation ring, now becomes material for patriotic preparedness promotion." Ironically, most of the on-board footage was shot on the U.S.S. *Arizona*, which was sunk at Pearl Harbor.

242 HIDDEN ENEMY (Mono, Jan) Howard Bretherton; *genre:* Spy; *location:* United States; *coding:* Nazi, WWII, Spy-Sab, Ger, Russ, WWI, FBI, War Mats, Prod, AF-N, Secret Plans, Russ-Ger Coop; *biases:* Anti-Espionage, Anti-Totalitarian.

A reporter (Warren Hull) and a female private investigator struggle with assorted spies for the formula of an experimental lightweight strategic metal with the strength of steel. Although no country is mentioned, the two spy gangs are respectively run by a lightly veiled German and a Russian. In all the confusion the newspaper man is fired for incompetence. But, by the end, he has won his job back by saving the girl and helping to expose the foreign espionage rings. It is only at the film's conclusion that the young lady reveals that she works for a patriotic organization: "...interested in finding out about undesirable aliens. They haven't forgotten the factories that were blown up and the American workmen that were killed in 1915 and 1916 ... through sabotage...."

243 HIS GIRL FRIDAY (Col, Jan) Howard Hawks; *genre:* Comedy; *location:* United States; *coding:* For Corr, WWII, Hitler, Stalin, FDR, AF-Russ, Blk, Ital; *bias:* Contraband Message.

Jokes about the war, Hitler, Stalin and the trials of one "Archie Leach" (Cary Grant's real name) are inserted into the frenetic dialogue of this remake of the 1931 UA film, *The Front Page*, based on the famous late 1920s Ben Hecht play. In this version, Grant plays the unscrupulous, fast-talking big city newspaper editor, Walter Burns, who desperately schemes to get his ace reporter (and former wife) to cover a politically sensitive execution.

244 HOUSE ACROSS THE BAY (UA, Mar) Archie Mayo; *genre:* Crime; *location:* United States; *coding:* Blk, Chi, Latin Am, Arms Dealers, AF-Fr, FBI, Hist Am; *biases:* Pro-French, Contraband Message.

This Walter Wanger production featured Joan Bennett and the quintessential gangster, George Raft. After Raft is sent to Alcatraz, his wife, played by Miss Bennett, is befriended by an aircraft designer/manufacturer played by Walter Pidgeon. Three French observers watch a compatriot take his plane on a test flight. Impressed with its performance, they place an order for 200 "combat" versions of the plane. The film was released during the winter of 1940 when, in fact, the French government was making large military purchases, particularly of aircraft, from the United States. A year earlier, in January, a nationwide controversy arose after the revelation of the death of an official of the French Air Ministry in the crash of a test flight of one of America's newest bombers.

245 THE HOWARDS OF VIRGINIA (Col, Sept) Frank Lloyd; *genre:* Historical Drama; *location:* United States; *coding:* Blk, Am Icons, Hist Am, Collab, AF-A, AF-Brit; *bias:* Pro-American.

The class struggle in colonial America is resolved in this flagwaver that takes place during the revolution. *New York Times* film critic Bosley Crowther concluded a favorable review with this comment: "As a stern and sobering reminder of our liberal tradition, it is more contemporary than a political speech."

246 THE INVISIBLE WOMAN (Univ, Dec) A. Edward Sutherland; *genre:* Comedy/Fantasy; *location:* United States; *coding:* Draft Avoid; *bias:* Contraband Message.

A campy John Barrymore plays a professor with an invisibility machine who hires a pretty model to help with his experiments.

At one point he is on the phone in his lab while the invisible model cavorts around in the nude. When he asks what she is doing, the lady responds: "I'm dodging the draft." Released in late 1940, this was probably the first feature film to refer to the newly implemented national conscription act.

247 IRENE (RKO, May) Herbert Wilcox; *genre:* Drama; *location:* United States; *coding:* Stalin, Hitler, Blk, WWII; *bias:* Contraband Message.

An Irish working girl with a flair for interior decorating is secretly maneuvered into New York society by a playboy admirer. Irene becomes the new social sensation of the Park Avenue set when she appears at a benefit in a gay nineties era gown. At the premiere of a Broadway revue in her honor, the opening newsreel spoof, "Moviebone News," makes references to both Stalin and Hitler.

248 ISLE OF DESTINY (RKO, Mar) Elmer Clifton; *genre:* Adventure; *location:* Pacific; *coding:* AF-MC, Arms Dealers; *bias:* Pro-Military.

A couple of Marines stationed on a Cinecolor South Seas island fall in love with an aviatrix who lands her amphibious plane on the wrong side of their island. The leader of a gun smuggling gang kidnaps her in order to distract the lovesick leathernecks while his ring removes a cache of weapons from the island for shipment to China. The Marines save the girl and break up the racket.

249 KNUTE ROCKNE—ALL AMERICAN (WB, Oct) Lloyd Bacon; *genre:* Biography; *location:* United States; *coding:* Nor, Am Icons, WWI, AF-A, Blk; *bias:* Pro-American.

Another national hero is resurrected to promote Americanism. An immigrant from Norway (part of Sweden prior to WWI; occupied by Germany in April 1940), he works as a chemist on synthetic rubber, fights bravely in the U.S. Army during the first World War and then coaches the famous Notre Dame football team until his tragic death in a 1931 plane crash. What is most interesting, though, is the speech Knute (Pat O'Brien) delivers to a Senate Committee investigating football: "[All boys have a] natural spirit of combat.... In Europe and elsewhere it manifests itself in continuous revolution and wars.... The most dangerous thing in American life today is that we're getting soft."

250 THE LONG VOYAGE HOME (UA, Nov) John Ford; *genre:* War Drama; *locations:* Great Britain, Atlantic, United States, Caribbean; *coding:* WWII, AF-A, War Mats, Nazi, AF-Brit, Brit, Fifth Col, Blk, Pol, AF-Ger; *biases:* Pro-Intervention, Pro-British.

The spiritually enervated international crew of a tramp steamer carrying munitions to war-torn Britain bravely endure an air attack by unseen (and unidentified) German planes while in the "war zone.". A disgraced former British officer redeems himself during the assault by rallying his frightened shipmates on the unarmed vessel. Mortally wounded by a German plane (which casts an ominous black shadow across its victim), he defiantly throws a boat hook at his attacker before collapsing into a lifeboat. The boat's tarpaulin blows over him like a shroud and then director Ford superimposes a Union Jack over the corpse. Loosely adapted from four Eugene O'Neill one-act plays, the film is more a story about the passions of men than a depiction of war. Yet, to quote Andrew Sarris from his book, *The John Ford Movie Mystery:* "Producer Walter Wanger, Ford and Nichols [the screenwriter] were all outspokenly anti-Hitler in this period, and thus *The Long Voyage Home* constituted a conscious tribute to Britain in its darkest hour."

251 LOVE THY NEIGHBOR (Para, Dec) Mark Sandrich; *genre:* Comedy; *location:* United States; *coding:* Blk, WWII; *bias:* Contraband Message.

The famous Fred Allen-Jack Benny radio feud was transposed to film in this work. Benny steals an entertainment act from Allen's show and then starts dating Allen's niece. When she decides to join Benny's show in Florida, it is the last straw. Allen, armed with a shotgun, chases the two in a speedboat (the sound of car brakes screeching and skidding tires being used for comic effect). As Allen fires away, Benny comments to the girl, played by Mary Martin: "I knew they should have painted the American flag on this boat." This is a reference to American merchant ships painting the stars and stripes on their sides to avoid being attacked by German U-Boats.

252 THE MAN I MARRIED aka I MARRIED A NAZI (TCF, Aug) Irving Pichel; *genre:* Drama; *locations:* United States, Germany; *coding:* Jew, Hitler, For Corr, Span Civ, AF-Ger, Stalin, Czech, Atroc-Conc, Nazi, Atroc, WWI, Jap, Goebbels, Am Icons, Chamberlain, Brit, Fr, Munich, Aust, Quota, Pac; *bias:* Anti-Nazi.

Based on a magazine story, this film specifically ridicules Hitler (frequently pejoratively referred to as "Shicky," as in "Schickelgruber") and the Nazis. An art critic and her German-American husband (Francis Lederer) visit the Third Reich with their small son in 1938. Largely through her eyes and those of a friendly American journalist (Lloyd Nolan) whom she has met, we witness how the German people have become mesmerized by chauvinism and blatant bigotry (anti–Semitism is dealt with explicitly). Having just attended a Nazi party rally, the correspondent makes a telling observation, ... "We [Americans] can still laugh at ourselves. These poor boys over here have lost their sense of humor, if they ever had any—and any nation that doesn't know how to laugh is dangerous." The wife, played by Joan Bennett, watches helplessly as her husband zealously embraces the regimentation and brutality of the regime. It is only after her husband's Jewish antecedents are revealed by his father that Joan and her son are allowed to return to the United States.

253 THE MAN WHO TALKED TOO MUCH (WB, Jul) Vincent Sherman; *genre:* Drama; *location:* United States; *coding:* Ital, Am Icons, FBI, WWII; *bias:* Contraband Message.

A smart defense attorney is having a hard time collecting his fees. His secretary offers the following topical explanation: "It's the European situation. Money seems to have gone into hiding." The lawyer's financial situation improves when he gets the goods on a gangster.

254 THE MAN WHO WOULDN'T TALK (TCF, Feb) David Burton; *genre:* Crime; *location:* United States; *coding:* AF-A, Fr, Ger, Latin Am, Spy-Sab, WWI; *biases:* Anti-German, Anti-Espionage.

A mysterious man confesses to the murder of prominent New York businessman Frederick Keller. During the trial, it is revealed that the defendant's real name is Frank Stetson (Lloyd Nolan). As a soldier in the U.S. Army 20 years before, Stetson had been sentenced to death in France for espionage (but had escaped). Stetson remains silent until another witness testifies that Keller had framed Stetson, at which time Stetson takes the stand. In flashback, he relates how Keller (Onslow Stevens) admitted his guilt when Stetson finally trackd him down: "I was born in Germany ... I became a [U.S.] citizen. I joined your Army because I could serve the Fatherland better that way." Stetson accuses him of betraying the "liberty and protection" that America had granted him, and Keller pulls a gun. In the struggle, Keller is killed.

255 MANHATTAN HEARTBEAT (TCF, Jul) David Burton; *genre:* Drama; *location:* United States; *coding:* Chi, Prod, AF-AC, Secret Weapon, Blk, Latin Am; *bias:* Pro-Military.

This was a remake of the 1931 Fox film, *Bad Girl.* Returning to New York from a vacation camp, a young airplane mechanic meets the girl who will become his wife. In an attempt to get ahead, he unsuccessfully bids for the purchase of a small aircraft plant. Soon after their marriage she announces they are expecting. Fearful for her health, he volunteers to put a new bomber

through its test flights, in order to raise the money necessary to engage a noted obstetrician.

256 THE MARINES FLY HIGH (RKO, Feb) G. Nicholls, Jr., B. Stoloff; *genre:* Adventure; *location:* Latin America; *coding:* AF-A, AF-N, AF-MC, Latin Am; *bias:* Pro-Military.

In the not so distant "past" gung-ho airborne Marines commanding local "Nationalistas" reestablish "law and order" in an anonymous Central American republic by blasting the hell out of "bandits" led by an American expatriot who calls himself "El Vengador." For reasons that are never clearly defined, the Thompson machine gun wielding El Vengador seeks to start a "revolution." But the main story features the beautiful young plantation owner's choice between the two handsome Marine Corps officers. The Marines made three major interventions during the first third of the century: the Dominican Republic (1916–1924), Haiti (1915–1934) and Nicaragua (1912–1913). After 1927 the Marines had a substantial air presence in Nicaragua that was engaged in heavy air to ground tactical support against the Sandino rebel forces.

257 MEN AGAINST THE SKY (RKO, Sept) Leslie Goodwins; *genre:* Drama; *location:* United States; *coding:* Secret Weapon, Prod, AF-AC; *bias:* Pro-Military.

A washed-up stunt flyer, played by Richard Dix, helps ghost the plans for a new "pursuit ship" that his younger sister is working on. The owners of the aircraft factory push forward the testing of a prototype in hopes of winning a government and/or a "foreign contract." When the original test pilot refuses to dive the plane, the old barnstormer, Phil, takes her up. The plane is wrecked and he is permanently grounded. Another, improved, model is rapidly produced. It is demonstrated by a military pilot before a mission headed by a Col. Sanders (in mufti). But following a successful test run, the plane's landing gear will not go down completely. Phil redeems himself by going up in a second plane and manually lowering the wheels. Unfortunately, for him, his parachute is torn when he attempts to jump clear of the plane.

258 MERCY PLANE (PDC, Jul) Richard Harlan; *genre:* Drama; *location:* United States; *coding:* Secret Weapon, AF-A, AF-N, Prod, FBI, War Mats, Collab; *bias:* Anti-Espionage.

A daredevil pilot and his aviatrix rival break up a criminal ring stealing privately owned planes for unspecified foreign powers. The thieves attempt to heist a newly designed hospital plane equipped with an invention that enables it to use short runways.

259 MILLIONAIRES IN PRISON (RKO, Jul) Ray McCarey; *genre:* Comedy/Drama; *location:* United States; *coding:* Comm, WWII, Nazi, *bias:* Contraband Message.

A couple of amiable ex-brokers are among a group of well-heeled prisoners sent to the penitentiary. Soon afterwards, they are promoting stocks for a worthless copper mine among their fellow inmates, ... "the war will send the stock real high.... Because of the war there's a government demand for copper...." When experiments to find a cure for Malta Fever using prisoner volunteers is publicized, the warden begins receiving letters accusing him of being a communist, Nazi, etc.

260 MONEY AND THE WOMAN (WB, Aug) William K. Howard; *genre:* Crime; *location:* United States; *coding:* WWII, AF-A, Fifth Col, Blk, Hist Am; *bias:* Contraband Message.

A young bank vice president becomes involved with the beautiful wife of an embezzling employee. In one scene the executive has a conversation with his black servant, George Washington Jones, after Jones asks him what is in the newspaper. The banker responds that there is "nothing in it but war news" and adds that he may soon have to join the army. Jones mumbles that he will join the "fifth column ... [because] all they do is talkin'."

261 THE MORTAL STORM (MGM, Jun) Frank Borzage; *genre:* Drama; *locations:* Germany, Austria; *coding:* Jew, Resist, Austr Atroc-Conc Nazi, Hitler, Ref, Atroc, Pacifism, Comm; *bias:* Anti-Nazi.

This motion picture deals explicitly with the tragic impact of the Nazi regime on a "non-Aryan" (Jewish) professor and his family in 1933, who live in a small university town in the Bavarian Alps. When Dr. Roth (Frank Morgan), whose name "doesn't sound very well to German ears" anymore, scoffs at the concept of differences in racial blood types, he is shouted down by newly brownshirted students who overnight, have abandoned the traditional intellectual tolerance of the university. A book burning follows soon afterwards in which the works of such authors as Heinrich Heine and Albert Einstein (who happen to be Jews) are ritualistically consigned to the flames. From then on the professor is mercilessly hounded by the Nazis and eventually sent to a concentration camp (where he will later die). His daughter (Margaret Sullivan) is subsequently killed while attempting to escape across the border with her pacifist lover (James Stewart) into Austria. As in *Four Sons* and *The Man I Married*, both q.v., this film addresses the problem of a family divided by conflicting attitudes towards the Nazi state (the professor's stepsons join the Brownshirts).

262 MURDER IN THE AIR (WB, Jun) Lewis Seiler; *genre:* Spy; *location:* United States; *coding:* FDR, WWII, Intell Serv, Peace Organ, Spy-Sab, Collab, Russ-Ger Coop, FBI, AF-N, War Mats, Prod, Sino-Jap War, Neutrality Act, League Nat, Mil Exer, Fifth Col; *bias:* Anti-Espionage.

Following a montage of acts of sabotage, this film begins with a Congressional Investigating Committee (read Dies Committee), discussing the extent of foreign espionage in this country. It was the fourth and final film in a series (the first, *Secret Service of the Air* was released in 1939) featuring the heroics of "Brass" Bancroft, a former Army Air Corps lieutenant, now in the employ of the Secret Service. In the lead role, Ronald Reagan assumes the identity of a spy accidentally killed in a train wreck. He is thus able to infiltrate an espionage ring and make contact with its leader. Brass is ordered to board the Navy's dirigible disguised as a sailor, in order to examine a new anti-plane "inertia projector" (an instrument capable of depriving all electrical objects within a radius of four miles of their power). While on board, he discovers another enemy agent, who is working as a civilian official, trying to steal the weapon's blueprints. During a storm the spy makes off with the plans. But once the dirigible is safely secured Brass and his sidekick, "Gabby," are able with the projector, to shoot down the plane in which the foreign agents are fleeing. Working title: *The Enemy Within.*

263 MURDER OVER NEW YORK (TCF, Dec) Harry Lachman; *genre:* Crime; *location:* United States; *coding:* Brit, Intell Serv, Blk, Spy-Sab, Fifth Col, Secret Weapon, WWII, War Mats; *biases:* Anti-Espionage, Pro-British.

While in New York for a policemen's convention, Chan tracks down a group of saboteurs who are working for an unnamed country attempting to disrupt the shipment of a new American bomber to Britain. One of the weapons employed by the enemy agents is a lethal gas called "tetragene." The designer of the bomber assures Chan: "If we build enough of these planes there won't be anything to worry about from the rest of the world."

264 MY LITTLE CHICKADEE (Univ, Feb) Edward Cline; *genre:* Comedy/Western; *location:* United States; *coding:* Chamberlain; *bias:* Contraband Message.

In this western farce starring Mae West and W. C. Fields, the bulbous-nosed prestidigitator, who is carrying an umbrella, gets entangled with an old maid when he boards a train. After they are disengaged, she asks him if his umbrella is broken. W. C. responds: "No, you can't break it. It's a genuine Chamberlain." At the time the umbrella had become a symbol that was inextricably linked to British Prime Minister Neville Chamberlain (1937–May 1940). Mae West later makes a "propaganda" crack when she notices "I am a good girl" written on a classroom blackboard.

265 MYSTERY SEA RAIDER (Para, Aug) Edward Dmytryk; *genre:* War Drama/Combat; *locations:* United States, Atlantic, Caribbean; *coding:* AF-Ger, AF-Brit, Spy-Sab, Nazi, WWII, Hitler, Fr, Brit, Neth; *bias:* Anti-German.

In an obvious recreation of the actual U-Boat sinking of the British liner *Athenia*, this film opens with the torpedoing of an unarmed passenger ship only hours after Britain's declaration of war with Germany. Soon afterwards, Nazi agents surreptitiously arrange for a tramp steamer, the *S.S. Apache*, to leave New York harbor and be commandeered on the high seas by the German navy for use as a raider. The plot soon centers around a belligerent group of seamen, including Americans, imprisoned aboard the converted raider after their ship was torpedoed by a U-Boat in the Caribbean. The raider's crew efficiently responds to a plethora of gutteral commands delivered by officers heavily bedecked with swastikas and iron crosses. But the *Motion Picture Herald* review notes that "there is no denouncing of Hitler or Nazism or Germany in the manner of other war films of contemporary distribution and no atrocities are depicted." Eventually, the raider is sunk by a Royal Navy cruiser. A good deal of topical newsreel footage of German naval vessels is worked into the film. The story was at least partially based upon the actual German seizure in October 1939 of the American ship, *City of Flint.*

266 NO TIME FOR COMEDY (WB, Jul) William Keighley; *genre:* Drama; *location:* United States; *coding:* WWII, Blk; *bias:* Anti-Fascist.

In this film adaptation of a 1939 anti-fascist/anti-war play by S. N. Behrman, a popular playwright (James Stewart) of light comedies attempts to produce a serious drama. After the play flops his wife supportively urges him to use the weapon of satire to make a comment upon the problems of the world; that creative artists have a duty to involve themselves in world issues in an era of "war" and "dictatorship;" that now (1940) is no time for comedy. Yet, ironically, all the specific references to the Spanish Civil War and to fascism contained in the Behrman play were deleted from the motion picture.

267 NORTHWEST PASSAGE (MGM, Feb) King Vidor; *genre:* Historical Drama/Combat; *location:* United States; *coding:* Fr, Atroc, US-Brit Coop, Blk, AF-A, Am Icons, Hist Am, AF-Brit; *bias:* Pro-American.

Major Rogers, Spencer Tracy sporting buckskin, marches across the Technicolor landscape of 18th century North America. Amidst almost continuous martial music, his volunteer colonial commandos, assisted by their British allies, conquer the frontier and slaughter the Indians. The graphically violent climactic battle scene at the Indians' camp is a precursor to the vicious anti–Japanese combat sequences in such WWII films as *Gung Ho!* (Un, 1943).

268 THE NOTORIOUS ELINOR LEE (Ind, Jan) Oscar Micheaux; *genre:* Drama; *location:* United States; *coding:* Blk, Ital, Ger, Fr, WWII, AF-N; *biases:* Anti-Fascist, Contraband Message.

This Micheaux Pictures production touts "a Great All Star COLORED CAST" in its opening titles. The story centers around Golden Gloves champion Benny Blue (Robert Earl Jones) whose professional contract has been acquired by Mrs. Lee, a lady who has made her fortune in the numbers racket. She makes a deal with Italian gangsters to build up Blue to a heavyweight championship bout and then force him to take a dive. The "Brown Bombshell from Chicago" subsequently beats Italian boxer Olivia Hererra. But he is defeated in a match with an arrogant German pugilist named Hans Wagner. Blue fights his way back to earn a second bout with Wagner. Mrs. Lee employs a pretty young lady to vamp Blue and is persuaded that she has succeeded in convincing him to lay down in an early round of the championship fight. However, Blue is too proud to disgrace his race. To paraphrase a white reporter's pre-fight comments, the black "keg of dynamite" proceeds to defeat the "egotistical Aryan." Soon afterwards the *Harlem News* reports that Elinor Lee has been "Shot to Death by Gang Bullets." Benny Blue was obviously meant to be Joe Louis, affectionately known by his fans as the "Brown Bomber," who was heavyweight champion of the world form 1937 to 1949. In June 1935 Louis had actually defeated Mussolini's champion, Primo Canera (the victory was particularly significant to the many black Americans who identified with Italian occupied "little Ethiopia"). As the so-called representative of an "inferior race and country," Louis' 1938 defeat of Nazi boxer Max Schmeling during the first round of their second encounter was even a sweeter victory. During a newspaper montage tracing Benny Blue's comeback there are numerous topical front page stories referring to the war, including one about the U.S. interning "Teuton Vessels." With possible irony intended, the uncredited actor who plays Wagner's trainer has a pronounced New York Jewish accent.

269 PASSPORT TO ALCATRAZ (Col, Jun) Lewis D. Collins; *genre:* Spy; *locations:* United States, Europe; *coding:* Spy-Sab, War Mats, Blk, Quota, Dipl, WWII; *bias:* Anti-Espionage.

The espionage agency of an unspecified European nation (their accented, monocle-wearing coordinator is addressed as "His Excellency") is obtaining doctored passports from an agent in the United States to smuggle their saboteurs into America. They are particularly interested in disrupting the production and shipment overseas of the explosive gas called nitropine. Special agent George Hollister (Jack Holt) assumes the identity of a captured enemy agent in order to penetrate the "alien" spy network operating out of New York City. In the meantime, Hollister's partner falls in love with Karol, a foreign national whose illegal status led her to be duped by the sabotage ring, headed by an executive officer of the company manufacturing the nitropine. There are no specific references to the war or to the belligerents involved.

270 PHANTOM RAIDERS (MGM, Jun) Jacques Tourneur; *genre:* Crime; *location:* Panama; *coding:* AF-Ger, Blk, Jap, WWII, Brit, AF-N; *bias:* Pro-Intervention.

This was the second MGM film featuring Walter Pidgeon as detective Nick Carter. The action centers around the unexplained disappearances at sea of insured ships with cargoes destined for Britain, after they pass through the Panama Canal. It is rumored that a "Raider" is responsible. With the help of his wacky beekeeping assistant, Bartholomew, Nick discovers that a criminal is setting off by remote control bombs planted on the ships while they were docked in the Canal Zone. The current war is simply used as a convenient cover for the lethal racket. In early 1939 the U.S. Government began to allow American-owned ships to change their registry to Panamanian, so as to avoid the "carry" restrictions on "cash and carry."

271 THE PHANTOM SUBMARINE (Col, Dec) Charles Barton; *genre:* Spy; *locations:* United States, Caribbean; *coding:* AF-N, Spy-Sab, For Corr, Fr?, Chin, Ital?, Hist Am, WWII, Neutrality Act, Intell Serv; *bias:* Anti-Espionage.

The salvage ship *Retriever* heads for an area near the Panama Canal looking for sunken gold. Those aboard include a sinister crewman, ex–Navy diver Paul Sinclair and a stowaway. This illegal passenger is Madeleine, a newspaperwoman who has been secretly recruited by the U.S. Navy to investigate the movements of a mysterious submarine that has been reported in those waters. While en route, the vessel is sabotaged by the ugly sailor, who then jumps ship and is picked up by a submarine. The *Retriever* is forced to put in at an island near the canal which is inhabited by a wealthy middle-aged foreigner with a pencil mustache named Henri Jerome (actually an enemy agent, possibly meant to be Vichy). Following repairs and an attempt upon Paul's life, the ship reaches the treasure site. While on the ocean floor, Paul discovers that mines have been surreptitiously laid to obstruct the defense of the canal. When Paul surfaces, he is greeted by Jerome and members of the sub's crew who have seized the *Retriever*. A U.S. Navy gunboat appears and saves the American captives. The *Variety* review noted that the film "has a good peg on which to hang the [publicity] campaign, what with Axis under-sea warfare now in full swing and getting headline mention." Interestingly, the studio synopsis indicated that the film's locale was originally intended to be the Philippine Islands.

272 PUBLIC DEB NO. 1 (TCF, Sept) Gregory Ratoff; *genre:* Comedy/Drama; *location:* United States; *coding:* Vets, Stalin, Hist Am, Hitler, Latin Am, Am Icons, Russ-Finn War, AF-N, Comm; *biases:* Anti-Soviet, Pro-American.

Penny Cooper (Brenda Joyce), the "Cooper Soup" heiress, has become a "swimming pool Bolshevik," who, among other things, denounces "Hitler as [a] foe of communism." She then encounters Alan (George Murphy), a down and out waiter, espousing the American way, who is not above giving her a good spanking for her misguided beliefs. She is not impressed, but her uncle is. The waiter is hired as a vice president of the soup company! But, it is not until Penny learns of the Soviet invasion of Finland that she returns to the capitalist fold and embraces Alan in matrimony.

273 THE RAMPARTS WE WATCH (RKO, Aug) Louis De Rochemont; *genre:* Drama (sem-doc); *locations:* United States, Europe; *coding:* Spy-Sab, WWI, Hitler, FDR, Churchill, Hist Am, Blk, AF-Brit, Bonds, Draft, AF-Ger, War Mats, WWII, AF-A, AF-N, Dipl, Pacifism, Belg, Am Icons, Resist, Aust, Am Vol, AF-MC, Pol, Goering; *biases:* Pro-Intervention, Pro-British.

This was a film adaptation of the 1939 book written by (Major) George Fielding Eliot. Using documentary footage and re-enacted scenes, U.S. history and the American way of life are chronicled from 1914 to 1940 (although no mention is made of the Treaty of Versailles or the League of Na-

tions). Americanism and the need for a strong defense are stressed, while pacifism is attacked. The central story deals with the effects of the first World War upon a small American town (the "American Community"). One young man goes to France as a volunteer flyer in the Lafayette Escadrille and returns home in a coffin. At a moving memorial service his father indicates that he believes his son's sacrifice was necessary. The film is pro-British and decidedly anti-German. An obvious precursor to the style used in Capra's *Why We Fight* series, extensive footage from the 1940 German propaganda motion picture *Baptism of Fire* is included near the film's conclusion. Released during the 1940 presidential election, the political bias of the film's creators is made unambiguous when a shot is inserted of doughboy Wendell Wilkie's military identification card.

274 SAFARI (Para, Jun) Edward H. Griffith; *genre:* Drama; *locations:* Atlantic, Africa; *coding:* Span Civ, AF-W, AF-Chi, Ger, Blk, Sino-Jap War, Am Vol, Brit, WWII; *biases:* Anti-Fascist, Anti-German.

Linda (Madeleine Carroll) tries to forget her former beau (who was an aviator killed in Spain) by accompanying an arrogant German, Baron de Courland, on a jungle jaunt in West Africa. But American white hunter Jim Logan (Douglas Fairbanks, Jr.) would rather go to Europe to fight in the war than head the Baron's hunting safari. During the remaining reels of the film, Jim, who poignantly reveals to Linda that he fought as a volunteer with the Chinese in the Sino-Japanese War, falls in love with and saves our heroine from a progressively blatant racist and ruthlessly jealous latent fascist.

275 SAILOR'S LADY (TCF, Jul) Allan Dwan; *genre:* Comedy; *locations:* United States, Atlantic; *coding:* AF-N, Mil Exer, AF-MC; *bias:* Pro-Military.

While participating in Pacific Fleet night maneuvers, a naval captain must contend with a crying one-year-old female stowaway. Perhaps the noise of the guns disturbs her? Actually, it's an errant safety pin. The major action then switches away from guns to the attempt to discover who among the crew's 1st Division may be the father. Some newsreel footage of the battleship *USS Dakota* and the fleet is used.

276 SANTA FE TRAIL (WB, Dec) Michael Curtiz; *genre:* Historical Drama; *location:* United States; *coding:* Mil School, Spy-Sab, Hist Am, Am Icons, AF-A, blk; *biases:* Pro-American, Pro-Military.

This is a travesty of American history that, among other things, is highly uncharitable to the abolitionists of the pre–Civil War era. Nevertheless, the film's pitch against their "radical ... propaganda" and the politicizing of the Army touched on issues as relevant to 1940 as to the 1850s.

277 SAPS AT SEA (UA, May) Gordon Douglas; *genre:* Comedy; *location:* United States; *coding:* Spy-Sab, AF-N, Ger; *biases:* Anti-Espionage, Contraband Message.

This Laurel and Hardy comedy begins with the two comedians working in a horn factory; the strain causes Ollie to have a nervous breakdown, so they buy a small boat so he can recover in peace. In one scene, a newspaper story is shown: "Convict Nick Grainger, Notorious International Spy Whose Sensational Escape and Theft of Naval Plans Causes Nationwide Concern." The photo of Grainger (Dick Cramer) depicts him wearing a monocle (German linkage), but when he shows up in person and hides out on the boys' boat, he seems to be a stereotypical Hollywood gangster (with no accent, no monocle, no indication that he is an "international spy").

278 SATURDAY'S CHILDREN (WB, May) Vincent Sherman; *genre:* Drama; *location:* United States; *coding:* Ital, WWII, *bias:* Contraband Message.

Based on a Depression play by Maxwell Anderson, this updated cinematic version deals with a young married couple in New York City whose fragile domestic situation is threatened when the mail order company for whom they work reduces its expenses in order to make up for a business slowdown resulting from shipping losses incurred by the war. The wife's dumb girlfriend remarks that the war is "silly" and adds there would probably be no such conflicts if Europeans "just went to a couple of football games on weekends...." Ironically, the inventor/idealist husband (John Garfield) wants to start a new life through a job in the Philippines.

279 THE SEA HAWK (WB, Aug) Michael Curtiz; *genre:* Historical Drama; *locations:* Great Britain, Latin America; *coding:* Dipl, AF-Brit, Spy-Sab, Blk; *biases:* Pro-Intervention, Pro-British.

This Errol Flynn swashbuckler opens with the shadow of lugubrious King Philip II of Spain looming over a map of the world. He consults with his ministers: "...with our arms sweeping over Africa, the Near East ... invincible everywhere but on our own doorstep ... a puny rockbound island ... gives aid to our enemies ... we will never keep northern Europe in submission until we have a reckoning with England ... with England conquered nothing can stand in our way."

A diplomat is dispatched to team up with a sinister collaborationist and undermine the English state while Philip proceeds to prepare his Armada. Meanwhile, Queen Eliza-

beth resists the importunities of Geoffrey Thorpe and his "Sea Hawks" to arm against the Spaniards. In fact, it is only after Flynn escapes from the New World with proof of Spanish treachery that she abandons appeasement. Released during the German Blitz and the invasion scare of Britain, and Italian advances in North America, contemporary parallels were obvious. British prints of *The Sea Hawk* contained a concluding speech by Elizabeth that was not included in the U.S. version. She talks about preparing the country for a war that "none of us wants." The final shots of this version show wooden masts flying the Union Jack dissolving to Britain's modern battle fleet majestically plowing through the waves.

280 SEVEN SINNERS (Univ, Oct) Tay Garnett; *genre:* Drama; *location:* Pacific; *coding:* Am Icons, AF-N, Chi, Home Def; *bias:* Pro-Military.

An island-hopping honky tonk singer named Bijou, played to the hilt by Marlene Dietrich, makes a handsome Lieutenant of the U.S. Navy (John Wayne) temporarily forget his duty. The American governor of Boni Komba tells her boss to get her to back off, "The Navy already has plenty of destroyers." When the smoke clears at the "Seven Sinners Cafe," she has taken a powder. Even Bijou realizes that Uncle Sam is more important than carnal lust. By order of the Navy Department, Boni Komba conducts regular practice blackouts.

281 SKI PATROL (Univ, May) Lew Landers; *genre:* War Drama; *locations:* Germany, Finland; *coding:* Ger, Am Vol, WWI, WWII, Italo-Eth War, Sino-Jap War, Russo-Finn War, Pol, Czech, Austr, Pac, AF-W, AF-Russ, AF-Finn, Comm, AF-Ger, AF-Jap; *biases:* Anti-Soviet, Pacifist.

This film opens with scenes of the winter sports competition at the 1936 Olympics in Germany—a Russian wins the gold; a Finn the silver; an American the bronze. Immediately following the awards ceremony, in which the head of the American Committee applauds the international spirit of friendship demonstrated by its young participants and pointedly condemns the "barbarism" of war, a montage sequence portrays the series of conflicts that led to the outbreak of World War II (the Spanish Civil War and Soviet participation in the invasion of Poland are notably absent). During a betrothal party in an idyllic Finnish village, the people are informed that their nation was "bombed without warning" and that the men of the district have been mobilized. A strategic mountain fortress is defended by the Finnish skier (Philip Dorn) and his fellow villagers. Significantly, the American Olympic ski competitor and a Pole named Jan Sikor-

sky (the president of the Polish exile government in London was General Wladyslav Sikorski) have joined the Finns as volunteers. In reality, about 11,500 foreign volunteers aided the Finns, including 300 Americans. A Finnish Nobel prize winner sacrifices his life to wipe out an attacking Soviet parachute patrol and a pacifist later goes mad after shooting an escaping enemy prisoner. The Russian winner of the Olympic ski marathon—who only won as a result of his Finnish rival's sacrifice—is one of the commanders of Soviet forces attempting to destroy the Finns. Having failed in direct assaults, the Russian troops tunnel beneath the Finns in order to blow up the fortification. A desperate attack commanded by the Finnish skier leads to the destruction of the Soviet tunnel and the death of both his Russian and American skiing competitors. The senior Finnish commander offers an ambiguous eulogy at the film's conclusion: "Forgive them father, for they know not what they've done. The victory is theirs', but they couldn't have realized the cost to them, and to us. The flower of our youth, trampled by their mad envy.... And to what end Lord?" It should be noted that, in reality, the Soviet Union had *not* participated in the 1936 Olympics.

282 SKY BANDITS (Mono, Apr) Ralph Staub; *genre:* Adventure/Western; *location:* Canada; *coding:* Secret Weapon; *bias:* Contraband Message.

Sergeant Renfrew and his sidekick Kelly of the RCMP swing into action once again in this Monogram "B" picture. They investigate the mysterious disappearance of planes carrying gold from a Yukon mine. It turns out that a scientist, believing he was developing a new anti-aircraft weapon for his country, has actually helped a gang of thieves increase the range of their radio-beam weapon which causes the gold planes to crash.

283 SKY MURDER (MGM, Sept) George B. Seitz; *genre:* Crime; *location:* United States; *coding:* Fifth Col, FBI, Atroc-Conc, AF-AC, Am Icons; *bias:* Anti-Fascist.

This was the third film in the "Nick Carter" mystery series. A young woman of German origin is threatened with reprisals against her family unless she aids a Nazi-inspired (although never specifically identified) "movement" in the U.S. (the Nazis used the term movement—"bewegen"—to describe themselves). One of their leaflets is featured early in the film: "Don't let them dope you with Democracy pills! The world needs a new medicine and we have it! You can be one of our leaders if you join now!"

Nick (Walter Pidgeon) comes to the aid of the woman—and the U.S. government—by tracking down the power-mad, rich young leader of the group who fancies himself the future dictator of America, and is using a printing company as a front. Carter dismisses the members of the "cause" as "rats" and "wackies."

284 SON OF MONTE CRISTO (UA, Nov) Rowland V. Lee; *genre:* Adventure; *location:* Europe; *coding:* Spy-Sab, Dipl, Resist, Russ-Ger Coop; *bias:* Anti-Totalitarian.

The 19th-century Balkan Ruritania of "Lichtenburg" is menaced by "more powerful neighbors" that, to quote the *Variety* review, give this motion picture "some telling touches of present day European diplomatic phenagling." A heel-clicking, German-accented General Gurko Lanen (George Sanders) plots a coup with the aid of a secret treaty with Russia. A insouciant young Count of Monte Cristo (read "England"), using the *nom de guerre* of the "Torch of Liberty," secretly helps the local underground subvert the machinations of Lanen. The linkages with the contemporary Nazi-Soviet Pact are unmistakable.

285 SON OF THE NAVY (Mono, Mar) William Nigh; *genre:* Comedy/Drama; *location:* United States; *coding:* AF-N; *bias:* Pro-Military.

The U.S. Naval bases at San Pedro and San Francisco provide a topical background to this story of a runaway orphan who "adopts" a Navy petty officer as his father and the daughter of the man's ship commander as his mother.

286 STAR DUST (TCF, Apr) Walter Lang; *genre:* Comedy/Drama; *location:* United States; *coding:* Blk, Fr, AF-AC; *biases:* Contraband Message, Pro-Military.

A former silent movie star, played by Roland Young, is now a talent scout for Amalgamated Studios. When his latest three recruits arrive in Hollywood for screen tests with a broken nose, a cold and a phoney Dorothy Lamour look, respectively, he utters "sabotage" in despair. Later, he wrangles a star role in a Napoleonic romance for the girl (Linda Darnell) he found in a small town coffee shop by splicing-in her screen test into a Fox Movietone newsreel shown to studio bigwigs at Grauman's Chinese Theatre. The Movietone News segment opens with Lowell Thomas extolling the testing of the Army Air Corps' latest fighter with a "top speed for sky battle."

287 STRIKE UP THE BAND (MGM, Sept) Busby Berkeley; *genre:* Musical Comedy; *location:* United States; *coding:* Am Icons, Latin Am, AF-N, Blk; *bias:* Pro-American.

Another Rooney/Garland vehicle with a lot of dancing and singing, but very little plot. Nevertheless, contemporary events were quite clearly on the director's mind. In one number Gershwin is proclaimed to be "as good as Beethoven and Bach" and that American music is "best of all." In another number, "La Conga," Judy makes a pro-South American bid decked out like Carmen Miranda. And in the martial grand finale, Mickey struts out in a naval officer's uniform and winds up floating on the screen beside July in tableau form with the fluttering stars and stripes superimposed.

288 SUSAN AND GOD (MGM, Jun) George Cukor; *genre:* Drama; *location:* United States; *coding:* Brit; *biases:* Pacifist, Contraband Message.

Susan (Joan Crawford) is a fickle society lady who returns from England happily announcing to one and all that she has found God by embracing a religious movement that promises earthly joy through total confession. Susan responds to the skepticism of her astonished friends by labeling them "hard-boiled worldlings." The new religious zealot adds that "civilization is a failure" and that the "movement [is]... the only thing in the world to stop war."

289 THREE FACES WEST aka THE REFUGEE (Rep, Jul) Bernard Vorhaus; *genre:* Drama; *location:* United States; *coding:* Austr, Ref, Czech, FDR, Russ-Ger Coop, Russ, Nazi; *biases:* Pro-American, Anti-Nazi.

A refugee Viennese surgeon and his daughter join a group of North Dakota farmers on their trek from the Dust Bowl to Oregon. Because she yearns for the boy left behind, John Wayne's advances are spurned. But then she is visited by the old beau, Eric. He has become an enthusiast of the "new Reich" and wants her to leave America with him. She decides to remain and marry the Duke.

290 TIN PAN ALLEY (TCF, Nov) Walter Lang; *genre:* Musical Comedy; *locations:* United States, Great Britain; *coding:* Brit, Blk, WWI, AF-A, Am Icons; *bias:* Pro-Intervention.

A couple of down and out vaudevillians refuse to do a war song because they do not believe America will enter the World War. But then Wilson declares war and so, naturally, they join up. Their girlfriend, meanwhile, is with a group entertaining troops in London. One of the featured songs is "America, I Love You." Like the majority of the American films of this period with a WWI motif, it was ineluctably related to contemporary events.

291 VIGIL IN THE NIGHT (RKO, Feb) George Stevens; *genre:* Drama; *location:* Great Britain; *coding:* WWII, Home Def, AF-Brit; *biases:* Contraband Message, Pro-British.

This is a medical tearjerker starring Carole Lombard as a dedicated nurse that takes place in England during the immediate prewar period. The original ending featuring Prime Minister Chamberlain's announcement of war was cut. In early 1940, when the film was completed, RKO executives were still apparently reluctant to directly address the war. This largely negated a series of subtle references to the conflict in Europe which included a recruiting poster in a scene and an increasing number of men appearing in uniform as the film progressed. While engaged in a struggle against an epidemic the noble heroine states: "You can't sign a peace treaty with disease." And soon afterwards a frustrated hospital administrator justifies limited hospital expenditures when he blurts out: "Do you realize that we're as close to war as we'll ever be?"

292 WATERLOO BRIDGE (MGM, May) Mervyn LeRoy; *genre:* Drama; *location:* Great Britain; *coding:* Home Def, Goering, Chamberlain, WWI, WWII, Ital, Russ?, AF-Brit; *biases:* Pacifist, Pro-British.

On the evening of September 3, 1939, the day Britain entered the war against Germany, a gray haired colonel, played by Robert Taylor, gets out of his staff car at the Waterloo Bridge and reminisces (via an extended flashback) about a young ballerina (Vivian Leigh) with whom he had fallen in love during a first World War Zeppelin raid on London. A whirlwind romance is cut short when he is recalled to France. After she is misinformed of his death in action, her world collapses. The dashing captain returns, but for her it is too late. At the beginning a series of documentary shots is incorporated into the film that includes footage of English children being evacuated from London. Based on the 1930 play by Robert E. Sherwood, an earlier film version had been produced by Universal in 1931; James Whale director.

293 WOMEN IN WAR (Rep, Jun) John H. Auer; *genre:* War Drama; *locations:* Great Britain, France; *coding:* AF-RAF, Bonds, WWI, WWII, AF-Brit, AF-W, AF-Ger, Fr; *bias:* Pro-British.

During a London blackout an irresponsible socialite named Pamela played by the popular British actress, Wendy Barrie, accidentally kills a drunken Army captain while defending her honor. They had attended a celebration of the sinking of the German pocket battleship Graf Spee (the damaged ship was scuttled by her crew off Montevideo on December 17, 1939, after a running battle with the Royal Navy. Because of war tensions her trial does not go well. But then a middle-aged woman named O'Neill, whom Pamela does not know, arranges her enlistment in the Overseas Nursing Corps to help Pamela avoid a conviction. After the usual training sequences, Pamela is shipped out to France with a group of nurses under the command of the mysterious Miss O'Neill. While crossing the English Channel their transport comes under German aerial assault. Pamela's relations with her cohorts do not improve after they are stationed in a village near the front, particularly since one of her fellow nurses mistakenly believes that Pamela is trying to steal her fiance. Desiring revenge, this nurse deliberately drives an ambulance with Pamela as a passenger into a British artillery barrage. Through shot and shell Miss O'Neill comes to the rescue and reveals that she is Pamela's mother (played by Elsie Janis, famous for her traveling one-woman show entertaining America's Doughboys in France during World War I). This film in some ways resembles Paramount's 1931 release, *The Mad Parade*.

294 ZANZIBAR (Univ, Mar) Harold Schuster; genre: Adventure; locations: Great Britain, Africa; coding: Dipl, Arab, WWI, WWII, Brit, Blk, Ger, Corr, Spy-Sab, AF-Brit; bias: Pro-British.

Somewhere in British East Africa, femme hunter/explorer Jan Browning (Lola Lane) searches for the sacred skull of a revered tribal sultan. By virtue of a special clause in the Versailles Treaty the Germans had been ordered to hand over the skull from their former colony to the British government. The Germans claimed they never held the relic. Now it is believed by British authorities that the skull has been secretly returned to a hostile chief to lead an uprising—which would tie-up British troops who "could be put to better use in troublesome times like these." It is alleged that whoever possesses the skull controls the natives. Therefore, the British deem it vital to the Empire that the artifact does not fall into enemy hands. With the aid of an American adventurer (James Craig), Jan overcomes hungry lions, hostile natives, an active volcano (with footage borrowed from Universal's 1931 release, *East of Borneo*) and a murderous spy, before finally escaping with the skull. The spy, ambiguously named Koski, is played by Eduardo Cianelli. During the brief period that Koski gains possession of the skull, he madly proclaims: "With this skull, my country will rule the continent."

1941

295 ACCENT ON LOVE (TCF, July) Ray McCarey; genre: Drama; location: United States; coding: Port?, FDR, Austr, Am Icons,

Hist Am, Ref, Collab, Fifth Col; bias: Pro-American.

The son-in-law of a rich and greedy business executive abandons his well-paid management position and begins to earn his keep digging ditches alongside the masses on a WPA project. He learns a lot about the living conditions of the working class, and also receives a heavy dose of Americanism from the patriotic immigrant laborers. FDR is lionized and the term "fifth columnist" is used.

296 ADVENTURE IN WASHINGTON (Col, May) Alfred Green; genre: Drama; location: United States; coding: AF-N, AF-MC, Am Icons, Blk, FDR, Hist Am, Latin Am, Nat Def, WWI, WWII; biases: Pro-American, Pro-Democracy.

A member (Herbert Marshall) of the important Senate subcommittee on Appropriations must contend with a nosy lady radio commentator as well as his new Senate page, a troublesome adolescent named Marty. Just as the kid begins to take his responsibilities seriously, a fellow Senator complains that a cloakroom confidence was betrayed. Marty is held responsible and dismissed. Bitter at having been unjustly charged, Marty visits a shady lobbyist and discloses the contents of a defense bill. When aviation stocks soar, the Senator is accused of being the source of the leak and is brought before an investigating committee. Marty, hearing this on the radio, hitchhikes back to Washington and confesses. After being reinstated by his fellow pages, a tearful Marty—with the U.S. flag in the background—recites the "American's Creed."

297 AFFECTIONATELY YOURS (WB, May) Lloyd Bacon; genre: Comedy/Drama; locations: Portugal, United States; coding: Atroc, Collab?, Appeasement, Blk, Nazi, WWII, Russ, For Corr, Fr; biases: Anti-Soviet, Anti-Nazi, Contraband Message.

Ricky Mayberry (Dennis Morgan), foreign correspondent for the *New York Record* returns home from Moscow. His editor wants to send him back to Europe, but Mayberry is tired of trying to "outwit the censors" and is also attempting to win back his ex-wife. At dinner, his former spouse is surprised to learn that Ricky was in Moscow during the purges. Ricky sardonically adds, "and I was in France on that sad day they forgot to blow up the bridges" (referring to bridges over the Meuse River, which in May '40 were *not* destroyed, thus allowing German troops to advance).

298 ALL THAT MONEY CAN BUY aka THE DEVIL & DANIEL WEBSTER (RKO, Oct) William Dieterle; genre: Fantasy; location: United States; coding: Hist Am, Am Icons, Collab, Ger, Vet?; bias: Pro-American.

Based on Stephen Vincent Benet's *The Devil and Daniel Webster*, this film takes place in early 19th century New England. Walter Huston plays the devil, Mr. Scratch, who tricks the Faust-like yokel named Jabez Stone into selling his soul for a horde of Hessian gold (the evil German linkage). In the final reel Daniel Webster (Edward Arnold) comes to the rescue. His oration about freedom and the struggle to maintain the American ideal wins over a "jury of the damned" (infamous Americans, including a shame-faced Benedict Arnold), thus saving Jabez. Webster's speech had a direct message for the 1941 audience: "Freedom isn't just a big word, it is the morning and the bread and the risen sun. It was for freedom we came to these shores in boats.... [A] new thing has come, a free man ... and when the whips of the oppressors are broken and their names forgotten and destroyed, free men will be talking and walking under a free star. Yes, we have planted freedom in this earth.... [Y]ou're Americans all, you can't be on the side of the oppressor.... Don't let this country go to the devil! God bless this country and the men who made it free."

299 ANDY HARDY'S PRIVATE SECRETARY (MGM, Feb) George B. Seitz; genre: Comedy; location: United States; coding: Hist Am, Draft, Lat Am, WWII?; bias: Pro-American.

Andy is so busy organizing the various aspects of his high school's senior graduation that he nearly flunks. Andy complains: "I was drafted." The young Hardy also arranges jobs for a brother and sister whose father is down on his luck. It seems the war ruined the man's European based tourist agency.

300 THE BIG STORE (MGM, Jun) Charles Riesner; genre: comedy; location: United States; coding: Hist Am, WWI, Chi, AF-N, Jew, Draft, Ital, WWII, Blk, Bonds; bias: Contraband Message.

During a song and dance routine in this Marx Brothers film, Groucho, playing department store detective Wolf J. Flywheel, musically dallies with "an American Navy girl—every night two sailors wait to convoy her home." (Note: With the passage of Lend Lease in March 1941, convoying of American merchant vessels became a major issue between pro-interventionists and the isolationists.) During the bed-buying sequence with the Italian stereotype (Henry Armetta), Groucho makes a crack about fecund Giuseppi knowing the "draft numbers" of all his kids. Later, a boastful Groucho tells a group of reporters and cameramen that his exploits as a detective will "shove the war news to the second page."

301 BILLY THE KID (MGM, May) David Miller; genre: Western; location:

United States; *coding:* AF-A?, Latin Am, Am Icons, Brit, Hist Am; *biases:* Pro-American, Anti-Fascist.

Between 1939 and 1941 a number of American western icons were invoked and/or portrayed in film as combating local pseudo-fascists for control over territory. Two more recent examples were *Young Bill Hickok* (Rep, 1940) and *The Son of Davy Crockett* (Col., 1941). *Billy the Kid* stands out because the outlaw hero, largely removed from his legend, is portrayed as a man of conscience who eventually makes the moral decision to join forces with an English rancher named Keating in confronting local fascist-like thugs working for a vicious killer named Hicky. They are determined to disrupt the business of the rancher, who has a contract to deliver beef to the U.S. Army. The noble Keating assures Billy that "when good people get together not even a Hannibal or a Napoleon can prevail." Nevertheless, the free press in the nearby township of Lincoln is wrecked by the thugs after the editor challenges Hicky and they later murder the unarmed Keating. At this point, the local newspaper man joins the forces of "law and order" to destroy the fascist henchmen, explaining "I'm a man of peace, but not at any price." This was a World War I era pacifist phrase that had been resurrected by pro-interventionists in 1941 as a pejorative term to be used to stigmatize their opponents.

302 THE BLONDE FROM SINGAPORE (Col, Oct) Edward Dmytryk; *genre:* Romance/Comedy; *location:* Pacific; *coding:* AF-RAF; *bias:* Pro-British.

This is a romantic comedy whose cast includes a flier who has turned to pearl-diving in order to buy a plane and join the Royal Air Force.

303 THE BODY DISAPPEARS (WB, Dec) D. Ross Lederman; *genre:* Comedy/Fantasy; *location:* United States; *coding:* Blk, Draft, AF-A; *bias:* Contraband Message.

Another crazy professor invents an invisibility formula. While conducting one of his experiments he excitedly proclaims: "Think of it, invisible men, thousands of them invading enemy territory. And no army in the world can combat them!" Willie, his black servant, is not all that impressed. In fact, earlier in the film, when the professor had insisted that Willie remain in the lab, the reluctant assistant had muttered: "Oh, Oh, why couldn't I have been drafted?"

304 BOWERY BLITZKREIG (Mono, Aug) Wallace Fox; *genre:* Comedy/Drama; *location:* United States; *coding:* WWII, Chi, Hist Am, Blk, Draft, AF-A; *bias:* Contraband Message.

The usual "East Side Kids" stuff is featured in this film. This time it centers around

some criminals trying to get Muggs to throw a boxing match. In addition to the title, the motion picture contains a few cracks relating to the world crisis. These include one about a "blackout" when referring to Scrunno, the African-American member of the Kids' gang.

305 BUCK PRIVATES (Univ, Jan) Arthur Lubin; *genre:* Comedy/Training; *location:* United States; *coding:* Draft, AF-A, FDR, Nat Def; Am Icons, Mil Exer, Latin Am, Hist Am, USO, WWI; *bias:* Pro-Military.

The Selective Service Act of 1940 went into effect on October 16th. Released only three months later, this farce was promoted as "The First Picture About Uncle Sam's Millions of Rookies Heading for Army Camp Life!" It featured Abbott and Costello in their first starring film roles. While in flight from a policeman, they pause to sign up with a friendly recruiting officer. Abbott and Costello have the usual trouble adjusting to military life. They perform a rifle drill parody which has a long tradition going back at least as far as Chaplin's 1918 classic, *Shoulder Arms*. The Andrews Sisters don "camp hostess" uniforms and follow the boys to their training base. Between entertaining the troops with such popular tunes as "The Boogie Woogie Bugle Boy of Company B," the sisters find time to fall in love with some of America's new soldiers. This major box office hit for the studio was an obvious attempt to popularize the draft. Sequel: *Buck Privates Come Home* (Un, 1947).

306 BULLETS FOR O'HARA (WB, July) William K. Howard; *genre:* Crime; *location:* United States; *coding:* WWII; *bias:* Contraband Message.

Joan Perry marries Anthony Quinn, but divorces him when she finds out he is a crook. She marries detective Roger Pryor in an attempt to lure the jealous Quinn out of hiding, but Quinn and his men kidnap Perry and plan to flee to Cuba. While waiting for a boat, one of Quinn's men turns on the radio and catches the end of a news broadcast: "—declaring certain Red Sea and African ports no longer in the war zone and thereby removing the restriction of American commerce to those areas." This refers to Roosevelt's declaration of April 1941, which circumvented the Neutrality Act and allowed Lend-Lease shipments to be delivered directly to British forces fighting the Germans in North America.

307 BURMA CONVOY (Univ, Oct) Noel M. Smith; *genre:* War Drama; *location:* Burma; *coding:* War Mats, AF-Brit, Am Vol, AF-Chi, Sino-Jap War, Spy-Sab, Brit; *biases:* Pro-Intervention, Anti-Japanese.

A group of drivers, led by an American named Cliff Weldon (Charles Bickford),

take trucks over the Burma Road to Chungking loaded with food and munitions for the "embattled Army of China." During one trip they are strafed by a biplane with no discernible markings (Japan is never identified as the enemy). Cliff, who had planned to return to the U.S., decides to stay when his younger brother is murdered by a spy. Along with an aide of the "Generalissimo" sent to investigate the information leaks, Cliff discovers that the trucking company owner is responsible for passing on convoy schedules to the enemy and of plotting with Eurasian "guerrillas" (the Japanese were in reality sending weapons through Thailand to Burmese rebels to disrupt the road) to hijack the latest convoy. Cliff and his Chinese sidekick gather up an armed posse of drivers on layover. Joined by a contingent of British Military Police, they catch up with their mates in time to dispose of the hijackers. The Burma Road was hand-hewn by over 100,000 coolies between 1937 and 1938; in December 1938 supplies—largely from the U.S.—were delivered through the British colony of Burma to China. On July 18, 1940, under Japanese pressure, Britain closed the Burma Road, but it was reopened three months later. Lend-Lease was extended to China on May 6, 1941.

308 BUZZY AND THE PHANTOM PINTO (Ind, May) Richard C. Kahn; *genre:* Western; *location:* United States; *coding:* Spy-Sab, War Mats; *bias:* Pro-American.

The star of this low budget independent feature is Buzzy Henry, a juvenile cowboy. The *Motion Picture Herald* review of this "Kiddie Western" concludes with a summary that makes a topical linkage: "The story concerns the efforts of a clique of bad men to obtain some grazing land, which conceals beneath its worthless surface a rich chemical deposit. The chief culprit is portrayed as a teutonic toned gent with a hand kissing habit and a following of boot clicking stooges. 'Buzzy' is mainly responsible for rounding up the villains, whom he classifies as 'un–American.'"

309 CADET GIRL TCF, Nov) Ray McCarey, *genre:* Musical Comedy; *location:* United States; *coding:* WWII, Mil School, AF-A, Latin Am, Good Neighbor; *bias:* Pro-Military.

A West Point cadet (George Montgomery) on leave in Texas falls in love with a local swing band vocalist. One of her songs—"She's a Good Neighbor"—contains pro-Latin American lyrics. The cadet is so impressed by the singing blonde (Carole Landis) that he plans to give up his military career. But in the fifth and last song of the film, "Uncle Sam Gets Around," she patriotically communicates to him that their love will have to wait until he graduates from the U.S. Military Academy. Lyrics include: "We don't like tyrants and we don't like war/ But We've got things worth fighting for./ It won't be fun but it's got to be done/ It's a fight for the U.S.A. and the U.S. Way."

310 CAUGHT IN THE DRAFT (Para, Jul) David Butler; *genre:* Comedy/ Training; *location:* United States; *coding:* WWI, Ger, Am Icons, Draft, AF-A, Draft Avoid, Mil Exer, AF-N, WWII, FDR, AF-AC, Blk, Hist Am, AF-W, AF-Ger; *bias:* Pro-Military.

Fatuous Hollywood star Don Bolton (Bob Hope) plays a sergeant in a World War I era combat film but, at home, the 32-year-old actor worries about the various conscription bills being debated before the Congress. When he is led to believe the age limit will be 40, Don pursues a pretty Army colonel's daughter, Tony (Dorothy Lamour), for an exemption. But when a bill is passed requiring all males between the ages of 21 and 31 to register for the draft, Don figures he is safe and tries to back out of their engagement. A planned fake enlistment to impress Tony and the final age limit being set at 35 lead to Don tricking himself into the Army. After several misadventures in training camp, Don displays heroism during maneuvers and thereby proves that he is worthy of Tony's affection. Political profundities include cutting a Wendell Wilkie button out of a dead fish while on KP. Wilkie, a Republican non-interventionist/internationalist, ran against Roosevelt in the 1940 presidential election. His support of conscription facilitated the passage of the Selective Service Act in August 1940.

311 CHARLIE CHAN IN RIO (TCF, Sept) Harry Lachman; *genre:* Crime; *location:* Brazil; *coding:* Chi, Draft, WWII, AF-A, Latin Am; *biases:* Pro-Intervention, Pro-Military, Contraband Message.

This was the Chan series' bid for South American friendship. The film contains several flashy cabaret scenes as well as featuring a lot of the Latin music. In this mystery, Charlie and his slang-talking "number 1 son," Jimmy, are in Rio attempting to track down a murderess. And eventually they succeed in delivering to the Brazilian police *her* killer. But the film does not end until after Jimmy receives his draft notice: "With me in it, Pop, the war's in the bag." Charlie smiles and adds: "It's a cinch."

312 CHEERS FOR MISS BISHOP (UA, Feb) Tay Garnett; *genre:* Drama; *location:* United States; *coding:* Ital, Am Icons, WWI, Hitler, Hist Am, AF-A, Nazi; *bias:* Pro-American.

Martha Scott plays a woman who dedicates her life to education and the promotion of the American way at a small mid-

western college. At one point a student of Scandinavian descent recites the Declaration of Independence. In her final year of teaching at Midwestern an elderly Miss Bishop wearily relates to her grandniece about having to deal with an irate father of a student who "caught his son reading *Mein Kampf* and blamed it on me." The toast Miss Bishop offers at a banquet honoring her retirement had an unmistakable message in 1941: "Wisdom is the first cousin of freedom. And freedom is the glory of our nation.... She's young, she's growing too fast, she makes mistakes—but somehow she manages to keep her people free—may she always."

313 CITIZEN KANE (RKO, Sept) Orson Welles; *genre:* Drama/ Biography; *location:* United States; *coding:* Blk, WWI, Comm, Fascism, Hist Am, Brit, Fr, Ger, Ital, World Crisis, Jap?, Am Icon, Russ, Hitler, Jew, For Corr; *biases:* Anti-Fascist, Contraband Message.

The dangers of demagoguery are pointed out through the recounting of the life of a power-hungry newspaper magnate. Hitler is portrayed standing next to Kane on a Berchtes-gaden-like balcony in the famous ten minute "News on the March" parody of the "March of Time" newsreel sequence.

314 COME LIVE WITH ME (MGM, Jan) Clarence Brown; *genre:* Comedy/Drama; *location:* United States: *coding:* Austr, Ref, Quota; *bias:* Pro-American.

Hedy Lamarr plays "Johnny Jones," an Austrian refugee in America with an expired passport. She fears deportation because her father was "liquidated." An arranged business marriage to indigent writer Bill Smith (James Stewart) resolves the foreign crisis but leads to a domestic crisis. Naturally, true love conquers all. This film bears a slight plot resemblance to the 1937 Columbia release, *When You're In Love.*

315 CONFESSIONS OF BOSTON BLACKIE (Col, Dec) Edward Dmytryk; *genre:* Crime; *location:* United States; *coding:* Nazi, Blk; *biases:* Contraband Message, Anti-Nazi.

Boston Blackie is suspected of murder when a crooked art dealer is shot during an auction. The dead man's body is hidden inside a fake statue. Blackie exposes the real murderer and recovers the real statue. At one point in the film, Blackie's friend Arthur Manleder is accosted on the street by a tough cop, who raps his arm with a billy club and pulls a gun on him. Manleder remarks, "You've got a little Gestapo in you."

316 CONFIRM OR DENY (TCF, Dec) Archie Mayo; *genre:* War Drama; *location:* Great Britain; *coding:* Russ, Dipl, Home Def, Blk, For Corr, WWII, Hitler, Finn,

AF-Ger, Musso, AF-Brit, Chamberlain, AF-RAF, WWI, Russ-Ger Coop; *biases:* Pro-British, Pro-Intervention.

The direction of this film had been started by Fritz Lang, but was completed by Mayo after the former fell ill. The script was based on a story written by Henry Wales and Sam Fuller. The opening title states: "This is London—September, 1940." Yank Mitchell (Don Ameche) is the American editor of "Consolidated Press." His English girlfriend (Joan Bennett) is a teletypist working for the MOI (Ministry of Information). Constantly frustrated by censorship, Yank is so obsessed with getting the scoop on the German invasion plans for Britain that he arranges for messages to be sent from the continent by carrier pigeon. Eventually, while trapped with his girl and an unexploded ("Hitler Kommt" chalked on its fin) in his blitzed office building, Yank receives the information. But he is dissuaded from sending it on to the States when he learns an English boy, played by Roddy McDowell was killed by a bomb after taking the message (a symbolic bulldog at his side). In this late year film release Hollywood no longer pulled its punches. Hitler is referred to as a "rat" and claims are made that he travels in an armored train bearing Red Cross insignia (Hitler did use an armored headquarters train, ironically called "Amerika," during the Polish and Yugoslav campaigns). Operation Sea-Lion, Hitler's plan for the invasion of England, reached a high state of readiness between July and September of 1940. Postponed in October, it was never seriously reconsidered after the Germans launched their attack upon the Soviet Union in June 1941.

317 CRIMINALS WITHIN (PRC, Jun) Joseph H. Lewis; *genre:* Spy; *location:* United States; *coding:* USO, AF-A, Secret Weapon, Spy-Sab, Collab, Blk; Draft; *biases:* Anti-Espionage, Pro-Military.

A gang of foreign agents have infiltrated a U.S. Army base. In an attempt to steal the formula of a new explosive they murder a chemist working for the Army. The chemist's avenging brother, who is an Army corporal played by Eric Linden, and a young newspaper woman eventually succeed in exposing the spy ring. The foreign agents on base include a traitorous sergeant and the troop's favorite recreation hall hostess, a beautiful blonde named Alma. A "colored" duo played by Bernice Pilot and Dudley Dickerson provide the comedy relief.

318 THE DEADLY GAME (Mono, July) Phil Rosen; *genre:* Spy; *location:* United States; *coding:* Spy-Sab, Nazi, FBI, Secret Weapon, WWII; *biases:* Anti-German, Anti-Espionage.

FBI agents decipher a message from German headquarters ordering the assassination of a doctor working on the invention of a night air raid detector. However, before they can reach the doctor's lab, German agents destroy it and kidnap the doctor. FBI agent Barry Scott (Charles Farrell), in decoding another message, discovers that a new spy is being sent to this country. He takes the spy's place, but is later exposed. He and the doctor are rescued by Hoover's boys, just in the nick of time.

319 DEVIL DOGS OF THE AIR (Rerel '35) (WB, Jun) Lloyd Bacon; *genre:* Training; *locations:* United States, Pacific; *coding:* Latin Am, Mil Exer, Hist Am, AF-MC, AF-N; *bias:* Pro-Military.

Aided by some technical assistance from the Navy, this re-release is a frolicsome adventure featuring flying Marines. Wiseguy Thomas Jefferson O'Toole (James Cagney) learns the value of discipline the hard way. A lot of footage of the San Diego Naval Base and the fleet on maneuvers (featuring the 6th Marine Air Wing, operating from the USS *Saratoga* and flying Boeing F4-B4 fighter-bombers) is incorporated into the film. The film has preparedness undertones.

320 THE DEVIL PAYS OFF (Rep, Nov) John H. Auer; *genre:* Drama; *locations:* Cuba, United States, Atlantic; *coding:* US-Brit Coop, Spy-Sab, WWII, AF-N, Atroc, Ger, Intell Serv; *biases:* Pro-Intervention, Anti-German.

The plot of this motion picture centers around the efforts of a cashiered Naval officer to obtain sufficient evidence to convict a shipping magnate of delivering ships to unspecified foreign powers. The vessels had been originally sold to the United States government for use in supplying Great Britain. The magnate and his cohorts have Germanic names.

321 DIVE BOMBER (WB, Aug) Michael Curtiz; *genre:* Adventure; *locations:* United States, Pacific; *coding:* War Mats, Am Icons, AF-N, AF-MC, WWII, AF-RAF, Natl Def, Am Vol, AF-AC, AF-Ger; *bias:* Pro-Military.

Errol Flynn stars as a young naval flight surgeon in this big budget color production. In spite of initial pilot opposition, he and his medical cohorts relentlessly pursue a solution to the problem of "blackout." Eventually, veteran pilot Fred MacMurray is won over to the vital necessity of research on flight safety systems. After learning he will be permanently grounded for medical reasons, he embarks on a fatal test flight of a new pressurized suit. His only regret is getting "yanked right before the main event." Most of the film was shot at the Naval Air Station in San Diego. Other scenes took place

at Pensacola and on board the carrier USS *Enterprise.*

322 DOCTOR KILDARE'S WEDDING DAY (MGM, Aug) Harold S. Bucquet; *genre:* Drama; *location:* United States; *coding:* Ital, WWII, AF-A, AF-N, AF-MC, Blk; *bias:* Contraband Message.

Midway through this episode of MGM's ongoing B-series medical drama, Dr. Gillespie is visited by an Italian (possibly refugee) conductor who is concerned that he may be going deaf. The avuncular doctor comments, "I can't think of anything more important right now than to keep your talent alive for a troubled world." There is an unusually large number of uniformed people representing all the military services portrayed in street scenes and at the train station. Although, by the summer of 1941, this was a common experience in real life, it would not be until the following spring that American films with a contemporary setting would regularly populate public crowd scenes with large numbers of extras playing military personnel. Universal's *Keep 'Em Flying*, q.v., is another 1941 film including such scenes.

323 DOUBLE TROUBLE (Mono, Nov) William West; *genre:* Comedy: *location:* United States; *coding:* Ref, WWII, Brit; *bias:* Contraband Message.

Harry Langdon and Charles Rogers star as the Prattle Brothers in this slapstick farce. They are brought to America as child refugees from war-torn England. Their benefactor, the owner of the Whitmore Bean Cannery, puts them to work at the plant though, when he discovers the "youngsters" are two dim-witted adults. The factory is threatened with bankruptcy after Langdon unwittingly allows a $100,000 bracelet to be sealed into one of the cans. But the publicity manager starts a sales boom by promoting the "canned diamonds." The boys eventually find the bracelet and the PR man gets the boss's daughter.

324 DOWN IN SAN DIEGO (MGM, Sept) Robert B. Sinclair; *genre:* Spy; *locations:* United States, Pacific; *coding:* Spy-Sab, Secret Weapon, AF-N, AF-MC, Hitler, Am Icons, Draft, Blk, AF-A, V, FBI, FDR?, Nazi; *biases:* Anti-German, Anti-Espionage.

Al Haines (Dan Dailey) enlists in the Marine Corps rather than be drafted. But his old gangster buddies, most of whom have German accents and surnames, control Al by convincing him that he killed a man during a night of heavy drinking. Al's younger sister, her high school buddies and Spot the dog follow their Marine to San Diego after they learn he may be in trouble. In the process of snooping around, the kids fall afoul of the enemy agents. Al, who has meanwhile confessed to the authorities, confronts the

spies, only to learn they have kidnapped his sister and her boyfriend. Al is instructed to steal one of the Navy's new torpedo boats that the Marines have been guarding and drive it out to a German freighter waiting off the coast. Al is mortally wounded when he recklessly approaches the armed ship to pick up the two youngsters who have jumped overboard. Three Navy planes that have followed Al attack and destroy the German ship. It was in the same month as this film's release that FDR publicly initiated an undeclared naval war against any Axis vessels entering the "defensive waters" of the United States patrolled by the American military.

325 ELLERY QUEEN'S PENTHOUSE MYSTERY (Col, Mar) James P. Hogan; *genre:* Crime; *locations:* United States, China; *coding:* Blk, Chi, Ref, Sino-Jap War?, Ital; *bias:* Contraband Message.

When not involved in bickering with his secretary/girlfriend, Nicki (Margaret Lindsay), Ellery Queen (Ralph Bellamy) solves a couple of murders. These deaths are directly related to the struggle for possession of a valuable jewel collection from China. It has been secretly brought into the States by a ventriloquist in order to raise money to aid starving Chinese refugees, presumably victimized by the war with Japan (the Sino-Japanese War is never specifically mentioned; but it is obliquely referred to in comments about the Chinese government being unable to adequately finance its starving people at this time). The mysterious Count Brett (Eduardo Ciannelli) is one of the heavies.

326 EMERGENCY LANDING (PRC, May) William Beaudine; *genre:* Spy, Comedy; *location:* United States; *coding:* Latin Am, Spy-Sab, Secret Weapon, AF-AC, Ger, WWII, War Mats; *biases:* Anti-Espionage, Anti-German.

A test pilot and a weather bureau observer develop a robot controlled plane. They convince the owner of the Lambert Airplane Factory, who has grown rich with a backlog of war orders, to allow them to conduct tests. Unfortunately, two foreign agents with Germanic names (Karl and Otto) sabotage the experimental plane. The boys, discredited, are sent off to a weather station in the desert. Soon afterwards, the same enemy agents steal a Lambert bomber from the factory and just happen to crash near the isolated weather station. With the aid of their robot device, the exiles apprehend the surviving agent who is trying to escape in the pilot's plane. In a hilarious conclusion the local sheriff, a midget, arrests the bewildered enemy agent.

327 THE FACE BEHIND THE MASK (Col, Jan) Robert Florey; *genre:* Crime; *location:* United States; *coding:* Ref, Am Icons, Quotas; *bias:* Contraband Message.

This film begins with a printed title card: "Just a few years ago—when a voyage to America meant adventure and not flight ... when a quota was a number—and not a lottery prize to be captured by a lucky few...." Peter Lorre is a Hungarian immigrant whose face is horribly scarred in a fire; he turns to crime to make enough money to have plastic surgery. Indications are that references to Lorre's status as a "refugee" were dropped from the film, and the printed card at the film's beginning made an effort to set it in an undefined "past" (although the settings are all contemporary U.S.).

328 FATHER TAKES A WIFE (RKO, Oct) Jack Hively; *genre:* Comedy; *locations:* United States, Mexico; *coding:* Russ, Latin Am, Draft Avoid, Quotas; *bias:* Contraband Message.

This is a light farce centering around the head of a shipping firm who falls in love with a glamorous actress, played by Gloria Swanson. In response to his son's incredulity at his announcement of marital plans, "senior" facetiously responds that it is in order "to avoid the draft." Aside from a passing reference to immigration quotas, the contemporary crisis is scrupulously avoided thereafter.

329 FEDERAL FUGITIVES (PRC, Mar) William Beaudine; *genre:* Spy; *location:* United States; *coding:* Hist Am, Spy-Sab, AF-AC, FBI, Secret Weapon, Ger, Collab, Fifth Col, Intell Serv; *biases:* Anti-German, Anti-Espionage.

Army Intelligence officer Captain James Madison, with the cooperation of an aircraft plant executive, secretly negotiates with foreign agents operating in the nation's capital for their acquisition of the plans for a newly designed American plastic training plane. With the critical inside help of a female member of the spy ring, who is innocently involved, Captain Madison is able to apprehend the spies and the corrupt lobbyist who is in league with them. Dr. Haskel, the leader of the foreign agents, whose real name is Otto Lieberman, plunges to his death down an elevator shaft while attempting to escape.

330 FLIGHT COMMAND (MGM, Jan) Frank Borzage; *genre:* Training; *location:* United States; *coding:* AF-N, Natl Def, WWII, Mil Exer, Chi, AF-RAF, Dunkirk; *bias:* Pro-Military.

An ensign, fresh out of flight school at Pensacola, played by Robert Taylor, must prove himself in the prestigious Hellcat Naval Fighter Squadron No. 8. Newsreel footage of the carrier USS *Enterprise*, musically accompanied by the "Eyes of the Fleet," is included in an obvious attempt to promote the new National Defense Program. Between war maneuvers on the carrier, a new device

for landing in the fog is tested. At a cocktail party, the fighting at Dunkirk is discussed.

331 FLIGHT FROM DESTINY (WB, Feb) Vincent Sherman; *genre:* Drama; *location:* United States; *coding:* Blk, WWII?, Hitler?; *bias:* Anti-Totalitarian.

A college professor who learns that he has only six months to live comes up with a theory about committing a murder to eliminate a menace to society. When a colleague suggests a dictator, the professor delivers the following monologue: "A dictator is a symbol. His death wouldn't be of any benefit for society without the death of the system that created him."

332 FLYING BLIND (Para, Aug) Frank McDonald; *genre:* Comedy; *location:* United States; *coding:* Spy-Sab, Secret Weapon, Ger?; *bias:* Anti-Espionage.

This is basically a comedy about a small time airline service that ferries couples planning to marry from Los Angeles to Las Vegas. Somewhere along the line they get involved with some foreign agents who are attempting to steal a new airplane transformer vital to National Defense.

333 FLYING CADETS (Univ, Oct) Erle Kenton; *genre:* Drama/ Training; *location:* United States; *coding:* AF-AC?, WWI, *bias:* Pro-Military.

In order to attract government cadets, a small time flying school owner enlists a World War I hero named Rocky to be an instructor. The climax comes when Rocky tests two new training planes designed by the young owner. During 1941, with the aid of civilian flying schools, the Army Air Corps had trained 11,000 pilots.

334 FLYING WILD (Mono, Mar) William West; *genre:* Spy; *location:* United States; *coding:* Blk, Spy-Sab, Prod, Secret Weapon, Collab, Fifth Col; *bias:* Anti-Espionage.

This B-film played on the national preparedness furor sweeping the country and the concomitant fear of sabotage of America's growing national defense industry. East Side Kid Mugsy (Leo Gorcey) drives his buddies, including a black youngster, to an aircraft plant. That same day, Mugsy helps save the plant's test pilot from the wreckage of the company's latest pursuit plane prototype. When Danny learns it is the result of sabotage he asks his father, the plant manager, if it is the work of foreigners. He is told: "That's the peculiar part of un–American activities.... The most vicious offenders are often born in America and just don't know what they're doing." The Kids participate in a scheme to entrap the "rats" that threaten America's security by letting it be known that Danny possesses plans of the company's new bombsight. This succeeds in flushing out the nefarious Dr. Nagle and his

gang. Danny is captured in the process, but the spies soon discover that the plans he carries are of an obsolete aircraft model. The spies are still able to acquire the real bombsight plans. They attempt to smuggle out the stolen plans wrapped in the bandages of a "patient" sent in the doctor's ambulance plane to a non-existent hospital located near the border. But the Kids, led by Mugsy, are able to "blitzkrieg" the "fifth column" doctor aboard his plane.

335 FORCED LANDING (Para, Jul) Gordon Wiles; *genre:* Spy; *locations:* Pacific, United States; *coding:* Spy-Sab, Russ, Latin Am, Am Vol, Collab, Fifth Col, Am Icons; *bias:* Pro-Intervention.

An American pilot (Richard Arlen) is hired by Mosaque, a Pacific Island republic (presumably located off the South American coast) to ferry supplies to a defensive fortifications project. When not wooing the daughter (Eva Gabor in her film debut) of a Dutch construction engineer, he is forced to combat some local "fifth columnists" trying to sabotage the buildup of their nation's defenses.

336 THE GANG'S ALL HERE (Mono, Jun) Jean Yarbrough; *genre:* Comedy/Crime; *location:* United States; *coding:* Appeasement, Chi, Blk, Sino-Jap War, War Mats; *biases:* Pro-Intervention, Contraband Message.

A couple of drivers, Frankie (Frankie Darro) and Jeff (Mantan Moreland) become involved in a conflict between competing trucking outfits. During the hijacking of their vehicle, Jeff implores, "Don't hit me, I'm for appeasement!" Later, when the villain's truck is stopped by the police, he explains to them that "we're carrying medical supplies for the war relief ship leaving for China in the morning."

337 THE GAY FALCON (RKO, Oct) Irving Reis; *genre:* Crime; *location:* United States; *coding:* Chi, WWII, US-Brit Coop; *biases:* Pro-Intervention, Contraband Message.

The Falcon, played by George Sanders, attends a "War Relief Ball" with his fiancée. A fatuous society matron exclaims, "Sort of lend-lease for democracy, you know!" as she steals away the Falcon for a dance. A jewel theft and murders ensue.

338 THE GET-AWAY (MGM, Jun) Edward Buzzell; *genre:* Crime; *location:* United States; *coding:* FBI, Natl Def, Blk, Chi; *bias:* Contraband Message.

A G-man impersonates a criminal in prison in order to befriend a notorious mobster whose gang has been responsible for a series of payroll robberies at defense plants. They "crash out" together. In spite of falling in love with the criminal's sister, the Fed eventually gets his man. In an opening radio broadcast the announcer states that the gang's activities are more dangerous than the "subversive activities and sabotage" discussed in previous broadcasts. Except for the topical linkage, this film was almost an exact remake of the 1935 MGM release, *Public Hero No. 1.*

339 A GIRL, A GUY AND A GOB (RKO, Mar) Richard Wallace; *genre:* Comedy; *location:* United States; *coding:* AF-N, Latin Am, Am Icons; *bias:* Pro-Military.

"I got an awful itch to do another hitch in Uncle Sam's Navy." Nevertheless, for 1941, the Navy is strictly incidental to this film. Planning to leave the Navy, the wrestling gunner, "Coffee Cup," played by George Murphy, spends virtually the entire film conning money and pursuing Lucille Ball. But in the end, he surrenders her to the nice rich guy and happily returns to the Navy's battleship grey bosom (accompanied by the strains of "Columbia, the Gem of the Ocean"). We even get a brief rear screen shot of the fleet as he and his mates return to his ship aboard a gig.

340 GREAT GUNS (TCF, Oct) Monty Banks; *genre:* Comedy/Training; *location:* United States; *coding:* AF-AC, AF-A, Draft, Mil Exer, Blk, V, WWI, Am Icons; *bias:* Pro-Military.

House servants Laurel and Hardy enlist in the army to keep an eye on their pampered millionaire boss, Dan Forrester, who has just been drafted. They wind up at a Cavalry base in Texas where the standard training shenanigans and accompanying love story follow. Stan and Ollie are subsequently "captured" during the division's annual maneuvers (newsreel footage of the September Army war games in Louisiana incorporated). The jeep in which they drive has a "...—" painted on its side. The boys are freed with the aid of their pet crow, Penelope, and a combat ready, democratized Dan.

341 THE GREAT LIE (WB, Apr) Edmund Goulding; *genre:* Drama; *location:* United States; *coding:* Blk, Hist Am, Fr, Lat Am, Nat Def, AF-A; *biases:* Contraband Message, Pro-American.

A playboy flier (George Brent) thinks he has married a concert pianist (Mary Astor), but is informed that her divorce was not final. With second thoughts about the selfish artist, he visits his loving old flame (Bette Davis) on her Maryland farm. Following some high camp thirties style melodrama, he marries the right girl. Soon afterwards he flies down to Brazil on a secret mission for the government concerning "hemisphere defense." When it is thought that he has died in the Brazilian jungles, his wife convinces the pregnant pianist to surrender her child to her. The viewer is treated to additional

cinematic histrionics when our intrepid aviator returns to his wife and new son.

342 THE GREAT MR. NOBODY (WB, Dec) Ben Stoloff; *genre:* Comedy; *location:* United States; *coding:* AF-A, Draft, Am Icons; *biases:* Pro-Military, Contraband Message.

"Dreamy" Smith (Eddie Albert) is the nice guy who helps out everyone except himself. His girlfriend waits patiently for a proposal. As a reward for his many unsung deeds, Dreamy receives the monthly Valor Award from his employer, *The Express* newspaper. He is then handed a letter from the government. Smiling, Dreamy turns toward his girl and says, "Wonderful news, Mary. You'll have to wait awhile longer [to get married]. I've been drafted!" He then runs over to the American flag and salutes it. "You're in the Army Now" plays on the soundtrack.

343 H. M. PULHAM, ESQ. (MGM, Dec) King Vidor; *genre:* Romance/Drama; *locations:* United States, France; *coding:* WWI, WWII, AF-A, Hist Am, AF-Ger, AF-MC, Jew?, Nazi, FDR; *biases:* Contraband Message, Preparedness.

A Boston banker's staid life is unsettled by both a call from a former lover and an assignment by his Harvard schoolmates to write a class history for their 25th reunion. In a series of flashbacks, the man, played by Robert Young, reminisces about his life. At one point he writes, ... "After graduation I attended the first Plattsburg camp and was with the AEF [American Expeditionary Force] in France." In the brief scene that follows, he and his men engage in combat with the "Heinies." After a troubled night, the banker sees the morning paper headlines reading: "Nazis Warn Roosevelt." Fleeing the "war news" and his wife, he meets the old girlfriend for lunch. They share a bottle of champagne and then depart again to fulfill the obligations due their respective families. The Plattsburg camp was a private officers' training project initiated by preparedness advocates—mostly Harvard alumni in 1915. Sixteen thousand men eventually attended the camp located in upstate New York. In the spring of 1940, the Plattsburg concept was revived and quickly approved. Five hundred men were sent to the reopened camp in July. The passage of a peacetime draft in the late summer precluded the continuation of the program.

344 HELLZAPOPPIN' (Univ, Dec) H. C. Potter; *genre:* Comedy; *location:* United States; *coding:* Draft, AF-A, Prod, Russ?, Blk, Latin Am, Draft Avoid?, Hist Am; *bias:* Contraband Message.

Ole Olsen and Chic Johnson arrive on stage by cab following a wild opening sequence from their Broadway hit "Hellza-

poppin'," which features a hell with gleeful devils roasting shapely girls on spits. When Ole identifies himself to Chic as secret service agent #25266, a nearby devil declares that number to be his draft number, rips off his devil's outfit to reveal an army uniform and marches away. During a discussion over changes in the script, Chic asks the deadpan screenwriter (Elisah Cook, Jr.) how old he is. "Twenty-three," is the reply. To which Chic quips, "That's a patriotic age. Uncle Sam needs young men like you." The writer quickly asserts that he would prefer to be twenty-nine (presumably beyond the draft age at the time of the film's production). The remainder of this zany motion picture is full of additional one-liners and sight gags—a few of which actually work. However, direct reference to contemporary world events disappear after the first fifteen minutes.

345 HENRY ALDRICH FOR PRESIDENT (Para, Dec) Hugh Bennett; *genre:* Comedy; *location:* United States; *coding:* Draft, FDR?, Blk; *biases:* Pro-Democracy, Contraband Message.

Based on a popular radio series, Henry Aldrich's cinematic debut was Paramount's answer to MGM's Hardy family series. The naive teen Henry is duped into running against the school's rich kid for the class presidency. When Henry explains his candidacy to his father by stating he was "practically drafted," the elder Aldrich testily responds, ..."in that case you won't need any campaign funds or headquarters." At the local ice cream parlor Henry's opponent is treating the rest of the class to free sodas. The faithful girl that Henry ignores enters and berates her classmates as "...suckers [for] falling for this cheap bribery ... are you the friends of this snob, this small town plutocrat...?" The annoyed candidate refers to her outburst as "dirty propaganda." What transpires next is unclear. One version has the camera cutting away from the girl at this point. Another source has noted that the girl's speech continues with the following, "Let's not forget, folks, that this is wartime and we're fighting dictator powers. America can use every plug it can get, especially from fresh-faced, vibrant youth, to plug its democratic system." Since the film was released late in 1941, it may be that the more topical sentence was inserted in some prints after Pearl Harbor.

346 HOLD BACK THE DAWN (Para, Sept) Mitchell Leisen; *genre:* Drama; *locations:* United States, Mexico; *coding:* Dipl, Rom, Jew, Latin Am, Ger, Neth, WWII, Ref, Quota, Am Icons, Hist Am, FDR, Fr, Good Neighbor, Aust, Vet; *bias:* Pro-American.

A jaded Rumanian gigolo (Charles Boyer) flees France after the German invasion. Arriving in Mexico, he soon becomes despondent due to a lack of funds and the inability to acquire a U.S. visa. His soulmates include a visibly pregnant Austrian who desperately wants her child to be born in America (during this period there was a virtual taboo on realistic portrayals of pregnancy in Hollywood film; one could conclude that this character was included to dramatically emphasize the plight of refugees). He finds financial security and, eventually, true love by landing an American schoolteacher. What makes this film even more interesting in that all but the final sequence is related by Boyer's character to "Mr. Saxon" (played by the film's actual director, Mitchell Leisen), on a Paramount sound stage during the shooting of a scene from *I Wanted Wings*, q.v., with Veronica Lake.

347 HONOLULU LU (Col, Dec) Charles Barton; *genre:* comedy; *location:* United States; *coding:* AF-N, Lat Am, Spy-Sab; *bias:* Pro-Military.

A Latin American swindler (Leo Carrillo) and his niece, Consuela (Lupe Velez), check in at Honolulu's most exclusive hotel. Annoyed with her uncle's latest scam, Consuela goes off on her own and gets a job in a burlesque theatre, a favorite hangout of the U.S. Fleet. Under the stage name of "Honolulu Lu," Consuela is adopted by three sailors, and begins a romance with one of them. At a charity contest for "Miss Honolulu," sponsored by a society matron that Lu's uncle is attempting to swindle, Consuela is spotted by her uncle. To keep her from hindering his scheme, he reports that she is an international spy. When the police arrive to arrest her, the sailors riot. Uncle then confesses and Lu's Spanish style hula wins the contest. According to Columbia's Press Book, a deliberate appeal to the Latin American audience was made by having Lupe Velez and Leo Carrillo deliver Spanish jokes in between their English lines.

348 HORROR ISLAND (Univ, Mar) George Waggner; *genre:* Crime; *location:* United States; *coding:* Bonds, AF-N, Lat Am; *biases:* Pro-Military, Contraband Message.

Promoter Bill Martin's latest scheme to get out of debt involves organizing excursions to an uninhabited island he owns off the Florida coast. Treasure hunting and murder ensue. Bill comes through unscathed and falls hopelessly in love. In addition, a government agent arrives on the island and offers to purchase it for a naval base.

349 HUDSON'S BAY (TCF, Jan) Irving Pichel; *genre:* Adventure; *locations:* Canada, Great Britain; *coding:* WWII, Brit, Fr; *biases:* Pro-British, Pro-French.

Paul Muni and his monstrous sidekick, "Gooseberry," are roguish fur traders in late 17th century New France (Canada). Their accents are egregious. They team up with a British subject and eventually, with the aid of his contacts in London, form the Hudson's Bay Company. The film is definitely pro-French and even more pro-Canadian (a co-belligerent with Britain against the Axis). In a revealingly ambiguous monologue, Muni states: "This country, Canada, like a pretty woman, needs a big strong fellow.... Those fellows live in Europe crazy. They fight all the time for a little piece of dirt."

350 I WANTED WINGS (Para, May) Mitchell Leisen; *genre:* Training/Drama; *location:* United States; *coding:* Home Def, For Corr, Blk, Hist Am, AF-AC, Mil Exer, WWII, Nazi; *biases:* Pro-Military, Preparedness.

Although the *MPH* Review stated that *I Wanted Wings* is "never a preachment, never propaganda," the film's opening title solemnly declares that "America today watches her skies with grave concern" and through her growing air corps "the Nation is building the upper battlements of its defense." Paramount's top box office draw of 1941 probably owed less of its financial success to patriotism and more to the highly publicized appearance in the cast of Veronica Lake, a new long-tressed actress dubbed the "Blond Bomber" in the studio's media campaign. The story centers around the lives of three socially disparate pilot trainees. The blue blood, Jefferson Young, III (Ray Milland), eventually finds happiness with a lady photographer. She shows him a composite photo of the ideal American airman, "Joe Yankee," and comments, "You'll never catch this guy goosestepping in a colored shirt with his arm stretched out." But the working class cadet (William Holden), must overcome assorted personal crises created by Lake's sultry bad girl before he is given a second chance to win the coveted wings of a pilot in the U.S. Army Air Corps. There is extensive actual footage, including the first interior shots shown to the public, of America's top-of-the-line bomber, the B-17 "Flying Fortress."

351 ICE CAPADES (Rep, Aug) Joseph Santley; *genre:* Comedy; *location:* United States; *coding:* AF-A, WWII, Draft, Draft Avoid, Latin Am, Brit, Ger, Czech, Am Icons, Good Neighbor; *bias:* Pro-American.

A cameraman for the National Newsreel Company gets into trouble when he promotes footage he shot of a beautiful girl (Vera Hruba) skating in a local park as that of a touring Swiss star. On that basis the producer of the Ice Capades had previously signed her without an audition. When she refuses to cooperate, the newsreel company

is sued. It turns out that she is an illegal alien from Sweden who is fearful of deportation. Contemporary references appear in several of the comic exchanges between the cameraman's sidekick, played by Jerry Colonna and the man-hungry character portrayed by Barbara Jo Allen. For instance, when Barbara suggests marriage to Jerry over the phone, he delivers the following response: "What a horrible way of dodging the draft."

352 IN THE NAVY (Univ, May) Arthur Lubin; *genre:* Comedy/Training; *locations:* United States, Pacific; *coding:* AF-N, Blk, Am Icons, Fil, WWII; *bias:* Pro-Military.

A plug for *Buck Privates*, q.v., is made during the opening credits of this film. Songboy Russ Raymond (Dick Powell) joins the Navy under an alias in order to escape his over-adoring female fans. While in training in San Diego and, later, aboard the battleship *USS Alabama* bound for Pearl Harbor, he must suffer as an aggressive female photographer and the antics of Abbot and Costello (in April 1940 the Pacific Fleet was ordered to remain indefinitely in Hawaii). Possible future military foes of Uncle Sam are twice musically warned, in the title song: "Any galoot who wants a dispute, will get it in the neck." The Andrews Sisters, wearing ridiculous operetta-style uniforms with oversized epaulettes, entertain the naval trainees in San Diego with a musical number whose lyrics include: "These are perilous times.../ To protect us from any and all possible enemies.../ While there's still a world left to see,/ You're off to sea to see the world."

353 INTERNATIONAL LADY (UA, Sept) Tim Whelan; *genre:* Spy; *locations:* Great Britain, United States, Portugal, Canada; *coding:* AF-Ger, Intell Serv, Dipl, US-Brit Coop, WWII, Goering, Ref, Nor, FBI, Am Vol, FDR, Brit, Spy-Sab, Ger, War Mats, Collab, Am Icons, AF-Brit, Nazi; *biases:* Pro-Intervention, Anti-Espionage, Anti-German.

Carla Nilson (Ilona Massey), a singing Axis agent who claims to be a Norwegian refugee, leaves war-torn London to make contact with a gang of Nazi saboteurs and spies operating in New York City. Carla's songs are coded so that when she makes broadcasts for a chocolate manufacturer's radio show, the Germans are alerted to exactly when and where flights of American-built "Flying Fortresses" are departing for Britain. A Scotland Yard man (Basil Rathbone) and an FBI agent (George Brent) join forces to break up the gang of enemy agents, which includes a doctor perfecting a chemical additive which will sabotage the planes' engines. Carla changes her tune after falling in love with her handsome FBI nemesis. The musical code-used-by-spies motif was not new: *Dishonored* (Para., 1931),

Madame Spy (Univ., 1934), *The Lady Vanishes* (Gaumont, 1938), for example.

354 INTERNATIONAL SQUADRON (WB, Oct) Lothar Mendes, Lewis Seiler; *genre:* War Drama; *locations:* United States, Great Britain; *coding:* Home Def, Am Vol, AF-RAF, War Mats, US-Brit Coop, WWII, AF-Ger, Free Fr, AF-A, Hitler, Churchill, Czech, Pol, Belg, Latin Am, Am Icons; *biases:* Pro-Intervention, Pro-British.

This was a militarized remake of the 1936 Howard Hawks' film *Ceiling Zero* (WB). The *Motion Picture Herald* review noted: "Here are today's thrills for today's audiences." American test pilot Jimmy Grant (Ronald Reagan) flies the first "Saunders" bomber to Britain. There, the girl-chasing Jimmy refuses the entreaties of some old flying buddies to enlist in the RAF, but changes his mind after witnessing the death of a child during the London Blitz. Jimmy joins the RAF's International Squadron, but his irresponsibility indirectly leads to the death of a compatriot who was flying a mission to which Jimmy has been assigned. Jimmy redeems himself by bumping a pal from a near-suicidal bombing mission over France. He perishes in a ball of fire after vanquishing a group of "Jerry" (German) fighters. Documentary footage, including shots of German aircraft and their crews in action, was integrated into the film's combat sequences.

355 JUNGLE MAN (PRC, Oct) Harry Fraser; *genre:* Drama; *location:* Africa; *coding:* WWII, Blk; *bias:* Contraband Message.

A jaded American girl named Betty and her fiance come to Africa to visit her missionary uncle and search for treasure in the fabled Dead City. But then Betty meets and falls in love with a handsome doctor, played by Buster Crabbe. The doctor, called Junga by the natives, has worked five years to perfect a serum to cure the "dread Malaka fever." When Betty is stricken with the fever Junga must dive for the serum in the hulk of a sunken ship. The first experimental batch, produced in the United States, was lost when the ship was torpedoed by a German U-Boat while unloading its cargo onto lighters.

356 KEEP 'EM FLYING (Univ, Nov) Arthur Lubin; *genre:* Comedy/Training; *location:* United States; *coding:* AF-AC, AF-N, AF-MC, USO, V, Am Icons; *bias:* Pro-Military.

In their third service film, Abbott and Costello (after a joke about *Buck Privates*, q.v.) collide with the expanding Army Air Corps and twin sisters played by Martha Raye. Though unskilled, the boys are allowed to become "grease monkeys" after Lou delivers an impassioned patriotic monologue: "There must be something for a lit-

tle guy like me to do ... in the biggest team we've ever had." During the carnival sequence the number of extras in uniforms, representing the three major services, is conspicuously large. In the concluding musical number we are treated to singing airmen with planes flying overhead in complimentary 'V' for victory formations. With an increasingly martial atmosphere developing in America the phrase, "Keep 'Em Flying," had become a popular (and patriotic) form of greeting by the summer of 1941.

357 KING OF THE ZOMBIES (Mono, May) Jean Yarbrough; *genre:* Fantasy/Comedy; *location:* Caribbean; *coding:* Blk, Spy-Sab, Ger, Ref, AF-N, Atroc, Collab, Secret Plans, AF-AC; *bias:* Anti-Espionage.

The *Motion Picture Herald* review noted: "Although the story is treated seriously ... it is as a comedy rather than as a thriller that it succeeds." A meteorologist (Dick Purcell) and his black valet (Mantan Moreland) are passengers on an Army plane that crashes on an island near Puerto Rico. A mysterious Dr. Sangre (Henry Victor; a regular Nazi villain in both British and Hollywood films), his wife and niece come to their aid. But it turns out that the doctor with a heavy accent is a master of zombies, hypnotist and foreign agent. In fact, Sangre has already imprisoned an Admiral whose plane crashed on the island a week earlier and is attempting to extract from him Navy defense plans for the Panama Canal. Eventually the supernatural forces are patriotically overcome. Monogram used zombies under foreign (Nazi) influence once again in the 1943 release, *Revenge of the Zombies*, q.v.

358 LADY BE GOOD (MGM, Sept) Norman Z. McLeod; *genre:* Musical Comedy; *location:* United States; *coding:* Hist Am, Chi, Ital, Fr, Blk, WWII; *biases:* Anti-German, Contraband Message.

This film features a song-writing team (Ann Sothern and Robert Young) that cannot quite get its romantic rhythm together. In the middle of the film a Jerome Kern-Oscar Hammerstein song obliquely referring to the German occupation of France is performed. "The Last Time I Saw Paris" is introduced as a "tender and affectionate salute to a lost city": "The last time I saw Paris/ Her heart was warm and gay/ No matter how they change her/ I'll remember her that way."

359 THE LADY EVE (Para, Mar) Preston Sturges; *genre:* Comedy; *locations:* Latin America, Atlantic, United States; *coding:* Brit, WWII, Hitler, Hist Am, Ital; *bias:* Contraband Message.

This is a romantic farce featuring Barbara Stanwyck as a femme fatale con artist and Henry Fonda as the rich ingenue. There are

a couple of comments about the boats not "running," i.e., passenger ships not crossing the Atlantic due to the submarine threat. In addition, Fonda's man Friday, Mr. Morgatroy, ("Muggsy") with a coatbrush held above his lip, imitates Hitler as he does a German double-talk routine.

360 LAND OF LIBERTY [made for '39 World's Fair] (MGM, Jan) Cecil B. DeMille (ed.); *genre:* Historical Drama; *location:* United States; *coding:* Blk, Hist Am, Am Icons, WWI, Jap, Italo-Eth War, Musso, AF-Ger, Hitler, Good Neighbor, Brit, FDR, League Nat; *bias:* Pro-American.

Beginning with the Revolution, this compilation film sponsored by the Motion Picture Producers and Distributers of America, Inc., tells America's story by using selected scenes from 112 features and shorts. Some of the films used were *The Big Parade* (MGM), *The President Vanishes* (Para.) *Drums Along the Mohawk*, q.v. and *Mr. Smith Goes to Washington*, q.v. The post 1900 section is predominantly composed of newsreel footage. Shots of Mussolini, Hitler and the Japanese invasion of Manchuria are included. At the film's conclusion God and FDR are invoked. The film was originally shown at the 1939 World's Fair. It was subsequently cut from 138 to 98 minutes and released by MGM with profits designated for war relief.

361 LET'S GO COLLEGIATE (Mono, Sept) Jean Yarbrough; *genre:* Musical Comedy; *location:* United States; *coding:* Chi, Blk, Draft, AF-A; *biases:* Pro-Military, Contraband Message.

Two fraternity brothers promise their favorite coeds that their college will have a winning rowing team. Unfortunately, their number one boatman has just been drafted, so they pick up a brawny truck driver named Herk and pass him off as the star athlete. After helping the team win Herk is arrested by the police for his involvement in a bank robbery. To cover their hoax the frat boys announce that their top rower was "drafted" by the government. This late 1941 release was the only pre-war film to directly refer to a man being drafted out of college.

362 LOOK WHO'S LAUGHING (RKO, Nov) Allan Dwan; *genre:* Comedy; *location:* United States; *coding:* AF-A, FDR-E, Fr, Latin Am, Prod, US-Brit Coop; *biases:* Pro-Intervention, Contraband Message.

Charlie McCarthy, with an assist from Edgar Bergen, flies into Wistful Vista to save Fibber McGee and Molly from disgrace and financial disaster. The term "sabotage" is used several times, the "Marseillaise" is played, and Charlie receives a quarter for a chocolate soda under the "Lend-Lease Plan." The Lend-Lease Act became law on March 11, 1941. It authorized the President to sell, transfer, lease, etc., war equipment and commodities to the "government of any country whose defense the President deems vital to the defense of the United States."

363 LOUISIANA PURCHASE (Para, Dec) Irving Cummings; *genre:* Musical Comedy; *location:* United States; *coding:* Austr, Blk, Latin Am, FDR, FDR-E, Draft, Ref, FBI, WWII, Hitler?, Musso?; *bias:* Pro-American.

In this Technicolor version of a Broadway hit, Bob Hope plays Jim Taylor, a shady small-time politico in Louisiana. He is designated as the fall guy by four nervous New Orleans grafters when it is learned that the head of a Senate committee investigating corruption will be visiting the state. With the reluctant aid of a couple of ladies, Jim compromises the bumbling senator. One of the ladies is a beautiful young refugee from Vienna who is trying to raise the money needed to purchase a passport for her mother. In one scene the Senator states: "Every time I think of Washington [D.C.], I cry." Jim retorts: "I know a couple of guys in Europe [Hitler and Mussolini] who feel the same way." In another scene, in which Jim has been stripped of all his clothes, he quips, "Here I am, caught in the draft again" (an "in" joke referring to Hope's earlier 1941 Paramount release, *Caught in the Draft*, q.v.).

364 LOVE CRAZY (MGM, May) Jack Conway; *genre:* Comedy; *location:* United States; *coding:* Hist Am, Blk, Span Civ; *bias:* Contraband Message.

A happily married couple, played by William Powell and Myrna Loy, is about to celebrate their fourth wedding anniversary when their domestic tranquillity is shattered by the arrival of the wife's domineering mother. After the missus demands a divorce, the husband hatches a series of mad schemes to prevent it, including impersonating Lincoln and appearing in drag as his spinster sister. In one of the many comic altercations, the Spanish Loyalist rallying cry is invoked, "They Shall Not Pass!" A "propaganda" crack is also made.

365 LUCKY DEVILS (Univ, Jan) Lew Landers; *genre:* Spy; *location:* United States; *coding:* Spy-Sab, Ger, Secret Weapon, FBI; *biases:* Anti-Espionage, Anti-German.

Mercury Newsreel's number one cameraman, Dick McManus (Richard Arlen), is almost fired after his cinematic pursuits lead to the crash of a secret robot bomber. In his continued quest for scoops, Dick does manage to get his teletypist girlfriend fired. Returning to the office late one night, he and his pal Andy (Andy Devine) discover two men rifling the Mercury film files for shots the camera crew had taken of a strategic dam.

Ritter and Berko, who are foreign agents, escape with the films they need to complete their sabotage plans. After a few plot twists, Dick and Andy are able to capture the foreign agents and turn them over to the FBI. The two heroes are rewarded with the resolution of their romantic difficulties.

366 LYDIA (UA, Sept) Julien Duvivier; *genre:* Drama; *location:* United States; *coding:* World Crisis, Hist Am, Am Icons, WWII?, V?; *bias:* Pro-American.

Only at the beginning of this nostalgic romantic melodrama is the present allowed to intrude. Over the radio we hear, along with actor Joseph Cotten, the Mayor of New York City dedicating a new orphanage: "In this era of destruction ... above all the flags of destruction in the world today ... the flag of humanity still flies high [in America]...."

367 MAN AT LARGE (TCF, Sept) Eugene Forde; *genre:* Spy; *locations:* Canada, United States; *coding:* Nazi, AF-Ger, FBI, Spy-Sab, AF-N, Collab, Fifth Col, Ital, WWII, US-Brit Coop, AF-Brit, Intell Serv; *biases:* Anti-Nazi, Pro-British, Anti-Espionage.

British Naval Intelligence fakes the escape of a captured *Luftwaffe* pilot from a Canadian internment camp. An FBI agent (George Reeves) posing as a newsman and a British agent pretending to be the "Nazi ace," Colonel von Rahn, successfully use the ruse to infiltrate an enemy espionage ring in America reporting on the formation of convoys to Britain. Despite the unintended sabotage of a vivacious female reporter named Dallas, it is only a matter of a few reels before the G-Man and his British cohort are able to neutralize the ruthless spies. The predominantly German spy ring thinks nothing of murdering an Italian member, Dr. Cataloni, when they learn he has been identified by the FBI. The terms "Nazi" and "fifth columnist" are repeatedly invoked throughout the film, particularly by Dallas. In January 1941 a German air force lieutenant jumped from a train in Canada carrying POWs and escaped to the United States. The American press exploited the story after the pilot was picked up by authorities.

368 A MAN BETRAYED aka WHEEL OF FORTUNE (Rep, Feb) John H. Auer; *genre:* Drama; *location:* United States; *coding:* Ital, Hitler, Musso, Draft, WWII, AF-A; *biases:* Anti-Nazi, Contraband Message.

A hick lawyer (John Wayne) comes to the big city to solve the murder of a hometown college basketball player. There are references to the draft and to the German bombing of London. The fascist leaders also rate a couple of cracks, including one that alludes to the realities of the so-called "Pact of Steel" alliance between Germany and Italy: "Came-

ron's got me sewed-up tighter than Hitler has Mussolini."

369 MAN HUNT (TCF, Jun) Fritz Lang; *genre:* Adventure; *locations:* Great Britain, Germany, Denmark; *coding:* Hitler, Nazi, Spy-Sab, Dipl, Pol, Den, Atroc, Appeasement, AF-Ger, WWII, AF-Brit, AF-RAF; *biases:* Anti-Nazi, Pro-British.

In July of 1939, Alan Thorndike (Walter Pidgeon), a world famous English hunter, is captured by the Nazis following an apparent attempt to assassinate their *Fuhrer* at Berchtesgarden. When his monocled interrogator (George Sanders) threatens him with death, the hunter calmly assures the arrogant Nazi that it was "only a sporting stalk" of the "strutting little Caesar." The "decadent" Englishman is then tortured in an attempt to force him to sign a false confession. He manages to escape, but is pursued by malevolent Nazis across Europe, through the film noir streets of London and, finally, to a burrow in the Scottish countryside. Having survived these encounters and with his nation now at war with Hitler's regime, Captain Thorndike is shown at the film's conclusion parachuting into Germany with a sniper's rifle. An offscreen narrator intones that "this time, he clearly knows his purpose...."

370 MARRIED BACHELOR (MGM, Oct) Edward Buzzell; *genre:* Comedy; *location:* United States; *coding:* WWII, Jap, Draft Avoid; *bias:* Contraband Message.

After separating from his wife, a man becomes an overnight celebrity with the publication, under his name, of an eccentric professor's book entitled, *A Bachelor Looks At Marriage*. Because the book receives a "bigger spread in the paper than the war" the alleged author, "Dr." Randolph Haven, goes on the lecture circuit. During a question and answer segment on a radio broadcast, he takes a call from a woman complaining about her husband's drinking; she claims he only married her "to avoid the draft." Guess who is the show's next caller? Interestingly, the masquerading doctor has a Japanese houseboy. Although Japanese servants had been very chic in mid–30s films, such an appearance in late 1941 is highly unusual.

371 MATA HARI (Re-r '31) (MGM, June) George Fitzmaurice; *genre:* Spy; *location:* France; *coding:* WWI, AF-Fr, AF-Ger, AF-Russ, Spy-Sab; *bias:* Pacifist.

This was another topical re-release. This time it concerns the infamous World War I female German spy, Mati Hari, played by the inimitable Greta Garbo.

372 MEET BOSTON BLACKIE (Col, Feb) Robert Florey; *genre:* Crime/Spy; *location:* United States; *coding:* Spy-Sab, Secret Weapon, Draft, AF-N, Neth; *bias:* Anti-Espionage.

This was the first of thirteen B-films starring Chester Morris as "Boston Blackie," the former safecracker turned wisecracker. Though preferring to work on his own, he frequently gives aid to the fatuous forces of the law. Returning to New York aboard an oceanliner from Europe, Blackie becomes implicated in robbery and murder. In his attempt to clear himself he uncovers the Coney Island headquarters of a spy ring. With an assist from his friendly police nemesis, the murderous foreign agents, who were attempting to smuggle a dive bombing site out of the country, are apprehended.

373 MEET JOHN DOE (WB, May) Frank Capra; *genre:* Drama; *location:* United States; *coding:* Indig Fasc Org, AF-A, Am Icons, Hist Am, WWII, Blk, Chi, Fifth Col, FDR?, WWI, Mil School; *biases:* Anti-Fascist, Pro-American.

This is a troubling exploration of the inherent weaknesses of American democracy that questions the very values Capra had repeatedly promoted in such films as *Mr. Deeds Goes to Town* (1936) and *Mr. Smith Goes to Washington* (1939), q.v. The rise of fascism is obviously viewed here as presenting a unique threat to American values. The incipient home style totalitarianism is personified by the corpulent business magnate, D. B. Norton, and his para-military apparatus can only be defeated by a free and united citizenry. John Doe's (Gary Cooper) radio speech, written by the lady reporter who created him, encapsulates this theme: "We're the people and we're tough.... A free people can beat the world at anything— from war to tiddly-winks ... [if we] tear down the fences of hate and prejudice.... Wake up John Doe—you're the hope of the world."

374 MEXICAN SPITFIRE'S BABY (RKO, Nov) Leslie Goodwins; *genre:* Comedy; *location:* United States; *coding:* Brit, Fr, WWI, WWII, Ref, Latin Am; *bias:* Contraband Message.

Uncle Matt cables dipsomaniacal Lord Epping in England (both characters are played by Leon Errol) to bring over a "war orphan" for the newlywed Spitfire to adopt. But pandemonium ensues when the Lord stumbles off the trans-Atlantic Clipper with a buxom blonde French girl named Fifi who was orphaned by the "last war."

375 MICHAEL SHAYNE, PRIVATE DETECTIVE (TCF, Jan) Eugene Forde; *genre:* Crime; *location:* United States; *coding:* Draft, Brit; *bias:* Contraband Message.

This was the premiere episode in the Fox B-series starring Lloyd Nolan as an Irish-American investigator. In this film he becomes embroiled in a gambling related murder while trying to keep the daughter of a client, the racing commissioner, out of trouble. The police visit her home in search of Shayne. The following exchange takes place at the door between Chief Painter and the middle-aged English butler, Ponsby:

Painter: We're from headquarters.
Ponsby: I'm over the conscription age.
Painter: Police headquarters!
Ponsby: Oh, the cops, Madam.

376 MILLION DOLLAR BABY (WB, May) Curtis Bernhardt; *genre:* Comedy/Drama; *locations:* Switzerland, United States; *coding:* WWII, Fifth Col, Am Icons, Nat Def, Ital, Hist Am, Blk, Belg; *biases:* Pro-American, Anti-Espionage, Contraband Message.

Cornelia Wheelwright (May Robson), a cantankerous wealthy American living in neutral Switzerland, is informed by her lawyer that her father made his fortune over thirty years ago by defrauding his business partner. Despite the lawyer's concerns about war conditions, the elderly lady immediately arranges to return to America aboard the Clipper out of Lisbon in order to arrange a meeting with the partner's heirs. When Cornelia's pompous manner with an American customs officer leads to a body search, the flabbergasted dowager asks if she is suspected of being a Fifth Columnist. The only heir is Pamela McAllister, a young girl who works as a vegetable cutter demonstrator at a department store: "It cuts cucumbers into five-point stars suitable for patriotic salads...." After Pamela gives away the million dollars given her by Cornelia so that she and her musician/composer boyfriend can make it on their own, Cornelia tells her lawyer: "I've just discovered America.... It's youngsters like that, that make you have faith in the future."

377 MISTER DYNAMITE (Univ, Mar) Jack Rawlins; *genre:* Spy; *location:* United States; *coding:* FBI, Can, Spy-Sab, War Mats, Prod, Am-Brit, Am Icons; *bias:* Anti-Espionage.

The star pitcher (Lloyd Nolan) of the World Series-bound "St. Louis Robins" becomes involved in espionage when he meets a girl named Vicki (Irene Hervey) at a gaming concession in New York City's "Bagdad" section. Vicki and her murdered compatriot are Canadian agents battling it out with enemy saboteurs responsible for the destruction of several munitions plants. The spies, led by Paul (Robert Armstrong), use a ventriloquist's dummy to transmit their signals (refer to *Mr. Moto's Last Warning*; 1939). The baseball player successfully comes to Vicki's aid and then goes off to pitch his team to the championship. There had actually been a major munitions factory explo-

sion in New Jersey in late 1940 in which sabotage was suspected. Continuing public fears of fifth columnist activities would culminate in a 1941 Memorial Day sabotage scare.

378 MOON OVER MIAMI (TCF, July) Walter Lang; *genre:* Musical Comedy; *location:* United States; *coding:* Latin Am, Draft; *bias:* Contraband Message.

Two young sisters from Texas, played by Betty Grable and Carol Landis, arrive in a Technicolor Florida in search of rich husbands. Grable winds up with a charming, but penniless, Don Ameche, while her sibling lands a millionaire played by Robert Cummings. There is the usual Conga number at the nightclub and a topical crack about one of the male leads getting "caught in the draft."

379 MURDER ON LENNOX AVE (Ind, ?) Arthur Dreifuss; *genre:* Crime; *location:* United States; *coding:* WWI, Blk, Vets, WWII?; *bias:* Contraband Message.

A "Better Business League" is promoted in Harlem to help fight for the "future of our race." One of its members is a proud black veteran of WWI who marches in uniform on "Decoration Day" (Memorial Day). At the beginning of the film, a jazz band practicing in an apartment building leads to a scuffle between an enraged tenant and a member of the band. While separating the two a cop asks: "What's the matter with you boys? Ain't there enough strife in this world without you boys starting a private war?"

380 MY LIFE WITH CAROLINE (RKO, Aug) Lewis Milestone; *genre:* Comedy; *location:* United States; *coding:* WWII, Latin Am, Pol, Ref, Churchill; *biases:* Pro-British, Contraband Message.

An urbane New York publisher, played by Ronald Colman, relates to audience in flashback form how he must handle his flighty wife's periodic romantic encounters with rich, young men. The *Variety* review concludes with the following observation: "Unusual—and perhaps a bit objectionable to those who don't like their propaganda smeared between halves of a domestic comedy—is an extraneous scene which finds Colman (a Britisher) fondling a bulldog. "I don't know your name," he says to the tough-looking pooch, "so I'll call you Winston." The scene is preceded by a flourish of "Hail Britannia" on the soundtrack and concludes with Colman shaking the dog's paw.

381 MYSTERY SHIP (Col, Sept) Lew Landers; *genre:* War Drama; *location:* United States, Atlantic; *coding:* Spy-Sab, Ger, WWII, War Mats, Brit, AF-N, FBI, For Corr; *bias:* Anti-German.

A couple of G-Men are secretly assigned to escort a group of criminal aliens imprisoned aboard a ship who are being deported to an unnamed country across the Atlantic war zone. Many of the aliens have Germanic surnames. They are led by Condor (as in vulture; Hitler's Kondor Legion that fought in Spain), who engineers their escape and violent seizure of the ship. Condor then forces the head G-Man's reporter fiancee, who had stowed away to get a story, to send a coded wireless message to representatives of an unspecified foreign power (obviously meant to be Germany). But our star G-Man, played by Paul Kelly, has meanwhile hidden in a field ambulance strapped to the deck that is equipped with a portable radio and answers the message by instructing the ship to rendezvous with a convoy off the Portuguese coast. When the ship arrives at the designated point it is greeted by several American destroyers and the undesirable aliens are recaptured. In fact, a U.S. naval squadron based in French Mediterranean ports that was established in 1936 to evacuate American citizens in Spain and keep an eye on troubled Europe remained on station until October 1940.

382 NAVAL ACADEMY (Col, May) Erle C. Kenton; *genre:* Drama; *location:* United States; *coding:* WWI, AF-N, Mil School; *bias:* Pro-Military.

Three freshmen, including a naval brat whose father was a World War I hero, enter the State Naval Academy preparatory school. The usual rights of passage take place. To quote the film's pressbook: "During the course of the ... picture, the three lads learn the true meaning of democracy and soon realize a youngster owes as great a duty to his fellows and to his country as he does himself."

383 NAVY BLUES (WB, Sept) Lloyd Bacon; *genre:* Musical Comedy; *location:* United States; *coding:* AF-A, AF-MC, Jap, Chi, Am Icons, FDR, Spy-Sab, AF-N, Latin Am, Natl Def; *bias:* Pro-Military.

Jack Oakie and Jack Haley play a couple of hustling, spendthrift gobs on the *USS Cleveland* who bet themselves into big trouble. In order to prevent a premature sea burial planned by swindled shipmates, they must convince the fleet's top "gun pointer," a former hog farmer, to re-enlist. Along the way, several songs are introduced and both the female leads are falsely arrested for spying on Hawaiian naval facilities.

384 NEVER GIVE A SUCKER AN EVEN BREAK (Univ, Oct) Edward Cline; *genre:* Comedy; *locations:* United States, Russia; *coding:* Russ, Nazi; *bias:* Contraband Message.

W. C. Fields, playing himself, relates a mad tale of romantic adventures in a mythical kingdom to a film producer at the "Esoteric" studios. In one scene of this farce, a

couple of goosestepping Nazis make a brief and unexplained appearance.

385 NICE GIRL? (Univ, Feb) William A. Seiter; *genre:* Drama; *location:* United States; *coding:* AF-AC, Am Icons, Brit?; *biases:* Pro-American, Pro-Military.

Deanna Durbin's small town nice girl reputation is in jeopardy when she falls for an older out of town city slicker played by Franchot Tone. Needless to say, the local beau wins out. The film concludes with a 4th of July celebration in which Deanna patriotically sings "Thank You America" to a group of soldiers from the air corps.

386 NO GREATER SIN (Ind, Fall) William Nigh; *genre:* Drama; *location:* United States; *coding:* Hist Am, Natl Def, Prod, AF-A, Fifth Col; *bias:* Pro-American.

A small midwestern town rapidly develops into a thriving industrial center due to "National Defense" contracts. To service the needs of the workers and of the soldiers at a nearby base an enterprising gangster has set up an entertainment complex at the edge of town known as the "Owl's Nest." The new health commissioner has his suspicions. He enlists the aid of a lady reporter and alerts the other local authorities. They are quick to cooperate. The military commander states: "While the Army is mechanizing its units, these women are motorizing their trade. They're the Army's own Fifth Column." But is it through the plight of a newlywed plant worker that the problem of social diseases is dramatized and the community properly educated. Congress passed the May Act, which empowered the military to police cities near bases and also gave them authority to close businesses involved in the vice trade.

387 ONE FOOT IN HEAVEN (WB, Nov) Irving Rapper; *genre:* Biography; *locations:* United States, Canada; *coding:* WWI, AF-A, Hist Am, Am Icons; *bias:* Pro-American.

Based on the actual experiences of Rev. William Spence (Fredric March) between 1904 and the mid–1920s, this episodic film portrays the story of a man who gets the "call" and becomes a Methodist minister. During World War I, Spence becomes the chaplain at a large U.S. Army facility. When his flag-waving parishioners visit his home to celebrate the Armistice, Spence solemnly reminds them of the men who will not return to America from the battlefields and then prays that their children will never be forced to go to war. But at the conclusion of his prayer, the minister intones that if we "must defend our democratic way of life [again, that God will] give us the strength."

388 ONE NIGHT IN LISBON (Para, Jun) Edward H. Griffith; *genre:* War Drama; *locations:* Great Britain, Portugal; *coding:*

AF-Ger, AF-W, Dipl, Brit, Intell Serv, Home Def, Spy-Sab, WWII, AF-Brit, AM Vol, War Mats, Hitler, Greek, Ital, Churchill, US-Brit Coop, Fr, Ger, Spa; *biases:* Pro-Intervention, Pro-British.

With the aid of duck calls, an American bomber ferry pilot in London named Houston (Fred MacMurray) courts a general's driver played by Madeleine Carroll. The film includes a suggestion that Hitler is mad and takes a mild swipe at the Italians when Houston is told by a Greek restaurant owner that they do not serve spaghetti, but do have "victory noodle strings." Minor complications arise for our Texan pilot and his new English lady when they become involved in espionage while on an Iberian tryst. At the film's conclusion, the spurned British suitor of Miss Carroll is told by a government official: "Nothing is more important than that England and America should hold fast to each other."

389 OUT OF THE FOG (WB, Jun) Anatole Litvak); *genre:* Drama; *location:* United States; *coding:* Jew, Russ, Nor, Lat Am, Hist Am, Am Icons, AF-A; *bias:* Anti-Fascist.

Allegorical—based on an Irwin Shaw play, *The Gentle People.* Out of the fog one dreary night along the docks in Brooklyn a man in a black trenchcoat with a menacing smile enters a small diner. Most of the habitues soon run out to observe a burning boat. The stranger Goff (John Garfield), meanwhile, goes back to the kitchen and makes friendly overtures to the Scandinavian cook (John Qualen). He is particularly interested in the small fishing boat Olaf co-owns with his Jewish tailor friend. Goff confidently assures the timid cook that it is not their boat that is on fire. The next evening Goff confronts the two fishermen at the docks and informs them that he is the "Admiral Dewey of Brooklyn" who will protect their boat from pirates for five dollars a week—or else. Goodwin, the tailor played by Thomas Mitchell, protests at first, but then reluctantly agrees to pay-off the fascistic gangster. Before long, though, Goff has entranced the tailor's daughter (Ida Lupino) and demands the kindly man's life's savings in order to take her on a trip to Havana. When Goff comes for the money, he mocks the tailor and cook with a fascist salute. After the tailor attempts to get help from the law Goff beats him with a rubber hose. Pushed to the brink, the Scandinavian and his Jewish friend plot to eliminate their tormentor. When Olaf warily states all he has ever wanted is peace, the tailor responds that you cannot appease "airplanes with bombs and men with guns in their pockets." Tricked onto the boat of the two fishermen whom he alludes to as "inferior people," they try to kill him. But these simple, ordinary men, lack the killer instinct. Nonetheless, Goff drowns when he tumbles overboard while struggling with his antagonists.

390 PAPER BULLETS (PRC, Jun) Phil Rosen; *genre:* Drama; *location:* United States; *coding:* Prod, Blk; *bias:* Contraband Message.

The daughter of an ex-con loses her job at a factory that has just "started defense orders" because she cannot be bonded. She turns to crime and later becomes involved in political corruption. Sentenced to a long term in prison, her aircraft engineer husband promises to wait.

391 PARACHUTE BATTALION (RKO, Sept) Leslie Goodwins; *genre:* Training; *location:* United States; *coding:* World Crisis, AF-A, Am Icons, Mil Exer, WWI, AF-AC; *bias:* Pro-Military.

The son (Edmund O'Brien) of the commanding officer, a rich college football hero (Robert Preston) and a hillbilly (Buddy Ebsen) are among the new recruits who are accepted for training to become paratroopers in the rapidly expanding U.S. Army. Between choruses of "The Parachute Infantry," the usual bonding through shared adversity takes place. The center of romantic interest is the daughter (Nancy Kelly) of the base Master Sergeant (Harry Carey). Although the "last war" is mentioned and the new paratroopers attack an "enemy village" during summer maneuvers, no reference is made to the second World War. This film was made with the direct assistance of the 501st Parachute Battalion at Fort Benning, Georgia. A Major Fite was also credited with contributing to the screenplay.

392 THE PENALTY (MGM, Mar) Harold S. Bucquet; *genre:* Crime; *location:* United States; *coding:* AF-N, FBI, WWII?, AF-AC; *biases:* Pro-Military, Contraband Message.

Rusty, the spoiled son of a gangster on the lam, is placed by the court in the custody of a farm family. The embittered teen resents his rural hosts and runs away. The local school teacher comes along and gives Rusty a ride. Rusty confides his plans to "join the Navy.... I want to get in the fighting right away." Returned to the farm, Rusty is eventually won over through the selfless love of the family. When cantankerous "Grandpop" (Lionel Barrymore) learns that Rusty can fly an airplane, they talk of joining the Flying Corps. Rusty's comment about the Navy may have been an early allusion to the growing possibilities of a naval war with the Germans. And, in fact, as a result of its expanded convoy duties, the first hostile exchange between a U.S. Navy destroyer and a German

U-boat took place in April (a month after the film's release).

393 PLAYMATES (RKO, Dec) David Butler; *genre:* Musical Comedy; *location:* United States; *coding:* Am Icons, Latin Am, USO, Draft, WWII; *bias:* Pro-American.

Another "adventure of the band farce," this post–Pearl Harbor release features Kay Kyser and his orchestra. Similar band films include *Second Chorus* (Par.) from 1940 with Artie Shaw's group and the Glen Miller Band in 1941 in *Sun Valley Serenade,* q.v. In the film's opening club number, Kay and the guys swing to "Thank Your Lucky Stars and Stripes." The lyrics include these lines: "...there's so much to be thankful for these days ... If you live right, if you get to sleep at night ... If you feel free, if there's sugar in your tea ... If you can sing, and believe in anything ... If you can have shoes, and can say the things you choose ... if you think its worth your while to save it, wave it ... you can thank your lucky Stars and Stripes."

The simple plot centers around Shakespearean actor John Barrymore (playing himself) who is forced to do a show with Kay in order to pay his back taxes. The IRS man reminds Barrymore that "Uncle Sam is in no mood for trifling at this moment."

394 POT O' GOLD (UA, Apr) George Marshall; *genre:* Musical Comedy; *locations:* United States, Canada; *coding:* AF-MC, WWI, Hist Am, Chi, Blk, Draft, Latin Am; *biases:* Pro-Military, Contraband Message.

An eccentric small town music store operator named James Hamilton Haskell (James Stewart) is visited by his rich uncle, a successful health food manufacturer from New York City. The film centers around the efforts of James to cajole the crusty music-hating uncle into putting a friend's swing band on the old man's radio show. While in jail for hitting his uncle with a ripe tomato, James (on harmonica) and his cellmates perform an extended rendition of Irving Berlin's World War I doughboy song "You Gotta Get Up in the Morning." When a $1000 weekly giveaway is announced as a promotion for the radio show, they are informed by a government representative that it must be conducted in such a way that people from all over the country are given an equal chance. One suggestion offered is to have a drawing and to borrow the "glass bowl they used for the draft numbers." This was a direct reference to the draft lottery that was conducted on October 30, 1940. Incidentally, actor Stewart would enter the armed forces in the summer.

395 POWER DIVE (Para, Apr) James Hogan; *genre:* Adventure; *location:* United States; *coding:* Secret Weapon, AF-AC; *bias:* Pro-Military.

Test pilot balderdash concerning a new speed plane, a "geodetic—plastic plane," is given a fillip by its preparedness undertones. The Army accepts the plane, the pilot gains fame and the kid brother gets the girl.

396 PUBLIC ENEMIES (Rep, Oct) Albert S. Rogell; *genre:* Drama; *location:* United States; *coding:* Hitler, Musso, Fr, WWII, Chi, Brit, Fifth Col, Ger, Hess; *biases:* Contraband Message, Anti-Fascist.

Bill Raymond, a hot-shot police reporter, falls in love with a pretty heiress and tangles with some gangsters who are involved in smuggling aliens. Bill excitedly tells his editor: "I'm on the trail of the biggest story since Hess landed in England." Bill also notes that Bonnie, his society girl, had once been engaged to a European baron named Eric. But, one day Bonnie attended a military parade and was repulsed by the hatred and arrogance she saw in the eyes of the thousands of marching men. Bill, with the aid of a couple ex-boxer pals, rescues Bonnie after she is kidnapped by the gangsters. At one point Bill looks at Bonnie's legs and states: "You're being patriotic, wearing rayon stockings." After the Roosevelt administration embargoed oil and scrap iron supplies to Japan in the summer of 1941, the Japanese suspended silk shipments to the United States.

397 RAGE IN HEAVEN (MGM, Mar) R. Sinclair, W.S. Van Dyke; *genre:* Drama; *locations:* Great Britain, France; *coding:* Brit, Ref; *bias:* Contraband Message.

In the late 1930s, the young owner of the Monrell Steel mills escapes from the French mental hospital where he has been confined. He returns home to Britain where his family is unaware of his condition. Philip Monrell quickly charms and marries his mother's secretary, a beautiful European "refugee," played by Ingrid Bergman. Philip's mental state begins to deteriorate again, providing the melodramatic grist to propel the film through its remaining reels.

398 RAIDERS OF THE DESERT (Univ, Jul) Jack Rawlins; *genre:* Adventure; *location:* Mid East; *coding:* Arab, Am Vol, Collab, Fifth Col, War Mats, AF-Brit?; *bias:* Anti-Fascist.

In this action comedy, two Americans jump ship and proceed to a modern, progressive city in the Arabian desert which is run by an American expatriot. A native chieftain complains about the introduction of democracy and with the aid of his men attempts to drive the Americans out and enslave the people. The chieftain is aided by traitors working within the city. But with the aid of his American compatriots, our expatriot do-gooder is able to overcome the evil fascist types.

399 RISE AND SHINE (TCF, Nov) Allan Dwan; *genre:* Musical Comedy; *location:* United States; *coding:* WWII; *bias:* Contraband Message.

The cheer for the dumb football hero, played by Jack Oakie, is "Hail to our one man Blitz - Boly Baoleuciecwez!" He is kidnapped by gangsters in order to prevent him from playing.

400 ROAD SHOW (UA, Jan) H. Roach, H. Roach, Jr., G. Douglas; *genre:* Comedy; *location:* United States; *coding:* Blk, Span Civ; *bias:* Contraband Message.

Millionaire Drago Gaines has been wrongfully committed to the "Hopedale Club— For the Rest of Your Life" mental institution by a vindictive relative interested in controlling his estate. Drago escapes the asylum with a nutty "Colonel" played by Adolphe Menjou. The two fugitives join a bankrupt carnival owned by a sympathetic young lady (Carole Landis). The film concludes with a riot at the show's encampment when rival carnies try to take over. As a watermelon mortar is rigged to defend against the invaders, the Colonel melodramatically disclaims, "They shall not pass!"

401 ROAD TO ZANZIBAR (Para, Apr) Victor Schertzing; *genre:* Comedy; *location:* Africa; *coding:* Ital, Fr, Brit, Blk, Draft; *bias:* Contraband Message.

This was the second in the series of "Road" films starring Bob Hope and Bing Crosby as a couple of wise-cracking connivers. This time they are working carnival side shows in Africa (why not?). After selling the bogus diamond mine for $5,000 to a bad-tempered criminal type, the boys are forced to head for the interior. Along the way, they meet with a couple of lady Brooklynites and some hungry cannibals. A running gag is Crosby coming up with assorted mad schemes that are invariably dangerous to his partner's health. When Hope ("Fearless" Frazier) is rigged-up as a human cannonball at the side show, he quips: "Listen, I don't mind being drafted, but not as ammunition." "Sabotage" and "propaganda" cracks are also delivered by Hope.

402 ROAR OF THE PRESS (Mono, Apr) Phil Rosen; *genre:* Comedy; *location:* United States; *coding:* Prod, Pac, Fifth Col, Natl Def, Spy-Sab, Ger; *bias:* Anti-Espionage.

Wally Williams (Wallace Ford), a recently married police reporter in New York City, neglects his new wife while investigating the murder of Henderson, the pacifist leader of the Guard America Committee. In the process, he unveils a group of foreign agents (including the German-accented Detmar) who are engaging in the sabotage of national defense industries. After Wally and his wife are

kidnapped by the gang of fifth columnists, some of his fellow reporters and a gangster pal assist the police in rescuing the pair and capturing the saboteurs. It is revealed that the foreign agents had pushed Henderson out of his high rise office window after he learned they were using the Guard America Committee as a front for their activities.

403 ROOKIES ON PARADE (Rep, Apr) Joseph Santley; *genre:* Musical Comedy; *location:* United States; *coding:* AF-A, Draft, USO; *bias:* Pro-Military.

A down-and-out songwriter (Bob Crosby, bandleader brother of Bing) gets caught in the draft. He puts on an Army show out of pure greed, but abandons exploiting it after patriotic words from Army officials. The film's musical numbers include the title song, "You'll Never Get Rich," and "The Army Builds Men."

404 RUGGLES OF RED GAP (Re-r '35) (Para, July) Leo McCarey; *genre:* Comedy; *locations:* Great Britain, United States; *coding:* Brit, Hist Am, Am Icons, Blk; *biases:* Pro-American, Pro-British.

In this timely re-issue the perfect British butler, Marmaduke Ruggles (Charles Laughton), is lost in a card game by his aristocratic employer to an American nouveau rich. He goes to Red Gap, Washington in early 20th century America with his new "governor" where he is introduced to the democratic way of life. But he becomes discouraged and leaves "service." Friends of his take him to a saloon and implore him to stay in the "land of opportunity" where all are created equal, as Lincoln said at Gettysburg. However, no one at the saloon can recall just what Lincoln did say. That is, with the exception of Ruggles, who proceeds to eloquently render the speech. He then decides to stay and open a restaurant, the "Anglo-American Grill."

405 SAILORS ON LEAVE (Rep, Sept) Albert S. Rogell; *genre:* Comedy; *locations:* United States, Pacific; *coding:* Hist Am, AF-N, Chi, Am Icons; *bias:* Pro-Military.

This is another typical service film from the period. An elaborate interfleet bet is rigged by some sailors to get out of debt. It involves an "inheritance" conditional upon marriage. Naturally, all ends well when the "allergic to girls" gob actually falls in love. In one sequence, a super-patriotic Chinese cab driver nearly causes a wreck by saluting the American flag while he is driving!

406 THE SAINT IN PALM SPRINGS (RKO, Jan) Jack Hively; *genre:* Crime; *location:* United States; *coding:* WWI, AF-A, Ger, Spy-Sab, Ref, WWII; *bias:* Contraband Message.

Simon Templar (George Sanders) goes to the California desert resort to deliver three rare stamps worth $200,000 to their heir,

Elna Johnson. Her uncle had smuggled them out of the "old country" in Europe only to be murdered in New York. The Saint asks an old pickpocket buddy turned hotel dick why the heiress is working as a tennis instructor: "they was [rich] ... but then they got blitzkrieged or something." After a couple more murders, the stamps changing hands several times, and numerous flirtations, everything is sorted out.

407 SCOTLAND YARD (TCF, Apr) *genre:* Spy; *location:* Great Britain; *coding:* WWII, Spy-Sab, AF-Brit, Nor, Churchill, Nazi, AF-Ger, AF-Fr, Hitler, Belg, Ital, Latin Am, Dunkirk; *biases:* Anti-Espionage, Pro-British, Anti-German.

Most of the action takes place amidst a London wracked by the Blitz (the German bombing of St. Paul's Cathedral is specifically referred to and actual newsreel footage of its destruction is shown). An infamous jewel thief, Dakin Barrolles, played by the handsome English actor, Henry Wilcoxson, has fought bravely as an officer under an assumed name in both Norway and in France. With his face disfigured at Dunkirk, Dakin receives plastic surgery in a British military hospital that results in his looking identical to the missing in action Sir John Lasher, a prominent London banker in civilian life. Then blackmailing enemy spies who know the real Sir John is in a German POW camp enter the scene. Their leader, posing as a house servant, insists that the phony bank president order a large shipment of gold bullion: "Our country needs gold to bolster her credit in South America." For God and country our protagonist calls in his old Scotland Yard nemesis. For his patriotic efforts, Dakin is spared jail and allowed "to have a crack at those Jerries again." While in London Lady Sandra Lasher makes a point of patronizing the restaurant of a naturalized Italian friend. Later, at the Lasher country home, she is portrayed taking in children evacuated from London.

408 SERGEANT YORK (WB, Sept) Howard Hawks; *genre:* Biography, Training/Combat; *locations:* United States, France; *coding:* AF-Fr, Pacifism, Draft Avoid, WWI, Draft, Hist Am, Am Icons, Jew, AF-Brit, AF-A, AF-Ger; *biases:* Pro-American, Pro-Military, Anti-German.

This was an obvious cinematic attempt to overcome resistance to the new Selective Service Act. It makes use of the true story of a backwoods conscientious objector who went on to become a World War I hero. After a special furlough from training camp during which York (Gary Cooper) was given President Wilson's *History of the United States* to read, the soldier reports back to his commanding officer and solemnly states, "I guess

I'm a stayin' in this here army." York's closest companion in the Army is a Jew from the Bronx. Secretary of State Cordell Hull (1933–1944), a Tennessee congressman during the First World War, is portrayed in the film on three separate occasions. *Sergeant York* became the top money grosser of the year. It was promoted in a "V Campaign" by the interventionists. They were probably particularly pleased with the sentiments expressed by a British Tommy to York in the trenches: "You know, you Yanks got here just in the nick of time." Warner Bros.' publicity campaign for this film did not pull its punches: "[Sergeant York] comes to the screen ... [as] the result of World War II's menacing threat to democracy."

409 SHADOW OF THE THIN MAN (MGM, Nov) W. S. Van Dyke; *genre:* Crime; *location:* United States; *coding:* ?; *bias:* contraband Message.

The only topical reference in this comic crime series entry was the billing in the opening credits for "Major" W. S. Van Dyke, the film's director.

410 SINGAPORE WOMAN (WB, May) Jean Negulesco; *genre:* Drama; *location:* Singapore; *coding:* Brit, WWII, Prod, Russ; *bias:* Contraband Message.

An attractive American widow (Brenda Marshall) with a shaky past falls in love with a rubber plantation owner in Singapore. When he tells his English friend about a major business loan he received, the Britisher congratulates him and adds: "Now you'll really be able to help the defense program. They need that rubber in the States." The young lady prepares to reopen some tin mines that had been part of her late husband's estate. But then the supposedly dead spouse makes an appearance, complimenting her on her mining activities; "With this war and everything, the tin business ought to be flourishing." The blackmailing husband later drives off to be conveniently killed in a car wreck.

411 SIS HOPKINS (Rep, Apr) Joseph Santley; *genre:* Musical Comedy; *coding:* Blk, AF-A, Am Icons; *bias:* Pro-American.

Judy Canova plays Sis Hopkins, a talented hayseed who is adopted by her rich big-city uncle who foots the bill for her education at the State College. While traveling by train to school, Sis admonishes some of her fellow students who have been joking about the "rubes" they have seen working in the fields. Sis informs them that "those guys put potatoes on your tables" and then sings the patriotic "That Ain't Hay (It's the USA)." The topical lyrics include the following as the train passes one of the nation's new army bases: "They're a mighty big expense ... part of our national defense." As the star of a campus revue, Sis will later perform this song a second time for the show's finale. While she sings, students dressed as farmers, factory workers and soldiers march down the aisles of the theatre and onto the center of the stage.

412 SKYLARK (Para, Nov) Mark Sandrich; *genre:* Comedy; *location:* United States; *coding:* Span Civ, Pol, Fr, Sino-Jap War, Latin Am, Good Neighbor, WWII; *bias:* Pro-American.

Claudette Colbert plays a wife who becomes increasingly frustrated by her husband's overzealous promotion of his business interests. A domestic squabble on the subway results in a stereotypical socialist worker in leather cap petulantly pronouncing (East European accent) that they should be ashamed to: "...a time like this. With all the agony in Spain, Poland ... laid out ..., France ... a shamble, China ... rumbling like an earthquake." Following the divorce, her ex-husband has a hangover that is "longer than the Burma Road." Eventually, though, the errant lovers are reunited aboard a ship in Havana bound for South America. It seems he has found a higher calling as a representative for the U.S. government in discussions concerning "hemisphere defense."

413 SMILIN' THROUGH (MGM, Sept) Frank Borzage; *genre:* Drama; *location:* Great Britain; *coding:* Am Vol, AF-Brit, Brit, WWI; *bias:* Pro-British.

A Victorian Englishman is left an embittered man after his sweetheart is accidentally killed on their wedding day by a jealous lover. While the one man goes to America, the other retires to his small country estate. Aside from his memories, his only love is for the niece he has raised, played by Jeanette MacDonald. Following the outbreak of the first World War the local vicar proudly becomes an Army chaplain and the niece begins entertaining the troops at the nearby canteen. Trouble arises when the son of his former rival arrives from America to join the British Army. A developing affair between the niece and the handsome American (Gene Raymond) leads to an estrangement from her uncle. Having been disabled doing "my bit" on the front, the American returns to England to claim the woman he loves. This Technicolor version of a melodrama which had been filmed twice before, in 1922 and 1932, contains an obvious subtext promoting Anglo-British cooperation. In response to an inquiry as to why he plans to join up the American states: "Well I'm half English, and a scrap's a scrap."

414 THE SMILING GHOST (WB, Sept) Lewis Seiler; *genre:* Crime; *location:* United States; *coding:* Blk, Draft; *bias:* Contraband Message.

This formula mystery features a haunted house and an heiress whose fiancés keep dying. When a man hired to pose as her fiance helps find the murderer, and then reveals his love for a lady reporter, the aunt of the flustered heiress delivers the following topical line: "Why worry? He'd probably have been drafted right in the middle of the honeymoon."

415 SO ENDS OUR NIGHT (UA, Feb) John Cromwell; *genre:* Drama; *locations:* Germany, Czechoslovakia, France, Austria; *coding:* AF-Ger, Spy-Sab, Resist, Hitler, Ref, Jew, Russ, Nazi, Atroc-Conc; *bias:* Anti-Nazi.

This film was based on a contemporaneous Remarque novel, *Flotsam*. The story centers around a group of refugees in flight from Germany before the beginning of the Second World War. Because they have been denied passports by the Nazis, they are hounded and driven from country to country. Fredric March plays an anti-Nazi former German military officer who joins the political nomads following his escape from a concentration camp. He attaches himself to a young Jewish couple. But then he learns that his wife, whom he had left behind in Germany, is desperately ill. After promising the Nazis to betray his German cohorts, he is allowed to visit his wife in the hospital. Following her death he leaps through a window, carrying his Gestapo tormentor along with him. While in France, having finally procured passports, the young lovers make plans to take a boat to America.

416 SOUTH OF PANAMA (PRC, May) Jean Yarbrough; *genre:* Spy; *location:* Panama; *coding:* AF-Brit, Secret Weapon, Spy-Sab, Latin Am, AF-A; *bias:* Anti-Espionage.

Although the film has nothing to do with the British, it was dedicated to the RAF. The plot centers around a new camouflage paint for airplanes invented by the hero and the attempts of foreign agents to steal its formula. During Army demonstrations conducted in Panama the good guys and gals overcome the opposition and even have time to introduce a new song.

417 SPOOKS RUN WILD (Mono, Oct) Phil Rosen; *genre:* Comedy/Drama; *location:* United States; *coding:* Blk, Draft, Ital?, AF-Ger; *bias:* Contraband Message.

As the result of a philanthropic gesture, the East Side kids are rounded up by the cops to be sent to "camp." Danny quips: "What, we've been drafted?" Later, while in the woods, Huntz Hall is plagued by vicious flying insects, one of whom he angrily mutters must be a "Messerschmitt." Eventually their summer adventures lead them to a haunted house occupied by none other than Bela Lugosi. His menacing Dracula-like, demeanor results in his being compared to a "dictator."

418 SULLIVAN'S TRAVELS (Par, Dec) Preston Sturges; *genre:* Comedy/Drama; *location:* United States; *coding:* WWI, Blk, Chi, Comm, AF-A, Hitler, Isolation?, Am Icons; *bias:* Pro-American.

John L. Sullivan (Joel McCrea), a successful Hollywood director of comedies, insists that, "with the world committing suicide," he wants to make a socially significant film. In order to capture the pulse of the American people, he sets out on the road disguised as a hobo. After experiencing soup lines and flop houses, and doing a stint in a chain gang on a phony murder rap, Sullivan concludes that in this "cockeyed caravan," what the masses really want and need is laughter. There is a specific reference to "the war in Europe" and the second-billed feature at a small town movie theatre he attends is entitled: *The Buzzard of Berlin*. In this late 1941 release, there is mention of a chain gang member thinking he was Charles Lindberg, that could be construed as linking Lindberg and his support of the isolationist America First Committee to criminal insanity.

419 SUN VALLEY SERENADE (TCF, Aug) H. Bruce Humberstone; *genre:* Musical Comedy; *locations:* United States, Canada; *coding:* Ger, Am Icons, Ref, Draft, Blk, WWII, Nor; *biases:* Anti-German, Contraband Message.

John Payne and the Glenn Miller Band get a gig in Sun Valley. But before John can head West he is served papers to appear to adopt a "refugee" for whom he had earlier applied as part of a publicity stunt. He is assigned "No. 36," a beautiful Norwegian girl played by Sonja Henie: "When the war came, first I lost my father and—then I lost my house." Despite a domestic singing rival, Sonja and her skiing win out. When sour beef is ordered by someone in German the comment is made: "Sounds terrible." And one of the film's seven songs is entitled: "The World is Waiting to Waltz Again."

420 SUNDOWN (UA, Oct) Henry Hathaway; *genre:* War Drama; *locations:* Africa, Great Britain; *coding:* Dipl, Spy-Sab, Blk, WWII, AF-Brit, AF-Ital, Italo-Eth War, War Mats, Ger, Arab, Can, Neth, Nor, WWI; *bias:* Pro-British.

A British outpost in East Africa commanded by a Canadian (Bruce Cabot) must contend with a native uprising inspired by outside forces (clearly Nazi, although not named as such). The pasta-loving cook at the outpost is a friendly Italian POW, presumably captured during the British defeat of Mussolini's army in neighboring Ethiopia in the spring of 1940. Zia (Gene Tierney), a supposedly half-breed native girl, becomes involved in smuggling arms through her caravan supply network. Interestingly, at the film's end a bishop delivers a sermon in a bomb-damaged church back in England, linking religion and the military: "Who waits with faith, waits with victory." The motion picture was produced by Walter Wanger. Note: in late 1940 the British had captured a large number of Italian soldiers in North Africa, along with vast stores of pasta.

421 SWING IT SOLDIER (Univ, Nov) Harold Young; *genre:* Musical Comedy; *location:* United States; *coding:* Draft, AF-A, AF-N, Nat Def, Lat Am; *bias:* Pro-Military.

An Army trainee named Jerry (middle-aged actor Ken Murray) is discharged six months earlier than his tent mate. Jerry is commissioned by his pal to look after the latter's pregnant wife. Complications arise because the wife—who is also a radio personality—has a twin sister (both roles played by real-life radio singing star, Frances Langford). Although released in early November, this film was obviously completed before the end of August, the month in which the original 12-month obligation for Selective Service was extended by Congress to 30 months. In the opening scene, the only one to take place in training camp, the typically obnoxious sergeant warns the two draftees that even though Jerry's "year's up tomorrow," he could still be sent to the guardhouse if they continue to listen to their portable radio after taps. When Jerry first returns to the offices of the ad agency where he had worked, he salutes all the uniformed workers (such as the doorman and the elevator boy). But when the agency secretary, Brenda (of the man-hungry comedy radio team of Brenda and Corbina), suggests a kiss for the "hero," Jerry declines: "Listen, I just did my duty for my country). "The Boogie Woogie Bugle Boy of Company B" is played in the background during a scene at a nightclub (none of the patrons are in military uniform).

422 TANKS A MILLION (UA, Sept) Fred Guiol; *genre:* Training/Comedy; *location:* United States; *coding:* USO, AF-A, Draft, Draft Avoid, Hist Am, Am Icons; *bias:* Pro-Military.

There are a few mules, but no tanks in this film. A wide-eyed draftee named Dodo Doubleday (William Tracy) has a photographic memory. While in training camp, the enthusiastic new enlisted man repeatedly demonstrates this special talent to the chagrin of his compatriots and a dim-witted career sergeant (Joe Sawyer). Having put on the new base commander's tunic while attempting to clean the garment, Dodo is grabbed to deliver a nationwide radio speech by the colonel to America's newest soldiers. After a nervous beginning, Dodo rises to the occasion, assuring the men that Uncle Sam needs them and concluding with the following: "In the words of John Paul Jones, we haven't begun to fight. But when we do, zowie!" Colonel Barkley is about to send Dodo to the guardhouse for taking his place when the officer receives a call from Washington, D.C., congratulating him on his "timely ... man to man" speech to the troops. Dodo's girlfriend, who is visiting the camp in the uniform of the "Buddies Entertainment League," is also impressed. This fifty minute feature was one of the first in a series of "Streamliners" produced by Hal Roach. In a 1942 sequel to *Tanks a Million* entitled *About Face*, Dodo wins his sergeant's stripes.

423 THAT HAMILTON WOMAN aka LADY HAMILTON (UA, Apr) Alexander Korda; *genre:* Biography; *locations:* France, Great Britain, Italy, Atlantic; *coding:* Brit, AF-Fr, Hist Am, Russ?, Dipl, AF-Brit, Ital; *biases:* Anti-Totalitarian, Pro-British.

Though short of funds, Korda came to the States, at Winston Churchill's request, to make this romantic epic. England fighting "alone" against Napoleon is unambiguously paralleled with Britain facing Hitler without allies in early 1941. Nelson's statement, addressed to the Lords of the Admiralty, has inescapable implications: "You cannot make peace with dictators; you have to destroy them—wipe them out!" Nelson's victories over the French fleet also reflected recent events. Because the British feared that the French fleet might fall under German control, the greater part of the French naval forces that had fled to North Africa following Hitler's conquest of metropolitan France were neutralized by the Royal Navy in July 1940. The Italians receive a rather mild barb via Lady Hamilton's mother when she jokingly refers to the henpecked King of Naples as a lover of macaroni. Vivien Leigh stars in the title role as the ill-fated mistress of the famous British admiral (played by Laurence Olivier).

424 THAT NIGHT IN RIO (TCF, Apr) Irving Cummings; *genre:* Musical Comedy; *locations:* Brazil, Argentina; *coding:* Latin Am, Nazi, Comm, Isolationist; *bias:* Pro-American.

This film epitomizes Hollywood's late 1930s, early 1940s attempt at wooing Latin America. Two earlier examples are *Juarez* (1939, WB), q.v., and *Down Argentine Way* (1940, 20th Fox), q.v. This effort was at least partially inspired by F.D.R.'s resurrection of his "Good Neighbor Policy." Carmen Miranda opens the garish all studio color production with a lively performance in Portuguese of "Chica, Chica, Boom, Chic." She is joined by her entertainer boyfriend Don Ameche dressed in pseudo-American naval whites and singing: "My friends, I extend felicitations to our South American relations.

May we never leave behind us all the common ties that bind us. A hundred and thirty million people send their regards to you...."

425 THAT UNCERTAIN FEELING
(UA, Apr, Ernst Lubitsch; *genre:* Comedy; *location:* United States; *coding:* Nazi, Comm, Isolationist; *biases:* Pro-Intervention, Contraband Message.

The "Happy Bakers" marital life has begun to come apart. When the wife falls for a screwball composer-pianist, the husband decides he must take a stand. The pianist, played with verve by Burgess Meredith, proclaims he is an individualist who is against everything, "communism, fascism, Naziism, capitalism...." When the two men first confront each other over their mutual love for the fey Mrs. Baker (Merle Oberon) the eccentric artist steadfastly announces to his rival, "I'm not going to fight." Mr. Baker (Melvyn Douglas) sarcastically responds to the repeated pacifistic assertions, "I understand, you're an isolationist." By the time of this film's release the term "isolationist" was increasingly becoming a pejorative epithet in America.

426 THEY DARE NOT LOVE (Col, Apr) James Whale, C. Vidor (uncr); *genre:* Drama; *locations:* Austria, Atlantic, United States; *coding:* Austr, Belg, AF-Ger, Resist, Spy-Sab, Nazi, Atroc-Conc, Hitler, Atroc, AF-Brit, WWII; *bias:* Anti-Nazi.

In 1938, following the German occupation of Austria (*Anschluss*), nobleman Kurt von Rotenberg (George Brent) and his commoner girlfriend Marta (Martha Scott) emigrate to America to escape Nazi persecution. Nevertheless, they are relentlessly pursued by the Gestapo. Kurt is tricked into agreeing to return, in exchange for the freedom of some (nonexistent) hostages. Marta joins Kurt on the ship, and they are married, planning to have eight days of happiness before the ship docks in Germany. With the help of the ship's anti-Nazi captain, the couple is rescued at the last possible moment by a British warship on the first day of WWII.

427 THEY MET IN ARGENTINA
(RKO, Apr) Leslie Goodwins, Jack Hively; *genre:* Musical Comedy; *locations:* United States, Argentina; *coding:* AF-N, Latin Am, Good Neighbor; *bias:* Pro-American.

A racehorse purchase is the excuse used to bring a couple of American cowpokes to sunny gay Argentina. One of them, played by a young gangling Buddy Ebsen, is amazed at how well the natives speak English. The film opens with a blatant musical pitch for inter-hemispheric cooperation. Written by Rogers and Hart it is entitled: "North America Meet South America" a portion of the lyrics include the following: "A senorita and a jolly tar/ Gauchos and Yanks mix at the bar

.../ North America meet South America/ There's only one America now."

428 THEY MET IN BOMBAY (MGM, Jun) Clarence Brown; *genre:* Adventure; *locations:* India, China; *coding:* Chi, AF-Brit, AF-Jap, Can, Sino-Jap War; *biases:* Anti-Japanese, Pro-British.

This was the *only* pre–Pearl Harbor fiction film to specifically portray the Japanese in a military adversarial relationship with occidentals. Gerald, an amiable jewel thief from Canada, played by Clark Gable, and his future lady accomplice spend the first third of this film in India separately plotting the heist of a valuable necklace. They subsequently wind up together on the lam in Hong Kong. In order to raise some cash, Gerald devises a scheme that requires his donning a British officer's uniform. While in this disguise, he is picked up by military authorities who send him off to command the evacuation of Chinese civilians from a town in the interior threatened by the invasion of the Japanese army. While they are attempting to leave the town, Japanese troops in armored cars arrive and demand all Chinese evacuees ("spies") be left behind. In the skirmish with the bloodthirsty "Japs" that ensues, the ersatz "Captain Huston" blows up several machine gun nests and saves the day. Afterwards, a wounded Gerald receives the Victoria Cross, even though His Majesty's representatives know he will be trading in his Sam Brown belt for prison stripes. Gerald vows to return and enlist. Hong Kong became a major conduit of military supplies to Chinese forces after the outbreak of the Sino-Japanese War. In the fall of 1938 the Japanese launched a campaign that effectively cut off the British colony from the interior of China.

429 THREE GIRLS ABOUT TOWN
(Col, Oct) Leigh Jason; *genre:* Comedy; *location:* United States; *coding:* Hitler, Natl Def, Pro, Fifth Col, Comm; *biases:* Pro-American, Contraband Message.

Seeking to avoid negative publicity, two Los Angeles convention hostesses and their manager try to secretly remove the body of a man they believe was murdered in their hotel. Meanwhile, a heated labor meeting concerning a proposed machinists' strike in the defense industry is taking place in the building's conference room. When Tommy, the reporter boyfriend of one of the hostesses, happens upon the scene, he complains to the lady that he cannot be concerned with her petty problems while "Hitler's in our front yard." After Tommy reminds the labor negotiators that the country is facing a "national emergency," they patriotically agree to a settlement. Later, when the police think Tommy is involved in the alleged murder and nab him, he yells: "Say, you guys think

you're in Germany?" In June 1941, there was a major aircraft industry strike on the West coast during which FDR sent troops to occupy the factories (invoking his recently declared state of "Unlimited National Emergency").

430 THREE SONS O' GUNS (WB, Aug) Ben Stoloff; *genre:* Comedy/Drama; *location:* United States; *coding:* Draft, Russ?, Hist Am, AF-A, Draft Avoid; *bias:* Pro-Military.

A widow (Irene Rich) and her three irresponsible sons are featured in this topical satire. Charlie (Wayne Morris), the only son who works regularly, keeps being fired for playing his trombone on the job. When the Conscription Act goes into effect, the three fill out their questionnaires requesting exemptions. At their draft board hearing they are defending their exemptions, including one based on an illegal marriage, when lovable Aunt Lottie (Marjorie Rambeau) appears, exposes their schemes, and then delivers a patriotic speech. Later, after completing training camp, their mother discovers Uncle Sam's discipline has made good boys out of her wayward brood. In fact, her three sons enjoy Army life so much that they have all decided to sign up for another year (the draft was not extended until the month of this film's release). Charlie is now the company bugler. This was the only prewar film to deal directly with draft avoidance. The early 1942 release, *Young America* (TCF), took a more somber view toward such activities.

431 TOM, DICK, AND HARRY (RKO, Apr) Garson Kanin; *genre:* Comedy; *location:* United States; *coding:* Hitler; *biases:* Anti-Nazi, Contraband Message.

Telephone operator Ginger Rogers agonizes considerably before choosing Mr. Right. However, at the beginning of the film no such indecision is displayed by either Rogers or her date (George Murphy) in regards to Adolf Hitler. Departing from a movie theatre, Ginger and George hear Hitler's voice and "Sieg Heils!" as the newsreel plays. They respond with loud, teeth-clenched hisses. This was actually not an unusual occurrence during film showings in occupied Europe—until the authorities began leaving the house lights on to spot the culprits.

432 TOP SERGEANT MULLIGAN (Mono, Oct) Jean Yarbrough; *genre:* Comedy/Training; *location:* United States; *coding:* AF-A, Blk, FDR; *bias:* Pro-Military.

This military service promo features the song, "$21 a Day—Once a Month." Two partners in an unsuccessful drug store join the army to escape their debt collector (Nat Pendleton). Guess who is their training camp sergeant? In one sequence the black comedian named Wonderful Smith, playing himself, has an amusing conversation with "the President."

433 TWO-FACED WOMAN (MGM, Nov) George Cukor; *genre:* Comedy; *location:* United States; *coding:* Ref, Draft, WWII; *bias:* Contraband Message.

A ski instructress, played by Greta Garbo, who fears she may be losing her husband to another woman, poses as her spirited twin sister. In the amusing restaurant scene, Garbo's naughty other half tells the husband: "I caught the last boat out [from Lisbon] ... I'm a penniless refugee." The draft is also mentioned.

434 UNDERGROUND (WB, Jun) Vincent Sherman; *genre:* Resistance; *location:* Germany; *coding:* WWI, Goering, Nazi, Resist, Nor, WWII, AF-Ger, Hitler, Goebbels, Hess, Pol, Himmler, Atroc-Conc, Atroc; *bias:* Anti-Nazi.

An anti-Nazi resistance group in Berlin making, among other things, clandestine "Voice of Freedom" radio broadcasts from a truck, is featured. The plot centers around the Francken brothers. Kurt (Jeffrey Lynn) is a former soldier who, after losing an arm during the invasion of Norway (April 1940), returns home and becomes a Nazi brownshirt. His older brother Eric (Philip Dorn), is the secret underground leader. Kurt's love for a pretty violinist, who is also a member of the resistance, clashes with his loyalty to the Party, and thus creates a moral dilemma. Colonel Heller (Martin Kosleck) of the Gestapo enlists Eric's assistance in silencing the illegal radio. After unwittingly betraying his older brother and witnessing the brutality of the Gestapo, Kurt decides to carry on the cause against the Nazi regime. As a demoralized Eric is escorted to the guillotine (sometimes actually used by the Nazis against political prisoners), his faith in humanity is restored when he hears the brother's voice break into the Nazi broadcast of the event and attack the regime.

435 UNFINISHED BUSINESS (Univ, Aug) Gregory La Cava; *genre:* Romantic Comedy; *location:* United States; *coding:* AF-A, FDR, Blk, WWI, Vet; *biases:* Contraband Message, Pro-Military.

Small-town girl Irene Dunne is seduced on the train to New York by rich Preston Foster, who promptly forgets her. Dunne marries Foster's semi-alcoholic brother Robert Montgomery on the rebound. She eventually falls in love with Montgomery, but is still unsure of her feelings for Foster. Montgomery sees her kissing Foster ("testing" to see if she still loves him—she does not), and leaves. He joins the Army, which makes a man of him. A year later, he comes home and finds that Dunne has given birth to their child, and they reconcile. It is clearly indi-

cated that Montgomery *joins* the Army, rather than being drafted, which is logical since the bulk of the film apparently takes place in 1940. When Montgomery comes home on leave, he discovers his portly butler (Eugene Pallette) wearing *his* World War I uniform.

436 UP JUMPED THE DEVIL (Ind, ?) *genre:* Comedy; *location:* United States; *coding:* Blk, Ital-Eth War; *bias:* Contraband Message.

Two jailbirds in this all black production are paroled on the condition that they find jobs. At the home of the well-to-do Mrs. Brown, they are hired as the butler and the maid, Mantan Moreland in drag as the latter. During a bazaar for "Aid to Abysinnia" at Mrs. Brown's, her pearl necklace is stolen. The lady's new employees become heroes when they track down the culprit.

437 VIRGINIA (Para, Feb) Edward H. Griffith; *genre:* Drama; *location:* United States; *coding:* WWI, Blk, WWII, Atroc-Conc, Am Icons; *biases:* Pro-American, Contraband Message.

Charlotte (Madeleine Carroll), who has been living in New York, returns to her family home in idyllic Technicolor Virginia. Despite contemporary trappings, we are then subjected to stale Civil War era sectional drivel for the next one and a half hours. There is, however, a brief bit of interesting dialogue that takes place near the middle of the film during an otherwise boring scene between Charlotte and her Southern gentleman farmer beau, "Stonewall" Elliott (Fred MacMurray). He refers to the use of the money from selling her home to go back to New York as buying "your way into a concentration camp." And he then sardonically compares her fallacious belief that the Civil War was fought to emancipate the slaves with other "phoney ... war slogans ... like make the world safe for democracy.... Remember that one?"

438 WASHINGTON MELODRAMA (MGM, Apr) S. Sylvan Simon; *genre:* Drama; *location:* United States; *coding:* Ref, AF-Ital, WWII, Nazi, Am Icons, Ital, Musso, Fr, Latin Am; *bias:* Pro-Intervention.

Calvin Claymore, the millionaire leader of a movement to raise money to send food to children orphaned and/or displaced by the European War, is campaigning for his cause in Washington, D.C. But support for the "Feed Europe Bill" is opposed by his future son-in-law and editor of the "Washington Tabloid." In a radio broadcast the latter states that: "Claymore and his associates are playing squarely into the hands of the dictators.... This bill ... would send food into territories which have been conquered by Germany ... and [would] ... lighten the burden of our enemies."

In an earlier discussion concerning rumors from Europe, this somewhat wishful comment is made *vis-à-vis* the Italians and their German allies: "Benito's boys are getting fed up with goose-stepping." The plot then concentrates on murder and blackmail. In fact, it is not until the last few minutes of the film that Claymore is able to resume his altruistic appeal before the Senate Foreign Relations Committee. In the late summer of 1940, Herbert Hoover created the "National Committee on Food for the Five Small Democracies." Interventionists opposed his plan as a form of indirect aid to the Nazis.

439 WEEKEND FOR THREE (RKO, Dec) Irving Reis; *genre:* Comedy; *location:* United States; *coding:* WWII, World Crisis; *bias:* Contraband Message.

A young married couple is plagued by a rambunctious weekend guest who is enamored of the wife. Several weeks later the young couple are emotionally and physically exhausted. Early one morning the guest puts a golf ball through their bedroom window. The husband wearily comments: "And they said invasion would be impossible."

440 WEST POINT WIDOW (Para, Jun) Robert Siodmak; *genre:* Drama; *location:* United States; *coding:* AF-A, Mil School, Blk, AF-N; *bias:* Pro-Military.

Nurse Nancy Hull (Anne Shirley) secretly married a West Point cadet. Two years later she has a daughter, while he has become a football star and found himself a new lady. Meanwhile, a doctor that works at Nancy's hospital has fallen in love with her. What is the solution in times of world crisis and the era of the Hays office? Nancy allows the newly commissioned officer to serve his country unhindered while she leaves for strategic Panama with her new husband, the Army Medical Corp's latest recruit.

441 THE WILD MAN OF BORNEO (MGM, Jan) Robert B. Sinclair; *genre:* Comedy/Drama; *location:* United States; *coding:* Isolationist; *bias:* Contraband Message.

In this turn of the century period piece, an unsuccessful medicine man takes his long neglected daughter to New York City. At a theatrical boarding house, the braggart passes himself off as an actor. Upon hearing a disturbance in the parlor he sanctimoniously tells his daughter, "With regard to other people's problems, my dear, I always maintain an attitude of strict isolation."

442 A WOMAN'S FACE (MGM, May) George Cukor; *genre:* Drama; *location:* Sweden; *coding:* WWII, Collab; *biases:* Anti-Fascist, Contraband Message.

Anna Holm (Joan Crawford), who was badly scarred on one side of her face in a childhood accident, leads a gang of blackmailers in the Swedish capital of Stockholm.

Desperate for love, she becomes entangled with a scheming, haughty aristocrat, Torsten Barring (Conrad Veidt), in a murder plot. But when her face is restored by plastic surgery, she has a change of heart and falls in love with the intended victim. A *New York Times* film critic thought, "...the film becomes pretentious when it infers that its villain is a Swedish Quislingist." For while propositioning Anna, Torsten states: "...This is 1941 ... the times are ripe ... what others have done in other countries, I can do here. Because ... the world belongs to the devil and I know how to serve him if I can only get the power—power!"

443 WORLD PREMIERE (Para, Aug) Ted Tetzlaff; *genre:* Comedy/Spy; *locations:* Italy, Germany, United States; *coding:* Spy-Sab, Atroc-Conc?, Atroc, Hitler, WWII, Nazi, Ital, Ger, AF-RAF, Jap, Blk; *bias:* Anti-Fascist.

Two German agents and an Italian fellow traveler team up in an attempt to sabotage the release of a Hollywood "propaganda picture" they consider to be slanderous to the fascist cause. One of the Germans, a Nazi blowhard, and his fatuous Italian colleague sneak onto the studio lot and are quickly hired by casting to impersonate foreign spies! But the bungling fascist partners are no match for the maniacal film director played by John Barrymore.

444 A YANK IN THE RAF (TCF, Oct) Henry King; *genre:* War Drama/Combat; *locations:* United States, Great Britain, Canada, Netherlands, France; *coding:* US-Brit Coop, Home Def, AF-RAF, Neutrality Act, WWII, Am Vol, Hitler, Atroc-Conc, Am Icons, Fr, War Mats, AF-Ger, Dunkirk; *biases:* Pro-Intervention, Pro-British.

Some of the scenes in the air and at RAF bases were filmed by a British crew led by Ronald Neame. While ferrying bombers to the embattled British, a cocky Yank played by Tyrone Power runs into an old flame, a leggy singer played by Betty Grable. Power, whose character is named Tim Baker, joins the RAF in order to be able to hang around. Instead, he gets a taste of what war is really like and acquires a healthy respect for the British. Near the end of the film a determined and vengeful Baker zooms high over Dunkirk in a Spitfire shooting down Nazis: "That's for Roger.... That's for the Corporal.... This one's just for me." According to Norman Kagan in *The War Film* the British specifically requested the upbeat ending that follows. This film was produced by Darryl F. Zanuck.

445 YOU BELONG TO ME (Col, Oct) Wesley Ruggles; *genre:* Comedy; *location:* United States; *coding:* Blk, Nazi, Jew, Latin Am; *biases:* Contraband Message, Anti-Nazi.

An idle millionaire (Henry Fonda) collides on a ski slope with a pretty physician played by Barbara Stanwyck. Following their marriage, he becomes resentful of his new wife's commitment to her patients. She refers to his lovemaking on the morning after they wed as "sabotage" designed to prevent her from going to work. Later, after he has made a fool of himself in a jealous outburst at a party, his wife calls him a "one man Gestapo." Marital bliss and social responsibility are achieved after he agrees to finance a bankrupt hospital.

446 YOU'LL NEVER GET RICH (Col, Sept) Sidney Lanfield; *genre:* Training/Comedy; *location:* United States; *coding:* USO, Draft, AF-A, Blk, Am Icons, WWII?; *bias:* Pro-Military.

With a Cole Porter score, "selectee" Fred Astaire dances his way through boot camp and into the heart of Rita Hayworth. Clapped into the guardhouse for accidentally hitting his sergeant, Fred passes the time by tapping to a bluesy "Since I Kissed My Baby Goodbye," as musically rendered by some incarcerated black soldiers (The Delta Rhythm Boys). Fred's "Wedding Cake Walk" song and "Dance Militaire" routine with Rita atop a papier mache tank is an inspired finale.

447 YOU'RE IN THE ARMY NOW (WB, Dec) Lewis; *genre:* Training/Comedy; *location:* United States; *coding:* WWI, AF-Ger, Draft, AF-A, AF-N, USO, Blk, Hitler?, Am Icons, Hist Am, WWII; *bias:* Pro-Military.

Released in late December 1941, this film gave comedian Jimmy Durante his turn at enlisting in the Army, with Phil Silvers along for the duration. A malfunctioning vacuum cleaner ("Whirlaway"—a joking reference to the 1941 Triple Crown winner) and a run-away obsolete tank provide the moving props. Despite the fact that Durante mistakenly *enlisted* in the service while trying to sell the recruiting sergeant a vacuum (and was therefore *not* a draftee), the Schnozzola's Apache dance (in drag!) featuring the song "I'm Glad My Number was Called," included the following lyrics: "I want to be prepared when Uncle Sam puts on the show,/ Just like my dad, when my dad was a lad,/ I'm glad my number was called."

448 YOU'RE OUT OF LUCK (Mono, Jan) Howard Bretherton; *genre:* Crime; *location:* United States; *coding:* Blk, Draft; *biases:* Pro-Military, Contraband Message.

An elevator operator (Frankie Darro) and a black janitor (Mantan Moreland) get mixed up in several murders involving a gambling ring. Darro's brother, a police detective, tells them they can help the police solve the case. Jeff (Moreland) asks if this means they will be helping the government. Told yes, he exclaims: "It happened at last—we's been conscripted!"

449 ZIS BOOM BAH (Mono, Nov) William Nigh; *genre:* Musical; *location:* United States; *coding:* WWII, AF-A, Am Icons; *biases:* Pro-Military, Contraband Message.

Grace Hayes had long ago surrendered custody of her son, Peter, to her late husband's parents, but she continued to contribute to his support via her stage singing career. Without Peter's knowledge, she visits Midwick, the small college he attends. She learns that her son has become extravagant and egotistical. Furthermore, the college is on the verge of bankruptcy. She cuts Peter's allowance to bring him to his senses, and then helps the students stage a musical show to raise money for the school. Peter and his mother are reconciled when he helps out with the fund-raiser. Two of the show's musical numbers are topical: "It Makes No Difference When You're in the Army," and the finale, "Miss America." The latter number presents the boy students in Army uniforms and the girls in two-piece bathing suits, and includes lyrics like: "When Miss America steps out with Uncle Sam, she's out with the best man in the land." Surprisingly, the draft is never mentioned in this film.

Part Two

Waging War, 1942–1945

15. Fighting Fascism on the Cinematic Front: The Seductive Language and Imagery of Film Propaganda

"An American will fight for only three things—for a woman, for himself and for a better world."—Foreword to China Girl *(TCF, 1943)*

Entertainment pictures presumably could reach a mass audience impervious to carefully reasoned writing. OWI believed this could be accomplished if propaganda messages were 'casually and naturally introduced into the ordinary dialogue, business and scenes which constitute the bulk of film footage.' By making the war pervasive in the depiction of ordinary lives, the movies would show that the country was united, with everyone participating equally.[1]

The American motion picture industry was in the media forefront of the nation's struggle to defeat the Axis. The media, most particularly the film industry, which between 1942 and 1945 averaged a weekly paid attendance of over 85 million (plus free screenings on military bases for millions of servicemen), fabricated a set of images that unobtrusively, yet relentlessly, reinforced the values and world view of American society. This was no small task, especially considering that the predominantly pleasure-seeking film audience was more or less ideologically disengaged, even at a moment of grave national crisis.

Although the particulars vary widely, the artistic portrayal of good and evil is both universal and perennial. But when a nation is directly endangered and its leaders believe that their society's ideological integrity is imperiled, images of reality, particularly the symbolism of good and evil, may be radically manipulated in order to accommodate political exigencies.

By reconstructing the totality of war-relevant American motion pictures—a significant aspect of the popular culture of the Second World War—we can attempt to "reconstruct ... [the] attitudes, values, and reactions ... of those no longer able

to speak to us directly."[2] Over 800 of the more than 1500 Hollywood feature films released between January 1, 1942 and September 30, 1945 have been identified in this study as containing some reference to the Second World War. The authors contend that the relevant (war-oriented) content of these motion pictures accurately reflects the cultural consensus of American society of the period. These films present a reassuring image of a unified American people and their allies, united in the fight against evil militaristic dictatorships. By doing so, the film industry significantly contributed to the destruction of fascism and also paved the way for the creation of a free and democratic postwar world.

Hollywood, as the dominant public entertainment medium of the era, developed and exploited code words and images which created associative linkages possessing the potential for audience manipulation. By helping to create or perpetuate common symbols, behavior models, and stereotypes through repetitive presentation, the mass media—particularly film—contributed to the forging of a national consensus. The various media in the United States during World

139

War II, actively encouraged by the Office of War Information, supported each other's presentations. The total war atmosphere created by millions of posters, radio announcements, and print ads exhorting Americans to collect scrap metal, donate blood, buy War Bonds, and to be wary of spies, was reinforced by the textual content of fictional wartime films.[3] Simply put, although the majority of American citizens never served in the armed forces, the war was all but inescapable.

For example, many of the same posters encountered in everyday life—on billboards, at work, or above the local drugstore's lunch counter—also appear in feature motion pictures of the period. Some wartime films contain a plug for War Bonds and stamps following their end credits, often duplicating the popular Bonds poster featuring a Revolutionary War-era Minuteman carrying his musket. Reminders to buy War Bonds even appear at the end of many films which are not war-relevant, such as *Shine on Harvest Moon* (WB, 1943). Other well-known posters were incorporated into film sets. For example, the anti-espionage "Loose Lips Sink Ships" poster is displayed on the wall of an Army canteen in *Seven Days Leave* (RKO, 1942). Among the numerous war posters seen at a scrap depot in *The Falcon in Danger* (RKO, 1943) is the emotionally provocative "Avenge December 7" (Pearl Harbor).

James Montgomery Flagg's famous World War One recruiting poster—Uncle Sam pointing at the viewer, with the slogan "I Want You For the U.S. Army"—may also be seen in a number of WWII-era films.[4] In *Mr. Lucky* (RKO, 1943) it is innovatively incorporated into the *mise-en-scène*: "Uncle Sam" seems to be following the draft-dodging hero (Cary Grant): the poster periodically appears in the background, particularly in over-the-shoulder shots, mutely appealing to Grant's conscience and demanding that he accept the responsibility of serving his country.

Wartime fictional film propaganda is essentially a relentless battle utilizing words and images as weapons—a series of encounters with an audience that has been willingly seduced by the enticements of dramatic entertainment. These encounters would appear to have had a cumulative impact. Therefore, we are primarily concerned with the phenomenon of the total film viewing experience, rather than the supposed influence of any particular motion picture upon the public.

Analyzing films in a collective sense some fifty years after their original release can provide an idea of what the attitudes of the public were at a particular historical moment. But conclusions drawn about an individual film's impact on its original audience can be quite misleading—especially when the films chosen for such scholarly attention (usually unduly emphasizing form and often ignoring the historical context) are invariably well-produced "A" features.

The vast majority of the American moviegoing public in the early 1940s was not reading *The New York Times* film reviews, nor viewing only critically acclaimed features or big-budget productions—they were *also* watching hundreds of "B"

pictures (and short subjects, and cartoons, and newsreels). The claims made in this book are based on patterns observed after examining the content of a very large sample, representing *all* identified war-relevant fictional motion pictures of feature-length.

The immediate film screening experience results in instantaneous gratification (or sometimes aggravation) at a low level of individual psychic risk; aroused emotions usually dissipate quickly, once the film ends and the viewer leaves the darkened theatre. For instance, many contemporary male viewers might briefly have identified with Errol Flynn, dashing lover of sexy Ann Sheridan and fearless killer of Nazis in *Edge of Darkness* (a popular 1943 release glorifying the Norwegian resistance). But it is highly unlikely that any of these Walter Mittys ran out of the movie theatre and murdered the local German delicatessen owner!

Can the film viewing experience and its affects be accurately gauged in historical perspective? Because of the very limited and unsystematic audience research conducted during the period, the answer would have to be no. But one can make reasoned observations through an examination of the content of a significant number of films in a specific time period.

For propaganda to be effective it must have a basis in or be compatible with the cultural/political preconceptions or inclinations of its primary target audience. Any single film's impact, in a significant or measurable way, is highly debatable and nearly impossible to accurately assess. Motion pictures would therefore appear to be less efficient in effecting immediate radical behavioral changes than in reinforcing preexisting attitudes of the public. Most people in a functioning democratic society will dismiss blatant attempts via the mass media at political cajolery. They tend to be more receptive to subtle persuasion—particularly when sugarcoated in a typical film melodrama, comedy, or adventure.

Film propaganda can also defuse existing or potential tensions, particularly in times of crisis, by stressing the commonality of experience—such as rationing problems—in a fictional format. Americans tend to be suspicious of, or even actively resist, being told what to do, or how to think and act. But a receptive climate for a specific political message can be created through repeated motifs, which by appearing in multiple films may begin to have a subtle impact upon the viewer.

For example, anti–Semitism certainly still existed in this nation at the time of America's entrance into the war against Hitler's Germany. To help neutralize anti–Semitic sentiments, the motion picture industry *could* have produced a number of films with Jewish heroes openly arguing for racial equality, respect, and compassion. While Hollywood placed no premium on subtlety, such a blatant frontal assault would have too obviously telegraphed the films' intentions, with the possibility of an audience backlash. Instead, what actually took place in a number of war-relevant films released between 1942 and 1945 was the presentation of a few obviously Jewish characters

Bataan (MGM, 1943): A multi-ethnic squad fights for democracy. Here we have white (Robert Taylor, Lloyd Nolan), black (Kenneth Spencer) and Filipino (J. Alex Havier). Jewish Sgt. Feingold has stepped out for a moment.

(usually in supporting roles), whose Jewishness was not over-emphasized. These cinematic Jews are deliberately portrayed as average Americans, who at some dramatic point may espouse the virtues of democracy or act heroically. Sometimes the latter is an act of individual bravery, but more often it is presented as taking place within a group—most particularly as a manifestation of the collective patriotism of a combat unit. Examples of this sort of "peripheral propaganda" include characters such as Chips Abrams (Sam Levene) in *Action in the North Atlantic* (WB, 1943), Corporal Jake Feingold (Thomas Mitchell) in *Bataan* (MGM, 1943), and Lt. Wayne Greenbaum (Levene again) in *The Purple Heart* (TCF, 1944).

Or consider, for instance, the fact that a substantial percentage of WWII motion pictures in a contemporary setting show "average" people eating well? A message of reassurance was thereby imparted to the contemporary movie audience that were compelled to cope with food rationing in real life.

The controversy with regards to wartime Anglo-American relations surrounding the release of *Objective Burma!* (WB,

1945) is also instructive.[5] The dominant British contribution to combat operations in the Burma military theatre is largely ignored in the film (to the chagrin of British audiences): only a British liaison officer at headquarters and two Ghurkas assigned to the mission are portrayed. This was perhaps an unfortunate mistake (in a diplomatic sense), but it was largely irrelevant to the film's producers and their primary audience, the American public. Along with several other combat and resistance-theme motion pictures released in the United States during 1945, *Objective Burma!* represented a climax of vituperation directed at the Japanese enemy, with whom we were currently engaged in the final phase of a bloody series of island campaigns. And, most important of all, it was widely believed that sometime in early 1946, the military forces of the United States (with only nominal direct assistance from the Allies) would have to stage a very costly invasion of the Japanese home islands. In the world so assiduously created in such an overtly propagandistic work as *Objective Burma!*, it is no more desirable to confuse or dilute the positive message of America's struggle with Japan (by depicting major British characters contributing to the fight) than it would be to humanize the enemy.

Nevertheless, despite the obvious intensity of racial hatred developed in a few well-known films, such as *Guadalcanal Diary* (TCF, 1943) and *Objective Burma!*, these motion pictures could be viewed as aberrations if it were not for the literally hundreds of casual pejorative references to the Japanese that appear in scores of additional wartime releases, including many films otherwise considered politically innocuous (refer to Chapter 19 for a discussion of film images of the Japanese, Germans, and Italians).

When one becomes aware of the vast and complex interrelationship between films, reality, attitudes, and beliefs, one can begin to grasp the true potential impact of fictional American film propaganda in its totality during the Second World War. Can anyone born after the war recreate the feelings of John or Mary Doe exiting a movie theatre in 1940s America, or measure the impact of a particular film upon them? The cumulative effect of images presented over a period of time most likely reinforced our national resolve to win the war and allayed fears about the conflict in the collective subconscious of the audience.

Ultimately, assuming a certain degree of predisposition/ preexisting biases, an audience must be seduced, *not* assaulted by propaganda. The motion picture is an ideal medium through which to achieve the former. For seduction is inherently a more delicate, complicated, and lengthy process—and because of that its mechanisms are far less easily recognized, properly assessed, and understood.

The U.S. Government and Film Propaganda

There was *no* U.S. government agency of propaganda that dictated the content of feature films during WWII. However, the Office of War Information, Bureau of Motion Pictures, did provide a rather cryptic list of guidelines (periodically updated) to the film industry, with "suggestions" concerning the presentation of America's war aims. While the OWI systematically monitored the content of Hollywood productions beginning in April 1942, it had limited regulatory power. The OWI's only direct influence was the power to reduce a film's profitability by restricting the foreign distribution of "unsuitable" films. While the movie studios usually acquiesced to OWI recommendations, there was never any formal industry-wide agreement with the government on what or what not to show on America's movie screens.

A rare example of a film project that was aborted largely as a result of OWI objections was "Bushido." A 26-page synopsis of a novel by Alexander Pernikoff was submitted for OWI review by Twentieth Century–Fox in the spring of 1943: the story describes the Japanese occupation of Manchuria as related by the lead character, a White Russian collaborator. The concluding paragraph of the OWI report, dated 7 September

1943 reads: "A serious problem from the standpoint of distribution overseas, is raised by the story's sympathetic presentation of a collaborationist.... A victim of blackmail, the hero serves the Japanese as a spy and becomes a party to the most heinous crimes against the people. To suggest that such an individual is more to be pitied than despised would be to minimize the real heroes of conquered countries.... Any presentation of a collaborationist as a hero is in direct contradiction to the War Information program."[6] Fox dropped the project.

One finished film which had its release delayed till 1946 primarily as a result of OWI objections was *Cinderella Jones* (WB). The OWI pointed out that its suggestions made after an October 1943 review of the script had been ignored in the finished product. The film starred Joan Leslie as a defense worker who must marry a brainy man by a certain date in order to receive an inheritance. The OWI's September 3, 1944, formal Recommendation notes: "Dated in wartime, the film contains frequent references to our war effort which are included only for comedy effect and might appear in poor taste to overseas audiences.... [A] finale showing an Army convoy on the highway blocking the hero and heroine's plans for elopement … [is an example] which could contribute to an altogether unfortunate projection of American life. Because these problems are not mitigated in any way by the pseudo-farcical treatment, this film is unsuitable not only for special distribution in liberated areas, but also for general distribution overseas."

While changes requested by the government were usually made by the studios, the U.S. government never ordered Hollywood to include war propaganda in its fictional features as happened in England, where the Ministry of Information exercised very strong control over the media.[7] Hollywood was not precluded nor discouraged from fulfilling its primary task of making a profit by successfully entertaining the public. But on its own accord, Hollywood unhesitatingly engaged in celluloid combat with the Axis. Was its propaganda campaign a cinematic war waged to win the hearts and minds of the American people? Or was its aim to bolster the morale of the United States and her allies? Perhaps the American film industry self-consciously attempted to define and rationalize the war aims of the United Nations in order to strengthen the ideological defenses of democracy against the insidious threat of fascism. But did Hollywood deliberately set out to spread hatred of the enemy and justify killing on a massive scale? Or did the worldwide conflict simply provide a topical background for business as usual, with the familiar villains in standard film genres being temporarily replaced by our Axis enemies?

Actually, a clearly defined consensus or "grand plan" on how to fight the Axis on film was never established. Instead, while making full use of the technological and artistic panoply available to them, with varying degrees of ideological intensity, America's motion picture industry enthusiastically mobilized its vast resources, but basically muddled through the infinite challenges of making films in a total war environment.

Tarzan Triumphs (RKO Radio, 1943): Nazi troops invade the jungle kingdom of "Polandria." Queen Frances Gifford is upset at the rough treatment of one of her subjects.

Portraying the Enemy

After Pearl Harbor, the enemy's point of view was effectively silenced in America. Thus the definition of fascism and the reasons behind the enemy's actions were "explained" by Hollywood. To American film audiences, the enemy became as it was fictionally depicted on the screen. Its image consisting of negative truths, half-truths, and pure distortions, the enemy—the "Other"—often became oversimplified and stereotyped. After exposure to a number of war films, an American viewer would probably have agreed with Jane's assessment of the enemy in *Tarzan Triumphs* (RKO, 1943): "Germans, now called Nazis ... [are] more savage than the beasts of the jungle."

Hollywood's weapons against the Axis were a repetitive series of negative words/phrases and visual images of the Nazis and Japanese, versus an idealized representation of America as all that was good and righteous. While a clearly defined ideological discussion was seldom engaged, a concentrated propaganda barrage was directed at domestic complacency. The audience was inundated by the force of an unending stream of rhetoric and visually "loaded" scenes contrasting our humanity with Axis inhumanity; a free world comprised of democratic nations versus an enslaved, fascist-dominated world.

With regards to the Germans, prejudicial clichés established by the mass media during World War I—Prussian brush haircut, monocle, Heidelburg dueling scar, draconian measures to subdue civilian populations—had the symbols and personalities of the Nazi state tacked on to create the evil Nazi Other. As for the Japanese, a generalized prewar Asian stereotype was crudely supplemented by glasses, buckteeth and the mordantly delivered "so sorry." While the Germans and their Nazi masters were frequently referred to in American films by personal names, the onscreen Japanese enemy usually appeared as anonymous phantoms who were called the "Japs" or "Nips" (not uncommonly augmented by a racial slur such as "little yellow").

Those films presenting recurring pejorative references directed at our enemies are the most clearly illustrative examples of crude propaganda. The raw number of films listed in Appendix C with five or more negative references to the Japanese is similar to the total number with anti–Nazi references. However, there is no mistaking the bias of vituperative intensity as applied to the Japanese—much of which, particularly in films portraying combat or resistance, had distinct racist overtones. Fifty-five anti–Japanese films with an average of 11 negative references were identified versus 48 anti–Nazi films with an average of 8 negative references. Overall, 242 films contained overt references to the Nazis, while 236 included mention of Japan (Italy, the third member of the Axis—at least until 1943—trailed with only 95 references).

The wartime image of the Nazis, Japanese, and Italians is discussed in greater detail in the chapter dealing with the Axis powers. However, a brief discussion of the basic propaganda tools utilized by Hollywood filmmakers in this regard illustrates the uneven combination of the superficial and the ideological, the reasoned and the emotional, which make up film images of the enemy during WWII.

The Nazis are shown to be the heirs of the Prussian militarists who were the instigators of World War I. They are anti-religion, anti-intellectualism, anti-family. The German people are under Hitler's spell or are held captive in their nation, helpless under the Nazis' cruel reign. Stereotypical German traits like punctuality, efficiency, and a desire for "order" have been perverted and taken to extremes.

The Japanese are fanatically anti–Western, and their ideals, mores, and beliefs are diametrically opposed to the Judeo-Christian ethics embraced by most Americans. Although Japanese characters are rarely portrayed in the same depth as film Nazis, there are similarities between the two fascist systems: anti-intellectualism, extreme nationalism, a desire for power and conquest. While the Nazis are often cruel and ruthless, most of their atrocities are performed with a specific purpose in mind, such as to obtain information or to cow the citizens of an occupied country (the Holocaust does not directly figure in any wartime feature film); Japanese atrocities, on the other hand, are depicted as barbaric and senseless, and sadism seems to be an ingrained Japanese national characteristic.

These portraits of the enemy are created by a judicious blend of visual images, dialogue, music, and plot. The Nazis were particularly enamored of symbolism and ritual, and wartime films use the Nazis' own symbols against them. The "Heil Hitler!" salute was tailor-made for mockery: it becomes "Heil Heel" in *Remember Pearl Harbor!* (Republic, 1942) and Hitler himself says "Heil me!" in *The Devil with Hitler* (UA, 1943). The semantic association of "Heil" with "heel" was made in *The Daring Young Man* (Columbia, 1942)—"Who'd drink to that heel [Hitler]?"—and in the opening titles of *The Devil with Hitler*: "Once upon a time there were three heels…"

The swastika, an ancient symbol adopted by the Nazis as their emblem, took on a sinister aura (and has retained it ever since).[8] Numerous films feature swastikas superimposed on maps or globes, signifying the Nazis' desire to conquer the world. In *The Navy Comes Through* (RKO, 1942), the swastika flag is raised by an American merchant ship to fool German U-boats—but before raising the hated banner, an American crewman spits on it! For pure symbolic reductionism, *Once Upon a Honeymoon* (RKO, 1942) cannot be bested: in prewar Europe, a disillusioned American bitterly comments on a pair of Hitler's henchmen: "I wouldn't trust those two swastikas as far as I could throw Goering."[9]

German words which came into common usage during the war include "blitzkrieg" (from "blitz"—lightning and "krieg"—war), and "Panzer" (meaning armor, generally referring to tanks). Americans swiftly adopted these words and turned them on the Axis. The RAF suitor of a young American woman boasts of his "emotional blitzkrieg" in *Thumbs Up* (Republic, 1943). An Australian airman played by Errol Flynn in *Desperate Journey* (WB, 1942) tells a Nazi officer: "[Your] blitzkriegs have stopped blitzing," and in the same film there is a threat to "kick you right in the middle of your goosestep." The Germans at Dunkirk were caught with their "Panzers down," one character remarks (while playing with toy tanks) in *All Through the Night* (WB, 1942). Even the term "Nazi" (itself a contraction of the German initials for National Socialist German Workers Party) is subjected to ridicule: "Nazi" is easily corrupted to "nazty" (nasty), as in *That Nazty Nuisance* (UA, 1943), and in *My Favorite Blonde* (Paramount, 1942).

The cinematic use of the iconographic imagery of Japan and Nazi Germany occasionally eliminates any need for direct confrontation with human beings. The Rising Sun painted across the top of a floating mine is all that is required to simultaneously identify it with Japan, and to impart a sense of imminent danger in *Minesweeper* (Paramount, 1943). A Chinese resistance leader unequivocally displays his intentions to destroy the forces of Japanese occupation by shredding a Rising Sun flag in *Dragon Seed* (MGM, 1944). Actress Beulah Bondi, playing a middle-aged teacher in *Back to Bataan* (RKO, 1945), enters her one-room schoolhouse that has just been liberated by the Filipino resistance, immediately tears down the flag of Japan, and uses it as a rag to wipe the Japanese calligraphy off the blackboard!

While the Axis leaders—Hitler, Mussolini, and Hirohito (and sometimes Tojo)—are frequently vilified and scorned in film dialogue (and in the case of the first two men, are impersonated in feature films a number of times)—there are also a number of examples in which the *image* of the leader is desecrated or destroyed as a visual symbol of their impending downfall. A portrait of Hitler lies neglected in the rubble of a bombed German headquarters building in *The Master Race* (RKO, 1944), and a painting of Emperor Hirohito similarly

Top: *The Devil with Hitler* (UA, 1942): Satan (Alan Mowbray) is disgusted with the ineptitude of the Axis trio: Hitler (Bobby Watson), Suki-Yaki (George E. Stone), and Mussolini (Joe Devlin). Bottom: *The Navy Comes Through* (RKO Radio, 1942): Desi Arnaz (second from left) is the Cuban-born member of a Navy gun crew serving on a merchant ship. His shipmates are (left to right) Frank Fenton, Pat O'Brien, Jackie Cooper, and Lee Bonnell.

All Through the Night (Warner Bros., 1942): A den of Nazi spies, right in New York City. Seated: Conrad Veidt. Others, left to right: Peter Lorre, Kaaren Verne, Judith Anderson.

rests in bomb debris at end of *Behind the Rising Sun* (RKO, 1943). *The Wife Takes a Flyer* (Columbia, 1942) includes a double-edged incident, showing both the ruthless nature of fascism and the scorn which all freedom-loving people feel for dictators: a Dutch citizen is sentenced to death by the Nazis for painting the (buck) teeth and (slanted) eyes of Hirohito over a picture of Hitler!

Signs, Symbols and Messages

Repetition is an important component of film propaganda. Ideally, filmmakers would like to use preexisting images, words or symbols which already have a meaning for film audiences; at other times, a new symbol has to be created or an old one altered to serve a new purpose. Second World War films contain numerous examples of both types of "signs." Additionally, concepts and ideas were tailored to serve the war aims of Hollywood: motherhood, American history, baseball,

religion, democracy—all had appeared many times in pre-war motion pictures. But during WWII, all of these "American symbols" (and more) were converted to weapons to be used against the Axis.

Perhaps the most familiar symbol of the Second World War is the "V for Victory." Whether expressed digitally (holding two spread fingers aloft), verbally, visually, or even musically (the first four notes of Beethoven's Fifth Symphony, which coincidentally spell out "V" in Morse code), the "V" was the ubiquitous symbol of the Allies. One of its earliest incarnations was Prime Minister Winston Churchill's famous hand gesture, and his speech before the House of Commons on May 13, 1940:

What is our aim? ... one word ... It is victory; victory at all costs ... victory, however long and hard the road may be, for without victory, there is no survival.[10]

The V was a bold expression exuding national confidence and by the latter half of 1942 was omnipresent in the United

Top: *Dragon Seed* (MGM, 1944): "Chinese" Katharine Hepburn and Turhan Bey watch their fellow villagers at work in this adaptation of a Pearl S. Buck novel about China's struggle against the Japanese invaders. Bottom: *Behind the Rising Sun* (RKO Radio, 1943): Pacifist Japanese J. Carrol Naish tries to restrain his militaristic son (Tom Neal). This was one of the few wartime films to show "good" Japanese characters. At left: Don Douglas.

To Be or Not to Be (UA, 1942): Tom Dugan (as "Hitler"), Jack Benny, and Robert Stack are Polish patriots disguised as Nazis in this popular film. Charles Halton, at far left, looks suspicious. Lionel Atwill can be glimpsed between Dugan and Benny.

States, appearing in countless variations on war posters, the "Win the War" Eagle 3-cent stamps, beamed in Morse code from the radio tower logo of RKO-Radio Pictures at the beginning of nearly every one of the studio's films (through early 1945), and even on some wartime Christmas wrapping paper![11] In one form or another the "V for Victory" appeared in at least 41 fictional feature films released during 1942, and 29 more the following year.

The V for Victory was a powerful antidote to the unavoidable reality of the initial Axis military successes and an expression of faith in the certainty of final Allied victory. It was a dramatic symbol of Allied resilience and reassurance of the ultimate retribution that would be visited upon our enemies. When boldly painted over a German proclamation in *To Be or Not to Be* (UA, 1942) and a similar sign in *Commandos Strike at Dawn* (Columbia, 1943), the message is clear: though the Nazis may have overrun most of Europe, they would never subdue the spirit of the enslaved citizens of the occupied nations and their fighting Allies. Germany cannot escape revenge; her conquest of Europe will be ephemeral—

hence the power of the final gesture of a dying British pilot in *Desperate Journey*, who gives the V sign after being assured by his fellow crewmen that they destroyed their military target in occupied Poland. But as the momentum of actual Allied victories inexorably mounted throughout 1943 and thereafter, the symbolic power of the "V for Victory" increasingly diminished. Thus, by the final year of the war it was redundant and appeared in only eight American feature films.

A similar, although less widespread symbol was the "thumbs up" sign, often associated with airmen, and with Great Britain. Indeed, the gesture is used as the title for a 1943 Republic musical set in England, *Thumbs Up*, which praises the war work of British civilians. It also appears in *Eagle Squadron, God Is My Co-Pilot, We've Never Been Licked,* and *Bombardier,* all aviation films. Crewmen from a sunken Allied tanker flash the "thumbs up" sign as a German U-boat shines a spotlight on their lifeboat; evacuated Norwegian villagers give the same signal, promising to return to free their homeland from Nazi occupation. And in *Sahara* (Columbia, 1943), after chasing and killing an escaping Nazi prisoner, Tambul (Rex Ingram)

Desperate Journey (WB, 1942): The crew of a downed RAF bomber escapes from Nazi captivity disguised as German soldiers. Left to right: Alan Hale, Arthur Kennedy, Errol Flynn, Ronald Sinclair, and American volunteer Ronald Reagan.

gives Joe Gunn (Humphrey Bogart) the "thumbs up" to signify "mission accomplished," before succumbing to his own wounds.

After the "V," perhaps the most frequently used symbol (or combination of symbols) is the American flag icon, and related images, names, and historical documents, such as the Statue of Liberty, the Declaration of Independence, "Uncle Sam," George Washington, Abraham Lincoln, the Liberty Bell, and so on:

Always an important patriotic emblem in a country that pledged allegiance to its flag and sang of its origins in the national anthem, the Stars and Stripes took on a new symbolic weight during World War II.... In 1943, Congress legalized a Flag Code, mandating rituals of usage that confirmed the status of the flag as a quasi-sacred object, a focus for unity in a nation lacking the cohesive factors of shared race or religion.... [It] meant country, honor, Main Street, apple pie—all the things for which the soldier fought.[12]

Images of the American flag are, as would be expected, very frequently found in wartime films. *Keeper of the Flame*

(MGM, 1942) and *Action in the North Atlantic* (WB, 1943), for example, conclude with a shot of "Old Glory." *Commandos Strike at Dawn* (Columbia, 1943) and *None Shall Escape* (Columbia, 1944) both end with shots of *all* the flags of the United Nations, the American flag of course prominently displayed (*The Black Parachute*, also produced by Columbia Pictures, uses a lesser version of this image, although the Union Jack and the Nationalist Chinese flag are visible alongside the U.S. flag). To symbolize wartime alliance, the U.S. and Mexican flags are juxtaposed in the musical finale of *Hands Across the Border* (Republic, 1943), and the British Union Jack and the Stars and Stripes *both* hang in a *British* aircraft factory in *Thumbs Up*.

In *Guadalcanal Diary* (TCF, 1943), a Marine's small, personal American flag—carried wherever he has seen action in service of his country—replaces a huge Rising Sun flag which had flown over a Japanese base. Both *Yankee Doodle Dandy* (WB, 1942) and *Holiday Inn* (Paramount, 1942) contain musical numbers with patriotic motifs—in the former, of course,

Eagle Squadron (Universal, 1942): Yank in the RAF Robert Stack takes a tour of London during the Blitz; his British guide is Diana Barrymore.

George M. Cohan's "You're a Grand Old Flag." An elderly Filipino schoolmaster refuses to take down the *American* flag that flies in front of his school, and is hanged by the invading Japanese for his act of defiance. There are many other examples, including scenes of the Pledge of Allegiance and renditions of the "Star Spangled Banner." What was the flag to Americans? A symbol of their freedom, their democracy, of national pride and unity. "Flag-waving" was one of the easiest propaganda tools to use during the war: it never failed to command respect.

The Statue of Liberty was another American icon used to stoke the fires of patriotic fervor in film audiences. Among the films the Statue's image appears in are *Saboteur* (Universal, 1942), in which the film's hero (Robert Cummings) fights an Axis agent on the statue's torch-holding arm, and *Since You Went Away* (UA, 1944), where a female worker at a defense plant talks of her visit to the Statue of Liberty and recites the

Emma Lazarus poem inscribed on the statue's tablet. The woman is a refugee from Eastern Europe, which makes her devotion to the ideals of liberty—embodied by the Statue of Liberty—all the more touching.

The Statue of Liberty is included in the background montage during "Freedom Song" from *Holiday Inn*; the "George Washington, Jr." patriotic ballet montage in *Yankee Doodle Dandy* concludes with George M. Cohan's father (Walter Huston) costumed as Uncle Sam and his mother (Rosemary DeCamp) dressed as the Statue of Liberty (aka "Miss Liberty"). Not to be outdone, Mount Rushmore serves as the backdrop for "Old Glory," sung by Bing Crosby in *Star Spangled Rhythm* (Paramount, 1942).

Ironically, another often-used symbol of America was only a few years old when the war began. The Golden Gate Bridge, completed in the 1930s, nonetheless took on an iconic life of its own during the war, symbolizing the gate through

Commandos Strike at Dawn (Columbia, 1943): A "baseball" image is cleverly incorporated into the poster art for this film, which actually deals with British commandos and the Norwegian resistance.

which thousands of servicemen would pass on their way to combat in the Pacific, and (the lucky ones) on their way back home. In *You Came Along* (Paramount, 1945), *Air Force* (WB, 1943), and *Thirty Seconds Over Tokyo* (MGM, 1945), military airplanes fly over (or under!) the famous span. Ships or sub-

marines going out to or coming back from the war pass under the bridge in *Destination Tokyo*, *The Fighting Seabees*, *Stand by for Action*, and *So Proudly We Hail*. In *Seven Days Ashore* (RKO, 1944), a merchant ship (which has successfully rammed a Japanese submarine) is named the *SS Golden Gate*.

From the quintessential patriotic symbol—the flag—to the quintessential American sport—baseball—is not such a large leap. Nor is it so far from baseball to one of the most familiar commercial icons of the era, Coca-Cola. Hollywood utilized both baseball *and* Coke as symbols of the American spirit in its wartime features.

Baseball (and to a lesser extent, football) became a popular wartime symbol of America for several reasons. First, baseball is "the national pastime," a sport invented in the United States and more popular in this country than in any other. Furthermore, baseball embodies a number of American ideals: it is a sport which allows for individual expression but which requires a team effort; it is played on a green field, symbolizing the pastoral virtues and natural resources of America; it is played by adults as well as children, and to some degree represents an innocent, fun-loving nation—but the desire to win is present in all players, and they exert all of their energies to triumph. Baseball becomes almost a secular religion for Americans: kids grow up with it—some later become its priests (professional players), and of these, the stars achieve secular "sainthood," like Lou Gehrig and Babe Ruth. The rest of America forms the congregation and regularly attends services—either at the stadium or over the radio.

Wartime films utilizing the baseball-as-America metaphor include *Pride of the Yankees* (WB, 1942), *It Happened in Flatbush* (TCF, 1942), and *Ladies' Day* (RKO, 1942). These three films all deal with professional baseball, a sport that was seriously affected by the war (many of the best players enlisted or were drafted). However, baseball also turns up in such unlikely films as *Wilson* (TCF, 1944), *Woman of the Year*, and *Block Busters* (Monogram, 1944). In the latter film, the East Side Kids use baseball as the means of socializing a young French refugee to his temporary home. In *Guadalcanal Diary*, the battle-weary Marines huddle around a radio hoping to hear the results of games being played "back home."

There are also indirect baseball references in a number of wartime films. Brooklyn, home of the Dodgers, becomes a symbol of America (along with Texas). Brooklyn natives are typical Americans, the "common man," and there are few films dealing with the armed forces that do *not* feature at least one "guy from Brooklyn" (often William Bendix), and more often than not this character is a Dodgers' fan. In *The Devil with Hitler*, a spy returns to Germany from the United States with the following information: "The Brooklyn Dodgers are a cinch to win." The baseball *cap* even becomes a symbol of America in these films, representing the citizen-as-soldier, as compared to the strictly uniformed Nazis and Japanese (and even our British allies).

Top: *Air Force* (Warner Bros., 1943): The crew of the bomber "Mary Ann" scramble to take off from the Philippines in the face of a Japanese attack. Bottom: *Thirty Seconds Over Tokyo* (MGM, 1945): Chinese guerrillas rescue Capt. Ted Lawson (Van Johnson), whose airplane crashes in China after the Doolittle Raid on Tokyo.

Wing and a Prayer (TCF, 1944): Naval aviator Dana Andrews prepares to pilot his torpedo bomber against the Japanese fleet.

The baseball and football metaphor is explicitly utilized in films like *Smith of Minnesota* (Columbia, 1942), and *Spirit of Stanford* (Columbia, 1942), in which real-life collegiate sports heroes join "Uncle Sam's team" for the duration. The team concept is also spelled out in *Hollywood Canteen* (WB, 1944), when the black Golden Gate Quartet sings "The General Jumped At Dawn," with lyrics such as: "The general had a groovy crew/ A million lads and I'm telling you/ There were white men, black men, on the beam/ A real solid All-American team."

The Purple Heart (TCF, 1944) contains an almost subliminal allusion to the idea of a wartime team. If one includes the Chinese patriot who becomes an "honorary" member of the crew, the imprisoned American flyers on trial for their lives in Japan total nine, exactly the number needed for a baseball team. The men have their individual chances "at the plate" as they are interrogated and tortured by the Japanese, but they stick together and at the end win a moral victory over the enemy by virtue of their teamwork (not a single member breaks down and confesses).

Although it may seem odd that a soft drink could become a wartime symbol, Coca-Cola—another American invention—is used in just that manner. In the days before "product placement" became big business, the appearance of actual brand names in films was relatively rare. However, Coke transcended this practice, and became a symbol of America, of normalcy. In *Wing and a Prayer* (TCF, 1944), a veteran pilot who has shot down several Japanese planes is toasted in the ship's mess by a colleague for "subtracting Zeroes." Since liquor had been banned on U.S. Navy vessels since before WWI, what does the airman use for his gesture? A Coke. Coke machines appear in barracks or canteens in *Thirty Seconds Over Tokyo* and *Winged Victory*. A German girl, working in Germany's spy-filled New York consulate in *Margin for Error*, shows that she is truly a friend of America by drinking a Coke. Other "Coke" scenes appear in films like *Two Girls and a Sailor* and *Back to Bataan*.

Wartime propaganda made use of many symbols, from the

Winged Victory (TCF, 1944): Air Corps cadet Don Taylor faces his superior officers (including a WAC) during training. Notice the Coke machine in the background.

common (Coca-Cola and baseball) to the sublime—motherhood, and religion. In each case, these icons, concepts, or symbols became particularly embued with the wartime mentality. Films were no longer content to say simply "Motherhood is good." Now, films must say "Motherhood is good and that is why the war must be won."

Hollywood was never afraid of sentiment, and evoking the image of American (and Allied) motherhood was a strong weapon used against the forces of fascism. Wartime films are filled with stalwart mothers: *Since You Went Away, The Human Comedy, Mrs. Miniver, The Sullivans, The White Cliffs of Dover*, to name but a few. In *This Is the Army* (WB, 1943), a woman loses her older son in the attack on Pearl Harbor; when her next-oldest expresses his desire to join up, she resists. Why must *she* risk another child? But by the end of the film, she realizes that the war is a just cause, and that every American family will be called upon to sacrifice many times. Turning to her son, she gives him her blessing, and says "Give it to them!" In *Tender Comrade* (RKO, 1943), Ginger Rogers tells her infant son that his father (her husband, killed in action), died

to make a better world for children to live in. Ted Lawson (Van Johnson), preparing for the Doolittle bombing raid on Tokyo in *Thirty Seconds Over Tokyo*, expresses some doubt about the possible deaths of Japanese civilians, but he justifies his mission because, if he does not bomb Tokyo, the Japanese might soon be dropping bombs on his pregnant wife back in the United States!

Mothers of the free nations support the war for various reasons, but one major point made repeatedly in wartime films is that the sanctity of the family is threatened by fascism, a concept illustrated many times. Not only are men, women, and children killed by the Axis, families are separated, children indoctrinated with fascist ideas, and women are raped and abused by fascist soldiers. Loss of intellectual, political, social and economic freedom is bad enough, but when the Nazis and Japanese assail the family unit, they have gone too far!

Like motherhood, religion is enlisted in the anti-fascist crusade. Essentially, wartime films assert that God is on *our* side: the Nazis have created their own religion, the cult of Fuehrer-

Margin for Error (TCF, 1942): Before America's entry into the war, German consul Otto Preminger looks askance at his Jewish protector, New York policeman Milton Berle. Also seated: Joan Bennett, Carl Esmond. Note the portrait of Hitler on the wall.

worship, and the Japanese are warlike "heathen," possessed by the cult of "bushido."[13] While few if any films feature explicit divine intervention on the side of the Allies, the religious faith of Allied soldiers and civilians is visible in many ways.

For instance, Roman Catholics are shown making the sign of the cross in *Manila Calling* and *Objective Burma!*, just before going into combat against the "godless" Japanese; the re-release version of *The Sign of the Cross* features a new prologue in which a Catholic priest *and* a Protestant priest drop leaflets on occupied Rome. The Lord's Prayer is used for dramatic effect in *Gung Ho!* and *Lifeboat*; verses from the 27th Psalm conclude *Since You Went Away*—"Be of good courage, and he shall strengthen your heart, all ye that trust in the Lord." The primary musical *leitmotif* of the resistance film *Edge of Darkness* is the hymn "A Mighty Fortress is Our God," ironically written by a German, Martin Luther.

Another sign that God is on the side of the democracies is the frequent appearance of positive clerical figures. These are not persecuted figures in occupied countries—although there are plenty of those—but rather "muscular Christians"

actively taking part in the war effort, whether in combat or on the home front. *China's Little Devils* (Monogram, 1945) and *God Is My Co-Pilot* (WB, 1945) both feature American missionaries in China who staunchly support anti–Japanese operations. Preston Foster is a Marine Corps chaplain who risks his life along with his fellow leathernecks in *Guadalcanal Diary*. The stirring climax of *Mrs. Miniver* (MGM, 1942) depicts vicar Henry Wilcoxon (a former DeMille hero, hardly a weakling or pacifist) speaking to his parishioners in his bombed-out church: Wilcoxon does not preach passive acquiescence or forgiveness, he assures his listeners (and the film's audience) that justice will prevail. Rabbi David (Richard Hale) in *None Shall Escape* does not go meekly with his fellow Jews when the Nazis order them deported (presumably to death camps)—he stands up and urges his people to fight, to resist the Nazis with all their might, to die if they must but not to submit to fascist tyranny. There are many other films which, overtly and otherwise, reinforce the idea that the war is being fought not only for democracy, but is also a moral crusade against the forces of darkness.

Top: *The Human Comedy* (MGM, 1943): What we're fighting for—Mom's home cooking. William Saroyan's sentimental tale of the American home front featured, left to right: Donna Reed, Mickey Rooney, Dorothy Morris (note the home-canning jar in her hand) and Fay Bainter. Bottom: *Mrs. Miniver* (MGM, 1942): Mrs. Miniver (Greer Garson) greets her husband (Walter Pidgeon), who has just returned from helping evacuate Allied soldiers at Dunkirk.

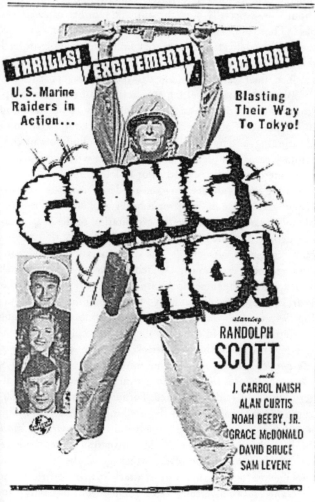

NIOTA THEATRE

Niota, Tennessee

Saturday Night, Dec. 5th.

Doors Open 7:30 P.M. — Adm. 15c and 25c Tax Inc.

THRILLS! EXCITEMENT! ACTION!

U. S. Marine Raiders in Action...

Blasting Their Way To Tokyo!

GUNG HO!

starring

RANDOLPH SCOTT

with

J. CARROL NAISH
ALAN CURTIS
NOAH BEERY, JR.
GRACE McDONALD
DAVID BRUCE
SAM LEVENE

Gung Ho! (Universal, 1943): Randolph Scott trains a group of Marines, then leads them on a raid on Japanese-held Makin Island.

Why We Fight and How We Fight

Few Americans, particularly after seeing an assortment of war films, would question the need to win the war. As previously noted, WWII was presented as a war against fascism, and fascism was identified as an unholy alliance of the godless Nazis and Japanese. But the basic answer to the question "What are we fighting for," would probably have been, "Freedom." President Franklin D. Roosevelt codified this in his "Four Freedoms" speech, citing "freedom from want, freedom of worship, freedom from fear, and freedom of speech," as the goals we were seeking.

In support of this concept, Hollywood depicted the war as a choice between slavery and freedom, perhaps also taking a cue from the "Century of the Common Man" speech by Vice President Henry A. Wallace, delivered in May 1942: in this speech, Wallace made a point of the "slave world-free world" dichotomy the war had created. During dramatic high points of relevant films, it is pointed out that a failure to defeat the Axis will result in continued slavery for occupied nations and the future enslavement of the remainder of the "free world" (including, ironically, the USSR!).

This message is explicitly delivered in numerous wartime films. The resistance circulates a provocative leaflet in an occupied village in *This Land Is Mine* (RKO, 1943): "Do Not Believe in the Generosity of the Conquerors. If they are not driven out of our land it means generations of slavery for our people." In the midwestern small town of *Happy Land* (TCF, 1943), a radio broadcast announcing the Nazi invasion of Poland provokes an emotional outburst from an old man who bitterly recalls America's earlier encounter with the Kaiser's Germany: "same old bunch of gangsters trying to make slaves ...." An Army deserter (Alan Ladd) in *Lucky Jordan* (Paramount, 1942) is warned that if America loses the war "we'll end up ... Nazi slaves." In *Underground Agent* (Columbia, 1942), a Mexican-American named Miguel, mortally wounded by Axis spies, makes a dying patriotic speech affirming his faith in America, where all people are "free men, not slaves." American civilians resisting the Japanese occupation of the Philippines make a final defiant broadcast over a captured enemy radio at the end of *Manila Calling*: "...blood of Americans and Filipinos flowed together ... our sacrifices wrecked the timetable [of the] warlords of Tokyo [in this] fight between a slave world and a free world."

Similarly, the process of democracy is demonstrated in several wartime films, a clear contrast with the brutal dictatorships in occupied countries or Axis nations themselves. Civilians in combat areas exercise their democratic rights: they *vote* to take over a Japanese broadcast station in *Manila Calling*; shipwreck survivors *vote* to place a rescued German seaman in charge of their lives (based on his superior knowledge) in *Lifeboat*; nurses and female volunteers democratically decide to stay with the wounded on Bataan rather than be evacuated, in *Cry Havoc!* (ironically, in a similar film, *So Proudly We Hail!*, the women are Army nurses and receive evacuation *orders* which they must obey). French convicts, escaping from the literal prison of Devil's Island in *Passage to Marseilles*, make a group decision about their future: they decide to fight on the side of the Free French.

Even military personnel, faced with extraordinary circumstances, behave like democratic Americans and vote on a course of action: in *The Purple Heart* captured U.S. airmen

China's Little Devils (Monogram, 1945): Child actor "Ducky" Louie plays a young Chinese boy who resists the Japanese invaders of his country, assisted by missionary Harry Carey and Flying Tiger Paul Kelly.

are given the choice between death or imprisonment by the Japanese. When the "undemocratic horde [gives them the right of] majority rule," the Americans vote to stay silent about the origin of their flight, thus condemning themselves to death in the service of a higher ideal. The multinational tank crew in *Sahara* makes a collective decision to stay and fight after a patriotic speech by Sgt. Joe Gunn (Humphrey Bogart). Crew members from a sunken vessel make a group decision to sign on a new Liberty Ship in *Action in the North Atlantic*; when one man wavers, his mates are irritated but their anger is defused by another sailor's defense of the right to free speech. Later, one character says "Liberty" ships are well named. In *The Impostor* (Universal, 1944), French soldiers bound for a Vichy outpost in Africa seize their transport ship and sail for Free French territory instead.

In each of these examples, individuals and groups arrive at the "right" decision on their own, by a democratic process. The government does not have to make the decisions for them,

and their decisions are not made in fear of later retribution. Citizens of a democratic country are not only free, they can be counted on to act morally when a choice needs to be made.

In addition to explaining the issues at stake in the war, Hollywood also addressed some of the moral implications involved in the *process* of winning the war.

A critical aspect in regard to the American audience was the overwhelming belief that the U.S and the Allies would ultimately achieve total victory. Most Americans had little doubt about this, especially once the difficult summer of 1942 was past. Therefore, a persistent problem facing the media was the need to deliver a message that simultaneously reinforced this confidence while making it clear that without continued sacrifice, final victory would be delayed or even jeopardized—complacency would prolong the sacrifices of our men overseas. However, this message was continually complicated by the evidence of abundance throughout the country, in spite of rationing, and by the relatively light overall number of U.S. military casualties (despite intense fighting with the Japanese on numerous Pacific islands) prior to late 1943.

One means of defusing the tendency towards complacency was the use of "emotional heavy artillery."[14] The most obvious example would be the exploitation of the Pearl Harbor debacle in wartime films. Although the idea that the attack represented America's lack of preparation or even incompetence is assiduously avoided by Hollywood, the sneak attack by the Japanese upon America's Pacific Fleet base at Pearl Harbor is invoked at least 44 times in films released during 1942 (and 35 times the following year). Scenes depicting the Japanese air raid itself, or alleged fifth columnist activities designed to facilitate the attack, appear in *Remember Pearl Harbor!*, *Submarine Raider* (Columbia, 1942), *Air Force* (WB, 1943) and *This Is the Army*. Sometimes only the gruesome aftermath of the raid is indicated. For instance, a transport carrying Army nurses bypasses the smoking naval base and joins a convoy headed for the Philippines in *So Proudly We Hail!* Marine raiders are given added incentive to slaughter the Japanese as they pass some of the wreckage of the fleet (actual footage inserted) on their way to attack a Japanese-held island in *Gung Ho!* (Universal, 1943). Such images not only subconsciously reminded Americans that the Japanese were an enemy whose military power was to be respected, they also reminded audiences that the debt had not yet been paid in full, *and* reinforced the resolve for a complete, unconditional victory.

The push for final victory involved adoption of tactics which had to be justified or glossed over. Nazi atrocities and Japanese actions are played to the hilt, but the massive Allied bombing of Axis and occupied nations is treated gingerly. It is always presented as a grim necessity, and the damage and injury to civilians is minimized.

In *Bombardier*, for instance, a pre-war demonstration of "precision bombing" is praised, not only for its greater

This Is the Army (WB, 1943): Boxing champion Joe Louis appears as himself in this production number. Most appearances of black servicemen in wartime Hollywood were in such non-action roles.

efficiency in destroying enemy targets, but for its humanity, since civilian targets will be spared. The aircrews preparing for the Tokyo raid in *Thirty Seconds Over Tokyo* are specifically directed to *military* targets on the Japanese home islands. *Bomber's Moon* and *Desperate Journey* begin with Allied bombing raids that are again specifically directed at military targets only.

There is a brief reference to the "thousand-plane raids" staged on Germany by Allied bombers in *The Navy Comes Through*, but since this comes from a Nazi U-boat captain, audiences could easily discount his description of the damage wrought on German cities.[15]

Surprisingly, a few films do show the effects of Allied bombing. *Enemy of Women* (Monogram, 1944), a fictionalized biography of Nazi Propaganda Minister Goebbels, features a scene in which Goebbels makes a radio speech discounting the effects of Allied bombs—while ordinary Germans labor to clean up the rubble after a raid! *Women in Bondage* (Monogram, 1944) depicts the bombing of Germany in a positive

light, since the bombs "mercifully" kill an anti–Nazi German woman who is being pressured to bear children in service of the Reich. *Behind the Rising Sun* (RKO, 1943) shows some of the results of Allied bombing of the home islands of Japan, but again this is seen as justified—in fact, the protagonist of the film, a Japanese father, prays for the bombs to destroy the Japanese militarists![16]

Son of Lassie (MGM, 1945) contains a puzzling sequence which, significantly, seems to have passed without comment at the time of the film's release. Allied planes bomb a peaceful Norwegian village in occupied Norway, a village which has *no* visible German fortifications, *no* war industry, and *no* obvious mines or other sources of aid to the Nazi war machine. Numerous civilians are killed, apparently only to provide a *deus ex machina* for the escape of downed RAF flyer Peter Lawford!

None of these films, understandably, shows much sympathy for the inhabitants of Axis and occupied countries who are on the receiving end of Allied bombs, and no mention is

Stand By for Action (MGM, 1942): Tough sailor Brian Donlevy is not impressed by the dapper reservist Robert Taylor.

made of the effects of the so-called "round-the-clock" bombing of Germany by the Allies, which began in January 1943 (American bombers by day, British bombers by night),[17] nor of the fire-bombing of Hamburg (July 1943) and Dresden (February 1945), nor of the horrendous toll bombs took on Japanese cities (on March 10, 1945, Tokyo was fire-bombed and over 130,000 people were killed or injured).[18]

Inhabitants of an occupied country actually *approve* of Allied bombing of their nation in *This Land Is Mine*. While sitting in an air raid shelter in their village, one character asks: "Why don't they bomb Germany?" Louise (Maureen O'Hara), replies: "Every factory and railroad in Europe *is* Germany ... until the Germans are driven out," the bombers are "our friends in the sky."

The same standard applied, to a lesser degree, in naval warfare. While in reality American submarines decimated the Japanese merchant fleet, U.S. submarines in wartime films destroy military targets only. On the other hand, American civilians are the victims of *Japanese* sub attacks in a number of films, including *The Amazing Mrs. Halliday* (Universal,

1943), *Stand By for Action* (MGM, 1942) and *Submarine Raider*.

The general impression seems to have been that the Nazis and Japanese were getting what was coming to them, and that "collateral damage" (to homes, churches, universities, hospitals, etc.) was unfortunate but no worse than the Nazis and Japanese had already done to *us*, and *would still do*, given the chance.

Such feelings also carry over into the general disregard for *enemy* lives which appears in many wartime films. Nazis and Japanese are slaughtered in film after film, but only in legitimate pursuit of Allied goals. There are few if any examples of Allied characters killing in rage, or solely for revenge. Two of the very few "cold-blooded" killings which appear in wartime films occur in *Passage to Marseilles* and *Destination Tokyo*. In the first film, Humphrey Bogart machine-guns the survivors of a German plane which has been shot down, avenging the death of his ship's cabin boy, who was killed by the strafing Nazi aircraft. Similarly, in the latter film a downed Japanese pilot is shot by a submarine crew member, but only after treacherously stabbing an American sailor who was trying to rescue him from the sea.

On the other hand, no false mercy is shown to Axis soldiers. The Allies use all of their might, every weapon at their disposal, to crush the fascist oppressors. The depersonalization of Nazis and—particularly—Japanese soldiers makes their deaths easier to take. As discussed in the chapter detailing images of the Enemy, treating the enemy as "vermin" who must be "exterminated" eliminates a great deal of the moral opprobrium attached to wholesale killing. Furthermore, the outrageous atrocities committed at every opportunity by the Enemy, and their militaristic track record "prove" that the war must be ruthlessly prosecuted to achieve final, total victory.

Conclusions

The Second World War represents perhaps the epitome of film as propaganda. Never before or since has the medium been so powerful, so widespread, and so united in its goals. With more than forty years of filmmaking experience behind it, the film industry knew all of the "tricks." The Enemy was clearly identifiable, and could be portrayed in simple, dialectical terms. The other media, the U.S. government, and the film audience willingly cooperated in the process: the other media contained the same themes and messages; there were few dissenting voices and no channels for the Enemy's viewpoint to be heard.

Did the results justify the expenditure of time and effort? Would the American people have supported the war effort as wholeheartedly had the film industry *ignored* the war, concentrating instead on escapist entertainment? Probably not—while WWII was widely viewed as a "just" war, it was too easy for some Americans to evade their responsibilities, to hope that the "other guy" would pick up the slack. The film industry alone did not sell Bonds, collect scrap, enlist soldiers and sailors, or contribute in a thousand ways to the war effort—but it did its part.

16. Reluctant Heroes: America's Armed Forces as Depicted in Films

They were, as a group, unwilling, nonmilitaristic heroes.[1]
"Even in uniform, they're still civilians. "—This Is The Army *(WB, 1943)*

The mental image many Americans have of the Second World War, fifty years after its conclusion, consists of war film clichés, often from postwar releases (*Battleground*—1949, *Sands of Iwo Jima*—1949, *The Longest Day*—1962) or television programs (like *Combat*).[2] As time passes and WWII veterans and those who lived through the war as civilians become a dwindling part of the U.S. population, the war becomes much more of a secondhand "memory," and there are fewer firsthand participants around to correct erroneous impressions.

But watching films released between 1942 and 1945—or reading books and magazines printed during this period—cannot be relied upon for completely accurate information about WWII, especially if such popular culture products are not placed in perspective. Indeed, in the depiction of the men and women of the armed forces, wartime films present only one side of the story.

During the Second World War there was a particular image of the armed forces which was acceptable for motion pictures, an image that owed more to the film industry and the government's concept of what would best serve the nation's war goals than it did to any reflection of reality.

If there are relatively few memorable Combat films from the war years, the reasons are these: the government (and thus the film industry) did not wish to portray extensive scenes of realistic battle, showing American servicemen dying or being seriously wounded; furthermore, WWII was to some extent a "long distance" war, with air and naval forces carrying a large burden, particularly in the early years of the conflict, which mitigated against films featuring depictions of "personal" combat between Americans and enemy soldiers; and finally, while the war was on, the film industry was operating under wartime shortages of material and personnel, limiting the scope of potential war films. After the cessation of hostilities, many of these obstacles were removed, and large-scale war films were once again possible, although a Combat film "boom" never developed.

Thus, films made during the war that focus on the military are often as interesting for what they do *not* show as for what does appear on screen. While there are myriad references to the armed forces of the United States in Hollywood's wartime films (references to the U.S. Army exceed any other coding term in our study, and Navy references are fourth overall), motion pictures actually focusing on the military—those containing sustained scenes of training and combat—are relatively few in number. For instance, just 30 feature films of the period are classified in the Filmography as dealing in any significant way with the training of service personnel.

Presumably due to their greater visibility, combat-oriented films have consistently received an inordinate amount of attention in previous film studies.[3] But less than 50 films are classified under the Combat genre (a few of which, such as *The Immortal Sergeant*—TCF, 1943—exclusively feature the armed forces of our Allies and are thereby discussed in Chapter 18) and only about half of these are predominantly set in a combat environment. For example, out of eight films classified in the Combat genre in 1942, two contain very limited (naval) battle footage—*Submarine Raider* (Columbia), and *Stand by for Action* (MGM). Only a single Combat film from 1942 features ground units of the United States armed forces in action—the gallant defense by the Marines of an isolated Pacific base, as depicted in *Wake Island* (Paramount).

Thus, our discussion of the image of the armed forces in wartime films is actually much broader than the traditional Combat film genre, encompassing a far greater number of films which feature soldiers, sailors, and airmen who are *not* actually fighting the enemy.

Jitterbugs in Uniform

The most frequent wartime fictional film appearance of men and women in America's armed forces is in a non-combat situation. Many are simply uniformed props in crowd scenes, appearing on the street, in nightclubs, and in train stations, bus stations and airports. Nearly half are never shown carrying a weapon or interacting with a weapons system. In fact, during 1942 and 1943, servicemen and women are just as likely to be portrayed fighting spies or saboteurs on the home front (refer to Chapter 21) as engaging in hostilities with organized military units of the Axis.

Overall, they are even more apt to be actively engaged in sexual combat—that is, servicemen and women in film are at greater risk of losing their hearts than their lives. For instance, when newly furloughed Pacific naval veteran Windy (Sonny Tufts) is pressed for details about his combat experiences in "the Slot" (1942–1943 Solomon Islands campaign) in *Here Come the WAVES* (Paramount, 1944), Windy dryly cuts off his inquisitive civilian pal: "The only battle I'm interested in tonight is the battle of the sexes." In *Crash Dive* (TCF, 1943) the extended campaign of romantic conquest of a schoolteacher (Anne Baxter) conducted by a U. S. Navy officer, played by sex symbol Tyrone Power, takes place between a couple of comparatively short combat sequences.

On occasion our fighting men are shown battling over a woman before ever engaging the enemy. Such a subplot is delivered in the form of comic relief in *Gung Ho!* (Universal, 1943). During the first half of the film, two young Marines (Noah Beery Jr. and David Bruce), when not training for a raid against a Japanese-held island, employ various tactics to gain a romantic advantage with the girl from back home (who

as a defense worker has conveniently relocated near their San Diego base).

In Training films, rivalry over the girl is usually the major source of dramatic conflict. In *There's Something About a Soldier* (Columbia, 1943), taking place at an anti-aircraft artillery training facility for officers, the base secretary (Jean Parker)—described at one point as a "90 millimeter sensation"—is the primary object of contention between soldiers Tom Neal and Bruce Bennett.

Sometimes, the American military man, while still stationed in the States, is compelled to fend off a romantic assault by the opposite sex. Johnny Cabot (Bing Crosby), a popular crooner who has enlisted in the Navy, is blitzkrieged by a busload of admiring female defense workers while on guard duty at the naval base gate in *Here Come the WAVES* (the screenwriters may have been inspired by stories of similar incidents occurring when Clark Gable was at the Army Air Force Training Center in Miami Beach).[4] *Bring on the Girls* (Paramount, 1945) depicts the romantic interactions between two sailors (Eddie Bracken and Sonny Tufts) and two nightclub employees (Veronica Lake and Marjorie Reynolds). *Seven Days Leave* and *Star Spangled Rhythm* (Paramount, 1942) are two examples of films highlighting the stateside romantic adventures of servicemen on leave.

Servicemen appearing in Hollywood's feature films who are stationed or furloughed in non-combat areas act out in a culturally acceptable form the fantasies of the millions of men in uniform—sexual fantasies and dreams of homecoming. A sexually deprived G.I. in a Quonset hut in Alaska is admiring a wall full of pinups when a starlet from a touring show enters (as if by magic) and begins dancing with him. His mates quickly form a line to wait their turn for a spin with the pretty blonde. The final shot of this scene from *Follow the Boys* (Universal, 1944) shows the young performer wearing heavy boots in order to protect her feet.[5] A USO show at the base canteen in *Seven Days Leave* (RKO, 1942) features a happy fat soldier in khaki athletically cutting the rug with the featured Latin female singer. The "canteen" films inform soldiers that "your uniform is your ticket," and no civilians are allowed (except as workers and hostesses).

Wartime movie audiences—both male and female—may have felt that a soldier on the screen chasing skirts was as much or more entertaining than watching a soldier fighting America's enemies. This viewing experience helped satisfy a basic need, fulfilling the fantasies of lonesome men and women. Facing a definite shortage of available males, single women made the song "They're Either Too Young or Too Old" (from *Thank Your Lucky Stars*—WB, 1943) a popular hit during the war. In the context of the war, particularly with regard to Training and Combat films, there were limited opportunities for male/female relationships to develop. Thus the moviegoer was presented with assorted, artificially created wartime situations bringing men and women together.

Iceland (TCF, 1942): the ubiquitous "V" for Victory takes form at the finale of this film. Sonja Henie has the point position.

Servicemen are most likely to encounter women who had some connection with the military themselves: women working in secretarial capacities on military bases—*Bombardier*, *Thunder Birds*, et al.—and relatives living on or near the base—in *Destroyer*, for example—and nurses (*To the Shores of Tripoli*). Even a stateside hospital can be a way station to romance, as in *Bride by Mistake*, *Christmas in Connecticut*, and *Thrill of a Romance*, although not all of the females involved are nurses. *Iceland* (TCF, 1942), and *Doughboys in Ireland* (Columbia, 1943) contain romances between American servicemen stationed overseas and local women. Another popular wartime meeting place (in films, at least) is the "canteen," officially sponsored or otherwise. A considerable number of these films were released in 1943–44, and most had some sort of romantic plot: *Stage Door Canteen* (UA, 1943), *Salute for Three* (Paramount, 1943), *Hollywood Canteen* (WB, 1944), *Cowboy Canteen* (Columbia, 1944), *She's a Sweetheart* (Columbia, 1944), and so on.

There are surprisingly few instances in wartime films of a soldier visiting an established girlfriend while on leave; instead, the romantic action usually occurs with a new girl—the typical wartime whirlwind romance. These rapid courtships—usually culminating in marriage or at least an "understanding"—are an acceptable, moral alternative to the (taboo) portrayal of one night stands (*The Miracle of Morgan's Creek* is something of an exception, although the filmmakers were forced to include scenes referring to a quickie marriage between Trudy Kockenlocker and the never-seen "Pvt. Ratskiwatski"). Wartime film examples include *The Clock* (MGM, 1945), *Music in Manhattan* (RKO, 1944), *Anchors Aweigh* (MGM, 1945), *Pillow to Post* (WB, 1945), *Those Endearing Young Charms* (RKO, 1945), and *Thrill of a Romance* (MGM, 1945).

Thrill of a Romance is mildly risqué, featuring as it does a budding love relationship between a wounded veteran (Van Johnson) and a *married* woman (Esther Williams). However, Williams is a bride in name only, since her husband (a) never consummated their marriage, having been called away to Washington on government business, and since (b) his divorce from a previous wife was never finalized, so his marriage to Williams is not legal, after all. Civilians were not the only ones whose marriages went unconsummated due to the exigencies

Salute for Three (Paramount, 1943): Compare the pose on this ad mat with the famous Grable pinup. Hollywood often combined sex with patriotism to sell its wartime product.

of wartime: *One Thrilling Night* (Monogram, 1942), *G.I. Honeymoon* (Monogram, 1945), *Murder on the Waterfront* (WB, 1943), and *Army Wives* (Monogram, 1945) all concern frustrated soldier-husbands who have to leave their equally frustrated brides before enjoying the nuptial bed.

In Hollywood films, to a certain extent as in real life, the war simultaneously separated people and brought them together. Difficult separations are only portrayed in the relatively small number of films featuring happily married couples (*Tender Comrade* and *Thirty Seconds Over Tokyo*, most prominently). But most Hollywood wartime leads are unmarried, and thus the war is presented as a grand adventure providing a unique opportunity to meet new people.

Encounters with prostitutes, a not uncommon wartime occurrence for servicemen, are alluded to in only a few mo-

tion pictures. An amusing example occurs at the beginning of *Star Spangled Rhythm*. Three gobs who have just disembarked from their ship—after months away from home—pass right by three available "working girls" without even noticing them. As the women look at each another in amazement, the sailors instead pause to gaze longingly at a Paramount Pictures billboard promoting "Glamour Squad," a fictitious film featuring a cheesecake line in swimsuits.

The subject of prostitution is matter-of-factly treated in *Stage Door Canteen*: a career Army sergeant expresses surprise when he is assured he will not get "rolled" in the popular and "decent" servicemen's club (presumably unlike his experiences in sleazy bars and nightclubs). *Action in the North Atlantic* (WB, 1943) is more revealing with regards to prostitution, in a gritty scene between a Merchant Marine captain and his first

Stage Door Canteen (UA, 1943): Just before shipping out, soldiers Lon McCallister and Michael Harrison (later known as Sunset Carson) visit the Stage Door Canteen, where they meet celebrities like Katharine Cornell and Aline MacMahon.

mate (Humphrey Bogart). The mate has spent the night with Pearl (Julie Bishop); the captain comes to Pearl's apartment in the early morning hours to inform Bogart he is needed aboard their new ship, and treats Pearl insultingly, assuming she is a prostitute. When Bogart casually informs the captain that the couple is "spliced," the latter makes amends by giving Pearl his wife's phone number.

By way of apology to the offended Pearl, the captain also tells her that in recent years the sailors had seen unpleasant things while "hangin' around" Axis ports. This only makes sense within the context of the film if one recalls the wartime trend of linking female spies with sex. In an earlier scene in a smoke-filled waterfront dive, Bogart knocks out a drunk who is loudly blathering about troop movements, both to prevent any spy from taking advantage of the situation, and so that he can listen to Pearl's singing.

Battlefield romances between a nurse and a serviceman, often culminating in marriage and a single evening's consummation, occur in a number of Combat genre films. In addition to simply providing a standard Hollywood romantic in-terlude, their inclusion was probably also intended as a symbolic antidote to the hatred and killing depicted in combat-oriented motion pictures.

In *So Proudly We Hail!*, the military couple (Claudette Colbert and George Reeves) share their special night in an anti-aircraft gun emplacement on Corregidor. After the two lovers finish the bottle of wine given them as a wedding gift, it is symbolically broken over the barrel of the gun. The groom departs on a dangerous mission the next morning and does not return.[6] War correspondent Ernie Pyle gives away the bride (another nurse) in *The Story of G.I. Joe* (UA, 1945); the ceremony in a gutted church on the Italian front has just been completed when the wedding party must take cover to avoid incoming German shells. The couple spend their honeymoon in the back of an ambulance. The groom is later reported killed in action.

Some form of warfront romance takes place in several other films, involving civilians and military personnel. Examples include *Flying Tigers* (Republic, 1942), *Corregidor* (PRC, 1943), *The Fighting Seabees* (Republic, 1944) and *Back*

A Bell for Adano (TCF, 1945): American occupation officer John Hodiak supervises the installation of a new town bell in the Italian village he commands.

to Bataan (RKO, 1945). Interestingly enough, few wartime Combat films hint at romantic or sexual relations between American servicemen and women from foreign countries. Two films set in Italy do suggest this: *A Bell for Adano* (TCF, 1945) and *The Story of G.I. Joe*. Since Italy was widely considered a country which had been "liberated" from fascist rule—rather than a captured enemy country—the Italians were viewed somewhat positively. Furthermore, the liaisons in these two films are not central to the films' plots.[7] In a way, Hollywood's reluctance is understandable—the industry (and the U.S. government) would not want soldiers to ship out *expecting* to find willing sexual partners in combat areas, nor would filmmakers want to needlessly worry wives, girlfriends, and mothers in the audience. A number of *post*-war films about WWII, on the other hand, do portray such romances.

The dramatic action in many wartime motion pictures largely unfolds in and around military bases and involves men on leave from combat theatres. On a number of occasions, the single significant indication of future potential combat for the leads (as opposed to exposure to a veteran's battle experiences

through a brief prologue, flashback, or dialogue reference) is the concluding footage in which the men are shown "shipping out." This invariably includes a scene or montage portraying uniformed men proudly marching off and embarking upon some form of transport (train, ship) that will convey them to one of the war fronts. A final embrace with the heroine, the American flag fluttering, and a patriotic medley or romantically inspirational song (such as "My Shining Hour" in *The Sky's the Limit*, RKO, 1943) are virtually *de rigueur*: *Private Buckaroo* (Universal, 1942), *Seven Days Leave*, *To the Shores of Tripoli* (TCF, 1942), *This Is the Army* (WB, 1943), and *Here Come the WAVES* all contain such scenes. Sometimes, as in *This Is the Army*, a symbolic reaffirmation of faith in the future of the nation is demonstrated by a quickie marriage ceremony immediately before departure.

Few wartime films address the topic of marriage problems caused by the war. *The Impatient Years* (Columbia, 1944) makes a rare reference to war-related divorce, and even this situation is (of course) straightened out in the end. *Marriage Is a Private Affair* (MGM, 1944) also treats this topic in a

So Proudly We Hail! (Paramount, 1943): American nurses share the hard times during the Japanese invasion of the Philippines. Paulette Goddard and Claudette Colbert at right.

romantic-comedy manner: Lana Turner finds John Hodiak less romantic and dashing when he doffs his uniform in order to supervise a defense plant making crucial war materials. She nearly strays (Hodiak's rival is a handsome man—James Craig—*still* in uniform), but remains faithful to her husband (who manages to return to active duty, anyway). There are a number of home front-oriented films detailing some of the problems among service wives left behind to run their home, supervise children, and (in some cases) hold down a job, but in most of these films—*Tender Comrade, Since You Went Away,* et al.—the husband is rarely seen and thus the military component of the equation is minimized.[8]

Most likely due to the difficulty and expense of realistically staging battle footage, many so-called Combat films include extended training sequences in the United States. As a result, the essential bonding of the major male characters is developed in a relatively benign venue. This locale also permits the logical introduction of a female character, usually resulting in a romantic rivalry between two male leads. During the subsequent combat phase of the film, one of the men (who

has often displayed some moral flaw) is either killed or severely wounded performing a heroic deed, thereby resolving the dramatic problem of who will be rewarded with the girl back home. Variations on this theme are essential to the plots of such films as *Aerial Gunner* (Paramount, 1943), *Bombardier* (RKO, 1943), *Gung Ho!,* and *The Fighting Seabees* (Republic, 1944).

Scenes of military maneuvers and "war games," a popular topic in 1940 and 1941, are relatively rare during the war.[9] There are only six such references coded in 1942, and six for the whole remainder of the war. *Two Yanks in Trinidad* (Columbia), for instance, an early 1942 release, features an extensive sequence of maneuvers on a Caribbean island, once again making use of newsreel footage from U.S. Army maneuvers in the summer of 1941.

Some wartime Training films such as *Aerial Gunner* (Paramount, 1943) and *The Navy Way* (Paramount, 1944) spend a considerable amount of time and footage on actual training, while at the other end of the spectrum, *Bring on the Girls* has about *one minute* of training footage! *Bombardier* begins in

Aerial Gunner (Paramount, 1943): Richard Arlen demonstrates the operation of a machine gun as Jimmy Lydon, Chester Morris, and Dick Purcell (standing center, left to right) watch. This film was shot on location at the Aerial Gunnery School in Harlingen, Texas.

the prewar period, then carries its protagonists into actual combat (briefly). This film is one of the few to feature a training accident that results in death—most of the other Training genre films (as well as Combat films with training sequences) never allude to the possibility that servicemen might be injured or killed even *before* they meet the enemy.[10]

Combat training exercises appear in a few films, such as *Gung Ho!, Marine Raiders, Thirty Seconds Over Tokyo* (the pilots have to learn to fly a heavy bomber off a carrier deck), and *Wing and a Prayer*. Naval "shakedown" cruises are depicted in *Stand by for Action* and *Destroyer*. In the latter film, the *John Paul Jones* actually *fails*, and is assigned to the ignominious duty of delivering mail to the Aleutians! Fortunately for the crew's pride, they manage to run into Japanese planes and submarines even in this backwater.

We Did It Before, And We Can Do It Again

One of the cherished concepts of wartime American society was the notion of a nation of "citizen-soldiers." America, protected as it is by two large oceans on the East and West, and with (more or less) friendly neighbors on its North and South, prided itself in *not* maintaining a large standing army. When Germany invaded Poland at the beginning of September 1939, the United States Army had less than 200,000 men in its ranks, and was rated 17th in the world.[11] Emergency measures over the next 8 months increased its strength to 242,000, still a relatively small force.[12]

The peacetime draft (which got underway in October 1940) and its wartime continuation brought over 10 million Americans into the armed forces of the nation. Hollywood films simultaneously reflect and obscure the fact that the wartime armed forces were mostly made up of draftees—acknowledging this by portraying the overwhelming number of servicemen in films as *non*-professional soldiers, but rarely mentioning the fact that most of these civilians were *drafted* into the service.

While most of the men (and virtually all of the women) in uniform in wartime films are newcomers to the ranks, in many films a seasoned veteran is on hand to guide them, serving as father-figures, mentors, even older brothers who—despite an outward gruffness—gradually realize that these "rookies" can become good soldiers.

Bataan (MGM, 1942) contains several examples of co-operation between veterans and newcomers. Capt. Lassiter (Lee Bowman), the original commander of the group, is a 1940 West Point graduate: in other words, a green professional soldier. However, the rest of the group is split between old-timers and rookies. The veterans include Sgt. Dane (Robert Taylor), Cpl. Feingold (Thomas Mitchell), and Cpl. Todd (Lloyd Nolan); the latter, although he claims he enlisted fairly recently, is actually a veteran who deserted and reenlisted under a new name. Aside from the two Filipino soldiers, the other men are new to the service, including one conscientious objector who "enlisted" as a non-combatant,[13] and a member of the California National Guard (the National Guard was federalized in the fall of 1940).[14]

Lassiter, the officer, is killed fairly quickly and Sgt. Dane takes command (even before he was killed, Lassiter had been relying on Dane's advice). Although he wishes he had "real soldiers," by the end of the film Dane sees the veterans *and* the newcomers acquit themselves gallantly, even the displaced Navy man (Purckett)—who refuses a chance to escape, saying "I joined up for the duration, which ain't yet"—and the conscientious objector. Experience tells: Dane is the last man alive at the film's conclusion (but will presumably soon be killed), while Todd and Feingold are among the last to die (Purckett stays alive longer than any of the newcomers). But *Bataan* makes it clear that *all* Americans (and Filipinos, too) can become effective warriors when democratic ideals are at stake: a ragtag group of citizen-soldiers and professionals delays a much larger force for a significant amount of time, winning at least a moral victory in the tradition of the Alamo.

Other films follow the same pattern, although as the war went on, veterans no longer appeared in such large numbers. This was also true in real life; just before Pearl Harbor, the Army consisted of 520,000 "regulars," 256,000 National Guardsmen, and 712,000 draftees. If the half million "regulars" in the fall of 1941 are considered the "professional" Army, then by the end of the war they were out-numbered almost 20 to 1 by draftees.[15]

Thus, "old-timers" or "re-treads" like WWI veterans "Boley" Boleslavski (Edward G. Robinson) in *Destroyer*, Henry Johnson (Walter Brennan) in *Stand by for Action*, "Dixie" Smith (Randolph Scott) in *To the Shores of Tripoli*, and Rob-

bie White (Harry Carey) in *Air Force*, become less and less prominent after 1943. Older men still appear, but generally as high-ranking officers, like Lt. Col. James Doolittle (Spencer Tracy) in *Thirty Seconds Over Tokyo* (1945).

Another, related trend which appears in a large number of 1942–43 releases but virtually disappears later in the war is the linkage, on a personal level, between WWI and WWII. *This Is the Army* begins in the First World War; when WWII breaks out, the offspring of the "doughboys" follow in their fathers' footsteps (ironically, they are whipped into shape by the *same* sergeant, Alan Hale, who apparently never managed to get promoted in the atrophied peacetime Army). Dixie Smith, in *To the Shores of Tripoli*, takes a personal interest in young Chris Winters (John Payne), because the older man served with Winter's father in WWI. In *Hail the Conquering Hero* (Paramount, 1944), Woodrow Wilson Truesmith (Eddie Bracken) never knew his father, a Marine hero who died in battle on the day Woodrow was born in 1918; Woodrow grew up idolizing the Marines and his late father, and is crushed when physical problems keep him from following in his father's footsteps. A similar problem plagues crooner Johnny Cabot (Bing Crosby) in *Here Come the WAVES*, but he manages to get into the Navy when the physical requirements are lowered, thus fulfilling his dream of continuing the Cabot naval tradition.

Both Boley Boleslavski and Henry Johnson, in *Destroyer* and *Stand by for Action*, yearn to serve on the same ship (or its namesake) that they served on in the First World War, and both get their wish. Boleslavski, however, in an unusual plot development for the period, clashes with his younger shipmates instead of acting as their advisor. He redeems himself during combat, and then decides to step aside and allow the new generation of sailors to fight the rest of the war.

Several films of 1942–1943 address the problems faced by older soldiers in the "new" armed forces. *Salute to the Marines* features Wallace Beery as a veteran Marine who retires prior to Pearl Harbor, when he is not chosen for duty in China. Having served only between the wars, he has never had the opportunity to win a combat ribbon, and is now considered too old for active duty. However, he makes his contribution by training Filipino soldiers, and goes down fighting when Japan invades the Philippines (his daughter, in uniform as a Woman Marine, accepts his decoration posthumously). *The Bugle Sounds* (MGM, 1942), another Beery vehicle, depicts the phaseout of the horse cavalry and the rapid mechanization of the Army in 1940–41 (this film was made prior to Pearl Harbor, and features a vaguely identified spy but no combat action). Beery finished up the war with *another* such role, *This Man's Navy* (MGM, 1945), as a veteran Navy man flying anti-submarine patrols in blimps.

Destroyer (Columbia, 1943): Glenn Ford, Regis Toomey, and Edward G. Robinson hang on as their battered ship rams a Japanese submarine in the northern Pacific.

Uncle Sam Wants You

As noted in the previous section, Hollywood films depict the wartime armed forces as largely manned by non-career soldiers, while at the same time avoiding the question of *how* these civilians got into the Army in the first place. If there is any discussion of the matter, the overwhelming majority of film servicemen say they "enlisted," "volunteered," or "joined up." Almost no one ever says "they got me," "I was drafted," "my number was called," etc.

This had not always been the case. As discussed in Chapter 13, there was a minor boom in draft-theme films in 1941, including a significant number of comedies, *Buck Privates* (Universal) and *Caught in the Draft* (Paramount) chief among these. After all, America was not at war yet, and being drafted into the armed forces was therefore something of a lark, a chance to be "one of the boys," meet pretty young women, feel patriotic, and yet not really risk one's life.

In the first few months of 1942, films with references to

the draft continued to be released. Most of these seem to have been produced or at least planned prior to America's entry into the war, for their treatment of the topic is still quite frivolous. *Private Buckaroo* is a good example. Trumpeter Harry James has his number called, and reports for duty like a patriotic citizen. His band, bereft of their leader, enlists to be with him!

For the rest of the war, draft references fall into two categories. There are jokes about the draft in films that have little or no military content: in *Over My Dead Body* (TCF, 1942), comedian Milton Berle, playing a mystery writer, discovers a murder victim and remarks, "Definitely 4-F."[16] Most of the 52 references in 1943 films would be of this offhand nature, mostly comedic in tone.

However, some films deal with the draft in other ways. For example, there are a few films about draft avoidance (or "draft dodging"). *Mr. Lucky* (RKO, 1943) and *Lucky Jordan* (Paramount, 1942) are two examples. In the first film, Cary Grant plays a professional gambler who assumes the identity

Salute to the Marines (MGM, 1943): As Japanese forces close in, retired Marine Wallace Beery—wearing his "dress blues" jacket—prepares to make a last stand in the Philippines. At left, his Filipino friend Keye Luke, and his wife (Fay Bainter).

of a dead Greek crewman on his gambling ship in order to avoid the draft; by the end of the film, however, Grant has seen the error of his ways and announces his intention to serve (albeit in the Merchant Marine). Alan Ladd, in *Lucky Jordan*, is another criminal who is drafted; he actually reports for basic training, but deserts at the first opportunity. Once again, basic decency triumphs over selfishness, and Ladd returns to uniform for the duration. It is interesting to note that in both of these films the protagonists—while played by handsome leading men—are criminals (or quasi-criminals) in civilian life, so that their initial reluctance to serve in the armed forces does not come as a real shock.

The Very Thought of You (WB, 1944) includes a supporting character who flaunts his "4-F" status, and is otherwise generally an unpleasant and obnoxious person. When, at the end of the film, he is re-classified "1-A," the prospect of his being drafted is viewed as valid punishment! Danny Kaye tries to avoid the draft in *Up in Arms* (RKO, 1944), but not out of cowardice or anti-patriotic feelings: he is a hypochondriac,

and honestly believes he is not physically able to serve. The Army doctors feel otherwise, and Kaye eventually becomes an inadvertent war hero, accidentally capturing a horde of Japanese soldiers! There are a few other films featuring draft dodgers, although generally in subsidiary roles: *Young America* (TCF, 1942) and *Junior Army* (Columbia, 1942), for instance.

While not specifically linked with the draft and draft dodging, several films do touch on related topics: desertion, and conscientious objectors. Almost the only example of a stated American conscientious objector appears in *Bataan*, the character of Hardy. Conscientious objectors, if drafted, were given two choices: they could serve in the armed forces but as noncombatants (Hardy is a medic), or carry out "alternative service" in civilian camps.[17] *The Hour Before the Dawn* (Paramount, 1944), set in England, stars Franchot Tone as a British conscientious objector. Since he is morally opposed to killing, Tone is ordered to work on a farm in lieu of military service. Notably, in both of these films, the "pacifist" views of the characters are discarded by the end of the film: enraged at the death of Lt. Bentley (who crashes an airplane full of dynamite into a bridge), Hardy runs straight at the Japanese, tossing grenades until he is shot and killed; the Tone character kills his treacherous wife (a Nazi spy, played by Veronica Lake), then joins the RAF as a gunner!

Desertion is another topic treated very briefly in wartime films. Some films feature characters who go AWOL (absent without leave), or contemplate doing so, mostly for legitimate personal reasons (in *Here Come the WAVES*, Johnny Cabot wants to go AWOL from an easy stateside job so he can get into combat!), but actual desertion is depicted very rarely. As noted above, Alan Ladd deserts in *Lucky Jordan*, but repents, so technically he was only AWOL. In *This Above All* (TCF, 1942), British soldier Tyrone Power deserts but changes *his* mind, influenced by Joan Fontaine (playing a society woman who has joined the armed forces to do her bit), and a priest. *Ladies Courageous* (Universal, 1944) contains an unusual scene in which the women observe a "group of Army deserters being sent to Leavenworth," including the former lover of one of the women, shown on a train in shackles. But for the most part, although there were 43,000 conscientious objectors and 350,000 cases of draft evasion and desertion, Hollywood preferred to accentuate the positive and dwell on more pleasant aspects of the war.[18]

As for the draft itself, *Adventures of a Rookie* (RKO, 1943) is the only film released in 1943 focusing on draftees. A rather unfunny vehicle for the Wally Brown-Alan Carney comedy team, the film opens with nightclub singer Brown (the dumb skinny one) receiving his draft notice; at camp he meets Carney (the dumb fat one), as well as rich draftee Richard Martin.[19] The film follows their "adventures" in basic training, including frequent clashes with their irascible sergeant, but they never make it into action. Later that year, however, they do, in the sequel, *Rookies in Burma* (RKO), albeit in the same humorous vein as *Up in Arms*.[20]

1944 saw a slight upsurge in the number of films about draftees, reflecting increased draft calls upon the civilian population in real life. One of these films was *Mr. Winkle Goes to War* (Columbia, 1944), a rare film showing older men being drafted. In reality, the armed forces preferred younger men; the original peacetime draft registered males between the ages of 21 and 36, but within a few months the Army asked for revisions in the law, since "rejections at induction stations and the results of boot-camp experiences convinced the army that draftees over the age of 26 were virtually worthless."[21] In *Mr. Winkle Goes to War*, mild-mannered Winkle (Edward G. Robinson, over 50 years old at the time), is drafted and reports for duty without complaint. This film is almost the only dramatic wartime film depicting induction, training, and combat as experienced by draftees. The rigors of boot camp are portrayed, as Winkle struggles to become a good soldier. Even when an executive order is promulgated exempting men over

the age of 38 from the draft, Winkle declines his release from the Army.[22] He ships out with his comrades, and demonstrates his bravery in combat in the Pacific.[23]

Mr. Winkle Goes to War is one of the very few films which specifically identifies draftees in combat. There are apparently some draftees among the crew in *Destroyer*, but this is not clearly stated. By the spring of 1942, the Navy, due to losses and rapid expansion, was forced to strip shore facilities of experienced petty officers to man their ships at sea; it began accepting men from the draft in 1943. There is an interesting, if brief scene in *Destroyer* featuring Leo Gorcey as one of the young sailors. During a medical/psychological exam, he is asked "Do you like girls?" This was an actual question asked of draftees and recruits, in an attempt to weed out homosexuals in the military.[24] *The Story of G.I. Joe* (UA, 1945), also presumably contains draftees in its Army unit, although no major point is made of this fact.

Basically, Hollywood seemed reluctant to state the obvious: millions of men were being drafted, and many of those were going into combat, where they stood a chance of being wounded or killed. Perhaps it was felt that stating this (or showing it) in films would be bad for morale and lead to a greater incidence of draft evasion or desertion. But Combat films *had* to show casualties in order to maintain some semblance of verisimilitude (although even here great restraint was exercised), so the only way out of such a dilemma was to avoid the topic of the draft insofar as combat units were concerned. Furthermore, having a heroic character state that he "volunteered" for the fight against fascism only made him *more* heroic; a hero who "waited" to be drafted was not quite as patriotic.[25]

The Boy Next Door on the All-American Team

In wartime Hollywood, the American soldier remains the "kid" from next door, not a hard-bitten professional soldier.[26] In one of his "Fireside Chats," President Franklin D. Roosevelt referred to the "sons of the new world" who were going into battle against the evil forces of the New Order.[27] This average guy reluctantly becomes a trained killer for the duration, and is either ennobled by the experience of combat or dies heroically. A hero's death insures that the martyr's buddies can return to the land of the Brooklyn Dodgers, hamburgers, dreamy girls with creamy complexions, and a postwar America ready to indulge in an orgy of ostentatious consumerism.

America is portrayed as reluctantly entering the war—even members of the professional military class are shown to be "defenders" rather than war-mongers. In *Wake Island*, Marine veteran "Smacksie" Randall (William Bendix) is prepared to return to civilian life: his "hitch" is up. Proudly dressed in civvies, including a Panama hat, Randall is shocked to learn of the attack on Pearl Harbor—which puts him right back into uniform. Similarly, Chris Winters (John Payne) in *To the Shores of Tripoli*, fed up with Marine life, prepares to leave the service only to have Pearl Harbor change his mind. *The Fighting Seabees* can be viewed as something of an allegory: non-military construction workers (=the average American) are trying to do their jobs when they are attacked by the Japanese, despite being unarmed non-combatants (=the attack on Pearl Harbor before war was declared). At first the workers try to take matters into their own hands (by arming themselves and fighting back), but only manage to spoil the U.S. military's plan to ambush some Japanese raiders. Matters are resolved, however, when the Seabees (Naval Construction Battalions) are formed, and the workers learn military discipline (=civilians reluctantly accept the draft, and become trained soldiers).

Along with the image of a military largely composed of civilians, there are a number of films in which at some point American civilians take up arms against the enemy. Most examples of this phenomenon take place in 1942 films—*Wake Island*, *A Yank on the Burma Road* (MGM, 1942) and *Manila Calling*. After this, civilians who want to fight the Axis are either in the armed forces or are fighting on the home front. There is no room for "freelance" anti-fascists in a total war effort.

However, submitting to military training and discipline does not make the average American an unthinking robot or fanatic, a la Hitler's Nazi soldiers or the "Banzai"–shrieking Japanese fighting men. G.I. Joe, while a competent, brave soldier, remains an average, friendly, even naive figure. One way of showing this is to portray the soldiers in their free time, enjoying pleasures of the younger generation: swing music, ice cream, young romance, practical jokes.

Robert Walker epitomizes the wartime "kid" image of American soldiers. Born in 1914 but looking younger than his actual age, Walker was under contract to MGM, where he essayed "kid soldier" roles in a number of well-known war films: *Bataan*, *See Here, Private Hargrove*, *The Clock*, *Since You Went Away* (on loan to David O. Selznick), and *Thirty Seconds Over Tokyo*. In *Bataan*, he is the gum-chewing Purckett, a stranded Navy man who regales his new-found comrades with tales of his myriad civilian occupations: theatre usher, mechanic, cowboy, cornet player, etc. As noted earlier, Purckett refuses a chance to escape when it is offered, and later writes a letter to his "mum," before catching a sniper's bullet and dying. As the hapless rookie Marion Hargrove in *See Here, Private Hargrove* (and its post–September 1945 sequel, *What Next, Corporal Hargrove?*), Walker embodies the eager but inept, likeable American boy/man who must be molded into a fighting soldier "for the duration" by a tough Army sergeant. Compared to other, older actors who frequently took on wartime roles, like Brian Donlevy, William Bendix, and even John Wayne, it is difficult to imagine Walker in any sort of prewar occu-

pation, with a home and family. He seems to have come straight from the farm/small town/high school/corner drugstore into the armed forces.

In addition to the depiction of America's soldiers as eager and inexperienced young men, other humanizing touches appear in a number of films. For instance, American military men are often linked with children, either their own or foreign surrogates. In *A Guy Named Joe* (MGM, 1944), Pete (Spencer Tracy) crash lands at his air base in Britain after a bombing mission over Germany. He is greeted at the edge of the airfield by an awestruck group of English youngsters. Although Pete has probably just killed many people—including women and children—during the raid (the strategic policy of area bombing led to massive collateral damage), these cheerful urchins ignore the war aspect of his job and ply him with questions about the joy of flying. Thus, the inherent innocence of the children is transferred to the flyer through his relationship with them.

In the opening sequence of *Bataan* an anonymous American soldier is shown carrying a little Filipino girl on his shoulder, as both civilians and military personnel flee from the advancing Japanese. Following an enemy aerial attack, the two are linked in death by an eerie tableaux: a mound of rubble with only his cap and her hand sticking out. The cocky new pilot in *Flying Tigers* (Republic, 1942), Woody (John Carroll), who boasts about the number of $500 bonuses he has earned for shooting down "Japs," nonetheless visits the local hospital and later entertains the Chinese kids with magic tricks during a Japanese air raid. In *Stand by for Action*, the crew of an American destroyer rescues a group of women and their children whose evacuation ship from Honolulu has been sunk by the Japanese. Between changes of diapers on the deck of this combat vessel, a few of the sailors musically entertain the babies with a folksy rendition of "In Your Uncle Samuel's Navy." Before the ship can reach the U.S., the pharmacist's mate has to deliver a new baby (a "stowaway"), while the rest of the crew torpedoes and sinks an attacking enemy battleship! Other films in which Americans take young children under their wing include *China's Little Devils* (Monogram, 1945), *Back to Bataan* (RKO, 1945), and *The Story of Dr. Wassell* (Paramount, 1944).

The innocence of children, and by extension the guiltlessness of wartime America, is clearly indicated in a scene set in the officer's quarters of a submarine on a dangerous secret mission in *Destination Tokyo* (WB, 1944). The executive officer boasts to the new junior officer about the sub's successful attack against a Japanese convoy the previous year; the USS *Copperfin*'s captain (Cary Grant), is asked what *his* "biggest kick" of the last year was. The captain solemnly relates that the most important event in his life that year was taking his son Michael to the hometown barbershop for the boy's first haircut!

The theme of childlike innocence is enhanced in a number of Combat films through the introduction of cute little animal mascots. They are often mongrel pups (symbolic of the youthful multi-ethnic American units) or physically small dogs. Skipper, a dog who looks like FDR's dog "Fala," delivers a litter to her proud Marine godfathers between Japanese attacks in *Wake Island*. A debate concerning the puppies' paternity even provides a brief moment of comic relief between combat sequences. "Tripoli" (as in "To the Shores of Tripoli," from the Marine Corps Hymn), is given by the beseiged Marine garrison of Wake Island to a bomber crew headed for the Philippines in *Air Force* (WB, 1943). The little dog, the surrogate child of the doomed Marines, has been taught to bark whenever someone says "Moto" (a reference to the character of "Mr. Moto," a Japanese detective played by Peter Lorre in a number of prewar films). "Peaches," the kitten mascot of a merchant ship in *Action in the North Atlantic* (WB, 1943), dies when the vessel is sunk by a U-Boat. Embarking on his new ship, a surviving crew member swears to teach Peaches' replacement, "Thomas," how to swim. A battle-hardened unit in *The Story of G.I. Joe* (UA, 1945) collectively adopts the mongrel dog "Ayrab," after his owner, the youngest member of their unit, is killed in North Africa. The dog accompanies the G.I.s to Italy.

As mentioned in Chapter 15, one frequent wartime "American icon" was the game of baseball. Once again, although baseball is a game enjoyed by many Americans of all ages, those who play it are mostly young men, and the "team" analogy was easily transferred in Hollywood films to the armed forces. Not only are there overt references to baseball (and football, and other sports) in wartime films—in *Guadalcanal Diary*, Marines enmeshed in mortal combat with the Japanese take time out to listen to the radio, hoping to hear the World Series' score—there are also numerous parallels drawn between war and sports. In *The Navy Comes Through*, a sailor comments on a battle with a German U-Boat: "We sure knocked that Heinie out of the box." Later, he shoots down a German plane: "That's for making me miss the World Series." The Marines in *Gung Ho!* are trained to be a "team for killing [Japs]." In the battle for Makin Island, tough kid "Montana" (from Brooklyn) makes a broken-field run through enemy fire to toss grenades into a Japanese machine-gun nest, scoring a metaphoric touchdown for his "teammates" (several of whom have been killed or wounded trying to knock out the enemy emplacement).

Another aspect of the team concept is the depiction of American military units composed of widely divergent types of American males. Virtually all of the armed forces of the United States were rigidly segregated prior to WWII, and while some of the barriers were removed during the war, complete integration was not achieved until the postwar period. Thus, *racial* homogeneity is still the order of the day in most Combat genre films. The major exceptions are discussed in Chapter 17 (dealing with Black images in wartime film), and in the Chinese section of Chapter 18.

On the other hand, Hollywood took pains to include as wide a spectrum of regional, ethnic, and social types as possible in its filmic armed forces. There are at least two major reasons for this: first, existing stereotypes could easily be penciled in for various parts, always a favorite shortcut of filmmakers; however, during wartime it was equally important to make a statement about national solidarity, and one clear way of doing so was to include as many different Americans as possible in the egalitarian ranks of the armed forces.

Thus, in war films one sees the usual regional characters: the guy from Brooklyn (sometimes doing double duty, as a Jewish-American); the farm boy from the Middle West; the guy from Texas; the young man of East European ancestry, usually from Chicago, Milwaukee, or Pittsburgh; some Boston Irish; a Southerner or two, sometimes poor, sometimes Southern aristocracy. Occasionally, a Hispanic character or an immigrant or refugee (from Russia, Germany, Austria) is included for a touch of ethnic diversity. Of course, there are plenty of white Anglo-Saxons to fill in the ranks.

Specific religious denominations are rarely identified, aside from the obvious Jew/Christian dichotomy, and the occasional visible Catholic.[28] While religion plays an important part in many wartime films, Hollywood chose to elevate such discussions above individual religious groups, preferring to cast its films in a "good vs. evil" light, i.e. "God is on our side because the Axis is evil." While religious persecution is frequently attributed to the Axis and shown on screen, about the only reference to religious intolerance or discrimination in the United States occurs in *Pride of the Marines*, in which a Jewish character alludes to prejudice he has experienced.[29] Otherwise, Christians and Jews unite in a common cause: in *Guadalcanal Diary* an ecumenical service is attended by Marines on a troop transport, including Sammy Kline, the son of a cantor, who joins in the singing of "Rock of Ages."

All socio-economic levels are represented in the armed forces. Rich and socially prominent characters appear in *Adventures of a Rookie* and *The Eve of St. Mark*; a movie star becomes a Naval aviator in *Wing and a Prayer*; a middle-aged newspaper editor joins up in *Over 21*; an engineer becomes a pilot in *You Came Along*; peacetime lawyers become wartime warriors in *Pilot No. 5* and *The Purple Heart*; former teachers (including a college professor) appear in uniform in *Objective, Burma!* and *You Came Along*. At the other end of the continuum are working-class characters like "Pig Iron" in *Gung Ho!*, Al Schmid in *Pride of the Marines*, and humble bank clerk Winkle in *Mr. Winkle Goes to War*. There are also characters who were either too young to have settled on a career in the prewar period, or whose studies were interrupted by the war. The implication is obvious: the war for democracy is being fought democratically.

Similarly, the American military is depicted as a more or less classless organization. Military discipline is observed, but there is no distinctive "officer class" in evidence. In fact,

Pride of the Marines (Warner Bros., 1945): On Guadalcanal, Dane Clark, Anthony Caruso, and John Garfield await a Japanese attack. Note the shamrock and Star of David on their machine gun, illustrating the "military melting pot" concept.

wartime films deemphasize the role of professional officers, and few films feature developed characters with the rank of Major and above. Protagonists of wartime films are much more likely to be privates, corporals, sergeants, and lieutenants (since virtually all American pilots were officers, a disproportionate number of captains and lieutenants appear in air-oriented films).

Sergeant was almost an ideal rank for wartime film protagonists. As a non-commissioned officer, a sergeant could command others, thus assuming stature and responsibility worthy of the leading character in a film. Furthermore, the rank was appropriate for the age of available actors. And, importantly, sergeants were *fighting* men, who participate in combat action directly, rather than sitting at headquarters and *planning* battles. Noted sergeants of the era include Sgt. Joe Gunn (Humphrey Bogart) in *Sahara*, Sgt. Dane (Robert Taylor) in *Bataan*, and Sgt.-Major Bailey (Wallace Beery) in *Salute to the Marines*. Captain Nelson (Errol flynn) in *Objective, Burma!* is one of the rare officers actually seen personally fighting the enemy.[30]

In the Navy and Air Corps, there was some "rank inflation," and protagonists are usually officers, like "Irish" Quincannon (John Ridgely in *Air Force*), Lt. Ted Lawson (Van Johnson in *Thirty Seconds Over Tokyo*), Lt. Ward Stewart (Tyrone Power in *Crash Dive*), and Captain Cassidy (Cary Grant in *Destination Tokyo*). Nonetheless, these characters are all mid-level military figures, who demonstrate the "qualities of simultaneous earthiness, averageness, special powers, and authority ... but ... shares the common soldiers' distrust of, and run-ins with, authority."[31] Furthermore, in air-combat films in particular, the officers *are* on the firing line with the enlisted men, usually piloting the plane, and thus actively participating in combat and sharing in the danger.

Higher-ranking officers are rarely portrayed in any detail. Even Spencer Tracy, as Lt. Col. James Doolittle in *Thirty Seconds Over Tokyo*, really has only a few choice scenes. Doolittle is also one of the few real-life American military figures to be impersonated on screen during the war: General Stilwell (Erville Alderson in *Objective, Burma!*) and Claire Chennault (Raymond Massey in *God Is My Co-Pilot*) are two others (although Chennault does *not* appear in *Flying Tigers* or *China's Little Devils*, two other American Volunteer Group films). General Eisenhower is referred to a few times during the war, and while General MacArthur's name is frequently invoked (due to the large number of film references to the Philippines), he is not impersonated.[32]

While officers above the junior grades are rarely personalized, at least they are not attacked or portrayed as martinets or war-mongers. A rare example of anti-officer sentiment is voiced in *Thousands Cheer*, when disgruntled soldier Gene Kelly says "Privates don't mix with officers or their families because we're not good enough." However, his irritation arises chiefly because he does not like being in the Army in the first place, and because he is in love with an officer's daughter (Kathryn Grayson), not because of anything specific that has been done to him. Indeed, the officer in question (John Boles) is portrayed as a loving father and a sympathetic leader of men.

Most other films, when the matter is brought up at all, show high-ranking officers as concerned, intelligent, and serious about their job. There are few examples of rank-based discrimination or prejudice; if anything, Hollywood stressed that the opposite was true. For instance, in *I'll Be Seeing You*, a sergeant is introduced to a lieutenant at a New Year's dance. The teenage girl who introduces them wonders if the non-com should salute his superior officer. Spying the combat ribbons and the Purple Heart on the sergeant's uniform, the young lieutenant replies, "No, *I* should salute *him*." A young woman who snobbishly wants to date only officers—in *Since You Went Away*—is admonished by Anne (Claudette Colbert) for her undemocratic attitude.

In the Meantime, Darling features a scene on a crowded train in which a pompous, influential, and wealthy businessman (Eugene Pallette) is told off by a serviceman. "War—the great leveler," Pallette grumbles. Although the sequence is humorous in tone, Hollywood was serious in its attitude towards the military: the forces of democracy *were* democratic.

The Private Life of the G.I.

Many wartime films depict servicemen in their off-duty hours. In fact, there are probably more films showing servicemen in canteens, nightclubs, concerts, USO shows, and so on, than films showing them in combat action! In line with the discussion in the previous section of this chapter, such images were intended to reinforce the concept of the American soldier (sailor, Marine, etc.) as a "normal" human being, *not* a mindless killing machine (even servicemen back from combat action—with a few notable exceptions—seem to shrug off the experience and behave normally).

This did not necessarily mean Hollywood's image of American soldiers was a *realistic* one. Most filmmakers willingly followed government advice, such as these "requests" made by the War Department:

American soldiers shall be represented to the public in dignified terms only ... sex jokes [and] allusions [should] not give American parents the idea that Army life bears any resemblance to *What Price Glory* or *The Cockeyed World* of regretfully-too-recent memory.[33]

For instance, there are few scenes depicting servicemen drinking, and even fewer showing drunkenness. While "service" films of the 1930s virtually always feature scenes set in waterfront dives (usually culminating in a brawl), such antics were left behind in wartime. The "canteen" films are conspicuously "dry." Nothing untoward ever occurs in these places of sanctioned entertainment: the hostesses are forbidden to date the guests (so not even a hint of sexual hijinks goes on), only soft drinks and food are served, no fights break out, and everything is quite innocent.[34]

A few films show alcohol actually being consumed, but in moderation: servicemen drink beer at a bar in *Mr. Winkle Goes to War*[35]; in *Here Come the WAVES*, Johnny orders a frozen daiquiri at a restaurant, but he does not drink it (he tosses the ice down the back of a woman's low-cut dress, in order to get his friend out of the way); soldiers and girls are shown in a beer hall in *See Here, Private Hargrove*, but they are more interested in dancing and singing than drinking; *You Came Along* (Paramount, 1945) shows servicemen (on a bond tour) with drinks in a cocktail lounge, but no drunkenness.[36]

The Story of G.I. Joe is a bit more realistic: the soldiers consume both alcohol and tobacco products—including cigars and chewing tobacco—on the Cassino front in Italy; they have liquor and turkey for Christmas dinner! *Miracle of Morgan's Creek* takes as its basic premise the idea that servicemen get drunk and have sexual flings with willing young women on the eve of their departure for active duty (although few of these carousing soldiers are actually ever seen). *Main Street After Dark* (MGM, 1945) features a criminal gang that robs drunken servicemen, but the emphasis is on the crooks and the police rather than the inebriated victims.

Only a very few films hint at the possibility of friction, even violence on the home front between servicemen and civilians: in *Janie* (WB, 1944), for instance, the jealous civilian boyfriend of a teenage girl *wants* to punch the soldier who is stealing his girl's affection. But he can not—soldiers and civilians *do not* fight, they must cooperate in order to win the war. However, by the end of the film the boyfriend has joined the Navy, so he now *can* scrap with his Army rival! *Jive Junction* (PRC, 1943) depicts the jealous rage of high school boys whose girlfriends are being monopolized by servicemen at the Jive Junction canteen, but this does not lead to violence (as soon as some slightly older women are recruited to act as hostesses, the soldiers drop the teenage girls!).

Inter-service rivalry is presented in extremely muted fashion. After *About Face* (UA, 1942), which was probably completed prior to Pearl Harbor (it was released in April), the next film featuring an inter-service fight was *Abroad with Two Yanks* (UA, 1944), in which two Marines (Dennis O'Keefe and William Bendix) punch out two GIs—because the two Marines are in drag (as part of a camp show), and the soldiers try to pick them up!

Otherwise, while the Marines toss a few friendly jibes at the Army (in *Marine Raiders*, for example, Marines on a Pacific island are relieved by the Army; the leathernecks stage a fake air raid and steal supplies from the fresh troops), virtually all branches of the service get along splendidly, acting like perfect gentlemen and good patriots, and cooperating when necessary to defeat the Axis forces. *Thirty Seconds Over Tokyo* makes a particular point of this: Army Air Force pilots are first trained to take off from a carrier by a Navy liaison officer, then are transported by the Navy to the jumping-off spot for their raid on Tokyo. As the Army planes soar into the sky, the sailors cheer and wish them luck.

Although most wartime films portray American servicemen as impossibly decent, clean-living All-American boys at heart, they are still top-notch soldiers. The bowdlerizing of their escapades while on leave was deliberate, and was due not only to the Production Code (since, after all, drunkenness and drunken brawls had appeared in prewar films and continued to appear in wartime films in *other* contexts), but also to a feeling that the American serviceman had to be depicted as an exemplar, a worthy representative of the Allies. Furthermore, Hollywood filmmakers were at all times conscious of their audience, and went out of their way to avoid showing unpleasant aspects of the war, unless some moral lesson could be extracted from them.

The Most Dangerous Game

Most of the Combat films released during the war were set in the Pacific Theatre of war. A "hunt" metaphor is frequently employed in these films—America's servicemen become uniformed Frank Bucks (a famed white hunter whose jungle exploits capturing wild animals had been featured in several films; his motto was "Bring 'Em Back Alive"). They proceed as if on safari, treating the enemy like beasts in the jungle. But these hunter-soldiers' motto is hardly as humane as Buck's: the Marine commander's instructions to his men in *Gung Ho!* before a raid on a fortified Japanese island are more apt: "[N]ot a Jap alive by sunset."

"Native" scouts are actually employed to help track down the Japanese in several films, including *Sergeant Mike* (Columbia, 1944), *Marine Raiders*, *The Fighting Seabees* and *Guadalcanal Diary*. The eponymous Sergeant Mike of the first film, an Army dog, actually helps his fellow GIs sniff out machine-gunners on an enemy-held island. Japanese snipers are routinely shot out of trees like squirrels in *Guadalcanal Diary*,

Gung Ho!, *Fighting Seabees*, *Bataan*, *Mr. Winkle Goes to War*, and other films. In *Guadalcanal Diary*, after shooting at a Japanese sniper, a Marine from Brooklyn states: "I swear I could see his buck teeth." A newspaper headline in *Destroyer*, describing a naval battle with the Japanese, shows the hunt metaphor was not limited to jungle encounters: "U. S. Destroyer Rams Sub; Bags Six Planes." This type of analogy was actually used in real-life: during the invasion of Saipan in the summer of 1944, Japanese planes were shot down in such enormous numbers that the action was dubbed "the Great Marianas Turkey Shoot."[37]

In many Pacific war films, specific references are made to "hunting" the Japanese. In both *Gung Ho!* and *Guadalcanal Diary*, Marines about to land on Japanese-held islands are exhorted with the cry of "Good Hunting!" In *Pride of the Marines*, Al Schmid (John Garfield) comments, shortly after learning of the attack upon Pearl Harbor: "You know, I bet it would be more fun shooting Japs than bears." A Marine facetiously refers to his buddy in *Guadalcanal Diary* as "Sergeant York" for his style of shooting at the enemy. Imitating the mannerisms of Gary Cooper playing the WWI hero in the film *Sergeant York* (WB, 1941), the man wets the sight of his gun before firing, and makes a turkey gobble sound, enticing a Japanese soldier to raise his head and be shot.

The wartime films dealing with the famous Flying Tigers unit reinforce the hunt metaphor each time their fighter planes are shown—the P-40 aircraft they fly is distinctively marked with a painted "shark" nose. The concept of the white hunter with his trophies is even more clearly implied when a new member of the Flying Tigers, Capt. Robert Lee Scott in *God Is My Co-Pilot*, returns from his first combat mission (in which he killed many of the enemy), and orders that the spinner of his P-40 be painted white. Near the end of the film, after he has defeated his arch nemesis, a wise-cracking Japanese ace called Tokyo Joe, Lee returns triumphantly to base carrying the dead Japanese pilot's samurai sword, like a hunting trophy. In the same film, General Chennault marks down on a bridge-game score pad the number of Japanese planes his Flying Tigers have shot down.

The acquisition of battle trophies, or "war souvenirs" as they were usually referred to at the time, was a preoccupation of many real-life servicemen. In its more extreme form it would include the collection of body parts (particularly ears)—a notorious incident was the skull of a Japanese soldier sent home to a girlfriend (there was a posed photo of her with it in *Life* magazine).[38] That such trophies were common currency in the United States by the middle of the war is reflected in *The Doughgirls* (WB, 1944): a fatuous radio correspondent presents the epaulettes from a Japanese officer's uniform as a wedding gift to a young couple. An inexperienced Marine is nearly killed by a sniper when he tries to retrieve a dead officer's samurai sword in *Guadalcanal Diary*. After slaughtering the garrison of a Japanese radar station, a folded-up

The Doughgirls (WB, 1944): A Russian woman sniper (Eve Arden), on a goodwill tour of the U.S.A., recruits an Orthodox priest for the rooftop wedding of her American friends—Craig Stevens, Alexis Smith, John Ridgely, Ann Sheridan, Jack Carson, and Jane Wyman.

battle flag is removed by an American Ranger without incident from an enemy officer's corpse in *Objective Burma!* And one of the first acts by a teenaged combat veteran upon returning home in *SNAFU* (Columbia—released after September, 1945) is to matter-of-factly place his captured Japanese flag above the family mantelpiece.

The dehumanization of the Japanese enemy added to the "hunt" analogy. In *The Fighting Seabees*, an American says: "We're not fighting men any more, we're fighting animals. That's why we got to change the rules." Like 19th-century buffalo hunters, American soldiers fire until their guns are red-hot, slaughtering Japanese soldiers by the hundreds. The final battle scene in *Guadalcanal Diary* shows what amounts to an American tank roundup of the last major pocket of Japanese resistance on the island. Flushed out of the jungle onto a beach, the fleeing enemy troops are mercilessly wiped out, their bodies left floating in the surf.

The taking of Japanese prisoners of war by American armed forces is portrayed in only two films, *Guadalcanal Diary*

and *Up in Arms* (not classified as a Combat film). After all, hunters do not *capture* their prey, they kill it. Japanese military wounded (only briefly depicted as sheet-covered lumps on cots in a segregated ward) are treated in a single Combat genre film, *So Proudly We Hail!*. Most of the scene in the ward consists of a series of tight close-ups on an American nurse (Veronica Lake), who overcomes her desire to murder the helpless men under her care in revenge for the death of her fiancé at Pearl Harbor. A treacherous Japanese officer captured by Chinese guerrillas is medically treated in an American medical missionary's clinic in *China Sky* (RKO, 1945).

There are many fewer examples of this type of hunting analogy in films dealing with the Nazis.[39] In the first place, there were almost no Combat films released during the war in which American ground forces fought German troops. However, an even stronger reason seems to be the perceived difference between the Germans and Japanese, as discussed at greater length in the chapter dealing with images of the enemy. The German soldiers were fanatics, but human; furthermore, most combat took place in at least semi-civilized areas, rather than Pacific jungle islands. Actions which, while gruesome, seemed just and routine in the Pacific, were unheard of in European warfare.

"You Never Touched Me!" or Oh, Death, Where Is Thy Sting?

The depiction of violence on movie screens has become extremely graphic in recent years. Years ago, individuals were shot and died with (at most) a delicate spot of blood on their shirt (usually not even a bullet hole!). An exploding blood "squib" in *Only the Valiant* (1951) was a major revelation; *Bonnie and Clyde* (1967) and *The Wild Bunch* (1969) ushered in slow-motion death on film, and the wonders of film technology have brought even more realistic and detailed gore and violence to the screen in the past two decades.

But in the 1930s and 1940s, on-screen traumatic injury and death was depicted as a comparatively sanitary dramatic event. Extreme, deliberate restraint was exercised during the war: American servicemen who made the supreme sacrifice are always left physically intact, frequently permitted to have some final moments with their comrades, and often make some defiant gesture directed at their enemies. A dignified expiration meant that fear was rarely expressed and that the only indication of mortal wounds would be a dirty uniform or bandages and a little blood on the lips.

Even relatively realistic Combat films like *Guadalcanal Diary* and *Bataan* are extremely restrained in the actual depiction of death and injury on the battlefield. In *Cry Havoc*, a wounded soldier (played by Robert Mitchum) dies peacefully in the arms of volunteer nurse Connie (Ella Raines). Similarly, Maximo (Ducky Louie), in *Back to Bataan*, survives a brutal interrogation by Japanese soldiers *and* a plunge over a cliff in a truck, living long enough to make an exit speech and then gracefully expire in the presence of John Wayne and Beulah Bondi.

The deaths in *Bataan* take place either off-screen (one of the Filipino soldiers is tortured and killed by the Japanese), or are relatively quick and (apparently) painless. Ramirez (Desi Arnaz) does not even die of battle wounds, passing away in a malarial delirium: yet he makes a final confession to an imagined priest, and dies quietly, with no battle sounds to interrupt his passing. Aviator Bentley (George Murphy) is mortally wounded prior to his suicidal crash into a bridge, but he manages to hide this from the other men, showing little or no pain—he finally expires in a literal explosion of glory. The only death with significant on-screen impact is the (presumed) beheading of Eeps, the black soldier, who receives a samurai sword blow to the neck and screams in agony.

Even if the film conventions of the day had allowed for more graphic portrayals of American death and injury, the industry would almost certainly have censored itself, or been urged by the government to downplay the concept of battlefield death or mutilation. Photographs of American dead were routinely withheld from publication, not only out of respect for the dead, but to avoid demoralizing civilians and servicemen who had yet to see action.[40] A *Life* magazine photo-essay from 1943, "Battle of Buna," contains many graphic photographs of dead Japanese soldiers, but waits until the final page to show an artfully composed shot of rows of crosses adorning American graves. The Japanese die grotesquely contorted in the mud; Americans are neatly lined up, out of sight, with Christian symbols of the resurrection marking their resting place.

A few films push the boundaries a bit, although the mayhem is usually described rather than shown. After viewing a photograph of three dead GIs ambushed by the Japanese, one character in *Objective Burma!* remarks that the bodies will soon "play host to every fly in Burma." The fate of Lt. Hewitt at the hands of the Japanese in *Marine Raiders* is bluntly reported: tied between several trees, his hands and feet have been cut off. At the conclusion of *Bombardier*, U.S. airman Buck Oliver (Randolph Scott) has been severely beaten by his Japanese captors, but still has the strength to escape, steal a vehicle, and cause a fiery crash that draws the attention of his airmen friends, flying overhead. They bomb the site, wiping out the Japanese camp (and instantly avenging Oliver).

Oliver's sacrifice is similar to the glorious suicides depicted in *Remember Pearl Harbor!* (Republic, 1942), *Appointment in Berlin* (Columbia, 1943), *We've Never Been Licked* (Universal, 1943), *Pilot No. 5*, and *Sabotage Squad* (Columbia, 1942), among other films. The first four films deliberately evoke the "memory" of the famous "Colin Kelly" story—Kelly, a U.S. aviator, in the early days of the war allegedly crashed his plane into a Japanese battleship, sinking it.[41] In *Wing and a Prayer*, a Navy flyer deliberately crashes his plane into the path of a torpedo that is bearing down on "his" carrier, saving the Navy ship at the cost of his own life. Mass "banzai" charges in the name of the Emperor, ritual suicide (*seppuku* or *hara kiri*), and kamikaze attacks by the Japanese are scorned as the acts of fanatics—but when it is an American who sacrifices his life, taking large numbers of "Nips" with him, the act is ennobling, to say the least. As author John Hersey wrote:

Most military suicides [by Allied servicemen] have been isolated acts of mad courage. The Japanese have done something no other nation in the world would be capable of doing. They have systematized suicide, they have nationalized a morbid, sickly act.[42]

Death in battle is frequently inspirational. In *Tender Comrade*, war widow Ginger Rogers tells her infant son that his father died so children all over the world could be free; in *The Human Comedy* a final letter from soldier Marcus arrives at his family's home: as if from the grave, Marcus (who has been killed in action) writes that the war is a righteous one, and his sacrifice was not in vain. Even execution can be seen as a victory of sorts: in *The Purple Heart*, the captured American airmen "defeat" the Japanese by refusing to identify their base for the bombing of Japan. Although they are sentenced to death, the Americans have won, not only demonstrating moral superiority over the enemy, but also humiliating the Japanese military establishment (so much so that one of the arrogant Japanese officers commits suicide over his loss of face).

Wartime films treat American deaths solemnly. A number of the Combat genre films contain moving death and burial scenes. In *Bataan*, as Captain Lassiter is buried, Private Eeps—who was studying to be a "preacher," but is now a demolitions expert—says a prayer for him. Mike Connors (Tom Tully) is buried at sea, wrapped in the American flag, in *Destination Tokyo* (*The Navy Comes Through* and *Action in the North Atlantic* also contain sea burial scenes). *Guadalcanal Diary* features a memorial service, where a long row of crosses signifies gallant men and comrades, "not statistics." As the survivors contemplate the terrible cost of freedom, the long-awaited American airplanes appear overhead, a sign that the tide has finally turned for the Allies. *God Is My Co-Pilot* and *Air Force* both feature scenes of dying aviators in the hospital, their friends and crew members in attendance as the heroic men slip peacefully into oblivion.[43]

While American soldiers pass away quickly and painlessly on the battlefield (or in the hospital), not so America's military opponents, particularly the Japanese. The fate of Japanese military personnel was monotonously predictable—DEATH, as graphic as possible for the period. Although images of the Japanese are discussed in more detail in Chapter 19, it is worth mentioning here that numerous films feature blood-spattered grimaces (in close-up) and screams of agony (particularly Japanese pilots trapped in the cockpits of their flaming airplanes), as the evil ones are exterminated.

Meeting the Enemy on the Field of Battle

Hollywood's wartime Combat films run the gamut from impossibly bloodless and fantastic, to reasonably grim and realistic. Actual combat between friendly and enemy forces occupies a rather small percentage of time even in Combat genre films: most of the footage is consumed with training for battle, traveling to the scene of battle, waiting for the battle to begin, lulls between scenes of battle, and the aftermath of battle. Even combat takes on different forms: ground, air, and naval, with variations within each type.

Aerial combat—as opposed to bombing—is a very personalized experience in war films. There are close-up reaction shots of the pilots in opposing cockpits—a microcosm of the war, a visual dialectic, the stalwart American and his bestial adversary. Even the depersonalized Japanese occasionally take

on a human face: *God Is My Co-Pilot*, for instance, features a running feud between "Tokyo Joe" (Richard Loo) and the pilots of the American Volunteer Group, notably Robert Lee Scott (Dennis Morgan). The Japanese ace taunts his opponents over the radio, using American slang like his propaganda counterpart Tokyo Rose. The Flying Tigers talk back to him, but only at the end does Scott manage to destroy the enemy pilot.

Bomber's Moon (TCF, 1943) features a war film staple: enemy treachery repaid. In this case, Nazi pilot von Streicher (Martin Kosleck) attacks a damaged Allied bomber limping back to England after a raid. American Jeff Dakin (George Montgomery) tells his crewmen to bail out, and Von Streicher ruthlessly machine-guns one of the parachutists. At the end of the film, Dakin—flying a stolen German plane—shoots down von Streicher, avenging the dead crewman (who happened to be Dakin's younger brother), and saving Winston Churchill as well (von Streicher was on his way to ambush the Prime Minister's train).

The enemy's disregard for the rules of civilized warfare is demonstrated over and over again in wartime films. The Japanese make particularly heavy use of snipers, camouflage, sneak attacks, ambushes, and false deaths and surrenders. When American defeats are recreated—generally the loss of the Philippines, as in *Salute to the Marines*, *Bataan*, *So Proudly We Hail!*, *Cry Havoc*, *Manila Calling*, and *Corregidor*—the Japanese win only through overwhelming force of numbers, ruthless battle tactics, and these "unfair" tricks. Furthermore, such victories are always Pyrrhic: despite the fact that all of the above films were made and released before the United States recaptured the Philippines, the gallant sacrifice of the Americans and Filipinos is treated as a victory, and the loss of the Philippines is perceived as merely a temporary setback.

The only wartime film to show extensive European ground combat activities by American forces is *The Story of G.I. Joe*, and it falls clearly in the realistic end of the spectrum. Postwar combat films and television shows have made scenes of urban combat familiar, but at the time the house-to-house battles, sniper attacks, and images of ruined towns and villages were new and unique. The film, while it has sentimental aspects, is unusually forthright in certain ways. For example, one of the primary characters, Lt. Walker (Robert Mitchum), is killed towards the end of the film. The audience has seen Walker and his men go from North Africa to Sicily to Italy, and has watched Walker mature (he is even promoted from Lieutenant to Captain in the course of the film). His death thus comes as a profound shock. The good guys really *can* get killed! And Walker's death is not a glorious, cathartic climax to the film: his body is brought down on the back of a donkey from the mountains where he died; members of his unit pay their respects to him before marching off to the next battle, one in a long series of battles which must be fought and won before the Axis is destroyed.

Other members of the unit are also killed in the course of the film, and the immediate or delayed retribution usually meted out to those who kill Americans is absent. The Germans kill us, we kill them, but the personal aspect, the revenge aspect, is absent. The only exception to this occurs when a German sniper, hiding in a church tower, is killed after shooting at the Americans. However, there is even a slight degree of sympathy shown for this character—his falling body becomes entangled in the bell ropes, causing the bells to symbolically toll for him.

Wartime films depicting naval combat are, as a whole, somewhat more realistic than ground combat pictures. It is difficult to personalize naval combat (although there are still inserts of dying Japanese pilots and sailors), and the concern with the mechanical operation of the ship makes American sailors seem less individualized and more team-oriented than the largely personalized members of ground combat teams.

For instance, *Wing and a Prayer* contains some fairly intense and impressive scenes of naval warfare, concentrating on the dangers to men on shipboard—flying shell fragments, fire, explosions—as well as the noise and confusion of battle. Even a film like *Destroyer* with strong individual roles—Edward G. Robinson and Glenn Ford star—manages to seem rather gritty and tough in the battle scenes.

This is not to say *all* naval combat films are paragons of realism, and there were lines beyond which Hollywood would not venture. For instance, in only two wartime films are major American ships sunk by direct enemy action: *The Sullivans* (TCF, 1944), which has a brief scene of the destruction of the *Juneau*, and a munitions ship is torpedoed in *Pacific Rendezvous* (MGM, 1942) (in *Minesweeper*, a U.S. ship is sunk by a Japanese mine). *Destination Tokyo*, while it at least has no "love interest," crams practically every possible outlandish occurrence into *one* submarine mission (and a "secret mission" at that): an emergency medical operation on board, depth-charges, sinkings of Japanese ships, a strafing by a Japanese plane (which is shot down and the pilot rescued, although he is killed after he stabs an American crewman), and so on.

Films like these may have garnered hoots from combat veterans, but as long as the enemy was not portrayed as *either* excessively strong *or* excessively weak, and as long as Allied servicemen were depicted in the best possible light, and as long as there was some pro-democracy message inserted somewhere, the film industry and the government were happy.

California, Here We Come

The fact that most G.I.s remained emphatically civilians at heart, tied to the world they had left, is best demonstrated by the way they stayed in contact with that world.[44]

One major aspect of Hollywood's wartime soldiers is the notion that the Americans are fighting primarily for their *Americanness*: for the right to be Americans, to do the things Americans do, and to enjoy the things Americans enjoy—chewing gum, cigarettes, Coca Cola, baseball, hotdogs, hamburgers, etc. The war is not a war of aggression, to acquire territory or natural resources—the average American has no desire to dominate or exploit other countries, even enemy nations. The Americans simply want to destroy the military capacity of the Axis, eliminate their totalitarian leaderships and convert them to democracy—all in the hope that, most importantly, the GIs can be rapidly demobilized and sent home. They want "unconditional victory and unconditional homecoming."[45]

American servicemen are repeatedly portrayed as men who are "doing a job," a job that must be done so they can *go home*. In *Wake Island*, Major Caton (Brian Donlevy) says: "[we] fight to destroy destruction—that's our job." In *God Is My Co-Pilot*, a reference to "the job" of winning the war is followed by a cut to workers at a defense plant in Robert Lee Scott's Georgia hometown. An off-screen narrator in *The Human Comedy* says that the soldiers of America are "not unafraid [but they have] accepted the necessity to dismiss their fear... They have a great inner strength of men who know the risk and danger of the work they must do...." Naval officer Tony (Joseph Cotten) in *Since You Went Away*, tells Anne (Claudette Colbert) that he did not join the Navy for the "Four Freedoms," but for "good 'ol home sweet home."

Whenever such discussion arises in a wartime film, American military personnel emphatically express their desire to return to civilian life—there is *never* talk of a postwar *military* career, not even by regular Army soldiers. The obvious message is that the United States is a non-militaristic society, forced into a dirty job by Axis plans to dominate the world.

Conversations held during a lull in combat are invariably related to home and prospects of returning to the States. Such moments are particularly effective (sometimes still emotionally moving to a viewer decades later) in *Destination Tokyo*, *Guadalcanal Diary* and *Objective Burma!*. Soldiers and sailors carry memories of home with them into the war zone: in *Guadalcanal Diary*, a Marine carries a photo of his wife and child in his helmet; Mike, the sailor treacherously stabbed by a Japanese pilot in *Destination Tokyo*, cherished a phonograph record of his family; similarly, in *The Story of G.I. Joe*, Sgt. Warnick (Freddie Steele), frantically searches for a record-player in war-ravaged Italy, so he can play a recording of the voice of the son he has never seen.[46]

In *Follow the Boys*, Jeanette MacDonald sings "I'll See You In My Dreams," during a visit to a military hospital. She tells the injured men to close their eyes and think of home: one soldier with bandages over his eyes dreams of his mother, another of his wife and child. Marcus (Van Johnson), the soldier son in *The Human Comedy*, hails from Ithaca, California.

Even though he is serving his country in a foreign land, his heart is home with his family and his girlfriend. Marcus's friend Tobey marvels: "We're both in the Army, but you've never left home." In a letter to his brother Homer (Mickey Rooney), Marcus writes: "I am proud that I am serving my country, which to me is Ithaca, our home...." And after Marcus has died in action, Tobey—who has no family of his own—pays a visit to Ithaca, to meet Marcus's mother, sister, brother, and girlfriend. When he arrives, he says "I'm home."[47]

There are other, less dramatic reminders of the ultimate desire and destination of American servicemen. Songs like "California, Here I Come," and "Deep in the Heart of Texas" are more than cheerful popular tunes: for those in the Pacific theatre of war, the former is used to cue the return to America from the war zone, as in *So Proudly We Hail!*, *The Very Thought of You*, and *Back to Bataan*. "Deep in the Heart of Texas," a 1942 hit, is heard in a number of films; the infectious clapping chorus is echoed by machine-guns in *Thirty Seconds Over Tokyo* and *Wing and a Prayer*.

The folks at home are also thinking about their men in the service. A number of films feature framed photographs of men in uniform, usually in a spot of honor on the mantle or table. Service flags, signifying men in the service (a blue star for each serviceman, a gold star for a family member killed in action), are proudly displayed. Letters from soldiers are anxiously awaited and, once received, are read and re-read. These letters bring the soldier home, at least in spirit, and bring the civilians closer to the war effort.[48]

One particularly strong evocation of "home" occurs in a number of wartime films—the celebration of Christmas. *Holiday Inn* (Paramount, 1942) while acknowledging all of America's important holidays, strikes a whole range of emotional chords with its musical presentation of "White Christmas." Seated at a piano before a fireplace, with a lovely blonde (*not a sexy pinup*) by his side, Bing Crosby's unaffected rendition of the Irving Berlin song simultaneously evokes nostalgic memories of a peaceful past (perhaps idealized by many, having just experienced a decade-long Depression) and wishes for a brighter postwar future. The snow-covered landscape of the idyllic Christmas experience juxtaposed with the warmth and safety inside the traditional home epitomizes the collective image of a national home worth fighting for. The emotional impact of this film must have been particularly strong for families separated by the war, with some members serving abroad (often under threat of sudden death) on ships or in far-off places with unpronounceable names.[49]

Other films also utilize the Christmas holiday as a reaffirmation of the values of the American home and family. The concluding scene of *Since You Went Away* features a family and friends gathered in the living room of their home on Christmas Eve. The evening is at first rather sad, since the head of the family has been reported missing in action—but as the film ends, Anne receives a call, and learns her husband is alive

and well. A WWI Christmas is celebrated in no man's land in *Army Surgeon* (RKO, 1942). Christmas is celebrated at sea in *Destination Tokyo*; the Christmas gift of knives for the ship's cook later becomes the gift of life when they are fashioned into surgical instruments used in an emergency operation. In *So Proudly We Hail!*, soldiers and nurses on their way to the Pacific in December 1942 celebrate Christmas on their ship with a party and a Christmas tree. *I'll Be Seeing You* deals with the return to the heartland of the United States by a wounded soldier (Joseph Cotten) for the Christmas holidays, in the company of a furloughed convict (Ginger Rogers).

In *Winged Victory*, servicemen on a Pacific island are treated to a Christmas show, and receive packages distributed by Santa Claus. The gifts—tangible links to home—include a painting of one man's hometown Main Street, and a photograph of another soldier's child. The celebration is disrupted by a Japanese air raid, yet another example of the callous Axis disregard for religion and decency. The defenders of *Wake Island* turn the tables on the enemy however, marking bombs as "Christmas presents" for the Japanese foe.

Keep Your Powder Dry : The Women Warriors of WWII

Clear-headed WACs handle the high pressure routine of an overseas headquarters as calmly as if they were in an office back home.... WACs do every job—little or big—with a thrilling competence that awakens respect in the eyes of even the ablest G.I. ... For wherever they serve—around the world and back—WACs are doing a job. A gallant, soldier's job. Making a glorious war record![50]

Although a few American women served in the military during World War I—among them the Navy's Yeomen (F)s—only nurses had been in continuous service with the U.S. armed forces since 1901.[51] Beginning in 1941, uniforms for American women began to take on importance, both as status symbols and as a statement of support for the U.S. Army that was being rapidly expanded by the draft. Most of the popular draft films released by Hollywood during 1941, including *Buck Privates* (Universal) and *You'll Never Get Rich* (Paramount), feature attractive young women in various "Camp Hostess" uniforms, helping ease the transition into military life for the hundreds of thousands of men recently selected for military service.

Because of bureaucratic confusion and foot-dragging on the part of the military, authorization for women's branches of the various services did not begin until the spring of 1942. Nevertheless, several 1942 film releases feature the preexisting Army Nurse Corps in action, most notably *Army Surgeon*. But the first film to portray uniformed women other than nurses was Columbia's August 1942 release, *Blondie for Victory*. A "Victory Fashion Show" finale includes women in the uniforms of a score of official and volunteer organizations,

Blondie for Victory (Columbia, 1942): Blondie (Penny Singleton) and another member of the (fictitious) Women's Home Army spot a suspicious character lurking in the woods.

including the Volunteer Ambulance Service, the newly established WAACs, the Women's Ferry Pilot Service, and "Parachute Nurses," a fictional branch of the service dreamed up by Columbia and featured in *Parachute Nurse*, another 1942 film.

In addition to American women serving in one of the branches of the U. S. military, the Armed Forces-Women (AF-W) coding in the Filmography includes volunteer nursing auxiliaries such as the Red Cross, and British and Russian women serving their respective countries in an official military capacity. One hundred forty-nine wartime films contain some reference to women in the armed services. However, about half the time these women are not developed characters, but are instead shown in crowd scenes in hotel lobbies, train stations, and nightclubs. In the latter, they usually appear seated at tables with other military people and dancing with servicemen. One good example appears in a crowded Washington hotel lounge scene in *Crash Dive*.

In the first two years of the war, most of the developed American servicewomen characters are nurses, a "traditional" occupation for women, even during wartime. Films like *Cry Havoc* and *So Proudly We Hail!* are the female equivalents of *Bataan* and *Wake Island*, and the women are depicted as strong and dedicated to their profession.

As the war went on, the armed forces realized that women could accomplish a good many tasks heretofore done by men, thus freeing up men for combat duty. The WAACS (Women's Army Auxiliary Corps) was established in May 1942 (the name was changed to WAC in July 1943). The WAVES (Women Accepted for Volunteer Emergency Services) was formed by the Navy in July 1942, and by the summer of 1945 over 8,000 officers and 73,000 "other ranks" had been enlisted. The Marine Corps Women's Reserve was officially formed in February 1943. Other services included the SPARS (women Coast Guard), established in November 1942 (over 8,000 women were actively serving in the Coast Guard by June 1944). The WAFS (the Women's Auxiliary Ferrying Service) and WASPs (Women's Air Force Service Pilots) are featured in several films:

these women ferried planes from factories, towed targets for gunnery practice, etc., but were (unfairly) not accorded full military status. Uniformed women from other nations—particularly Great Britain, Australia, and the Soviet Union—appear in one or more wartime releases. As a reflection of the need to enlist more women, references to women in the service are the only branch of the American military to show a statistical increase in coded references for 1944 (increasing from 44 references in 1943 to 52 references in 1944; for 1945, references to AF-W rank fourth among *all* war-specific coding terms).

These films present a variety of messages: in addition to overtly hailing women's contribution to the war effort, there is a possible subtext for younger non-working women at home—become active on the home front or risk being drafted into the service (although there was no draft for women, for a time there was talk about creating a "civilian" draft to force non-soldiers into essential war work, but this never came about). There are specific references to this possibility in *Ladies Courageous* and *Three Little Sisters* (Republic, 1944); and a woman defense worker makes a speech in a night club in *Priorities on Parade* (Paramount, 1942), asserting that it is smart for women to do defense work, because otherwise they might have to fight.[52] Women in uniform are also useful in wartime films for touches of romance and humor, although it is surprising to note that they are generally treated with respect and not made the butt of jokes (as were, for example, air raid wardens) or treated as mere sex objects for male characters.

Here Come the WAVES, while a musical comedy, actually depicts WAVES in a fairly serious fashion. There is footage of a real-life boot camp at the Hunter College training facility in the Bronx; later, the WAVES are shown assisting in the instruction of male gunners, acting as air traffic controllers, and in other military occupations. *Ladies Courageous* is chiefly concerned with the WASPS' campaign seeking permission for women ferry pilots to fly military airplanes outside the continental United States. However, in one scene a male serviceman grumbles about having a woman flight instructor. "A woman taught you how to walk, didn't she?" the instructor replies (this echoes a scene in *Priorities on Parade*, where a female welder is assigned to teach a new male employee the rudiments of his job—"If Hitler knew about this he'd give up!" the man states).

Women Marines are rarely shown in wartime films, but in *Salute to the Marines*, Sergeant Helen Bailey (Marilyn Maxwell) accepts a medal which has been posthumously awarded to her Marine father (Wallace Beery) for his heroic actions during the Japanese invasion of the Philippines. The presence of female personnel at the Marine Corps' training facilities in San Diego is greeted with skepticism by a couple of male leathernecks in *Marine Raiders*. Observing the ladies marching across the parade ground, one of the two combat

veterans comments wryly that the women have "outmaneuvered" them.

Unlike their male counterparts, most of the women's uniformed services had little or no cadre of experienced "soldiers" to draw upon. Few films show non-working women entering the service directly from high school or college. Most portray mature women who already have careers—as in *Here Come the WAVES*, which shows a woman working in advertising answering the call, and depicts a twin sister musical act (both played by Betty Hutton) enlisting. *Parachute Nurse* depicts nurses abandoning a civilian hospital to enlist en masse (in real-life, there was a shortage of trained nurses in civilian hospitals during the war), although they explain that a new class of student nurses will soon arrive to take their place.

The commanders of the women's units are usually middle-aged types, gruff and businesslike but capable of showing maternal compassion to the young women entrusted to their care. Capt. Marsh (Fay Bainter) in *Cry Havoc*, Capt. "Ma" McGregor in *So Proudly We Hail!*, and Lt. Col. Spottiswoode (Agnes Moorehead) in *Keep Your Powder Dry*, for instance, are highly capable administrators, but are human beings as well. Captain Morgan (Lauretta M. Schimmoler) in *Parachute Nurse* is a bit more mannish than most, a short-haired veteran of the "last war," but is nonetheless a good officer who forces one nurse to resign because the young woman's bad attitude is ruining morale, and then cooks up a scheme to keep a *good* nurse in the unit.

While wartime films illustrate women's ability to carry out many military tasks, they also reassure American audiences that our women would not be asked to engage in combat themselves (in *Parachute Nurse*, the women are given parachute training in order to assist military "units" that are unreachable any other way, but are not shown receiving weapons instruction).[53] In reality, the only women who served at or even near the front lines were nurses and a few WACS, and Hollywood films follow suit.

Nurses and WACS are shown in a combat area in *Four Jills and a Jeep* (TCF, 1944), and—along with a troupe of entertainers—endure an air attack. Other nurses are shown in forward areas (or on ships sailing into the combat zone) in *The Story of G.I. Joe*, *The Navy Comes Through*, *Army Surgeon*, *Yanks Ahoy*, *Up in Arms*, and *The Story of Dr. Wassell*, among other films. Women die serving their country in *So Proudly We Hail!* and *Ladies Courageous*, and are taken prisoner by the Japanese in *Cry Havoc*, *Corregidor*, and *First Yank into Tokyo* (RKO, 1945).

For the most part, films focusing on women in the armed forces depict them as capable, patriotic Americans, willing to make some sacrifices for the war effort. While romance appears in many of these films, only rarely are there hints that joining the WACS or WAVES was *primarily* a means by which young women could meet eligible young men. Like the wartime image of men in the armed forces, American women

Keep Your Powder Dry (MGM, 1945): WAC Susan Peters tries to convince fellow soldier Lana Turner to keep a stiff upper lip.

join up "for the duration" only—the war is something which must be won as quickly as possible, so that everyone can get back to their normal lives.

They Also Served

As a glance at the coding statistics reveals, references to the armed forces of the United States are weighted strongly towards the two main services, the Army (343 references) and the Navy (258 references). There are also a significant number of references to the Marine Corps (108), and to the Air Corps (117—although at the time the Air Corps was part of the Army, it has been coded separately since there is a major distinction between images of the aviators and of the ground forces). However, there were other services involved in America's war effort.

The Coast Guard, technically under Treasury Department jurisdiction, was largely ignored by Hollywood during

the war. Not a single new feature film focusing on the Coast Guard was released in the 1942–45 period (an edited feature-length version of the prewar Republic serial, *SOS Coast Guard* came out in 1942); only 17 motion pictures have been identified containing some reference to this branch of the armed forces (*one* in 1945).[54] Perhaps the normal coastal patrol activities associated with the service were considered too prosaic for wartime audiences. Additionally, most of the Coast Guard's larger ocean-going vessels and cutters, and their crews, were placed under the jurisdiction of the Navy for the duration (primarily to be used as convoy escorts). A fact noted in passing in *Guadalcanal Diary* at the pre-invasion briefing, is that the "Navy and Coast Guard will put us ashore." Thus, cinematically stimulating activities that could be credited to the Coast Guard were extremely limited.

Close-in patrols by light craft and coastal surveillance were the main duties allotted to the Coast Guard. A picket vessel in operation before the war intercepts some Japanese agents who have seized an American tugboat in *City Without Men* (Columbia, 1943). An actual wartime shortage of small

Ladies of Washington (TCF, 1944): Trudy Marshall shows off her SPAR (Coast Guard) uniform to two friends. Notice the gas rationing sticker on the car's windshield.

patrol vessels is reflected in *Enemy Agents Meet Ellery Queen* (Columbia, 1942): at the beginning of the film, Ellery is traveling home on a train after donating his yacht to the Coast Guard (armed civilian craft manned by the Coast Guard Reserve, so-called Coastal Pickets, patrolled the Atlantic and Gulf coasts between the summer of 1942 and 1943).

The only wartime film depicting members of the Coast Guard in action against the enemy is *They Came to Blow Up America* (TCF, 1943). In this film, a young Coast Guardsman patrolling a beach intercepts some Nazi saboteurs who have just landed from a U-Boat.[55] Ironically, throughout the first year of America's participation in the war, coastal patrols were conducted as much to keep people from witnessing the gory flotsam of the Battle of Atlantic which was washing up on shore, as they were for security purposes.[56]

Ladies of Washington, a B-picture released by Twentieth Century–Fox in mid–1944, features several members of the Coast Guard, although the film is a spy drama. Interestingly, Trudy Marshall is cast as a pretty young ensign in the SPARS (an acronym formed from the Coast Guard motto, "Semper

Paratus," meaning "Always Ready"). But the film barely alludes to her clerical responsibilities and instead dwells upon her romance with a handsome medical doctor.[57] A reference to a woman joining the SPARS is also included in Monogram's 1944 release, *Lady, Let's Dance.*

The Merchant Marine, whose members were usually portrayed in prewar films as bar-brawling toughs, was given a patriotic makeover by wartime Hollywood.[58] The civilians operating our merchant vessels deserved it—over 60,000 died delivering supplies to America's armed services and the Allies, and transporting U. S. servicemen overseas. Thirty-four wartime feature films contain references to the Merchant Marine. *Action in the North Atlantic* and *Tampico* (TCF, 1944) are the most significant war-relevant films. Both contain climactic scenes in which the valiant crews of merchant vessels ram their damaged ships into menacing German U-boats that had torpedoed them. *U-Boat Prisoner* (Columbia, 1944) features a sequence in which a convoy straggler teams up with its destroyer escort to sink a German U-boat (aided by a Merchant seaman being held prisoner on the sub itself).

Combat, or the effects of combat, is portrayed in a relatively large number of those films in which the Merchant Marine is represented. In addition to the above-mentioned encounters with enemy naval vessels, in *The Navy Comes Through* a freighter carrying munitions to England tangles repeatedly with the German Navy (the Navy gun crew on board is ably assisted by the civilian sailors). And although the action is not shown, the U-boat that torpedoed the protagonists' ship in *Lifeboat* (TCF, 1944) is itself destroyed by Merchant Marine shellfire when it surfaces to finish its victim off with its deck gun.

A more subtle means of acknowledging the wartime contribution of the Merchant Marine was the eventual issuing of uniforms, much like those of the Navy, to officers. The ship's captain played by Edward G. Robinson in *Tampico* wears such a uniform, as does Walter Reed, playing the husband of "Mexican Spitfire" Lupe Velez in *Mexican Spitfire's Blessed Event* (RKO, 1943).

Several motion pictures featuring the American Merchant Marine include scenes in which members of the crew must endure the consequences of their ship being torpedoed. In PRC's *Submarine Base*, a merchant seaman survives his second sinking only to wind up on a small island secretly controlled by Nazi agents. On another obscure island, torpedoed Merchant seamen team up with a magician to harass the visiting Adolf Hitler and his Axis cohorts in *That Nasty Nuisance* (UA, 1943). Alfred Hitchcock's better-known *Lifeboat*, taking place entirely within the confines of the titular craft, focuses on the travails of surviving crew members and passengers from a merchant vessel sunk by a German U-boat. The Allied civilians eventually discover that they have been betrayed by the German officer they had rescued and then allowed to command their boat. *Lifeboat* includes the rather gruesome amputation of a seaman's mangled leg, without anesthetic, using a clasp knife.

Action in the North Atlantic features a close-knit, ethnically mixed crew in which the officers and unionized seamen are largely treated as equals. Having survived an ordeal aboard a lifeboat after their tanker is sunk by a U-boat, the crew signs up together to serve aboard a new Liberty ship. Their first cruise is as part of a convoy making the infamous Murmansk Run to Russia. During the trip they are engaged in almost constant battle with the armed forces of the Third Reich. But ultimately the American civilians triumph, sinking the same U-boat that had torpedoed their tanker and killing the Nazi sailors who had viciously terrorized the helpless survivors of the earlier encounter.

Conclusions

During the Second World War, with over 12 million men and women serving in the armed forces of the United States,

Tampico (TCF, 1944): Merchant Marine captain Edward G. Robinson commands an oil tanker in the Gulf of Mexico. Betrayed by a spy, his ship is sunk by a German U-boat.

many if not most Americans had a friend, relative, or acquaintance in uniform. In addition, within a relatively short period of time the civilian population was inundated with war news and information of all types. Youngsters made model airplanes and memorized the "silhouettes" of friendly and enemy aircraft; some people kept war maps in their homes, plotting every advance and setback; young women soon knew the various uniforms and ranks of all the services, worn by boyfriends, brothers, cousins, fathers, and potential beaus; children played "war" games in back yards and vacant lots.

Hollywood could not deceive such knowledgeable audiences with unrealistic, fanciful depictions of American men and women in the service, unless the deceptions were willingly accepted by audiences. What if few WACS looked like Lana Turner in *Keep Your Powder Dry*? What if the nurses on Bataan in *So Proudly We Hail!* are just a bit too well coiffed for their desperate situation? What if the likelihood of an American tank crew (*Sahara*) being in North Africa well before "Operation Torch" (November 1942) was rather small? What if the ethnic mix of soldiers in the various Combat films was a bit too well balanced to seem realistic? These were minor inaccuracies, done to enhance the entertainment value of the films.

Hollywood had a message to deliver along with entertainment—feature films are not documentaries, and the melodrama, coincidences, inaccuracies, and deliberate obfuscations were part of this message. Audiences knew they were watching fictional stories, and enjoyed them. Films said the United States and its Allies would win because we were *right*—our soldiers were fighting the good fight. The audience left the theatre reassured, patriotically inspired, and entertained.

17. "We're in This Together": America's Minorities and the War Effort

1. It's Our Country Too: Blacks in Wartime

No one had expected it, and no one intended it, but [World War Two was] the watershed of the post-emancipation struggle for equality.[1]

Hollywood and other popular media, in accordance with the wishes of the U.S. government, made a point of portraying the American war effort as universal: men, women, children, teenagers, senior citizens, foreign-born and native-born, all did their part to defeat the Axis. The few cynics or naysayers were depicted as criminals, traitors, or worse, but were definitively identified as isolated exceptions. No *class* of American was singled out as *un*patriotic. All Americans were encouraged to support the war effort, regardless of their sex, age, or race:

As a counter to whatever incipient fifth column might have been lurking within the poisonous weeds which race hatred had fostered, government press agents mounted a noisy propaganda campaign.[2]

As part of this campaign, the U.S. government produced several documentaries dealing with black participation in the war effort: *The Negro Soldier* (1944), and *The Negro Sailor* (produced in 1945, but not released until 1946). A privately produced documentary, *We've Come a Long Way* (1943), depicted both uniformed and home front activities of black Americans.[3]

In keeping with this theme, Hollywood also began to utilize black Americans—and foreign blacks, in some instances—in ways it had never before considered feasible. Blacks, according to American films of the wartime era, were pitching in just like everyone else, both on the front lines and on the home front.

However, as with wartime images of Chinese and Latin American characters, depictions of blacks during the war are frequently fleeting, token, humorous, and all too often just as racially stereotyped as pre-war film characterizations.

A very few films may be singled out as pioneering new, positive and mature black characters—or just black characters free to be normal human beings, stripped of the stereotypical dialect and actions which were the identifying marks of Hollywood's black images. While these films do indicate an attitudinal change, and bear discussion, the majority of the war-relevant films containing black characters depict them in isolated musical numbers, or as domestic servants, railroad redcaps or porters, and in other minor roles.[4]

Similarly, in "real" life some strides were made in racial equality during the war, but all was far from calm on the home front. Blacks who took advantage of the boom in wartime industrial production discovered discrimination in the workplace, discrimination in housing, and discrimination in the new regions of the country (California and the industrial Midwest, in particular) to which they relocated. Racial unrest exploded into violence in Detroit in the spring of 1942, but the most serious race riots of the war occurred in 1943. Newark, Philadelphia, and Mobile all suffered civil unrest, while Detroit was hit hardest, 35 people perishing in the Belle Isle riots of June 1943.[5] None of this, obviously, was even hinted at in Hollywood films of the period.

Black references are third in overall numbers for the 1942–1945 period, after references to the U.S. Army and to Shortages:

	1942	1943	1944	1945	Total
Black	92	100	64	35	291
AF-Black	2	19	7	2	30

Appearances of black characters in war-relevant films seem numerically quite imposing, but this is rather misleading, since these high numbers do not translate into a major revolution in black screen images. Still, there are some interesting exceptions, almost all a direct result of the war. Wartime films containing more than a brief appearance of a black character fall into three broad categories: films featuring blacks in the armed forces; films featuring blacks on the home front; and films in which the black characters do not deal with the war directly, although the films themselves make some reference to the conflict.

The last category, while it may not seem a particularly fertile area for a changed racial depiction, includes such films as *Syncopation* (RKO, 1942). William Dieterle directed this effort to trace the history of jazz, as related through the career of white trumpeter Jackie Cooper. However, the black contribution to jazz is not minimized, and Todd Duncan appears as Cooper's black mentor, Reggie. The black roles are for the most part non-stereotyped and an unusual air of equality pervades the film. A number of other films of the period feature black musical performances, sometimes with war-relevant numbers, but just as often not, and generally no effort was made to present black characters as anything other than part of a musical interlude. For these reasons, *Syncopation* is quite unusual for its time.

Cabin in the Sky (MGM, 1943), while perpetuating some hoary black stereotypes, was still a rarity, a prestige all-black release from a major studio, showcasing the talents of Lena Horne (who made musical appearances in MGM's major musicals but rarely received a dramatic part), Eddie "Rochester" Anderson, Ethel Waters, Louis Armstrong, and nearly every other black player of significance in the period.

Revenge of the Zombies (Monogram, 1943) went to the other extreme, from MGM to Monogram, but it did contain one of Mantan Moreland's better performances. Moreland frequently stole the show from his white co-stars, and contributed considerably to the success of the Monogram Charlie Chan series.[6] Monogram was also home to the East Side Kids films, featuring "Sunshine" Sammy Morrison (until 1943). Morrison, while occasionally the butt of casual racial remarks, is portrayed as an equal member of the "gang," and is not subjected to servile or demeaning tasks solely based on his race.

To Have and Have Not (WB, 1945) is an interesting film, set on the Caribbean island of Martinique in 1940. The plot of the film revolves around American charter boat captain Morgan (Humphrey Bogart) and his unwilling involvement with a group of Free French adherents who wish to escape from the Vichy-dominated island. There are no black characters of real significance, but there are many black extras in the crowd scenes—including black French sailors and black gendarmes—going about their daily lives in a perfectly normal way. Frenchy's bar is that rarity in Hollywood films of the 1930s and 1940s (and even later), an *integrated* nightclub-restaurant! Blacks appear as *customers*, sitting at tables and conversing, not merely serving drinks or playing in the orchestra

(there is also one scene where Morgan and Slim—Lauren Bacall—duck into a black saloon to avoid Vichy police).[7] This vision of an integrated but still "civilized" society is quite a change from Hollywood films set in the United States, where blacks appear in very small numbers, and those films set in Africa, where blacks are present in large numbers but are virtually always shown as semi-civilized (at best) "natives" or servants.

Films about blacks on the home front strive to present black characters as patriotic, willing participants in wartime activities. However, these films are not numerous, and actual depictions of blacks involved in home front or home defense activities are very rare.

In the Meantime, Darling (TCF, 1944), for instance, features Clarence Muse (unbilled, despite a substantial role, while many lesser characters *are* given billing) as the "handyman" at a hotel catering to the wives of Army officers from a nearby training camp. Muse is wise, friendly, respectful—the perfect servant. His connection with the war effort (besides helping to run the hotel) is through his son, who is in the Army. Muse receives a letter from his son after a long delay, and explains to one of the guests that while he (Muse) has been writing frequently, his son has never replied until now. This sets the audience up for a dramatic scene, perhaps with Muse receiving news that his son has been killed, wounded, or decorated for valor, but the film drops this plotline cold, and the son is never again referred to.

Sherlock Holmes in Washington (Universal, 1943) contains a brief scene in which, after a reference is made to a Navy pilot, a black train porter proudly states: "My boy's in the Army—he's going to be a pilot, too." The first all-black Air Corps unit was formed in the fall of 1941, with black pilots and black ground personnel.[8] However, no other feature film of the period even hints that blacks were serving as military pilots.

Since You Went Away (UA, 1944), the quintessential American "home front" film, depicts another loyal black retainer, in this case Hattie McDaniel. McDaniel, Claudette Colbert's maid, leaves when the family can no longer afford to pay her salary. However, she soon returns to work for the family after hours (without pay). McDaniel—although a positive character—is very much a "stereotypical maid ... still the faithful black servant of *Gone with the Wind*."[9] This film also includes a brief glimpse of a black soldier at a train station with his wife and child, an unusual "humanizing" touch for the period.

Marching On (Independent, 1943), a rarely seen all-black feature, depicts a black family involved in the war effort: "You're a junior air raid warden and I'm sewing for the Red Cross," a mother remarks to her daughter. *Hit Parade of 1943* (Republic, 1943) shows a black civil defense worker, and black women waiting for a bus to take them to work in a defense factory, although all of this appears in a musical production number.

Casablanca (Warner Bros., 1943): Sam (Dooley Wilson) plays it again for Humphrey Bogart and Ingrid Bergman.

Lifeboat (TCF, 1944), includes a black steward (Canada Lee) among the survivors of a ship which has been sunk by a German submarine. Lee is generally portrayed as the equal of the others in the lifeboat—in fact, he is given the chance to "vote" along with the other survivors to decide the fate of the U-boat captain who has been captured (although he declines this opportunity)—but is still initially identified as a servant and is a subordinate, even deferential character.[10] John Steinbeck's impression of the character, after seeing the film, was strongly negative: "He was angered that instead of the dignified man in his script Joe had been changed 'to a stock comedy Negro.'"[11] This seems a bit of an overreaction, but perhaps Steinbeck had envisioned a much more assertive figure.

Casablanca (WB, 1943) is another "in-between" film, neither home front nor military in nature. Dooley Wilson, the ubiquitous "Sam," is Humphrey Bogart's friend and confidante, but there is still a clear distinction between the white employer and his black employee. *Reunion in France* (MGM, 1942) contains an interesting sequence set in Paris after the

German occupation (but before America's entry into the war). A black jazz player in a nightclub sings "I'll Be Glad When You're Dead, You Rascal You," and adds—"and Adolf, too!"[12]

Film depictions of blacks in the armed forces are rather more frequent than illustrations of blacks specifically involved in home front activities, but there are still few films showing black servicemen in action. This, at least for the first several years of the war, reflects actual American military practice. During the first year of the Selective Service system, only 7,000 blacks were drafted, nationwide—local draft boards, up through 1943, consistently showed a preference for white males.[13] Nonetheless, blacks were able to *enlist*, and by December 1941 there were 100,000 blacks in the U.S. Army.[14] The Army, Navy, and Marine Corps were all segregated at the war's outset: this blatant segregation of the armed forces (and the inferior facilities assigned to black service personnel) led to a series of violent altercations between white and black troops, beginning in 1941.[15]

As the war went on, whites—even those who believed in

white supremacy and segregation—realized that discrimination against blacks in the armed forces was counter-productive to the war effort. The need for more military manpower overcame any lingering racist sentiments, and by the end of 1943, blacks "were taken into the military in numbers reflecting their population base."[16] This in turn forced a reduction in segregation on troop trains and ships, and in various military facilities. While many black soldiers were placed in logistics and supply units (such as the well-known Red Ball Express), by the end of the war black and white Army combat units were operating in close cooperation.

The other services went even further: the Navy, which for years allowed blacks to serve on ships only as mess attendants, began to commission black officers at the end of 1943; the Coast Guard commissioned over 700 blacks during WWII, and the Merchant Marine was more or less fully integrated.[17]

During wartime, black servicemen appear in musical numbers in such films as *Star Spangled Rhythm* (Paramount, 1942—Eddie "Rochester" Anderson), *This Is the Army* (WB, 1943—Joe Louis),[18] *Hit Parade of 1943* (1943), and *The Heat's On* (Columbia, 1943).[19] *Reveille with Beverly* (Columbia, 1943) features a black sailor in one scene. A black soldier—prominently displaying the Distinguished Service Cross—appears in *Stage Door Canteen* (UA, 1943). Other black servicemen are briefly shown in *Stand by for Action* (MGM, 1942), *Gung Ho!* (Universal, 1943), and *Guadalcanal Diary* (TCF, 1943), among other films.

Follow the Boys (Universal, 1944) contains a sequence in which the Louis Jordan band (a black swing group) entertains a group of black soldiers. *Stormy Weather* (TCF, 1943) is an interesting film, starring Bill "Bojangles" Robinson. It begins with his discharge from the Army at the end of WWI[20], and follows his career (in rather fictionalized form) to 1943, when he is seen entertaining black troops. These last two films demonstrate how segregation—even in entertainment—was routine and not deemed worthy of comment (in *Follow the Boys*, George Raft joins the Jordan band and dances for the black troops on the back of a flatbed truck, but the whole "performance" is impromptu and reinforces, probably unintentionally, the second-class status accorded black troops).[21]

Marching On, mentioned above, was partially shot at Fort Huachuca, Arizona, and contains actual footage of black soldiers in training (with black non-coms and white officers).[22] The plot centers around Rodney Tucker Jr. (Hugh Martin), who refuses to enlist in the armed forces despite the patriotic entreaties of his mother and his Spanish-American War veteran grandfather. Tucker voices the opinion that the war is no concern of American blacks, but a black soldier insists: "This is just as much our country as anybody else's." Tucker is drafted, but deliberately does poorly in training and maneuvers. He finally goes AWOL and heads for home, but after a brief encounter with his long-lost father (an amnesiac WWI

Marching On! (Independent, 1943): This rather crude poster reflects the low production values of this all-black film. However, *Marching On!* does contain some interesting scenes of actual black soldiers training at Fort Huachuca, Arizona.

veteran who promptly dies), Tucker and his grandfather stumble across a nest of Japanese spies. The older man is mortally wounded, but says as he dies: "The Lord has been good to me—he let me have one more fight for my country." Tucker undergoes an attitude adjustment: "They gave me another chance to prove that I'm an American too, that my blood is as red as ... anyone else."

While cheap and crude—even compared to other independent all-black films of the period[23]—*Marching On* does raise some interesting points about black participation in the war effort. Tucker's reluctance to serve initially seems to be compounded of equal parts of selfishness and cowardice; he later deserts in a jealous rage over his girlfriend's alleged preference for another soldier. However, his unspoken attitude is that the United States deserves little allegiance from blacks, who are the victims of discrimination, and that the Axis powers are at war with *white* America. The murderous Japanese spy ring and a heat-induced hallucination about a Nazi invasion of America combine to make Tucker realize that fascists are the enemies of *all* Americans.

Three major studio films feature black military characters in significant roles: *Bataan* (MGM, 1943), *Crash Dive* (TCF, 1943), and *Sahara* (Columbia, 1943). The films all present their black characters in a positive, non-stereotyped manner, each within a different context.

Sahara features Rex Ingram as Tambul, a Sudanese (British colonial) soldier who teams up with American Humphrey Bogart and a multi-national tank crew. Foreign nations had utilized black units—usually from their colonial possessions—for a number of years, and such units were depicted from time to time in motion pictures. *The World Moves On* (Fox, 1934) shows black colonial troops in action in WWI, although the primary black character in the film is the ultra-stereotype, Stepin Fetchit. Fetchit follows his white employee into the Army (presumably as a kind of valet, since he is *not* assigned to an all-black unit), and is surprised to discover black Senegalese (French colonials) soldiers at the front. Later, these blacks are shown fighting in conjunction with white troops in the film's battle scenes. *Drums of the Desert* (Monogram, 1940) portrays a Senegalese paratroop unit under the command of a white French Foreign Legion officer (Ralph Byrd), in a contemporary setting (Mantan Moreland plays a black sergeant from Harlem).

Ingram, one of the most dignified and respected black actors of the period, had earlier appeared in a number of films, including major roles in *The Green Pastures* (WB, 1936), *The Adventures of Huckleberry Finn* (MGM, 1939), *The Thief of Bagdad* (UA, 1940), and *Cabin in the Sky* (MGM, 1943). Much of the stature accorded to Tambul in *Sahara* may be attributed to Ingram's screen presence, but the role of Tambul is "an extraordinarily well-conceived and well-written part."[24] Tambul is "an integral part of a brave group, a comrade, a man on a level with his fellow-soldiers,"[25] not a servant. He speaks precise, if mildly stilted English, and at no point is demeaned or made into a comic figure.

Tambul and his Italian prisoner (J. Carrol Naish) join Sgt. Gunn (Humphrey Bogart), and the motley group of soldiers Gunn has collected around his lone tank (including two Britons, an Irishman, a South African, a Free Frenchman, and two Americans—one each from Brooklyn and Texas, naturally). A short time later, the tank shoots down a German plane and the pilot is captured. The German aviator objects to being searched by Tambul, a member of "an inferior race." This racist comment and a later remark by the Nazi (he calls Tambul a "neger"—German for "Negro" but easily understood by American audiences as "nigger"—in a disparaging tone) elicit a strong response from the usually taciturn Gunn: "Wipe that smile off your face or I'll knock your teeth through the top of your head."

The Allied soldiers take possession of an abandoned mosque which contains a waterhole (Tambul assumes the role of their guide, since he possesses detailed knowledge of the desert). However, the well is almost dry; when the German prisoner tries to escape and warn his fellow soldiers of this (killing the Italian in the process), Tambul chases him down and kills him, preserving the secret at the cost of his own life, "possibly the first time that a Hollywood producer has ever allowed the spectacle of a Negro vanquishing a white man in fair combat to appear in a film."[26] This is also the most "gallant" death depicted in the film—most of the other men's deaths are far less spectacular and visible (Tambul even gives the "thumbs up" to Gunn as he dies, indicating that the Nazi was not able to reveal their secret).

Earlier, Tambul is shown in friendly discourse with Waco (Bruce Bennett), the white Texan. Waco offers Tambul a cigarette; Tambul, mildly surprised, accepts it. Waco says he was a farmer before the war; Tambul volunteers the information that he is a career soldier, as his father and grandfather were. When Waco asks him about the practice of polygamy among "Mohammedans," Tambul says Muslims are allowed to have up to four wives, but that he, personally, has only one. "You sure learn a lot in the Army," Waco says. "Yes, we both have much to learn from each other," Tambul replies.

Like the character of Tambul in *Sahara*, Private Wesley Eeps in *Bataan* is "accidentally integrated" into a white unit by the exigencies of war. In the early days of 1942, American and Filipino troops are retreating in the face of the Japanese invasion of the Philippines. Sgt. Bill Dane (Robert Taylor) and a hastily assembled group of men are assigned to destroy a bridge over a ravine, then hold off the Japanese for as long as possible, giving the main body of American forces a chance to form defensive positions behind them. Among the soldiers are several Filipinos, a Mexican-American from California, and black demolition expert Eeps.

Eeps, played by singer and stage actor Kenneth Spencer (who had previously appeared in *Cabin in the Sky*), is given individual traits but is *not* excessively stereotyped.[27] He is introduced, shirtless, humming what seems to be a "spiritual."[28] Later, he reveals he was "studying to be a preacher" before he enlisted in the Army, and he says a prayer over the first of the group to die. Eeps does his job competently, is treated as an equal by the other men, and survives until almost the end of the film (a testament to his importance—in Hollywood films, "disposable," marginalized characters are usually killed off quickly).

Eeps' death is among the most memorable in the film, and is depicted in a fairly shocking and grotesque manner for the period: while bayoneting a Japanese soldier, Eeps is killed by a samurai-sword wielding officer, who chops at the back of his neck. Eeps screams and there is almost a freeze-frame of his anguished face as the blade sinks into his flesh.

Both *Sahara* and *Bataan* pay black soldiers the ultimate

compliment of presenting them as "one of the gang." As one critic noted, "Not by one lapse does director Tay Garnett differentiate in his treatment of the white soldiers and the Negro."[29] *Bataan* is perhaps the more surprising film, since its black soldier is American; "foreign" blacks such as Tambul in *Sahara* might exist outside expected stereotypical boundaries, but to show an American black as the equal of whites was quite shocking in its day.

Crash Dive is more conventional, if only because it takes place within a more conventional context. Ben Carter, as Navy mess attendant Oliver Cromwell Jones, is presented positively, and his friendship with the older, white CPO McDonnell (James Gleason) is very different than the usual master-servant relationship. McDonnell is suffering from a heart ailment, which he hides from Naval officials to avoid a medical discharge. Jones learns of his friend's illness, but refrains from revealing McDonnell's secret.

Jones is definitely not, by any stretch of the imagination, comic relief (although his scenes with Gleason are at times humorous); he does not speak in dialect, roll his eyes, or otherwise exhibit Stepin Fechit-like traits. Throughout the film his actions are admirable; he even goes along on a dangerous commando mission (as the other men blacken their faces in preparation for the raid, Jones says "I'm the only born commando here") with McDonnell, Lt. Ward (Tyrone Power), and other Navy personnel. In fact, Jones and Ward are the last two men to leave the enemy island, swimming underwater to safety.[30]

Overall, *Crash Dive* presents Jones as a normal, realistic, and believable human being, no mean feat for the time period. If his character is slightly less heroic and manly than Tambul and Wesley Eeps, it may be because Jones is initially shown in a subordinate, non-combatant role, rather than appearing as a fighting man from the outset in situations of almost constant peril (a great deal of *Crash Dive* takes place in the United States; *Sahara* and *Bataan* are set entirely in combat zones). However, Jones's occupation accurately reflects the Navy's situation at the time of the film's production, and Jones rises *above* his subordinate role. By extension, therefore, the armed forces' policy of segregating blacks in "service" units is shown to be a mistake, since blacks are as brave and competent as their white counterparts when they are allowed to be.[31]

Although in the majority of war-relevant films, Hollywood relegates blacks to bit parts, it should nonetheless be noted that exceptional efforts such as *Sahara*, *Crash Dive*, and *Bataan* depict blacks in a way few if any pre-war Hollywood films were able to. These outstanding exceptions are the films which paved the way for post-war efforts towards a more realistic portrayal of blacks.

2. Pan-Americana: Latin Americans and WWII Hollywood

"Imagine that: Mexico fighting on the same side as the gringos!" Pedro Armendáriz in Soy Puro Mexicano, *a 1942 Mexican propaganda feature.*

Hollywood's treatment of Latin Americans during the war is somewhat similar to its portrayal of blacks and of Chinese characters. For the purpose of showing international and interracial cooperation, token Latin American characters appear in a number of films. Lip service is paid to our "Good Neighbors" and hemispheric solidarity against fascism. Latin music, popular in Hollywood films for a number of years, was now politically correct as well. However, films set in and dealing with Latin America actually decline in number and importance from the immediate pre-war period, and Latin America is increasingly seen as a rather irrelevant backwater to the war.

The first Latin American nations to join the Allies were the smaller Central American and Caribbean countries, closely linked to the United States economically: "these declarations [of war] were of only nuisance value to the Allied cause. They had been made to please Uncle Sam."[32] Their chief contribution to the war effort was geographic, providing the United States with friendly land for air and naval bases.

Mexico declared war on the Axis powers in May 1942, after the notorious sinking of two Mexican oil tankers by U-boats. Mexico's abundant mineral resources fueled the Allied war machine; however, 250,000 Mexican residents of the United States also served in the U.S. armed forces, including 14,000 who actually saw combat.[33] The Mexican Navy patrolled the Gulf of Mexico, and the Mexican Air Force sent a fighter squadron (Squadron 201) to the Pacific, where it participated in the liberation of the Philippines, beginning in June 1945.[34]

Brazil was the only other Latin American country to send troops overseas to fight (although Cuba patrolled its section of the Caribbean, once even sinking a German U-boat). As with Mexico, German submarine warfare caused Brazil to actively enter the conflict. In August 1942, a Brazilian troop ship was sunk by a U-boat with the loss of 300 lives; in the next six days, three more ships were sunk, and at the end of that month Brazil declared war on Germany and Italy (but not Japan).[35] In addition to eventually accepting patrol duties for the South Atlantic, Brazil sent infantry troops to Italy where they saw combat, beginning in September 1944.[36]

Little if any of this appears in Hollywood's wartime productions.[37] While as the chart below indicates, coding references to Latin America are numerous, many of these references are minor:

1942	1943	1944	1945	Total
42	38	35	18	= 133

Latin American references in Hollywood's wartime productions range from largely non-war relevant musical numbers to the inclusion of Latin American characters in multinational and multiracial military groupings.

The latter type of depiction is the most clearly war-related. Examples of the token Latin soldier/sailor/Marine include Desi Arnaz both in *The Navy Comes Through* (MGM, 1942) and *Bataan* (MGM, 1943). In the first film, Arnaz plays Pat Tarriba, a Cuban-born member of a Navy gun crew serving on a Merchant Marine ship. He speaks with an accent and is recognizably "ethnic," but is not particularly separated from the rest of the crew (the only other "foreign" character is an Austrian seaman who is called "Dutch"). Arnaz's character in *Bataan*, Private Felix Ramirez, has a few distinctive scenes. He is identified as a Mexican-American from California, a member of the National Guard rather than a Regular Army soldier. In one scene, Ramirez picks up a swing music broadcast on an old radio, and enthusiastically says, "That's Tommy Dorsey from Hollywood—he sends me!" He also describes his hot rod back home, and tough Sgt. Dane (Robert Taylor) calls him a "jitterbug kid." Interestingly enough, Ramirez dies of malaria, the only member of the unit *not* killed by the Japanese.[38]

Bombardier (RKO, 1943) and *Guadalcanal Diary* (TCF, 1943) also portray Latin members of the U.S. armed forces. Richard Martin is cast as Ignatius "Chito" Rafferty in the first film—interestingly enough, Martin later translated this character to the Old West, first in *West of the Pecos* (RKO, 1945) and then in a series of Tim Holt Westerns for RKO, from 1947 to 1952. Rafferty is tall, handsome, romantically inclined, speaks with an accent, and makes a point to refer to his Irish-Mexican heritage. However, he is not a major character in *Bombardier*. *Guadalcanal Diary* features Anthony Quinn (who in real life *was* Irish-Mexican) as Jesús "Soose" Alvarez, a Mexican-American Marine comrade of Lloyd Nolan and William Bendix. Alvarez speaks with an accent and is personalized with some individual traits, but is not a blatant stereotype. He is just one more Marine in a polyglot group of Marines—a typical Hollywood "universal platoon"[39]—with nicknames like "Taxi," "Hook," "Chicken," "Butch," and "Tex."[40] Alvarez is prominently featured in several sequences, killing Japanese soldiers in hand-to-hand combat, then escaping overwhelming odds by swimming away underwater. In his final scene, Alvarez throws his knife at one attacking Japanese soldier and laughs wildly, but is shot and killed by another enemy soldier.

There is also a wounded Mexican-American veteran named Juan in one sequence of *Pride of the Marines* (WB, 1945). Sitting in a wheelchair during a discussion, Juan is offended when one of the wounded soldiers asserts that he does not want "others" taking jobs away from him, "like the Mexicans." The man apologizes to Juan, who is, after all, a fellow serviceman, but Juan realizes that the war has only temporarily put a halt to discrimination (in fact, this sentiment is verbalized by one of the other soldiers in the group, a Jew).

In *Girl from Monterrey* (PRC, 1943), Alberto (Anthony Caruso) is a Mexican boxer brought to the United States by his sister Lita (Armida), a singer. Late in the film, Alberto disappears for a time. When he shows up again, he tells Lita he went to Mexico City to enlist; Lita proudly announces that she has given two men to the armed forces—her brother Alberto to the Mexican Army, and her boyfriend Jerry to the U.S. Army.

Related to the Latin military characters are those Latin Americans assisting the Allied cause in other active ways, usually as secret agents. *The Falcon's Brother* (RKO, 1942), which introduced Tom Conway as the successor to his real-life brother George Sanders, begins with the arrival of a boat from South America. Sanders and Conway uncover a gang of Nazi agents; later, Sanders is killed saving a Latin delegate to a Pan-American conference from an Axis assassination attempt, but Conway helps defeat the spies (and inherits the lead role in the series). Two Mexican secret agents, including one played by George J. Lewis, help the brothers in their battle against the fascists.[41]

The cast of *Underground Agent* (Columbia, 1942) includes Julian Rivero as Miguel, who assists telephone expert Lee Graham (Bruce Bennett) in foiling a Nazi spy plan to tap the phones of defense plants. Miguel, captured by the Axis agents, is tortured in an attempt to make him reveal the workings of the "scrambler" installed by Graham. Refusing to talk, Miguel is killed by the Nazis, but not before he makes a patriotic speech: "Here we live [as] free men, not slaves like you ... You will not find many in America who will trade their freedom for the darkness you bring on the world." In an earlier sequence, Miguel's entire family appears, singing the praises of freedom and democracy.

Tampico (TCF, 1944) also contains some Mexican agents, although the film is rather disappointing in its scanty depiction of inter-American cooperation during the war. For example, no mention is made of Mexican naval units providing any coast guard or sub-chasing chores in the Gulf of Mexico; the only Mexican military figure portrayed in detail is Nestor Paiva, playing a surly and suspicious Mexican naval commander who questions Merchant Marine captain Edward G. Robinson after Robinson's ship has been torpedoed. The port of Tampico itself is typical Hollywood fantasy, a mixture of sleazy waterfront dives and singing and dancing Latins (who in virtually every instance seem more Spanish than Mexican).

However, Robinson is aided in the destruction of a Nazi spy ring by secret agents Valdez (Marc Lawrence)—a sailor who seems villainous until the final section of the film—and Dolores (Mona Maris)—a sultry *femme fatale* (who vamps virtually every officer from Robinson's ship)—and, apparently (although it is not clear) by a Mexican government official who is their superior officer. As is usual for Hollywood, however, it takes a two-fisted American amateur to uncover spies that the professional intelligence service could not catch.

A few films promote Pan-American solidarity more or less indirectly. *Undercover Man* (Paramount, 1942) is a routine Hopalong Cassidy period Western about a band of outlaws raiding both Mexico and the United States. Cassidy (William Boyd) teams up with Don Tomás Gonzáles (Antonio Moreno) to capture the bandits. The film contains "endless unsubtle lines of dialogue about the need for Anglos and Latinos to be 'good neighbors,'"[42] obvious references to the Roosevelt Good Neighbor Policy. The film does, on the other hand, contain two comic Mexican stereotypes: the fat, lazy Miguel (Chris-Pin Martin), and the fat cook Rosita (Eva Puig).

Hands Across the Border (Republic, 1944), despite a promising title, does not spend any time on inter–American cooperation, although Duncan Renaldo has a supporting role as a Hispanic ranch foreman. The musical finale, illustrating the Hoagy Carmichael title song, is largely irrelevant to the rest of the film, but does strongly promote U.S.-Mexican friendship in an abstract, musical production number format.[43]

Girl Trouble (TCF, 1942), a contemporary comedy, stars Don Ameche as the owner of a Venezuelan rubber plantation who travels to the United States for a development loan. He falls in love with a rich young woman (Joan Bennett) posing as a maid. While Ameche's Latin identity is only marginally relevant, in a way this film at least reflects Latin America's chief wartime role, as a source of raw materials for the United States.

Pan-Americana (RKO, 1945), a contemporary musical, concerns a picture magazine's quest for beauty-contest candidates from the Americas. There are scenes set in Cuba, Mexico, and Brazil, and second-echelon Latin musical performers (no Carmen Miranda or Xavier Cugat here) are seen in various "specialty" acts. However, the only significant Latin character is "Lupita" (played by Isabelita), who tries to enter the contest, and finally gets in as the representative from Brooklyn! Portrayals of the other contestants are reduced to the skimpiest national and sexual stereotypes.

By far the most numerous Latin American references during the war are those with little direct war-relevance. Generally, they consist of musical performances by Hollywood's Latin contingent, particularly Carmen Miranda, José Iturbi, and Xavier Cugat, and appearances in supporting roles by Latin actors and actresses such as Lupe Vélez, Armida, Tito Guízar, and others.[44] The Latin-inspired musical numbers are sometimes war-relevant (or at least promote Pan-American solidarity), but are just as often *non*-relevant. The large number of such songs should not be attributed directly to the war, but more to the contemporary public taste, aided and abetted by pre-war Hollywood's Latin American efforts:

Latin music's mass popularity was developing from the beginning of the decade. An extremely important part was played by Hollywood ... these musicals greatly advanced the spread of Latin rhythms and melodies into American culture ... the 1940s film musicals both reflected and augmented Latin music's popularity in hybrid forms that made it more acceptable to American audiences...[45]

However, many of these musical numbers also reinforce standard stereotypes about Latinos, who had no pressure group to ensure their "protection" from pre-war stereotyping. In this, Latin Americans were more closely related to blacks in Hollywood films, also largely relegated to their usual status of servants and service personnel; the Chinese, on the other hand, had the OWI to "suggest" to producers that houseboy and laundryman roles were inappropriate for a "fighting Ally."

Fortunately for Latin Americans, their Hollywood-imposed stereotype was far milder than either the black or Chinese images. Fortunate, because—despite claims of Good Neighborliness and Pan-American cooperation—the image of Latin Americans in Hollywood films was relatively unaffected by the war.

18. "United Nations": Hollywood's Portrayal of America's Allies

While the majority of war-relevant films made in the United States deal with the war's impact on Americans, a conscious effort was made by Hollywood—encouraged by the U.S. government—to portray the contributions of the Allied nations in the struggle against fascism.

There are frequent verbal and visual references to our Allies, and a significant number of films *focusing* on other nations, some even omitting U.S. characters entirely. In retrospect this seems a bit surprising, but may in part be attributed to Hollywood's traditional desire to internationalize its product: neither the British nor the Russian film industry would have been likely to produce films about *America's* exploits during the war, although (at least in British films) U.S. characters do appear from time to time.

The term "United Nations," as used in films of the period, does not refer to the organization which now goes by that name (and which was not formally constituted until 1945). Rather, the term was a euphemism or verbal shorthand for those countries actively opposing the Axis. On January 1, 1942, a "Declaration of United Nations" was signed in Washington by 26 countries,[1] "engaged in a common struggle against savage and brutal forces seeking to subjugate the world." The signatories pledged to employ their full resources against the Tripartite Pact members (Germany, Italy, and Japan) "with which such government is at war" (a loophole for the USSR, which was *not* at war with Japan), and all agreed not to sign a separate peace.[2]

The League of Nations fiasco notwithstanding, the concept and term "United Nations" caught on with the American public, and references to the UN concept of concerted international cooperation appear in at least 27 war-relevant films (the banner year for such references was 1943, with 12). While specific references to the best-known Allies (Great Britain, Russia, China) are most frequent, other Allied nations and multinational groupings appear in a number of films.

In *Mexican Spitfire's Elephant* (RKO, 1943), for instance, a benefit show for a war relief organization showcases a "Mexican" dance team,[3] Dutch dancers, a Cossack (Russian) choir, and a Chinese magician; the show is put together by Americans and Britons. Fibber McGee and Molly host refugee children from virtually *every* Allied and occupied nation in *Heavenly Days* (RKO, 1944). And the same shot—of "United Nations" flags—closes *Commandos Strike at Dawn* (Columbia, 1943) and opens *None Shall Escape* (Columbia, 1944). The latter film, which begins in the post-war period, depicts a Nazi war criminal's trial before a multinational tribunal (with black and Asian members).

Military cooperation is also in evidence in some films, although most such depictions are rather informal in manner—in other words, large-scale official cooperation between military forces of different nations is referred to, but in practice is rarely shown. Instead, the Allies are personalized, as in *Sahara* (Columbia, 1943). Humphrey Bogart is a tough American soldier (with a tough name: "Joe Gunn") who teams up with a multinational (British empire, French, Sudanese, American) tank crew. Similarly, Errol Flynn and his paratroopers are aided by Chinese and Indian (Ghurka) soldiers in *Objective, Burma!* (WB, 1945). *Escape in the Desert* (WB, 1945) depicts servicemen from many Allied nations in a brief airport scene. Military men (and women) of various nations can also be spotted in several "canteen" films, particularly *Stage Door Canteen* (UA, 1943).

There are also "international squadron" type films, usually featuring Americans enlisted in Allied armed forces (as in *Desperate Journey*, WB, 1942), although these are generally set prior to America's declaration of war on the Axis. *Desperate Journey*, *Sahara* and *Immortal Sergeant* (TCF, 1943), all depict multinational units drawn from the British Empire (and former colonies, such as the United States): English, Canadian, Australian, Scots, Irish, and even South African soldiers team up to battle the Axis.

In many of these films nationality is drawn with the broadest possible strokes, or else effaced almost entirely (cf. Lyle Talbot as a Canadian in *They Raid by Night*, PRC, 1942). However, the concept of the United Nations was still strong, and some of the most stirring moments in Hollywood war films occur when Allied unity and determination are highlighted. One such moment is the climactic musical number in *Thousands Cheer* (MGM, 1944), as Kathryn Grayson sings the "United Nations Hymn" against a background of national flags. At times like this, film audiences could truly believe that a united effort against fascism was merely the first step towards a new era of peace and international cooperation.

Britain and Its Empire

American identification with Britain's fate hardly wavered, despite the stress and tension. No one was more roundly criticized than the British, yet no other people ever supplanted the preference that Americans felt for the British when compared with other nations.[4]

By far the most numerous film references to America's Allies are those concerning Great Britain, as the following chart illustrates:

Code	1942	1943	1944	1945	Total
Britain	78	54	30	15	177
Russia	35	52	36	13	136
China[5]	42	35	24	20	121

Furthermore, related terms are similarly weighted in favor of our British cousins. A comparison of references to the Allied leaders, for instance, shows Winston Churchill running second only to Franklin Delano Roosevelt, with Josef Stalin and Chiang Kai-shek far behind:

	1942	1943	1944	1945	Total
FDR	35	37	22	9	103
Churchill	13	16	8	4	41
Stalin	2	8	5	3	18
Chiang	9	3	3	3	18

Another noteworthy point is that many more Hollywood films feature *significant* British characters than of any other Allied nation. This is certainly due at least in part to pragmatic factors, such as the availability of British performers in Hollywood, America's pre-Pearl Harbor bias towards Britain (which undoubtedly explains the high number of British-oriented films in 1942, since many of these were already in production or pre-production prior to December 1941)[6], and the language and cultural connections between the two nations, which simplified production matters (sets and costumes were much simpler to prepare than those for films set in China or Russia, for instance).

Films dealing with Great Britain and British characters may be very roughly broken down into three categories: films about the British armed forces; films about the British home front (or those set in Britain which extol the virtues of that nation); and films featuring British characters outside England.

Most of the films of all three types portray British characters in a somewhat stereotyped manner—although the overall impression is positive—reinforcing the "stiff upper lip" attitude, the class structure, and—when relevant—the general air of bemusement Britons have when confronted with brash Americans.

Soldiers of the King: The British Military

The British military was cited quite frequently during the war years, as the following statistics indicate:

Code	1942	1943	1944	1945	Total
AF-Brit[7]	22	31	17	6	76
AF-RAF	24	18	6	6	54

However, the majority of films referencing the armed forces of Great Britain do so in a minor way: uniformed characters appear in crowd scenes, or the RAF drops parachutists behind enemy lines, and so on. Films actually dealing with the British military in action were, understandably, rather rare in Hollywood during the war, since American audiences preferred to see films about their *own* armed forces in action.

A number of the exceptions occur early in the conflict, and many of these hedge their bets by casting American stars and/or featuring them as American *characters* serving in the British armed forces. *A Yank in the RAF* (TCF, 1941) is a pre–Pearl Harbor example of this, with Tyrone Power as the eponymous American flyer helping out during the Battle of Britain. Similar characters appear in *Desperate Journey* (WB, 1942—Ronald Reagan), *Reunion in France* (MGM, 1942—John Wayne), *Eagle Squadron* (Universal, 1942—Robert Stack), *Paris Calling* (Universal, 1942—Randolph Scott), and *The Purple V* (Republic, 1943—John Archer).[8] However, only *Eagle Squadron* actually deals with regular combat by the RAF: the other pictures are basically escape films about downed pilots behind enemy lines.

The Royal Air Force, which gained worldwide fame during the Battle of Britain in 1940, remained popular in Hollywood films throughout the war. However, films dealing specifically with the RAF are concentrated in the 1941–1942 period, when they were the "only game in town." After this point, the RAF appears mostly in a supporting role (dropping supplies to the Norwegian resistance in *The Moon Is Down*, TCF 1943, for instance), or in more films about downed pilots behind enemy lines, such as *The Wife Takes a Flyer* (Columbia, 1942), in which Franchot Tone is shot down over Holland.

Great Britain landed regular troops in Norway in April 1940 in a vain attempt to repel the German invasion. However, the campaign was unsuccessful for a variety of reasons, among them insufficient planning and last-minute changes in the plans which had been made. By the middle of June, the British troops had been withdrawn, and Norway was in German hands. However, from this point on, the British began a series of regular raids along the Norwegian coast, lasting well into 1944.[9]

As their exploits came to the attention of the American public, the British "Commandos" were highlighted in several films. *They Raid by Night* (PRC, 1942) is a very cheaply made film featuring a multinational team (Lyle Talbot as a Canadian, Charles Rogers as a stereotypical Cockney, and George Neise as a Free Norwegian officer) attempting to smuggle a Norwegian general out of occupied Norway. The Commandos stage a raid on German fortifications in Norway (courtesy of some stock footage), and pick up the team. *Commandos Strike at Dawn* (Columbia, 1943) is a substantially more elaborate production in the same setting. Paul Muni escapes from Norway after stabbing a Nazi officer; he arrives in England with news of a secret airbase, then participates in a British Commando raid back to his country to destroy it. *First Comes Courage* (Columbia, 1943) chiefly concerns a scout (Brian Aherne) for a planned Commando raid who is trying to escape from the Nazis with information needed for the attack. With the aid of Norwegian patriot Merle Oberon, he does so. *Son of Lassie* (MGM, 1945) also takes place in Norway, but is another film about the adventures of a downed RAF pilot (Peter Lawford), rather than British Commandos.

In *Eagle Squadron* (Universal, 1942), American RAF pilot Robert Stack redeems his earlier blunders by traveling to France on a Commando raid and stealing a new German fighter plane. Real-life raids into occupied France—against Calais (July 1940), and Dieppe (August 1942)—are alluded to in several films, including *The Gorilla Man* (WB, 1943), *Tonight We Raid Calais* (TCF 1943), and *The White Cliffs of Dover* (MGM, 1944). The latter film is historically somewhat more interesting than the others, since it depicts an actual Allied setback.

On August 19, 1942, British troops landed in Dieppe, a French channel port. This was not an attempt at a full-scale invasion, nor even to establish an Allied beachhead. The troops—Canadian, British, and Free French—were to attack and destroy German fortifications and gather information. However, the landing was strongly opposed by the Germans, and the Allied troops suffered serious casualties.[10] The British film *Next of Kin* (released with added footage in the United States by Universal in 1943), while allegedly portraying a raid on submarine pens in Norville, reproduces some aspects of the Dieppe raid and suggests that the attack was betrayed by "loose talk" in England.

The White Cliffs of Dover begins with an American nurse (Irene Dunne) waiting for the wounded to return to England from the Dieppe raid. Her son (Peter Lawford) is one of the soldiers injured in action, and he succumbs to his wounds in the hospital. Ironically, the film suggests that Lawford was conceived in Dieppe during World War One, when Dunne and her British Army husband met there on leave. The scenes of the raid do not consume a great deal of the film's footage, but the fact that such a notorious British defeat is mentioned at all is rather interesting.

A number of other films feature the British military in some detail, *Immortal Sergeant* (TCF, 1943) chief among these. However, since its chief protagonist is identified as a Canadian, this film will be discussed in that section. *The Story of Dr. Wassell* (Paramount, 1944) contains one sequence in which American Navy personnel hitch a ride with British troops on Java: these troops are portrayed quite positively (as are some Dutch soldiers), but they are not the central focus of the film. *Secrets of Scotland Yard* (Republic, 1944), while not strictly a military film, deals with the British Cipher Bureau, and *Appointment in Berlin* (Columbia, 1943) stars George Sanders as a cashiered British officer who goes undercover in Nazi Germany to serve his country. Franchot Tone is a British Army corporal cut off from his unit in North Africa in *Five Graves to Cairo* (Paramount, 1943); however, he spends most of the film disguised as a club-footed waiter in a seedy desert hotel!

Ironically, very little attention is paid to the British Royal Navy in this period. There are several reasons for this: first, the RAF and the Battle of Britain were considered inherently more "romantic" and exciting than the Royal Navy and the Battle of the Atlantic (after all, the RAF pilots were based in Britain, which allowed for romance and drama in their off-hours; Navy ships were at sea in an all-male environment for long periods of time). Also, the RAF's "International" or "Eagle Squadron" provided the perfect excuse for American characters to appear, definitely a plus as far as Hollywood was concerned. A few British naval films made the rounds in American theatres—*In Which We Serve*, and *San Demetrio, London*—and *Two Tickets to London* (Universal, 1943) features an American crewman on a British *merchant* vessel, but for the most part the RAF got the lion's share of the film glory during WWII.

On the whole, Hollywood depicted our British Allies as making a valuable, but peripheral, contribution to the actual fighting. Far more interest was shown in the everyday life of civilian Britons in wartime.

Stiff Upper Lip: The British Home Front

... the Minivers became an exemplary family, a model for Americans. They set an example to which others should aspire ... The point is that, in wartime, one ought to behave like Kay Miniver....[11]

As mentioned above, Hollywood found it relatively easy to make films set in England. However, this ease of production would have meant little if American audiences had not been willing to accept English settings and characters. In many ways, England serves as a surrogate for America, different but not "foreign," and much closer to the actual war.

Even films which were not specifically about British home front activities found an English setting convenient: *Ministry*

of Fear (Paramount, 1944), *London Blackout Murders* (Republic, 1943), *The Brighton Strangler* (RKO, 1945), *The Mysterious Doctor* (WB, 1943), and *Return of the Vampire* (Columbia, 1943), among others, *could* have been set in the United States with some minor plot adjustments. However, England's proximity to Europe allowed for the inclusion of blackouts, bombings, spies, and the like, which would have been much less plausible in a U.S. setting.

More to the point are directly war-oriented films of the *Mrs. Miniver* (MGM, 1942) mold. While this MGM production remains the quintessential British home front film, other examples include *Thumbs Up* (Republic, 1943), *Tonight and Every Night* (Columbia, 1945), *This Above All* (TCF, 1942), and *Forever and a Day* (RKO, 1943).

All of these films purport to show Americans how "ordinary" Britons deal with the war on a daily basis: *Mrs. Miniver* even begins with the printed claim that it is the story of an "average English middle-class family." However, the film quickly shows that Hollywood was hardly portraying "average" Britons: the Minivers have a large house, at least two servants, and a boat. Indeed, the film clearly identifies at least three social strata: the aristocracy (Lady Belden), the upper middle class (the Minivers), and the working class (the Miniver's servants, Mr. Ballard the stationmaster). The friendly, paternalistic relationship between the first two levels and the service sector cannot disguise the strict class distinctions which exist, although there is some indication that the worn-out aristocracy is relinquishing its social and political leadership to persons of the Miniver's social level.

This Above All (TCF, 1942) addresses the English social structure more directly, as wealthy Joan Fontaine joins the WAAFs despite her family's objections. She meets working-class deserter Tyrone Power, who is rehabilitated both by her concern and through the efforts of a church rector (the clergy were generally considered upper-middle class socially). Inspired by his social "betters," Power redeems himself during the Blitz.

Forever and a Day tells the story of a London house from its construction in 1804 to the present day, and in doing so presents the audience with heavy doses of "There'll Always Be an England"-style propaganda (*A Yank at Eton*, MGM, 1942, also contains similar sentiments, which were more prevalent in pre–1942 Hollywood). As is often the case, both upper class and working class characters are depicted, and while the servants are often portrayed as sly and/or disdainful of their employers (Charles Laughton as a butler, for instance), the image of England as a country of rigid class structures is still present.

This social stratification, the continued existence of the British monarchy, and the existence of British imperial colonies such as India presented an obstacle to wholehearted American acceptance of Great Britain as a "democratic" partner in the fight against fascism:

This relationship was complex and ambivalent. On the one hand, Americans were fascinated by British traditions and institutions ... On the other hand, there was a deep conviction that Britain was not a genuine democracy.[12]

Nonetheless, Hollywood criticized Great Britain only obliquely, if at all, concentrating instead on the human-interest side of England's struggle. Again, *Mrs. Miniver* serves as the best example. Greer Garson as Mrs. Miniver is the perfect wife and mother: beautiful, capable, rational, and reasonable. She stands up to an armed German fugitive (a member of the Luftwaffe whose plane has crashed nearby) and to the formidable Lady Belden. She is loved by all, and by extension is the ideal British woman, the result of proper "breeding." Everyone else in the film is also idealized, although not to Kay Miniver's level: Clem Miniver (Walter Pidgeon) is good-humored, handsome, and brave; Lady Belden is gruff but kindhearted; the Vicar is stalwart and friendly; stationmaster Ballard is respectful but maintains his own self-respect; Vincent Miniver changes from a rather arrogant college boy to an RAF pilot; and so on. When the Miniver's house is bombed, they make the best of it; at the final church service, the dead are mourned but there is no defeatism evident in the faces of the survivors. American audiences, fairly secure in the knowledge that *they* would never have to face the war on such intimate terms, adopted the brave Britons as their stand-ins.

A number of films took this concept a step further, by inserting Americans into the British home front milieu. In these films it is the Americans who learn *from* the Britons how to cope with war. *The Canterville Ghost* (MGM, 1944) not only pokes fun at the British aristocracy—little Margaret O'Brien is the "lady of the manor" to whom everyone must pay homage—it depicts Robert Young as an American soldier whose "hereditary" cowardice must be overcome. It is, through a combination of pep talks from O'Brien and supernatural assistance from Charles Laughton, the ghost.

Thumbs Up (Republic, 1943) stars Brenda Joyce as Louise Latimer, an American performer who hires on at a British defense plant in a scheme to get a part in a musical show which will feature only defense workers in its cast. Louise makes friends with her fellow workers (and falls in love with an RAF officer); she is chosen for the musical, but when her perfidy is revealed and her friends desert her, Louise changes her mind and returns to the plant for the duration. Throughout the film, Louise's "American" ways are contrasted with British manners, but the essential compatibility of the two nations is convincingly portrayed.[13] One musical number—"Who Are the British"—consists of a roll call of famous Britons (from Shakespeare down to Winston Churchill), interspersed with phrases like "Hail to the island with its fighting sons so true ... They're a fearless fighting crew."

Tonight and Every Night (Columbia, 1945) has a similar premise: Rosalind Bruce (Rita Hayworth) travels to London before the war and gets a job in a musical show. When war comes she discovers the courage and fortitude of the British people, and takes on some of it herself. Even the death of Rosalind's best friend in a German bombing attack and the departure of her RAF fiancé for India cannot stop the show from going on (the film's "Hat Box Theatre" was based on the real-life Windmill Theatre, which *did* continue to function, even during the height of the Blitz). The musical production number built around the title song begins with a simulated newsreel depicting "typical Britons, some of whom are invited to step out and join in the number, moving from screen to stage. People from all walks of life sing out in affirmation of the wartime spirit."[14]

The King's Men: British Characters

There are many examples of Hollywood films of the war period featuring British characters outside of England. Some of these are simply caricatures with little or no relevance to the war (the tippling "Lord Epping" in the *Mexican Spitfire* series, for instance, is hardly a positive Allied image). Others, however, serve as representatives of British (and therefore, Allied) ideals.

Nineteen forty-two saw a handful of films featuring beautiful female British secret agents, usually linked with American leading men: *Secret Agent of Japan* (TCF—Lynn Bari); *My Favorite Blonde* (Paramount—Madeleine Carroll); *Dangerously They Live* (WB—Nancy Coleman); and *Escape from Hong Kong* (Universal—Marjorie Lord). These characters are significant because there are relatively few wartime films depicting *American* female secret agents in foreign locales, although several Russian women agents turn up (*Miss V from Moscow*, PRC, 1942, and *Background to Danger*, WB, 1943), and a Dutch woman agent appears in *Destination Unknown* (Universal, 1942).

Similarly, British children, often as refugees, appear in a number of Hollywood films: *Journey for Margaret* (MGM, 1942), *On the Sunny Side* (TCF, 1942), *Junior Army* (Columbia, 1942), and *Heavenly Days* (RKO, 1944). In *The Boy from Stalingrad* (Columbia, 1943), a British boy joins a group of Russian children after his father is shot by the Nazis. The children wage their own guerrilla war against the invaders, and the British boy sacrifices himself to help the others escape.

Finally, there are films which simply present admirable British characters, allowing their nationality and actions to speak for themselves. Monty Woolley, in *The Pied Piper* (TCF, 1942), playing on his established image as a curmudgeon with a heart of gold, escorts a group of abandoned/orphaned children to freedom from Nazi-occupied France. *None but the Lonely Heart* (RKO, 1944), while only peripherally war-relevant, is a strong drama featuring Ethel Barrymore, Cary Grant, and Barry Fitzgerald as mother, son, and surrogate father, respectively. Bordering on outright farce, *Passport to Destiny*

(RKO, 1944) stars Elsa Lanchester as a feisty London char-woman who hikes across Europe in an effort to kill Hitler, buoyed by the belief she has a lucky charm which protects her from harm. The Sherlock Holmes films of this period—some war-oriented, others not—take pains to emphasize the "Britishness" of the detective, as in the final scene of *Sherlock Holmes and the Secret Weapon* (Universal, 1942), when Holmes quotes Shakespeare's "This England" speech.

The Empire Strikes: Canada and Australia

Films about the British armed forces often depict units made up of Britons, Scots, Irish (presumably Northern Irish, since Eire was neutral), Canadians, and Anzacs (Australians and New Zealanders), with occasional contributions from India, South Africa, and other African possessions. The political relations between these countries and Great Britain were varied (some were colonial possessions, others were self-governing Dominions), but Hollywood paid little attention to this. In reality, such mixed units were not extremely common, although forces from various countries would often fight in the same theater of war.

The following chart shows the coded references to Australia and Canada in war-relevant films of the period:

	1942	1943	1944	1945	Total
Australia	7	12	6	0	25
AF-Austral	0	3	5	0	8
Canada	12	10	0	3	25
AF-Canada	6	5	1	1	13

These numbers are rather low, and films focusing on Canadians and Australians are even rarer. While the lead in *They Raid by Night* is identified as a Canadian, his nationality is not relevant to the plot of the film (it seems to have been a convenient ploy to explain the presence of American actor Lyle Talbot in the role). Don Terry plays a Canadian intelligence agent in *Unseen Enemy* (Universal, 1942), a film set in the pre–Pearl Harbor period. In this instance, Terry's nationality is an excuse for his anti–Nazi actions in a period of American neutrality.

Immortal Sergeant, one of the few Hollywood films to concentrate on the actions of a British ground forces unit, stars Henry Fonda as a Canadian corporal who assumes command of his unit when their sergeant (Thomas Mitchell) is mortally wounded. Set in North Africa, the film depicts the British Army's clashes with Italian and German forces. Once again, Fonda's Canadian nationality seems to have been a plot device to account for his lack of a British accent.

Three films which do concentrate on Canada's contribution to the war effort are *Captains of the Clouds* (WB, 1942), *Corvette K-225* (Universal, 1943), and *Northern Pursuit* (WB, 1943). The first film stars James Cagney as a Canadian bush

pilot who joins the Royal Canadian Air Force after hearing a radio speech by Winston Churchill. Cagney's brash attitude results in a training accident and his dismissal from the service, but he reenlists as a ferry pilot under a false name, and sacrifices his life by crashing his unarmed plane into a German fighter. Cagney, unthinkable as a Briton, *could* essay the role of a Canadian, a nationality viewed by Americans as less formal and more "Americanized" than Britons. The film also makes reference to Canada's natural resources and wilderness (in fact, *They Raid by Night* also refers to the Canadian protagonist's experience in the logging industry). On the whole, however, the film is little different in concept than *A Yank in the RAF* (TCF, 1941), in which American Tyrone Power follows a similar route from Canada to England.

Corvette K-225, on the other hand, is a bit unusual since it concentrates on Canada's naval forces and their role in escorting Atlantic convoys. The filmmakers shot extensive documentary footage for this film, and the result is a straightforward account of the title ship's missions, under the command of Randolph Scott (again, a convincing Canadian only by virtue of the relatively amorphous Canadian image in the American mind). However, there is no great difference between the characters and incidents in this film and those concentrating on the U.S. Navy, like *Destroyer* (Columbia, 1943), although the actual footage is interesting to watch.

Northern Pursuit deals with the Royal Canadian Mounted Police rather than the Canadian armed forces; New Zealand native Errol Flynn appears as a Canadian policeman on the trail of Nazis in the "Great White North." While the film is a far cry from the cross-Canada odyssey shown in *The 49th Parallel* (a 1941 British film designed to portray the wide diversity of Canadian people), it does contain some points of interest. For example, the Nazis try to foment dissension among Canadian Indians (a ploy they tried on Arabs in the Middle East in other films), insisting that life under the "New Order" will be more equitable for minorities.

Australia fared even less well in Hollywood. While Australia as a location was utilized for several films, and while Australians show up in other films (albeit mostly as background characters, as in *Around the World*, RKO, 1943), films dealing significantly with Australia are very few in number. There were pragmatic reasons for this: the Australian accent is much more pronounced than the Canadian (at least to American ears), and it would consequently be harder for American actors to "pass" (although sometimes the Aussie accent was dispensed with entirely). Additionally, since most Australian troops served in the Pacific theater, there were fewer opportunities for "occupied country" films, or appearances of Australian soldiers in canteens, street scenes, and the like, although *Around the World* contains a scene in which Kay Kyser and his band sing and play "Waltzing Matilda" for a Australian military audience.[15]

Doctor Gillespie's New Assistant (MGM, 1942) portrays

three young doctors, all assisting the kindly Gillespie in the absence of young Dr. Kildare: one is a Chinese-American, one is just plain All-American (Van Johnson), and one is an Australian Army doctor (Richard Quine) temporarily detached from duty. These minor appearances seem a bit unfair, since in reality Australia more than did its part during the war: "With a population of only seven million, the nation still managed an armed forces of over half a million in early 1945."[16]

One film which does single out Australia is *The Man from Down Under* (MGM, 1943), a vehicle for Charles Laughton. WWI veteran Jocko (Laughton), takes two Belgian orphans back to Australia with him to raise as his own children. Turned down for service in WWII for medical reasons, Jocko nonetheless demonstrates his bravery during a Japanese air raid on the city of Darwin (while Australia never underwent a "blitz" on the scale of London, some cities were subjected to Japanese air strikes during the early years of the war in the Pacific).

Abroad with Two Yanks (UA, 1944) is set in Australia, but chiefly deals with the adventures of two U.S. Marines (Dennis O'Keefe and William Bendix) on "rest and recreation" leave there. There is an Australian airman (played by John Loder), and an Australian woman (Helen Walker), who serves as the romantic bone of contention between the men. In one scene, the Marines give an Australian sergeant a Japanese medal as a souvenir, as if the Australian was a non-fighting civilian. However, Loder's character is depicted as having been in combat and he is positively portrayed.

Marine Raiders (RKO, 1944), also has as its protagonist an American Marine (Robert Ryan) on leave in Australia. The film spends a little time on the Australian people, who are chiefly represented by Ruth Hussey (with no particular accent) as an Australian WAAF (there is also a reference to her brothers, who are fighting in North Africa). Ryan falls in love with Hussey and they agree to marry. However, he is wounded during a Japanese air raid, and his Marine superior (Pat O'Brien) has him shipped back to the United States. Ryan finally gets back to Australia and marries Hussey before leaving to fight the Japanese once more. It is very difficult to find anything particularly "Australian" about the characters or settings in *Marine Raiders* (no kangaroos, koala bears, Aussie bush hats or "Waltzing Matilda")—Australia could very well be England, if Ryan was in the Army or the Air Corps rather than the Marines, and was fighting the Germans rather than the Japanese. Hussey could be Australian, British, or American for all the difference it makes to the film.

Uncle Joe Stalin and His People

The prowess of the Red Army kept the Russians high in popular esteem up to the close of the Second World War... But admiration for Russia as a fighting ally had never diminished suspicion of Communism as a social and political creed.[17]

During World War II, America's two major right-wing/totalitarian/militaristic enemies—Japan and Germany—were rather quickly and easily stigmatized as the racially repugnant "little Jap monkeys," and the quintessentially arrogant, black-shirted Nazis. But what was to be done with the established image (now incompatible with political "reality") of our new *left*-wing/totalitarian/militaristic *ally*, the Soviet Union?

During the period between the world wars, "Red" Russia, the only successful national communist state, had become inextricably linked with the cause of international communism and its ideological challenge to capitalist democracies. Hence, the USSR, its foreign representatives, and any domestic group or individual espousing communism or socialism, were major targets of popular artistic vilification and/or satire (especially during periods of political stress) in the United States (this was in addition to *official* government criticism of the Soviet Union and Communism).

The new need to acceptably portray the communist Russians as our "brothers-in-arms" was particularly difficult to achieve since intense anti–Soviet sentiment had flared up between mid–1939 and mid–1941.[18] The direct cause of this was the infamous Nazi-Soviet Pact of August 1939, and the invasion of Poland by Hitler and Stalin the following month. The image of the Soviet Union had been tainted even more by the Red Army's attack on "little" Finland during the winter of 1939–1940. This latter action created a huge public outcry in America and almost led to direct British intervention against Russia.

The cinematic reaction in America to the Soviet invasion of Finland was comparatively rapid for the industry. Within six months of Finland's defeat in March 1940, Universal released *Ski Patrol*, a film that unequivocally attacked the communist behemoth's aggression.[19] It was only after Hitler's June 1941 invasion of Russia that anti–Soviet/anti-communist works—such as *Ski Patrol* and MGM's better-known 1940 Christmas season release *Comrade X*—ceased to be produced in the U.S.[20]

But at the end of 1941, America suddenly found itself involved in the most vicious of world wars and a partner in an anti-fascist alliance of convenience with both Great Britain and the USSR. The U.S.A. shared many deep cultural ties with the former nation, not the least of which were a common language and a compatible, closely related political system. As for the Soviet Union, the spiritual center of world communism for the past two decades, it had been tirelessly disparaged as the semi-barbaric mother of an alien and very dangerous ideology. Now the goal of the American government was to quickly dissipate, or at the very least neutralize, residual fears and hostilities towards the Soviet Union and communism, and to generate and encourage enthusiastic support for the military efforts of the Soviet Union against Hitler's Wehrmacht.[21]

This changing policy is pinpointed in a rather unusual

sequence in *Foreign Agent* (Monogram, 1942). One of the leaders of a Nazi-sponsored "peace" organization located in Los Angeles makes an isolationist speech in a public park: "Today we are shouting the praises of Soviet Russia for their heroism and their military achievements. What a sad commentary on the democracies of our forefathers. I don't like Soviet Russia and I wouldn't raise a finger to help her." His speech evokes unfriendly mutters from the crowd of onlookers, and a heavily accented emigrant from Russia climbs up on the platform to refute the man's assertions.

The speech—which could have been *positively* delivered in a Hollywood film just a year earlier (or a few years later)—and the speaker are clearly discredited. The speaker is on the payroll of a Nazi spy ring; the audience of everyday Americans in the park loudly disagrees with him; and a recent emigrant to America shows that *he* is a better citizen than the native-born agitator because he recognizes the agitator's right to free speech. The speech is abruptly terminated when FBI agents arrive and arrest the speaker on charges of sedition!

Research has identified 136 American fictional feature films released during the war which refer to our Russian ally (all but two in a positive manner), but only eight deal exclusively with or prominently feature the Russians—*Miss V from Moscow* (PRC, 1942), *The Boy from Stalingrad* (Columbia, 1943), *Mission to Moscow* (WB, 1943), *The North Star* (RKO, 1943), *Song of Russia* (MGM, 1943), *Days of Glory* (RKO, 1944), *Three Russian Girls* (UA, 1944), and *Counter-Attack* (Col., 1945). All of these films were released between December 1942 and April 1945 (a month before the Third Reich's capitulation).

The initial step in the wartime reconstruction of the image of Russia was to ensure that negative references to the Soviet Union and communism disappeared from America films. But the heart of the solution was the redirection of the mental gaze of the audience by transferring the evil images formerly associated with the communist Satan to our current military adversaries *and*, most importantly, to project the positive cinematic iconography of American traits and ideals[22] onto the current motion picture representations of the Russian people (*not* the Soviet State).

Thus, the Nazis and Japanese are given the role of godless, sadistic villains, and the Russian people are recast as friendly pseudo-Americans: "After Russia became an ally, Hollywood presented the former villain from a favorable, people-are-the-same perspective."[23] The *Russian* people (not the Soviets, remember) are depicted as simple, honest people who love the same things Americans do: home, family, friends, freedom. The two major examples of this glorification of the Russian people—specifically the peasantry—by making them seem more like *us*, are *The North Star* and *Song of Russia*.

There were various other ways in which Hollywood attempted to humanize our Russian allies. What better demonstrates the compatibility of the Russians and Americans than

an international romance? *Ninotchka* (MGM, 1939) presented human, likeable Russian Greta Garbo in love with Westerner Melvyn Douglas, *but* it severely criticized the Soviet system. Under wartime political circumstances, the first was allowable, even preferable, but the latter was forbidden. American cinema reflected the new sensitivities of the U.S. government by "bleaching the red" out of communism on movie screens. Thus, any discussion of ideology is avoided, and personal characteristics and relationships are emphasized. Both *Song of Russia* and *Three Russian Girls* focus on visiting Americans (Robert Taylor, Kent Smith) who meet and fall in love with Russian women (Susan Peters, Anna Sten), but there is no discussion of the Soviet political system in either film. There is a hint of romance between an American flyer and a female Soviet secret agent in *Miss V from Moscow*,[24] and another Soviet woman spy is romantically linked with American George Raft in *Background to Danger* (WB, 1943). Russian Army medic Annabella escapes from a German prison camp with American pilot George Montgomery in *Bomber's Moon* (TCF, 1943), and a romance develops between the Wisconsin native and the blonde Soviet "bombshell" (Annabella does use the term "comrade" several times in the film, but otherwise the ideological differences between the Soviet and American are subsumed in their romance). Eve Arden, portraying a "Russian Sergeant York" on a tour of the United States, has no love interest in *The Doughgirls* (WB, 1944), but she does facilitate the triple marriage of her American friends, bringing a Russian Orthodox priest to their hotel for the ceremony.[25]

This latter film also clearly shows how Hollywood sidestepped ideological facets of the Soviet system in order to foster goodwill in American audiences. One of the strongest criticisms of Russian communism was its atheistic nature, which earned it the undying enmity of the Catholic Church. Yet in *The Doughgirls*, visiting Soviet soldier Arden knows where to find an Orthodox priest in Washington, D.C.! In *Song of Russia*, Taylor and Peters are married in an Orthodox church ceremony.[26] Tamara Toumanova, an entertainer separated from her government-sponsored troupe in *Days of Glory*, joins a group of Russian guerrillas (operating under official Soviet direction, *not* an autonomous underground group), but the crucifix she prominently wears around her neck at all times does not seem to bother them at all.

Another humanizing ploy was the inclusion of Russian "culture" in Hollywood films. After 1942, Russian music began to appear in American films, although it never achieved the same level of popularity as the Latin American conga/rumba/samba. Traditional Russian folk music conveniently circumvented the issue of communism and the Soviet state, while positively portraying a happy Russian people (as opposed to the dour or even murderous anarchist/Bolshevik stereotype).[27] For instance, a medley of Russian folk songs is featured in Universal's 1943 release, *His Butler's Sister*, which starred Deanna Durbin. Extended scenes of happy Russian peasants dancing

Top: *The Boy from Stalingrad* (Columbia, 1943): A group of Russian children, aided by a stranded British teenager, oppose the Nazi invasion of Russia. Bottom: *The North Star* (RKO Radio, 1943): Russian Air Force aviator Dana Andrews with some peasants from his hometown, who fight the Nazis in their own way. Left to right: Andrews, Walter Brennan, Farley Granger, Jane Withers.

Top: *Song of Russia* (MGM, 1943): The Russians were not all "godless Communists," at least during World War Two. American visitor Robert Taylor marries Russian Susan Peters in a Russian Orthodox church. Bottom: *Days of Glory* (RKO Radio, 1944): Tamara Toumanova and the population of a Russian village are forced to watch the Nazis execute a young partisan.

and singing appear in both *The North Star* and *Song of Russia*. Russian classical music, particularly that of the pre-revolutionary composer Tchaikovsky, is also used prominently in a number of relevant films. *Song of Russia* actually features the Soviet music school established at the famous composer's birthplace.

In addition to noble Russian peasants and brave Russian women soldiers and spies, Hollywood presented a number of emigrant Russian and Russian-American characters, often depicting them as apolitical, humorous eccentrics. This type of Russian was epitomized by the bushy-haired actor billed as the "Mad Russian," Bert Gordon, who had a rather short-lived film career. One of his wartime vehicles was *Laugh Your Blues Away* (Columbia, 1942). Leonid Kinskey and Mischa Auer also repeatedly portrayed comical (but usually positive) Russian, Russian-American, or "generic Slavic" characters. Both of these actors had extensive pre-war careers playing similar characters; during the war Kinskey was featured in *Somewhere I'll Find You* (MGM, 1942) and *The Fighting Seabees* (Republic, 1944), while Auer played "himself" on a USO tour in *Around the World* (RKO, 1943), among other films.

Such ploys helped favorably dispose Americans towards the Russians, but there were still some dangerous topics which had to be dealt with, disposed of, or ignored. The Soviet invasion of Poland in conjunction with Nazis is never mentioned in a wartime American fictional film. However, in the notorious *Mission to Moscow*, a rationale for the Nazi-Soviet Pact is provided which includes a negative portrayal of the Polish government. An outrageously contrived justification for the Soviet attack upon Finland is also given.

The well-known anti-communist rhetoric of the Nazis, and their propaganda explaining the invasion of the Soviet Union as a western anti–Bolshevik crusade, seldom appear in American films. Even the Nazi fanatic in *The North Star* never makes pejorative references to communism. Two brief, but nevertheless explicit, references to Nazi anti-communism are made in the resistance films *Hangmen Also Die* (UA, 1943) and *Paris After Dark* (TCF, 1943). Only one American film, *Desperate Journey* (WB, 1942), acknowledges that Nazi Germany's allies participated in the war against the Soviets—specifically, a joke is made about the Italian contribution to the campaign. It would thus appear that any mention of officially sanctioned Axis anti-communism was to be avoided, even when it would have helped clarify the reasons for the viciousness of the monumental campaign on the Eastern front. Apparently, it was felt that such references could evoke memories of pre-war, anti–Soviet attitudes in America.

In fact, most of the relatively few references to the horrendous Russo-German war on the Eastern front either mention Germany's heavy casualties or emphasize the Nazis' fear of the Russian Army. For instance, some Nazi censors in *Berlin Correspondent* (TCF, 1942) are punished for their incompetence by being sent to Russia. There are various verbal references to the gallant defense of Stalingrad, and in *The North Star* the extent of German losses in Russia is demonstrated by the German military doctor's (Erich von Stroheim) forcible use of Russian children as blood donors for his casualties.

Three Russian Girls (UA, 1944): Russia's women warriors captured the public's attention during WWII—in this film, three nurses help hold off the German invasion of Russia, aided by an American test pilot.

Hollywood attempted to reshape the artistic reality of Soviet Russia in the American public's mind. Although more than likely developed on an *ad hoc* basis, one may detect a fairly sophisticated methodology for incrementally readjusting the conventional cinematic perceptions of communism in order to accommodate our Russian ally.[28] A closer examination of a few representative films illustrates these points.

Two of the more obvious pro–Soviet films to be produced in America are the obscure *Miss V from Moscow* and the much better known *The North Star*. The two other motion pictures analyzed, *Jack London* (UA, 1943) and *The Male Animal* (TCF, 1942) have not been critically connected before with the reshaping of attitudes toward the Soviet Union during the wartime alliance.[29] Released in early 1942, *The Male Animal* was based on a satiric stage play by James Thurber and Elliot Nugent. A direct attack upon hysterical red-baiting at the small "Midwestern University," its timing could not have been more fortuitous: in the process of condemning anti-communist witch-hunters it also specifically links their methods to fascism.[30] The film thus begins to shift the evil attached to the old communist bogeyman to that of the new enemy, fascism (without ever mentioning the Soviet Union or Nazi Germany). In fact, it is probably the first wartime feature film to do this (and the last to actually deal with America's perceptions of communism as opposed to perceptions of our Russian communist *ally*). *The Male Animal* is unique in yet another way. It is one of the last American films released during the war to employ the use of the term "red" in the pejorative political sense. The term "red," as a designator for Russia, was apparently considered so politically loaded by Hollywood that during the war it is used only in a positive political cinematic manner, in a limited number of references to the Soviet ("Red") Army.[31]

The crucial issue in *The Male Animal* concerns a professor of English (Henry Fonda) who wants to read to his class a letter written by the 1920s anarchist Bartolomeo Vanzetti. He is opposed by Eugene Pallette (a fat-capitalist stereotype), the red-baiting head of the Board of Trustees. During a rally for the football team, Pallette is portrayed as a fascistic Huey Long-type demagogue. When Fonda, who has favorably compared Vanzetti's letter to the writings of Abraham Lincoln, finally reads it aloud, it turns out to be the innocuous, apolitical reflections of a simple man. His opponents are silenced. With Sousa's rousing "Stars and Stripes Forever" pounding away in the background, the satiric parting shot of the film takes place the next day as Pallette petulantly accuses the campus intellectual of being a "fascist" when the student fails to enthusiastically cheer the home team! The subtext here is that the "red menace" was false, whereas the threat from the extreme right to the American ideal is very real.

The first wartime American film to prominently feature our Soviet ally was *Miss V from Moscow* (released in December 1942). Despite its poor production qualities, this spy film provides today's viewer with an insight into the transformation of America's perception of the Soviet Union during World War II.

For instance, the film immediately, yet quite subtly turns the tables on negative images of the Soviets (such as those so hilariously parodied in *Ninotchka*). *Miss V* opens with the usual stock footage of Red Square, and cuts to the sterile atmosphere of a Soviet bureaucrat's office (the requisite portrait of Stalin in the background). But instead of a dour, masculine Greta Garbo and her brusque supervisor Bela Lugosi, the smiling Vera (Lola Lane, one of America's small-town sweetheart Lane sisters from the popular Warner's "Daughters" series) is intro-

duced. Stalin's favorite secret agent, Vera is not to wreak havoc among the capitalists, but to aid them in the struggle against fascism: she is to go to occupied France and obtain information on the German U-Boat campaign against American convoys carrying Lend Lease supplies to beleaguered Russia.

Vera, or "Miss V" (for Allied victory), armed only with an identifying two-franc piece, arrives in Paris. The rest of the film centers around Vera's attempts to acquire information while assuming the identity of a deceased look-alike German agent. Her contacts with the enemy allow the reinforcement of negative images of barbarous Nazi fanatics (torturers and hostage takers, for example). At the same time, Vera is teamed up with the Free French underground (a proxy for the Soviet partisans), and with two RAF pilots (one British, one American) stranded after a commando raid (signifying: the Allies taking the war to the German-controlled continent). Another Russian agent is also operating in Paris, and he sacrifices his life during a Nazi raid on the agents' hideout, dying as he transmits vital information back to Russia.

Two final points need to be made with regard to *Miss V* and the manipulation of American perceptions of the Soviet Union. First, the fatuous local Nazi commander boasts that the new German offensive in the east will culminate in the Nazis linking up with "our yellow Aryan brothers." The implication is that if America does not at least support the Soviets with military supplies, such an anti-democratic union would pose an even greater threat to the U.S. in the Pacific theater.

Secondly, as a result of information obtained by Vera, Soviet submarines help save an American convoy on the Murmansk run (given that this sequence is constructed entirely out of grainy stock footage, the exact contribution of the Russians is not clear). To emphasize this point even further, Vera's supervisor in Russia says "this achievement is symbolic of the cooperation and unity between our great nations." There was in fact a good deal of U.S. public resentment that the Soviets were not doing enough to protect our supply shipments to them. Therefore, this fictional scenario would appear to be an attempt to dissipate such negative feelings in America.[32] In effect, the concept of the Soviet Union fighting largely alone against the Germans was cinematically altered to create an image of the Soviets fully and willingly cooperating with the Allies in order to defeat the Third Reich.[33]

Whereas the other feature films so far discussed worked to transfer anti-communist/Russian traits to the German fascists, United Artist's 1943 autumn release, *Jack London*, reasserts the image of the "yellow peril"—while indirectly neutralizing the "red menace" concept—by sympathetically portraying Russian soldiers brutalized by their Japanese captors during the Russo-Japanese War of 1904–1905.[34] In the process, the concept of the Soviets actively fighting our Japanese enemy is subliminally asserted. The film deliberately obscures the fact that throughout most of World War II the Soviet Union and Japan conscientiously observed a neutrality pact.[35]

Blood on the Sun (UA, 1945): In 1920s Tokyo, investigative reporter James Cagney is about to fall victim to a sneak attack by a giant Japanese officer (played by Los Angeles policeman Jack Halloran).

Jack London depicts the famous American author's escapades in Asia as a correspondent reporting on the Russo-Japanese conflict. The role of war correspondent immediately links London (Michael O'Shea) with such contemporary journalists as Ernie Pyle, and with numerous fictional reporters who oppose fascism, in films like Hitchcock's *Foreign Correspondent* (UA, 1940), *Somewhere I'll Find You* (MGM, 1942), and *Blood on the Sun* (UA, 1945).

Jack London thus provides an ideal vehicle to positively portray pre-Soviet (non-communist) Russians as victims of the vicious Japanese who had initiated the war with a "surprise attack" on Port Arthur (a Pearl Harbor linkage). It touches upon many of the major themes more openly developed in such blatantly pro–Soviet American films as *The North Star* and *Song of Russia*.

An example of such a motif is that of the Russians as peace-loving innocents forced into armed conflict with warmongering neighbors. This is achieved by portraying a duplicitous, effeminate Japanese diplomat, and pompous "Banzai"-shouting Japanese officers (making fascist-like salutes)

who gloat over the sinking of the Russian Pacific Fleet (accomplished by making a sneak attack on Vladivostok and Port Arthur). This not only makes the linkage with Pearl Harbor, but also with the recurrent theme of treacherous Japanese diplomacy as depicted in numerous American wartime films, e.g., *Wake Island* (Paramount, 1942).

While still in Manchuria, London also observes Russian prisoners-of-war being marched off under appalling conditions (these prisoners are later massacred by their captors), and that the Japanese are using Krupp field howitzers. The former reinforces images of Japanese brutality and shows the Russians suffering under a nation allied to her current enemy.[36] The latter helps implant the concept of a long term relationship between Germany and Japan.

RKO's *The North Star* was released in the fall of 1943. Along with a few other films, such as *Mission to Moscow*, *Song of Russia*, *Days of Glory* and *Counter-Attack*, it represents the high point of Hollywood's favorable representation of the Soviet Union during the Second World War. The notorious *Mission to Moscow* is unique in that it slavishly white-washes the totalitarian communist regime, including an outrageous apologia for the well-publicized Stalinist purges of 1937–1938. That film aside, *The North Star* perhaps represents the most blatantly pro–Russian film produced in wartime America.

Furthermore, *The North Star* is the most important of these films because it is so successful at cinematically transferring (re-coding) the positive images of America onto the Soviets. In essence, it is not a Russian village/commune in the Ukraine that is violated by the Nazi war machine but "Anytown" in the Midwest, USA, "where simple, almost American-like folk, fought for freedom against the Nazi enslavers."[37]

In fact, although it is made clear the village is a commune and that the film is set in Russia, few overt images of the prewar image of communism are presented. Instead of a portrait of Stalin in Rodian's home, there is one of Pushkin. Aside from the hammer and sickle flag above the town hall, the only specific reference to the political ideology of the Soviet regime is the occasional use of the term "comrade."[38]

To the uplifting strains of an Aaron Copland score,[39] the viewer of *The North Star* is introduced to a sunny agricultural community in June 1941 where healthy, happy, singing farm workers are busily harvesting the winter wheat. The initial atmosphere (established largely through the *mise en scene*) is of abundance, harmony and peace.

The old village philosopher Karp (played by America's perennial old man, Walter Brennan) drives his horse-drawn cart through the pristine, well-constructed (on a Hollywood backlot) village. Passing by numerous sunflowers, cheerful school children and a flock of fat geese, Karp encounters and thereby introduces us to the film's other leads. The most important is Dr. Kurin, a famous pathologist who has chosen to settle down in the village. Significantly, Dr. Kurin is played by Walter Huston, who had played American presidents (including Lincoln) in several films over the past fifteen years, the father of George M. Cohan in *Yankee Doodle Dandy* (WB, 1942), and—earlier in 1943—a Norwegian village doctor in Warners' anti–Nazi film, *Edge of Darkness*. Incidentally, neither he nor any other member of the cast speak with Russian accents. Additionally, although the cast includes many well-known actors, there are no glamorous stars.

Karp's peregrinations also take him past the home of Boris (chairman of the local Soviet, who vaguely resembles Stalin). Boris's two sons are Kolya (Dana Andrews), an air force bombardier on leave, and Damian (Farley Granger), who has just earned a university scholarship. Kolya's status—home on leave—emphasizes that Russia is not expecting war in the near future. Though obviously proud of his rank of lieutenant (he is always seen in uniform), Kolya is not in any way portrayed as militaristic. Nor, despite several nationalistic remarks, is Kolya shown to be ideologically motivated.

Rodian's two young daughters and Boris's sons join the villagers that evening in a ridiculous ten-minute interlude of robust folk dancing and singing. The following morning the two couples head off on a walking tour to Kiev. After teaming up with Karp, the four lie in the hay of the old man's wagon and wistfully sing of peace and the universal aspirations of idealistic youth: "We're the younger generation ... the future of the nation...."

These idyllic pleasures are shattered when the travelers, along with many other peasants on the road, are ruthlessly bombed and strafed by German planes on the opening day of Hitler's invasion of mother Russia (another allegorical Pearl Harbor). A peasant's corpse is observed entangled in a fallen telephone pole, and a little boy from the village bleeds to death from his wounds (the bleeding of children is a major motif of *The North Star*).

The village is aerially assaulted soon afterwards. Following the attack, the villagers gather, as their leaders, including the local military commander, address them over the radio. They are exhorted to resist the Germans by destroying their crops or becoming guerrillas. As the "Internationale" (probably the first time the Communist anthem was played in its entirety in a fictional American film) begins to swell in the background, they do *not* vow to defend the Russian communist state, but instead collectively swear the "Partisan Oath" to save their people from "fascist slavery."

Those individuals chosen to remain in the village stoically proceed to burn all that is of value in order to deny it to the advancing Germans. Reminiscent of Paul Revere's ride, the villagers are apprised of the Germans' imminent arrival by a girl on horseback yelling: "The Germans are coming!" Interestingly, a film released earlier in 1943, *In Our Time* (WB), portrays the peasants on a Polish aristocrat's estate similarly preparing for the arrival of the Wehrmacht.

Meanwhile, Kolya makes his way to the nearest air force base, and carries out several bombing sorties against the enemy. When anti-aircraft fire disables his plane and kills the other members of his crew, Kolya sacrificially plunges the bomber into a column of German tanks.[40]

Significantly, *The North Star* is one of the few American full-length fictional films to portray a unit of the regular Soviet armed forces in direct combat with the Germans. Aside from some stock footage in *Miss V from Moscow* and *Three Russian Girls*, and a few scenes in *Counter-Attack*, all other military action in pro–Soviet WWII American commercial motion pictures features partisan bands and individuals. Apparently the Red Army could be occasionally mentioned and even receive snippets of praise from afar, but could never be shown fighting the Germans in organized combat between regular units. Yet the largest battles in military history, involving millions of men and thousands of tanks and aircraft, were taking place on the Eastern Front throughout 1943.[41]

Informed by Dr. Kurin that the Germans are using the village children for transfusions, the guerrillas, mounted on horses like the cavalry coming to the rescue in a Hollywood Western, recapture their village from the Nazis. As the battle rages, Dr. Kirin picks up a gun lying beside the corpse of the school principal and confronts the callous German doctor, von Harden (Eric von Stroheim). Although contemptuous of his fanatical Nazi cohort, von Harden condones the means used by the Hitler regime to achieve its goals, including forced transfusions from children for the German wounded. Old Dr. Kurin does not condemn fascism from a communist point of view, but with the moral outrage of civilized man. He then shoots the German surgeon.

In the final scene of *The North Star*, Marina (played by Anne Baxter), the older daughter of Rodian, reflects on the losses of her people, including the death of her younger sister and the blinding of her boyfriend Damian. She delivers a speech similar to Ma Joad's famous "We're the people" soliloquy from *The Grapes of Wrath* (TCF, 1940). Thus, the Russian peoples' struggle, bleached politically white by their sacrifices and the selective editing of the American film industry, becomes inextricably linked with the positive image of Heartland, USA, and the iconography of the American Constitution: "Things will be better some day ... the earth belongs to us, the people, and we will fight for it." In the cinematic reality of America in 1943 the Russian "we" of *The North Star* had become us—but only for the duration.

The Eagle and the Dragon: China[42]

...how wide was the gulf between reality and the idealized portraits of Chiang Kai-shek and his country... display[ed] in America.[43]

One of the most astounding results of the coming of World War Two was the reversal of America's image of China and the Chinese. In some ways, this is even more startling than the way America suddenly embraced Communist Russia as a valued ally, since public attitudes towards China were primarily based on race, rather than politics or ideology. It is much easier to rationalize away political differences in the face of a common foe than it is to erase years of racial bias, and yet the American media did its best to do so where China was concerned. However, as with many aspects of the war, Hollywood managed to give the impression of complying with the "party line," while continuing to perpetuate old stereotypes.

Prior to 1937, the image of Asians in Hollywood cinema was largely confined to the Chinese. Chinese characters in American films generally fell into one of three categories: the sinister Oriental (Fu Manchu and his clones, as well as various warlords and their henchmen), the Oriental sage (Charlie Chan and other proverb-spouting characters), and the comic waiter-laundryman-houseboy (exemplified by the ever-smiling Willie Fung). There were also a number of examples of the alluring—but often dangerous—Chinese *femme fatale*. After the full-scale Japanese invasion of China in 1937, pub-

lic opinion shifted to the side of the Chinese, and films showing sympathy for the Chinese side began to appear. Some of these films even featured Chinese characters in significant (although supporting) roles.

This favorable disposition towards China peaked in 1942 and 1943, as "an image of Chiang Kai-shek's China as a heroic and democratic bastion of freedom" poured out of U.S. government channels, and was echoed by the media:

Generalissimo Chiang Kai-shek [is] the philosopher-soldier at the head of his 450,000,000 people ... From the leader down to the humblest private ... the Chinese army has distinguished itself by superb acts of united heroism. It has fought the Japanese for five long years....[44]

The following chart illustrates the strong support given in Hollywood films to China, particularly in the first two years America was in the war:

Code	1942	1943	1944	1945	Total
China	42	35	24	20	121
AF-China	7	7	5	5	24

1942 stands out as the banner year for China in Hollywood—Chiang Kai-shek was elevated to the status of a world leader, and the Chinese Army became our gallant fighting ally (despite the fact "that the Chinese Army was scarcely employed at all in fighting the Japanese").[45]

As time went on, however, blind support for Chiang and Nationalist China began to slip.[46] Lip service was still paid to China as one of the major Allied powers, but in reality the United States paid little attention to Chiang, gave him relatively little aid, and for the most part assumed China would do no more than play the role of a swamp in which large numbers of Japanese troops would remain mired, thus keeping them out of action elsewhere. However, even to the end of the war:

American admiration for China and for Chiang Kai-shek in particular still proved to be too deep-seated, too independent of the facts of the situation to disappear entirely.[47]

Hollywood went along with the program, lauding China's contribution to the cause of freedom. Nearly every studio made at least one strongly pro–Chinese film, and Chinese actors like Benson Fong, Keye Luke, and Victor Sen Yung found steady employment playing Nationalist Chinese agents and soldiers (unfortunately, actors Richard Loo and Philip Ahn, of more "sinister" facial aspect, were stuck with villainous Japanese roles more often than not).

However, Hollywood was not quite ready to entrust major Asian roles to Asian actors. The WWII-era Charlie Chan was Sidney Toler, a Caucasian born in Missouri; the leads in *Dragon Seed* (MGM, 1944) were played by Katharine Hepburn and Turhan Bey (a Turk); the major positive Chinese roles in *China Sky* (RKO, 1945) were portrayed by Anglo actors (Anthony Quinn, Carol Thurston), while the villainous roles went to Asians (Loo and Ahn). Even some major *Japanese* roles went to non–Asian actors: Frank Puglia (*Escape from Hong Kong*, Universal 1942), Harold Huber (*Little Tokyo, U.S.A.* TCF, and *Lady from Chungking* PRC, both 1942), J. Carrol Naish and Tom Neal (*Behind the Rising Sun*, RKO 1943).

Casting Chinese and Anglo actors in Chinese and Japanese roles blurred distinctions between races and nationalities, and seems quite confusing today. How can Anglo characters curse the Japanese as "squint-eyed, yellow monkeys" in one breath, and laud Chiang Kai-shek and his Chinese forces in the next moment? This was also disturbing at the time to the Office of War Information, which frequently asked Hollywood studios to tone down racial attacks on the Japanese foe for just such reasons.[48] In *Night Plane from Chungking* (Paramount, 1943), a strong anti-racist comment is delivered by Ellen Drew, when opportunistic businessman Otto Kruger abruptly calls their Chinese driver "boy"—"The Chinese are no longer 'boy,'" she reminds him.

WWII films about China, with very few exceptions, tend to feature Anglo characters in leading roles, reducing the Chinese to subsidiary parts. Some films go to extremes: *Escape to Hong Kong*, set entirely in that city in December 1941, does not feature a single significant Chinese character! The only two Asians with more than one line of dialogue are two Japanese characters *posing* as Chinese! This film actually has the audacity—after virtually ignoring China and the Chinese for the previous hour—to conclude with the line, "Chiang Kai-shek, here we come!"[49]

Other films with Chinese settings but relatively little interaction with specific Chinese characters include *Flying Tigers* (Republic, 1942), *Halfway to Shanghai* (Universal, 1942), *Around the World* (RKO, 1943), and *The Amazing Mrs. Holliday* (Universal, 1943). In the latter film, Deanna Durbin escapes from war-ravaged China with nine orphans—including *one* Chinese baby! Loretta Young shepherds a group of Chinese schoolgirls through the battle-torn countryside in *China* (Paramount, 1943), but the real heroics are performed by the cynical American Alan Ladd and his sidekick William Bendix. At the climax, Ladd stalls for time until Chinese guerrillas can plant explosive charges, which then destroy a Japanese military unit (and Ladd).

Minor Chinese characters appear in a number of films. Many of these are Chinese-Americans, whose undeniable patriotism was often used for comic, ironic, and patriotic effect. *To the Shores of Tripoli* (TCF, 1942), for instance, depicts a Chinese man cheering a parade of U.S. Marines, holding a U.S. flag and a sign reading "Me Chinese" (presumably so he will not be mistaken for a Japanese-American and "relocated"). The protagonists of *Escape in the Fog* (Columbia, 1945) escape from a Nazi death trap by projecting the words "Hail Japan" on a glass door, which is then smashed by patriotic Chinese-Americans! A heroic Chinese-American doctor from Brooklyn (Keye Luke again) appears in *Doctor Gillespie's New Assistant* (MGM, 1942) and *Three Men in White* (MGM, 1944).

A Chinese houseboy in *The Falcon Strikes Back* (RKO, 1943) makes a remark about the common cause of China and the United States. A Chinese-American soldier is seen playing cards with white soldiers on a train in *The Human Comedy* (MGM, 1943).

More significant Chinese roles may be found in relatively early films like *Bombs Over Burma* and *Lady from Chungking* (both PRC, 1942). Chinese-American actress Anna May Wong received top-billing in each of these films: in the first, she is sent to Burma to determine who has been leaking information to the Japanese about the Burma Road (the land route from the Burma railhead to Kunming, China, by which China received outside aid—it was cut by Japan in April 1942).[50] *Lady from Chungking* is even more interesting, as Wong plays a Chinese noblewoman who leads anti–Japanese guerrillas by night.[51] The guerillas rescue two downed Flying Tiger pilots, and Wong provides them—at the cost of her own life—with information about a planned Japanese assault on Chungking (the Nationalist capital), which is then foiled by the Allies. Wong, a former Paramount star, was virtually the only Asian performer to receive top-billing in a Hollywood film in the sound era.[52]

Dragon Seed, based on a novel by Pearl S. Buck, was the closest Hollywood would come to presenting a completely *Chinese* story, with Chinese protagonists and no Anglo leading characters. The impact, of course, is somewhat marred by the failure to cast *any* Chinese actors in the leading roles, which were assumed by Katharine Hepburn, Turhan Bey, Walter Huston, Aline MacMahon, and Akim Tamiroff, but it is difficult to fault Hollywood too strongly—would American audiences have gone to see a film starring Benson Fong, Anna May Wong, Keye Luke, Chester Gan, and Richard Loo?

Despite the rather antiseptic view of Chinese life and its deliberately obscure political orientation, the film is good Allied propaganda:

To the OWI *Dragon Seed* was a notable contribution to the war effort—a film that would show Americans that the Chinese understood what they were fighting for and that they were willing to die for freedom.[53]

The Chinese are recognizably human; no mean feat, given Hollywood's usual view of non–Western societies. The audience sympathizes with their plight, as men are murdered and women raped by the invading Japanese. Hepburn, a politically aware village woman, takes the rather drastic step of poisoning a troop of Japanese soldiers, but, coming after the countless atrocities of the "devil dwarves," her actions are perceived as fully justified. Nor are the Chinese completely whitewashed into propaganda poster images (they are "glamorized" but not to the extent of the unbelievable Russian "peasants" of *The North Star* and *Song of Russia*)—weasel Akim Tamiroff collaborates with the Japanese, a role akin to that of French collaborator Hume Cronyn in *The Cross of Lorraine* (MGM, 1944) or Norwegian collaborator Charles Dingle in *Edge of Darkness* (WB, 1943).

For the most part, however, Hollywood continued to use Chinese characters as foils for Anglo protagonists. Victor Sen Yung is an overeager, comic Chinese lawyer in *Secret Agent of Japan*, revealed at the climax to be an agent of the Nationalist Chinese, who saves the hero and heroine, and recruits the hero (Preston Foster) into the Chinese Army. Philip Ahn (for once in a positive role) portrays Gary Cooper's faithful retainer in *The Story of Dr. Wassell* (Paramount, 1944), assisting Cooper in his scientific research in China, then joining the U.S. Navy in Cooper's honor after Pearl Harbor!

Chinese guerrillas save American airmen after the bombing raid on Tokyo in *The Purple Heart* (TCF, 1944) and *Thirty Seconds Over Tokyo* (MGM, 1945). In the former film, Benson Fong kills his own father, a traitorous Chinese village leader who betrayed the airmen to Japan. For this act, Fong is rewarded by being named an honorary member of the squadron (and presumably suffers the same fate—execution—as the flyers). *Thirty Seconds Over Tokyo* features Fong again, this time as the Westernized son of a Chinese doctor who treats the injured flyers. The Chinese characters in this film are generally treated with dignity and respect, although there is still a patronizing air about the China sequences, with its scenes of kindly British missionaries caring for Chinese children (and child-like adults).[54]

China's Little Devils (Monogram, 1945) was one of the last major China-theme films. "Ducky" Louie, a young Chinese-American boy, plays the leader of a gang of Chinese children who harass the Japanese. Louie also appeared in *Back to Bataan* (RKO, 1945) and *China Sky* (RKO, 1945) in similar roles. In *China's Little Devils*, Louie is called "Little Butch," after his friend, Flying Tiger pilot Big Butch (Paul Kelly). When an American missionary (Harry Carey) says that he will not change his pacifist ideals even though the United States has entered the war against Japan, the Chinese boy replies, "*I've been at war all my life.*" Little Butch eventually loses his life in the struggle against Japan, the missionary finally puts his pacifism on hold for the duration, and Big Butch bombs Tokyo in memory of his Chinese namesake.

While the Chinese Army is mentioned in a number of films, it is rarely shown in action (guerrilla groups are featured more often). Chinese air cadets—in the United States for training—are saluted in *Stage Door Canteen* (UA, 1943) and in *Thunder Birds* (TCF, 1942), but they are not singled out for individual attention (the latter film contains a *very* oblique hint that a Chinese cadet is dating an American girl). As the examples cited earlier attest, Chinese "guerrillas" bear the brunt of offensive action in most Hollywood wartime presentations, aided (and often led) by Anglo characters. In *A Yank on the Burma Road* (MGM, 1942), American cab driver Joe (Barry Nelson) agrees to lead a Chinese attack on a Japanese stronghold, in exchange for the freedom of the German-American husband of a woman (Laraine Day) he has befriended.

Robert Preston is in apparent command of Chinese reg-

ular air transport units in *Night Plane from Chungking* (Paramount, 1943). This film portrays the Chinese military as professional and competent. Victor Sen Yung is Preston's sidekick (although they have the equal rank of Captain). An aged Chinese noblewoman, en route to a "secret mission" in India for the Nationalist government, also appears in this film.

Ironically, perhaps the most positive Chinese character in Hollywood wartime films is one who had existed before the war, and who would continue to exist afterwards: Charlie Chan. A number of the pre-war Chan films (released at the time through Twentieth Century–Fox) had some war relevance, beginning with *Charlie Chan at the Olympics* (TCF, 1937), set in Hitler's Germany. When the Chan series moved to Monogram in 1944, the Chinese-American detective was re-introduced as a government agent, with an office in Washington, D.C. (Monogram repeatedly used an exterior stock footage shot of an impressive building for "Secret Service Headquarters," apparently undisturbed by the California state flag prominently flying out front!).

In the first Monogram Chan, *Charlie Chan in the Secret Service*, Chan has a portrait of Chiang Kai-shek on the wall of his office, along with a similar picture of Franklin D. Roosevelt. He disposes of a group of spies who are trying to steal plans for a new torpedo.

Throughout the series, Chan is depicted as shrewd, good-natured, a family man, brave, and intellectually superior to every other character—regardless of race or nationality—in the films. He is stereotyped, but only to the extent that he uses stilted English (but certainly not incorrect or pidgin English), and in the frequent "Chinese" proverbs he utters upon the least provocation. Chan's various "sons" (and in at least *Secret Service*, a daughter as well) are completely Americanized.[55]

An OWI reviewer disliked the script of *Secret Service* submitted for review, feeling the depiction of Chan and his children would offend the Chinese. The script was read by the Chinese consul in Los Angeles at the request of the studio and the OWI; the consul had no objection, and Monogram proceeded with the series. The OWI, misreading the Chan character entirely, still refused to issue an export license so the film could be shown overseas.[56]

Unlike the British, Russian, and other Allied characters appearing in Hollywood productions of the war years, Chinese characters are defined not only by their status as an Ally, but also by their racial identity and their filmic past. Even with the best of intentions, Hollywood could not completely break free of its ingrained racial conventions, and as a result the Chinese were more often praised than seen.

Under the Cross of Lorraine: Free French

References to France in Hollywood films of the war period are numerous; however, in consideration of France as an

"Ally" for purposes of this chapter, many of these references are not applicable. France had the singular distinction of being, at various times (and sometimes simultaneously), a fighting Ally, an occupied country, and even an enemy.

Germany's invasion of France began in May 1940. By the end of the month, the British Army had been trapped on the beaches at Dunkirk and miraculously rescued; many of France's soldiers were not so fortunate.[57] In June, Italy joined the fray on the side of Nazi Germany, and a short time later, French leader Marshal Pétain asked for an armistice. Pétain formed a government, based in Vichy, which controlled approximately 40% of France; the Nazis occupied the rest.

Despite the impression given in Hollywood films, the Vichy government was not always considered a German puppet. In fact, the United States government continued to deal with Vichy for some time afterwards (the Germans occupied the Vichy portion of France in November 1942, ending even the pretense of a separate government). However, almost from the first, references to Vichy in American films were negative.

Perhaps the most anti–Vichy film is *To Have and Have Not* (WB, 1945), which depicts the struggle between Free French adherents and the Vichy administration on the Caribbean island of Martinique in 1940. The Vichy government controlled the French islands in this area until July 1943, when control was ceded to Free French authorities.[58] The Vichy police are the fascistic villains of this film; in an early scene, a plainclothesman records the names of Americans Harry Morgan (Humphrey Bogart) and his client Johnson because he overheard Johnson make a "disparaging reference to Vichy." Later, the Vichy agents have a running gun battle with the Free French (who are only trying to flee the island, not overthrow the Vichy government), and Vichy sailors pursue Morgan's boat, opening fire and wounding one of his passengers. There are also scenes featuring sinister interrogations by Vichy police officials Dan Seymour and Sheldon Leonard, both well-known to Hollywood audiences as gangster-types.

Most Hollywood films dealing with France focus on the life of Frenchmen under German occupation, and on the Resistance. Since this topic is covered in Chapter 20, we shall focus here on references to the Free French military, considered part of the Allied armed forces.

Charles de Gaulle, a career military man, had been promoted to general and named a junior member of the French Cabinet during the German offensive of 1940. When Reynaud, head of the French government, resigned and the aged Marshal Pétain took over with the intention of signing an armistice with Hitler, de Gaulle left France to continue the struggle. On June 18, 1940, he broadcast an appeal from England for Frenchmen to ignore the armistice. Not only were there armed forces in France which had not been defeated, France also had a large Navy and many colonial possessions which had not been touched by the Nazi war machine.

At the end of June 1940, Winston Churchill recognized de Gaulle as "leader of all free Frenchmen, wherever they may be, who rally to him in support of the Allied cause," and official British government recognition followed in August.[59]

A struggle ensued between de Gaulle's forces and those Frenchmen overseas who remained loyal to the "legal" Vichy government. France's African colonies were the scene of much political maneuvering and some bloodshed. At the end of September 1940, Free French troops—aided by the British Royal Navy—tried to capture the West African port of Dakar, but were repulsed after heavy fighting. Nonetheless, the Free French were making their presence felt: "by late fall, de Gaulle had an estimated 30,000 men under arms, prepared to kill Germans and Italians in the name of France."[60]

The United States government resisted the temptation to recognize the Free French, even after the attack on Pearl Harbor and America's entry into the war on the side of the Allies. In the spring and summer of 1942, the U.S. government established *de facto* relations with the Free French, without severing relations with Vichy or making any promises to de Gaulle about his political status after the liberation of France. Eventually, of course, the United States was forced to recognize de Gaulle as the legitimate head of the French government (in October 1944), but a residue of bitterness remained on both sides.

All of this was mostly irrelevant to the popular media. The Free French were colorful Allies, and were exalted in much the same way as Chiang Kai-shek and his Chinese forces. The relative paucity of references in Hollywood films may be attributed to the fact that the Free French forces were operating in theatres of war which were not "boxoffice" (such as Africa), and to the greater dramatic potential in French "resistance" stories.

Several Hollywood films highlight the conflict between Free France and Vichy, pitting Frenchman against Frenchman. *To Have and Have Not*, discussed earlier, is a good example of this. *Night Plane from Chungking* features a French soldier who is on his way to join de Gaulle, although he carries a Vichy passport (American pilot Robert Preston practically hisses when he says "Vichy," a good example of America's attitude towards the collaborators). This character proves his trustworthiness, sacrificing his own life to enable his companions to escape from their Japanese captors.

In *Passage to Marseilles* (WB, 1944), Free French sympathizers try to prevent a ship loaded with nickel from falling into Vichy hands (including Sydney Greenstreet as "Duval," perhaps an allusion to Vichy official Pierre *Laval*). After they do so, Humphrey Bogart joins the Free French air force for raids over his occupied homeland. *Casablanca* (WB, 1943), of course, ends with Bogart and French colonial policeman Claude Rains (a Vichy government employee) leaving to join the Free French forces in Brazzaville, capital of Free French Africa.

The Cross of Lorraine (MGM, 1944), although it takes its title from the symbol of Free France, deals with escaped French prisoners of war who join the Resistance forces in France, rather than the uniformed Free French armed forces (who operated outside France until D-Day). The various Resistance groups in France agreed to cooperate until liberation, and were more or less united under de Gaulle in the National Resistance Council. After the liberation of Paris, however, de Gaulle froze them out, fearful of Communist influence and unwilling to share political power with the various Resistance factions. A Free French saboteur (not a member of the Resistance) makes a brief appearance in *Uncertain Glory* (WB, 1944), and Jean Pierre Aumont is detached from Free French military duty in Africa for undercover work in his native France in *Assignment in Brittany* (MGM, 1943). Virginia Bruce is identified as a Free French secret agent working in the Middle East in *Action in Arabia* (RKO, 1944).

A few films do contain images of the Free French armed forces. In addition to the brief military reference in *Assignment in Brittany*, noted above, a Free French flyer (Paul Henreid—although Austrian, he was Hollywood's all-purpose "good European" during the war) and his RAF comrades are pursued by the Nazis in *Joan of Paris* (RKO, 1942).

Africa was the location of most Free French military action until D-Day, and two films concentrate on this aspect of de Gaulle's forces.[61] *Jungle Siren* (PRC, 1942) stars Buster Crabbe as an American engineer with the Free French forces (he has the rank of Captain), scouting locations for an airfield and combating Nazi-inspired native rebellions. He is assisted by his Brooklyn-born sidekick (Paul Bryar) and a lithesome native girl (stripper Ann Corio).

The Impostor (Universal, 1944) is somewhat more serious in nature. French expatriate Jean Gabin plays the lead in this film, which was produced, directed, and written by fellow Frenchman Julien Duvivier. Gabin escapes a date with the guillotine due to a fortuitous Nazi air raid. Assuming the identity of a dead French soldier, he boards a ship bound for Dakar, the Vichy stronghold in Africa. However, the troops have a change of heart after hearing a de Gaulle radio broadcast, and the ship sails to Free French Equatorial Africa instead. Gabin proves his bravery in battle against the Axis, but his imposture is revealed. Given another chance, Gabin sac-

rifices his life to silence a machine gun nest threatening his comrades, and dies a Free Frenchman.

Hollywood images of the Free French military, while few and far between, were almost entirely positive. However, they were probably not numerous enough to make any particular impact on the filmgoing audience.

The "Little" Allies

As a final note, other "Allies" are depicted or referred to in a number of films, although rarely in detail. As noted earlier, a "Free Norwegian" officer (George Neise) appears in a major role in *They Raid by Night*, and a "Free Polish" pilot (Robert Stack) has a significant part in *To Be or Not to Be* (although he is not seen acting in his military capacity in the film). References to the Dutch military (again, as opposed to the Resistance forces in occupied Holland) may be found in *The London Blackout Murders* (Republic, 1943), *Pilot Number Five* (MGM, 1943), and in *The Story of Dr. Wassell*. In the latter film, a Dutch officer (Carl Esmond) serving in Java, reports via radio about a Japanese amphibious landing, remaining at his post until he is killed. The protagonist of *Escape in the Desert* is a Dutch pilot (Philip Dorn—another frequent "good European" in wartime Hollywood features) who, after serving in Europe, volunteers to "finish the job" against fascism by fighting the Japanese.[62] Paul Henreid is a Dutch secret agent on duty in Lisbon in *The Conspirators* (WB, 1944), and Dutch agents Gale Sondergaard and Gilbert Roland operate in New York in *Enemy Agents Meet Ellery Queen* (Columbia, 1942). Latin American—usually Mexican or Brazilian—military characters appear in a few films of the period, as discussed in Chapter 17.

However, the military contributions of the "minor" Allies were generally not deemed of enough interest to attract Hollywood's attention. Once the United States entered the war, U.S. forces drew the lion's share of attention in *all* American media, and Hollywood was no exception. Nonetheless, the films featuring Allied characters or references do provide an interesting insight into American attitudes of the war years.

19. Images Americans Loved to Hate: Germans, Japanese and Italians on Screen

[B]oth the Germans and Italians were seen as caricatures of a political ideology that did not contaminate the entirety of their ethnic identity, nor extend itself to the Americans of German or Italian descent. The Japanese, contrariwise, were depicted in the most barbarous fashion.[1]

[W]e viewed the war with the Japanese as a race war, and the war with the Germans as an ideological war. When we disliked Germans, it was the Nazis we meant. When we disliked the Japanese, it was all of them.[2]

The Japanese attack on Pearl Harbor was not only a military surprise, it also came as a profound psychological shock to the American people. For well over a year prior to the "day that will live in infamy," many Americans—actively encouraged by Hollywood and other popular media—had begun to accept the inevitability of war against the forces of European fascism, chiefly Nazi Germany.[3] Yet, when President Franklin D. Roosevelt announced to Congress and the American people on December 8, 1941, that we were at war, our enemy was the Empire of Japan. Three days later, America would also be in armed conflict with the remaining members of the Tripartite Pact, but only because Hitler and Mussolini, living up to the terms of their alliance with Japan, formally declared war upon the United States on December 11th.

Once the war began, there was a need to understand why we were fighting, and who our enemies were. This was most economically achieved by glorifying the virtues of American democracy, and by graphically specifying the evils that must be destroyed in order to preserve our way of life. Motion pictures were one major means by which the codification of good and evil was disseminated during World War II.

1. The Nazty Nuisance

The Germans were recognized to be human beings, but of a perverse type, cold, diagrammatic, pedantic, unimaginative, and thoroughly sinister.[4]

Many Germans were disaffected from Nazism; in turn, qualities of fanaticism and arrogance were ascribed and restricted to Gestapo or SS officials. In short, there were Nazis and there were also good Germans.[5]

From a propaganda point of view, Nazi Germany, as a clearly defined, ideologically antithetical opponent, was an almost ideal wartime enemy. America's deadly struggle with Hitler's Third Reich could be viewed and reinforced in terms of a simple dichotomy—the democratic common man versus the militaristic superman. The image of the physically and mentally flawed Nazi leadership, obviously counter to the Aryan ideal espoused in their polemical diatribes, was repeatedly exploited in American films as a potent symbol of the inherent contradictions of National Socialism.[6]

But the German population, with whom most Americans shared a common western heritage, was not generally targeted by Hollywood filmmakers as the enemy. The power-hungry Hitler and his crazy ideology are shown to have misled the German people and placed them under a deadly spell: "the enemy was the Nazis—militaristic leaders who forced their way of life on the Germans."[7] So, during the World War II years, there evolved upon America's movie screens a complex set of co-existing images representing the citizens of Hitler's Germany—the honest, straightforward common German, helpless against the ruthless dictatorship of the bombastic, perverted Nazi fanatic Hitler, his fellow fascists, and the op-

portunistic or misguided German people/soldiers aiding his plan for world domination through military conquest.

The threat of the Third Reich is not so much defined in ideological terms, but in terms of a free world versus an empire seized through the military might of the Wehrmacht and enslaved by ruthless Blackshirted Nazi administrators. As a consequence, while the Japanese were primarily stigmatized as a racial opponent, the real and potential threat of racist Nazi theories was largely ignored in America's wartime films.

A key element in Hollywood's formulation of the German enemy in 1942–1945 lies in a critical linkage between the militaristic Prussian stereotype established and reinforced through American propaganda (including many commercial feature films) during the First World War, and the contemporary image of a Nazi elite devoted to a power-crazed dictator named Adolf Hitler. The Third Reich's heritage is made clear in *Berlin Correspondent* (TCF, 1942) when Gestapo Colonel Karl von Rau (Martin Kosleck) tells his admiring secretary: "Although I'm a Nazi, I was born a Prussian Junker."

Additionally, there are frequent filmic references to the previous American, British and French encounter with the Kaiser's militaristic Germany in the "last war" (this linkage could not be utilized in anti–Japanese or anti–Italian film propaganda, since both Italy and Japan were on the *Allied* side during WWI; some use was made, however, of Japan's rapid rise to militarism beginning with the Russo-Japanese War of 1904–1905). There are 136 film references to the First World War in the 1942–1945 period—the subtext being that this is the second time in just over twenty years that Americans have been forced to embark upon a crusade in the name of western democracy against an authoritarian coalition—led by Germany—seeking world domination.[8] Consequently, many American motion pictures suggest that the only way of guaranteeing a permanent solution to this recurrent threat to world peace is the total destruction of the military powers possessed by such belligerently anti-democratic regimes—hence the appeal of FDR's declaration in 1943 to accept only "unconditional surrender" from the Axis powers.

The concept of war guilt, i.e., of fascist leaders instigating a world war despite a lack of legitimate provocation, is asserted in a number of films that portray the Nazis as systematically militarizing their country and deliberately undermining democratic governments during the years immediately prior to the outbreak of World War II. The notorious *Hitler's Children* (RKO, 1943), among other things, depicts the Nazi educational system as indoctrinating German youth to spy and kill. *Margin for Error* (TCF, 1943) centers around a major Nazi sabotage organization in prewar America operated out of the German consulate in New York City. RKO's 1942 release, *Once Upon a Honeymoon*, features an Austrian aristocrat, a secret Nazi representative, who visits all the countries targeted for conquest by Hitler, making contact with individuals willing to betray their nations (a swastika clock is repeatedly used to symbolize Hitler's timetable). *Secrets of Scotland Yard* (Republic, 1944) posits the idea that the German military, realizing that British Intelligence helped cause their downfall in WWI, planted a long-hidden "mole" in the British Cipher Bureau in preparation for WWII. This means, of course, that they *knew* there was going to be a "next war" all along.

Prewar armaments preparations, the underlying culpability of Prussian militarism, and the Nazi corruption of German youth are all illustrated in *The White Cliffs of Dover* (MGM, 1944). In a scene set in Britain during the mid–1930s, two aristocratic German boys are guests at the home of an upper class English family. Playing outside with the family's son, they express their admiration of the house's large flat lawn—not for its aesthetic value, but because it would make an excellent field upon which to land gliders! Responding to concerns expressed by the English parents, the German boys claim that their father's armaments plants are only making non-military items. After further questioning, they emphatically deny Germany was defeated in the last war and ominously assert that the new Germany "will win next time."

While there are only a few films which make a direct connection between Kaiser Wilhelm and Hitler—*Sherlock Holmes in Washington* (Universal, 1943) and *Watch on the Rhine* (WB, 1943) for example—oblique linkages are also apparent in such films as *Friendly Enemies* (UA, 1942), a First World War drama featuring middle-class German immigrants living in America. In the most dramatic scene of the long and rather boring biopic, *Wilson* (TCF, 1944), both the Kaiser and Imperial Germany are lambasted by the American President. Having recently been informed about German machinations in Mexico (the Zimmermann telegram affair), Wilson (Alexander Knox) histrionically accuses Germany of being "the most evil and autocratic power this world has ever seen."

The parallels between the American film treatment of the Kaiser in World War I and that of Hitler during the Second World War are rather interesting, but are not that startling. After all, for many leaders of the Hollywood industry this was their second bout in the propaganda war with Germany. The Warner Brothers had produced and William Nigh had directed *My Four Years in Germany* (First National, 1918), and one of Raoul Walsh's earliest directorial efforts was rabidly anti-German *The Prussian Cur* (Fox, 1918).

There are a number of similarities between the earlier cinematic bashing of the Kaiser and his entourage and the WWII film attacks directed at Hitler and his Nazi cronies. Just as there had been exploitation of the Kaiser's withered arm, many WWII films mock the "Heil Hitler" salute. At one point Hitler wearily "Heils" himself in *The Devil with Hitler*! In *The Wife Takes a Flyer*, a Hitler-happy Nazi major has "Heiled" so much that an aide has to massage his exhausted elbow.

The Kaiser, Hitler, and their associates are virtually always portrayed in uniform, frequently with the Iron Cross and assorted other medals pinned on their chests. The Kaiser had his foolish and degenerate Crown Prince, Hitler the womanizing Goebbels and the obese, drug-addicted Goering. Both the Chaplinesque Hitler mustache and the Kaiser's trademark W-shaped mustache are ceaselessly caricatured in film and other popular media. Both men are also portrayed as power-mad dictators who order the invasion of peaceful countries and condone brutal atrocities committed to repress the conquered peoples.

In contrast to the conflict with Japan in the Pacific, which is depicted as a war to exterminate the menacing yellow hordes of an Asian nation, the European war against the German-dominated fascist alliance becomes a struggle whose primary purpose is to purge the world of an evil ideology and its fanatical militarist proponents. As a result, there are a number of films which target Hitler and other Nazi leaders, operating under the theory that the evil is concentrated at the top of the hierarchy, not in the German people. One such example appears in *They Live in Fear* (Columbia, 1944), the story of an anti–Nazi teenager (whose family is also anti–Nazi) who seizes the opportunity to come to the United States. Speaking to citizens of his adopted nation, the boy says "in Germany, the individual is an inmate in an institution." This type of outlook was officially frowned upon by the U.S. government: the OWI repeatedly criticized studios whose films showed "good Germans," fearing that sympathy for the German people could lead to demands for a "soft peace."

Nonetheless, Hollywood concentrates on Nazi officials and officers, not the German population, as the guilty parties. A hit team of American gangsters successfully carries out its mission after being parachuted into Germany in *Hitler — Dead or Alive* (Charles House Prods., 1943). This low-budget potboiler has a clean-shaven (thus unrecognizable) Fuehrer (courtesy of the gangsters), cowering before a wall as he is shot by his own bodyguards. In the deliberately ambiguous conclusion of *The Strange Death of Adolf Hitler* (Universal, 1943), Germany's leader presumably dies at the hands of a lookalike assassin. In *Passport to Destiny* (RKO, 1944), a British cleaning lady (Elsa Lanchester) makes her way to Berlin, intent on assassinating Hitler and ending the war.

The actual 1942 assassination of Reinhard Heydrich, the Nazi overlord of the occupied Czech state, is recreated in two films, *Hangmen Also Die* (UA, 1943) and *Hitler's Madman* (MGM, 1943). In the former, Heydrich's swishing demeanor is obviously meant to imply that he is a homosexual. In the latter film, as suggested in the title, Hitler's overseer is characterized (to excess) by John Carradine as both a psychopath and a (hetero)sexual deviant.[9] In both films, therefore, the assassination of Heydrich is depicted as not only strategically important to the war effort (which it really was not), but as morally correct.

In *None Shall Escape* (Columbia, 1944), an unrepentant

Hotel Berlin (Warner Bros., 1945): As Germany crumbles, General von Dahnwitz (Raymond Massey), weighs his options. To flee to South America or not to flee? His blonde companion is Andrea King.

captured Nazi official named Grimm (Alexander Knox), who had been forced to flee his German-Polish border village in the years after World War I following an attempted rape, is tried by an international tribunal for war crimes perpetrated against the same village during the German occupation of Poland.[10] The Nazi fanatic (George Coulouris) of *The Master Race* (RKO, 1944), secretly placed as an agent provocateur in a Belgian village recently liberated from the Germans, is swiftly tried and executed by an Allied firing squad after his true identity and deadly activities are revealed.

Germans who become Nazis may be brutal and arrogant, but—unlike the Japanese enemy—they are of the same racial stock as most Americans, and, in many cases, capable of redemption: "it somehow seemed easier to regard Germany as a temporary enemy, its people redeemable once the Nazis were overthrown."[11] Hitler and the Nazi leadership are consistently portrayed in wartime American films as symbolic corrupters of a western culture. This implicitly absolves most other Germans—except the industrialists, the aristocracy and the officer class that sold out to the Nazis—of war guilt and "crimes against humanity." National Socialism becomes cinematically defined as a perverse ideology used by a criminal elite to manipulate the German population into supporting the Nazis' mad attempt to dominate the world.

While the Japanese were invariably stereotyped as one-dimensional, many facets of German characters—sometimes even Nazis—were shown. The number of wartime films set in Germany with all or predominantly German casts of characters, is surprisingly large, including *The Seventh Cross, Address Unknown, Enemy of Women, Women in Bondage, The Hitler Gang,* and *Hotel Berlin,* to name a few.[12] In contrast, only four Hollywood films of this period take place mostly in Japan: *Behind the Rising Sun, First Yank into Tokyo, The Purple Heart,* and *Blood on the Sun.* And only the first of these concentrates on the Japanese people rather than the adventures of Americans in Japan.

Films about Germany and the Germans virtually all contain anti–Nazi characters. In *The Seventh Cross* (MGM, 1944),

First Yank Into Tokyo (RKO Radio, 1945): American Tom Neal submits to plastic surgery so he can infiltrate a Japanese POW camp and rescue a scientist. Barbara Hale is a captive nurse who keeps his secret.

a German political prisoner (possibly meant to be a socialist) played by Spencer Tracy, escapes the country in 1936 with the assistance of a working-class friend (Hume Cronyn), even though the armaments factory worker has benefited from full employment and family-support legislation under Nazi rule. Another example is a German POW in *The Master Race*. He had participated in atrocities in Russia, but expiates his crimes by helping to restore a war-damaged village church in Belgium. He is later treated sympathetically when he exposes a Nazi agent before expiring from burns (the result of a fire deliberately set by hardcore Nazis). The German soldier who was a miner in civilian life in *Counter-Attack* (Columbia, 1945) is eventually persuaded by his Soviet captor to re-embrace working-class solidarity and betray his ruthless, fanatical commanding officer. The distinguishing feature of a young poetry-reading German soldier in *The Moon Is Down* (TCF, 1943) is his unwillingness to kill and torture in the name of Adolf Hitler.

An interesting example also occurs in *Berlin Correspondent* (TCF, 1942). Karen (Virginia Gilmore) is Gestapo Colonel von

Rau's assistant. She willingly undertakes the job of exposing the German "traitor" who is passing confidential information to an American correspondent (this occurs prior to Pearl Harbor). When her father expresses his distaste for her job, and for the Nazi regime, she says that older people just can not understand the New Order. But it is actually Karen who does not realize what Nazism truly means. When her father turns out to be the informant—and is arrested by von Rau—Karen undergoes a change of heart and becomes a "good German," eventually escaping to freedom with the American (Dana Andrews).[13]

Nazi apostates also appear in *Underground* (WB, 1941),[14] *Hitler's Children* (RKO, 1943) and *None Shall Escape*. In the latter two films, young Nazi officers, having witnessed the Nazi persecution of the women they loved, renounce that ideology even though it means their deaths. In *The North Star* (RKO, 1943) a German Army medical officer (Erich von Stroheim) shows his contempt for a Nazi colleague when he pointedly remarks that he studied surgery under a great doctor, who happened to be Jewish. The Nazi officer portrayed in *The Pied Piper* (TCF, 1942), played with verve by Otto Preminger, shows a crack in his Nazi facade when he arranges for his half-Jewish niece to accompany a group of refugees fleeing to England from German-occupied France.

Obviously, few Nazis were pictured so humanistically. "They are not men, but robots trained for killing, without soul or heart," wrote one contemporary author in a non-fiction book.[15] The smart, but evil, fanatics in *Hitler's Madman* and in *Chetniks* (TCF, 1943) show a willingness to kill, even murdering their fellow ideologues. Rivalries between German military officers and their Nazi counterparts, usually involving power and women, invariably result in the death of one or both of the parties. This is strikingly evident in *Hostages* (Paramount, 1943), wherein internecine struggles involving the seized properties of a Czech collaborator allow a resistance leader to escape the authorities. In order to cover up this failure, a Nazi is murdered by his German Army cohort. In the latter half of *The Hitler Gang* (Paramount, 1944), during which the bloody Nazi purge of June 1933 is recreated, Goering and Himmler compare respective death lists and coldly agree to have Strasser, an early Nazi leader, assassinated. Hitler, at Goebbels' urging, also actively joins in the purge and apparently shoots his former mentor, the homosexual SA leader Ernst Roehm. Goebbels, himself, is portrayed as initially being on the purge list of some rival Nazis leaders in the pseudo-biographical Monogram release, *Enemy of Women* (1944).

The killing and betraying of their own by Nazis occurs repeatedly in wartime American films: *Invisible Agent, Nazi Agent, The Master Race, Once Upon a Honeymoon,* and *Daring Young Man,* for instance. When arrogant Gestapo officer von Rau in *Berlin Correspondent* betrays the Nazi cause in the expectation of receiving the sexual favors of a young blonde, his jealous secretary reports him to his superior (thereby condemning him to death). As von Rau is arrested, he protests: "I'm a loyal Party member." Looking triumphant, his scorned secretary coldly responds: "Perhaps they'll write it on your tombstone."

The leading Nazi agent in *Background to Danger* (WB, 1943), played with exaggerated repulsiveness by Sidney Greenstreet, fails in his mission to trick neutral Turkey into joining the Axis alliance, and is met at the airport by an SS escort—it is intimated he will be executed upon his return to Germany by order of the "Hangman" Himmler.

Broken Axis

With America at war with both Germany and Japan, it was patriotic, as well as economical, to create villains with dual affiliations, thereby suggesting complicity between Germany and Japan.[16]

There are 38 wartime motion pictures which portray or refer to cooperation between the Axis partners—including such films as *Bombs Over Burma* (PRC, 1942), *The Devil with Hitler* (UA, 1942), *Little Tokyo, USA* (TCF, 1942), and *Salute to the Marines* (MGM, 1943). Some form of distrust leading to dissension between the supposedly cooperating members of the Axis partnership invariably takes place in these films. In *The Devil with Hitler*, it remains on a benignly comical level, similar to the tone established in Chaplin's 1940 classic, *The Great Dictator* (UA)—both films feature a number of ridiculous encounters between caricatures of Hitler and Mussolini. In many of the other such films, the alleged partners in world conquest are more apt to harm each other than their democratic enemies.

Baron Akito (Peter Lorre) actually kills his Nazi counterpart in *Invisible Agent* (Universal, 1942) for allowing a list with the names of Axis agents in America to pass into the Allies' hands. Disgusted with the German for having refused to restore his honor by committing suicide, Akito wipes his knife clean of the Nazi's blood on the man's swastika armband. Similarly, in *Lure of the Islands* (Monogram, 1942), the Japanese member of an Axis team shoots his Nazi counterpart in the back when the German flatly rejects his associate's demand to atone for the failure of their mission by committing suicide. On several occasions in *Busses Roar* (WB, 1942), a German agent working with Japanese spies on a sabotage operation in the United States sarcastically refers to his Japanese associate as "Mr. Cherry Blossom." Perhaps this relationship between the Axis partners is best described in *The Purple Heart* (TCF, 1944). A Russian correspondent attending the trial of American flyers in Tokyo remarks that the Japanese think of America and England as "belligerent enemies" and consider the Germans "friendly enemies."

Germans, on several occasions, are also portrayed murdering their Italian allies. A captured Luftwaffe pilot, an arrogant Aryan stereotype who has displayed Nazi fanaticism, coldly kills his Italian fellow-prisoner in *Sahara* (Columbia, 1943) when the latter, who has called Hitler a "maniac," indicates he plans to cooperate with their Allied captors. At one point in *Five Graves to Cairo* (Paramount, 1943) a German officer offhandedly mentions to an Italian general on Rommel's staff that an Italian soldier was shot outside their field headquarters for stealing water.

The Italians are repeatedly portrayed as militarily useless to their Axis partner and thus are treated as expendable by the Germans. In *Background to Danger* (WB, 1943), a Nazi agent actually tosses a bomb into the Italian Embassy in Ankara! It is all part of a covert campaign to convince neutral Turkey that the Soviets are planning to undermine their government and that the only way to protect themselves from a Russian invasion is to join the Axis. Nazi spies literally stab an Italian agent in the back in *Spy Train* (Monogram, 1943).

On more than one occasion Nazi buffoons/automatons

The Hitler Gang (Paramount, 1944): Paramount's attempt at a Nazi Party history, with Bobby Watson again playing Adolf Hitler. Standing at right, Roman Bohnen, as Ernst Roehm.

are exposed as inherently cowardly when their power relationship with another is reversed. After his arrest by the Gestapo, the corpulent blackshirted Heiser in *Invisible Agent*, for example, denounces his fellow Nazis and is willing to betray state secrets to his invisible American cellmate in an attempt to save his life. In *The Hitler Gang*, the Fuehrer himself is portrayed as pathetically craven after the failed Munich *putsch* of 1923: the police arrest him when he emerges from his hiding place in a wardrobe closet. During Heydrich's deathbed scene in *Hitler's Madman*, the mortally wounded Nazi overlord begs for morphine and screams he does not want to die for Hitler. To Himmler, standing at his bedside, Heydrich predicts the Nazis will lose the war because they were too weak—they did not kill enough!

Interestingly, there are far fewer film examples of the use of negative terms for Germans, such as "Kraut," "Jerry," "Fritz," or "Heinie" (all coded under Nazi) than to "Jap" for the Japanese. Statistically, the overall number of films with references to Nazis is slightly larger than the number of films

containing such references to the Japanese (242 to 236). But the cumulative numbers of *pejorative* references and their obviously racially prejudiced content are far more intense when applied to the Japanese than when directed at the Nazis. There are only a limited number of references to the Germans/Nazis at the same level as the vicious talk of hunting and killing the Japanese expressed countless times by wartime American film characters (see Chapter 16). Thus, the description of a dead German as a "good Jerry" in *Reunion in France* (MGM, 1943) is comparatively unusual.

Images of Evil

By early 1942 the prevailing Hollywood image of Nazi Germany was a montage of accouterments and stereotypical affectations, many of which had their origins in the propaganda films released during the First World War—shaved heads, "Heidelberg" scars (facial; from fencing duels in college),

Five Graves to Cairo (RKO Radio, 1943): Erich von Stroheim, cast as Field Marshal Erwin Rommel, recreated the "Prussian officer" role he developed during World War One. Franchot Tone and Anne Baxter are impressed.

monocles, Lugers, riding crops, heel-clicking, arrogant Junker officers with a "von" before their surnames, iron crosses, jackboots, and goosestepping. The black uniform (including jodhpurs and Sam Browne belt) of the SS, the swastika (usually on an armband or displayed as a flag), a predilection for the employment of torture devices, and the iconography associated with Hitlerism, particularly the "Heil Hitler" salute, are the main additional non-plot means by which the theme of Nazism is established in American motion pictures released throughout the war. The distinctive German steel helmet and its associative linkages with German military aggression and atrocities committed during both world wars—even if many of the World War I era stories were later proven to be apochryphal—reinforce the concept of a brutal German army that traditionally carried out the orders of the state without question.

All that was needed to complete the picture was an actor with a guttural voice or at least an affected continental accent. Actors frequently cast as Nazis during the war include Martin Kosleck, John Carradine, George Coulouris, and such authentic "German" types as Kurt Kreuger (in real life, Swiss), Hans Schumm, Arno Frey, Ivan Triesault (who was really Estonian), Otto Preminger, Walter Slezak, and Helmut Dantine (these three actually Austrian), and Sig Rumann (who was often a comical Nazi). Supporting roles were often filled by character actors and bit players like Lionel Royce, William von Brincken, Frederick Giermann, Otto Reichow, Kurt Katch, Robert O. Davis, Hans von Morhart, Hans von Twardowski, and Henry Victor.[17]

The unflattering impersonation of Field Marshal Rommel by Erich von Stroheim in *Five Graves to Cairo*, while contrary to the well-publicized personality traits of the famous soldier (who was not a member of the Nazi Party and was openly admired by many of his contemporary foes), convincingly conformed to the American film image of the characteristically arrogant German/Nazi officer. For instance, the marshal's baton that Rommel was frequently shown carrying in newsreel footage has been replaced in the film with a riding crop.

Stroheim had established his film persona portraying enemy officers committing atrocities in such notoriously anti–German World War I American films as *Hearts of the World* (Griffith, 1918), and *The Hun Within* (Paramount-Artcraft, 1918). In *The North Star* (RKO, 1943) von Stroheim, playing a jaded German Army medical officer, first appears riding in an open staff car with a Nazi colleague in the vanguard of the forces invading Russia. However, this initial impression, bolstered by the actor's reputation and the surname of his character (von Harden) is later confused by his identity as a doctor (he even wears a Red Cross armband instead of a swastika), and by the political contradictions that will later be bitterly expressed by the vain military surgeon.

German officers traveling in open staff cars symbolize a military elite and would remind many in the contemporary audience of actual footage showing Hitler in his custom black Mercedes — particularly the oft-used scene of his grand entrance into Nuremburg, lifted from Leni Reifenstahl's 1934 *Triumph des Willens*. Mechanized troops, Nazi automatons in machines, sub–Hitlers in staff cars, make similar entrances into peaceful villages, violating their idyllic bliss in *Commandos Strike at Dawn*, *The North Star*, *None Shall Escape* and *The Pied Piper*. In *Hitler's Madman*, Heydrich, in *his* black Mercedes, disrupts an innocuous traditional blessing of the peasants' fields and has the officiating priest shot.

The iconographic fetishism centering around the swastika associated with National Socialism is brilliantly evoked on film in *Reunion in France*. During a dinner party at which Nazi officials and their French collaborators have gathered to celebrate, there is an overhead shot of a candle-lit swastika-shaped dinner table, with Wagnerian music playing on the soundtrack, a macabre display of Nazi kitsch. Conjuring up images of Nazi torchlight processions, it also symbolizes the unequal nature of an unholy union.

The most evil cinematic Nazis are usually portrayed in the black uniform of the SS (usually referred to as members of the dreaded secret police, the Gestapo—although they were separate organizations, Hollywood made little distinction between the two),[18] wearing swastika armbands, and sometimes also the Adolf Hitler band near the sleeve cuff (indicating extreme loyalty through membership in Hitler's personal bodyguard). This not only accentuates their ideological uniformity, but additionally creates an associative linkage of fascism with death by being attired from head to toe in black. In fact, several of these villainous film Nazis are further sartorially adorned with the death's head, or *totenkopf*, insignia at the center of their cap band. Unless some member of the Allies steals their uniform for the purpose of disguise, Nazis (except spies) virtually never appear on screen in civilian clothes. These individuals are thus immediately visually identifiable as Nazis and separated from all other humans by their uniform. Because of the obvious association with militarism created by the uniform and the inevitable instigation of atrocities by those characters so dressed, the screen Nazis epitomize demonological imagery.

These blackshirted Gestapo officials are invariably portrayed issuing orders, plotting, interrogating prisoners, etc., while ensconced in cavernous sterile offices adorned with Nazi Party paraphernalia. Instead of such traditional German iconography as the Imperial Eagle, or images of Bismarck and Goethe, the room is usually cluttered with swastikas on a flag or banner, and a Hitler portrait or bust. Good examples of Party-approved interior decorating appear in *Berlin Correspondent*, *Desperate Journey*, and *First Comes Courage* (Columbia, 1943). Even Nazi spy hideouts in the United States come equipped with the ubiquitous Hitler portrait, as seen in *All Through the Night* (WB, 1942) and *Cowboy Commandos* (Monogram, 1943), for instance.

Along with the usual Nazi icons in the offices of Party officials, a globe or world map on the wall is frequently included in the decor. This is a crude, but effective, means of visually reinforcing the concept that the Nazis desire to conquer the world (after all wasn't the Nazi slogan: "Today Germany; Tomorrow the World"?). Hitler's suite prominently features a large metallic sphere, symbolizing the globe, with a swastika suspended inside it, in *The Hitler Gang*.[19] At the Berlin headquarters of Nazi espionage in *They Came to Blow Up America* (TCF, 1943) the commander's office displays a world map with a bullseye over the United States!

The Nazi predilection for iconographic display made it easy for the American film industry to contribute to the wartime demonization of their Party symbols. The visual debunking of the Nazis in motion pictures was a particularly effective means of employing topical humor as a propaganda weapon. When East Side kid Huntz Hall comes down with "German measles" at the conclusion of *Ghosts on the Loose* (Monogram, 1942), his spots are in the shape of little swastikas. National Socialism is innovatively put down during the scene in *Invisible Agent* where the unseen American hero (made invisible by a drug injection) makes a fatuous Nazi functionary named Heiser repeatedly spill food over the Nazi regalia encompassing his fat girth. The flustered German quite accurately exclaims that it is an "insult to the entire Nazi Party!"

Even the names assigned to Nazi characters have meaningful connotations in wartime Hollywood. The most common and obvious is the prefix "von," an aristocratic signifier. The individual is therefore immediately stigmatized as inherently un-democratic. A few examples: Baron Hugo von Detner (*Nazi Agent*), von Beck (*The Master Race*), Sig von Aschenhausen (*Above Suspicion*), and General von Bodenbach (*The Black Parachute*). There are also names which take on double meanings, perhaps because the name itself has an ulterior connotation. For instance, the evil German commandant of *Till We Meet Again* (Paramount, 1944), Major Krupp, has a surname that was the family name of *the* major German armaments industrial dynasty. Captain Koenig, the Nazi commandant of the Norwegian fishing village of Trollness in *Edge of Darkness* (WB, 1943), has a name which means "king" in German. Early in the film the audience is introduced to Koenig beside a scale model of the village telling a visitor about his "kingdom" and boasting about his "master plan" for occupied territories.

There are also names which sound like other English words: for instance, von *Hard*en in *The North Star*, and von Keller (while meaning "cellar" in German, it also sounds like "killer") in both *This Land Is Mine* and *Northern Pursuit*. The name of the spy Fauscheim in *They Got Me Covered* evokes "faux" (false), and Wilhelm Grimm in *None Shall Escape* is as dour as his name. Some names simply *sound* brutal and unpleasant: Strasser[20] (*Casablanca*), von Rau (*Berlin Correspondent*), von Streger (*My Favorite Blonde*), Blecher and von Ramme (*Watch on the Rhine*), and of course, the unforgettable Anton Schugg of *Counter Espionage*.

Der Fuehrer's Face

The omnipresence of Hitler's image and the swastika make it appear the Fuehrer is participating in and condoning the brutal acts depicted being carried out by members of the Party and military officers. *Berlin Correspondent* opens with the shadow of the swastika looming behind the title and credits. In 1943 alone, Hitler is referred to in 71 war-relevant films. Overall, Hitler is the most often cited individual in the 1942–1945 period, and the eighth most frequently coded reference term overall (in contrast to Hitler's 190 references, Franklin D. Roosevelt is only cited in 103 films). This directed film audience animus upon Hitler and Nazis and away from ordinary Germans—remove the Nazis and Germany will be good again.

The leader image of Hitler is attacked in a number of films. For instance, with obvious irony intended, he is impersonated by a Jewish actor named Bronski in *To Be or Not to Be*. In *The Devil with Hitler* the Nazi leader literally winds up in Hell, demanding to take charge! A chimpanzee made-up to look like Hitler appears in the hilarious Spike Jones number "Schicklegruber," performed in *Meet the People* (MGM, 1944).

Hitler's mustache itself becomes a focal point of the Nazi demonology in a number of films: the dedicated Nazi officer in *The Moon Is Down* is visually set apart (stigmatized) from the professional German military commander by his Hitler mustache. The musical finale of *Priorities on Parade*, which takes place in a defense plant, includes lyrics referring to the workers happily paying 25 cents to watch newsreels of planes they built dropping bombs: "As long as they drop on that mus-

tache [Hitler], I'll go along fighting this fight even if they don't pay me cash."

The unintelligible (to the majority of Americans) words and harshly grating delivery of Hitler's speeches seemed like the rantings of a lunatic. His wild gesticulating and exaggerated facial gestures were simultaneously annoying and amusing. Translated snippets of his rhetoric, full of Nazi catchphrases about the master race and a racially purified Germany's need for more living space, were both offensive and seemingly ridiculous. After all, did the Austrian-born Hitler really fit the bill as a paragon of the blond haired, blue-eyed Ayran superman?

Many of Hollywood's wartime releases contain verbal and visual attacks aimed directly at Hitler. Most insinuate or flatly assert that the Nazi leader is a madman. *The Hitler Gang* begins at the end of WWI, as German Army corporal Hitler is treated for blindness at a military hospital. Although Hitler blames the (temporary) loss of his eyesight on his battle wounds, one of the Army doctors pronounces it "hysterical" blindness. Later in the film, Hitler consults with an astrologer, and follows this quack's advice about his political career. His advisors Himmler and Goebbels chafe at Hitler's irrational actions and frequent tantrums, but they play cleverly on his jealousy and paranoia—first convincing him that his niece, Geli, is unfaithful (Hitler murders her), and later masterminding the "Night of the Long Knives" purge.

The commencement speaker at an officer's graduation ceremony near the end of *Over 21* (Columbia, 1945) reminds his audience of "the victory at Munich [in 1938] of a certain maniac." It is bitterly suggested in *City Without Men* (Columbia, 1943) by a lawyer defending an innocent man charged with aiding foreign agents, that the prewar actions of Hitler should have led to the Fuehrer's incarceration in a lunatic asylum.[21]

Hitler's tantrums and rages are frequently depicted or referred to, often humorously, as in *Miracle at Morgan's Creek* (Paramount, 1944), when he learns of the birth of sextuplets in the United States. Mental hospital director Sig Rumann makes a joke about Hitler needing his "professional services" in *Berlin Correspondent*, but quickly withdraws his remark. To quote a war crimes trial witness in *None Shall Escape*: "How could anyone take that hysterical paperhanger seriously?" This was perhaps the primary underlying question inherent in wartime American films that deal with Hitler. It is in the cinematic treatment regarding questions of Hitler's sanity and his dubious socio-economic background that there are significant differences with the earlier motion pictures portraying his autocratic predecessor, Kaiser Wilhelm (or, as he was familiarly called in America, "Kaiser Bill"—who, while shown to be ruthless and desirous of power, was still a member of European royalty).

There are numerous disparaging film references of an apocryphal nature to Hitler as a pre–World War I laborer, and to his questionable activities in Munich after the war and before he became the leader of the Nazi Party. The snide reference to the "former Munich paperhanger" in *The Conspirators* (WB, 1944) is a typical example of this line of personal attack. In a comical vein, Hitler is called a "cheap non-union house painter" in *The Devil with Hitler*.[22]

Questions are also raised regarding Hitler's legitimacy and the identity of his father (from a propaganda perspective it was largely irrelevant that it was actually his father who was illegitimate). These stories were the origin of the pejorative usage of "Schicklgruber," the maiden name of Hitler's paternal grandmother.[23] The name not only sounded queer to American ears but was obviously code for referring to the Fuehrer as a funny bastard. Lest the reader think this point is being overemphasized by the authors, it should be noted that in at least 22 American films released between 1942 and 1944 "Schicklgruber" is used to refer to Hitler. For example, a bent-over caricature of "Schicklgruber" is enthusiastically swatted on his backside by a group of kids in the Blondie series film *It's a Great Life* (Columbia, 1943). At one point in *Underground Agent* (Columbia, 1943), the hero addresses an Axis gang collectively as "you Schicklgrubers," and in *Watch on the Rhine*, the German military attache in Washington, D.C.—a career soldier, not a Nazi—makes a reference to the upstart Hitler as "Schicklgruber."[24]

On the whole, Hitler was almost universally disparaged in wartime Hollywood as a ranting, largely ineffectual madman. How such an incompetent bumbler could have captured control of the German nation, inspired fanatic loyalty in Nazi Party members, and commanded a military machine that captured most of Europe in less than two years, is not explained. *The Hitler Gang* and *The Master Race* suggest that Hitler was nothing more than a puppet of the German military-industrial complex, but there are still inherent contradictions in Hollywood's portrait of Hitler the buffoon, and the real-life power he possessed.

Nazi Ideology

While ideological matters are usually avoided in Hollywood feature films, some aspects of the Nazi ideology were depicted or discussed during the war. Most of these had some basis in actual Nazi doctrine; however, on screen the Nazis are generally presented as anti-democracy, anti-religion, and anti-family, rather than espousing a particular program of their own (other than Fuehrer-worship).

The expression of Nazi disdain for democracy, especially the so-called "decadent" democracies, becomes a cultural as well as political assault upon Americans' collective idealized conception of themselves. The "New Order," Hitler's fascist and totalitarian plan of government and society, even had a few proponents in England and the United States in the pre-

war years. However, Hollywood Nazis never discuss the advantages of *their* plan, they only criticize others (particularly America). A few examples illustrate the sarcasm and scorn heaped upon the democratic system in these wartime films.

For instance, in *The Great Impersonation* (Universal, 1942), one character remarks: "the day of decadent sentimentality is gone, a new order is here." The "degenerate democracies" of the West are referred to in *Edge of Darkness*, and the head of an Axis spy ring in *Underground Agent* scorns the "fumbling methods of democracies." *Saboteur* (Universal, 1942), although made prior to the outbreak of war (and thus rather hesitant to "name names"), features a home-grown fascist named Tobin (Otto Kruger), who has thrown in his lot with the Nazis. Tobin disdains the concept of democracy, the idea that each citizen has a vote and "all men are created equal." The Nazis appeal to his elitist, upper-class tastes.

In conjunction with this concept of Nazism as a dictatorship of an elite, there are a number of references to Nazi racism, not only regarding Jews, but other races and nationalities as well. In *This Land Is Mine*, Major von Keller refers to the United States as "a charming cocktail of Irish and Jews," and Americans are called "mongrels" in *Lucky Jordan*. The downed Nazi pilot in *Sahara* complains about being searched by a black Sudanese soldier.

Attacks on Jews appear with some frequency, although *None Shall Escape* contains the most detailed depiction of discrimination, violence, and deportation—as well as a graphic scene of a massacre. *Tomorrow, the World* features a Hitler Youth member who brings his anti–Semitism to the United States. In *This Land Is Mine*, Nazi doctrine is imparted to schoolchildren in an occupied nation, inspiring some students to assault one of their classmates and scrawl a "J" on his face. Similarly, in *Commandos Strike at Dawn*, a little Norwegian girl tells her father that a German officer criticized Jews and Poles in a presentation at her school.

The Hitler Gang, a history of the formative years of the Nazi movement, portrays Nazi anti–Semitism as a calculated policy decision, arrived at in an early meeting between Hitler and his advisors. They try to think of a scapegoat, a group upon which to focus their hate and thus provide a rallying point for prospective members. Various suggestions are made. Hitler rejects an assault on the Christian churches, saying the Church is too big to tackle at that moment. As for the Bolsheviks, the Nazis are "not ready for that yet." Finally, Himmler brings up the Jews, and thus the Nazi policy of anti–Semitism is born. Later, when Hitler begins to attack the Jews in public, some founding members of the Party protest this swing away from purely political concerns. But these dissenters are brutally suppressed by Nazi thugs.

Wartime films also contain a number of depictions of Nazi persecution of Christian churches and religious figures. While the post-war revelation of the horrors of the Holocaust tended to overshadow many of the Nazis' other atrocities, there was a determined attempt to subvert the Christian churches in Germany, instituting Nazism as the "state religion." This is again spelled out in *The Hitler Gang*, and also illustrated in *First Comes Courage*, in which a wedding is held before an "altar" featuring Nazi regalia and a copy of *Mein Kampf*. A Hitler Youth member in *They Live in Fear* tells his instructor he is reading "my Bible ... *Mein Kampf*." The teacher approves, since the book points out the "divine power of our Fuehrer."

Even the ubiquitous Iron Cross proudly worn by German officers could be seen as subliminally anti–Christian and blasphemous, a religious symbol awarded for martial skills involving death. Indeed, the very symbol of the Nazi Party—the *swastika*—is also known as a *hakenkreuz*, a "hooked" or "broken" cross. A Hitler Youth member in *They Live in Fear* notes that the Nazi swastika is the "cross doubled," and a sign of strength, while the Christian cross is a "sign of humility."

Individual Nazi atrocities against religious figures appear in a large number of wartime films, most of which are *not* directly related to the aforementioned plan to make Nazism a religion. Instead, these atrocities often occur in occupied nations, and serve to reinforce the image of the Nazis as evil, brutal, anti-religion, anti-*civilization*.

For instance, a Czech priest is callously shot while leading a religious procession in *Hitler's Madman* (Nazi official Heydrich also wipes his feet on the church banner!). Priests are also killed in *The Cross of Lorraine*, *This Land Is Mine*, *Hangmen Also Die*, and *The Hitler Gang*. A Nazi soldier shoots the Mother Superior of a convent in *Till We Meet Again*; at the end of this film, a Nazi officer threatens to send a young novice nun from the same convent to the German military brothels in Poland (mercifully, she is killed instead).

The latter film is just one of at least seven wartime productions featuring explicitly religious imagery in conjunction with Nazi (in one case, Japanese) atrocities: *The North Star*, *Edge of Darkness*, *Song of Russia*, *None Shall Escape*, and *Back to Bataan* (the Japanese example) are the other titles. Each of these films contains a scene in which a victim of Axis brutality is carried or held in a "Pieta"-like pose, evoking memories of the martyred Christ. *The Seventh Cross* contains even more blatant religious imagery—the Nazi concentration camp commandant orders the crucifixion of seven escaped prisoners. One by one, the seven crosses of the title are filled, until only the final one remains vacant.

Nazi assaults upon public education, a primary symbol of democratic states, are extremely significant. The village schoolhouse promotes associative linkages with the one-room schoolhouse of American history. To destroy the source of rational knowledge means the exclusion of the common man and the creation of an ideological elite. Book burnings, well-publicized in real life during the 1930s as examples of Nazi intolerance, appear in *Commandos Strike at Dawn* and *Edge of Darkness*, and are referred to in *Days of Glory*. In *Edge of Darkness*, the town schoolmaster is humiliated and turned out of his

home, which is then converted into a military blockhouse. Charles Laughton is an oppressed schoolteacher in *This Land Is Mine*, who is finally arrested by German troops while teaching about the rights of free men.[25] The Gestapo invade the American Colony school in Berlin on Memorial Day, 1939, in *Hitler's Children*. This film, based on a non-fiction work about the Nazi educational system (*Education for Death*), also contrasts the liberal education policies of the American school with the hate-filled instructional curriculum of Nazi schools.

A related topic addressed in a number of wartime films is the destruction of the family unit by the Nazis, both in Germany and in occupied nations. As with religion, the Nazis insisted that the Party was to take the place of the family. This is depicted in completely negative terms (there are no positive references to a feeling of comradeship, or family loyalty among Party members). Children are taught to inform on their parents and neighbors. The Nazis take children away from their families and raise them to be loyal to Hitler in *Hitler's Children*, *None Shall Escape*, and *The Strange Death of Adolf Hitler*. In *Tomorrow, the World*, a boy becomes a fanatic member of the Hitler Youth despite the fact that the Nazis killed his parents! A Hitler Youth member turns his own mother in for harboring defeatist ideas in *They Live in Fear*: she sadly says she's lost three sons, "one in Russia, one in Italy, and—him." *Bomber's Moon* features an obnoxious little boy, dressed in Hitler Youth regalia, who repeatedly spies on the protagonists of the film, a fleeing American pilot and female Russian medical officer. When he finally proves they are indeed enemies of the Reich, the boy stridently demands his reward!

The institution of marriage and normal sexuality are also under Nazi assault. Hitler is unmarried, but carries on an affair with his youthful niece Geli in *The Hitler Gang*, initially against her will (later, the film implies that he murders her). Goebbels, although a married man with children, is depicted as a womanizer in *Enemy of Women*, and his family is never shown. Wilhelm Grimm, the Nazi protagonist of *None Shall Escape*, is rejected by his fiancee when he returns from WWI; he later rapes a young girl and she commits suicide as a result.

Hitler's Children features a young woman who proudly sleeps with male Nazis and bears children out of wedlock, producing future soldiers for the Reich. The protagonist of *Women in Bondage* is a German woman whose husband has been severely wounded on the Russian front (he later dies). Nazi officials pressure her to bear children by other German soldiers.

Additionally, as discussed in the chapter on the Resistance films, there are numerous examples of lustful German soldiers assaulting women in occupied nations.[26] Their "rights" to these women are discussed in *The Strange Death of Adolf Hitler*. Koenig (Helmut Dantine) brings his Polish mistress (Nancy Coleman) from one conquered nation to another (Norway) in *Edge of Darkness*, treating her as nothing more than a piece of property, part of the spoils of war. Only very rarely—in *The Moon Is Down* and *The Wife Takes a Flyer*, for instance—do German soldiers respect the women they are attracted to (in several of these films, notably *The Moon Is Down* and *Edge of Darkness*, these "romantic" Germans are killed by the women they desire).

The Myth of the Superman

Are we not the supermen,
Aryan-pure supermen?
Jah, we is the supermen,
Super-duper supermen![27]

As with Adolf Hitler, Nazis in general were depicted in wartime films as brutal, evil, and ruthless, but also ineffectual, cowardly, and unintelligent. This could not entirely be reconciled with their recent military accomplishments, but it was calculated to remove any possible positive aspect of their characterization.

Such had not always been the case, at least in regards to the Wehrmacht (Army) and Luftwaffe (Air Force). Prior to 1942, the Nazis were unpopular in America, but the achievements of the German military machine earned at least grudging respect. This is evident as late as 1942 in films like *Grand Central Murder* (MGM), and *Remember the Day* (TCF), where the term "Panzer" is used to convey the impression of power, as in the phrase "You'd need a Panzer division to get through that crowd." This is a reflection of publicity given the "blitzkrieg," in which the German Army overran France, Belgium, Poland, and the Netherlands in relatively short order. The Luftwaffe is also depicted as a powerful force in films about the "Blitz" of London, with numerous scenes of mass destruction appearing in films like *Eagle Squadron* (Universal, 1942), and *A Journey for Margaret* (MGM, 1942). The word "blitz" became jargon for any fast, overwhelming action in romance, business, and sports (the term is still used today in football).

However, these references to the might of the German military machine were quickly suppressed once America joined the war. Indeed, there are very few films released in the 1942–1945 period which show German troops in combat. This reflects the actual situation in western Europe theater: American troops did not engage the Germans in ground combat until the invasion of North Africa (November 1942), so the Nazis were chiefly fighting the Russians on the Eastern front. After the African landings, the recapture of Europe was a long, slow process, beginning with the battle for Sicily (July 1943), the landings on the Italian mainland (September 1943), and finally, D-Day (June 1944), when Allied troops returned to France in force for the first time since Dunkirk (June 1940).

As a result, German soldiers in wartime films are mostly depicted in the role of occupation troops. This provides plenty of opportunities for atrocities and repression of the civilian population, as discussed in the Resistance chapter. In pitched battle with the partisan forces, the Germans either win by dint of overwhelming manpower and arms, or are slaughtered by the brave resistance fighters. While the Germans are ruthless in ruling their captured lands, they are often ineffectual. Individual Nazi characters are occasionally portrayed as efficient (in *Hitler's Madman*, Heydrich orders a rubber stamp of his signature so he can sign execution orders faster!), but for the most part even these characters are usually outwitted by Allied agents, downed airmen, and members of the Resistance.

As opposed to the usual negative and humorless treatment of Japanese film characters, Germans displaying unquestioning obedience to authority are as likely to be mocked as to be abhorred. There is the fatuous sergeant played by Sig Rumann in *Tarzan Triumphs* (RKO, 1943), whose favorite epithet is "swine!" Rumann, a middle-aged, German-born character actor, had earlier played an incompetent Gestapo man in the satiric United Artists release, *To Be or Not to Be* (UA, 1942). In *Berlin Correspondent*, Rumann is also an instrument of Nazi policy, as the director of a mental hospital whose "deranged" patients are deliberately killed (a clear reference to the euthanasia of "mental defectives," which was carried out in Germany well before the mass execution of Jews began).[28]

An SS commander portrayed by Raymond Massey in *Desperate Journey* (WB, 1942) is constantly frustrated by the cocky antics of a group of downed Allied fliers who have escaped captivity—Massey had a similar role as an ineffectual revolutionary French police chief attempting to entrap and eliminate his insouciant English nemesis in *The Scarlet Pimpernel* (London Films, 1934). Ironically, Massey would later portray a non-Nazi German officer in *Hotel Berlin* (WB, 1945), who is coerced into committing suicide by the Nazi hierarchy (perhaps a reference to the fate of Field Marshal Erwin Rommel, implicated in the July 20, 1944, plot to kill Hitler).

The *Motion Picture Herald*'s analysis of the leading Nazi in *The Wife Takes a Flyer* (Columbia, 1942) is amusingly informative. Played by the fortyish comedian Allyn Joslyn, Major Zellfritz (Fritz being slang for a German and "on the fritz" for being out of order) is described in the review as having "more swish than swastika" and as being a "dolt wielding a power beyond his intelligence to control, and mouthing the catchwords of the Nazi credo in futile misapplication to trivia."[29]

Film portrayals of actual Nazi leaders are careful to avoid any suggestion of decency. Both the film "biography" of Hitler and the Nazi Party—*The Hitler Gang*—and the film "biography" of Goebbels—*Enemy of Women*—begin after the protagonists are grown men. There are no scenes of boyhood or family life, no indication why these men became the monstrous dictator and his right-hand man.

As mentioned earlier, Hitler is mercilessly lampooned and caricatured. Goebbels and Goering are widely viewed as his closest associates, and thus come in for a good deal of criticism as well. A merchant ship captain in *U-Boat Prisoner*

(Columbia, 1944) says "a little paperhanger, a man with a club foot, and a strutting fathead have a lot to answer for."

Dr. Joseph Goebbels, Minister of Propaganda, frequently impersonated by Martin Kosleck (as early as *Confessions of a Nazi Spy*, 1939) is portrayed as a cadaverous, weasel-faced, club-footed plotter.[30] However, his role as spokesman for the Third Reich also provided opportunities for irony. At the end of *Enemy of Women*, having just survived a bomber raid that destroyed his own home, all Goebbels (Paul Andor) can do is deny the effectiveness of the Allies' strategic bombing campaign and impotently assert that Germany is destined to achieve final victory!

"Fatso" Goering is more often referred to, than impersonated. As head of the Luftwaffe, he became the butt of various jokes in this context, and his physical appearance (grossly overweight, heavily bemedaled) also served as fodder for Allied wisecracks.[31] In *The Hitler Gang*, he does appear on screen (played by Alexander Pope), and is treated even more harshly than Hitler or Goebbels. After the Munich "Beer Hall Putsch," the wounded Goering asks his wife for morphine to dull the pain. She says, "I can't bear to see you starting it *again*," indicating that Goering had previously had a drug abuse problem. Sent to a nursing home in Sweden to recover, he is next seen running amok ("Get the strait-jacket!"), and is finally sent to an insane asylum after he attacks a nurse in an attempt to obtain morphine. But when Hitler comes to power, who is named head of the Luftwaffe? Hermann Goering.

All of these images of Nazism, whether serious or comic, are intended to reinforce dislike and contempt for the enemy on the part of American audiences. The OWI was constantly warning filmmakers not to portray our enemies as invincible supermen *or* bumbling idiots: either extreme was misleading and possibly harmful. Consequently, Hollywood tried to portray the Nazis as evil and capable of doing great damage, but vulnerable when confronted by the forces of democracy. At times the monocles, goosestepping and heiling may have appeared more amusing than menacing, yet the threat posed by followers of Hitler's New Order was very real. The consequence of failing to defeat the Third Reich was nothing less than the destruction of the democratic ideal held sacred by Americans.

2. Smiles of Deceit: The Cinematic Extermination of Japan

For most Americans, the war was about revenge against the Japanese. [32]

Pearl Harbor was not only the immediate cause for the United States' entrance into the Second World War, it also clearly defined for most Americans our primary enemy in the conflict. Revenge for the sneak "Jap" attack on the U.S. Pacific Fleet remained the paramount source of war motivation for many Americans. This would continue to be the case throughout the war, even though the "Europe First" policy of the Allies meant American casualties from combat with the *Germans* were beginning to mount by the latter part of 1942.[33]

This anti–Japanese feeling is displayed even in films set in the European theatre of war, such as *Action in the North Atlantic* (WB, 1943), *Desperate Journey* (WB, 1942) and *Journey for Margaret* (MGM, 1942); in each of these films, verbal attacks are delivered at the *Japanese* despite the fact that the visible enemy on screen is the Germans!

In fact, the last film mentioned above is one of nearly 50 references in 1942 explicitly evoking the collective American memory of the Pearl Harbor attack. Segments of FDR's "Day of Infamy" speech are heard in several films (as radio broadcasts), including *Flying Tigers* (Republic, 1942), *The Navy Comes Through* (RKO, 1942) and *God Is My Co-Pilot* (WB, 1945). At least two other films, *The Sullivans* (TCF, 1944) and *Pride of the Marines* (WB, 1945), show American families gathered for Sunday dinner when they hear the news over the radio about Pearl Harbor. The father (Thomas Mitchell) of the Sullivan boys sums it up: "No good dirty sneaks.... These Japs will be sorry they were born."

America's rage at the treacherous assault on Pearl Harbor—coming as it did before a formal declaration of war by Japan—is illustrated by the score of films containing explicit references to the Kurusu-Nomura diplomatic mission to Washington, D.C. The fact that Kurusu and Admiral Nomura delivered Japan's war message to U. S. Secretary of State Cordell Hull several hours *after* the bombing of Pearl Harbor was considered proof the Japanese were inherently sneaky and never to be trusted. Newsreel footage of the duo was reissued after Pearl Harbor, with new narration describing their apparently peaceful actions although they had "mass murder in their hearts."

Nearly half of these "Kurusu" films, including *Across the Pacific* (WB), *Little Tokyo USA* (TCF) and *The War Against Mrs. Hadley* (MGM), were released in 1942. At the beginning of *Remember Pearl Harbor!* (Republic, 1942), an American reporter in Manila "interviews" Kurusu about his peace mission to Washington (courtesy of rather crude intercutting between *studio* footage of the reporter and *newsreel* footage of the Japanese diplomat). In *Salute to the Marines* (MGM, 1942), retired U.S. Marine Wallace Beery, referring to Kurusu's "peace" mission *before* the attack on Pearl Harbor, presciently remarks: "I wouldn't believe that there little bow-legged, four-eyed monkey if he was standing on a stack of Bibles as high as the Washington Monument." While defending their isolated American outpost against Japanese invaders in *Wake Island* (Paramount, 1942), some Marines bitterly recall exchanging toasts to peace and to the Japanese Emperor with members of the Kurusu-Nomura mission (one of whom is portrayed as a buck-toothed, glasses-wearing caricature) while the diplomats' plane was at Wake for refueling on its way to Washington.

Sometimes the desire for revenge upon the Japanese for "starting the war" is motivated by highly personal reasons. One of the Marine pilots in *Wake Island* makes a suicidal bombing attack on the Japanese invasion fleet to avenge the death of his wife (an innocent civilian) in the Pearl Harbor raid (*Air Force* includes scenes of wounded women and children after the attack). Similarly, a nurse (played by Veronica Lake) in *So Proudly We Hail!* (Paramount, 1943) wants to "kill Japs" because her fiancé was strafed and killed as he tried to get to his fighter during the attack. In *The Sullivans*, one factor contributing to the five brothers' enlistment in the U.S. Navy is the loss of a neighbor's son in the explosion of the battleship *Arizona* at Pearl Harbor. Similarly, a Marine volunteering for a special mission in *Gung Ho!* (Universal, 1943) does so because his brother had been killed during the attack on the Hawaiian naval base: "They didn't find enough of him to bury." Don Barry's suicidal attack on an invading Japanese force in the Philippines in *Remember Pearl Harbor!* is made in memory of an Army friend (killed by Japanese spies), *and* in the honor of another buddy's father, who has just been killed at Pearl Harbor.

Although it was the primary such reference, "Remember Pearl Harbor!" was not the only rallying cry for Americans in 1942 and 1943. Several films invoke the memory of Wake Island, which fell to the Japanese on December 25, 1941. Less than 400 Marines held out against 13 Japanese assaults before succumbing to vastly superior numbers.[34] One of Edward G. Robinson's Army buddies in *Mr. Winkle Goes to War* (Columbia, 1944) expresses the desire to "strangle ... [a] Jap" for his brother, a member of the ill-fated garrison on Wake Island. That wish becomes his final act during an engagement with the enemy on a Pacific island. *Busses Roar* (WB, 1942) concludes with its Marine hero melodramatically punching a Japanese spy in the face, in memory of his fallen leatherneck comrades on Wake Island.

A number of other war-related motion pictures feature the conversion of formerly politically apathetic individuals to active resistance against the Axis after learning of Japan's surprise December 1941 assaults on Pearl Harbor, the Philippines, and Hong Kong: *Invisible Agent* (Universal, 1942), *Secret Agent of Japan* (TCF, 1942), *Mug Town* (Monogram, 1942), *To the Shores of Tripoli* (TCF, 1942), *Two Yanks in Trinidad* (Columbia, 1942) and *Pride of the Marines* (WB, 1945) are just a few examples.

As illustrated by the title of one film, *Betrayal from the East* (RKO, 1945), many Americans felt the Japanese attack was a form of unmitigated oriental knavery against a peaceful, trusting and essentially altruistic American people.[35] Quite a few films thus make a point of featuring an evil Japanese officer who has been exposed to the culture of the United States (a number of highly placed Japanese, including Admiral Yamamato and Foreign Minister Matsuoka, had in fact spent time in the United States; most films using this theme

feature Japanese officers who received their college educations here). But instead of showing gratitude or even an understanding of Americans, these supposedly cosmopolitan and enlightened Japanese are cruel and disdainful enemies.

Samurai (Cavalcade Pictures, 1945) tells the story of a Japanese orphan who is raised in California, but abandons his adopted country and becomes a militaristic Japanese agent who spends his time planning the invasion of California! The theme of Japanese "ingratitude" is also particularly strong in *Behind the Rising Sun* (RKO, 1943), *We've Never Been Licked* (Universal, 1943), *The Purple Heart* (TCF, 1944) and *First Yank Into Tokyo* (RKO, 1945).

In *Behind the Rising Sun*, a Japanese graduate (Tom Neal) of Cornell University actively participates in atrocities perpetrated by Japan's forces in China against the civilian population. *The Purple Heart* features captured American airmen who are prosecuted by a pompous Japanese officer (Richard Loo), while their court-appointed Japanese lawyer lets them know his professional credentials include a degree from Princeton in 1931 (the year Japan initiated imperial acts of aggression against China by seizing Manchuria). Loo also plays a college student in *Betrayal from the East*—his role as a Stanford football cheerleader allows him to travel around the West Coast and keep in contact with his spy ring! And in *First Yank Into Tokyo*, the American-educated, football-loving Japanese officer (again played by Richard Loo) who commanded troops during the Bataan Death March, abuses Western inmates of a prison camp on the Japanese home islands, forcing them to work in a munitions factory. *We've Never Been Licked* actually portrays Japanese students involved in prewar espionage while attending the prestigious private military college, Texas A&M.

The shock of the brilliantly executed attack upon Pearl Harbor and the series of Japanese victories against the western colonial empires in the Pacific during the first six months of the war was compounded by the generally held racist misconception that the Japanese were inherently incapable of mastering western technology and military science—particularly ironic in light of the Japanese defeat of Russia in 1905. This belief lent credence to the theory that Japan's victories were only possible through treachery, misuse of western education and technology, and help from their German allies.[36]

A number of films, for instance, mention the United States' sale of strategic materials (particularly scrap metal) to Japan, a practice that continued until mid-1941. This economic policy is strongly condemned (in hindsight) as having given the Japanese weapons which were then used on Americans.

In *So Proudly We Hail!*, concern is voiced at a field hospital on Bataan about a soldier's wounds becoming infected, but an Army surgeon states: "Not likely — probably good American steel." After an American submarine captain and a young sailor disarm an unexploded Japanese aerial bomb wedged between the deck and the hull of their submarine in

Destination Tokyo, the officer (Cary Grant) bitterly notes: "It [the fuse] has 'Made in the USA' stamped on it." A crew member on a bombing mission in *Aerial Gunner* (Paramount, 1943) claims they should dedicate their bombs to his uncle, explaining that the man formerly sold scrap iron to the Japanese. Another airman jauntily responds: "Let's give 'em some *free!*"[37] In *God Is My Co-Pilot*, a cocky Japanese ace named Tokyo Joe (Richard Loo) flies over a Flying Tigers airbase and taunts his American opponents: "Come on up and get a load of that scrap metal you sold us." When Japanese tanks appear during the offensive in the Philippines in *Salute to the Marines*, retired Marine Wallace Beery is not surprised: "What do you think they've been doing with that scrap iron we sold them, taking it for their anemia?"

In spite of the proven effectiveness of such Japanese military equipment as the Zero fighter and the oxygen-powered Long Lance torpedo (which was superior to any U.S. torpedo of the period), "Made in Japan" retained its preexisting negative connotations throughout the war—appearing in several films, such as *The Princess and the Pirate* (RKO, 1944) and *It Ain't Hay* (Universal, 1943). An insidious linkage is made between inferior products and an inferior race in *Abroad with Two Yanks* (UA, 1944) when a Marine on leave in Australia disparages the quality of a pair of souvenir binoculars: "These glasses are as squint-eyed as that Jap I took 'em off of."

This negative attitude toward the technological capabilities of the Japanese is also reflected in Columbia's early 1943 release, *Two-Man Submarine*. Apparently only German agents can adequately understand the work of Allied scientists on a Pacific island who are attempting to perfect a penicillin formula. The Nazis ask their Japanese "partners" only to provide a submarine for their proposed getaway with the purloined formula.[38]

Such assertions illustrate the second significant component (after outrage about Pearl Harbor) of America's anti–Japanese attitude during the war—racism. This was a tenuous matter at best, given the conflicting allegiances of Japan and China, both Asian nations—Japan was our enemy but China was our ally; Hirohito and Tojo were bad, but Chiang Kaishek was good—so the Japanese were to be disparaged as a *nationality* and a *culture* rather than a *race*. Hollywood attempted to tone down overt racial comments, while concentrating its attacks on Japanese society. This met with mixed success, particularly in the first year of the war when anti–Japanese sentiment was at its peak.

Examples of Hollywood's deliberate attacks on Japan's culture include *Mountain Rhythm* (Republic, 1942), in which the hillbilly Weaver family occupies the home of a Japanese farming family that has been "relocated" to an internment camp. The Weavers are so infuriated by the short and uncomfortable (to them) furnishings, that they make a bonfire out of them the next day! Japanese food is denigrated in several films: in *Guadalcanal Diary*, a Marine knocks over a table

with rice cakes in disgust; in *Marine Raiders*, the comic cook (Frank McHugh) calls a stew made with captured "Jap" food "Yaki Suki," and another Marine throws in his old boot for "flavor."

Even these "cultural" references are undeniably tinged with racism—wartime films dealing with Germany rarely criticize German culture (in fact, there are a number of references to the Nazi *suppression* of German culture), and while Italians are often caricatured as an opera-loving, spaghetti-eating nation, no particular attacks are launched on either opera or Italian food.

The level of vituperation directed at the Japanese enemy is extremely high in wartime American films. More than 50 motion pictures with five or more pejorative references to the Japanese (most often the words "Japs" and "Nips") have been identified—averaging more than 10 negative references per film. Five of these motion pictures contain over thirty instances of verbal abuse directed at the Japanese, while *Manila Calling* (TCF, 1942), *Air Force* (WB, 1943) and *Guadalcanal Diary* (TCF, 1943) each reach a count of at least thirty-five! Whereas many of the "Nazi" or "Hitler" coding references are self-referents delivered by German characters (such as the familiar "Heil Hitler" salutation), the overwhelming majority of coding references to Japanese are unequivocally negative racial slurs (most frequently delivered in Combat genre films). When combined with the many casual pejorative references (there were a total of 85 films with a "Japanese" coding in 1942; 15 of these with five or more negative references), American movie audiences were being subjected to an unrelenting rhetorical barrage of contempt for our Japanese enemy.

In addition to the recurrent use of "Jap" and "Nip," the Japanese were frequently dehumanized by literally comparing them with animals (usually simians), insects and vermin (almost always rats).[39] The racial aspects of these slurs are reaffirmed by linking these verbal assaults with such racially derogatory expressions as "little" (in stature), "buck-toothed," "yellow," "bow-legged" and "slant-eyed." The resulting compound negatives include "slant-eyed baboon" in *Escape from Hong Kong* (Universal, 1942), "bow-legged baboon" in *Lure of the Islands* (Monogram, 1942), and the lurid invective used by career Marine sergeant Wallace Beery in *Salute to the Marines*: he refers to the Japanese as "little yellow mustard-colored monkeys" (these remarks despite the fact that he has been working with and training Filipino soldiers, apparently harboring no such racial prejudice against *them*; he says "You're just as good Americans as anybody [born in the USA].").

In *Busses Roar*, another Marine sergeant explains to a black porter that his gun is for "little slant-eyed yellow-bellied sharks" (with a double meaning for yellow: Asian *and* cowardly). An insect/analogy variation on the longtime fear of menacing yellow hordes is the following comment, made in *China Girl* (TCF, 1943): "Don't be surprised if in the near future they [the Japanese Army] are ... crawling all over Burma like eight million bedbugs in green pants."[40] In *Marine Raiders*, a Marine responds to the taunts of unseen "Japs" with: "You dirty bunch of dog meat." *Prisoner of Japan* (PRC, 1942) contains the choice comparison of the Japanese to "slimy sea snails."

Numerous American films include positive and sympathetic portrayals of anti–Nazi Germans and German-Americans—frequently as members of a traditional family whose values as well as their physical well-being are threatened by the ideological paladins of the Nazi state. But only one war-time American motion picture, *Behind the Rising Sun*, develops any sympathetic Japanese characters.

Little Tokyo, USA implicitly criticizes the Japanese family: spy Satsuma (Abner Biberman), beats his young son after the boy brags about his father's powerful radio, and suggests that the boy could even be killed if he lets any more information slip out. Teru (June Duprez), Satsuma's grown "daughter" is used as bait to lure American detective Steele (Preston Foster) into a trap, and is then coldly murdered by Axis agent Hendricks to frame the policeman. In *Behind the Rising Sun*, the militaristic protagonist voices his approval of the Japanese practice of selling their daughters into prostitution.

Ironically, the rabidly anti–Japanese *Little Tokyo, USA* is one of only two Hollywood releases to (briefly) show a patriotic Japanese-American. This character (played by Richard Loo in one of his few positive roles of the war years) helps uncover Japanese espionage activities in the U.S., and is rewarded by never being seen alive again, having been promptly decapitated by enemy agents, the "accepted Black Dragon method of eliminating people."[41]

For that matter, most Japanese characters in wartime Hollywood are seldom developed at all—unlike a number of their evil Nazi counterparts, they largely remain stereotyped abstractions. One need only attempt to find a Japanese equivalent of the distinctive German officers portrayed by Erich von Stroheim in *Five Graves to Cairo* and *The North Star* (RKO, 1943), or the Nazis portrayed by Conrad Veidt in *Casablanca* and *Nazi Agent* (MGM, 1942). A few of the exceptions to this include the young Cornell-educated Japanese officer in *Behind the Rising Sun*, the Japanese secret agent played by Peter Lorre in *Invisible Agent*, the characterization of Tojo by Robert Armstrong in *Blood on the Sun* (UA, 1945), and Richard Loo's portrayal of "Tokyo Joe" in *God Is My Co-Pilot*.

Most often, though, wartime cinematic portrayals of the Japanese enemy are little more than vicious racial stereotypes. A few of the most outrageous examples include the "Banzai"-shouting, samurai sword-wielding fanatics disrupting a courtroom in *The Purple Heart* (TCF, 1944) and the cruelly lecherous Japanese officer, played by Anglo actor Harold Huber, in *Lady from Chungking* (PRC, 1942) and again in *Dragon Seed* (MGM, 1944). Other white actors who appeared in Japanese roles during the war include Abner Biberman, Peter Lorre, Mike Mazurki, Noel Madison, Ernest Dorian, J. Carrol Naish, I. Stanford Jolley, Ivan Lebedeff, George E. Stone,

Prisoner of Japan (PRC, 1942): Action-packed three-sheet poster for this tale of Japanese treachery in the Pacific.

and Johnny Arthur. Ironically, the two Asian actors who most commonly portrayed evil Japanese were Chinese-American actor Richard Loo and Korean-American actor Philip Ahn.[42]

There are also a number of films which—while featuring Japan as the primary enemy—show few if any Japanese characters in detail. *Bataan*, for instance, shows the invading Japanese in long shot, as shadowy figures only half-seen amid jungle foliage, or in brief shots during furious battle scenes. *Manila Calling* and *Marine Raiders* follow a similar pattern, and films concentrating on naval and air warfare—*Destination Tokyo, Air Force, Wing and a Prayer*, for instance—are often content with brief shots of Japanese pilots (usually in their death throes as their plane is shot down) and anonymous naval crewmen scrambling into action.

Unlike the ubiquitous Hitler and Mussolini impersonations during the war (Hitler's name appears in the *title* of six wartime feature films!), Japan's two primary bogeymen—Emperor Hirohito and Premier Hideki Tojo—were more often referred to than depicted. Emperor Hirohito is referred to over forty times in war-relevant Hollywood releases. Although Tojo's name is invoked only half as many times as his emperor's, he is more frequently verbally abused. For instance, in *The Fighting Seabees* (Republic, 1944) the Japanese enemy is pejoratively referred to as "Tojo and his bug-eyed baboons." In *The Sullivans*, one of five sons serving on a cruiser in the Pacific, writes home: "Tell Papa to save up a good quid [of chewing tobacco] and maybe we can fix it so he can spit it right in Tojo's eye." A serious portrayal of Tojo—widely seen as one of the chief architects of Japan's militarist clique—appears in *Blood on the Sun*, set in 1920s Japan.

Hirohito is impersonated, briefly, as a buck-toothed caricature wearing glasses, with a painted rising sun on his chest, standing alongside Hitler and Mussolini during a musical number in *Star Spangled Rhythm* (Paramount, 1942). This is apparently the only time a Hollywood actor impersonated the Japanese Emperor during the war. An image (a painting, photo, or caricature) of Hirohito appears in a few other films, including *Behind the Rising Sun, Pilot No. 5* and *Government Girl* (RKO, 1943). A particularly unflattering interpretation, pairing him with a likeness of Hitler on a dart board, appears in the latter film. The heads of all three Axis leaders are portrayed on a "test your strength" machine at a war bonds rally in *Mountain Rhythm* (Republic, 1942). The top prize is awarded only to those who have the power to propel the metal ball to "Hirohito" at the top—his eyes roll and his hair pops up when his head is hit.

Although Hirohito could be the butt of sarcastic remarks and jokes, direct suggestions of death for the Emperor, such as fitting him for a "wooden kimono" (i.e., a coffin) in a musical number from *Panama Hattie*, are comparatively rare. Another example occurs when, in a pointed musical gesture, Louis Armstrong's "I'll Be Glad When You're Dead, You Rascal You" is "dedicated to Hirohito" on a radio request show in *Reveille with Beverly* (Republic, 1943).[43] This general reluctance to have an actor impersonate the Emperor or to openly call for his demise may reflect an early decision on the part of American officials to preserve the institution of the Emperor. Otherwise, it is difficult to understand why Hirohito was not abused as regularly as Hitler and Mussolini—indeed, in sev-

eral films (notably *The Devil with Hitler* and *That Nazty Nuisance*—UA, 1942 and 1943) Hitler and Mussolini are joined by a Japanese character who is pointedly *not* the Emperor.[44] In the first film "Suki Yaki" (George E. Stone) is identified as a diplomat from the Japanese war department, and in the latter "Suki Yaki" is portrayed as an effete Japanese general (played by the whiny-voiced Johnny Arthur; for a time this character is mistakenly believed to have been turned into an orangutan by a magic trick).

These thinly veiled (sometimes not even that) racial attacks on the Japanese are often cloaked in terms of Japan's militaristic bent and blamed on their "foreign" culture. Hollywood seized upon examples of Japanese "barbarism" and "atrocities," embellishing them and blaming them on the "code of *Bushido*," which, like Nazism, would have to be eradicated after the war by the victorious Allies in order to prevent Japan from repeatedly posing a threat to world peace.

Virtually every wartime Hollywood film dealing with Japan contains one or more "atrocities" (or at the very least, specific references to such acts).[45] In our study, "atrocity" is defined as any act depicted as being contrary to the rules of "civilized" nations. These include torture, murder, execution of civilians (or military personnel without cause), abuse of prisoners, and so on:

An endless stream of evidence ranging from atrocities to suicidal tactics could be cited ... to substantiate the belief that the Japanese were a uniquely contemptible and formidable foe who deserved no mercy and virtually demanded extermination.[46]

Some of these atrocities are meant to display Japanese "barbarism," as the Japanese actively attack institutions of Western civilization. For instance, the Japanese bomb or attack hospitals and churches and show disrespect and hostility towards religion in *Corregidor* (PRC, 1943), *Salute to the Marines, Air Force, China Sky, The Story of Dr. Wassell,* and *China's Little Devils*, among other films. A Japanese Christian is persecuted in *Behind the Rising Sun* (a film that "hit a new high in atrocities").[47] Western missionaries oppose Japanese aggression in *China's Little Devils* and *Flying Tigers*. A school principal in the Philippines is hung from a flagpole in *Back to Bataan*.

Other atrocities are more personal in nature. Women are raped, or threatened with rape, in *Behind the Rising Sun, China, Dragon Seed,* and *So Proudly We Hail!*. The "Rape of Nanking," which occurred in 1937, is cited several times. Civilians, including women and children, are killed, brutalized, sexually assaulted, tortured and given opium-laced candy (*Behind the Rising Sun, Dragon Seed, China's Little Devils, China, Back to Bataan*).

Near the beginning of *Flying Tigers*, a Chinese child is shown eating at an aid station near the airfield, next to crates labeled "United China Relief." Suddenly, Japanese bombers raid the field; when the smoke clears, there is a shot of the injured child crying amidst the debris.[48] A similar shot occurs in *Bataan*: a refugee column is passing by, and one American soldier is shown carrying a little Filipino girl on his shoulders. After a Japanese attack from the air, all that remains is a pile of rubble with her hand sticking out, and the G.I.'s cap lying nearby.

Japan's brutal treatment of Allied soldiers and prisoners of war is depicted in a number of films. Even an escapist comedy like the Danny Kaye vehicle *Up in Arms* (RKO, 1944) features a sequence in which the hapless Kaye is captured and tortured by Japanese soldiers (although he turns the tables and winds up taking them all prisoner). In *Marine Raiders*, Robert Ryan loses control of his emotions when he finds a friend tied to a tree (openly imitating crucifixion)—his hands and feet have been chopped off. More mutilation victims appear (obliquely shown, of course) in *Objective Burma!* (WB, 1945), and a dying soldier begs to be killed by his own comrades after falling victim to Japanese torture. One of the Filipino soldiers who tries to cross the Japanese lines in *Bataan* is caught and tortured to death, his butchered remains left hanging for his comrades to find.

Prisoners of war are tortured in *Bombardier* and *The Purple Heart*. The Bataan "Death March," which occurred after the fall of the Philippines in early 1942, did not become common knowledge in the United States until the following year. It is recreated in *Back to Bataan*, as tired, hungry, and wounded men are driven mercilessly by brutal Japanese guards, then shot or bayoneted when they drop from exhaustion.[49] *First Yank Into Tokyo* is largely set in a Japanese POW camp, where the prisoners are forced into slave labor. In *God Is My Co-Pilot*, a prison camp scene features Japanese guards abusing men, women and children. To illustrate the fact that Japanese militarism was no recent phenomenon, *Jack London* (UA, 1943) depicts Japanese mistreatment (and outright mass execution) of Russian prisoners during the Russo-Japanese War.

Close analysis of several films shows Hollywood's careful orchestration of its attacks on Japan. *Back to Bataan* and *Behind the Rising Sun* demonstrate two aspects of the treatment of the Japanese enemy during the war.

Back to Bataan is a Combat/Resistance film and, like many such pictures, depersonalizes the Japanese. In all of the battle scenes the Japanese are mowed down mercilessly, often at long distance. American and Filipino defeats take place offscreen (very few Allied soldiers are killed or wounded in the battle scenes), and the overall impression is of a Japanese horde, easily killed but capable of overwhelming our defenses simply by weight of numbers.

Individualized Japanese characters appear in a few scenes, but no single character stands out or appears in more than a couple of sequences. For example, General Homma (Leonard Strong) is introduced (drinking, in the company of three geishas); he tells Dalisay Delgado—whom he believes to be a collaborator—that the Japanese look on the Filipinos as their "nieces and nephews." But he warns her ominously that the

Japanese will be strict masters. Homma appears again after the Allied guerrillas have become increasingly successful in their raids on the occupying forces. In an interesting scene, he queries his officers (Richard Loo and Philip Ahn) about their failure to stop the attacks, flashing a reflection from the blade of his dagger in their faces as he speaks. However, he never appears again in the film. In real life, General Homma was in command of the Philippines at the time of the Bataan Death March, and was executed after the war for his part in the atrocities.

Abner Biberman has a flashy scene as the brutal Japanese captain who hangs the Filipino school principal when the old man refuses to haul down the American flag, but he is seen only once more, this time being hung by the guerrillas from the same flagpole. Ahn and Loo appear briefly in several scenes, but are not personalized to any extent. Benson Fong is cast as another Japanese officer, again without any particular distinguishing traits. "Prince Ito" (Harold Fong), who represents the Imperial Family at the Philippines Independence celebration, is a crude stereotype: short of stature, thick glasses, heavily bemedaled uniform, thick accent. He appears only in the independence day sequence.

The absence of a chief villain—such as those which appear in many anti–Nazi resistance films—tends to undermine the film's impact in some ways. True, the Japanese are shown to be ruthless and brutal (including: rape, shooting civilian hostages in reprisal for resistance acts, hanging the schoolteacher, torturing a young Filipino boy, mistreating prisoners) but these atrocities seem relatively mild since they are performed by anonymous (indeed, in most cases *faceless*) Japanese soldiers. On the other hand, this tends to support the concept that *all* Japanese are bloodthirsty, sneaky, cruel, and untrustworthy, and avoids the Nazi/good German dichotomy found in many films set in Europe.

There are some interesting touches in *Back to Bataan*: the Japanese decide to grant "independence" to the Philippines (the U.S. had already promised, as the film notes, that the Philippines would be freed on July 4, 1946), but chiefly as a propaganda ploy (the ceremony is broadcast on the radio and filmed by the Japanese). In several scenes, the Japanese refer to the Filipinos as fellow Asians who have been "exploited" by the white man, a racial theme which was also mentioned in *Little Tokyo, USA*, and *Blood on the Sun*.[50]

Behind the Rising Sun, on the other hand, is one of the very few wartime films set in Japan, and practically the only film to concentrate on Japanese characters (there are a few non–Asian characters in the film—Americans O'Hara, an engineer, and Sarah, a reporter; a Russian, Boris; and a German, Max—but the film focuses on Taro, played by Tom Neal). The film bears some similarity to *Hitler's Children* (both films were written by Emmett Lavery and directed by Edward Dmytryk), but whereas *Hitler's Children* is just one of a number of films set in Germany which feature developed German characters,

Behind the Rising Sun is practically alone in transposing this formula to Japan.

Taro (Tom Neal) is the son of a powerful Japanese publisher (J. Carrol Naish), who returns to Japan from college (Cornell) in the United States in 1936. The day he arrives, Japanese militarists murder liberal minister Takayashi, the latest in a series of political assassinations which have gradually been eroding the liberal opposition to the militarist clique. Taro is called up for military duty after the war in China breaks out in earnest (1937). At first, Taro is shocked by the atrocities committed by Japanese troops: women and children are abused, opium-laced food is doled out to the Chinese people. However, he gradually becomes callous—in one scene, he closes his office window to shut out the screams of women and children—and then joins in as an active participant in the brutal subjugation of China. By 1941, even Taro's father says "My son is nothing more than a savage." Taro joins the air corps, and when war is declared on the United States, he is overjoyed. However, he is killed when his fighter is shot down during an Allied air raid on Tokyo.

Taro's character is virtually an inversion of Karl Bruner (Tim Holt) in *Hitler's Children*. Taro moves away from his pro–Western stance (he sings a college song while bathing, and wears a robe with a large "C" embroidered on it), eventually becoming imperialistic, racist, and militaristic. Karl, indoctrinated into Nazism by the Hitler Youth movement, gradually comes to realize that his beliefs are wrong, largely through his relationship with Anna (Bonita Granville). Taro, on the other hand, is *not* redeemed by the humanistic views of his girlfriend, Tana (Margo); in fact, when she is arrested by the "Thought Police" after the attack on Pearl Harbor, Taro coldly testifies against her at her trial!

A comparison of the two films' treatment of the "enemy" protagonists indicates Hollywood's differing views of Germany and Japan. Karl represents the German people under the influence of Nazism; he is "saved" by his love for Anna, thus demonstrating that the Germans are not intrinsically evil. Taro, on the other hand, first appears showing the benefits of his Western education, but this positive veneer is gradually stripped away and his essential nature—and by inference, that of the Japanese people—is revealed.

Taro's father, who narrates the film in flashback, also undergoes a metamorphosis during the course of the film, but is at all times presented as an atypical Japanese. He expresses no preference for either the liberals or militarists during the 1936 disturbances. He is a product of the "feudal society" still prevalent in Japan, one of the "great families" which dominates the country. However, he sees his son gradually becoming less human under the influence of the Japanese war machine, and apologizes to O'Hara for Taro's behavior: "Today my son is nothing more than a savage." After Taro's death, Naish commits suicide, and the film ends with his words: "To whatever gods are left in this world, destroy us as we have destroyed others … destroy us before it is too late."

Behind the Rising Sun, in addition to its unusually detailed portraits of Taro, Tana, and Taro's father, contains a number of other interesting details calculated to cast Japanese society in an unfavorable light. While there are some comparisons between the Japanese militarists and the Nazis—the "Thought Police," atrocities, racist attitudes and imperialistic goals—the national character of all Japan is also criticized. For example, a harmless baseball game (played for fun in Brooklyn, one character remarks) becomes a "military exercise" in the "warrior state" of Japan. Later, in a scene very similar to ones in *The Purple Heart* and *Jack London*, news of the Marco Polo Bridge incident (which signaled the outbreak of open hostilities between Japan and China in July 1937) sparks a raucous demonstration by Japanese soldiers in a bar: they shoot at the bottles behind the bar, perform a wild "samurai sword dance," and wildly shout "Banzai!" Japanese contempt for other nations is openly expressed by several characters. In one scene, Taro's superior officer tells him "the Chinese are just so many animals"; later, Taro cheers the attack on Pearl Harbor as the beginning of the "white war." As mentioned earlier, *Behind the Rising Sun* also features a number of atrocities, including rape and murder, abuse of women and children, and torture (needles under the fingernails, crucifixion). All of these point to the Japanese as a "naturally" barbaric race, and suggest that the militarists are merely exploiting these tendencies rather than brainwashing an entire nation.[51]

If Hollywood thus identified the Japanese as a barbaric race capable of committing war crimes and atrocities, it is not surprising that the Japanese enemy in wartime films are treated with a greater degree of callousness than either Germans or Italians. While, as discussed earlier, Emperor Hirohito is treated relatively mildly, there are no such reservations about killing his subjects who were defending his empire.

Reactions to the downing of Japanese aircraft in two different films, *Air Force* and *Destination Tokyo*, are illustrative. In the former, the gunner responsible for the kill, played by John Garfield, icily states: "Fryin' Jap going down." In the latter film, after witnessing the flaming crash of a Japanese floatplane from the deck of a submarine, the ship's cook also makes a "fried Jap" crack to a mate. In *Manila Calling* (TCF, 1942), a Japanese pilot who is shot down and rolls out of the cockpit dead is referred to as "one good Jap." During a briefing in preparation for an air raid in *God Is My Co-Pilot*, a large sign reading "Kill or Be Killed" is display on a wall.

The belief that the war against Japan called for virtual extermination of the Japanese was reinforced in a number of other ways. For instance, in many combat films there are scenes of Japanese aircraft crashing in flames, shot down by Allied planes or anti-aircraft gunners. The Japanese pilots are sometimes shown screaming, bleeding, or slumped over in their cockpit (at other times, in *Cry "Havoc"* for example, they are not depicted at all), but they are never shown parachuting to safety. In contrast, there are a number of films in which

Allied pilots parachute from damaged planes (but not always with happy results, as in *Bomber's Moon*, where a crewman is gunned down by a Nazi flyer), and even German pilots occasionally "hit the silk" (as in *Sahara*).

Further examples of the "kill every Jap" mentality (the stated purpose of the Makin Island raid by the Marines in *Gung Ho!* is to wipe out every Japanese soldier on the island—and then leave!) may be found in the brutal and often unusual means used to kill Japanese soldiers in wartime films. Even heavy construction equipment is used against Japanese troops: in *The Fighting Seabees*, John Wayne topples a gas tank with a bulldozer, immolating an advancing formation of soldiers; in *Mr. Winkle Goes to War*, Edward G. Robinson rolls over a Japanese machine gun nest in *his* bulldozer; in *Gung Ho!*, a commandeered steamroller is used to crush Japanese soldiers. In both *Gung Ho!* and *Guadalcanal Diary*, knives and bayonets are specifically used to kill Japanese soldiers at close quarters, and Filipino bolos are used effectively in *Salute to the Marines* and *Back to Bataan*. Conversely, combat films like *Back to Bataan*, *Bataan*, *Pride of the Marines*, *Guadalacanal Diary*, *Marine Raiders* and *Wake Island* feature wholesale slaughter of enemy troops, who foolishly (or fanatically) charge in the face of American machine guns and other weaponry only to be killed in massive numbers.[52] The very scale of such slaughter dehumanizes the Japanese, who are depicted as zealous worshippers of the Emperor, willing (even eager) to die in battle.

Even humorous remarks reflect the American desire to punish the Japanese people for their treacherous war-mongering. A little boy in *Busses Roar* expresses the desire to grow up and become a pilot so he can "knock off those Japs." Similarly, in *Rationing*, another young boy pretends he is a tail-gunner and says "I got 12 Japs so far." A song from *Panama Hattie* (MGM, 1942) includes the lines: "After the war's over, on our honeymoon, we could go to China, the Philippines, Australia, India. I'll even show you where Japan used to be!"

It has been argued that the depth of hatred caused by the attack on Pearl Harbor—combined with the racial aspect of the conflict—not only contributed to American attitudes towards the Japanese (encouraged by and reflected in Hollywood films of the period), but also affected the conduct of the war itself. The belief that the Japanese were barbaric, uncivilized, even sub-human—reinforced by atrocity stories—may not have directly resulted in the atomic bombing of Nagasaki and Hiroshima, but the perception of Japan as a nation of "fanatics" who would fight to the bitter end was certainly a contributing factor in the decision to use these weapons rather than mount a conventional invasion of the home islands.[53]

3. The Mocking of Mussolini

"Italians are not like Germans—only the body wears a uniform, not the soul." Sahara *(Columbia, 1943)*

Unlike the overwhelmingly negative film portrayals of Japanese and Japanese-Americans, Italians and Italian-Americans are portrayed in a very ambivalent manner in wartime Hollywood. References to Italy in films range from negative portrayals of Italy's buffoonish dictator Benito Mussolini, and disparaging references to the Italian armed forces and secret service, to neutral and even positive depictions of Italian-Americans.

The wide disparity in these images may be explained in several ways: first, there were many Italian-Americans in the United States, and virtually all were loyal citizens, many serving with distinction in the U.S. armed forces. On Columbus Day 1942, President Roosevelt lifted the "enemy alien" status from Italian-Americans.[54] Furthermore, the racial aspect of anti–Japanese attitudes was largely absent when referring to Italy and Italians. Additionally, Mussolini's fascist legions were neither feared nor respected from a military standpoint, and therefore were not considered a significant threat to the United States. Mussolini himself was viewed chiefly as a blustering henchman of Hitler.[55]

Since the Allies were at war with Italy, and given the generally negative images of Japanese-Americans and German-Americans, it is rather surprising to discover the number of *favorable* references in wartime films to Italian-Americans. Only in *Pilot Number 5* (MGM, 1943), in a prewar setting, is an Italian-American portrayed as an admirer of Mussolini. In contrast, an Italian-American in *My Son, the Hero* (PRC, 1943) vociferously attacks Mussolini and resents being called an "enemy alien." *The Racket Man* (Columbia, 1944) features an Italian-American Army sergeant who is killed overseas, thus inspiring the film's protagonist to become a better soldier. Lt. Canelli (Richard Conte) of the ill-fated captured American bomber crew of *Purple Heart* (TCF, 1944) is also portrayed heroically during their torture and trial in Japan.[56] The ethnic Italian crew member on the submarine *Copperfin* in *Destination Tokyo* (WB, 1943) is named Toscanini (a direct linkage with the famous Italian conductor Arturo Toscanini, an outspoken anti-fascist, who fled Mussolini's Italy before the outbreak of World War II). An Italian-American who owns a boarding house in *Good Luck, Mr. Yates* (Columbia, 1943) has a young son who enthusiastically champions the Allied cause.

A number of other Italian-American characters appear during the war; they are almost always depicted in the usual, pre-war stereotypical manner, as heavily accented, voluble barbers, grocers or pushcart vendors, waiters, and so forth. Henry Armetta, Gino Corrado and other character actors found that their roles were little changed despite the fact that the United States was at war with Italy. These roles are not exactly positive, but neither are they negatively skewed due to the current political situation.

There is virtually no exploitation during the war of such negative terms as "wop," "dago" and "guinea." However, there is an occasional use of the Italian gangster stereotype, but usually without any direct political connotations, e.g., *Baby Face Morgan* (PRC, 1942), *A Yank on the Burma Road* (MGM, 1942) and *Truck Busters* (WB, 1942).

In a few spy films featuring Axis agents, the Italian or Italian-American participant is similar to his early 1930s gangster progenitor, though inclined to be the least politically motivated member of the spy ring and less violence-prone than his comrades. Italian-Americans working with Nazi spies are usually portrayed as incompetent, unenthusiastic, cowardly effetes and as self-serving gangsters, such as the Italian spies in *Joan of Ozark* (Republic, 1942) and *Busses Roar* (WB, 1942). To bolster his ideological commitment to the Axis, the Italian member of the spy ring in *Underground Agent* (Columbia, 1942), is reminded that failure to carry out his duties could lead to unpleasant consequences for his family in Italy. An Italian spy working in Washington, D.C. in *They Got Me Covered* (RKO, 1943) owns a florist shop and a beauty salon. The single act of violence that this man (Eduardo Cianelli) commits is to slap his male secretary when the flunky fails to decipher information recorded in shorthand by an American stenographer. Frank Puglia plays an escaped Italian POW in *The Boogie Man Will Get You* (Columbia, 1942)—he boasts, not of how many Allied planes he shot down, but how many planes were shot out from under *him*! His plans to transform himself into a "human bomb" and blow up a U.S. defense installation fail miserably.

Compared to the vilification of the "Nazis" and the "Japs," there is no equivalent criticism of the Italians as a people or even of Italian fascism—except as personified by the posturing, fez-wearing Benito Mussolini (virtually all references to Mussolini are pejorative, e.g., a basket of food brought to a Dutch woman by a Nazi in *The Wife Takes a Flyer* includes "baloney from Mussolini"). While Hitler is often portrayed as sinister or mad, Mussolini is always caricatured as a buffoon or a toady of the Fuehrer—in *The Devil with Hitler*, *That Nazty Nuisance*, *They Got Me Covered* and *Meet the People* (MGM, 1944), for instance.[57] Mussolini (Joe Devlin) actually implores the Fuehrer in *The Devil with Hitler* to let him have *Italy* (his own country!)—if not the boot, at least the heel! In this film and its sequel, *That Nazty Nuisance*, Hitler, Mussolini, and Japanese envoy "Suki-Yaki" are depicted as mutually distrustful plotters. One of the funniest moments in *They Got Me Covered* occurs when an American reporter (Bob Hope), flying home from Russia, remarks: "You can't trust Hitler—he would doublecross his best friend." From another seat in the back of the airliner, a disgruntled Mussolini (Joe Devlin again) stands up and says "You're telling me!"

In *Meet the People*, released after Mussolini was deposed in July 1943, a typically bizarre Spike Jones musical number features a heavily accented caricature of Il Duce imploring a chimpanzee dressed up as Hitler: "What's-a happened to the big-ga blitz?" After the monkey, whom Mussolini refers to as "Schicklegruber," steals his fascist ally's medals and pants,

Mussolini continues singing: "You promise me Spain, the Mediterranean, Tripoli and-a France. I lose-a Spain, the Mediterranean—I even lose-a my pants!" Even an Italian soldier (played by J. Carrol Naish) in *Sahara* comments: "Mussolini is not so clever like Hitler—he can dress his Italians up only to *look* like thieves, cheats, murderers. He cannot, like Hitler, make them feel like that. He cannot, like Hitler, scrape from the conscience the knowledge [that] right is right, wrong is wrong."

Mussolini's "Pact of Steel"[58] with Hitler's Germany would have been more aptly named, in the opinion of most Americans, the pact of overcooked pasta. Italy's General Sebastiano, a frustrated aesthete (played by Fortunio Bonanova) in *Five Graves to Cairo* (Paramount, 1943), actually makes a suggestion to Field Marshal Rommel (Erich von Stroheim) that the best way of negotiating with the Allies is to send cooks with macaroni instead of diplomats! This image of the Italian military as bumbling and un-warlike was repeated in many films.

During the entire war, members of the Italian armed forces are portrayed or referred to only 17 times, compared to 94 references to the Japanese armed forces and 152 German military references. Despite significant military action in North Africa, Sicily and southern Italy during 1942 and 1943, American armed forces are never portrayed on film in actual combat with Italians. In fact, Italian soldiers (called "Eye-ties" by the British) are shown fighting honorably in only a single motion picture release—*Immortal Sergeant* (TCF, 1943)—against British Tommies in Libya. None of the Italians surrender; none survive a short but intense desert skirmish between the two forces. *Immortal Sergeant* is also unique in that it shows the Italian air force in action—a damaged fighter-bomber, its cockpit engulfed in flames, apparently deliberately crashing into a British truck (the scene is particularly ambiguous because there are none of the standard Hollywood cockpit-interior reaction shots of the pilot).[59]

A Bell for Adano (TCF, 1945) is based on a 1944 John Hersey novel about the American occupation of a Sicilian village. The film contains a particularly poignant scene when a group of bedraggled, repatriated Italian soldiers returns to the village. The widow of Giorgio, one of their compatriots, is told about her husband's death. Although he was an anti-fascist, Giorgio patriotically joined the Italian Army in 1940 to fight for Italy. At the imminent approach of the American Army, most of his fellow soldiers began to drink and verbally abuse Mussolini. After Giorgio called them traitors and shouted that "the only chance for our nation's honor is to fight," he was pelted with bottles and shot to death by his own men!

Hollywood films also show German military personnel disparaging their allies. The captured Italian soldier in *Sahara*—portrayed as basically a good sort—is murdered by a Nazi prisoner when the Italian refuses to participate in an escape attempt.

In *Chetniks* (TCF, 1943), a Yugoslav guerrilla leader, General Draja Mihailovitch (Philip Dorn), leads an attack by his horsemen on an Italian Army motorized supply column. They quickly subdue the feeble resistance mounted by a few of the Italian troops. The Italian commanding officer (Nestor Paiva) remains seated in the back of his touring car, neither issuing orders, nor firing his pistol; he quickly raises his hands in surrender. The fat and cowardly major, when interrogated, must examine his papers to even find out what the convoy is transporting!

Mihailovitch, noting that his guerrillas cannot operate the captured vehicles on the "thin blood" of Italians, calls German headquarters and audaciously offers to ransom the Nazis' allies for gasoline. The Italian major does not appear to be insulted by these negotiations, but insists *he* be ransomed for no less than fifty gallons of gas. Mihailovitch settles for ten gallons of low test from the aggravated general at German headquarters, who only agrees to the deal after being reminded by a Nazi political officer: "We can't afford to insult Italy openly, just yet" (the film takes place in the months immediately following the spring 1941 Axis conquest of the Balkan state). The Italians are never seen or even referred to again in the film.

Chetniks is the only American film released during the war to portray the Italian Army as a force of occupation, but the Italians are not even shown administering their considerable area of control in the Balkans. Consequently, Italians are never portrayed cinematically committing atrocities against civilians or their military opponents.[60]

In comparisons between members of the Italian armed forces and their German allies, the Italians repeatedly come up short. In *Desperate Journey* (WB, 1942) Allied airmen joke that "three picked Italian infantry divisions" fighting with the Germans in Russia must be advancing to *Rome!*[61] A group of frightened Italian soldiers are actually shown begging to surrender to an American civilian in order to escape their German allies in *Cairo* (MGM, 1942). The Italian soldier in *Sahara* is captured by Tambul (Rex Ingram) so the black Sudanese would have someone to carry his equipment! When tank commander Gunn (Humphrey Bogart) refuses to take the

prisoner along—"I'm not taking on a load of spaghetti"—the Italian follows his captors on foot through the desert until they relent. To some degree, these Hollywood images were based on reality, as Italian soldiers readily abandoned the futile defense of Mussolini's fascism: "You can't work up a good hate against soldiers who are surrendering to you so fast you have to take them by appointment," wrote G.I. cartoonist Bill Mauldin.[62]

There are only a few passing references to Italy's attempted invasion of Greece in the fall of 1940. Mussolini launched an ill-prepared assault upon Greece in October 1940 that led to a military disaster for the Italians, who then had to be "bailed out" by Hitler's German troops. An oblique allusion to the event is made in *The Big Street* (RKO, 1942): someone jokingly points out that a certain individual was made as welcome "as the Italian ambassador to Greece."[63] A snippet of information on the event during a radio news broadcast is heard in the background of a scene in *Mister Lucky* (RKO, 1943).

A Yank in Libya (PRC, 1942), an adventure film taking place in the Italian colony—where a series of major battles between Mussolini's fascist forces and their German allies of the Afrika Korps and the British were fought between 1940 and 1943—makes no mention at all of Italy. The greater portion of *The Story of G.I. Joe* (UA, 1945) takes place in Italy, but shows American soldiers in battle only with German troops (the Germans had occupied Italy in September 1943, following Mussolini's ouster in July). As in *A Bell for Adano*, the defeated Italian civilians in *The Story of G.I. Joe* are portrayed sympathetically, as "liberated" civilians rather than citizens of a defeated enemy.

Reflecting the public perception of an ineffectual enemy, Hollywood's Italian foes were thus most often distinguished by their lack of a sustained and memorable presence. Ultimately, the inherent sham of Italian Fascism was exemplified in American movie theatres by the virtual absence of its cinematic presentation.

20. Soldiers Without Uniforms: Wartime Resistance Films

The men and women of the Resistance were soldiers without uniforms and almost without arms, fighting for freedom and democracy, not for empire.[1]

In all the occupied countries there are men and women, and even little children, who have never stopped fighting, never stopped resisting, never stopped proving to the Nazis that their so-called new order will never be enforced upon free peoples.—President Franklin D. Roosevelt[2]

The wartime "Resistance" films are consistent and deliberate in their portrayal of life under Axis occupation. In the absence of large-scale American military activities in the Eu-

ropean theatre of war, Resistance films depict direct conflict with the Nazis. In a war intellectually conceived as the united forces of democracy versus fascism, Resistance films show people of other nations contributing to the war effort. Resistance films also provide the perfect opportunity for the portrayal of Nazi and Japanese ruthlessness, brutality, and antidemocratic actions, illustrating the reasons why fascism must be destroyed, enhancing the righteousness of the Allied cause and justifying the demand for unconditional surrender.

Active European resistance was rather limited in scope until mid-1943,[3] and the stress of occupation severely damaged social cohesion in the occupied nations—however, these realities were largely ignored in favor of action plots in which the enemy (particularly the pompous and brutal Nazi stereotype) is almost always bested. To those interested in promoting popular support for America's war effort, Hollywood's screen images often created a paradox: on the one hand, the cinematic portrayal of a sadistic, but petty and bureaucratic, enemy, frequently suffering heavy casualties (the German occupation garrisons in three 1943 releases—*The Edge of Darkness, The North Star,* and *Tarzan Triumphs*—are annihilated); versus the reality of a highly motivated and deadly opponent (already in possession of most of the European continent) which posed a bona fide threat to western democratic values and the American way of life. An obviously troubled OWI worried that unrealistic stories could be misleading the American public.[4]

Although many Resistance films make a pretense of nationalism, only a token effort is made to effect a realistic recreation of native cultures on screen. Instead, most of the films' characters are Hollywood "generic foreigners," embodying idealized American traits and values. Speeches made by resistance martyrs are invariably filled with defiance against the enemy Other and declarations affirming Allied unity, while invocations of a specific nationalistic spirit are comparatively muted.

Thus, the Norwegian scholar in *Edge of Darkness* (WB, 1943) makes universal humanistic allusions when confronting the Nazis, rather than glorifying his nation's heroes. A French teenager is arrested by the Gestapo in *Paris After Dark* (TCF, 1943), while attempting to flee the Nazis' compulsory labor program and join the Free French forces. Before being shot by an irritated Nazi officer, he briefly exhorts workers in a German-run munitions complex with a "United Nations" plea: "They [the Germans] can't run their factories with dead Frenchmen ... Take their guns away from them! They can't win. The Allies are in Africa ... The Russians are still in Stalingrad ... Stand up together—united—Vive la France!"

By downplaying national specificity, Hollywood's wartime Resistance films evoke the image of ordinary American citizens fighting the Nazis and Japanese. This was probably intended to heighten identification with, and sympathy for, the populations of the occupied countries. Furthermore, with the exception of a few Combat films, most wartime scenes of armed conflict with the Nazis appear in the Resistance genre. Such surrogate combat distracted American audiences from the reality of American casualties and subliminally reduced the sense of urgency for the opening of a Second Front on the European continent. Instead of the actuality of thousands of Allied planes being destroyed (and their crews killed or captured) while participating in the strategic bombing of occupied Europe and Germany, downed airmen are repeatedly portrayed teaming up on the ground with the resistance, as in *Desperate Journey* (WB, 1942), *Joan of Paris* (RKO, 1942), *Paris Calling* (Universal, 1942), *Bomber's Moon* (TCF, 1943), and *The Purple V* (Republic, 1943). These American and British airmen symbolically become the first wave of the armies preparing to liberate the Axis-enslaved continent.

In the minds of most Americans, there were three "Europes": England (irrelevant for resistance film purposes), a cosmopolitan continental Europe (=Paris), and a pastoral land of bucolic, simple country folk. The latter image was reinforced to some degree by the large number of Americans who were either immigrants or the children of immigrants, with lingering ties to (and nostalgia for) the "old" country. The majority of Resistance genre films take place in rural settings, or in small towns or villages. A reflection of the fictionalized, romanticized European vision held by many American moviegoers, such locales proved ideal in eliciting sympathy for the protagonists, thus establishing an emotional connection between the film audience and the resisters.

Occupied populations are not only brutalized by their human oppressors, but also by the technology of mechanized warfare. Machines became psychological, as well as physical, tools of war. That these tools are possessed by the tormentors and not available to the tormented is illustrated in *None Shall Escape* (Columbia, 1944), as mechanized units roar by a peasant wagon while entering a newly conquered Polish border town. A similar scene marks the beginning of the Nazi takeover of a small Norwegian village in *Commandos Strike at Dawn* (Columbia, 1942). The prelude to the savage Japanese occupation of a Chinese village in *Dragon Seed* (MGM, 1944) is visually established by daily bomber attacks interrupting the harvest—the day the planes stop flying overhead, a motorized column of the "devil dwarfs," the Rising Sun emblazoned on their vehicles, enters the village. The aerial bombing of peasant carts peaceably traveling down a sunlit road—and the smoking carnage that results—dramatically heralds the opening of Hitler's invasion of the Soviet Union in *The North Star* (RKO, 1943). And heavily armed German parachutists, uniformed harbingers of a brutal ideology employing western military technology, violate an idyllic, politically neutral jungle kingdom in *Tarzan Triumphs* (RKO, 1943).

Even in a city setting, the atmosphere of Resistance films is usually not realistically urban. For instance, there are almost no bustling crowds or street scenes filled with people. The action instead, takes place in a small café or a home, places interchangeable with those in a village. This focus on the bucolic serves to romanticize the occupied countries and to downplay the urban worker connection with Communism, which was important in terms of garnering support for our Russian war allies.[5]

In order to emphasize democratic nationalism and not inordinately detract from the melodrama, most characters in Resistance films are neither directly nor indirectly identified with a specific political group. However, the Communist link is suggested in one of the more urban-oriented films, *Paris After Dark* where the resisters refer to their "committee" meetings, and a German radio broadcast denounces "the so-called underground [as] ... nothing but a small group of Jews and Communists."

A more subtle intimation of an urban resistance group's Communist orientation appears in *Hostages* (Paramount, 1943). A prominent member of the Prague-based leadership committee is a middle-aged baker named Maria—played by Katina Paxinou, a Greek actress who somewhat resembled "La Pasionara," the famous Spanish Communist leader during the 1936–39 Spanish Civil War (indeed, Paxinou portrays a similar character in *For Whom the Bell Tolls*, set during this conflict).

Though formerly a professional engineer, the hero of *Watch on the Rhine*, Kurt Mueller (Paul Lukas), convalescing in 1940 America, defines his "trade" as fighting fascism. Kurt's identification with the working class and his "premature anti-fascism" imply a left-wing orientation. This is reinforced by additional references he makes to fighting para-military Nazi Brownshirts during the 1931 elections in Germany, and to joining other Germans fighting alongside anti-fascist Italians in the Spanish Civil War.[6]

Chinese Communist affiliations are suggested in *Dragon Seed* through the selective use of certain words and phrases, as well as by specific actions. For instance, the village collaborator (Akim Tamiroff) is disdainfully referred to by a young resistance leader as a "running dog." This same leader also paraphrases Mao when commenting on the Japanese invaders: "[T]heir words came out of the mouths of guns." As had actually occurred in the Soviet Union during the Nazi invasion, inhabitants of the province flee the advancing Japanese, dismantling and taking with them a factory from a nearby town. Later, returning from the so-called "free land" (i.e., the Red Chinese-controlled sector of China), they bring a message from the "High Command" (not stated, but obviously Mao, *not* the Nationalist Chinese or Chiang Kai-shek): "We must work together like the fingers in one hand ... we must track down this enemy and kill him." At the film's conclusion, acting upon orders from the High Command, the peasants collectively torch the fields they had been forced by the Japanese to sow, so as to prevent the fruits of their harvest being used to feed the hated enemy (a Soviet-style scorched earth policy).

Exile governments, particularly monarchies, are largely ignored in Resistance films. This is due in part to the distaste many Americans felt toward the more dictatorial regents in Europe. For instance, King Leopold of Belgium, who stayed behind and attempted accommodation with the Nazis, would not have elicited much sympathy from a 1940s American audience. Events in Greece and Yugoslavia, both suffering from civil wars (between various ethnic groups, and Communist and non–Communist factions) in conjunction with the Second World War, would have detracted from the concept of a unified peoples' war. However, in Black Parachute (Columbia, 1944), the people of a fictional Balkan country are victimized by a fake monarch who makes propaganda broadcasts urging collaboration with the Nazis. Towards the end of the film, one of the resisters blows up himself and a troop of Nazi soldiers, shouting "Long live the King!" This sentiment did not win the film any points with the OWI—the government reviewers had already requested extensive re-writes, but still felt that it was counter-productive to show the Allies supporting a monarchy (even one located in a non-existent country).[7]

France, Norway and China were the countries most frequently used as settings for Resistance films (14 out of 29), while no motion pictures classified in the Filmography under this genre take place in Belgium, Denmark, Greece or the Netherlands. One Resistance film, *Black Parachute*, as noted above, is situated in an unnamed country in eastern Europe.[8] *Chetniks* takes place in Yugoslavia. Three other relevant wartime films portray the Soviet partisans in action in the USSR.

France and the United States have a long, traditional association, going back to America's war for independence. The shared ideology of the French "Declaration of the Rights of Man" with the United States' "Declaration of Independence" is unabashedly affirmed in the opening clauses of the former document (affirming the equality of all mankind), which are poignantly read aloud in a classroom at the end of *This Land Is Mine* (RKO, 1943). Additionally, France is a country whose culture and society were familiar to many Americans from popular culture (including pre-war films).

Norway, while less familiar, presented an idyllic rural image. Even the name of the fishing village of *Troll*ness in *Edge of Darkness*, conjures mental associations with the mischievous dwarves of Scandinavian mythology. In addition to the advantage of a (white) Northern European population, Norway was not tarnished by a nasty internal conflict, such as the civil war in Greece, which raised the spectre of Communism. Alone among its Scandinavian neighbors, Norway actively resisted the Nazi yoke. It was also the scene of a brief, but vicious, military campaign in the spring of 1940 between a British-French expeditionary force and the invading German forces (see Chapter 5).[9]

China was the ultimate Asian peasant society, whose regular and irregular armed forces had been struggling against Japanese invaders since 1937. The strong China lobby in the United States, spearheaded by *Time* magazine publisher Henry Luce, helped publicize China's "gallant" struggle. The very real divisions among the Chinese themselves were completely whitewashed in wartime propaganda: if any group or leader is mentioned, it is the Nationalists under Chiang Kai-shek, but many Chinese films prefer to skip *any* specific reference. China, in wartime films at least, is depicted as united against the Japanese.

European cities serving as venues for Resistance films include Paris (more often than any other city), Warsaw (*To Be or Not to Be*, UA, 1942) and Prague (*Hostages*, Paramount, 1943 and *Hitler's Madman*, MGM, 1943). Interestingly, Hollywood manipulates the associative linkages created by the visual evocation of the romanticized images of these cities. For example, shots of the traditional landmarks of Paris, such as the Eiffel Tower and Champs-Elysees, are either totally absent from the films or only appear briefly to set the scene—as in *Reunion in France* (MGM, 1943) and *Paris Calling* (Universal, 1942).

The opening scene of *Paris After Dark* does contain a fleeting shot of the Eiffel Tower while the "Marseillaise" plays on the soundtrack, but this is immediately juxtaposed with a shot of a black swastika and the well-known newsreel footage of the conquering German Army entering Paris. The prewar "City of Light" is figuratively plunged into the darkness of Nazi occupation. Additionally, much of the remaining action in this and other relevant films quite literally takes place in the blackness of the urban night, presaging the *film noir* style associated with postwar Hollywood (*Reunion in France* is a particularly good example). This cinematic atmosphere is obviously deliberate, in order to paint a bleak picture of the fallen cities and accentuate the brutality exercised by the Nazi conquerors upon the subdued populations. It also expresses in visual terms the "darkened continent" analogy that FDR had used to describe occupied Europe in his April 28, 1942, Fireside Chat.[10]

With the exception of *Watch on the Rhine*, which is set in the prewar (1940) United States, all of the nearly thirty films categorized under the Resistance *genre* take place in an Axis-occupied country or in Germany itself. These films invariably portray cruelty and exploitation by the occupying power or ruling party, which leads to escalating violence on the part of the normally benign native population. In all but one film classified under the Resistance genre, Axis soldiers or officials are killed by resisters. The exception is *The Seventh Cross* (MGM, 1944), a tale of escape from a concentration camp in 1936 Germany.

All of the wartime motion pictures taking place in Axis-occupied countries feature resistance operations. The local heroes and heroines resist from the start by plotting to disrupt the efficiency of the occupation government. However, their activities usually do not become violent until the Nazis commit cruel acts of repression. The typical Resistance film scenario initially portrays passive non-compliance or petty opposition (or meetings to discuss such actions) by the occupied population.

In *Edge of Darkness*, the German occupation of the village of Trollness is irksome but not violent, yet the Norwegians constantly express their hatred of the Nazis: "The individual man must stand up to you like a rock," an old scholar tells the local German commander. "We'll fight until we push the last one of you into the sea," is the bitter rejoinder made by one of the Norwegian women to a German soldier who has gently expressed a liking for her. The "V for Victory" symbol is painted over a Nazi sign in *Commandos Strike at Dawn*, and over a German occupation proclamation in *To Be or Not to Be*, another form of passive resistance to Axis rule.

Eventually, however, the Axis occupation becomes too much to bear, and the inhabitants of the occupied countries can no longer refrain from violence. Actions taken by Nazi forces in wartime Resistance films include the seizure of private homes in *Days of Glory*, *Reunion in France*, and *The Moon Is Down*; a school is taken over for a military hospital in *The North Star*; a synagogue becomes a stable in *None Shall Escape*; the meager possessions of Chinese peasants are looted in *Dragon Seed*; in the dead of Russian winter, German soldiers take clothes from the citizens, even the scarf from an old woman (*Days of Glory*)! The fascist invaders take food from the starving populace for their own use in *Chetniks*, *Reunion in France*, *Commandos Strike at Dawn*, and *Dragon Seed*. In *Sahara*, a Free French soldier says the Nazis took the cows from his village so the children had no milk.

The "natural resources" of the occupied countries include the women. There are numerous examples of sexual assault and harassment by Nazi and Japanese officials, officers, and enlisted men. In *Tarzan Triumphs*, the arrogant colonel who leads the Nazi expedition to Polandria accosts Princess Zandra (Frances Gifford) while extolling the "new era" of the Third Reich. One of Zandra's subjects who tries to save her from the Nazi's lecherous advances is shot. The Polish mistress of a Nazi officer is considered human war booty in *Edge of Darkness*; a French nun is condemned to serve in a military brothel for her resistance activities in *Till We Meet Again* (although she is spared this fate and dies instead). Karen, a young Norwegian woman, is raped by a German soldier after being dragged out of the village church in *Edge of Darkness*; there is a cut to laughing Germans at the inn that serves as their headquarters. Young French female resisters standing before a firing squad are offered their lives if they "volunteer" to "entertain" German troops, in the resistance sequence of *Gangway for Tomorrow* (RKO, 1943).

Japanese rape of Chinese civilians is depicted (in oblique 1940s film style, of course) in *Dragon Seed* and *China* (in the latter film, it is a young schoolgirl who is brutally assaulted). American nurses in a Japanese POW camp are harassed by their captors in *First Yank Into Tokyo*, and a nurse in *So Proudly We Hail!* tells her comrades that she was in Nanking when the Japanese took over, raping women who were told it was "an honor to serve the Emperor."

Forced labor is also a potent symbol of Axis occupation

in wartime resistance films, reinforcing the idea of the fascists "enslaving" formerly free people. During the war, millions of foreign workers were employed in Germany, some "voluntarily" and some who were coerced (by various means) into leaving their occupied land in order to maintain the German war machine. Actual "slave" labor also existed, as inmates of concentration camps were forced to perform hard labor until they dropped from hunger, exhaustion, and illness.[11]

Deportation to Germany for wartime labor, or forced labor on military projects in the occupied nations themselves appears or is referred to in *None Shall Escape, The Moon Is Down, Paris After Dark, Till We Meet Again, Reunion in France, Hitler's Madman*, and other films. In *Cross of Lorraine*, news of an impending mass deportation to Germany leads to a violent uprising in a French village. In *Son of Lassie*, a large number of civilians are shown working—under armed German supervision—on a coastal battery site in Norway. One fisherman says this is good "practice for digging [the Germans'] graves."[12] The natives of the fictional African country of Polandria are forced to clear land for a Nazi airstrip in *Tarzan Triumphs*. The Polandrians are "bad fighters, but good workers," one Nazi remarks. Examples also appear in the Asian resistance films: Koreans and American POWs are forced to work in a Japanese munitions plant in *First Yank Into Tokyo*, and Chinese guerrillas attack the Japanese soldiers who are seizing men for forced labor in *Dragon Seed*.

Actions like these lead to stronger resistance, which in turn provokes heinous reprisals that escalate the resistance to an active mode and result in even bloodier counter-measures by the Nazis. Although some of the local populace may initially be reluctant to actively oppose their conquerors, many (usually all) eventually join the fight, either due to moral pressure or because of increasing Nazi savagery against the populace. In the process, there are political conversions, the discovery of personal courage, and the elimination of collaborators (by both sides).

Initial acts of violent rebellion include the sabotage of a mine and the destruction of a collaborator's store in *The Moon Is Down*; another mine is blown up in *Hitler's Madman*; a troop train is sabotaged in *Uncertain Glory*; more trains are blown up and convoys are ambushed in *The Black Parachute*; yet more trains are wrecked in *This Land Is Mine* and *Desperate Journey*—in the latter film, this results in a back-up of rolling stock which becomes a target for Allied bombers. A munitions dump is blown up in *Hostages* and an Italian convoy is ambushed and captured in *Chetniks*. Acts of industrial sabotage include the dumping of kerosene into a batch of canned fish (destined for Germany) in *Edge of Darkness*. Plans are made to wreck German tanks with old parts in *Hangmen Also Die*, and a munitions factory is blown up in *First Yank Into Tokyo*.

Naturally, these actions generate brutal responses on the part of the occupying forces. Nearly every film set in an oc-

cupied country contains one or more examples of Nazi and Japanese "atrocities." Life under Axis rule is not only portrayed as drab, strict, and unpleasant, the brutality of the occupiers makes it unbearable. There are numerous scenes of torture, summary executions, casual cruelties, sexual harassment, and economic exploitation. Those who strike back are ruthlessly suppressed; resistance activities bring massive reprisals.

In *Till We Meet Again*, a laundress is tortured with a hot iron; Nazis break the arms of a woman for information in *The North Star*; hostages are taken to be shot in reprisal for an act of sabotage in *Uncertain Glory*. In *The Black Parachute*, the German commander (John Carradine), who says "Perhaps I'm an artist of destruction," orders the seizure of 100 hostages—specifying "men, women, and children"—and says every second one should be shot. A young guerrilla fighter is captured, tortured, then hanged in front of a crowd of villagers in *Days of Glory* (RKO, 1944). There is a mass hanging of old men, women and children in *China's Little Devils* (Monogram, 1945).

Many Resistance films contain powerfully emotive execution scenes. In *Hangmen Also Die*, in reprisal for the Rienhardt Heydrich assassination (May 1942), all the men of the Czech village of Lidice, including a priest and a Jew, are shot. *They Raid by Night* (PRC, 1942) opens with an execution by firing squad. *Back to Bataan* features the hanging of a Filipino school principal on the school's own flagpole![13] Chinese are lynched and others are shot down, en masse, by Japanese machine guns in *Dragon Seed*. In *China Girl*, the Japanese execute "spies," and the film's American hero later escapes by crawling through a trench filled with the corpses of those who were shot. In *Lady from Chungking* (PRC, 1942), General Kaimura (Harold Huber) orders the destruction of a whole village in reprisal for a guerrilla attack.

Collective gestures of defiance are particularly strong in such execution scenes—there are raised fists and cries of "long life to Czechoslovakia" before a firing squad does its work in *Hostages*; the "V for victory" sign is flashed in *Hangmen Also Die* (UA, 1943) by the soon-to-be-executed villagers taken as hostages in reprisal for the assassination of Reichsmarshal of Czechoslovakia Heydrich. Before his summary execution, partisan Joseph (Art Smith) in *The Black Parachute* spits in the face of a Nazi officer.

Most of these atrocities are carried out without any vestige of the usual German concern for legal niceties. *This Land Is Mine* is one of the few films to depict a trial in an occupied country (collaborationist officials appear to be cooperating with the Nazis). The Nazis usually dispense with due process and swiftly execute those who transgress. Public executions are cruel displays of power meant to demoralize potential opposition—in real life, this practice was at least partially successful. But in Hollywood's vision the martyrs always provide inspiration for further acts of resistance, usually on a significant scale: "every one of us they execute wins a battle for our cause," says one character in *This Land Is Mine*. The pragmatic German colonel in *The Moon Is Down* opposes unnecessary reprisals, based on his experiences in the First World War: "A dead relative really arms an enemy."

Little cinematic time is expended in portraying the overwhelming number of individuals who are simply trying to survive the ordeal of occupation. The cowardly teacher played by Charles Laughton in *This Land Is Mine* is a rare exception—and even he experiences a patriotic conversion after a prolonged moral struggle. The wife (Ruth Gordon) of the town doctor in *Edge of Darkness* wants to deny the unpleasant realities of the occupation of her Norwegian village, but is eventually moved by the force of events to join her husband (Walter Huston) in supporting the resistance. In the same film, her son, who had earlier collaborated with the enemy, runs in front of German machine gunners in order to warn rebelling villagers of an ambush.

Resistance films make the point of virtually unanimous opposition to the Axis by deliberately including scenes of women and children actively participating in resistance activities.

The Boy from Stalingrad (Columbia, 1943) is entirely focused on a juvenile group—including a girl and a British boy—resisting the Nazi invasion of Russia. *China's Little Devils* is also youth-oriented: Chinese boy "Little Butch" (named after a Flying Tiger pilot), leads a group of children against the Japanese. In a grim ending, Little Butch is caught and executed, becoming another martyr for the democratic cause.[14] Even Tarzan's son "Boy" (Johnny Sheffield) shoots a Nazi in *Tarzan Triumphs*.

Teenagers are featured in both *Days of Glory* and *The North Star* in active resistance roles. In the latter film, Damian (Farley Granger) and Clavdia (Jane Withers) are observing a German convoy. In order to create a diversion so their friends can escape with a cartload of weapons, the two young people attack the Nazis, killing some before a grenade leaves Damian blinded and Clavdia dead. A German soldier comes to see who had the temerity to attack them: "a dead kid and a fat girl ... dangerous enemy...."

Women are also portrayed as combatants in resistance films. An old woman uses a torch to guide RAF bombers to the site of a Nazi-controlled mine in *The Moon Is Down*. This film also features a woman who kills a German soldier with scissors. Karen (Anne Sheridan), an active resister in *Edge of Darkness*, is the sniper who kills a German soldier attempting to haul down the Norwegian flag at the film's conclusion. Women are also active participants in the spontaneous village rebellion in *The Cross of Lorraine*.

Olga (Jeanne Bates) is a member of the resistance in *The Black Parachute*. She not only actively takes part in the ambush of Nazi trains and motorcades, she spies on the occupying forces by posing as a maid in their headquarters. Even after her father is caught and executed as a partisan, Olga continues to fight the Nazis. At the film's conclusion, she leaps in front of a Nazi's gun, taking the bullet intended for King Stephen, giving her life for the cause (well, not exactly the cause of democracy, but at least the cause of freedom from Nazi tyranny).

Lady from Chungking features Anna May Wong as a female resistance leader who masterminds intelligence-gathering and anti–Japanese actions. She kills a Japanese officer but also pays with her life. In *Dragon Seed*, Jade (Katherine Hepburn) is a Chinese woman who acts as the conscience of her village, alerting them to the danger of the Japanese invasion, and later poisoning a Japanese officer. Dalisay Delgado (Feli Franquelli) poses as a pro–Japanese Filipino in *Back to Bataan*, but is actually passing information to the resistance forces.

Other strong female resisters—played by glamorous Hollywood stars—include Maureen O'Hara in *This Land Is Mine*, Joan Crawford in *Reunion in France*, and Merle Oberon in *First Comes Courage*. The use of women and children as resistance fighters reinforces the theme of fascism's threat to the family. Not only are families affected by the occupation forces while living together under fascism, they are often separated by the war. In *Paris After Dark*, the wife of a French POW assumes a leading role in the resistance while he is in a prison camp, and continues the struggle when he returns home, a worn-out and defeated man.[15]

Romance and happiness are delayed or even destroyed by the war and by dedication to the cause of resistance. Films like *Edge of Darkness* (the Errol Flynn and Anne Sheridan couple), *Back to Bataan* (Anthony Quinn and Feli Franquelli) eschew the traditional Hollywood happy ending for an ambiguous "maybe after the war we'll be able to live a normal life" statement, or worse: the death of one or both romantic partners is depicted in *Commandos Strike at Dawn*, *The North Star*, and *Days of Glory*. In all of these films, resistance to the invaders is deemed more important than one's personal happiness—self-sacrifice is praised, and American audiences (undoubtedly including many women whose husbands or boyfriends were away at war) could empathize even further with those living under fascist domination.

The resisters are, more often than not, a collective of concerned neighbors versus the evil Other. These people are not ideologues, but are motivated by a mixture of vaguely defined patriotism (more anti-fascist and pro-freedom than ideological or nationalistic) and romanticism. Portrayed as heroic warriors, sometimes in vaguely national garb (such as Russian peasant blouses or worker's leather caps), the populations of entire villages are shown rising up against their oppressors in a number of films, including *Edge of Darkness*, *The Cross of Lorraine*, *Dragon Seed* and *The North Star*.

In both *Edge of Darkness* and *The North Star*, in stark contrast to the mechanized Wehrmacht, villagers attack and overwhelm the enemy by a collective force of will. Literally trampling over the local collaborator, an armed phalanx of determined Norwegians throw themselves upon their German oppressors during the horrific conclusion of *Edge of Darkness*. One man pulls the pins on two grenades and jumps into a German machine gun nest. Some of his compatriots make a frenzied dash in a horsedrawn cart up to the German's heavily fortified headquarters, using the primitive vehicle as a platform from which to launch a barrage of grenades at the enemy defenders.

Russian partisans abandon their hidden forest camp to exact revenge upon the savage Nazi occupiers of their commune in *The North Star*. Spearheading the climactic attack are men who crawl up to the village through the adjacent cornfields and then literally spring up from the soil of Mother Russia to ambush the Germans' defensive positions. Mounted guerrillas, shouting and tossing grenades, descend upon the desperate German garrison now trapped in the village of North Star. Other partisans (who have been waiting for a cartload of rifles to be delivered) follow on foot and, along with the peasants who had been forced to endure the brutal occupation, use clubs and weapons from the dead to finish off the Nazis.

A brilliantly choreographed scene symbolizing spontaneously aroused mass contempt for the Germans occurs in response to a metaphorical execution in *Edge of Darkness*. After the village scholar is publicly humiliated and his books (his life) are destroyed by the Nazi occupiers, a powerful sequence worthy of Sergei Eisenstein, the Soviet originator of politically provocative cinematic montage, follows. On each side of the human square the Germans have formed around the persecuted man and his burning books, the enraged villagers successively advance (with ballet-like precision) en masse up to the pointed line of the German soldiers' fixed bayonets.

As the stakes for the Nazis rise with increased resistance, the brutality and mounting pressure begin to test the depths of many Germans' devotion to the New Order. The web of contradictions often takes its toll on those who retain some vestiges of humanity. The end result in a number of scenarios is the same for the German occupier—madness or death. Maddened by loneliness, exacerbated by the unwillingness of the people in a remote Norwegian village to socialize with their occupiers, a sensitive young German officer in *The Moon Is Down* visits the widow of a recently executed man. Dressed in her black mourning clothes, she stoically listens to the disturbed man as if he is a troublesome child and, after he proclaims his love for her, she casually suggests they go upstairs. The emotionally understated climax of this scene occurs when the audience sees the woman secretively removing a large pair of shears from a sewing basket. The grisly outcome is left to the imagination of the viewer. In the Resistance film genre, the oppressors are no longer a faceless enemy (as in many Combat genre films), but are characters with names, interacting on a personal basis with the oppressed. The motivations behind atrocities are thereby revealed, crudely creating an ideological dialectic. An example would be the several explicit scenes of

book burning and mistreatment of intellectuals. The idea of educated individuals freely expressing their thoughts among equals is antithetical to the self-proclaimed Nazi supermen who have imposed their New Order on an unwilling populace.

Nazi anti-intellectualism is repeatedly portrayed in Resistance films. In *Edge of Darkness* a defiant elderly scholar who refuses to passively obey a German order to vacate his home—which is to be used as a blockhouse—is roughed up and then publicly humiliated by the enraged Nazi commander, Captain Koenig: [There's] no room for philosophers [in the New Order]." Nazi disrespect for culture is graphically demonstrated in *Song of Russia* (MGM, 1944) when the invading German armies indiscriminately bomb Tschaikowskoye, the village birthplace of the composer Tchaikovsky and home of a small music school. The elderly school president is discovered wandering amid the ruins in shock, a shattered violin in his hands (the morbid "Pathetique" playing on the soundtrack). And a former professor belonging to a partisan band in *Days of Glory* refers to the Nazis deliberately setting fire to a Russian library.[16]

In *Hitler's Madman*, Reinhard Heydrich (John Carradine) interrupts a lecture at the University of Prague, announcing the closing of the institution, then orders the male students to be sent to labor battalions. The female students are to be given medical examinations to assess their suitability for "entertaining" troops at the front (movie code for being forced into prostitution).[17] In *This Land Is Mine*, the town mayor, anxious to appease the Germans, pressures the scholarly school principal to censor text books. The principal, in a poignantly understated scene, instructs his teachers to carry out a "delicate surgical operation" by tearing out selected pages from their history texts—beginning with Charlemagne. One teacher, played by Maureen O'Hara, tells students in her class to keep the pages—one day they will be replaced (when France is free).[18]

Resistance in the Far East

Most non–European resistance films are set in China; only three are located elsewhere, *Manila Calling* (TCF, 1942) and *Back to Bataan* (RKO, 1945) in the Philippines, and *Tarzan Triumphs*, in the mythical African kingdom of "Polandria."[19] In comparison with the portrayal of the mostly self-reliant resisters in Europe, filmic resistance in other war theatres is far more apt to be directed or dominated by Americans. There are at least two basic reasons for this. First, American audiences were not likely to flock to films featuring all-Asian casts, regardless of their positive feelings about our Chinese allies. Also, there was the commonly held notion that non-whites were less capable of defending themselves. As a result, only one Pacific theatre resistance film, *Dragon Seed* (MGM,

1944), has absolutely no American characters.[20] And even *Dragon Seed* makes an oblique reference to American aid in a comment referring to "foreign writing" on a guerrilla's gun: "A wise man does not question the origin of gifts."[21]

But in *Manila Calling*, for example, the Filipino characters are subsidiary to the Americans, although it is their country that is being invaded![22] Most of the Filipinos in this film are members of the "Scouts," the American-officered military organization. The film depicts American civilians broadcasting over a captured Japanese radio station located on a mesa so the "Japs ... can't use [it] to feed [the] natives their lying propaganda." In other words, the Filipinos are childlike and might be unduly influenced by enemy broadcasts. The Americans then decide to restore the radio facilities in order to use them as a "weapon ... [to] put courage back into the hearts of beaten people."

Back to Bataan (RKO, 1945) features John Wayne as an American officer who leads a motley group of American and Filipino guerrillas against the Japanese. Wayne uses Anthony Quinn, the grandson and namesake of a famous Filipino hero, as a figurehead to rally Filipino support—but it is the American who commands the group.[23] Most of the Filipinos are depicted as at least partially Americanized: a Filipino school principal is hung for refusing to take down the *American* flag flying in front of his school. The Filipino children are taught about American ideals of freedom and democracy (and talk about American things like hot dogs and baseball).

Even *Lady from Chungking* (PRC, 1942), which stars Anna May Wong as a strong Chinese resistance leader, includes two Flying Tiger pilots to carry out an important act. Aided in their escape from behind Japanese lines by the Chinese resistance, the American pilots return to their base with detailed information on enemy troop train movements prior to a planned assault on Chungking, China's wartime capital.

Evoking comparisons to the insensitive treatment of other minorities in earlier American films, Asians performing vital wartime service go largely unrecognized on the screen. They are all but invisible, seldom receiving so much as a nod or a "thank you." To American filmmakers, Asians were expendable, unless they were Americanized, even when they performed heroic deeds. Maximo (Ducky Louie), a Filipino boy who has proudly adopted American culture, dies in the arms of his American teacher in *Back to Bataan* after making the supreme sacrifice to prevent his American-led guerrilla band from being ambushed by the Japanese. But when two unidentified Filipinos make a suicidal attack upon a Japanese tank at the end of the same film, their death is treated matter-of-factly. If this had been Sergeant Goldberg and his pal from the U.S.A. attacking an armored car with grenades, as in *Salute to the Marines* (MGM, 1943), there would have probably been at least a moment of recognition and a sense of loss.

One exception is the prominent role of a Chinese guerrilla leader, played by Anthony Quinn, in *China Sky* (RKO,

1945). Quinn is depicted as a strong, independent guerrilla leader who cares for his men and is determined to play his part in freeing China from Japanese domination. However, when critical decisions need to be made, the Quinn character usually defers to the civilian American doctor (Randolph Scott) in a nearby village.

Within these constraints, however, Hollywood films still at least pay lip service to the idea that the Chinese and Filipinos (and to a lesser extent Koreans and other Asians under Japanese domination) are resisting the enemy with all their might. In *Bombs Over Burma*, Lin Ying, a Chinese agent, observes men feverishly working to repair a damaged road: [T]heir work is never done. If the road to Burma is out, there will be a road from India—from Russia. If there is no road for trucks, we'll carry supplies on our backs. China will never be conquered."

Chinese guerrillas or irregular troops appear in *China* (Paramount, 1943), *30 Seconds Over Tokyo* (MGM, 1945), and a number of other films, but are rarely the center of attention. *First Yank Into Tokyo* features active resistance by Koreans, a country occupied by Japan for many years. The Koreans arrange to smuggle an American agent into Japan—one member of the underground resigning himself to almost certain death to carry out this task—then assist the American in his mission (to extract a scientist from a POW camp), blowing up a munitions plant in the bargain. There is even a slight hint of the plight of Koreans *in* Japan, where they are considered inferior and are discriminated against.

Back to Bataan deals entirely with Filipino resistance to the Japanese, albeit under American direction. This film does attempt to depict the almost unanimous resolve of the Filipino people to defeat the Japanese invaders. Some of the scenes resemble European resistance films, portraying an outwardly submissive population that is nonetheless constantly scheming to undermine the Japanese occupation forces.

If one can overlook the paternalism which plays a large part in these Asian resistance films, there are still indications that Hollywood felt that the Chinese, Filipinos, and Koreans were as eager to obtain their freedom as the French, Norwegians, and other Europeans. The differences in the filmic depiction of European and Asian resistance can mostly be attributed to racial similarities/differences between the intended audience for the film and the people being portrayed—white, Anglo-Saxon American filmgoers were simply more interested in the plight of other Caucasians.

Defending the Motherland: The Russian Resistance

While Soviet Russia was one of the Allies during the war, and while pro–Soviet propaganda attempted to erase the prewar anti–Red attitudes of many Americans (see Chapter 5), few wartime films depict the Soviet armed forces in combat action. Instead, there are several major films (and some minor ones) highlighting the Russian "resistance" forces fighting the Nazis.

In reality, there was very little "underground" resistance in Russia, at least as the term is used in other Resistance genre films. The Soviet government kept close tabs on all guerrilla groups operating behind enemy lines; the "resistance" forces were for the most part merely extensions of the regular Soviet Army, receiving their orders regularly and coordinating their actions with the main forces. The Soviets did not want any "freelance" guerrilla groups operating on Russian soil, for fear that these organizations would later prove a threat to the Communist government.

Most of the wartime films dealing with the Russian resistance show the guerrilla groups operating as an extension of the Red Army. Due to the vast scale of the Russo-German war theatre, in which most of the territory was continuously at risk, a significant portion of the European Russian population remained on the front lines (or behind enemy lines, as the Germans advanced) and were thereby universally drafted as fighting auxiliaries into the armed forces of the Soviet Union. This is most dramatically exemplified by the villagers collectively taking the "Partisan Oath" on the first day of the Nazi invasion of their country (June 22, 1941) in *The North Star*.

The two major Russian resistance films are *The North Star* and *Days of Glory*—neither film contains any characters other than Russians and Germans. *The Boy from Stalingrad* and *Song of Russia*, on the other hand, do feature "Allies" (a British boy and an American musician, respectively), but do not present these characters in the same supervisory position as Asian resistance films like *Back to Bataan*. While official U.S. assistance to Russia is not ignored in films like *Three Russian Girls*, *Action in the North Atlantic*, and even *Miss V from Moscow*, it is extremely muted or entirely absent in the Russian Resistance films.

As a result, the Russians are depicted as competent, fiercely nationalistic and anti-fascist, and entirely united in their determination to win the war. No collaborators appear in Russian resistance films: in the context of Soviet Russia, collaboration would indirectly raise the issue of anti-communism, suggesting that the collaborators were willing to cooperate with the Nazis as the lesser of two evils (as actually happened in the Ukraine).[24] The image of a united Soviet people is even more closely adhered to than in the Chinese films, which do occasionally feature collaborators (*Dragon Seed* and *The Purple Heart*, for instance).

Virtually all wartime films set in Russia portray it as the ultimate European peasant society. There are almost no urban scenes and therefore the heroic Russian stand against the prolonged Nazi siege of Leningrad is ignored, except for *Three Russian Girls* (which was a remake of a Soviet film). The victory at Stalingrad is referred to in numerous films, but resistance of people in and around the city is not depicted. Even *The Boy from Stalingrad* is only peripherally involved with the Stalingrad campaign and it is unclear whether any of the resisting children are actually supposed to be from the city named after the Soviet leader.

Thus, the portrait of Russian resistance that emerges in these films is that of a united peasantry, directed from afar by the Red Army, ceaselessly battling the Nazi invaders of their peaceful land. Women and children's roles in resistance activities are highlighted. In *Song of Russia*, children are taught to make Molotov Cocktails in music school; only those under 12 years of age are evacuated—all others are to remain and resist the German advance. A Soviet partisan woman sniper, using a silenced rifle, is actually shown killing a German soldier at the beginning of *Days of Glory*. A ballerina (Tamara Toumanova) who is forced by circumstances to join a partisan group, reluctantly kills a German prisoner who tries to escape, and then becomes a full-fledged guerrilla. This film also features a teenaged boy and girl who are members of the group and are given adult responsibilities. *The North Star* is the story of one Russian village (a farming collective), and depicts old men, women, and young people engaged in active resistance to the German invaders.

"Scorched Earth," mainly a Soviet phenomenon, is shown to be the ultimate expression of a collective will to resist. There are scenes of Russians burning the fields they planted and torching their homes in *The North Star*, *Song of Russia*, and *The Boy from Stalingrad*, thereby denying the Nazis any resources to exploit and affirming the Russian people's total commitment to cause of Allied victory. This concept appears in other wartime films set in Poland (*In Our Time*), China (*Dragon Seed*), and France (*The Cross of Lorraine*).

The Russian resistance films are an odd mixture of reality (the status of the guerrilla groups) and fantasy (the portrayal of the Russian peasants, the suppression of any real discussion of the Soviet political system). As could be expected, Hollywood chose to "accentuate the positive and eliminate the negative," a decision that would prove rather embarrassing to a number of filmmakers a few short years later.

Friendly Enemies: Resistance Activities in Fascist Countries

Four films, one set in the United States, one set in prewar Germany, and two in wartime Germany deal specifically with German opponents of Hitler's regime. However, at least 14 more (with a Resistance coding) portray some form of German opposition to the Nazis in their plots. As mentioned in Chapter 6, the "good German" concept was not heartily endorsed by the United States government, for fear that such a feeling would lead to a demands for a "soft" peace.

However, Hollywood's image of Nazi Germany as a kind of giant prison camp ruled by a Nazi minority actually went to the other extreme, crediting "good Germans" with a more active resistance to Hitler than the historical record corroborates. An old man in *Berlin Correspondent* (TCF, 1942) explains to his daughter (who works for the Gestapo) why he provides information about Germany's military operations to an American radio broadcaster: "We in Germany are imprisoned by our government. There is no escape."

Why were the studios willing to directly contravene government policy? The large number of Americans of German ancestry probably had some influence on this decision. While virtually *all* Japanese in wartime films are sinister villains, the Japanese-American population in the United States was quite small (and mostly interned!); not so with the many hundreds of thousands of German-Americans, whose loyalty to the United States was rarely questioned. Films suggesting that everyone in Germany was an ardent Nazi would hardly have pleased these paying customers. Consequently, wartime films pay special attention to the "ordinary" German citizens who hate Hitler and his henchmen.

In fact, virtually every film that takes place in the Third Reich contains either active German resisters or some act of defiance against the regime. A dramatic example of an individual anti-fascist act appears in *Enemy of Women* (Monogram, 1944): a wounded German soldier in a hospital responds to the visiting Propaganda Minister Goebbels' disparaging remarks about democracies by calling him a "Liar!" The heroine of *Women in Bondage* (Monogram, 1944), a war widow being pressured to breed with an SS officer for the glory of the Reich, sacrifices her life in order to help guide Allied bombers to a German munitions plant. In *The Purple V* (Republic, 1943), a German professor (intellectuals are often active resisters, particularly in German resistance films) helps a downed Allied airman escape from Germany by dressing in a stolen Nazi uniform; he helps his daughter and the American get away, but the old man is killed, and his dying gesture of defiance is to rip off the swastika armband.

They Live in Fear (Columbia, 1944) opens with a sequence in a German school. The Hitler Youth students are harangued by their Brownshirt instructor, and one of the teenagers, Paul Graffen, nearly betrays his anti-Nazi sentiments. When he gets home, Paul tells his father he cannot take much more of such constant Nazi indoctrination. But his father warns him that Paul's deception is all that stands between his family and a "death camp." When the Hitler Youth are taken to Dachau on a kind of "field trip" and are ordered to execute some prisoners with shovels, Paul only pretends to kill his victim. The grateful man writes Paul a letter of introduction to a fellow academic in the United States, and Paul takes this opportunity to escape from Nazi Germany once and for all.

Most German resisters act out of individual conscience,

and are not often depicted as part of an organization. Additionally, German resistance in wartime films comes mainly in the form of "secondary" resistance, i.e., aid to Allied airmen, soldiers, or spies. In *The Purple V*, the downed American airman (John Archer) can be identified by a "V"-shaped tattoo on his wrist. After marking his own wrist with the same symbol, an anti–Nazi German deliberately sacrifices himself to assist the American. A young German woman helps an RAF crew escape after their bomber is shot down in *Dangerous Journey* (WB, 1942). There is little organized anti–Nazi opposition in evidence. In fact, the two films which most clearly depict German anti-fascist organizations are *Hitler—Beast of Berlin* (PDC, 1939) and *Underground* (WB, 1941), both made before America entered the war.

There are no films that portray active resistance (such as sabotage or aiding Allied spies or airmen) by Japanese citizens against their authoritarian regime. Indeed, it is the *Korean* resistance, operating both in occupied Korea and in Japan itself, that assists an American agent in *First Yank Into Tokyo* (RKO, 1945). In *Behind the Rising Sun* (RKO, 1943), a Japanese cabinet member (J. Carrol Naish) is horrified to learn his prospective daughter-in-law was tortured by the Japanese Thought Police. After his son, who has been dehumanized by war, is killed in combat, the politician ritualistically commits suicide following an appeal to his gods for the purification of Japan through the elimination of its militaristic leadership by Allied bombs! In contrast to this single example, the legitimacy of the fascist government of Germany is repeatedly called into question by elements of the indigenous population which resist its authority. However, active resistance to one's own government, even a fascistic one, invariably leads to a martyr's death or exile.

Direct references to anti-fascist Italians opposing Mussolini's regime occur in just three films: the prewar *Sundown* (UA, 1941),[25] *Pilot No. 5* (MGM, 1943), and *Sahara* (Columbia, 1943). The subject is broached more obliquely in the otherwise didactic *Watch on the Rhine*. While traveling on a train to Washington, D.C., the motion picture's anti-fascist German hero, Kurt Muller, engages a young Italian-American couple in conversation, during which it is mentioned with pride that both Italians and Germans fought in the International Brigades against the fascist forces in Spain.

The former mayor of Adano, in *A Bell for Adano* (TCF, 1945), who claims to be anti-fascist, greets the American commander of the Italian village's Allied administration government with a fascist salute! But the mayor is portrayed as an opportunistic fool, not a political fanatic. And the only reminder of Mussolini is a faded spot on the wall of the Town Hall where the portrait of Il Duce once hung.

Only a single film, *Chetniks*, contains a brief scene depicting resistance activities directed against Italian occupying forces, when an Italian supply column is attacked by the noncommunist Yugoslav guerrillas led by Draja Mihailovitch.

There are *no* motion pictures that portray Italian occupiers in any way interacting with indigenous civilians and, therefore, there are no scenes of Italian troops and their fascist auxiliaries (including Mussolini's secret police, the OVRA) committing atrocities.

Collaborators

The opposite of resistance *to* the enemy was collaboration *with* the enemy. These individuals are not Axis agents planted in a country prior to invasion, but are citizens of that country who—for one reason or another—decide to throw in their lot with the Nazis or Japanese occupiers of their nation.

Occasionally these "traitors" are actually patriots in disguise, enduring the scorn of their fellow countrymen in order to acquire important information and to help defeat the enemy from within, as in *Reunion in France* (MGM, 1942) and *First Comes Courage* (Columbia, 1943). In *First Comes Courage* the Norwegian heroine (Merle Oberon) actually marries a Nazi major, known to enjoy torturing political prisoners, sacrificing her "honor" for the cause of democracy.

But generally those who collaborate in wartime films are actually working with the enemy, either out of self-interest and greed, ideological agreement (very rarely),[26] or a misguided belief that "going along" with the fascists is the only way to survive. However, sincere but naive attempts at rational accommodation with the Nazis by conquered peoples are ultimately futile—and usually result in tragedy.

There are some collaborators whose motives are differentiated from the filmic norm. The selfish, domineering mother (Una O'Connor) of Albert Lory (Charles Laughton) in *This Land Is Mine* is introduced in the film with a (presumably) black market bottle of milk wrapped in newspaper which reads "Hitler Speaks," presaging her later actions. Mrs. Lory betrays a French resister to the Germans in order to save her weak son, but this eventually leads to his final conversion, arrest, and (presumably) to his death. In *Hitler's Madman*, Bauer (Ludwig Stossel), an ethnic German mayor in Czechoslovakia, proudly and vocally supports the SS and even enthusiastically invokes Hitler's *Mein Kampf*. But upon learning of the death of both her sons (in the German Army) on the Russian front, the mayor's wife discloses the route of Heydrich's motorcade to the Czech resistance, leading to the Reichsmarshal's assassination.

Most collaborators are depicted as isolated individuals who are motivated by the desire for power and money. The student resistance leader in *Dragon Seed* contemptuously describes a merchant collaborator to his fellow villagers: "This man loves his cash box above his country." In *Edge of Darkness*, cannery owner and collaborator Kaspar is shown actually smiling and smoking a cigar in the company of the German occupiers, while his brother-in-law and niece are among the Norwegian hostages digging their own graves before being shot!

There are no known wartime film examples of indigenous Nazi-inspired parties in occupied countries, such as Vidkun Quisling's fascist Hurd Party in Norway. However, in *The Moon Is Down*, the Germans occupy a mining village without opposition due to the activities of a fifth columnist, and the German commander comments: "Corell has proved himself as one of the best of Mr. Quisling's operatives." Corell's fascist membership is further suggested by a trip he makes to Berlin and, later, by his participation in the execution of a Norwegian. Yet, Corell is never shown in any type of Party uniform. In fact, he usually wears a black suit and bowler hat, more suggestive of an undertaker or businessman. An indirect linkage to Norwegian fascism is created by the use of Quisling's name as a pejorative term in a number of films. For example, in its adjectival form, "quisling" is repeatedly used throughout *Edge of Darkness*.

The only collaborationist government to be directly attacked by Hollywood is Vichy France.[27] There are coded references to Vichy, virtually always negative in tone, in at least 16 films between 1942 and 1945. A bottle of Vichy water, as opposed to Champagne, is symbolically tossed into a wastebasket in the famous concluding scene of *Casablanca*. This film evokes real issues in its depiction of Frenchmen who are reluctantly cooperating with Vichy—as the "legal" government—yet who dislike the Nazis and resent their influence. At the film's conclusion, of course, the Vichy police chief (Claude Rains) decides to give up his job and join the Free French forces.

Other examples of official French cooperation with the Germans appear in several films. Men clad in what appear to be Garde Mobile uniforms are present at the courtroom scene in *This Land Is Mine*. There are also Vichy police in *To Have and Have Not*, set on a French Caribbean island. In this film, the Vichy henchmen are the villains, performing their anti–Free French duties with brutal zeal.

Paul Lukas plays a French policeman working under German supervision in *Uncertain Glory*. Although Lukas is a patriotic Frenchman, he goes through the motions of serving the Germans. His Gestapo superior disparages his ability, and even threatens to include him in the group of French hostages seized in retaliation, unless the perpetrators of an act of sabotage are arrested. Lukas convinces a French criminal (Errol Flynn) already sentenced to death to claim responsibility, thus saving the hostages.[28]

While the major French "collaborationist" politicians are never impersonated in wartime films, there are a number of direct references and allusions to Marshal Petain and Pierre Laval. Petain's portrait appears in several films, including *To Have and Have Not*, *Casablanca*, and *Passage to Marseilles*; in *The Cross of Lorraine*, the World War I military hero is referred to as an old man "in the hands of barbarians." Laval's name is linked with that of Norwegian traitor Quisling in

Reunion in France. Passage to Marseilles features a Vichy sympathizer named Duval (Sydney Greenstreet), which may be an allusion to Laval. Basil Rathbone portrays a French politician who collaborates with the Germans in *Paris Calling*, but he is not specifically identified as a Vichy official.

The few local politicians in occupied countries who are shown willingly cooperating with Axis occupation authorities are almost never shown giving the "Heil Hitler" or "Banzai" salutes— one exception occurs in the opening scene of *Hangmen Also Die*, as Heydrich's entourage, including collaborators, all perform the Nazi salutation. This absence of overt fascist allegiance seems to indicate that most collaborators have no ingrained affinity with their new masters, but are simply going along out of self-interest.

In virtually all of the Resistance films, the collaborators pay for their treason in the end. In *Back to Bataan*, a Filipino collaborationist mayor complains to his Japanese masters that his life has been threatened by the resistance and that little is being done to protect him. Sure enough, he is stabbed to death a short time later. Kaspar, the cannery owner in *The Moon Is Down*, is discovered wandering the streets of Trollness by a German patrol which is investigating the massacre of the occupation garrison. Driven insane by his ordeal, the babbling traitor is coldly shot by the Nazi soldiers. In *Commandos Strike at Dawn* a collaborator who has betrayed his fellow Norwegians to the Germans, is in turn denounced by his wife, even though she knows it will mean his death. He is drowned like a dog by his fellow villagers (including some of his relatives) when he tries to betray the resisters, secretly summoning a waiting German patrol craft with a dog whistle (an excellent example of crudely effective wartime symbolism, i.e., the Germans=fascist dogs). The obsequious Chinese provincial governor who betrayed a group of American flyers to the Japanese in *The Purple Heart* is stabbed to death by his own son! One of the Americans spits on the corpse as it is carried out of court, and the flyers later elect the son an honorary member of their group. In *Hangmen Also Die*, the cowardly collaborator (Gene Lockhart) is shot in the back by SS, and crawls up some church steps before expiring, in a scene which is evocative of the death of Rico in *Little Caesar* (WB, 1930).

A few collaborators re-convert and perform acts of redemption. Unable to endure the stigma associated with aiding the German occupiers and fearful that he might betray others, a Frenchman (George Sanders) in *This Land Is Mine* shoots himself. A village mayor in occupied France named Vitrey (the surname implying the vitreous nature of his obsequious behavior towards the Germans) atones for his political sins by preventing the Nazis from violating the honor of a novice nun who has helped an American flyer escape from the Nazis in *Till We Meet Again*.

Conclusions

Free men can't start a war, but once it's started they can fight on in defeat. Herdmen, followers of a dictator, can't do that. So it is always herdmen who win battles and the free men who win wars.[29]

The wartime Resistance films are a carefully crafted genre: in a single motion picture, filmmakers portray Nazi atrocities, unselfish sacrifice, united action, and Allied solidarity. American movie audiences could be expected to learn from the ordeals that citizens of occupied countries were being subjected to, and to appreciate the brave response of these oppressed people. The ideals of freedom and democracy are presented as international, and the evils of fascism are shown to be widespread.

The reality of the situation in occupied Europe and Asia was irrelevant; the fact that Russian peasants probably did not look or act like those in *The North Star* was also beside the point. The Resistance films, like most wartime productions, were not intended to be documentary representations—their purpose was to entertain and to instill in wartime audiences a proper attitude towards the war.

21. Loose Lips Sink Ships: Spies, Saboteurs and Traitors

Mr. Industrialist, are you prepared to cope with the grim and deadly menace of sabotage? Do you imagine that the skilled agents of Germany, Italy and Japan will permit you to produce weapons of war—weapons which will bring about the defeat of these nations—without making every desperate effort to stop such production?[1]

For more than a decade, Japanese mass espionage was carried out in the United States and her territorial outposts while a complacent America literally slept at the switch ... on our own Pacific Coast there toiled a vast army of volunteer spies.... Little Tokyo, U.S.A. *(TCF, 1942)*

The spy/saboteur films of the World War II era are numerous, varied, and often unsubtle.[2] According to Hollywood,
Axis spies were as thick as fleas in the years before Pearl Harbor, and their nefarious plots continued to threaten the war
effort throughout the war. Cautionary slogans like "Loose Lips
Sink Ships," and the government's censorship of soldiers' mail
reinforced the public's belief that the spy menace was real and
threatening.

Yet, when confronted with such fears, the government
(and particularly the FBI, charged with stopping enemy activities within the United States) consistently denied the existence of a serious problem. There were a few spies in pre-
war America, the FBI had to admit. Indeed, the publicity
garnered by the notorious breakup of German spy rings in 1938
and 1941 fueled American indignation against the Axis even
before the attack on Pearl Harbor.[3] However, these matters
were well under control by December 1941, according to the
FBI. The public was not so sure.

In June 1942, Nazi Germany sent eight agents to the
United States in U-boats with orders to attack defense plants
in Philadelphia, New York, East St. Louis, and Alcoa, Tennessee.[4] However, the first four saboteurs, landing on a Long
Island beach, were spotted by a Coast Guard patrolman. A
short time later, one of the Germans surrendered to federal
authorities, informing on his companions. All were arrested and
six were executed. This episode, fictionalized in *They Came to
Blow Up America* (TCF, 1943), merely reinforced America's
belief in the spy and saboteur threat.[5] How else could the Japanese have caught us so unprepared at Pearl Harbor? What else
could explain the accidents and fires at defense plants?

Vainly, the government protested:

We have had isolated cases of mischief to military goods in process
of manufacture; but according to the F.B.I. not a single case can with
certainty be traced back to the German, Italian, or Japanese war machines.[6]

Today, it seems that there was a middle ground between
Hollywood's tales of lurking spies and saboteurs and the FBI's
staunch declaration that America was safe. There *were* unusual
occurrences at defense plants and in other vital areas, even
after Pearl Harbor. And while *most* may be blamed on carelessness, accidents, and personal malice:

the German documents show indelibly that, contrary to all indignant protestations and phony disclaimers, the Abwehr [German military intelligence] was in the sabotage business in the United States
on a substantial scale throughout the war.[7]

Regardless of the real truth of the matter, what is certain
is that Hollywood films represented the spy/saboteur menace
as real and serious, particularly in the first two years of war.
As the following charts indicate, the totals for Spy Coding references and Spy Genre films are very high in 1942 (Spy/Sabo-
teur was the second most frequently cited coding term of that
year), but decreased dramatically as the war went on:

	1942	1943	1944	1945	Total
Spy *Coding*	94	60	22	8	184
Spy *Genre*	55	19	7	2	83
% of war-relevant films	21%	8%	4%	2%	10%

It can be seen that the incidence of spy/saboteur *coding*
is much higher than films considered as Spy *genre* films (or hy-
brids, like spy comedies). While the totals drop significantly
for both in 1944–45, brief coding references to spies or sabotage may be found in a number of films, but Spy genre films
are very scarce in this period, less than one-third the total of
films containing spy/saboteur coding.

The films of primary interest in this study are the Spy
genre films, films containing significant plots or sub-plots
about spies or saboteurs. Most of the films discussed in this
chapter are 1942–43 releases, the peak years for such films in
Hollywood. Many 1942 releases were, if not actually produced, at least conceived in 1941 before America's entry into
the war. As noted in Part One, the popularity of spy films
had soared in the 1939–1941 period, and by 1941 Hollywood
was no longer even bothering to disguise its Allied sympathies.[8]

Consequently, a number of 1942 spy films are only peripherally related to the *United States*' war effort: these include
films set overseas, and films which involve American aid to
Great Britain. Films which include or mention the attack on
Pearl Harbor, often as the climactic event, form a sort of middle ground or transition between pre-war style spy films and
true wartime spy films.

Among the films set overseas is *The Great Impersonation*
(Universal, 1942), an updated version of a WWI-theme novel.
Ralph Bellamy plays a German officer recruited to substitute
for his exact double, a British nobleman, thus paving the way
for his penetration into the upper echelons of British military
planning. *Sherlock Holmes and the Secret Weapon* and *Sherlock
Holmes and the Voice of Terror* (both Universal, 1942) are set
in wartime England, as is *Counter-Espionage* (Columbia, 1942).
These films not only have British settings, but most also feature British protagonists, another sign that Hollywood was
not quite geared up for the war.

Africa, the Middle East, and the Far East (including the
South Pacific) are also popular spy haunts, as depicted in *Bombs
Over Burma* (Columbia, 1942), *Law of the Jungle* (Monogram,
1942), *Drums of the Congo* (Universal, 1942), *Cairo* (MGM,
1942), *Lure of the Islands* (Monogram, 1942), *Jungle Siren*
(PRC, 1942), and *A Yank in Libya* (PRC, 1942). The latter
two films have the Nazis trying to foment "native" rebellions
against the Allies. Given the Nazis' well-known racial policies,
these films may seem rather farfetched today, but in real life
the Nazis were not averse to supporting (and encouraging or
even suggesting) rebellions, particularly in areas where the Allies would be inconvenienced by civil unrest (stories of a Nazi
alliance with the Irish Republican Army make good reading

but the actual results of such cooperation were slight). The Japanese were also involved in this type of activity, cloaking it under the category of Asian resistance to white colonialism (ignoring the fact that many countries under Japanese imperial domination—Korea, Manchuria, the Philippines, and so forth—were themselves racially Asian). The Indian separatist Chandra Bose threw in his lot with Japan, and a puppet government was established in the Philippines (the latter is alluded to in *Back to Bataan*, RKO 1945).

American aid to Britain "short of war" was a fact of life from the latter part of 1940. In real life and in Hollywood, this aid was the target of Axis skullduggery. Saboteurs try to destroy a Lend-Lease shipment of tanks in *The Bugle Sounds* (MGM, 1942). In *Careful, Soft Shoulder* (TCF, 1942), *Dangerously They Live* (WB, 1942), *Nazi Agent* (MGM, 1942), *Spy Ship* (WB, 1942), and *Who Done It?* (Universal, 1942), among other films, details of convoys to Great Britain are sought by Axis agents. *My Favorite Blonde* (Paramount, 1942) teams bumbling American vaudeville performer Bob Hope with British agent Madeleine Carroll, who is being pursued by Nazis because she knows when Lend-Lease bombers to England are scheduled to leave. All of these films could have easily been released in 1941, and many were undoubtedly conceived in that year.[9]

Films which work in the attack on Pearl Harbor are interesting, and somewhat more timely than the previously discussed spy pictures. One thing these Pearl Harbor films have in common is the sense that the war between the Axis and the United States had already been joined prior to December 7, 1941, but that it took the Japanese attack to make most Americans (including the protagonists of some of these films) realize this fact.

Secret Agent of Japan (TCF, 1942) and *Escape from Hong Kong* (Universal, 1942), are two films with very similar plotlines. Both films involve expatriate Americans in China (*Secret Agent of Japan* takes place in Shanghai) who become involved with a female British agent and are pitted against German and Japanese spies. Both films culminate with the December, 1941, Japanese attacks on U.S. and British Pacific possessions (in *Secret Agent of Japan* news of the Pearl Harbor bombing arrives towards the end of the film; in *Escape from Hong Kong*, the initial Japanese attack on Hong Kong is recreated at the climax). In both films the American protagonist is transformed from a detached and "neutral" observer to an active participant in the war, ending with the hero's stated intention to join forces with Chiang Kai-shek's Nationalist Chinese. Except for the last-minute inclusion of the Pearl Harbor/Hong Kong attacks, however, both of these films are very pre-war in style and content.

Remember Pearl Harbor! (Republic, 1942), *Stand by All Networks* (Columbia, 1942), and *Texas to Bataan* (Monogram, 1942) also bring in the Pearl Harbor attack at various points in their narratives. The latter film actually transpires almost

entirely before December 7, 1941, as the three "Range Busters" encounter saboteurs out west, then escort a shipment of horses for the Army to the Philippines. After wiping out a spy ring in Manila, the cowboys return to the States, but news of the attack on Pearl Harbor inspires them to join the armed forces so they can finish the job they have already started.

Stand by All Networks is the story of broadcaster Bob Fallon (John Beal), who is fired from his job for his pre–Pearl Harbor "alarmist" views. The Japanese attack proves his point; Bob tracks down a clandestine Axis radio, saves a troopship from sabotage, and is soon back on the air. *Remember Pearl Harbor!* takes place in the Philippines; three Army men face fifth columnists in the pay of Japan, *and* a German spy posing as a Dutchman. After news of the attack on Pearl Harbor, Lucky Smith (Don Barry) crashes a stolen Japanese plane into a Japanese warship participating in the invasion of the Philippines.

Perhaps the most detailed spy film utilizing Pearl Harbor in its plot is *Little Tokyo, U.S.A.*. The film begins with a montage of Japanese spy activity in the United States, accompanied by narration describing the pre-war preparations of Japan. Takimura (Harold Huber), a Japanese-American importer, visits Tokyo and is appointed head of spy activities on the West Coast, replacing an admiral whose military expertise is needed elsewhere.[10] Takimura and his fellow conspirators—including a German-American named Marsten—assemble maps and diagrams of vital defense facilities, steal plans for new aircraft, and eagerly await the day of reckoning. Suspicious police detective Mike Steele (Preston Foster, who had already opposed German and Japanese agents in *Secret Agent of Japan*) disagrees with his girlfriend, anti-war broadcaster Maris Hanover (Brenda Joyce):

MARIS: Why don't you give up the idea that every Japanese gardener is an Army officer, and enjoy life?
MIKE: Don't kid yourself that there isn't a Jap spy ring right here in Little Tokyo—and they're getting ready for something.

Steele, framed for murder by the Japanese agents, is languishing in jail when Pearl Harbor is attacked. Although most Japanese nationals are taken into custody as enemy aliens, Japanese-Americans like Takimura are still free, preparing for the "next phase" of Japan's attack: the Aleutians, western Canada, and then the West Coast of the United States. Steele escapes from jail and tricks Takimura—and his Anglo henchman Hendricks (Don Douglas), the manager of the radio station where Maris works—into confessing their traitorous intentions. The spies are arrested by the police (Takimura tries to commit suicide but Steele stops him). The film ends with stock footage of the evacuation of *all* Japanese-Americans from the West Coast. The newly converted Maris makes a final news broadcast, admitting that "unfortunately ... the loyal must suffer inconvenience along with the disloyal."

Little Tokyo, U.S.A. is a fairly lurid and uncompromising

Texas to Bataan (Monogram, 1942): In 1942, Hollywood saw spies and saboteurs everywhere, even out West. The "Range Busters" wrapped up a spy ring in Texas, then defeated another in Manila, just before Pearl Harbor.

indictment of Japanese spying and sabotage[11] but its final form is actually *milder* than originally intended. After strong protests from the Office of War Information and others, 20th Century–Fox made a few changes.[12] Takimura states that "most" Japanese-Americans are loyal to the United States; one positive Japanese-American character is depicted—Oshima (Richard Loo), who, in response to Steele's question about his loyalty, states, "I'm an American." He agrees to help Steele track down a hidden spy radio, and is murdered (beheaded, "the accepted Black Dragon method of eliminating people") for his patriotic efforts. On the whole, however, most Japanese residents of the United States shown in the film—citizens or not—are depicted as actual or potential spies and saboteurs.

The duplicity of the Japanese characters is illustrated in a number of ways. A young Japanese boy, whose boasting initially alerts Steele to the presence of a powerful spy radio trans-

mitter in the area, is severely beaten by his father (a spy) for talking. Later, when questioned by Steele, the boy refuses to talk, out of fear and "loyalty to the Emperor." In another sequence, a Japanese man and woman loudly insist upon their constitutional "rights" when Steele tries to learn the whereabouts of his friend Oshima (the OWI was not too happy with Steele's tough statement: "The only warrant I need is my badge"). Finally, after the attack on Pearl Harbor, the Japanese-American community hypocritically throws itself into the war effort, selling bonds ("Buy a Bomber to Beat Japan") and putting up signs in their shop windows reading "We Are Loyal U.S. Citizens." But as *Little Tokyo, U.S.A.* clearly shows, this is merely a front for their sinister espionage plans.

The fear of a "fifth column" in the United States was present from 1939 through 1941; the activities of the German-American Bund were "exposed" in *Confessions of a Nazi Spy*

(Warner Bros., 1939), and other films of the pre–Pearl Harbor period also feature both foreign-born and native fascists. After Pearl Harbor, these fears resurfaced for a time. Particularly suspect were Japanese-Americans in Hawaii and California, as *Little Tokyo, U.S.A.* shows, but German-Americans and Italian-Americans also came in for their share of suspicion.

But Hollywood did not stress the traitorous potential of these groups with nearly as much vigor. *Margin for Error* (TCF, 1942) includes a German-American Bundist in its cast, but he is depicted as foolish and vain, and is belittled even by his Nazi superiors. Indeed, German-Americans are often seen as patriotic anti–Nazis, despite pressure placed on them by agents of "the Fatherland." *Waterfront* (Monogram, 1944) concerns a German-American who is blackmailed into helping Nazi spies by threats to his family, still trapped in Germany. In *The Phantom Plainsmen* (Republic, 1942), a Nazi operative similarly threatens a German-American with news that the Gestapo has his grandson in custody. *Nazi Agent* (MGM, 1942) features a German-American refugee who is forced to aid enemy spies by his twin brother, a fanatical Nazi (both roles played by Conrad Veidt, a German exile). The good brother eventually kills his evil twin and assumes his identity, in the hopes of somehow aiding the Allied cause.[13]

A few similarities in the initial group of wartime spy films should be obvious: the spies are usually a mixed Axis team of Germans and Japanese, with occasional Italian assistance. There are also traitors or collaborators from Allied nations—Chinese, British, Dutch, and American, or at least characters *posing* as Allied nationals—working with or for the Axis agents. Sometimes these collaborators are working for money only, but at other times they are home-grown fascists, associating with the Nazis and Japanese out of sincere sympathy for the Axis cause. Occasionally, they are both. Examples of such characters, in addition to Hendricks of *Little Tokyo, U.S.A.*, are Tobin (Otto Kruger) in *Saboteur* (Universal, 1942), and Lorenz (Sydney Greenstreet) in *Across the Pacific* (WB, 1942). Other collaborators appear in *Careful, Soft Shoulders* (TCF, 1942), *Riders of the Northland* (Columbia, 1942), *Texas Manhunt* (PRC, 1942), *The Lady Has Plans* (Paramount, 1942), and *Lucky Jordan* (Paramount, 1943), among other films.[14]

In the latter two films, American gangsters conspire to steal secret plans, with the intention of selling them to the Axis. This type of collaboration, a holdover theme from the pre-war years, almost entirely disappeared after 1942. Any hint that an American, even a criminal, would willingly cooperate with the enemies of his country was considered a forbidden topic. In *Seven Miles from Alcatraz* (RKO, 1943), an escaped convict refuses to deal with Nazi spies, saying "We're hoodlums, but we're *American* hoodlums." One of the gangsters who helps defeat the Nazi spy ring in *All Through the Night* proudly says, "The *people* did it."

One of the more interesting "collaborator" films of 1942

is *Spy Ship*. Irene Manning plays Pamela Mitchell, a spokesperson for the "American Above All" committee. Mitchell is identified as a wealthy aviatrix: it is obvious the filmmakers were making a not-so-subtle reference to real-life pilot Charles Lindbergh, the most famous member of the isolationist America First Committee. However, apparently fearful of a lawsuit—given the nature of the film's "female Lindbergh"—*Spy Ship* makes enough changes in the character to avoid a direct comparison. Pamela Mitchell is not only an isolationist (the film transpires just before Pearl Harbor), she is also a traitor whose public speeches contain coded references to Lend-Lease convoy sailing dates, for the use of prowling German U-boats! Pamela is murdered by the Nazi spy chief, and the rest of the enemy agents are eventually rounded up.

The gimmick of passing coded information via a public speech (sometimes over the radio and sometimes in a song) was hardly original: other films using variations on this idea include *The 39 Steps* (British, 1935), *Meet Boston Blackie* (Columbia, 1941), *Who Done It?* (Universal, 1942), *King of the Cowboys* (Republic, 1943), and many others. Allied agents also make use of this trick more than once, notably in *Paris Calling* (Universal, 1942), in which a piano in a French cafe is connected to a secret radio transmitter!

After the plethora of spy films in 1942, Hollywood seemingly began to tire of the subject. There are still a significant number of spy plots and references in 1943, but 1944 and 1945 show a steep decline. Interestingly enough, perhaps in response to the government's campaign downplaying the wartime *domestic* spy menace, at least three of the films in these last two years are set in the pre–Pearl Harbor period, and at least six are set in foreign locales.

Thus, spy and saboteur films set during WWII in the continental United States were by and large produced during a relatively short period, although a substantial number accumulated during this interval. While spies and saboteurs were virtually interchangeable in the public mind, for the sake of this chapter the two types of enemy agents will be discussed separately. However, many of the films combine the two activities, and plots used in one type of film were often easily transposed to the other. Generalizations about saboteur films apply equally to spy films, and vice versa.

Sabotage

Most Americans realized that the industrial might of our nation was going to be the factor which would tip the scales in favor of the Allies. Thus, sabotage was seen as a potential Axis weapon, and Hollywood films of the period contain a high number of sabotage references. Among the favorite targets of saboteurs in these films are defense plants (particularly aircraft plants and shipyards), oil refineries, mines, ships and trains (loaded with food, war materials, and troops), the

Panama Canal and other waterways, and food supplies (crops and cattle herds). However, the Nazis and their henchmen rarely accomplish their task: in nearly every film, they are apprehended before actually causing severe damage to their targets.

But this is not always the case. *Saboteur* (Universal, 1942), begins with a fatal fire at an aircraft plant in California. Later, the same gang tries to sabotage a warship being launched in New York, but their plans just barely go awry (earlier, one of the saboteurs briefly smiles when he sees a photograph of the *Normandie*, a French liner which burned in New York while being refitted as a warship; the intimation is that *this* was his work).[15]

King of the Cowboys is an odd film, since the sabotage ring is unidentified—there are *no* references to the Nazis or Japanese, and all the members of the gang are American. However, regardless of their origin, they do cause a string of fires and explosions before Roy Rogers tracks them down. In *Timber* (Universal, 1942) and *Texas Manhunt* (PRC, 1942), saboteurs disrupt timber and beef production, respectively, but no major, crippling blows are struck before the heroes arrive on the scene.

More often, the saboteurs are thwarted by vigilant Americans. Sometimes these heroes are just citizens who stumble onto enemy agents, but frequently the saboteurs are defeated by official or semi-official representatives of the government. This may have been one way of reassuring Americans that the FBI and other counter-spy agencies were on the job.

Secret Command (Columbia, 1944), one of the last wartime sabotage films, stars Pat O'Brien as a government agent assigned to work undercover in a shipyard. He poses as a worker in order to expose the sabotage ring headed by a member of the Gestapo (that the Gestapo was a Nazi organization chiefly concerned with *internal* security did not bother Hollywood—few Americans would have recognized "Abwehr," the name of the German intelligence agency, but *everyone* knew about the Gestapo). Bruce Bennett tangles with saboteurs in *Sabotage Squad* and *Underground Agent* (both Columbia, 1942). In the first film he is a member of the police "subversives" squad,[16] and in the latter film he is a telephone company operative brought into the case by the government. FBI agent George Sanders adopts an entirely new identity and travels to Germany in *They Came to Blow Up America*. After training as a saboteur, he is sent back to the United States in a U-boat. Through his testimony, his fellow saboteurs and many other Nazi spies in America are captured.[17] After undergoing a fake court-martial to establish his *bona fides*, Army officer Humphrey Bogart saves the Panama Canal from destruction at the hands of Japanese agents in *Across the Pacific* (Warner Bros., 1942).

Even semi-official representatives of the government help foil sabotage. Laurel and Hardy, rejected by the Army, become civil defense workers in *Air Raid Wardens* (TCF, 1943). They

are too inept even for this duty, but manage to defeat a Nazi gang plotting the destruction of a magnesium plant.[18] In *War Dogs* (Monogram, 1942), a security guard (a WWI veteran) sacrifices his life to prevent saboteurs from blowing up the defense plant he is guarding.[19]

This is not to belittle the anti-spy/saboteur efforts of the common man in wartime Hollywood. Aircraft plant worker Robert Cummings in *Saboteur* travels across the entire continent, not only to clear himself of a charge of sabotage and murder, but also to shatter the sabotage gang itself before it can do any more harm. Intern John Garfield is unwittingly enmeshed in espionage in *Dangerously They Live*, and he also manages to come out on top, as does reporter Richard Travis in *Spy Train*. Ordinary, decent men, with no special counter-espionage, military, or law enforcement training, they nonetheless rise to the occasion. In a way, this could be construed as an allusion to the United States itself: while not a militaristic culture (as, for example, Germany and Japan are portrayed), the United States does what it must in time of danger to prevail over the forces of evil.

And not only stalwart leading men and women prove themselves capable of heroism when faced with the specter of sabotage and espionage: many film comedians encounter Axis agents, including the Ritz Brothers (*Behind the Eight Ball*, Universal 1942), Abbott and Costello (*Who Done It*, and *Rio Rita*, MGM 1942), Judy Canova (*Joan of Ozark*, 1942), Joe E. Brown (*Joan of Ozark* and *The Daring Young Man*, Columbia 1942), Bob Hope (*My Favorite Blonde*, and *They Got Me Covered*, Paramount 1943), the East Side Kids (*Ghosts on the Loose*, Monogram 1943 and *Let's Get Tough*, Monogram 1942), and Red Skelton (*I Dood It*, MGM 1943), in addition to the previously mentioned Laurel and Hardy encounter with saboteurs in *Air Raid Wardens*. There are also comic spy films of a somewhat higher class, such as *Cairo* (MGM, 1942) with Jeanette MacDonald, and those of rather lower quality (*Hillbilly Blitzkrieg*, Monogram 1942).

Most of these films begin with the protagonist (or protagonists) *accidentally* stumbling across Axis agents. In *Ghosts on the Loose*, the East Side Kids decide to fix up the house where Glimpy's sister (Ava Gardner!) is going to live after she is married. They go to the house next door by mistake, and run afoul of a Nazi spy ring. In *Joan of Ozark*, mountain girl Judy Canova unwittingly foils a Nazi plot when she shoots a pigeon the spies use to carry their messages. The Ritz Brothers are last-minute replacements at a rural theatre, which just happens to be located in a barn housing Nazi radio apparatus (*Behind the Eight Ball*). As fantastically unreal as these films are, they suggest several things: first, that even the most idiotic American is more than a match for enemy spies and saboteurs; second, that enemy agents are, by and large, bumbling incompetents.

On the whole, therefore, Hollywood played it safe. Saboteurs are out there, threatening America's war industries and

War Dogs (Monogram, 1942): Billy Lee makes the ultimate sacrifice, giving up his best friend to be trained as an Army dog.

natural resources. But America's counter-espionage agencies, police forces, and even everyday Americans are capable of stopping the Axis saboteurs in their tracks.

Spies

In addition to sabotaging America's factories, enemy agents were involved in a number of other nefarious schemes, at least according to Hollywood. There are many films in which spies attempt to obtain plans for new weapons or inventions, a frequent pre-war plot device. Films of this type include *A Date with the Falcon* (RKO, 1942—a formula for synthetic diamonds), *Dawn Express* (PRC, 1942—a formula for a gasoline additive), *Eyes in the Night* (MGM, 1942—another "secret formula"), *Foreign Agent* (Monogram, 1942—plans for an anti-aircraft searchlight filter), *Hillbilly Blitzkrieg* (rocket plans), *The Lady Has Plans* (Paramount, 1942—plans for a new torpedo), *Lucky Jordan* (Paramount, 1942—new tank

armor), *Joe Smith—American* (MGM, 1942—a new bombsight), *Sherlock Holmes and the Secret Weapon* (Universal, 1942—*another* new bombsight), *Ship Ahoy* (MGM, 1942—a new magnetic mine), *Bombardier* (RKO, 1943—*another* new bombsight), *We've Never Been Licked* (RKO, 1943—another "secret formula"), and so forth.

Ironically, the Norden bombsight had *already* been obtained by German agents, who stole the plans piecemeal over a period of several years in the late 1930s.[20] A great deal of technical information had been spirited out of the United States in the 1930s by German agents: some of it was obtained through theft and bribery, but a good deal was simply culled from technical journals and reports which were available to the general public.

Films of this sort continue to appear throughout the war, although in greatly reduced numbers. As late as 1945, films like *Escape in the Fog* (Columbia), *The Jade Mask*, and *The Scarlet Clue* (both Monogram) revolve around spies who try to obtain secret plans, formulae, and reports.

Most spy films of the period make little effort to realistically portray spy activities.[21] In fact, most films pay little attention to the mechanics of spying at all—movie spies usually kill, threaten, or kidnap people in an attempt to obtain the desired secrets; there is relatively little stealthy surveillance, complicated burglary, or secret micro-photography. Few Hollywood films address the mundane aspects of spying as well as *Next of Kin* (Universal, 1943), a British film released in the United States with an added prologue spoken by J. Edgar Hoover. In this film, spies, in such simple ways as eavesdropping on everyday conversations, collect enough information to ambush a British commando raid on France. Although *Action in the North Atlantic* contains scenes of a shady character asking for ship movement information in a waterfront bar, Hollywood films generally prefer to emphasize the action, adventure, and mystery aspects of the spy genre over the technical details of espionage.[22]

Secrets of Scotland Yard (Republic, 1944) at least makes an attempt to be different. Set in England shortly after Hitler's invasion of Poland in 1939, the film deals with the British Cipher Bureau, responsible for cracking the Nazi codes. However, shortly after the First World War, the Germans are farseeing enough to plant a double-agent in the British agency, and the search for this "mole" is the focus of the film. There is also a modicum of attention paid to the actual code-breaking chores of the bureau. The film hardly eschews melodrama altogether, though: the plot hinges on identical twin brothers (both played by Edgar Barrier), with one taking the other's place in the bureau, after the first man's murder at the hands of Axis agents.

A somewhat similar film is *Pacific Rendezvous* (MGM, 1942). Lee Bowman goes to work in the Office of Naval Intelligence code room, deciphering German and Japanese radio messages. He learns the Axis partners are coordinating their espionage efforts and pinpointing American convoys in the Pacific. Bowman's superior officer is murdered by his mistress, who is actually a spy. Captured by the spy ring and threatened with death if he does not decipher a coded dispatch so it can be relayed to the Axis, Bowman plants a call for help in the message, which is then intercepted by Naval Intelligence, and the FBI rounds up the spy ring.

Enemy agents in wartime Hollywood do not restrict themselves to stealing secret plans. Despite what would seem to be the necessity of keeping their presence and activities hidden, spies cannot resist trying a little propaganda from time to time. In *Ghosts on the Loose*, Bela Lugosi and his gang are turning out pro–Nazi pamphlets ("How to Destroy the Allies" and "What the New Order Means to You") on a printing press hidden in the basement of a "haunted" house. The Axis agents in *Rio Rita* are a bit more level-headed: their propaganda is aimed at Mexico, historically a nation with a strong anti–U.S. bias (although an Allied nation in WWII), and they even try to convince a popular Latin singing star to cooperate with

them in the plot. The spy ring in *Foreign Agent* tries a little bit of everything: under the auspices of a front organization called the "North American Peace Association," the agents preach isolationism and anti-war sentiments. They also try to steal a searchlight-filter invention, thus paving the way for a successful Japanese bombing raid on Los Angeles!

There are Axis attempts to foment uprisings among the "natives" in Africa and the Middle East, mentioned earlier; in *Northern Pursuit* (Warner Bros., 1943), the Nazis try to enlist Canadian Indians in their battle against the Allies, and also plan to bomb waterways and canals between the United States and Canada. Finally, Axis agents even try counterfeiting War Savings Stamps—in *Secrets of the Underground* (Republic, 1942)—as well as bonds and U.S. currency—in *I Escaped from the Gestapo* (Monogram, 1943)—in an attempt to disrupt the American war economy.

But nothing worked. In film after film, spy after spy—sinister, bumbling, murderous—succumbs to his or her own ineptitude, the vigilance of Allied counter-spies, the accidental intervention of everyday Americans, and the treachery or incompetence of their own accomplices. Perhaps the FBI was right: America *was* safe from spies and saboteurs.

Spies for Our Side

It is rather surprising to discover that very few films about American or other Allied spies were made *during* the war. In 1946, three major films about the topic were released: *O.S.S.* (Paramount—with Alan Ladd), *Cloak and Dagger* (Warner Bros.—with Gary Cooper), and *13 Rue Madeleine* (TCF—with James Cagney). But in wartime Hollywood, most Allied intelligence agents are shown participating in *counter*-espionage duties in the United States, in England, or in neutral countries (these references are generally coded as "Intelligence Service" and total only 46 for the whole war, about 25% of the Spy/Sab totals).

There are a few exceptions. A number of Resistance films, like the aforementioned *Paris Calling*, contain sequences in which the citizens of an occupied country pass information to the Allied armed forces (another good example is *Assignment in Brittany*, MGM 1943). *Miss V from Moscow* (PRC, 1942) deals with a Russian secret agent on duty in occupied France. Vera Morova (Lola Lane) cooperates with the resistance and two stranded Allied airmen to obtain information about U-boats, thus saving a Lend-Lease convoy bound for Russia. A number of the films dealing with Allied airmen downed behind enemy lines feature some incidental espionage/sabotage action. For example, *The Purple V* (Republic, 1943), concerns an American with the RAF who crashes in Germany. Donning the uniform of a German flyer as a disguise, the American comes into possession of a secret report destined for Hitler. Thus, the film becomes not only the story of his attempt to escape from Nazi Germany, but also to escape *with* the report.

There are several films about British intelligence agents at work in hostile territory. *Assignment in Berlin* (Columbia, 1943) stars George Sanders as a British officer cashiered in 1938 for his outspoken criticism of the Munich Pact. Recruited as a Nazi spy, he is actually a double agent, working for British Intelligence. Pretending to betray military secrets, Sanders is arrested and imprisoned. This solidifies his position with the Nazis, who bring him to Germany upon his release from prison. Sanders becomes a "Lord Haw-Haw" style propaganda broadcaster, but his radio messages to England really contain coded information for British Intelligence. His biggest scoop is news of the impending German invasion of England, and Sanders actually steals an airplane and crashes it into the invasion fleet, lighting the way for an RAF bombing attack.

Tonight We Raid Calais (TCF, 1943) features John Sutton as a British Commando who is selected by military intelligence for a secret mission in occupied France. He must locate a German tank factory located in the middle of a number of "dummy" factories so the RAF can bomb the real one. He is aided in his quest by members of the French Resistance.

Above Suspicion (MGM, 1943) is set before war actually breaks out, in 1939. American professor Fred MacMurray and his wife Joan Crawford are enlisted by British Intelligence—since they are "harmless" neutrals and thus *above suspicion*—to travel to Germany and find out what has happened to a British secret agent. Although the couple has adventures and narrow escapes galore, they are not official intelligence agents and are not, strictly speaking, operating in an enemy country.

Films like *Background to Danger* (Warner Bros., 1943) and *Passport to Suez* (Columbia, 1943) are "in-between" films, set in neutral countries (Turkey and Egypt).[23] They are better described as films of international intrigue like *Casablanca* (Warner Bros., 1943) and *The Conspirators* (Warners Bros., 1944), rather than films about Allied spies on intelligence-gathering missions in enemy territory.

One of the few wartime films to meet *those* criteria is *Invisible Agent* (Universal, 1942). Jon Hall is the grandson of the man who discovered the secret of invisibility. After Nazi and Japanese spies try to steal the formula from him, Hall (following the attack on Pearl Harbor) agrees to become an invisible spy for America. He parachutes into Germany on a mission to obtain a master list of Japanese spies in the United States (lists of enemy agents also figure in *Secret Agent of Japan*, and *They Got Me Covered*). He is aided by an anti–Nazi German (Albert Basserman) and a British spy (Ilona Massey). Hall also discovers plans for a massive German air raid on New York City, and foils the project by stealing one of the loaded bombers and destroying the crowded airfield.

Invisible Agent is quite lighthearted, despite its scenes of sinister Nazis and Japanese threatening torture. Hall's invisibility not only reinforces the concept of the Allies as innately superior to our enemies, it also provides a perfect opportunity for scenes in which the Nazis are portrayed as clumsy buffoons.

Additionally, the rivalry between the German and Japanese Axis "partners" (Peter Lorre is the chief Japanese agent, Baron Ikito and Sir Cedric Hardwicke is his Nazi opposite number) is ironically humorous. It eventually breaks out in open conflict, and Ikito kills his Nazi counterpart, then commits suicide. This is just one of a number of spy films in which the Axis partners argue, compete, and even openly fight among themselves. In *They Got Me Covered*, the enemy spies (German, Italian, and Japanese) race to interpret a shorthand notebook before their "allies" do; in *Spy Train* (Monogram, 1943), an Italian agent is literally stabbed in the back by Nazi spies.[24]

For the most part, therefore, between 1942 and 1945, the word "spy" was almost automatically and pejoratively applied to Axis agents. The Allies, it seemed, did not have to lower themselves to spying or sabotage to beat the enemy: our armed forces were enough. It was only the enemy who had to resort to sneaky, underhanded spying and sabotage in an attempt to gain an unfair advantage. When necessary, ordinary Americans rise to the occasion and carry out espionage and counterespionage duties, proving themselves in every way a match for the sinister professional spies of Germany and Japan—a fitting parallel to the concept of the American "citizen-soldier" who, when aroused by injustice or treachery (for example, the attack on Pearl Harbor), becomes a formidable foe, equal in every way to the permanent military establishment of our foes (see Chapter 16).

This is certainly an unrealistic view of warfare, but it is one which stacks the decks, morally, in favor of the Allies. And, after all, this was only to be expected of propaganda films: there was no room for moral ambiguity in wartime Hollywood.

22. Scrap Happy: Home Front Activities on Film

"Those poor civilians, they're having a tough time, having to give up their gas and tires and sugar, having to buy bonds ..."—a sarcastic Cpl. Barney Todd (Lloyd Nolan) in Bataan *(MGM, 1943)*

The typical American family was one which was donating blood, buying bonds, saving its tin cans and fats, collecting old newspapers and hunting up scrap metal...[1]

The coding category "Home Front" in the filmography encompasses a number of references to domestic participation in the war effort. While civil defense and other quasi-military activities are excluded (these are coded as "Home Defense"), there were many other war-related programs, organizations, and activities through which Americans "did their bit." These included buying War Bonds and Stamps,[2] donating blood to the Red Cross, participating in scrap drives, organizing and attending functions for various charities, and planting Victory Gardens.

The following chart illustrates the Home Front coding statistics by year:

	1942	1943	1944	1945	Total
Home Front:	26	45	32	10	113

As can be seen, Home Front references reach a peak in 1943, the first year Hollywood's releases had all been *produced* during wartime. The annual total drops off in the following two years, reinforcing the opinion that "community involvement in the war followed the same curve as war production, paralleling its spectacular rise and subsequent decline."[3]

It is interesting to note that, even in the peak year of 1943, there are few films *about* the home front in America. Passing references far outweigh plots dealing with Bonds, Victory Gardens, or Red Cross activities. There was simply not enough dramatic interest in such mundane, daily trivia, important as it may have been to those involved and to the war effort. However, unlike Hollywood's treatment of some other war-related topics—such as Home Defense—Home Front activities are rarely ridiculed. Even passing comments about Bonds, the Red Cross, etc., are given serious intonations. There are jokes, of course, but Hollywood knew better than to suggest that Bonds were not necessary, or that the Red Cross was a waste of time.[4]

There are a number of dramatic films set in the United States which more or less take the war as their starting point. *Rationing* (MGM, 1944), discussed in Chapter 11, is one such effort. *The Human Comedy* (MGM, 1943) is also clearly an attempt to show the war's effect on every day life in America. However, the one film which tries, more or less successfully, to encompass the entire "Home Front" experience is *Since You Went Away* (UA, 1944), in which "a single household serves as a microcosm of the war effort."[5]

Since You Went Away, long and sentimental, depicts the lives of the Hilton family, whose head (the father, Tim) is away at war. Anne Hilton (Claudette Colbert) and her two daughters, 17-year-old Jane (Jennifer Jones) and 13-year-old Brig (Shirley Temple), have to endure the financial hardships caused by Tim's sudden reduction in earnings (in civilian life he was an advertising executive, upper-middle class), as well as deal with rationing, shortages, and all of the other daily intrusions of the war.

In relatively short order, the Hiltons fire their maid (she continues to work for them in her spare time, for free) and take in a boarder (the gruff but kind-hearted Col. Smollett—Monty Woolley); their neighbor Mrs. Hawkins plans a dance for airmen from a nearby base; Brig plants a Victory Garden; Anne gets a job as a welder in a war plant; Jane postpones college, becomes a nurse's aide, and gets engaged to soldier Bill (Robert Walker), who is later killed in action; Tim is reported missing in action; Jane goes to work in a veteran's hospital; Tim is found, safe and sound. There are also plenty of "background" references, such as refugees, wounded soldiers, travel restrictions, blacks in the armed forces, historical references to Lincoln and the Civil War, *ad infinitum*. The film tries to be "the definitive cinematic statement about domestic life during the war."[6]

If anything, *Since You Went Away* is a bit too overblown and sentimental, and the fact that virtually *every* aspect of the home front is experienced by the Hilton family is rather hard to swallow. However, the film is powerful and certainly takes its home front issues more seriously than many lesser films.

Most other Hollywood productions did not attempt to weave an entire film around home front activities. Instead, topics such as War Bonds, Victory Gardens, and the Red Cross were used to give topical relevance to otherwise routine comedies, dramas, musicals, mysteries, and other genre efforts.

Any Bonds Today?

Bonds were one way the government financed its war effort. Taxes were another, but while Congress continually argued about the best way to levy and collect taxes, bonds were unarguably popular. During the First World War, Liberty Bonds had been sold in large quantities. In 1940, Congress authorized the issuance of a "defense bond," and the first Defense Savings Bonds—intended to finance America's rearmament in the face of growing world strife—went on sale in May 1941.[7]

"After Pearl Harbor the monthly sale of bonds tripled, bringing in more than a billion dollars a month,"[8] although the Defense Bond soon gave way to the War Bond. During the war, there were seven separate bond issuances (each a numbered "War Loan Drive"). All seven were oversubscribed, although many of the bonds were purchased by financial institutions and other corporate bodies, frustrating the U.S. government's plans to "sop up individual purchasing power and put a brake on inflation ... the individual quotas were never met, while institutional quotas were always over-subscribed."[9]

The Treasury Department enlisted the aid of Hollywood figures and other celebrities to sell bonds:

As in the First World War, show business celebrities were the most effective salesmen of bonds ... the bond drives grew increasingly vulgar and stunt-ridden....[10]

At least 71 films in the 1942–1943 period make some reference to Bonds, ranging from nearly subliminal glimpses of promotional posters in the background of a shot (*Hit the Ice* and *Shadow of a Doubt*, both Universal, 1943), to the devotion of major elements of the plot to the topic. Bonds references drop sharply in the 1944–1945 period, totaling only 41 for these two years, although bonds were still being promoted and sold by the government (there was even a post-hostilities "Victory Loan" drive). Numerically, 1943 was the peak year for bond references (46), followed by 1944 (27), but films utilizing bonds in their plots are more prevalent in the first two years of war.

In *Home in Wyomin'* (Republic, 1942), Gene Autry sings "Any Bonds Today," a song written by Irving Berlin.[11] Celebrities are shown selling bonds in *Ladies Day* (RKO, 1943—a movie star, played by Lupe Velez), *The Sky's the Limit* (RKO, 1943—a Flying Tiger ace, played by Fred Astaire), and *You Came Along* (Paramount, 1945—three war heroes, including Bob Cummings). In the latter film, a bond tour takes the Air Corps officers across the country in 10 days, but they spend most of their time womanizing in the various cities they visit. The film is literally plastered with bonds posters, but the three "heroes" do not take their duties very seriously, and the local bond-drive officials are presented as pompous, self-important businessmen. The importance of buying bonds is hardly mentioned in this late entry in the "bond tour" sub-genre.

In *My Son, the Hero* (PRC, 1943), a well-known war correspondent makes a bond-selling tour of the United States. He visits his father (Roscoe Karns), carrying $100,000 in cash from bond sales (it seems unlikely that the Treasury Department would entrust the cash from bond sales to their celebrity salespeople, but in this film they do). The cash is subsequently "lost" (wagered on a horse) by Karns and his cronies, but all ends well, and the money is recovered and turned over to the government.

Bond rallies, often held in defense plants, stadiums, and other public places, usually featured speeches and entertainment, all calculated to encourage people to buy War Bonds. Such rallies are depicted in *Carolina Blues* (Columbia, 1944), *Sing a Jingle* (Universal, 1944), and *Between Two Women* (MGM, 1945). In *The Gang's All Here* (MGM, 1943), admission to a fancy party at a palatial estate is the purchase of $5,000 in War Bonds. *A Gentle Gangster* (Republic, 1943) begins with a minister criticizing his church congregation for

their failure to buy enough War Bonds. The film's protagonist, chairman of the local Bond drive, mounts the pulpit and makes a speech, urging his fellow citizens to "whip out our dollars and slash the enemy across his ugly face." A major scene in *Mountain Rhythm* (Republic, 1943) is a bond-selling contest between the hillbilly Weaver Family and the students at an exclusive prep school.

As mentioned earlier, there are a few films which directly involve War Bonds in their plots. Several of these are crime films: *Secrets of the Underground* (Republic, 1942), depicts the actions of a Nazi spy ring that produces counterfeit War Savings Stamps. This seems to be a rather minor bit of sabotage, since the denominations ($.10 up to $5.00, which could be accumulated in small booklets until the total reached $18.75, the amount needed to purchase a $25.00 bond) were so small that the money thus denied the U.S. government would hardly make a difference in the war effort. In *The Falcon Strikes Back* (RKO, 1943), Gay Lawrence is framed for the theft of $250,000 in War Bonds, a perfect example of Hollywood's inclusion of a war-relevant element in a standard mystery plot. But for the most part, references to War Bonds in Hollywood films were just that—references.[12]

Digging for Victory: Victory Gardens

Government agencies, 4-H groups, and public schools all promoted cultivation of home gardens from the moment of Pearl Harbor. It became almost unpatriotic for people living in middle America not to have a victory plot beside the family home....[13]

Although not as ubiquitous as Bond references, depictions of—and verbal references to—Victory Gardens appear with some frequency during the war years in Hollywood productions. However, Victory Gardens are even less dramatic than War Bonds, so there are virtually no films with a major plot emphasis on home gardens. *In the Meantime, Darling* (TCF, 1944) depicts a hotel's communal Victory Garden plot, managed by the wives of Army officers, but this figures in several scenes at the most. Other Victory Garden references are more fleeting, including jokes and songs, as in *It's in the Bag* (UA, 1945), and *And the Angels Sing* (Paramount, 1944). Shirley Temple's character cultivates a Victory Garden in *Since You Went Away*; Cliff Edwards tries to grow a Victory Garden on a small plot of ground outside a lighthouse in *Seven Miles from Alcatraz* (RKO, 1943). And a left-handed reference to Victory Gardens appears in *Wing and a Prayer* (TCF, 1944), as a crew member on an aircraft carrier carefully tends a *hydroponics* garden on the ship!

In real life, Victory Gardens became popular in 1942, but really made an impact on the home front in 1943:

Whether it was patriotism or a means to supplement the family larder Victory Gardens produced 8,000,000 tons of food from 20,000,00 individual plots during 1943, enough production to make a difference in national food supplies.[14]

However, as with a number of other home front activities, participation in the Victory Garden boom fell off significantly in 1944 and 1945. Ironically, the additional food harvested from these gardens did not result in a significant decrease in the redemption of food ration coupons—the public continued to use all of their coupons, every month, stockpiling the food they did not consume. But Victory Gardens did provide fresh vegetables for variety in the diet of Americans on the home front, and gave participating gardeners a feeling of accomplishment and patriotism.

Scrap Happy

For all these drives the slogan was "Give Till It Hurts." So people gave ... the zest for the scrap drives was so high that the bungling and the swindles went almost unnoticed. People were simply glad to take part.[15]

Despite America's natural resources and great industrial strength, the country was not self-sufficient in all areas. Rationing and shortages (discussed in Chapter 24) sometimes resulted from the diversion of materials to the war effort, but in other cases were the result of a curtailment in imports. A great deal of effort was directed towards finding alternative methods of producing silk, rubber, and other needed materials, but this was generally the realm of a few scientists. The American people made *their* contribution by recycling paper, metal, even waste fats from the kitchen: it was the era of the scrap drives.

Today's environmentally conscious recyclers turn in their used household waste in an effort to "save the earth," but during WWII, citizens actively sought out needed materials, stripping their homes, garages, attics, and vacant lots in the name of the war effort. It was one way every American could contribute to winning the war, and did not require even the money needed to buy a war bond.[16]

The scrap drive mania began even before America officially entered the war. In the summer of 1941, the government asked citizens to donate 10,000 tons of aluminum, to be converted into airplanes for national defense. The U.S. public reacted with enthusiasm, turning in *70,000* tons of the metal. Unfortunately, it was then discovered that only "virgin" aluminum could be used to make warplanes, but the public had at least shown its willingness to sacrifice household wares for a good cause.[17]

During the war, the primary materials collected in scrap drives were rubber, paper, and metal. Sometimes the mania for recycling went to extremes: in *He Hired the Boss* (TCF, 1943), patriotic Stuart Erwin collects the tinfoil inner wrappers from cigarette packages! This foil, squashed into a ball, eventually helps Erwin defeat a gang of thieves.

Other Hollywood films use scrap drives as the source of various plot twists. Fred MacMurray, a car dealer whose business has been "Closed for the Duration," instead collects scrap metal at his car lot, and unearths a magic lamp (complete with genie) in a batch of donations, in *Where Do We Go from Here?* (Paramount, 1945). A valuable clue is uncovered in a box of scrap in *The Falcon in Danger* (RKO, 1943). One character remarks that this "salvage depot" is where "corkscrews [are turned] into battleships."

However, scrap drive references in most Hollywood films are less important and distinctive, but are rarely depicted as foolish or useless. As with other Home Front coding, scrap drive references dwindle in 1944 and 1945—again reflecting the general decline in participation in real life[18]—but the subject is still treated with respect.

The Red Cross and War Relief

References in Hollywood wartime films to the Red Cross generally come in two forms: signs, posters, and other manifestations of the Red Cross logo, often exhortations to donate blood, and in references to "first aid courses."[19] The Red Cross, of course, performed many additional duties during the war, from traveler's aid to refugee relief and liaison with prisoners of war, but Hollywood generally relegated these aspects of this organization to the background. In *The Master Race* (RKO, 1944), for instance, Red Cross parcels are prominently displayed in one scene, arriving for distribution to destitute Belgians just after their village has been liberated by Allied troops. However, no special mention is made of this.

There are also a number of wartime films featuring dances, musical shows, and other activities for the "benefit" of various war charities. Sometimes these are given the names of actual organizations, while others have fictitious names or are referred to generically as "War Relief."

Mexican Spitfire's Elephant (RKO, 1942) contains both types of Home Front references. As the film opens, Carmelita (Lupe Velez) is practicing first aid on her Uncle Matt (Leon Errol), in preparation for her "Red X" (as she calls its) class. The main plot revolves around a war relief show—consisting of various "United Nations" acts, including a Chinese magician and Dutch dancers—for an unspecified war charity purpose.

First aid references also appear in *The War Against Mrs. Hadley* (MGM, 1942), *The Powers Girl* (UA, 1943), and *The Youngest Profession* (MGM, 1943), among other films. Interestingly enough, this is one Home Front area treated humorously in some films, although in 1942 the subject was hardly considered trivial by most Americans:

There was a near-mania for first-aid instruction. The best-selling book of 1942 sold more than 8,000,000 copies. But because it was considered a pamphlet, it never appeared on best-seller lists. It was the official Red Cross handbook on first aid.[20]

However, first aid instruction—at least linked with the war effort—is often depicted as an outlet for the misguided zeal of foolish women and children, who practice bandaging family members and household pets. Perhaps because the war was geographically so far removed from the U.S. mainland—thereby reducing the chances that anyone would ever *use* first aid for a war-related injury—it was easier to spoof this basically noble impulse. The OWI film reviewer reporting on *Princess O'Rourke* (WB, 1943), describes a scene in which female Red Cross volunteers:

pounced upon the unwitting victim with 'sadistic glee' and displayed a presumably comic ineptitude with bandages and blankets.[21]

A nearly identical scene appears in *Blondie for Victory* (Columbia, 1942), as Blondie demonstrates her newly won knowledge for an eager audience of housewives, with Dagwood as the "injured person" who is soon completely mummified in bandages.

More "professional" Red Cross functions are treated with more respect. The Jennifer Jones character in *Since You Went Away* becomes a nurses' aide, and recites the Red Cross pledge at the stirring "capping" ceremony. She later goes to work in a veteran's hospital, tending to injured soldiers, and angrily defends this job as vitally important to the snobbish Mrs. Hawkins. Other film nurses of the period are almost without exception portrayed as competent, professional, and selfless.

War Relief functions are also occasionally shown in a lighter vein, although it is never suggested that the money raised would be misspent. *Mister Lucky* (RKO, 1943) contains

several examples, including the humorous sequence wherein Cary Grant learns to knit! Knitted scarves, sweaters and other items were often produced by patriotic home frontiers, for shipment to servicemen and refugees; in *True to Life* (Paramount, 1943), a family's youngest daughter is "knittin' a mitten for Britain."

The central plot of *Mister Lucky* involves Grant's efforts to swindle a War Relief organization out of its money; he helps the group set up a "casino night," but changes his mind about absconding with the proceeds, having discovered the true meaning of the fight against fascism.

Various other films feature charity events, among them *One Mysterious Night* (Columbia, 1944), *Chip Off the Old Block* (Universal, 1944), *The Gang's All Here* (MGM, 1943) and *Saboteur* (Universal, 1942). Sometimes these events coincide with the sale of War Bonds, or are musical presentations with one or two war-relevant numbers within a generally non-relevant framework. While details and statistics about this type of activity in real life on the home front are hard to come by, it is safe to say that Hollywood was exaggerating just a bit in its depiction of gala benefit dances and casino nights for War Relief.

The general impression given in Hollywood films of the period is, however, a very positive image of American participation in Home Front activities. Some of this was a deliberate attempt to encourage audiences to participate in such activities, but in many ways the films of WWII reflect the fact that many Americans *were* involved on the Home Front, in many ways.

23. Soldiers of the Home Front: The Battle of Production

More than any other war in history, World War II was a battle of production ... It was clear that we were playing a game of catch-up, and it was equally clear that the side with the most bombs, aircraft and weaponry would be the side that won the war.[1]

In retrospect, Allied victory appears to have been virtually inevitable once the United States entered the war. North America's industrial centers were untouched by enemy bombs or shells, and—unlike the besieged and vulnerable munitions factories of Germany and Japan—America's factories actually increased their output as the war went on:

War production peaked in November, 1943.... More than two-thirds of all goods produced ... were for the war. Ships were being delivered at the rate of six a day....[2]

The U.S. government, fully realizing the importance of America's factories, spent a good deal of time and effort reinforcing the concept of the factory worker as a vital part of the

Allied war machine. Hollywood paid lip service to this concept in many of its wartime films, as the following chart shows:

	1942	1943	1944	1945	Total
Production	66	68	61	21	216

These numbers are significant, but as shall be seen, Hollywood found factories and production topics of relatively little dramatic interest, and films about war work often revolve around spies and saboteurs, or take an unrealistic, musical comedy view of defense plants.

More significantly, a number of wartime films clearly indicate that working in a defense plant was a "second class" contribution to the war effort—a *real* man would join the armed forces, leaving women, blacks, and "4-Fs" to make the guns, planes, tanks, and bullets. Ironically:

With an overall death rate of 5 per 1,000 the military was a safer place to be than at home, where the death rate was more than twice as high and where the death and injury rates were higher still in war industries.[3]

In real life, the defense worker vs. soldier drama was played out between the War Manpower Commission—in charge of civilian employment—and the U.S. military and its "supplier," the Selective Service System. The armed forces, constantly pressing for more men, fought against occupational draft deferments, while industry struggled to keep its factories running as its male workers were drafted away.[4]

"Production" references in Hollywood wartime films generally fall into two categories: passing comments about "war work," often in a joking tone, and films which actually feature characters involved in war production jobs. There are numerous examples of the former, with cracks about "Grandma working the swing shift at Lockheed" and "lady welders," referring to the supposedly humorous side of defense work.

Peripheral references to production also occur in films like *Youth Runs Wild* (RKO, 1944). In this film, juvenile delinquents try to steal tires from the parking lot of a defense plant, knowing the factory workers can get a "priority" on replacements (so they can continue to commute to work).

Films actually dealing with war work often focus on melodramatic, romantic, or comedic aspects of production (or the workers' lives) rather than the job itself. This seems only logical, given Hollywood's primary function as entertainment for the mass audience. Films in this vein include *Saboteur* (Universal, 1942), which begins in an aircraft plant but quickly turns into a cross-country adventure (as Robert Cummings tries to track down the man who started a fatal fire), and *Joe Smith, American* (MGM, 1942), starring Robert Young as another ill-fated defense worker (who is kidnapped by spies and tortured for the knowledge he possesses about a new bombsight). *Gangway for Tomorrow* (RKO, 1943) deals with the lives of a group of defense workers who participate in a carpool. None of these films really addresses the protagonists' work in their respective industries, merely using defense work as a timely backdrop for their individual stories.

Wings for the Eagle (WB, 1942) spends somewhat more time on production. Beginning prior to Pearl Harbor, the film is set at a Lockheed aircraft plant in California. Among the workers at the factory are Dennis Morgan, Jack Carson, and George Tobias. Tobias, an immigrant, loses his job because he is not a U.S. citizen, but is re-hired after getting his citizenship papers; his son, meanwhile, joins the Air Corps and is killed when Japan invades the Philippines. Morgan, originally portrayed as a draft evader (keeping his "essential" Lockheed job), enlists and goes into the Air Corps, avenging Tobias's son by shooting down two Japanese airplanes. As in a 1943 film, RKO's *The Sky's the Limit*, there is a ceremony marking a production milestone (in *Wings for the Eagle*, the 2,000th bomber produced at the plant).

Another film concentrating even more closely on production (but including romance and drama as well, of course) is *Man from Frisco* (Republic, 1944). Loosely based on Henry J. Kaiser's "Liberty Ship" plan, this film also begins in the pre–Pearl Harbor period. Matt Braddock (Michael O'Shea) has an idea to increase ship production by pre-fabricating sections of the hull, superstructure, etc., but runs into opposition from the shipbuilding establishment, and the town where the shipyard is located. Pearl Harbor brings the people together in common cause, but a fatal accident caused by a faulty weld nearly ruins Matt's plans.[5] However, his idea has caught on, the first ship is completed on time, and Matt leaves to start prefabricated shipyards all over the country.

Man from Frisco contains a number of "production" clichés which are prevalent in wartime films: the workforce includes women as well as men, and workers of foreign extraction (in this case Italian, Irish, Russian, and Latin American). There are problems concerning inadequate housing for the new workers. One of the women workers gets the news her husband has been killed in action. There are various delays, problems, even accidents, but in the end the production goal is accomplished, and the workers cheerfully pull together to do their part for the war effort. Where this film breaks the mold, however, is in its central character, Matt Braddock. Braddock, a young leading man type, not only completes the job in this plant, he makes plans to establish more shipyards; in other words, he *stays* in production.

This was quite a departure for wartime Hollywood. Men in defense work are shown as either too old to fight (Brian Donlevy, in *An American Romance*, MGM, 1944, is a retired manufacturer who comes back to work to run an aircraft factory), or they work in plants or shipyards only after they are rejected by the armed forces: Allan Jones in *Sing a Jingle* (Universal, 1944), Eddie Bracken in *Hail the Conquering Hero* (Paramount, 1944), and Jess Barker in *Good Luck, Mr. Yates* (Columbia, 1943), for instance. In the latter two films the protagonist *pretends* to be in the service, ashamed of his 4-F status and his relegation to defense work.

In *Alaska Highway* (Paramount, 1943), Richard Arlen refuses to join his father's construction crew building the vital Al-Can Highway (between the United States and Alaska, through Canada), because he'd rather "sling lead at the Japs." He changes his mind, not because he is convinced of the necessity of the job, but because he is romantically pursuing Jean Parker. Ex-convicts staff a factory in *City of Silent Men* (PRC, 1942); in *The Chance of a Lifetime* (Columbia, 1943), *convicts* are given work-release to work in defense plants.[6]

Reinforcing the idea that factory work in wartime was the venue of old men, 4-Fs, women, comedians, minorities, and those physically unable to fight, are the numerous films in which employees of defense plants eagerly abandon (or try to abandon) their jobs for military service. This was an attempt to distance the protagonists of these films from the audience's general perception of defense workers:

There was no little talk of the factories being full of draft dodgers. Yet factory walls were covered with posters urging workers not to enlist. Repeatedly they were told they could serve their country best by staying where they were. It was their patriotic responsibility to wait to be drafted. They were told such things by management and government. But no one bothered to tell the rest of the country.[7]

As mentioned earlier, Dennis Morgan has a change of heart and leaves his factory job in *Wings for the Eagle*, but his example is eagerly followed by many other film characters. These include *Destroyer* (Columbia, 1943—Edward G. Robinson is a welder, a WWI veteran, who rejoins the Navy so he can serve on the ship he just helped build), *Hers to Hold* (Universal, 1943—Joseph Cotten is a former Flying Tiger working at a aircraft plant while waiting for his Air Corps commission to come through), *Hoosier Holiday* (Republic, 1943—the "Hoosier Hotshots" desperately want to quit their farm jobs and join the Air Corps, but their local draft board will not let them!), *The Sky's the Limit* (RKO, 1943—former Flying Tiger Fred Astaire turns down a job from a negatively portrayed defense contractor), *Rosie the Riveter* (Republic, 1944—Frank Albertson leaves his defense job for the Marines), and *Secret Command* (Columbia, 1944—Pat O'Brien works undercover at a shipyard to catch a Nazi saboteur, then joins the service to make a "real" contribution to the war effort).[8]

There are many more examples of this simultaneous denigration of production work/glorification of military service. While the value of serving in the armed forces could not be underrated—particularly by Hollywood—it is difficult to see why defense work was cast in such an unsatisfactory light. Eddie Bracken's character in *Bring on the Girls* (Paramount, 1945) quits his defense plant job to join the Navy, despite his lawyer's insistence that Bracken is "a vital war worker where you are." "Vital?" Bracken retorts, "All I do is take bolts from one box and put them in another. Then I take washers and change them from one box to another. Then the nuts! A six-year-old child could do it."[9] Later in the same film, a young woman, referring to her elderly, deaf fiancé, says "He's not much to look at, but all the good men are in the service."

Audiences undoubtedly cheered the heroic actions of film soldiers, sailors, and airmen, but most would have wondered at the sanity of characters like John Hodiak in *Marriage Is a Private Affair* (MGM, 1944). Army pilot Hodiak is discharged so he can supervise a critical factory production process, but spends the whole film pulling strings to get back into the service, and finally gets his wish: he is shipped overseas, away from his beautiful young wife (Lana Turner)!

In this type of film, defense workers other than the protagonist are rarely highlighted, except as passing examples of the "melting pot" cliche noted in *Man from Frisco*: whenever workers are characterized in some detail, there are almost always examples of older men, immigrants or workers of foreign descent, and women (blacks sometimes appear, but are rarely singled out; in reality, blacks entered the industrial labor force in great numbers during the war, but were subjected to discrimination in hiring and promotion, leading to serious racial strife in 1943).

Rosie the Riveter at Work and Play

One of the cliches which emerged fairly early in Hollywood war films was the generic female war worker, better known today as "Rosie the Riveter" (the title of Norman Rockwell's well-known painting, featuring a hefty female defense worker with a rivet gun—and one foot resting on a copy of *Mein Kampf*). Passing references to, and direct depictions of female factory workers (usually in aircraft plants, but sometimes shipyards or munitions plants) were almost wholly new to Hollywood films; prior to the war, working women were virtually always shown in female-dominated professions, including nursing, secretarial and office work, and teaching.

The following chart shows references to "Female Labor" in Hollywood films between 1942 and 1945. Films were coded in this way whenever a female character was depicted either in a directly war-oriented civilian profession (usually female factory workers), or when a female character was depicted in a previously male-dominated profession (a frequent Hollywood wartime example was the female cabdriver).

	1942	1943	1944	1945	Total
Fem Labor	17	45	41	17	120

These numbers are not at first glance impressively high, unless one realizes that virtually *none* of these references would have appeared in pre-war films. Hollywood was establishing a brand new stereotype, one that in fact was somewhat based on fact: the United States work force went from 24% female in 1940 to 33% female in 1944. By the summer of 1944, nearly 37% of the nation's war workers were women.[10]

Once again, Hollywood often chose to look at the comedic or melodramatic aspects of women's employment, both in the defense industry and elsewhere.[11] *Swing Shift Maisie* (MGM, 1943) is an interesting film which shows some insight into the wartime factory as a small community of its own, with classes and clubs for the workers in their free time. However, Maisie (Ann Sothern) gets little work done, spending most of her time pursuing a handsome test pilot (James Craig) and fending off the plots of jealous fellow worker Jean Rogers. Maisie is employed in a defense plant in the opening scenes of *Maisie Goes to Reno* (MGM, 1944), but she develops a nervous tic from overwork and is sent to Reno for a vacation (this film also features an all-girl orchestra, a popular wartime motif).

Republic won the right to produce "the" *Rosie the Riveter* film (1944), but once again any serious problems faced by

Rosie the Riveter (Republic, 1944): Jane Frazee and Vera Vague, wearing their aircraft plant ID tags, read a letter. Carl "Alfalfa" Switzer looks on.

women war workers are relegated to the background. Rosie (Jane Frazee) works in an aircraft plant, but her problems mostly concern her jealous boyfriend, a plant executive, who objects to her working, and the tribulations of sharing a room (platonically, of course) with male war workers (the women work the day shift, the men work the night shift).

In *Beautiful but Broke* (Columbia, 1944), an all-girl band breaks up because two of its leaders decide to become defense workers (inspired by romance, not necessarily through any particular patriotic motive). Claudette Colbert goes to work in a shipyard in *Since You Went Away* (UA, 1944) for both patriotic and financial reasons.

Thumbs Up (Republic, 1943), although a musical, is actually one of the more serious attempts to portray women in defense work (although, as usual, little time was spent showing them actually *working*). Set in England, the film stars Brenda Joyce and Elsa Lanchester as Louise, an American singer and Emmy, a Cockney chorus girl, respectively, who hire on at an aircraft factory. After a montage sequence depicting their training, the two women are given an orientation to their jobs by a female supervisor: "This is where they manufacture gray hairs for that nasty man in Germany." The supervisor points out other women working in the factory, and admits that the job is often difficult and boring, but it is one that has to be done. While Louise and Emmy work in an all-female section (under a male foreman), the factory's work force is made up of both male and female employees, and no distinction is made about the difficulty or worthiness of their duties or their competence (this film is also rare in the almost total absence of any "cheesecake" scenes involving its female characters).

Women government workers are also singled out in Hollywood's wartime productions. *Government Girl* (RKO, 1943) and *Dixie Dugan* (TCF, 1943) are two good examples. These films often combine humor about the housing shortage in Washington, D.C. with comments on wartime bureaucracy, but the female roles are most often familiar secretarial positions, and the plots concentrate on their love lives rather than their work.

Unlike their male counterparts, women war workers in Hollywood films do not often yearn for a more active (i.e., uniformed) role in the war effort. Indeed, leaving their homes to work in factories is seen as a major sacrifice and contribution to the war effort by women. There are numerous references to women "freeing up" or "replacing" male factory workers who have joined the armed forces. Even those women who take non-defense plant jobs are seen as occupying positions of men who are fighting or working for victory: in *Dixie Dugan*, for example, the heroine first appears driving a cab , replacing a male driver who is now working in a defense plant. When it is discovered that she has no driver's license, Dixie goes on to a government war job.

In addition, while Hollywood makes much of the humorous aspects of women incongruously working as cabdrivers, welders, riveters, mechanics, and so on, wartime films strongly suggest that these women are fully competent in their newly assumed roles. Part of this positive assertion was undoubtedly due to a reluctance to undermine the audience's faith in our defense plants by showing bumbling women workers; however, the general impression one gets upon viewing these films is that women are *capable* of doing nearly any job as well as a man. In *Priorities on Parade* (Paramount, 1942), a new male employee is apprenticed to a female welder. He initially protests ("If Hitler knew about this he'd just give up!"), but soon learns his new mentor knows her stuff.

Two rather rare examples of women workers who are not wholly competent appear in *Rosie the Riveter* and *Swing Shift Maisie*. In the first film, Rosie, on her first day at work, is shown clumsily spraying the foreman with a paint sprayer (earning her a transfer to riveting, thereby making the film's title accurate). In *Swing Shift Maisie*, a careless worker's loose hair becomes entangled in a machine, but this is shown to be a direct result of her negligence (and the character involved is otherwise negatively portrayed). *Two* industrial accidents occur in *Thumbs Up*—in the first, Louise refuses to tie her hair up tightly in a scarf, and the kerchief's loose fabric is snatched up in a drill press (as in *Swing Shift Maisie*, a female's pride in her appearance causes trouble). Later, a female worker is seriously hurt while working on the landing gear of a plane under construction, but this accident is actually caused by the carelessness of a *male* supervisor!

This public demonstration of female ability makes the postwar anti-female backlash all the more ironic—industries unceremoniously fired female workers to make jobs for returning male veterans, and Hollywood moved into its *film noir* phase, featuring calculating, manipulative, dangerous females.

An Overall Is a Uniform Too: Farm Labor

If America's factories were turning out the armaments of war, America's farms were equally important, supplying food for the domestic population, the armed forces, and much of the still-free world. Despite this obvious importance, a farm labor shortage developed during the war, as young men joined the military or simply left the farm for better-paying jobs in heavy industry. Politicians from agricultural areas began to complain to Washington, and in November 1942 Congress passed an amendment to the Selective Service law which gave draft deferments to many farmers.[12]

At least 18 films made between 1942 and 1945 address the farm-labor shortage (coded as "Production—Farm"). Several—including *Hoosier Holiday* (1943) and *The Eve of St. Mark* (TCF, 1944)—depict young farmers who want to join the armed forces but are dissuaded because their services are needed on the farm. Another film in this vein is *Jamboree* (Republic, 1944). A musical group (Freddie Fisher's band) goes to work on a farm to learn how to play "rural"-style music in preparation for a radio job. However, when they try to quit and return to the big city (having mastered the required cornball musical style), the farm owner (Ruth Terry) refuses to give them their "Availability Certificates." The War Manpower Commission had instituted a program whereby employers (chiefly in manufacturing) would not hire a worker unless he or she could produce a "certificate of availability," which indicated the worker "had not left another war job to seek higher pay."[13] In *Jamboree*, the band members stay on to harvest the bean crop, and are then released by their boss (in an ironic twist ending, the female farmer and her sisters get the radio job, and Fisher and his band decide to take over the farm!).

Hollywood, taking its cue from various public statements by President Roosevelt, also promoted voluntary farm labor by non-farming "civilians" as a way of keeping the bread basket producing at full capacity. *Junior Army* (Columbia, 1942) is one of the first films to deal with this theme, but the concept really became popular in films of 1943 and 1944. *Harvest Melody* (PRC, 1943), *Cowboy Canteen* (Columbia, 1944) and *Twilight on the Prairie* (Universal, 1944) depict the farm-labor efforts of entertainers, but teenagers were most often portrayed as part-time farm laborers: *Jive Junction* (PRC, 1943), *Mountain Rhythm* (Republic, 1943), *Teen Age* (Continental, 1944), *Moonlight in Vermont* (Universal, 1943), *They Live in Fear* (Columbia, 1944) and *Song of the Open Road* (UA, 1944) are good examples. In the latter film, young movie actress Jane Powell runs away from her regimented life as an actress to help young people harvest crops in California. Then, to save a crop from destruction, she enlists her Hollywood friends—including W.C. Fields and Edgar Bergen—to publicize the need for temporary laborers. *Pin Up Girl* (TCF, 1944) does not depict any such activities, but the song "Yankee Doodle Hoedown" is a direct appeal for volunteer farm labor as a means of aiding the war effort.

It is interesting to note that these "farm labor" films did not try to link "Victory Gardens" (personal gardens supplementing the food supply of individual families) with the

Swing Shift Maisie (MGM, 1943): Maisie (Ann Sothern) neglects her factory duties to chat with a handsome test pilot (James Craig).

actual farm production needs. The emphasis was very clearly on the *mass* production (generally harvesting) of food, not for personal consumption, but for the war effort: in *Teen Age*, several boys apologize for appearing in their work clothes, but are reassured: "Farmer uniforms are mighty important right now."

Conclusions

In summary, Hollywood paid lip service to the idea that America's factories are an integral part of the war effort, and that defense workers were doing an invaluable patriotic duty by making the guns, planes, and tanks needed by America's fighting men. However, relatively few films addressed the topic of war production directly, choosing to focus on the private lives of defense workers away from the job. Furthermore, Hollywood's obvious bias towards military service resulted in films which imply that defense work is a poor substitute for active duty, at least for male workers.

24. Deprivation for the Duration: Rationing and Shortages

As can be seen from the following chart, one of the most frequent coding terms found in the Filmography is "Shortages," indicating that a reference to war-related shortages or rationing may be found in the film:

Year	# of Citations	% of War-Rel Films
1942	82	30%
1943	118	45%
1944	74	36%
1945[1]	39	39%
TOTALS	313	37%

Shortage references are the fifth most prevalent war reference in 1942 films, the most numerous type of reference in 1943, and are second only to references to the U.S. Army in 1944 and 1945. For the entire war, Shortage references are also second overall to Army references (see *Top Ten Annual Coding Terms* in the Appendices).

In many instances the Shortage reference is the only war reference to be found in films which could be (and probably were, at the time) considered "non-topical." This indicates how quickly Americans adjusted to and accepted (although perhaps not cheerfully) the privations brought on by the war. While United States' territory was, with a few notable exceptions, physically untouched by the conflict, and while many but not all families contributed one or more members to the armed forces, virtually *all* Americans were affected by war-related shortages and rationing.

Shortages—in real life and in films—fell into several categories. Most visible were shortages of consumer goods. Some of these shortages were directly attributable to the war: rubber, for instance, was mostly obtained from the Far East, and this area was either under Japanese domination or in the immediate battle zone for most of the war. Ninety-eight percent of America's crude rubber supplies were thus cut off in one blow.[2] The rubber shortage led to another, far-reaching shortage: gasoline. Except for a period in 1942 when German submarines caused spot shortages of gasoline by sinking tankers off the Atlantic coast, gasoline was rationed chiefly to conserve rubber tires, not because the fuel itself was in particularly short supply (although regional shortages, caused by unequal consumption, would continue to plague the country throughout the war and result in regional differences in the basic ration).

Since tires and gasoline were among the first major consumer commodities to be rationed, and since this struck deeply at America's love affair with the "freedom" of the open road, references to rubber and gasoline shortages and rationing constitute a very large number of the Shortage references, particularly in 1942 and 1943.

In *X Marks the Spot* (Republic, 1942) and *No Place for a Lady* (Columbia, 1943), murders are committed over stockpiles of tires. In *Rubber Racketeers* (Monogram, 1942), Ricardo Cortez portrays a former bootlegger who finds the tire shortage to his liking. His gang steals and re-sells new tires on the black market, and also sells inferior retreads which lead to a fatal accident.

Most of the tire/gas references, however, are humorous, often exaggerated comments about the inflated value of tires: in *Highways by Night* (RKO, 1942), one character says, "I've had a terrible experience!" Another man replies, "Me too, I just tried to get a new inner tube." In *A Desperate Chance for Ellery Queen* (Columbia, 1942), a man "checks" his tires at the hat check counter of a nightclub. A luxury car is priced at $16,000 in *Lucky Legs* (Columbia, 1942), but it costs $20,000 "with tires." After a car accident in *Blondie for Victory* (Columbia, 1942), Mr. Dithers anxiously asks Dagwood, not about any possible injuries, but about the condition of his tires.

In addition to gasoline rationing, the government tried to reduce wear on tires by promoting carpooling (*Gangway for Tomorrow*, RKO 1943, is about the private lives of a group of Americans who "share the ride" to the defense plant where they work), and by instituting a national speed limit of 35 miles per hour. However, neither of these were as powerful as the simple fact that gasoline *was* rationed and that new tires were *very* difficult to obtain.

Rationing (MGM, 1944), an unusual film which both pokes fun at shortages and rationing (and the concomitant government bureaucracy) and yet justifies their existence, opens as grocer Wallace Beery drives towards the small town of Tuttleton—the road signs indicate Tuttleton is "1/3 Gallon" away, then "1/8 Gallon" away, instead of the normal mileage indicators. Running out of gas, Beery has to push his car into town. He offers to give the local gas station proprietor some ration coupons "next week" in exchange for some gas now, but the greedy man counters with an offer to sell him fuel for an inflated black market price of fifty cents a gallon.

Gasoline rationing stickers are visible on many, but not all automobiles in Hollywood films of the war period. While the exact ration varied during the war, the basic classes of stickers were fairly consistent: "A" stickers received the lowest ration, and were issued for private automobiles used for "pleasure" or non-essential driving; "B" stickers were for "essential" travel (such as commuting to work), and received more gasoline per week; "C" stickers were given the highest ration.[3]

The *Motion Picture Herald* commented on the difficulties faced by filmmakers with regards to ration stickers:

To omit stickers is to ignore gas rationing, which is the opposite of the friendly cooperation which the Government expects of the motion picture. To use an "A" sticker is to invite customers ... to break into a babble of comments regarding plausibility, if not to snicker. To use a "B" sticker is to invite a louder babble, and a "C" sticker is a risk no producer has ventured thus far. The placement of whatever sticker is decided upon is a problem in itself [given] the differences in ruling on that point prevailing in different localities....[4]

In most cases, ration stickers seem to show up primarily on actual automobiles, not on the mockup windshield/front seat props used for most in-car dialogue scenes. However, there are examples of "real" cars appearing *sans* ration stickers in films, presumably because these cars were studio property, never taken off the lot. But aside from a joke or two in 1942, ration stickers themselves are rarely discussed in wartime films, although gas rationing itself continues to be mentioned throughout the war.

The "point rationing" system also served as the source of a number of contemporary references in Hollywood films. Food was assigned various "point values," and consumers were required to provide ration coupons with the proper number of points in order to purchase these items. Other items were rationed by the issuance of coupons. Shoes, for example, were rationed beginning in February 1943. Each individual was allotted one stamp, valid for four months, which had to be presented when purchasing shoes. In *The Chance of a Lifetime* (Columbia, 1943), the Runt (George E. Stone) hears a policeman's shoes squeaking and says: "I know the sound of his 18s—I mean the size, not the coupon" (Stamp 18 in War Ra-

Rubber Racketeers (Monogram, 1942): The black market in tires attracted organized crime, according to this King Brothers production starring Ricardo Cortez as a gangster who deals in "hot" rubber.

tion Book One was designated for one pair of shoes from June until October 1943).[5]

A popular topic in wartime Hollywood productions is the invention (usually by crackpot inventors) of "synthetic rubber." The U.S. government promoted the planting of guayule, a plant from which rubber could be obtained, but this made no significant dent in the national shortage. Attempts to chemically produce rubber are referred to in *Miss Annie Rooney* (UA, 1942), *So This Is Washington* (RKO, 1943), and *True to Life* (Paramount, 1943). Synthetic gasoline and silk are also fantasy inventions seen as solutions to real-life shortages, as depicted in *Here We Go Again* (RKO, 1942), and *What a Blonde!* (RKO, 1945), for example.

In addition to shortages caused by the physical inaccessibility of materials, there were shortages caused by America's diversion of materials to the war effort. One good example of this was the rapid conversion of many typewriter factories to war work, beginning in March 1942 (as mentioned in *Practically Yours*, Paramount, 1944). Typewriters, new and used, thus became a scarce commodity, with priority given to organizations engaged in war work. Wristwatches were also particularly hard to obtain.

Automobile factories were enjoined from producing civilian vehicles "for the duration"—thus, Fred MacMurray, since he is unable to sell any cars, is forced to convert his automobile dealership into a scrap metal drive headquarters in *Where Do We Go from Here?* (Paramount, 1945).[6] Similarly, in *Stars on Parade* (Columbia, 1944), a group of young Hollywood hopefuls, planning a show to highlight their talents, rents a building that formerly housed an automobile dealership. *Truck Busters* (WB, 1943) deals with a gangland attempt to create a trucking monopoly by wrecking their small competitors, realizing that replacement trucks will be virtually impossible to obtain. A shipyard worker in *Teen Age* (Continental, 1944), celebrates a production milestone at the shipyard by going out and buying a car—a *used* car, but one which still runs well, the script carefully notes.

Sugar and meat are commodities which are also frequently referred to in Hollywood's wartime productions. Sugar was the first foodstuff to be controlled during the war, national rationing going into effect at the beginning of May 1942. There were several reasons for this step: most sugar was imported from Cuba, Puerto Rico, Hawaii, the Philippines, and other overseas locations. The war cut off some of these sources, and restricted the shipping available for transport of raw sugar from others. As the war went on, domestic production (particularly of beet sugar) increased, but labor shortages affected sugar refineries, transportation was still a problem, and the armed forces became a major consumer, competing with the domestic market. Additionally, the government encouraged home canning (to offset the drop in availability of commercially canned foodstuffs), and even more sugar was needed for this process.

Sugar shortage/rationing references are most noticeable in 1942 and 1943 productions, when the topic was relatively new to audiences. In *House of Errors* (PRC, 1942), Harry Langdon keeps his sugar in a safe! Sugar references, mostly humorous, also appear in *Blondie for Victory* (Columbia, 1942), *The Old Homestead* (Republic, 1942), *Never a Dull Moment* (Universal, 1943), *A Night for Crime* (PRC, 1943), and *Smart Alecks* (Monogram, 1942), among other titles.

Meat rationing is another frequently mentioned topic in Hollywood films. In the fall of 1942, the government took steps to regulate the slaughter and distribution of meat, realizing that the demand for 1943 would far outstrip the supply. Much of this increase was, obviously, due to the needs of the armed forces (and related, war-oriented markets such as Lend-Lease). In 1941, non-civilian sources purchased just over 5 percent of the U.S. meat supply; this share was projected to increase to 28 percent by 1943.[7] Meat and fats rationing was instituted at the end of March 1943.

True to Life (Paramount, 1943): Victor Moore as a typical (for Hollywood) WWII air raid warden—bumbling, officious, and incompetent. Hardly an endorsement for the Office of Civil Defense.

Meat rationing continued throughout the war, but was a complex and varied program. At times, the available supply was in excess of the projected demand, and various cuts and types of meat were reduced to "no points" (i.e., were not rationed). Pork was relatively plentiful throughout the war, but beef—particularly the more expensive cuts—was often in short supply, especially in the East, far from the major cattle-producing sections of the country.

Hollywood was more or less cognizant of this, and comments about "meat shortages" are often pointed and specific (characters more often desire "a nice steak" than "a nice ham hock" or "a nice leg of lamb"). Generalized jokes about meat shortages and rationing are usually along the lines of a remark in *The Ghost and the Guest* (PRC, 1943): "This place is busier than a meat market with meat!" *Black Market Rustlers* (Monogram, 1943) is, predictably, a Western about rustlers stealing cattle—but in wartime, the cattle are now even *more* valuable. *Rationing*, while it touches on nearly every aspect of the wartime rationing program, particularly focuses on meat shortages, rationing, and the black market. Wallace Beery uncovers a gang which buys cattle, slaughters them, falsely stamps the beef with a "USDA Inspected" stamp, and sells the meat to unsuspecting (but carnivorous) customers.

Hollywood rarely hints that food rationing is sending any Americans to bed hungry. Indeed, there are numerous scenes featuring home-cooked meals, preparation for meals, meals in restaurants, and so on—there is almost never any indication that food is not readily available.[8] Some delicacies, yes, but "plain, everyday food," no. This mirrors real life, where rationing and shortages seriously inconvenienced some consumers, but food was generally available, although the selection was restricted.

There were also shortages which could not necessarily be called "material." In certain parts of the country, housing was in very short supply due to the wartime production boom. *Rosie the Riveter* (Republic, 1944) takes this shortage as its premise: the film opens with a montage of "No Vacancy" signs, people converting gas stations and stores to living quarters, and so on. Defense workers Frank Alberton, Frank Jenks, Vera Vague, and Jane Frazee all claim the last vacant room in a boarding house, and are forced to occupy the room in shifts.

Washington, D.C., became the center of the nation's war bureaucracy, and a number of films poke fun at the shortage of accommodations in the capital (the joke was that D.C. stood for "Damn Crowded"): *Government Girl* (RKO, 1943), *The Doughgirls* (WB, 1944), *Johnny Doesn't Live Here Anymore* (Monogram, 1944), and *The More the Merrier* (Columbia, 1943), to name a few. Once again, comic and romantic complications result from the struggle for living space.

The "manpower shortage" was also a serious subject which was treated somewhat humorously by Hollywood. With millions of men drafted into military service, factories, farms, and other businesses were forced to hire those too young, too old, or—in the case of women and minorities—those previously not considered "suitable" for employment. Of course, Hollywood saw a different side of this, as Bette Davis laments in "They're Either Too Young or Too Old" in *Thank Your Lucky Stars* (WB, 1943), in which the "manpower shortage" is converted into a "man shortage" with romantic implications uppermost in women's minds. The "man shortage" is also the central focus of *You Can't Ration Love* (Paramount, 1944): college girls set up a "point system" for dates with the few eligible and attractive male students. Due to the draft and the boom in war production, "many coed colleges became 75 to 90 percent female 'for the duration.'"[9]

Similarly, the "servant shortage"—which would seem to be of interest only to those in the upper brackets of society—was considered hilarious by Hollywood, as evidenced by films like *My Kingdom for a Cook* (Columbia, 1943), *Mister Muggs Steps Out* (Monogram, 1943), *Make Your Own Bed* (WB, 1944), and *Standing Room Only* (Paramount, 1944—which combines both the housing shortage in wartime D.C. *and* the servant shortage). Domestic servants, it seemed, were being both patriotic and self-serving by leaving their menial positions as butlers, maids, cooks, and chauffeurs to work in defense plants or enlist in the armed forces.[10]

Other inconveniences of wartime also fall into the "shortage" category. The difficulty in traveling from one part of the country to another during wartime is mentioned in a number of films. This leads to comic complications in *Music in Manhattan* (RKO, 1944), as Anne Shirley is forced to pose as the wife of a famous war hero (Philip Terry) in order to obtain a plane ticket to Washington; in *Pillow to Post* (WB, 1945) Ida Lupino poses as the wife of an Army officer in order to qualify for a motel room! During the war, "nonessential travel" was discouraged by the government, but even legitimate civilian travelers were often hindered by the priority given to servicemen and those engaged in essential, war-related travel. Scenes in overcrowded trains appear in films such as *In the Meantime, Darling* (TCF, 1944) and *The Thin Man Goes Home* (MGM, 1945). In the first film, pompous businessman Eugene Pallette, traveling on a crowded train to attend his daughter's wedding, is criticized by a fellow passenger, a soldier, who calls him "Butch." "War, the great leveler," Pallette grumbles.

As the war went on, Americans seemed to take the shortages and rationing in stride, and strident films such as *Rubber Racketeers* ceased to appear. While the percentage of war-relevant films with Shortage references in 1944–45 averages 37%, these references become less frequent, and often almost subliminal (ration stickers on car windshields, for instance).

Hollywood—and, by extension, most Americans—saw shortages and rationing as annoying but necessary evils which had to be put up with in order to win the war. Hoarding was decried as unpatriotic. Films which specifically mention hoarding include *Rationing* (a man buys more flour than he could possibly use, claiming "I'm just trying to buy this stuff so the hoarders won't get it"), *Tender Comrade* (RKO, 1943—a woman admits hoarding lipstick), and *The Heavenly Body* (MGM, 1943—an astrologer's hoarded canned goods are exposed).

Black market operators were considered criminals in films. This was somewhat more extreme than public opinion in real life:

The behavior of many persons was often different when the discussion shifted from the general objectives of price and rationing control to actual specifics of everyday life. People receiving black market goods often did not ask further questions, and many were tolerant of black market activity if it involved petty price increases and small quantities of rationed commodities.[11]

Most Hollywood films dealing with the black market depict hardened criminals *entering* the black market as an alternative to their former crooked endeavors, rather than formerly honest individuals (such as the local butcher or grocer) turning to the black market as a way of making money (or retaining the good will and patronage of long-time customers). Even the venal gas station proprietor in *Rationing* is merely a dupe of the black market meat ring run by "real" gangsters.[12]

However, *complaining* about the rationing program and war-induced shortages is seen as the right of every American. *Rationing*, as noted earlier, is very critical of the involved government bureaucracy and red tape surrounding rationing; a running gag features a farmer (Milton Parsons), who repeatedly appears with larger and larger piles of forms in an effort to get exemptions from some regulations. One of the comic highlights of the film is a weary Wallace Beery's retelling of "Little Red Riding Hood," intermingled with ration jargon: "Grandmother is frozen by the OPA ... because meat is a perishable commodity, Grandmother will be eaten first."[13]

However, Beery's reply to a woman who demands to know how she and her husband can get a "good dinner" in spite of the shortages and rationing regulations, summarizes the reasons Americans were willing to forego their usual consumption of meat, sugar, gasoline, and other rationed items, at least "for the duration":

First of all you take a steak away from a Marine down in Guadalcanal and cook it with some potatoes that should go to one of the Coast Guardsmen on the Aleutian Islands; then you add some fresh vegetables from the mess of our troops down in Northern Africa, and add a couple of pounds of butter that you were going to send to some sailors on a submarine, with two cups of coffee that belongs to an aviator in the South Pacific.

Patriotic and didactic statements like this appear frequently in Hollywood's wartime productions, but rarely in connection with rationing and shortages. Shortages and rationing are more often the butt of jokes than a serious wartime topic in Hollywood films.

25. "Turn Out That Light!": Home Defense

A familiar figure in Hollywood films of the war years is the air raid warden, strolling the darkened streets of America's towns and cities in his white "doughboy"-style helmet with the triangular Civil Defense emblem, warning careless homeowners that a light—which could attract enemy bombers—is visible. Like many of the other Home Front topics, Hollywood depicts Home Defense measures as both ridiculous and patriotic, an ambivalent portrayal at best.

The following chart demonstrates how Home Defense references reach their peak in 1943, then drop off drastically as the war receded from America's shores:

Year	# of References	% of War-Rel Films
1942	37	13%
1943	53	20%
1944	14	7%
1945[1]	2	2%
Totals	106	13%

Home Defense references in Hollywood films range from actual depictions of home defense measures—including air raid wardens, airplane spotters, and the like—to verbal references to "blackouts," a term referring to a defensive measure which quickly became associated with other topics. Also included in this category are references to men's and women's auxiliary organizations, and other quasi-military activities on the home front.[2]

However, the most frequent Home Defense references are those alluding to air raid wardens and "blackouts." Naturally, the attack on Pearl Harbor made many Americans nervous about enemy planes (widespread press coverage of the London Blitz added to this atmosphere), as Steven Spielberg's *1941* (Universal-Columbia, 1979) later comically illustrated.

Depictions of air raid wardens are most prevalent in 1943; the term "blackout" persists throughout the war, although it is often applied to completely non-topical situations (see, for example, *The Last Horseman*, Columbia, and *Detective Kitty O'Day*, Monogram, both 1944).

The Office of Civilian Defense was formed in May 1941, initially headed by Fiorello La Guardia, mayor of New York City. By the end of the year (when America was actually at war) there were 6,000 local Civil Defense councils with more than one million volunteer members.[3] Local jurisdictions formed their own civil defense organizations, and other, more specific national organizations—like the Civilian Air Warning System—also contributed to America's defense in some way. Most such activities went into high gear only after Pearl Harbor, and, after a period of near-hysteria, settled into a routine. By the middle of 1943, it was obvious that the mainland United States was in no danger, and public attention drifted to other topics.

Ironically, even during the period of the greatest participation and interest, America's air raid wardens are almost always portrayed in a comical light by Hollywood, as earnest but over-zealous and occasionally self-important civilians, often those too old or otherwise unfit for military service.[4]

In *Air Raid Wardens* (TCF, 1943), for instance, Laurel and Hardy are rejected by the armed forces, so they become civil defense volunteers instead. However, their incompetence is obvious at even this level, and they are forced to resign their positions as air raid wardens (redeeming themselves in the end by capturing Nazi saboteurs). Similarly, Stuart Erwin works off his frustrations over his 4-F draft status by becoming an air raid warden in *He Hired the Boss* (TCF, 1943). Victor Moore's antics as a warden in *True to Life* (Paramount, 1943) are a running joke in the film, as he runs into the street ordering pedestrians to "lie down in the gutter!" Warden Charlie Ruggles in *Dixie Dugan* (TCF, 1943) accidentally sets off an incendiary bomb that burns through several floors of his apartment house while attempting to demonstrate the best means of extinguishing it! James Craig is a handsome and conscientious air raid warden in *The Heavenly Body* (MGM, 1943), but the film itself is a romantic comedy. Craig is identified as a former war correspondent who picked up a "bug" while overseas, and now makes his contribution to the war effort in this manner.

As with defense workers, civil defense is often shown to be the place where women, older men and other minorities can make a war contribution: Martha Scott is an air raid warden in *Hi Diddle Diddle* (UA, 1943), the elderly Lum and Abner are wardens in *So This Is Washington* (RKO, 1943), middle-aged Leon Errol becomes a warden in *The Mexican Spitfire's Elephant* (RKO, 1942), and there is a black air raid warden shown in one sequence of *The Hit Parade of 1943* (Republic, 1943). The latter portrayal is of some historical interest, since Eleanor Roosevelt had made it her personal business to see that blacks were allowed to participate in the national civil defense program.[5] Sometimes these depictions are just another opportunity to poke fun at the over-zealous and inept: in *Princess O'Rourke* (WB, 1943), "the women in a civil defense unit delighted in staging too frequent air raid drills."[6]

While "blackout" jokes are tossed in frequently throughout the war—Jack Benny asks his wife, "When did you buy this house, in a blackout?" in *George Washington Slept Here* (WB, 1942)—blackouts and air raid drills actually figure prominently in the plots of a number of 1942 and 1943 films. Many of these are mysteries, since crime obviously flourishes in the dark: *After Midnight with Boston Blackie* (Columbia, 1943), *The Falcon in Danger* (RKO, 1943), *The London Blackout Murders* (Republic, 1943), *No Place for a Lady* (Columbia, 1943), *Quiet Please, Murder* (TCF, 1943), and *Pacific Blackout* (Paramount, 1942) all contain significant "blackout" scenes. *A Night for Crime* (PRC, 1943) begins with the announcement of a blackout in Los Angeles, and a montage shows the neon signs of the famed Hollywood nightspots winking out. The film ends with another, identical blackout, and an air raid warden chastising the hero and heroine for leaving their car's headlights on.

Unfortunately, real life did not necessarily mirror Hollywood's preoccupation with "blackout" security. Most blackout precautions were intended to foil German and Japanese bombers,[7] but while enemy aircraft never seriously threatened the U.S. mainland, German U-boats were extremely active off the Atlantic coast in 1942, and "during the first three months after Pearl Harbor the United States practiced no darkening discipline whatever [on the Atlantic seaboard]."[8] Even after early 1942, military authorities were reluctant to order coastal communities to black out their lights (which silhouetted mer-

chant ships, making them easy targets for submarines), partly due to a false impression about the capabilities of German U-boats, and partly due to protests from business interests who did not want to inconvenience tourists![9]

Other Home Defense activities are covered in Hollywood's wartime productions. Some are shown in a serious, or at least semi-serious light. For instance, *Cowboy in the Clouds* (Columbia, 1943) is a relatively straight adventure drama about the Civil Air Patrol, a civilian organization of private pilots who flew patrol duty (generally along the Mexican border or anti-submarine patrols off the coasts) and otherwise freed military pilots for active service. *Raiders of Sunset Pass* (Republic, 1943), deals with a wholly fictional organization, the Women's Auxiliary Plains Service (WAPS). To replace cowboys serving in the armed forces, government agent John Paul Revere (Eddie Dew) recruits the rough-riding daughters of cattle ranchers to ride herd against rustlers. Although fanciful, this Western at least portrays the women as capable and serious about their home defense duties.

Many wartime films, however, choose to poke fun at the various "auxiliary" organizations formed during the war. While the Red Cross is the focus of some humor, Hollywood reserved true ridicule for fictional home defense organizations.

Blondie for Victory (Columbia, 1942) is an early example. Blondie joins the "Housewives of America," who wear military-style uniforms but generally restrict their activities to fund-raising and other home front activities. *Tramp, Tramp, Tramp* (Columbia, 1942) portrays Jackie Gleason and Jack Durant as two patriotic idiots who are turned down by the Army. They form their own "Home Defense Army," filling its ranks with other 4-Fs (including a midget). The idea inexplicably catches on and units are formed across the nation. Feckless tenor Dennis Day tries to drill some female militia in *Sleepy Lagoon* (Republic, 1943), with predictably comic results. A women's organization in *Those Endearing Young Charms* (RKO, 1945) bears the unwieldy name of the "Women's Uptown 84th Street Auxiliary War Relief Association."

On the whole, Hollywood shows little appreciation for the efforts of American civilians participating in home defense measures. For every serious air raid warden like James Craig in *The Heavenly Body*, there are numerous comic, inept, and overbearing air raid wardens shouting "Put out that light!" For every serious film about civilian defense such as *Cowboy in the Clouds*, there are others depicting amateur soldiers, both male and female, proudly dressed in outlandish uniforms but accomplishing nothing. These films may or may not have reflected the general attitude of Americans towards civilian defense—given the high levels of participation in the early years of the war, this is questionable—but the impression one gains today from watching Hollywood films of the war years is that civilian defense was the last refuge of the pompous and dim-witted.

26. The Junior Army and Youth Running Wild

To absorb the excess energies of students who wanted to join in the war effort, a High School Victory Corps was created in the summer of 1942 ... for the most part they were kept busy with parades, scrap drives, bond sales, and calisthenics.[1]

In the midst of a war ... it was considered particularly unfortunate that large numbers of young people on the home front were engaging in conduct believed deleterious both to themselves and the community.[2]

Beginning in the late '30s, Hollywood began to pay more attention to the youth of America. This is not to say there had not been youthful film stars before this time—Shirley Temple is one obvious exception—or that films dealing with young people were not being made. But slowly, for no single outstanding reason, Hollywood came to realize that an American youth culture was developing, and films began to reflect this. Mickey Rooney (MGM), Judy Garland (MGM), Bonita Granville (Warner Brothers, then RKO), Deanna Durbin (Universal), Jane Withers (Republic, after spending her childhood at Fox), Virginia Weidler (MGM), Jimmy "Henry Aldrich" Lydon (Paramount, then Republic), Donald O'Connor (Universal), the East Side Kids (Monogram), Jane Powell (MGM), and other performers in their teens moved from supporting roles to starring roles, and it was their screen "parents" who became incidental to the plot. Jitterbugging, jive-talking "teenagers" had arrived.[3]

In its portrayal of American youth during World War Two, Hollywood was caught between conflicting loyalties: on the one hand, it was politically correct to laud the contributions of young people on the home front; on the other, Hollywood was forever on the lookout for exploitable topics with the potential for box-office success, and juvenile delinquency was especially "hot" during the war. Consequently, wartime Hollywood presents a contradictory portrait of American youth. Most young people are patriotic and active in home front activities, but there are a number of films highlighting juvenile delinquency, which is often directly attributed to the war. There are also films dealing with the effect of the war on children of other nations, depicting them as sneaky villains (Hitler Youth types), brave refugees, and daring, underage guerrilla fighters.

By far the most numerous "juvenile" theme films are those containing positive portraits of American youth on the home front. Very early in the war, films like *Junior Army* (Columbia, 1942) and *Johnny Doughboy* (Republic, 1942) promote contributions by young people to the war effort. In the first film, a teenage British refugee (Freddie Bartholomew) befriends a budding juvenile delinquent (Billy Halop). They both attend a military school, whose students participate in scrap metal drives and help harvest crops. Halop's attitude is

bad at first, but when he sees an old pal (Huntz Hall) in the company of a Nazi saboteur, he throws in with Uncle Sam for the duration.

In the latter film, Jane Withers plays a dual role, as a young movie star and her double. The actress runs away from Hollywood, and the double has to take over her chores; however, when the "Junior Victory Caravan" is formed to entertain troops and sell bonds, the double convinces the *real* star to come back to do her bit.

Song of the Open Road (UA, 1944) is quite similar to *Johnny Doughboy* in plot: youthful star Jane Powell leaves her hectic life in the film capital, and joins the teenage "U.S. Crops Corps," which helps harvest fruits and vegetables. At the climax, Jane uses her Hollywood contacts to save a crop from ruin. Additional films about young people helping harvest crops include *Mountain Rhythm* (Republic, 1943; students at a prep school also sell bonds and unite with the hillbilly Weavers to expose an Axis agent—the principal of their school!), *Jive Junction* (PRC, 1943), *They Live in Fear* (Columbia, 1944), and *Moonlight in Vermont* (Universal, 1943).

Other early motion pictures about young people contain some war relevance, although it is often restricted to a musical number or two, as in *Babes on Broadway* (MGM, 1942), *Youth on Parade* (Republic, 1942), and *Mister Big* (Universal, 1943). Some films are a bit more war-oriented in their "let's put on a show" mentality: high school students in *Jive Junction* open a "canteen" and form a band to entertain troops; a high school senior is convinced to stay in school and put on a USO show for the military in *Cinderella Swings It* (RKO, 1943); and military prep school students stage a show for Navy Relief in *Chip Off the Old Block* (Universal, 1944).

Some films portray rather more active and personal contributions to the war effort. Given the manpower shortage due to the draft, young people found a number of jobs open to them in their formerly "free" time. In *Top Man* (Universal, 1943), Donald O'Connor organizes his junior college classmates to work in the local defense plant after school (on shortened, four-hour shifts—an actual practice in many plants). Jennifer Jones becomes a nurse's aide in *Since You Went Away* (UA, 1944). The East Side Kids are hired at a department store to replace drafted employees in *Keep 'Em Slugging*

(Monogram, 1943), and Mickey Rooney gets a job as a telegraph messenger to help support his family (his father is dead and his older brother is in the service) in *The Human Comedy* (MGM, 1943).

Young women often felt it was their duty to help keep up the morale of the armed forces. In *Meet Miss Bobby Socks* (Columbia, 1944) and *Three Little Sisters* (Republic, 1944), young girls write letters to soldiers (although the soldiers are naturally somewhat disappointed to learn, as the plot always has them do, that their pen-pals are "jail bait"—however, the girls usually have older, attractive sisters who step in and provide romantic recreation).[4] Some young women went even further in their "patriotic" duty:

The bus depots of the larger cities and towns were crowded with teen-age girls, variously called Victory Girls, Patriotutes, Cuddle Bunnies and Round-Heels. Hauled in by the police, they protested that they were performing a patriotic service, maintaining military morale. Some were as young as twelve years old.[5]

Obviously, Hollywood was not going to depict *this* kind of home front activity by juveniles, although *Janie* (WB, 1944) and *The Miracle of Morgan's Creek* (Paramount, 1944) hint at it in a typically "innocent" way. In the first film, the small town of Hortonville is turned upside down when an Army detachment arrives for training. The high school-age girls of the town are particularly attracted to the young soldiers, much to the chagrin of the town boys. Preston Sturges carries the matter a bit further in *Miracle* (although Betty Hutton is hardly an adolescent), as Hutton plainly states that she considers it her duty to make soldiers "happy" before they ship out. She winds up pregnant, a fairly good indication of *what* she does to make them happy.[6]

Another portrayal of youth affected by the war appears in films dealing with refugees. While being displaced from one's home is certainly not a pleasant experience, the refugee children in films like *Junior Army, Journey for Margaret* (MGM, 1942), *On the Sunny Side* (TCF, 1942), *Silver Skates* (Monogram, 1943), *Block Busters* (Monogram, 1944), and *Heavenly Days* (RKO, 1944), are all positively depicted. These children are brave, friendly, and confident; while the war has hurt them, it has not defeated them. Even the loss of loved ones and forceable evacuation from their homes has not crushed their spirit.

Even more indomitable are those children shown actively resisting the Axis powers. As discussed in Chapter 7, the films featuring child warriors include *The Boy from Stalingrad* (Columbia, 1943), *The North Star* (RKO, 1943), *Days of Glory* (RKO, 1944), *China's Little Devils* (Monogram, 1945), and *Back to Bataan* (RKO, 1945). It is interesting to note, furthermore, that the usual Hollywood prohibition against killing children is largely dispensed with in these films: in virtually every example, one or more of the youthful protagonists is killed by the enemy. This is certainly one way of demonstrating the heroic nature of these children, and a surefire method

of gaining sympathy for the Allies and fanning hatred of the Axis.[7]

However, not all Hollywood films of the war period contain positive images of youth. There are a few films dealing with the Hitler Youth organization. *Hitler's Children* (RKO, 1943) was the first and most successful, although its primary male character (Tim Holt) is not exactly a child (he was 24 years old when the film was released). However, the film—based on a nonfiction book entitled *Education for Death*—does go into some detail concerning the ideological indoctrination of German children under the Nazi regime.[8]

Hitler Youth members arrive in America in *They Live in Fear* and *Tomorrow, the World* (UA, 1944). In the first film, Paul Graffen joins the Hitler Youth to divert suspicion from his anti–Nazi family. When the young Nazis are ordered to kill some concentration camp inmates at Dachau with shovels (a "post-graduate course in Nazi cruelty"), Paul balks. The man he spares shows his gratitude by giving the teenager a letter of introduction to a high school principal in the United States. Paul travels to America and becomes a real son of democracy despite various travails, at the end of the film announcing his intention to join the Army, and become a U.S. citizen. This film contains a fair amount of footage dedicated to the war-related activities of Paul's classmates, including one scene in which two high school girls in Red Cross uniforms and two teenage boys dressed as soldiers promote a blood drive. Paul himself establishes a babysitting service, presumably to help out families in which both parents are working in defense plants (although this is not specifically stated).

Skip Homeier, on the other hand, is a true Nazi who enters the United States under false pretenses in *Tomorrow, the World*. Anti-Semitic, sneaky, and violent, the 12-year-old Hitler fan even tries to steal secret plans from his American guardian, then attacks the man's daughter when he is discovered. At the end, some hope for his rehabilitation is suggested, but for most of the film Homeier (who originated the role in the stage version on Broadway) is a real "Bad Seed."

Wartime juvenile delinquency films, on the other hand, usually portray American youth as victims of the social upheaval caused by the war, rather than as innately evil, or politically unreliable. There was, as one writer put it:

…a staggering rise in juvenile delinquency … Much of the problem could be traced to the fact that there was no explicit place in the war effort for youngsters below draft age. There was also the parental neglect attendant on the wartime disruptions of everyday life … juvenile delinquency … rose steadily during the war.…[9]

Even relatively mild films like *My Pal, Wolf* (RKO, 1944) and *Twice Blessed* (MGM, 1945) make references to delinquency on the home front. Gretchen Anstey is too young to be a "Cuddle Bunny" or a juvenile delinquent in *My Pal, Wolf*, but she *is* neglected by her parents (her father is an industrialist, her mother a business executive), and is left in the care of a strict governess, which results in various types of domestic trouble. *Twice Blessed* shows no troubled teens, but Gail Patrick—cast as a well-known adult "authority" on women's issues—makes a speech referring to the "startling increase in juvenile delinquency since the war."

The biggest difference in juvenile delinquency films of WWII and those made before (and after) the conflict is the direct connection between the war and delinquency. In *Kid Dynamite* (Monogram, 1943), a judge admonishes the East Side Kids for leading useless, trouble-making lives during a period of national emergency. The Kids had heard lectures like this before, but without the patriotic slant; this time, it works, and the boys cease their loafing and join the armed forces.

The prime year for wartime juvenile delinquency films was 1944, however. At least five motion pictures with war-relevant aspects directly address the subject; two other films, *Delinquent Daughters* and *I Accuse My Parents* (both PRC, 1944) deal with similar topics, although their war-relevance has not been determined.[10] The five major juvenile delinquent films are *Faces in the Fog* (Republic), *Where Are Your Children?* and *Are These Our Parents?* (both Monogram), *Youth Runs Wild* (RKO), and *Teen Age* (Continental Pictures).

Are These Our Parents?, a follow-up to Monogram's successful *Where Are Your Children?*, has the least war-relevant content of the quartet. Noel Neill is a rich girl who runs away from the fancy boarding school she has been placed in by her uncaring, high-society mother. Neill takes up with Richard Byron, a working-class teenager (Byron says "between the plant, school and the garage, I work 16 hours [a day]"). Byron is angry and depressed because his father, a foreman in an aircraft plant, has been neglecting his work and family in order to run around with a "loose woman." Byron's father shows him a roll of bills he won at the racetrack, after skipping a day of work, and Byron responds: "The boys at the front will appreciate you too, for the delay." The two teenagers are accused of the murder of a nightclub owner, and the juvenile officer blames Neill and Byron's parents for neglecting their parental duties. The real killer confesses to the crime, and the teens are reunited with their repentant mother and father, respectively.

Faces in the Fog also features war worker parents and their wayward children. Mary (Jane Withers) is neglected by her parents, who work in a defense plant and fail to exercise proper parental control; Joe's father is also a war worker, but he is a better parent. However, Joe drops out of school after being falsely accused of a crime, and decides to join the Army. He and Mary get married, and spend their honeymoon in a hotel room. Mary's father, not realizing the teenagers are married, is outraged and shoots Joe. Mary has to lie about her marriage to save her father from jail.

Where Are Your Children? and *Youth Runs Wild* make the linkage between the war and social problems even more clearly (parents who are too busy to pay attention to their children were not unique to WWII). *Where Are Your Children?* is set in California, where Judy (Gale Storm)'s family has moved to work in the shipyards. Judy and Danny (Jackie Cooper) become sweethearts; they also fall prey to the evils of the roadhouse, and are picked up by juvenile authorities. Danny joins the Navy. Judy travels to San Diego with some other young people to see him. However, she does not know that she is in with a bad crowd until there is an argument at a gas station over ration coupons. Judy leaves the others and makes it to San Diego in time to see Danny ship out. She is later arrested as an accomplice in the gas station altercation (the attendant was killed). Judy, acquitted of complicity in the crime, decides to work in a day care center for children of defense workers, doing her bit for the war effort until Danny comes home.

This film hits a number of war-time themes in addition to juvenile delinquency: population dislocation (often in search of high-paying defense jobs), family disruption, rationing, and lack of child care for defense workers. While Judy and Danny keep to the straight and narrow—both eventually making concrete contributions to the war effort—the other young people in the film are not as fortunate.

Youth Runs Wild, a Val Lewton production for RKO Radio, portrays some similar problems. The film was apparently inspired by a *Look* magazine article entitled "Are These Our Children?" as well as an RKO short subject, "Children of Mars."[11] The project was given to Lewton's unit, originally under the title of the magazine article (which had, coincidentally, been used by RKO already, in 1931). *The Dangerous Age* was an interim title; after cuts and some re-shooting, the film was finally released as *Youth Runs Wild*.[12]

Teenager Frankie (Glenn Vernon) wants to leave school and become a defense worker; his brother-in-law Danny (Kent Smith) is in the service, and his parents work in defense plants, so he feels left out of the war effort. He and two pals are caught stealing tires from cars parked at a defense plant, and paroled in the custody of Danny (who has returned home, wounded in action). Frankie's neighbor and girlfriend Sarah (Tessa Brind) is treated like a servant by her parents, also war workers, who spend their off hours playing cards and drinking. Sarah moves in with Toddy (Bonita Granville), an older girl, and gets a job in "Rocky's" (a sleazy roadhouse). Frankie sees her there with a soldier, and a brawl ensues. Toddy is fatally injured in the fight (ironically, due to some jiu-jitsu that Frankie and his friends learned from Danny). Frankie is shipped off to a forestry camp by the authorities, and Sarah decides to clean up her act and wait for him. Danny and his wife, meanwhile, opens a day care center for children of war workers to "siphon off some of the excessive youthful energies" that get them into trouble.[13]

Once again, children with no direct involvement in the war effort feel left out, and wander into delinquency and worse. They become easy prey for older criminals. Frankie sees his entire family making a contribution; Sarah is treated poorly by her working parents. The boys see a young child crying in the back seat of a car in the parking lot of the defense plant; with no organized child care available, the child's parents are forced to bring their offspring to work (a concern also addressed in *Where Are Your Children?*).

Perhaps the earliest of these juvenile delinquent films was the independent exploitation film *Teen Age*, copyrighted in 1943 but considered a 1944 film in this study due to the difficulty of pinpointing a specific release date. It is remarkably similar to the others of this genre, beginning with a juvenile court official admonishing parents for neglecting their children. The stories of a number of teenagers unfold, including that of Dan Murray (Johnny Duncan), member of a "car-stripping" gang.[14] Dan eventually sees the error of his ways, but dies tragically. The other teens have their lives directed into more positive avenues: a girl goes to business col-

lege, then gets an administrative job in a shipyard; two boys are sent to work on a farm to help with the crops, learning the value of honest work and helping the war effort in their own way. Even Dan Murray's ex-convict father (Wheeler Oakman) straightens out his life and goes to work in a shipyard.

As noted earlier, juvenile delinquency themes had appeared earlier and would reappear later, but linking delinquency with the war was peculiar to the World War II years. On more than one occasion, characters—even in films not directly dealing with juvenile delinquency—state that the war is being fought for the next generation, the young people. These motion pictures place the blame on adults, and suggest that adults must take the responsibility for supervising their children, raising them to be good, productive citizens, so that the efforts of the armed forces fighting fascism will not be in vain.

27. Two Hour Furloughs: The Lighter Side

Let's have more light comedies and musicals and less Nazis.... Patrons want escapist entertainment, rather than to be reminded of the actualities of today. We want more comedies and musicals. People want to laugh.[1]

Conventional wisdom has it that Hollywood's version of the Second World War was glamorous and unrealistic. However, a significant number of films seriously address the issues of the day with a minimum of glamour and slickness. But many wartime films DO seem to be "pure" escapism, concentrating on humor, music, and beautiful women. What purpose did *these* films serve? Were they made only to give audiences a break from grim reality, or were they contributing in their own way to the fulfillment of America's war aims?

Our research shows that 1945 was the first year since 1942 in which the majority of Hollywood films released were *not* relevant in some way to the war (38% of films released from January through September 1945 had war-relevant content, compared to an average 56% for each of the three preceding years; see Appendix A). This movement away from "war" films was deliberate, instituted by the studio heads both as a response to exhibitor complaints about too many war-oriented features in 1943, and in an effort to avoid having a surplus of war films on hand when peace arrived.[2] However, even during the peak war years of 1943–44, Hollywood made deliberately escapist fare, films which would "give the public a chance to forget the war when they come into the theatre."[3] But some of these films had a hidden agenda—like a pleasant-tasting breakfast cereal which is also "good for you," many escapist films are not only entertaining, but also make their own contributions—in their own way—to the war effort.

1. Something for the Boys: Wartime Musicals

The upswing in the production of musicals is in part a consequence of the demand for films to make the populace happy while in the theatre, away from a world of reality hedged around with unhappiness of varied kind far and near.[4]

Soldiers overseas do not like war or propaganda pictures ... Musical and girl shows are first preference of the men ... with comedies second.[5]

Hollywood musicals, after Westerns and other period pictures, may seem the least likely place to find war-oriented film content. However, well over 100 musicals released in the 1942–1945 period contain some war-relevant material. As Allen L. Woll states:

World War II revived the musical and gave it a sense of mission. It became streamlined in form and committed to the task of winning the war in the hearts and minds of the American people.[6]

In what ways did the musical film contribute to the war effort? Even the term "musical" is a bit vague, encompassing as it does a variety of styles and formats. Most wartime musicals follow the traditional musical comedy model, consisting of a series of musical and comedy performances (sometimes relevant to the plot, sometimes not) within a plot (substantial or perfunctory) that hopefully provides some semblance of continuity. But there are also a few musical *dramas*—including *Tonight and Every Night* (Columbia, 1945) and *Follow the*

Boys (Universal, 1944)—containing musical numbers and comic relief, but essentially dramatic films with musical interludes.

Hollywood's wartime musicals serve three main purposes. First, those musicals which directly address the war—whether as the main point of the film, or in one specific musical number—work towards the same aims as non-musical films. That is, they contain general patriotic messages, reinforcing pride in America (and its Allies); they promote democratic ideals, and enumerate the purposes and goals of the war effort; and they stress the importance of teamwork over individual self-interest. They also treat specific war-related issues, including military recruitment, the home front, and war production.

A second important purpose of wartime musicals is to showcase glamorous settings, gorgeous costumes, and beautiful women. While an argument could be made that satisfying the desires of the "male gaze" has always been a predominant goal of Hollywood filmmakers, this was never so noticeable as during the war. However, in addition to the obvious—men, especially servicemen, enjoyed looking at attractive women—there were also other reasons for this conspicuous display of glamour and sex. All audiences—men, women, and children—could be expected to derive some pleasure from lavish musical numbers, fancy costumes, colorful sets, and cheerful music. Hollywood musicals present a world much more cheerful and glamorous than real life.

The third purpose of wartime musicals combines elements of the first two. Musicals contain a pleasant image of America (the overwhelming majority of such films are set in the United States) and the world. Idealized images of home, of factories, of farms, of military training camps, of women, of families—these all appear in wartime musicals, even those which are ostensibly "realistic" or at least more serious in tone. The war exists in some of these musicals, but is absent in even more. There is little mention of death, and while wartime leave-takings occur, postwar reunions are virtually guaranteed. These nostalgic films depict a happier world than that which exists outside the theatre, a world which existed before the war (many films are set in pre–WWI America, for instance) and which *will* exist again when the war is over.

Musicals with a Message

This Is the Army (WB, 1943) is one example of the way musicals handled war themes. While this film is about as "war-oriented" as a film can be, it contains surprisingly little propaganda, and even overtly patriotic songs are downplayed. Many of the songs in the film come from Irving Berlin's World War One camp musical "Yip Yip Yaphank," and from its WWII counterpart, "This Is the Army." Originally written for a military audience, they poke fun at Army life ("This Is the Army, Mr. Jones," "Oh, How I Hate to Get Up in the Morn-

ing"). There are also some outright ballads ("I Left My Heart at the Stage Door Canteen") and songs that are completely irrelevant to the war like "My Sweetie," and "Mandy," an enormous ministrel-themed production number. "God Bless America" (sung by Kate Smith), and the finale ("This Time for Certain") are among the relatively few songs in the film which could be categorized as patriotic and directly war-oriented.

The dramatic plot, such as it is, boils down to a few sporadic areas of conflict: will Johnny (Ronald Reagan) marry Eileen (Joan Leslie) before he is sent overseas, and will a mother accept the decision of her son to enlist in the Air Corps after the death of his older brother at Pearl Harbor? The answer to both questions is, of course, yes: the women reaffirm their belief in ultimate victory and the just nature of our cause. "Give it to them," Ted's mother tells her surviving son, and Eileen (who has joined the Red Cross Auxiliary and shows up at the end of the film in a uniform of her own) lays it on the line to the vacillating Johnny: "You don't know what the war is all about—we're a free people, fighting to remain free. We're all in this fight together, women as well as men. Let's share our responsibilities."

Thus, the message delivered by *This Is the Army* is twofold. The first message, in the musical and comedy sequences, is that the Army is a lot of fun, even though you may be crippled in combat (like Jerry Jones—Johnny's father—in WWI), or shot down in flames (like Ted at Pearl Harbor). The second message, which appears in the *very* brief dramatic scenes, is the standard "what we're fighting for" plug, which is surprisingly effective although diluted by the film's format.

Thousands Cheer (MGM, 1944) also addresses the issues of war in its dramatic portions—which are substantially longer than the "plot" sections of *This Is the Army*. The film follows the lives of two young people, Kathryn (Kathryn Grayson) and Eddie (Gene Kelly). While Grayson gets to sing and Kelly gets to dance, most of the specialty numbers are presented within the context of military camp shows, and include performances by Kay Kyser and his band, Mickey Rooney, Judy Garland, and Eleanor Powell. The plot segments contrast the attitudes of the romantic leads towards the war: Kathryn voluntarily puts her career as a concert singer on hold in order to "do her part" for the war effort; she joins her father, an Army colonel, and helps stage a colossal camp show for the troops. Eddie, on the other hand, is resentful that he has been drafted away from his civilian occupation (circus aerialist), and wants to get out of the infantry and into the more glamorous Air Corps. By the end of the film, however, Eddie has seen the light—he realizes (courtesy of an object lesson learned while practicing his old act on the flying trapeze, helped out by some tough talk from Grayson) that "team work" is needed to win the war.

The "team" concept is present in a number of other wartime musicals. *Hollywood Canteen* (WB, 1944) contains a number by the black Golden Gate Quartet in which the singers refer to an "all-American team effort" ("The General Jumped at Dawn"). In *Priorities on Parade* (Paramount, 1942) the focus is on the home front, but the message is similar to that of *Thousands Cheer*—self-interest must be suppressed for the duration, since it will take teamwork to win the war. Johnny Johnston and his swing band try to cash in on the war production boom by entertaining war workers at a defense plant. However, they are co-opted into working in the plant itself (playing music on the side), a circumstance that does not exactly please Johnston, particularly when he is assigned to learn his job under the supervision of a female welder (Betty Rhodes). But Rhodes, out of her welder's mask and overalls, turns out to be pretty cute, and Johnston's attitude about war work improves considerably.

Other films which offer a musical comedy look at defense plants—a clear metaphor for national "teamwork" between civilians and soldiers—include *Star Spangled Rhythm*, *Rosie the Riveter* (Republic, 1943), *Hit Parade of 1943* (Republic, 1943), and *Joan of Ozark* (Republic, 1942). The film-makers manage to kill two birds with one stone in these films: they make working in a defense plant look like fun, and manage to include numerous chorus girls in abbreviated "work clothes," exposing vast expanses of skin. Audiences knew, of course, that such images were fantastically unreal, but the message was delivered nonetheless.

"On the Swing Shift" (*Star Spangled Rhythm*) is actually presented as a musical number being shot for a film, and features not only scantily clad females but dozens of brawny male performers as beefcake for women viewers! In *Jam Session*, the "No Name Jive" number includes a female chorus in tight shorts backing the beauteous Ann Miller, wielding oil cans, hammers and riveting guns. Even Judy Canova, the epitome of the plain but decent All-American girl, is indirectly glamorized in the "Lady From Lockheed" number in *Joan of Ozark*. While she wears a welder's mask (with a bonnet on it), she is accompanied by chorus girls in silver two-piece overalls.

A significant number of musicals are directly concerned with the armed forces, like *This Is the Army*, discussed above:

The film musical of the 1940s, with the soldier as the central figure, became a giant enlistment poster, encouraging American citizens to either enlist or accept the draft without resentment or fear.[7]

Understandably, military-theme musicals are generally light in tone. No one, least of all men in the service (or about to go into the service) was interested in heavy drama and a constant reminder of what they were about to face. Instead, films like *Bring on the Girls* (Paramount, 1945), *Anchors Aweigh* (MGM, 1945), and *Private Buckaroo* (Universal, 1942) concentrate on the romance and comedy inherent in military service.

Bring on the Girls would at first seem to be a wartime musical not unlike *Thousands Cheer* or *Priorities on Parade*: defense worker Eddie Bracken (actually he *owns* the factory and several more, but works in a menial job at the plant) joins the Navy, and the rest of the film deals with his military training. But this summary is very misleading: there is *one* dialogue reference to Tokyo, and a single newspaper headline mentions "Nazis," but otherwise there are almost no allusions to the war, our enemies, or what we are fighting for. In fact, Bracken joins the Navy *not* out of a sense of patriotism, but—as he clearly states—to avoid gold-digging women who want to marry him for his money![8]

From the Navy's point of view, this film is either a great recruiting tool or a complete farce. After Bracken enlists, he is first seen on a bus traveling to sunny Miami (the happy sailors are singing "Uncle Sammy's in Miami"). The new recruits (including such veteran movie smart-alecks as Frank Faylen, Huntz Hall, and Dave Willock) live in Miami's swankiest hotel, spend their free time at the posh Coral Club, and never undertake any duties more rigorous than mopping the floor! There is a *one-minute* montage of naval training (stock footage), but other than a passing mention in one dialogue scene that they are going on "active duty," no reference is made to the fact that these sailors will soon be fighting for democracy.

Bring on the Girls much more closely resembles pre-war "service musicals" like *Give Me a Sailor* (Paramount, 1938) and *The Singing Marine* (WB, 1937) than it does *This Is the Army* or *Stage Door Canteen*. But this does not mean *Bring on the Girls* serves no purpose—in addition to making Navy life seem like great fun, it is an excellent example of the lavish "girl show" musical, designed primarily to showcase beautiful (and scantily clad) females.

Here Come the WAVES (Paramount, 1944), *Star Spangled Rhythm*, and *Anchors Aweigh* also make the Navy look like a pretty soft touch. In the first film, Bing Crosby and Sonny Tufts spend their time in the Navy producing a stage show promoting WAVE recruiting, although they are both anxious to get away from this soft, stateside job surrounded by women, and want to see combat action![9] The latter two films are "sailors on leave" stories, both coincidentally set in glamorous Hollywood. Join the Navy and see the stars—or join *any* service and see the stars, as *Stage Door Canteen* and *Hollywood Canteen* illustrate.

The Navy was not alone in its musical comedy fantasy world. The Army was also a fun place to be during wartime, according to Hollywood. *Hey, Rookie* (Columbia, 1944) is reminiscent of *This Is the Army*: this time it is showbiz veteran Larry Parks who is assigned to produce a "soldiers' show," rather than Ronald Reagan.[10] Unlike the earlier film, where Reagan's show is depicted as massive and lavish, Parks has a very limited budget. Once again, however, the show's tone is impressively optimistic. Songs include "It's Great to be in Uniform," and "It's a Helluva, Swelluva, Helluva Life in the Army."

Private Buckaroo works a variation on *Priorities on Parade*: instead of a swing band working in a defense plant, Harry James and his orchestra are drafted into the Army (actually, Harry is drafted and his pals enlist to be with him!). The Andrews Sisters reprise their roles as camp hostesses from *Buck Privates* (Universal, 1941), and sing "Don't Sit Under the Apple Tree With Anyone Else But Me." This song suggests that the girlfriends of soldiers might be tempted to stray during wartime, but the *second* verse (the girlfriends' answer) warns soldiers to watch out for women "on foreign shores." While there were very few available women on Guadalcanal or in North Africa, at least a song like this *suggests* that there *might* be.

Up in Arms (RKO, 1944) goes a step further with such fantasizing. A troopship, bound for the Pacific Theatre of War, is also carrying Army nurses. As the ship pulls out, there is a panning cheesecake shot of the smiling nurses on deck, every one glamorously coiffed and made-up. Later, they relax on deck in revealing bathing suits and sun suits, and the sea voyage into the combat zone takes on the aspect of a summer cruise.

Hollywood musicals also inform current and prospective soldiers that they need not even make the effort to visit the local canteen and search out entertainment, because the stars will bring it to them. *Four Jills in a Jeep* (TCF, 1944), *Follow the Boys* (Universal, 1944), and *Around the World* (RKO, 1943), among other films, deal with traveling USO and other military entertainment units.

Follow the Boys, a drama with musical and comedy sequences rather than a musical comedy, concludes with the death of Tony (George Raft), a movie dancer who has been rejected by the Army due to an old leg injury. To compensate for his rejection, he sets up an organization which supplies entertainment to military installations. Tony perishes on the way to an Australian tour when his ship is torpedoed (he is apparently the *only* casualty—talk about bad luck! Even the Andrew Sisters survive!). However, his wife and the rest of the show business world vow to carry on his work.

Around the World also ends on a somber note: after traveling with Kay Kyser and his troupe through Australia, China, and Egypt, young singer Marcy McGuire learns that her father, an Army officer she was hoping to meet while on the tour, has been killed in action. Bravely, Marcy sings "Great News in the Making," alluding to the end of hostilities and a better world to come.

While neither of these films features any major military characters, *Four Jills in a Jeep* adds a male soldier as romantic interest for Carole Landis, who is one of the four "Jills" of the title, female performers touring military bases in Europe and North Africa. As in *Hollywood Canteen*, the soldier finds romance with a movie star.[11] It *probably* wouldn't happen, audiences knew, but it was something to think about.

Another war-relevant aspect of wartime musicals is their open glorification of America, the American way, and the virtues of democracy. Some films demonstrating these sentiments have contemporary settings, some do not. Some refer directly to the war, some do not. *Yankee Doodle Dandy* (WB, 1942) is probably the best-known flag-waver of the war years, but films like *Holiday Inn* (Paramount, 1942) also celebrate the American way of life. "God Bless America," sung by Kate Smith, is one of the more serious songs—and thus one of the most effective—in *This Is the Army*. *Born to Sing* (MGM, 1942) features the "Ballad for Americans," and *She's a Sweetheart* (Columbia, 1944) includes "The American Prayer."

Pride in America extends to America's wartime allies.

Tonight and Every Night, a Rita Hayworth vehicle, contrasts the glamorous stage performances at a London theatre with the impact of war on the performers and audiences. Early in the film, star Rita Hayworth, the rest of the cast of the show, *and* the show's audience have to take shelter when an air raid interrupts the festivities. But there's a bright side, since this is the way Hayworth meets RAF pilot Lee Bowman, who becomes her fiancé. The film celebrates the formidable staying power of the British people (Hayworth, however, plays a visiting American), but the true moral of the story is "the show must go on"—the title of the film refers to the nightly performances at the theatre, which were never canceled despite the Blitz. Even when her two closest friends and fellow actors are killed in an air raid, Hayworth, inheriting some of their stiff upper lip, carries bravely on.

Thumbs Up (Republic, 1943) was almost a dry run for *Tonight and Every Night*, and also bears a strong resemblance to *Priorities on Parade*. American performer Brenda Joyce wants to become a star on the British stage, but the only way she can get a break is to go to work at a defense plant, hoping to be "discovered" by a producer casting a musical featuring only defense workers. She is offered a big contract through the connivance of the show's associate producer, but chooses to stay in defense work for the duration, convinced by her RAF boyfriend and her plucky fellow workers that this is the thing to do.

Thumbs Up features the song "Who Are the British?" Sung by Gertrude Niesen to a crowd of workers in the aircraft plant's cafeteria (in front of huge British and U.S. flags), the lyrics cite famous Britons, including Shakespeare, Kipling, Beatrice Lillie, Lord Mountbatten, Generals Montgomery and Wavell, and concludes with a reference to Winston Churchill (at this point the camera tilts up to a photograph of Churchill on the wall).[12] Most of the other songs in the film are not war-oriented, although the finale—a reprise of a song entitled "From Here On In" which has already been sung *twice* before—has new, optimistic lyrics:

> From here on in,
> It should be easy sledding...
> We're on the victory track.[13]

Although the heyday of the "Latin American musical" actually came before America's entrance into the war,[14] there are many Latin-themed song and dance numbers in Hollywood's wartime musicals. Carmen Miranda became a star, appearing in *The Gang's All Here* (TCF, 1943) and *Something for the Boys* (TCF, 1944), among other films. Xavier Cugat and José Iturbi were also frequent musical "guests" during this period. Terms like "Good Neighbor" and "Americans all" fly thick and fast, but most of the Latin American numbers are only peripherally war-oriented, if at all.

Hands Across the Border (Republic, 1944), concludes with a modestly staged production number illustrating the title tune, a plug for inter-American cooperation (specifically Mexican-American; the film's plot has almost nothing to do with this theme, however). *Brazil* (Republic, 1944—oddly enough, starring *Mexican* singer Tito Guizar) and *Pan-Americana* (RKO, 1945) are among the few wartime musicals with a preponderance of Latin American songs rather than a mere token musical number.

The other Allies are occasionally represented by isolated musical numbers (like "You Can't Brush Off a Russian," from *Sweethearts of the U.S.A.*—Monogram, 1944), or in omnibus production numbers such as the "Victory Polka" finale of *Jam Session* (Columbia, 1944), featuring fighting men (and chorus girls) representing various Allied nations, and the climactic "United Nations on the March" from *Thousands Cheer*.

Thus, in spite of their relentlessly cheerful and unrealistic plots and settings, these war-oriented musicals do their best to support the war effort, keeping morale high and conveying optimistic, patriotic messages.

Bring on the Girls

> Bring on the girls, clear the decks for action;
> Bring on the girls, they're the main attraction.
> Why does the sailor go to the USO—
> Not for tea and cakes.
> So if you're smart and have a heart,
> Give 'em Veronica Lake.
> And if you want morale, let me tell you pal
> Better dress it up in curls.[15]

As sexist as it may seem today, during WWII the display of attractive women in revealing costumes was considered "good for morale." In *So Proudly We Hail!* (Paramount, 1943), Army nurse Paulette Goddard preserves her black negligee throughout the Philippines campaign, because it "keeps [her] morale up." In *Here Come the WAVES*, Betty Hutton and her twin sister (also Betty Hutton) are nightclub performers; when one of the sisters announces her intention to join the WAVES, her partner objects: "We're doing more for morale [where we are] than Dorothy Lamour's sarong." In *I'll Be Seeing You* (Paramount, 1945), teenager Barbara (Shirley Temple) responds to her mother's concerns about a low-cut dress: "For your information, Mother, this neckline is a morale builder."

Among the enduring icons of the war are the famed Betty Grable bathing suit and Rita Hayworth negligee pinup photos, often cited as "morale-boosters" for men in the armed forces. Sex not only sold films, it was considered patriotic! In spite of the strictures of the Production Code, musicals of the war era make a deliberate point of emphasizing "cheesecake" shots to an extent rarely seen before or since.

Separated from their homes, wives, and girlfriends, men in the armed forces fantasized about better times when the war would be over. Pinups were a visual reminder, if not of actual lovers or acquaintances, at least of sex and romance, two things soldiers in wartime desire but usually cannot have. With humorous overstatement, films like *Guadalcanal Diary*, *Gung Ho!*, *Busses Roar*, and *Up in Arms* illustrate the soldier's attachment to "his" pinup girl.

In *Up in Arms*, a tough soldier named Blackie dreams of his favorite, Veronica Lake, while in a bunk on a troopship. However, it is his unfortunate neighbor (Danny Kaye) who winds up entangled in the G.I.'s sleepy embrace! A similar scene occurs in *Star Spangled Rhythm*—a soldier in a tent sings "That Old Black Magic" to a photo of Vera Zorina. The photo comes to life as Zorina (in an extremely revealing costume) dances across a snow-covered landscape, and the soldier's amorous reactions to this daydream prove irritating to his tent-mate. William Bendix is seriously attached to *his* pinup photograph of Betty Grable in *Guadalcanal Diary*.

Pin Up Girl (TCF, 1944), starring Betty Grable, capitalizes on her offscreen fame as a favorite of the armed forces. The famous pinup pose appears (as an artist's rendering) behind the opening credits, and the photo itself appears as part of the plot at least three times. Grable is a good-hearted USO canteen hostess in the Midwest who comes to Washington as a government stenographer, falls in love with a Navy man (a "hero of Guadalcanal"), and becomes a star performer. Grable's charms are revealed in several musical numbers, and there is also some cheesecake from the "Skating Vanities" (chorus girls on skates), and even Martha Raye!

The title song in *Cover Girl* (Columbia, 1944) serves as an excuse to parade beautiful models, and in *Bring on the Girls* the song "How'd You Like to Take My Picture" features various women in stereotypical pinup poses (in a bubble bath, on the beach, undressing in the boudoir, and so on). These films (and their advertising) deliberately set out to emulate the image of the well-known "Vargas" and "Petty" girls, seen in magazines and on calendars across the nation.

It should not come as a surprise that many of the favorite pinup stars of WWII were primarily musical performers: Betty Grable, Ann Miller, Rita Hayworth, and Esther Williams (although Williams was a swimmer, her starring vehicles were generally musical comedies). Other actresses whose sex appeal made them popular with male audiences included Veronica Lake, Dorothy Lamour, and Ann Sheridan, all of whom appeared in one or more wartime musicals, despite their personal lack of musical ability.

Grable's wartime career was chiefly spent in musicals with little or no war relevance, often period pictures: *Song of the Islands, Springtime in the Rockies, Footlight Serenade, Coney Island, Sweet Rosie O'Grady, Diamond Horseshoe* (also known as *Billy Rose's Diamond Horseshoe*), and *The Dolly Sisters*. Only *Pin Up Girl*, out of eight Grable films released between 1942 and 1945, contains significant war-relevant content. As Fox's top star of the era, her films were almost always lavish Technicolor productions, and Fox was reluctant to limit their appeal and longevity by including a great deal of topical material. Nonetheless, the films *all* include many musical numbers designed to display Grable's physical charms to their best advantage.

In *Coney Island*, for instance, Grable's legs and hourglass figure are showcased in numerous musical numbers. In one sequence, impresario George Montgomery strips the extraneous frills, feathers, and ruffles from Grable's costume, gradually exposing more of her famous body.

Both of Rita Hayworth's wartime Columbia films are directly related to the war—*Cover Girl* and *Tonight and Every Night*—but the studio was careful to include the type of sumptuous production numbers audiences expected. B-picture stalwart Ann Miller appeared in nine musicals between 1942 and 1945, two for Paramount in 1942, and then seven straight for Columbia. Many of these contain some war material, but *Priorities on Parade, True to the Army*, and *Reveille with Beverly* are the most directly relevant. Once again, the musical numbers were considered the most important aspect of her films, and Miller is frequently showcased in abbreviated costumes and relatively lavish settings, as in the "Cooperate with Your Air Raid Warden" number in *Priorities on Parade*.

Some of the cheesecake musicals are contemporary, war-oriented films, but even non-topical musicals play their part in displaying the female form. With the South Pacific a major theatre of war, films like *Pardon My Sarong* (Universal, 1942), *Rhythm of the Islands* (Universal, 1943), *Rainbow Island* (Paramount, 1944), *Song of the Islands* (TCF, 1942), *Song of the Sarong* (Universal, 1945), and *Tahiti Honey* (Republic, 1943) automatically become fantasies set in pre-war (and by inference, postwar) paradise. *Song of the Islands*, a more or less contemporary film set in Hawaii, not only ignores the war but also fails to show *any* Navy sailors! Dorothy Lamour, by virtue of her pre-war films, was closely associated with this genre. As the "sarong girl," she even parodies herself in a cheesecake number in *Star Spangled Rhythm*, "A Sweater, A Sarong, and a Peekaboo Bang."

Other atypical settings for cheesecake footage include period films like *Shine On, Harvest Moon* (WB, 1944): the Technicolor finale to this black and white musical biography of Nora Bayes (Ann Sheridan) is a production number sung to the title tune, and features chorus girls dressed as various fruits and vegetables! The opening sequence of *This Is the Army*, set in 1917, features George Murphy singing "My Sweetie," accompanied by a bevy of chorines (although these are the last

to be seen in the film—the "chorus girls" in the film's other numbers are played by male soldiers in drag!).

The ice-skating musical and the swimming musical were two other sub-genres designed to titillate male audiences. In the former, Sonja Henie (for 20th Century–Fox), Vera Hruba Ralston (for Republic), and Belita (for Monogram) all show plenty of leg as they whirl across the ice in films like *Iceland* (TCF, 1942), *Wintertime* (TCF, 1943), *Ice Capades Review* (Republic, 1942), *Lake Placid Serenade* (Republic, 1944), *Lady, Let's Dance* (Monogram, 1944) and *Silver Skates* (Monogram, 1943).

Esther Williams was the sole female swimming movie star of the war years. Backed by MGM, her career began to gather momentum during the war as she showed her form in *Bathing Beauty* (MGM, 1944), *Ziegfeld Follies* (MGM, 1944), and *Thrill of a Romance* (MGM, 1945). The first of these films is particularly notable for its cheesecake-oriented camerawork: in the spectacular water ballet finale, an underwater camera focuses on the spread legs of female swimmers!

In addition to musicals starring attractive "pinup" stars, there are films whose cheesecake quotient is filled by attractive chorus girls. *Rosie the Riveter* (Republic, 1944) stars Jane Frazee, an attractive young woman singer, but no Betty Grable. However, the finale, during which Frazee sings the title tune, features a scantily clad chorus, which is also prominently featured in the advertising for this film.

Bring on the Girls stars Veronica Lake, Eddie Bracken, Sonny Tufts, and Marjorie Reynolds; the first two do no singing or dancing during the film, while Tufts and Lord have several songs each. However, the film is filled with cheesecake images. Indeed, as the credits roll, the title song is sung by a continuous parade of attractive women who walk directly up to the camera, presenting their images in close-up for the audience. When Bracken and his sailor friends go to the swanky Coral Club, they are greeted by a hatcheck girl and a cigarette girl (Yvonne DeCarlo and Veronica Lake), both in abbreviated costumes—short skirts and halter tops. The first musical number is the previously mentioned "How Would You Like to Take My Picture," a series of cheesecake tableaux (including a modified striptease by a female defense worker). The next major production number begins with Marjorie Reynolds and a male dancer, but then opens up to feature an assortment of chorus girls in pastel costumes (showing off the Technicolor hues). Yet another sequence is set at Bracken's home, where he is giving a pool party; naturally, shots of women in bathing suits are prominent.

Such films were obviously popular with male audiences, but one should not infer that women disliked musicals, even those with a high cheesecake quotient (a significant percentage of the whole). Betty Grable was one of the top ten box-office figures from 1942 through 1951, a distinction she would not have been able to attain if her appeal was solely to male audiences.[16] Musicals appealed to all ages, sexes, and classes, or at least they tried to. The escapist plots, popular music, well-staged dances, lavish settings and color (for the larger-budget films), all had definite appeal to wartime film audiences.

The cheesecake in musicals was just an added bonus for the men, particularly those whose lives had been disrupted by the war. They could see beautiful women, dream about them, fantasize about coming home from the war to wives or sweethearts—above all, they could, for a while, forget about the male-dominated world of regimentation, orders, uniforms, and possible injury or death.

Thoughts of Home

The third major contribution of wartime musicals is perhaps the least obvious. The settings, plots, characterizations, and overall attitude and outlook of these films were designed to reassure American audiences of the validity of the American way, to remind them of what it meant to be an American, and to suggest that the war was but a transitory cloud which would soon yield to a brighter future.

One good example of the way musicals provide reassurance to audiences occurs in *The Gang's All Here* (TCF, 1943). Alice Faye is a singer in love with soldier James Ellison. In one sequence, Faye sings "No Love, No Nothing," an "answer" song to the cautionary "Don't Sit Under the Apple Tree with Anyone Else but Me." Costumed as a housewife, on a stage set representing a small apartment, Faye—ironing clothes!—makes it clear that she will wait for her soldier to return from the war, and there will be no fooling around in the meantime. This is an image of unshakable loyalty and enduring domesticity. Similar sentiments are expressed in "I Promise You (A Faithful Heart)," sung in *Here Come the WAVES*, and in "Don't Forget the Girl Back Home," heard in *Three Little Sisters* (Republic, 1944).

Certainly the directly war-relevant musicals contribute to this attitude, but the *non*-relevant musicals are also important. A glance at the musicals released in 1942–1945 shows a significant number of period films, including a surprisingly large number situated in the pre–World War *One* era, ranging from the 1890s through the first decade of the 20th century.

Twentieth Century–Fox was a prime source for these "Gay Nineties" films, which take audiences back to a period of enormous growth and vitality in America. The Civil War was over, and the First World War was yet to come (the Spanish-American War, if mentioned in these films at all, is portrayed as a quick, painless, glorious victory). Songs and costumes of the period were quaint but still close enough to contemporary tastes to please 1940s audiences. The outside world does not intrude on American happiness.

My Gal Sal (TCF, 1942) is an early example of these "good

times" films.[17] Rita Hayworth and Victor Mature are the romantic leads, Mature playing a songwriter and Hayworth a stage performer, which allows for plentiful songs and dances. Their romance has its rocky points, but the film is not a serious drama. *Coney Island* (TCF, 1943) features Betty Grable as an entertainer at the turn of the century, with George Montgomery and Cesar Romero as rivals for her hand. One critic correctly identified this film as an "antidote to the grim realities at the front."[18] *Hello, Frisco, Hello* (TCF, 1943) stars John Payne as a San Francisco impresario who headlines Alice Faye in his new musical show. Grable is back again as a singer and dancer, in *Sweet Rosie O'Grady* (TCF, 1943), another turn of the century tale. She finished up the war years with *Diamond Horseshoe* and *The Dolly Sisters* (1945), both period musicals. *Irish Eyes Are Smiling* (TCF, 1944) is a vehicle for singer Dick Haymes, cast as an Irish-American songwriter in the early 1900s; June Haver is his showgirl love interest. And so on and so forth.

The other studios were not as fixated on this period as Fox was, but MGM did produce one of the best examples of wartime nostalgia, *Meet Me in St. Louis* (1944). If any film could reassure Americans that things would be "all right," it was this enormously popular and sentimental family tale starring Judy Garland and Margaret O'Brien. Universal contributed *Bowery to Broadway* (1944) and *The Merry Monahans* (1944); the latter film actually carries its showbiz-family tale through the end of WWI. Warner Brothers spent a lot of time and money on *Shine On, Harvest Moon* (1944), a fictionalized biography of singer Nora Bayes (Ann Sheridan) and songwriter Jack Norworth (Dennis Morgan). Republic Pictures made *Atlantic City* (1944), another film spanning the pre-to-post WWI era.

There are also similar films set slightly later in time—as well as a few placed even earlier, such as *Dixie* (Paramount, 1943), a Civil War-era vehicle starring Bing Crosby, and *Can't Help Singing* (Universal, 1944), a musical Western with Deanna Durbin. The "1920s" musicals have the advantage of showing postwar (post–WWI, in this case) conditions, thereby reassuring contemporary audiences that things would be even better after the war. *Show Business* (RKO, 1944), a fictionalized "biography" of Eddie Cantor, *Stormy Weather* (TCF, 1943), a fictionalized "biography" of Bill Robinson, *Broadway* (Universal, 1942), a fictionalized "biography" of George Raft, and *Greenwich Village* (TCF, 1944), are all good examples of this type of film.

Is Everybody Happy? (Columbia, 1943) takes particular advantage of its setting to make a point for wartime audiences. Ted Lewis, playing himself, tells a story (in flashback) to a young soldier and his girlfriend. During WWI, a young man and woman are undecided about marriage, but eventually go ahead and tie the knot anyway. Despite a wartime injury which ends his piano career (shades of *This Is the Army*, where George Murphy's dancing career is ruined by a war injury), the young man switches to trumpet and becomes successful. At the end of the film (after plenty of vintage songs), Lewis reveals that the WWI couple were the parents of the WWII soldier! The moral of the story? Go ahead and make plans, the war will not last forever and even a wartime injury can be overcome.

Most period musicals are not directly war-relevant, but the message is still the same. America will survive. Think of the good old days—they will be back, but even better than before.[19]

Musicals, therefore, should not be dismissed as irrelevant to the war effort simply because their content seems frivolous or escapist. These attitudes were rightly seen as making an important contribution to both civilian and military morale by the very nature of their escapism, which was neither random nor accidental.

2. Smiling Through: Comedy in War Films

Pearl Harbor had been caught napping and Singapore collapsed from over-confidence—but fear not: a Parisian piano player or a Broadway Runyonite or a Washington stenographer can outwit the Gestapo any day.[20]

As with musicals, wartime comedies were a double-edged weapon. On the one hand, comedies are obviously escapist fare, specifically designed to lighten the hearts of moviegoers, if only for the duration of the film. Comedies are supposed to make people laugh and feel better, a noble goal at any time, but particularly so in times of crisis or stress. Under the general category of "improving morale," comedies did their duty. But, again as with musicals, wartime comedy films could and did serve other, more specific war-related purposes.

For instance, as discussed in the chapter on propaganda, films mocking the enemy contributed to the nation's war effort, although some observers felt that too much ridicule of Hitler, Mussolini, the Japanese, etc., was actually counterproductive. But other aspects of film comedy were also war-relevant.

For instance, a good many of the wartime references to shortages and rationing are comedic in tone. As noted in Chapter 24, films trod a fine line between traditional American "griping" and outright criticism of the rationing system. The freedom to gripe, complain, bitch—whatever the term— is cherished by Americans both on an individual level and on a larger scale (demonstrations, for instance, could be considered a "mass gripe"). Of course Americans disliked shortages and rationing, and jokes about the heightened value of tires, sugar, and silk stockings abound in WWII Hollywood. But there are few jokes which make hoarding or dealing in black market goods seem acceptable, and even fewer which suggest that the rationing system is unfair or unnecessary.

Even the film most directly concerned with (and critical of) the rationing bureaucracy—*Rationing* (MGM, 1944)—

clearly brands hoarders and black marketeers as venal and unpatriotic. Problems with the rationing system, including reams of government red tape and confusing regulations, are accepted as "typical" government bungling and overkill, but the need for some sort of system is explicitly championed, even by those at its mercy (like beleaguered storekeeper Wallace Beery).

Rationing and shortages were taken in stride and became the butt of jokes rather than the subject of bitter recriminations. Americans were not faced with the same strictures as Britons, and our English cousins were holding up, were they not? American ingenuity in the face of shortages is demonstrated, often with comic overtones in a number of films. In *Lady Bodyguard* (Paramount, 1943), a rural gas station's gas pumps are now labeled "Barley" and "Oats," as *real* horsepower makes a comeback. *Miracle at Morgan's Creek* (Paramount, 1944) demonstrates that rationing has its benefits: a highly alcoholic punch with a few lemons floating in it becomes the patriotic "Victory Lemonade: Save Sugar For Victory."

Such references—and similar jokes about blackouts, air raid wardens, Red Cross classes and other home defense and home front activities—show that Americans were taking the *war* seriously, but that they did not have to taken *themselves* (or stuffy bureaucrats, officious air raid wardens, and self-important "Women's Home Auxiliary" members) seriously. In *Blondie for Victory* (Columbia, 1942), a defense worker husband complains that his wife is spending too much time on *her* war activities with the "Housewives of America," and is neglecting her duties at home: "I work at the airplane plant all day and eat hash every night." *True to Life* (Paramount, 1943) features Victor Moore as an addled civil defense warden who— mistakenly believing an air raid has been signaled—repeatedly dashes into the street and attempts to make passersby lie down in the gutter!

The war did not necessarily keep anyone from having a good time, as long as they made a contribution to the war effort while they were doing so. The countless bond rallies, benefits for war relief funds, and camp shows depicted in wartime films have a serious goal—support for the Allied war effort— but the participants in these activities are almost always shown to be enjoying themselves. Not only are they receiving the satisfaction of knowing that their efforts are patriotic, the very act of "pitching in" is pleasant.

Song of the Open Road (UA, 1944) is a good example. In this film, juvenile movie star Jane Powell runs away from the drudgery of filmmaking, and joins a group of youngsters who help harvest crops. What could be construed as menial labor is instead portrayed as healthy outdoor fun in the company of cheerful, new-found friends. To save an endangered orange crop, Jane rallies her Hollywood friends (like W.C. Fields and Edgar Bergen) to provide live entertainment for the volunteer crop pickers. *Harvest Melody* (PRC, 1943) is very similar in its depiction of farm labor in musical comedy terms.

Putting one's personal tastes aside, the *Blondie* series from Columbia provides a good example of how war relevance is included in innocuous situation comedies. A good many of the *Blondie* films released between 1942 and 1945 contain topical material: some of the entries are heavily skewed towards the war (*Blondie for Victory*, 1942), while others are not as directly relevant (*Blondie's Blessed Event*, 1942, *Footlight Glamour* and *It's a Great Life*—both 1943—for example). While Dagwood is never called to serve in the armed forces (presumably because he is engaged in essential war work with Dithers Construction, or because he is the "sole support" of Blondie and his two children), the Bumsteads do their patriotic part—buying bonds, contributing to scrap drives, observing rationing regulations, etc. Sometimes the war intrudes on their lives—it has an impact on Dagwood's job, for instance—but the Bumsteads can handle it. And if the *Bumsteads* (idiotic Dagwood and bossy Blondie) can handle it, *any* American family could handle it.

While comedies set on the home front were intended to minimize the negative impact of the war on American life, one would not expect to find many comedies about life in the armed forces during wartime. There are a number of films—outright comedies and films with comic overtones—released throughout the war which focus on individual soldiers, sailors, or airmen on leave, in training, or preparing to leave for active duty: *Seven Days Leave* (RKO, 1942), *Moonlight and Cactus* (Universal, 1944), *Sailor's Holiday* (Columbia, 1944), and *Seven Days Ashore* (RKO, 1944), for instance. These films all feature characters who are *in* the service (although generally they are not portrayed as career military men), but the films are not *about* their lives in the service.

Early in the conflict, *One Thrilling Night* (Monogram, 1942) utilizes the war as the backdrop for a comedy: a newly-wed couple's one-night honeymoon (the husband has to report for active duty the next day) is constantly disrupted by various events. As the husband departs, his frustrated wife says "Darn those Japs!" Such films continue to be made throughout the war, although the emphasis shifts from outright farce to a more sedate blend of romance, comedy and drama: *Pillow to Post* (WB, 1945) and *The Impatient Years* (Columbia, 1944), for instance.

However, outright "service comedies" in the *Buck Privates* vein are concentrated largely in 1942. Many of these films were made or at least written prior to Pearl Harbor, and treat the Army (and Navy, Air Corps, etc.) humorously. Among the 1942 entries in this comic sub-genre are *About Face*, *Fall In*, and *Hayfoot* (all UA), *Private Snuffy Smith* and *Hillbilly Blitzkrieg* (both Monogram), *Two Yanks in Trinidad* (Columbia), and *True to the Army* (Paramount). Most of these films make little or no reference to the war, or (at best) feature bumbling Axis spies.

1943 saw a much smaller crop of such films, including *Yanks Ahoy* (UA), *Let's Face It* (Paramount), and RKO's Brown and Carney pair, *Adventures of a Rookie* and *Rookies in Burma*. These films for the most part at least acknowledge the fact that America was at war, although only Brown and Carney actually got overseas and into combat of a sort (in *Rookies in Burma*). Otherwise, the soldier stars of these comedies have to make do with submarines lurking off the coast (*Fall In* and *Let's Face It*), or are outright imitations of *Buck Privates* (i.e., restricting themselves to training and maneuvers—*Adventures of a Rookie*). *See Here, Private Hargrove* (MGM, 1944) is one of the last wartime examples of these training camp comedies, and it was actually based on a 1942 bestseller.[21]

Humor also appears as a component of non-comedy films, including the grim and realistic Combat films. Virtually every example of this genre includes one or more characters who make sardonic wisecracks, or otherwise lighten the tone of the film for a moment or two. Sonny Tufts as the hard-luck Marine in *So Proudly We Hail!* (Paramount, 1943), William Bendix as the tough Brooklyn cabbie in *Guadalcanal Diary* (TCF, 1943), even Wallace Beery in the leading role of the retired Marine sergeant in *Salute to the Marines* (MGM, 1943)—these are all serious films, and the actors mentioned are not merely "comic relief." Instead, they represent the brash, confident side of America, unimpressed by the military might of the Axis and determined to "finish the job" as quickly as possible.[22]

Some of this "combat humor" is black—the notorious "fried Jap going down!" remark in *Air Force* (WB, 1943), for example—and is aimed at the enemy. However, almost as often the humor is self-directed. Members of his Marine unit constantly complain about Frank McHugh's cooking in *Marine Raiders* (RKO, 1944)—and this bit of humor occurs in a film which features a Marine who has been crucified, his hands and feet chopped off, by the Japanese![23]

The rivalry between branches of the armed forces provides moments of humor in *Guadalcanal Diary* (TCF, 1943) and in *Marine Raiders*: the Marines chide the Army for arriving "late" when the GIs land to replace the leathernecks. David Bruce and Noah Beery Jr. play half-brothers who are friendly romantic rivals in *Gung Ho!* (Universal, 1943), and their constant bickering is used to lighten the tone of this combat film. When the Marines go into action, however, Bruce takes Beery's place in an assault on a machine gun nest and is killed.

Even on the battlefield, Americans (and our Allies) display their sense of humor, a visible sign of confidence in ultimate victory. Representatives of democracy have a right to crack jokes, to smile, to poke fun at their friends and their government. This is in direct contrast to film images of the enemy, who are almost always portrayed as unsmiling and grim, as befits their status as America's evil opponents, doomed to defeat. Occasionally a Nazi or a Japanese character will crack a smile: but this usually comes while they are plotting some nefarious act or committing an atrocity, and in almost every case their sadistic glee is violently repaid in very short order.

Wartime musicals and comedies, called by some "escapist entertainment" and an "antidote to grim reality," nonetheless managed to contribute to the war effort, often in a more sub- tle manner than blatant wartime propaganda films. Their mes- sages are often unstated, but clear, and their optimistic atti- tude was shared and appreciated by film audiences.

28. When the War Is Over: Postwar Planning

[There was] ... the daunting memory of what had followed the last war ... a collapse of the coun- try's social, political and economic order. Yet ... people were far from downcast. On the contrary, they felt themselves to be standing at the threshold of a promising new era.[1]

"Our guys are out fighting in countries they never even heard of for a lot of foreigners who'll turn on us like a pack of wolves the minute it's over."—Tender Comrade *(RKO, 1943)*

America began to plan for the postwar period almost be- fore hostilities had begun. While the exact outcome of the war was not known, most Americans felt our country would never be defeated and occupied by the Axis powers, and that the fighting would eventually end. Win, lose, or draw—the con- cept of demanding "unconditional surrender" of the Axis was only agreed upon at the Casablanca conference in January 1943—there would be a postwar.[2]

Postwar Planning in the United States was published in April 1942 by the private Twentieth Century Fund, and sum- marized the activities of various government and private or- ganizations in postwar planning. If this seems a bit early in the war to be thinking of the postwar period, it should be noted that this book was actually a revision of a pamphlet first issued in July 1941![3]

In August 1941, the Atlantic Charter was signed by Frank- lin D. Roosevelt and Winston Churchill; among other state- ments, this declaration contained the phrases :

after the final destruction of the Nazi tyranny, they hope to see es- tablished a peace which will afford to all nations the means of dwelling safely within their own boundaries ... in freedom from fear and want.[4]

In the fall of 1942, a War Crimes Commission was estab- lished by the Allies, looking forward to the end of the war when those responsible would be brought to justice.[5] The United Nations Food Conference, which opened in May 1943, pro- duced a proclamation "in full confidence of victory," and made plans for an international food organization to alleviate world hunger.[6] At the Teheran Conference, Roosevelt, Churchill and Stalin issued a statement, dated December 1943, referring to "the peace that will follow."[7] A Congressional act, passed in October 1944, renamed the Office of War Mobilization as the Office of War Mobilization and Reconversion.[8] Indeed, by the spring of 1944, more than one million veterans had returned to civilian life, and the total number of employed Americans had dropped more than a million in just six months.[9]

Hostilities in Europe officially ceased on 5 May 1945, and the Germans signed the surrender documents on May 7; "V-E Day" was the next day, May 8, 1945.[10] Japan accepted the surrender terms of the Allies on 14 August 1945 ("V-J Day"), and the official documents were signed on board the battleship *Missouri* in Yokohama harbor on September 2, 1945.[11] The Second World War had ended.

However, for the American public, the end had been an- ticipated much earlier. While government planning for post- war readjustment was wisely begun well in advance of the ac- tual end of hostilities, the government was disturbed by the change in public attitudes, beginning in 1944. In November 1944, General Eisenhower held a press conference and warned the American public that the Nazis were not yet beaten, de- spite the steady advances of the Allied forces into Germany. He obliquely asked Americans on the home front to continue to produce war materials and buy War Bonds to support the armed forces.[12]

But after D-Day, the writing was on the wall (although the German counter-offensive known as the Battle of the Bulge in December 1944 threw a scare into everyone), and it was difficult to maintain the same fever pitch of patriotism as in 1942 and 1943. Even after the defeat of Germany, Japan fought on, and no one knew how long it would take to beat that na- tion. As Allied troops moved closer and closer to the Japanese home islands, the fighting grew bloodier:

To counteract the apparent complacency at home, the Navy asked people to take their 1945 vacations on the West Coast and visit the ports ther.... What they saw was the debris of the battle for Oki- nawa—ship after ship gutted, burned, torn open, blood-stained.... But still the Red Cross appealed in vain for volunteers to prepare sur- gical dressings. Army planes futilely leafleted boomtowns with hand- bills begging workers to sign on at local war plants. America was not so much complacent, however, as tired.[13]

Postwar references, while never extremely numerous, ap- pear fairly early in Hollywood films, and peak in 1944, well before the cessation of hostilities:

	1942	1943	1944	1945		Total
Postwar	9	11	23	18	=	61

References to the postwar period in wartime films fall into several categories. A number of films contain the standard "we'll meet again when the war is over" routine, *Three Russian Girls* (UA, 1944) and *Marine Raiders* (RKO, 1944), for example. In the first film, these sentiments are expressed by a Russian nurse (Anna Sten) and her American pilot boyfriend (Kent Smith). In all likelihood, of course, Sten's character will probably be sent to a reeducation camp after the war for fraternizing with an American, but in 1944 the Russians were our Allies, and everyone hoped the postwar period would see a continuation of the same "friendly spirit of cooperation."

Several films address the problem of war criminals. *None Shall Escape* (Columbia, 1944) is a highly interesting film which begins with a postwar war crimes trial before an international (and multi-racial, including black and Asian judges) tribunal in Poland. Nazi officer Wilhelm Grimm (Alexander Knox—who ironically had the title role in *Wilson* for 20th Century–Fox the same year) is accused of various atrocities, and there are flashbacks showing Grimm's return from World War One as a wounded German veteran, his gradual conversion to National Socialism, and his brutal repression of the Polish village under his control. The title refers to "all the Wilhelm Grimms" who will, the film asserts, be hunted down and arrested. This film seems almost uncanny in its prediction of the Nuremberg Trials; however, the Allies had already stated their intention to try "war criminals" after the cessation of hostilities, and *None Shall Escape* merely elaborates on this theme.

The Master Race (RKO, 1944) is slightly different, taking place in Belgium after the Allied liberation of the country, but before the war officially ends (news comes of the surrender of Germany in this *1944* release after two-thirds of the film has passed). Colonel Von Beck (George Coulouris), a Nazi officer, poses as a Belgian concentration camp inmate (even shooting himself in the leg to add veracity to his story) and is "freed" by American soldiers. He sets out to sow dissension and distrust among the Belgians and the liberating forces. What distinguishes *The Master Race* from another "liberation" film like *A Bell for Adano* (TCF, 1945—set in Italy) is Von Beck's fanatical insistence that, although "this war" is over, the Germans will rise again.

This motion picture, which includes documentary footage of the D-Day invasion, was completed just three weeks after the Normandy landings. In many ways it is remarkably accurate in its depiction of the immediate postwar period: the Belgian village is administered by a joint U.S.-British occupation force (a Russian Army medical officer, liberated from the concentration camp nearby, lends his assistance); at the end of the film, the U.S. military commander says he will be leaving to work with the occupation troops in Germany. The shat-

tered Belgian town must try to rebuild not only its buildings, but its economy, and the lives of the survivors. Von Beck tries to ruin the healing process, but is eventually exposed, summarily tried (as a spy), and shot.

Unrepentant Nazis appear with some frequency in Hollywood's postwar films, but it is a little surprising to see this theme propounded as early as 1944. Interestingly enough, *The Master Race* indicates the Nazi Party was merely a tool of an aristocratic caste of German nationalists; in the opening scene, von Beck hands out false identity papers to German diplomats, soldiers, and industrialists so they can go underground, while a portrait of Hitler is carelessly discarded on the floor, and the Nazis are dismissed as past their usefulness.

Hotel Berlin (WB, 1945) also deals with Nazis who plan to evade the inevitable postwar punishment. General von Dahnwitz (Raymond Massey), the "Butcher of Kharkov," whose name appears on the "Allied war criminal list," eventually decides *not* to flee Berlin (he is later forced to commit suicide for his part in a plot to depose Hitler); however, Baron von Stetten (Henry Daniell) vows "We will be back," and makes plans to flee via submarine to America, where he will assume command of the Nazi underground.

Destination Tokyo (WB, 1944) does not specifically refer to postwar trials, but it does make a statement that the war is being fought to "wipe out a system that puts daggers in 5-year-old's hands," a reference to militaristic aspects of Japanese society and politics. The war crimes trials of Japanese officials were not as well publicized as the Nuremberg Trials in Germany, but the Allies did hold the Japanese militarists responsible for various wartime atrocities, as well as their part in starting World War Two.[14]

There are a few films which mention reconversion of American society (and particularly the economy) to a peace footing, a subject which consumed the attention of the government and industry in real life, but was not sufficiently dramatic to concern Hollywood. *Heavenly Days* (RKO, 1944), a vehicle for the radio team of Fibber McGee and Molly (Jim and Marion Jordan), begins with the married couple traveling to Washington, D.C. to visit relatives. Eventually, McGee gets a government job in a postwar planning agency, the "Coordinator of Public Morale in the Postwar Era," depicted as a typical Federal government boondoggle. In *The Affairs of Susan* (Paramount, 1945), one of Susan's suitors is working for the government, planning for the reconversion of aircraft plants to civilian use.

Even these minor references indicate the breadth of Washington's concern about the postwar period. Economically, the wartime boom could easily become a postwar bust: "For many, the end of the war would indeed mean hello, peace, good-bye, job."[15] *Atlantic City* (Republic, 1944), a period musical, includes a brief World War I sequence. Afterwards, the film's protagonist (Brad Taylor), an entrepreneur, pitches the idea of a "Miss America" contest to Atlantic City businessmen, stating: "In these postwar times, with the inevitable economic readjustment, we've got to have something *big* to sell."

While there was little direct mention of the role of women in the postwar world, this was another matter of interest to the government and industry:

From 3,000,000 to 4,000,000 women will have answered the call to service in American industry during the war ... A portion of these new recruits will return to their homes after the emergency is over. But a large number will need or want permanent employment ... Will discriminations be raised against them when labor ceases to be a scarce commodity? Will a concerted drive be made to put the woman back in "her place" or will the working woman—professional, skilled, and unskilled—be given a role becoming her capacities in the post-war world?[16]

Most Hollywood films showing women at work in defense plants—or in other, traditionally male occupations—depict them as capable, and happy with their work. Only rarely, as in *Since You Went Away* (UA, 1944) are women forced to go to work for financial reasons (and despite this, Claudette Colbert discovers she likes being a welder, although it is clear *she* will gladly give up her job when her husband returns). Some films, like *Lady in the Dark* (Paramount, 1944), not-so-subtly suggest that a woman's place is in the home, but for the most part Hollywood dodges the issue of women's role in the postwar era.

The two biggest postwar themes discussed in Hollywood's war-era films are the purpose of the world conflict and the treatment of veterans—"what we're fighting for," and "those who fought."

The immediate goal of the Allies was, of course, the defeat of fascist Germany, Italy, Japan, and their associates. This was self-evident, and needed no explanation or elaboration. However, a number of Hollywood films expand upon this basic goal. The war is being fought for "freedom," "democracy," and a "better world," especially a better world for "our children." One soldier in *Eve of St. Mark* (TCF, 1945), remembering his childhood in the Depression, says: "We're not just fighting Japs. We're fighting so that in 1950 our kids won't have to steal potatoes out of a box car."

Two little-known films from 1942, *Lady from Chungking* (PRC) and *Youth on Parade* (Republic), contain early, abstract references to the postwar world. In *Lady from Chungking*, Chinese patriot Kwan Mei (Anna May Wong) says: "the force of peace will prevail until the world is again sane and beautiful." *Youth on Parade* is a college musical, and contains a lecture and a song indicating that the postwar world will be the responsibility of the younger generation: "It's kids like us who'll win this fuss, and make the peace—no more Versailles Treaties, 'cause it's proven they don't last." In other words, the resolution of the First World War was a faulty one, leading to the rise of Hitler, and this must not happen again. *Thunder Birds* (TCF), another 1942 release, also criticizes the outcome of WWI: a British pilot trainee says he does not want to fight

for "some empty victory," but wants "to help it really mean something *this time*."[17]

As the war went on, these sentiments continue to appear in various Hollywood films. In *The Story of G.I. Joe* (UA, 1945), correspondent Ernie Pyle (Burgess Meredith) writes: "Surely, something good must come out of this. I hope we can rejoice in victory so that another great war can never be possible."

The White Cliffs of Dover (MGM, 1944) contains a deathbed statement by a young British soldier (Peter Lawford) about the creation of a "new world" and "a peace that will stick." This film spans both World Wars—Lawford's father is killed just before the Armistice in WWI—and contains an ironic scene (set in the early 1930s) in which two German youngsters visiting England claim that Germany will win "next time." In *Over 21* (Columbia, 1945), a newspaper editor (Alexander Knox) agrees that "a couple of bad boys [Hitler and Mussolini, presumably] started this thing ... but what worries me is the 'bad boys' of the next generation. The world won't survive the next war."

For the most part, however, Hollywood films of the period rarely go beyond such vague statements. The errors of the World War I postwar period will not be repeated; the occupied nations will be freed; peace and democracy will reign supreme; children will grow up in a free world, dictators and militarists will be punished for their crimes against humanity. There are a few oblique references to improvement in racial equality (*Youth on Parade*) and women's rights (*Twice Blessed*, MGM, 1945), but Hollywood chose not to get too specific about social, economic, and political goals for the postwar world, just to be on the safe side.

On the other hand, Hollywood—and the rest of America—makes it very clear that returning veterans will be rewarded for their sacrifices:

Readjustment, despite the aid of a grateful nation, often proved to be rocky ... America certainly did not let the veterans down ... By 1945 a grateful nation would help a veteran buy a home, set himself up in business, take up farming, go to college, learn a trade, finish high school or get a government job.[18]

Perhaps the quintessential "returning veteran" films are the 1946 releases *The Best Years of Our Lives* and *Till the End of Time* (both RKO). These motion pictures cover nearly every veteran's problem Hollywood could conceive of: physical disability, psychological trauma, broken marriages, employment problems, and so on. However, Hollywood had been addressing many of these problems as early as 1944.

My Buddy (Republic, 1944) is one of the more interesting returning-veteran films, explicitly linking the two World Wars. Irish priest Father Jim Donnelly (John Litel) tells a government Postwar Planning Committee about the fate of Eddie Ballinger (Don Barry), a WWI veteran who turned to crime after failing to find gainful employment in the postwar period. Ballinger serves a prison term, then goes back into the rackets and is eventually gunned down by the police. Although similar plots had been used before—*They Gave Him a Gun* (MGM, 1937) and *The Roaring Twenties* (WB, 1939), for instance—*My Buddy* uses Ballinger's story to press for greater consideration for veterans in the post–WWII period.

The film is surprisingly effective despite its short running time. Back from the war (where his pal is killed by a German sniper just moments before news of the Armistice reaches their trench), Eddie admits to his girlfriend that "the war changes a guy ... over there we lived for the moment." His old employer cannot afford to take him back—in an uncompromising montage sequence, Eddie searches for work but finds only signs reading "No Help Wanted," while "You're in the Army Now" plays (in a minor key) in the background. Stooping to pick up a discarded cigarette butt, Eddie is confronted by an old Army friend. "What are we, excess baggage?" Eddie asks. "Didn't they figure we'd be coming back some day? Couldn't they have planned something?"

In a pool hall operated by bootlegger Oberta, Eddie overhears a man at the next table. "There's enough jobs for us Americans. The trouble is the country's full of foreigners. And they're the ones doing all the beefing. They're never satisfied." When Eddie calls him a liar, the man accuses Eddie of being "another one of those agitators." After a brawl—in which the other man is knocked out—Eddie is offered a job by Oberta. He resists as long as he can, but, frustrated and angry, finally hires on with the gangster.

After a brush with the police, Eddie is convicted and sent to prison for five years. On the day of his release, a friendly guard warns Eddie not to waste his life. "I was over there, too," the guard says, and things were tough when he returned, too. He wanted to be an architect—now he's a prison guard. "But I'm still going to be an architect some day." Eddie says it's too late: "All I asked for was a job; and I got five years in this hole."

Eddie's attempts to avenge himself on Oberta result in his own death at the hands of the police. Father Donnelly wraps up his story, and the listening politicians are impressed. Senator Henry equivocates just a bit, saying "Of course, Eddie Ballinger was not typical of the boys who fought in the last war, nor is he typical of our boys today." But, as a montage of marching men and women appears on the screen, he adds: "However, all of our gallant men and women in the armed forces can rest assured that the people of American will this time have plans ready for their return and will not let them down!"

As noted above, soldiers were being discharged from the service in significant numbers as early as 1944, and wounded veterans had come home even earlier.[19] Hollywood films of the period contain a number of such characters. For obvious reasons, wounded veterans in Hollywood films were rarely seriously disabled: Gene Kelly dances up a storm in *Cover Girl* (Columbia, 1944); Richard Arlen goes to work as a lumberjack in *Timber Queen* (Paramount, 1944); Kent Smith opens a youth recreation center in *Youth Runs Wild* (RKO, 1944); Dennis O'Keefe even manages to get back *into* the service at the end of *Sensations of 1945* (UA, 1944); Charles Drake makes a joke about his artificial leg in *You Came Along* (Paramount, 1945)—and no wonder, since most of the time he forgets even to limp *slightly!*[20] Ted Lawson (Van Johnson) loses his leg in the aftermath of a bombing raid on Tokyo in *Thirty Seconds Over Tokyo* (MGM, 1945); while he is in China, Lawson's injuries are depicted as quite serious, but once he returns to the United States, the loss of a leg is downplayed almost to the level of a minor wound (his superior officer insists that Lawson will be able to stay in the service and perform important functions; Lawson's wife is just glad he is alive). Also, the motion picture ends almost immediately upon his reunion with his wife, thus evading the necessity of showing Lawson's adjustment to his loss.

This is understandable: first, the protagonist of a Hollywood film generally had to be physically fit; second, it was considered detrimental to public morale to dwell on soldiers returning from combat missing an arm or a leg, or blinded, or shell-shocked.

There are a few exceptions. *Pride of the Marines* (WB, 1945), based on a true story, features John Garfield as Marine Al Schmid, blinded in battle on Guadalcanal. The film is surprisingly frank in its depiction of Schmid's initial bitterness. He refuses to cooperate with authorities (they want to award him the Navy Cross), and rejects his friends and their attempts to help him. Eventually, however, Schmid changes his mind and decides to accept the decoration in the name of his comrades who lost their lives fighting the Japanese; he reconciles with his sweetheart and his old friends, and the film even ends with a suggestion that his physical condition may improve.

This motion picture also contains an interesting sequence set in a military hospital in San Diego. A group of wounded veterans discusses their lives after the war. One says *his* father was a First World War veteran who ended up selling apples on the corner during the Depression. Another makes a reference to outsiders—like Mexicans—taking jobs away from Americans, forgetting for a moment that a Mexican-American soldier is seated nearby in a wheelchair. A Jewish veteran—wounded with Schmid on Guadalcanal—reminds the other men that at least *they* will not be discriminated against because of their religion. However, there are some positive statements about "fighting for a better world," and making America "work [together] in peace like we did in war," so "no new Hitler" will be able to menace their children (this last statement is made by a veteran who says he plans to study law under the G.I. Bill, and then go into politics).

While *Pride of the Marines* contains the most seriously wounded returning-veteran protagonist of the war era,[21] there are a few films which, rather surprisingly, feature veterans with psychological problems caused by the war. In *Identity Unknown* (Republic, 1945), Richard Arlen is a veteran with amnesia—although amnesia was usually seen by Hollywood as a minor, actually rather interesting condition. *I'll Be Seeing You* (UA, 1945) stars Joseph Cotten as a soldier who was physically wounded (a bayonet wound), but who is also psychologically scarred by the trauma of combat. *When the Lights Go on Again* (PRC, 1944) combines *all* of these: Marine Ted Benson (James Lydon) is given home leave to recover from a wound *and* battle fatigue, then contracts amnesia as the result of an accident on the way home! All three of these servicemen, by the way, manage to overcome their emotional and psychological problems and presumably live happily ever after.

Other returning-veteran's problems are touched on in *The Impatient Years* (Columbia, 1944) and *Duffy's Tavern* (Paramount, 1945). The latter film involves a scheme to raise money for a factory to be staffed by returning veterans, an indirect comment on the postwar employment problem. *The Impatient Years*, although it is a comedy and features Lee Bowman as a serviceman only *temporarily* home from the war, hints at family problems awaiting the veterans' return.

In this film, Andy Anderson (Bowman) returns on convalescent leave (again, no visible evidence of his wounds), only to discover that his wife Jane (Jean Arthur), whom he met and married a few days before he was shipped overseas, is practically a stranger to him. He is also a new father, but his young child does not know him. Furthermore, Andy is jealous of his wife's friendship with civilian Henry Fairchild, a boarder in their home. The couple quarrels constantly, and finally applies for a divorce. However, the judge (Edgar Buchanan), realizing this is a problem many returning veterans will face after the war, orders Andy and Jane to recreate, step by step, their whirlwind courtship. They do, and fall back in love, just before Andy is declared fit for duty and sent into combat once more.

While *The Impatient Years* is a romantic comedy with a happy ending (although one could imagine Andy returning home *after* the war to face the same problem all over again!), it makes a number of valid points. Even though Andy and Jane are both decent human beings, they had rushed into marriage after a brief romance, only later to learn how little they knew about each other. The film also indicates that the experience of combat had an affect on Andy's outlook on life—civilians can never know what he went through, and he is a different person than the carefree Andy who wooed and wedded Jane. Andy suspects that his wife has been unfaithful to him (although these fears are groundless; she had assigned a number of *platonic* husbandly duties to Fairchild, the boarder). This was a common fear among servicemen, and one which was not wholly unfounded: "The strain of separation made even the most devoted serviceman's wife susceptible to the chance of temporary emotional solace with other men."[22]

Made while the war was still being fought, *The Impatient Years* is not as explicit as *The Best Years of Our Lives*, which clearly depicts the breakup of Virginia Mayo's marriage to returning veteran Dana Andrews. However, the rather illogical happy ending aside, it still contains a rather pessimistic picture of the domestic problems awaiting returning veterans.

Overall, Hollywood's wartime references to the postwar world are generally positive and optimistic, but are often vague and peripheral to the plots of the films they appear in. Perhaps Hollywood felt discussions of postwar goals and problems were not appropriate topics for entertainment films, and were best left to documentary and government filmmakers.

When postwar problems are discussed in wartime films, there is often a surprising frankness (although tempered by a happy ending, more often than not) not usually associated with upbeat, morale-building themes. However, these motion pictures are certainly in the minority. For the most part, the end of the war is eagerly anticipated as a chance to return to a normal, peaceful, happy and prosperous life in a world finally freed of the horrors of totalitarianism.

Filmography to Part Two

This preliminary section contains the following material: Abbreviations used in the Filmography and statistical analyses of information found in the Filmography. For information on the differences between this filmography and that of the 1937–1941 period, see page 81.

Abbreviations Used in the Filmography

AF: Armed Forces/ appearance or explicit reference to national armies, navies, air forces, militia, etc. Sub-codes AF-A, AF-N, AF-MC, AF-CG, AF-AC refer to *U.S.* Army, Navy, Marine Corps, Coast Guard, and Air Corps *only* (while the Air Corps was renamed the Army Air *Force*, for ease of coding we have retained the earlier initials); AF-W refers to women in uniformed services (of all nations), including military nurses; all armed forces of other nations (any branch, except for AF-RAF) are identified as AF-GER, AF-BRIT, AF-CHI, AF-JAP, etc. AF-FT refers to Armed Forces-Flying Tigers (American Volunteer Group in China, 1941); AF-RAF refers to the Royal Air Force of Great Britain. AF-MER refers to the U.S. Merchant Marine, not strictly a branch of the armed forces, but one which during the war was awarded quasi-military status. AF-BLK refers to any black serviceman or woman in the uniformed services of any country.

Am Vol: American Volunteers/ depiction or explicit reference to U.S. citizens participating in foreign conflicts. Does not include those characters who are inadvertently drawn into wars, rebellions, etc. by virtue of being in the "wrong place at the wrong time."

Appeasement: Reference to prewar policy of the British government under Prime Minister Neville Chamberlain (and Americans who endorsed the policy) which encouraged accommodation with Nazi Germany out of fear of another world war. After September 1939 was used pejoratively.

Arab: Arab/ depiction of Arab nationals.

Atroc: Atrocity/ depiction or explicit reference to war crimes and other actions which go beyond acceptable bounds of warfare, law enforcement, and political action. For example, massacres, execution without trial, torture.

Atroc-Conc: Atrocity-Concentration Camp/ depiction or explicit reference to concentration camps (not necessarily death camps, as in Nazi Germany, but these are included).

Austral: Australia/ depiction of Australian national or reference to Australia.

Austr: Austria/ depiction of Austrian national or reference to Austria.

Belg: Belgium/ depiction of Belgian national or reference to Belgium.

Blk: Black/ appearance of any black character of any nationality.

Blk Mkt: Black Market/ reference to or depiction of illegal activities involving rationed goods.

Bonds: Bonds/ reference to or depiction of war bonds (called defense bonds prior to 1942) or stamps (including solicitation to buy), the U.S. government's means of financing the war. Also includes references to "Liberty Bonds," sold during WWI.

Brit: British/ appearance of characters identified as being British nationals (including England, Scotland), or explicit reference to Great Britain.

Can: Canada/ depiction of Canadian national or explicit reference to Canada.

Chamberlain: Chamberlain/ depiction or explicit reference to Neville Chamberlain, Prime Minister of Great Britain from 1937 to 1940.

Chi: Chinese/ appearance of character of Chinese race or a specific reference to China.

Chiang: Chiang Kai-shek/ depiction or explicit reference to leader of Nationalist Chinese forces, Generalissimo Chiang Kai-shek.

Churchill: Churchill/ depiction or explicit reference to Winston Churchill, Prime Minister of Great Britain from 1940–1945.

Collab: Collaborator/ appearance or explicit reference to a citizen of one nation who is in sympathy with or in the employ of a foreign enemy. Includes references to "traitors," "fifth columnists," and the German-American Bund organization.

Czech: Czechoslovakia/ depiction of Czech national or reference to Czechoslovakia.

De Gaulle: Charles De Gaulle/ explicit reference to French military officer who headed the "Free French" (also called the "Fighting French") forces with the Allies.

Den: Denmark/ explicit reference to Denmark or depiction of Danish national.

Dipl: Diplomat/ appearance of character in diplomatic corps.

Draft: Draft/ reference to conscription in the U.S.

Draft Avoid: Draft Avoidance/ reference to attempts to avoid military service, registering for draft, etc.

Dunkirk: Dunkirk/ recreation of or reference to evacuation of British Expeditionary Force from the French port of Dunkirk in 1940.

Eisenhower: Dwight D. Eisenhower/ reference to U.S. general, commander of Allied forces in European theater of war.

Ethiopia: Ethiopia/ reference to Ethiopia, attacked by Italian forces in 1937 and liberated by British troops in 1941. Also included are references to the leader of Ethiopia, Haile Selassie.

FBI: Federal Bureau of Investigation/ depiction of FBI agent or explicit reference to operations of FBI.

FDR: Franklin D. Roosevelt/ explicit reference to the President of the United States during this period.

FDR-E: Eleanor Roosevelt/ explicit reference to the First Lady of the United States during this period.

Fem Lab: Female Labor/ depiction of or explicit reference to women working in previously male occupations as a result of the war.

Fil: Filipino/ depiction of Philippine national or reference to Philippines.

Fin: Finland/ depiction of Finnish national or reference to Finland.

Fr: French/ appearance of character identified as French national.

Free Fr: Free French/ reference to French government-in-exile established after fall of France in 1940. Also known as the "Fighting French" for a time (to distinguish them from the Vichy French, who had reached an accommodation with Nazi Germany).

Ger: German/ appearance or explicit reference to German nationals or people of German descent.

Ger-Am: German-American/ appearance or explicit reference to U.S. citizens of German heritage.

Goebbels: Goebbels/ explicit reference to Franz Josef Goebbels, Nazi Minister of Propaganda.

Goering: Goering/ explicit reference to Field Marshal Hermann Goering, head of German Luftwaffe.

Grk: Greek/ depiction of Greek national or person of Greek descent, or reference to Greece.

Hess: Rudolf Hess/ appearance or reference to Hitler's deputy fuehrer, who defected to the Allies (flying to Scotland) in 1942.

Heydrich: Reinhold Heydrich/ appearance or reference to the Nazi SS official assassinated in Czechoslovakia in 1942.

Himmler: Heinrich Himmler/ appearance or reference to head of the Nazi SS.

Hirohito: Emperor Hirohito/ appearance or specific reference to the Emperor of Japan during the war years; includes references to "the Emperor" or "the Mikado."

Hist Am: Historical American/ appearance or explicit reference to historical American figures such as former presidents (Lincoln, Washington), generals (Custer, Pershing), or statesmen.

Hitler: Adolf Hitler/ appearance or explicit reference to German leader of this period. Note: A reference to "Hitler" or "Mussolini" is NOT double-coded as "German," or "Italian." "Schickelgruber" and "Fuehrer" are also coded as Hitler references.

Home Def: Home Defense/ reference to or depiction of civilian preparations for national defense, including air raid wardens, plane spotters, etc.

Home Front: Home Front/ reference to or depiction of non-civil defense, war-related activities in the United States. Includes scrap drives, fund-raising activities.

Iceland: Iceland/ depiction of Icelandic national or explicit reference to Iceland, occupied by U.S. troops in 1941.

Ind: India/ appearance of Indian national or explicit reference to India.

Intell Serv: Intelligence Service/ reference to official intelligence organizations such as military intelligence, usually in counterspy or military espionage operations. FBI is not included in this coding.

Isolat: Isolationist/ reference to U.S. attitudes opposing intervention in foreign wars.

Ital: Italian/ appearance of character identified as Italian national or of Italian descent.

Jap: Japanese/appearance or explicit reference to Japanese nationals or actions of Japan as a nation. Explicit verbal references to "Japs," and "Nips" are also coded this way.

Jap-Am Reloc: Japanese-American Relocation/ depiction of or reference to evacuation of Japanese-Americans to relocation camps during WWII.

Jap-Ger Coop: Japanese-German Cooperation/ depiction or reference to military or intelligence cooperation between official representatives of Axis nations.

Jap-Ger-Ital Coop: Japanese-German-Italian Cooperation/ depiction or reference to cooperation between Axis partners.

Jew: Jew/ appearance of character identified as a Jew.

Juv: Juvenile/ depiction of juveniles involved in war effort; includes children working officially (with the resistance, or involved in home defense or home front activities), or those unofficially affected by the war. Also includes depiction or explicit reference to juvenile delinquency caused by wartime conditions.

Kor: Korea/ reference to Korea or depiction of Korean national.

Laval: Pierre Laval/ reference to French politician who served in the Vichy government and was regarded as a collaborator by many.

League/Nat: League of Nations/ reference to League of Nations, international organization which was a forerunner to the United Nations.

Latin Am: Latin American/ appearance of character of Hispanic background. Includes Mexicans, Brazilians, Argentines, Cubans, etc.

MacArthur: Douglas MacArthur/ reference to U.S. general, commander of military forces in the Philippines until the Japanese conquest, then commander of ground forces in the Pacific theater of operations.

Mex: Mexico/ used only to code references to Mexico or in Armed Forces connection; Mexican characters are coded as Latin Am.

Mil Exer: Military Exercises/ depiction or explicit reference to military maneuvers or training.

Mil School: Military School/ depiction of or reference to military school or academy.

Munich: Munich Crisis/ reference to the threat to world peace precipitated by Hitler's preparations for the invasion of Czechoslovakia in the spring of 1938, ostensibly to protect the Sudeten German minority. In September 1938, an agreement was signed ceding the Sudetenland to Germany.

Musso: Mussolini/ depiction or explicit reference to Italian leader of this period; includes verbal references to "Il Duce."

Nazi: Nazi/ explicit reference to Nazi party. Includes depiction of swastikas. Also includes verbal references to Nazi institutions such as the Gestapo (secret police) and the SS.

Neth: Netherlands/ depiction of Dutch national or reference to Netherlands or Dutch possessions.

Nor: Norway/ reference to Norway or depiction of Norwegian national.

Pacifist: Pacifist/ reference to anti-war attitudes.

Pearl Harb: Pearl Harbor/ depiction of or explicit reference to the Japanese attack on Pearl Harbor on December 7, 1941.

Petain: Henri Philippe Petain/ French military official who became the figurehead leader of the Vichy government (see Vichy).

Pol: Poland/ reference to Poland or depiction of Polish national or person of Polish descent.

Port: Portugal/ reference to Portugal or Portuguese national.

Postwar: Postwar/ reference to postwar events, situation, planning, and/or goals.

POW: Prisoner of War/ reference to non-civilian individuals held captive by opposing side.

Prod: Production/ depiction or explicit reference to industries producing war materials; also references to obtaining raw materials for such production, including mining, logging, and so on.

Prod-Farm: Production-Farm/ depiction or explicit reference to farm labor aimed at food production during wartime.

Ref: Refugee/ depiction or explicit reference to persons forced to flee their home countries due to war or political oppression.

Resist: Resistance/ depiction or explicit reference to forces fighting fascist or totalitarian governments, either in occupied nations or enemy countries themselves. Does not refer to national armed forces, except in the case where the country in question has surrendered and resistance forces continue to fight.

Rom: Romania/ also "Rumania." Reference to Romania or depiction of Romanian national.

Rommel: Rommel/ depiction of or reference to Erwin Rommel, German general (later Field Marshal), commander of German forces in North Africa (the Afrika Korps), then commander of German troops in France at the time of the D-Day invasion.

Russ: Russian/ appearance of character identified as Russian national, or explicit reference to actions of Russian nation.

Russ-Ger Co-op: Russian-German Cooperation/ reference to non-agression pact signed by Stalin and Hitler; also includes depiction of Russian and German nationals acting as allies.

Short: Shortage/ Reference to shortages of materials due to the war; also includes references to official rationing of materials.

Sino-Jap War: Sino-Japanese War/ explicit reference to 1937 Japanese invasion of China and subsequent fighting there.

Sp: Spain/ depiction of Spanish national or reference to Spain.

Span Civ: Spanish Civil War/ explicit reference to war in Spain, 1936–1939.

Spy-Sab: Spy-Saboteur/ appearance of character depicted as enemy national engaged in intelligence or sabotage operations in a friendly country (i.e., no FRIENDLY agents included).

Stalin: Josef Stalin/ reference to leader of USSR.

Swed: Sweden/ depiction of Swedish national or reference to Sweden.

Switz: Switzerland/ depiction of Swiss national or reference to Switzerland.

Tojo: Hideki Tojo/ reference to Japanese general, head of militarist faction, who served as the Prime Minister of Japan during WWII.

UN: United Nations/ reference to Allied cooperation and postwar planning, although the actual United Nations organization was not formed until after the war.

US-Brit Coop: US-British Cooperation/ depiction or explicit reference to official or semi-official cooperation between governments of U.S. and Great Britain, or individuals acting on their behalf. Includes references to "Lend-Lease."

US-Chi Coop: US-Chinese Cooperation/ depiction or explicit reference to official or semi-official cooperation between the United States and China.

US-Mex Coop: US-Mexican Cooperation/ depiction or explicit reference to official or semi-official cooperation between the United States and Mexico.

US-Russ Coop: US-Russia Cooperation/ depiction or explicit reference to official or semi-official cooperation between the United States and the USSR.

USO: United Service Organization/ reference to organization providing recreational activities for servicemen. Also includes canteens, camp shows, etc. regardless of sponsoring organization.

V: "V"/ depiction of capital letter V when used to signify Allied Victory. Includes the "three dots and dash" Morse code, and opening notes of Beethoven's Fifth Symphony.

Vet: Veteran/ explicit reference or depiction of character identified as U.S. veteran of previous war (WWI, Spanish-American War, Civil War).

Vichy: Vichy France/ reference to French government, based in Vichy, established after the German invasion of France. Generally seen as a puppet of the Nazis, the Vichy zone was later occupied by the Germans.

War Corr: War Correspondent/ appearance of character identified as a working journalist, news cameraman, newsreel photographer, radio reporter, etc. covering the war fronts.

WWI: World War One/ explicit reference to First World War.

Yugo: Yugoslavia/ depiction of Yugoslavian national or explicit reference to Yugoslavia.

War Related American Films, 1942–1945

		1942	1943	1944	1945	Total
Columbia						
	relevant:	32	34	35	16	117
	released:	58	48	49	35	190
	relevant percent:	55%	71%	71%	46%	62%
MGM						
	relevant:	36	24	19	15	94
	released:	55	29	28	23	135
	relevant percent:	65%	83%	68%	65%	69%
Monogram						
	relevant:	24	17	17	10	68
	released:	45	37	45	26	153
	relevant percent:	53%	46%	38%	38%	44%
Paramount						
	relevant:	20	20	22	6	68
	released:	43	24	35	13	115
	relevant percent:	47%	83%	63%	46%	59%
PRC						
	relevant:	24	17	5	3	49
	released:	44	29	31	21	125
	relevant percent:	55%	59%	16%	14%	39%
Republic						
	relevant:	19	19	15	8	61
	released:	48	51	50	38	187
	relevant percent:	40%	37%	30%	21%	33%
RKO						
	relevant:	22	37	20	14	93
	released:	35	45	32	23	135
	relevant percent:	63%	82%	63%	61%	69%

20th C.-Fox						
relevant:	29	23	20	6	78
released:	52	31	27	18	128
relevant percent:	56%	74%	74%	33%	61%
Warner Bros.						
relevant:	21	17	17	11	66
released:	31	20	19	13	83
relevant percent:	68%	85%	89%	85%	80%
United Artists						
relevant:	10	10	11	7	38
released:	20	25	22	11	78
relevant percent:	50%	40%	50%	64%	49%
Universal						
relevant:	32	34	18	2	86
released:	62	58	53	38	211
relevant percent:	52%	59%	34%	5%	41%

Totals:

1942:

relevant films	269
released films	493
relevant percent	55%

1943:

relevant films	252
released films	397
relevant percent	63%

1944:

relevant films	199
released films	391
relevant percent	51%

1945:

relevant films	98
released films	259
relevant percent	38%

Totals:

relevant films	818
released films	1540
relevant percent	53%

NOTES: Totals for 1945 are for films released through September 30, 1945 only.

These statistics cover only American films released by the major companies in the United States; independent films, foreign films, and re-releases, although they are included in the filmography if war-relevant, and are included in the coding statistics, are not counted in the above totals.

Yearly Survey of Films' War Relevancy

	Degree of Relevance					
Year	*1*	*1.5*	*2*	*2.5*	*3*	*Average*
1942	88 films	35	45	16	88	*2*
percent of war-relevant films	33%	12%	17%	6%	33%	
1943	51 films	48	38	23	96	*2.1*
percent of war-relevant films	20%	19%	15%	9%	38%	
1944	40 films	31	36	30	65	*2.1*
percent of war-relevant films	21%	14%	18%	14%	32%	
1945	31 films	19	20	10	20	*1.8*
percent of war-relevant films	32%	18%	20%	10%	20%	

Totals	1	1.5	2	2.5	3
number of films:	210	133	139	79	269
percent of war relevant films	25%	16%	17%	10%	32%

Overall Average Degree of Relevance: 2

The above analyses ("War Related American Films, 1942–1945" and "Yearly Survey of Films' War Relevancy") illustrate the pervasiveness of World War II in the American consciousness. For the entire period, 53 percent of all feature-length, fictional motion pictures produced in the United States and released by the 11 major studios contained war-relevant material. Thirty two percent of these films have been rated "highly relevant" (3), while another 26 percent received "moderately relevant" (2) to "moderately-highly relevant" (2.5) ratings.

From 1942 to 1945, over 330 Westerns were released, 22 percent of the total output of Hollywood studios: fewer than 10 percent of these films have been identified as containing any war-relevant material. If all Westerns (relevant or not) were excluded from this study, the overall percentage of war-relevant films would increase dramatically.

More than 80 percent of the releases of the "Big Five" Studios (MGM, Paramount, RKO Radio, 20th Century–Fox, Warner Bros.) in 1943 contained topical material. In contrast, films released by the three smallest organizations—Monogram, Republic, PRC—averaged only 44 percent relevancy (largely due to the nonrelevance of the Western genre, a staple of these companies). As could be expected, the totals for January through September 1945 demonstrate a continued shift away from topical subjects. After more than three years of war, American audiences wanted escapist topics. Nonetheless, 38 percent of the films (45 percent of non–Westerns) contained war-relevant material, and 20 percent of these films received "highly relevant" (3) ratings. Fifty percent of the war-relevant films were "moderately relevant" or above.

Frequency of Topical References in Films, 1942–1945*

Coding Term	1942	1943	1944	1945	Total
AF-Army	96	105	93	49	343
AF-Air Corps	25	41	30	21	117
AF-Australian	0	3	5	0	8
AF-Black	2	19	7	2	30
AF-British	22	31	17	6	76
AF-Canadian	6	5	1	1	13
AF-Chinese	7	7	5	5	24
AF-Coast Guard	7	5	4	1	17
AF-Filipino	2	3	1	1	7
AF-Free French	1	0	4	1	6
AF-French	1	9	8	2	20
AF-Flying Tigers	4	7	1	2	14
AF-German	52	54	31	15	152
AF-Italian	3	9	4	1	17
AF-Japanese	26	32	24	12	94
AF-Marine Corps	31	33	31	13	108
AF-Merchant Marine	6	12	12	4	34
AF-Navy	69	79	72	38	258
AF-Neth	1	2	3	1	7
AF-Royal Air Force	24	18	6	6	54
AF-Russian	4	9	8	3	24
AF-Women	23	44	52	30	149
American Volunteer	12	9	3	0	24
Appeasement	1	4	2	0	7
Arab	3	8	6	2	19

*A diskette with the raw coding data for the films in Part Two may be obtained from the authors.

Coding Term	1942	1943	1944	1945	Total
Atrocity	27	50	19	10	106
Atrocity—					
Concentration Camp	19	22	18	2	61
Australia	7	12	6	0	25
Austria	11	5	7	1	24
Belgium	5	8	4	0	17
Black	92	100	64	35	291
Black Market	8	12	7	3	30
Bonds	25	46	27	14	112
Britain	78	54	30	15	177
Canada	12	10	0	3	25
China	42	35	24	20	121
Chiang Kai-shek	9	3	3	3	18
Churchill	13	16	8	4	41
Collaborator	66	47	23	5	141
Czechoslovakia	8	18	11	0	37
De Gaulle	3	3	4	1	11
Denmark	5	2	1	0	8
Diplomat	16	13	6	4	39
Draft	44	52	34	8	138
Draft Avoidance	7	3	3	0	13
Dunkirk	6	6	1	2	15
Eisenhower	0	1	1	4	6
Ethiopia	3	3	0	0	6
FBI	43	23	16	3	85
FDR	35	37	22	9	103
FDR-Eleanor	3	2	2	0	7
Female Labor	17	45	41	17	120
Filipino	13	10	3	5	31
French	38	37	18	8	101
Free French	4	12	7	3	26
Germany	43	30	18	8	99
German-American	14	7	7	2	30
Goebbels	8	7	5	0	20
Goering	10	12	7	2	31
Greek	7	10	5	0	22
Hess	6	3	2	0	11
Himmler	7	8	3	1	19
Hirohito	17	15	5	8	45
Historical American	41	40	28	12	121
Hitler	69	71	39	11	190
Home Defense	37	53	14	2	106
Home Front	26	45	32	10	113
Iceland	3	0	0	0	3
India	2	1	0	3	6
Intelligence Service	30	11	3	2	46
Isolationist	7	6	2	0	15
Italian	32	30	21	12	95
Japan	85	69	53	29	236
Japanese-German					
Cooperation	21	7	3	1	32

Coding Term	1942	1943	1944	1945	Total
Japanese-German-Italian Cooperation	4	2	0	0	6
Jew	15	30	23	9	77
Juvenile	19	23	26	5	73
Latin America	42	38	35	18	133
Laval	2	3	3	0	8
League of Nations	1	5	1	1	8
MacArthur	10	12	7	4	33
Military Exercise	6	3	3	0	12
Military School	9	10	6	3	28
Munich Crisis	1	6	1	0	8
Mussolini	10	18	6	2	36
Nazi	84	91	52	15	242
Netherlands	19	18	8	1	46
Norway	12	15	3	2	32
Pacifist	5	4	2	2	13
Pearl Harbor	44	35	14	8	101
Petain	0	2	3	1	6
Poland	24	20	9	5	58
Postwar	9	11	23	18	61
POW	4	10	8	6	28
Production	66	68	61	21	216
Production—Farm	2	6	9	1	18
Refugee	21	22	20	4	67
Resistance	17	33	19	11	80
Romania	2	4	0	0	6
Rommel	1	4	2	2	9
Russia	35	52	36	13	136
Shortages	82	118	74	39	313
Sino-Japanese War	3	3	0	1	7
Spanish Civil War	7	8	3	0	18
Spy-Saboteur	94	60	22	8	184
Stalin	2	8	5	3	18
Tojo	3	4	12	4	23
United Nations	4	12	11	0	27
US-British Cooperation	27	10	4	2	43
US-Chinese Cooperation	3	1	0	0	4
US-Russian Cooperation	3	4	4	1	12
USO	18	25	28	10	81
V for Victory	41	29	22	8	100
Veteran	6	4	9	5	24
Vichy France	8	5	2	1	16
War Correspondent	17	15	10	8	50
World War One	47	48	33	8	136

NOTES: only those coding terms which totalled five references (or accumulated three references in any single year) are included on this chart. The following terms are listed in the Filmography but did not meet the criteria for inclusion on the chart:

SPAIN   JAPANESE-AMERICAN RELOCATION
AF-NORWEGIAN   KOREA
CHAMBERLAIN   RUSSIAN-GERMAN COOPERATION
SWEDEN   YUGOSLAVIA

FINLAND   SWITZERLAND
HEYDRICH   TURKEY
US-MEXICAN COOPERATION

Top Five Annual Coding Terms

(Note: since BLACK references were only occasionally war-relevant, that category is not counted in this chart, although the totals are listed for comparison purposes)

1942:	AF-ARMY	96	1944:	AF-ARMY	93
	SPY-SAB	94		SHORTAGES	74
	JAP	85		AF-NAVY	72
	NAZI	84		PRODUCTION	61
	SHORTAGES	82		NAZI	52
	(BLACKS	92)		(BLACKS	64)
1943:	SHORTAGES	118	1945:	AF-ARMY	49
	AF-ARMY	105		SHORTAGES	39
	NAZI	91		AF-NAVY	38
	AF-NAVY	79		AF-WOMEN	30
	HITLER	71		JAP	29
	(BLACKS	100)		(BLACKS	35)

Top Ten Overall Coding Terms

AF-ARMY	343
SHORTAGES	313
BLACKS	291
AF-NAVY	258
NAZI	242
JAP	236
PRODUCTION	214
HITLER	190
SPY-SABOTEUR	184
BRITAIN	177

Not every coding term is necessarily always war relevant. Various ethnic, national and racial terms are also coded, and these are not always used in a topical manner; many appearances of black characters in war-relevant films are not war-relevant in and of themselves.

It is beyond the scope of this study to weight each appearance of a coding term. A verbal reference to "Hitler" was coded as one reference, and a film in which Hitler is a major character (as in *The Devil with Hitler*, UA, 1942) was also coded as one reference.

One hundred and sixteen coding terms met the minimum criteria for inclusion in this analysis. Twenty-one of these terms had 100 or more references, indicating the term appeared in at least 12 percent of war-relevant films. It is interesting to note that most of these terms are directly war oriented: only Blacks, Britain, China, Latin America, and Russia are coding terms used nontopically with any frequency. The other terms are either directly war relevant by definition—Bonds, Armed Forces-German, Nazi, Draft—or are predominately used in conjunction with the war (Female Labor, Japan).

Frequency of Pejorative References in Films, 1942–1945

This analysis represents a selected sample of wartime films containing pejorative references to the Nazis and Japanese. It is designed to give an idea of the depth and breadth of pejorative references to the enemy appearing in wartime feature films.

NOTE: Pejorative references coded as NAZI include "Nazis," "Fascist," Jerries," "Heinies," "SS," "Gestapo," "Krauts," "Huns," and "Boche."

Pejorative references coded as JAP include "Japs," "Nips," "Yellow—," "Slant-eyed—" "Buck-tooth," "Apes," "Little—," "Bow-legged—," "Devil dwarves" (usually in films based on Pearl Buck novels).

Pejorative References to Nazis (films with 5 or more)

1942:	Total References		
PARIS CALLING	15	ACTION IN THE NORTH ATLANTIC	5
REUNION IN FRANCE	15	BACKGROUND TO DANGER	5
SECRET ENEMIES	10	HITLER'S CHILDREN	5
SHERLOCK HOLMES AND		SEVEN MILES FROM ALCATRAZ	5
THE VOICE OF TERROR	10	SONG OF RUSSIA	5
MISS V FROM MOSCOW	10	THEY GOT ME COVERED	5
DESPERATE JOURNEY	5	WILD HORSE RUSTLERS	5
DARING YOUNG MAN	5	BOMBER'S MOON	5
ENEMY AGENTS MEET		1944:	
ELLERY QUEEN	5	THE CONSPIRATORS	20
INVISIBLE AGENT	5	MAKE YOUR OWN BED	15
THE NAVY COMES THROUGH	5	THE MASTER RACE	15
ONCE UPON A HONEYMOON	5	THE CROSS OF LORRAINE	10
VALLEY OF HUNTED MEN	5	DAYS OF GLORY	10
1943:		PASSAGE TO MARSEILLES	10
ASSIGNMENT IN BRITTANY	15	THEY LIVE IN FEAR	10
HITLER'S MADMAN	15	U-BOAT PRISONER	10
PARIS AFTER DARK	15	ADDRESS UNKNOWN	5
CHETNIKS!	10	ENEMY OF WOMEN	5
FIRST COMES COURAGE	10	MINISTRY OF FEAR	5
HITLER—DEAD OR ALIVE	10	MR. SKEFFINGTON	5
NORTHERN PURSUIT	10	NONE SHALL ESCAPE	5
SAHARA	10	WATERFRONT	5
THEY CAME TO BLOW UP AMERICA	10	1945:	
WATCH ON THE RHINE	10	HOTEL BERLIN	10
EDGE OF DARKNESS	10	BETRAYAL FROM THE EAST	5
		ESCAPE IN THE DESERT	5

Pejorative References to Japanese (films with 5 or more)

1942:	Total References		
MANILA CALLING	35	SOMEWHERE I'LL FIND YOU	10
ESCAPE FROM HONG KONG	15	STAND BY FOR ACTION	10
SECRET AGENT OF JAPAN	15	CHINA	10
FLYING TIGERS	10	FOREIGN AGENT	5
JOAN OF OZARK	10	LITTLE TOKYO, U.S.A.	5
LADY FROM CHUNGKING	10	LURE OF THE ISLANDS	5
PRISONER OF JAPAN	10	REMEMBER PEARL HARBOR!	5
		WAKE ISLAND	5

1943:

GUADALCANAL DIARY	40
AIR FORCE	35
BATAAN	30
GUNG HO!	20
SALUTE TO THE MARINES	15
SO PROUDLY WE HAIL!	15
CHINA GIRL	10
FLIGHT FOR FREEDOM	10
CORREGIDOR	5
MINESWEEPER	5
NIGHT PLANE FROM CHUNGKING	5
PILOT NO. 5	5
ROOKIES IN BURMA	5
STAGE DOOR CANTEEN	5
THAT NAZTY NUISANCE	5
WE'VE NEVER BEEN LICKED	5

1944:

WING AND A PRAYER	20
DESTINATION TOKYO	20
THE FIGHTING SEABEES	20
MARINE RAIDERS	20
THE STORY OF DR. WASSELL	15
EVE OF ST. MARK	10
ABROAD WITH TWO YANKS	5
CRY HAVOC	5
THE DOUGHGIRLS	5
DRAGON SEED	5
HAIL THE CONQUERING HERO	5
THE PURPLE HEART	5
SERGEANT MIKE	5
SEVEN DAYS ASHORE	5
THE VERY THOUGHT OF YOU	5

1945:

BACK TO BATAAN	30
OBJECTIVE, BURMA!	25
FIRST YANK IN TOKYO	25
GOD IS MY CO-PILOT	25
PRIDE OF THE MARINES	20
BETRAYAL FROM THE EAST	15
CHINA SKY	15
THIRTY SECONDS OVER TOKYO	15
THIS MAN'S NAVY	5

Pejorative References to the Enemy: Total Films

NAZI ref=	5–9	10–14	15–19	20–24	25–34	35+
1942:	7	3	2			
1943:	8	8	3			
1944:	7	5	2			
1945:	2	1				
Totals:	24	17	7			

Average Number of References per Film:

1942:	8 (12 films/95 references)
1943:	8 (19 films/165 references)
1944:	8 (14 films/115 references)
1945:	7 (3 films/20 references)
Overall:	8 (48 films/395 references)

JAP ref=	5–9	10–14	15–19	20–24	25–34	35+
1942:	6	6	2			1
1943:	8	2	2	1	1	2
1944:	10	2		3		
1945:	1	0	3	1	4	
Totals:	25	10	7	5	5	3

Average Number of References per Film:

1942:	10 (15 films/155 references)
1943:	13 (16 films/215 references)
1944:	9 (15 films/130 references)
1945:	19 (9 films/175 references)
Overall:	12 (55 films/675 references)

Filmographic Entries, 1942–1945

1942

450 ABOUT FACE (UA, Apr) Kurt Neumann; *genre:* Comedy; *location:* United States; *coding:* Prod, AF-A, Pol?, Home Def, Blk, Fem Lab, AF-MC, AF-N; *relevance:* 1.5.

This was the second film in a series of low-budget barracks comedies produced by Hal Roach featuring the competitive antics of an over-achieving draftee named Dodo Double-day (William Tracy) and a dumb Army lifer, Sergeant Ames (Joe Sawyer). While on leave, the newly promoted young Sergeant Double-day and his hard-boiled nemesis attend a meeting of the local Girls' Home Defense League. Jealous of the attention Dodo is receiving and angered at being referred to as an "old army mule" by a society matron, Sergeant Ames leaves in a huff. He returns with a girl and shanghais Dodo to an Army-Navy dance. An interservice riot in the parking lot ensues when Ames crashes their hired vehicle into a sailor's car (such disagreements between branches of the service were VERY rare in wartime films; this film was probably written before Pearl Harbor). Refer to *Tanks a Million* (UA, 1941), q.v., and *Fall In* (UA, 1942), q.v. Dodo and his veteran buddies would get together after the war in *Here Comes Trouble* (UA, 1948).

451 ACROSS THE PACIFIC (WB, Sept); John Huston; *genre:* Spy; *locations:* United States, Canada, Panama; *coding:* AF-A, AF-N, AF-Can, Nazi, Jap-Am?, Jap, AF-Jap, Hirohito, Ger-Jap Coop, Pearl Harb, Intell Serv, Mil School, Dipl, FDR, Chiang, Fil, Chi, Spy-Sab, Collab, Hist Am; *relevance:* 3.

After a rigged court-martial, U.S. Army officer Rick Leland (Humphrey Bogart) makes contact with a Japanese espionage ring aboard a ship bound for Panama. In order to gain their confidence, Rick acquires detailed aerial defense information for the Canal Zone. The suspicious Japanese and their Occidental collaborator seize the plans from Rick and prepare to launch an air attack upon the Panama Canal from a secret base located on a plantation in the interior. Rick foils the enemy's plans. The Axis agents include a jive-talking Japanese-American (Keye Luke) and a flabby German-American(?) intellectual, portrayed by Sidney Greenstreet, who admires Japanese militarism. Mary Astor is the love interest, thus

reuniting three of the principals from *The Maltese Falcon* (WB, 1941) with director Huston. Vincent Sherman completed this film when Huston went into the Army (where he made a number of government war documentaries).

452 THE AFFAIRS OF MARTHA (MGM, Aug) Jules Dassin; *genre:* Comedy; *location:* United States; *coding:* Latin AM, Nazi, Short?; *relevance:* 1.

Martha (Marsha Hunt), the family cook, uses a pseudonym when she writes a reputedly scandalous book about her wealthy employers and their friends entitled *Kitchen's Eye View*. The local ladies, while complaining about the difficulties of getting help in wartime, organize to discover who the culprit is. Meanwhile, Martha's downstairs friends rally to her side against the "Gestapo" tactics of their bosses.

453 A-HAUNTING WE WILL GO (TCF, Aug) Alfred Werker; *genre:* Comedy; *location:* United States; *coding:* Jap, Nazi, Short, Blk; *relevance:* 1.

Laurel and Hardy are trying to thumb a ride to Florida after being tossed out of jail where they had served time on a vagrancy charge. Laurel reads a paper that features a headline about the Japanese and Nazis. The boys are subsequently picked up by a couple of gangsters who dupe them into escorting a coffin on a train trip. It gets accidentally switched with a coffin used in a traveling magic act. Meanwhile, the boys are hired by the magician, the Great Dante (playing himself), as comic relief for his show. In one routine on stage they are cruelly tricked by the illusion of a T-bone steak (a rare commodity in wartime USA). Surprisingly, there are no uniformed servicemen in view at the train station.

454 ALIAS BOSTON BLACKIE (Col., Apr) Lew Landers; *genre:* Crime; *location:* United States; *coding:* Atroc-Conc, Draft, Nazi; *relevance:* 1.

Boston Blackie (Chester Morris) and the cast of a Broadway show put on a Christmas Eve show in prison. However, Joe (Larry Parks), the brother of one of the chorus girls and a convict at the prison, escapes disguised as a clown. He wants to get even with the men who framed him. Blackie is blamed for the escape, and when one of the criminals is murdered, Blackie has to clear Joe's name. At one point, Blackie shows up in a stolen police uniform, and his friend Arthur Manleder says, "You've been drafted!" There are

also dialogue references to "concentration camp," and Blackie's sidekick Runt refers to a policeman as the "Gestapo." This type of humorous references to Nazi activities—directed at Americans—would largely disappear as the war went on.

455 ALL THROUGH THE NIGHT (WB, Jan) Vincent Sherman; *genre:* Spy; *location:* United States; *coding:* V, FBI, Dunkirk, AF-N, AF-RAF, Ger-Am, Hitler, Goering, Himmler?, Nazi, AF-Ger, Blk, Spy-Sab, Collab, Atroc-Conc; *relevance:* 3.

A New York gangster named Gloves (a tongue-in-cheek performance by Humphrey Bogart) pursues a group of fifth columnists (including Conrad Veidt, Judith Anderson, and Peter Lorre) after they murder the German-American deli owner who made Gloves' favorite cheesecake. Gloves, his gang (including Frank McHugh, Jackie Gleason, and Phil Silvers), and other members of New York's underworld (a black and a Chinese character are in on the final battle) unite to break up a secret meeting in which the Nazis are plotting various acts of sabotage. At the climax, Gloves struggles with the Nazi ringleader in a powerboat loaded with explosives that is speeding towards an anchored U.S. Navy warship. In the nick of time Gloves bails out and the boat explodes, killing the spy but missing the battleship. When one of the patriotic hoods is asked who broke up the Nazi spy ring, he proudly replies, "The *people* did." Several of the saboteurs are clubbed over the head with a baseball bat and have Vs chalked upon their backs: "It's about time someone knocked those heels on their Axis." Among the principal players, Veidt, Kaaren Verne (Bogart's love interest), and Lorre were all expatriate Germans.

456 ALWAYS IN MY HEART (WB, Mar) Jo Graham; *genre:* Drama; *location:* United States; *coding:* USO, AF-N, AF-A, Blk, Collab, USO, Latin Am, Ital, AF-CG; *relevance:* 1.

Walter Huston returns to his family in a West Coast fishing town after spending many years in prison. He organizes the harmonica players at the local cannery into a symphony-like group to play at USO benefits on military bases.

457 ANDY HARDY'S DOUBLE LIFE (MGM, Dec*) George B. Seitz; *genre:* Comedy/Drama; *location:* United States; *coding:* Home Def, Blk, AF-A, Short; *relevance:* 1.

Andy (Mickey Rooney) is planning to go to college. The usual financial and female problems arise. At one point, while talking jive to his befuddled father, Andy refers to someone being AWOL. Judge Hardy (Lewis Stone) asks if this means the individual has deserted from the Army. "No," Andy replies, it stands for "a wolf on the loose." Later, Andy explains to the two young ladies with whom he has been flirting that since Wainwright College is not coed he is facing a four-year "smooch blackout." It is interesting to note that, despite the date of this film's release, America's favorite teenager makes no references to the draft.

458 ARMY SURGEON (RKO, Dec) A. Edward Sutherland; *genre:* War/Drama; *locations:* Pacific, France; *coding:* WWI, Fr, Atroc, AF-Ger, Jap, AF-A, AF-Mer, AF-W, Pearl Harb; *relevance:* 3.

A hospital ship in a convoy comes under attack somewhere in the Pacific. This leads to an extended flashback relating the World War I experiences shared by the head surgeon (James Ellison) and senior nurse (Jane Wyatt). Included are a German aerial attack on an ambulance and a dramatic rescue of a wounded soldier in "no man's land." An "all clear" horn returns the story to the present. The comic sergeant from Brooklyn, who had also served in the last war, has to be restrained from beating up a merchant seaman who makes a defeatist-sounding comment. The sergeant then boasts: "[we're going to treat the enemy] like he was the umpire back in Brooklyn" (a typical Hollywood ploy: briefly introducing and then quickly terminating an ideological conversation). This was the first wartime American film to portray women of the Army Nurse Corps (founded in 1901) in combat.

459 ATLANTIC CONVOY (Col., July) Lew Landers; *genre:* Spy; *locations:* N. Atlantic, Iceland; *coding:* AF-MC, Juv, Collab, AF-A, AF-AC, Hitler, AF-Ger, Nazi?, Fr, Brit, Spy-Sab, Ref, Iceland, Pol, Nor; *relevance:* 3.

Weatherman Carl Hansen (John Beal) works with the U. S. coastal air patrol in Iceland. Because of his uncanny ability to predict when Allied merchant vessels will be attacked, Hansen is suspected of providing information to the Germans. In an attempt to prove his innocence, Hansen volunteers to accompany a pilot on a mission to rescue some English "evacuees" and their nurse, stranded on a life raft. When the pilot, Captain Morgan (Bruce Bennett), is injured landing their floatplane, Hansen is forced to fly the aircraft back to Iceland. This only increases the suspicions of military authorities, since no one knew he could fly. Hansen's fingerprints are sent to Washington, and reveal that Hansen is really an AWOL Marine. Hansen flees, and with the aid of one of the

evacuees, actually a Nazi cabin boy, makes contact with a fishing/spy boat. On board they meet Nazi U-Boat commander von Smith who, years earlier, posing as a Pole, stole the plans of a remote control device invented by Hansen. Now, in order to sink a munitions ship in the harbor, the Germans need Hansen's expertise. Von Smith: "When we ram this tub [the fishing boat] into her she'll blow this outpost of democracy off the map." Hansen is able to signal Captain Morgan, and together they dispose of the Nazi threat. Virginia Field has the leading female role, cast as a nurse.

460 BABES ON BROADWAY (MGM, Jan) Busby Berkeley; *genre:* Musical/Comedy; *location:* United States; *coding:* Ital, Ger, FDR, Latin Am, Ref, Chi, Brit, Fr, Hist Am, Aust, Neth; *relevance:* 2.

This Busby Berkeley extravaganza features Mickey Rooney and Judy Garland as young Broadway hopefuls who stage their own show in order to raise enough money to send some settlement kids to the country. One of the major production numbers is dedicated to the British "Tommy." Judy also sings a patriotic solo tune entitled "FDR Jones" (adapted from the WPA musical, "Pins and Needles"), and some evacuated British children are given a chance to communicate with their parents via a radio broadcast to the embattled isle. Judy serenades them with: "Chin Up, Cheerio, Carry on." The lyrics include the following line: "Hang onto your wits...we'll turn the Blitz on the Fritz." Between 1939 and 1940 some 5,000 British children were evacuated to the United States and several of the Commonwealth nations. During 1941 NBC had actually arranged some well publicized radio hook-ups with England between evacuees and their parents. A similar transatlantic radio scene is enacted in TCF's February release, *On the Sunny Side*, q.v.

461 BABY FACE MORGAN (PRC, Sept) Arthur Dreifuss; *genre:* Crime/Comedy; *location:* United States; *coding:* Jap, Short, Collab, FBI, Ital; *relevance:* 1.

In this gangster spoof, the small-town son (Richard Cromwell) of a dead gang leader is put in charge of the Acme Protection Agency, a front for the mob's insurance racket. Now under the control of a gangster named "Doc" Rogers, the naive youth—dubbed Baby Face— is coached to become a killer. When one of the gang's henchmen expresses concern about the FBI, Doc responds: "The FBI is too busy slapping the Japs and rounding up the Bundists." Baby Face finds a girl and goes straight. The Amerika-Deutscher Volksbund, or German-American Bund, under the leadership of Fritz Kuhn, was an independent Nazi organization established in

1936. Unflattering portrayals of Bund leaders appear in *Margin for Error*, q.v., and in *Hotel Berlin*, q.v.

462 BEHIND THE EIGHT BALL (Univ., Dec.) Edward F. Cline; *genre:* Comedy; *location:* United States; *coding:* Short, Spy-Sab, Blk Mkt; *relevance:* 1.5.

After the Ritz Brothers are kicked out of the nightclub where they had been working, they gratefully accept an offer from a young woman (Carol Bruce) to star at a summer theatre in a converted barn, unaware that the guest stars in two previous performances have been murdered on stage! While hitchhiking to the sticks, the zany brothers make various jokes about shortages and the black market. During the show, the boys inadvertently discover Axis spies making wireless broadcasts from a secret room behind the stage. A new member of the Sonny Dunham Band is exposed as the killer (he has a gun in his clarinet!), who was trying to scare the show away from the theatre so the spies could work unmolested.

463 BELLS OF CAPISTRANO (Rep., Sept.) William Morgan; *genre:* Western; *location:* United States; *coding:* WWI?, Hist Am; *relevance:* 1.

The head of the Johnson Rodeo is trying to gain possession of the struggling World Wide Rodeo by marrying its pretty owner, Jennifer (Virginia Grey). Gene Autry joins the young lady's show, quickly exposes Johnson's true intentions, and financially stabilizes World Wide when his popularity wins the rodeo show a series of excellent contracts. The film concludes with a patriotic pageant. Gene begins by singing the opening stanza of a World War One-vintage chauvinistic song, directed at immigrants, entitled "Don't Bite the Hand That's Feeding You." He then recites the "Uncle Sammy Patter," with lines like: "America is singing...let peace and freedom ring." A background chorus begins singing "America the Beautiful" as the camera pans past each state flag and finally centers on the Stars and Stripes. This was Autry's last new film for the duration (he went into the Air Corps).

464 BERLIN CORRESPONDENT (TCF, Sept.) Eugene Forde; *genre:* War/Drama; *locations:* Germany, Switzerland, United States; *coding:* War Corr, Atroc, Resist, AF-Ger, Rommel, Pearl Harb, Brit, AF-RAF, Nazi, Hitler, Dipl, Russ, Ger, Collab, Atroc-Conc, Jap?, Ital, Goebbels, Himmler; *relevance:* 3.

It is November 1941 and British planes are bombing the German capital. Under the watchful eyes of two Nazi censors, Bill Roberts (second-billed Dana Andrews, sporting a pencil-thin moustache), the *New York Chronicle*'s Berlin correspondent, makes a seemingly innocuous radio broadcast to America. But his colleagues in New York are able to decode his real scoop: the German Army is taking a beating in Russia. After Col. Von Rau (Martin Kosleck) of the Gestapo reads the *Chronicle*, he orders the censors sent to the Russian front (references to German defeats on the Eastern front and Nazi fears of the Red Army would frequently appear in American wartime films). Von Rau uses Karen (Virginia Gilmore), his attractive employee, to vamp Bill and discover the source of his information. Unfortunately for Karen, it turns out to be her aged father! Bill and the repentant Karen help her father escape to Switzerland, using Bill's passport. After the attack on Pearl Harbor, the Nazis kidnap Bill, put him in a concentration camp and replace him with a double who makes anti-war broadcasts. With the aid of Karen and Von Rau's jealous assistant (Mona Maris), Bill is able to escape the Third Reich, disguised as a Nazi officer. This B-picture has some interesting points, including a fairly explicit discussion of the Nazi policy of euthanasia for "mental defectives."

465 THE BIG STREET (RKO, Sept.) Irving Reis; *genre:* Drama; *location:* United States; *coding:* Blk, Jew, Ital, Latin Am, Grk, FBI; *relevance:* 1.

Based on a Damon Runyon story: a sentimental Broadway nightclub waiter (Henry Fonda) falls in love with a glamorous singer who has been paralyzed in an altercation with a drunken admirer. Lucille Ball plays the pompous former star who selfishly accepts the waiter's help while scorning his love. Some gangster friends provide comic relief. After taking her "highness" to Florida, a visiting friend comments, "...we were received [by her] like the Italian ambassador in Greece." Mussolini's troops had launched an unprovoked attack upon Greece in October 1940.

466 BLACK DRAGONS (Mono, Mar) William Nigh; *genre:* Spy; *locations:* Japanese, United States; *coding:* Dipl, Nazi, Prod, Jap, Hitler, Hirohito, FBI, Collab, Pearl Harb, Ger-Jap Coop; *relevance:* 3.

Nazi plastic surgeon Dr. Melcher (Bela Lugosi) is engaged (before Pearl Harbor) by the Japanese Black Dragon Society to transform six of their members into living likenesses of American industrialists who have been secretly murdered by the organization. Following the successful operations, Dr. Melcher tells the Japanese that it is an honor to help "destroy the archaic democracies." They promptly throw him in jail. Melcher swears to the Japanese "apes" that "the Fuehrer will wipe you off the face of the earth!" The bulk of the film takes place in America immediately following the attack on Pearl Har-

bor. The FBI tracks down the crazed Melcher who, following his escape from the Japanese, comes to America and systematically slays the six phony captains of industry. Several American films would depict dissent among the Axis partners, e.g., *Busses Roar* (WB, 1942) and *Invisible Agent* (Univ, 1942) q.v. There actually was a nationalist Japanese group founded in 1901 called the Black Dragon Society (referred to in a few other films, including *Little Tokyo, USA* and *The Purple Heart*, q.v.). The working title for this film was the racially provocative "Yellow Menace."

467 BLONDIE FOR VICTORY (Col., Aug) Frank R. Strayer; *genre:* Comedy; *location:* United States; *coding:* Juv, USO, Short, Blk Mkt?, Jap, Chi?, Brit?, Collab, Spy-Sab?, V, Home Fr, Home Def, AF-A, AF-N?, AF-W, AF-AC, Bonds?, Prod, Prod-Farm, Fem Lab; *relevance:* 3.

Although it is never clearly specified in this entry, Dagwood (Arthur Lake) is apparently engaged in war-essential work at Mr. Dithers' architectural firm (presumably the construction of housing for defense workers, since civilian construction was drastically curtailed for the duration). After a particularly stressful day, Dagwood goes home to seek relief from his war-accelerated job. Instead, he is assaulted by his family's home front activities. For instance, Blondie (Penny Singleton) and the "Housewives of America" are meeting in his living room, and they eagerly practice first aid on the helpless Dagwood. Son Alexander and his friend Alvin (aided by Daisy and her puppies) are collecting money for the war effort (the dogs carry kegs marked "Buy a Bomb" and "Buy a Bullet"), and Dagwood is conned into donating. Since Blondie is spending so much time on her extracurricular activities, Dagwood is forced to handle the housework in addition to his day job. However, after a hectic experience with a false "saboteur," the Housewives of America agree that their true contribution to the war effort is the maintenance of America's home life. Lip service is paid to women who are directly involved in the war, from defense plant workers and Red Cross employees to women in the military (there is a "Defense Fashion Show" featuring various uniformed women, and a concluding montage sequence depicts these women once more).

468 BLONDIE GOES TO COLLEGE (Col., Jan) Frank Strayer; *genre:* Comedy; *location:* United States; *coding:* Juv, Mil School, Prod, AF-A, Draft; *relevance:* 1.

Dagwood's enthusiasm for college football inspires him to attend college for a semester. Since he and Blondie decide to attend college together, they place Baby Dumpling

in a military prep school, the Calhoun Academy. When the Bumsteads register at Leighton College they learn its star football player has been drafted. By the end of the semester Dagwood has come up with a "revolutionary" idea for new construction, Blondie is pregnant again and Baby Dumpling is a sergeant with the proud moniker of "Old Scrap Iron."

469 BLONDIE'S BLESSED EVENT (Col., Apr) Frank Strayer; *genre:* Comedy; *location:* United States; *coding:* Bonds, V, AF-A, AF-MC, Short, Prod, FBI, Hist Am; *relevance:* 1.5.

A nervous Dagwood is sent to an architect's convention in Chicago to get him away from Blondie during the final stages of her pregnancy (although she certainly does not *appear* pregnant at all). With the aid of an eccentric and impoverished playwright (Hans Conreid), Dagwood delivers a provocative speech at the convention declaring that people should dispense with the services of architects. The playwright moves in with the Bumsteads and turns their lives upside-down. The overwhelmingly negative response to his speech results in Dagwood being fired by Mr. Dithers. However, a man from the government's priority board, impressed by Dagwood's innovative ideas for "victory" construction (he suggested substituting a mixture of soybeans and potato peels for steel and concrete), offers him a job (this aspect of Dagwood's speech is not mentioned until the final scenes of the film—possibly representing a last-minute script revision to add topicality to the film). When Mr. Dithers finds out about the offer, he protests that he is a patriotic bond-buying citizen whose "new junior partner," Dagwood, is indispensable to his company. In one scene, son Alexander—jealous of his new baby sister—writes a note saying he is running away from home to join the Army (but upon second thought, he crosses this out and writes "the Marines").

470 BLUE, WHITE AND PERFECT (TCF, Jan) Herbert I. Leeds; *genre:* Spy/Crime; *locations:* United States, Pacific; *coding:* Ger, Prod, FBI, Nazi, Spy-Sab, Collab, Russ?, Latin Am; *relevance:* 2.5.

Detective Michael Shayne (Lloyd Nolan) is hired as a riveter by the Thomas Aircraft Corporation to help uncover a German spy ring suspected of sabotaging the war effort. But Shayne is dismissed by the owner after a large shipment of industrial diamonds is stolen. While pursuing the case on his own, Mike learns the spies concealed the diamonds in the bottom hems of dresses shipped to Honolulu. Aboard the steamer bound for Hawaii, and in Honolulu, the detective relentlessly chases after the Nazi spies. An FBI agent is also on their trail. Mike is ultimately able to rout the enemy agents after he convinces a female dress company employee they are not simply thieves, but "spies [who] steal industrial diamonds bound for German factories."

471 BOMBAY CLIPPER (Univ., Feb) John Rawlings; *genre:* Spy/Crime; *locations:* India, Singapore, Fil; *coding:* Brit, Spy-Sab, Ger?, US-Brit Coop, Prod, War Corr, Ind; *relevance:* 2.

Jim Wilson (William Gargan), correspondent of the Amalgamated News Service in India, is assigned to find out why several million dollars in diamonds are being sent to the United States aboard a Clipper plane. A series of mysterious robberies and murders follows. Jim finally learns the stones are being consigned to America to be cut into precision machine dies for Britain's war industry. Jim receives the packet of diamonds from a dying courier. Foreign spies then seize the plane and head for a rendezvous with a submarine. Jim and another Clipper passenger overcome the conspirators.

472 BOMBS OVER BURMA (PRC, June) Joseph H. Lewis; *genre:* War/Drama; *locations:* Burma, China; *coding:* AF-Chi, Am Vol, Collab, AF-FT?, Chi, Brit, Russ, Jap, AF-Jap, AF-Ger, Chiang, Atroc, Spy-Sab, Intell Serv, Jap-Ger Coop; *relevance:* 3.

A Chinese school teacher named Lin Ying, played by Anna May Wong, is sent as a secret agent to discover who is leaking information about Burma Road convoys to the Japanese. She boards a bus for Chungking, along with several American volunteer workers and an Englishman, Sir Roger. A tough American mechanic, Slim, explains why he is helping the Chinese: "I figure China is learning ... to hit back at big bullies... till the last one o' them is dead. Them coolies out there in the mud an' rain, well, them guys are all blood brothers of mine." The bus passengers are bombed and strafed along the way and forced to take refuge in a monastery. A scheme involving a fake convoy flushes out the spy. It turns out Sir Roger is actually an officer in German military intelligence. The plot of this film is quite similar to *Night Plane to Chungking*, q.v.

473 THE BOOGIE MAN WILL GET YOU (Col., Oct) Lew Landers; *genre:* Comedy; *location:* United States; *coding:* Prod, Draft, Ger, Spy-Sab, AF-A, POW, Short, Jap, AF-Ital; *relevance:* 1.

Boris Karloff plays a nutty professor ensconced in the cellar of an old New England inn who is experimenting with electricity in hopes of creating a flying superman who can "destroy Berlin [and] ... throttle Tokyo." To pay off his debts he sells the hotel, except his laboratory in the basement, to a young

woman (Jeff Donnell) who wants to convert the dilapidated building into a tourist attraction. Continued experiments in the basement lead to several apparently fatal miscalculations. Bedlam occurs when an Italian aviator who has escaped from a Canadian prison camp, Baciagalupi (the surname resembles a well known phrase of derision in Italian—Frank Puglia plays the role), bursts into the lab with dynamite strapped to his body. The mad, self-proclaimed "human bomb," who boasts of having had nineteen planes shot out from under him, plans to blow up a nearby munitions plant. Then some of Karloff's failed subjects revive. Peter Lorre is also in the cast.

474 BORN TO SING (MGM, Mar) Edward Ludwig; *genre:* Musical Comedy; *location:* United States; *coding:* Juv, Hist Am, Pol, Fin, Czech, Chi, Russ, Brit, Fr, Jew FDR, Collab, V, Blk, Latin Am, Short, Hitler, Nazi, FBI; *relevance:* 1.5.

Following his discharge from the state reformatory, Leo Gorcey rejoins his friends (including Virginia Weidler). They prevent a despondent song writer, who was cheated by a Broadway producer, from committing suicide. In a plot to get the writer's money back, the youngsters run afoul of the law. With the aid of a sympathetic gangster, they escape from the police and take refuge in an old beer hall that had once been a German-American Bund meeting place. With the gangster's further assistance, they get their talented juvenile associates to perform the song writer's show before the Broadway opening of the crooked producer's version. The film's final production number, "Ballad For Americans," is a rousing patriotic piece (originally heard in the Federal Theatre Project's show "Sing For Your Supper"), separately directed by Busby Berkeley, plugging national unity.

475 BOSS OF BIG TOWN (PRC, Dec) Arthur Dreifuss; *genre:* Crime; *location:* United States; *coding:* Spy-Sab, USO, Short, Blk Mkt, Home Fr, AF-?; *relevance:* 2.

Mike Lynn (John Litel), the two-fisted manager of a large West Coast food market, combats local racketeers who attempt to force price hikes in defiance of wartime government regulations. Intimidation and local political corruption lead to Lynn's dismissal from the central market. But with the aid of the police, Mike has a showdown with Jeffrey Moore, the "Big Boss" of the racketeers: "Talk about the the fifth column—you've invented a new one—the sixth column. With food one of the most important items for our morale, you stand behind the flag cheating the people... They ought to hang you for treason." In a speech delivered in March, FDR had warned about the potential dan-

gers of a "sixth column" on the home front.

476 BOSTON BLACKIE GOES HOLLYWOOD (Col., Nov) Michael Gordon; *genre:* Crime; *location:* United States; *coding:* Draft, AF-Russ, AF-A, Blk, Nazi, Home Def; *relevance:* 1.

When the famous Monterey diamond is stolen, Inspector Farraday (Richard Lane) immediately suspects his old antagonist, ex-crook Boston Blackie (Chester Morris). Blackie, his pal the Runt (George E. Stone), Farraday and Farraday's dumb assistant Matthews travel to Hollywood in pursuit of the jewel. There are a number of minor war references in the film. In one scene, Matthews claims he's a "class A [police] officer," and the Runt replies: "Yeah, class 1-A, and I wish you were in it." Blackie asks Farraday if he has "been taking lessons from the Gestapo," and says *if* he had the stolen diamond, "I'd hire the Russian Army to guard it."

477 BROADWAY (Univ., May) William A. Seiter; *genre:* Musical; *location:* United States; *coding:* MacArthur, Home Fr; *relevance:* 1.

George Raft, playing himself, visits New York City and recalls his start in show business as a hoofer in a Twenties speakeasy. When Raft arrives in New York he announces that he has left Hollywood on business for Uncle Sam (an unspecified patriotic gesture). As Raft wanders down Broadway he sees all the lighted neon signs (contrary to the official dim-out policy at the time). Later, he reads a newspaper with the headline: "MacArthur Launches New Attack."

478 BROADWAY BIG SHOT (PRC, Feb) William Beaudine; *genre:* Crime; *location:* United States; *coding:* —; *relevance:* 1.

Jimmy O'Brien (Ralph Byrd) is a crime reporter, as well as a local campus gridiron hero, who arranges his phony incarceration in the state prison in order to get a big story on a notorious inmate. Before being discharged with the story and the affections of the warden's daughter, Jimmy wins an election to the presidency of the inmate's union. Windy, the losing candidate, stuttering delivers a little speech in the warden's office: "Dat symbol of democracy has once more been hoid—even though we are confined in peen-al ser-ve-tude, we still ex-er-cise our un-alienable rights. In de face of cat-ta-klis-mic condition of half de world dis is nothin' short of plen-phlemonal."

479 THE BUGLE SOUNDS (MGM, Jan) S. Sylvan Simon; *genre:* Training-Spy; *location:* United States; *coding:* Intell Serv, Hist Am, Mil Exer, Spy, AF-A, AF-N, Blk, FBI, WWI, Vet, Collab, US-Brit Coop, Spy-Sab, Draft; *relevance:* 2.5.

"Hap" Doan (Wallace Beery), a career Army sergeant and a decorated WWI veteran, is dismayed to learn his cavalry regiment is to be fully mechanized and composed of twenty per cent "selectees" (a pre-war euphemism for draftees). But when his commanding colonel reminds him of the "national emergency," Hap pitches in to train the new men and prepare them for summer maneuvers. During the unloading of some new armored vehicles from a train, an explosion destroys a tank and mortally wounds Hap's beloved horse. Hap goes on a drinking binge that leads to his court martial. As a civilian, the supposedly disgruntled Hap is approached by saboteurs (masterminded by George Bancroft) to help them in the destruction of a Lend Lease shipment of tanks. Hap, who is actually working for military intelligence, prevents the enemy agents from carrying out their plans. *Variety* noted that the "views of hundreds of armored cars, trucks, and tanks in action are reassuring evidence that Uncle Sam's cavalry forces have been transformed into capable fighting chauffeurs."

480 BUSSES ROAR (WB, Sept) D. Ross Lederman; *genre:* Spy; *location:* United States; *coding:* AF-Jap, FBI, AF-MC, AF-N, AF-A, Jap, Ital, Nazi, Jap-Ger Coop, Spy-Sab, Intell Serv, Prod, WWI, Bonds, Home Fr, Blk, Pearl Harb; *relevance:* 3.

A Japanese sabotage ring on the West Coast, assisted by a German spy and an Italian gangster, plants a time bomb aboard a passenger bus traveling through a military industrial zone. Their plan is to illuminate the area by creating a large fire, thus enabling a Japanese submarine waiting offshore to shell nearby defense plants. The bus passengers (a typical American melting pot mixture, including a counter-espionage agent posing as a bum, an elderly couple, a black porter—Willie Best—and a Marine sergeant—Richard Travis), foil the plans of the enemy saboteurs. On several occasions the leader of the Japanese ring and the German agent question each other's abilities. At one point the German derisively refers to his Japanese counterpart as "Mr. Cherry Blossom." When his girl asks the heroic sergeant why he joined the Marines, he patriotically responds by invoking Pearl Harbor and his father's participation in the "last war." On February 12, 1942, the Japanese submarine I-17 had surfaced off the California coast near Santa Barbara and shelled an oil refinery. One odd aspect of this film is the presence of enemy aliens walking around in the "restricted zone" of southern California where, in real life, they would not have been allowed.

481 CAIRO (MGM, Sept.) W.S. Van Dyke; *genre:* Spy-Comedy; *locations:* United States, Egypt; *coding:* Brit, FBI, War Corr, V, Jap-Ger Coop?, FDR, AF-Ital, Nazi, Hitler, Spy-Sab, Jap, Ital, Blk, Home Fr, AF-A, AF-Brit, Arab, WWI; *relevance:* 3.

This film's dedication announces that it is intended to be a parody of the spy drama. It also spoofs the screen persona of its star, Jeanette MacDonald. Homer Smith (Robert Young) of the Cavity Rock, California *Times Leader* has been sent to the Near East to do a series called "The Small Town Looks at the War." His ship is torpedoed and he washes ashore in Libya. He finds himself stranded in the desert with a Nazi agent (played by Reginald Owen) who claims to be a member of British Intelligence. When Homer accidentally discharges a gun, a group of hysterical Italian soldiers appears and begs to surrender before their German allies catch them! The remainder of the picture's plot centers around Homer and his escapades in Cairo with a homesick American movie actress (MacDonald), whom he mistakenly believes to be working with the Nazis. She thinks likewise of him. Together with the British authorities, they eventually help prevent the real enemy agents from using a bomb-laden radio-controlled airplane to blow up a troop transport.

482 CALL OUT THE MARINES (RKO, Feb) F. Ryan, W. Hamilton; *genre:* Spy-Comedy; *location:* United States; *coding:* AF-N, Spy-Sab, Latin Am, AF-MC; *relevance:* 2.

Two ex-sergeants, played by Victor McLaglen and Edmond Lowe, rejoin the Marines and help breakup a spy ring attempting to steal war plans. A couple of musical pitches promoting cooperation with our South American neighbors are included. This was the last action comedy featuring the original Quirt and Flagg performers from the 1926 classic, *What Price Glory?* (although the characters use different names in this film, probably for legal reasons).

483 CALLING DR. GILLESPIE (MGM, Aug) Harold S. Bucquet; *genre:* Drama; *location:* United States; *coding:* Neth, AF-?; *relevance:* 1.

A disagreement between a young woman (Donna Reed) and her boyfriend (Phil Brown) triggers the young man's latent psychotic tendencies. He goes on a rampage and before he is apprehended, he makes an unsuccessful attempt on the life of Dr. Gillespie (Lionel Barrymore). Gillespie's assistant in this film is Dr. Gerniede (Philip Dorn), from Holland, who wants to transfer from surgery to psychiatry: "My father was a surgeon in Holland ... and I wanted to please him. But now with the world in frenzy, our chief medical problem is nervous and mental disorders. I want more than ever to help." After Brown is carted away, Reed finds a new boyfriend—in uniform. There are some indications that this film was completed fairly early in 1942: Brown makes a reference to working in a factory making automobiles in Detroit, and later buys a new car, both of which date the film, since civilian automobiles were not produced after February 1942, and automobile rationing went into effect almost at once.

484 CANAL ZONE (Col., Mar) Lew Landers; *genre:* War/Drama; *location:* Panama; *coding:* AF-AC, AF-MC, US-Brit Coop?; *relevance:* 2.5.

This film is set prior to the attack on Pearl Harbor. An old banana shipping station in Panama has been converted into a relay station for American bombers being flown to Africa by civilian pilots. Commander Merrill (Chester Morris), an ex-military flier, is in charge of the men who will ferry B-17s across the Atlantic. The latest group of trainees is composed of the usual cross-section of Americans, including a southern farm boy, an ex-Marine, a former baseball player with the Brooklyn Dodgers, and a society playboy named Ames (John Hubbard). Ames' recklessness eventually results in the accidental death of the ex-farmer. But he is able to redeem himself by rescuing another comrade who has crashed in the jungle. Announcing he plans to sign up with the U.S. Army Air Corps for some real action, Ames joins the squadron for a flight to Africa. Free French-controlled French Equatorial Africa had become a major conduit of American supplies for British forces in Egypt.

485 CAPTAINS OF THE CLOUDS (WB, Feb) Michael Curtiz; *genre:* Training-Adventure; *locations:* Canada, Britain; *coding:* Can, Fr, Am Vol, US-Brit Coop, Dunkirk, Nazi, AF-Ger, Jap, Hitler, Chi, Latin Am, Churchill, Chiang, WWI, AF-Rcaf, AF-Can, Brit, Austral; *relevance:* 3.

James Cagney plays a cocky Canadian bush pilot named Johnny who joins the Royal Canadian Air Force after listening to a radio broadcast of Churchill's defiant speech in the wake of the Dunkirk evacuation. Turned down for combat duty due to his age, he becomes a flight instructor, but his unorthodox training methods lead to the severe injury of an American trainee and a subsequent court martial. Sometime later, under the assumed name of a buddy killed in a flying accident, Johnny joins a group of replacement pilots ferrying American-built bombers to England. As they are approaching the British coast, the unarmed squadron is attacked by a German fighter. To save his mates, Johnny makes a suicidal crash into the "Heinie" plane. The redemption by sacrificial death of a flawed hero is used in at least two other 1942 film releases, *Flying Tigers* and *Remem-*

ber Pearl Harbor!, q.v. By special agreement, the bulk of Commonwealth wartime training of airmen was conducted in Canada. Much of the film was shot in Ontario at actual RCAF training bases (RCAF Air Marshal and WWI ace "Billy" Bishop appears in this footage, at graduation exercises for air cadets). This was the first Technicolor film with WWII combat scenes.

486 CAREFUL, SOFT SHOULDER (TCF, Sept) Oliver H.P. Garrett; *genre:* Spy; *location:* United States; *coding:* Pearl Harb, Hist Am, Spy-Sab, Intell Serv, Ger-Jap Coop, Short, WWI, FDR, Hirohito, Jap, Collab, Nazi, AF-N; *relevance:* 3.

A fatuous young socialite named Connie (Virginia Bruce) glibly tells a playboy companion at a Washington party that she would make a good spy. A fat Nazi collaborator, Mr. Fortune, representing himself as a member of the Secret Service working in counterespionage, later approaches Connie and dupes her into wheedling some convoy codes from the playboy's father, a naval attache. But the U. S. Navy is wise to Fortune and his co-conspirators. The secret information the spies wired to their compatriots leads a German U-boat patrol straight into an American naval ambush.

487 CASTLE IN THE DESERT (TCF, Feb) Harry Lachman; *genre:* Crime; *location:* United States; *coding:* Ital, AF-A, Chi, Span Civ; *relevance:* 1.

While on vacation in the Mojave Desert, Charlie Chan (Sidney Toler) becomes involved with a series of murders at the secluded mansion of an eccentric millionaire, a descendant of the infamous Borgia family. Charlie is assisted by his "Number Two" son (Victor Sen Yung), on leave from the U. S. Army Signal Corps. Chan's son had gladly received his draft notice at the end of the 1941 release, *Charlie Chan in Rio*, q.v. About twenty-two per cent of eligible Chinese-American males were eventually drafted or enlisted in the armed forces in WWII (nearly 14,000 total).

488 CITY OF SILENT MEN (PRC, Oct) William Nigh; *genre:* Crime; *location:* United States; *coding:* Ger?, Prod, Home Fr, AF-A; *relevance:* 1.5.

Two unemployed ex-convicts (including Frank Albertson) run into trouble in a small town when they are unable to pay for their lunch. The mayor intervenes, setting them up in business by reopening an old canning factory. He tells the judge it will help the U. S. government in the war effort by using worthy former convicts to help ease the labor shortage. Prejudice in the community, stirred-up by a man named Muller, is ultimately overcome.

489 THE CORPSE VANISHES (Mono, May) Wallace Fox; *genre:* Horror; *location:* United States; *coding:* Russ, Short, Ref?, *relevance:* 1.

A mad scientist (Bela Lugosi) sends orchids perfumed with a trance-inducing drug to young brides for their weddings. He later steals the supposedly dead bodies and drains them of an unspecified fluid at his secret laboratory in order to restore his aging wife's youthful beauty. Pat (Luana Walters), an attractive young society columnist, tracks down the story. The newspaper's photographer (Vince Barnett) comments that he has enough film to "cover the Russian front."

There is also a pointed but oblique reference to rubber rationing.

490 COUNTER-ESPIONAGE (Col., Sept) Edward Dmytryk; *genre:* Spy; *location:* Britain; *coding:* Prod, Short, V, US-Brit Coop, FDR, Brit, Churchill, Nazi, Hitler, Spy-Sab, Intell Serv, Home Def; *relevance:* 3.

In the midst of a German air raid on London, the plans for Britain's secret "Beam Detector" are stolen from the home of Sir Stafford Hart, head of British Intelligence. During the Scotland Yard investigation a cufflink is found that connects the notorious American jewel thief, Michael Lanyard, alias the Lone Wolf, to the crime. But the Lone Wolf (Warren William) is actually working with the British as a counter-espionage agent to help expose a German spy ring. The fanatical leader of the Nazi gang, who ruthlessly shoots one of his own men in the back to retrieve the plans from the Lone Wolf, is captured and informed that the plans he transmitted to Berlin over a radio-photo mechanism were bogus.

491 CRIMINAL INVESTIGATOR (Mono, Oct) Jean Yarbrough; *genre:* Crime; *location:* United States; *coding:* AF-A, Draft; *relevance:* 1.

Pat Martin (Robert Lowery), a cocky cub reporter, wins a spot on an important newspaper after scooping his rivals. Impudently disdaining police assistance, he investigates the murder of a showgirl who was the widow of a millionaire. When asked by his new editor why he is not in the Army, Pat responds that he has flat feet.

492 DANGER IN THE PACIFIC (Univ, July) Lewis D. Collins; *genre:* Adventure; *locations:* Pacific, United States; *coding:* AF-A; AF-RAF, Nazi, AF-Jap, Jap, Brit, Intell Serv, Spy-Sab, Jap-Ger Coop, Collab, US-Brit Coop; *relevance:* 3.

Doctor David Lynd (Don Terry), an American scientist-explorer, is persuaded by a British Intelligence officer to postpone his marriage to a wealthy aviatrix and undertake an expedition into the jungles of a Pacific island. Accompanied by his pal and camera-man, Andy Parker (Andy Devine), they use the cover of searching for a new drug to locate a secret Axis munitions compound on the island. No sooner have the Americans transmitted this information than natives working for a German-accented agent (Edgar Barrier) capture them. A message sent by the agent to a Japanese invasion fleet is intercepted by the British. Bombers destroy the secret base just in time to chase off a native firing squad and save the heroes.

493 DANGEROUSLY THEY LIVE (WB, Feb) Robert Florey; *genre:* Spy; *location:* United States; *coding:* Bonds, USO, AF-Can, AF-RAF, Intell Serv, AF-Ger, Blk, FBI, Brit, Spy-Sab, Collab, Hitler, Nazi, Goering, Himmler, US-Brit Coop, Atroc-Conc; *relevance:* 3.

In New York City, Nazi agents kidnap Jane Greystone (Nancy Coleman) of British Intelligence, who is known to have memorized information about a convoy leaving Halifax for England. Jane's attempts to escape from her captors lead to an auto accident. At the hospital, a famous psychiatrist (who is a really a Nazi—played by Raymond Massey), diagnoses her as suffering from amnesia—she will need treatment at his private sanitarium. Jane enlists the aid of a skeptical intern, Michael Lewis (John Garfield). By the time he realizes Jane is who she claims to be, they are both prisoners. Through the use of drugs and torture, the Nazi agents apparently succeed in forcing Jane to reveal the planned route of the convoy. Mike overcomes their captors and Jane contacts British Intelligence so that bombers can attack the U-Boat wolf pack now gathered at the *false* position she gave.

494 THE DARING YOUNG MAN (Col, Oct) Frank Strayer; *genre:* Spy-Comedy; *location:* United States; *coding:* Spy-Sab, Short, AF-A, AF-N, AF-MC, AF-AC, FBI, Hitler, Nazi, AF-Ger, Russ?, Latin Am?, FDR, Blk, Jap; *relevance:* 2.5.

Joe E. Brown plays Jonathan Peckinpaw, a meek businessman who lives with his grandmother (Brown in drag). Three neighboring Nazi spies (Hans, Kurt, and Marlene—among them, Lloyd Bridges) blow up his shop in the process of liquidating an associate. Jonathan falls in love with Ann Minter (Marguerite Chapman), a newspaper reporter covering the explosion. He tries to enlist to win her affection, but is turned down by the Army, Marines, Navy *and* Air Corps as a physical wreck. Jonathan takes up bowling(!) to improve his physique. The use of a radio-controlled ball, designed by a local hustler, results in Jonathan again crossing paths with the spies. In discussing their plans, one Nazi carelessly remarks to his colleagues: "That sounds Kosher." After an embarrassed pause, the nervous man gasps: "Did I say that? Heil Hitler! Heil Hitler! Heil Hitler!"

495 A DATE WITH THE FALCON (RKO, Jan) Irving Reis; *genre:* Crime; *location:* United States; *coding:* Spy-Sab, Rom, Blk, Prod; *relevance:* 1.5.

A scientist named Samson has invented a synthetic diamond "that will be of vital value to the nation's defense industry." Soon after giving a demonstration to associates in New York City, Samson is found dead in his hotel room. Inspector O'Hara suspects the Falcon (George Sanders), but grants the debonaire detective 12 hours to clear his name by solving the case. In doing so, the Falcon discovers the man's identical twin brother, and runs into assorted criminals interested in the synthetic diamond formula. The only reference to espionage is an allusion to the formula being valuable "in the hands of an unscrupulous party." The female crook (spy?; never specified) is identified as being from Romania—an ally of Nazi Germany at the time.

496 THE DAWN EXPRESS [aka NAZI SPY RING] (PRC, Mar) Albert Herman; *genre:* Spy; *location:* United States; *coding:* FBI, Spy-Sab, Nazi, Hitler, Ref, Short, Draft, Pol, Prod; *relevance:* 3.

Buddies Tom Fielding (William Bakewell) and Robert Norton (Michael Whalen) are working at a research laboratory on a new additive, a couple of drops of which doubles the power of a gallon of gas. Tom is entrapped by a blonde who claims to be a Polish refugee. Actually she is German and a member of a gang of Nazi spies. Sex and threats to his family induce Tom to procure the formula for the spies. Meanwhile, G-Men enlist the aid of Bob in attempting to thwart the enemy agents. At the end, Bob flees in a plane with the Nazi leader and tricks him into incorrectly mixing the formula, which leads to an explosion that destroys their aircraft.

497 A DESPERATE CHANCE FOR ELLERY QUEEN (Col, May) James Hogan; *genre:* Crime; *location:* United States; *coding:* AF-A, AF-N, Short; *relevance:* 1.

Ellery Queen (William Gargan) visits San Francisco and becomes involved in murder and a counterfeiting operation working out of a nightclub which is a front for a gambling den. At one point a short, belligerent man collects his hat from the club's coat check room and then shouts: "Haven't you forgotten something?" The clerk apologizes and hands over a couple of automobile tires! Interestingly, although numerous uniformed extras appear in street scenes, no military personnel are portrayed as patrons of the club where the illegal gambling takes place.

Due to rubber shortages incurred by Japanese conquests, tires were one of the first items to be rationed by the government.

498 DESPERATE JOURNEY (WB, Sept) Raoul Walsh; *genre:* Adventure/Combat; *locations:* Britain, Germany, Poland, Netherlands; *coding:* Dunkirk, Resist, Spy-Sab?, FDR, V, Latin Am, US-Brit Coop, Austral, Can, FR, WWI, Hitler, Goering, Nazi, Jap, AF-Ital, AF-Raf, POW, Russ, Brit, Churchill, Pol; *relevance:* 3.

In this wild yarn Errol Flynn swashbuckles the Nazis. After the Polish resistance blows up a vital rail line, an RAF bomber is sent to attack the backed-up rolling stock. Presumably taking place just before the United States enters the conflict, the international crew includes an American bombardier named Johnny (Ronald Reagan) and a Canadian navigator (Arthur Kennedy). Following the successful bombing raid, the crippled plane is forced to crash land. The surviving crew members are captured and menacingly interrogated by Nazi stereotypes. After Johnny discovers the monocle-wearing Nazi officer (Raymond Massey)—who had boasted of the German "iron fist"—has a "glass jaw," the boys escape and embark on an odyssey across occupied Europe. Along the way they witness a hospital train "jammed with the wounded from the Eastern Front," and get an assist from the German underground. They return to England in a captured plane. The Flynn character, an Aussie named Terry, concludes by stating: "Now for Australia and a crack at those Japs" (apparently meaning the Pacific war has broken out in the meantime).

499 DESTINATION UNKNOWN (Univ, Oct) Ray Taylor; *genre:* Spy; *location:* China; *coding:* Ger-Jap Coop, Resist, Pearl Harb, AF-FT, Jap, AF-Jap, Atroc, Chiang, Chi, Russ, Nazi, AF-Neth, Brit, Spy-Sab; *relevance:* 3.

This spy drama occurs in occupied "China shortly before the U.S. was treacherously attacked by Japan." A Dutch intelligence agent posing as a White Russian exile, Elena Voranoff (Irene Hervey), and an American flyer (William Gargan) on a secret mission for the Chinese are both trying to retrieve the Russian crown jewels that the Soviet government used to pay China for a shipment of antimony for war production. Two Britons and some Chinese guerrillas assist them in thwarting the concerted opposition of the Japanese Military Police and a German agent named Karl Renner.

500 THE DEVIL WITH HITLER (UA, Oct) Gordon Douglas; *genre:* Fantasy/Comedy; *location:* Germany, "Hell"; *coding:* AF-Ger, Hitler, Musso, Jap, V, Nazi, Hess, Spy-Sab, Ger-Jap-Ital Coop, Atroc-

Conc; *relevance:* 3.

This was a Hal Roach "Headliner" (a short feature): an opening title announces the story begins and ends in Hell and that it concerns "three heels" named Hitler, Mussolini and Suki Yaki (from the Japanese War Department). The Board of Directors in Hell view a Hitler speech on a television screen and decide they want to replace the Devil with the Fuehrer. The Devil (Alan Mowbray), claiming that "Schicklegruber is just a flash in the pan," is given 48 hours on earth to save his job by getting Hitler (Bobby Watson) to perform a good deed. The invisible Devil enters Hitler's bathroom, gets the valet fired by sabotaging the Fuehrer's bubble bath and then materializes, introducing himself as "Gesatan," the new valet. Slapstick between the Axis partners includes a routine where the three wind up sleeping together out of mutual fear and distrust, following their individual attempts to take out life insurance policies (from Lloyd's of London) on each other. After forcing Hitler to free a young couple he planned to execute as spies, the Devil triumphantly returns to Hell. But the maniacal Fuehrer appears, demanding to rule both the underworld *and* the outer world. The Board of Directors gives Hitler the job. The title of this film and its climax are reminiscent of a World War I propaganda film, *To Hell with the Kaiser* (Metro, 1918). Roach produced a sequel in 1943, *That Nazty Nuisance*, q.v.

501 DOCTOR BROADWAY (Para, June) Anton [Anthony] Mann; *genre:* Crime; *location:* United States; *coding:* Draft, Ital?; *relevance:* 1.

Dr. Broadway (MacDonald Carey), who helps the local New York characters and is loved by them, turns detective when some Manhattan gangsters frame him on a murder charge. Although the film would appear to be taking place in the wartime present, the Great White Way is not dimmed out. When the doctor crawls out on a high window ledge to rescue the heroine, whom he believes to be crazy, he tells her: "I'm a pigeon—one of Uncle Sam's pigeons. They've been drafting us pigeons, too."

502 DOCTOR GILLESPIE'S NEW ASSISTANT (MGM, Dec) Willis Goldbeck; *genre:* Drama; *location:* United States; *coding:* Prod, Short, Blk, Austral, Chi, Fil, AF-MC, AF-W, Draft, Jap, Brit; *relevance:* 1.5.

This was the second in the "Dr. Gillespie" series after MGM discarded Dr. Kildare, a result of Kildare actor Lew Ayres declaring himself a conscientious objector. The film goes out of its way to prove its patriotic credentials. For instance, wheelchair-bound Dr. Gillespie tells the head surgeon he would like to join the Marines (newsreel footage had been released showing 64-year-old actor Lionel Barrymore, crippled by arthritis, registering for the draft!). When the new interns are welcomed to the staff, it is reverently mentioned that a former surgeon was on Bataan and that several nurses are now in the military. The three new interns are all preparing to go to war: an Australian army doctor who wants to learn about the new sulfa drugs before returning home; a Chinese-American (Keye Luke) waiting for his passport to go and help his people resist the Japanese; and Dr. Adams (Van Johnson) from Kansas City, who proudly displays his draft notice. Ironically, in real life Van Johnson (who played sevicemen *many* times during the war and afterwards) was 4-F.

503 DRUMS OF THE CONGO (Univ, July) Christy Cabanne; *genre:* Adventure; *location:* Africa; *coding:* Blk, AF-A, Spy-Sab, Intell Serv, Prod, Collab; *relevance:* 2.

When U.S. Army Intelligence discovers the existence of a huge meteorite in Africa (presumably the Belgian Congo), Captain Kirk Armstrong (Don Terry) is sent to bargain for its acquisition from the tribe that guards it. It has been determined that the meteorite, known as the "Viao Mezi," contains a valuable alloy for the manufacture of precision war instruments. Along the way, Captain Armstrong must deal with enemy agents who are also interested in the stone, including a female spy and a murderous native henchman. Factual note: the Belgian Congo would later become a prime source for uranium ore for the United States.

504 DUKE OF THE NAVY (PRC, Jan) William Beaudine; *genre:* Comedy; *location:* United States; *coding:* AF-N, Blk, Hitler; *relevance:* 1.

Obviously produced prior to Pearl Harbor, this film is set in pre-war Florida. Navy man Duke (Ralph Byrd) and his pal Cookie are broke, but they are staked to a vacation in a fancy hotel by a friendly rich woman. Mistaken for rich people themselves, they attract the attention of the "General," a swindler who offers to sell them a treasure map. The map costs $2,000 and the treasure is worth a million dollars: "That's 500 to 1," one character says, "I'd take those odds on Hitler winning the war." There are peripheral references to "government" construction taking place on Caribbean islands, perhaps referring to the September 1940 arrangement with Britain (the U.S. sent them fifty WWI-vintage destroyers, and the English gave the Americans rights to establish naval bases on a number of islands).

505 EAGLE SQUADRON (Univ, May) Arthur Lubin; *genre:* Training/Combat; *locations:* Britain, France; *coding:* Churchill, Brit, Atroc, Postwar, Am Vol, AF-Brit, AF-RAF, AF-W, US-Brit Coop, WWI, AF-Ger, Pol, Ref, Nazi, Pearl Harb, War Corr, FR, Short; *relevance:* 3.

In a foreword spoken by war correspondent Quentin Reynolds, the American film audience is informed that "this is the story of some of our countrymen who did not wait to be stabbed in the back.... [and] went to England where they became famous as the Eagle Squadron ... [they found that the British] were our kind of people with our ideals and our hatred of tyranny." During the London Blitz, new recruits, including Chuck Brewer (Robert Stack) and a Polish-American named Borowsky (Edgar Barrier), join RAF Fighter Squadron 71, made up of American volunteers. In a sweep over occupied France they take a beating from a patrol of new German "Leopard" planes. Chuck is initially angered by the apparent callousness of the British towards their casualties. Later experiences with his WAAF girlfriend (Diana Barrymore) during a bombing raid on London, in which a hospital is hit, help him to begin to understand the true nature of British reserve. Chuck distinguishes himself in a commando raid on a Luftwaffe airfield in France, stealing one of the Nazi's new airplanes equipped with a special detection device, and flying it back to England. Universal sent a unit to England to film the actual Eagle Squadron's activities, and British combat footage (taken from the gun cameras of British fighters) was incorporated into the motion picture. In reality, over a score of American pilots did join the RAF before the United States entered the war. Most of these were transferred to the U.S. 8th Air Force in 1942. *Eagle Squadron* had its London premiere in July 1942 and was seen by actual squadron members (who felt that the film did not give the British enough credit).

506 ENEMY AGENTS MEET ELLERY QUEEN (Col, July) James Hogan; *genre:* Spy-Crime; *location:* United States; *coding:* AF-Ger, Nazi, Short, AF-MC, AF-A, AF-N, AF-CG, V, Hitler, Nazi, Resist, Russ?, Neth, FBI, Jap, Collab?, Pearl Harb, Blk; *relevance:* 3.

On the train trip back from New London where he had donated his yacht to the Coast Guard, Ellery Queen (William Gargan) becomes involved in murder. It turns out that a shipment of Egyptian relics on the train includes a mummy case full of diamonds destined for the Dutch resistance (represented by Gale Sondergaard and Gilbert Roland). Nazi agents attempt to seize the jewels and send them to Germany on a U-boat: "These diamonds will give our Fuehrer many more weapons to wipe out your stupid democracy." Ellery and girlfriend Nikki (Margaret Lindsay), with an assist from some Marines, capture the Nazi spy ring, based in a New York health club. This was Columbia's final Ellery Queen entry.

507 ESCAPE FROM HONG KONG (Univ, May) William Nigh; *genre:* Spy/War Drama; *location:* Hong Kong; *coding:* US-Brit Coop, Spy-Sab, Ger, Intell Serv, Pol, Neth, Chi, Latin Am, Jap, Ger-Jap Coop, Brit, Chiang, Hitler, Nazi, Pearl Harb; *relevance:* 3.

Rusty (Don Terry), Pancho (Leo Carrillo) and Blimp (Andy Devine), a vaudeville act from America called "The Three Sharpshooters," are performing at a Hong Kong theatre. In the midst of the show, Valerie (Marjorie Lord), a British agent posing as an enemy agent, is arrested by the military police in a shootout with a known Nazi operative. The three Americans come to the aid of the pretty spy when she is exposed by a traitor named Major Reeves (actually a German named von Metz). Reeves and a Japanese cohort are after the Anglo-Chinese defense plans for resistance to a possible Japanese invasion. Valerie and her American allies make a dramatic escape in a speedboat to the Chinese mainland as the Japanese launch their assault upon Hong Kong. Japanese military forces attacked the neutral enclave of Hong Kong, the "Lisbon of the Far East," on December 8, 1941. The small British colony's garrison surrendered on the 25th.

508 EYES IN THE NIGHT (MGM, Sept) Fred Zinnemann; *genre:* Crime; *location:* United States; *coding:* AF-A, Blk, Spy-Sab, Short, Prod, Collab, Nazi?; *relevance:* 2.5.

This film was based on a novel by Bayard Kendrick, one of a series featuring a blind detective. Duncan Maclain, played by Edward Arnold, helps an old friend (Ann Harding) out in a murder case. The murder is directly tied to attempts by Nazi agents to steal the secret formula of a war-related product developed by her scientist husband. A sequel was released in 1945, *The Hidden Eye*, q.v.

509 THE FALCON'S BROTHER (RKO, Nov) Stanley Logan; *genre:* Spy/Crime; *location:* United States; *coding:* Hitler, Latin Am, V, Spy-Sab, Collab, Home Def, Chi, Dipl, Ger, Pearl Harb, Short, FBI, Intell Serv, US-Mex Coop; *relevance:* 3.

Gay Lawrence (George Sanders), the Falcon, becomes involved in Nazi intrigue when he goes to meet his brother Tom (played by Tom Conway, the real-life brother of George Sanders), arriving from South America on a ship. A man has been murdered on the ship, and the police believe it is the Falcon's brother—however, Tom arrives by airplane, and tells Gay that he was drugged and dropped off the ship in Bermuda. While investigating the mystery, the Falcon is injured and spends most of the film in bed (offscreen), but Tom takes his brother's place as a sleuth, assisted by Lefty, the Falcon's sidekick. They investigate a dress shop featuring a special "Victory Dress" ("designed with a minimum of material") and find a clue that leads them to the studio of a fashion photographer. Before the photographer is mysteriously murdered, they learn from him that specially composed photos on magazine covers are used to disseminate coded messages to Nazi agents throughout the country. A pair of Mexican government agents (posing as a dance team) assists the Lawrence brothers in solving the case. The spy ring plans to assassinate a Latin American envoy attending a Pan-American solidarity conference. Gay is fatally shot while saving the life of the diplomat, but the spies are captured and Axis agents all over Latin America are rounded up. Tom Lawrence says he will carry on as the Falcon (and Conway *did* assume the role of the Falcon for nine more films).

510 FALL IN (UA, Nov) Kurt Neumann; *genre:* Training/Comedy; *location:* United States; *coding:* Draft, Hist Am, Collab, AF-A, Spy-Sab, V, Hitler; *relevance:* 3.

Camp Carver's commanding officer explains to the assembled non-coms that, due to the extension of the draft, there will be an immediate need for new officers. Dodo Doubleday (William Tracy) is one of those selected, while the old timer Sgt. Ames (Joe Sawyer) is not. Doubleday proves his leadership abilities by creating a smart unit out of a group of barefooted hillbilly recruits. On a payday weekend Doubleday and his men are assigned MP duty. Most of the servicemen and local girls, including Dodo's sweetheart, gather at a recreation center set up at the mansion of Arnold Benedict (get it?). While on the phone to Dodo, his girl discovers that the house is bugged to glean military secrets. A brawl erupts between the exposed Nazi agents and their guests. The local ladies contribute to the fight with a Coke bottle catapult. Doubleday and Ames crash into the secret basement radio center and discover information that will lead to the roundup of a coast to coast espionage network.

511 FIGHT ON MARINES (Ind, ?) Louis Gasnier; *genre:* Spy; *location:* United States; *coding:* AF-MC, Spy-Sab; *relevance:* 2.

This obscure independent (George Hirliman) production was released by Astor Pictures—an outfit specializing in re-releases and exploitation films—on the states' rights market. Little information is available on this film, which was ignored by the major trade publications, but it stars Wallace Ford and Grant Withers as Marines who become involved with spies. It was shot in Florida.

512 THE FLEET'S IN (Para, Jan*) Victor Schertzinger; *genre:* Musical Comedy; *location:* United States; *coding:* AF-MC, Hist Am, AF-N, Home Def, Latin Am, Blk, Draft; *relevance:* 1.5.

A shy gob, played by William Holden, acquires the reputation of a Lothario when he is photographed with a movie star at a servicemen's show. This leads to his shipmates betting large sums of money that he can publicly kiss "The Countess" (Dorothy Lamour), an entertainer at San Francisco's popular Swingland club, who gives sailors the cold shoulder. True romance overcomes the inevitable misunderstandings. A comment by the hero to the Countess illustrates that this film was in the can before Pearl Harbor: "I'll be back in a few months—that is, if things clear up."

The plot of this motion picture is similar to that of Republic's 1941 release, *Sailors on Leave*, q.v. and *Lady Be Careful* (Paramount, 1936).

513 FLIGHT LIEUTENANT (Col, July) Sidney Salkow; *genre:* Drama; *locations:* United States, Latin America; *coding:* Hist Am, WWI, AF-AC, Latin Am; *relevance:* 1.5.

Pat O'Brien plays a veteran World War I ace and civilian air hero who crashes his plane while intoxicated, killing his co-pilot. Disgraced, he leaves his son in the custody of a trusted lawyer friend and takes a job with a broken-down airline in Dutch Guiana. Several years later, during America's pre-war defense build up, O'Brien returns to the United States and joins the Air Corps under an assumed name as a mechanic. His son (played by Glenn Ford), who has become an Army test pilot, is stationed at the same air base. When O'Brien learns the young lieutenant is scheduled to fly a prototype aircraft—which has been rushed into testing by our entrance into the war—he takes it up himself and is killed when it falls apart in a dive. There were a number of films released during the Thirties that featured washed-up pilots flying in South America, i.e., *Sky Giant* (RKO, 1938) and *Only Angels Have Wings* (Col., 1939).

514 FLY BY NIGHT (Para, Jan) Robert Siodmak; *genre:* Spy; *location:* United States; *coding:* Spy-Sab, Ger; *relevance:* 3.

Doctor Jeff Burton (Richard Carlson) becomes involved in romance and adventure when he runs out of gas near a sanitarium, the hideout of a gang of Axis spies. An escapee forces Jeff to drive him back to the man's apartment, only to be mortally wounded by one of the spies who has been following them. Before the escapee dies, he gives Jeff a baggage check for a package containing the model of a secret weapon developed by Professor Langer, a famous scientist held captive by the enemy agents. Now suspected of murder by the police, Jeff kidnaps a pretty commercial artist (Nancy Kelly) to aid in his flight from the law. Feigning insanity, Jeff is admitted to the sanitarium and locates the imprisoned professor. When the spy leader, Dr. Sturm, discovers Jeff's true identity, the Axis agents force him to turn over the weapon model. In a gruesome conclusion, unaware that the device was designed to emit rays that destroy eyesight, the spies are subsequently all blinded when Sturm insists on its demonstration.

515 FLYING TIGERS (Rep, Oct) David Miller; *genre:* Combat; *locations:* China, Burma; *coding:* Hirohito, Atroc, AF-FT, AF-Brit, AF-Chi, AF-A?, Dipl, AF-Jap, Jap, V?, Am Vol, Ref, US-Chi Coop, FDR, Pearl Harb, Chi, Brit, Chiang; *relevance:* 3.

The famous American Volunteer Group (AVG), flying their shark-nosed P40s for the Chinese against the Japanese, is composed of the usual cross-section of U.S. society, including a gum-chewing Brooklynite, a burntout flyer with an alcohol problem, and a good old boy from Alabama. Their commander is played by the quintessential All-American, John Wayne. There is also a handsome, irresponsible newcomer, Woody (John Carroll), who frequently reminds his fellow pilots that he is motivated solely by the $500 bonus for shooting down "Japs." Woody quickly becomes an ace, but his disregard of teamwork eventually leads to the death of one of his comrades. Soon after learning of the attack on Pearl Harbor, Woody undertakes (by hiding in a plane without permission) a dangerous bombing mission against a strategically important bridge and redeems himself when he crashes the TNT-laden plane, crippled by defensive fire, into a Japanese supply train. In actuality, the AVG (under the leadership of General Claire L. Chennault) began operations in late 1941. In spite of remarkable success against superior Japanese forces during the spring of 1942, the organization was officially disbanded and its responsibilities absorbed by the U. S. Air Corps on July 4, 1942. *No* reference is made in this film to RAF operations in the same combat theatre. Other films dealing with the Flying Tigers include *Lady from Chungking* (1943), *The Sky's the Limit* (1943), and *God Is My Co-Pilot* (1945), all q.v. This film's plot strongly resembles a prewar Warner Brothers release, *International Squadron*, q.v. Republic Pictures claimed that no actual airplanes were used in this film—just miniatures and full-sized mockups only capable of taxiing along the ground.

516 FOR ME AND MY GAL (MGM, Sept) Busby Berkeley; *genre:* Musical Drama; *locations:* France, United States; *coding:* Draft Avoid, AF-N, AF-A, Ger, Draft, AF-MC, WWI, Bonds, V, USO; *relevance:* 2.

The opening of the *Film Daily* review of this motion picture is a good example of how the martial spirit of the times permeated the industry: "The current Judy Garland vehicle ... has the power of a tank and the speed and flexibility of a wide-open jeep." The plot centers around a young vaudeville dancing couple whose career and love life are interrupted by America's entrance into World War I. In order to be able to keep a cherished engagement at the Palace Theatre, Harry (Gene Kelly), as a means of evading the draft, closes the lid of a traveling trunk on his hand. Jo (Garland), whose brother has just been killed in action in France, leaves Harry in disgust. Harry restores his self-esteem and wins back Jo by serving valiantly at the front as an ambulance driver (an ending allegedly reshot by the studio to make Kelly's character more heroic).

517 FOREIGN AGENT (Mono, Oct) William Beaudine; *genre:* Spy; *location:* United States; *coding:* Isolat, Ger, Ger-Am, FDR, AF-A, AF-N, Spy-Sab, Nazi, Jap, Ital?, AF-Jap, Blk, Chi, Russ, Austral, Pol, Prod, Short, Bonds, Draft, V, Goebbels, Goering, Hitler, FBI, Collab, Jap-Ger-Ital Coop; *relevance:* 3.

An Axis spy ring on the west coast is engaged in disseminating anti-war, pro–isolationist propaganda. The head of the spy ring, Dr. Werner (Hans Schumm), has a German accent and wears a monocle. His associates include a gangster (possibly an Italian-American), a German-American, and a Japanese (ludicrously overplayed by Ivan Lebedeff). Werner also bankrolls the isolationist North American Peace Association. The enemy gang is particularly interested in procuring the plans for a newly developed anti-aircraft searchlight filter. They murder the inventor, but fail to find the plans. Mitzi (Gale Storm), the inventor's daughter, her boyfriend (John Shelton), and the FBI foil the foreign agents, who are making plans to assist in a Japanese air raid on Los Angeles. Mitzi, a movie actress, also sings at a waterfront club. One of the numbers she performs is "It's Taps for the Japs," in which she refers to the Japanese as a "sneaky race" and as "dirty devils."

518 FOUR JACKS AND A JILL (RKO, Feb*) Jack Hively; *genre:* Musical Comedy; *location:* United States; *coding:* AF-Ger, AF-N, Latin Am, Blk, Ref?; *relevance:* 1.5.

When their female singer is forced by her gangster boyfriend to resign, four musicians (including Ray Bolger and Eddie Foy, Jr.) hire Anne Shirley as her replacement. However, complications ensue when King Stephan of Aregal (Desi Arnaz) falls in love with her. The king is reportedly "in exile" in the United States because he is "still afraid some of those foreign agents will knock him off." As it develops, Arnaz is just posing as the king, anyway. There is also a dialogue reference to a "one-man panzer division."

519 FRIENDLY ENEMIES (UA, June) Allan Dwan; *genre:* Spy; *location:* United States; *coding:* Ger, Jew?, WWI, Spy-Sab, AF-A, FBI?, Ger-Am; *relevance:* 3.

In this period film, two elderly German-Americans have lived and prospered in the United States for the past forty years. But their friendship is strained by the outbreak of war in Europe in 1914. Pfeiffer (Charles Winninger), a wealthy brewery owner, is still nostalgic for the fatherland; Block (Charlie Ruggles—intended to be a German-Jew?) is a millionaire banker who has become a hundred-percent American. With the United States about to enter the conflict against the Central Powers, Pfeiffer's son secretly joins the Army. In the meantime, the old man has contributed $50,000 to a German emissary (Otto Kruger) to supposedly help stop the "persecution" of Germans in America. The money is actually being funneled to an espionage ring. When, in the spring of 1918, Pfeiffer is informed his money was used to blow up a troop transport on which his son was traveling, he joins forces with Block and the Secret Service to capture the responsible German spies. This film was based on a 1918 play which, in one of its road companies, starred Winninger and Lew Fields as the two friends (Winninger appeared in the Block role in the stage version, rather than the part of Pfeiffer he essayed on screen). In 1925, a silent film version was produced, starring Lew Fields and Joseph Weber.

520 GALLANT LADY (PRC, June) William Beaudine; *genre:* Drama; *location:* United States; *coding:* Blk, AF-A, Bonds; *relevance:* 1.

A woman doctor (Rose Hobart) escapes from the southern prison where she had been incarcerated following her conviction for a mercy killing. She finally clears her name by rescuing several people injured in a bus accident. In the town where she has taken refuge there are several War Bonds posters in shop windows.

521 THE GAY SISTERS (WB, Aug) Irving Rapper; *genre:* Drama; *locations:* United States, France; *coding:* Brit, WWI, AF-Raf, AF-A, V; *relevance:* 1.5.

Three sisters—Barbara Stanwyck, Nancy Coleman, and Geraldine Fitzgerald—refuse to sell their old New York mansion to make way for an entertainment complex. The story is framed by events that take place in both the First World War (their mother went down on the *Lusitania* and their father was killed in France while fighting with the A.E.F.) and the Second World War. One of the sisters (Fitzgerald), who had returned to America because she was bored with her English husband, goes back to Britain after learning of his death while flying in combat with the RAF.

522 GEORGE WASHINGTON SLEPT HERE (WB, Nov) William Keighley; *genre:* Comedy; *location:* United States; *coding:* Short, Home Def, Blk, Hist Am, FDR-E, US-Brit Coop; *relevance:* 1.5.

A New York City couple move from their high rise apartment to a dilapidated colonial era farmhouse. The rest of the film centers around their costly restoration efforts. There are several references to the war. When the husband, played by Jack Benny, first observes the home his wife (Ann Sheridan) had purchased he sarcastically inquires: "When did you buy this house—during a blackout?"

523 GET HEP TO LOVE (Univ, Oct) Charles Lamont; *genre:* Musical Comedy; *location:* United States; *coding:* Juv, AF-AC, Short; *relevance:* 1.

Little Doris Stanley (Gloria Jean), an adolescent concert singer, finds herself in a foundling home after fleeing from her money-grubbing aunt. She finagles her adoption by a childless rich couple from a small town in Massachusetts. While detectives search the country for her, Doris becomes actively involved in the local high school scene. She sets her romantic sights on jalopy-driving, jive-talking Jimmy Arnold (Donald O'Connor). When he ruins a hard-to-replace tire, she serenades him with a song entitled "Let's Hitch A Horse To The Automobile." The war-related lyrics include the following: "Our nation needs its gasoline; the situation's pretty keen; so hitch your auto to a horse." It is later determined that the aunt has no legal rights over Doris.

524 GIRL TROUBLE (TCF, Oct) Harold Schuster; *genre:* Comedy; *location:* United States; *coding:* AF-A, Home Fr, Short, Brit, Bonds, Latin Am, Prod; *relevance:* 2.

Don Ameche is a Venezuelan playboy named Pedro Sullivan who travels to New York to obtain a loan for his rubber plantation. He rents an apartment from a beautiful socialite (Joan Bennett) who poses as the maid. Despite its numerous topical references, the OWI complained that the film displayed a rather lackadaisical attitude toward the war. Even the *MPH* trade review noted that *Girl Trouble* contains "overdrawn portraits of the idle rich in the war effort." Pedro almost loses the loan for the expansion of production of a strategic raw material because of the personal whims of a rich leader of the rubber industry.

525 GIVE OUT, SISTERS (Univ, Sept) Edward F. Cline; *genre:* Musical Comedy; *location:* United States; *coding:* Short; *relevance:* 1.

A group of kids from a dancing school, including an heiress (Grace McDonald), is pressed into service at a nightclub. The Andrews Sisters play the three disapproving spinster aunts of the young heiress! A topical crack is made about the rich teenaged girl being "worth her weight in rubber." It is indicated in the credits that one of the numbers performed in this jitterbug musical was co-written by a Pvt. Sid Robbins.

526 GRAND CENTRAL MURDER (MGM, May) S. Sylvan Simon; *genre:* Crime; *location:* United States; *coding:* AF-Ger, Blk; *relevance:* 1.

Between train departures and arrivals, a murder is committed and solved at New York's Grand Central Station. Van Heflin is the detective hero, and Virginia Grey is his wife. In response to a personal threat, Grey retorts: "You and what Panzer division?" Otherwise, there are no overt war references.

527 THE GREAT IMPERSONATION (Univ, Dec) John Rawlins; *genre:* Spy; *locations:* Africa, Germany, Britain, France; *coding:* Intell Serv, AF-Ger, AF-Brit, Hitler, Spy-Sab, Home Def, Hess, Collab, Blk, Nazi, Brit, AF-Brit, Austr, Fr; *relevance:* 3.

In French West Africa, immediately prior to the outbreak of war, a dissolute English aristocrat named Sir Edward Dominey is rescued by a look-alike German baron (both characters are played by Ralph Bellamy). When hostilities begin, the baron decides to kill Dominey, report to espionage headquarters in Berlin with a proposal to impersonate the British peer, and then proceed to Britain. Back in England, the seemingly rehabilitated Dominey returns to his wife (Evelyn Ankers) and, through her family's connections, is given a high position in the Home Defense department. He soon receives instructions from the Nazi spy leader in Britain to make contact with the underground pro–German movement in Scotland. A jealous former lover of the baron's (now also a German spy) tips off British Intelligence, but Dominey convinces them that *he* killed the German aristocrat and that he is impersonating the baron in order to expose German agents operating in Britain. Dominey is allowed to take a copy of the Home Guard's defense plans to Germany. Convinced they can succeed with their invasion plans, the Germans arrange to send

Rudolph Hess on a secret mission to organize the "Quislings" in Britain. After the information concerning Hess' capture is leaked to the press, Dominey is forced to make a daring escape from Germany. E. Phillips Oppenheim's 1920 novel had been filmed twice before, most recently by Universal in 1935, with Edmund Lowe as the star.

528 HALFWAY TO SHANGHAI (Univ, Sept) John Rawlins; *genre:* Spy; *locations:* Burma, Shanghai; *coding:* Am Vol, Collab, AF-Brit, US-Chi Coop, Hitler, Nazi, UN, War Corr, Spy-Sab, Brit, Chi; *relevance:* 3.

On a train headed for Rangoon, two Gestapo agents, Zerta and Otto, are pursuing a renegade Nazi spy. In the spy's possession is a map showing the locations of China's munitions dumps along the Burma Road. Baxton (Kent Taylor), an American engineer working on the Burma Road, and Vicki (Irene Hervey), an old flame whom he had met two years earlier in Shanghai, provide the romantic angle. Zerta murders the man with the map, receiving unexpected aid from a pro–Nazi American newspaperwoman. Burma's colonial police kill the Gestapo agents, recover the map and arrest the Hitler-loving female as an "enemy of the United Nations." The United Nations was a term coined by FDR that originally referred to the international coalition fighting the Axis— *not* to the world organization that was chartered in 1945. The OWI was not displeased with this film, but regretted the "silly, giggling" characterizations of the Chinese.

529 HAYFOOT (UA, Jan) Fred Guiol; *genre:* Training/Comedy; *location:* United States; *coding:* AF-A; *relevance:* 1.5.

Largely due to his photographic memory, Private Dodo Doubleday (William Tracy) of *Tanks a Million* (UA, 1941), *About Face*, and *Fall In*, q.v., is promoted to Top Sergeant. This particularly chagrins regular Army sergeants Ames and Cobbs. When they discover Doubleday has an aversion to guns, the two veteran non-coms perceive a chance to discredit the new sergeant before the colonel and his pretty daughter. The usual shenanigans follow, with Dodo eventually outwitting his rivals.

530 HELLO ANNAPOLIS (Col, Apr) Charles Barton; *genre:* Training; *location:* United States; *coding:* Mil School; Prod; WWI; FDR, Nazi, AF-N; *relevance:* 1.

In the immediate prewar years, two midshipmen—one from a wealthy shipbuilding family (Tom Brown) and the other an enlisted man (Larry Parks) who has won an appointment to the Academy—compete for the affections of a Navy brat (Jean Parker). She favors the richer of the two, Bill. Nonetheless, Bill is not fully acceptable to her until he loses his cynical attitude towards service

life. This attitude leads to his being "silenced" by the entire student body. In one scene, Bill's roommates ignore him while listening to an FDR radio speech in which the president condemns the "Nazis." The Columbia Press Sheet touted the studio's research into the use of Annapolis "slanguage" in the film's dialogue. For instance, local girls are referred to as "crabs."

531 HER CARDBOARD LOVER (MGM, June) George Cukor; *genre:* Comedy; *location:* United States; *coding:* Ger?, Latin Am, Blk; *relevance:* 1.

A beautiful but enigmatic lady (Norma Shearer) hires an infatuated song writer (Robert Taylor), who has gone into debt at a gambling casino, to pose as her lover in order to make her fiancé (George Sanders) jealous. The two men eventually come to blows in a hotel basement after finding themselves together in an elevator. The night manager excitedly tells the house dick: "There's a blitzkrieg in the basement."

532 HERE WE GO AGAIN (RKO, Oct) Allan Dwan; *genre:* Comedy; *location:* United States; *coding:* AF-A, Latin Am, Vet?, Brit, Home Fr, Bonds, Short, Draft, Blk, WWI, Prod; *relevance:* 2.

Fibber and Molly McGee (Jim and Marian Jordan) go on a second honeymoon at the expensive Silver Tip Lodge. Fibber's typical bungling lands them in the bridal suite, for which he has insufficient funds. Meanwhile, scientist Edgar Bergen and his wooden sidekick, Charlie McCarthy, are camping nearby while conducting a search for a rare silk-producing moth. To avoid being exposed as a deadbeat by Molly's ex-beau Otis Cadwalader (Harold Peary), Fibber agrees to use his friendship with Bergen to persuade the eccentric scientist to invest in a synthetic gas formula developed by Otis. The gas substitute ruins engines and the moth's silk turns out to be brittle. But when the formula is accidentally spilt on the moth silk—! There are numerous topical references in this lightweight comedy featuring a number of popular radio stars. The motion picture's plot resembles that of *Miss Annie Rooney*, released earlier in the year by United Artists.

533 HI, NEIGHBOR (Rep, July) Charles Lamont; *genre:* Musical Comedy; *location:* United States; *coding:* Blk, Short, Home Def; *relevance:* 1.

The kids attending a backwoods agricultural college alienate their wealthy benefactress. Therefore, in order to raise the funds needed for the construction of new buildings, they decide to convert the campus into a resort during the summer break. Birdie, a black maid, makes one of only a few war references with the following exclamation relating to the critical rubber shortage: "Bless my hand-me-down girdle." Jean Parker and John Archer were the adult leads.

534 HIGHWAYS BY NIGHT (RKO, Oct) Peter Godfrey; *genre:* Drama; *location:* United States; *coding:* Latin Am, AF-N, Short, Prod; *relevance:* 1.5.

Tommy Van Steel (Richard Carlson) is a sober, intelligent and very wealthy young man who refuses to involve himself in the ordinary business matters of the Van Steele motorboat works. While Tommy doodles with the plans of a new engine for naval "mosquito boats," worldly Uncle Ben informs his nephew that he needs to acquire the "common touch." After a night on the town, a hungover Tommy finds himself in a ditch wearing the clothes of a murdered gangster. He hitches a ride with a young woman (Jane Randolph) whose family owns a small trucking business. Tommy goes to work for them as a wage earner. He later helps the truckers overcome some gangsters, including the one who had killed the man whose identity he had assumed. Tommy, having proven himself to be a regular guy, now plans to marry right away, since he will be entering the U. S. Navy in a couple of weeks.

535 HILLBILLY BLITZKREIG (Mono, Aug) Roy Mack; *genre:* Comedy; *location:* United States; *coding:* Spy-Sab, Short, Ger, Jap, AF-A, Prod; *relevance:* 2.5.

Ornery hillbilly Private Snuffy Smith (Bud Duncan) accompanies his long suffering sergeant, Homer Gatling (Edgar Kennedy), on a detail to the Smokey Mountains of Tennessee. They have been assigned to guard a new rocket invention of interest to the Army. Ekkers, the head of a Nazi spy ring, orders his agent Marlene to acquire the rocket's plans by vamping the overweight Snuffy. She returns, instead, with the plans for a whiskey still! Led personally by Ekkers, the spies proceed to the barn where the rocket model is being kept. After the Nazi agents are rounded up, Snuffy and the sergeant are accidentally launched while sitting astride the rocket: "Next stop, Tokyo!" This appalling film, based on the characters from the *Barney Google* comic strip (still running, but now under the *Snuffy Smith* name), provoked the following comment from the OWI: "If we want foreign peoples to receive a true picture of the U. S. Army, we shall not export this film."

536 HOLIDAY INN (Para, June*) Mark Sandrich; *genre:* Musical; *location:* United States; *coding:* Hist Am, Blk, Prod, AF-?; *relevance:* 1.5.

Fred Astaire and Bing Crosby were teamed for the first time in this summertime smash hit about two showbiz pals and their ongoing competition for their female counterparts

(Marjorie Reynolds and Virginia Dale). Irving Berlin composed the dozen or so numbers for the film, including the war-oriented "Song of Freedom," and the Oscar-winning "White Christmas." The latter piece would appear to have uniquely evoked wartime America's nostalgia for the mythic rural past in a peacetime USA.

537 HOME IN WYOMIN' (Rep, Apr) William Morgan; *genre:* Western; *location:* United States; *coding:* Bonds; *relevance:* 1.5.

Western music radio star Gene Autry returns to his Wyoming home town to assist a friend with his rodeo. While there, Gene also solves a couple of murders. The film opens with an extended scene in a New York broadcasting studio as Autry sings Irving Berlin's "Any Bonds Today?": "Here comes the freedom man / Can't make tomorrow's plan / Not unless you buy a share of freedom today." Republic studios proudly promoted their singing cowboy as the first motion picture star to aid the United States Bond campaign by directly plugging bonds in a feature film.

538 HOUSE OF ERRORS (PRC, Apr) Bernard B. Ray; *genre:* Comedy; *location:* United States; *coding:* Prod, Short, Vet, Brit?; *relevance:* 2.

In his final starring role in a feature film, Harry Langdon plays one of two newspaper delivery "boys" (the other is Charles Rogers) who are fired for incompetence. They try to be reporters and attempt to get a story about the inventor of a new machine gun. Posing as a valet and butler in order to gain access to the inventor's home, the two suffer various domestic misadventures. These include an encounter with some thieves who are interested in the gun's prototype, kept in the laboratory. In one scene reflecting wartime shortages, Harry's character is portrayed surreptitiously opening a concealed library safe containing sugar cubes for his coffee.

539 I LIVE ON DANGER (Para, July*) Sam White; *genre:* Crime; *location:* United States; *coding:* Brit, V, War Corr, Iceland; *relevance:* 1.5.

Chester Morris plays a radio reporter angling for a coveted war correspondent assignment in London. However, his competitor for the spot has the edge because of his "scoop on the occupation of Iceland" (American troops began relieving the British garrison in July 1941). Morris gets his chance to make an impression on the boss after he stumbles upon a murder plot. When he is awarded the London job, his assistant, comically attired as an air raid warden, flashes the "V for victory" sign. But Morris turns the assignment down so that he can help absolve his girlfriend's brother of the murder charge.

540 I WAS FRAMED (WB, Apr) D.

Ross Lederman; *genre:* Crime; *location:* United States; *coding:* AF-N, Blk, Short, AF-A; *relevance:* 1.

A big city newspaper reporter (Michael Ames) is framed and placed in jail for attempting to expose a crooked mayoral candidate. He escapes and is ultimately absolved by the law. In the small town where he settles under an assumed name, a little girl is always playing war games. A man says to her: "Too bad you aren't a boy, so you could join Uncle Sam's army when you grow up."

541 ICE CAPADES REVUE (Rep, Dec) Bernard Vorhaus; *genre:* Musical Comedy; *location:* United States; *coding:* Ref, Short, Draft, V, AF-A, AF-CG, AF-AC, AF-N, AF-MC, Czech; *relevance:* 2.

Ann, a pretty New England farm girl (Ellen Drew) inherits a nearly bankrupt ice show from her late uncle. With the supposed backing of an astrology nut, played by Jerry Colonna, they go to Ann's farm to rehearse. The female star, Czech skater Vera Hruba, in an obvious allusion to the war, solemnly informs Ann that this is her chance to start all over in a new country. With unpaid creditors planning to foreclose, the skaters manage to put on a show that so impresses the president of the Rink Manager's Association that they are awarded a major contract. The finale is a military-inspired display featuring a medley of martial tunes. As five men dressed in the uniforms of each of the services enter the rink, the skaters execute an elaborate routine ending with a V formation (cf *Iceland*, q.v.).

542 ICELAND (TCF, Oct) H. Bruce Humberstone; *genre:* Musical Comedy; *location:* Iceland; *coding:* Draft, AF-A, AF-N, AF-MC, Iceland, FDR, V; *relevance:* 2.

The U. S. Marines land in Iceland and are warmly greeted by the natives. As they march through the streets of Reykjavik, the Sammy Kaye orchestra's female vocalist sings "You Can't Say No To A Soldier." The suggestive lyrics are concluded by a gravel-voiced male singer: "So you better give in if you want them to win—for you." Katina, a local girl played by Sonja Henie, embraces this musical advice and relentlessly pursues a handsome Marine corporal (John Payne). Following the inevitable nuptials, Katina performs a skating finale that includes a V formation, accompanied by the Marine Corps Hymn and a concluding chorus of "Let's Bring New Glory To Old Glory." The Marines were first sent to Iceland in July 1941; they were replaced by a U.S. Army division in March 1942.

543 INSIDE THE LAW (PRC, May) Hamilton MacFadden; *genre:* Comedy/Drama; *location:* United States; *coding:* Bonds; *relevance:* 1.

A group of crooks, under the tutelege of Wallace Ford, arrange for some of the gang to be employed in a small town bank they plan to rob. In the process, they discover its vaults are virtually empty. To remedy the situation the gangsters come up with various schemes to get the locals to deposit cash in the bank. At one point the bank's owner admonishes his fellow citizens: "Don't forget to buy Defense Bonds." The $70,000 deposited disappears, but is later returned after some of the mob "get religion" while attending a church service.

544 INVISIBLE AGENT (Univ, July) Edwin Marin; *genre:* Spy/Fantasy; *locations:* United States, Germany, Britain; *coding:* AF-Brit?, Intell Serv, Ger, AF-Raf, AF-Chi, AF-Ger, Fr, Den, Nor, Neth, Dipl, Free Fr?, US-Brit Coop, Hitler, Nazi, Hess, Tojo, Jap, Spy-Sab, FBI, Resist, Russ, Goering, Goebbels, Jap-Ger Coop, Pearl Harb, Atroc; *relevance:* 3.

An American, Frank Raymond (Jon Hall), possesses a secret invisibility formula. He is prevailed upon by Allied leaders to parachute into Germany for the purpose of obtaining vital information. Frank is assisted by a beautiful blonde (Ilona Massey) working for British Intelligence, and by the German resistance. J. Edward Bromberg plays a fat, cowardly Nazi martinet obsessed both with Massey and his own self-promotion. In his invisible state, Frank is able to outwit malicious Gestapo and Japanese agents, destroy German bombers poised for a one-way raid upon New York City (a Spring 1942 *Life* magazine article had portrayed a possible German bombing raid upon the East Coast), and escape to England with a list of Axis agents operating in America. Several incidents in the film portray distrust between the Axis partners, culminating in Japan's Baron Akito (Peter Lorre) killing his Nazi counterpart (Sir Cedric Hardwicke) for losing the list of agents' names.

545 ISLE OF MISSING MEN (Mono, Sept) Richard Oswald; *genre:* Crime; *location:* Pacific; *coding:* Blk?, AF-Jap, AF-N, Atroc-Conc, Ref, Austr, Jap; *relevance:* 2.

The S.S. *Bombay* is somewhere in the Pacific heading for the penal island of Caruba. Passengers include a lady "who never gives a hint that she was in Rangoon when the Japs bombed it flat" (Jan.-Feb. 1942) and an elderly Austrian refugee writer named Heller. He is later killed when a Japanese plane makes a bombing run on the ship. The heroine (Helen Gilbert), the wife of a convict on Caruba, is planning to help her husband escape. But she falls in love with the governor (John Howard) of the island. Her husband is conveniently killed while endeavoring to escape aboard a freighter that carries a war cargo.

546 IT HAPPENED IN FLATBUSH (TCF, May*) Ray McCarey; *genre:* Comedy; *location:* United States; *coding:* AF-A?; *relevance:* 1.

Lloyd Nolan plays Maguire, a baseball manager with a checkered past who leads the Brooklyn Dodgers to the World Series' championship, with the aid of a rookie ballplayer (George Holmes). A typically rambunctious Brooklyn altercation over an umpire's call leads to a courtroom scene. Maguire delivers the following war-related plea to the judge: "Can we punish a man for displaying a spirit that the whole country could use today—the spirit of patriotism? Mr. O'Doul isn't just a citizen of Brooklyn, he's a good American. He doesn't see in Shaughnessy here just a man with whom he's had a quarrel. No—he sees in him an enemy of the community, a rat.... Don't forget, judge, if Brooklyn were invaded by an enemy tomorrow, it's men like O'Doul who'd be the first in the barricades to defend it."

547 JOAN OF OZARK (Rep, Aug) Joseph Santley; *genre:* Spy/Comedy; *location:* United States; *coding:* AF-A, Atroc-Conc, Free Fr, Vichy, Den, Nor, Pol, Czech, Russ, Brit, Belg, Fr, Grk, V, Postwar, Hist Am, Draft, Spy-Sab, Collab, Blk, Jew?, Nazi, Hitler, Goebbels, Himmler, Hirohito, Jap, AF-Jap, Jap-Ger-Ital Coop, AF-Ger, Short, Prod, Fem Lab; FBI, Ital; *relevance:* 2.5.

Mountain girl Judy Hull (Judy Canova) inadvertently shoots a pigeon carrying a secret message from a couple of Axis agents posing as hillbillies. When Judy turns it in to the FBI she is hailed by the press as "Public Patriot No. 1." A Nazi spy leader who operates the swanky Club 76 as a front, sends an unwitting theatrical agent (Joe E. Brown) to the sticks to sign up Judy as an entertainer. The Nazi wants to liquidate the girl. Other members of the spy ring include a foolish Italian and a sinister Japanese; the latter is arrested following an attempt to kill Judy on the day she arrives in town. Judy becomes a hit when she makes her stage debut on July 4th singing a war-related number: "Lady From Lockheed." Judy later muffs the official christening of a new bomber on its maiden flight. Learning the champagne bottle has been filled with explosives by the enemy agents, Judy flies up in a second plane to retrieve the dangling, unbroken bottle. She then drops the glass bomb on a Japanese submarine that just happens to be cruising below on the surface.

548 JOAN OF PARIS (RKO, Feb) Robert Stevenson; *genre:* War Drama; *locations:* France, Britain; *coding:* AF-Ger, Fr, AF-Raf, Free Fr, Hitler, Nazi, Resist, Atroc, Spy-Sab; *relevance:* 3.

A young Parisian barmaid (Michele Morgan), whose patron saint is Joan of Arc, aids a stranded Free French flyer (Paul Henreid) and his four RAF companions (including Alan Ladd) to escape the Gestapo in occupied France (in real life, helping downed Allied airmen escape capture and imprisonment was a major function of the Resistance in France in the early years of the war). In order to accomplish this, she makes contact with the underground, led by an elderly female British agent (May Robson, then in her 80s, in her final film role). With the Nazis closing in, Joan patriotically diverts the Gestapo chief away from the flyers, knowing it will lead to a firing squad for herself. The hulking, menacing head of the Gestapo, played by Laird Cregar, is appropriately named Herr Funk. This film has some similarities with *Nurse Edith Cavell* (RKO, 1939.)

549 JOE SMITH, AMERICAN (MGM, Feb) Richard Thorpe; *genre:* War Drama; *location:* United States; *coding:* Prod, V, Spy-Sab, FBI?, Hist Am, Nazi?, AF-AC, AF-Raf, AF-A, Atroc, Draft, Nor, Austria, Chi; *relevance:* 3.

Prior to America's entrance into the war, Joe Smith, the average working man (portrayed by Robert Young), is employed at an aircraft plant. He is selected to work in a segregated section of the factory on a top-secret bombsight. One evening, Joe is kidnapped by foreign agents. In a darkened house on the outskirts of town, his faceless inquisitors first offer Joe a bribe, then grill him mercilessly, and finally torture the worker for his technical information. To withstand the pain, Joe concentrates on happy memories of his family—meeting the woman he would marry (Marsha Hunt), the birth of his son, and so on. He is also inspired by the his son's earlier references to Nathan Hale, a hero of the American Revolution. Joe makes his escape when the frustrated agents take him out of the house with the intent of killing him. Joe's ability to recall minute details, such as certain noises he heard while traveling blindfolded, facilitates the capture of the spies. The leader of the ring turns out to be one of the executives at the aircraft plant. There are several points of interest in this film: made before Pearl Harbor, it never specifically identifies the spies' origin (Noel Madison is billed on the credits as "Schricker," a Germanic name, but is not called by this name in the film itself). However, in an interesting touch, the letter "N" on a car's hubcap (for Nash, a manufacturer of the period) spins when the car is driven and takes on the appearance of a swastika. Joe himself is identified as the American-born son of Norwegian and Austrian parents, both countries under Nazi domination at the time of the film's release.

550 JOHNNY DOUGHBOY (Rep, Dec) John H. Auer; *genre:* Musical Comedy; *location:* United States; *coding:* Juv?, WWI, AF-A, FDR, MacArthur, Bonds, V, USO; *relevance:* 2.

When young film star Ann Winters (Jane Withers) turns sixteen and is signed by her agent to yet another juvenile role, she runs away. Penelope, the president of an Ann Winters fan club, arrives in Hollywood and since she is Ann's exact double, is pressed into service by the desperate agent. Penelope is approached by a group of the star's friends who are organizing an entertainment show for servicemen dubbed the "Junior Victory Caravan." Penelope, realizing the value of the show to the war effort, cajoles Ann's confidante into revealing the star's whereabouts. She travels to the mountain lodge hideaway and persuades Ann to do her patriotic duty.

551 JOURNEY FOR MARGARET (MGM, Dec) W.S. Van Dyke; *genre:* War Drama; *locations:* Britain, United States; *coding:* Juv, Munich, AF-Raf, Dipl, Ref, Fr, Neth, Czech, Austria, Jap, Ital, AF-Ger, Hitler, Nazi, Ethiopia, Span Civ, War Corr, Brit, Pearl Harb, Home Def; *relevance:* 3.

American war correspondent Johnny Herbert (Robert Young) and his pregnant wife (Laraine Day) escape the fall of France, only to be subjected to the dangers of the German blitz of London during the Battle of Britain (July–October 1940). Johnny's wife returns alone to the United States after suffering a miscarriage resulting from injuries received during a bombing raid. A hardened Johnny visits a war orphan's home for a story. But it is only when he witnesses a crazed mother clutching her dead child amidst another Luftwaffe attack, that Johnny gets truly "mad" at the Nazis. He becomes involved in the lives of two homeless children traumatized by the war. The little boy and girl are inseparable, so Johnny adopts both before flying back to America. The film introduced the movie-going public to a five-year-old actress named Margaret O'Brien. This film was based on a book by correspondent William L. White, which told the true story of his experiences during the Blitz.

552 JUNGLE SIREN (PRC, Aug) Sam Newfield; *genre:* Adventure; *location:* Africa; *coding:* Jap, AF-AC?, Blk, Hitler, Nazi, Degaulle, AF-Free Fr, Spy-Sab, Collab; *relevance:* 2.

Captain Gary Hart (Buster Crabbe) and Sergeant Mike Jenkins (from Brooklyn—played by Paul Bryar) are American engineers with the Free French army in Africa. They are sent into the interior to conduct a survey for an Allied airfield and to foil the activities of the local native chief, a known "Nazi Quisling." Herr Lukas, the Hitler-loving German agent in the area, manipulates the fat ignorant chief into sabotaging the American's efforts and threatening their lives. With the aid of a swarthy sarong-clad native girl named Kuhlaya, played by real-life stripper Ann Corio, the heroes are eventually able to successfully complete their mission.

553 JUNIOR ARMY (Col, Nov) Lew Landers; *genre:* War Drama; *location:* United States; *coding:* AF-Ger?, Juv, WWI, Mil School, Hist Am, Draft, Draft Avoid, Ref, Spy-Sab, Collab, Brit, Blk, Nazi, Home Fr, Prod-Farm, AF-A, AF-N; *relevance:* 2.

A well-educated teenaged English refugee, Freddie Hewlett (Freddie Bartholomew), befriends a tough gang kid named Jimmie Fletcher (Billy Halop). Freddie suffers from a fear of airplanes—his parents were killed in the Blitz, and he was trapped in the rubble of his home for two days. Freddie shelters Jimmie from the law and then uses his influence to have the ruffian admitted with him to the Pearson Military Academy. Jimmie resists the discipline and spirit of the academy, and deserts when threatened with a court martial. While on the run, he encounters his draft-dodging former gang leader (Huntz Hall) accompanied by an escaped Nazi saboteur ("landed from a submarine"). They try to force Jimmie to help them steal the school's training plane to facilitate their escape. His patriotism finally aroused, Jimmie heroically assists in the capture of the villains. The "Junior Army" of the title does not refer to the military school, but to another organization, glimpsed only briefly. In mid 1942, the High School Victory Corps was organized to encourage secondary school activities designed to promote the war effort.

554 JUST OFF BROADWAY (TCF, Sept) Herbert I. Leeds; *genre:* Crime; *location:* United States; *coding:* Home Fr, Chi, Jap; *relevance:* 1.

Private detective Michael Shayne (Lloyd Nolan) is a member of a sequestered jury trying a woman for murder. One evening he sneaks out of the jury room and, in collaboration with a girl reporter covering the story, is able to track down crucial information pertaining to the case. On several occasions Shayne admonishes individuals not to divulge something by invoking the ubiquitous war-inspired rhyme: "A Slip of the Lip Might Sink a Ship." With apparently unintended irony re its racial implications, a tour guide on a trip through Chinatown states: "See that license in the window? That's a Jap-hunting license." Signs offering a license to kill Japanese actually appeared in America in 1942, particularly on the West Coast.

555 KEEPER OF THE FLAME (MGM, Dec) George Cukor; *genre:* Drama; *location:* United States; *coding:* Atroc-Conc, WWI, Hist Am, Hitler, Ger, Fr, Pol, War Corr, Jew, Blk, Spy-Sab; *relevance:* 2.

In the period before Pearl Harbor: Steven O'Malley (Spencer Tracy), a jaded foreign correspondent just back from war-torn Europe, joins the crowd of reporters gathered at a rural hotel to cover the death of a great American politician whom he admired, Robert Forrest. With some difficulty, O'Malley wrangles a personal interview with Forrest's enigmatic widow Christine (Katherine Hepburn). He pierces her initial reticence, only to learn that Forrest's Forward America Association was actually a subversive fascist organization: "When I first married him he was as much a part of this country as Lincoln.... But he envied the dictators and thought that all governments of the people and by the people were soon to perish from the earth." She reluctantly agrees to allow O'Malley to print the truth about her late husband (including the fact that she bears some responsibility for his death in a car wreck). In response to her concern regarding its potentially negative impact upon the American people, O'Malley asserts: "He was their enemy, and they must know it.... They want the truth, and they can take it." Christine is murdered by her late husband's secretary (a proto-fascist himself), and the film ends with a montage of O'Malley's articles and his book about Claire. This very dark and atmospheric film is shot in a pseudo-Gothic style.

556 KID GLOVE KILLER (MGM, Apr) Fred Zinnemann; *genre:* Crime; *location:* United States; *coding:* AF-AC, Latin Am, Fem Lab, Prod; *relevance:* 1.

A crime lab scientist (Van Heflin) and his female assistant (Marsha Hunt) exploit the latest technology to discover the person who murdered the city's reform mayor with a car bomb. The killer, the scientist's best friend and rival for his assistant's love, had been compromised by an association with gangsters. The two scientists start working on a new case, whose victim was bludgeoned to death by his sweetheart—a female blacksmith at a plane factory.

557 KLONDIKE FURY (Mono, Mar) William K. Howard; *genre:* Adventure; *location:* United States; *coding:* WWI, Russ, US-Russ Coop, *relevance:* 1.

Doctor John Mandre (Edmund Lowe), a brain surgeon, is discredited after the death of a patient during a delicate operation. Having served as a pilot during World War I, he joins the civilian-manned airplane ferrying service shuttling military aircraft destined for the Soviet Union to Alaska (in real life, these duties were carried out by the Ferry Division of the Air Transport Command). On a return flight the doctor crashes in the Klondike. Mandre is picked up and taken to an isolated trading post. Before leaving, he performs the same delicate brain surgery in order to save a local man with a severe head injury. Eight airfields between North Dakota and Fairbanks, Alaska were established during World War II to ferry Lend Lease planes to the Russians. By the end of hostilities, Soviet pilots had taken delivery of over 8000 American aircraft flown to Alaska by civilian pilots.

558 LADY FROM CHUNGKING (PRC, Dec) William Nigh; *genre:* Resist Drama; *location:* China; *coding:* Ger, Postwar, Atroc, Hirohito, Jap, AF-Jap, Russ, Chiang, Chi, FDR, Hitler, Vichy, AF-FT, Resist, Pearl Harb; *relevance:* 3.

A Chinese noblewoman, Kwan Mei (Anna May Wong), her true identity concealed, works as a peasant in the rice fields by day and leads Chinese guerrillas by night. The guerrillas protect two downed American pilots of the Flying Tigers and later help them escape from the Japanese-occupied area. Kwan Mei exploits her feminine wiles, with the added aid of a bottle of French champagne (from Vichy), to inveigle the cruel and puerile Japanese General Kaimura (Harold Huber) into discussing details of troop train movements in preparation for a planned assault on Chungking, China's wartime capital. With this information, the two American airmen are able to direct a Flying Tiger raid upon the train. Kwan Mei fatally wounds the general, who, in turn, orders her execution. Kwan Mei begins to speak defiantly, and even after she is shot, her disembodied spirit rises and declares that "You cannot kill me. You cannot kill China.... for the soul of China is eternal. When I die, a million will take my place ... China's destiny is victory ... out of the ashes of ruin and old hatreds, the force of peace will prevail." This film also portrays an obsequious German businessman dealing with the Japanese (and selling guns to the Chinese guerrillas at the same time) and contains an oblique allusion to the Russo-Japanese Neutrality Pact (which went into effect in April 1941 and was scrupulously observed by both parties until August 1945): an "entertainer" (Mae Clarke) tells General Kaimura that her mother was American and her father was Russian. "Officially, that is no good," he replies.

559 LADY GANGSTER (WB, June) Florian Roberts; *genre:* Crime; *location:* United States; *coding:* Blk, Hitler, Atroc-Conc, AF-A, AF-AC; *relevance:* 1.

A failed young actress named Dot (Faye Emerson) becomes involved with mobsters in a bank heist. She is apprehended, but not before the loot is hidden. Dot winds up in women's prison. During the trial she falls in love with the handsome district attorney (Frank Wilcox). One of her hard-boiled prison mates comments: "I'd play [ball] with anybody but Hitler to get out of this hole." Robert Florey directed this film under a pseudonym.

560 THE LADY HAS PLANS (Para, Jan*) Sidney Lanfield; *genre:* Spy; *locations:* United States, Portuguese; *coding:* Ger, Dipl, AF-Raf, Intell Serv, US-Brit Coop, Collab, AF-N, Nazi, Spy-Sab, V, FBI, Brit, War Corr; *relevance:* 3.

American racketeers steal some naval plans and have them copied in invisible ink onto the back of Rita Lenox (Paulette Goddard). She is to impersonate Sidney Royce (also Paulette Goddard), a well-known newspaperwoman scheduled to fly to neutral Lisbon, take the lady's place on the Clipper and sell the plans to waiting Nazi agents. Things do not work out that way, however, with Sidney innocently arriving in Lisbon to join radio broadcaster Ken Harper (Ray Milland). Sidney is bewildered when she is mysteriously approached by both the Nazi consul and an English diplomat. Ken teams up with the British to rescue Sidney from the late-coming Rita. Before the sinister Nazis are neutralized, they are able to make a photo of Rita's back to be sent to Berlin. But the resourceful Ken had earlier drugged Rita and replaced the plans on her back with "V for Victory." A similar plot device had been used in MGM's 1934 release, *Stamboul Quest*.

561 LADY IN A JAM (Univ, June) Gregory La Cava; *genre:* Comedy; *location:* United States; *coding:* Prod?; *relevance:* 1.

Irene Dunne is a rich young woman who has squandered her fortune. Her financial advisor asks psychiatrist Patric Knowles to study her on the sly, and he signs on as her chauffeur. Dunne and Knowles leave New York to visit Dunne's grandmother in the West. The old lady offers Dunne a share in a gold mine she believes might pay off. Knowles "salts" the mine with gold to bolster Dunne's confidence, but the plot backfires when a gold rush ensues and the government steps in to assay the mine. However, they discover something even more valuable—mercury ore, a vital war material, so Dunne recovers her fortune and becomes romantically involved with Knowles.

562 LARCENY INC. (WB, May) Lloyd Bacon; *genre:* Comedy; *location:* United States; *coding:* V, Short, Bonds; *relevance:* 1.

Fresh out of Sing Sing, three ex-cons are unsuccessful in obtaining a legitimate bank loan to finance a dog track deal. Pressure Maxwell, played with panache by Edward G. Robinson, the brains of the larcenous trio, has an inspiration—buy the luggage shop next door to the bank so that they can tunnel into its vault. Comic complications develop when a fast-talking salesman (Jack Carson) enters their newly acquired store. Promotional gimmicks include a "V for Volume" sale (promotions using the "Victory" motif were very popular during the war, especially in 1942 and 1943).

563 LAUGH YOUR BLUES AWAY (Col, Nov) Charles Barton; *genre:* Comedy; *location:* United States; *coding:* V, Short, Russ; *relevance:* 1.

Radio's bushy-haired "Mad Russian," Bert Gordon, and popular model Jinx Falkenberg are featured in this Columbia B-picture. The story centers around the efforts of a society-conscious matron named Westerly to find a rich mate for her son after he has announced his heretical intentions of obtaining a regular job. With matrimony in mind, Mrs. Westerly throws a posh party for some wealthy western friends with an eligible daughter. When the other invited guests renege, she is forced to hire some actors, including Boris Rascalnikoff (Gordon) posing as a Russian prince. The Westerly doorbell chimes out the Beethoven's Fifth, "... -," the V for Victory theme.

564 LAW OF THE JUNGLE (Mono, Feb) Jean Yarbrough; *genre:* Adventure; *location:* Africa; *coding:* Collab, Intell Serv, Blk, Ger, Spy-Sab, Brit; *relevance:* 2.

Nona Brooks (Arline Judge) sings in a cafe in British Rhodesia owned by a Nazi collaborator. Two foreign agents who have been stirring up trouble among the natives murder a British Intelligence officer who has written a report on their activities. Fearing trouble, Nona flees into the jungle, inadvertently carrying the report in her belongings. She joins a safari led by an American scientist (John King). The Axis agents, determined to retrieve the document, pose as British officials and waylay the expedition at a native village. Fortunately, the explorer's black servant (Mantan Moreland) is a lodge brother of the native chief.

565 LET'S GET TOUGH (Mono, May) Wallace Fox; *genre:* Spy-Crime; *location:* United States; *coding:* Juv, Ger, Intell Serv, Jap, Tojo?, AF-A, AF-N, AF-MC, Nazi, Blk, Chi, FBI?, Jap-Ger Coop, Spy-Sab; *relevance:* 3.

Patriotically aroused by the advent of war, the East Side Kids (including Bobby Jordan, Leo Gorcey, Huntz Hall, and "Sunshine" Sammy Morrison) unsuccessfully try to enlist in the armed services. The dejected kids later break into a Chinese shop, believing it to be owned by a Japanese, and find the corpse of its owner. They are apprehended by the police while exiting the premises. At the same time, Phil (Tom Brown), the older brother of East Side Kid Danny, is meeting with German and Japanese agents in the rear of Matsui's Tea Company. Phil had been dishonorably discharged from the Navy for subversive activities and is now in league with the Axis spy ring. While attempting to make amends to the Chinese shop owner's widow, the Kids stumble upon clues that eventually will lead them to Matsui (Philip Ahn). They penetrate the basement of his business and break up a masked ceremony of the Black Dragon Society. Phil, who is actually working as a double agent, lends a hand.

566 LIFE BEGINS AT 8:30 (TCF, Dec) Irving Pichel; *genre:* Drama; *location:* United States; *coding:* Blk, Hist Am, Russ?, Ital, Spy-Sab; *relevance:* 1.

A once famous actor, played by Monty Woolley, is reduced through alcohol abuse to working as a department store Santa in New York City. He becomes totally dependent upon his club-footed daughter (Ida Lupino) after he is fired on Christmas Eve. Matters become even worse when an Italian restaurant owner arrives with the police to collect a $100-plus liquor tab. After the Italian leaves with his money, Woolley shouts: "When this country is forced to the scorched earth policy, I should like the privilege of putting a match to that man!" His problems are solved when he accepts an offer of marriage from a wealthy admirer. Because of the obvious draft age of the daughter's boyfriend (Cornel Wilde) and the total absence of uniforms in the street scenes, it may be assumed that this film was completed early in the year but its release had been delayed.

567 LITTLE TOKYO, U.S.A. (TCF, Aug) Otto Brower; *genre:* Spy; *locations:* United States, Japan; *coding:* Isolat, Prod, FDR, AF-N, AF-CG, Collab, Ger-Am, Jap-Am Reloc, Atroc, Jap, Hirohito, AF-Jap, Fil, Can, Jap-Ger Coop, Pearl Harb, Spy-Sab, Hitler, Bonds, Home Fr; *relevance:* 3.

Preston Foster plays detective Mike Steele, whose beat is the Japanese section of Los Angeles. Shortly before December 7th, he is warned about fifth columnist activities in the community. He enlists the aid of a loyal Japanese-American (who is then murdered by the spy ring). Steele is soon on the trail of an espionage group that includes ethnic Japanese, a German-American, and an American traitor. When Steele gets too close to the truth, the spies frame him for murder. With the help of a pickpocket friend and a lady radio announcer, Steele is able to escape from jail and confront the spies. Confident that Steele will be killed, the American traitor boasts of his activities. The police rush in and arrest the Axis agents. Steele strikes

the Japanese spy leader (played by Harold Huber), declaiming: "That's for Pearl Harbor! You slant-eyed...." (Note: The OWI reviewer deplored this use of "Gestapo" methods by Steele) In an epilogue, actual newsreel footage is shown of the "mass evacuation" (forced relocation in March 1942) of Japanese-Americans from the West Coast. Steele's girlfriend (Brenda Joyce) delivers an accompanying radio commentary which includes the following apologia inserted at the insistance of the OWI: "Unfortunately, in time of war, the loyal must suffer inconvenience with the disloyal" (the OWI's problems with the script of this film led the government agency to more closely scrutinize Hollywood films in the pre-production stages). Among the film's numerous pejorative racial references are a couple examples of the infamous "so solly" line delivered by a sneering Japanese.

568 THE LIVING GHOST (Mono, Nov) William Beaudine; *genre:* Crime/Horror; *location:* United States; *coding:* Short, Home Def; *relevance:* 1.

Detective Trayne (James Dunn) pursues a madman posing as a doctor, who paralyzes the brains of his victims. The only war references are a crack about the rubber shortage and a signboard outside of a real estate office that reads: "Justice of the Peace, Deputy Sheriff, Air Raid Warden, Realtor."

569 THE LONE RIDER IN CHEYENNE (PRC, Mar) Sam Newfield; *genre:* Western; *location:* United States; *coding:* Pearl Harb, Hist Am, Bonds; *relevance:* 1.

This is a typical low-budget horse opera which appears to take place in the mythical post-Civil War west. However, there is one anachronistic scene in a saloon, as cowboy star George Houston asks the piano player to accompany him while he sings the following: "The West will remember Custer ... and will remember Pearl Harbor.... Buy Defense Bonds.... to avenge December 7th." The crowd at the saloon responds with lively applause. Around the time of this film's release, Defense Bonds (first offered in May 1941) were renamed War Bonds.

570 LUCKY JORDAN (Para, Nov*) Frank Tuttle; *genre:* Crime; *location:* United States; *coding:* Draft Avoid, AF-N, AF-A, Draft, Nazi, FBI, Short, Bonds, USO, Spy-Sab, Collab, Atroc, Aust, AF-W, Ger, Neth, AF-Ger, WWI, Fr, Ital?, Blk, Prod, Jap, Pol; *relevance:* 3.

Alan Ladd plays the title character, a gangster who is drafted into the Army. Lucky goes AWOL, kidnapping a pretty canteen girl (Helen Walker) when she attempts to persuade him to return: "If we lose [the war] we'll end up Nazi slaves." Back in New York City, Lucky discovers his old mob has gone

into the new and more lucrative racket of supplying "foreign lugs" with military information. Lucky remains patriotically indifferent until some Nazis rough up the motherly, gin-swilling old lady who has provided him with a hiding place. When he confronts the Nazis, their sadistic, monocle-wearing leader offers Lucky $100,000 for a report on new tank armor. Lucky spurns them: "Till I ran up against you, Nazi was just a word in the newspapers to me.... Now it's another way to spell cockroach." Lucky is tortured. The FBI arrests the spies and Lucky is allowed to rejoin his Army outfit. The OWI analyst noted that the: "distinction between a Nazi and an American is a Hollywood cliché at the moment.... which ... contains the implication that Nazism could never be an American phenomenon .... [T]hese films.... encourage a dangerous sense of our own immunity, and instill in us a misconception of the enemy."

571 LUCKY LEGS (Col, Oct) Charles Barton; *genre:* Comedy; *location:* United States; *coding:* AF-A, AF-N, AF-MC, Short; *relevance:* 1.

Gloria Carroll (Jinx Falkenberg), a long-legged chorus girl, is bequeathed a million dollars by the playboy who had produced her last show. She is immediately besieged for money by assorted characters. A salesman tells her the cost of a car is "$16,000 — $20,000 with tires." A gangster, from whom the money was actually stolen, tries to retrieve it through trickery. A handsome attorney comes to the rescue and wins Gloria's love. The war-related song "Three Little Sisters" is performed in the show.

572 LURE OF THE ISLANDS (Mono, July) Jean Yarbrough; *genre:* Adventure; *location:* Pacific; *coding:* Laval, Spy-Sab, Draft Avoid, Draft, Jap, Hirohito, AF-Jap, Blk, Vichy?, FBI, Hitler, Nazi, Collab, Jap-Ger Coop, AF-MC; *relevance:* 3.

FBI agents Wally (Robert Lowery) and Jinx (Big Boy Williams) land on the French Pacific island of Tanukai disguised as shipwrecked sailors. They are in search of possible fifth columnist activities. The local commandant (Ivan Lebedeff), who pretends to be French, is actually a Nazi. He and his assistant, Laval (a deliberate reference to Vichy leader Pierre Laval?), are communicating with the Japanese. A half-breed native girl named Tana, played by burlesque queen Margie Hart, helps the boys elude the suspicious commandant and foil the plans for a Japanese aerial landing. Tana even joins the FBI men with a machete to expedite the dispatching of the Japanese commandos who survived the crash of their plane. She calls them "bowlegged baboons." The Japanese officer in charge of the ill-fated assault shoots the commandant in the back when the Nazi refuses to commit suicide. That the FBI had no jurisdiction on French islands in the Pacific was apparently of little consequence to Monogram Pictures.

573 THE MAD MONSTER (PRC, May) Sam Newfield; *genre:* Horror; *location:* United States; *coding:* AF, Prod; *relevance:* 1.

George Zucco plays a crazed scientist who has developed a formula that turns men into wolf monsters. The film opens with the doctor in his lab, ranting about his discovery as images of his detractors appear superimposed on the screen: "Our armed forces are locked in combat with a savage horde who fight with fanatical fury. But that ... will avail them nothing when I place my new serum at the disposal of the War Department." This is never mentioned again, and Zucco's sole wolfman (Glenn Strange) eventually proves his undoing.

574 MADAME SPY (Univ, Dec) Roy William Neill; *genre:* Spy; *locations:* United States, Europ; *coding:* AF-Ger, AF-N, Collab, FBI, Intell Serv, Prod, Jap, Nazi, Spy-Sab, Chi, Brit, Russ, Latin Am, Austral, AF-CG, AF-A, AF-AC, V, WWI; *relevance:* 3.

A famous war correspondent, David Bannister (Don Porter), marries the glamorous Joan (Constance Bennett) while in Europe: the church is bombed as the wedding concludes. David's job takes them on a worldwide tour of various war fronts. The couple's ship is sunk by a German submarine on their return voyage. In New York City, David is concerned about the shady characters with whom his wife associates. David's broadcasts urge the American people to support the war effort. A series of suspicious murders occur. After further investigation, David follows his wife to the farmhouse hideaway of a group of Nazi spies. David is captured but he is saved from execution by the eccentric caretaker (Jimmy Conlin). It is revealed that David's wife is an American counter-intelligence agent who helped round up a spy ring. David and Joan make a final broadcast: "You defeatists, obstructionists, calamity-howlers, watch out. The people aren't going to put up with your kind of sabotage any more."

575 MAISIE GETS HER MAN (MGM, June) Roy Del Ruth; *genre:* Comedy; *location:* United States; *coding:* AF-A, Short, Blk, FDR, USO; *relevance:* 1.5.

Ann Sothern's Maisie series character, a vaudeville trouper, is out of a job after she is almost killed by a temperamental knife thrower. She winds up in Chicago working as a receptionist at a sleazy office building catering to theatrical agents and entrepreneurs of questionable honesty. While there,

she meets a hick (played by Red Skelton), who is trying to break into stand-up comedy. Following an opening night fiasco and a false arrest of the aspiring comedian, Maisie gets back on stage with a tour group doing benefits at Army camps. Guess who is a private in the audience?

576 THE MAJOR AND THE MINOR (Para, Sept*) Billy Wilder; *genre:* Comedy; *location:* United States; *coding:* Hist Am, Juv, AF-Ger, Fr, Neth, Belg, Resist?, AF-A, AF-N, Brit, Mil School, Blk, Pol, Ital, Home Def; *relevance:* 1.5.

Short of funds, Sue Applegate (Ginger Rogers) poses as a pigtailed twelve year old at New York's Grand Central Station to buy a half-fare train ticket back to Iowa. To get past skeptical conductors, little "Susu" enlists the aid of unsuspecting Major Kirby (Ray Milland). He is traveling to the midwest for a teaching assignment at a boys' military academy. During a three day layover at the academy the predictable comic misadventures occur. These include a series of encounters between Susu and her cadet escorts in which the "innocent little Panzer Divisions in sheep's clothing" employ nearly identical sexual gambits by describing the German army's conquest of France. Before she is chased away by the Major's jealous fiancee, Sue is able to finagle his cherished transfer to active duty in the Army. On his way to the West Coast for embarkation to an overseas assignment, the Major makes a stop in Iowa. A printed title situates this film in May 1941; in the opening sequence, Rogers (working for a home hair-treatment company) visits the lecherous Robert Benchley, who tells her his wife is at her "air raid drill" class. "She keeps telling me we're going to get into this war," Benchley adds.

577 THE MALE ANIMAL (WB, Apr) Elliott Nugent; *genre:* Comedy; *location:* United States; *coding:* Blk, Russ, AF-AC, Hist Am, Ital, Latin Am; *relevance:* 2.

A timid English professor (Henry Fonda) at a midwestern university comically overcomes an old romantic rival for his wife while fighting a serious battle with a red-baiting board of directors for the right to read a letter by Bartolomeo Vanzetti (of Sacco and Vanzetti) in his class. In the process, the mini Red Scare of 1939-1940 is repudiated, fascism is condemned and Americanism is reaffirmed: "[In] this muddled world ... we hold the fortress of free thought and free speech." Based on a play by James Thurber and Elliott Nugent.

578 THE MAN IN THE TRUNK (TCF, Oct) Malcolm St. Clair; *genre:* Crime/Comedy; *location:* United States; *coding:* AF-N; *relevance:* 1.

The man in the trunk has been dead for

ten years, the victim of a murder. A chorus girl named Peggy (Lynn Roberts) buys the trunk at an auction; when she later opens it, the ghost of the man (Raymond Walburn) appears. He helps her lawyer boyfriend (George Holmes), who represents the man convicted of the murder, discover the actual killer. At the film's conclusion, the lawyer bids Peggy farewell as he leaves to join the Navy, and says: "Peggy, when I come back, will you dance for me instead of the public?"

579 THE MAN WHO CAME TO DINNER (WB, Jan) William Keighley; *genre:* Comedy; *location:* United States; *coding:* Blk, Ethiopia, FBI, Chi, FDR-E, Churchill, Prod, Fem Lab, AF-A; *relevance:* 1.

An acerbic radio celebrity named Whiteside (a caricature of Alexander Woolcott, played by Monty Woolley) injures himself in a midwestern home while on a lecture tour. Told he will be confined to a wheelchair for several weeks, Whiteside proceeds to apply his malevolent wit in such a manner as to intimidate all those about him (including Bette Davis, Ann Sheridan, and Jimmy Durante). There are numerous comments about contemporary events, as well as references to such familiar personalities as Winston Churchill and Eleanor Roosevelt. After putting up with Whiteside for nearly a month, his harried private nurse (Mary Wickes) declares she is leaving the profession and going to work in a munitions factory.

580 THE MAN WHO WOULDN'T DIE (TCF, May) Herbert I. Leeds; *genre:* Crime; *location:* United States; *coding:* AF-A, Short; *relevance:* 1.

Detective Michael Shayne is hired to pose as the husband of a millionaire's daughter and discover who is attempting to kill off members of the family. The villain turns out to be a supposedly dead man who is in league with the rich man's young second wife. Observing one of the killers with a revolver, Shayne inquires: "Planning to go into the Army?" "No," replies the man, "shooting is only a hobby." There are several other topical references, including some which relate to the tire shortage. For instance, the killer attempts to escape in the local police chief's car. "Take a shot at his tires," Shayne suggests. "*His* tires? Those are *my* tires," the chief says. "Can't get any more."

581 MANILA CALLING (TCF, Oct) Herbert I. Leeds; *genre:* Resist; *location:* Philippines; *coding:* Resist, Pearl Harb, Collab, Russ, Chi, Fil, Hitler, Nazi, Jap, Hirohito, AF-Jap, Atroc, Austria, Ger, Prod, Latin Am, MacArthur, AF-A; *relevance:* 3.

A guerrilla band made up of American radio men and Filipinos—including Lloyd

Nolan, Carole Landis (a stranded entertainer), and Cornel Wilde—becomes isolated on the island of Mindanao by the Japanese conquest of the Philippines. Incensed by the "Jap lies" broadcast over the "Japanese Friendship Station," the guerrillas capture an enemy radio transmitter located on a former American plantation. Resisting several vicious counter-attacks and periodic sniping in which most of the guerrillas are killed, the radio installation is repaired. During the final Japanese assault, the survivors heroically broadcast a message of defiance and encouragement to the people: "We've got to work together. They're doing it in Russia and China and the Balkans. Their guerrillas haven't been stopped yet.... Resist! ... MacArthur promised that he'd be back." This film is crowded with war propaganda, including numerous racial slurs upon the Japanese, such as referring to them as "yellow monkeys."

582 A MAN'S WORLD (Col, Sept) Charles Barton; *genre:* Crime; *locations:* United States, Latin America?; *coding:* Prod, Collab, Short, Spy-Sab, Jap; *relevance:* 2.

After nurse Mona Jackson (Marguerite Chapman) witnesses the gangland murder of one of her patients, she is promptly kidnapped, placed upon a freighter, and dropped off at a remote chromite mining town (in an unnamed country rich in mineral deposits needed for national defense). There, she is more or less under house arrest at a saloon that "entertains" the miners (i.e., a brothel). The other girls immediately ask Mona if she brought any nylons (in short supply during wartime). Blossom (Wynne Gibson), the owner of the establishment, informs Mona that it is their patriotic duty to help the war effort by keeping the miners happy. Later, Blossom agrees to restrict saloon hours so the miners can be rested enough to work. The foreman adds it will help "Take the yap out of the Japs." Some saboteurs at the mine are subsequently discovered and violently dispatched. Mona falls in love with the mine foreman (William Wright) while nursing his wounds.

583 THE MAYOR OF 44TH STREET (RKO, May) Alfred E. Green; *genre:* Crime/Musical; *location:* United States; *coding:* Juv, AF-Jap, FBI, Blk, Chi; *relevance:* 1.

Joe (George Murphy) is the operator of a dance band booking agency whose former proprietor (now in jail) used the business as a front for an extortion racket. Nevertheless, Joe and his girlfriend (Anne Shirley) create a successful legitimate business until teenage hoodlum Bits and his jitterbugging gang start disrupting shows. Life becomes further complicated for Joe when the gangster (former star Richard Barthelmess) is paroled and

seeks to restart his racket with the assistance of Bits. Eventually, even Bits is appalled by the strong arm tactics and allies himself with Joe in order to bring about the gangster's downfall. A newspaper that features a story about the bombing of a dance hall includes an additional front page headline: "3000 Japanese Troops Arrive In China."

584 MEN OF SAN QUENTIN (PRC, May) Martin Mooney, M. King; *genre:* Drama; *location:* United States; *coding:* Bonds, Prod; *relevance:* 1.

A new warden (J. Anthony Hughes) institutes humanitarian reforms at a formerly corrupt prison. There are minor references to the inmates buying bonds and doing vital defense work.

585 MEN OF TEXAS (Univ, July) Ray Enright; *genre:* Western; *location:* United States; *coding:* War Corr?, AF-A, Hist Am; *relevance:* 1.

In the latter half of 1865, the star reporter (Robert Stack) and photographer (Leo Carrillo) for the *Chicago Daily Herald* are sent to Texas to investigate continued civil unrest between Union occupation troops and returning Confederate soldiers. The wartime-influenced flag-waving script (*Variety:* "with undertone of patriotic message apparent throughout the latter half") culminates with a final fadeout as the ghost of Sam Houston proclaims: "Today's America needs men who will defend, not destroy, her unity, her freedom, her democracy."

586 MEXICAN SPITFIRE SEES A GHOST (RKO, June) Leslie Goodwins; *genre:* Comedy; *location:* United States; *coding:* Collab, Blk, Latin Am, Brit, Can; *relevance:* 1.

Leon Errol's dipsomaniacal Lord Epping character is in need of capital. The wealthy Fitzpatten siblings of Canada are interested, but when they arrive in America, Epping has departed for Canada to hunt moose. Uncle Matt, also played by Errol, performs his usual series impersonation of the English lord to keep the Fitzpattens from leaving. While trying to adjust Matt's hairpiece disguise, Carmelita (Lupe Velez) makes a crack about him looking "just like a fifth columnist." Most of the remaining action of the film takes place in a supposedly haunted house (a gang of crooks is operating out of the basement).

587 MEXICAN SPITFIRE'S ELEPHANT (RKO, Sept) Leslie Goodwins; *genre:* Comedy; *location:* United States; *coding:* Ital, Latin Am, Brit, Home Def, Home Fr, UN, Russ, Chi, Neth; *relevance:* 2.

Lord and Lady Epping visit New York City to aid Aunt Della (Elisabeth Risdon) with her war relief drive. Aboard ship they unwittingly become involved with crooks

trying to smuggle a jewel into the country inside an onyx elephant. The usual complications arise when the temperamental Carmelita, played by Lupe Velez, spots her husband dancing with the pretty lady crook at the Epping's hotel. Two of the principals are involved in additional war activities: Carmelita is preparing to take first aid classes and Uncle Matt (Leon Errol) becomes an air raid warden.

588 MISS ANNIE ROONEY (UA, May) Edwin L. Marin; *genre:* Comedy; *location:* United States; *coding:* AF-N, Prod, Short, Chi, Fr; *relevance:* 1.5.

Annie is a jitterbugging adolescent played by Shirley Temple. Her high school boyfriend drives a jalopy with "Blitz Buggy" painted on the door (this was a short-lived name for the vehicle entering service in late 1940, that has since become known as the Jeep). Annie's unemployed father (William Gargan) has invented a formula that he claims will make rubber out of milkweed. He later crashes a formal party Annie is attending and unsuccessfully tries to demonstrate the process to the host, the president of the Consolidated Rubber Company. The Rooneys are humiliated. But the next day they receive a visit from the firm's president who proceeds to make Mr. Rooney a cash offer. It turns out that the solution, when applied to rug material (on which it was spilled at the industrialist's home), creates the perfect tread material for battle tanks.

589 MISS V. FROM MOSCOW (PRC, Nov) Albert Herman; *genre:* Spy; *locations:* France, Russia, Atlantic; *coding:* Intell Serv, AF-Raf, Jap, AF-Russ, Spy-Sab, AF-Ger, Fr, Brit, Czech, Pol, Resist, Am Vol, AF-Mer, AF-N?, Russ, Stalin?, Nazi, Hitler, Ger, Collab, Atroc, Atroc-Conc, Ger-Am, V, Jap-Ger Coop, US-Russ Coop; *relevance:* 3.

In an opening sequence obviously modeled on *Ninotchka* (1939), Vera Morova (Lola Lane), a Russian intelligence agent, is summoned to Counter-Espionage Headquarters in Moscow. The commissar in charge sends her to Paris on a secret assignment to impersonate a Nazi spy whom she closely resembles. With the help of the French resistance and two young RAF flyers (one American and one British), stranded in France after participating in a commando raid, she outwits the brutal Gestapo in occupied France. Using her feminine wiles to obtain information from the womanizing Col. Heinrick, Vera sends a wireless message to Moscow. Spies in America have alerted the Germans to a Russia-bound American convoy, and German submarines, operating out of French bases, are poised to destroy it. Vera's information allows the Allies to save the convoy from destruction. The commissar in charge is happy: "This achievement is symbolic of the cooperation and unity between our great nations." [There is some question as to whether this film is set before or after Pearl Harbor—Steve Worth (Howard Banks) is an American serving with the RAF, which would place the film prior to the official U.S. entry into the war, but convoys of war material to Russia did not begin until 1942.] In one scene, the pompous Heinrick refers to "our yellow Aryan brothers" (the Japanese). He later informs Vera that "The Russian army is annihilated." "What, again?" she replies. There is also an *unintentionally* humorous sequence in which Heinrick and Vera attend a speech by Hitler (who appears in documentary footage, with dubbed-in German dialogue); Heinrick eagerly repeats (in English) everything Hitler says, including references to the "unspeakable Russian vermin," while Vera tries to look interested.

590 MISTER WISE GUY (Mono, Feb) William Nigh; *genre:* Comedy/Drama; *location:* United States; *coding:* Chi, AF-A, Draft, Blk, Jap, Home Def; *relevance:* 2.

The East Side Kids are sent to reform school after becoming implicated in the gangland hijacking of a wine truck. They are visited by Danny's older brother Bill (Douglas Fowley), a former guard who is about to enter the Army. But Bill is unjustly convicted of murder and sentenced to die. The boys break out of the reformatory to help prove his innocence. There are several pro-conscription references woven into the plot, which would tend to indicate that this film was in the can before Pearl Harbor. The scene where the kids watch a newsreel about a "Giant Clipper" escaping "Jap Raiders" was probably a last-minute insertion.

591 MRS. MINIVER (MGM, Aug) William Wyler; *genre:* War Drama; *location:* Britain; *coding:* Dunkirk, Brit, AF-Brit, AF-RAF, AF-W, Pol, Fr, Nor, Neth, AF-Ger, Span Civ, V, Hitler, Goering, Goebbels, Nazi, Home Def, Musso, Collab, Atroc; *relevance:* 3.

A middle class family in an English village stoically copes with the onslaught of the second World War. When the vicar solemnly announced in church that Britain and Germany are at war, the congregation displays no surprise or panic and quietly disperses. Later, Mrs. Miniver (Greer Garson), her husband (Walter Pidgeon) away in his small boat participating in the evacuation of Dunkirk, calmly handles a downed Luftwaffe airman, a fanatical Nazi, whom she finds in her garden. After an air raid in which several villagers, including Mrs. Miniver's new daughter-in-law, are killed, the congregation gathers in their bomb-damaged church and listens to the vicar declare in an inspirational

sermon that the war is now the "people's war."

592 MUG TOWN (Univ, Dec) Ray Taylor; *genre:* Crime/Comedy; *location:* United States; *coding:* AF-A, Jap, Short, Home Def, Pearl Harb, Draft; *relevance:* 2.

The "Dead End Kids" (Universal's version of the East Side Kids) lose a pal while freight hopping across the country. The four surviving toughs visit the small town where the deceased boy's mother lives and find a "soft spot." One of them, Tommy (Billy Halop), gets a job at the town's service station. He replaces a local boy who recently enlisted. When Tommy is asked whether he plans to join the Army, he delivers a tirade about this country never showing any interest in *him*. The other kids later help Tommy avoid being framed for the theft of some furs. Soon after the Pearl Harbor attack, all four young men march into the mother's living room wearing Army uniforms. Tommy looks straight into the camera, points his finger at the audience and states: "And we're not kidding!"

593 THE MUMMY'S TOMB (Univ, Oct) Harold Young; *genre:* Horror; *locations:* United States, Egypt; *coding:* Draft?, Russ, AF-A; *relevance:* 1.

In this sequel to *The Mummy's Hand* (1940), the latest incarnation of the dynasty of high priests sworn to preserve the mummy of Kharis (Lon Chaney, Jr.) helps the Mummy in America to kill off those individuals who violated his tomb during an archaeological expedition. A reporter assigned to the murder case comments: "I had my choice of covering this story or the Russian front. I chose this."

594 MURDER IN THE BIG HOUSE (WB, Apr) B. Reeves Eason; *genre:* Crime; *location:* United States; *coding:* —; *relevance:* 1.

A cub reporter (Van Johnson) and his female sidekick (Faye Emerson) uncover a murder ring in the state penitentiary which prevents death row inmates from making politically damaging final confessions. In the offices of their paper, the *Morning News*, is a large "War Map."

595 MY FAVORITE BLONDE (Para, Mar*) Sidney Lanfield; *genre:* Comedy; *location:* United States; *coding:* Intell Serv, Blk, AF-Raf, US-Brit Coop, Spy-Sab, Brit, Nazi, V; *relevance:* 2.5.

Bob Hope plays a struggling vaudeville actor in pre-war America who is the straight man to a trained penguin. While traveling on a train between shows, he encounters a beautiful British agent (Madeleine Carroll) and helps her elude a band of Nazi spies. The object of the enemy's attention is a jeweled scarab containing a microscopically engraved

code detailing the flight schedule of 150 Hudson bombers being sent to Britain under Lend Lease. This film seems to spoof Hitchcock's 1935 thriller, *The Thirty-Nine Steps* (Gaumont).

596 MY FAVORITE SPY (RKO, June) Tay Garnett; *genre:* Musical Comedy/Spy; *location:* United States; *coding:* Intell Serv, Ger, AF-Ger, US-Brit Coop?, Draft, Spy-Sab, AF-A, AF-MC, AF-N; *relevance:* 2.5.

Band leader Kay Kyser is forced to postpone his nuptials when he is unexpectedly called up for military service. It turns out that the Army made a mistake—fortunately for the Army, since Kyser turns out to be an incompetent officer, ruining a gas training drill (a rare WWII reference to gas warfare, which was widely used in WWI). The Army does offer Kay a secret counter-intelligence job in order to help them trap an espionage group believed to be using a popular nightclub as a front. Kay returns to his band at the "Orchid Room," while the news is leaked that he was rejected by the Army for flat feet. Kay is soon dodging the bullets of Nazi spies. Kay's government-supplied "wife" (a blonde agent played by Jane Wyman), who describes herself as coming under the Lend-Lease Act, is not appreciated by his real fiancée. The OWI commented: "It is too bad that the U.S. Secret Service has to be so ridiculous while the enemy has everything very neatly and efficiently planned, and is only outwitted in the end through an accident."

597 MY SISTER EILEEN (Col, Sept) Alexander Hall; *genre:* Comedy; *location:* United States; *coding:* Home Def, AF-Mer, Grk?; *relevance:* 1.

The Sherwood sisters (played by Rosalind Russell and Janet Blair) leave Columbus, Ohio, and lease a basement apartment in Greenwich Village from an eccentric artist. On their first evening in New York City, the girls' little apartment is invaded by a host of zany characters, including a shady businessman who, when told to leave, pompously informs them he is the local air raid warden.

598 NATIVE LAND* (Ind, May) Leo Hurwitz, P. Strand; *genre:* Drama; *location:* United States; *coding:* Blk, FDR, Hitler; *relevance:* 1.

This independent release from left-wing Frontier Films was purportedly based upon material presented at the U.S. Senate Civil Liberties Committee hearings of 1938. The film is a semi-documentary work that mixes acted scenes with newsreel footage and is accompanied by an off-screen narration delivered by black activist and singer Paul Robeson. In several separate episodes, including one of black and white sharecroppers being brutalized for attempting to organize, and another of a big city union victimized by industrial espionage, the abuses of the Bill of Rights by "fascist-minded corporations" are condemned. *Native Land* concludes with the narrator lauding the strength of the American people for winning their freedom from abroad and exhorting them to unite to combat the "enemies from within."

599 THE NAVY COMES THROUGH (RKO, Oct) A. Edward Sutherland; *genre:* Combat; *locations:* United States, North Atlantic; *coding:* Mil School, AF-Mer, AF-AC, Jap, Hitler, Nazi, Goering, AF-W, AF-N, AF-MC, Ref, Resist, AF-Ger, Latin Am, FDR, V, Pearl Harb, Spy-Sab, Hist Am, Austria; *relevance:* 3.

A naval gunnery crew (Pat O'Brien, George Murphy, Jackie Cooper, and a Cuban played by Desi Arnaz), mans an armed merchant ship making the Atlantic run. After dodging a U-boat and shooting down a couple of Nazi bombers, the rich "quiz kid" on board deciphers a coded wireless message that enables them to intercept and capture a German submarine supply ship. With the German language skills provided by an anti–Nazi Austrian crew member (who insists on identifying himself as Dutch; played by Carl Esmond, who in real life *was* Austrian), they lure two U-boats to their doom—it could happen only in Hollywood's version of the Battle of the Atlantic.

600 NAZI AGENT [aka SALUTE TO COURAGE] (MGM, Mar) Jules Dassin; *genre:* Spy; *location:* United States; *coding:* AF-Ger, Jew, Dipl, Ger-Am, Ref, AF-N, AF-A?, FBI, Fr, Blk, Spy-Sab, Collab, Hitler, Nazi, AF-Brit, Ital, Resist; *relevance:* 3.

An intellectual German-American refugee is forced by his monocle-wearing Nazi twin brother (both roles played by Conrad Veidt) to assist a group of spy-saboteurs working out of the (prewar) German consulate in New York City. Their main activities are directed at convoys bound for Britain. Determined to expose the foreign agents, the good German kills his Nazi brother and assumes the man's identity as the head of the spy ring. In order to carry on the struggle against the Third Reich and to protect some friends, he allows himself to be deported by the FBI with the rest of the consular staff. At one point a character mentions that the music of Mendelssohn (a Jew), heard on a car radio, is forbidden in Germany. Both this film and *Margin for Error* deal with pre-war German espionage rings headquartered in the German consulate in New York.

601 NEATH BROOKLYN BRIDGE (Mono, Nov) Wallace Fox; *genre:* Comedy/Drama; *location:* United States; *coding:* AF-N, Short, Blk, Ital, Draft, Blk Mkt?, Juv?; *relevance:* 1.5.

The East Side Kids rescue a teenage girl (Anne Gillis) from her abusive stepfather, but are framed for murder when the man is later found dead. Eventually, a local gangster (Marc Lawrence) is exposed as the real killer. The girl makes plans to marry Butch (Noah Beery Jr.), a former East Side Kid who is now in the Navy. There are a number of topical dialogue references: for instance, Glimpy (Huntz Hall) calls an Italian street vendor a "war profiteer" because he is charging $.17 a pound for tomatoes and has "no ceiling," and the gangster is making plans to rob a warehouse full of silk, presumably to sell the scarce material on the black market.

602 THE NIGHT BEFORE THE DIVORCE (TCF, Mar) Robert Siodmak; *genre:* Comedy/Drama; *location:* United States; *coding:* —; *relevance:* 1.

A married couple break up because the wife (Lynn Bari) is better at almost everything, including golf. She starts dating an older pianist, only to become a prime suspect when he is mysteriously murdered. The ex (Joseph Allen, Jr.) returns to her side to help resolve the crisis. At one point the heroine informs her husband that he has subtlety, "like a dictator's promise."

603 NIGHTMARE (Univ, Nov) Tim Whelan; *genre:* Spy; *location:* Britain; *coding:* AF-Ger, Collab, Intell Serv?, US-Brit Coop?, Spy-Sab, Nazi, Brit, Churchill, Short, AF-Brit, AF-A; *relevance:* 3.

Daniel Shane (Brian Donlevy), an American gambler, is put out of business when the Luftwaffe bombs his Soho club. Shane is left with only the tuxedo he is wearing and a steamship ticket for the U.S.—he is planning to return to join the Army. On his way to the docks, Shane gets caught in a storm and obtains shelter by breaking into the home of Leslie Stafford (Diana Barrymore). After discovering him, Leslie insists that Shane repay her for the food he has stolen by removing the body of her dead husband from the study. Later, when the police become involved, the two drive to the Scottish castle of Leslie's cousin Abbington. Eventually, they learn that Abbington is the leader of a Nazi espionage ring that has been placing cases of Scotch loaded with explosives in ships en route to the United States.

604 THE OLD HOMESTEAD (Rep, Aug) Frank MacDonald; *genre:* Crime; *location:* United States; *coding:* Fem Lab, Home Fr, Short; *relevance:* 1.5.

"The Weavers," a country music family, live in the small town of Farmington. In the process of attempting to stop a crime wave, Mayor Elviry becomes mixed-up with gangsters. Police Chief Abner finally breaks up the racketeering by arresting the mob for violating the sugar rationing regulations. In one of the musical numbers sung at the local nightery, the farmers are encouraged to "Dig, Dig, Dig for Victory."

605 ON THE SUNNY SIDE (TCF, Feb) Harold Schuster; *genre:* War/Drama; *locations:* United States, Britain; *coding:* Juv, Fr, AF-Ger, Brit, AF-Raf, Prod, US-Brit Coop, Ref; *relevance:* 2.

An English adolescent (Roddy McDowall) is sent as an evacuee to the United States for the duration of the war. He joins the Andrews family of suburban Cleveland and quickly adjusts to American slang and the ubiquitous hotdogs. Since his father is a pilot in the RAF, young Hugh gets a lot of attention from the neighborhood kids. So much so that young Don Andrews becomes a little jealous of his English guest. But this problem is resolved and British-American friendship is symbolically reaffirmed when the two team up to defeat the local bully and his stooge (an allegorical Hitler and Mussolini?). An interesting comment is made by Mr. Andrews to his wife soon after Hugh arrives at their home: "I've got the factory running full blast making supplies for England. I'll do anything in the world to help her win the war, but I'll be darned if I'll turn myself into an afternoon tea drinker." This film was copyrighted in December 1941.

606 ONCE UPON A HONEYMOON (RKO, Nov) Leo McCarey; *genre:* Comedy/Drama; *locations:* Austria, Norway, France, Poland, Czechoslavakia; *coding:* Austr, Spy-Sab, Belg, Fr, Short, Goebbels, AF-Pol, Nor, Fr, Czech, Pol, War Corr, Dipl, AF-Ger, Hitler, Himmler, Nazi, Hess, Goering, Collab, Jew, Atroc-Conc, Neth; *relevance:* 3.

A former burlesque queen from Brooklyn, played by Ginger Rogers, sets her romantic sights on a cosmopolitan Austrian baron (Walter Slezak). Following their marriage in Austria in 1938, the couple honeymoon in all the western countries subsequently conquered by Hitler. An insouciant American radio corespondent named Pat O'Toole (Cary Grant) follows them around Europe in order to confirm his suspicion that the Baron is actually a secret agent and Hitler's point man, negotiating with Nazi sympathizers in those countries. The Nazi persecution of Jews is explicitly dealt with during the Polish sequence of this motion picture. On board a liner bound for the United States after the fall of France, the politically awakened heroine terminates her Nazi husband's planned "goodwill mission" to America by pushing him overboard.

607 ONE THRILLING NIGHT (Mono, June) William Beaudine; *genre:* Crime; *location:* United States; *coding:* AF-A, Short, Jap; *relevance:* 2.

Newlyweds Millie and Horace Jason

(Wanda McKay and John Beal) arrive in New York for a one-night honeymoon, since he is scheduled to leave the next morning to join the Army. Complications arise when they discover a gangster locked in a trunk in their hotel room. By the time things are straightened out, the room clerk makes their six o'clock wake-up call. Millie sits up in bed pouting: "Darn those Japs!"

608 ORCHESTRA WIVES (TCF, Sept) Archie Mayo; *genre:* Musical; *location:* United States; *coding:* AF-AC, AF-N, Blk, Jap; *relevance:* 1.5.

A small town girl (Ann Rutherford) marries a trumpet player (George Montgomery) in the touring "Glenn Morrison" (played by Glenn Miller) band. Problems with a vampish female vocalist must be overcome. Numbers performed by the popular swing band include the Academy Award winning "I've Got a Gal in Kalamazoo" and the topically oriented opening number "People Like You and Me," with lyrics like: "Uncle Sam'll see you through, We'll have to roll up our sleeves, Tighten our belts, But through the dark we'll see, The lady with the liberty light..." Throughout the tour the band does not encounter any significant wartime travel difficulties—*no* uniforms are evident in a train sequence, and the train itself is not overcrowded. There are large numbers of teenagers and young adults shown listening to the band on its tour stops, but only one or two token uniforms in each scene (although the pre-war setting is not specified, this film is intended to represent the Miller band's actual history between 1937–1941). The song "That's Sabotage," credited onscreen, is not heard in the film, and was apparently cut. The uncredited Nicholas Brothers, in tails, demonstrate their famous flying splits during the band's peformance at a swank nightclub. This film went into production in March 1942; the Miller band broke up in September, as leader Miller joined the Army Air Force (as a bandleader). He later died in an airplane crash over the English Channel in 1944.

609 PACIFIC BLACKOUT [aka **MIDNIGHT ANGEL**] (Para, Jan) Ralph Murphy; *genre:* Spy; *location:* United States; *coding:* Fr, AF-A, Mil Exer?, Home Def, Spy-Sab, Home Fr, Prod, Nazi, Vichy; *relevance:* 3.

As air raid sirens blare for a blackout in a large West Coast city, the young engineer who invented a new anti-aircraft range finder, Robert Draper (Robert Preston), is sentenced to death for the murder of a co-worker. During the simulated bomber raid, the police van crashes and Draper escapes. Mary Jones (Martha O'Driscoll), a sympathetic telephone operator Draper meets in the park, helps the fugitive track down the French nightclub singer, Marie, whose perjured testimony helped to convict him. They find her murdered, but a letter on her dressing room table reveals that her associate, Ronnel, is a spy determined to steal or destroy the range finder. The letter also indicates that Marie has falsely testified because Ronnel threatened the lives of her parents in occupied France. Draper and Mary go to the munitions factory where his device is stored. At the plant they capture Ronnel's confederate, trap him into a confession, and learn that one of the American aircraft participating in the exercise has been secretly loaded with real bombs. Although the bomber's radio has been sabotaged, Draper is able to signal its pilot with a searchlight using Morse code.

610 PACIFIC RENDEZVOUS (MGM, June) George Sidney; *genre:* Spy; *location:* Pacific, United States; *coding:* Fr, Brit, FBI, AF-Russ, Spy-Sab, Intell Serv, AF-MC, AF-N, AF-A, Jap, Ger, War Corr, AF-Jap, Home Fr, Chi, FDR, Blk, Hist Am, AF-W?, Hitler, Nazi, Fem Lab Russ, Russ-US Coop, Jap-Ger Coop; *relevance:* 3.

While waiting to receive his commission, Gordon (Lee Bowman), a former war correspondent and author of a book on codes, meets Elaine Carter (Jean Rogers), the silly niece of a navy bigwig, at a war benefit in Washington, D.C. Soon afterwards, the new lieutenant is assigned to the decoding room of the Office of Naval Intelligence (ONI) to decipher Japanese and German shortwave messages. Gordon eventually cracks the code and learns in a deciphered message that, via an espionage network, information on American convoys in the Pacific is being exchanged between the Axis partners. Gordon's superior officer, Commander Brennan, is shot by his mistress, Olivia Kerlov, when he discovers she is a spy. Olivia then reports to the German espionage headquarters operating out of her hotel. Gordon becomes suspicious of Olivia and goes to her room. There, he and Elaine (who had followed him) are captured and threatened with death if Gordon does not decode a U.S. message so it can be sent on to the Germans. Knowing the ONI is monitoring all such transmissions, Gordon mixes in a call for help. The FBI raid the hotel. The OWI expressed a concern that this film might "give a false impression of the haphazard way in which our intelligence departments work and of the kind of people who work in them." The film was an updated remake of MGM's 1935 release, *Rendezvous* (based on a novel by the renowned cryptographer, Herbert O. Yardley).

611 THE PALM BEACH STORY (Para, Nov*) Preston Sturges; *genre:* Comedy; *location:* United States; *coding:* Blk, AF-A, FDR, Brit?; *relevance:* 1.

Gerry Jeffers (Claudette Colbert), the wife of a struggling engineer, leaves her husband (Joel McCrea) and heads for Florida. On the train, she encounters an eccentric millionaire, played by Rudy Vallee, who promptly falls in love with her. When her husband rejoins her in Florida, Gerry introduces him to the millionaire as her brother. In this outrageous satire upon the idle rich (the display of wasteful extravagance irritated the OWI reviewers, who suggested that the numerous sailors on a yacht could have been better employed in the Navy), romantic complications are resolved by the last minute introduction of twin siblings of the couple. Although the *Variety* review states that there is "not a hint of the war," a few topical references are actually made in the film. For instance, the millionaire's sister, a princess by marriage, states that she wants her husband to be an American: "It seems more patriotic."

612 PANAMA HATTIE (MGM, Sept) Norman McLeod; *genre:* Musical Comedy; *location:* Panama; *coding:* Hirohito, Home Fr, AF-A, AF-N, Blk, Jap, Musso, Hitler, Latin Am, FDR, Spy-Sab, Draft, Russ, Brit, Short, Home Fr, Postwar, Chi, Fil, Austria, Ind, Neth, Fr, Den?; *relevance:* 3.

This motion picture was based on a 1940 Broadway musical hit starring Ethel Merman. In the topically loaded film version, Ann Sothern plays Hattie Maloney, a flashy entertainer with a heart of gold who performs at Phil's Place in the Canal Zone. Although Hattie is in love with an Army sergeant, she is protected by three crazy gobs who are habitués of the cafe: Red, Rags and Rowdy (Red Skelton, "Rags" Ragland and Ben Blue). Problems arise when the sergeant's daughter, the product of a mismatch with a blueblood, pays a visit. Meanwhile, the three sailors track down a couple of German spies who have a lab in a mysterious house honeycombed with secret panels. The final musical production number includes the following bloodthirsty lyrics: "We've got a wooden kimono [coffin] for the Mikado / We've got a mausoleum for Mussoleum [sic] / We'll pickle Shicklegruber for the coroner's exam / For we're out to carve our monogram / On the son-of-a-gun who picks on Uncle Sam!"

613 THE PANTHER'S CLAW (PRC, Apr) William Beaudine; *genre:* Crime; *location:* United States; *coding:* AF-N, AF-A, Bonds, Ital, Blk, WWI, Ref?; *relevance:* 1.5

This film was based on a mystery novel by Anthony Abbot, and seems to have been intended as the first in a series featuring Sidney Blackmer as sleuth Thatcher Colt, but no sequels ever materialized. Mild-mannered

Everett P. Digberry (Byron Foulger) is suspected of the murder of Hungarian opera star Nina Politza, but the real killer is "Captain" Walters, her manager. There are a number of topical references, although none are central to the plot. In one scene, Digberry protests his treatment by the police: "I pay my taxes, I've got two nephews in the Navy, and I'm buying a government bond every month." Walters claims he was with the "Fighting 69th," during WWI, but Colt exposes this as a lie: "There weren't any *rats* in the Fighting 69th." And Colt's assistant (Rick Vallin) is scheduled to report for induction in the armed services.

614 PARACHUTE NURSE (Col, June) Charles Barton; *genre*: Training; *location*: United States; *coding*: WWI, Chi?, Jap, AF-Ger, AF-A?, AF-W, Short, Ger-Am; *relevance*: 3.

A printed title at the beginning of this film states: "While this story is pure fiction, the idea is real and vital" and the motion picture is dedicated to the "gallant women preparing to play their part in the defense of the United States." In fact, no such womens' parachute unit would ever be organized by the U.S. Army (the film never states that the "Aerial Nurse Corps of America" is affiliated with the Army, but this is apparently the idea). The film portrays a group of bored young civilian nurses who are patriotically inspired by a "paranurse" to sign up for training in the new Nurses Parachute Corps. During her first day in camp, a late-arriving, silly Southern nurse and the matronly captain have the following exchange: the recruit says she want to "help win this war ... fightin' with parasites." "You mean parachutes?" the captain asks. "Ma'm, when you're fightin' with Japs, you're fightin' with parasites." Gretchen, a sensitive German-American shunned by most of her fellow trainees because her brother is a Vice Air Marshal in the Luftwaffe, commits suicide (in a graphic scene) by deliberately failing to pull her ripcord on their first jump. Following the usual barracks melodramatics, the survivors line up for graduation exercises on the parade ground, the superimposed Stars and Stripes fluttering in the breeze. Although the film never explicitly states that the nurses are being trained for combat duty, the film hints at this possible deployment (which, in real life, never came). Another 1942 Columbia release, *Blondie for Victory*, q.v., also makes reference to "parachute nurses." Columbia contractee Marguerite Chapman was top-billed, with William Wright as one of the women's instructors.

615 PARIS CALLING (Univ, Jan) Edwin L. Marin; *genre*: War Drama; *locations*: France, Britain; *coding*: Spy-Sab, V, Resist, Am Vol, Span Civ, Sino-Jap War, Jap, Vichy, DeGaulle?, AF-Brit, AF-Raf, AF-Ger, Hitler, Nazi, Collab, Atroc, Brit, Fr, Chi, Nor, Resist; *relevance*: 3.

Marianne (Austrian actress Elisabeth Bergner) is a wealthy Parisian who flees the French capital with her mother and thousands of other civilians during the German invasion. Her mother dies of shock after a German bomber attack upon their refugee column, so Marianne returns to Paris and joins the newly organized underground. Meanwhile, Texan Nicholas Jordan (Randolph Scott) is flying missions with the RAF over France. He is a veteran of both the Spanish Civil War and the Sino-Japanese War (note that the hero of Hemingway's Spanish Civil War novel *For Whom the Bell Tolls* is named Robert Jordan). After being shot down and stranded behind German lines, Nick finds his way to the cafe headquarters of the resistance, where Marianne plays coded messages for a secret wireless on the piano. Before British commandos finally come to the rescue, Nick is captured and undergoes a brutal interrogation by the whip-wielding Blackshirts of the Gestapo. Marianne is forced to kill her former lover, a collaborationist. There are some similarities between this film and *Reunion in France*, q.v. The refugee-strafing scene is a good example of Hollywood imparting terrorist motives to the Axis; in reality, there was no deliberate policy of attacks on refugee columns, although isolated incidents did occur. After the fall of France in 1940, around 8 million refugees fled from the north of France and Belgium towards the unoccupied zone in the south.

616 PHANTOM KILLER (Mono, Oct) William Beaudine; *genre*: Crime; *location*: United States; *coding*: Fr, Jap; *relevance*: 1.

John Harrison, a prominent citizen who is allegedly a deaf mute, is suspected by the local assistant district attorney (Dick Purcell) of killing several finance men. But it takes the sleuthing of the District Attorney's skeptical reporter girlfriend (Joan Woodbury) to prove Harrison is the actual murderer. She discovers he had used a mute twin brother for his alibi. Early in the film, when the newslady tries to persuade her boyfriend to give up his idea that Harrison is the guilty man, she notes that the DA is alone in his belief and that the others cannot all be wrong. The DA snaps back: "That's what they said about fifty million Frenchmen and look where they are." This film is a remake of *The Sphinx* (Monogram, 1933).

617 THE PHANTOM PLAINSMEN (Rep, June) John English; *genre*: Western; *location*: United States; *coding*: Pacifist, Nazi, Atroc?, AF-Ger, Ger, Collab, *relevance*: 2.

During the immediate pre-WWII period the Three Mesquiteers (in this film: Bob Steele, Tom Tyler, and Rufe Davis) are working for Cap Marvin, an old horse rancher. Cap is a pacifist and always stipulates in his contracts that his stock shall not be resold for military purposes. However, Kurt Redman, manager of the local Cattleman's Exchange, is secretly working for the Nazis and shipping the horses purchased from Marvin to Germany. When the Mesquiteers stumble upon this information they aprise their employer of the situation. Cap announces he will no longer do business with Redman, but the Nazi collaborator informs the man that his grandson, who had been studying overseas, is being held by the Gestapo. The cowboy trio go to work on the indigenous Nazi and his associates. The Three Mesquiteers had dealt with enemy agents once before in their 1938 release, *Pals of the Saddle*, q.v.

618 THE PIED PIPER (TCF, Aug) Irving Pichel; *genre*: War Drama; *locations*: France, Britain; *coding*: Juv, AF-Raf, Belg?, Ger-Am, League Nat, WWI, AF-Ger, AF-Brit, Jew, Atroc-Conc, Nazi, Hitler, Churchill, Ref, Dunkirk, DeGaulle, AF-Fr, Atroc, Fr, Neth, Brit, Intell Serv; *relevance*: 3.

A vacationing elderly Englishman named Howard (Monty Woolley, sporting a beret), who has an aversion to children, becomes stranded in France following the German invasion. As Howard struggles to reach the coast in an attempt to return to Britain, he acquires, to his growing dismay, an entourage of abandoned and orphaned kids (including Roddy McDowall). They travel across the country by car, train, bus, boat, in a cart, and on foot, finally reaching their destination, the Channel coast. As the group is about to board a small fishing boat to make the hazardous Channel crossing, they are arrested by the Nazis. Despite threats, Howard remains defiant. The SS major in charge, played by Otto Preminger, is impressed. The major arranges for their safe passage on the condition that his part-Jewish niece be allowed to accompany them on their voyage. When the German asks Howard if his niece, as a Jew, would be welcome in the United States, the Englishman replies that thousands of refugee children have been accepted, and there "have never been any conditions that I know of, as to color, race or religion." An interesting point: one of the children is entrusted to Howard's care by a woman who is going to join her husband (the child's father) at the League of Nations headquarters. The League had drastically reduced its staff in 1939, but was not officially disbanded until after the war, when it was superseded by the United Nations organization.

619 PITTSBURGH (Univ, Dec) Lewis Seiler; *genre:* War Drama; *location:* United States; *coding:* FDR, V, AF-A, Prod, Fem Lab, Pearl Harb, Jap, Home Fr, Nazi, Pol, V; *relevance:* 2.5.

In the early 1930s, Pitt and Cash (John Wayne and Randolph Scott), goaded by an ambitious, pretty "Hunky" named Josie (Marlene Dietrich), quit their jobs as coal miners and form an independent company. After marriage to the heiress of a wealthy steel magnate, Pitt's increasingly high-handed methods with the union lead to his downfall. Later, when America enters the war, the outcast Pitt goes to work at his former partner's company as a common laborer. Pitt's labor-saving ideas, designed to increase war production, bring him to Cash's attention and lead to a reconciliation. The film is framed with an opening patriotic speech/pep talk by Cash to the assembled war workers and a concluding offscreen narration delivered by an old friend of the two men, promoting capital-labor unity and active female participation in the war effort: "Millions of.... men and women ... to feed the supply lines to the courageous Americans fighting on battlefronts all over the earth."

620 POLICE BULLETS (Mono, Sept) Jean Yarbrough; *genre:* Crime; *location:* United States; *coding:* Short, Nazi; *relevance:* 1.

John Reilly (John Archer), head of a protection racket, is warned by his lawyer of an impending federal investigation for tax evasion. He hires a gullible professor (Milburn Stone) with a photographic mind to memorize all his accounts and then destroys the ledgers. As Reilly is burning all his books, his henchman asks him if he's been "playing Nazi." Donna (Joan Marsh), who is working for the police, learns of Reilly's scheme. Before she can bring the professor to the police, a rival gang kidnaps both of them. All the racketeers are eventually rounded up. There are a number of other wartime references, including several about the rubber shortage.

621 THE POSTMAN DIDN'T RING (TCF, July) Harold Schuster; *genre:* Comedy/Drama; *location:* United States; *coding:* Draft, Short, Prod-Farm, Hist Am, FDR, *relevance:* 1.5.

When a government mail sack missing for fifty years is recovered by postal authorities, an attempt is made to distribute its contents to the addressees or their heirs. In a small western farming community, the local store owner Dan Carter (Richard Travis), who has gone into debt to help the farmers increase their crop production for the war effort, is about to be foreclosed by the ruthless Harwood banking family. Dan says: "This is fascism, one man directing the policy of this bank." He receives one of the misplaced pieces of mail—a letter from his grandfather to his father, both deceased, containing now-controlling shares in the Harwood bank. Dan becomes chairman of the board and makes the bank's resources available to his needy neighbors. Just as he is about to leave on his honeymoon, Dan happily accepts his notice from the draft board.

622 POWDER TOWN (RKO, May) Rowland V. Lee; *genre:* War/Drama; *location:* United States; *coding:* Prod, Spy-Sab, FBI; *relevance:* 2.

A professor (Edmond O'Brien) experimenting with a secret explosive formula goes to work at a new munitions plant in a town that is rapidly expanding due to defense contracts. He runs into comic conflict with the tough Irish foreman (played by Victor McLaglen). Some spies of unspecified nationality attempt to steal the formula, but the scientist and the working man team up to foil their efforts.

623 THE PRIDE OF THE YANKEES (RKO, July*) Sam Wood; *genre:* Biography; *location:* United States; *coding:* Hist Am, AF, Blk, Ger-Am?; *relevance:* 1.5.

This sentimental film biography of the legendary New York Yankee first baseman Lou Gehrig (played by Gary Cooper) opens with a printed prologue suggesting that "the thousands of young Americans [in 1942] on far-flung fields of battle" should be inspired by a "hero of the peaceful paths of everyday life" and his valiant struggle against an incurable disease (which led to Gehrig's death in June 1941). There is also an exchange that had unmistakable contemporary significance for servicemen and their families—an idealistic character played by Walter Brennan defines a hero as "a guy that does his job." Gehrig's humble origins in an immigrant family (presumably German-Americans, although this is not specifically stated), his rise to team captain of a world champion team, and his romantically quaint marriage are chronicled. The emotionally wrenching day in 1939 when Gehrig delivers his farewell address to his fans—"People all say I've had a bad break. But today—today I consider myself the luckiest man on the face of the earth"—is faithfully recreated (with the added emotional punch of Babe Ruth, playing himself, in the background).

624 PRIORITIES ON PARADE (Para, July) Albert Rogell; *genre:* Musical Comedy; *location:* United States; *coding:* Home Def, Latin Am?, AF-AC, AF-N, AF-A, Musso, Hitler, Churchill, Fem Lab, Prod, Jap, Home Fr, Bonds, Short, Pearl Harb; *relevance:* 3.

Johnny Draper (Jonnie Johnston) and his swing band visit the Eagle Aircraft Factory in hopes of being paid to entertain the war workers. Instead, the personnel manager assigns them to various jobs in the factory. Johnny is made an apprentice to a tough woman welder (Betty Rhodes). Johnny tells her that "if Hitler knew about this he'd give up!" She testily responds that a girl can do more than just rock a cradle. Johnny and his band practice during their lunch break (usually only twenty or thirty minutes in actual war factories). The band becomes such a hit that they are placed on the night shift to musically stimulate the workers. Publicity about their morale-boosting show leads to an offer of a Broadway contract. But the band turns it down in order to keep working for Uncle Sam. The final number of the show is about payday for war workers: "A lot of it goes for taxes.... war bonds, a little of it for me, but I don't mind.... I want a big payday over Tokyo." With the exception of Ann Miller (who performs a number in a boudoir setting entitled "Cooperate with Your Air Raid Warden"), the cast leads were mostly radio personalities. The *Variety* review sarcastically dismissed this film as "just another of the misfortunes of war." A couple of months after this film's release, Universal produced a cartoon with a similar theme, *Yankee Doodle Swing Shift*.

625 PRISONER OF JAPAN [aka ISLE OF FORGOTTEN SINS] (PRC, June) Arthur Ripley; *genre:* War Drama; *location:* Pacific; *coding:* Spy-Sab, AF-Jap, Pacifist, Atroc, Juv, Latin Am?, Jap, Pearl Harb, AF-N, AF-MC; *relevance:* 3.

David Bowman (Alan Baxter), an alcoholic American and an avowed pacifist, has been imprisoned in his own house on a small island in the South Pacific. His former astronomy teacher, Matsuru (Ernest Dorian), is a Japanese agent who sends messages about the location of American convoys to his superiors from a secret underground radio room. Toni (Gertrude Michael), a tough American entertainer trying to get back to the States, lands on the island. She quickly sizes up the "Little Rising Sons" as spies, but is also captured. After Matsuru murders a native boy, David attacks the enemy agent and seizes his gun. Matsuru arrogantly tells David: "Put away that gun. It is not your nature to kill." David shoots and mortally wounds the enemy agent. David and Toni lock themselves in the radio bunker, pledge their mutual love and then make radio contact with an important American convoy, directing its escorting battleship to fire upon their location. As the shells begin to slam into the island, the two reach out for each other and, just as their fingers touch, the scene is obliterated by a huge explosion (director Arthur Ripley's 1944 film *Voice in the Wind*, q.v., has a similar "artistic" and unhappy ending). Edgar G. Ulmer wrote the screen story and later claimed (in an interview with Peter Bogdanovich) to have directed a significant part of this film. The basic premise of the film—a white couple held hostage by an "oriental" despot—also appears in *East of Borneo* (Universal, 1931) and *The General Died at Dawn* (Paramount, 1936).

626 PRIVATE BUCKAROO (Univ, June) Edward F. Cline; *genre:* Musical Comedy; *location:* United States; *coding:* Pacifist?, Home Fr, WWI?, AF-W, AF-A, AF-MC, Prod, FDR, Draft, USO, Nazi, Jap, Short, Blk, Bonds; *relevance:* 3.

When Harry James is drafted, the rest of his band joins up and goes with him to training camp. Harry is pleased, but his manager is not, reminding the popular trumpeter of his contract. The manager is told Uncle Sam has the priority. As in Universal's popular 1941 release, *Buck Privates*, q.v., the Andrews Sisters portray USO entertainers. One of the numbers the girls sing is "Six Jerks in a Jeep." Naturally, Harry is appointed company bugler. The USO stages a show for the soldiers before they are shipped out, including a musical skit directed at defense workers: "If we expect them to win we'll have to dig in ... The boys in khaki and blue are all depending on you." The soldiers are ordered to march to their transports during the show, and the Andrews Sisters vocally accompany the departing men with "Johnny Get Your Gun Again." Another number, sung to the tune of the WWI hit "Mademoiselle from Armentieres," refers to the "Monkey Men from Tokyo." A concluding montage mixes shots of the men boarding ships and scenes of war production. The USO (United Service Organizations), the "Home Away From Home" for American servicemen, was operating over 425 clubs in the States by the spring of 1942, and 3,000 by the end of the war.

627 PRIVATE SNUFFY SMITH [aka **SNUFFY SMITH, YARDBIRD**] (Mono, Jan) Edward Cline; *genre:* Comedy; *location:* United States; *coding:* Mil Exer, Draft?, AF-A; *relevance:* 1.5.

This was the first motion picture based upon the hillbilly character from a popular comic strip, "Barney Google and Snuffy Smith." After finagling his way into the Army, middle-aged Snuffy (Bud Duncan) is discharged when a model of the service's latest range-finder he was guarding is stolen. The revolutionary range-finder is later retrieved and used to help win the war games for the commanding general's "Red Army." During the maneuvers our hillbilly hero saves the life of an Army sergeant. As a result, the general allows Snuffy to re-enlist as a custo-

dial worker, called a "yard bird" in army slang. *Hillbilly Blitzkreig*, q.v., was a sequel with more direct war-relevance.

628 THE REMARKABLE ANDREW (Para, May) Stuart Heisler; *genre:* Historical drama, Fantasy; *location:* United States; *coding:* AF-A, Hist Am, Austral, Czech, Russ, Fr, Ch, Jap, Italy, AF-Brit, Ger, Jew; *relevance:* 2.

In June 1941 Andrew Long (William Holden), the young and amiable bookkeeper for the purchasing department of Shale City, is framed by corrupt politicians who are looting the small town's treasury. The ghost of Andrew's lifelong hero, General Andrew Jackson (Brian Donlevy, in full military regalia), comes to his aid. When the rye-drinking Jackson's blunt methods fail to get Long out of jail he calls a war council composed of a few of his old cronies, including General George Washington, Chief Justice John Marshall and Jesse James. An additional member of the group is the very common and irascable Pvt. Smith of the Continental Army, a humorously symbolic G.I. Joe. The cause of democracy is thereafter valiantly and eloquently defended, leading to Andrew's acquittal. With the war in mind, one OWI analyst commented that the film "is a brilliant example of how movingly the screen can bring to life the great democratic traditions which are the strength and hope of America and of the world to be." The screenplay of this film, which was in production prior to America's entrance into the war, was written by Dalton Trumbo.

629 REMEMBER PEARL HARBOR! (Rep, May) Joseph Santley; *genre:* Spy/Adventure; *locations:* Philippines, United States; *coding:* Ger, AF-N, War Corr, MacArthur, Hist Am?, Latin Am, Dipl, US-Brit Coop?, AF-Jap, AF-A, AF-FIL?, Spy-Sab, Collab, Nazi, Atroc-Conc, Jap-Ger Coop, Ger, Pearl Harb, WWI, Jap, Hitler, Fil, Neth; *relevance:* 3.

An opening title announces this film is dedicated to the gallant men, both Americans and Filipinos, who sacrificed their lives in the battle for freedom. This is followed by actual newsreel footage of Japanese ambassador Kurusu on his final peace mission to the United States (November 1941). Three Army pals in the Philippines tangle with fifth columnists working for the Japanese. A Nazi spy, posing as a Dutchman (Sig Ruman), is also plotting against American interests. The womanizing "Lucky" Smith (Donald M. Barry), who escapes from the guardhouse where he was being held for neglect of duty (one of his friends is killed by spies while Lucky is visiting the soldier's sister), goes after the enemy agents when he learns of the attack on Pearl Harbor. The fifth columnists

join forces with an advance party of Japanese soldiers who have landed at a plantation owned by the "Dutchman." A battle ensues between the invaders and American troops. Lucky commandeers one of the Japanese planes and makes a suicide dive into a Japanese battleship supporting the troop landings: he shouts "Remember Pearl Harbor, you dirty rats!" (The film does not explain how Lucky learned to fly). The film concludes with a ceremony in which Lucky is posthumously awarded a medal (this takes place *before* the Philippines fell to the Japanese, and in fact the film never mentions this, since it was completed before the final surrender of Corregidor in May 1942).

630 REMEMBER THE DAY (TCF, Jan) Henry King; *genre:* Drama; *location:* United States; *coding:* Belg, AF-Ger, Hist Am, Am Vol, AF-Can; *relevance:* 1.

An aging and very proud high school teacher (Claudette Colbert), who lost her husband in the First World War, visits the hotel in the nation's capital where a former pupil is scheduled to give a presidential campaign speech. Somewhat bewildered upon entering the bustling Mayflower Hotel, she queries a young lady working at the gift shop as to whether it is too late to get into the banquet hall where the speech is to be delivered. The girl responds: "Well, if you have your own Panzer division you might make it." There are similarities between this film and United Artist's 1941 release, *Cheers for Miss Bishop*, q.v.

631 REUNION IN FRANCE (MGM, Dec*) Jules Dassin; *genre:* War Drama; *location:* France; *coding:* Laval, AF-Ger, Blk, Hitler, Nazi, Goering, Atroc, Atroc-Conc, Jew, Ger, Intell Serv, US-Brit Coop?, Am Vol, Collab, Vichy, Fr, WWI, POW, AF-Raf, V, Pol; *relevance:* 3.

The film begins in May 1940. Rich Frenchwoman Michele (Joan Crawford) is engaged to industrialist Robert (Philip Dorn), but he cannot spend much time with her because France is at war. Returning to Paris after the Nazis have occupied the city, she learns her palatial home has been requisitioned for German use (she is allotted one room in the basement). She gets a job with the dressmaker she formerly patronized. When Michele meets Robert again, she learns he has become a collaborator with the Nazis, and refuses to share his luxurious life, earned at the expense of France. One evening, she meets Pat (John Wayne) on the street; he is injured and weary, and she takes him back to her room to elude the Gestapo agents and gendarmes who are on his trail. Pat is an American RAF pilot, shot down over France. Escaping from a concentration camp, he made his way to Paris but has no papers or money. Michele returns to Robert, telling him she wants to leave France; she claims Pat is an American student trapped in the country and asks if he can be issued papers as her chauffeur. Robert agrees, but then he apparently reneges and sends her off in a German staff car. The driver is actually a British agent disguised as a German, and Michele is driven to a remote airfield. A plane lands to take her and Pat to England, but Michele discovers Robert is actually working for the Allies. She returns to Paris to stay with him and assist him in his work. See *Paris Calling*, q.v., and *Joan of Paris*, q.v., for very similar plots.

632 RHYTHM PARADE (Mono, Dec) Howard Bretherton, Dave Gould; *genre:* Musical Comedy; *location:* United States; *coding:* Blk, Latin Am?, Hitler, Musso, Hirohito, Jap, Home Fr, Draft, AF-W, Brit, Russ; *relevance:* 2.

Sally (Gale Storm), a singer in a nightclub girlie revue, is spotted by a promoter and offered a chance to perform in a Broadway show. But another singer is jealous and tries to spoil her chances by revealing that Sally is taking care of an eight-month-old child (actually the daughter of her sister, who is in Honolulu). War references in the film include a crack about one of the showgirls being so dumb "she thinks a jeep is a female Jap," a Victory Garden musical number and a final patriotic bump and grind routine offered by the revue, allegedly promoting women in the military: "Here's an army of a different kind ... a petticoat army ... Mama sniping Jappers ... Daddy home changing diapers."

633 RIDE 'EM COWBOY (Univ, Feb) Arthur Lubin; *genre:* Comedy; *location:* United States; *coding:* Blk, Brit; *relevance:* 1.

Abbott and Costello, who have been selling peanuts and hotdogs at a New York rodeo, wind up as cowboys at the Lazy S Dude Ranch after a dispute with their boss. As they get off the train, a sign at the local Indian reservation says: "Contribute Bundles to Albuquerque." This is the only direct war reference in the film, which was made during the summer of 1941, and is a parody of the widely supported 1940-1941 "Bundles For Britain" campaign in the United States, in which American volunteers knitted garments to be sent to the British. Reflecting the growing nationalistic spirit of the times, there is a Frontier Day Celebration at the film's conclusion in which most of the cast rides in on horses and carrying American flags.

634 RIDERS OF THE NORTHLAND (Col, June) William Berke; *genre:* Western; *location:* United States; *coding:* AF-Ger, Spy-Sab, AF-AC, AF-A, Collab, Ger, Short; *relevance:* 2.5.

Texas Ranger Steve Bowie (played by Charles Starrett; surnames of historical Americans were popular in films during the war) is anxious to do his bit for the war effort by joining the armed forces. "I want a crack at those men who say all men are NOT created equal," Steve says. But his Ranger commander informs Bowie that men like himself are needed by the government in Alaska to prevent enemy activities in that strategically vital territory: "Enemy agents are as dangerous as a nest of rattlesnakes." Bowie and two sidekicks travel to an Alaskan ranch to investigate the murder of a former Ranger who had been sending reports to the government. It is not long before they encounter a gang of collaborators working with a sinister U-Boat commander (Martin Kosleck), preparing secret runways and munitions dumps for a planned assault upon the United States.

635 RIGHT TO THE HEART (TCF, Jan) Eugene Forde; *genre:* Comedy Romance; *location:* United States; *coding:* Short, Chi; *relevance:* 1.

Socialite John T. Bromley III (Joseph Allen Jr.) wants to become a boxer. Over his parents' objections, he goes to Killian's camp to train, and there falls in love with Jenny, Killian's daughter. In one scene, a rural character is looking at a magazine: "Glamour girls they call them. Huh! I got an old magazine inside with Lillian Russell in tights. They don't wear them long tights nowadays. Must be a war shortage." In fact, silk stockings (and even nylon replacements) were so scarce during wartime that "leg makeup" appeared, and women were reduced to drawing "seams" on the backs of their legs to make it look like they were wearing stockings!

636 RIO RITA (MGM, Apr) S. Sylvan Simon; *genre:* Musical Comedy; *location:* United States; *coding:* Latin Am, Hitler, Nazi, Short, Spy-Sab; *relevance:* 2.

Abbott and Costello (on loan from Universal) are fired from a pet shop job in the city and hide in the trunk of a car that is driven to a Texas dude ranch located near the Mexican border. The ranch manager (Tom Conway) is the leader of a Nazi spy ring who is attempting to dupe a popular Latin radio singer (Kathryn Grayson), with the help of an alluring female agent, into aiding their cause. The boys and the ranch owner (John Carroll), a childhood sweetheart of the singer, foil the Nazis' plans. One amusing scene portrays a Nazi flunky giving a fascist salute to a donkey. The animal had swallowed a spy radio disguised as an apple, and the radio is now broadcasting a Hitler speech! This film was based on a Ziegfeld stage show which was also the basis for a 1929 film (both earlier versions were obviously without the

Nazi spy plot). The spy aspects of this version of *Rio Rita* were lifted from an early script for *Lost in a Harem* (which was made later in the war *without* any war content).

637 ROAD TO MOROCCO (Para, Oct*) David Butler; *genre:* Comedy; *locations:* Africa, United States; *coding:* Arab, Blk, Short, Nazi, Jap, Chi, Russ, Stalin, Brit; *relevance:* 1.

In their third "Road" film, the wisecracking duo of Bing Crosby and Bob Hope expend the usual series quota of topical references. After the freighter on which they are traveling explodes, the boys find themselves stranded in an Arab town on the Mediterranean coast. A montage of news reports about the sinking includes Japanese, Chinese and Russian broadcasts. One of the Chinese announcers wears an "I Am Chinese" button to insure that he is not mistaken for our Japanese enemy. The bulk of the film's plot centers around the problems the two American adventurers face when they become involved with a beautiful princess (Dorothy Lamour) who is matrimonially inclined, but who must also still deal with her discarded fiance, a violently jealous sheik. In early 1944 the OWI would not allow this film to be distributed overseas without the deletion of the radio announcer scene.

638 ROLLING DOWN THE GREAT DIVIDE (PRC, Apr) Peter Stewart; *genre:* Western; *location:* United States; *coding:* AF-A, Prod; *relevance:* 1.5.

"War has come to our country again" and so the Texas Rangers are attempting to do their bit by supplying the Army with the horses it needs. Local thieves would also like a piece of the action. A couple of singing cowboys (Bill "Radio" Boyd and Art Davis) at a border cafe and a government agent break up the gang of horse rustlers. The OWI was unimpressed: "An inexpensive horse opera into whose plot has been woven a patriotic war-time [sic] theme. Except for the fact that the horses were to be sold and used by the U. S. Army, the picture has no timely significance at all." The Army was still purchasing large numbers of horses in the spring of 1941 to maintain several cavalry units. Only the results of the first large-scale peacetime maneuvers during the summer of 1941, and reports of the massive armored warfare on the Russian front finally convinced the U.S. Army leadership to endorse full-scale mechanization. *The Bugle Sounds*, q.v., dealt with the Army's replacement of horses by motorized vehicles. Note: Peter Stewart is a pseudonym for director Sam Newfield.

639 RUBBER RACKETEERS (Mono, June) Harold Young; *genre:* Crime; *location:* United States; *coding:* Blk Mkt?, Blk?, Prod, Short, Chi, AF-A; *relevance:* 2.5.

Just out of prison, a former bootlegger (Ricardo Cortez) adapts to wartime America by embarking on a new racket—stealing and marketing new tires, and selling used tires his gang has improperly retreaded with contraband crude rubber. When a defense plant worker is killed in an auto crash caused by one of the gang's defective retreads, his fellow workers set out to expose the racket. In a topical twist on the gangster genre, the leader's henchmen turn on their boss in the name of patriotism. His Chinese servant then enlists in the Army.

640 SABOTAGE SQUAD (Col, Aug) Lew Landers; *genre:* Spy; *location:* United States; *coding:* AF-Ger?, AF-A, Spy-Sab, Collab, Prod, Short, Nazi, Hitler, Draft, Draft Avoid, FBI, Intell Serv, Atroc-Conc, Chi; *relevance:* 3.

Eddie Miller (Edward Norris), a small time gambler, has a brawl with Army recruiting officers when he is rejected because of a bad heart. Following his release from jail, Eddie takes a job in a bookie joint in order to repay his bail bond, which was posted by John Cronin (Bruce Bennett), a policeman and Eddie's rival for the hand of Edith (Kay Harris). Edith is a manicurist in Conrad's barber shop, which is really a front for a Nazi spy ring. Eddie's pickpocket friend steals a wallet from a wealthy customer of the shop; inside the wallet is a "condor" medallion that is the identifying symbol of the head of the enemy gang. Eventually, Eddie and his friend track the enemy agents to a warehouse, and see a truck being loaded with explosives in order to destroy an aircraft factory. Eddie indignantly tells the saboteurs: "You Nazi boys ought to have more sense than to try to play games with America." Eddie hijacks the truck, taking the spy leader (Sidney Blackmer) along for the ride. For reasons not entirely clear, Eddie fatally wrecks the truck (why did he not just stop? Print sources suggest Eddie crashed the truck to avoid hitting a troop truck, but this scene does not appear in the finished film—he just *wrecks*). At a posthumous awards ceremony it is stated that Eddie was working undercover for the police subversive detail, "whether he knew it or not."

641 SABOTEUR (Univ, Apr) Alfred Hitchcock; *genre:* Spy; *location:* United States; *coding:* Pacifist, Ger?, Ital?, AF-N, AF-A, Fem Lab, Prod, V, Ref, Jap, Spy-Sab, Collab, FBI; *relevance:* 3.

Barry Kane (Robert Cummings) is a West Coast aircraft factory worker who is suspected of sabotage following a lunchtime fire in one of the plant's hangars. A buddy is killed in the fire and, with the FBI after him, Barry pursues a mysterious co-worker named Fry (Norman Lloyd) whom he believes to be the real saboteur. A cross country chase ensues; Barry picks up an initially skeptical young lady (Priscilla Lane) along the way (Hitchcock mimicking the successful formula of his 1935 British film classic, *The Thirty-Nine Steps*). In New York City Barry confronts Tobin (Otto Kruger), the cynical leader of the fifth columnists, who disparages the "moron millions" of America. Barry patriotically retorts: "We're not soft! We're plenty strong! We'll win no matter what you guys do." The famous suspense scene atop the Statue of Liberty encompasses Barry's climactic encounter with the saboteur Fry.

642 SCATTERGOOD SURVIVES A MURDER (RKO, Oct) Christy Cabanne; *genre:* Comedy; *location:* United States; *coding:* Blk, Home Def; *relevance:* 1.

This was the penultimate motion picture in the radio series spinoff (begun in 1941) featuring pudgy Guy Kibbee as Scattergood Baines, the wise and avuncular owner of Coldriver's general store. When the town's two rich old maid sisters are murdered, leaving their fortune to their house cat, Scattergood helps "Dunker" Gillson, an aspiring young newspaper reporter, solve the crime. At one point Dunker drives his noisy old car up to the general store. In response to the mechanical racket, Scattergood's black assistant shrieks "Air Raid!" and flees the premises.

643 SECRET AGENT OF JAPAN (TCF, Apr) Irving Pichel; *genre:* Spy; *location:* China; *coding:* Dipl, Am Vol, Rom, Intell Serv, AF-N, Tojo, AF-Jap, Jap, Neth, Fr, Jap-Ger Coop, Brit, Russ, Ital, Ger, AF-Ger, AF-Chi, Chiang, Chi, Pearl Harb, US-Brit Coop, Spy-Sab, Collab, Atroc, WWI; *relevance:* 3.

Early in December 1941, at the Bar Dixie in Shanghai (under Japanese occupation), an international group of businessmen discusses the possibility of war between Japan and the United States. A man with a German accent claims the Japanese are already providing bases for German sea raiders and that "American aid to England is being sunk in the Pacific." It is not long before the bar's American owner, Ray Bonnell (Preston Foster), becomes involved in intrigue with an attractive young Briton named Kay Murdock (Lynn Bari). Hauled before the sinister head of Japanese police, Saito, Ray is forced to listen while his business partner is tortured to death. It seems the police would like to retrieve a coded list of Japanese agents working in Honolulu. After escaping from the Japanese, Ray is aided by Kay, actually a British agent, in delivering the information to Naval Intelligence. Ray's supposed Romanian friend, Alec (Steve Geray), turns out to be a German agent working with the Japa-

nese. With the announcement of the attack upon Pearl Harbor, a Chinese friend arranges for the couple's flight from Shanghai to avoid their internment. Ray plans to join the Chinese Army.

644 SECRET ENEMIES (WB, Oct) Ben Stoloff; *genre:* Spy; *location:* United States; *coding:* AF-Ger, Atroc-Conc, Ger-Am, Ger, Nazi, Hitler, Home Def, FBI, Spy-Sab, Draft, Pearl Harb, AF-N; *relevance:* 3.

A young attorney (Craig Stevens) joins the FBI just after Pearl Harbor, when he learns his best friend, a government agent, has been mysteriously murdered by poison gas in a hotel room. The new agent and his cohorts track down the Nazi spy ring responsible for their comrade's death. The ring is operating out of a hotel in New York City owned by a German-American. The spy leader threatens to put the hotel owner's wife, who is in Germany, in a concentration camp: "Your loyalty belongs to the country where you were born, to the race whose blood flows through your veins. Once a German, always a German!" The hero's former fiancee (Faye Emerson) is revealed to be the spouse of the head spy. There are definite similarities between the plot of this film and that of Warner Brother's 1935 release, *G-Men*.

645 SECRETS OF THE UNDERGROUND (Rep, Dec) William Morgan; *genre:* Spy; *location:* United States; *coding:* Ger?, Spy-Sab, Bonds, Fr, Ref, Collab, AF-W, War Corr, Nazi; *relevance:* 2.5.

Paul Panois, a renowned French artist, escapes the German occupation of his country, only to be blackmailed by a Nazi spy ring in America. Either he agrees to engrave plates for the counterfeiting of U. S. War Saving Stamps or the Gestapo will torture his imprisoned daughter in France. After Paul learns his daughter has eluded her captors, he flees with the plates from the spies' dairy farm hideout and contacts the New York district attorney. When Panois is later murdered, an assistant DA (John Hubbard) and his reporter girlfriend (Virginia Grey) set out to solve the case. At the dairy, the killer and leader of the spies, Maurice, the pudgy little effeminate owner of a fashionable gown shop, is captured, with the help of the local Women's Defense Corps. In a macabre touch, several customers who become suspicious of Maurice's activities are murdered, and their corpses incorporated into his patriotic window displays!

646 SEVEN DAYS LEAVE (RKO, Nov) Tim Whelan; *genre:* Musical Comedy; *location:* United States; *coding:* Mil Exer, FDR, Chi, Home Fr, Latin Am, Jap, Short, AF-A, AF-N, AF-W, USO, Bonds, Draft, Mil School, Blk; *relevance:* 2.5.

Following war maneuvers, the men of Company G receive seven days leave. While on a bar binge with his mates, handsome Johnny Gray (Victor Mature) learns from the Great Gildersleeve (Harold Peary, crossing over from another RKO series) that he has one week to marry the descendant of his grandfather's Civil War rival, in order to fulfill the stipulations of a will bequeathing him $100,000. During a whirlwind romance with the initially unresponsive lady (played by Lucille Ball), many popular radio acts of the day are featured. Johnny employs "military tactics" to overcome the lady's resistance. At the climax, Johnny and his army buddies board a transport to go overseas, and Johnny bids his new bride farewell: "Look darling, I may not kill many of our enemies, but I'm certainly going to confuse a lot of them."

647 SHANGHAI GESTURE (UA, Feb) Josef von Sternberg; *genre:* Drama; *location:* China; *coding:* Brit, Chi, Blk, Russ; *relevance:* 1.

Based on a 1920s play by John Colton: an international assortment of the dregs of the earth is gathered in Shanghai at the notorious "Madame Gin Sling's" casino. Completed before American entry into the war, one cannot help thinking the film was meant, at least partly, as an allegory on the current disastrous state of the world. The opening titles refer to Shanghai's international settlement and allude to China's difficulties with Japan (although the film is apparently meant to take place prior to the Japanese occupation of the city in 1937). Ona Munson is Madame Gin Sling, and Gene Tierney plays her adopted daughter.

648 SHEPHERD OF THE OZARKS (Rep, Mar) Frank McDonald; *genre:* Drama; *location:* United States; *coding:* AF-A, AF-N, Home Fr, Prod, AF-AC; *relevance:* 2.

This film opens with an off-screen narrator extolling America's defense production, accompanied by a montage of armed forces maneuvers and armaments factories. The narrator concludes with a promotion of aluminum drives, "[for] the eagles of democracy fly on wings of aluminum."

Jimmy Maloney (Frank Albertson), an Army Air Corps pilot, bails out over the Ozark Mountains and finds himself marooned in isolated Weaverville (the Weaver brothers and Elviry comprising its leading citizens). While waiting for transport out, Jimmy falls in love with a country girl. Jimmy's father, the wealthy owner of an aluminum company, arrives a few days later. During his stay, the greedy Mr. Maloney discovers that the rural community is located on rich aluminum bauxite ore deposits. When Jimmy learns of his father's attempts to profit on a metal vital to national defense,

he arranges for government agents to visit Weaverville. The senior Maloney's activities have so alienated the mountain folks that no one will sell their property. At this point some Army units hold maneuvers in the area and, thinking the United States is under attack from the "enemy," the mountaineers resist the invasion. Jimmy arrives and clears up matters. The now patriotically aroused people willingly agree to sell their land. The plot of this film is somewhat reminiscent of *In Old Monterey* (Republic, 1939), q.v.

649 SHERLOCK HOLMES AND THE SECRET WEAPON (Univ, Dec*) Roy William Neill; *genre:* Spy; *locations:* Britain, Switzerland; *coding:* Nazi, Spy-Sab, Home Def, Hitler, AF-W, Brit, AF-Raf, Switz, Atroc; *relevance:* 3.

This film is often listed as a 1942 release but the official release date in the *Motion Picture Herald* is March 1943. Sherlock Holmes (Basil Rathbone) agrees to escort Dr. Tobel from Switzerland to England; the scientist has invented a new type of bombsight he wishes to give to the Allies. In London, Dr. Moriarity (Lionel Atwill) kidnaps Tobel, but the inventor had split his design into four pieces, giving one to each of four scientists. Holmes and Moriarity race to find the men; Moriarity kills the first three and steals their portion of the plans, but Holmes beats him to the fourth and final man. Moriarity is killed trying to escape. Moriarity is not identified as a Nazi agent (although some German spies do appear in the film)— he plans to *sell* the bombsight to Germany, a variation on a plot device more often used in the 1937-41 period (but still utilized throughout the war), of a "freelance" spy or gangster willing to deal with the highest bidder for stolen plans.

650 SHERLOCK HOLMES AND THE VOICE OF TERROR (Univ, Sept) John Rawlins; *genre:* Spy; *location:* Britain; *coding:* Intell Serv, Nazi, WWI, V, AF-Brit, AF-Raf, AF-W, AF-Ger, Hitler, Spy-Sab, Brit, Home Def, Collab, US-Brit Coop, Postwar?; *relevance:* 3.

All Britain is being taunted by the self-described Nazi "Voice of Terror" who, over a secret transmitter, interrupts radio communications and gleefully describes his organization's acts of sabotage. Despite objections from military leaders, Sherlock Holmes (Basil Rathbone) is engaged by British Intelligence's Inner Council to ferret out the enemy agents. With the aid of Kitty (Evelyn Ankers), a Cockney prostitute, and her various Limehouse district friends and "professional" clients, Holmes eventually succeeds in trapping the saboteurs at their headquarters located in the south of England in an abandoned church. The enemy agents are

dressed in their Nazi uniforms, preparing a welcome for the German invasion fleet. The Voice of Terror turns out to be the head of the British Inner Council, Sir Evan Barham (Reginald Denny)! It is revealed that the real Barham was executed twenty years earlier while a prisoner of war, and his identity was assumed by a German agent. Among several patriotic homilies delivered throughout the film is a promotion of class solidarity in wartime by Kitty: "There's only one side, England! No matter how high or low we are, we're all on the same team. We've all got the same goal—Victory!" Factual note: one of Nazi Germany's actual propaganda broadcasters (in addition to the well-known "Lord Haw Haw" and "Axis Sally") was called "the Voice of Scotland."

651 SHE'S IN THE ARMY (Mono, May) Jean Yarbrough; *genre:* Comedy; *location:* United States; *coding:* AF-N, AF-W; *relevance:* 2.

Diane Jordan (Veda Ann Borg), a debutante singer at a New York night club, joins the Women's Ambulance Corps for the publicity (nearly 25,000 women, mostly in California, actually volunteered for the Women's Ambulance and Defense Corps of America—which was *not* a branch of the U. S. Army). A gossip columnist bets Diane $5000 she cannot last through the organization's six week training camp. Diane does have a hard time taking camp seriously, until she falls in love with a Navy officer (Lyle Talbot). But the camp commander learns of the wager and expels Diane from the Corps. Diane is later reinstated after she saves a comrade from a barracks fire. Diane's winnings are donated to the corps for the purchase of an ambulance. Refer to *Thumbs Up* (Republic, 1943) and *Keep Your Powder Dry* (MGM, 1945), both q.v., for somewhat similar plotlines.

652 SHIP AHOY (MGM, May) Edward Buzzell; *genre:* Musical Comedy; *locations:* Caribbean, United States; *coding:* Blk, AF-N, AF-W, FBI, Spy-Sab, Latin Am, Ital, Jap, Nazi?, Ger-Ital-Jap Coop; *relevance:* 2.

Axis agents dupe the dancing star of an American show troupe (Eleanor Powell) into smuggling a miniature magnetic mine concealed in a portable radio out of the country. During the course of a voyage to Puerto Rico, FBI agents and a hypochondriac short story writer, played by Red Skelton, clear the lady and foil the spies. The final musical number presents the two stars and their sidekicks marching out of a Navy recruiting station while singing the "Last Call For Love." The Tommy Dorsey Band (with Frank Sinatra as the vocalist) also appears in this film.

653 SING YOUR WORRIES AWAY (RKO, Mar) A. Edward Sutherland; *genre:*

Musical Comedy; *location:* United States; *coding:* Isolat; *relevance:* 1.

"Chow," a nutty songwriter played by Bert Lahr, gets into trouble with gangsters interested in his recent inheritance of $3,000,000. Near the end of the film, Chow and his pal Tommy are strapped to ice blocks heading for a spinning saw in an ice house. With resignation, Tommy informs Chow that no one appears to have heard their desperate screams for help. Chow responds: "I guess we're a couple of 'ice-olationists.'" This insipid motion picture was obviously in the can prior to the attack upon Pearl Harbor.

654 SLEEPYTIME GAL (Rep, Mar) Albert S. Rogell; *genre:* Comedy; *location:* United States; *coding:* Russ, Nazi, Grk; *relevance:* 1.

Popular radio comedienne and hillbilly singer Judy Canova plays a young lady named Bessie who is mistaken for a nightclub entertainer targeted for a gangland assassination. At one point Bessie and a friend are locked in an air conditioning room with the controls set at freezing. When the efficiency of this method of killing is challenged, the responsible gangster confidently asserts: "By this time the two are probably stiffer than a Nazi in Russia."

655 SMART ALECKS (Mono, Aug) Wallace Fox; *genre:* Comedy/Drama; *location:* United States; *coding:* USO, Hitler, Short, Blk; *relevance:* 1.5.

The East Side Kids learn that Hank (Gabriel Dell), one of their pals, has fallen in with some bank robbers, including Butch (Maxie Rosenbloom). Hank is arrested and sent to prison. Danny (Bobby Jordan) helps the police catch Butch and gets a $200 reward. He plans to use it to buy baseball uniforms for the gang, but they misunderstand and steal the money from him. Butch and his partner escape from prison and beat Danny up. A brain operation saves Danny, Hank wins a pardon for helping capture Butch again, and the Kids buy the uniforms after all. There are numerous dialogue references to shortages and rationing in this film; additionally, in one scene the brutish Butch is described as wolfing his food "like Hitler was in Brooklyn."

656 SMITH OF MINNESOTA (Col, Oct) Lew Landers; *genre:* Biography; *location:* United States; *coding:* FDR?, AF-N, AF-A, Home Fr, MacArthur, Mil School, Grk?; *relevance:* 1.5.

Real life college athletic star Bruce Smith plays himself in this football film. The plot has the Columbia studio putting Smith under contract and assigning a scenarist to write a story in which there is *not* a last-minute game-winning touchdown. The writer visits Smith's hometown in search of an angle.

Smith's friends and relatives tell about his exemplary life as a student-athlete. Smith appears in Navy uniform at the conclusion. The writer says to Smith: "We can't keep the U. S. Navy waiting while we talk about movies.... You're joining another team." The football hero respectfully replies: "They've got a great captain [FDR]." In one scene, the owner of the town's lunch counter (a naturalized citizen, possibly from Greece) mentions two of his sons who are in the Army.

657 SOMEWHERE I'LL FIND YOU (MGM, Sept) Wesley Ruggles; *genre:* War Drama; *locations:* United States, Philippines, Indochina; *coding:* Fil, AF-A, Atroc, Isolat, Russ, Brit, Pol, Fr, Ref, Dipl, Span Civ, Vichy, Appease, MacArthur, AF-W, AF-Fil, Chi, Blk, Ger, Nazi, Jap, Hirohito, AF-Jap, Pearl Harb, Czech, War Corr, Austria; *relevance:* 3.

For the third time since 1938, MGM cast Clark Gable as a foreign correspondent (*Too Hot to Handle*, 1938 and *Comrade X*, 1940, q.v.). Jonny Davis (Gable) is recalled from Germany in the fall of 1941 by his isolationist editor for sending "war mongering" reports to the paper. Jonny, asked how he found Berlin, responds: "Strictly by the sense of smell." Jonny falls in love with Paula (Lana Turner), a reporter who is engaged to his younger brother Kirk. Paula goes to Indo-China on assignment and disappears; Jonny and his brother follow, and find her smuggling Chinese babies from the war zone into Vichy-controlled but Japanese-occupied Indo-China (Japanese troops were allowed into the country to "protect" it in 1940). The trio travels to the Philippines, and when the Japanese attack, Kirk joins the Army and Paula becomes a Red Cross volunteer. Later, on Bataan, Kirk is killed opposing a Japanese landing; Jonny and Paula are reunited. They calmly face death together during a Japanese assault as Jonny dictates a final inspirational story for America: "Brown men and white men fought together, and when their blood ran together it was the same color.... The battle of Bataan was lost by Japan ... Remember Tokyo, there's more to come!" This was Clark Gable's last film before he joined the Army Air Corps; his wife, Carole Lombard, lost her life in an airplane crash (she was on a bond-selling tour) while Gable was making this film.

658 SOUTH OF SANTA FE (Rep, Feb) Joseph Kane; *genre:* Western; *location:* United States; *coding:* Prod; *relevance:* 1.

Carol Stevens (Linda Hayes) owns an undeveloped gold mine near Whitaker City. Because there are no "priorities" on gold mining machinery she is unable to interest three financiers in backing its operation. The Vaqueros, a group of cowboys who want to

"keep the old West alive," try to help Carol by inviting the wealthy entrepreneurs for a weekend in the traditional West. On a visit to the mine they discover that it has tungsten content, and therefore is valuable to war production. One of the investors tells Carol: "Uncle Sam will thank you for this." Some big city gangsters, armed with machine guns and an airplane, kidnap the financiers and hold them for ransom. Between songs by the Vaqueros' leader, Roy Rogers, the six-shooting cowboys rescue the kidnap victims.

659 THE SPIRIT OF STANFORD (Col, Oct) Charles Barton; *genre:* Biography, Drama; *location:* United States; *coding:* Bonds, AF-N, Hitler, Musso; *relevance:* 1.

This was Columbia's second fall release that featured an actual football star (see *Smith of Minnesota*, q.v.). Stanford's All-American quarterback, Frankie Albert, plays the cocky campus football hero who selfishly quits his college team before the crucial game of his final season, fearing a loss will hurt his value as a professional. But when Frankie learns his roommate is seriously ill, he returns and helps win the game. At the film's conclusion the recovered roommate informs two freshmen that Frankie Albert is not playing football in 1942: "There's a bigger game going on in the world. He's trying out for Uncle Sam's team—the Navy. And if he makes it they'll know he's in to win."

660 SPRINGTIME IN THE ROCKIES (TCF, Nov) Irving Cummings; *genre:* Musical Comedy; *locations:* Canada, United States; *coding:* Can, Latin Am, Home Def, FBI; *relevance:* 1.

A dance team, played by Betty Grable and John Payne, break up in New York and then romantically reconcile at a Canadian resort. In this garish Technicolor musical Carmen Miranda comes along as a Good Neighbor token. The film opens with a blackout in New York City and closes with a Broadway show number featuring a combination of the Samba and jitterbug entitled the "Pan-Americana Jubilee."

661 SPY SHIP (WB, Aug) B. Reeves Eason; *genre:* Spy; *location:* United States; *coding:* Isolat, Collab, Spy-Sab, US-Brit Coop, Jap, AF-Ger, Hitler, Pacifist?, Ger-Jap Coop, FBI, AF-Mer, AF-CG, AF-N, AF-W, AF-Jap, Brit, Can, Ital?, Ger, Pearl Harb, *relevance:* 3.

Pamela Mitchell (Irene Manning), a wealthy aviatrix, is a prominent member of the America-Above-All Committee (AAA), which is actually a fifth columnist front. During the week before Pearl Harbor she is wrapping up a lecture tour on "Why We Should Stay Out Of The War." Her speeches contain coded information for the Germans about convoys to Britain that she has obtained from her fiancé, who works for a maritime insurance company. Columnist Ward Prescott (Craig Stevens), suspecting Pamela is a traitor, enlists the aid of her half-sister Sue (Maris Wrixon). Martin Oster, head of the Nazi organization and a former lover of Pamela's, arrives from Honolulu. When Pamela refuses to surrender letters that link them together, he kills her. Ward and Sue trail Oster and his gang to an interned Danish freighter on which the spies plan to leave the country. The police are notified and, after a fierce gun battle, the enemy agents are apprehended. It is not too difficult to make connections between the fictional Pamela and the AAA, and the real-life isolationist America First Committee and their most famous advocate, aviator Charles Lindbergh. However, there was also a real-life female flyer named Laura Ingalls who was convicted and sentenced to prison in early 1942 on charges of being an unregistered Nazi agent. The film is a loose remake of *Fog Over Frisco* (WB, 1934), a crime drama starring Bette Davis.

662 STAND BY ALL NETWORKS (Col, Oct) Lew Landers; *genre:* Spy; *location:* United States; *coding:* Spy-Sab, Pearl Harb, FBI, Home Def, AF-A, Nor; *relevance:* 2.5.

Prewar America's hottest on-the-spot radio announcer, Bob Fallon (John Beal), warns the public that many of the disasters he covers are the work of saboteurs: "It's about time we wake up. You know what sabotage did for Norway." Ben is fired for being an alarmist. Ben's investigator, Monty, is murdered after discovering the Axis ring responsible for the wave of destruction. Before Ben and his girlfriend Fran (Florence Rice) can check out the list of names Monty sent, Pearl Harbor is bombed (the standard newsreel footage is shown). Then, using an announcer who mimics Ben's voice, the saboteurs begin to broadcast fake reports that discredit civil defense procedures. Ben traces the source of these specious radio transmissions to an old showboat. Captured by the Axis agents, Ben and Fran are set adrift in the showboat which has been wired with explosives timed to detonate when the boat passes near a loading troopship. Ben is able to disarm the bomb just in time. After being reinstated by his radio station, Ben learns Fran is a government agent.

663 STAND BY FOR ACTION (MGM, Dec) Robert Z. Leonard; *genre:* Combat; *locations:* United States, Pacific; *coding:* AF-Brit, Jap, Blk, AF-Ger, AF-Jap, AF-Blk, AF-MC, AF-N, Pearl Harb, FDR, WWI, Vet, Fil, Prod, Fem Lab?, Hist Am; *relevance:* 3.

A fun-loving Harvard grad turned Navy officer (Robert Taylor) is removed from the tennis courts of California after Pearl Harbor and assigned to a newly re-commissioned World War One vintage destroyer, the *USS Warren*. It is commanded by a man who "fought his way up" (Brian Donlevy) and is manned by the usual mixed lot, including a crusty old sailor played by Walter Brennan, who faced the "Heinies" while serving on the *Warren* during the last war. While escorting a convoy to the mainland, they pick up civilian survivors (including women and children) from a ship sunk by a Japanese submarine (in real life, about 30,000 women and children, mostly military dependents, were evacuated from Hawaii after the attack on Pearl Harbor, although none of these ships were sunk). Sometime later, the Ivy League lieutenant learns the full realities of war when the *Warren* engages and torpedoes a Japanese battleship menacing the convoy. The frustrated American admiral (Charles Laughton) in command can only observe the action with binoculars since his flagship was damaged from a "sneak punch by a slant-eyed Beelzebub."

664 STAR SPANGLED RHYTHM (Para, Dec*) George Marshall; *genre:* Musical Comedy; *location:* United States; *coding:* AF-Blk, Fem Lab, Hist Am, Home Def, USO?, Jap, Ital, Collab, Hitler, Musso, Hirohito, Blk, Prod, Bonds, AF-N, AF-A, AF-MC, Short; *relevance:* 3.

This all-star Paramount musical received special roadshow release in late 1942, before going into general release the following year. Sailor Johnny Webster (Eddie Bracken) and his pals get shore leave in Los Angeles. They eagerly set out for the Paramount studios, where Johnny's father Pop (Victor Moore) is the head man—or so Pop had written. Actually, Pop is just the gate guard. Learning that his son is on the way, Pop and studio employee Polly (Betty Hutton) concoct a plan to have Pop impersonate studio head DeSoto (his name is a spoof of the then-current Paramount head of production Buddy DeSylva; Paramount chairman Y. Frank Freeman is called "Frank Fremont"). The scheme comes off successfully, but Johnny decides to have Pop sponsor a big show at the Canteen auditorium, at which time Johnny will marry Polly. Pop and Polly try to round up some Paramount stars, but DeSoto learns of their plot and fires them both. However, Polly manages to spread the word and the movie stars show up to put on a show for the servicemen. During Bing Crosby's final, patriotic number, "Old Glory," the sailors are recalled to their ship in preparation for sailing (see *Private Buckaroo*, q.v.). Guest stars include Paulette Goddard, Dorothy Lamour, Veronica Lake (these three doing a number entitled "A Sweater, A Sarong and a Peekaboo Bang"), William Bendix, Bob Hope, Preston Sturges, Cecil B. DeMille, Fred MacMurray, Eddie "Rochester" Anderson, Dick Powell, Mary Martin, and Alan Ladd (the trailer for the film boasted "More stars than in the flag").

665 THE STRANGE CASE OF DR. RX (Univ, Apr) William Nigh; *genre:* Crime; *location:* United States; *coding:* Blk, Short; *relevance:* 1.

Five men previously acquitted of various criminal charges due to incompetent prosecution are later murdered by a mysterious avenger. The killer turns out to be a crazed criminal lawyer (Samuel S. Hinds) who turns his poison-dart fountain pen on himself when the law closes in. During a craps game with a black servant (Mantan Moreland, who else?), a dimwitted police sergeant, played by Shemp Howard, offers a hunk of aluminum to cover his bet. He assures his skeptical opponent that the metal is badly needed by the government. Patric Knowles and Anne Gwynne were the romantic leads.

666 SUBMARINE RAIDER (Col, June) Lew Landers; *genre:* Combat; *locations:* Pacific, United States; *coding:* Spy-Sab, AF-Jap, Jew, Pearl Harb, AF-N, FBI; *relevance:* 3.

Taking place during December 6-7, 1941, this was the first Hollywood motion picture to re-enact the attack upon Pearl Harbor. The American submarine *Sea Serpent* picks up a pretty young woman (Marguerite Chapman) who is the sole survivor from a yacht that was sunk by a Japanese aircraft carrier headed for Hawaiian waters. When the submarine commander (John Howard) hears her story, he attempts to warn Pearl Harbor. However, the captain of the Japanese carrier jams the sub's signals and sends his pilot son into the air on a one way mission to sink the *Sea Serpent*. Meanwhile, the sub commander's brother, a government agent, is murdered while investigating mysterious activities around Honolulu (after the infamous raid there were many rumors of fifth columnists working on the island; one claimed arrows had been cut in the cane fields pointing to the naval base). Surfacing on the morning of the seventh, the crew of the *Sea Serpent* hear the wireless reports of the bombing of Pearl Harbor. They avenge their countrymen by ambushing the enemy carrier. The submarine crew and their lady passenger drink a toast to the remainder of the Imperial Japanese Navy: "Bottoms Up!" Ads for the film included the phrase "Fling defiance and shells into the fiendish face of Nippon's fury!" John Howard later served during the war, receiving the Navy Cross for valor.

667 SUNDAY PUNCH (MGM, May) David Miller; *genre:* Comedy/Drama; *location:* United States; *coding:* Draft; *relevance:* 1.

Love blossoms between a landlady's jaded daughter (Jean Rogers) and a disillusioned college dropout (William Lundigan) at a Brooklyn boarding house catering to aspiring boxers. The new Swedish janitor (Dan Dailey) is discovered to have a "punch like a ninety ton tank." Later on, another of the boxing boys, played by Leo Gorcey, proudly proclaims that he has been drafted by "my Uncle Sam."

668 SWEATER GIRL (Para, May*) William Clemens; *genre:* Musical Comedy/Crime; *location:* United States; *coding:* AF-A; *relevance:* 1.

A group of college kids attempt to put on a musical show, but members of the cast keep getting killed. Eddie Bracken plays the wisecracking campus hero who eventually exposes the murderer among them. He then announces his enlistment in the U. S. Army. One of the film's songs, "I Don't Want To Walk Without You," became a wartime hit.

669 SWEETHEART OF THE FLEET (Col, May) Charles Barton; *genre:* Musical Comedy; *location:* United States; *coding:* USO, Short, WWI, Pearl Harb, AF-N; *relevance:* 2.

Publicist Phoebe Weyms (Joan Davis), whose agency's top client sponsors a radio show called "A Blind Date With Romance," talks the local Navy recruiting station into participating in a publicity stunt. At a giant USO rally for the Navy, the two "mystery girls" who sing on the show will be revealed and proclaimed "Sweethearts of the Fleet." Problems arise when Phoebe learns that the singers, Brenda and Cobina (radio comics playing themselves), are so unattractive that personal appearances are not recommended. Phoebe finds two models to pose as the Blind Date girls, while persuading Brenda and Cobina to cooperate with behind-the-curtain singing. Phoebe promises to find them two sailor escorts. One of the selected escorts warily comments they "won't let Pearl Harbor happen twice." Brenda and Cobina's looks had also been the butt of a joke in *Caught in the Draft* (Paramount, 1941).

670 SYNCOPATION (RKO, May) William Dieterle; *genre:* Musical; *location:* United States; *coding:* AF-A, WWI, Bonds, USO, Hist Am, Jew?, Blk; *relevance:* 1.

The evolution of modern jazz from its African roots, the slave experience, the "colored" music of early 20th Century New Orleans and Chicago, the black influence upon white musicians beginning around World War I, and finally to the popular swing bands of 1940s America, is traced in *Syncopation*.

It is particularly noteworthy that, without ever being preachy, a strong message for racial cooperation is presented throughout this film. For instance, the starring white trumpeter (Jackie Cooper), whose career parallels the development of jazz, is inspired by a black trumpeter, Reggie (Todd Duncan—probably intended to represent Louis Armstrong). Reggie's mentor was a man named King Jeffers (obviously meant to be the famous King Oliver). In one scene, black jazz musicians who have traveled north from New Orleans perform at a Liberty Bonds rally in Chicago during the First World War.

671 TAKE MY LIFE [aka **MURDER RAP**] * (Ind, July) ?; *genre:* Drama; *location:* United States; *coding:* Blk, AF-A, AF-Blk; *relevance:* 1.

In this all-black feature, a Goldseal production released by Toddy-Consolidated, the "Harlem Dead End Kids" abandon their lifestyle of petty crime in order to join the U. S. Army.

672 TALES OF MANHATTAN (TCF, Aug) Julien Duvivier; *genre:* Drama; *location:* United States; *coding:* Bonds, WWI, Blk, Chi, AF-A; *relevance:* 1.

This is a multi-story film which follows a man's dress coat from its original owner to its final resting place (on a scarecrow). The war references all appear in the section starring Edward G. Robinson, George Sanders, and Henry Hull (other stories feature Charles Boyer, Henry Fonda, Rita Hayworth, Paul Robeson, and other players; a sequence with W.C. Fields was deleted prior to release).

Robinson is a down-on-his-luck lawyer who attends his Yale (Class of 1917) reunion wearing the coat. The first topical reference occurs when Robinson's invitation—marked return to sender, addressee unknown—is shown: "Buy Defense Bonds" is stamped across the envelope. Later, at the reunion, there are references to Robinson's Army training after his graduation (i.e., for World War One). He is also asked about his recent activities, and he says he just got in from "China" (actually, he had been in Chinatown), and someone asks him about the "fighting" there.

673 THE TALK OF THE TOWN (RKO, Aug) George Stevens; *genre:* Comedy Drama; *location:* United States; *coding:* Pol?, Blk; *relevance:* 1.

An anti-management worker, played by Cary Grant, is on the lam after being falsely accused of arson and murder when his foreman is thought to have died during a suspicious factory fire. As the "gardener" for a sympathetic school teacher (Jean Arthur) who has provided him refuge, he becomes friends with a Supreme Court nominee (Ronald Colman) renting the teacher's home

for the summer. The future Supreme Court justice later helps save the worker from a lynch mob. In an impassioned speech before the mob, the idealistic jurist condemns their violence and adds, with contemporary significance, that the law "is your finest possession ... It makes you free men in a free country. Think of a world [that is now] crying for this very law."

674 TEN GENTLEMEN FROM WEST POINT (TCF, June) Henry Hathaway; *genre:* Historical Drama; *location:* United States; *coding:* Mil School, Fr, WWI, Blk, MacArthur, Hist Am; *relevance:* 1.

The first class of cadets at the U. S. Military Academy go through their patriotic paces in Hollywood's version of early 19th-Century America. Initial training is so severe that only ten cadets from the original company remain (including George Montgomery and John Sutton). After the usual social leveling in the barracks and strategy lessons from an avuncular French instructor, the young men are given the chance to do a little Indian fighting against Tecumseh. Famous future graduates of West Point, including Generals Custer, Pershing and Douglas MacArthur are paid homage at the film's conclusion.

675 TENNESSEE JOHNSON (MGM, Dec*) William Dieterle; *genre:* Biography; *location:* United States; *coding:* AF-A?, Fr?, Blk, Latin Am, Hist Am; *relevance:* 1.

The life of Andrew Johnson is portrayed from the time he fled Tennessee in 1830 as an apprenticed tailor until his return to the Senate after serving as President of the United States. The greater part of the film centers around Johnson's (Van Heflin) struggles with the radical Republican leader, Thaddeus Stevens (Lionel Barrymore), culminating in the President's impeachment. Johnson's speech in his defense before the Senate was depicted by Hollywood in such a way as to contain inescapable contemporary allusions: "If [during Reconstruction] we continue a divided nation, the day will come when still stronger armies and fleets from overseas [than Napoleon III's] will conquer and enslave not only our Central and South American brethren, but ourselves as well. As our forefathers knew: 'United we stand; divided we fall.'" At the request of the OWI, scenes with Barrymore were re-shot to soften the character of Stevens, a rabid abolitionist, who was originally depicted in a much more villainous fashion.

676 TEXAS MANHUNT (PRC, Jan) Peter Stewart; *genre:* Western; *location:* United States; *coding:* Spy-Sab, Ger, AF-A, Short, Collab, Prod; *relevance:* 3.

A German-accented foreign agent named Reuther (Arno Frey) recruits a band of saboteurs in the American West to destroy enough cattle so that beef supplies to the U. S. Army are threatened: "Your reward will be a high place in the New Order.... I will reach you often to make sure your new patriotism has not wavered." Federal Marshall Lee Clark (Lee Powell) is sent to Texas by the U. S. Department of Agriculture to investigate the cattle sabotage. With the help of a pretty girl (Julie Duncan) and the local radio gossips, known as the "Winchells of the Prairie" (as in Walter Winchell; played by Bill "Radio" Boyd and Art Davis), Lee is able to round up the enemy agents responsible for creating the meat crisis.

677 TEXAS TO BATAAN (Mono, Oct) Robert Tansey; *genre:* Western/Spy; *locations:* United States, Philippines; *coding:* AF-A, Jap, FBI, Hitler, Musso, Jap, Nazi, Fil, Spy-Sab, Collab, Jap-Ger Coop, Pearl Harb, Prod; *relevance:* 3.

The Range Busters (John King, David Sharpe, and Max Terhune) and their wooden dummy sidekick, Elmer, take on Axis agents in the months immediately preceding America's entry into the war. These agents, led by a sneaky little Japanese man, are first encountered while attempting to sabotage a rancher's beef contract with the U.S. Army. Because of the earlier difficulties, the Range Busters escort a shipment of horses from the identical rancher to the U.S. Cavalry in the Philippines. While there, the boys have a violent altercation with members of the same enemy spy ring. Back in Texas, the Range Busters are preparing to attend church when the radio broadcasts news of the attack on Pearl Harbor. The boys indicate they plan to join up, and are told by a rancher friend: "And this time, go all the way to Tokyo."

678 THAT OTHER WOMAN (TCF, Nov) Ray McCarey; *genre:* Comedy; *location:* United States; *coding:* Bonds, Short, Home Fr, AF-A, AF-N; *relevance:* 1.5.

A young woman named Emily (Virginia Gilmore) works overtime to matrimonially entrap her playboy boss (James Ellison), a construction engineer. With the assistance of her aunt, a strategy is devised to ease out Emily's main rival while enhancing her own sex appeal. A subtle indication of wartime conditions is the large number of servicemen depicted in street scenes. Among the more overt references to the war is a sequence in which Emily informs her boss that she has had ten percent deducted from his salary to purchase War Bonds.

679 THEY ALL KISSED THE BRIDE (Col, June) Alexander Hall; *genre:* Comedy; *location:* United States; *coding:* AF-MC, Short, Jap; *relevance:* 1.

Joan Crawford portrays a tough businesswoman in charge of the Drew Transportation Company, which builds and operates trucks. She falls in love with a crusading reporter, played by Melvyn Douglas, who has written a series of articles exposing some of her underhanded methods. When confronted with information concerning her use of labor spies, Crawford delivers a classic example of war-inspired casual racism: "When I want a sneak, I'll hire the best—I'll get a Jap." Under the sway of her reporter lover, Crawford's character becomes a more humane employer.

680 THEY DIED WITH THEIR BOOTS ON (WB, Jan) Raoul Walsh; *genre:* Biography, Historical Drama; *location:* United States; *coding:* Brit, Blk, Hist Am, AF-A; *relevance:* 1.

With Errol Flynn playing the gallant "Long Hair," General George Armstrong Custer, this was another Hollywood picture that wreaked havoc with American history. The message is hyperbolic Americanism and promilitarism. The film deliberately downplays sectionalism during the Civil War episodes (unlike the 1940 WB release, *Santa Fe Trail*, q.v.). It blames political machinations and greed for starting an Indian war. But most interestingly, the film creates an entirely fictional ex–British officer, Lt. "Queens Own" Butler (George P. Huntley, Jr.), who deliberately turns down an offer to leave the Battle of the Little Big Horn in order to stand by his American compatriots to the bitter end. Lest one think current events were not on the minds of the studio heads, the following excerpt from a Warner Brothers interoffice memo dated May 13, 1941, from Aeneas MacKenzie to Hal Wallis, is informative: "I need not mention that this picture will be released at a moment when thousands of youths are being trained for commissions, and when hundreds of new and traditionless units are being formed. If we can inspire these to some appreciation of a great officer and a great regiment in their own Service, we shall have accomplished our mission."

681 THEY RAID BY NIGHT (PRC, June) Spencer G. Bennet; *genre:* Combat-Resistance; *locations:* Norway, Britain; *coding:* V, Can, AF-Nor, Nor, Brit, AF-Ger, Resist, AF-Brit, Hitler, Himmler, Nazi, Collab, Atroc; *relevance:* 3.

A Canadian-born British Army commando (Lyle Talbot) leads a small team that parachute into occupied Norway to rescue a Norwegian general held captive by the Nazis. A beautiful quisling's (June Duprez) betrayal results in the capture and torture of a member of the resistance and nearly leads to the failure of the mission. The Norwegian general is eventually brought to the coast where the raiders successfully rendezvous with a party of British commandos. The "...-" of Beethoven's Fifth Symphony is used on several occasions throughout the film. There had been two successful large-scale British raids upon the German garrison on Norway's Lofoten Islands in March and December of 1941.

682 THIS ABOVE ALL (TCF, July) Anatole Litvak; *genre:* War/Drama; *location:* Britain; *coding:* Dunkirk, AF-Ger, WWI?, AF-Brit, Brit, AF-W, Home Def, Hitler, Russ?, Jew?, Postwar; *relevance:* 3.

Prue Cathaway (Joan Fontaine), the daughter of a wealthy London surgeon, volunteers for the WAAFs over the class-biased objections of her matronly aunt. Prue says: "You and people like you are a worse danger to us than Hitler.... [Y]ou fear [the war] because the common men who are doing the fighting may suddenly begin to doubt the importance of risking their lives [to satisfy your selfish whims]." While in training camp, Prue meets Clive (Tyrone Power), an embittered lower-class man who is recovering from a wound he received at Dunkirk, but who has since become a deserter. Later, taking refuge from the Home Guard in a vicarage, Clive is bolstered by a talk with the church rector, himself a disabled veteran. Returning to London, Clive proves his bravery by rescuing a mother and child trapped in a building bombed by the Germans during the Blitz. This film was based on a novel by Eric Knight, author of *Lassie, Come Home*.

683 THIS GUN FOR HIRE (Para, Mar*) Frank Tuttle; *genre:* Crime/Spy; *location:* United States; *coding:* Pearl Harb?, Prod, Blk, Jap, Spy-Sab, Collab, Hist Am, Home Def; *relevance:* 2.

In his first starring role, Alan Ladd plays Raven, a professional killer who unwittingly becomes involved with an enemy collaborator. At about the same time, a singing magician, played by Veronica Lake, is enlisted by a senator to help him expose suspected fifth columnist activities. She encounters Raven on a train. He is fleeing the police, having been double-crossed by his employer. Later, she learns he worked for the wealthy industrialist (Tully Marshall) believed to be collaborating with the enemy. When their paths cross again, the lady magician arouses the killer's patriotism by convincing him that he was used to acquire a poison gas formula that was sold to the enemy: "Tomorrow they'll ship it back in bombs. Japanese breakfast food for America ... This war is everybody's business." Raven eventually helps defeat the treacherous millionaire, but pays with his own life. Based on a novel by Graham Greene, this film also features Brian Donlevy and Laird Cregar.

684 THROUGH DIFFERENT EYES (TCF, June) Thomas Z. Loring; *genre:*

Crime; *location:* United States; *coding:* Blk, Short, *relevance:* 1.

Veteran District Attorney Steve Pettijohn (Frank Craven) lectures a class of law students on the risks of accepting circumstantial evidence by citing the example of a recent murder case in which he was involved. In the course of relating the story, Pettijohn refers to having "to drive slowly to save tires."

685 THUNDER BIRDS (TCF, Nov) William A. Wellman; *genre:* Training; *location:* United States; *coding:* Postwar?, AF-AC, AF-A, US-Brit Coop?, USO, AF-Brit, AF-Chi, AF-Ger, Short, Sino-Jap War, Home Def, Atroc, Churchill, WWI, Jap; *relevance:* 3.

Allied air cadets receive their flight training at a military-sponsored civilian air base in Arizona (much of the film was shot on location at actual training fields near Scottsdale and Mesa). The daughter of a local rancher (Gene Tierney) is romantically torn between a young English trainee (John Sutton) and his middle-aged American instructor (Preston Foster). The former has left medical school to fly a bomber and thus avenge the death of his brother, shot down during a mission over Germany. After winning the heart of the American girl, the future RAF pilot tells her that he does not wish to be a "butcher up there, killing men for some empty victory," but that for the sake of the postwar world he wants "to help make it really mean something this time." Although Chinese flyers are praised at both the beginning and the end of this Technicolor film, none of the friendly Chinese cadets portrayed are individualized. RAF training in the United States began in June 1941. Trivia note: a photo of director Wellman appears in the film, identified as the WWI pilot-father of the John Sutton character (Wellman, a real-life WWI flyer, also directed *Wings*, 1926).

686 TIMBER (Univ, Aug) Christy Cabanne; *genre:* Adventure; *location:* United States; *coding:* Prod, Spy-Sab, Collab, FBI; *relevance:* 2.

A lumber camp owner is ordered by the government to speed up production or lose his war contract. The camp has been plagued by unexplained accidents and work slow-ups. The mill boss, named Quebec (Leo Carrillo), and the chief (Andy Devine) of the wood crews team up with a couple of undercover FBI men (including Dan Dailey) to track down the enemy agents responsible for the acts of sabotage (including the dangerous disabling of lumber trucks).

687 TISH (MGM, Sept) S. Sylvan Simon; *genre:* Comedy/Drama; *locations:* Canada, United States; *coding:* AF-AC?, Am Vol, Blk, Draft, Ital; *relevance:* 1.5.

Three old spinsters (Marjorie Main, ZaSu Pitts, and Aline MacMahon) meddle in the love life of a small town girl. The young lady (Virginia Grey) eventually makes the right romantic choice and secretly marries her childhood sweetheart (Lee Bowman), Main's nephew. She later leaves town to join her new husband when he becomes a bomber ferry pilot in Canada. Main's choice for Bowman was Susan Peters, who married Richard Quine instead. Quine is drafted and later killed in action, and Peters dies in childbirth. Main takes the baby home to raise.

688 TO BE OR NOT TO BE (UA, Mar) Ernst Lubitsch; *genre:* Comedy/Drama; *locations:* Poland, Britain; *coding:* AF-Raf, Spy-Sab, AF-Ger, Hitler, Nazi, Goering, Jew, Resist, V, Atroc-Conc, Hess, Pol, AF-W; *relevance:* 3.

A second-rate Shakespearean theatre troupe in Warsaw is preparing an anti–Nazi play when the Germans invade their country. The largely Jewish cast, headed by ham actor Joseph Tura (played by Jack Benny), soon become involved in resistance activities. They must prevent a German spy, who had been posing as a patriotic Polish professor, from revealing to the Gestapo the names of the Polish underground leaders and the families of Poles who are fighting with the British (Robert Stack appears as a Polish flyer with the RAF). To fool the Gestapo, Tura impersonates the professor. He borrows lines from the unstaged play to give color to his role. Having foiled the idiotic Nazis, several of the actors (including a Jew made up as Hitler) escape to England in a stolen German plane. They are approached by two farmers armed with pitchforks after parachuting over Scotland: "First it was Hess; now him [Hitler]." (Deputy Fuehrer Rudolph Hess had flown to Britain and parachuted over Scotland on May 10, 1941.) This film was released soon after the death of female lead Carole Lombard, who was killed in an airplane crash while on a Bond tour. *To Be or Not to Be* was remade, over 40 years later, by actor-director Mel Brooks, who took the Jack Benny role.

689 TO THE SHORES OF TRIPOLI (TCF, Apr) H. Bruce Humberstone; *genre:* Training; *location:* United States; *coding:* Hist Am?, AF-N, AF-MC, AF-W, V, Pearl Harb, Jap, Fil, Chi, WWI, FDR, Latin Am; *relevance:* 3.

John Payne plays a brash playboy who joins the Marine Corps in 1941. His training takes place at the Marine's San Diego base, under a tough sergeant (Randolph Scott) with whom his father had served during the first World War. After the usual altercation with his sergeant, the new recruit redeems himself by saving the non-com's life during a repair operation on a floating gunnery target. Nevertheless, the new hero elects to leave the service. But as he grabs a cab with his girl (a nurse; played by Maureen O'Hara) the radio announces the "surprise Japanese attack on Pearl Harbor." He jumps out of the cab and rejoins his mates, who just happen to be marching down the street to board a waiting transport ship. They pass an Asian man who is enthusiastically waving an American flag and wearing a hand lettered sign reading: "Me Chinese." This Technicolor picture was released during the height of anti–Japanese hysteria in the nation, and proved to be one of Fox's most profitable films of the season.

690 TOMORROW WE LIVE (PRC, Sept) Edgar G. Ulmer; *genre:* Crime; *location:* United States; *coding:* Blk Mkt, Hitler, Short, AF-A?; *relevance:* 2.

Old Pop Bronson, an ex-con who runs a desert lunchroom in Arizona, is blackmailed by a gangster known as the "Ghost" (Ricardo Cortez) into fronting for a black market operation in stolen tires. Pop's daughter (Jean Parker) and her boyfriend, Lt. Bob Lord, come to the rescue. Bob informs the gang leader that he is a lot like Hitler. The Ghost petulantly replies: "Hitler! Why he's a cheap amateur." The gangster then proceeds to explain to Bob why he is better than Hitler.

691 TOP SERGEANT (Univ, June) Christy Cabanne; *genre:* Training; *location:* United States; *coding:* Mil Exer, AF-A, FBI; *relevance:* ?

Another Don Terry-Leo Carrillo-Andy Devine vehicle (see also *Escape from Hong Kong* and *Unseen Enemy*, q.v.). Four soldiers en route to camp in a jeep have an encounter with a group of bank bandits fleeing a posse of deputy sheriffs. When the smoke clears three of the gunmen and the kid brother of Sergeant Manson (Terry) are dead. The surviving bandit, Al Bennett, escapes and later joins the army. His Top Sergeant is none other than the unsuspecting Manson. Bennett's negligence during maneuvers leads to the death of several GIs and the exposure of his criminal past. Manson is sent on to Officer's Training School.

692 TORPEDO BOAT (Para, Jan*) John Rawlins; *genre:* Adventure; *location:* United States; *coding:* AF-MC, AF-N, Prod; *relevance:* 1.5.

A couple of dare-devil pals, Skimmer and Tommy (Richard Arlen and Phillip Terry), design a smaller, faster and stronger naval craft than the fleet's standard PT Boat. Having largely overcome the standard cash flow problem and rivalry for the ladies, the two are given a chance to show off their test model to officers of the U. S. Navy. However, ignoring Tommy's warnings, Skimmer pushes the boat beyond its limitations, resulting in Tommy's death when the engine explodes. Skimmer atones for his recklessness by sacrificing a second test model to prevent a barge from crashing into another experimental boat being driven by his girl (Jean Parker). When Skimmer awakens in the hospital, she is by his side and he is informed of the Navy's acceptance of his design.

693 A TRAGEDY AT MIDNIGHT (Rep, Feb) Joseph Santley; *genre:* Crime; *location:* United States; *coding:* Chi, Ger; *relevance:* 1.

An amateur sleuth (John Howard) in the Thin Man tradition, has a radio show on which he frequently broadcasts solutions to current murder mysteries. When he and his wife (Margaret Lindsay) find the corpse of a young girl in an apartment loaned to them, the oft-ridiculed police are more than glad to pin the rap on him. The only reference to the war is contained in a bit of dialogue delivered by the harried radio station representative when he tries to make up a program for an unfilled hour slot: "Put in anything—animal acts, German bands. No! Don't get German bands."

694 THE TRAITOR WITHIN (Rep, Dec) Frank McDonald; *genre:* Drama; *location:* United States; *coding:* WWI, Short?, Ger-Am; *relevance:* 1.

Don Barry is the truckdriver boyfriend of Jean Parker. Parker's father (George Cleveland) is always bragging about his WWI heroics, which (he says) were wrongly attributed to the current mayor of the town. Parker meets a German—now an American citizen—who tells her that her father is telling the truth. Parker gets Barry to blackmail the mayor into giving him a new truck, but pushes it too far by threatening to reveal the truth to the opposition party. The mayor commits suicide, and the whole plot comes out.

695 TRAMP, TRAMP, TRAMP (Col, Mar) Charles Barton; *genre:* Comedy; *location:* United States; *coding:* WWI, Blk, Russ, Nazi, FDR, AF-Ger, Spy-Sab, Draft, AF-A, Home Def; *relevance:* 2.

When Bellville's boys depart to become "draftees," Hank (Jackie Gleason) and Jed (Jack Durant), the town's barbers, face financial ruin. The Mutt and Jeff-like duo try to enlist, but fail the Army's physical (Hank cannot read the eye chart because he is illiterate—ironically, in 1941 the armed forces discovered that one of five men examined for the draft were unable to read). Still desiring to help out Uncle Sam, they form a Home Defense army with other "rejectees," drilling in the backyard of a widow whose son was killed in the "last war." Their attempts at taking photos of training result in

the two being arrested as spies. The colonel, who is from their hometown, clears them. Publicity about the Home Defense Army leads to units being established across the nation. A group of notorious gangsters join up in order to evade the law. As a result, they passively endure the periodic harrasments of a midget sergeant and the idiocies of "commander" Hank. When a local newspaperwoman confirms the mob's murderous activities, Hank and Jed uphold the honor of their Boy Scout-style uniforms by bagging the criminals beneath their tent and holding them for the police. This film would appear to have been completed prior to America's entrance into the war.

696 TRUE TO THE ARMY (Para, Mar*) Albert S. Rogell; *genre:* Comedy; *location:* United States; *coding:* Draft, AF-A, V, US-Brit Coop; *relevance:* 2.

Daisy Hawkins (Judy Canova) is a circus performer who witnesses a gangland killing. In an attempt to avoid the mob, she flees to the nearby Army camp where her boyfriend, played by Jerry Colonna, is the head pigeon trainer. Predictable complications arise after Daisy is transformed into a new Army private. The latter part of the film is made up of a series of routines performed at a huge show for the servicemen. The general's daughter (Ann Miller) tap dances to the beat of machine-gunning. Daisy then comes on stage and, while singing "I'm Wacky for Khaki," shoots the menacing gangsters who have dispersed throughout the crowd. The finale portrays the principals singing in front of a V formation of saluting soldiers. This was a remake of *She Loves Me Not* (Paramount, 1934), a college musical starring Bing Crosby and Miriam Hopkins, and was in turn remade as *How to be Very Very Popular* (TCF, 1955).

697 TWIN BEDS (UA, Apr) Tim Whelan; *genre:* Comedy; *location:* United States; *coding:* AF-A, USO, Russ, AF-N, Blk, Latin Am; *relevance:* 2.

Quarrelsome newlyweds, played by George Brent and Joan Bennett, do not have a proper honeymoon because the wife has joined the USO (as a "colonel") and immediately begins devoting her time to such things as "Kisses For Soldiers" at charity balls. Their married life becomes even more strained when the wife has twin beds installed in their bedroom and a crazy Russian singer (Mischa Auer) moves in as their neighbor.

698 TWO YANKS IN TRINIDAD (Col, Mar) Gregory Ratoff; *genre:* Comedy; *locations:* Caribbean, United States; *coding:* Mil Exer, Brit?, Blk, AF-A, AF-N, Collab, Atroc, Pearl Harb, Jap, Latin Am, Fil, Draft; *relevance:* 2.

When two racketeers, played by Brian

Donlevy and Pat O'Brien, have a falling out, the latter joins the U. S. Army to escape the vengeance of the former. Donlevy and his two bodyguards also enlist and follow O'Brien to his station on Trinidad (one of the bases leased to America by the British in the fall of 1940 in exchange for fifty World War I vintage destroyers—the Trinidad base became operational in August 1941, and was an important link in the South American shipping route). The people of Trinidad enthusiastically welcome the U.S. soldiers to their island. The new GIs unwittingly become involved with a displaced American gangster who owns the local nightclub, and who secretly sells fuel oil to "foreign submarines" (not seen, and never specified as German). Donlevy plans to desert, until he is informed of the Japanese assaults upon Pearl Harbor and Manila. He then teams up with O'Brien to blow up the gangster's oil tanker, using a floating mine towed behind a smaller boat. The two are promoted to the rank of sergeant but are also sentenced to the brig! This fairly elaborate and well-produced film was almost certainly conceived before Pearl Harbor (the finale seems tacked-on), and strongly resembles pre-war films like *Buck Privates* (1941)—there is even a comic, irascible sergeant (Donald MacBride) and extensive footage of military maneuvers.

699 UNDERCOVER MAN (UA, Oct) Lesley Selander; *genre:* Western; *location:* United States; *coding:* Latin Am, US-Mex Coop; *relevance:* 1.

This is a typical period (late 1800s) Hopalong Cassidy (William Boyd) western. Sporadic raids on both sides of the United States-Mexican border have led to mutual antagonism among the local people. Hopalong is called in to round up the gang responsible for the raids and to re-establish harmony between the two nationalities. There are several references to being "good neighbors" in the film. The OWI referred to this "propaganda" as anachronistic, "but it is too obvious to be missed."

700 UNDERGROUND AGENT (Col, Dec) Michael Gordon; *genre:* Spy; *location:* United States; *coding:* Pearl Harb, Fem Lab, AF-A, Churchill, Hitler, Ital, Jap, Ger, Ital-Jap-Ger Coop, Spy-Sab, Collab, Latin Am, Atroc, Prod; *relevance:* 3.

When it is discovered that Axis saboteurs have been tapping into the phone lines of defense plants, Lee Graham (Bruce Bennett) of the telephone company is called in. Lee puts together a team and with their help he devises a word scrambler. But the boarding house in which they live turns out to be a front for the Axis ring led by a German agent named Miller (Rhys Williams). A patriotic Mexican-American assistant of Lee's, Miguel, is subsequently tortured by the evil Miller in an attempt to force him to betray the secret of the scrambler. Dying, Miguel delivers an impassioned speech in defense of democracy: "Here we live like free men; not slaves like you ... You will not find many in the Americas who will trade their freedom for the darkness you bring on the world." The Axis agents, including the usual reluctant Italian participant, are rounded up. With his work completed on the home front, Lee prepares to enter the Army so that he can "take a look at Tokyo through a gun sight." The OWI commented: "The film stops in its tracks at regular intervals to allow [Miguel and his family] to say [how much they love America]—with saccharine emphasis."

701 UNSEEN ENEMY (Univ, Apr) John Rawlins; *genre:* Spy; *locations:* United States, Canada; *coding:* Isolat, Dipl, Jap, AF-Jap, AF-Can, AF-Brit, AF-Mer?, Can, Ital, AF-Ger, Ital-Ger-Jap Coop, Hitler, Musso, Spy-Sab, Intell Serv, Prod; *relevance:* 3.

A rabidly propagandistic prologue identifying this film as taking place in the fall of 1941 refers to the Japanese as the "treacherous hordes of the rising sun." A Canadian intelligence officer (played by Don Terry) poses as a Nazi at a prison camp in order to learn about an Axis spy ring in San Francisco. A captured German sea raider captain has been ordered to join the spies following his planned escape. Waiting for the captain in San Francisco is a crew of Axis seamen smuggled into the country to man an interned Japanese ship. The enemy agents intend to hijack the ship and convert it into a raider, which will prey upon America's west coast shipping. A harbor patrol detective (Andy Devine) teams up with the Canadian to defeat the Axis enemy. They are further assisted by a loyal Italian-American (Leo Carrillo), who after realizing he has been duped by the spies into helping provide them with a front, turns on his former business colleagues. Before the United States entered the war, there was some pro–Mussolini sentiment among Italian-Americans; however, after the attack on Pearl Harbor, Italian-American *anti*-fascist organizations by the hundreds were formed. The government never seriously doubted the loyalty of Americans of Italian or German descent *as a class*, unlike the blanket distrust of Japanese-American citizens (which lead to their "relocation").

702 VALLEY OF HUNTED MEN (Rep, Nov) John English; *genre:* Western/Spy; *locations:* United States, Canada; *coding:* AF-Ger, Spy-Sab, AF-Can, Hitler, Nazi, Ref, Pearl Harb, Short, Collab, Ital, POW, Jap, Ger, Ger-Am, Prod; *relevance:* 3.

Three Nazi flyers escape from a Canadian internment camp in the fall of 1941 and flee across the border to Montana. They ruthlessly kill several locals, including a store owner who insults the Fuehrer. A posse is formed by the citizens of Valley City to track down the murderers. The posse kills two Nazis and mistakenly believes it has eliminated the third. Posing as the nephew of Dr. Steiner (Edward Van Sloan), a refugee scientist who has smuggled to America a secret formula for rubber extraction from culebra plants, the surviving Nazi flyer (Roland Varno) plots with German-American Bundists to sabotage Steiner's experiments. On the day of the Pearl Harbor attack, the culebra plants that local ranchers planted in cooperation with Steiner are destroyed. The doctor is suspected by the ranchers of selling out the United States to his fatherland. The Three Mesquiteers (Bob Steele, Tom Tyler, Jimmie Dodd) come to Steiner's rescue and nab the Nazi villains.

703 WAKE ISLAND (Para, Aug*) John Farrow; *genre:* Combat; *location:* Pacific; *coding:* Dipl, AF-N, AF-MC, Hitler, Goebbels, Spy-Sab?, Atroc?, Hist Am, Jap, Hirohito, AF-Jap, FDR, Pearl Harb, Russ, Pol, Chi, Ital, WWI; *relevance:* 3.

In the latter half of 1941, U. S. Marines and a civilian construction crew work feverishly to complete the fortifications on a small Pacific island outpost. In late November they briefly host the infamous Japanese peace delegation led by Kurusu when it makes a stopover on the journey to Washington, D.C. Immediately following the Pearl Harbor attack, Japanese naval forces lay seige to Wake. Among the Marine defenders is a Polish aircraft mechanic whose family was caught in Warsaw during the German invasion, and a pilot whose wife was killed at Pearl Harbor. Comic relief is provided by two career Marines, played by William Bendix and Robert Preston. When the Japanese make their first landing attempt upon the island, Bunker Hill is invoked as the Marines are ordered to hold their fire until seeing the "whites of their eyes." The pilot of the island's last aircraft is coldly machine-gunned by a Japanese flyer after bailing out. In the final scene the civilian contracting engineer (Macdonald Carey) and the Marine commander (played by Brian Donlevy) are shown fighting side by side as the Japanese overwhelm the last defensive position on Wake (the island was defended Dec. 8-23, 1941). Director John Farrow shot this film just after his release from combat duty with the Canadian Navy. This was one of the most popular box-office films of 1942, and was nominated for four Academy Awards.

704 THE WAR AGAINST MRS. HADLEY (MGM, Sept) Harold S. Bucquet; *genre:* War/Drama; *location:* United States; *coding:* Blk, AF-AC?, Pearl Harb, Draft, USO, AF-A, Home Def, V, Fil, FDR, MacArthur, Short, Nazi, Austral, Home Fr, Jap; *relevance:* 3.

Stella Hadley (Fay Bainter), a fatuous wealthy widow living in the nation's capital, would prefer to ignore the fact that the United States has entered the war. But the war ineluctably intrudes upon her life. Among other things, her butler becomes an air raid warden, her son is drafted, her daughter marries a working-class sergeant, and her best friend Cecelia begins reneging on social engagements in order to take first aid courses. Mrs. Hadley is not fully converted into an informed and conscientious citizen until she learns that her son has won the Distinguished Service Cross for wiping out a Japanese machine gun nest. Cecelia comments that "those Japs and Nazis better look out, now that Stella's in the war."

705 WAR DOGS [aka PRIDE OF THE ARMY] (Mono, Nov) S. Roy Luby; *genre:* War/Drama; *location:* United States; *coding:* Juv, Postwar?, Pearl Harb, AF-A, AF-MC, Prod, Fem Lab, WWI, Spy-Sab; *relevance:* 3.

In a small eastern town a young social worker and a juvenile court judge attempt to help a motherless adolescent named Billy Freeman (Billy Lee), whose father is an alcoholic First World War veteran. Mr. Freeman, a former Marine captain, is turned down when he tries to re-enlist. But Billy's police dog (wartime euphemism for German shepherd) Pal, is accepted for training to become an Army Patrol Dog. Billy tearfully tells Pal to "Remember Pearl Harbor" when he leaves his canine friend at the "Dogs For Defense" training camp. Mr. Freeman is meanwhile given a job at a war plant. Later, Billy's father proves himself a hero by sacrificing his life to dispose of a bomb thrown at the factory by saboteurs. Plant guards, with the assistance of Pal, capture the enemy agents. The judge and the social worker marry and adopt Billy: "This time we're going to fix it so you don't have to win a war—ever!" The U. S. Army, with the assistance of the civilian sponsored Dogs For Defense organization, recruited and trained about 50,000 canines during the war. The "K-9" Corps was officially formed in 1942. Juvenile lead Billy Lee had earlier appeared in another popular "boy and his dog" film, *The Biscuit Eater* (Paramount, 1940).

706 WE WERE DANCING (MGM, Mar) Robert Z. Leonard; *genre:* Comedy; *location:* United States; *coding:* Jew?, Pol, Austria, Ital, Brit, Neth, Chi, Blk; *relevance:* 1.

A penniless Polish princess (Norma Shearer) and a Polish gigolo (Melvyn Douglas) secretly elope from a party at which her engagement to a wealthy American is to be announced. They allude to being refugees as a result of Hitler's invasion of their homeland. The sophisticated couple survive by being "professional guests" at the homes of philistine families. That is, until the word gets around that the two are married. A domestic crisis arises when the husband decides to find a real job.

707 WHAT'S COOKIN' (Univ, Feb)
Edward F. Cline; *genre:* Musical Comedy; *location:* United States; *coding:* AF-A, Jap, Home Def; *relevance:* 2.

Marvo the Magician (Leo Carrillo) helps a group of youngsters who call themselves "The Jiving Jacks and Jills," put together a song and dance act. With the added assistance of the little rich girl next door, the aspiring performers are signed up for a radio show with established stars, including the Andrews Sisters. The show is sponsored by the rich girl's aunt, the head of an organization called "All-American Food." Soldiers from an artillery unit stationed nearby attend the program's debut. "I'll Pray For You," sung by the Andrews Sisters, contains wartime allusions; "Pack Up Your Troubles," a WWI-vintage song, is also heard. The final scene of the film portrays the rich girl's harried uncle throwing a plate (on the back of which is inscribed: "Made in Japan") to the floor. The last shot before the end titles roll shows feet trampling over the printing on the shattered crockery.

708 WHERE TRAILS END (Mono, Apr)
Robert E. Tansey; *genre:* Western/Spy; *location:* United States; *coding:* Spy-Sab, Prod, Collab; *relevance:* 2.

A U. S. Marshal, played by Tom Keene, is assigned to help the people in a valley who are being run off their ranches by a gang of terrorists. It turns out that the vital war mineral tungsten has been discovered in the valley and enemy agents want to gain control of the land before this information is revealed.

709 WHISTLING IN DIXIE (MGM, Dec)
S. Sylvan Simon; *genre:* Comedy/Crime; *location:* United States; *coding:* Blk?, Jap, Short; *relevance:* 1.

Wally Benton (Red Skelton) is a popular New York radio mystery show detective known to his listeners as "The Fox." After completing a show in which the Fox foils a saboteur named "Otto," Wally prepares to leave town on his honeymoon. But when his fiancee, Carol (Ann Rutherford), receives a scarab pin from a former sorority sister, she insists they first visit the girl's home in Georgia. This leads the couple to adventure and intrigue centered around a stash of gold hidden in the powder magazine of a Civil War era fort. Wally delivers a few cracks with regards to wartime shortages. There is also the following exchange with Carol when he opens the package containing the scarab:

WALLY: What I've always wanted, a Japanese beetle.
CAROL: What makes you think it's a Japanese beetle?
WALLY: It's got a yellow belly.

This film was a sequel to *Whistling in the Dark* (MGM, 1941).

710 WHITE CARGO (MGM, Sept)
Richard Thorpe; *genre:* Adventure; *location:* Africa; *coding:* Blk, Brit, Short, Jap; *relevance:* 1.

White plantation overseers at an African rubber station in 1910 are driven crazy by the heat and a scheming half-breed native girl named Tondelayo (Hedy Lamarr). The motion picture opens with a brief scene in the wartime present. The head boss flies in to visit the station. When the manager states that the native workers will want to celebrate, the boss responds: "All celebrations are off, and all leaves ... for the duration.... With the Japs in Malaya, we need rubber and more rubber." He goes on to say that increasing production without access to new equipment means they will have to recruit more labor, like in the old days.

711 WHO DONE IT? (Univ, Nov)
Erle C. Kenton; *genre:* Comedy; *location:* United States; *coding:* FBI, Hist Am, Short, Home Def, Russ, Czech, WWI, Spy-Sab, Nazi; *relevance:* 1.5.

Abbott and Costello play soda jerks who are aspiring radio writers. One evening they are given a chance to meet Colonel Andrews, the head of the "GBS" network, following the broadcast of his "America on the Air" show. But just as the Colonel announces he has a vital message for all Americans he is mysteriously killed. The boys, along with a professor friend and his girl, track down the murderer. In the process, they discover Andrews was about to expose an enemy agent who used the broadcast to send coded messages relaying convoy positions to the Nazis. While working at the Radio City drug store, Abbott and Costello perform a couple of war-oriented gags. For instance, when Abbott asks for three lumps of sugar in his coffee, Costello tells him to turn his back and then dunks a sugar cube tied to a string three times into the coffee cup.

712 THE WIFE TAKES A FLYER (Col, Apr)
Richard Wallace; *genre:* Comedy; *location:* Netherlands; *coding:* Fr, AF-Raf, AF-Ger, Nor, Pol, Den, Neth, AF-Ger, Hitler, Nazi, Russ, Musso, Ital, V, Atroc-Conc, Resist, Belg, Hirohito, Jap, Brit; *relevance:* 3.

RAF pilot Chris Reynolds (Franchot Tone) takes refuge in Anita Waverman's home after being shot down over Nazi-occupied Holland. The Dutch family represents him to the fatuous Hitler-heiling Nazi billeted in their home, Major Zellfritz (Allyn Joslyn—wearing a monocle and pitching his voice lower than normal), as the mad husband of Anita (Joan Bennett). By day, the Nazi drops propaganda leaflets over England, and at night he assiduously attempts to seduce Anita. One evening, the Major brings a basket full of food from the various conquered countries for dinner with Anita. She points to the chicken and asks where he got the "bird." Zellfritz replies: "*All* the countries give us the bird." After being captured and sentenced to death by the Nazis, Chris is able to escape during an air raid alarm, steal Zellfritz's uniform and fly off to England with Anita in the Major's plane. The film's conclusion shows Zellfritz walking away from the camera with "The End" superimposed on the seat of his pants. The OWI analyst noted: "It is true that it is hard to hate Major Zellfritz at whom you laugh so heartily; however it is also true that movie-goers do not flock to the depressing, hate-stirring, anti–Nazi films."

713 WINGS FOR THE EAGLE (WB, July)
Lloyd Bacon; *genre:* War/Drama; *locations:* United States, Pacific?; *coding:* Draft, Ger, Isolat, Draft, Draft Avoid, US-Brit Coop, FDR?, Churchill, UN?, WWI, AF-AC, AF-A, Prod, Pearl Harb, Chi, Fil, Jap, Nazi, Fem Lab; *relevance:* 3.

Largely taking place in the year before Pearl Harbor, this film deals with defense production at a Lockheed aircraft plant in California. Featured workers include Corky Jones (Dennis Morgan), who attempts to escape the draft via an "essential defense work" exemption, and Jake Hanso (George Tobias), a patriotic alien crew boss who loses his job because he never obtained his citizenship papers. Soon after December 7th, Jake takes his oath of citizenship and is reinstated at Lockheed. On the very day the workers celebrate the 2000th bomber to come off the line, Jake receives a telegram informing him that his son, an Army pilot serving in the Philippines, was killed in action. Corky has meanwhile had a change of heart, enlisted and been awarded his commission in the Army Air Corps. Somewhere over the Pacific, he and his bomber crew avenge Jake's son by shooting down two Japanese planes. In one scene, midgets are shown working in confined spaces in the tail sections of airplanes under construction, a practice which actually occurred in real life.

714 WOMAN OF THE YEAR (MGM, Feb)
George Stevens; *genre:* Comedy/Drama; *location:* United States; *coding:* Juv, Blk,

Yugo, Chi, Nor?, Latin Am?, Churchill, FDR, FDR-E, Ref, Vichy, Hitler, Hess, Nazi, Chiang, Span Civ, Atroc-Conc, Russ, Grk; *relevance:* 2.5.

Sam, a sports writer, and Tess, an aggressive female political columnist (Spencer Tracy and Katharine Hepburn), working for the same New York newspaper, fall in love, marry and then overcome their differences. With a witty script by Ring Lardner, Jr., this film could be construed as symbolically affirming a united front against the militarist regimes by juxtaposing the liberal intellectual Tesses of society with the baseball-loving Sams of America. Tess is the emancipated Fifth Avenue blueblood who has been crusading to resist fascism since the Spanish Civil War, but Sam is the guy in the street who instinctively understands that a little Greek refugee boy needs committed love rather than a lot of expensive toys. The motion picture is full of contemporary references, such as Sam commenting to a friend that "she [Tess] don't talk to anybody that hasn't signed a non-aggression pact."

715 X MARKS THE SPOT (Rep, Nov) George Sherman; *genre:* Crime; *location:* United States; *coding:* Blk Mkt, Short, AF-A, Intell Serv, Home Def; *relevance:* 1.5.

Eddie Delaney, a young private detective, is about to receive his commission in Army Intelligence when he learns his police sergeant father has been killed during a warehouse heist. With the aid of Lt. Decker (Dick Purcell) of the Homicide Squad, Eddie sets out to find the murderers. Suspicion begins to fall on Eddie, following his discovery of additional bodies. Eddie's sleuthing finally leads him to the warehouse, which is full of tires being sold on the black market. The "head boss" of the racket, Lt. Decker, appears and attempts to kill Eddie. The police, having been alerted by Eddie's girlfriend, arrive and arrest the gang. The OWI analysis expressed indignation that the film did *not* "show that Americans who either buy or sell in the Black Market are traitors aiding the enemy." It concluded that *"X Marks the Spot* is an example of a film using a vital war problem as a convenient peg on which to hang a gangster melodrama. It is the kind of film the OWI does not want to see made."

716 A YANK AT ETON (MGM, Sept) Norman Taurog; *genre:* Drama; *locations:* Britain, United States; *coding:* Brit, Hist Am, US-Brit Coop; *relevance:* 1.

Timothy Dennis (Mickey Rooney) is a typical American high schooler who is "deported" before the war to Britain's most prestigious prep school when his widowed mother marries a wealthy Englishman. In a timely revision of the MGM-British studio release, *A Yank at Oxford* (1938), but with younger participants, the impulsive Timothy learns to appreciate the value of America's kinship with our more restrained English brethren. One sequence, in which the avuncular headmaster (Edmund Gwenn) welcomes Timothy back after having run away, is particularly noteworthy. The headmaster quotes Thomas Jefferson to the youthful American: "With Great Britain on our side we need not fear the whole world. With her, then, we should most sedulously cherish a cordial friendship, and nothing would tend more to knit our affections ... than to be fighting once more, side by side in the same cause."

717 A YANK IN LIBYA (PRC, July) Albert Herman; *genre:* Adventure; *location:* North Africa; *coding:* Spy-Sab, Intell Serv, US-Brit Coop, Hitler, Himmler, Nazi, Hirohito, Russ, Grk, Austral, War Corr, AF-Brit, Brit, Arab, Collab; *relevance:* 3.

Mike Malone (Walter Woolf King), an American correspondent in Libya, uncovers a Nazi conspiracy to incite the Arabs near a British garrison to revolt. Mike barely escapes from the Arabs with one of the guns supplied them by the Germans. When he reports this to the local British consul (topbilled H.B. Warner), Mike is dismissed as a meddler. Mike then meets a crazy Brooklynite (comedian Parkyarkarkus) posing as an Arab peddler. The supposed peddler is actually working for British intelligence, who are fully aware of the Nazi plot. The flustered British consul tells a compatriot that Malone is "more of a nuisance than a fifth column and an Arab revolt rolled into one." In spite of Malone's continued interference, and with the aid of a loyal Arab chieftain, the attempted uprising is suppressed and the responsible Nazi agent slain. Interestingly, there is no textual indication that Libya had been an Italian possession, nor that it was still the scene of an ongoing military campaign at the time of the film's release.

718 A YANK ON THE BURMA ROAD (MGM, Jan) George Seitz; *genre:* War/Drama; *locations:* United States, Burma, China; *coding:* US-Chi Coop, Am Vol, Brit, Ger-Jap Coop?, Hist Am, Sino-Jap War, Chiang, Chi, AF-Chi, Resist, Collab, AF-Jap, Jap, WWI, Ger-Am?, Eth?, Pearl Harb, Ital, Span Civ; *relevance:* 3.

At the opening of the film a rolling title appears: "This is the story of one American who tackled Japan a little before the rest of us ... And what he started, the rest of the Yanks will finish!" A New York cabbie named Joe Tracy (Barry Nelson) receives a lot of publicity when he captures the notorious Spinaldi brothers. As a result, he is invited by the Chinese Benevolent Society to lead a convoy carrying medical supplies over the Burma Road to Chungking. While in Rangoon, Joe meets Gail Farwood (Laraine Day) and agrees to take her along. What Gail initially fails to tell Joe is that her German-American husband, who had been flying for the Japanese, is a captive of Chinese guerrillas. Harrassed by Japanese aircraft, the convoy arrives at a bombed-out village where they witness the suffering of Chinese civilians. They are informed of the Pearl Harbor attack. In exchange for Gail's husband's life, Joe agrees to lead the local guerrillas in an assault upon a Japanese-occupied town that commands the road. During the battle, the traitorous spouse is (conveniently) killed. After taking the town, a smiling Joe tells his Chinese allies to: "Bring on some more Japs." Informed the road is now clear to Chungking, Joe confidantly adds: "We're not stoppin'.... We're headin' for Tokyo, Yokohama and points east!" Released about a month after the fall of Wake Island, Joe's penultimate comment mimics the famous radio message attributed to that doomed island garrison: "Send us more Japs." The character of Joe Tracy was inspired by Daniel Arnstein, a Chicago cabdriver who, as the United States "commissioner" to the Burma Road, was credited with breaking the bottleneck of transport and supplies.

719 YANKEE DOODLE DANDY (WB, May) Michael Curtiz; *genre:* Biographical Musical; *location:* United States; *coding:* Brit, Ger, Hist Am, USO, Jew, Short, AF-N, AF-W?, AF-A, FDR, FDR-E, Fr, Hirohito, Hitler, Jap, Blk, WWI, Vet; *relevance:* 2.

This musical biography of George M. Cohan (James Cagney) begins as Cohan is summoned to the White House by the President (a thinly disguised FDR impersonation). Cohan, who is appearing in a play about a president (*I'd Rather Be Right*), thinks he may have offended the Chief Executive: "It's wartime—it may be treason. I may get shot for this." However, the President merely wants to present the Congressional Medal of Honor to Cohan for his contribution to "the American spirit." The President says Cohan's WWI song "Over There" was "just as powerful a weapon as any cannon, as any battleship we had ... Today, we're all soldiers, we're all on the front." Most of the film is a flashback of Cohan's life and career in show business. In one sequence, he tries to enlist in the Army in WWI but is turned down because he is 39 years old. Instead, he writes "Over There" and this song becomes his contribution to the war effort. The film ends with a company of soldiers marching past the White House singing "Over There." The premiere of this film was pushed forward several months (from July to May 1942) because

Warner Brothers was afraid Cohan—who was dying of cancer—would not live to see its release. He did, and in fact lived until November 1942.

720 THE YANKS ARE COMING (PRC, Nov) Alexis Thurn-Taxis; *genre:* Musical; *location:* United States; *coding:* AF-N, AF-AC, AF-A, AF-MC, Short, V, UN, FDR, MacArthur, Nazi, Fr, Pol, Den, Nor, Neth, AF-Brit, AF-Russ, AF-Chi, Belg, Draft, Ital, Jap, Prod, Fem Lab?, USO; *relevance:* 3.

The members of a popular band (Henry King and his Orchestra) join the Army after their crooner, Bob Reynolds, turns down a Hollywood contract in order to enlist. Only Gil Whitney, the band leader, resists, declaring his brother is "sucker" enough for one family. But even Gil changes his tune when he receives a telegram that Bob has been killed in action. Once in uniform, the band is quickly reconstituted to rehearse for a big canteen show. There are numerous war-oriented posters visible on the walls of the hall, including one which reads "Little Japs Have Big Ears," and the ubiquitous "Zip Your Lip." Four of the songs played in the film are war oriented. "There Will Be No Blackout Of Democracy" was inspired by an FDR speech and includes the lyrics: "This nation is united as it was never before; we all see eye to eye ... We have the solemn vow of Franklin D." This motion picture, which is loaded with topical references, is framed by a pro-filmic patriotic prologue and epilogue which the OWI uncharitably described as "a pretentious parenthesis in which to enclose a film of skimpy dimensions."

721 YOU CAN'T ESCAPE FOREVER (WB, Oct) Jo Graham; *genre:* Crime; *location:* United States; *coding:* AF-N?, AF-A, MacArthur, Short, Blk Mkt, Prod, Fem Lab, FBI, Collab; *relevance:* 1.5.

The dynamic managing editor of the *News Chronicle*, "Mitch" Mitchell (George Brent), is demoted by his publisher for printing an unsubstantiated story about the local political boss. As the new writer of the Prudence Maddox "Bewildered Hearts" column, Mitch spices things up in order to get fired. Instead, his fresh approach boosts circulation. One client's letter leads Mitch to investigate a Lonely Hearts Club. Mitch discovers the club is a front for a black market operation in bootleg tires and hijacked sugar that is controlled by the cousin of Boss Greer. With an assist from the Army, Mitch sees to it that Greer and his associates are arrested.

722 YOUNG AMERICA (TCF, Feb) Louis King; *genre:* Drama; *location:* United States; *coding:* Juv, AF-A, Draft, Draft Avoid, FBI, Blk; *relevance:* 1.

Jane (Jane Withers), the spoiled teenage daughter of a New York stock broker, is exiled to her grandmother's farm in the midwest. After reluctantly agreeing to raise a bull for 4-H competition, she begins to love the virtues of rural life. Topicality intrudes by way of a young man on the lam who is using a false name in an attempt to evade conscription. When the G-Men come for him, the draft dodger (played by William Tracy) claims he can now be deferred as a farmer. One of the feds responds: "They've got horses in the Army—and there's lots of farming to do around horses." In the can before Pearl Harbor, this motion picture reflected a continuing resistance to the draft that was only halted by our sudden entrance into the war.

723 YOUTH ON PARADE (Rep, Oct) Albert S. Rogell; *genre:* Musical Comedy; *location:* United States; *coding:* Juv, Short, Postwar, Draft, Draft Avoid, WWI, AF-N, AF-A, AF-AC, Hitler, Prod; *relevance:* 2.

The jitterbugging, jiving students (including Ruth Terry, Martha O'Driscoll, and Tom Brown) of Cotchatootamee College rebel against psychology professor Payne's system of replacing their names with numbers. They perpetuate a hoax to discredit the system by creating an imaginary student of high intelligence. Complications arise when the students are forced to produce "Patty Flynn, No. 79." The deception is eventually exposed, but it matters little amidst the patriotic fervor created by the college musical show which climaxes the film. The show's primary number, "You Got To Study, Buddy," is war related: "We need brains. / 'Cause pen and ink and guys who think / Can build more planes... / It's kids like us who'll win this fuss / And make the peace / No more Versailles treaties, / 'Cause it's proven they don't last" The mention of Versailles in the lyrics is one of the earliest cinematic references to a postwar world. They reinforce the message that had been previously inserted in a lecture delivered by Professor Payne (John Hubbard): "The peace ... is going to be *your* baby.... It's going to take the kind of minds that can see clearly through all the fogs of selfishness and vengeance and racial prejudice."

1943

724 ABOVE SUSPICION (MGM, Sept) Richard Thorpe; *genre:* War/Drama; *locations:* Britain, France, Germany, Italy; *coding:* Intell Serv, AF-Ger, Ger, Hitler, Home Def, Nazi, Goering, Goebbels, Spy-Sab, US-Brit Coop, Atroc, Atroc-Conc, Fr, Pol, Brit, Resist, Musso, AF-Ital, WWI, Himmler, Austria; *relevance:* 3.

In the spring of 1939, an American professor at Oxford, Richard Miles (Fred MacMurray) and his bride are secretly enlisted by the British Foreign Office to seek out a missing agent while on their continental honeymoon. The agent had been in Germany attempting to learn about a "secret weapon," the German magnetic mine (Germany actually had developed a magnetic mine which caused the loss of a number of British ships early in the war, until countermeasures were developed). The couple follows a trail of leads to a book shop in southern Germany, where they learn the agent is posing as a collector of chessmen. They discover that his home is occupied by a German count (Basil Rathbone), in actuality a Gestapo man. Frances Miles (Joan Crawford) is later brutally interrogated by the Nazis. Richard eludes the Gestapo and is eventually able to rescue both his wife and the British agent, who was also held captive. The trio drive across the border into Italy, the two men dressed in Nazi uniforms and Frances hidden in the trunk. Since the United States was at war with Italy at the time of the film's release, this ending provides another example of the distinction made by most Americans between the Nazi regime and their fascist ally. The OWI analyst dismissed *Above Suspicion* as: "[little] more than a glorified chase. It says nothing and does nothing except divert."

725 ACTION IN THE NORTH ATLANTIC (WB, June) Lloyd Bacon; *genre:* Combat; *locations:* United States, Canada, North Atlantic, Russia; *coding:* AF-Mer, AF-Ger, WWI, Russ, FDR, Jew, Home Def, Jap, V, Atroc, Hitler, Nazi, Free Fr, Bonds, USO, AF-Blk, Pol, Czech, Nor, Neth, Chi, Can, Austral, Latin Am, UN, AF-A, AF-N, AF-AC, AF-Can, AF-Russ, Hist Am, US-Russ Coop, Prod, Fem Lab; *relevance:* 3.

An American tanker manned by the usual ethnic mix (captained by Raymond Massey) is torpedoed. The U-boat then surfaces and rams the crew's lifeboat. Over a week later the survivors are rescued by the U.S. Navy. Back in New York, bosun's mate O'Hara (Alan Hale) sends a raspberry to Hitler over the radio. Following a reminder about democracy from the avuncular Jewish crew member (Sam Levene), the surviving shipmates sign on to man a new Liberty ship, the *Sea Witch*. They join a giant Allied convoy headed for Murmansk (in real life, some of these convoys suffered up to 50% casualties on the trip). During a German wolfpack attack, the *Sea Witch* leaves the convoy to lure away one of the attacking U-boats. After several days of being stalked by the Nazi sub (commanded by a scar-faced stereotype), and undergoing aerial attacks by the Luftwaffe, the ship lies dead in the water. When the U-boat surfaces to finish off the *Sea Witch*, the Americans, under the acting command of Chief Mate Joe Rossi (Humphrey Bogart), raise enough steam to ram their nemesis. Escorted by Soviet fighter planes, the freighter limps into Murmansk to the cheers of the Russians (including women dockworkers). With a script by John Howard Lawson, frequent use of Soviet style montage, and the evident influence of Noel Coward's *In Which We Serve* (1942), this is a classic example of cinematic war propaganda.

726 ADVENTURE IN IRAQ (WB, Oct) D. Ross Lederman; *genre:* War/Drama; *location:* Iraq; *coding:* Arab, AF-Brit, Collab, Brit, AF-Ft, AF-AC, Spy-Sab, WWI, Hitler, Nazi, Blk; *relevance:* 2.5.

An American veteran of the Flying Tigers, a dissolute Englishman, and the latter's wife are traveling across the Iraqi desert when their aircraft runs out of fuel. They become captives of a pro–Axis Arab tribe. The western-educated sheik states: "We have been offered an attractive treaty by Herr Hitler." The sheik, whose three brothers are about to be executed as spies by the British, offers to spare the woman (Ruth Ford) if she will sleep with him. The American flyer (Warren Douglas) and his English compatriot (John Loder) manage to make a wireless call for help before the Arabs kill the Englishman. Just as the American pilot is about to be tortured to death, a U.S. Army Air Corps squadron comes to the rescue. There had actually been an unsuccessful pro–German coup against British forces based in Iraq in May of 1941. This film was a remake of *The Green Goddess*, filmed in 1923 and 1930. The OWI would not allow this version to be shown overseas, fearing it might offend British or Middle Eastern audiences.

727 ADVENTURES OF A ROOKIE (RKO, Aug*) Leslie Goodwins; *genre:* Training/Comedy; *location:* United States; *coding:* WWI, Mil Exer, AF-A, AF-N, AF-W, Home Fr, Prod, Draft, Short, V; *relevance:* 2.

RKO's Abbott and Costello imitators, Alan Carney and Wally Brown, play a truck driver and a small-time nightclub entertainer who are drafted. As in several previous service comedies, there is also a rich draftee (Richard Martin) to play straight man. The usual shenanigans take place with the frustrated drill sergeant. On their first pass from camp the three recruits are invited to a house party. But they are quarantined when it is believed they have been exposed to scarlet fever. The suspicious sergeant barges in on the boys and their female hosts, and is also quarantined. They are all released, only to get lost trying to find their unit on field maneuvers. The rookies finally rejoin their outfit in time to be shipped overseas (see *Rookies in Burma*, q.v.).

728 AERIAL GUNNER (Para, June*) William H. Pine; *genre:* Training/Combat; *locations:* United States, Pacific; *coding:* Nazi, AF-Brit, AM Vol?, Jap, AF-Jap, Draft, AF-AC, Pearl Harb, Dunkirk; *relevance:* 3.

The last bomber of a raiding mission returns to its South Pacific airfield. Severely damaged, two of its four crew members are dead and one is missing. From his hospital bed the wounded pilot, Lt. John Davis (Richard Arlen), tells the base commander the story of his lost crewmate, Sgt. Foxy Pattis (Chester Morris). John and Foxy grew up together, but had a falling out. John subsequently enlisted, while his embittered estranged friend waited to be drafted. They wound up together again at an Army gunnery school in Texas. During training, Foxy, an instructor, was determined to satisfy his grudge against John. This was compounded by the usual rivalry for a young lady's affections. Sometime later, Foxy was assigned to John's aircrew as a tail gunner. Following the successful bombing mission, delivering "scrap iron" to a Japanese island base, their plane was attacked by enemy fighters and forced down. As the surviving crew members attempted to make repairs, Japanese soldiers ambushed them. Foxy sacrificially held the enemy off with a machine gun so that the others could escape. Much of this Pine-Thomas production was shot at the Aerial Gunnery School in Harlingen, Texas, and the film was given its world premiere there.

729 AFTER MIDNIGHT WITH BOSTON BLACKIE (Col, Mar) Lew Landers; *genre:* Crime; *location:* United States; *coding:* AF-N, Draft, Short, Home Def, Prod, AF-W, AF-A, AF-MC, Blk; *relevance:* 1.5.

One of Boston Blackie's old friends is released from prison. The man wants to make sure his grown daughter gets some diamonds he has hidden away, but he is kidnapped and murdered by some former associates. The daughter asks Blackie to help her. Blackie (Chester Morris) eventually captures the criminals and retrieves the diamonds. There are numerous soldiers, sailors, and uniformed women in street scenes, on a train, and at a bus station. Blackie's rich friend Arthur Manleder complains about the servant shortage: "My butler-chauffeur's 1-A in the Army, my cook's got a better job in a munitions factory." Several scenes take place during a "trial blackout" of New York City (including the ubiquitous air raid warden who says "Douse that light"), and there are references to gasoline and rubber rationing, although only one car (a cab) displays a ration sticker. In this film Boston Blackie's real name is revealed to be Horatio Black!

730 AIR FORCE (WB, Mar) Howard Hawks; *genre:* Combat; *locations:* United States, Pacific, Philippines, Australia; *coding:* Blk, Spy-Sab, Austral, AF-Jap, AF-N, AF-A, Pearl Harb, AF-AC, AF-MC, AF-W, Fil, Russ, FDR, MacArthur, Jew, Collab, Atroc, Hist Am, WWI, Dipl; *relevance:* 3.

This classic combat film features the crew of a B-17, named the "Mary Ann," as they fly from San Francisco across the Pacific. The crew includes an Irish-American officer, a cynical Polish-American (John Garfield), a Jewish cabbie from Brooklyn (George Tobias), a midwestern farmer, an idealistic small-town kid, and an avuncular middle-aged sergeant (Harry Carey). The "Mary Ann" lands in Hawaii amidst the Japanese attack on Pearl Harbor, encountering fifth columnist snipers on the ground (in real life, a flight of B-17s from the mainland *did* arrive during the Japanese attack, although they were not attacked by fifth columnists). The B-17 later arrives at Wake, where its crew commiserates with the island's defenders and is told by the Marine commander to: "Send us more Japs." In the Philippines, the "Mary Ann" is damaged during an air raid on Clark Field. Rather than abandon their ship, the crew, with the help of the men on the base, makes emergency repairs and barely escape attacking Japanese troops. As the "Mary Ann" approaches Australia, an enemy invasion fleet is spotted. After reporting its position, the B-17 participates in a massive aerial assault upon the Japanese armada. *Air Force* is the ultimate example of an *anabasis* in which the righteous side is advancing in retreat. It concludes with the plane's crew being briefed before taking part in a revenge raid upon Tokyo (allusion to the Doolittle raid?). The number of invectives directed at the Japanese is particularly high (35). The exterior scenes for this film were filmed mostly in Florida, with the full cooperation of the Army Air Corps.

731 AIR RAID WARDENS (MGM, Apr) A. Edward Sutherland; *genre:* Comedy; *location:* United States; *coding:* Hitler, Pearl Harb, AF-A, AF-N, AF-MC, Spy-Sab, Nazi, Jap, Bonds, Home Def, Home Fr, Russ, Neth, Chi, Prod; *relevance:* 3.

Immediately after Pearl Harbor, the struggling small-town business team of Laurel and Hardy attempts to enlist. After being turned down by Uncle Sam, the dejected boys are reluctantly included in the Air Raid

Warden Service. Meanwhile, they find a new partner for their failing bicycle shop—but he just happens to be an enemy agent. A new magnesium plant under construction nearby is of particular interest to the spy and his Nazi associates. Following a disastrous air raid drill performance, Laurel and Hardy are obliged to surrender their civil defense equipment. Overhearing the spies speaking German, the comic duo is able to restore their standing in the community by preventing the Nazis from destroying the new plant. An open-mouthed Hitler portrait in the spy's hideout is used for one of the few successful gags in the film. Over five and a half million Americans participated in civil defense activities during the war.

732 ALASKA HIGHWAY (Para, June*) Frank McDonald; *genre:* Adventure; *locations:* United States, Canada; *coding:* AF-MC, AF-A, Can, Short, Pearl Harb, Jap; *relevance:* 2.

Pop Ormsby returns to his West Coast construction company from a trip to Washington with a contract to build a highway linking the continental United States to its Alaskan territory and a commission as an Army engineer. All of his employees agree to sign on except his eldest son, Woody (Richard Arlen), who wants to "sling lead at the Japs, not mud." A pretty girl (Jean Parker) changes Woody's mind. He joins the construction team with the military rank of sergeant. The "uniformed Paul Bunyans" wrestle with the elements, doubling their efforts when Pop receives a telegram reporting Japanese landings on the Aleutian Islands (Kiska and Attu in June 1942). Six months after the project is begun, representatives of the American and Canadian governments are shown (in newsreel footage) cutting the tape officially marking the opening of the new highway. In fact, though barely acknowledged in the film, the highway sliced through over 1500 miles of northwestern Canada. The ALCAN Highway, as it came to be known, was actually completed between March and October of 1942. Over 40,000 U.S. troops and civilian workers eventually worked on the highway and related projects during the war (and actually served as the *de facto* defenders of the area, since Canada had no troops nearby). The contribution to the project of all-black construction battalions is ignored in this film. While the film's advertising billed the highway as "America's Victory Boulevard," by the time the road was completed the Japanese threat to Alaska was largely over. The OWI felt the film was "misguided," since the plot centered around the battle between Woody and his younger brother over the girl.

733 ALWAYS A BRIDESMAID (Univ,

Sept) Erle C. Kenton; *genre:* Musical Comedy; *location:* United States; *coding:* Short, Blk Mkt?, *relevance:* 1.5.

Tony (Patric Knowles), an assistant district attorney, and Linda (Grace McDonald), a private detective, are independently assigned to investigate a lonely hearts club that is a front for unscrupulous promoters of illegally manufactured goods. In one scene, various people battle for a radio microphone. A character named Colonel Winchester grabs hold of it and attempts to auction off stock in his phony synthetic rubber business. Later, the squabbling Andrews Sisters, who work for Tony, and the "Jiving Jacks and Jills" invade Nick's cafe for a jitterbug exhibition. Nick wants to know why the "zootsuit commandos" are "blitzing the place."

734 THE AMAZING MRS. HOLLI-DAY (Univ, Feb) Bruce Manning; *genre:* War Drama; *locations:* United States, China, Burma, Pacific; *coding:* Juv, AF-Jap, Ref, Jap, Home Fr, AF-A, AF-N, AF-Mer, Atroc, Chi, AF-Chi; *relevance:* 3.

Ruth (Deanna Durbin), a young American in China living with her missionary uncle, becomes the guardian of a mixed-nationalities group of orphaned children after the Japanese bomb their village. Ruth and her charges, eight white children and a Chinese baby, reach a port in Burma and stow away on a cargo ship attempting to run the Japanese blockade. The ship is torpedoed, but Ruth, the ship's steward and eight of the children escape on a raft. After being rescued and taken to San Francisco, the only way Ruth can get the children past immigration is to let them think she is the wife of the missing ship owner. Ruth and the kids are installed in the magnate's Nob Hill mansion, where the drab missionary girl is transformed into a stunning young woman and the rowdy children are convinced to expend some of their energy on a victory garden. A few weeks later, Ruth is singing at a China relief party when the shipping magnate (Harry Davenport) and the ninth child appear at the door. His son (Edmond O'Brien), who has fallen in love with Ruth, smoothes things over. French director Jean Renoir was originally assigned to this film but had to withdraw due to illness. He was replaced by producer Manning, who took on double duty.

735 THE APE MAN (Mono, Feb) William Beaudine; *genre:* Horror; *location:* United States; *coding:* Short, AF-A, AF-N, Blk Mkt?, Fem Lab, Blk, FDR?, Draft; *relevance:* 1.5.

A scientist (Bela Lugosi) is the subject of an experiment in which he transforms himself into a man-beast by injecting the spinal fluid of a gorilla into his body. When Lu-

gosi realizes the horror of what he has done (he cannot walk upright, and has a lot more body hair), he attempts to return to normal by obtaining human spinal fluid from people he murders. Wallace Ford is a cocky reporter—he has received his draft notice to report to the Navy in 30 days—who teams with photographer Louise Currie (she has replaced a male photographer who joined the Signal Corps) to solve the case. There are several references to gasoline rationing and shortages, including an oblique reference to the black market ("bootleg gas").

736 APPOINTMENT IN BERLIN (Col, July) Alfred E. Green; *genre:* Spy; *locations:* Germany, Britain, France; *coding:* Munich, Appease, WWI, US-Brit Coop?, Neth, Brit, AF-Brit, AF-Fr, Fr, Nor, Chi, Belg, Eth, War Corr, Vichy, Resist, Hitler, Himmler, Nazi, Collab, Atroc-Conc, Span, Swed, AF-Raf, Dipl, Goering, Goebbels, Spy-Sab, Intell Serv, Dunkirk, Chamberlain; *relevance:* 3.

Disturbed by the 1938 Munich Pact, RAF Wing-Commander Keith Wilson (George Sanders) goes on a drinking binge, publicly attacking the "great magician, Hitler, [who] … makes mice of Englishmen." After his prompt court martial, Wilson is secretly enlisted as a counter-espionage agent by British Intelligence. Wilson allows himself to be entrapped through gambling debts by a German spy ring and arranges to give them a photo of the plans of a new aerial torpedo. With the cooperation of Scotland Yard, Wilson is arrested while turning it over and is imprisoned. Upon his release in 1940, Wilson is contacted by the Nazis. They arrange his secret passage to Germany, where he begins making Lord Haw Haw-like broadcasts as the "Voice of Truth." Although his broadcasts appear to be propaganda, they actually contain coded messages for British Intelligence. With the help of a female British agent (Gale Sondergaard), two American correspondents, and the German resistance, news of an impending German invasion of Britain is sent out. Wilson, in a stolen German plane, makes a suicide dive into an oil tank complex, next to the assembled invasion fleet, exposing the armada to attacking RAF bombers. Plans for the German invasion of Britain are also referred to in *Confirm or Deny* (TCF, 1941), and *The Gorilla Man* (WB, 1943), q.v.

737 AROUND THE WORLD (RKO, Nov*) Allan Dwan; *genre:* Musical Comedy; *locations:* Africa, China, Australia, India, Egypt; *coding:* FDR?, Short, AF-Blk, Ger, Bonds, Spy-Sab, AF-A, AF-N, AF-MC, AF-W, AF-AC, AF-Austral, Blk, Hist Am, Home Def, Hist Am, USO, UN, Chi, Brit, Russ, AF-Brit, AF-Chi, Draft; *relevance:* 3.

The Kay Kyser band and assorted show business friends make a three-continent tour entertaining Allied armed forces. The flimsy plot is held together by songs and gags. A thin sub-plot involves comedian Mischa Auer and Kay becoming involved with some Nazi spies. A young singer named Marcy McGuire stows away with the tour in the hope of meeting her father (an officer). After Marcy learns he was killed aboard a torpedoed transport, she performs in the tour's final production number singing "Great News" (with actual footage of a GI crowd inserted): "Old Glory's on display / Great news is in the making... / Great things are on the way... / Going to sing till that victory day." In real life, Kyser and his organization devoted a great deal of time to entertaining service personnel: his band played 1,500 camp shows during the war years!

738 ASSIGNMENT IN BRITTANY (MGM, Apr) Jack Conway; *genre:* Resist; *locations:* France, North Africa, Britain; *coding:* Arab, Collab, AF-Ger, Resist, Free Fr, Fr, WWI, Hitler, Nazi, Atroc, Atroc-Conc, AF-Brit, Intell Serv; *relevance:* 3.

Pierre Metard (Jean Pierre Aumont), a Free French officer who helped break up a German plot to start an Arab revolt in North Africa, is ordered to London. Assigned to British Intelligence, Captain Metard is given plastic surgery so that he can assume the identity of a Frenchman from a village near a secret German submarine base. Posing as the villager, Metard pinpoints the U-boat pens. Before he can make contact with Britain, Metard is betrayed by the former lover (Signe Hasso) of the man he is impersonating (she is a Nazi collaborator). Having survived torture, Metard is rescued by the resistance. Following a successful raid by British commandos, Metard and the local girl (Susan Peters) whom he has come to love, leave France with the survivors (the "Marseillaise" roaring on the soundtrack). The idea of a secret agent undergoing plastic surgery in order to impersonate an enemy was also used in *Lancer Spy* (TCF, 1937) and *First Yank Into Tokyo* (RKO, 1945), q.v.

739 BACKGROUND TO DANGER (WB, July) Raoul Walsh; *genre:* War Drama; *locations:* Turkey, Germany, Syria, *coding:* Rom, Bulg, Ital, Atroc, Laval, Vichy, Dipl, Spy-Sab, Collab, Nor, AF-Brit, Blk, Austria, Churchill, Stalin, FDR, Turk, Pol, Russ, Czech, Free Fr, AF-Fr, Atroc, Hitler, Himmler, Nazi, Hist Am, US-Russ Coop; *relevance:* 2.5.

Joe Barton (George Raft), a gum-chewing American adventurer working for the U.S. government, becomes enmeshed in the conspiracies of assorted foreign agents. Their activities revolve around Nazi attempts to manipulate neutral Turkey into declaring war on the Allies. Joe joins forces with a beautiful Soviet agent named Natasha (Brenda Marshall) in order to successfully prevent the Nazis from disseminating phony documents purported to be the secret plans for the Russian invasion of Turkey. Sidney Greenstreet plays the increasingly frustrated Nazi heavy. At the end, Joe and Natasha are preparing to fly to Cairo together so as to further "cement Russian-American relations." "Hitler's ambassador of treachery and deceit," Franz von Papen, is mentioned by name in the film but is not portrayed.

740 BATAAN (MGM, June) Tay Garnett; *genre:* Combat; *location:* Philippines; *coding:* Draft, Mil School, Short, Jap, AF-Jap, Jew, Pacifist, AF-A, AF-N, AF-W, AF-AC, AF-Blk, Latin Am, Bonds, Atroc, Fil; *relevance:* 3.

Although studio-bound, this is the quintessential American combat film from WWII. A "mixed crew" of thirteen volunteers making a last stand against the Japanese onslaught touches upon basic American mythology. But some of the many racial barbs go beyond hysterical propaganda to the utterly absurd. For example, the following warning is given by the sergeant in command (Robert Taylor) to his men: "Those no-tail baboons ... are skillful.... They have all the best trees [for snipers] marked on the maps." The group includes the rare portrayal of a black soldier who heroically participates in combat. There is also a scene depicting a wounded pilot (George Murphy) deliberately crashing his plane into a bridge the Japanese are relentlessly repairing. This is reminiscent of the climactic episode in the 1942 release, *Flying Tigers*, q.v. The penultimate battle sequence in *Bataan*, featuring hand-to-hand fighting against screaming, bayonet-wielding Japanese troops (heightened at dramatic points by speeded-up footage) in the primal mist-shrouded jungle, is probably the most effective fictional combat footage to be produced by an American studio during the war. The OWI described the film as "extraordinarily grim and realistic.... It tells us without compromise or melodramatics what war is and what the enemy is.... [The Japanese] are not merely men in the uniform of the enemy but dauntless, treacherous fighters, the sort who feign death in order to rise stealthily and stab in the back."

741 BEHIND PRISON WALLS (PRC, Mar) Steve Sekely; *genre:* Comedy/Drama; *location:* United States; *coding:* Prod, Short, Jew, Ital; *relevance:* 1.5.

Steel magnate James J. MacGlennan and his idealistic (socialist) son John (Alan Baxter) are sentenced to prison for "withholding essential war material" for personal use.

Webb, the ruthless vice-president, tries to take over MacGlennan Enterprises in their absence. When John is pardoned for revealing the truth about their misuse of steel rations, "J.J." places his son in charge, hoping John's "crack-brained" theories will ruin Webb's plans. A newly mature John moderates his more radical concepts, revitalizes the business and removes Webb. In the process, John convinces his father that it actually pays for management to team up with the workers, the so-called "little fellow." Due to the muddled delivery of this message, the OWI felt the film's "propagandistic value [is] doubtful."

742 BEHIND THE RISING SUN (RKO, July*) Edward Dmytryk; *genre:* War/Drama; *locations:* Japan, China, Burma; *coding:* Dipl, FDR, Atroc, War Corr, Swe, Pol, Russ, Sino-Jap War, Hirohito, Jap, AF-Jap, Spy-Sab, AF-AC, Nazi, Ger, AF-N, Chi, Pearl Harbor; *relevance:* 3.

In the bombed ruins of 1943 Tokyo, a Japanese diplomat (J. Carrol Naish), mourning the combat death of his Cornell-educated son (Tom Neal) and preparing to commit hari kari, tells the tragic story (in flashback) of his family's participation in the militarization of their island nation. Beginning in the mid-1930s, this personalized tale interweaves actual historical events with the lives of his family and a group of occidental friends. The foreign acquaintances include a female American correspondent and a jovial Russian agent. The beloved son, whom the diplomat had encouraged to join the Imperial Japanese Army, becomes a brutal fanatic. As an officer in China, he commits atrocities (including condoning the use of opium to further enslave the civilian population). While on leave, he testifies at a spy trial against his fiancee (Margo) and their accused American friends (menaced by guards with bamboo rods). Despite graphic scenes depicting the torture of the defendants (the *Variety* review stated it gave "American audiences plenty to hiss about"), this film did sympathetically portray a few Japanese characters. It is also one of the rare American motion pictures to make reference to the Neutrality Pact between Japan and the USSR. The OWI refused a request by RKO to shoot footage in Japanese relocation centers for *Behind the Rising Sun*. Tom Neal donned Japanese makeup again in *First Yank Into Tokyo* (1945), q.v.

743 BEST FOOT FORWARD (MGM, Oct) Edward Buzzell; *genre:* Musical Comedy; *location:* United States; *coding:* Mil School, Blk Mkt, Home Fr, AF-A, AF-FT, Draft, Short, FDR, Churchill, V, Chi; *relevance:* 1.5.

As a publicity stunt, a glamorous Hollywood star (Lucille Ball, essentially playing herself) accepts an invitation to the senior prom of a private midwestern military academy. This is basically a formula musical (in Technicolor) with a few topical references thrown into the dialogue. For instance, after Miss Ball is mobbed and stripped to her lingerie by a group of the boys' dates seeking souvenirs, she responds to an offer of a coat with the following quip: "Oh no, no raincoat. Those kids might be collecting scrap rubber too."

744 BLACK MARKET RUSTLERS (Mono, Aug) S. Roy Luby; *genre:* Western; *location:* United States; *coding:* AF?, Collab, Short, Home Fr, Blk Mkt; *relevance:* 1.5.

"Crash" Corrigan and his two pals (the "Range Busters") are called to the ranching community of Winston by the local Cattle Man's Association following a series of cattle thefts and murders by black marketeers. The "Fifth Column racketeers" are rounded up within a short time by the good guys. As sidekick Alibi (Max Terhune) exits the jail, he dumps the criminals' guns in a "Scrap Drive" box. Crash then turns to the camera and directly addresses the film audience: "There's more than one way to win this battle on the home front … One is to buy [meat] from honest dealers." Wartime cattle rustling was a real problem. The individuals involved usually operated out of trucks, literally slaughtering their prey on the run. The Range Busters had helped to protect the government's meat supply from cattle rustlers in a Spanish-American War setting in the 1941 release *Tonto Basin Outlaws*.

745 THE BLACK RAVEN (PRC, June*) Sam Newfield; *genre:* Crime; *location:* United States; *coding:* Short, AF-MC; *relevance:* 1.

A former crook (George Zucco) runs the Black Raven, a hostelry on the American side of the Canadian border. He specializes in smuggling "hot guys" into Canada. During one stormy night, a number of guests on the lam arrive. But in the morning only an eloping couple (Wanda McKay and Bob Livingston, billed under the name "Robert Randall" for some reason) are left alive. To quote the OWI analysis: "The presence of 'A' and 'B' [gas rationing] stickers on automobile windshields and the girl's remark that her father 'would call out the Marines, if he could, to keep us from getting married,' constitute the only notice this film takes of the present world conflict."

746 BOMBARDIER (RKO, May*) Richard Wallace; *genre:* Training/Combat; *locations:* United States, Pacific, Japan; *coding:* Pacifist, Atroc, AF-Raf, Jap, AF-Jap, AF-Ger, Draft, Hitler, AF-AC, AF-N, Latin Am, POW, Spy-Sab, Pearl Harb; *relevance:* 3.

The episodic nature of this film may have something to do with it being in pre-production prior to December 7th. Following an introduction by an Army Air Corps general, it opens with a pre-war scene in which American officers are debating the merits of dive bombing versus high-level bombing. The usual romantic rivalries between the leads (Randolph Scott and Pat O'Brien) and training sequences of ethnically mixed crews are then portrayed. For added excitement, there is a brief interlude about a spy attempting to obtain America's secret bombsight (the unnamed Norden bombsight). There is also an unusual scene of a trainee, the son of a pacifist, who visits the chaplain to express his concern over the ethics of possibly bombing civilians. After Pearl Harbor, the bomber squadron is transported to an "island base" from which it launches an attack on the Japanese home islands (presumably another allusion to the Doolittle raid). The lead B-17 is shot down before dropping its flares. The survivors of the crew are immediately tortured for information by their Japanese captors. Two of the Americans escape and martyr themselves by torching a truck, lighting up the target area for their comrades flying above in the main attack formation.

747 BOMBER'S MOON (TCF, Aug) Charles Fuhr; *genre:* War/Drama; *locations:* Belgium, Germany, Netherlands, Britain; *coding:* Neth, Jew, AF-Ger, AF-Raf, Resist, US-Russ Coop, US-Brit Coop, Hitler, Goering, Goebbels, Czech?, Ger, Russ, AF-Russ, AF-AC, AF-W, Nazi, Juv, Am Vol, Atroc, Atroc-Conc, POW, Churchill; *relevance:* 3.

A damaged RAF bomber commanded by an American, Captain Jeff Dakin (George Montgomery), is attacked by a fighter while limping back to Britain after a raid over Germany. The sadistic Nazi pilot (Martin Kosleck) machine-guns the bombardier (Dakin's brother) as he bails out (see *Wake Island* for a similar incident). Dakin stays in the plane and makes a forced landing in Belgium. He is captured and sent to a POW camp in Germany. During a night air raid, Dakin, a man who claims to be a Czech army officer (Kent Taylor), and a Russian army medic (a woman, played by Annabella) escape. The attractive "Alec" directs them to a Frankfurt economist, the leader of the German underground, whom she had met before the war. After killing the "Czech," who is actually a Gestapo agent, the two escapees cross into Holland with false papers. A Dutch fisherman helps Alec reach Britain by sea with valuable documents. Dakin infiltrates a nearby Luftwaffe base, steals an enemy fighter and shoots down a captured British Spitfire (piloted by the Nazi who had attacked his

bomber). The Germans were planning to use the Spitfire to attack a train on which Churchill was known to be traveling. Dakin lands safely in England. A negative OWI review included the following observation on this rather short B-picture: "This type of presentation conveys the idea that the Nazis are pushovers for any American, and is not calculated to give the American public a clear picture of the real problems facing our fighting men."

748 THE BOY FROM STALINGRAD (Col, May) Sidney Salkow; *genre:* Resist; *location:* Russia; *coding:* Juv, AF-Ger, AF-W?, Brit, Resist, Nazi, Russ, AF-Russ; *relevance:* 3.

In the fall of 1942, some Russian peasant children are helping with the grain harvest when the invading German Army turns and thrusts towards nearby Stalingrad. Caught between the advancing Nazis and the retreating Red Army, the youngsters attempt to flee after setting fire to the fields. Several of the children, including a girl named Nadya, take refuge in a cellar in an abandoned bomb-ravaged village. Along the way, they save an unconscious English teenager. When Tommy revives, he tells the little group that he is an ally, the son of a British engineer shot by the Nazis for helping to blow up the Dnieper Dam. Vowing "the only good Nazi is a dead Nazi," the children embark upon a guerrilla campaign to harrass the Germans. When the bemused Nazis finally close in on the little band, Tommy enters their camp and sacrificially pulls the pin on a grenade. The youngsters' activities have delayed the German advance by two precious days, allowing for a Russian counter-offensive to be mounted. The two surviving guerrillas are decorated by the Red Army. Interestingly enough, the Soviets had produced a series of films during the 1920s featuring Russian children fighting (for the Communists, of course) during the Revolution; the first film was entitled *Little Red Devils*. The epic battle for Stalingrad began in August 1942 and ended in February 1943 with the total capitulation of the remnants of the German 6th Army.

749 CABIN IN THE SKY (MGM, Apr) Vincent Minnelli; *genre:* Musical Comedy/Fantasy; *location:* United States; *coding:* Hitler?, Blk, Draft, Short; *relevance:* 1.5.

Little Joe, a gambling womanizer played by Eddie "Rochester" Anderson, is reformed by a dream of his own death in which Lucifer Jr. and the Lord's General battle for his soul. During the six months he is allotted to redeem himself, Little Joe encounters many temptations sent by Lucifer Jr., including the beauteous Georgia Brown (Lena Horne). Lucifer Jr. refers to her as a "black marketeer" and at another point tells the Lord's General that "Little Joe's been 1-A on our list for a long time."

750 CALABOOSE (UA, Jan) Hal Roach, Jr.; *genre:* Comedy Western; *location:* United States; *coding:* AF-A, AF-W, Home Fr?, Prod; *relevance:* 1.5.

In this western "Streamliner" (a short feature produced by Hal Roach, Jr.), two young cowboys, Jim and Pidge (Jimmy Rogers and Noah Beery, Jr.), get a job loading horses for shipment to the army. But their incompetence leads to a mass escape of the animals. Later, Pidge, attracted to the sheriff's niece, arranges for his own arrest so that she can "reform" him. One attempt at topical humor particularly annoyed the OWI: "A group of uniformed women, no doubt meant to burlesque such groups as the A.W.V.S. [American Women's Voluntary Services; founded in January 1940], act too silly to be funny and are in bad taste in these war times.... [W]hile the group ... is not named, they are treated as if they were nitwits."

751 CAPTIVE WILD WOMAN (Univ, Apr*) Edward Dmytryk; *genre:* Horror; *location:* United States; *coding:* Short; *relevance:* 1.

Doctor Sigmund Walters (John Carradine) is a mad scientist trying to create a superior race. He murders his nurse and then implants her brain into a stolen circus orangutan named Cheela. Cheela is metamorphosized into the beautiful Paula Dupree (Acquanetta). Seemingly well behaved, Paula reverts to her ape-like ways when she discovers her beloved animal trainer, Fred, kissing his fiancee. On a stormy night, Cheela/Paula kills the scientist and returns to the circus, just in time to sacrificially save Fred from some escaped lions. At an earlier point in the film, while Fred is serving up the big cats' meal, he makes the following comment to a colleague: "I'll feed them—but you must explain the Meatless Tuesdays to them!" Carradine, who frequently portrayed Nazi officers during the war years, is not identified here specifically as a German—however, his comments about "racial improvement" (the reason for his experiments) were probably intended to link him with the "Master Race" theorists of the Third Reich.

752 CASABLANCA (WB, Jan) Michael Curtiz; *genre:* War/Drama; *locations:* North Africa, France; *coding:* Ger, Blk, Am Vol, Vichy, Petain, Isolat, Eth, Nor, Neth, Czech, Arab, Chi?, Jew?, Bulg, Pearl Harb?, Resist, Span Civ, WWI, Hitler, Nazi, AF-Ger, AF-Ital, Free Fr, De Gaulle, Fr, AF-Fr, Yugo, Atroc-Conc; *relevance:* 3.

In late 1941 in Vichy-controlled Morocco, Casablanca has become a way station for people fleeing the German conquests (Ger-

many opened consulates in Casablanca and Algiers in September 1941 in an effort to exert greater control in North Africa). At the popular Rick's Cafe, owned by a cynical American (Humphrey Bogart), almost everyone (from almost everywhere) is plotting to go somewhere else, particularly since the Nazis are trying to coerce the local Vichy officials into bending to their will. The obnoxious Major Strasser (Conrad Veidt) of the Gestapo, is particularly interested in having the French detain a fugitive Czech resistance hero, Victor Lazlo (Paul Henreid), recently escaped from a concentration camp (he has a scar over one eye, presumably from Nazi beatings). Rick, however, remains aloof—explaining when he is introduced by the Vichy police chief (Claude Rains) to Strasser: "I stick my neck out for nobody. I'm the only cause I'm interested in." But then the beautiful Ilsa (Ingrid Bergman) enters his "gin joint" and wistfully asks black pianist Sam (Dooley Wilson) to play "As Time Goes By." She is a Norwegian refugee married to Lazlo, but she had a passionate affair with Rick in Paris during the spring of 1940. Rick overcomes his bitterness against her for abandoning him in France, ends his self-imposed isolation from the world's problems, and nobly agrees to help Ilsa and her husband get away from the Nazis. With his will restored, Rick, who had previously actively resisted fascism in Ethiopia and Spain, kills Major Strasser at the airport when the German tries to prevent the couple's plane from departing. Rick and the French police chief walk off together to join the Free French garrison in Brazzaville (since the film is set before Pearl Harbor, Bogart's character is not obliged to return to America to fight). Interestingly, although identified as Czech, Lazlo is portrayed as a leader of a politically correct pan-European resistance movement. Nevertheless, the OWI was uncomfortable with the positive portrayal of Rains' Vichy police official (the U.S. government's policy toward Vichy was extremely ambiguous).

753 THE CHANCE OF A LIFETIME (Col, Oct) William Castle; *genre:* Crime; *location:* United States; *coding:* AF-MC, Jap, Short, Prod; *relevance:* 1.5.

With his own criminal past in mind, Boston Blackie petitions the state governor and prison authorities to parole worthy inmates with needed skills to "step into our factories and augment the war effort." Despite Inspector Farraday's objections, the warden endorses the idea. A pilot program is approved after Blackie's millionaire friend, Arthur Manleder, pledges to employ the men in his defense-oriented machine tool factory. One of the convicts, on family leave, recovers the hidden cash from an old robbery. Trouble

starts when the two men with whom he pulled the heist demand their shares. After one crook is accidentally killed, Blackie takes the heat from the police so that the program will not be cancelled. In the final scene, Manleder helps capture the crooks, and Blackie says his friend is "like the United States Marines." "Only [the crook] landed first," Manleder replies. "Well, someone has to land first, so the Marines can land first and run them off—you know, like the Japs."

754 CHATTERBOX (Rep, Apr) Joseph Santley; *genre:* Comedy; *location:* United States; *coding:* Blk, Short, Latin Am, V; *relevance:* 1.5.

Joe E. Brown plays a well-known cowboy radio star named Rex Vane, who is awarded a movie contract by Mammoth Pictures. Problems develop after the newspapers expose him as a "phony" with an aversion to horses. Taking advantage of the publicity, the tyrannical owner of Mammoth insists Rex complete their picture. Through a series of accidents Rex redeems himself, wins back the loyalty of his fans and marries Judy Boggs (Judy Canova), his leading lady. During a barbecue at the "Victory Ranch," the Mills Brothers, dressed as cooks, sing and play "Sweet Lucy Brown." A large "V" is displayed above their stove. Judy stuffs herself with hotdogs at the party, even though they are known to give her hiccups. She explains: "Tomorrow is Meatless Tuesday and it'll give me something to remember."

755 CHETNIKS! (THE FIGHTING GUERRILLAS) (TCF, Feb) Louis King; *genre:* Resist; *location:* Yugoslavia; *coding:* Atroc, Nazi, AF-Ital, Hitler, Resist, Atroc-Conc, Musso, AF-Ger, Czech, Brit, Nor, Grk, Den, POW, Yugo, Belg, Neth, Fr; *relevance:* 3.

Opening with newsreel shots of the April 1941 German offensive against Yugoslavia, this film portrays alleged wartime incidents involving General Draza Mihailovich (Philip Dorn), the real-life leader of the non-communist resistance known as the Chetniks (the rival Communist guerrillas were led by Tito, who became the post-war leader of the country). At a local command center of the German occupation army, General von Baur rants about the Chetnik "bandits" to his Gestapo counterpart, Colonel Brockner (regular Nazi heavy Martin Kosleck). In the mountains, the Chetniks capture an Italian supply column. The partisans contact the Germans to exchange the frightened Italians for gasoline. Before agreeing to negotiate for the freedom of his Axis partners, General von Baur contemptuously states: "I wouldn't give ten marks for Mussolini himself! Never ... for useless Italians!" In an attempt to force Mihailovich's wife (living in town under a false name) to surrender, the Nazis halt food supplies to the village. In one scene, after stuffing herself with food in front of her students, the Nazi schoolteacher compels the children to sing the "Horst Wessel Song." In a final attempt to force the Chetniks to disband, the Nazis threaten to execute all the people of Mihailovich's home village. With the help of Natalia, a partisan working under cover as Brockner's secretary, the Chetniks destroy the German forces and rescue the villagers. The fact that the Italians had a separate occupation zone is only alluded to in the film. The OWI reviewer found the inconsistency of the actors' accents disconcerting.

756 CHINA (Para, Mar*) John Farrow; *genre:* War/Drama; *location:* China; *coding:* Juv, Am Vol, Resist, Jap, AF-Jap, Chi, AF-Chi, Intell Serv, Atroc, Chiang, Hirohito, AF-W, Ref, Ital, Ger, Pearl Harb; *relevance:* 3.

In the fall of 1941, Jones (Alan Ladd), sales representative in China for an American oil company, is only interested in making money from his best customers, the Japanese. During his travels he runs into American teacher Carolyn (Loretta Young). She is escorting a group of coeds to a university where they "have an appointment with the destiny of China." Jones reluctantly agrees to give them a lift in his truck. At a farmhouse, some Japanese soldiers burst in, killing a peasant mother holding a baby orphan (nicknamed "Donald Duck" by the Americans), and raping one of the students. Jones dispatches the unrepentent perpetrators: "I just shot three Japs … and I've got no more feelings about them if they were flies in a manure heap." Won over to the cause, Jones later briefly halts an advancing Japanese division by casually engaging its pompous general in conversation about American cigarettes, the recent attack on Pearl Harbor, and democracy. Having bought the time needed by Chinese guerrillas to mine the mountainside above, Jones nonchalantly flicks his cigarette butt into the face of the general a moment before the exploding mountain buries them beneath a gigantic landslide. Significantly, Carolyn had actively participated in this event by helping the guerrillas to place the dynamite charges. The film's final shot shows her determined face superimposed with the *Chinese* flag. The OWI was pleased, both with Jones' conversion and with the presentation of the Chinese guerrillas as "realistic and intelligent."

757 CHINA GIRL (TCF, Jan) Henry Hathaway; *genre:* War/Drama; *locations:* China, Burma; *coding:* War Corr, AF-Jap, Can, US-Chi Coop, Russ, Chi, Juv, Jap, Atroc, Spy-Sab, Pearl Harb, AF-FT; *relevance:* 3.

In late 1941, Johnny Williams (George Montgomery), an American news photographer in China, is detained by Japanese occupation forces. While mass executions of civilians, described by the Japanese governor as "spies," take place in a nearby field, Johnny is offered money to photograph the Burma Road. He refuses. Expecting to be shot in the morning, Johnny and another Western prisoner escape. In their flight they must crawl through a ditch filled with the corpses of the recently executed. Commandeering a Japanese plane, the two reach the base of the Flying Tigers. There, Johnny selfishly resists being recruited by the American volunteer flyers, falls in love with a half-Chinese girl (played by Gene Tierney), and becomes involved in espionage. Unbeknownst to him, a document he stole from the Japanese contains in code the particulars of the planned attack on Pearl Harbor. During a Japanese aerial attack, both the girl and her father are killed while reading an inspirational poem to his class of Chinese students. With a little boy feeding the ammunition to a machine gun, a vengeful Johnny shoots down one of the enemy planes. Like *China*, q.v., this film shows an initially neutral American's conversion to anti-fascism. *China Girl* begins with a foreword stating: "An American will fight for only 3 things—for a woman, for himself, and for a better world."

758 CINDERELLA SWINGS IT (RKO, Jan) Christy Cabanne; *genre:* Comedy/Drama; *location:* United States; *coding:* Blk, Draft?, Russ, USO, AF-A, FDR, Home Fr, Hist Am, Home Def; *relevance:* 2.

In the last edition of the Scattergood Baines film series, the friendly old sage (Guy Kibbee) of Coldriver encourages high school senior Tommy to gather local talent and put on a USO show for the Army. Tommy, discouraged by his family's insistence that he finish school before joining up, is told by Scattergood that President Roosevelt wants young boys to complete their educations. Scattergood also promotes the stardom of a young lady with operatic training by persuading her to "swing it" for the service benefit. The finale of the USO show is a patriotic song entitled "The Flag Is Still There, Mr. Key."

759 CITY WITHOUT MEN (Col, Jan) Sidney Salkow; *genre:* War/Drama; *location:* United States; *coding:* AF-Jap, Hitler, Pearl Harb, AF-A, AF-CG, AF-N, Hirohito, Jap, Appease, Spy-Sab, Latin Am, Chi, Short; *relevance:* 2.5.

In the summer of 1941, West Coast tugboat pilot Tom Adams (Michael Duane), about to be commissioned in the Navy, is tricked by two Japanese into picking them up from a freighter called the *Hanseatic*.

When a Coast Guard cutter approaches, the armed Japanese force Tom to make a run for it. The tug is overtaken and Tom is later convicted of smuggling aliens, despite his lawyer's impassioned speech against "appeasement"—"When Hitler marched into the Rhineland, we could have put him in an insane asylum." Tom's fiancee, Nancy (Linda Darnell), moves into a boarding house near the prison. When Tom learns of the attack on Pearl Harbor, he inspires his fellow convicts to petition for parole to join the Army. After they are turned down, one of the prisoners ruminates: "I was gonna take a powder—a keg of powder right down Hirohito's smokestack." Nancy reads about an "Axis Raider" masquerading as the freighter *Hanseatic* and is able to muster political pressure to win Tom's release. In the final shot, Tom is shown in a naval ensign's uniform embracing Nancy. The OWI dismissed this film as "implausible claptrap."

760 CLANCY STREET BOYS (Mono, Apr) William Beaudine; *genre:* Comedy/Drama; *location:* United States; *coding:* Juv, Jew?, Latin Am?, Blk, Bonds, Draft, Short, Prod, Fem Lab, AF-A; *relevance:* 1.5.

A rich rancher friend and benefactor of the McGinnis family, affectionately known as "Uncle Pete," visits New York City after selling a thousand head of cattle to the U. S. Army. This creates a crisis for Muggs (Leo Gorcey) and his mother, since Uncle Pete has been sending checks for the care of seven children, six boys and a girl. Muggs persuades his East Side gang to pose as the nonexistent siblings, with Glimpy (Huntz Hall) in drag as sister "Annabelle." Muggs explains to Uncle Pete that Annabelle is a riveter in a defense plant. Predictable complications and a few additional war cracks follow.

761 COMMANDOS STRIKE AT DAWN (Col, Jan) John Farrow; *genre:* Resist/Combat; *locations:* Norway, Britain; *coding:* Nor, V, AF-Nor, Intell Serv, Belg, Neth, Pol, Fr, UN, League Nat, AF-Ger, Resist, Atroc, Nazi, Czech, Jew, AF-Brit, AF-W, AF-Can, Russ, Brit, Collab; *relevance:* 3.

In the early summer of 1939, British admiral Bowen (Sir Cedric Hardwicke), his son, and daughter Judith vacation in a small Norwegian town. Judith (Anna Lee) falls in love with the village scientist, a widower named Eric Toresen (Paul Muni). But before they can meet again, the Germans invade and occupy Norway (the spring of 1940). Book burnings, executions, anti–Semitism, etc., convert the once docile villagers into determined resisters, pledging to "kill or be killed." Eric stabs a German officer and, while hiding from his pursuers, discovers a secret airbase under construction. Eric escapes in a small boat to Britain. When the

English are informed about the field, they realize that it will pose a threat to their Russian convoys. Eric, who has been reunited with Judith, agrees to guide a commando raid led by Admiral Bowen's son. Both men are killed, but the base is destroyed and many of the oppressed villagers, including Eric's daughter, are rescued. The OWI was pleased: "This film points out the need of liberty and the horror of occupation, and as such serves as a lesson to everyone." Location footage for this film was shot in Newfoundland, with real Canadian troops standing in as the commandos.

762 CORREGIDOR (PRC, Mar) William Nigh; *genre:* Combat; *location:* Philippines; *coding:* Atroc, Hist Am, Jap, AF-Jap, AF-AC, AF-A, AF-W, Blk, Fil, AF-Fil, Short, Prod, POW, Pearl Harb; *relevance:* 3.

Royce, a woman doctor played by Elissa Landi, arrives in the Philippines on December 6, 1941, to marry a medical researcher. The next day, the Japanese bomb the church in which the wedding has just been held. The newlyweds flee with the troops to Bataan (in real life, almost 26,000 civilians joined more than 80,000 troops in the exodus to the peninsula). They are later evacuated to the island fortress of Corregidor, known as "the Rock." An old colleague, whom Royce still loves, is working there. The three doctors help tend the mounting casualties resulting from unrelenting enemy attacks. Her husband is killed during a bombing raid and Royce is evacuated on the last plane out before the capitulation of Corregidor (in April). A final message is broadcast to America: "The jig is up.... Everyone is bawling like a baby.... We will be waiting for you guys to help." Ironically, the only Filipino character to be singled out in the film, an officer incapacitated by malaria, is portrayed shooting himself on the road to Bataan. Eleven thousand, five hundred Americans and Filipinos took refuge on Corregidor, which finally fell to the Japanese on May 19, 1942.

763 CORVETTE K-225 (Univ, Oct) Richard Rosson; *genre:* Combat; *locations:* Canada, North Atlantic; *coding:* AF-Ger, AF-Brit, AF-Raf, Prod, AF-Can, AF-W, Hist Am, Hitler, Nazi, UN, Churchill, Brit, Can, Nor, Fr, Russ; *relevance:* 3.

Lt. Commander MacClain (Randolph Scott) of the Royal Canadian Navy is one of several survivors of a sunken corvette. He bitterly reports to headquarters that a U-Boat with a black cross on its conning tower surfaced and began machine-gunning the sailors in their lifeboats. While awaiting the completion of a new vessel, MacClain becomes romantically involved with Joyce (Ella Raines), the sister of a fallen comrade. Soon after accepting command of the K-225,

MacClain attends a briefing for a convoy leaving for England from Halifax. Among the many nationalities represented is a female Soviet ship captain. During the Atlantic crossing, the convoy is assaulted by German aircraft and submarines. Following the sinking of a merchant ship, the K-225 forces the attacking U-boat to the surface (it is the one with the black cross), engages it in a gun duel and then rams it. Stokey, a crusty old sailor played by Barry Fitzgerald, proclaims: "These rats will never strafe another lifeboat." The damaged K-225 is cheered when it limps into port escorted by the RAF. There are a number of similarities between this film and Warner's earlier release, *Action in the North Atlantic,* q.v. Note: the Canadian ship's mascot (a dog) is named "Milton," perhaps a linkage to the "mother country" of Great Britain via a reference to the poet John Milton (*Paradise Lost*).

764 COSMO JONES IN "CRIME SMASHER" (Mono, Jan) James Tinling; *genre:* Crime; *location:* United States; *coding:* Blk, Bonds, Home Def, Short; *relevance:* 1.5.

Cosmo Jones (Frank Graham), an amateur criminologist, helps policemen Edgar Kennedy and Richard Cromwell foil two rival gangs that have been terrorizing the city with robberies and kidnappings. This film was based on a CBS radio show, but Monogram was unable to spin it off into a successful film series, a la Columbia's "Crime Doctor" and "Whistler" films. The war relevance in this film is restricted to one glimpse of a gasoline ration sticker, several War Bonds posters on walls, and a few minor dialogue references, including one to a "dimout" (similar to a blackout, only not as complete). In one scene, Mantan Moreland (playing Jones' assistant), tells several gangsters not to bother looking for the missing ransom money on *him*: "I ain't got no money in my pockets—I spent it all for War Bonds!"

765 COWBOY COMMANDOS (Mono, June) S. Roy Luby; *genre:* Western Spy; *location:* United States; *coding:* Ital?, Bonds, Hitler, Nazi, Spy-Sab, Collab, Prod; *relevance:* 3.

The three Range Busters (Ray Corrigan, Denny Moore, and Max Terhune) and a lady friend (Evelyn Finley) leave their rodeo War Bonds drive and return home to track down some saboteurs who have been interfering with production at a magnesium mine vital to the war effort. The headquarters of the saboteurs is a swastika-festooned room hidden behind the local bar. Their leader is a man named Werner and one of his henchmen is called Mario (however, the latter character, played by Western veteran Frank Ellis, neither dresses nor speaks like an Ital-

ian). They are assisted by traitorous American mine foreman Fraser. After clicking his empty pistol at a "Wanted For Murder" poster of Hitler, cowboy Slim sings: "I'm goin' to get Der Fuehrer, sure as shootin' ... With a noose around his head and his body full of lead, I'll deliver him as dead as dead can be." Led by "Crash" Corrigan on his white horse, the "Cowboy Commandos" literally ride down the saboteurs. Under OWI pressure, the deputized cowboys replaced a scripted vigilante group. The film begins with Evelyn Finley demonstrating trick riding, then addressing the audience directly: "Please don't applaud, ladies and gentlemen. Applause won't keep this flag flying or our boys fighting ... Before you leave here today, buy War Bonds and Stamps."

766 COWBOY IN MANHATTAN (Univ, May) Frank Woodruff; *genre:* Musical Comedy; *location:* United States; *coding:* AF-W, AF-A; *relevance:* 1.5.

A glib producer cons a group of Texas hotel owners into backing a Broadway show about their state as a promotional stunt for Texas. When ticket sales fall short, he hires a young Texas songwriter (Robert Paige) to pose as a wealthy cattle baron who so admires the blonde leading lady (played by popular singer Frances Langford) that he buys all the seats for the opening night. Complications arise when the two actually fall in love. The show's grand finale features the war-oriented song, "Private Cowboy Jones." While the leading lady sings, the cowboys on stage go behind screens and change into Army uniforms. The chorus girls do the same, returning to the stage as WAACs. One dialogue reference to lynching was not appreciated by the OWI.

767 COWBOY IN THE CLOUDS (Col, Dec) Benjamin Kline; *genre:* Adventure; *location:* United States; *coding:* Home Def, Jap; *relevance:* 2.

Civil Air Patrol pilot Glen Avery makes a forced landing near the ranch run by Steve Kendall (Charles Starrett). Steve's comic sidekick Cannonball (Dub Taylor), initially thinks Glen is a Japanese spy. The CAP pilot is flying across the state, trying to enlist civilian support for the home defense project, but has been adamantly opposed by Amos Fowler, the state's biggest cattleman. Steve decides to help the CAP, particularly after meeting pretty CAP pilot Dorrie (Julie Duncan). A series of successful benefit performances for the CAP further antagonize Fowler, but the rich man changes his attitude when Steve and his men rescue Dorrie, after her plane crashes in the midst of a forest fire. Dorrie is revealed to be Fowler's daughter. The Civil Air Patrol was founded in 1942 as a civilian auxiliary to the Army

Air Corps, and performed invaluable patrol duties, particularly along the Mexican border, thus freeing Army pilots for more important duties. Approximately 40,000 civilian flyers served during the war.

768 CRASH DIVE (TCF, May) Archie Mayo; *genre:* Combat/War Drama; *locations:* United States, North Atlantic; *coding:* Dipl, AF-N, Hist Am?, AF-Ger, AF-A, AF-Blk, AF-W, Russ, Chi, Pearl Harb, Mil School, Short, WWI, Nazi, USO; *relevance:* 3.

Lt. Ward Stewart (Tyrone Power), a well-connected young PT Boat commander, is reassigned to the submarine service. As the new executive officer on the USS *Corsair*, he comes under the command of Dewey Connors (Dana Andrews). Although Ward makes it clear he would prefer to command a torpedo boat, both he and Dewey share a mutual interest in a pretty schoolteacher played by Anne Baxter. Between extended romantic interludes, including scenes in wartime Washington, the USS *Corsair* encounters and sinks a German mine-laying "Q-Boat" (a warship camouflaged as a neutral noncombatant). In the final reels the American submarine goes on a mission to find and destroy the base from which the Q-Ship had operated. Ward leads the attacking landing party. The raiders include a heroic black cook (Ben Carter) and a hard-boiled veteran (James Gleason) of the First World War. The latter stays behind and sacrifices himself so that the others may escape. In Technicolor.

769 CRAZY HOUSE (Univ, Oct) Edward F. Cline; *genre:* Comedy; *location:* United States; *coding:* AF-W, Home Def, Draft, AF-N, AF-A, AF-Ger, Blk, V, Latin Am, Short, Collab; *relevance:* 1.5.

Comedians Olsen and Johnson decide to produce their own film, which leads to predictable mayhem. There are a number of minor topical references, including signs and posters, and a few remarks about rationing ("Are butter and egg men rationed?"), and the like. In one scene set on the Universal Pictures lot, Alan Curtis is shown making a war movie in which he shoots some Nazi soldiers. Other Universal stars appearing in cameos are Basil Rathbone and Nigel Bruce (as Sherlock Holmes and Dr. Watson).

770 CRIME DOCTOR (Col, June) Michael Gordon; *genre:* Crime; *location:* United States; *coding:* Vet, WWI, Short, AF-A, AF-N?, AF-Mer?, League Nat, Hist Am; *relevance:* 2.

In 1932, gangster Phil Morgan (Warner Baxter) is slugged and tossed from a moving car by his cohorts, irritated that Morgan has hidden the loot from a recent robbery. Morgan survives, but with amnesia. Taken in by a sympathetic doctor, Morgan (calling himself Robert Ordway) starts his life over. By 1943, he is a doctor himself, specializing in psychology; he is a frequent visitor to the state prison, where he treats the inmates. Ordway's work does not go unnoticed, and he is appointed head of the parole board. However, his old gang returns and Ordway eventually turns himself in for his crimes, but is given a suspended sentence. This film was the first in a series based on a radio show. There are a number of minor war references, but one sequence is particularly relevant. Ordway meets Wheeler (Leon Ames), a former Army officer who served with distinction in WWI; now in prison, Wheeler repeatedly tries to escape, hopeful of fighting in WWII. Ordway directs the man's efforts elsewhere: Wheeler drills and trains his fellow inmates in military matters, and is eventually given a parole. Exactly *why* officials felt training prisoners in close-order drill and other military techniques was beneficial to the war effort is never made clear, although in real life over 100,000 ex-felons *did* eventually serve in the armed forces after their release from prison.

771 THE CRYSTAL BALL (UA, Jan) Elliot Nugent; *genre:* Crime/Drama; *location:* United States; *coding:* AF-N, Prod, Short; *relevance:* 1.5.

Toni, a failed beauty contestant from Texas (played by Paulette Goddard) is stranded in New York City. She is befriended by Madame Zenobia, a crystal gazer working with a crooked real estate man in an attempt to swindle a rich widow. While disguised as Zenobia at a Navy Relief bazaar, Toni meets Brod (Ray Milland), the widow's handsome lawyer. Toni decides that Brod is her man. Romantic impediments include a federal investigator who accuses Brod of sabotage for purchasing property for the widow on which the government wants to build a defense plant. The OWI felt the story was "implausible and stupid," further noting that "the war cracks are pointless and dragged in only for their timeliness." This film was produced by Paramount but sold to United Artists for release.

772 THE DANCING MASTERS (TCF, Nov) Mal St. Clair; *genre:* Comedy; *location:* United States; *coding:* AF-A, Prod, Short; *relevance:* 1.5.

Laurel and Hardy are the operators of the "Arthur Hurry" dancing school. Oliver teaches a jive class, while Stanley, in drag, conducts ballet lessons. The boyfriend of their best student has invented a "ray gun" that will "revolutionize modern warfare." But the girl's industrialist father and a rival suitor attempt to gain control of the military device in order to increase the profits from their war production concerns. When the inven-tor is indisposed, the boys step in to help demonstrate the weapon before a group of government agents. In the process of acquiring the financial backing of the government, the comic duo blows up the home of the greedy industrialist.

773 DANGER! WOMEN AT WORK (PRC, Aug) Sam Newfield; *genre:* Comedy; *location:* United States; *coding:* Fem Lab, Short; *relevance:* 1.5.

In this "topical mirth maker" three girl-friends in Los Angeles are doing their bit for the war effort. Pert drives a taxi, while Terry and Marie work at a gas station. When Terry (Patsy Kelly) inherits a ten-ton truck from her uncle, she and her pals go into the commercial hauling business. Some trucker boyfriends arrange for their boss to pay the girls a hundred dollars to carry a load of magnesium from Las Vegas to Los Angeles. But, to conform to wartime regulations barring trucks from traveling empty, the girls must first find something to haul to Las Vegas. This leads to various comic misadventures when the ladies agree to transport the paraphernalia of a gang of professional gamblers.

774 DESTROYER (Col, Sept) William A. Seiter; *genre:* Training/Combat; *locations:* United States, Pacific; *coding:* Mil Exer, AF-Jap, WWI, AF-N, AF-Brit, Prod, Home Fr, Hist Am, Tojo, Jap, Nazi, Chi, Fr, USO, Mil School, Fem Lab?; *relevance:* 3.

Steve "Boley" Boleslavski (Edward G. Robinson) is a welder working on a new destroyer being built to replace the World War I vintage *John Paul Jones*, recently lost in the Pacific. Boley becomes a real nuisance to his fellow laborers due to his insistance upon perfection. Only at the launching of the new *Jones* does Boley reveal that he had served on its namesake in the last war. Boley rejoins the Navy and, following a stint working with new recruits at the San Diego Naval Training Center, wrangles an assignment as chief boatswain's mate on the *Jones*. Obsessed with the good old days, Boley proceeds to alienate most of his "new Navy" crewmates (particularly the young Chief Petty Officer he replaces, played by Glenn Ford). After two failed shakedown cruises, the captain demotes Boley and the *Jones* is humiliatingly assigned to the Aleutians mail run. While in the northern Pacific, the *Jones* is torpedoed in an attack by Japanese planes. With the ship dead in the water and stalked by an enemy submarine, it is Boley's patriotic faith—and skill with a welder's torch—that enable the *Jones* to raise enough steam to ram the Japanese craft. Having won the crew's respect and instilled them with pride in the "best tin can in the fleet," Boley steps aside so that the younger men can finish the war. Interestingly enough, there were several well-known incidents of U.S. warships ramming enemy submarines which occurred *after* the release of this film!

775 DIXIE DUGAN (TCF, Mar) Otto Brower; *genre:* Comedy; *location:* United States; *coding:* Blk, Hist Am, FDR?, Prod, Fem Lab, Short, Home Fr, Home Def, Hitler?, Nazi, Draft, Draft Avoid, FBI?, Spy-Sab, Collab, Chi, Chiang, Can, Brit, AF-A, AF-N, AF-MC, AF-W; *relevance:* 3.

The film opens with a montage of wartime Washington, concluding with a series of shots of various government agency acronymns (WPA, WPB, OPM) on office doorways. The final shot in the sequence is the freshly lettered MOWPFW (Mobilization of Women Power for War). Its chief, former industrialist Roger Hudson (James Ellison), grabs a taxi to go to a radio broadcast. The incompetent cabbie is perky Dixie Dugan (Lola Andrews), who has replaced her boyfriend Matt, now working in a defense plant. After listening to Hudson's radio speech, Dixie applies for a civil service job. Guess who becomes Hudson's new secretary? To get rid of Dixie (because his fiancee is jealous), Hudson assigns her to conduct a survey. Dixie collects the data and submits an innovative report on how to best utilize female labor. When Hudson refuses to look at it, Dixie complains to an anti-administration newspaper chain. However, Hudson reads her report and persuades a senator to promote it over the radio, heading off the hostile "exposé" of his agency. Dixie becomes a national heroine and the newspaper chain reluctantly presents her with an "Americanism" award. The film includes some actual second-unit location footage shot in Washington, D.C., surprising for a B picture of the period. Charlie Ruggles plays Dixie's father, a typical, bumbling air raid warden who accidentally sets off an incendiary bomb in their apartment building! The title character was based on a popular comic strip of the period.

776 DOCTOR GILLESPIE'S CRIMINAL CASE (MGM, Nov) Willis Goldbeck; *genre:* Drama; *location:* United States; *coding:* Blk?, AF-A, AF-N, Hitler, Pearl Harb, Jap, Prod, Short, Chi; *relevance:* 1.5.

A young lady who has fallen in love with an Army sergeant visits her old friend Dr. Gillespie (Lionel Barrymore) for reassurance concerning her criminally insane husband. On her behalf, Dr. Gillespie goes to the state penitentiary, only to be kidnapped by the man during a prison break. Finally acknowledging his sickness, the husband deliberately runs into a barrage of police bullets. One of the subplots centers around the efforts of the hospital staff to rehabilitate an embittered man whose legs were shot off by a strafing

enemy plane at Pearl Harbor. In the final scene he waltzes on his new artificial legs at the doctor's birthday party.

777 DOUGHBOYS IN IRELAND (Col, Oct) Lew Landers; *genre:* War/Drama; *locations:* United States, Ireland; *coding:* AF-Brit?, Brit?, Draft, AF-A, USO; *relevance:* 3.

Danny O'Keefe (played by Kenny Baker, a Dick Powell look-alike who was the regular vocalist on the Jack Benny radio show prior to Dennis Day), the band leader and tenor at the Club Shamrock in New York City, is inducted into the Army, along with three other members of his orchestra. Gloria (Lynn Merrick), the blonde vocalist, promises to write Danny regularly. She then delegates her elderly secretary to conduct the correspondence. Following training camp, Danny and his mates are shipped off to Ireland. On sentry duty Danny has an encounter with a fiery Irish lass named Molly Callahan (Jeff Donnell). After some of her relatives have an altercation with American soldiers, Danny is able to smooth things over by singing some Irish ballads. A developing romance between Danny and Molly is interrupted by the appearance of Gloria, who is touring with a USO camp show. But when Danny is severely wounded while participating in a commando raid, it is Molly who is by his bedside when he awakens in the hospital. Large numbers of American troops began arriving in Northern Ireland in January 1942. The Irish Free State (Eire) remained neutral throughout the war. The OWI criticized this film as "a sloppy musical [which] could not be taken in any way as a factual account of what our troops are doing in Ireland."

778 DUBARRY WAS A LADY (MGM, June) Roy Del Ruth; *genre:* Comedy/Fantasy; *locations:* United States, France; *coding:* Short, Blk, Home Fr, Prod, Fem Lab, Home Def, Bonds, FDR?, FBI; *relevance:* 1.5.

Lenny (Red Skelton) is a hat check clerk at a New York club who wins the Irish Sweepstakes. It goes to his head and he makes a play for a showgirl named May (Lucille Ball). Lenny is given a Mickey Finn and hallucinates that he is King Louis XV in 18th century France. May becomes the pompadoured Madame DuBarry and her boyfriend a revolutionary attempting to seize Louis' throne. When Lenny revives, the tax man is waiting for him. This Technicolor film was just a vehicle for Skelton's comic routines and numerous displays of female pulchritude. War-oriented gags include the following response to Lenny asking why his hat check replacement was not a girl: "You can't get any, they're all working in the shipyard."

779 EDGE OF DARKNESS (WB, Apr)

Lewis Milestone; *genre:* Resist; *location:* Norway; *coding:* Resist, Intell Serv, AF-Ger, AF-Nor, Hitler, Nazi, FDR, Churchill, AF-Brit, Nor, Belg, Neth, Fr, Russ, Collab, Atroc, Atroc-Conc, Pol, Brit; *relevance:* 3.

When a German patrol is sent to investigate the strange silence from the occupation garrison at Trollness, they find mounds of corpses and the Norwegian flag defiantly flying. As the captain in command dictates his report, he stands by the body of the former commandant, Captain Koenig (Austrian actor Helmut Dantine in one of his numerous Nazi roles, cf *Mrs. Miniver*, q.v.). An extended flashback is initiated: Koenig boasts to visiting SS Major Ruck that it is easy to suppress petty sabotage by the villagers. He identifies the leading local troublemaker as fisherman Gunnar Brogge (Errol Flynn). Gunnar is preparing to flee to England when a wounded man staggers into his work shack and gasps out a report on a failed uprising in a nearby town. Gunnar resolves to stay and urge his fellow villagers to actively resist. Soon afterwards, they learn Ruck is actually a British agent who can arrange a submarine arms delivery. A fat collaborationist (referred to repeatedly as a "Quisling") alerts the Nazis of possible armed resistance. In retaliation, Koenig notifies the townspeople that his men will begin to occupy their homes. A series of escalating incidents, including the burning of the local schoolteacher's books, the rape of Gunnar's sweetheart Karin, and the seizing of hostages propel the people into open rebellion. Returning to the present, a German soldier is shot from the adjacent woods as he is raising the swastika flag. Many of the women of Trollness are portrayed actively participating in resistance acitivities, including carrying and using arms (the sniper who kills the German soldier is Karin, played by Ann Sheridan). The *Motion Picture Herald* called this rather grim film "an icy shower turned loose on the audience in the hope of driving home what this war is about." Twentieth Century–Fox also addressed the Norwegian resistance in its March release, *The Moon Is Down*, q.v.

780 EYES OF THE UNDERWORLD (Univ, Jan) Roy William Neill; *genre:* Crime; *location:* United States; *coding:* Short, Blk Mkt, FDR, Bonds, AF-A; *relevance:* 1.5.

Richard Dix plays a dedicated police chief who had once served a prison term. Racketeers, in league with corrupt officials, have him investigated by the state while they deal in hot tires on the black market. The gangsters are eventually arrested and the honest police chief is exonerated. At a police party in which two officers who have joined the Army are honored, a "Buy Bonds" poster is displayed on the wall.

781 THE FALCON AND THE CO-EDS (RKO, Nov*) William Clemens; *genre:* Crime; *location:* United States; *coding:* Short, Bonds, Latin Am?; *relevance:* 1.

The daughter of an old friend asks the Falcon (Tom Conway) to investigate the suspicious death of a faculty member at an exclusive girls' boarding school. Another murder occurs, but the Falcon exposes a neurotic teacher as the killer before she commits a third homicide. A large billboard featuring an American flag and an exhortation to buy war bonds and stamps may be seen in one shot, and an "A" ration sticker (on a private car), a "T" ration sticker (on a public bus) and possibly a "C" ration sticker (on the school's station wagon) may be seen.

782 THE FALCON IN DANGER (RKO, July) William Clemens; *genre:* Crime; *location:* United States; *coding:* Short, Prod, Fem Lab, Home Def, Pearl Harb; *relevance:* 2.

The debonair detective, who is about to get married, is asked to help solve the mystery of an airliner that had crashed with no one aboard. Palmer, a wealthy industrialist, his male secretary, the pilot and $100,000 in securities are missing. The millionaire, whose businesses include scrap salvage, returns home a few days later. Palmer claims he was kidnapped and robbed by armed men and forced to parachute out of the plane with them. He then escaped from a farmhouse where he had been held captive. The Falcon determines that Palmer faked the incident after killing his secretary, who had discovered that Palmer was responsible for his financial ruin. One scene takes place during a "dim-out" and there are several references to wartime shortages.

783 THE FALCON STRIKES BACK (RKO, May) Edward Dmytryk; *genre:* Crime; *location:* United States; *coding:* AF-A, War Corr, Collab, Latin Am, Fem Lab?, Ref, Nazi, Chi, Home Fr, Bonds, Short, Rommel, Draft; *relevance:* 1.5.

A gang of racketeers steals $250,000 worth of War Bonds, deliberately leaving clues that will incriminate the Falcon (Tom Conway). The young crime-solver had once discovered the evidence used to convict a gang member. When the Falcon takes the skeptical Inspector to the bar where he claims to have been slugged, they find a sign that reads: "Volunteer Knitters of America—Enroll Here." It later turns out that the place is a front for the crooks. The Falcon is arrested, but escapes. With the help of his friend Goldy, the Falcon proceeds to the mountain lodge headquarters of the gang and solves the case. At one point Jerry, a Chinese houseboy, says to Miss Gregory (an American): "Your people and mine have a common cause."

784 THE FALLEN SPARROW (RKO, Aug*) Richard Wallace; *genre:* War/Drama; *location:* United States; *coding:* Am Vol, Atroc, Spy-Sab, Collab?, Span Civ, Hitler, Nazi, Ref, Russ, Nor, Fr; *relevance:* 3.

In the fall of 1940 a tormented veteran of the International Brigades in Spain, held captive by the fascists for two years, returns to New York City to find the murderers of a friend. Kit (John Garfield) was tortured to reveal the whereabouts of a Nazi battle flag (of the unnamed Kondor Legion) captured by his brigade. Kit knows the Nazis killed his friend in order to get him to come out of hiding. The Nazis link themselves to a refugee organization and use a beautiful woman (Maureen O'Hara) as bait. Led by the sadistic cripple (Walter Slezak) who had tortured him in Spain, they almost succeed in breaking Kit in America. But Kit, both psychologically and physically overcomes his oppressors: "Before I let that little man [Hitler retrieve the banner] … I'll burn in hell." In the dramatic confrontation with his club-footed nemesis, who taunts him by stating: "You lack the brutality to kill in cold blood," Kit calmly pumps five shells into the man. RKO created a similar climactic scene for their film glorifying Russian partisans, *The North Star*, q.v. One OWI reviewer described *The Fallen Sparrow* as the "first Hollywood film to correctly evaluate the war in Spain as an assault of the Axis and its sympathizers on democracy everywhere."

785 FALSE FACES (Rep, May) George Sherman; *genre:* Crime; *location:* United States; *coding:* MacArthur, FDR; *relevance:* 1.

Circumstantial evidence points to the playboy son of a district attorney when a nightclub singer is murdered. The real killer is tracked down by the DA. The wayward son is chastened by the ordeal. This film is linked to the war by photos of MacArthur and FDR in the DA's office.

786 FIRST COMES COURAGE (Col, July) Dorothy Arzner; *genre:* War Drama/Resist; *locations:* Norway, Britain; *coding:* AF-Ger, Resist, Hitler, Nazi, Atroc, Brit, AF-Brit, Collab, Nor, Intell Serv; *relevance:* 3.

Despite being called a traitor by fellow villagers, Nicole Larson (Merle Oberon) consorts with a pompous Nazi major in occupied Norway. Nicole is actually a spy who forwards information from the boastful officer to British Intelligence. The British send an agent to coordinate a commando raid on an ammunition dump and to assassinate the increasingly suspicious Nazi. The English captain (Brian Aherne), an old love of Nicole's, is wounded and captured. Before he can be tortured, Nicole engineers his escape. In an attempt to keep her cover, Nicole consents to marry the Nazi. But the major has become acquainted with her activities and informs her that she will be the victim of an "unfortunate automobile accident."

The gallant captain returns and shoots the Nazi as commandos assault their target. On the beach Nicole refuses to embark for England with the surviving raiders: "I must go back. I'm the widow of a German hero. I'm above suspicion now."

787 FIVE GRAVES TO CAIRO (Para, May*) Billy Wilder; *genre:* Spy; *location:* Egypt; *coding:* AF-Raf, Pacifist, Laval, Dunkirk, AF-Brit, Hitler, Hess, Nazi, AF-Ger, Rommel, Fr, AF-Fr, AF-Ital, Musso, Arab, Spy-Sab, Atroc, Pol, Neth, Grk, Russ, Belg, Churchill, Atroc-Conc, Jap, Appease?, Munich; *relevance:* 3.

In June 1942, the British are retreating before Rommel's Afrika Korps (the Afrika Korps was sent to bolster the Italians, who had been defeated by the British in North Africa in 1941). Corporal John Bramble (Franchot Tone) abandons his disabled tank and staggers into a dingy roadside hotel. The nervous Egyptian owner (Akim Tamiroff) hides Bramble when Rommel's advance detail arrives. Assuming the identity of the hotel's deceased waiter, who was a Nazi secret agent, and overcoming the Anglophobia of the French maid (Anne Baxter), Bramble is able to discover the mystery of the "Five Graves"—supply caches secretly prepositioned before the war by an archeological expedition led by a disguised Rommel. Forced to kill a Nazi who uncovers his ruse, Bramble is allowed to pass through German lines when the French girl unexpectedly sacrifices herself by claiming she shot the officer. After the German defeat at El Alamein, Bramble, now a 2nd lieutenant, returns to the hotel and visits her grave. The arrogant Rommel, played by Erich von Stroheim, mercilessly patronizes the opera-singing Italian general on his staff. The Italian (Fortunio Bonanova) petulantly remarks: "A nation that belches cannot understand a nation that sings."

788 FLIGHT FOR FREEDOM (RKO, Feb*) Lothar Mendes; *genre:* Drama; *locations:* United States, Pacific; *coding:* Postwar, FDR, AF-MC, AF-N, Ital, Brit, Blk, V?, Spy-Sab, Isolat, Tojo, Jap, Pearl Harb; *relevance:* 2.

In 1942 a U. S. naval task force launches planes "loaded with America's answer to December 7th" against one of the Japanese-controlled islands. The lead bomber, flown by Randy Britton (Fred MacMurray), radios the fleet that all targets are pinpointed. An off-screen narrator concludes that this offensive would have been impossible without the courageous efforts of a lady in the 1930s.

During the ensuing extended flashback we learn about the life of famous aviatrix Toni Carter (Rosalind Russell). She agrees to a Navy request to crash on a round-the-world flight near some islands the "sons of heaven" are believed to have fortified. The Navy could then reconnoiter the area while conducting rescue operations. A malevolent Japanese agent informs Toni at her final stopover that he knows about the plans and the pre-arranged crash site, so she takes her plane up and flies till it runs out of gas. Back in the present, her former lover Randy leads his squadron in the attack. This fictional biography was obviously based on the life of Amelia Earhart, whose plane was lost mysteriously over the Pacific in July 1937. Her flight was not really part of a U.S. plot to map the Pacific, although some Navy ships were positioned in the area to assist her in case of an emergency.

789 FOLLIES GIRL (PRC, July) William Rowland; *genre:* Musical Comedy; *location:* United States; *coding:* AF-A, Ital?; *relevance:* 1.5.

When a talented costume designer (Wendy Barrie) is dismissed by her company, a friend arranges for her to sell her creations to the manager of a burlesque house. The show, with the girls in their spectacular new outfits and including the patriotic number, "Keep the Flag Flying, America," is a hit. An Army private on leave meets and falls in love with the designer. But then she learns he is the son of her former employer. Friends of the two reunite them at a wild party given for servicemen.

790 FOOTLIGHT GLAMOUR (Col, Sept) Frank Strayer; *genre:* Comedy; *location:* United States; *coding:* Prod, Short, Fem Lab, Free Fr, Brit, USO, AF-A?, AF-Brit?; *relevance:* 2.

J. C. Dithers Construction is in trouble because it built fifty housing units at a remote location where Dagwood claimed a new defense plant would be built (that will teach Dithers to listen to Dagwood!). Salvation seems to approach when Mr. Dithers' friend, tool manufacturer Randolph Wheeler, pays an unexpected visit. But instead of looking for a new factory site, the man is in town to find a place to keep his stagestruck daughter Vicki away from an opportunistic theatre director. The Bumsteads are selected to be her hosts (Blondie makes an uncharacteristically negative comment when she first hears of this: "You know how scarce food is." The U.S. government frowned on such comments, preferring to emphasize that plenty of food was available, but that certain *kinds* of food were rationed). Dithers then attempts to persuade Wheeler that it is his patriotic duty to build a new defense plant

in the area, near the housing site. In spite of her father's protests, Vicki plans to put on a play (to benefit the USO) in which she, Blondie, and Dagwood will star. As expected, Dagwood makes a shambles of the production and Vicki loses her taste for the stage. There are a reasonable number of topical references in this film, including a scene in which young Alexander Bumstead and his friend Alvin dress up as British Commandos.

791 FOR WHOM THE BELL TOLLS (Para, July*) Sam Wood; *genre:* War/Drama; *location:* Spain; *coding:* Span Civ, Am Vol, Ref, Russ, Nazi-orig rel vers, Brit-orig rel vers, Fr-orig rel vers, Span, AF-W, Am Vol, Stalin?, War Corr-orig rel vers, AF-Ital-orig rel vers, AF-Ger-orig rel vers; *relevance:* 2.

This film adaptation of Ernest Hemingway's 1940 novel was first assigned to Cecil B. DeMille. But the big-budget Technicolor project was later given to producer/director Sam Wood. Due to interference from the State Department in 1942 (desiring to keep Franco neutral during the war, it pressured Paramount into submitting the film to a Spanish representative for approval), the motion picture's content was largely de-politicized. Nevertheless, the substance of the novel was retained in the nearly three-hour-long original release version. However, Paramount cut about thirty minutes for the film's Fall re-release, removing most of the remaining political dialogue (for instance, all direct references to the Germans, fascism and communism were deleted). In 1937 Spain, on the eve of a major offensive, American Robert Jordan (Gary Cooper) is sent on a special mission for the "Republic" to meet a partisan band and blow up a strategic mountain bridge. The leader of the band, Pablo (Akim Tamiroff), is reluctant to take the risks, but he is pressured into supporting the operation by the strong-willed Pilar (actress Katina Paxinou—the character resembles the Spanish Loyalist heroine, La Pasionara). When Jordan is asked why he came to Spain, the former college instructor states: "A man fights for what he believes in" (but what constitutes his political convictions is never defined). Jordan falls in love with Maria (Ingrid Bergman), who was traumatized when the "Nationalists" (i.e., Franco's forces) took her town, killed the Republican mayor (her father), shaved the heads of the Republican women, and raped her. At great sacrifice, the small band of guerrillas succeeds in destroying the bridge, unaware the offensive has been canceled. As the survivors make their escape, Jordan, whose leg is broken, stays behind with a machine gun to cover their retreat. Thinking of Maria, Jordan shoots at approaching Nationalist troops (firing directly into the camera lens).

792 FOREVER AND A DAY (RKO, Mar) Rene Clair, Frank Lloyd, Victor Saville, Edmund Goulding, Cedric Hardwicke, Robert Stevenson, Herbert Wilcox; *genre:* Drama; *location:* Britain; *coding:* AF-Ger, WWI, US-Brit Coop, Brit, Home Def, Churchill, War Corr, AF-A, AF-Brit, Nazi; *relevance:* 2.

Based on an idea by Sir Cedric Hardwicke, this unique Anglo-American production had seven directors and over seventy name actors (including virtually the entire British contingent in Hollywood). RKO distributed it at cost and contributed the profits to assorted war charities. Preparing to return to America after covering the Blitz for his newspaper, Gates T. Pomfret receives cabled instructions from his British-born father to sell the Trimble-Pomfret house in London. Gates reaches the home as an air raid begins. In the cellar shelter he meets Lady Lesley Trimble, who would like to keep the house in the family. Annoyed by Gate's frivolous attitude, the young lady recounts the old building's history (in a series of flashbacks) illustrating the English spirit from 1804 to 1940. These include an ancestor who died at the Battle of Trafalgar in 1805 and a direct American descendent of his who came to London in 1917 as a Doughboy and was later killed in action in France. Just as Lesley is finishing her story, a bomb wrecks the house. As she and Gates emerge safely from the shelter they agree to rebuild it—together. Among the performers appearing are Charles Laughton, C. Aubrey Smith (whose portrait graces the house and even survives the Blitz), Buster Keaton, Ray Milland, Nigel Bruce, and Donald Crisp.

793 FUGITIVE FROM SONORA (Rep, July) Howard Bretherton; *genre:* Western; *location:* United States; *coding:* Short; *relevance:* 1.

In this period western, cowboy star Don "Red" Barry plays the dual role of a reformed outlaw and his twin brother, a parson preaching salvation on the frontier. Together they help settle a range war between cattlemen and homesteaders. One rancher anachronistically justifies his claim by stating he has "priority grazing rights."

794 THE GANG'S ALL HERE (TCF, Dec) Busby Berkeley; *genre:* Musical Comedy; *locations:* United States, Pacific; *coding:* AF-A, AF-N, Fem Lab, Jap, Latin Am, Blk, AF-MC, AF-Ger, AF-Jap, AF-AC, MacArthur, Spy-Sab, Bonds, Short; *relevance:* 2.5.

An Army sergeant (James Ellison) from a wealthy family must choose between a socialite and an entertainer with a heart of gold (Alice Faye). Comic relief is provided by Carmen Miranda and Edward Everett Horton. Musical numbers choreographed by

Busby Berkeley, including Miranda's famous "The Lady With the Tutti Frutti Hat," which featured a fleshy chorus line wielding huge phallic bananas, must have made this Technicolor film a big hit with the GIs. Although there are numerous topical references, the $5000 War Bonds Admission for the Benefit Show at a luxurious estate that caps the film would appear to be an egregious example of conspicuous consumption in times of alleged deprivation and national sacrifice. The OWI noted this, but found most objectionable a sequence that juxtaposes a frivolous race track scene with Miranda dissolving into a fleeting combat scene in the Pacific.

795 GANGWAY FOR TOMORROW (RKO, Nov*) John H. Auer; *genre:* War/Drama; *locations:* United States, France; *coding:* Blk, AF-Ger, MacArthur, Draft, Jap, AF-A, AF-AC, AF-W, Atroc?, Fem Lab, Prod, Prod-Farm, Hitler, Nazi, Collab, Resist, Pearl Harb, Ref, Fr, Austral, Short; *relevance:* 3.

As part of a car pool, Jim Benson picks up five co-workers and drives them to their aircraft plant. Confessing that he has speculated with his wife about their backgrounds, Jim invites them all to Sunday dinner. When they gather in the car the next day his fellow workers lose themselves in reveries of their individual pasts. With offscreen narration and the use of flashbacks and internal flashbacks, their separate stories are depicted. For example, French refugee Lisette (Margo) recalls her life as a cafe singer while secretly working with the underground. Tricked by a "Quisling" and Nazi authorities into singing the "Marseillaise," she later escapes execution and warns the resistance of a traitor in their midst. She comes to the U.S. and is able to work in a defense plant because her father was an American citizen (so she is, too). Wellington (John Carradine) was an epicurian tramp who knew nothing about Pearl Harbor until hauled before a small town judge for vagrancy. The judge shames him by pointing out that Wellington does not have the right to a peaceful jail cell while his fellow Americans are sacrificing at home and abroad to win the war. Despite the occupations of the principals, not a single scene in this film is set inside the factory!

796 A GENTLE GANGSTER (Rep, May) Phil Rosen; *genre:* Drama; *location:* United States; *coding:* FDR, AF-A, AF-N, AF-AC, Prod, Bonds, Home Def, Home Fr; *relevance:* 1.5.

Reformed bootlegger Mike Hallit, an honest citizen of Elmdale for the past twenty years, eliminates a gambling place that a gangster attempts to establish in town. Participation in war activities is the measure of respectability in this community that has prospered from war production. In the film's opening scene, a reverend admonishes his congregation for falling behind in the purchase of War Bonds. Insurance salesman Mike is appointed chairman of the local Bond drive. He makes a speech from the pulpit: "[Bonds] are insurance against the loss of your freedom ... [E]very dollar lying idle in our pockets, is a direct help to the enemy ... We'd all like to personally take a crack at the dictators, but we can't ... So let's whip out our dollars and slash the enemy across his ugly face."

797 GET GOING (Univ, June) Jean Yarbrough; *genre:* Comedy; *location:* United States; *coding:* Nazi?, Spy-Sab, Short, AF-?; *relevance:* 3.

Judy King (Grace McDonald) flees her small town and goes to war-crowded Washington, D.C. In a women's boarding house Judy makes friends with Tillie, her scatter-brained, clothes-borrowing roommate (Vera Vague). Judy joins Tillie and some other boarders as a government typist, and becomes enamored with her agency's personnel director, Bob Carlton (Robert Paige). To get the attention of the aloof Bob, Judy deliberately casts suspicion upon her fitness to work with confidential documents. Before her ruse is discovered, Bob has several dates with her while carrying out his investigation. To teach her a lesson, Bob has Judy placed under mock arrest as a spy suspect. After Judy confesses, she joins her girlfriends at the popular Dutch Treat club, only to discover that the place is the headquarters of a real Nazi spy ring. In a wild free-for-all the enemy agents prove no match for Judy and her pals.

798 THE GHOST AND THE GUEST (PRC, Apr) William Nigh; *genre:* Comedy; *location:* United States; *coding:* Blk, Short, Home Fr; *relevance:* 1.

James Dunn and Florence Rice (and their black chauffeur Sam McDaniel) spend their honeymoon in a ramshackle farmhouse given to them as a wedding present. The farm belonged to a recently executed gangster, and the newlyweds get involved with the police and some of the gangster's former associates who are trying to locate hidden diamonds. At one point the bridegroom makes a Victory Garden crack, and he later complains about the confusion created by the other guests: "This place is busier than a meat market with meat!" A female telegraph messenger appears in one scene—women messengers, elevator operators, and cab drivers were frequently depicted in wartime films; a subtle reference to the absence of men who previously held most such positions.

799 THE GHOST SHIP (RKO, Dec*) Mark Robson; *genre:* Drama; *locations:* United States, Latin America; *coding:* Blk, Ger, Grk, Latin Am; *relevance:* 1.

Although promoted as a horror film since it came from the Val Lewton unit at RKO (*The Cat People, I Walked with a Zombie,* etc.), this was actually a psychological sea drama, not unlike *The Sea Wolf* (WB, 1941). Richard Dix commands a tramp steamer, and his new mate (Russell Wade) begins to suspect that Dix is actually insane. The film seems to be set in the pre-war period, but in one scene—set in a Central American port—a black sailor (calypso singer Sir Lancelot) is harassed by several German sailors, and replies "I'm a British subject, I am, and I'll not sing for you or any other Heinie." Wade comes to his shipmate's aid and is knocked out. This type of anti–German (but not specifically WWII-oriented) bias was more frequently used in films of the 1937-41 period.

800 GHOSTS ON THE LOOSE (Mono, July) William Beaudine; *genre:* Spy/Comedy; *location:* United States; *coding:* Juv, Draft, Spy-Sab, Blk, Home Fr, Nazi, Collab, Short, Prod?; *relevance:* 2.5.

The East Side Kids are determined to give Glimpy's sister (Ava Gardner in one of her earliest roles) a nice wedding. When the boys hear the newlywed's future home is in disrepair, they drive over to redecorate it. They mistakenly go to the house next door, which just happens to be the headquarters of a Nazi gang led by the evil Emil (Bela Lugosi). The Nazis try to scare off the boys by making the house appear to be haunted. But these plans backfire when the kids flee to the basement and discover a printing press and leaflets bearing titles such as "What The New Order Means To You" and "How to Destroy the Allies." Believing the press belongs to the bridegroom (Rick Vallin—identified as an "airplane engineer" to explain why he is not in the Army), the boys move it to the house actually owned by the innocent groom. A cat and mouse game ensues between the teenagers and the Nazis. The cops finally close in on the source of propaganda and arrest the Nazis. But Glimpy has caught the German measles (his face is covered with little swastikas) and so everyone is quarantined.

801 GILDERSLEEVE ON BROADWAY (RKO, Oct*) Gordon Douglas; *genre:* Comedy; *location:* United States; *coding:* Bonds, Fr, Latin Am, Home Def, Blk; *relevance:* 1.5.

It is spring in Summerfield and love is in the air. Leroy is so concerned that his guardian, "Uncle Mort" (Throckmorton P. Gildersleeve), will marry a local spinster that the adolescent stages a phony air raid drill to disrupt a potentially romantic encounter. Later, Gildersleeve travels to a druggist's convention in New York City to meet his niece's estranged fiance. While in the big city, he becomes involved with a blonde gold-digger and almost marries a rich widow. Between conga dances he escapes the blonde and gets the widow to sign a distribution contract which will benefit his druggist friend. There is not a single overt indication of the war during the scenes in New York.

802 GILDERSLEEVE'S BAD DAY (RKO, May*) Gordon Douglas; *genre:* Comedy; *location:* United States; *coding:* Blk, Short, Home Fr, USO, Prod, Latin Am; *relevance:* 2.

Gildersleeve, serving as foreman, lobbies his fellow jurors to reach a not guilty verdict for a safe cracker named Louie. Unbeknownst to Gildersleeve, Louie's pals had sent him an anonymous bribe offer. So, when $1000 arrives in the mail, his family suspects the worst. Various misadventures lead to Gildersleeve redeeming himself by capturing the crooks. War material is limited to a few references to shortages and an attempt to raise money for a servicemen's canteen. In one amusing scene, the judge drives up to Gildersleeve's with a carload of jurors on the "share-the-ride plan." Gildersleeve tells the man it would be improper for a judge to travel with the jurors, gets in the car, and then drives off leaving the befuddled judge standing on the sidewalk.

803 GIRL FROM MONTERREY (PRC, Oct) Wallace Fox; *genre:* Musical Comedy; *location:* United States; *coding:* Prod, AF-A?, AF-Mex, Latin Am, Short; *relevance:* 2.

Mexican singer Lita (Armida) has a brother, Alberto (Anthony Caruso) who becomes a successful prizefighter. However, Lita is romantically attracted to a rival fighter, Jerry (Terry Frost). Jerry's manager tries to use blonde bimbo Flossie (Veda Ann Borg) to vamp Alberto and keep him out of shape. Alberto disappears for a time, then returns and reveals he went to Mexico City to enlist in the armed forces of Mexico. Lita says she has now given two men to the army: Alberto to the Mexican Army, and Jerry to the U.S. Army. The title song makes references to rationing of gasoline and tires, and a song entitled "Jive Brother Jive" includes these phrases: "Swing out on land and on sea / Swing out for our liberty / Swing out and set the world free... / Give with hot rivets and bolts... / We've got a job to do."

804 THE GOOD FELLOWS (Para, Aug*) Jo Graham; *genre:* Comedy; *location:* United States; *coding:* AF-A; *relevance:* 1.

In a small midwestern town, Jim Helton (Cecil Kellaway) neglects his real estate business and his family through his absorption in lodge activities. Jim is eventually brought to the brink of financial ruin and a possible prison stint before a government representative arrives with the authority to lease an old orphanage Helton owns for an Army convalescent home.

805 GOOD LUCK, MR. YATES (Col, June) Ray Enright; *genre:* War/Drama; *location:* United States; *coding:* Mil School, Draft, Prod, Fem Lab, AF-A, AF-N, Spy-Sab, Hist Am, Pol, Short, Juv, FDR, Ital, Russ, Jap, V, AF-W, AF-Mer, AF-MC, AF-AC, Home Def, Draft Avoid, MacArthur, Ref, Nazi, Ger; *relevance:* 3.

Oliver Yates (Jess Barker), a popular instructor at a military school, receives a patriotic send-off when he leaves to join the Army. Rejected and reclassified 4-F due to a punctured eardrum, Yates obtains a shipyard defense job, and takes a room in a boarding house run by a patriotic Italian-American (Henry Armetta). To conceal his real job from his former pupils, Yates gets a newly enlisted friend to post his letters from training camp. Oliver falls in love with co-worker Ruth Jones (Claire Trevor), a lady welder who also lives at his boarding house. A romantic rival at the shipyard spreads the rumor that Yates is a Nazi spy in league with an elderly German refugee doctor. Mobbed by shipyard workers, Yates challenges his antagonist. During the struggle, a fire is started and the other man is trapped. Yates saves him from death and again becomes a "home front hero" in the eyes of his students. The boys beg Mr. Yates to resume teaching, but he decides to remain at the shipyard for the duration. A rare wartime example of a film in which the protagonist does not leave a defense plant for the military. In one scene, a shipyard worker is given a telegram after missing a day of work: "Thanks for your fine, loyal work in my behalf. Signed, Adolf Hitler."

806 GOOD MORNING, JUDGE (Univ, Apr*) Jean Yarbrough; *genre:* Comedy; *location:* United States; *coding:* Short, Blk, Fr; *relevance:* 1.

David Burton (Dennis O'Keefe), a New York music publisher, has unintentionally plagiarized the tune of his number one song hit, "Spellbound." In order to beat the resulting lawsuit, he slips a Mickey Finn to the female lawyer (Louise Albritton) for the plaintiffs. The two antagonists become lovers. There is a single reference to rationing.

807 THE GORILLA MAN (WB, Jan) D. Ross Lederman; *genre:* Spy; *location:* Britain; *coding:* Spy-Sab, Nazi, Bonds, Short, AF-Brit, Collab?, Intell Serv, Brit, Fr; *relevance:* 3.

Returning from a commando raid in occupied France, a shell-shocked Captain Craig Killian (John Loder) is taken to a sanitarium on England's south coast. The institution is operated by a trio of brutal Nazi agents who have been informed that Killian carries a vital message from a British Intelligence officer concerning the location of the planned German invasion of Britain (a serious possibility in the fall of 1940). The secret enemy agents pronounce Killian insane, so as to discredit the officer's report. Later, they murder two women and make it appear the captain is the killer. Killian escapes the mental hospital and, with the help of a sympathetic lady friend, is able to prove his sanity and exonerate himself.

808 GOVERNMENT GIRL (RKO, Nov*) Dudley Nichols; *genre:* War/Drama/Comedy; *location:* United States; *coding:* Blk, FBI, Spy-Sab, Ital?, AF-N, AF-MC, AF-AC, AF-W, Home Fr, Prod, Fem Lab, Pearl Harb, Draft, Churchill?, Hitler, Hirohito, AF-A, FDR, Russ, Short, Hist Am; *relevance:* 3.

Olivia De Havilland plays a secretary named Smokey at the War Construction Board, who works for an automotive industry genius (Sonny Tufts) brought to Washington to expedite the manufacture of bombers. By continually cutting red tape, he manages to alienate various special interests but increases production. He is summoned before a Senate investigating committee (the Senate Special Committee to Investigate the National Defense Program was formed in 1941, with Harry Truman as the chairman; it reportedly saved the taxpayers many millions of dollars by spotting waste and mismanagement). Smokey, who has fallen in love with her boss, makes a patriotic appeal before the committee: "And if the man who made [expanded bomber production] ... possible ... makes too many little mistakes to suit you, then as Lincoln said about General Grant, you better find some more men that made mistakes out of the same barrel!" The investigation is called off. Comic relief is provided by scenes in which the main characters cope with the crowded wartime conditions in the nation's capital. On the reverse side of a production chart in their office is a dart board with unflattering caricatures of Hitler and Hirohito.

809 THE GREAT GILDERSLEEVE (RKO, Jan) Gordon Douglas; *genre:* Comedy; *location:* United States; *coding:* Blk, Short, Home Fr; *relevance:* 1.

This was the first film in a series starring the rotund comedian Harold Peary on the screen in his radio persona, the blustering Throckmorton P. Gildersleeve of small town Summerville. He is the guardian of his niece and nephew. Judge Hooker, who controls their trust fund, uses his position in an attempt to force Gildersleeve into marrying his spinster sister. There are a few war-oriented cracks scattered throughout the film.

Birdie, the black maid played by Lillian Randolph, delivers the following one to a dieting Gildersleeve at dinner: "Here's something from your victory garden you can eat."

810 GUADALCANAL DIARY (TCF, May) Lewis Seiler; *genre:* Combat; *location:* Pacific; *coding:* Jew, AF-Blk, AF-A, AF-N, AF-MC, AF-CG, Home Fr, AF-Jap, Hirohito, Tojo, Jap, Latin Am, Austral, Jew, Atroc, War Corr, USO, Chi, Fil, POW, Hist Am, WWI; *relevance:* 3.

Based on the bestseller by war correspondent Richard Tregaskis, this combat classic skillfully interweaves offscreen narration with plot action to achieve a semi-documentary style. Aboard a transport in the Pacific in July 1942, the usual ethnic mix of soldiers (including a taxi driver from Brooklyn, played by William Bendix, and a Mexican-American, played by Anthony Quinn)—the spirit of America in Marine uniforms—prepares to make the first full scale landings against a Japanese-held island. While cleaning his rifle, Betty Grable fan "Taxi" (Bendix) holds up his non-regulation blackjack and states: "If it'll make the Japs happy to die for their emperor, I'm going to try to make them happy." After suffering many casualties as a result of their own inexperience and Japanese stealth, the Marines learn they must systematically carry out the distasteful job of eliminating the "tricky" enemy. In the tradition of *The Fighting 69th* (WB, 1940), a (Notre Dame graduate) chaplain (Preston Foster) is with the men to assure them of the justness of their cause. In a final paroxysm of violence, most of the surviving enemy garrison is driven onto the beach and slaughtered, their bodies left floating in the surf. *Guadalcanal Diary* contains at least thirty-five pejorative references to the Japanese. The OWI praised this "realistic" motion picture, and *The Film Daily* called it "a superb tonic for the nation's morale." One of the incidents in the film is obviously based on the well-publicized "Goetge patrol" incident on Guadalcanal.

811 GUNG HO! (Univ, Dec) Ray Enright; *genre:* Training/Combat; *locations:* United States, Pacific; *coding:* Postwar, Fil, Grk, Jap, AF-Jap, Hist Am, Prod, Fem Lab, AF-MC, AF-N, Pearl Harb, Chi, Austral, Span Civ, Jew, Blk, AF-Blk, Short, Atroc; *relevance:* 3.

In preparation for a Marine diversionary attack upon the Japanese-held island of Makin (which actually took place on August 17, 1942), Colonel Thorwald (Randolph Scott) interviews volunteers, looking for men who will be "killers." The group that eventually makes up his Raider Battalion include a poor kid from Pittsburgh nicknamed "Pig Iron" (Robert Mitchum), a hillbilly, a

fighting preacher, a Spanish Civil War veteran, and a Filipino whose sister was raped by the Japanese. Following intensive training and a cramped voyage aboard two submarines, the Marines make a surprise dawn landing. The colonel's final instructions are "[N]ot a Jap alive by sunset." There ensue the usual encounters with Japanese snipers and a treacherous false surrender. This film includes extensive and unusually graphic (for the time) scenes of hand to hand combat. As the surviving raiders gather with their wounded on the beach to return to the submarines, an offscreen narrator intones: "[T]hirty [comrades] have died for an ideal. We must live it."

812 HANGMEN ALSO DIE (UA, Mar) Fritz Lang; *genre:* Resist; *location:* Czechoslovakia; *coding:* Czech, AF-Ger, Brit, Russ, Jew, Hitler, Heydrich, Nazi, Resist, Collab, V, Atroc, Atroc-Conc; *relevance:* 3.

Reichs Protector Heydrich, known as the "Hangman" to the people, rules the occupied Czech state with an iron fist. At a meeting of Nazi officers and Czech officials, Heydrich announces that because the "swine at Skoda [have] refused to work" the Gestapo will run the Czech arms industry. After Heydrich is shot by a doctor in the resistance, the local Gestapo chief (Alexander Granach) takes draconian measures, including the seizure of 400 hostages (many are from the Czech elite—several of whom are later shot while defiantly singing "No Surrender"). The assassin (Brian Donlevy) offers to confess and then poison himself, but the underground leaders vote against it. Instead, they create an elaborate frameup of a fat collaborationist named Czaka (Gene Lockhart). Blackshirts pick up Czaka, release him and then shoot him down on the steps of a church. The Nazis know Czaka did not kill Heydrich, but in a secret report it is stated that to "save the face of the German occupational authority" they will accept him as the assassin and close the case. The film concludes with a large lettered "NOT" superimposed over a long shot of a city followed by a fade in to "The End." The retaliatory elimination of the Czech village of Lidice is never even alluded to in this film. Bertolt Brecht, at the time residing in Hollywood, contributed to the script for this film. See also *Hitler's Madman*, q.v.

813 HAPPY LAND (TCF, Dec) Irving Pichel; *genre:* War/Drama; *location:* United States; *coding:* Vet, Bonds, Hitler, AF-N, AF-A, AF-MC, Ger-Am, Blk, AF-Ger, WWI, Pol, Russ, Jap, Fem Lab, Draft, AF-Can; *relevance:* 2.5.

The idyllic existence of pharmacist Lew March of Hartfield (as in heartland), Iowa, is shattered when a teenaged Western Union

girl delivers a telegram informing him that his only son, Rusty, was "killed in action." The formerly kindly man (Don Ameche) becomes embittered and withdraws from the community. Then, on one of Lew's lonely walks, he is visited by the spirit of his Civil War veteran father, Gramps (Harry Carey). Together, they stroll through town and, via flashbacks, journey through their lives. Thus Lew comes to realize that his son's death had meaning, by helping to protect the American way of life. Gramps departs and a renewed Lew returns to his drugstore. A short while later a shipmate of Rusty's on leave who has no family appears. Lew takes the young man home. The OWI lauded this film's "effective portrayal of straight Americana."

814 HARVEST MELODY (PRC, Nov) Sam Newfield; *genre:* Musical Comedy; *location:* United States; *coding:* Prod-Farm, Fem Lab, Jap, Hitler, Prod, V, Juv, Short, AF, Eisenhower, FDR, Can, Brit, Fr, Latin Am; *relevance:* 2.5.

Tommy (Johnny Downs) and Janie come to Los Angeles to see the U.S. Government Employment Bureau about hiring farm workers. At a nightclub, they meet press agent Chuck Hammond (Sheldon Leonard), whose business is in trouble because the war news prevents him from acquiring the usual newspaper coverage for his clients, including the Radio Rogues, Eddie LeBaron and his orchestra, and rich widow Nancy DeWitt. Chuck offers his clients' services as farm laborers as a publicity stunt. Chuck and his volunteers are greeted by Tommy, his singing farmhands, and some college girls who are working during their vacation. Tommy tells them: "We here on the farm feel that a good one-third of the war belongs to us ... you're all soldiers on one of the fronts of the war." Chuck encourages a romance between Tommy and film star Gilda Parker (Rosemary Lane) to gain more publicity. Gilda is chosen president of the American Farm Clubs and takes her duties so seriously that she turns down the offer of a big movie contract. Tommy and Janie reunite at the finale. In one scene, a Radio Rogue impersonates Hitler (while white-washing a barn) and is tossed in a pig pen by his partners!

815 HE HIRED THE BOSS (TCF, Apr) Thomas Z. Loring; *genre:* Comedy; *location:* United States; *coding:* AF-A, Short, Bonds, Draft, Home Def, Blk Mkt; *relevance:* 2.5.

Hubert (Stuart Erwin) is a timid, fortyish, bookkeeper for the Bates' importing firm. He keeps waiting for a ten dollar raise in order to be able to marry the firm's stenographer. Hubert is very conscientious about homefront participation, collecting tin foil from cigarette packages, riding motor scooter to work, buying Bonds, becoming an Air Raid Warden, and so on. But when Hubert returns to his job after failing his final physical for the Army, the blustering Mr. Bates demotes him. Hubert's life changes following a property windfall and Bates' inability to pay a bank loan. Hubert takes over the firm by covering its debts. In an action-filled climax, the newly assertive Hubert, using his ubiquitous tin foil ball as a weapon, helps waylay a gang of silk thieves attempting to hijack stocks from the firm's warehouse.

816 HEADIN' FOR GOD'S COUNTRY (Rep, Aug) William Morgan; *genre:* War/Drama; *location:* United States; *coding:* AF-Jap, AF-AC, Spy-Sab, Jap, AF-N, Home Def; *relevance:* 3.

The inhabitants of Sunivak, an isolated Alaskan village, are not pleased when a stranger, Michael Banyan (William Lundigan), appears in the fall of 1941. Only Laurie Lane, who runs the weather station, and old Clem Adams, the town printer, befriend him. While Banyan is in jail for fighting, the tubes from Laurie's radio, the only one in town, are stolen. Banyan, to get even with the hostile townspeople, secretly prints a phony Seattle newspaper front page announcing America's entrance into the war. Banyan mocks the villagers' frantic defense preparations as organized by the cannery owner, Albert Ness, but then persuades them to adopt modern defensive measures. When a supply boat arrives with a recent newspaper, Banyan takes a dogsled out of town. Spotting a Japanese raiding party heading for Sunivak, he turns back and convinces Laurie to send an SOS over the wireless. The villagers, secure in their foxholes, release their dogs and rout the raiders. Banyan kills the traitorous Ness as the man attempts to seize the weather station. U. S. aircraft arrive in time to finish off the Japanese soldiers and sink their ship anchored in a nearby bay.

817 THE HEAT'S ON (Col, Dec) Gregory Ratoff; *genre:* Musical Comedy; *location:* United States; *coding:* Latin Am, Blk, Home Fr, AF-A, AF-Blk; *relevance:* 1.5.

This film opens during a performance of "Indiscretions," a floundering Broadway musical starring the sexy Fay Lawrence (Mae West). Desperate to attract an audience, the producer finagles a reform group known as "The Foundation," into attempting to close the "immoral" show. Unfortunately, the gimmick is too successful. Eventually, after the usual complications, a second and more successful show, "Tropicana," becomes a hit. Victor Moore, playing the wimpish brother of the society matron who runs the Foundation, solos on a Victory Garden number: They Looked So Pretty on the Envelope."

Also, well-known Forties pianist, Hazel Scott, performs a timely rendition of "The Caissons Go Rolling Along," while black soldiers and girls perform in a production number.

818 THE HEAVENLY BODY (MGM, Dec*) Alexander Hall; *genre:* Comedy; *location:* United States; *coding:* AF, AF-W, Russ, Blk, Home Def, Short, Home Fr, War Corr; *relevance:* 2.

The French-born wife (Hedy Lamarr) of an astronomer (William Powell) takes up astrology when her husband spends too much time studying his newly discovered comet. Lamarr is told by her star advisor that a handsome new man will come into her life; her flustered husband moves into his observatory: "I'll thank you to send my ration books." Two weeks later, the new Air Raid Warden (James Craig) knocks on Lamarr's door to warn her about a visible light in her bedroom window. This dark stranger (who picked up a "six-syllable fever" in North Africa as a war correspondent) is the predicted new man in Lamarr's life. When Powell feigns illness, a Russian doctor friend prescribes vodka, leading to a wild, drunken party. The astrologer turns out to be a hoarder, with over 3000 cans of food hidden in her basement. Powell and Lamarr reconcile, and Craig makes his rounds accompanied by his new dog.

819 HENRY ALDRICH GETS GLAMOUR (Para, Jan*) Hugh Bennett; *genre:* Comedy; *location:* United States; *coding:* Home Fr, Home Def, Jap, Short, AF-N; *relevance:* 1.5.

Centerville's favorite awkward teenaged son, Henry, acquires the scandalous reputation of being a "wolf." The rumor originates after Henry is photographed accidentally stumbling into the arms of Hollywood star Hilary Dane, visiting a nearby town to play in a Navy Relief show. Miss Dane eventually comes to Henry's rescue by making a public announcement that he is not a "wild … Casanova." Henry's best pal Dizzy, reflecting wartime conditions, is primarily concerned about his gas and tires when he loans Henry his car for a date.

820 HERE COMES KELLY (Mono, Sept) William Beaudine; *genre:* Comedy; *location:* United States; *coding:* Draft, Jew, Latin Am; *relevance:* 1.5.

Kelly (Eddie Quillan) cannot keep a job because of his temper. His friend Sammy Cohn gets him a job as a process server; Kelly has to deliver a subpoena to dancer Carmencita. Kelly and Sammy are given subpoenas for gangsters involved in an oil swindle, including one for the mysterious, unnamed leader. Kelly's girlfriend Margie is nearly seduced by a shady lawyer, but Kelly

exposes him as the oil swindle mastermind. Just as Kelly is about to marry Margie, he receives his induction notice. Kelly's mother consoles Margie: "Don't worry, the war will soon be over. He never held a job more than two months in his life."

821 HERS TO HOLD (Univ, July) Frank Ryan; *genre:* Romance; *location:* United States; *coding:* Home Fr, Short?, AF-AC, AF-FT, Chi, Jap, Prod, Fem Lab; *relevance:* 3.

Bill Morley (Joseph Cotten) returns to America after an eighteen-month stint in the Flying Tigers, in order to obtain his commission in the U. S. Army Air Corps. While waiting on the West Coast, Bill goes to the Vega aircraft plant to supervise tests of a wing flap he has designed. At a Red Cross Blood Bank, sparks fly when he meets Penelope Craig (Deanna Durbin), a wealthy debutante. Soon afterwards, "Penny" discards her designer clothes, dons denim and becomes a riveter at Vega. Having heard her sing at a party, Bill's pal Rosey persuades Penny to entertain the war workers at lunchtime. One of the songs she performs is the topical "Say A Prayer For The Boys Over There." The budding romance chills after Bill is notified of his commission in the Air Force. He does not want Penny to become another war widow at the plant. Rosey gets word through to Penny of Bill's imminent departure for overseas. She arrives at the airport in time to reaffirm their love. The OWI's yearly summary cited this film as one of three containing blatant scenes of "conspicuous consumption," something the government frowned upon.

822 HE'S MY GUY (Univ, Mar) Edward F. Cline; *genre:* Musical Comedy; *location:* United States; *coding:* Blk, V, Prod, Fem Lab, Bonds, AF-A, Short; *relevance:* 2.

The husband-wife team of Van Moore (Dick Foran) and Terry Allen (Irene Hervey) are struggling on the vaudeville circuit. They are visited by Madge (Joan Davis), a nutty ex-hoofer, now a riveter at a defense plant. The couple later separates and Terry takes a secretarial job in the personnel department of an aircraft factory. The plant, whose workers include many women, is experiencing numerous accidents. Terry tells her boss that stress may be a contributing factor and suggests that the workers be allowed a "chance to let off steam" in a talent show. Van is brought on board to stage the show, supposedly using only employee acts. The "Victory Vanities" show includes a number by the Mills Brothers and a song—"On the Old Assembly Line"—performed by Gertrude Niesen in a great cardboard V, with a chorus of fellow workers in accompaniment: "Pitch in...until our side comes out on top … [T]he job we do will mean a lot to some soldier who will be counting on me and you." The plant's president is so impressed by the show that he names Van and Terry co-directors of entertainment for all of his defense factories. Universal got more mileage out of "Boogie Woogie Bugle Boy" (first heard in *Buck Privates*, 1941) in this film.

823 HI BUDDY (Univ, Feb) Harold Young; *genre:* Musical Comedy; *location:* United States; *coding:* WWI?, AF-A, AF-N, AF-AC, AF-MC, AF-Blk, USO, Bonds; *relevance:* 3.

The "Hi, Buddy" clubhouse for slum kids is about to fold because potential donors are investing in War Bonds. Two of the adult "Buddies," fireman Johnny Blake (Robert Paige) and policeman Dave O'Connor (Dick Foran), who is about to join the Army, try to help. When Johnny is offered a singing spot on a popular radio show, *he* delays enlisting so that his earnings can be used to support the club. Johnny goes on a tour of Army camps with the show, unaware that his agent is embezzling his money. In the meantime, Dave learns of the club's continuing problems while on furlough and obtains permission to do a benefit show with his Army pals. After Johnny learns from Dave about the agent's deceit, the two buddies coerce the man into writing large checks at the benefit's various booths. In Dave's show the solidarity of all the services is stressed. Some tap dancing black soldiers participate in the "We're All In This Together" number. Johnny hurries to the nearest recruiting station and returns to deliver a final song for the benefit.

824 HI DIDDLE DIDDLE (UA, Aug) Andrew Stone; *genre:* Comedy; *location:* United States; *coding:* AF-N, Ital?, Russ?, AF-MC, Short, Prod, Fem Lab, Home Def, Hitler, Ger?; *relevance:* 2.5.

Sonny Phyffe (Dennis O'Keefe) is a sailor who plans to marry socialite Janie Prescott (Martha Scott). Because his ship was delayed, Sonny is late for the wedding breakfast (the guests had to all contribute ration coupons for the cake). "Colonel" Phyffe, a shady character, is living off his opera-singing wife. Various interruptions following the marriage, including Janie's Air Raid Warden service, delay the honeymoon until the last day of Sonny's leave. A Navy public relations officer informed United Artists that his service took a dim view of films "which exploit the uniform in violation of naval customs." In a titled forward, the audience is challenged to find the "propaganda" in the film. Perhaps it is the scene in which the opera singer and her friends musically abuse *Tannhauser*, causing her Wagner wallpaper to become animated and flee the room!

825 HI YA CHUM (Univ, Mar) Harold Young; *genre:* Comedy; *location:* United States; *coding:* AF-A?, Short, Prod, Russ, Home Fr; *relevance:* 2.

"The Three Madcaps" (the Ritz Brothers) are a flop in the "Fancies of 1943." With the show canceled, they head west for Hollywood in an old flivver. Their car expires in Mercury, California, a former ghost town whose mercury deposits have made it a wartime boomtown. Between stints washing dishes, the boys entertain the patrons at the "Workers' Club Restaurant." One atrocious war-oriented number they perform, "Pedalling Two on a Bike," is meant to encourage using bicycles as an alternate means of transportation. A gangster attempts to exploit the war stimulated wealth by establishing a gambling house. When some of his thugs, derisively referred to as an "army of occupation," attempt to destroy the restaurant, the Ritz Brothers neutralize them using napkins laced with laughing gas.

826 HI YA SAILOR (Univ, Oct) Jean Yarbrough; *genre:* Musical Comedy; *location:* United States; *coding:* AF-N?, USO, AF-Mer, Fem Lab; *relevance:* 2.

Bob Jackson (Donald Woods) persuades three of his Merchant Marine buddies to invest in the publication of a song he has composed. When the sailors dock in New York City they hail a cab driven by a pretty blonde, Pat Rogers, and begin a vain search for the song publisher. Trying to avoid paying their fare to Pat, the three duck into a servicemens' canteen where the singing star Annabelle is performing. Various adventures eventually lead to Annabelle plugging Bob's song and a legitimate publisher buying it. Female cabbies were a popular character type in wartime films, e.g., *In Society* (Univ., 1944); *Cover Girl* (Col., 1944). The actress who played Pat, Elyse Knox, was the daughter of Secretary of the Navy, Frank Knox.

827 HIGH EXPLOSIVE (Para, Mar*) Frank McDonald; *genre:* Adventure; *location:* United States; *coding:* Fem Lab?, Prod; *relevance:* 1.5.

After being kicked out of auto racing for bad sportsmanship, Buzz Mitchell (Chester Morris) goes to work as a driver for old friend Mike Douglas' nitroglycerin company. With war having just been declared, Buzz blusters patriotically about rescuing Mike's business by doing one of the most dangerous national defense jobs. A stunt-flying accident, for which Buzz is partially responsible, kills the younger brother of Mike's girlfriend. Buzz wants to leave, but Mike reminds him of his responsibility to America's victory program. When an oil well fire threatens a nearby munitions plant, a request is made to blow it out with nitro. Mike

and Buzz charter a plane, but when fog makes it impossible to land, Buzz tricks Mike into parachuting out and then crashes the nitro-loaded plane into the burning well. This film could be regarded as a civilian version of Republic's *Flying Tigers*, q.v.

828 HIGHER AND HIGHER (RKO, Dec*) Tim Whelan; *genre:* Musical; *location:* United States; *coding:* AF, Fr?, Blk; *relevance:* 1.

Mr. Drake (Leon Errol) is a former millionaire who is about to lose his mansion. When his wealthy friends refuse to help him out, his loyal servants—whom he has always treated as equals—come to Drake's aid. The first scheme to restore their former status (and recover their back wages) involves passing off the scullery maid (Michelle Morgan) as Drake's debutante daughter in order to marry her to a rich man. But the "count" turns out to be a phony. Financial salvation comes when they all work together to convert the mansion's wine cellar into a successful tavern. The singing boy next door was played by Frank Sinatra, in his first starring role. This muddled film concludes with a printed dedication: "To the families and friends of our men ... in the Armed Services." Perhaps RKO was a tad nervous about Sinatra's controversial draft deferment.

829 HIT PARADE OF 1943 [aka **CHANGE OF HEART**] (Rep, Mar) Albert S. Rogell; *genre:* Musical Comedy; *location:* United States; *coding:* AF-Blk, Draft?, Home Fr?, Hist Am?, AF-AC?, AF-A, AF-N, AF-MC, Short, Bonds, Home Def, Spy-Sab, Jap, AF-Ft, Latin Am, Blk, Prod, Fem Lab; *relevance:* 2.

Jill Wright (Susan Hayward), a midwest ingenue trying to break into the songwriting business, pays fifty dollars to the Miracle Song Publishing firm to plug her first work. But when she comes to New York City, Jill discovers that the charming company president, Rick Farrell (John Carroll), has changed the title and is promoting the song as his own. Jill agrees to ghost write some additional numbers, planning to get even later. A vindictive "other woman" creates further obstacles to a budding romance. On a Bond broadcast, Rick performs Jill's latest song, revealing to the public that she is the composer. One of the musical's seven songs, "Yankee Doodle Tan," performed by the black Golden Gate Quartet, is a patriotic paean to the armed services. In fact, there are numerous black specialty acts and musical performers featured throughout this film. The OWI comments on a major production number accompanied by Count Basie and his orchestra are noteworthy: "[It] includes two Negroes in sailor suits, four Negresses who are waiting for the Victory Bus which

will take them to the Swing Shift, two Negroes in Zoot Suits, a Negro policeman and
a Negro Air Raid Warden. This number
compliments and criticizes the Negroes. [It]
... is beautifully staged ... and ... indicate[s]
that Negroes are doing their share in war
work. But ... the government has registered
its disapproval of Zoot Suits [due to their
material-wasting length and wide lapels,
these suits, popular among black and Hispanic youth, were considered unpatriotic]."

830 HIT THE ICE (Univ, June*) Charles
Lamont; *genre:* Comedy; *location:* United
States; *coding:* Bonds, Home Def; *relevance:*
1.

Abbott and Costello are two sidewalk
photographers who accidentally take a photo
of some bank robbers. Fleeing from the
crooks, they wind up in a mountain cabin.
Although the plot is non-relevant, there is
one reference to a "blackout" and a Bonds
poster is shown.

831 HITLER—DEAD OR ALIVE (Ind,
Apr*) Nick Grinde; *genre:* War/Drama; *lo-
cations:* United States, Germany, Canada,
Britain; *coding:* Ger, AF-AC?, AF-Can, FR?,
V?, Jap, Russ, WWI, AF-Ger, AF-Raf,
Hitler, Nazi, Atroc-Conc, Musso, Resist; *rel-
evance:* 3.

In this far-fetched work, three ex-cons
(led by Ward Bond) sign a million dollar
contract with an American businessman to
either capture or kill Adolf Hitler. Arriving
in England as Canadian paratroopers, they
force their pilot on a training mission to fly
to Germany. The criminal trio and the pilot
hijack a truck, but are quickly picked up by
the Gestapo and interrogated at a concentration camp. The monocle-wearing Colonel
Hecht is aware of the true identity of the
"American swine," but is afraid there might
be some truth to their story about carrying
a special message for Hitler. Elsa, a dancer
with whom the colonel is enamored, is an
Allied secret agent working with the German underground. Hitler (Bobby Watson)
arrives at his nearby castle retreat (presumably Berchtesgaden). Elsa, who has been invited to entertain the Fuehrer, comes to the
castle with the Americans disguised as her
musicians. In a shoot out, "Schicklegruber"
is taken hostage. The Gestapo catch up with
the group and execute most of them, including a cowardly Hitler, who is not recognized because the Americans shaved off
his moustache and cut off his forelock.
Johnny, the pilot, escapes to America and is
shown flying a new bomber paid for by the
gangsters' reward money. The plot for this
film was inspired by an actual advertisement
which ran in *The New York Times* in May
1940, in which Dr. Samuel Church of the
Carnegie Institute offered $1,000,000 for

Hitler's capture and delivery ("alive, un-
wounded and unharmed") to the League of
Nations for trial.

832 HITLER'S CHILDREN (RKO,
Mar) Edward Dmytryk; *genre:* War/Drama;
location: Germany; *coding:* Juv, AF-Ger, Hitler, Goering, Goebbels, Nazi, Fr?, Brit, Spy-
Sab, League Nat, Ger, Ger-Am, WWI, Austria, Musso, Ital, Jew, V, Resist, Atroc,
Atroc-Conc, Czech, Pol, Hist Am; *relevance:*
3.

In 1933 Berlin, the humanity and freedom of the American Colony School is contrasted with the political indoctrination and
regimentation of the new Nazi Horst Wessel Schule. Hitler Youth Karl (Tim Holt) of
the latter falls in love with German-born
Anna (Bonita Granville) of the former. Several years later the Gestapo forcibly removes
all Jews, Poles, Russians and persons of German blood from the American school. Anna's
professor (Kent Smith) eventually finds her
working as an administrator at a camp for
girls "drafted" to have illegitimate children
for the state. Although she discourages the
professor's attempts to help her, Anna later
confesses to a blackshirted Karl that she does
not want to be a part of the Nazi's "diseased
new world." Anna is sent to a labor camp,
where her passive resistance leads to her being identified as a "dangerous agitator."
Threatened with sterilization, Anna escapes
and takes refuge in a cathedral. In the middle of the bishop's sermon, in which he questions the authority of Hitler, armed Nazis
enter and seize the girl. Anna is sentenced
to a public lashing. Karl, who has been ordered to supervise the punishment, intervenes. At a trial where Karl is expected to re-
cant over the radio, he tricks the Party by
exhorting his listeners to renounce the Nazis.
As Anna runs to his side, they are both shot
dead. The American professor, having heard
the broadcast over the public address system
at the airport, sadly boards a plane leaving
Germany. This film was based on a non-
fiction book by Gregor Ziemer, *Education
for Death*, which also served as the basis for
a 1943 Walt Disney cartoon of that title (released by RKO). In 1950, associate producer
Robert Golden, screenwriter Emmet Lavery,
and star Bonita Granville "remade" *Hitler's
Children* as an anti–Communist film, *Guilty
of Treason* (Eagle-Lion), which also contains
a scene in which Granville is whipped.

833 HITLER'S MADMAN [aka HIT-
LER'S HANGMAN] (MGM, June) Doug-
las Sirk; *genre:* Resist; *location:* Czechoslo-
vakia; *coding:* Hess, WWI, League Nat,
Czech, Hist Am, AF-Ger, AF-Raf, Brit,
Hitler, Heydrich, Nazi, Atroc, Atroc-Conc,
Resist, Collab, Himmler, Russ, Pol, Jew; *rel-
evance:* 3.

Unlike *Hangman Also Die*, this film version of the assassination of Reinhard Heydrich is closer to historical truth. And, whereas
the earlier film only features Heydrich in one
brief scene, John Carradine's bestial portrayal of the Nazi overseer of the occupied
Czech state is fully developed in *Hitler's
Madman*. Two scenes are particularly illustrative. In the first, Heydrich closes the University of Prague after disparaging a professor's lecture. He compels the male students
to "volunteer" for the Nazi Labor Legion,
and later lasciviously forces the women to
submit to medical examinations before sending them to the Russian front to "entertain"
German troops. The second sequence shows
Heydrich disrupting a peasant religious procession (a blessing of the wheat fields). The
blackshirted Nazi leader condemns the "illegal meeting," then wipes his boots on a sacred cloth. When the priest attempts to stop
Heydrich, he is ruthlessly shot down. The
villagers begin to commit acts of sabotage.
The German mayor's wife—whose two sons
were killed fighting in Russia—betrays Heydrich. A villager named Karel (Alan Curtis),
who has parachuted back into Czechoslovakia from Britain, leads an ambush of Heydrich's motorcade (May 27, 1942: three
Czechs trained by the British were the actual assassins). The mortally wounded Heydrich is visited by Himmler (a monocle-
wearing caricature, resembling the corpulent
Goering more than the actual Himmler).
Heydrich screams for morphine, declares he
does not want to die for the Fuehrer and
then prophesies that Germany will lose the
war "because we were too weak." Himmler
informs Hitler by phone that Heydrich "died
like a hero," and then orders the eradication
of the village of Lidice (suspected of harboring the assassins; this occurred on Sunday,
June 10, 1942). The men of the village, who
have been lined up against the churchyard
wall, are shot as they defiantly sing the Czech
National Anthem. The film is framed by a
recitation of Stephen Vincent Benet's poem
dedicated to the victims of the savage reprisals
(some 5,000 people were killed by the Nazis
in revenge for Heydrich's death). The concluding portion of the poem is delivered by
the superimposed spirits of the executed villagers. This film was originally produced by
Seymour Nebenzal for PRC, but was bought
by MGM for release.

834 HOOSIER HOLIDAY (Rep, Sept)
Frank McDonald; *genre:* Comedy; *location:*
United States; *coding:* Blk, AF-AC, Fem
Lab?, Draft, Prod-Farm; *relevance:* 2.

The five Baker boys (George Byron and
the musical "Hoosier Hot Shots") live and
work with their mother on a large midwestern farm. Although Fairchild, the head of

the local draft board, considers their occupation to be essential to the war effort, the brothers all wish to join the Army Air Corps. When the five singing daughters of Fairchild (Dale Evans and the "Music Maids") return home from finishing school, the boys determine that a collective romantic effort may force the hand of the girls' father. But the old man calls their bluff. The Baker boys have also recently been awarded a patriotic service flag for their farm work by the state governor. The brothers resign themselves to settling down on the home front for the duration.

835 HOSTAGES (Para, Aug*) Frank Tuttle; *genre:* Resist; *location:* Czechoslovakia; *coding:* AF-Ger, Hitler, Nazi, Atroc, Collab, Resist, Jew?, Czech, Pol; *relevance:* 3.

Purportedly based on fact, this film was adapted from a best selling 1942 novel. Perhaps casting William Bendix as a Czech resistance leader had something to do with its failure at the box office. When a drunken German officer drowns himself behind a Prague cafe, the Nazis round up the twenty-six customers of the restaurant as hostages. These include a wealthy collaborator (Oscar Homolka) and Janoshik (Bendix), the bungling washroom attendant. The death report is falsified as a murder by the two leading German occupation authorities, both of whom wish to confiscate the collaborator's coal business. The Prague underground mobilizes in a desperate attempt to rescue Janoshik, who is really Karl Vokosch, their leader. But the shrewd Vokosch escapes from the Nazis on his own. The remaining hostages are promptly shot. As Vokosch directs a new series of sabotage activities against German munitions dumps, the military "Protector" general learns of Janoshik's true identity. To cover himself, he kills his Nazi counterpart, Commissioner Rheinhardt (Paul Lukas). This film contains references to girls being forced to "entertain" German soldiers, which also occurs in *None Shall Escape* (Columbia, 1944), q.v., among other films.

836 HOW'S ABOUT IT? (Univ, Feb) Erle Kenton; *genre:* Musical Comedy; *location:* United States; *coding:* AF-N; *relevance:* 1.

This was another swing extravaganza showcasing the talents of the Andrews Sisters. They are elevator operators in a music publishing house who hope to get into show business. A romantic subplot centers around a young lady who accuses the handsome music publisher of plagiarizing her calendar poem for song lyrics. In a patriotic stage number finale the Andrews Sisters sing "Here Comes The Navy," with a battleship's gun turrets providing the background. *Born to Dance*, a 1936 MGM release starring Eleanor Powell, concluded similarly.

837 THE HUMAN COMEDY (MGM, June) Clarence Brown; *genre:* War/Drama; *location:* United States; *coding:* Juv, AF-N, Postwar?, Russ, Fil, Grk, Chi, AF-A, AF-AC, Short, Latin Am, Blk, Home Def, Prod, Un, FDR, Hist Am, Bonds, Jap; *relevance:* 2.5.

This highly sentimental work portrays a small town American family coping with the stress of war. With his father dead and his older brother in the Army, teenaged Homer McCauley (Mickey Rooney) helps support his family by taking a job as a telegram messenger. One of his first deliveries is a death notification from the War Department to a Mexican-American mother. Homer's brother Marcus McCauley (Van Johnson) is a typical GI who misses home, believes in God and country, and is not ashamed to admit his fear of death (although never pointedly addressed, management of this natural fear in soldiers facing combat was deemed critical to American morale by military authorities). In what becomes his final letter to Homer, Marcus writes: "I am proud that I am serving my country … I would rather there be no war, but as there is a war, I have long since made up my mind to be the finest soldier it is possible to be." On Homer's journey to bring the dreaded death notice telegram to his own mother, he is joined by Marcus' invalided Army buddy, Tobey (an orphan): "I'm home for good now … [Marcus] gave me more than life … he gave me a family." Homer tears up the telegram and enters the McCauley household, announcing: "The soldier has come home."

838 I DOOD IT (MGM, Sept) Vincent Minelli; *genre:* Comedy; *location:* United States; *coding:* Nazi, AF-Brit, Chi, Hist Am?, Free Fr, Home Def, US-Brit Coop, USO, Blk, Jew?, Short, Spy-Sab, Collab?, Draft, AF-N, AF-A; *relevance:* 2.

Red Skelton is a pants presser with a crush on Broadway star Eleanor Powell. Powell has a fight with her boyfriend and marries Skelton on the rebound, believing he is a rich potential backer for her next show. Skelton eventually foils a plot to blow up a warehouse full of Lend-Lease supplies, conveniently located next to the theater where Powell is performing. The sabotage plot is shoehorned into the final few moments of the film, but there are a number of topical jokes throughout, including references to rationing and the draft.

839 I ESCAPED FROM THE GESTAPO (Mono, May) Harold Young; *location:* United States; *coding:* Russ, Atroc, Jew, Ger-Jap Coop, AF-Ger, Goering, Hitler, Fem Lab, Prod, Ger, Blk, AF-A, AF-N, AF-MC, AF-Mer?, AF-AC, Spy-Sab, Collab, FBI, Nazi, Atroc; *relevance:* 2.

A forger (Dean Jagger) escapes from prison and is tortured into helping a gang of saboteurs produce counterfeit money and securities (the gang also holds his mother hostage). He engraves clues for the FBI on the false bills, and also—with the aid of another unwilling collaborator (Frances Farmer)—helps foil an enemy plot to blow up an oil refinery. John Carradine added yet another villainous Axis role to his credits, as the head of the spy ring. The opening of this film shows an animated Nazi "octopus" reaching out to grab the U.S.A.

840 IDAHO (Rep, Mar) Joseph Kane; *genre:* Western; *location:* United States; *coding:* Prod, Latin Am?; *relevance:* 1.

A judge wants to close down a gambling house established in a "boom town" because it sets a bad moral tone, and takes money from the "high-paid workers at the tungsten mine." Roy Rogers helps the judge and his pretty daughter (Virginia Grey) solve their problems. Tungsten was a strategic war material, and although the war is never specifically mentioned, the idea of a defense-industry "boom" affecting a small town was used frequently in Hollywood's war films.

841 IMMORTAL SERGEANT (TCF, Jan) John M. Stahl; *genre:* Combat; *locations:* North Africa, Britain; *coding:* AF-Raf, AF-Ger, AF-Brit, Can, Neth, Brit, Dunkirk, AF-Ital, AF-W, Fr, Nazi, Russ, Churchill?, Latin Am, War Corr, WWI; *relevance:* 3.

In North Africa, a British Army unit is stranded behind enemy lines. After an encounter with Italian planes, they ambush an Italian armored car. WWI veteran Sgt. Kelly (Thomas Mitchell) is mortally wounded; to avoid hindering the rest of the squad, he commits suicide. Before he does, he rouses the leadership qualities of the Canadian corporal (Henry Fonda). Fonda leads the men against German troops in a battle at an oasis. Unlike similar combat-oriented films (*Wake Island, Bataan, Air Force*), *Immortal Sergeant* includes a love interest—Maureen O'Hara, seen in flashbacks as the woman Fonda loves but is too shy to propose marriage to. At the end, toughened by his combat experiences, he manages to pop the question. Before the attack on the armored car, Sgt. Kelly calls the "Eye-ties" (British slang for Italians) "fools," for not posting proper sentries—a typical Hollywood disparagement of the prowess of Italy's armed forces. However, after the bloody encounter, one of the soldiers points out that the Italians did stand and make a fight of it (even though they were wiped out).

842 THE IRON MAJOR (RKO, Oct*) Ray Enright; *genre:* Biography; *locations:* United States, France; *coding:* Am Vol, Ger Hist Am, AF-MC, AF-AC, AF-W, AF-N WWI, AF-Ger, AF-A, Fr, Brit, Blk, Spy-Sab; *relevance:* 2.

Biography of Frank Cavanaugh (Pat O'Brien), a WWI hero who became a well-known college football coach of the 1920s and 1930s (at Holy Cross, Dartmouth, and Fordham). Ironically, Cavanaugh is at first opposed to the war, but enlists when the U.S. becomes a combatant. His bravery earns him the nickname of "the Iron Major," but he sustains injuries which—years later—cost him his eyesight and finally, his life. The film opens with a montage depicting Cavanaugh's seven grown children (six sons and a daughter) enlisting in the armed forces for World War Two. At the end of the film, another montage—of marching soldiers—is shown, with voiceover narration by Cavanaugh's friend, Father Tim Donovan (Robert Ryan): "[They will] carry on ... fighting for the same ideals ... on all the far-flung battlefields of the world ... for the heritage you helped give them."

843 IS EVERYBODY HAPPY? (Col, Oct) Charles Barton; *genre:* Biography; *location:* United States; *coding:* WWI, AF-A, Blk; *relevance:* 2.

Bandleader Ted Lewis (who plays himself) tells a soldier he meets at a camp show to marry his girlfriend right away: in flashback, the story of two of Lewis's friends is told, including the interruption of their romance by WWI. Finally, Lewis reveals that the couple were the parents of the soldier in question. Portions of at least 18 songs were included in this film, which ran just over 70 minutes in length.

844 IT AIN'T HAY (Univ, Mar) Erle C. Kenton; *genre:* Comedy; *location:* United States; *coding:* Jap, AF-A, AF-N, USO, AF-W, Home Fr?, Short, V, Blk; *relevance:* 2.

An Abbott and Costello film based on a Damon Runyon story. Costello befriends a young girl whose father owns a horse-drawn cab, but Lou is blamed when the horse dies. He accidentally replaces the horse with famous racehorse Teabiscuit. Naturally, there is a wild horserace at the conclusion. A soldier is included as love interest for the ingenue, and there are several topical gags. For instance, Lou is hit on the head with a flowerpot marked "Made in Japan" and says "That's the closest hit they'll ever make around here." There are also several references to the national speed limit of 35 mph, but oddly enough, no direct references to rationing (deleted verses from one of the songs *did* mention shortages; "To Hell with the Heil!" was also cut)—in fact there is *no* specific mention of the war. The film concludes with a variety show for servicemen at Camp Saratoga. The "Saratoga Canteen" number includes soldiers and a WAC on the stage.

845 IT COMES UP LOVE (Univ, Apr) Charles Lamont; *genre:* Musical Comedy; *location:* United States; *coding:* Short, Mil

School; *relevance:* 1.

Ian Hunter is an executive whose secretary (Louise Albritton) falls in love with him. She has a rival for his hand, however, and tries to win Hunter's two daughters (including Gloria Jean, Universal's attempt to recreate Deanna Durbin) over to her side. Donald O'Connor, on vacation from a private military academy, plays Gloria Jean's boyfriend. At one point, Albritton complains to Hunter that he is driving too slowly. Hunter responds, "In these days—[you] got to save tires."

846 IT'S A GREAT LIFE (Col, May) Frank Strayer; *genre:* Comedy; *location:* United States; *coding:* Hitler, Ref, Short, Prod?, Brit, AF-A, Draft; *relevance:* 1.5.

A Blondie series entry: Dagwood is sent to buy a house, but misunderstands and buys a *horse* instead. Mr. Dithers tells Dagwood he has to keep the horse (described as "a refugee from England"), and the $200 comes out of his own pocket. Blondie does not like this, but the Bumstead children think their new pet is great. The horse disrupts an important business meeting between Dithers and Mr. Brewster (Hugh Herbert): Brewster owns some land on which Dithers wants to build a "defense housing" project. Brewster is a horse-lover, and he invites Dagwood to a fox hunt. Slapstick ensues, but Brewster is so impressed that he makes the business deal with Dithers, and Dagwood gives Brewster the horse as a present. There are a number of references to shortages and rationing in this film. In an early scene, the Bumstead children pull a Tom Sawyer stunt: for the price of one cent, the neighborhood children get "10 Whams" at a caricature of a bent-over Hitler drawn on a sheet (hung in front of a rug which needs beating).

847 JACK LONDON (UA, Dec) Albert Santell; *genre:* Biography; *locations:* United States, China, Japan, Korea; *coding:* Dipl, War Corr, Brit, Ger, AF-Russ, AF-Jap, Jap, Blk, Grk, Prod, Chi, POW, Hist Am, Atroc; *relevance:* 2.

This biography of writer Jack London (Michael O'Shea) opens with the contemporary launching of the Liberty Ship *Jack London*, but also includes considerable footage dedicated to London's war correspondent activities during the Russo-Japanese War. This conflict is carefully depicted as a forerunner of Japan's imperialistic actions of the 1930s and 1940s. The Japanese are shown to be treacherous, effete, power-mad, and capable of mistreating and even murdering prisoners of war (the Russians are forced to march until they drop, and are then bayoneted, kicked, etc., in scenes which bring the Bataan Death March to mind—although the details of this were not made public until

January 1944). There is a sinister, racist "Captain Tanaka," perhaps a deliberate reference to the specious "Tanaka memo," allegedly a 1922 Japanese blueprint for conquest. A link with the Germans (the Japanese use German-made artillery) is also inserted. This was a relatively expensive Samuel Bronston production, released through United Artists. Susan Hayward plays London's wife.

848 JITTERBUGS (TCF, June) Mal St. Clair; *genre:* Comedy; *location:* United States; *coding:* V, Short; *relevance:* 1.5.

A rather tired and sad-looking Laurel and Hardy—playing the owners of a mechanical "Zoot Suit" band—help a young girl recover money from a gang of swindlers operating a showboat. A subplot involves a fake pill which supposedly changes water into gasoline; there are also references to rationing, shortages, and other topical subjects.

849 JIVE JUNCTION (PRC, Dec) Edgar G. Ulmer; *genre:* Musical; *location:* United States; *coding:* Blk Mkt, Ital, AF-A, AF-N, AF-W; Russ, USO, Bonds, Home Fr, Musso, Home Def, Prod, Prod-Farm, Juv; *relevance:* 2.

When his East Coast music school closes "for the duration," a teenager (Dickie Moore) enrolls at an "ordinary" California high school. His new classmates are more interested in "jive" than classical music. To add to the boy's misery, his pilot father is killed in action (with the United Ferry Command) in the Pacific. The high school girls decide to contribute to the war effort by forming a band ("The Girls Junior Canteen Orchestra"—with Moore as their musical director) and by opening a canteen for servicemen stationed nearby. The teenagers obtain the loan of a barn for their "Jive Junction" by helping harvest the orange crop. The club attracts Army personnel, but the soldiers monopolize the high school girls, and Moore is ostracized by his irate male classmates. However, he invites some older girls to serve as hostesses, and everything works out. The school band wins a national contest with their "original patriotic composition," and earn the opportunity to tour Army camps across the nation.

850 JOURNEY INTO FEAR (RKO, Feb) Norman Foster; *genre:* Spy; *locations:* Turkey, Russia; *coding:* WWI, Fr, Brit, Russ, AF-Russ, Stalin, Ref, Grk, Nazi, Spy-Sab, Turk; *relevance:* 2.5.

This film was originally completed in June 1942, but Orson Welles (who was the producer for RKO) directed additional footage and reshot the final sequence, and the recut film was not nationally released until early 1943. Engineer Howard Graham (Joseph Cotten) is nearly murdered in Turkey. Col. Haki (Welles—made up to resemble Josef

Stalin) of the Turkish police warns Graham the Nazis are after information he possesses. With the help of Haki, Kopeikin (Everett Sloane), and dancer Josette (Dolores Del Rio), Graham manages to board a steamer to make his escape. The ship has a widely varied passenger list: a Greek refugee widow and her son, a French woman married to a British man, and a German archeologist. However, Nazi assassin Banat is also on the ship, and he stalks the American. Graham is captured by the Nazis, but escapes. Banat chases him to a hotel ledge three stories above the street; Col. Haki saves Graham, and Banat falls to his death. Based on a novel by Eric Ambler (see also *Background to Danger*, q.v.).

851 KEEP 'EM SLUGGING (Univ, Apr) Christy Cabanne; *genre:* Drama; *location:* United States; *coding:* Draft, Jap, Ger, AF-A, Short, Home Fr; *relevance:* 2.

The Dead End Kids (whose personnel overlapped somewhat with Monogram's East Side Kids, later the Bowery Boys) get jobs at a department store, replacing men who have been drafted. One of the store managers works for a hijack gang, and he frames a Dead End Kid for robbery when the youngster refuses to go along with the crime. In the end, the criminals are defeated.

852 KID DYNAMITE (Mono, Feb) Wallace Fox; *genre:* War/Drama; *location:* United States; *coding:* Juv, Blk, Russ, Czech, Bonds, AF-N, AF-MC, AF-A, AF-W, Home Fr, Short, Jap, Nazi, Home Def, FDR, WWI, Atroc, Draft; *relevance:* 3.

Another East Side Kids entry: Danny (Bobby Jordan) takes Muggs' (Leo Gorcey) place in a boxing match when Mugs is kidnapped. However, Muggs thinks Danny was in on the plot, and Danny is thrown out of the gang. He enlists in the Army at the suggestion of an old man, who says Danny should join a gang "that is fighting ... bullies called Japs and Nazis." The rest of the Kids are chewed out by a woman judge for leading useless lives during a period of national emergency, and by the end of the film Muggs and Glimpy (Huntz Hall) have joined up as well. There are numerous references to the war (including posters, verbal comments, and so on), including a mention of the destruction of the Czech village of Lidice, in reprisal for the assassination of Heydrich (see *Hitler's Hangman, Hangmen Also Die*, q.v.).

853 KING OF THE COWBOYS (Rep, Apr) Joseph Kane; *genre:* Western/Spy; *location:* United States; *coding:* Prod?, Spy-Sab; *relevance:* 2.

Roy Rogers is asked to investigate a sabotage ring operating in a Western state (apparently Texas). The governor's male secretary is actually the brains behind the gang,

which operates out of a traveling tent show (an innocent member of the show remarks, "Every town we play has an explosion or fire."). Roy exposes the gang, then defuses a bomb set to blow up a railroad bridge as a supply train passes over it. Oddly enough for a 1943 film, the gang of saboteurs does *not* contain any foreigners and at no time does anyone refer to Germany, Japan, or even "the war" (in one scene, a business leader tells the governor "We factory owners have gone all out for defense," but this is the only direct reference to the war). If it were not for the frequent use of the term "sabotage," the crimes could be construed as unrelated to the war.

854 LADIES' DAY (RKO, Mar*) Leslie Goodwins; *genre:* Comedy; *location:* United States; *coding:* Bonds, V, Latin Am, Blk; *relevance:* 1.5.

A baseball player (Eddie Albert) marries a Latin movie star (Lupe Velez), whom he meets while she is selling War Bonds at the stadium. First, Albert cannot pitch while Velez is around, then (during the World Series) he cannot pitch UNLESS she is there! OWI reviewers remarked on the odd chronology of this film: the team wins the "1941" World Series, but Velez is shown selling *war* bonds (NOT defense bonds) prior to Pearl Harbor! There is also no mention of the draft, peacetime or otherwise.

855 LADY BODYGUARD (Para, Jan*) William Clemens; *genre:* Comedy; *location:* United States; *coding:* Blk Mkt?, Short, Home Def, FBI; *relevance:* 1.5.

As a publicity stunt, a test pilot (Eddie Albert) is given a free insurance policy, but the policy is mistakenly written for one *million* instead of one thousand dollars. The female insurance agent (Anne Shirley) responsible for selling the policy tries to get the pilot to cancel the deal—they get married instead. There are a number of war references in this comedy, including one scene in which three criminals accidentally fly an airplane into the Los Angeles area, causing a full-scale alert and anti-aircraft barrage.

856 LADY OF BURLESQUE (UA, Apr) William A. Wellman; *genre:* Crime; *location:* United States; *coding:* Ital, Jew, Home Def, Chi, Russ; *relevance:* 1.

Film version of the novel "The G-String Murders," credited to stripper Gypsy Rose Lee (but actually authored by mystery writer Craig Rice). The opening titles indicate that the film is set in the pre-war period, but there are several minor war references, including comments about the fighting ability of the Chinese (in the film, directed at a waiter, but obviously with a double meaning). Barbara Stanwyck stars as the sassy stripper.

857 A LADY TAKES A CHANCE (RKO, Aug*) William A. Seiter; *genre:* Romantic Comedy; *location:* United States; *coding:* Short, Latin Am, Blk; *relevance:* 1.5.

This film was produced independently and released through RKO, which may explain why it was rather hard to see until recently (it has now been colorized and is making the rounds). Jean Arthur leaves New York for a bus tour of the West, and falls in love with footloose cowboy John Wayne. At the end, he decides it is time to settle down after all. The film opens with a printed title: "Once upon a time ... It was so long ago that people drove sixty miles an hour, and skidded their tires, and drank three cups of coffee all at once, and ate big gobs of butter, and there were more fellows around than there were girls, and everybody was having a good time without knowing it. That's when our story happened, away back then ... in 1938. And here's hoping that 'Once upon a time' goes on again some quick tomorrow, only better." There are no other overt references to the war, but in one scene Jean Arthur cooks John Wayne a meal with lamb chops, and he protests "I like steak." However, he agrees that the lamb is tasty. Lamb and pork were not rationed as strictly as beef during the war, and this scene may have been an oblique suggestion to movie audiences to *try* other types of meat.

858 LASSIE COME HOME (MGM, Dec) Fred Wilcox; *genre:* Drama; *location:* Britain; *coding:* WWI, WWII, AF?, Brit; *relevance:* 1.

Although the plot of this Technicolor film is set in pre-war England, a printed preface dedicates the film to writer Eric Knight (who wrote the original book), who fought in World War One and was killed in World War Two (Knight, who had lived in the U.S. for years, joined the Army; after working with Frank Capra on the "Why We Fight" series, Knight was on assignment for Armed Forces Radio when he was killed in January 1943). Then, as the film opens, a narrator refers to the "people of Yorkshire in peace and war," and says "Lassie is Sam's only saleable possession in these dark, pre-war days of depression." Sam, Lassie's owner, was played by Donald Crisp. *Son of Lassie* (1945, q.v.) was much more directly war-oriented, as Lassie's son Laddie battles the Nazis in Norway.

859 LAW OF THE NORTHWEST (Col, May) William Berke; *genre:* Western; *location:* Canada; *coding:* Prod, Can; *relevance:* 1.

Canadian trapper Paul Darcey (Charles Starrett) opposes construction of a road connecting to the Alcan Highway (across Canada to Alaska—see *Alaska Highway*, q.v.). When the road supervisor is murdered, Paul is suspected, but the RCMP eventually discovers that a crooked contractor is trying to obtain control of a tungsten mine. Paul joins the armed forces at the end of the film.

860 LET'S FACE IT (Para, Aug*) Sidney Lanfield; *genre:* Comedy; *location:* United States; *coding:* AF-A, AF-Ger; *relevance:* 2.

Bob Hope and Betty Hutton star in this adaptation of a hit Broadway musical (which starred Danny Kaye) with songs by Cole Porter. Hope and two Army buddies agree to spend a weekend on Long Island with three housewives who want to make their husbands jealous. However, the husbands show up with three other women: the soldiers' girlfriends! At the climax, Hope causes a Nazi submarine to beach itself by "blinding" the periscope with his pocket mirror. Joe Sawyer appears again as a frustrated sergeant (see, for example, *Fall In* and *Tanks a Million*, q.v.).

861 LET'S HAVE FUN (Col, Mar) Charles Barton; *genre:* Comedy; *location:* United States; *coding:* Home Def, Russ, Nazi; *relevance:* 1.

"Mad Russian" Bert Gordon plays a good-hearted Russian who tries to help a down-and-out actor (John Beal), whose wife has died and left him with a young daughter. Gordon and a female agent (Margaret Lindsay) help the actor get a good role, but success goes to his head. At the end, everything is straightened out. Very minor topical references in this film: Boris (Gordon) sings the little girl to sleep with improvised nursery rhymes like "Eeney meeney miney moe, catch a Nazi by the toe." Leonid Kinsky also appears.

862 THE LONDON BLACKOUT MURDERS (Rep, Jan) George Sherman; *genre:* Spy/Crime; *location:* Britain; *coding:* AF-W, Brit, Home Def, Short, US-Brit Coop, AF-Brit, AF-Neth, Ger, Spy-Sab; *relevance:* 2.5.

Rawlings (John Abbott), a former doctor, murders a German saboteur during an air raid. Mary, who lives over the shop Rawlings owns, tells her Dutch soldier boyfriend she suspects Rawlings of the crime. Rawlings kills another Nazi agent before being arrested by Scotland Yard. At his trial, the killer admits he murdered his wife as well as the two saboteurs, then exposes the leader of enemy ring. However, the film hints that Rawlings will probably be executed for taking the law into his own hands. In reality, most Nazi agents in England were either taken into custody early in the war, or were known to British Intelligence and were used to feed false information to Germany.

863 THE MAD GHOUL (Univ, Nov) James Hogan; *genre:* Horror; *location:* United States; *coding:* Bonds, AF-A, Pearl Harb?; *relevance:* 1.

Dr. Morris (George Zucco) exposes his assistant Ted Allison (David Bruce) to an experimental gas which causes Ted to age prematurely and to become a zombie-like automaton. The only antidote (temporary) for this malady is a serum which must be obtained from a fresh human heart. Morris is in love with concert singer Isabel (Evelyn Ankers), Ted's fiancee, but she has fallen in love with Eric (Turhan Bey), her accompanist. Ted robs graves to obtain hearts for his serum, and Morris tries to use him to kill Eric. At the end, both Morris and Ted die of the effects of the gas. In one scene set in a hotel lobby, a large sign reads "HELP BUILD A BOMBER—BUY BONDS." Underneath, a desk decorated with flag bunting is set up, and a woman is selling bonds to a man. On the wall behind the desk is a very large photograph of what appear to be wrecked airplanes—perhaps a photo of the aftermath of Pearl Harbor? As the scene progresses, several Army officers walk by in the background.

864 THE MAN FROM DOWN UNDER (MGM, Dec) Robert Z. Leonard; *genre:* War/Drama; *locations:* France, Australia; *coding:* Munich, AF-Jap, Ger, AF-Austral, Belg, Pol, Jap, WWI, Ref, Pearl Harb, Austral; *relevance:* 2.5.

France, 1919: Australian soldier Jocko (Charles Laughton) smuggles two Belgian orphans back to Australia with him. Time passes, and Jocko, a boxer, raises the two children as his own. When WWII breaks out, Jocko tries to reenlist, but is turned down for medical reasons. Instead, he gets a construction job. Japanese bombers raid the city of Darwin, and when the crew of a downed plane seizes a hotel where his adopted daughter and Jocko's long-time girlfriend are caring for evacuated children, Jocko and a friend burst in and defeat the enemy. For his bravery, Jocko is given a commission in the Australian Army. Laughton's character here is somewhat similar to his role in *The Beachcomber* (1938).

865 MARCHING ON* [aka **WHERE'S MY MAN TO-NITE?**] (Ind, ?) Spencer Williams, Jr.; *genre:* Drama/Training; *location:* United States; *coding:* Hist Am, FDR, Fil?, Bonds, Home Fr, Home Def, WWI, Vet, Draft, USO, AF-Ger, Pearl Harb, AF-A, AF-W, AF-Blk, Blk, Spy-Sab, Hirohito, Jap; *relevance:* 3.

All-black film later re-released (with 20 additional minutes of unrelated musical footage) as Where's My Man To-Nite? Rodney Tucker Jr. (Hugh Martin) has a bad attitude towards military service, although his late father served in WWI and his grandfather constantly boasts about *his* service in the Spanish-American War. Rodney is drafted and sent to Fort Huachuca, Arizona (actual location footage) but deliberately does as poorly as possible in training. Jealous over his girlfriend's supposed relations with a sergeant, Rodney goes AWOL. Through an amazing coincidence, he finds his father, now an amnesiac bum who almost immediately dies. While wandering through the desert (trying to get home to Texas), Rodney hallucinates about a Nazi invasion of the United States. His grandfather finds him, but they stumble onto a nest of Japanese spies. In the struggle, Grandpa is killed but a detachment of black soldiers arrives to capture the enemy agents. Rodney straightens up: "They gave me another chance to prove that I'm an American, too." His girlfriend joins the WACs (there were a number of black women in the WACs, but they were largely under-utilized due to racial prejudice; most were assigned to the Army Service Forces, which was responsible for providing military personnel with food and clothing). Crudely made but interesting film.

866 MARGIN FOR ERROR (TCF, Feb) Otto Preminger; *genre:* Comedy/Drama; *location:* United States; *coding:* Ref, Russ, Pol?, Russ, Austria, Czech, FDR, WWI, Pearl Harb, Jew, Hitler, Goering, Nazi, AF-A, Churchill, Spy-Sab, Collab, Short, Ger, Ital, Dipl, Atroc-Conc, US-Brit Coop, Russ-Ger Coop; *relevance:* 3.

Based on a stage play by Claire Booth Luce; Milton Berle is Moe Finkelstein, a Jewish NY policeman assigned to guard the German consulate (this takes place prior to Pearl Harbor). The Nazi consul (Otto Preminger) is a dictatorial type with a Czech wife (Joan Bennett). Bennett is actually in love with Max (Carl Esmond), the consul's secretary. Preminger tries to get Max to commit suicide by revealing Max's Jewish heritage, but Moe convinces Max of the foolishness of Nazi ideas. Max decides to help the U.S. authorities capture a gang of Nazi saboteurs (one boasts: "This job's almost as big as the Black Tom explosion of the First World War"), and the consul is shot, stabbed AND poisoned. The film opens and closes on an American troop ship bound for Europe. Moe tells the story to the other troops, who are suspicious of fellow-soldier Max because of his foreign accent. When one of the men apologizes to Max, he replies: "We're all fighting for the same cause, for the same peace, for the same freedom, for the same country." Although Berle was top-billed, the film is more drama than comedy. The German Consulate in New York was a center for Nazi propaganda in the late 1930s, until the

U.S. government stepped in to restrict its activities.

867 THE MEADVILLE PATRIOT (Ind, ?) Ben K. Blake; *genre:* Drama; *location:* United States; *coding:* AF-A; *relevance:* 1.

An independently produced and distributed film with a cast of unknowns. Jim, former city editor at a big city newspaper, is turned down by the Army due to his poor physical condition. He takes the job of running the small-town "Meadville Patriot" paper and marries the niece of the paper's former editor. Jim and his wife are caught in a controversy over an attempt to introduce local prohibition, but the problems are eventually worked out, and Jim enlists in the Army.

868 THE MEANEST MAN IN THE WORLD (TCF, Feb) Sidney Lanfield; *genre:* Comedy; *location:* United States; *coding:* Blk, Prod, Hist Am, Fem Lab, Draft, Short?; *relevance:* 1.5.

Small-town lawyer Jack Benny is too nice for his own good. He decides to seek his fortune in the big city and then return to marry his sweetheart (Priscilla Lane), but his easy-going attitude keeps him penniless. His assistant (Eddie "Rochester" Anderson) advises Jack to cultivate the reputation of the meanest man in the world, but in the end he marries his girlfriend even though he's still poor-but-nice. There are no overt references in the film, but there are a few oblique dialogue comments: jokes about the "night shift at Lockheed," industrialist Henry Kaiser, Benny's "4-F credit rating," and so on.

869 MELODY PARADE (Mono, Aug) Arthur Dreifuss; *location:* United States; *coding:* Blk, Latin Am, AF-N, AF-A, Fr?, Prod, Fem Lab; *relevance:* 1.5.

Eddie Quillan works in Tim Ryan's failing nightclub. He tries to find a girl singer to bring in the customers; when wacky Irene Ryan shows up, Quillan and Ryan think she is an eccentric heiress and hire her. The real talent in the club is hatcheck girl Mary Beth Hughes. At least two war-oriented songs are included in this film: "The Woman Behind the Man Behind the Gun," and "Mr. and Mrs. Commando." The first song includes these lyrics: "Once they had so many dates / Life became a bore; / Now they're in defense work / Making bombers by the score."

870 MEXICAN SPITFIRE'S BLESSED EVENT (RKO, July?) Leslie Goodwins; *genre:* Comedy; *locations:* United States, Canada; *coding:* AF-AC, AF-Mer, Blk, Brit, WWI, Latin Am, Short, AF-A?; *relevance:* 2.

The final "Mexican Spitfire" series entry (star Lupe Velez returned to Mexico and made one more film before her untimely death in 1944) takes place at a Western-theme resort hotel in Arizona. The hotel is located near a military airfield, and Air Corps personnel appear in numerous crowd scenes. Carmelita's (Velez) husband (Walter Reed) is an officer in the Merchant Marine, on two weeks' leave. He tries to get Lord Epping (Leon Errol) to sign a contract, but faces stiff competition. Through a misunderstanding, Epping thinks Carmelita has just given birth, and he agrees to sign with her husband—but the "blessed event" is an ocelot cub, and Carmelita "borrows" a real baby, with predictable results. Trivia note: RKO's soon-to-be comedy team, Wally Brown and Alan Carney, both appear as employees of the hotel, but share no scenes together.

871 MINESWEEPER (Para, Nov*) William Berke; *genre:* Training/Combat; *location:* United States; *coding:* AF-Jap, AF-A, Jap, Prod, Mil School, AF-AC, Nazi, Pearl Harb, AF-N; *relevance:* 2.5.

Richard Arlen, a Navy officer who had deserted due to heavy gambling debts, rejoins the service after Pearl Harbor. Under an assumed name, he becomes a gunner's mate on a minesweeper. While trying to buy an engagement ring, Arlen misses his ship. His best friend takes his place and is killed when the ship hits a mine. Arlen considers deserting again, but instead volunteers for dangerous duty, learning the secret of a new Japanese mine at the cost of his own life.

872 MISSION TO MOSCOW (WB, May) Michael Curtiz; *genre:* Biography; *locations:* U.S., Britain, Russia, Germany, Poland; *coding:* Dipl, Hitler, Stalin, Russ, UN League Nat, Hist Am, Jew, Blk, Latin Am, Fem Lab, Munich, AF-Russ, AF-Brit, AF-W, AF-Chi, AF-N, AF-MC, AF-FR, Musso, Ital, Jap, AF-Jap, Collab, Pol, Span, Russ-Ger Coop, Jap-Ger Coop, Yugo, Austria, Czech, Ethiopia, Fr, Neth, Chi, Atroc, Brit, Fin, US-Brit Coop, Draft, Pearl Harb, FDR, Churchill, Isolat, Appease?, AF-Ger, Ger, Nazi, Hess, WWI, Laval, Chamberlain, Dunkirk, Nor, Den, Goering, FBI, Postwar; *relevance:* 3.

In retrospect, one of the most unusual films produced by Hollywood, this film was an adaptation of the 1941 best-seller by Joseph E. Davies, former ambassador to Russia, relating his experiences in the Soviet Union between 1936 and 1938. Walter Huston portrayed Davies in the film version (although Davies appeared on screen in a spoken prologue); other actors (chosen for their physical resemblance to their real-life counterparts) portrayed a number of other world leaders and noted statesmen including Stalin, Churchill, Haile Selassie, Litvinov, Bukharin, and Molotov. Franklin Roosevelt was obliquely played by Captain Jack Young (who also portrayed the President in *Yankee Doodle Dandy*, 1942, q.v.). The film was specifically designed as pro–Soviet, anti–Nazi propaganda, and deliberately distorts the historical record to portray Stalin (and Davies and FDR) in the best possible light. For example, the purge trials are specifically identified as necessary to protect the Soviet Union from "fifth columnists ... guilty of a conspiracy with the German and Japanese high commands to pave the way for an attack upon the Soviet state." The film whitewashes the Nazi-Soviet pact signed in 1939, implying that the "democracies [drove] Stalin into Hitler's arms," and that Russia merely used this as a breathing space to prepare for an inevitable war against Germany. An animated map shows Germany invading Poland, but ignores the Russian occupation of Polish territory. The Russian invasion of Finland is also dismissed in a facile manner: "Russia knew she was going to be attacked by Hitler so the Soviet leaders asked Finland's permission to occupy strategic positions to defend herself against German agression. She offered to give Finland twice as much territory in exchange, but Hitler's friend Mannerheim refused and the Red Army moved in" (it is never mentioned that Russia was expelled from the League of Nations for this invasion). Not merely a distortion of the facts for propaganda purposes, *Mission to Moscow* is an amazing revisionist portrait of Stalin and the Soviet Union's actions in the 1937-1941 period. During this period, Hollywood had produced a number of *anti*–Soviet films, including *Ninotchka* (MGM, 1939) and *Public Deb No.1* (TCF, 1940). Interestingly enough, the term "Communism" is only heard one time, in a speech by a German-American Bundist.

873 MISTER BIG (Univ, May) Charles Lamont; *genre:* Musical; *location:* United States; *coding:* Short, Blk?; *relevance:* 1.5.

Teen musical with Donald O'Connor and Gloria Jean as students at a performing-arts high school. They want to put on a "jiving" musical instead of "Antigone," which does not sit too well with the stuffy owner of the school. War relevance in this film is chiefly represented by one skit on point values and rationing.

874 MISTER LUCKY (RKO, May*) H.C. Potter; *genre:* War/Drama; *location:* United States; *coding:* Draft, Ref, Chi, Czech, Hist Am, AF-A, AF-Mer, AF-Raf, AF-Ital, AF-Ger, Resist?, Draft Avoid, Home Fr, Grk, Blk, Ref; *relevance:* 2.5.

1941: before Pearl Harbor, gangster Cary Grant owns a gambling ship, but needs money to move it to Cuba "for the duration." Upon receiving his draft notice, he switches identities with a dead Greek crewman who was

4-F. To obtain the money he needs, Grant convinces a group of society women (including Laraine Day) to finance their War Relief project with a "gambling night." He plans to steal the money and sail away. However, Grant falls in love with Day. Inspired by a patriotic letter from the Greek sailor's mother relating the story of their village's gallant opposition to the Nazis, Grant turns all of the money over to War Relief. He also turns his ship over the government, and joins the Merchant Marine to do his bit.

875 MISTER MUGGS STEPS OUT (Mono, Dec) William Beaudine; *genre:* Comedy; *location:* United States; *coding:* Draft, Short, Bonds, Fr; *relevance:* 1.

In order to replace servants who have been drafted, the rich Murray family employs ex-convicts; Muggs (Leo Gorcey) is hired as the chauffeur. The other East Side Kids help out by waxing the Murray's car, but Glimpy (Huntz Hall) warns against exerting too much effort: "They only got an 'A' card" (the lowest gas ration available). The OWI disliked the Murray's method of overcoming the wartime servant shortage.

876 THE MOON IS DOWN (TCF, Apr) Irving Pichel; *genre:* Resist; *location:* Norway; *coding:* AF-Ger, Nazi, Nor, AF-Nor, Hitler, Resist, Collab, WWI, Atroc, Brit, Belg, Fr, Pol, AF-Raf; *relevance:* 3.

Based on a John Steinbeck novel, this film deals with the German occupation of a small Norwegian mining town. The film begins with an interesting (pre-credits) sequence in which Hitler's ranting voice is heard over a map of Norway. His hand shakily crawls up the map and then pounds on it as he shouts in fury. Assisted by the traitorous acts of the owner of the general store, German paratroopers occupy the peaceful town (the sets from *How Green Was My Valley*, doing double duty) and the local militia is ruthlessly ambushed. The Germans insist that production of iron ore be stepped up, and expect the civil authorities to cooperate with them in maintaining order. However, a dispute at the mine leaves a German officer dead, and the man who killed him is sentenced to be executed. This only leads to further acts of rebellion by the villagers; even after five hostages are seized and shot, the resistance continues. The RAF bombs the mine, guided by an old woman carrying a torch; the British later drop explosives for the resistance—"It is a present from your friends to you, and from you to the enemy … there are many little uses you can find for it." The Germans begin to crack under the strain: one young officer says "I had a funny dream. I dreamt Hitler was crazy." He is later murdered by the widow of the first man to be executed. The Germans seize hostages and prepare to hang them, but suddenly explosions begin to go off all over town. The final shots show the Norwegian traitor and his Nazi allies staring about in fear and consternation. Sir Cedric Hardwicke portrays the German commander, a member of the officer class (i.e., generally *not* a Nazi) who does not believe in taking hostages or torturing prisoners to increase production in occupied countries, but is confronted with a hostile populace (led by Henry Travers and Lee J. Cobb) nonetheless.

877 MOONLIGHT IN VERMONT (Univ, Dec) Edward Lilley; *genre:* Musical Comedy; *location:* United States; *coding:* Juv, Prod-Farm; *relevance:* 1.5.

Gwen (Gloria Jean), a Vermont farm girl, enrolls at a performing arts school in New York City, but she has to go home to the farm when her Uncle Rufus is faced with ruin by a shortage of farm labor. Her friends from the school go with her to help harvest the crop, Gwen wins a $500 prize at a farm show for her cow, and is able to go back to school with her uncle's blessing. Another "farm labor" film (see also *Song of the Open Road*, 1944 and *Harvest Melody*, 1943, both q.v.).

878 THE MORE THE MERRIER (Col, May) George Stevens; *genre:* Comedy; *location:* United States; *coding:* AF-MC, AF-A, AF-W, Hist Am, FDR, FDR-E, Spy-Sab, Fem Lab, Postwar, Jew?, Latin Am, Jap, Hitler, Short, FBI, AF-N; *relevance:* 2.5.

Government worker Connie (Jean Arthur) decides to sub-let her spare room in order to help relieve the housing shortage in Washington. Mr. Dingle (Charles Coburn), a business tycoon, gets the room in spite of her objections. Dingle in turn shares his room with aircraft technician Joe (Joel McCrea—who enters carrying a propeller), temporarily assigned to Washington. Connie is engaged to a dull bureaucrat but wises up and marries Joe just before he joins the Army and ships out to North Africa. This is one of a handful of films poking fun at life in the nation's capital during the war. See, for instance, *Government Girl* and *Dixie Dugan*, q.v.

879 MOUNTAIN RHYTHM (Rep, Jan*) Frank McDonald; *genre:* Comedy/Drama; *location:* United States; *coding:* Juv, FDR, AF, Hitler, Hirohito, Jap, Musso, Bonds, Prod-Farm, FBI, Spy-Sab, Short, Jap-Am Reloc, WWI; *relevance:* 3.

The hillbilly Weaver family (a country-music group under contract to Republic in the late '30s and early '40s) "patriotically" takes over a California farm formerly belonging to a Japanese-American family (who are now in a "relocation" camp—the mailbox reads "U Ichi I Scratchi"). The farm is next to an exclusive prep school. The snobby schoolboys lose a bond-selling contest to the Weavers and have to help harvest the melon crop. The school headmaster is really an Axis agent (he wears a monocle, a sure tipoff) who hopes to sabotage the farm effort and sow class dissension in the United States. In the end, the Weavers, the schoolboys, and their parents unite to defeat the enemy agent and save the crops. This film is one of the few to address (even obliquely) the relocation of Japanese-Americans to camps in the interior of the U.S., and illustrates what happened to their homes and businesses when they were taken away (i.e., Anglo-Saxons took them over).

880 MURDER ON THE WATERFRONT (WB, Aug) B. Reeves Eason; *genre:* Crime; *location:* United States; *coding:* Short, AF-N, AF-MC, USO, Nazi, Collab, Spy-Sab, Atroc; *relevance:* 2.5.

A freighter loaded with gunsight parts—destined for the Aleutians—is preparing to depart from a West Coast port. A group of entertainers puts on a waterfront show for the sailors and Marines. One of the dancers is Gloria (Joan Winfield), the new bride of sailor Joe Davis (Warren Douglas). Technical expert Lewis is murdered by enemy agents in an attempt to discover the secret of the new gunsight thermostat, and Gloria and Joe (who had sneaked away to be alone) are suspects. The killer is finally revealed as turncoat officer Barnes. A remake of *Invisible Menace* (Warner Bros., 1938), which in turn was based on a play entitled "Without Warning."

881 MY FRIEND FLICKA (TCF, Apr) Harold Schuster; *genre:* Drama; *location:* United States; *coding:* Mil School?, AF-A; *relevance:* 1.

Roddy McDowall's father (Preston Foster) allows him to take care of one of the horses on their ranch. The boy chooses the "worst" horse but eventually grows to love it. There is one brief mention of the war, when Foster remarks that he may have to serve in the Army. In Technicolor.

882 MY KINGDOM FOR A COOK (Col, Aug) Richard Wallace; *genre:* Comedy; *locations:* Britain, United States; *coding:* Blk, Short?, AF-AC, Brit, FDR?; *relevance:* 1.5.

Crusty British author Charles Coburn (as "Rudyard Morley") and his grown daughter visit a small New England town where he is to make a speech as part of his "good will" tour of America. He lures the town's only decent cook away from her employer, the town's leading society matron. A feud erupts but Coburn comes to appreciate the hardworking Americans he meets in the town, and at the film's end he leaves for Washington to meet the President. A romantic subplot involves Coburn's daughter and the Army pilot son of the society woman.

883 MY SON, THE HERO (PRC, Apr) Edgar G. Ulmer; *genre:* Comedy/Drama; *location:* United States; *coding:* War Corr, Musso, Blk, Bonds, AF-AC, Jap, Ital; *relevance:* 2.

A variation on the "Apple Annie/Lady for a Day" theme: Roscoe Karns is a down-on-his-luck fight manager whose son is a famous war correspondent (he covered the Doolittle Raid on Tokyo). The young man is on a bond-selling tour, and is carrying nearly $100,000 in cash from sales of war bonds when he arrives to visit his father. To impress his son, Karns moves into a vacant beach house, and his pals pose as his "servants." Among his friends is Tony (Luis Alberni), an Italian-American who hates Mussolini and resents being called an "enemy alien." Karns bets some of the bond money on a horserace—he later thinks he has lost it, but it turns out his dopey boxer friend Maxie Rosenbloom actually bet on the wrong horse, which DID win the race.

884 THE MYSTERIOUS DOCTOR (WB, Aug) Ben Stoloff; *genre:* Crime/Spy; *location:* Britain; *coding:* AF-Brit, Home Def, Churchill, Prod, Hitler, Nazi, Collab, Brit; *relevance:* 1.5.

Sir Harry Leland (John Loder) is actually a German agent who has been murdering people and spreading tales of a headless ghost in a small British mining community. Leland wants to make sure the local tin mines are not reopened. Standard mystery film substituting a war-related motivation for the usual greed-driven crimes.

885 MYSTERY BROADCAST (Rep, Nov) George Sherman; *genre:* Crime; *location:* United States; *coding:* Collab, FDR, Latin Am?, Prod?, Fem Lab?; *relevance:* 1.

Two rival radio mystery-show hosts (Frank Albertson and Ruth Terry) try to solve a murder committed twelve years before, but several new murders occur before the killer is finally exposed. In one scene, Terry's producer threatens to call the show's sponsor about a format change he does not like, and Terry's sidekick (Mary Treen) calls him a "Quisling" (after the Norwegian Nazi leader blamed by many at the time for his country's swift capitulation to Germany). Treen also makes a remark about being on the "swing shift," although she is not a defense worker; Nils Asther plays a musician named "Ricky Moreno."

886 NEARLY EIGHTEEN (Mono, ?) Arthur Dreifuss; *genre:* Musical Comedy; *location:* United States; *coding:* AF-A?, Short?; *relevance:* 1.

Gale Storm plays a young woman who wants to get a job singing in a cafe but cannot be legally hired until she is 18 years old (she is a couple of months too young). She poses as a much younger girl in order to enroll in a private school for talented children, run by Bill Henry. Henry naturally falls in love with her, but is distressed because he thinks she is jailbait. In the end, everything works out. One song contains the cryptic line: "The kisses that I give are not the G.I. kind" (huh?). There are also definitely war-oriented posters on the walls of a malt shop, but are not clear enough to be specifically identified, and it is possible that a ration sticker is shown on a car windshield.

887 NEVER A DULL MOMENT (Univ, Nov) Edward Lilly; *genre:* Comedy; *location:* United States; *coding:* Blk, AF-?, Short, Prod, Home Def; *relevance:* 1.5.

Numerous topical gags appear in this Ritz Brothers vehicle, in which the brothers—the "Three Funny Bunnies"—are mistaken for gangsters and unwittingly participate in a jewel robbery. A typical Ritz Brothers topical gag: "Roses are red, violets are blue, sugar is sweet, but where can you get it?"

888 NEXT OF KIN * (added US footage) (Univ, May) Thorold Dickinson; *genre:* Spy; *locations:* Britain, France, Germany; *coding:* FBI, Brit, Nazi, Spy-Sab, AF-Brit, Nazi, Fr, Hitler, Ref, Neth, Spa, AF-Raf; *relevance:* 3.

For the U.S. release of this British film, FBI Director J. Edgar Hoover appeared in a newly filmed prologue. The picture deals with the ramifications of loose talk on the home front: German agents in England learn of a pending commando raid and are waiting for the soldiers when they land in France. Hoover's footage reinforced the message for U.S. audiences: "I hope this film will show you that no matter how unimportant you may feel in the war effort, you hold in your hands a life or death of an American soldier." Originally planned as a training film, *Next of Kin* became a popular commercial film in Britain, and was shown to U.S. troops stationed there. In addition to the added prologue, some cuts were made in the film for its U.S. release in order to reduce the appearance of British incompetence!

889 A NIGHT FOR CRIME (PRC, Feb) Alexis Thurntaxis; *genre:* Crime; *location:* United States; *coding:* FBI, Blk, Home Def, AF-A, Short; *relevance:* 1.5.

This film begins with a radio announcement of a blackout in Los Angeles. A montage shows famous Hollywood nightclub signs (Mocambo, Ciro's, etc.) blinking off. Joe Powell (Lyle Talbot), a studio publicity man, visits Susan Cooper (Glenda Farrell), a reporter and his erstwhile girlfriend. She is not impressed by his declarations of love: "They ought to ration that soft-soap as well as sugar." Susan's neighbor Ellen is strangled, and dumb-cop Hoffman suspects Joe and Susan. Meanwhile, Joe tries to locate Mona Harrison, an actress who has disappeared in the middle of shooting a film. Mona's body is discovered in Topanga Canyon by an air raid warden, but *new* scenes of her on film mysteriously appear in the producer's office. Joe and Susan track down another Mona Harrison in Reno—but it is really Mona's psychotic twin sister, who killed Mona so she could get into the movies. Joe informs Susan that he has enlisted, and Susan changes her frigid attitude, saying "I've always been crazy about a uniform!" There are quite a number of shortage and rationing jokes in this film, as well as the opening and closing blackout references.

890 NIGHT PLANE FROM CHUNGKING (Para, Jan*) Ralph Murphy; *genre:* War/Drama; *location:* China; *coding:* AF-Chi, AF-Jap, FDR, Chi, Chiang, Short?, AF-FT?, Russ, Fr, Neth?, Nazi, Jap, Jap-Nazi Coop, Vichy, Free Fr, DeGaulle, Spy-Sab, India; *relevance:* 3.

In the period before Pearl Harbor, six people (including Ellen Drew as the American secretary to an elderly Chinese woman, and Preston Foster as an American pilot working for the Chinese air force) are traveling across China by bus. The bus is wrecked and they are sent to India via airplane, but the plane is attacked by Japanese aircraft and has to crash-land. One of the group—a clergyman (Stephen Geray)—leads the group to a nearby monastery, but it is a trap, and the fake preacher turns out to be a Nazi agent. The group escapes with the aid of the American pilot and the self-sacrifice of a French officer (who has a Vichy passport but expresses support for DeGaulle's Free French). A loose remake of *Shanghai Express* (Paramount, 1932). The OWI noted: "The Chinese are sympathetically drawn. They are stoical, dignified, loyal, serious and intelligent. Madame Wu is said to have burned and demolished her own estate in China so that it would not fall into Japanese hands."

891 NO PLACE FOR A LADY (Col, Feb) James Hogan; *genre:* Crime; *location:* United States; *coding:* Short, Home Def, AF-A; *relevance:* 1.5.

Rich widow Mrs. Harris conspires with her boyfriend Eddie to defraud the insurance company: she has inherited $50,000 worth of new automobile tires from her late husband. Pulling a switch, they put a load of junk tires in the warehouse, which is then burned to the ground. Mrs. Harris wants the money, but says "I wouldn't worry, except for the war. I feel like a traitor." However, she is later murdered. Detective Jess Adair (William Gargan)—who is preparing to join the Army—investigates the crime. At one point Jess poses as an air-raid warden during a blackout. Most of the principals in this film were working off the final film of their contract with Columbia, where they had been appearing in the "Ellery Queen" series (which had been canceled).

892 NO TIME FOR LOVE (Para, Nov*) Mitchell Leisen; *genre:* Comedy; *location:* United States; *coding:* Short, Bonds, Blk, Ital; *relevance:* 1.

Claudette Colbert is a photographer for a national magazine working on a story about the construction of a tunnel. She becomes romantically involved with Fred MacMurray, a college-educated "sandhog" she hires as her assistant after she gets him fired. At one point Colbert fantasizes about MacMurray as "Superman," who saves her from a villain. Peripheral topical references only in this romantic comedy.

892 NOBODY'S DARLING (Rep, Aug*) Anthony Mann; *genre:* Drama; *location:* United States; *coding:* Short; *relevance:* 1.

Janie (Mary Lee) is a student at Pennington School, where the children of Hollywood stars are educated. Although her parents are glamorous performers, Janie is mousy and plain (although a talented singer). She tries to become fashionable and attractive so she can obtain the lead role in the upcoming school play, but the other students laugh, thinking she is joking. Upset, Janie runs away. Chuck, the student director/writer of the play, follows her in the school's station wagon. However, thieves steal the car's tires (an allusion to the rubber shortage), leaving the two teens stranded miles from a phone. The newspapers get wind of the story, playing up the "elopement" of the children of movie stars. This shocks Janie's mother into paying more attention to her maternal duties.

894 THE NORTH STAR (RKO, Oct*) Lewis Milestone; *genre:* Resist; *location:* Russia; *coding:* Juv, WWI, AF-Ger, AF-W?, AF-Russ, Russ, Nazi, Atroc, Jew, Resist; *relevance:* 3.

This film later became notorious (during the McCarthy era) as a pro–Russian propaganda piece written by "unfriendly witness" Lillian Hellman (although it was re-released in the 1950s, with added footage, as the *anti*–Soviet *Armored Attack*!). The Russian peasants are portrayed by friendly, All-American types such as Walter Huston, Walter Brennan, Dana Andrews, Anne Baxter, and Farley Granger, and the musical score was written by Aaron Copland, best-known as the composer of "American" symphonic music. Their peaceful farm collective is disrupted by the Nazi invasion of Russia. The men ride off to become guerrillas, and the women and children plan to implement the

"scorched earth" policy, but are forestalled by the arrival of occupation troops. German Army doctor Erich von Stroheim takes blood from the village children for wounded German soldiers. The partisans return and wipe out the Nazis, and the villagers burn their homes and march off to defeat the enemy. The film closely resembles other films about occupied countries, such as *Edge of Darkness*, *This Land Is Mine*, and so on. There is a rare depiction of Russia's armed forces in action: Andrews is a bombardier in the Russian air force, and proudly wears his uniform while visiting his home village before reporting for duty. On a mission, Andrews takes the controls of his crippled bomber when the pilot is killed, then makes a suicide dive into a German tank column.

895 NORTHERN PURSUIT (WB, Nov) Raoul Walsh; *genre:* War/Drama; *location:* Canada; *coding:* Ger, AF-Ger, Hitler, Nazi, WWI, Can, Brit, Fr, Pol, AF-Rcaf, Atroc, US-Brit Coop, Collab; *relevance:* 3.

In 1941, a U-boat lands a small party of German saboteurs in Canada. However, an avalanche wipes out the whole group, with the exception of their leader, Luftwaffe Colonel Von Keller (Helmut Dantine). Von Keller is captured by two Mounties, including Steve (Errol Flynn), whose parents were both German. When Steve does not bring the German in at once, the RCMP becomes suspicious. Later, Von Keller and several other Germans escape from an internment camp, joining up with civilian Ernst (Gene Lockhart) and some Eskimo guides. Steve is courtmartialed for hitting a fellow Mountie when his loyalty is questioned. Ernst brings him to Von Keller; they are going into the north, where Steve's skills will be helpful. To convince Steve to cooperate, the Nazis kidnap his fiancee Laura (Julie Bishop) and bring her along. Years before the war, the Nazis hid a disassembled plane and bombs in an abandoned mine. Now they plan to bomb strategic waterways and canals between Canada and the United States. Steve overcomes the Nazis and the wounded Von Keller crashes the plane and is killed. One interesting point about this film deals with the Indians: one Indian says his people have been "oppressed" by the British, and only the Germans can give the Indians their rights. Of course, the Nazis refer to the Indians as swine, and later shoot their Indian guide when he tries to get help. This theme was repeated a number of times with, variously, Africans, Arabs, and (with the Japanese in place of Germans) Asians. There are some similarities between this film and the British 1941 feature *The Invaders* (also known as *The 49th Parallel*).

896 OLD ACQUAINTANCE (WB,

Nov) Vincent Sherman; *genre:* Drama; *location:* United States; *coding:* AF-A, AF-N, Home Fr; *relevance:* 1.

Kit Marlowe (Bette Davis) and Millie Drake (Miriam Hopkins) are two women whose paths cross over the years. Millie is married to Preston, but her domineering ways break up the marriage; Kit is attracted to him, but she says the shadow of Millie would always be between them. They meet again in 1942: Preston is an Army officer. Kit's new boyfriend is Rudd, a younger man who is about to enter the Navy. Kit refuses Rudd's marriage proposal, then changes her mind, but it is too late: Rudd is in love with Preston's daughter Dierdre. At the end, Kit and Millie are left alone. Based on a stage play.

897 OVER MY DEAD BODY (TCF, Jan) Mal St. Clair; *genre:* Crime/Comedy; *location:* United States; *coding:* Short, Draft, AF-N, V, Chi?, Blk, Home Def; *relevance:* 1.

A stockbroker commits suicide in a situation identical to one in an unfinished story by mystery writer Jason (Milton Berle). In order to finish his story, Berle becomes a "suspect," but when the "suicide" is revealed to be murder, Berle has to solve the crime in order to clear himself. There are a few topical jokes in this film: for example, when Berle sees the dead body, he mutters, "Definitely 4-F."

898 PARIS AFTER DARK (TCF, Oct) Leonide Moguy; *genre:* Resist; *location:* France; *coding:* V?, Resist, WWI, Atroc-Conc, Collab, Hitler, Himmler, Nazi, Goebbels, Goering, Free Fr, DeGaulle, Brit, Stalin, Russ, Neth, Grk, Jew, POW, AF-Ger, Fr, AF-Fr, Atroc; *relevance:* 3.

French surgeon George Sanders masterminds a sabotage ring in occupied Paris. His assistant Brenda Marshall's husband (Philip Dorn), former editor of a workers' newspaper, has recently been released from a Nazi POW camp, and returns a defeatist. Marshall's younger brother George expresses his desire to join the "Fighting French" (aka the Free French). When he learns of the Allied landings in North Africa, George incites the workers at the factory, who have been threatened with forced-labor deportation to Germany: "Take their guns away from them, they can't win. The Allies are in Africa, next it'll be France." George is shot for his stand. Marshall shoots and wounds the German commandant responsible. Dorn, whose prison camp stretch has ruined his health, takes the rap for the attempted assassination, thereby saving the lives of 50 hostages who were to be shot in reprisal for the shooting. Germany used foreign laborers extensively during the war, taking them from its allies, from neutral nations, and from occupied countries (around 700,000 of these workers came from France); except for Jews and Soviet POWs, most of these workers were not slave labor, but varying degrees of political and economic pressure were applied to obtain manpower. After a first "draft" in early 1942, the Nazis placed additional demands on France for civilian workers in the summer, at which time many young men went into hiding, or joined the Resistance rather than be sent to Germany.

899 PASSPORT TO SUEZ (Col, Aug) Andre de Toth; *genre:* Spy; *location:* Egypt; *coding:* Spy-Sab, Collab, Jap, UN, Home Def, Brit, Short, Fr, Ref, AF-Brit, War Corr, Atroc; *relevance:* 3.

The Lone Wolf (Warren William) and his butler Jameson (Eric Blore) arrive in Egypt. They are blackmailed into helping Axis agents obtain defense plans to the Suez Canal. The Nazi spies try to escape, but the Lone Wolf strafes their car from an airplane, killing them. The Suez Canal was closed several times during the early years of the war when Axis planes dropped mines in the waterway, but with the defeat of German forces in North Africa the primary threat to the canal was removed.

900 THE PAYOFF (PRC, Jan) Arthur Dreifuss; *genre:* Crime; *location:* United States; *coding:* Nazi; *relevance:* 1.

Typical Hollywood reporter Lee Tracy solves the murder of a special prosecutor investigating the city's rackets. There is one brief war reference (to the "Gestapo") in the dialogue of this film.

901 PETTICOAT LARCENY (RKO, July*) Ben Holmes; *genre:* Comedy; *location:* United States; *coding:* —; *relevance:* 1.

Precocious 11-year-old radio star (Joan Carroll) wants to learn more about gangsters so she can improve her scripts, but is really kidnapped and has to be rescued by her press agent. One dialogue reference to "sabotage."

902 PILOT NO. 5 (MGM, June) George Sidney; *genre:* War/Drama; *locations:* United States, Pacific, Java; *coding:* AF-A, AF-Jap, Blk?, Pearl Harb, Hirohito, Jap, Draft, Musso, Ital, Resist, AF-AC, AF-N, Nazi, Prod, Fem Lab, Brit, Neth, AF-Neth, Span Civ, Eth; *relevance:* 3.

As Japanese forces close in on an island in the Dutch East Indies, Franchot Tone is chosen to fly a dangerous mission against the approaching enemy convoy in the Allies' sole remaining plane, assembled from parts salvaged from wrecked and disabled fighters. While Tone is gone, the other pilots (including his pal Gene Kelly) tell their commanding officer (from the Netherlands) the story of Tone's life: he was a young lawyer who became involved with a crooked polit-

ical machine in his home state, then turned against his boss but was ostracized by everyone, including his fiancee. Tone joins the Air Corps, reconciles with his girlfriend (Marsha Hunt), and is sent to the Pacific. At the end, he crashes his plane into a Japanese aircraft carrier when his jury-rigged bomb fails to release. This is another version of the "Colin Kelly" story which made the rounds in the early years of the war about the U.S. pilot who allegedly crashed into an enemy ship: see also *Appointment in Berlin*, and *We've Never Been Licked* (both q.v.). Note of interest: the crooked political machine Tone works for includes an Italian-American admirer of Mussolini, who has a large portrait of Mussolini (seated on horseback, giving the fascist salute) on his office wall.

903 POWER OF THE PRESS (Col, Jan) Lew Landers; *genre:* Drama; *location:* United States; *coding:* Churchill, Hitler, Short, Collab, Nazi, Ital, Jap; *relevance:* 2.

Small-town newspaper publisher Guy Kibbee crusades against abuses by the press, particularly the New York *Gazette*. Kibbee takes over when the *Gazette*'s publisher is murdered, but makes little headway against the paper's entrenched policies. The *Gazette* attacks a political enemy of Rankin, a minority owner of the paper (and the man behind the murder of Kibbee's predecessor). Incited by the article, a crowd burns a warehouse allegedly full of hoarded materials (but which actually contained secret Army supplies). Rankin is eventually exposed, and Kibbee editorializes against newspapers that use their power unwisely: these are the "truly dangerous Fifth Columnists."

904 THE POWERS GIRL (UA, Jan) Norman Z. McLeod; *genre:* Comedy; *location:* United States; *coding:* Home Def, Home Fr, AF-AC; *relevance:* 2.

Photographer Jerry Hendricks (George Murphy) snaps a photo of schoolteacher Ellen (Anne Shirley) in the arms of the town drunk (he had accidentally knocked her down and then picked her up). Ellen loses her job as a result of the "scandal" and travels to New York to join her sister Kay (Carole Landis). Jerry helps Kay get a job as a Powers model, and marries Ellen just before he joins the photographic division of the Air Corps. There are several other war references: John Powers (head of the model agency) is an air-raid warden, and there is a humorous first aid sequence.

905 PRINCESS O'ROURKE (WB, Oct) Norman Krasna; *genre:* Comedy; *location:* United States; *coding:* Ref, FDR, Home Fr, AF-AC, FBI; *relevance:* 2.

Princess Maria (Olivia DeHavilland) has fled from her occupied European kingdom to asylum in the United States. Lonely and

bored and under constant Secret Service protection, she finally escapes her sheltered life and poses as a poor refugee. She falls in love with commercial pilot Eddie O'Rourke (Robert Cummings) at a first aid class. There are romantic complications when Eddie refuses to give up his U.S. citizenship (in order to marry the princess), but the film climaxes with a midnight wedding at the White House. The couple is married by a Supreme Court Justice, and Eddie tips the witness a dollar (unknown to him, it was the President!). Eddie then goes into the Army Air Corps.

906 THE PURPLE V (Rep, Mar) George Sherman; *genre:* Resist; *locations:* Britain, Germany; *coding:* Resist, AF-Raf, AF-Ger, Hitler, Nazi, Rommel, Ger, V, Stalin, Hist Am, Himmler, Russ, Am Vol, Dipl; *relevance:* 3.

American RAF crewman Joe Thorne (John Archer) parachutes from his damaged plane so the pilot can make it back to England with the film of their recon flight. Joe lands in Germany, near the wreck of a German plane he had shot down. Donning the uniform of a dead Nazi flyer, Joe is given a secret report by a mortally injured military passenger to be delivered to Hitler. He hides out with a family of Germans he knew from his student days in Germany before the war (the father is an anti–Nazi professor, played by Fritz Kortner, a German stage actor who left Germany when Hitler came to power). The Gestapo learns about the fugitive American; to fool them, the German son of the family burns a "V" onto his wrist (to match Joe's tattoo), and is then shot while fleeing by German soldiers. Joe (who has burned off *his* "V" with acid), assumes the son's identity flees with Katti, the family's daughter. Aided by the sacrifice of the professor, they escape in a stolen plane with the secret report (about the supply problems of Rommel's Afrika Korps). In one scene, Joe talks with a German woman who mourns the death of her husband in Russia (this is one of the few times in a Hollywood film where an ordinary German citizen is seen expressing emotion about their war losses). The OWI congratulated Republic Pictures on this film: "This picture is of value to the government's war information program in that it dramatizes that there are German people who desire democracy and who believe in the common cause of the United Nations. There has been an inclination to overlook this in most films." In later years, however, the OWI frequently criticized films that were too "soft" on the German people (placing blame solely on the Nazis), and *The Purple V does* include at least one "average" German citizen (a nosy neighbor) who is pro-Nazi.

907 QUEEN OF BROADWAY (PRC, Mar) Sam Newfield; *genre:* Romance; *location:*

United States; *coding:* Short, Bonds, Blk; *relevance:* 1.

In order to adopt a little boy, a young woman (Rochelle Hudson) involved with sports betting agrees to marry a man (Buster Crabbe) who owns a football team. But after they are married, the couple realizes they *really* love each other. There are several brief topical references (rubber shortages, war stamps) in this comedy.

908 QUIET, PLEASE—MURDER (TCF, Mar) John Larkin; *genre:* Crime; *location:* United States; *coding:* Home Def, AF-A, Hitler, Goering, Collab, Nazi, Himmler; *relevance:* 2.

James Fleg (George Sanders) and Myra Blandy (Gail Patrick) steal a rare book from a library, killing a guard in the process. Myra sells a fake copy of the book to Cleaver, a Nazi agent buying valuable items for his government. Cleaver learns of the deception. McByrne (Richard Denning), a detective investigating the book theft, is smitten with Myra. She tricks him into meeting the irate Cleaver, each man believing the other is Fleg. They meet in the library, and the real Fleg kills Cleaver. McByrne eludes the murderer and his henchmen by turning on all of the building's lights, thereby alerting the air-raid warden and the police. The villains in this film could have easily been two sets of gangsters, but making Cleaver a Nazi gave the film a topical veneer.

909 RAIDERS OF SUNSET PASS (Rep, Dec) John English; *genre:* Western; *location:* United States; *coding:* Prod, Fem Lab, AF-A, Hist Am; *relevance:* 2.5.

Government agent John Paul Revere (Eddie Dew) is sent to cattle country to do something about the shortage of cowboys, which is hampering beef production. He forms the WAPS, made up of the daughters of ranchers, who can ride and rope as well as any cowboy. But the women are instructed to notify Revere via walkie-talkie if rustlers show up. The rustlers set traps to make it appear the women are incompetent. They also blackmail Dad Mathews, leader of the ranchers, into calling off the plan. Mathews, who has an old criminal record, is afraid his soldier son (due home on leave) will be ashamed of him. Revere and Frog (Smiley Burnette) defeat the rustlers and clear Mathews of the old charge against him.

910 REDHEAD FROM MANHATTAN (Col, May) Lew Landers; *genre:* Comedy; *location:* United States; *coding:* Spy-Sab, FBI, Latin Am, Nazi, Blk; *relevance:* 1.5.

When their ship is torpedoed off the East Coast, Rita (Lupe Velez) and Jimmy Randall (Michael Duane) reach shore on a life raft. They uncover a cache of money and weapons left by Nazi saboteurs. They keep the money

and travel to New York, where Rita meets her twin sister Elaine, a Broadway star. Elaine is secretly married and pregnant, so Rita substitutes for her, incognito. This causes trouble with their respective boyfriend and husband, but the trouble is eventually sorted out, and Rita plans to marry Jimmy.

911 RETURN OF THE VAMPIRE (Col, Nov) Lew Landers; *genre:* Horror; *location:* Britain; *coding:* Brit, Ref, Rom, AF-Ger, Atroc-Conc; *relevance:* 1.5.

London: in 1918, vampire Armand Tesla (Bela Lugosi) has a stake driven through his heart. His werewolf assistant Andreas (Matt Willis) regains human form. Twenty-three years later, Andreas is a lab assistant in the employ of Lady Jane (Frieda Inescort). When a Luftwaffe bombing raid unearths Tesla's body, two laborers unwittingly remove the stake, bringing the vampire back to life. Tesla takes the identity of Dr. Bruckner, a refugee from a German concentration camp, puts Andreas back under his spell, and plots revenge on Lady Jane, one of those who tracked him down in 1918. Tesla exerts hypnotic influence over Nicki (Nina Foch), fiancee of Lady Jane's son John. At the end, Andreas regains his will (with the aid of a handy crucifix). When Tesla is stunned by another bomb explosion, Andreas stakes him again, this time for good.

912 REVEILLE WITH BEVERLY (Col, Feb) Charles Barton; *genre:* Musical Comedy; *location:* United States; *coding:* AF-Blk, AF-A, AF-N, AF-W, Hirohito, Jap, Blk, Draft, Home Def, V, Hist Am, Short, Home Fr, Prod, Fem Lab, FDR, USO, UN; *relevance:* 3.

The entire Ross family is involved in the war effort: father is an air-raid warden, mother has a Victory Garden and saves her cooking grease, sister Evelyn is a riveter in an airplane factory, and brother Eddie is a soldier. Beverly Ross (Ann Miller) is a receptionist at a local radio station, but begins an early-morning radio show for the soldiers in a nearby Army camp, and becomes an Army favorite. Two soldiers, Barry and Andy, fall in love with her. Barry is rich, and Andy is his former chauffeur: to test the theory that women always fall for rich men, they switch identities. During a camp show, the troops are suddenly ordered to ship out; Beverly covers their departure by broadcasting as usual, and sends her best wishes to both Barry and Andy, en route to parts unknown. One of the requests Beverly receives for her show comes from Franklin Delano Lincoln Van Buren Jones, a black sailor on board a Navy ship, who asks for a Duke Ellington tune. The OWI commented on this scene: "This serves to remind us of the large number of our Negro citizens who are fighting on all

battle fronts, and to show that their service is appreciated as much as anybody else's."

913 REVENGE OF THE ZOMBIES (Mono, Sept) Steve Sekely; *genre:* Horror; *location:* United States; *coding:* Ger, Blk, FBI, Short; *relevance:* 2.5.

Learning of his sister Lila's death, Scott Warrington travels to his family home in Louisiana, accompanied by detective Larry (Robert Lowery), and his servant Jeff (Mantan Moreland). Dr. Von Altermann (John Carradine), Lila's husband, is really a Nazi scientist trying to create an army of zombies (he has only made about six so far, though). Lila is also one of the undead, but she will not respond to his commands. Larry, Scott, and Jeff, with the aid of Von Altermann's secretary Jennifer (Gale Storm), and a government agent (Bob Steele), manage to foil the plan. Zombie Lila drags Von Altermann into a pit of quicksand. According to OWI documents, the interracial zombie lineup was at the government's request: an all-black zombie crew would have suggested that blacks had a "lower mentality." Interestingly enough, Germany and the Nazis are never overtly mentioned, although Von Altermann's name and demeanor make his nationality quite obvious (his zombies also goose-step, a definite clue).

914 RHYTHM OF THE ISLANDS (Univ, Apr) Roy William Neill; *genre:* Musical Comedy; *location:* Pacific; *coding:* —; *relevance:* 1.

Before the war, two American entrepreneurs (Allan Jones and Andy Devine) on a Pacific island make a living staging fake "native" shows for tourists. They decide to sell their interest in the island and return to the United States, and the film deals with their efforts to do just that. The film opens with a title stating that people think of tropical islands "now" (1943) as a body of land surrounded by aircraft carriers, but before the war it was different. This is the only overt topical reference in this musical comedy.

915 RIDING HIGH (Para, Nov*) George Marshall; *genre:* Musical Comedy; *location:* United States; *coding:* Blk, Home Def, Prod?; *relevance:* 1.

Miner Victor Moore's daughter Dorothy Lamour comes to visit him. Dick Powell is a mining engineer. Dorothy, a former burlesque queen, puts on a show for the workers; Dick fights counterfeiters. One of the songs is topical: "He Loved Me Till the All Clear Came."

916 ROOKIES IN BURMA (RKO, Dec*) Leslie Goodwins; *genre:* Comedy; *locations:* Burma, Far East; *coding:* AF-Jap, AF-A, Jap, POW, Atroc-Conc, Brit; *relevance:* 3.

Wally Brown and Alan Carney (RKO's studio-created answer to Abbott and Costello) are soldiers captured by the Japanese (in reality, regular U.S. troops were not fighting in Burma at this time). They meet their top sergeant at the POW camp—he was caught while searching for *them* (this is a running gag throughout the film). While in the camp, Brown and Carney insult the Japanese guards in English, but make a mistake when they are called before an Oxford-educated Japanese officer, calling him a "bow-legged baboon" and other names before realizing their error! The sergeant, meanwhile, has been using double-talk to confuse the officer. The Army trio escapes and, together with two female American entertainers also hiding from the Japanese, manage to reach the Allied lines by using an elephant and a captured tank. This was a sequel to *Adventures of a Rookie*, q.v., but any further planned military escapades of the duo were forestalled by the OWI, which asked RKO to discontinue the series, since it portrayed American soldiers as imbeciles. Brown and Carney used the same character names ("Jerry Miles" and "Mike Strager") in most of their other RKO features, but *not*, interestingly enough, when they played merchant seamen in *Seven Days Ashore*, q.v.

917 SAHARA (Col, Oct) Zoltan Korda; *genre:* Combat; *location:* North Africa; *coding:* Prod, Arab, Atroc, Atroc-Conc, AF-A, AF-Brit, Dunkirk, Russ, Chi, Jap, Musso, AF-Ital, Hitler, Nazi, AF-Ger, Austral, AF-Blk, AF-Free Fr, POW, Span Civ, Resist; *relevance:* 3.

In June 1942, the British 8th Army is forced to retreat across the North African desert. Humphrey Bogart is a U.S. tank commander assigned to the British forces; his crew consists of a Texan (Bruce Bennett) and a soldier from Brooklyn. They pick up a group of Allied stragglers (at a field hospital which has been strafed by Nazi planes), including a Free French soldier, an Irishman, several Britons, and a South African. They later encounter a black Sudanese soldier (Rex Ingram), and an Italian POW (J. Carroll Naish). Bogart does not want to take Naish along, but eventually relents. The tank heads for a waterhole; on the way, they are attacked by a Nazi plane but shoot it down and take the pilot prisoner. The tank and its crew arrive at the ruins of an old mosque, but find the waterhole almost dry. Bogart and his men destroy the advance guard of a German unit which is also heading for the mosque. Bogart decides to lure the main force to the waterhole, buying time for the Allied forces. A pitched battle ensues; Bogart calls a truce and offers the Germans water if they surrender their weapons to him (they do not know the well is now dry). The German pilot kills the Italian soldier (a similar fate befalls

an Italian POW in *Sundown*, q.v., 1941), then tries to warn his comrades of Bogart's trick; Ingram chases him down and kills him, but is then shot to death by the Nazi troops. Finally, only Bogart and one British soldier are left defending the waterhole, but the Germans are driven by thirst to surrender. Fortunately for all, a German shell has reopened the well, and Bogart and his prisoners are soon greeted by the advancing Allied forces. This film was "suggested" by a Russian film entitled *The Thirteen* (set during the Russian Revolution), although it also bears similarities to *The Lost Patrol* (RKO, 1934), and even some Westerns.

918 SALUTE FOR THREE (Para, June*) Ralph Murphy; *genre:* Musical; *location:* United States; *coding:* USO, AF-A, AF-W; *relevance:* 2.5.

Radio singer Judy (Betty Jane Rhodes) is pushed into a fake "romance" with war hero Buzz (MacDonald Carey) by her press agent boyfriend Jimmy. They meet at the Manhattan Canteen (a club for servicemen) and fall in love for real, but Buzz walks out when he learns the relationship was merely a publicity stunt. However, Jimmy helps get Buzz and Judy back together, and even joins the armed forces himself at the end. The topical songs in this film include: "I'll Wait for You," "Left, Right," and "My Wife's a WAAC."

919 SALUTE TO THE MARINES (MGM, Sept) S. Sylvan Simon; *genre:* Drama/ Combat; *locations:* Philippines, United States; *coding:* Pacifist, Spy-Sab?, WWI, AF-Jap, Jap, AF-Brit, AF-N, Fil, Chi, Neth, Jew, Jap-Ger Coop, AF-MC, AF-W, AF-Mer, Hist Am, Mil Exer, Collab?, FDR, Dipl, Hitler, Nazi, Ger, Pearl Harb, Atroc; *relevance:* 3.

Well-produced (in Technicolor) Wallace Beery vehicle. At the San Diego Marine base in 1943, the commanding officer tells the latest group of young Marines the story of Marine William Bailey (Beery). There is a flashback to the Philippines, 1940. Sgt.-Major Bailey, a 29-year veteran of the Corps, is well known for his ability to train raw recruits. He is temporarily detached to serve the Philippine government, which will need trained troops when the islands become independent in 1945 (as originally scheduled; due to the war, the Philippines actually became an independent nation in 1946). While Bailey feels "them there Filipinos are too little to make good fighting men," he obeys orders. However, he asks the Colonel to make sure he (Bailey) can go to China if his battalion is transferred. The Colonel agrees. Bailey trains the Filipinos well, but both he and the Colonel are left behind when the Marine battalion is sent to China. Bailey, upset since he never had the chance to earn a combat

ribbon, retires. His wife and grown daughter live in Balligan, a Philippine town populated by "pacifist screwballs." Bailey does not fit in, but when, on December 7, the Japanese bomb the town and then land troops there, the ex-Marine takes charge (he also personally strangles the German agent who has been posing as the town's storekeeper). Bailey, a few Marines, and the trained Filipino irregulars hold off the Japanese until the Marines can blow the nearby Balligan bridge, denying the invading troops an easy road to Manila. However, Bailey, his wife, and the rest of his men are trapped on the enemy side of the lines, and will soon be overwhelmed by the Japanese. As the film returns to 1943, Bailey's daughter (Marilyn Maxwell)—now in the service herself—accepts her father's combat decoration. This film contains some of the most colorful anti–Japanese invective of the war, including "little bow-legged, four-eyed monkey," and "little yellow mustard-colored monkeys." The German agent also comes in for Bailey's criticism: "All the time you were just a dirty, crawling bilge rat, squealing about peace."

920 SARONG GIRL (Mono, June) Arthur Dreifuss; *genre:* Comedy; *location:* United States; *coding:* Bonds, Hist Am, V?, Spy-Sab?, Blk, Hitler, Short; *relevance:* 1.

Ann Corio is a stripper whose lawyer gets her released from jail by claiming Ann supports her poor, old mother. However, Ann does not really *have* a mother, so the lawyer finds an old lady (Mary Gordon) to pose as the exotic dancer's mom. After various romantic mixups, Corio marries the lawyer. There are a few minor topical remarks in this low-budget comedy musical, mostly courtesy of scatterbrained Irene Ryan. To a policeman, she complains, "You ought to be out trying to get some robbers or saboteurs." She also tells butler Mantan Moreland, "You sing just like Hitler." "Why, Hitler don't sing," he replies. "He will when we catch him," Ryan says.

921 SEVEN MILES FROM ALCATRAZ (RKO, Jan*) Edward Dmytryk; *genre:* Spy; *location:* United States; *coding:* AF-N, Pearl Harb, Draft, Short, Home Def, Home Fr, Hitler, Nazi, MacArthur, Prod, Spy-Sab, Atroc; *relevance:* 3.

Champ Larkin (James Craig) and Jimbo (Frank Jenks) escape from prison on Alcatraz Island. They take refuge at a lighthouse on another little island, run by Cap Porter (George Cleveland), his daughter Ann (Bonita Granville), and Stormy (Cliff Edwards). However, a group of Nazi spies arrives at the lighthouse, waiting to rendezvous with a German submarine (Hollywood fiction—no combat U-boats operated in the Pacific during WWII). Larkin is tough, but he finally agrees with Jimbo, who says "We're hoodlums but we're *American* hoodlums," and they team up to thrash the Nazis. Bonita Granville gets whipped again (see *Hitler's Children*, q.v.)!

922 SHADOW OF A DOUBT (Univ, Jan) Alfred Hitchcock; *genre:* Crime; *location:* United States; *coding:* Blk, AF-A, Bonds; *relevance:* 1.

Uncle Charlie (Joseph Cotten) is really the "Merry Widow" murderer who preys on middle-aged women. Visiting the town of Santa Rosa, he moves in with his relatives, including his young namesake (Teresa Wright). Detective MacDonald Carey finally tracks him down. There are no overt topical references, but servicemen may be seen on the street, there are bond posters on walls, and so on. This film seems to be set in 1941, prior to Pearl Harbor, and may be meant to suggest the "pre-war innocence" of America.

923 SHE HAS WHAT IT TAKES (Col, Apr) Charles Barton; *genre:* Musical Comedy; *location:* United States; *coding:* AF; *relevance:* 1.5.

Jinx Falkenberg pretends to be the daughter of a famous actress so she can get a part in a play. Tom Neal is a Broadway columnist taken in by her ruse, but there is still only one producer willing to take a chance on her. Friends of the famous actress raise enough money to put on the show. Reporter Constance Worth, jealous of Falkenberg's romance with Neal, plans to expose Falkenberg's real identity. However, Falkenberg's friends kidnap Worth until the show has begun. By that time it is too late, Falkenberg is a star. There is at least one topical musical number, "Let's March Together."

924 SHERLOCK HOLMES FACES DEATH (Univ, Sept) Roy William Neill; *genre:* Crime; *location:* Britain; *coding:* AF-AC, AF-Brit, Brit, Postwar, AF-Ger, POW, Jap, Nazi, Atroc-Conc; *relevance:* 1.5.

Hurlstone, the British estate of the Musgrave family, has been converted to a convalescent home for officers recovering from combat fatigue. One has recently escaped from a Japanese POW camp. Dr. Watson is the medical officer in charge. Sally Musgrave (Hillary Brooke) is in love with U.S. Army pilot Pat Vickery (Milburn Stone). Sally's older brothers are both murdered, with small holes appearing in their heads. Insp. Lestrade arrests Pat, but Sherlock Holmes arrives to take a hand, and exposes Watson's assistant Dr. Sexton as the real killer. Sexton wanted to marry Sally so he could control the Musgrave wealth (he had discovered an old land grant giving the family control of valuable British real estate). While driving back to London, Holmes comments on Sally's destruction of the document: "There's a new spirit abroad in the land … the time's coming when we shan't be able to kneel and thank God for blessings before our shining altars while men anywhere are kneeling in either physical or spiritual subjection. And, God willing, we'll live to see that day."

925 SHERLOCK HOLMES IN WASHINGTON (Univ, Apr) Roy William Neill; *genre:* Crime; *locations:* Portugal, United States; *coding:* Hist Am?, Brit, AF-N, AF-A, AF-Brit, Blk, AF-Blk, V, Churchill, WWI, Short, Home Def, Spy-Sab?; *relevance:* 3.

The final directly war-oriented Sherlock Holmes film. Holmes (Basil Rathbone) and Watson (Nigel Bruce) travel to Washington; a British agent, being pursued by Nazis, secretly passes a microfilm hidden in a matchbook cover to the unwitting Nancy (Marjorie Lord). The spies, led by George Zucco—posing as an antique shop owner—kidnap Nancy (knocking out her soldier-fiancé, played by John Archer, who later married Marjorie Lord in real life) but cannot find the film. Holmes solves the case and recovers the valuable information (which is never specifically identified). Zucco's character is named "Heinrich Hinkle," formerly an agent of the Kaiser, now serving the Nazis.

926 SILENT WITNESS (Mono, Jan) Jean Yarbrough; *genre:* Crime; *location:* United States; *coding:* Short, Blk, Blk Mkt; *relevance:* 1.

Lawyer Bruce Strong (Frank Albertson) wins an acquittal for the Manson brothers, accused of dealing in black market silk. Carlos, a disgruntled member of the gang, is mortally wounded by the Mansons but manages to speak to the District Attorney before he dies. The Mansons murder the D.A. to keep their secret, and frame Bruce for the killing. Bruce is eventually cleared by the combined efforts of his fiancee Betty (Maris Wrixon) and his dog, Ace.

927 SILVER SKATES (Mono, Feb) Leslie Goodwins; *genre:* Musical; *location:* United States; *coding:* Ref, Neth, Bonds, Blk, Short, AF-N; *relevance:* 1.

Patricia Morison's ice show is faced with disaster when skating star Belita threatens to quit. Morison's boyfriend (singer Kenny Baker) romances Belita to keep her with the show, but in the meantime Morison discovers a 10-year-old Dutch refugee who can skate, and makes her the star of the show instead. Morison and Baker reunite, and Belita decides to marry her boyfriend. Sonja Henie started a vogue for skating stars when she signed with 20th Century–Fox in the late 1930s; Belita (Monogram Pictures) and Vera Hruba Ralston (Republic Pictures) followed in her wake.

928 THE SKY'S THE LIMIT (RKO, Aug*) Edward H. Griffith; *genre:* War/ Drama/Musical; *locations:* United States, China; *coding:* AF-Chi, AF-Jap, AF-A?, Sino-Jap War?, AF-FT, AM-Vol?, AF-AC, AF-N, AF-MC, Ital, Blk, Draft, Prod, Fem Lab, Jap, FBI, Short, Brit, Russ, Chi, USO, UN, Home Def, Austral; *relevance:* 3.

Flying Tiger ace Fred Astaire and his buddies (Robert Ryan and Richard Davies) are sent to the U.S. on a bond-selling tour. Weary of hero-worship, Astaire dons civilian clothes and ducks out of the festivities. Joan Leslie, a magazine writer who wants to be a war correspondent, meets Astaire and falls for him even though she thinks he is a draft dodger (when he turns down the offer of a job with an aircraft manufacturer). The defense contractor is depicted in a rather negative fashion, an unusual portrayal for a Hollywood film of this period. Other points of interest include a Robert Benchley comic routine on production, and the dedication of the 10,000th bomber to be produced by a U.S. factory (by a lady riveter who is the widow of a Polish-American soldier killed on Bataan). Airmen on a U.S. bond tour also appear in *You Came Along* (1945), q.v.

929 SLEEPY LAGOON (Rep, Sept) Joseph Santley; *genre:* Comedy; *location:* United States; *coding:* Home Def, Short, Prod, Fem Lab, FDR, Jap, Musso, AF-N, Blk; *relevance:* 2.

The town of Sleepy Lagoon is caught up in the war-production boom. Judy Canova is elected mayor and hires her uncle to open an amusement park to provide clean diversion for the defense workers in their off-hours. However, Judy's uncle (Ernest Truex) is a front man for a gambling ring, and Judy has to defeat the crooks in order to keep her town clean. The sudden prosperity of war workers caused a number of problems on the home front: while salaries were relatively high, many consumer goods (cars, clothing, etc.) were unavailable due to war-time shortages. The government preferred to have the workers buy war bonds with their excess cash, rather than hoarding the money or spending it on scarce items or black-market luxuries.

930 SO PROUDLY WE HAIL! (Para, June*) Mark Sandrich; *genre:* Combat; *locations:* Philippines, Pacific, United States, Australia; *coding:* AF-A, AF-W, AF-Jap, WWI, Jap, Postwar, Pearl Harb, Tojo, Hirohito, AF-Fil, Fil, AF-MC, AF-N, Atroc, Chi, Jew?, Juv, MacArthur, Austral; *relevance:* 3.

A group of Army nurses, evacuated from Corregidor and flown to Australia, is now on a ship bound for the U.S. Nurse Lt. Janet Davidson (Claudette Colbert) is in a coma and shows no will to live, so her fellow nurses tell the ship's doctor her story. The nurses left San Francisco just before Pearl Harbor was attacked; they land at Bataan in the midst of the battle for the Philippines. Janet falls in love with medical technician John (George Reeves), while fellow nurse Joan (Paulette Goddard) teams up with Marine Kansas (Sonny Tufts). The nurses undergo great hardships. Olivia (Veronica Lake), whose fiance died at Pearl Harbor, sacrifices herself (by dropping a live grenade down her blouse and blowing up a troop of Japanese soldiers) so her comrades can escape to the island fortress of Corregidor. Word comes for the nurses to leave, but Janet refuses to go until she hears from John, who has gone on a mission to the main island. She goes into shock when a bomb explodes nearby, and is carried, comatose, to the evacuation ship. As the film ends, the doctor reads Janet a letter from John—stating he believes he will survive to see her again—and Janet begins to recover. This studio-bound film contains some interesting minor touches; the "feminine touch" comes to war with a sign on a foxhole—"This Foxhole Approved by Good Housekeeping." Also, there is a slightly bowdlerized reference to a contemporary rhyme, "The Battling Bastards of Bataan," here altered to "Battling *Orphans* of Bataan." There is a scene in which Lake's character considers killing wounded Japanese soldiers entrusted to her care, but relents (this is the reverse of a scene in *Bataan*, where Robert Walker hesitates at killing a Japanese adversary, then changes his mind when the soldier tries to kill *him*). There was some criticism of the makeup and wardrobe of the actresses in this film—for the most part, they looked *too* good, considering the hardships they were undergoing. However, there are some grim moments, and the evacuation under fire to Corregidor is extremely well staged. Although lip service is paid to the "gallant Filipino people," there are no significant Filipino characters in the cast.

931 SO THIS IS WASHINGTON (RKO, Aug*) Ray McCarey; *genre:* Comedy; *location:* United States; *coding:* Short, Home Def, Draft, AF-A, AF-N, AF-MC, AF-AC?, Blk, Prod, Fem Lab, Spy-Sab, Collab, Jap, Blk Mkt; *relevance:* 3.

Lum and Abner (Chester Lauck and Norris Goff, stars of the popular radio series—who were forced to don old-age makeup in order to play their characters on screen) travel to Washington to promote Abner's synthetic rubber invention. They visit an agency designed to bring the "common man" into the war effort, but Abner gets amnesia and forgets his formula! Since this is the only worthwhile invention brought to his office, the head of the agency tries desperately to bring Abner's memory back. The film begins in

Lum and Abner's general store in Arkansas, which is also the "Ration Board, Draft Board, Air Raid Warden Station," etc.

932 SOMETHING TO SHOUT ABOUT (Col, Feb) Gregory Ratoff; *genre:* Musical Comedy; *location:* United States; *coding:* Blk, UN, AF-?, Prod; *relevance:* 1.

Broadway producer Samson is offered the job of staging a show starring no-talent Donna Davis, who is financing the show herself. Press agent Ken (Don Ameche) urges Samson to substitute the talented Jeanie (Janet Blair) for Donna, but Donna withdraws her support when the show (starring herself) flops. Ken and Jeanie stage a vaudeville show instead. The show ends with a patriotic production number vaguely suggesting the benefit of "working together," and culminating with the unveiling of a huge U.S. flag, but apparently no other overt topical references.

933 SONG OF RUSSIA (MGM, Dec*) Gregory Ratoff; *genre:* War/Drama; *locations:* Russia, United States; *coding:* US-Sov Coop?, AF-Ger, Hitler, Stalin, AF-Russ, Russ, Resist, Nazi, Span Civ, Atroc?; *relevance:* 3.

John Meredith (Robert Taylor—who entered the Navy after completing work on this film) visits Russia to conduct a series of symphony concerts. He falls in love with music student Nadya Meschkov (Susan Peters), and they are married in a Russian Orthodox ceremony. When the Nazis invade Russia, Nadya visits her village—the birthplace of composer Tchaikovsky—and sees the people burn everything of value and take to the woods as guerrillas. John and Nadya reluctantly leave, realizing they can make a greater contribution to the war effort by raising funds through concerts in the United States. In one scene, John plays Tchaikovsky at (unspecified) Carnegie Hall—interestingly enough, Tchaikovsky himself played there in 1891. At the request of the OWI, the filmmakers deleted a dialogue reference to the Nazi-Soviet Pact (which reflected badly on Russia, now an Ally). The OWI was pleased, however, with the filmed verson of Stalin's "Scorched Earth" speech (July 3, 1941): "Stalin's delivery is markedly calm and poised, in extreme contrast to the Hitlerian school of hysterical ranting ... The sense of responsible leadership in Russia which this speech would aid in establishing would be most helpful." (Note: Stalin is not impersonated on-screen in the film; the speech is delivered by an off-screen voice.) Star Robert Taylor later criticized the film during the HUAC hearings of the late 1940s, claiming he was "forced" to make it, and that he considered it pro–Communist in nature.

934 SPY TRAIN (Mono, Sept) Harold Young; *genre:* Spy; *location:* United States;

coding: Home Fr, Bonds, AF-A, AF-MC, AF-N, Ger, Hitler, Goering, Nazi, AF-W?, Hist Am, Short, Home Def, Russ, Prod, Latin Am, V?, Atroc-Conc, War Corr, Spy-Sab, Ital, FBI?, Blk; *relevance:* 3.

War correspondent Bruce Grant (Richard Travis) decides to visit the country estate of his publisher in an effort to determine why the man has stopped printing Bruce's anti–Nazi articles. On the train with Bruce are Nazi spies trying to recover a briefcase full of secret papers, a time bomb in a suitcase, an Italian agent (who is literally stabbed in the back by a Nazi spy), and the publisher's daughter (Catherine Craig), who has mistakenly been given the case containing the bomb. The spies accidentally take the time bomb instead of secret papers, and are blown up when they get off the train. The publisher—who had been blackmailed by the Nazis (they threatened to publish a photo of his daughter consorting with Hitler and Goering—a fake, of course) into suppressing Bruce's articles—agrees to resume publication.

935 STAGE DOOR CANTEEN (UA, May*) Frank Borzage; *genre:* War/Drama/Musical; *location:* United States; *coding:* AF-Blk, Chi, Postwar, Hirohito, Jap, Hitler, Nazi, AF-Ger, Pearl Harb, Bonds, Home Def, WWI, AF-A, AF-N, AF-MC, AF-CG, Stalin, AF-Russ, Ital, FBI, Blk, Jew, AF-W, AF-Brit, AF-Chi, Brit, Short, Latin Am, Draft, UN, AF-Austral, AF-AC, Fr, MacArthur; *relevance:* 3.

Three soldiers waiting to be shipped out visit New York. They spend three evenings at the Stage Door Canteen, a serviceman's club operated by the American Theater organization (it is interesting to note that only enlisted men are seen enjoying the club's facilities—presumably, officers could afford to attend commercial establishments). The soldiers fall in love with three of the canteen hostesses, and promise to return for them after the war. Many stage and screen stars appear as themselves in the canteen sequences (including Gypsy Rose Lee—who does a very demure striptease—and Edgar Bergen, accompanied by a uniformed Charlie McCarthy), along with numerous bands and singers. One of the most stirring scenes is Sam Jaffe's introduction of a group of real Russian sailors (including a woman). The film runs well over two hours, and was produced by Sol Lesser. The three soldiers are played by Michael Harrison (later a Western star under the name Sunset Carson), William Terry, and Lon McCallister (their characters are all nicknamed after states: Texas, Dakota, California); their girlfriends are Cheryl Walker, Marjorie Riordan, and Dorothea Kent. The Stage Door Canteen opened its doors in March 1942, and a percentage of the film's profits were donated to the operation of the real-life canteen. A total of seven official "Stage Door Canteens" eventually opened, including one in London, in addition to the myriad USO clubs and other recreational centers.

936 STORMY WEATHER (TCF, July) Andrew Stone; *genre:* Biography/Musical; *location:* United States; *coding:* AF-Blk, Hist Am?, Blk, WWI, AF-A; *relevance:* 1.5.

Hollywoodized "biography" of dancer Bill Robinson tracing the period from his discharge from military service in France in 1918 (he says his unit won the "Croix de Guerre") until the present (1943), as he performs for a group of black servicemen preparing to ship out. Lena Horne is cast as his love interest, and Cab Calloway and Fats Waller also appear. Robinson was 65 years old when he made this film.

937 THE STRANGE DEATH OF ADOLF HITLER (Univ, Sept) James Hogan; *genre:* Resist; *locations:* Austria, Germany; *coding:* AF-Ger, Switz, Hitler, Nazi, Himmler, Resist, Russ, Dipl, Austria; *relevance:* 3.

Austrian Franz Huber (Ludwig Donath) is arrested by the Gestapo for mocking Hitler; he is transformed into Hitler's double via plastic surgery (they threaten to kill his wife and children unless he cooperates). His family is told he has been shot; his children are sent off to a Hitler Youth camp. His "widow" is accosted by German soldiers—she resists their advances and is taken to court. She meets and marries a Swiss diplomat. Huber plans to murder Hitler, and his wife joins the anti-Nazi underground with a similar intention. Hitler and Huber wind up at the same hotel, and one is killed—but which one?

938 A STRANGER IN TOWN (MGM, Apr) Roy Rowland; *genre:* Drama; *location:* United States; *coding:* —; *relevance:* 1.

An incognito Supreme Court justice Grant (Frank Morgan) visits a small town on a hunting trip. He is shocked to find a corrupt political machine in control of the town government and courts, but eventually straightens out the situation. There are no overt topical references, but Grant's concluding speech states that all citizens of a free country must be willing to fight to keep their nation free and united.

939 SUBMARINE ALERT (Para, June*) Frank McDonald; *genre:* Spy; *location:* United States; *coding:* Ital?, FBI, Jap-Ger Coop, AF-Jap, Jap, Spy-Sab, Hitler, Nazi, Ger, AF-N, Collab; *relevance:* 3.

Richard Arlen is an engineer working undercover for the FBI in an attempt to expose an Axis gang which is jamming radio transmissions and helping Japanese submarines sink Allied ships. Arlen's girlfriend (Wendy Barrie) is the daughter of a German professor killed by the Nazis. Some very poor model work hinders the effectiveness of this low-budget Pine-Thomas production.

940 SUBMARINE BASE (PRC, Sept) Albert Kelley; *genre:* War/Drama; *location:* Caribbean?; *coding:* Spy-Sab, AF-Ger, AF-Mer, Nazi, Collab, Latin Am?; *relevance:* 3.

Gangster Joe Morgan (Alan Baxter) and henchman Spike hide out on an island to "cool off." Taggart (John Litel), a Merchant Marine officer, arrives after his ship is torpedoed—he is a former policeman. A group of young women is also stranded on the island, and Morgan controls the only available boat. A U-boat appears and Morgan gives them supplies in exchange for a token (marked with a swastika) which can be redeemed at a store run by Nazi agent Kroll. However, Morgan actually planted a delayed-action bomb on the Nazi sub; when Kroll learns of this, he kills the gangster, but Morgan's past crimes are redeemed by his patriotic act. Alan Baxter also sacrificed his life for the Allied cause in *Prisoner of Japan* (PRC, 1942), q.v.

941 SWING FEVER (MGM, Nov*) Tim Whelan; *genre:* Musical; *location:* United States; *coding:* AF-A, AF-N, USO, Blk, Short, Russ?; *relevance:* 2.

Kay Kyser is a composer who can also hypnotize people. Marilyn Maxwell wants him to use his powers to convince a boxer that he cannot lose. In one scene, Kyser tells a nightclub audience his band has to leave to "entertain the service boys at a local canteen." The canteen contains a large number of jitterbugging servicemen, who besiege Kyser's female vocalist for autographs (and a few get kisses as well). One of the songs relates the vocalist's preference for a "guy in khaki" over a "guy in a tux."

942 SWING OUT THE BLUES (Col, Dec*) Mal St. Clair; *genre:* Musical Comedy; *location:* United States; *coding:* V, AF-Raf; *relevance:* 1.

Before the war, "The Four Vs" were partners with singer Rich (Bob Haymes). Rich marries Penny Carstairs (Lynn Merrick), but leaves her when he finds out Penny only married him to avoid marrying the man her aunt had chosen. Rich comes back in an RAF uniform, and makes up with Penny (who in the meantime has given birth to their son).

943 SWING SHIFT MAISIE (MGM, Oct) Norman Z. McLeod; *genre:* Comedy; *location:* United States; *coding:* MacArthur, Bonds, AF-A, AF-AC, Spy-Sab, Home Fr, Home Def, Short, WWI, Prod, Fem Lab, V, Hitler, Nazi, Blk, Draft, Jap, Ger-Am; *relevance:* 3.

Maisie (Ann Sothern) works in an aircraft factory. However, since she could not produce her birth certificate, Maisie had to lie to get her job. She was assisted by test pilot Breezy (James Craig), who asked how a long-time chorus girl could go to work in a factory. "He's my Uncle Sam too, you know!" Maisie replies. "If you can fly planes, then brother, I can build 'em." Fellow worker Jean Rogers falls in love with Breezy so she informs on Maisie to get her out of the way. Maisie is suspected of espionage, but in the end everything works out well. The film is mildly interesting in its depiction of defense plants as semi-enclosed worlds of their own, with clubs, lectures, and other planned activities for the defense workers. In one scene a worker—who ignored warnings about wearing her hair loose—gets her hair caught in a piece of machinery. Allegedly, industrial accidents caused by women imitating Veronica Lake's "peekaboo" hairstyle caused the government to ask the actress to change her coiffure!

944 SWING YOUR PARTNER (Rep, May) Frank McDonald; *genre:* Musical Comedy; *location:* United States; *coding:* Short, AF-A?; *relevance:* 1.

Dairy owner Miss Bird (Vera Vague) goes to work incognito in her own plant in order to discover the identity of an employee who insulted her. But working alongside "regular people" makes Miss Bird change her tyrannical ways. Musical comedy with topical references to rationing and shortages, but no direct plot involvement with the war.

945 TAHITI HONEY (Rep, Apr) John H. Auer; *genre:* Musical Comedy; *location:* Pacific; *coding:* Fr, AF-N, Russ?, Free Fr, Jap, Pearl Harb; *relevance:* 1.5.

In the period before Pearl Harbor, Mickey Monroe (Dennis O'Keefe) and his band are playing in Tahiti, but business is terrible. They meet Suzie (Simone Simon), a French singer who wants to get to the U.S. Mickey tells the rest of the band that Suzie has a Navy boyfriend waiting for her in the States, so they let her go along. Suzie meets Lt. Barton—who pretends to be her long-lost boyfriend—and Mickey is jealous, but eventually he and Suzie get together romantically. Mickey joins the Navy himself, in response to the bombing of Pearl Harbor.

946 TARZAN TRIUMPHS (RKO, Feb) William Thiele; *genre:* Resist; *locations:* Africa, Germany; *coding:* Isolat, Arab, Atroc, AF-Ger, Hitler, Nazi, V, Juv, Blk, Resist; *relevance:* 3.

Frances Gifford is the princess of a lost African civilization (significantly called "*Poland*ria") who asks Tarzan (Johnny Weissmuller) for help when a German military expedition invades her kingdom, formerly a "haven of peace." The Nazis want the nation's oil and mineral riches for their war effort. Tarzan is not too politically committed to the anti–fascist effort at first, but changes his mind when the Nazis commit various atrocities (including kidnapping and torturing Boy), and then enthusiastically begins to "Kill Nazis!" Cheetah makes a broadcast over the German's wireless set; when the ape's message is picked up in Berlin, the Nazis listening begin "Heiling" in response to the "personal message" from their Fuehrer! Jane, by the way, spends the entire film in England (thus avoiding a confrontatiion with the lovely Gifford).

947 TARZAN'S DESERT MYSTERY (RKO, Dec*) William Thiele; *genre:* Adventure; *location:* Africa; *coding:* Arab, Spy-Sab, AF-Brit, Ger, Brit, Rommel, Musso, Blk; *relevance:* 3.

Jane is in England for the duration, but she writes to Tarzan and asks him to find some rare jungle plants needed to produce a malaria cure. Tarzan has to cross a desert to obtain the plants; he runs into stage magician Nancy Kelly, who has been acting as an Allied courier to sheik Lloyd Corrigan. German agent Otto Kruger is up to no good, but Tarzan eventually steps in and straightens things out. This Tarzan episode was heavily recut and edited after early previews indicated that certain scenes were "too strong." The Mussolini reference occurs when a defiant Cheetah sticks out his jaw and has to be shooed away: "You Mussolini—scat!"

948 TENDER COMRADE (RKO, Dec*) Edward Dmytryk; *genre:* War/Drama; *location:* United States; *coding:* Dipl, Collab, FBI, AF-A, AF-N, Blk, Short, Blk Mkt, Pearl Harb, Hitler, Nazi, Home Fr, Fr, Brit, Belg, Postwar, Prod, Fem Lab, Jap, Resist, Ger-Am?; *relevance:* 3.

This film became notorious during the HUAC hearings in the post-war period, when Ginger Rogers' mother cited its alleged "Communist" message (i.e., women sharing resources in a group house). Ginger Rogers' soldier-husband (Robert Ryan) is shipped overseas, leaving her with an infant child. She moves into a house with other female defense workers, and each one has a story to tell: one has a husband in the Navy, one has a husband AND a son in the service, one never got to consummate her marriage with her soldier husband, and so on. The housemaid is a middle-aged, college-educated German refugee. At the end of the film, news arrives that Ryan has been killed in action, but Rogers and the others must carry on. Rogers tells her infant son that her husband "bought you the best world … with his life."

949 THANK YOUR LUCKY STARS (WB, Sept) David Butler; *genre:* Musical; *location:* United States; *coding:* AF-Blk, Ital, Blk, Russ, Latin Am, Jew, AF-N, AF-A, V, Draft, Brit, Home Fr, USO?; *relevance:* 2.

An all-star Warner Brothers musical. Producers S.Z. "Cuddles" Sakall and Edward Everett Horton are putting together a show. They try to sign up singer Dinah Shore under the nose of Eddie Cantor. Meanwhile, Dennis Morgan and Joan Leslie are bilked by a phony agent. Leslie meets Cantor lookalike "Joe Sampson" (also played by Cantor), a bus driver who lives in her apartment building. The real Cantor is ruining the show with his unreasonable demands, so Leslie has him kidnapped, substituting Joe. In turn, Joe puts Morgan in the show. On opening night, the real Cantor escapes and goes to the theater, but no one believes his story. Many Warner Brothers stars appear in musical numbers—one topical sequence features Bette Davis singing "They're Either Too Young or Too Old," about the wartime shortage of eligible men.

950 THAT NAZTY NUISANCE (UA, Aug) Glenn Tryon; *genre:* Comedy; *location:* Pacific; *coding:* Nazi, AF-Ital, AF-Ger, AF-Jap, AF-Mer, AF-Rac, Ger-Ital-Jap Coop, Arab?, Ref, Hitler, Goebbels, Musso, Jap; *relevance:* 3.

Hitler (Bobby Watson), Mussolini (Joe Devlin), Von Popoff (a reference to German diplomat Franz Von Papen), and Suki-Yaki (Johnny Arthur) visit a mythical tropical island in order to sign a treaty with the island's ruler (Ian Keith). Some American Merchant Marine sailors (including Frank Faylen and Emory Parnell) are stranded on the island. Faylen takes the place of a traveling magician, and apparently turns Suki-Yaki into an orangutan. At the end, the Americans seize a Nazi submarine and the three Axis leaders are shot out of the torpedo tubes. Bobby Watson played Hitler in a large number of films during the war (in fact, as late as 1950 he was cast as Hitler in RKO's *The Man He Found*, but his footage was scrapped and the film was reshot and released as *The Whip Hand*). This film was a followup to *The Devil with Hitler* (q.v.), although a different actor played the Japanese Suki-Yaki (note: these two short features were later combined and released as a single film under the title *The Devil with Hitler*).

951 THERE'S SOMETHING ABOUT A SOLDIER (Col, Dec*) Alfred E. Green; *genre:* Training; *location:* United States; *coding:* AF-A; *relevance:* 2.5.

Wally Williams (Tom Neal) and Jimmy Malloy (Bruce Bennett) attend the Anti-Aircraft Training School in North Carolina. Wally is a cynical and opportunistic ex-reporter; Jim has worked his way up from the ranks, and returned from active service in North Africa to attend the school. Both men fall for post secretary Carol Harkness; her brother was killed in action with Jim's unit. Jim is a hard worker; Wally is smart but lazy. After Carol's rebuke, Wally changes his ways, even accepting responsibility for a training accident that was not his fault. Jim does poorly on a math test just before graduation, and Wally tries to help him by changing the answers, but is caught and dismissed from the school. When Jim and Carol learn the truth, they bid a grateful goodbye to Wally, who has joined up as an enlisted man. Good example of the "training" genre, with the dual hero (one straight-arrow, one wise-guy) much in evidence.

952 THEY CAME TO BLOW UP AMERICA (TCF, May) Edward Ludwig; *genre:* Spy; *locations:* United States, Germany; *coding:* FDR, Blk, Churchill, Goering, Goebbels, Nazi, AF-CG, AF-N?, Austria, AF-Ger, Resist, Ger, Intell Serv, FBI, Collab, Ger-Am, Atroc-Conc, POW?, Hitler, Spy-Sab; *relevance:* 3.

Although a printed preface states this film was "NOT documented from the official records of the case," *They Came to Blow Up America* was clearly based on the 1942 apprehension of eight Nazi saboteurs, landed by submarine in Florida and Long Island, and on the case of double-agent William Seebold, who worked for the FBI while pretending to spy for the Nazis. The film begins in the offices of the FBI, where one agent complains that two of the eight Nazi saboteurs were *not* executed: "We're too soft. We could borrow a leaf from Hitler when it comes to dealing with our enemies." His supervisor (Ward Bond), tells the story of Carl Steelman (George Sanders), one of the "saboteurs" who turned state's evidence and had his life spared. Carl's story is related in flashback. Even his parents think he is a loyal member of the German-American Bund, but Carl is actually working for the FBI. When Ernst Reiter, another U.S. Nazi, is killed fleeing from the police, Carl takes his place and goes to Germany to train as a saboteur. While in Germany, he meets Helga, an Austrian who is spreading anti–Nazi propaganda, and helps her escape. He has a close call when Reiter's wife shows up and denounces him as a fake, but Carl manages to convince the local Gestapo commander that the woman is insane (she's committed to an asylum, and is later murdered to prevent her from talking when it turns out she was right!). The agents return to the United States in a U-boat, and are all arrested by the FBI. Carl is told he must continue to pose as a traitor, since his evidence would sound more convincing (why a court would believe a turncoat Nazi more than a loyal FBI agent is not explained)! Some actual documentary footage of the captured German agents is included at the finale. Carl's final job is the arrest of one of his father's German-American friends, who is actually a Nazi agent.

953 THEY GOT ME COVERED (RKO, Feb) David Butler; *genre:* Comedy/Spy; *locations:* United States, Russia; *coding:* Rom, Munich, Vichy, War Corr, Hitler, Nazi, Hirohito, Jap, Musso, Ital, Ger-Jap-Ital Coop, FBI, Prod, Fem Lab, Stalin, Russ, Spy-Sab, Collab, AF-A, AF-N, AF-MC, AF-W, FDR-E, Short, Blk, Petain, Home Def, USO, Chi, Draft, Hist Am; *relevance:* 3.

Foreign correspondent Bob Kittredge (Bob Hope) fails to report the Nazi invasion of the Soviet Union (he thought it was a parade). He is called back to Washington and fired (on the plane back, Bob says "You can't trust Hitler—he would doublecross his best friend!" A fez-wearing, uniformed Mussolini stands up from another seat in the plane and says, "You're telling me?"). A mysterious man named Vanescu offers to give Bob the inside story on Axis agents in America. The information is recorded in a government stenographer's notebook, which is stolen by a trio of Axis agents (one German, one Italian, one Japanese), but they cannot read her shorthand. Bob, still searching for Vanescu, is framed into looking like a fool, so no one will believe his stories, but in the end he manages to triumph. There are a number of jokes concerning conditions in wartime Washington. Dorothy Lamour was teamed with Bob Hope once more, after making a number of *Road* films with the comedian and Bing Crosby. Otto Preminger, Eduardo Cianelli, and Philip Ahn were the three enemy agents.

954 THIS IS THE ARMY (WB, Aug) Michael Curtiz; *genre:* Musical; *locations:* United States, France, Pacific; *coding:* AF-Blk, Brit?, V?, Postwar?, Pearl Harb, AF-A, AF-MC, AF-AC, Fr, Hist Am, Ger, Ital?, Pol, Czech, Jap, AF-Jap?, WWI, AF-W, AF-N, FDR, MacArthur, Draft, Blk, Jew, Bonds, Short, Nazi, Home Fr; *relevance:* 3.

This Technicolor film was based on a stage musical by Irving Berlin that toured with an all-soldier cast during the war (raising money for Army Relief), with additional material from his World War One musical show "Yip Yip Yaphank." During WWI, Broadway star George Murphy is drafted; he puts on a service show, and is then shipped overseas to fight, returning with a leg injury that terminates his career as a dancer. When WWII arrives, Murphy's son Ronald Reagan repeats his father's feat, staging a benefit show before leaving for the front (the final show is attended by the President of the United States, seen only in long shots). Many of the players in this film were servicemen on detached duty (see also 1944's *Winged Victory*,

q.v., for a similar "semi-official" film), freed to perform since profits from the movie were donated to the Army Relief fund (as with the play); the credits for this film list the actual service ranks of the personnel involved. Berlin himself makes a rare movie appearance in the film, dressed as a WWI doughboy and singing "Oh, How I Hate to Get Up in the Morning" (this number had also been performed in *Alexander's Ragtime Band*—TCF, 1938). A dramatic sub-plot in this film (which is mostly musical numbers) concerns Reagan's girlfriend (Joan Leslie), who wants to marry him. He is reluctant, however, fearing he will be killed and she will be a widow. At the end of the film, they do get married. The original play toured the U.S. between October 1942 and August 1943, and was later staged in London (November 1943), Italy, Egypt, Okinawa, and Hawaii.

955 THIS LAND IS MINE (RKO, Mar*) Jean Renoir; *genre:* Resist; *location:* France; *coding:* Brit, Postwar, Blk Mkt, Juv, AF-RAF, AF-Ger, Hitler, Nazi, Jew, Resist, Bonds, Collab, WWI, Fr, AF-Fr, AF-AC, Atroc; *relevance:* 3.

Set "somewhere in Europe" (obviously France): Charles Laughton is a cowardly schoolmaster in love with fellow teacher Maureen O'Hara. O'Hara's brother (Kent Smith), a member of the Resistance, tosses a grenade at a Nazi motorcade, killing one of the German motorcyclists. O'Hara covers for him, and Laughton has to back her up. The intellectual, Jewish principal of their school is one of ten hostages seized (and later executed) by the Nazis in an attempt to uncover the perpetrator. Laughton's mother (Una O'Connor) informs on Smith to collaborator George Sanders. Sanders turns Smith in, but later commits suicide in remorse. Laughton is charged with Sanders' death, but Nazi commander Walter Slezak offers to acquit him if Laughton promises to cooperate. Laughton pretends to go along, but makes a speech in court condemning the Nazis and the corruption of collaborationist officials, including the mayor. The next day he is arrested while reading to his students from France's seminal revolutionary document, "A Declaration of the Rights of Man [and of Citizens]" that begins by proclaiming that all men are born free and equal.

956 THREE HEARTS FOR JULIA (MGM, Feb) Richard Thorpe; *genre:* Romance; *locations:* United States, Portuguese; *coding:* AF-A, USO, Atroc-Conc, Fem Lab?, Blk, Hitler, Nazi, War Corr, Draft, Pol, Neth, Czech, Fem Lab?; *relevance:* 2.5.

Writer Jeff Seabrook (Melvyn Douglas) returns to America after two years in Europe. His wife Julia (Ann Sothern) tells him she wants to put her musical career ahead of

their marriage, so she is going to divorce him and marry someone else (she has a choice of two suitors). Jeff manages to win her back just before he departs for Army service. The OWI remarked: "There are many more or less hidden plugs for something that might be called the American Way of Life...." Among these are a Czech symphony conductor who finds American ways—while odd—preferable to those of Nazi-occupied Europe; additionally, the orchestra gives up Beethoven for arrangements of American folksongs when it tours Army camps (presumably because Beethoven was German—but what about the ubiquitous "V" of Beethoven's Fifth Symphony!?).

957 THUMBS UP (Rep, Sept) Joseph Santley; *genre:* Musical Drama; *location:* Britain; *coding:* AF-A, Blk, Brit, AF-RAF, AF-Brit, AF-W, US-Brit Coop, Free Fr, Churchill, Hitler, Musso, Hirohito?, Prod, Fem Lab, USO, Home Def, AF-N, Short; *relevance:* 3.

Louise (Brenda Joyce) is an American singer in the "American Bar," located in wartime London. Her erstwhile boyfriend Bert, a theatrical agent/producer, tells her that he cannot get her a role in a new musical because the British producer is determined to stage a "patriotic musical" employing only defense workers in the cast. Louise and Emmy (Elsa Lanchester), a Cockney chorus girl, get jobs in an aircraft plant. At first Louise is distressed by the hard work, but eventually she makes friends among the workers, and falls in love with the RAF supervisor at the factory, Douglas Heath (Richard Fraser). When tryouts for the stage show are held at the plant, Louise is selected. However, word leaks out about her plot, and the other workers ostracize her. Louise accepts the blame for an accident in which another woman worker is injured (although it was really Heath's fault), and resigns her post. She tells Bert that she does not deserve to represent defense workers in the show. Heath eventually tracks her down and they reconcile. The film concludes at the aircraft factory, as Louise and the other workers sing while Heath takes their latest aircraft on a test flight. In one amusing sequence, Louise dances the jitterbug while the inhabitants of a small British town look on. Suddenly, several jeep-loads of American GIs drive up. Spotting the dancers, they join in: "It's a monkey jump, gang!" Overhearing their incomprehensible jive talk, one British matron remarks that these soldiers must be "Free French."

958 TIGER FANGS (PRC, Sept) Sam Newfield; *genre:* Adventure/Spy; *locations:* United States, Far East; *coding:* Nazi, Jap, Brit?, Collab, Spy-Sab; *relevance:* 2.5.

Famous explorer Frank Buck (playing

himself) is sent to the Far East to investigate problems on rubber plantations. Nazi agents Gratz (Buck says Gratz "smells like a Hun") and Lang are shooting tigers with darts dipped in a drug which causes them to become maneaters, thus disrupting the flow of rubber to the Allies. Lang gets stuck with one of his own darts, and Gratz is squashed by an elephant, as Buck triumphs. The semidocumentary *Jungle Cavalcade* (RKO, 1941) was another Buck feature with some topical references.

959 TONIGHT WE RAID CALAIS (TCF, Apr) John Brahm; *genre:* War/Drama; *locations:* Britain, France; *coding:* WWI, AF-Fr, AF-Ger, Resist, Intell Serv, Brit, Fr, Free Fr, AF-Brit, AF-Raf, Hitler, Nazi, Collab, Atroc; *relevance:* 3.

British commando Carter (John Sutton) is sent on a secret mission to France to locate a German tank factory so the RAF can bomb it. He has to identify the real factory from among some dummy factories set up by the Germans. In France, Carter meets Bonnard (Lee J. Cobb), whose son died when the British sank the French fleet at Oran; because of this, Odette (Annabella), Bonnard's daughter, wants to turn Carter in to the Germans. Odette turns him in when the Nazis arrest her parents. However, the Nazis kill Bonnard anyway, and Odette helps Carter escape and light fires to pinpoint the tank factory. The RAF bombs the plant, Carter escapes to England, and Odette joins the Resistance to fight for her own country. The actual Calais raid occurred on 3-4 July 1940.

960 TOP MAN (Univ, Sept) Charles Lamont; *genre:* War/Drama; *location:* United States; *coding:* WWI, AF-N, AF-A, Prod, Fem Lab, Juv, Blk; *relevance:* 3.

Tom Warren (Richard Dix), a World War I-veteran flyer, is recommissioned in the Navy. He tells his teenaged son Don (Donald O'Connor) to be the "man of the family" until he returns. Don enlists his junior college friends to work in the local aircraft plant after school, and the plant wins an "E" pennant (for excellence in production). The school musical is staged at the plant to celebrate the award, and Don's father presents him with an honorary Navy medal for his idea.

961 TRUCK BUSTERS (WB, Feb) B. Reeves Eason; *genre:* Crime; *location:* United States; *coding:* Ital, Prod, Short, MacArthur, AF-A; *relevance:* 1.5.

Trucking magnate Gray goes into partnership with gangster Bonetti. The war means no new trucks are available for civilian use, and the two men plan to put small trucking companies out of business, thereby gaining a monopoly. Casey Dorgan (Richard Travis) opposes them, but is framed for murder by

Bonetti. He manages to clear himself, defeat the gangsters, marries his girlfriend, and joins the Army, all before the end of the film. Interestingly, the gangsters in this film are Italian, but no overt connection is made between this and the fact that Italy was a member of the Axis.

962 TRUE TO LIFE (Para, Aug*) George Marshall; *genre:* Comedy; *location:* United States; *coding:* Blk, AF-A?, AF-W, AF-N, Bonds, Prod, Home Def, Draft, Nazi, Short; *relevance:* 1.5.

Radio writers Fletcher (Franchot Tone) and Link (Dick Powell) have to come up with a new idea for a radio series (no excuse is given for neither man being in the armed forces). Link goes out looking for inspiration, and eventually moves in with the "ordinary" Porter family (they think he is out of work), making notes about their lives and relaying them to Fletcher for dramatization. The radio show is a hit, and Fletcher and Link fall in love with Bonnie Porter (Mary Martin). The Porters are at first offended when they discover their lives have been turned into a radio show, but learn to enjoy the fame. Bonnie and Link reconcile. Pop Porter (Victor Moore) is an over-zealous air-raid warden and inventor (one of his failed inventions is synthetic rubber). Bonnie's younger sister is shown "knittin' a mitten for Britain."

963 TWO-MAN SUBMARINE (Col, Mar*) Lew Landers; *genre:* War/Drama; *location:* Pacific; *coding:* AF-Ger, Prod, Spy-Sab, AF-Jap, Nazi, Jap-Ger Coop, Atroc, Austral; *relevance:* 3.

Jerry Evans (Tom Neal) is working on a "forgotten" Pacific island to produce the wonder drug "peninsulin" from mold which grows in a cave. Pat Benson (Ann Savage—later to co-star with Neal in the 1946 cult film *Detour*) parachutes onto the island as Jerry's replacement (he is scheduled to join the armed forces). When Jerry's supervisor is murdered by several Japanese who arrive in the titular two-man sub, Jerry burns the only copy of the "peninsulin" formula (after memorizing it, of course). Later, a German submarine arrives and the Nazis, led by the brutal Captain Von Spanger, also try to extract the secret formula via threats and torture. However, Jerry, Pat and a drunken Australian doctor (J. Carrol Naish) team up to defeat the Axis, albeit at the cost of the doctor's life. The OWI made a number of recommendations for changes in the script of this film, of which at least one was followed (the Australian character was included, to avoid having an all-U.S. cast of scientists). It is also interesting to note that Nazis were inserted into a story which should logically have used Japanese villains (the title subma-

rine *is* Japanese, but the Nazis are the main menace). Factual sidelights: British scientists developing penicillin considered the drug so potentially important that plans were made to destroy all traces of it in the event of a German invasion of England. Also, two-man Japanese submarines were used in the attack on Pearl Harbor, and one was in fact beached and captured—the ensuing publicity probably inspired the miniature submersible's inclusion in this film.

964 TWO SENORITAS FROM CHICAGO (Col, June) Frank Woodruff; *genre:* Comedy; *location:* United States; *coding:* AF-W, UN, Latin Am, Short, V; *relevance:* 1.5.

Daisy Baker (Joan Davis) wants to be a theatrical impresario. She passes off two hotel maids (Jinx Falkenberg and Ann Savage) as the Portuguese authors of a play (which she really found in a trash can). The hoax is exposed, but the musical becomes a hit nonetheless. There are topical jokes about rationing and shortages, and at least one war-related musical number about the United Nations defeating the Axis countries, featuring chorus girls in revealing uniforms.

965 TWO TICKETS TO LONDON (Univ, June) Edwin L. Marin; *genre:* War/Drama; *locations:* Britain, North Atlantic; *coding:* AF-Ger, Blk, Russ, Fr, Nazi, AF-Brit, AF-Rarf, Collab?, Brit, AF-Mer; *relevance:* 3.

American Merchant seaman Dan Driscoll (Alan Curtis) is a crewman on a British ship. When a U-boat sinks three ships in their convoy, Dan is accused of being a traitor. He escapes from custody after a train wreck in England, saving Jeanne (Michele Morgan), a young French woman, from the crash as well. In London, Jeanne, the widow of a British pilot, introduces Dan to her young son. The boy thinks Dan is his father. When Jeanne learns her brother was killed in Dan's convoy, she turns Dan over to the police, but Dan is acquitted in a trial, and is reunited with Jeanne just before his new ship sails.

966 TWO WEEKS TO LIVE (RKO, Feb) Mal St. Clair; *genre:* Comedy; *location:* United States; *coding:* AF-A, Ger, FBI, Spy-Sab, Short, Draft; *relevance:* 1.5.

Lum and Abner series entry: Abner is mistakenly told he has only a short time to live. In order to earn some money, he takes on a series of dangerous jobs. In one sequence, he plans to spend the night in a haunted house, but gets the address wrong and is mixed up with Nazis spies and the FBI. His final job is testing a rocketship to Mars, but the rocket lands in Mars, Iowa, instead. There are some minor topical references to rationing, the draft, and so on.

967 THE UNDER DOG (PRC, Nov*) William Nigh; *genre:* War/Drama; *location:*

United States; *coding:* Juv, AF-A, Spy-Sab, Nazi?, Prod, Jap, Short, Atroc; *relevance:* 3.

A young boy (Bobby Larson) is taunted by his peers because no one in his family is in the service. He offers his dog Hobo for the WAGS, but Hobo is rejected. However, the boy and his dog manage to defeat a gang of saboteurs who were planning to destroy the defense plant where the boy's father works. At the end of the film, the father joins the Army (yet another example of Hollywood placing a premium on military service over home front occupations—no matter how vital to the war effort—for males). There were several other wartime films dealing with "war dogs," including *War Dogs* (1942), and *My Pal, Wolf* (1944), both q.v., as well as the MGM cartoon *War Dogs* (1943), which satirized the "WOOFS." This film also contains references to the "idle wives" and "delinquent children" of war workers, and to the societal problems caused by the dislocation of families due to war work.

968 WATCH ON THE RHINE (WB, Sept) Herman Shumlin; *genre:* Resist; *locations:* United States, Mexico; *coding:* Juv, Ital, Dipl, Hitler, Nazi, Hist Am, Rom, Span Civ, Blk, Ref, WWI, Resist, Atroc?, Ger, Ger-Am, AF-Ger, Latin Am, Collab, Isolat?; *relevance:* 3.

This film was based on a stage play by Lillian Hellman, and the screenplay was written by Dashiell Hammett. Paul Lukas is the world-weary patriarch of the Muller family (a role he also played on Broadway) and Bette Davis is his American wife. In 1940, the Mullers emigrate to the U.S. from Germany with their three children, and move in with Davis's mother in Washington. Muller had been the second-ranking anti–Fascist in Germany, had fought with the International Brigades in Spain, and was a prisoner of the Gestapo for 6 months. A sleazy Rumanian (George Coulouris; Rumania became a satellite ally of Nazi Germany after its pro–Western king was forced to abdicate) discovers Muller's identity and plans to tip off Nazi agents in Washington, but Muller kills him. Lukas then departs for Germany in an attempt to rescue his anti–Hitler associate from the clutches of the Nazis.

969 WE'VE NEVER BEEN LICKED (Univ, Sept) John Rawlins; *genre:* Training/Combat; *locations:* United States, Japan, Pacific; *coding:* Ger, Ital?, Mil School, FDR, Munich, Czech, Sino-Jap War, WWI, Dipl, Chi, Fil, AF-A, AF-AC, AF-N, AF-Jap, Jap, Latin Am, Spy-Sab, Hitler, Hirohito, Musso, Blk, Draft, Atroc, Collab, Nazi, Brit?, Pearl Harb; *relevance:* 3.

A ceremony is held to honor the Texas A&M graduates now in the armed forces. Brad Craig's story is related in flashback

when his name is announced. As a freshman, Brad (Richard Quine) makes friends with Cyanide (Noah Beery Jr.), as well as Nina (Anne Gwynne). The constant hazing and strict discipline of the college make Brad want to drop out, but he changes his mind when counseled by science teacher Pop Lambert, Nina's father. He gradually earns the respect of his classmates, but—since he had lived in Japan during his youth—he also makes friends with two Japanese students and the school's Japanese gardener, and defends Japan's actions in the Pacific (pre-Pearl Harbor). Brad is assigned to guard a lab where a secret formula is being developed, but he is attacked and the formula is stolen. However, the formula was a fake. Brad tries to expose the spies (the Japanese students and gardener) by offering to sell them the *real* formula, but is caught and dismissed from school. He goes to Japan with his two "friends" and becomes a propaganda broadcaster for the enemy. Brad goes along as an observer on a Japanese carrier aircraft raid against the U.S. fleet in the Solomon Islands. When he hears Cyanide's voice on the radio (Cyanide is now a U.S. pilot), Brad kills the Japanese pilot and crashes his plane into a Japanese carrier. The film returns to the present, and Brad is awarded the Medal of Honor, posthumously. See *Appointment in Berlin*, q.v., for a very similar storyline.

970 WHAT'S BUZZIN' COUSIN? (Col, July) Charles Barton; *genre:* Musical Comedy; *location:* United States; *coding:* Musso, Hitler, Hirohito, Blk, Bonds, Draft, FDR, Short; *relevance:* 2.

Freddie Martin's band (with John Hubbard as the fictitious lead singer) arrives at a ghost-town hotel, now owned by four chorus girls, including Ann Miller. The boys in the band decide to help the girls make a go of the night spot, but patronage is sparse. However, Eddie "Rochester" Anderson thinks he has found gold in the hotel's Victory garden, and a gold rush ensues. The young women sell the hotel at a profit, and everyone is happy. Four of the ten songs in the film have some topical interest: Eddie "Rochester" Anderson sings one of them, "Short, Fat, and 4-F"; another is entitled "Three Little Mosquitoes," and calls for the squashing of Hitler, Mussolini, and Hirohito; "$18.75" refers to the amount of money one paid for a bond. There are also jokes about shortages and other war-relevant subjects.

971 WHEN JOHNNY COMES MARCHING HOME (Univ, Jan) Charles Lamont; *genre:* Musical Comedy; *location:* United States; *coding:* Vet, FBI, Mil School, AF-Blk, AF-A, AF-N, AF-MC, Blk, Short, Fem Lab; *relevance:* 3.

Marine hero Johnny Kovacs (Allan Jones) arrives home on furlough. In order to avoid all of the fanfare around his hero's welcome, Johnny takes a room at a boarding house and changes into civilian clothes. The young people at the house—especially Joyce (Jane Frazee)—think he is a nice guy, but then they begin to suspect he is a deserter, and snub him. At the end, everything turns out all right. Phil Spitalny's "all-girl" orchestra appears in the film.

972 WHISTLING IN BROOKLYN (MGM, Dec) S. Sylvan Simon; *genre:* Comedy; *location:* United States; *coding:* AF-N, Bonds, Nazi, Short, Home Fr; *relevance:* 1.5.

The third and last film featuring Red Skelton as radio detective "The Fox," otherwise known as Wally Benton. A murderer who signs himself "Constant Reader" is at large. Through a misunderstanding, the police think Wally is the killer. The rest of the film is an almost constant chase, with Wally fleeing from the police and from some gangsters. The real killer is finally apprehended. There are many topical gags and references in this film, although the plot is not war-relevant. For instance, when the police first come to arrest Wally, he says, "I was just kidding about that C-book [a high-priority gasoline ration] and that tire in my basement was an oversized teething ring" [since tires were rationed, hoarding them was considered unpatriotic]. The Brooklyn Dodgers, including Leo Durocher, appear as themselves in the film.

973 WILD HORSE RUSTLERS (PRC, Feb) Sam Newfield; *genre:* Western/Spy; *location:* United States; *coding:* Hitler, AF-A, Ger, FBI, Spy-Sab, Nazi, Jap, Collab, Atroc-Conc, AF-N, Prod; *relevance:* 3.

Tom (Bob Livingston) and Fuzzy (Al "Fuzzy" St. John) are horse-buyers for the U.S. Cavalry. The twin brother of the Flying Horse Ranch foreman is actually Hans, a Nazi agent. Tom and Fuzzy are framed for the murder of a ranch-hand, actually killed by Hans. Hans takes his brother's place, planning to murder the Army horses with poisoned hay. Tom and Fuzzy catch the Nazi agent when he forgets to remove his hat during the National Anthem, and free the innocent foreman. Fuzzy decides to join the Navy.

974 WINGS OVER THE PACIFIC (Mono, June*) Phil Rosen; *genre:* War/Drama; *location:* Pacific; *coding:* Dipl, Pearl Harb, Czech, Neth, Pol, Brit, Fr, Nor, WWI, AF-Ger, Hitler, Goering, Nazi, AF-Jap, Jap, Spy-Sab, FDR, Jap-Ger Coop, AF-AC?, AF-N; *relevance:* 3.

After a dogfight, an American pilot (Edward Norris) and his Nazi adversary both crash on a South Pacific island inhabited by Jim Butler, his daughter Nona (Inez

Cooper), and various "natives." The German pilot and a Nazi agent masquerading as a "Dutch" trader discover oil on the island, and plan to inform their allies, the Japanese. The friendly natives kill the trader, and the U.S. pilot defeats the Nazi flyer; when the Japanese arrive to take possession of the island, the natives wipe them out. The American contacts U.S. forces, who will make the island an Allied base of operations. In point of fact, the Luftwaffe never operated in the Pacific theatre of war.

975 WINTERTIME (TCF, Sept) John Brahm; *genre:* Musical Comedy; *locations:* United States, Canada; *coding:* Ref, Nor, Nazi, Can; *relevance:* 1.5.

In the period before Pearl Harbor, Freddy Austin (Cornel Wilde) owns a failing Canadian resort hotel. Norwegian industrialist Ostgaard and his daughter Nora (Sonja Henie) visit the hotel, and Freddy and Nora fall in love. Nora convinces her father to invest in the resort, and it becomes a moneymaker. When the Nazis invade Norway (April 1940) Ostgaard is ruined. Nora has the chance to make big money skating in a U.S. ice show, but cannot enter into the country because the immigration quota is filled. However, her financial and personal problems are solved when she marries Freddy. Immigration quotas were relaxed for refugees in 1939-40, but in June 1940 Congress passed the Russell Bill, which severely restricted the flow of refugees into the United States (additionally, as the battle of the Atlantic heated up, there were fewer spaces available on ships leaving Europe).

976 YANKS AHOY (UA, Aug) Kurt Neumann; *genre:* Comedy/Spy; *locations:* Pacific, United States; *coding:* AF-A, AF-W, AF-Jap, Short, Spy-Sab, AF-N; *relevance:* 3.

Dodo Doubleday (William Tracy) and Sgt. Ames (Joe Sawyer) are being shipped overseas. Dodo has a photographic memory, and when he sees mysterious flashing lights on shore, he tells the captain. They learn that an enemy agent is contacting a saboteur on the troop ship. Ames attacks a man he believes to be the saboteur, but it turns out to be the first mate! Dodo and Ames finally team up to capture a Japanese two-man submarine at the climax of the film. Several Japanese midget submarines had unsuccessfully participated in the attack on Pearl Harbor, and were a point of curiosity for U.S. audiences in several films (including *Two-Man Submarine*, q.v.).

977 YOUNG AND WILLING (Para, Jan) Edward H. Griffith; *genre:* Comedy; *location:* United States; *coding:* Isolat, AF-A, Draft, Home Fr; *relevance:* 1.5.

Six star-struck young people share a Greenwich Village apartment. They find a play written by a well-known producer, and convince him to give them parts in the show. The topical interest involves Tony and Marge: they are secretly married, but then Tony is drafted and this causes consternation, but all is finally resolved happily at the end.

978 YOUNG IDEAS (MGM, Nov) Jules Dassin; *genre:* Comedy; *locations:* United States, France?; *coding:* FR, Atroc; *relevance:* 1.

Josephine Evans (Mary Astor) writes a novel entitled *As I Knew Paris*, which tells "how recent history caught up with the simple people … of Paris." Jo marries Michael (Herbert Marshall), a professor of chemistry at a small college. Michael does not approve of the slightly risqué tone of the book. Jo replies: "The only thing that matters is whether or not the book leaves the reader determined that what I saw happen in France won't happen here!" Jo's two teenage children (by a previous marriage) try to break up the marriage to Michael, but then change their minds and try to keep Jo and Michael together. At the finale, Michael starts to spank Jo's son Jeff, who protests: "Now, look—no atrocities!" Oddly enough, the words "war," "Nazis," "Germany," "invasion," etc., are not used in the film, although the "recent history" of France could only refer to the German conquest.

979 THE YOUNGEST PROFESSION (MGM, June) Edward Buzzell; *genre:* Comedy; *location:* United States; *coding:* Ital, AF-W?, AF-A, AF-N, Blk, Hitler, Bonds, Jap, Home Fr, Hist Am; *relevance:* 2.

Virginia Weidler and her teenaged friends are autograph hounds in New York City, staking out Grand Central Station and the city's hotels, and cornering MGM stars like Lana Turner, Greer Garson, Robert Taylor, Walter Pidgeon, and William Powell. Meanwhile, Weidler's governess (Agnes Moorehead) thinks Weidler's father (Edward Arnold) is having an affair with his secretary, and tells Weidler so. Weidler sells one of her autograph albums and hires John Carroll to pose as a diplomat and make a play for her mother, hoping to make her father jealous. It works so well that Arnold and Carroll get in a fight at a Red Cross dance. Weidler runs away from home and joins the Salvation Army, but Arnold fires Moorehead, buys the autograph album back, and brings Weidler home. There are a good many peripheral topical references in this film, beginning with a large number of uniformed extras in crowd scenes (in fact, Robert Taylor is shown in his Navy uniform even in the credits). Weidler's mother is very active on the home front, participating in Red Cross activities, and there are a number of references to bonds and "war savings

stamps," as well as the usual joking remarks about Hitler and Japan.

980 YOU'RE A LUCKY FELLOW, MR. SMITH (Univ, Oct) Felix Feist; *genre:* Comedy; *location:* United States; *coding:* Blk, AF-A, Ital; *relevance:* 2.

The title comes from a popular song introduced by the Andrews Sisters in *Buck Privates* (1941, q.v.). Lynn Crandall (Evelyn Ankers) has to get married before her 24th birthday in order to inherit a large sum of money, so she travels to Chicago by train to meet her stuffy fiance. A group of soldiers, led by Tony (Allan Jones), board the train. Lynn's younger sister Peggy feigns measles to stop the marriage, and the train is quarantined. Lynn marries Tony to save her inheritance; when Tony finds out, he refuses to let her spend any of the money until she proves she is a responsible adult. At the end of the film they are happily reconciled. The OWI had suggested "playing down signs of extravagant spending in wartime," and the removal of a dialogue reference to "lynching," and these were both done.

1944

981 ABROAD WITH TWO YANKS (UA, Aug) Allan Dwan; *genre:* Comedy; *location:* Australia; *coding:* AF-Jap, AF-A, AF-MC, V, Tojo, Jap, MacArthur, USO, AF-Austral, Chi; *relevance:* 3.

William Bendix and Dennis O'Keefe are two Marines whose detachment is sent to Australia for rest and recreation after "chasing the Japs right into the sea." Bendix had saved the life of Australian pilot John Loder, and this earns the boys an entree into the home of Loder's friends, the Stuarts. Both Bendix and O'Keefe try to romance Joyce Stuart (Helen Walker), but it is Loder who wins her in the end. For much of the latter portion of the film both Bendix and O'Keefe are dressed as women (they were participating in the "Marine Follies" camp show), and the final scene shows them punching two GIs who try to pick them up!

982 ACTION IN ARABIA (RKO, Feb*) Leonide Moguy; *genre:* Adventure; *location:* Syria; *coding:* Arab, War Corr, UN, Nazi, Free Fr, Collab, Neth, Austria, Spy-Sab; *relevance:* 3.

George Sanders is a newspaperman in Damascus who uncovers a Nazi plot to cause an Arab uprising, thereby threatening the Suez Canal. He is aided by Virginia Bruce, an agent of the Free French forces, and by

Foreign Service official Robert Armstrong. The Nazis are led by Alan Napier. The film is set in 1941, before Pearl Harbor. Axis attempts to subvert the Middle East also appeared in *A Yank in Libya* (PRC, 1942) and *Adventure in Iraq* (WB, 1943), both q.v.

983 ADDRESS UNKNOWN (Col, Apr*) William C. Menzies; *genre:* Drama; *locations:* Germany, United States; *coding:* Hitler, Jew, Ger-Am, WWI, Nazi, Ger; *relevance:* 3.

Interesting film dealing with anti–Semitism in pre-war Germany, a subject rarely addressed during the war years (although the world knew of the Nazi's anti–Semitic policies, the extent of the Holocaust was not revealed until the war had ended)—the film includes a montage of Brownshirts persecuting German Jews. Martin Schultz (Paul Lukas) decides to go to Germany to further the art business he shares with Max Eisenstein (Morris Carnovsky); Max will stay in San Francisco to run the U.S. end of the partnership. Griselle (K.T. Stevens), Max's daughter, goes to Germany to study acting, leaving her former fiance Heinrich (played by Peter Van Eyck)—Martin's son—behind. Martin gradually comes under the spell of the burgeoning Nazi party, through the actions of his mentor, a Nazi Baron. As the campaign against the Jews mounts, Martin severs relations with Max. Meanwhile, Griselle has become a stage actress in Germany, but when she protests Nazi censorship of the play she is appearing in, she is exposed as a Jewess and is nearly killed by the hostile audience. Fleeing to Martin's home for safety—pursued across the countryside by Gestapo agents with dogs—she is turned away by her father's former partner, and is murdered by her persecutors. Martin is compromised by letters sent by his son (in Max's name) from the United States—the Nazis become suspicious of his apparent interest in "decadent" art. A final letter to Martin is returned to Max and Heinrich, stamped "Address Unknown." This film was based on a short story originally published in 1938.

984 THE ADVENTURES OF MARK TWAIN (WB, May*) Irving Rapper; *genre:* Biography; *locations:* United States, Britain, Austria, India; *relevance:* 1.

This biography of 19th-century writer Mark Twain (Fredric March) obviously contains no direct war references. However, Twain makes a speech in which he says democracy, freedom and tolerance must be defended "with the pen if possible or the sword if need be," so that Americans can be a "free and united people."

985 AN AMERICAN ROMANCE (MGM, Nov) King Vidor; *genre:* Drama; *location:* United States; *coding:* WWI, Draft, Prod, Fem Lab, AF-N, Pearl Harb, Jap, V, Hist Am; *relevance:* 2.

Fictional biography of fictional immigrant Stefan Dangos (shortened from Dangosbiblichek; played by Brian Donlevy), who rises from poor steelworker to automobile industry magnate. His oldest son, George Washington Dangos (all of Dangos' sons are named after famous Americans) is killed in the First World War; when WWII arrives, two of his grandsons become Naval airmen, and Stefan comes out of retirement to help solve production problems in the aircraft industry. Long and ambitious Technicolor film by King Vidor was not commercially successful.

986 AND THE ANGELS SING (Para, Apr*) George Marshall; *genre:* Musical; *location:* United States; *coding:* V, Home Fr, Pol, Ger-Am?; *relevance:* 1.5.

Four sisters (including Dorothy Lamour and Betty Hutton) become involved with a bandleader (Fred MacMurray)—he loves one, but a different one loves *him*. At least one topical song—about Victory Gardens—is heard in this film.

987 ARE THESE OUR PARENTS (Mono, July) William Nigh; *genre:* Drama; *location:* United States; *coding:* Juv, Prod, Russ, AF-N, AF-AC, Home Fr, Short?; *relevance:* 1.5.

Second in a mini-"series" of juvenile delinquent films from Monogram Pictures, following *Where Are Your Children?*, q.v. In this film, Noel Neill is a society girl who runs away from the fancy boarding school she has been placed in by her uncaring mother. She makes friends with Richard Byron, a young man whose father is neglecting his job in a defense plant to run around with a blonde floozy. The two teenagers become involved in the murder of a nightclub owner (a dissolute Russian—Ivan Lebedeff), but are eventually exonerated. The juvenile officer sharply criticizes their parents for neglecting to supervise the young people's activities. Several minor topical references.

988 ARSENIC AND OLD LACE (WB, Sept) Frank Capra; *genre:* Comedy; *location:* United States; *coding:* V, Home Def, Blk, FDR, Hist Am, AF-N?, Chi; *relevance:* 1.

Black comedy based on a hit play with Cary Grant as the bemused nephew of two murderous aunts (and a loony uncle who believes he is Teddy Roosevelt). Raymond Massey and Peter Lorre are the heavies. There are a number of minor topical references in this film, including "blackout," "V" (three dots and dash), and so on. This film was actually shot in late 1941, but Warner Bros. was contractually bound to withhold it from theatres until the Broadway production closed.

989 ATLANTIC CITY (Rep, Aug*) Ray McCarey; *genre:* Musical; *location:* United States; *coding:* Postwar, WWI, Blk, Bonds; *relevance:* 1.

Brad Taylor is an impresario who develops a nightclub in Atlantic City into a tourist attraction. This is a period film with a short section dealing with World War I: Brad and his sidekick (Jerry Colonna) join the Army, and Brad's girlfriend (Constance Moore) sells Liberty Bonds. After the war, Brad encourages the town's businessmen to accept his idea of a "Miss America" contest: "In these post-war times, with the inevitable economic readjustment, we've got to have something big to sell."

990 BATHING BEAUTY (MGM, May*) George Sidney; *genre:* Musical Comedy; *location:* United States; *coding:* Latin Am, Short; *relevance:* 1.

Technicolor MGM musical teaming Red Skelton and Esther Williams for the first time. Skelton is a songwriter secretly married to Williams; he "enrolls" in the all-girl's school where she teaches swimming so they can be together. Only a few minor topical references are included. The finale is an aquatic ballet with a swimming pool full of beautiful young women, a sure-fire bet to please the (male) audience, particularly servicemen.

991 BEAUTIFUL BUT BROKE (Col, Sept*) Charles Barton; *genre:* Comedy; *location:* United States; *coding:* AF-AC, Prod, Fem Lab, AF-A, AF-N, Short, Grk; *relevance:* 2.5.

Dottie Duncan (Joan Davis) becomes the manager of a talent agency when her boss joins the Marines. However, many of her client bands have broken up since their (male) musicians have joined the armed forces or are working in defense plants. Dottie arranges a job for an all-girl band, even though she does not *have* one as a client. She creates a female band which gets hired to play in Cleveland, but they are bumped from their train in Nevada when a group of pilots takes priority. Dottie then loses their train tickets. While waiting, two of the band become romantically involved with an engineer and an Army captain who are working at an armaments plant. The men try to get the band members to become defense workers rather than traveling musicians. At the end, the women decide defense work is more important than swing music. In one sequence, the band plays a benefit for a "baby station," where children of factory workers can be cared for while their mothers are working—absenteeism in defense plants among women workers was a major problem during the war, and could be attributed in part to the demands of homemaking, child care, and so on. The film opens with a sequence in which Dottie bids a tearful farewell to her dog, who is entering the Canine Corps! Jane Frazee sings one song about people who complain about the war, suggesting that they "Take the Door to the Left" (and get the heck out!).

992 BERMUDA MYSTERY (TCF, May) Benjamin Stoloff; *genre:* Crime; *location:* United States; *coding:* WWI, AF-A, Short, Prod?; *relevance:* 1.5.

Frank Martin is killed by a poisoned cigarette. Constance Martin (Ann Rutherford) hires Steve (Preston Foster), a private detective, to solve the crime. Martin and five friends, upon their discharge from the Army in WWI, agreed to meet once a year; at one of these annual meetings, they pooled their money to invest, with the proceeds to be split among the survivors. Now, members of the group are being mysteriously murdered. In one scene, Steve has a flat tire; he opens his trunk and discovers no spare, only a note: "Thanks for the tire. Let this be a lesson to you. Never leave your car unlocked."

993 BETWEEN TWO WORLDS (WB, May*) Edward Blatt; *genre:* Fantasy; *locations:* Britain, North Atlantic; *coding:* AF-Mer, Nazi, Home Def, Austria, War Corr, Free Fr, Brit; *relevance:* 1.5.

During the London Blitz, eight people (an actress, a cynical reporter played by John Garfield, a war profiteer, a Merchant Marine sailor, a rich man and his wife, a priest, and a middle-aged British woman) planning to leave England on a ship are killed when a bomb hits their taxi on the way to the docks. However, they do not know they are dead, and find themselves on a mysterious ship sailing to an unknown destination. They are joined by a shell-shocked former pianist (Paul Henreid) and his wife (Eleanor Parker) who committed suicide together. Eventually, they learn they are on their way to the "hereafter," and the Examiner (Sydney Greenstreet) sorts them out—some will go to Heaven, others to Hell. Henreid and Parker get second chances at life, however. This was the second filmed version of the play *Outward Bound*.

994 THE BIG NOISE (TCF, Oct) Mal St. Clair; *genre:* Comedy; *location:* United States; *coding:* Draft, Spy-Sab?, AF-A, Jap, Hitler, Nazi, Jap-Ger Coop, Russ, Blk, Short, Prod, Fem Lab; *relevance:* 3.

Laurel and Hardy are janitors who want to be detectives. They are mistakenly hired to protect Professor Hartley, inventor of a new super bomb. Hartley is pursued by crooks who want to steal the secret and sell it to the enemy. When the inventor leaves for Washington, he gives Stan and Ollie a decoy bomb, but it turns out to be the *real* one. They end up dropping it on an enemy submarine (with Japanese *and* Nazi officers

on board). This ending is somewhat similar to *Joan of Ozark* (Republic, 1942), q.v.

995 THE BLACK PARACHUTE (Col, May*) Lew Landers; *genre:* Resistance; *locations:* Europe, Britain, Switzerland; *coding:* AF-Ger, War Corr, Hitler, Resist, Spy-Sab, Collab, AF-?, Atroc, Nazi; *relevance:* 3.

Larry Parks, an American war correspondent, parachutes into a fictional European country occupied by the Nazis. The resistance wants to free their king (Jonathan Hale) from the enemy; meanwhile, the Nazis have an impostor king making propaganda broadcasts to his people. Parks, disguised as a Nazi officer, kills the impostor and takes his place. He is uncovered, but not before the real King is freed. Parks escapes, and the King broadcasts a message of hope to his country from exile. The OWI disliked the original script of this film, fearing it would be associated with the actual situation in Greece or Yugoslavia. Columbia Pictures made a number of changes to allay their concerns: Parks is not an official representative of the Allied governments, there is no mention of a "government in exile," and specific references to names or places in the Balkans are absent (the character names in the film are generic "foreign"—King Stephen, Olga, Marya, etc.). Parks is depicted working *with* the resistance, rather than solving the problems alone. However, the OWI still recommended against allowing this film to be shown overseas, because the resistance was supporting a monarchy rather than a democratic government! John Carradine plays a Nazi general, somewhat similar to his role as Heydrich in *Hitler's Hangman* q.v.

996 BLOCK BUSTERS (Mono, July) Wallace Fox; *genre:* Comedy/Drama; *location:* United States; *coding:* Juv, Jew, Blk, Hitler, Short, Fr, Russ, Chi, AF, Ref, Hist Am; *relevance:* 1.5.

East Side Kids entry in which a rich woman (who nonetheless remembers her poor roots) brings her French refugee grandson Jean down to the East Side to learn about American sports and experience life in a democracy. Muggs and Glimpy and the gang are suspicious of the foreign kid (he wears a beret, speaks with an accent, and fights with his feet), but in the end he joins their baseball team and hits the game-winning home run. The title of this film is also war-relevant ("block buster" referred to a huge, although conventional, type of bomb used by the Allies); earlier, the East Side Kids had appeared in *Bowery Blitzkreig* (1941), another topical title (although the film itself had nothing to do with the German "lightning war").

997 BOWERY CHAMPS (Mono, Dec) William Beaudine; *genre:* Comedy/Drama; *location:* United States; *coding:* Juv, Blk, AF-

A, Short, Russ, Draft, Hist Am, Home Fr, Home Def; *relevance:* 1.5.

Muggs (Leo Gorcey), Glimpy (Huntz Hall), and the other East Side Kids help clear dancer Gypsy Carmen of suspicion in the murder of her ex-husband. Danny (Bobby Jordan), uses his 12-hour pass from the Army to help clear up the case (a running gag in the film concerns everyone telling Danny, "The Army has done you a lot of good"). Muggs himself says "I just got my reduction [sic] papers," a typical Muggs malapropism. There are a few other topical remarks and gas rationing stickers appear on the windshields of a number of cars.

998 BRIDE BY MISTAKE (RKO, July*) Richard Wallace; *genre:* Comedy; *location:* United States; *coding:* AF-Ger, USO?, Short, Postwar, AF-N, AF-AC, Prod, Chiang; *relevance:* 2.

Norah (Laraine Day) switches places with her secretary Sylvia (Marsha Hunt) to avoid fortune-hunting suitors. Sylvia's husband Philip wants Norah to get married so he can take his wife with him to Washington where he is going to work. Norah's guardian arranges for Norah (posing as Sylvia) to work at an Army Air Force rest center. Norah falls for flyer Tony, but she is not sure if he loves her or Sylvia (who pretends to be the rich Norah). At the finale, Tony makes the right choice.

999 BROADWAY RHYTHM (MGM, Mar) Roy Del Ruth; *genre:* Musical; *location:* United States; *coding:* Blk, Latin Am, Jew, Short, V, FDR, FDR-E, Churchill, Prod, Fem Lab, Home Def, Home Fr; *relevance:* 2.5.

Producer Jonnie Demming (George Murphy) is putting on a play "with a message," but his retired vaudevillian father (Charles Winninger) thinks audiences want pure entertainment. He decides to put on his own show, taking Jonnie's star (and love interest) Helen (Ginny Simms—the former vocalist with Kay Kyser's orchestra, now a solo performer) with him. The rest of the film is made up of various musical and comedy numbers, with the thin plot sandwiched in between. Finally, everyone reconciles on stage at the end. There are a number of topical references, both visual and verbal. Impressionist Dean Murphy imitates Franklin D. Roosevelt and Eleanor Roosevelt, Wendell Wilkie, Winston Churchill, and a number of movie stars. In one scene from Jonnie's play, Trixie (Nancy Walker) portrays a female welder on the swing shift who sings "Milkman Keep Those Bottles Quiet."

1000 THE CANTERVILLE GHOST (MGM, May*) Jules Dassin; *genre:* Fantasy; *locations:* Britain, France; *coding:* Short, AF-Ger, Blk, AF-A, AF-Brit, Nazi, Brit, Prod, Fem Lab; *relevance:* 2.

In medieval times, cowardly knight Charles Laughton is cursed to roam the halls of his ancestral mansion until one of his descendants performs a brave deed. During WWII, a group of American Rangers is billetted at the castle, among them a distant relative of Laughton (Robert Young). On a commando mission to France, Young loses his nerve, freezing when one of his comrades is shot. However, he regains his courage with the help of young Margaret O'Brien, the current "lady" of the manor: when an unexploded bomb lands near the castle during a German air raid, Young tows it away behind a jeep, and it explodes harmlessly in the countryside. This gallant act frees Laughton from his curse and Charles the friendly ghost can pass over to the other side at last. This film spends a little time contrasting the boisterous American soldiers with their English allies—at a village dance, young O'Brien jitterbugs with one of the Rangers; another American soldier dances with a young woman who works in a factory making "Wellingtons" (British bombers, named after the "Iron Duke" who defeated Napoleon at Waterloo). There are a few similarities between this film and the 1944 British comedy *Don't Take It to Heart*.

1001 CAROLINA BLUES (Col, Dec*) Leigh Jason; *genre:* Musical Comedy; *location:* United States; *coding:* Prod, USO, Bonds, Blk, AF-N; *relevance:* 3.

Kay Kyser, leader of a popular band, hires Ann Miller as his new female singer. However, he thinks she is rich and has various preconceptions about rich people (they do not take work seriously, and so on), so that complications ensue. The band plays at bond rallies to raise money for a warship to be named after Kay's home town, Rocky Point, North Carolina. Victor Moore plays six roles.

1002 CHARLIE CHAN IN THE SECRET SERVICE (Mono, Feb) Phil Rosen; *genre:* Crime/Spy; *location:* United States; *coding:* Ger, FDR, Chiang, AF-AC, AF-N, AF-MC, Intell Serv, AF-Ger, Bonds, AF-Jap, Jap, Ref, Short, Chi, Blk, Spy-Sab, Collab?, Latin Am?, Prod; *relevance:* 2.

After Fox dropped the Chan series, producer Philip Krasne took the character to Monogram Pictures. An inventor is murdered in his own home, and his plans for a revolutionary new torpedo are stolen. Charlie Chan (Sidney Toler), his son (Benson Fong) and daughter (Marianne Quon) come to investigate. The killer is revealed as Von Vegon (Gene Stutenroth), who is apparently a Nazi agent (although this is not clearly stated). Von Vegon is killed by his accomplice, a flighty society matron (who had hidden the stolen plans in a miniature Statue of Liberty she made out of plaster). There are a number of topical jokes and remarks in the film, many delivered by Birmingham Brown (Mantan Moreland—in this film he plays a servant of the murderess, but later he became a regular in the series as Chan's chauffeur): for example, after his employer has been arrested for murder, Brown makes a phone call—"Is this the Manpower Commission? I'm wide open for a defense job!"

1003 CHIP OFF THE OLD BLOCK (Univ, Feb) Charles Lamont; *genre:* Musical Comedy; *location:* United States; *coding:* Mil School, Juv?, Brit, AF-N; *relevance:* 1.5.

Donald O'Connor is suspended from the Sperling Naval Academy prep school for two weeks. Visiting his naval officer father, he also meets Ann Blyth, a young girl from a theatrical family. Donald gets Ann a job singing in a Broadway show, to be premiered at the prep school as a benefit for the Navy Relief fund. In a sub-plot, Donald fears his father's meetings with a "foreigner" have something to do with espionage—but his father was just ordering a new sailboat for Donald's birthday. The OWI asked Universal to change two parts of the script: the birthday present was changed from a fuel-wasting speedboat to the economical sailboat, and a menial Chinese servant was deleted from the plot altogether (to avoid showing a fighting Ally in a subservient role).

1004 CHRISTMAS HOLIDAY (Univ, June*) Robert Siodmak; *genre:* Crime/Drama; *location:* United States; *coding:* AF-A, AF-N, AF-W; *relevance:* 1.5.

Based on a Somerset Maugham novel, this film marked a change of pace for singer Deanna Durbin. On Christmas Eve in New Orleans, Durbin tells a sympathetic serviceman (Dean Harens) the story of her marriage to a rotter (Gene Kelly). Just as Harens is preparing to leave, he learns Kelly has escaped from prison, where he has been serving a sentence for murder. The soldier and a reporter friend save Durbin from the clutches of Kelly, who is then killed by the police.

1005 THE CONSPIRATORS (WB, Oct) Jean Negulesco; *genre:* War/Drama; *locations:* Netherlands, Spain?, Portuguese; *coding:* Ref, Nor, Collab, Fr, Resist, Pol, Czech, Brit, Hitler, Goering, Nazi, Atroc-Conc, Atroc, Jap, AF-Ger, Austria Jew?, FDR, Laval, Neth, Resist; *relevance:* 3.

Warner Bros. tried to recapture the success of *Casablanca* with this tale of double-dealing espionage, set in neutral Portugal. Paul Henreid is a Dutch agent sent to Lisbon to meet Sydney Greenstreet, leader of an Allied spy ring (Greenstreet's character name is "Quintanilla," and he wears what appears to be a Hebrew prayer shawl in some scenes). The group also includes Peter Lorre, Hedy Lamarr, and Lamarr's husband (Victor Francen), a member of the German legation. One of the spies is murdered by the Nazis, and a coin used as identification is stolen. Francen is exposed as the traitor and killed; Henreid leaves on a secret mission, but he and Lamarr will meet again, someday. One point of interest: there are no significant U.S. characters in this film, which was cast almost entirely with foreign actors resident in Hollywood. Coins used as identification for secret agents also figured in the plots of *Miss V from Moscow* (1942) and *Sabotage Squad* (1942), q.v.

1006 COVER GIRL (Col, Mar*) Charles Vidor; *genre:* Musical; *location:* United States; *coding:* Vet, Fem Lab, AF-W, AF-A, AF-N, AF-MC, Draft, Short, Bonds, Nazi, USO; *relevance:* 2.

Rusty (Rita Hayworth) is a dancer at Danny McGuire's nightclub. Danny (Gene Kelly) is a wounded ex-serviceman (he makes a reference to being "shot up" in Libya) who is in love with Rusty. However, she wins a "Cover Girl" contest and is promoted as a Broadway star by John Coudair (Otto Kruger), who was in love with Rusty's grandmother forty years previously. Rusty becomes a hit in a show produced by Wheaton (Lee Bowman), while Danny closes his club and goes to off to "entertain at Army camps" with his pal Genius (Phil Silvers). Rusty agrees to marry Wheaton, but changes her mind at the last moment and reunites with Danny. Although the plot is not directly war-oriented, there are quite a few references to the war in this film, particularly jokes about rationing; there are also visual references in several production numbers, as in the "magazine cover" number. Rita Hayworth was Columbia's top musical star in this period, and *Cover Girl* was a lavish Technicolor production that was nominated for five Oscars (winning one: Best Score for a Musical Picture). The OWI reviewer made an astute observation: "From our point of view, it would have been better not to play the hero [Kelly] as a veteran discharged from the Army because of wounds, since he does some pretty athletic dancing throughout the film."

1007 COWBOY CANTEEN (Col, Feb) Lew Landers; *genre:* Musical Comedy; *location:* United States; *coding:* USO, AF-A, Draft, Jap, Blk, Fem Lab, Prod-Farm; *relevance:* 2.5.

Charles Starrett needs workers to take over his ranch after he goes into the Army. But he is disappointed to see Jane Frazee and her vaudeville troupe show up to work during their vacation, although Tex Ritter—Starrett's cousin—is happy to meet the attractive Jane. After various plot twists, Starrett changes his mind and proposes to Frazee, who accepts and agrees to wait for his return. The title comes from a country and western version of the "Stage Door Canteen," which is set up on the ranch to entertain troops stationed nearby. The OWI asked that a verbal reference to a "yellow Jap" be removed from the film (to avoid offending other Asians), but this was apparently not done.

1008 CRIME BY NIGHT (WB, Sept) William Clemens; *genre:* Crime/Spy; *location:* United States; *coding:* Blk, Spy-Sab, Collab, V, Prod, Home Fr; *relevance:* 2.5.

Private eye Sam Campbell (Jerome Cowan, promoted to leading-man status due to the manpower shortage in Hollywood) and his assistant Robbie (Jane Wyman) investigate a series of axe murders at a summer resort. One of the victims is an inventor whose chemical formulas are used in war work. Sam learns that Ann Marlow (Faye Emerson), although posing as a concert manager, is really the brains of an enemy spy ring (her "clients" are all conveniently located near defense plants). At the end, Sam remarks that Ann could "really kiss," and when Robbie gives him a kiss herself, an off-key musical quote from Beethoven's Fifth Symphony (...-) is heard.

1009 THE CROSS OF LORRAINE (MGM, Jan) Tay Garnett; *genre:* War/Drama-Resistance; *locations:* Germany, France; *coding:* Resist, AF-Fr, Petain, Hitler, Nazi, Goering, AF-Ger, Atroc-Conc, Atroc, Fr, Free Fr, DeGaulle, Chi, Russ, POW, Pol, Span Civ, Latin Am, Collab; *relevance:* 3.

This film is set in 1940, during the fall of France and afterwards. As the Germans invade France, the French Army accepts volunteers from Spanish Civil War refugees. Rodrigues (Joseph Calleia), a Chilean who fought against Fascism wherever the "people's armies were on the march," enlists. After the collapse of the French forces, Rodrigues is taken prisoner with a group of other soldiers, including Paul (Jean Pierre Aumont), Victor (Gene Kelly), and Andre (Hume Cronyn). They are sent to a POW camp where they meet the brutal guard Sgt. Berger (Peter Lorre). Andre, a former wine merchant who had business dealings with the Germans before the war, collaborates with the Nazis and is given a cushy job. Victor, on the other hand, refuses to cooperate and is thrown into solitary confinement (Berger kicks him in the head when Victor spits on him). The prisoners judge Andre guilty of collaboration, gag him, and throw him into the compound at night. The guards, thinking he is escaping, shoot him dead (a scene later repeated in *Stalag 17*, 1953). Paul escapes, taking Victor with him, although Victor is a broken man due to his POW ex-

periences. While they are hiding in a French village, the Nazis arrive to take 50 men for forced labor in Germany. Paul is wounded when he resists, but Victor regains his nerve, and the townspeople rise up to slaughter the German soldiers. Victor warns them that the Nazis will be back, so the townspeople burn their own homes and march off to join the Resistance. The Cross of Lorraine was the symbol of Joan of Arc, and was adopted by DeGaulle's Free French forces as a symbol of resistance to Nazi Germany. While utilized by propagandists as a symbol of the United Nations' opposition to the Axis, the Free French were never considered a full ally, and DeGaulle was often ignored by Roosevelt and Churchill when major decisions were made.

1010 CRY "HAVOC" (MGM, Feb) Richard Thorpe; *genre:* Combat; *location:* Philippines; *coding:* Jap, AF-W, AF-Jap, Fil, AF-Fil, Atroc, Atroc-Conc, Ref, Brit, Pearl Harb, AF-A, AF-MC, POW, MacArthur, FDR; *relevance:* 3.

In the period immediately after Pearl Harbor, the Japanese begin their invasion of the Philippines. A group of young American women—in civilian life a chorus girl, a dietician, a fashion writer, a cannery supervisor, several British students, and so on—volunteer to become nurses in a hospital on Bataan. They include Pat (Ann Sothern), and Grace (Joan Blondell). The women have to endure poor food, malaria, and Japanese bombs as they tend to the wounded and ill. When word comes that the advancing enemy cannot be stopped, the women are given the option to be evacuated to Corregidor, but they all decide to stay on Bataan, where they are needed most. Lt. Smith (Margaret Sullivan), an Army nurse, is secretly married to Lt. Holt, who is killed during the final, deliberate Japanese air strike on the hospital. The film ends as the women are taken prisoner by Japanese troops, who "had planned to march straight to California," but were slowed down by the gallant defense of the Philippines. The OWI had requested changes in the script before the film went into production, and while some were made, the final result was not entirely to the government's liking: the volunteers are characterized as "quarrelsome and petty," and this—although they are specifically *not* Army nurses—was felt to reflect badly on real-life Army nurses; additionally, little emphasis is placed on the contributions of the Filipino people themselves in the battle for their country, and the OWI complained of the "insignificant, minor role" Filipinos play in the film (one of the volunteer nurses is Filipino, but the major characters are all Americans). This film is somewhat reminiscent of

War Nurse (MGM, 1930). It could also be viewed as the female version of *Bataan*, q.v. Army nurses in the Philippines are also the topic of *So Proudly We Hail*, q.v.

1011 CYCLONE PRAIRIE RANGERS (Col, Nov) Benjamin Kline; *genre:* Western Spy; *location:* United States; *coding:* Bonds, Spy-Sab, Collab, Ger; *relevance:* 2.5.

Charles Starrett is a rodeo performer who is recalled from a bond-selling tour to investigate sabotage out West. Crops, food trains, and livestock are being destroyed by enemy agents. The head of the ring poses as a deaf-mute cobbler, but he and his confederates are smoked out by Starrett and comic sidekick Dub Taylor.

1012 DARK MOUNTAIN (Para, Sept*) William Berke; *genre:* Crime; *location:* United States; *coding:* Short, AF-W, Neth; *relevance:* 1.5.

Don Bradley (Robert Lowery) is a Forest Ranger stationed in a rural area. His friend Willie—in a "humorous" role reversal—has a girlfriend serving with the WACs in North Africa (*he* knits *her* a sweater). Don's former girlfriend Kay (Ellen Drew) has married Steve, a "wholesaler" (actually a gangster). After an aborted truck hijacking (there is an indication the stolen merchandise includes hard-to-get silk), Steve murders two of his henchmen to keep them from talking. Don lets Kay stay in a forest lodge, but Steve also shows up. When Don and Willie try to capture him, Steve uses Kay as a hostage, then escapes in Don's dynamite-laden jeep. The jeep crashes and explodes. Don and Kay are reunited. There are a few other minor references to shortages and other topical remarks. There is apparently no explanation given for Don *not* being in the armed forces.

1013 DARK WATERS (UA, Nov) Andre de Toth; *genre:* Crime; *location:* United States; *coding:* Jap, Blk; *relevance:* 1.

Gothic-style thriller with Merle Oberon as a young woman who visits her relatives on a Louisiana plantation in an attempt to recover from the shock of being on a ship that was torpedoed by the Japanese. However, Oberon's real aunt and uncle have been murdered and replaced by impostors, and the fakers try to get her to commit suicide so they can control the estate.

1014 DAYS OF GLORY (RKO, Apr*) Jacques Tourneur; *genre:* Resistance; *location:* Russia; *coding:* Juv, AF-Ger, Resist, Russ, AF-Russ, Atroc, Stalin, Jap, Hitler, Nazi, AF-W, Brit?; *relevance:* 3.

Gregory Peck is Vladimir, leader of a group of Russian guerrillas operating out of a forest headquarters. The other partisans include Fedor (Hugo Haas), who is always quarreling with Sasha (Alan Reed), former Oxford professor Semyon (Lowell Gilmore), and Yelena (Maria Palmer). Nina (Tamara Toumanova), a dancer who has become separated from her troupe, takes refuge with the band (the Soviet guerrillas pay no attention to the cross she wears around her neck, an anomaly in officially atheist Soviet Russia). At first she is considered a burden, but when a German prisoner tries to escape, Nina shoots him. Later, she takes part in a sabotage mission against a German train, and she and Vladimir fall in love. Maria is shot trying to sneak through the German lines with a message, so Nina takes her place. She is accompanied by young Mitya. Mitya is captured by the Nazis and interrogated. When he refuses to talk, he is taken to a makeshift gallows; before he is hung, Mitya smiles and shouts, "You cannot hang a nation ... Death to the Germans!" The partisans receive orders to stage a diversionary attack on the Nazis to set the stage for a major Red Army counterattack. During the battle, they sell their lives dearly, and the film ends as the narrator says "this is one reason why the hordes of Hitler fled...." Somewhat more realistic than *The North Star* q.v., although the story could have easily been translated to nearly any other occupied country. It also dispenses with any U.S. presence, unlike *Song of Russia*, and *Three Russian Girls*, both q.v. The ending—with lovers Peck and Toumanova facing certain death together— is reminiscent of the finales of *Somewhere I'll Find You*, *Corregidor*, and *Salute to the Marines* (all q.v.). The two recite the "Guerrilla's Creed" as they fight fascism to the very end.

1015 THE DESERT SONG (WB, Feb) Robert Florey; *genre:* Adventure; *locations:* Africa, Switzerland; *coding:* AF-Ital, AF-Fr, Laval, Arab, Span Civ, Vichy, De Gaulle, Hitler, Nazi, Resist, War Corr, Collab; *relevance:* 3.

Although shot in 1942, this film was not released until 1944, probably due to government concern about portraying the French in a bad light. The film is set in North Africa in 1939, where a German banking syndicate is financing construction of a railway through the desert to the port of Dakar. The corrupt Caid Yousseff forces his Arab subjects to work like slaves on the railroad, guarded by French troops. However, the mysterious El Khobar—in reality American bandleader Paul Hudson (Dennis Morgan)—has been raiding the construction sites. He kidnaps singer Margot (Irene Manning) in an attempt to draw French troops away from the Caid's palace. Paul also manages to convince French Col. Fontaine that he is being used by the Nazis. Fontaine kills the Caid, and the enslaved workers are freed. Paul gets Margot. *The Desert Song* was based on a 1926

operetta, and had previously been filmed (with obvious plot differences from this version) in 1929 and 1935. In Technicolor.

1016 DESTINATION TOKYO (WB, Jan) Delmer Daves; *genre:* Combat; *locations:* United States, Japan, Pacific; *coding:* Ital, AF-Jap, FDR, WWI, AF-N, AF-AC, Grk, Postwar, Appease?, Hist Am?, Tojo, Hirohito, Jap, Short, Chi, Russ, V, Bonds, Nazi, Collab; *relevance:* 3.

The U.S. submarine *Copperfin*, commanded by Cary Grant, sneaks into Tokyo Bay to obtain weather information for American bombers (the information is radioed to the aircraft carrier *Hornet*, which was the launching point for the Doolittle raid on Tokyo; see *Thirty Seconds Over Tokyo*, q.v.). The usual war film assortment of adventures occur: an emergency appendicitis operation on a sailor (based on an actual war-time incident which took place on the *USS Silversides* in December 1942, while the sub was submerged off the Solomons Islands), strafing and depth-charge attacks by the enemy, and the sinking of several Japanese ships with torpedos. In one scene, the sub attempts to rescue a Japanese pilot whose plane has been shot down; the pilot stabs a sailor in the back who was trying to assist him, and is gunned down. Although this is virtually the only scene which personalizes the enemy, the film makes a point of stressing the militaristic nature of Japanese society, especially the current generation. Referring to the dead sailor (Mike), Grant says many more Mikes will die until we "wipe out a system that puts daggers in five-year-old's hands." Along with *Air Force* and *Guadalcanal Diary*, this is one of the best "combat" films of the war years. Interestingly, none of these films contain any female roles of note, a realistic touch (given their settings) which belies the conventional wisdom that Hollywood *always* had to have a "love interest."

1017 DETECTIVE KITTY O'DAY (Mono, May) William Beaudine; *genre:* Crime; *location:* United States; *coding:* Home Def, Short, Hist Am; *relevance:* 1.

First in a brief series starring Jean Parker as Kitty O'Day, an amateur detective. Peter Cookson is Johnny Jones, her boyfriend and reluctant companion in sleuthing, and Tim Ryan portrays irascible police Inspector Clancy. In this film, Kitty is a secretary and her employer is murdered as part of a plot to steal $100,000 in securities. A ration sticker is briefly visible on a car windshield at one point, and Clancy's assistant Mike (Edward Gargan) says "I'm in a blackout" when Johnny drops a pair of pants over his head. Otherwise, there are no topical references in this film—particularly odd is the lack of

comment about Johnny *not* being in the service.

1018 DOUBLE EXPOSURE (Para, Dec) William Berke; *genre:* Crime; *location:* United States; *coding:* US-Russ Coop, Fem Lab?; *relevance:* 1.

Nancy Kelly goes to work as a photographer for Chester Morris at *Flick* magazine. She gets Morris to hire her boyfriend, Philip Terry, by claiming he is her brother. When the jealous Morris learns the truth, he assigns Terry to "get pictures on a ship leaving for Russia" (according to the Paramount pressbook). Ships bound for Russia from New York in 1944 were undoubtedly carrying Lend-Lease supplies, usually on the Murmansk run. With his rival out of the way, Morris can pursue Kelly romantically, although a murder mystery throws a few obstacles in their way.

1019 THE DOUGHGIRLS (WB, Nov) James V. Kern; *genre:* Comedy; *location:* United States; *coding:* AF-Jap, AF-Russ, Hist Am, FDR, FDR-E, Dipl?, Short, Home Fr, Tojo, Jap, Bonds, Stalin, Russ, Prod, Fem Lab, FBI, AF-A, AF-N, AF-MC, AF-AC, Resist, Nazi, US-Russ Coop, AF-W; *relevance:* 3.

This film was based on a stage play, which took the severe housing shortage in Washington D.C. as its comedic basis. Jack Carson, Jane Wyman, John Ridgely, Alexis Smith, Ann Sheridan, and Eve Arden (as a Russian woman sniper) are all forced to share a single hotel suite because of the lack of accommodations. The rooms have also been promised to pompous radio commentator Alan Mowbray. A priest (Russian Orthodox) is finally found who marries Carson-Wyman, Ridgely-Sheridan, and Smith-Craig Stevens (an AAF pilot preparing to go overseas). The OWI had little sense of humor when it came to poking fun at the wartime bureaucracy (of which it was a part): "A complete travesty on Washington in wartime— the housing situation, American women, the inefficiency of government bureaus, the FBI, the foreign celebrities, etc." The Arden character is perhaps the most interesting in the film, although she is rather stereotyped; at one point, she refers to Stalin as "the father of [our] country." In 1943, an actual female Russian sniper toured the United States—female snipers with high "body counts" are also alluded to in *Stage Door Canteen*, q.v., and in *Days of Glory*, q.v.

1020 DRAGON SEED (MGM, Aug) Jack Conway, Harold Bucquet; *genre:* Resistance; *location:* China; *coding:* AF-Jap, Atroc, Hirohito, Resist, Collab, Chi, AF-Chi; *relevance:* 3.

Pearl S. Buck's novel was turned into a 2 1/2 hour film with, as usual for Hollywood,

Caucasians taking all major Chinese roles. The film covers the period during which the Japanese invasion of China was escalating. Literate peasant Katharine Hepburn can see what is coming, but her fellow villagers (including Turhan Bey as her husband, as well as Walter Huston and Aline MacMahon) have to learn about atrocities and repression first hand. Akim Tamiroff collaborates with the invaders. Hepburn poisons a group of Japanese officers, and the whole village burns their crops and moves away, leaving nothing but scorched earth for the Japanese. The political situation in China is avoided almost entirely: no one mentions Chiang Kai-shek and the Nationalists or Mao Tse-tung and the Communists (although one character does paraphrase a statement by Mao). The term "Jap" is not used, with most characters referring to the Japanese invaders as the "enemy," or occasionally as the "devil dwarves" (this was a Pearl Buck trademark; actually, the Chinese characters for "bandit," "Japanese," and "dwarf" are practically identical). As in *Behind the Rising Sun*, q.v., the Japanese are linked with opium: they hand out candy spiked with opium to Chinese children. This was fact-based: beginning with the invasion of Manchuria in 1931–33, the Japanese deliberately revived the opium trade in China, both for profit and to undermine the Chinese people by increasing opium addiction.

1021 ENEMY OF WOMEN (Mono, Nov) Alfred Zeisler; *genre:* Biography; *locations:* Germany, Austria; *coding:* AF-AC, WWI, AF-Ger, Hitler, Goering, Himmler, Stalin, Russ, AF-Ger, Nazi, Goebbels, Ger, Austria, Jew, Rommel, Atroc-Conc, Pol; *relevance:* 3.

This pseudo-biography of Nazi propaganda minister Paul Joseph Goebbels (Paul Andor) deals largely with his pursuit of actress Maria (Claudia Drake). Goebbels arranges to make her a star with Ufa (the major German film studio), then has her father executed in a Nazi party purge when she scorns his advances and marries a young doctor. Maria and her husband flee to Austria, but return to Germany in an attempt to rescue Levine, her Jewish acting teacher. When her husband is arrested, Maria has to agree to become Goebbels' mistress in exchange for his freedom. But after her husband is freed, Maria is mercifully killed in an Allied air raid (saved from a fate worse than death by—death!). In real-life, Goebbels was in charge of the German film industry (among other propaganda functions). Although married, he was romantically linked with a number of Ufa actresses, including Lida Baarova, a Czech who came to Germany in 1936. As usual with most Holly-

wood biographies, actual historical incidents were used, but with little regard for factual accuracy or correct chronology. This film also depicts Nazi persecution of the Catholic church in Germany, something rarely mentioned in Hollywood films. This film was sub-titled "The Private Life of Dr. Paul Joseph Goebbels."

1022 THE EVE OF ST. MARK (TCF, May*) John M. Stahl; *genre:* Training/Combat; *locations:* United States, Philippines; *coding:* AF-Jap, Prod-Farm, Juv?, Draft, Hist Am, Pearl Harb, Fil, Tojo, Jap, AF-A, AF-N, AF-AC; *relevance:* 3.

This film was based on a Maxwell Anderson play produced on Broadway during the 1942-43 season. William Eythe is a farm boy who is drafted in 1940 and sent to the Philippines. When war breaks out, he is in the midst of the desperate fighting, along with a mixed platoon of "all-American" types, including Southern aristocrat Vincent Price. Back home, Eythe's mother and his girlfriend (Anne Baxter) pray for his survival. The squad takes a vote on whether to withdraw or keep up the resistance one more day, and the men agree to stay on. The Japanese attack once again. Eythe is reported missing in action; his commanding officer forwards part of a letter from Eythe to Baxter, adding that Eythe and some of the men escaped the Japanese attack (this ending is much more upbeat than the original play's conclusion). Eythe's younger brother wants to join the Army, but their father says he must stay home and keep the farm operating. The film is somewhat talky and philosophical, betraying its stage origins.

1023 EVER SINCE VENUS (Col, Oct*) Arthur Dreifuss; *genre:* Musical Comedy; *location:* United States; *coding:* AF-A, AF-N, Short, Fem Lab?, Blk, Latin Am, Fr; *relevance:* 1.

Ross Hunter (later a producer) invents a new lipstick, but he and his partners (Billy Gilbert and Fritz Feld) cannot market it on their own. With the assistance of Ann Savage, they convince industrialist Hugh Herbert to produce the cosmetic. Most of the action takes place in and around a cosmetics convention. There are a number of minor topical references in this film, but the omissions are extremely significant: *no* explanation is made for Hunter not being in the armed forces (he is a research chemist, but even the easy way out—saying his "day job" was in a defense plant—is not taken); *no* comment is made on any shortage in the cosmetic industry, and in fact Herbert is specifically identified as the owner of several *idle* factories, which can be opened up to produce the new lipstick (as if this was a priority!).

1024 FACES IN THE FOG (Rep, Nov) John English; *genre:* Drama; *location:* United States; *coding:* Home Fr, Juv, Prod, AF-A; *relevance:* 1.5.

Mary (Jane Withers) and Joe (Eric Sinclair) are two teenagers in love. Joe is falsely accused of a hit-and-run accident, and drops out of school to join the Army. He and Mary get married, but Mary's father does not know this. In an attempt to avenge his daughter's dishonor (the two young people spent the night in a motel together), the father shoots Joe. In order to get her father acquitted, Mary lies about her marriage. One of a handful of non-musical, dramatic films about the effect of the war on the home front. Both Mary and Joe's fathers work in a defense plant, but while Joe's parents still take time out for quality time with their son, Mary's mother and father are self-centered and do not properly supervise their children, leading to the kind of tragedy that occurs in the film.

1025 THE FALCON IN HOLLYWOOD (RKO, Mar*) Gordon Douglas; *genre:* Crime; *location:* United States; *coding:* Fem Lab; *relevance:* 1.

The Falcon travels to Hollywood for a vacation (he seems to spend a lot of time on vacation, especially considering he *has no job*—see also *The Falcon in San Francisco*, q.v.). When an actor is murdered, his ex-wife (Jean Brooks), now a studio fashion designer, is suspected. She is engaged to marry a movie director. The RKO studios served as the "sets" for this film. Veda Ann Borg appears as a wise-cracking female cab driver who helps the Falcon do his sleuthing.

1026 THE FALCON OUT WEST (RKO, Mar*) William Clemens; *genre:* Crime; *location:* United States; *coding:* Short, Ital?, Blk, Latin Am; *relevance:* 1.

A Texas playboy is murdered (with rattlesnake venom) in a New York nightclub. The Falcon (Tom Conway) trails the victim's fiancee back to Texas, and all of the other principals in the cast follow. There is an oblique reference to wartime conservation of fuel, when the Falcon offers to "share the ride" (a common catchphrase) in a stagecoach taking him from the train station to a ranch.

1027 THE FIGHTING SEABEES (Rep, Jan*) Edward Ludwig; *genre:* War Drama/Combat; *locations:* United States, Pacific; *coding:* War Corr, AF-A, AF-Jap, AF-MC, AF-N, AF-Blk, Tojo, Jap, Blk, AF-W, Austral, Jew?, Mil School, Pearl Harb, Russ, Atroc; *relevance:* 3.

Wedge Donovan (John Wayne) is the boss of a construction company which has been sending workers into the Pacific war zone. He is disturbed because his workers are exposed to Japanese fire, but are not allowed to shoot back (since this would make them combatants rather than civilians). Navy commander Bob Yarrow (Dennis O'Keefe) proposes special construction battalions *within* the armed forces, and he asks his girlfriend, reporter Constance Chesley (Susan Hayward), to convince Donovan to go along with the plan. While Yarrow is working on his plan, Donovan and his men (including a Russian-American played by Leonid Kinsky) are sent out again. Constance goes along to write a story about their work. However, when Donovan's men come under sniper fire once more, he issues weapons to them. This impetuous act ruins a military plan to ambush the Japanese troops, and Donovan is forced to admit his error. They return to the United States and the Seabees ("CB" for Construction Battalions) are formed, with Donovan receiving the rank of Lt. Commander. Their next job is the creation of an oil depot on a South Pacific island. The Japanese are present in force, and when Donovan's pal Eddie (William Frawley) is killed by a sniper's bullet, Donovan loads up his bulldozer with dynamite, ramming an oil tank and blowing up the Japanese troops (taking a fatal bullet wound in the process). The film's story of the formation of the Seabees is somewhat at variance with the facts, since organized Naval construction battalions were in action rather early in 1942.

1028 FOLLOW THE BOYS (Univ, Mar*) Eddie Sutherland; *genre:* War Drama; *locations:* United States, Britain, Pacific, Australia; *coding:* WWI, Draft, USO, UN, Pearl Harb, Home Fr, FBI, Latin Am, Jew, AF-Jap, Blk, AF-Blk, V, Hist Am, Jap, Bonds, AF-A, AF-W, AF-N, AF-MC, Short, Austral, Brit; *relevance:* 3.

Tony West (George Raft) is an ex-vaudeville dancer who becomes a Hollywood star through his association with dancer Gloria (Vera Zorina), whom he marries. When war comes, Tony is turned down due to a bum knee; his father, also an ex-vaudevillian, comes up with idea of entertaining the troops in the camps. Tony helps form the Hollywood Victory Committee, which soon develops into an enormous organization operating in the U.S. and overseas. Gloria does not take part in the activities because she is pregnant, although Tony does not know this, and they argue (in turn, Gloria does not know why Tony is not in the Army). Tony sails to Australia with a troupe of performers, but is killed when the ship is torpedoed. Back home, new mother Gloria throws herself into the activities of the Hollywood Victory Committee as a tribute to her late husband. There are many cameo and guest appearances in Universal's answer to *Stage Door Canteen* and *Thousands Cheer*, including the Andrews Sisters, Sophie Tucker, W.C. Fields, and others.

The Delta Rhythm Boys sing "The House I Live In," a song promoting racial and ethnic harmony. Orson Welles, aided by two GIs, saws Marlene Dietrich in half as part of his magic act (her legs stroll off stage by themselves!).

1029 FOLLOW THE LEADER (Mono, June) William Beaudine; *genre:* Comedy/ Drama; *locations:* United States, Pacific; *coding:* Juv, AF-A, Blk, Jew, Jap, Nazi, Musso, Short, Blk Mkt, Draft, Home Fr, Fr?; *relevance:* 2.

This film opens with a bizarre dream sequence in which Glimpy (Huntz Hall) is captured by cannibals (including former East Side Kid "Sunshine" Sammy Morrison) on a tropical island. Glimpy wakes up to find himself in barracks—he and Muggs (Leo Gorcey) are both in the Army. They go home on leave and help clear one of their pals of a false charge of robbery.

1030 FOUR JILLS IN A JEEP (TCF, Mar*) William A. Seiter; *genre:* War Drama; *locations:* Africa, Britain; *coding:* AF-N, AF-AC, AF-Mer?, Arab?, WWI?, USO, AF-W, AF-Brit, AF-A, FDR, Churchill, Latin Am, Nazi, Free Fr, Draft; *relevance:* 3.

Four Hollywood actresses—Kay Francis, Carole Landis, Martha Raye, and Mitzi Mayfair—travel to England and North Africa to entertain the troops. Phil Silvers is their driver. There are guest appearances by Jimmy Dorsey and his band, singer Dick Haymes (later criticized for receiving a draft deferment due to his Argentine citizenship), Alice Faye, Betty Grable, Carmen Miranda, and George Jessel. Landis actually married a soldier she met while on such a tour, and this film depicts the romance (in semifictional form). In one scene, GIs and WACs join the professionals in a musical number.

1031 GANGSTERS OF THE FRONTIER (PRC, Sept) Elmer Clifton; *genre:* Western; *location:* United States; *coding:* AF-W?; *relevance:* 1.

This is a period Western with Tex Ritter, Dave O'Brien, and Guy Wilkerson as the "Texas Rangers." Outlaws take over the town of Red Rock, forcing the townspeople to work in the nearby mines as slaves. The heroes and two women help round up the criminals. *The Motion Picture Herald* saw this film as an allegory about fascism, and felt the women were precursors of the WACS.

1032 THE GIRL IN THE CASE (Col, May*) William Berke; *genre:* Crime; *location:* United States; *coding:* Ger, Prod, Short, Spy-Sab?, FBI?; *relevance:* 1.5.

William Warner (Edmund Lowe) is a practicing lawyer, but his hobby and real love is locksmithing. Playboy Tommy Rockwood arranges to have Warner visit his home, in the hopes the lawyer can open a

steel chest. Warner refuses, but remarks on the resemblance between Rockwood's chest and one which was formerly in the German consulate. Later that night, Warner and his assistant Tuffy sneak into the house and open the chest. Inside is the formula for a new explosive. The next day Warner tries to return the paper to the chest, but is told the house actually belongs to John Heyser, a chemical firm executive. Heyser is Rockwood's step-father. Rockwood was blackmailing the older man, threatening to tip off the government. Heyser murders Rockwood and tries to blame it on Warner; he also tries to claim the formula is really for synthetic rubber. The police arrive in time to arrest the executive and prevent the formula from being turned over to the Axis.

1033 GOING MY WAY (Para, Feb*) Leo McCarey; *genre:* Drama; *location:* United States; *coding:* AF-AC, Ital, Blk, Juv, AF-A, Chi?; *relevance:* 1.5.

Bing Crosby is a Catholic priest sent to St. Dominic's, a run-down parish supervised by Barry Fitzgerald. The church is mortgaged, the parishioners are depressed, and the local young people are on the verge of becoming juvenile delinquents. Crosby organizes a youth choir, and one of his songs ("Swingin' on a Star") becomes a big hit, paying off the mortgage. The singing priest also promotes a romance between the son of the mortgage-holder and a young woman; the young man joins the Army Air Corps, and is sent to North Africa. Things are going well, but the church catches fire and burns down, so Crosby convinces opera star Rise Stevens to take the choir on tour, earning enough money to rebuild the church (although the bishop tells Fitzgerald construction will have to wait until "after the war"). Crosby leaves, his job done. This enormously popular film won the Academy Award for Best Picture, Best Director, Best Screenplay, Best Song, Best Actor (Crosby) and Best Supporting Actor (Fitzgerald).

1034 A GUY NAMED JOE (MGM, Feb) Victor Fleming; *genre:* Fantasy/War Drama; *locations:* Britain, Pacific, United States; *coding:* AF-Ger, Brit, Jap, Chi, AFK-AC, AF-W, AF-N, USO, Postwar, AF-Jap, Nazi; *relevance:* 3.

Unusual fantasy war film starring Spencer Tracy as Pete, an American bomber pilot who is killed attacking a German aircraft carrier (Hollywood fiction: Germany actually never had an operational carrier in action in WWII). His girlfriend Brenda (Irene Dunne), is also a flyer, and she is distraught over his death. Peter, however, goes to heaven and meets the "Boss" (Lionel Barrymore), who in life was a famous military general (there is some indication this character is supposed to represent General Billy Mitchell, an advocate of military air power). Pete is sent back to Earth to give a helping hand to flyers, including the cocky Ted (Van Johnson). Some time later, Ted has been transferred to the Pacific theatre; Brenda (a member of the Women's Ferry Service) and Pete's old friends Al (Ward Bond) and Nails (James Gleason) are also there. Brenda and Ted fall in love, although Brenda is still mourning for Pete. Ted is assigned to bomb a Japanese ammo dump; Pete is jealous, but after the Boss tells him Ted and others like him are "fighting for the freedom of the very air we breathe," Pete agrees to help. In a rather far-fetched climax, Brenda steals Ted's plane (Pete is in the back seat, guiding her) and flies the mission for him, blowing up the ammo dump and successfully returning to base. She finally lets go of Pete's memory, and embraces Ted. Pete walks down the field, hands in his pockets, as the Army Air Corps song plays. This film began shooting in February 1943, but the filming was interrupted for several months when Van Johnson suffered serious injuries in a motorcycle accident. Spencer Tracy urged MGM to wait for Johnson's recovery, and the film was finished in September 1943. Remade (in a contemporary setting) by Steven Spielberg as *Always* in 1989. Note that there is no "Joe" in this film (the title refers to the generic Air Corps' term for an "okay guy").

1035 HAIL THE CONQUERING HERO (Para, June*) Preston Sturges; *genre:* Comedy; *location:* United States; *coding:* Draft, AF-MC, AF-N, AF-A, AF-W, WWI, MacArthur, Hitler, Rommel?, Jap, Prod, Hist Am, Short, Bonds, V, Blk; *relevance:* 2.5.

Preston Sturges' followup to *The Miracle of Morgan's Creek*. Woodrow Lafayette Pershing Truesmith (Eddie Bracken) is the son of a WWI Marine hero, but has been turned down by the armed forces due to his hay fever. Instead, he is a shipyard worker in California, although everyone in his hometown believes he is a Marine. Six real Marines (including William Demarest and Freddie Steele), back from Guadalcanal, overhear his sad story in a bar and convince him to go home posing as a Marine hero to make his mother happy. However, the whole town is caught up in the deception, and Woodrow is proposed as a candidate for mayor. His opponent finds out the truth, but Woodrow himself confesses, an act of honesty that impresses the townspeople so much that they STILL want him for mayor.

1036 THE HAIRY APE (UA, May*) Alfred Santell; *genre:* Drama; *locations:* Portuguese, Atlantic, United States; *coding:* AF-A, Ref, AF-Mer, AF-N?, WWI, Jew, Brit?; *relevance:* 2.

Film version of a Eugene O'Neill play with a thin veneer of war-relevance. Hank (William Bendix) is the chief stoker on the S.S. *Amerigo*, an old freighter preparing to leave Lisbon for New York with war refugees on board. Hank is proud and tough—he boasts that *he* makes the ship go, since his crew fuels the boilers that power the ship. Among the passengers bound for America are Helen (Dorothy Comingore), who works for a relief organization, and her spoiled society friend Mildred (Susan Hayward). There is also an elderly couple, probably Polish Jews from their speech and appearance (the man is a classical violinist). As the convoy pulls out, Mildred flirts with Lazar (John Loder), the second engineer of the ship, who is a friend of Helen's. Mildred coaxes Lazar into showing her the boiler room, where Hank and his men are working furiously to keep the ship up to convoy speed. She is horrified by the spectacle of the sweaty stoker, and calls him a "hairy ape!" This causes Hank profound depression, and his work suffers. The *Amerigo* falls out of the convoy, but reaches New York safely. In the city, Hank finally confronts Mildred and demands to know why she insulted him. She is terrified, and faints, and Hank realizes she is only a woman, that her social status means nothing at this point. He leaves, his self-esteem restored. The S.S. *Amerigo* prepares to sail for Lisbon.

1037 HANDS ACROSS THE BORDER (Rep, Jan) Joseph Kane; *genre:* Western; *location:* United States; *coding:* Latin Am, AF-A; *relevance:* 1.5.

Roy Rogers goes to work on the Adams' family ranch; Kim Adams (Ruth Terry) is trying to win a government contract to supply Army horses, but is opposed by rival rancher Danvers. Roy saves Trigger from being shot as a killer horse, and wins a race (including a "simulated gas attack and combat zone") which clinches the contract for the good guys. The title has little to do with the plot—there is no real cross-border cooperation in the film (Duncan Renaldo has a supporting role as a Hispanic ranch foreman). The final musical production number does feature crossed U.S. and Mexican flags and simulated custom's offices with a painted "border," and lyrics referring to "hands that shake for democracy" and "we find it very easy to be Good Neighbors."

1038 HEAVENLY DAYS (RKO, Aug*) Howard Estabrook; *genre:* Comedy; *location:* United States; *coding:* AF-Raf, Juv, Short, AF-A, AF-N, AF-W, Blk, Ref, FBI, Jap, Neth, Brit, Belg, Fr, Postwar, Hitler, WWI, Hist Am, Home Fr, Pearl Harb, Churchill, Home Def, Czech, Grk, Chi, Russ; *relevance:* 2.

Radio characters Fibber McGee and Molly (Jim and Marian Jordan, married in real life as well as on the show) are invited to Washington, D.C. by one of Molly's relatives. Once there they become involved with the bureaucracy—Fibber, as an "average American" goes to work for a committee dealing with the "postwar situation"—and also adopt a houseful of refugee children from nearly every country occupied or threatened by the Axis.

1039 HENRY ALDRICH, BOY SCOUT (Para, Jan*) Hugh Bennett; *genre:* Comedy/Drama; *location:* United States; *coding:* Prod, Juv, Home Fr, AF-A; *relevance:* 1.

Henry is a Boy Scout patrol leader who accepts a "problem child" into his troop. The boy's father wants his son to straighten up—if he does, the father will relocate his plastics factory to Henry's town. The Boy Scouts reform the trouble-maker, Henry's patrol wins an "E" pennant (usually given to defense plants for excellence in production of war materials), and everyone is happy. Considerable propaganda for democratic ideals as personified by the Boy Scouts; also one reference to "commando tactics."

1040 HENRY ALDRICH'S LITTLE SECRET (Para, June) Hugh Bennett; *genre:* Comedy; *location:* ??; *coding:* Bonds; *relevance:* 1.

Henry Aldrich (Jimmy Lydon) is convinced that his father (John Litel), head of the Child Welfare Board, is making a mistake in charging a young woman with being an unfit mother. When the mother has to leave town to help her husband beat an unfair murder rap, Henry has to care for the baby. In what may have been intended as a parody of *Mr. Smith Goes to Washington* (Col., 1939), Henry filibusters in court to stall for time until the mother can return. A reporter calls in to report on the filibuster, and a War Bonds poster is shown on a wall.

1041 HERE COME THE WAVES (Para, Dec*) Mark Sandrich; *genre:* Musical Comedy; *location:* United States; *coding:* AF-W, Mil School, AF-MC, AF-N, AF-A, V, Fem Lab, Prod, Short, USO, Jap, AF-Jap, Latin Am, Blk?, WWI; *relevance:* 3.

Twins Susie and Rosemary Allison (both Betty Hutton) join the WAVES. Just before they graduate from training camp, the sisters run into old friend Windy (Sonny Tufts), visiting New York while his ship, the USS *Douglas* is being refitted (it had been torpedoed in the Pacific but was not sunk). Windy is friends with popular crooner Johnny Cabot (Bing Crosby), whose father was killed in action on the *Douglas* during WWI. Johnny cannot get into the Navy because he is color blind. Susie is a rabid Johnny Cabot fan, but

Rosemary cannot stand him. When the Navy lowers its physical requirements, Johnny finally enlists and is sent to San Diego for training. Susie and Rosemary are also assigned to the West Coast. Johnny joins the crew of the *Douglas*, still undergoing repairs but nearly ready for action. However, Susie does not want Johnny to ship out ("We need him on the home front!"), so she forges his name to a memo proposing a WAVES-recruiting show. Johnny accepts his assignment reluctantly. Rosemary, who has fallen in love with him, thinks Johnny sent the memo to stay out of combat. However, at the end Johnny and Windy pair off with Rosemary and Susie, respectively, the show is a success, and the two men rejoin the *Douglas*, now sailing back into action. This musical contains a few scenes highlighting WAVES on duty—in one scene, Rosemary is shown working as an air traffic controller, and the climactic musical number features a long montage of actual footage depicting WAVES working as trainers, secretaries, mechanics, and so on—but mostly the WAVES seems to be a way for women to meet cute sailors. The opening song states, "Join the boyfriend who's across the foam, help to bring him back home." *Here Come the WAVES* also includes several Johnny Mercer-Harold Arlen songs which would become classics: "That Old Black Magic" and "Accentuate the Positive" (the latter sung by Crosby and Tufts in blackface).

1042 HEY, ROOKIE (Col, Apr*) Charles Barton; *genre:* Musical Comedy; *location:* United States; *coding:* Draft, AF-A, AF-W, AF-N, USO, Blk, Arab; *relevance:* 3.

This film was based on a real-life touring soldiers' show. Broadway producer Larry Parks is drafted. He is coerced into producing a camp show in just three weeks, despite a lack of funds and minor inconveniences such as basic training, drill, maneuvers, and so on. His girl friend (Ann Miller) arrives with a USO troupe. One of the songs in this film is entitled "It's a Swelluva, Helluva Life in the Army." The musical climax is "He's Got a WAVE in His Hair (And a WAC on His Hands)," and features Ann Miller in a WAC uniform, who tells Parks, "It isn't a costume, it's a uniform—I'm in the Army now."

1043 HI BEAUTIFUL (Univ, Dec) Leslie Goodwins; *genre:* Comedy; *location:* United States; *coding:* AF-A, Postwar, Blk; *relevance:* 1.5.

Patty (Martha O'Driscoll), who works for a real-estate firm, finds soldier Jeff (Noah Beery Jr.) sleeping in the firm's model "postwar home." They eventually fall in love, and Patty's maid Millie (Hattie McDaniels) enters them in a contest as the "Happiest GI Couple." They win, but then have to pretend they are married and have children, a dog, and so on. At the end they decide to get married for real.

1044 THE HITLER GANG (Para, Apr*) John Farrow; *genre:* Biography; *locations:* Germany, Sweden; *coding:* Dipl?, Resist?, Hitler, Ger, AF-Ger, Austr, Atroc, Atroc-Conc?, WWI, League Nat, Himmler, Hess, Musso, Goebbels, Goering, Nazi, Juv, Heydrich, Jew, FDR, Stalin, Churchill, Chiang, AF-Chi, AF-Austral, AF-Russ, AF-Brit, AF-A, AF-N, UN, Fr, Brit, Pol; *relevance:* 3.

Paramount's attempt at a Hitler/Nazi Party biography, covering the period from 1918 to 1934: "in every detail it is true insofar as decency will permit." Adolf Hitler (Bobby Watson, Hollywood's most prolific Hitler impersonator, giving a more restrained performance here) is first seen in a hospital at the end of World War I. He claims he was blinded in a gas attack, but the military doctor attributes his blindness to hysteria. Later, Corporal Hitler is ordered to attend meetings of the German Workers' Party, to determine if the organization can be controlled by the Army leadership. With Army money, Hitler becomes leader of the Party, renamed the NSDAP (National Socialist People's Workers' Party), which gains converts by attacking Jews and Communists. The failed putsch of 1923 exposes Hitler as a coward (he hides in a closet but is later arrested and sent to prison), but he eventually comes to power as "der Fuehrer." The film ends with the 1934 purge of the party's paramilitary branch, the SA (the "Night of the Long Knives") and a montage of events leading up to the outbreak of war and beyond: "from then on we all know what happened." The final shot shows United Nations' soldiers marching ("good men of 55 nations"), symbolizing the battle against Fascism. Hitler and his Nazi associates are portrayed in an extremely negative manner, as weak and flawed human beings rather than monstrous supermen: Hitler is vain, boastful, and superstitious (he consults an astrologer for advice on his future). It is strongly implied that he murdered his 16-year-old niece/mistress Geli (after Himmler, Goering and Goebbels convince him she has been unfaithful). Goering is a drug addict; Goebbels is a scheming toady; Ernst Roehm is a homosexual (hinted at very discreetly). The Nazi movement is largely directed by the German military caste. This excellent political film is almost never seen today, which is a shame, since it is well-produced, written and directed.

1045 HOLLYWOOD CANTEEN (WB, Dec) Delmer Daves; *genre:* Musical/War Drama; *locations:* United States, Pacific; *coding:* Hitler, Blk, USO, Jap, Ital, Ger, AF-A, AF-N, AF-Blk, AF-AC, AF-Chi, AF-Russ, AF-Brit, Jew, Latin Am, AF-Austral, Chi, WWI, Free Fr, Nor, Neth, Den, Grk; *relevance:* 3.

Slim (Robert Hutton) is a wounded GI who returns to the U.S. from New Guinea on leave. On the ship, he meets a fellow soldier, a sergeant (Dane Clark), also wounded in action (Clark's character uses a cane for the rest of the film). After sightseeing in Los Angeles, Slim is told to visit the Hollywood Canteen—"your ticket is your uniform." Along with the other visiting servicemen, he meets stars like Joe E. Brown, Bette Davis, John Garfield, Eddie Cantor, Roy Rogers (and Trigger), the Andrews Sisters, and so on (interestingly enough, not all of these are Warner Bros. contractees). Bette Davis introduces Slim to Joan Leslie. The next day, Slim meets the Sergeant and tells him about the canteen and Joan Leslie, to the older man's disbelief. The two men return to the Canteen the next night, and Slim is the "millionth" serviceman to enter the club, winning a date with Joan Leslie as his prize! They have a wonderful night on the town. The next day, Slim and the Sergeant visit the Warner Brothers' studios, where a jealous Slim watches Joan play a love scene with Zachary Scott. That night, Slim is bid farewell by the crowd at the Canteen, and he says, "I just represent every fellow who's ever come here ... I might have been [from] the British Commonwealth ... a Chinese air cadet ... one of our good friends from Russia" (he also mentions black soldiers, Latin Americans, the Free French, and other Allied nations). Joan does not show up to say goodbye, so he leaves her a note. As his train is preparing to leave, Joan arrives, and Slim tells her he is in love with her. The real Hollywood Canteen, patterned after the Stage Door Canteen in New York, opened in October 1942. Bette Davis and John Garfield were among the organizers, and the final shot of the film is of Davis, saying "Wherever you go, our hearts go with you." Ann Sheridan was offered the Joan Leslie role in this film but turned it down, fearing it would encourage servicemen to believe they would find romance with the stars at the Canteen, rather than merely light refreshments and entertainment. Point of interest: in the REAL Hollywood Canteen, female service personnel were forced to watch the entertainment from the balcony, and were not allowed on the dance floor.

1046 THE HOUR BEFORE THE DAWN (Para, Feb*) Frank Tuttle; *genre:* War Drama; *location:* Britain; *coding:* Prod-Farm, AF-Ger, Brit, AF-Raf, Ref, Austria, Nazi, Spy-Sab, Home Fr, Pacifist; *relevance:* 3.

Franchot Tone is a wealthy young Englishman who has an aversion to killing (when he was young, he accidentally shot his pet dog). His father is a retired general, and his older brother is in the RAF. The family takes in Veronica Lake, a young Austrian refugee who becomes the family governess (for Tone's brother's child). When war breaks out, Tone is assigned to farm work since his status as a conscientious objector prevents him from serving in the armed forces. He marries Lake to prevent her from being evacuated as an enemy alien. However, Lake's true identity as a Nazi spy is exposed when German bombers try to destroy a secret airfield near the Tone estate. Tone kills his traitorous wife, and joins the RAF as a tail-gunner. Based on a novel by Somerset Maugham.

1047 I LOVE A SOLDIER (Para, Aug*) Mark Sandrich; *genre:* Romantic Comedy; *location:* United States; *coding:* Prod, Fem Lab, AF-A?, Nazi, Hitler, Jap, US-Brit Coop, Bonds; *relevance:* 2.5.

San Francisco shipyard welder Paulette Goddard falls in love with war hero Sonny Tufts. But Goddard does not want to marry a soldier during wartime; there is also the minor problem of Tufts' *current* wife, a rich woman whose manufacturer father was "mixed up with big Nazi concerns" before the war. But Tufts finally hears that his wife has divorced him, and he and Goddard tie the knot just before he ships out again. There was some controversy about Goddard's welding attire in this film (whether it was proper or not).

1048 THE IMPATIENT YEARS (Col, Sept) Irving Cummings; *genre:* Romantic Comedy; *location:* United States; *coding:* AF-AC, AF-N, AF-W, Chi, Short, Jap, Home Fr, Postwar; *relevance:* 2.

Andy (Lee Bowman) and Janie (Jean Arthur) knew each other only one day before they were married. The following day, Andy was shipped overseas with the Army. A year and a half later, Andy returns, but although they now have a baby, the couple does not get along well, and they file for divorce. The divorce court judge orders them to reenact the events leading up to their marriage, and this causes them to fall in love all over again. Comedic treatment of what would become a significant social problem after the war—the breakup of wartime marriages.

1049 THE IMPOSTOR (Univ, Feb*) Julien Duvivier; *genre:* Combat; *locations:* France, Africa; *coding:* AF-Fr, AF-Ger, AF-Ital, AF-Free Fr, AF-Blk, Dunkirk, Petain, WWI, Russ, De Gaulle, Nazi, Ref, Blk; *relevance:* 3.

1940: Clement (Jean Gabin) is a Frenchman sentenced to death for killing a police agent during a strike. However, a Nazi air raid allows him to escape from prison, and he assumes the identity of a dead French soldier. Along with a few other men, Clement—now known as Lafarge—boards a freighter destined for Dakar, in Africa. However, the men are inspired by a radio broadcast by Charles DeGaulle, and the ship diverts to French Equatorial Africa, a Free French enclave. Clement—after changing his mind about deserting—distinguishes himself in battle with the Italians, and helps construct a vital airfield. His deception is almost revealed when the fiancee (Ellen Drew) of the dead soldier arrives in Africa, but she allows him to continue when she sees how dedicated he is. However, Clement's imposture is exposed when another soldier arrives with the truth; Clement is reduced in rank and sent to a dangerous sector of the front, where he dies in battle against German troops. Gabin, who missed military mobilization during the German invasion of France in 1939 (he was making a film and was given a temporary deferment), left Vichy France in 1941 and went into exile in Hollywood. After making *Moontide* (TCF, 1942) and this film, he joined the Free French naval forces and served on several ships. In 1944 he transferred to the tank corps, seeing action in France and Germany, and was awarded the Croix de Guerre.

1050 IN OUR TIME (WB, Feb*) Vincent Sherman; *genre:* War Drama; *location:* Poland; *coding:* Jap, AF-Fr, Czech, Appease?, Chamberlain, Dipl?, Stalin, Russ, Pol, AF-Pol, Resist, AF-Ger, Hitler, Goering, Nazi, Nazi-Russ Coop, Brit; *relevance:* 3.

In 1939, two British women, Jennifer (Ida Lupino) and her foolish employer, Mrs. Bromley, arrive in Poland to buy antiques. Jennifer falls in love with Stephen (Paul Henreid), a member of the Polish aristocracy. They marry, and—with the aid of Stephen's uncle Leopold—begin to renovate the family estates, improving the lot of the peasants and instituting progressive management and agricultural methods. When the Nazis attack, Stephen joins his regiment but is wounded and sent home. As the war approaches the family estates, Jennifer, Stephen and Leopold burn the crops and leave to join the Polish forces still fighting the invaders. Among the symbols of Polish resistance to the Nazis in this film are Chopin's "Polonaise" (see *A Song to Remember*, 1945, q.v.), and defiant broadcasts by Warsaw radio: "Death to Fascism!"

1051 IN SOCIETY (Univ, Aug*) Jean Yarbrough; *genre:* Comedy; *location:* United States; *coding:* Fem Lab; *relevance:* 1.

Abbott and Costello vehicle, with the team as plumbers who are sent to a rich neighborhood on a job. The only topical relevance comes in the character of a female cab driver (a female barber is also featured in one scene).

1052 IN THE MEANTIME, DARLING (TCF, Oct) Otto Preminger; *genre:* Romance; *location:* United States; *coding:* Mil Exer, Short, Blk, Hirohito?, Jap, AF-W, AF-Blk, AF-MC?, Pearl Harb, Prod, Fem Lab, Juv, AF-A, Atroc-Conc, V, Home Fr; *relevance:* 3.

Jeanne Crain, the daughter of a rich businessman, marries Army Lt. Frank Latimore. They are forced to live in a seedy hotel near the base where Latimore's tank battalion is stationed. Crain finds it hard to adjust to life in the crowded hotel with its inconveniences and restrictions; she even tries to pull strings to get her husband a safe desk job, and buys a luxurious trailer for them to live in. The couple argues about this, but Latimore apologizes when he thinks Crain is pregnant. She is not, but they reconcile before Latimore is shipped out, and Crain realizes that everyone must make sacrifices if the war is to be won. Clarence Muse appears in the film as the hotel's black porter, whose son is serving in the armed forces. Fairly rare example of a wartime romance dealing with the adventures of a *married* couple (as opposed to a couple who get married or engaged at the *climax* of the film). While Victory Gardens are frequently mentioned in Hollywood films, they are not often shown—this film actually depicts a *communal* garden tended by the hotel's inhabitants.

1053 JAM SESSION (Col, May*) Charles Barton; *genre:* Musical Comedy; *location:* United States; *coding:* Prod, Latin Am, Short, Blk, V, UN, AF-A, AF-N, Ital, Bulg, Grk, Fem Lab, AF-Brit, AF-Neth, AF-Austral, AF-Russ, AF-Chi, AF-Mex; *relevance:* 2.

Ann Miller, a young woman from Kansas, wins a trip to Hollywood, but she cannot get a break in the the industry despite her dancing ability. One of her neighbors is struggling screenwriter Jess Barker. Ann impersonates a stenographer and tells him her life story as the basis for a screenplay. At the end, Ann gets a film role, and she and Barker fall in love. The finale of the film (and the sequence with the most topical relevance) is "The Victory Polka," in which Ann Miller appears as a defense worker (along with various chorus girls) on a factory set, singing "We know what the fight's about—now let's make our machinery shout!" There is a dissolve to chorus girls in various national outfits who dance with soldiers representing various Allied countries. The "No-Name Jive" number features chorus girls in factory worker outfits.

1054 JAMBOREE (Rep, May) Joseph Santley; *genre:* Musical Comedy; *location*

United States; *coding:* Prod-Farm, Fem Lab; *relevance:* 2.5.

Agent Joe Mason (George Byron) wants Freddie "Schnickelfritz" Fisher and his band to get a regular musical spot on the Jarvis radio show, but Jarvis wants to hire Ernest Tubb and his Texas Troubadors instead. Tubb's band members are working for Ruth Cartwright (Ruth Terry) and her sisters on their farm, but they quit and travel to the big city. Joe sends Fisher and his band to work on the farm so they can learn how to play Tubb's style of "rural" music. They do so well that Jarvis's assistant thinks they *are* Tubb's band and tries to hire them, but Ruth will not release them from their jobs on the farm until the crops are in. She refuses to grant them their "certificates of availability," needed to leave a war-related job for another position. After various complications, including a romance between Joe and Ruth, the crops are harvested and Ruth gives Fisher and the boys their release from work. However, Jarvis decides to hire Ruth and her musical sisters for his show, and *both* Tubbs' and Fisher's bands decide to stay on the farm! The concept of "Availability Certificates" was developed by the War Manpower Commission to prevent war workers from leaving jobs in vital industries for higher-paying jobs elsewhere.

1055 JANIE (WB, July*) Michael Curtiz; *genre:* Comedy; *location:* United States; *coding:* Juv, Ital?, Vet, FBI, AF-A, AF-MC, AF-N, AF-W, Draft, Short, WWI, Hitler, Home Fr, Latin Am, Blk, USO; *relevance:* 2.5.

The war has had an impact on the small town of Hortonville: some of the town's young men are in the service, the women join home front organizations like the Red Cross, and so on. But then news comes that the Army has chosen Hortonville as the site for maneuvers. Mr. Conway (Edward Arnold) is opposed to this—he recalls what happened on *his* last furlough in New York before going to France in 1918. And Conway has a teenage daughter, Janie (Joyce Reynolds). The Army does arrive, and Janie neglects her teenage boyfriend Scooper for 19-year-old Army private Dick Lawrence (Robert Hutton). This is repeated all over town, as the Hortonville girls are attracted to "men" in uniform. Dick and Janie plan a romantic evening alone (the adults are at an American Legion dance), but Scooper finds out and spreads the word that a giant party is being held in the Conway home. A grand melee results (and Scooper, who has enlisted in the Navy, gets in a fistfight with Dick), but everything is straightened out. The soldiers pull out the next day, and Conway heaves a sigh of relief—only to spot a train

full of Marines pulling into town! This adaptation of a play spawned a sequel, *Janie Gets Married* (1946).

1056 JOHNNY DOESN'T LIVE HERE ANYMORE (Mono, July) Joe May; *genre:* Comedy; *location:* United States; *coding:* Draft, Blk, Short, AF-A, AF-N, Postwar, Fem Lab; *relevance:* 2.5.

Kathie (Simone Simon) arrives in Washington to work for the war effort, but the girl she was going to room with has gotten married. Instead, Kathie convinces Johnny (William Terry) to sub-let his apartment to her, since he is going in the Army anyway. But Johnny had also given keys to 11 of his friends, male and female, and many of them show up at odd times. Kathie finally marries Johnny when he comes home on leave. An epilogue takes place in 1949. The film includes scenes of a "gremlin" (played by a midget).

1057 KANSAS CITY KITTY (Col, Sept*) Del Lord; *genre:* Musical Comedy; *location:* United States; *coding:* Blk?, Arab?; *relevance:* 1.

Joan Davis and Jane Frazee buy a song publishing firm, only to learn it is involved in a lawsuit over the hit tune "Kansas City Kitty." Another composer claims the song is plagiarized from his "Minnesota Minnie." Eventually, a classical piece pre-dating both pop songs is unearthed. One interesting point about this musical comedy: the OWI recommended, based on a review of the pre-production script, that several incidental war references be *deleted* from the film, since "none of the characters are shown as being concerned with the war." This was apparently not done, and the references remained.

1058 LADIES COURAGEOUS (Univ, Mar*) John Rawlins; *genre:* War Drama; *location:* United States; *coding:* Prod, Eisenhower, AF-Neth, Chi, AF-FT, Pearl Harb, AF-Ger, AF-Jap, AF-A, AF-W, AF-AC, AF-MC, Bonds, Russ, Churchill; *relevance:* 3.

The struggle of the Women's Auxiliary Ferrying Squadron to earn military status is dramatized in this film. The WAFS (later renamed the Womens' Air Force Service Pilots, or WASPS) was formed to release male pilots for combat duty. Their primary mission was to deliver airplanes from factories or airbases to the point of departure for combat. Noted aviatrix Jacqueline Cochran supervised the organization, which eventually numbered nearly 2,000 women flyers, 38 of whom were killed in the performance of their duties. The service was deactivated in December 1944. Loretta Young plays squadron leader Roberta Harper, who wants her organization upgraded from a civilian adjunct to a full branch of the Army; she also wants permission for female pilots to ferry planes outside of the U.S. Various accidents

and snafus jeopardize these goals, but Young finally wins recognition for her female flyers. As the film ends, the women prepare to ferry planes to a Pacific island in preparation for a "big push" against the Japanese.

1059 LADIES OF WASHINGTON (TCF, May*) Louis King; *genre:* War Drama; *location:* United States; *coding:* Isolat, Spy-Sab, AF-W, AF-CG, AF-A?, Blk, Short, Blk Mkt, Home Fr, Prod; *relevance:* 2.5.

The wartime bureaucracy in Washington is again highlighted in this film. Sheila Ryan wants to get even with the married man with whom she had an affair. He works for the government, and an Axis spy (Anthony Quinn) convinces her to steal valuable steel production figures in the man's safekeeping. However, the spy kills a guard and the rest of the plan falls apart. Ryan winds up in a mental institution at the climax. Trudy Marshall is top-billed as a SPAR (female Coast Guard member) friend of Ryan's whose doctor-boyfriend becomes unwittingly involved in the plot.

1060 THE LADY AND THE MONSTER (Rep, Mar*) George Sherman; *genre:* Horror; *location:* United States; *coding:* Short, Czech, Ger?, Latin Am; *relevance:* 1.

Erich von Stroheim plays Professor Franz Mueller in this version of the novel "Donovan's Brain." He removes the brain from the dead body of a financial magnate, but the brain soon begins to dominate von Stroheim's assistant (Richard Arlen), to the dismay of Vera Hruba Ralston. The only overt war reference in this film is an "A" ration sticker on the windshield of a station wagon (this same car appears in a number of other Republic films of the period—the sticker appears in shots of the "real" car, while mockups of the windshield, used for dialogue scenes, do NOT have it).

1061 LADY IN THE DARK (Para, Feb*) Mitchell Leisen; *genre:* Musical; *location:* United States; *coding:* Blk, AF-MC, FDR, Short, Fem Lab?; *relevance:* 1.5.

Lisa Elliott (Ginger Rogers) is the super-efficient editor of "Allure" magazine, assisted by effete photographer Russell (Mischa Auer), and Charlie Johnson (Ray Milland). Lisa thinks she is in love with Kendall (Warner Baxter), a middle-aged married man whose wife will not give him a divorce. Her family doctor suggests that she see a psychiatrist to determine the cause of her depression; she also complains about a song which keeps coming back to her. Eventually, Lisa succumbs to Charlie's attractions, and he takes the upper hand in running the magazine as well. There are three fantasy "dream" sequences in this lavish Technicolor film; in the first, Charlie appears as a Marine Corps sergeant in dress blues, who delivers a message from the President "for national unity." Otherwise, the topical references are very sparse. However, this film may be also seen as a relatively early plea for the postwar *removal* of women from "men's jobs" in the work force, suggesting in no uncertain terms that women get married, stay home, and "have babies."

1062 LADY, LET'S DANCE (Mono, Apr) Frank Woodruff; *genre:* Musical; *location:* United States; *coding:* AF-W, AF-A?, Draft, Latin Am, Ref, AF-CG; *relevance:* 2.

Jerry (James Ellison) promises to find a replacement dance partner for Manuelo, whose former partner joined the SPARs. He finds Belita, who can dance *and* ice skate. When Jerry sees how good Belita is, he sends her to star in another show in Chicago, and loses his job as a result. He is drafted. Later, Belita meets the wounded Jerry in a veteran's hospital and they are reunited. Belita was Monogram's ice-skating answer to Republic's Vera Hruba, and Fox's Sonja Henie (oddly enough, both Belita and Vera Hruba had skating parts in *Ice Capades*, 1941, although the star of the film was Dorothy Lewis, whose career never developed).

1063 LAKE PLACID SERENADE (Rep, Dec) Steve Sekeley; *genre:* Musical; *locations:* United States, Czechoslovakia; *coding:* Hist Am, Blk, AF-W, AF-AC, Brit, Prod?, Czech, Ref; *relevance:* 1.

Vera (Vera Hruba Ralston) wins an ice-skating competition in her native Czechoslovakia, and is invited to skate at the Lake Placid Winter Carnival (where Roy Rogers shows up to sing "Winter Wonderland"). However, when unspecified "enemies" invade her homeland, Vera goes to live with her industrialist American uncle and his two daughters. She also falls in love with Paul (Robert Livingston), who designs airfields for the Army. Vera Hruba came to the U.S. after losing to Sonja Henie in the Olympics skating competition. She later took the name of Ralston (after a breakfast cereal!) and married the head of Republic Pictures, Herbert J. Yates. The oddest thing about *Lake Placid Serenade* is its reluctance to "name names"— not only are the Germans never mentioned, but the war in Europe (the film is presumably set in 1939) is only referred to obliquely, as "the situation over there." And this in a 1944 film!

1064 THE LAST HORSEMAN (Col, Oct*) William Berke; *genre:* Western; *location:* United States; *coding:* Home Def; *relevance:* 1.

Period Western about cattle rustling, etc., with one topical (albeit anachronistic) joke: after he and sidekick Dub Taylor have been knocked out in a brawl, hero Russell Hayden says, "We were caught in a blackout."

1065 THE LAST RIDE (WB, Sept*) D. Ross Lederman; *genre:* Crime; *location:* United States; *coding:* Short, Home Fr, Blk Mkt; *relevance:* 2.

Police detective Harrigan (Richard Travis) is assigned to the case of a black market tire ring. He learns his younger brother and a crooked police captain are in on the racket. Harrigan pretends to take a bribe and is suspended from the force—he joins the gang, but is exposed. His younger brother saves him at the cost of his own life, and the black market in tires is smashed.

1066 LAURA (TCF, Oct*) Otto Preminger; *genre:* Crime; *location:* United States; *coding:* Short; *relevance:* 1.

Detective Mark McPherson (Dana Andrews) is assigned to investigate the murder of Laura Hunt (Gene Tierney). Among the people he interviews are Laura's mentor Waldo Lydecker (Clifton Webb), Laura's fiance Shelby (Vincent Price), and Ann Treadwell (Judith Anderson), who loves Shelby. McPherson falls in love with Laura via her portrait, and is shocked to learn she is actually alive: the murdered girl was someone else. Laura joins the other three people as suspects in the killing, but eventually Lydecker is exposed as the jealous killer. Very minor topical reference (a ration sticker) in this glossy romantic thriller.

1067 LIFEBOAT (TCF, Jan) Alfred Hitchcock; *genre:* War Drama; *location:* Atlantic; *coding:* Fr, War Corr, Ger-Am, Span Civ, Chi, Russ, Brit, Prod, Draft AF-Brit?, AF-Mer, AF-Ger, Hitler, Nazi, WWI, Atroc-Conc, Blk, Czech, Ref; *relevance:* 3.

John Steinbeck wrote the screen story for this film. A small group of people (the usual mix of classes: a millionaire—Henry Hull, a leftist sailor—John Hodiak, a black steward—Canada Lee, a reporter—Tallulah Bankhead, etc.) takes refuge in a lifeboat after their ship is sunk. They pick up the captain (Walter Slezak) of the U-boat that sank them, and—after a discussion—vote and decide to let him live. He betrays their trust by hoarding scarce food and water, and by trying to steer the lifeboat towards a rendezvous with a German submarine-supply ship. He is finally killed by the others. However, they see the German supply ship sunk by an Allied warship, and *another* German (a youthful sailor) is pulled from the ocean, so the debate begins all over again. The OWI was displeased with the original script for this film and requested many changes; for example, the sailor was originally a Spanish Civil War veteran; the millionaire was quoted as wishing to beat the British to the postwar markets in China, etc. These and other sections were altered or entirely removed to placate the government agency.

1068 LOST ANGEL (MGM, Jan) Roy Rowland; *genre:* Comedy/Drama; *location:* United States; *coding:* Jap, Chi, Kor, Juv; *relevance:* 1.

Margaret O'Brien is an orphan who has been raised "scientifically" by a group of doctors. After she's interviewed by reporter James Craig, she decides to run away and experience the outer world he told her about. Craig is forced to care for her when she shows up, and O'Brien repays him by promoting a romance between the newspaperman and Marsha Hunt. There are a few topical references: for example, child prodigy O'Brien knows the date of Japan's occupation of Korea.

1069 MADEMOISELLE FIFI (RKO, July*) Robert Wise; *genre:* Historical Drama; *location:* France; *coding:* AF-Ger, Fr, Resist, Collab; *relevance:* 2.

One of producer Val Lewton's few non-horror films for RKO, this was based on two stories by Guy de Maupassant: "Boule de Suif," and "Mademoiselle Fifi." During the Franco-Prussian War (1870-71), a group of French travelers is detained by Prussian soldiers. The Prussian commander orders Simone Simon, a humble laundress, to dine with him, although she hates the invaders of her country. Her traveling companions prevail upon her to accept so their trip can continue, but afterwards they shun her for "fraternizing" with the enemy. When the coach reaches its destination, Simone learns the girls at the laundry where she works are going to a Prussian army party. To avoid losing the military's business, Simon is forced to accompany them. At the party, she kills the Prussian officer she had met before. Meanwhile, one of the other stage passengers kills a Prussian soldier. He leaves to join the resistance, while Simon takes refuge in the village church. Fairly faithful adaptation of the two stories, although a deliberate effort is made to draw parallels between the Prussians and the Nazis, thus making the film a sort of allegory about the contemporary occupation of France.

1070 MAISIE GOES TO RENO (MGM, Sept) Harry Beaumont; *genre:* Comedy; *location:* United States; *coding:* Vet?, Bonds AF-W, AF-N, AF-MC, Short, FBI, AF-A Prod, Fem Lab, Draft; *relevance:* 2.

Maisie (Ann Sothern) is ordered to take a vacation from her job as a welder in a defense plant (she has developed a nervous twitch in her eye, which proves very embarassing since all of the men workers think she is winking at them). She goes to Reno and meets a soldier whose wife (Ava Gardner) is intent on divorcing him. However, it is all part of a plot by Gardner's relatives to gain control of her fortune. Maisie plays

Cupid and reunites the couple, falling for a demobilized war hero (John Hodiak) herself.

1071 MAKE YOUR OWN BED (WB, May*) Peter Godfrey; *genre:* Comedy; *location:* United States; *coding:* Short, AF, Spy-Sab, Hitler, Nazi, Prod, Home Fr, FBI; *relevance:* 2.5.

Jerry (Jack Carson) is a private eye hired by wealthy manufacturer Whirtle (Alan Hale) to "pose" as a butler and protect him from Nazi spies. Jerry's girlfriend Susan (Jane Wyman) is also hired, as a maid. However, Jerry and Susan do not know that Whirtle made up the whole story to get around the shortage of domestic help: he wants them to be *real* servants. But real spies and saboteurs become involved in a plot to steal Whirtle's munitions plant plans, and the FBI is finally called in to save the day.

1072 MAN FROM FRISCO (Rep, Apr*) Robert Florey; *genre:* War Drama; *location:* United States; *coding:* Prod, Fem Lab, AF-N, Ital, Russ, Latin Am, Pearl Harb, Draft; *relevance:* 2.5.

In the period before Pearl Harbor, Matt Braddock (Michael O'Shea) develops a plan to build pre-fabricated ships. His ideas run into opposition, until the Japanese attack puts the pressure on the shipbuilding industry. Various personal and technical problems intervene (including references to housing problems for defense workers, and the problem of child care for war workers), but Matt's process wins out, and at the end of the film he leaves to start new shipyards across the country. Real-life industrialist Henry Kaiser is the man credited with developing the "Liberty Ship" concept that Matt utilizes in this film. Kaiser's shipyards produced 30% of total U.S. tonnage in 1943; over 2700 Liberty Ships were built between 1941 and 1944.

1073 MARINE RAIDERS (RKO, June*) Harold Schuster; *genre:* Training/Combat; *locations:* United States, Australia, Pacific; *coding:* AF-CG, Chi, USO, AF-Jap, AF-N, AF-MC, AF-W, AF-A, Austral, AF-Austral, Tojo, Jap, Atroc, Pearl Harb, Bonds, Hitler; *relevance:* 3.

In September 1942, U.S. Marines are fighting on Guadalcanal. Robert Ryan captains a group of "paramarines," and his group is assigned to assist Pat O'Brien's regular Marines in an attack on Japanese reinforcements, recently landed by barge. Ryan temporarily loses control of himself when his lieutenant—caught behind enemy lines—is discovered tied between two trees, minus his hands and feet. Ryan blindly rushes toward the Japanese, wiping out a machine gun nest before O'Brien catches up, slapping him and ordering him to return to his men. After nu-

merous assaults, the Marines finally "annihilate" the Japanese troops. The Marines are relieved by Army troops in November 1942, and are sent to Australia for a rest. On his first day in Australia, the embittered Ryan meets Australian WAAF Ruth Hussey. They go for a drive into the countryside, where they fall in love. Although Ryan is reluctant to propose marriage since he knows he will soon be returning to combat, Hussey insists she wants to take the risk. However, during a Japanese bombing attack, Ryan is slightly wounded. O'Brien, learning of Ryan's romance with Hussey and misunderstanding, has his friend placed on a transport back to the U.S. This causes a rift between the two men. Back in San Diego, Ryan and O'Brien are assigned to train new Marines; when their outfit is ordered to ship out, Ryan is nearly left behind because the commanding general fears his experiences on Guadalcanal have made him unstable. O'Brien vouches for him; in Australia, Ryan and Hussey are reunited and married, and they make up with O'Brien. The Marines are sent to capture a Japanese-held island, and after much fighting manage to establish a beachhead. Hussey waits in Australia, doing her part to hasten the end of the war and her permanent reunion with Ryan.

1074 MARK OF THE WHISTLER (Col, Oct*) William Castle; *genre:* Crime; *location:* United States; *coding:* Short, AF, Russ; *relevance:* 1.

Richard Dix reads a newspaper story about unclaimed bank accounts. He is broke, but he figures out a way to pose as one of the depositors, and collects nearly $100,000. However, the real owner of the money had some enemies, and they nearly kill Dix—thinking he *is* that person—before they are foiled. There are only a few very minor topical references in this film: a poster featuring a serviceman in a drugstore window, and an oblique reference to the difficulty in obtaining transportation (in this case, a ticket on a train).

1075 MARRIAGE IS A PRIVATE AFFAIR (MGM, Oct) Robert Z. Leonard; *genre:* Romance; *location:* United States; *coding:* AF-AC, AF-W, AF-N, Prod, Short, Latin Am, Blk, Postwar?, Bonds, Austral; *relevance:* 2.5.

Lana Turner marries John Hodiak, an Army flyer. But when Hodiak is discharged from the service so he can supervise lensmaking at his factory, Turner finds out that being a housewife and expectant mother is not so glamorous. Lana is also attracted to former suitor James Craig, who is still in the service. Hodiak pulls strings to get back into the Army, and leaves for Australia. Turner changes her mind about divorce, and they patch things up via long-distance telephone.

Although Hollywood paid lip-service to the importance of industry in winning the war, few films dealt with men running the war plants—most male characters, as in this film, saw military service as the only way to "honorably" serve their country.

1076 THE MASTER RACE (RKO, Sept*) Herbert J. Biberman; *genre:* War Drama; *locations:* Belgium, Germany; *coding:* AF-A, AF-Ger, Resist, Belg, Jew, Ger, UN, US-Brit Coop, AF-Brit, AF-Russ, Collab, Spy-Sab?, Hitler, Nazi, Atroc-Conc, Atroc, Postwar, WWI, POW, US-Russ Coop; *relevance:* 3.

After the Allied landings in Normandy in June 1944, the Third Reich realizes it is doomed. Plans are made for fanatic Germans to go underground and plant the seeds of the next generation. One of these is Colonel Von Beck (George Coulouris), who shoots himself in the leg and impersonates a Belgian prisoner in a concentration camp. When the camp is liberated, Von Beck is allowed to return to "his" village, where he takes up residence with the wife of a dead Belgian collaborator. Administering the town are the U.S. Army commander, Major Phil Carson (Stanley Ridges), and his British counterpart; they are aided by a Russian Army doctor who was an inmate in the Nazi prison camp. A subplot involves Resistance fighter Frank (Lloyd Bridges), who returns "from the hills" to discover that his sister was raped by a Nazi soldier and has borne a child; Frank's girlfriend is the daughter of the dead collaborator. Von Beck, maintaining his Belgian disguise, tries to sow anti–Allied sentiment among the townspeople. The prison barracks where Nazi prisoners are kept is set afire at Von Beck's urging, and the undercover man also kills the collaborator's widow when she threatens to expose him. Von Beck is exposed anyway, when survivors of the fire recognize him as a fellow German; he makes a speech warning the Allies that "once again we are allowing you to *temporarily* take over your towns, your countries ... the third world war will hold no surprises for us." Major Carson replies: "We're not going to let you contaminate our lives any longer." Von Beck is tried and shot as a "spy" (the German surrender occurs during the film, and someone remarks "the war is half over," so presumably Von Beck's execution was legal). There are some similarities between this film and Samuel Fuller's *Verboten!* (coproduced by RKO shortly before it went out of business in 1959; the wartime "...-" logo appears on the release prints).

1077 MEET MISS BOBBY SOCKS (Col, Oct) Glenn Tryon; *genre:* Musical Comedy; *location:* United States; *coding:* Juv?, AF-A, Chi; *relevance:* 1.

Don (Bob Crosby) is discharged from the Army after being wounded in action. He comes back to the U.S. and looks up the girl who wrote him love letters while he was overseas, and who promised to get him work as a radio singer when he returned. Don is shocked to discover Susie (Louise Erickson) is only 15 years old, and has no way to get him a job. However, he is happy to meet Helen (Lynn Merrick), Susie's attractive older sister. Meanwhile, Susie and her friends plot a campaign to establish Don as the crooner idol of the teen set. Don reveals his true age (30) to Susie, and she decides to stick with her teenage boyfriend; Don and Helen get together.

1078 MEET THE PEOPLE (MGM, Apr*) Charles Reisner; *genre:* Musical Comedy; *location:* United States; *coding:* Nazi, Prod, Fem Lab, Hitler, Musso, Ital?, FDR, AF-A, Collab, Russ; *relevance:* 2.

Dick Powell's play about life in a shipyard has been overly glamorized by its female star, Lucille Ball. Powell suggests she work in a real shipyard to see what life is really like. Ball does, but then gets caught in a job freeze and cannot quit (see *Jamboree,* q.v.). The play is finally produced as a factory show to celebrate the launching of of a new Liberty ship. Spike Jones and his City Slickers entertain the workers with a song entitled "Schickelgruber," in which a Mussolini impersonator sings to a chimpanzee made up to resemble Adolf Hitler: "What's-a happened to the bigga-blitz ... put the skids on the Fritz.... You say you make-a me king some day, and now it seems Mussolini-a Queen of the May."

1079 THE MERRY MONAHANS (Univ, Sept) Charles Lamont; *genre:* Musical; *location:* United States; *coding:* WWI, Bonds; *relevance:* 1.

1899: Vaudeville performer Pete Monahan (Jack Oakie) is tricked into marrying chorus girl Rose, although he really loves his partner Lillian (Rosemary DeCamp). Pete's two children from this marriage eventually grow old enough to join the act, as the Three Merry Monahans. In 1917, Pete's son (Donald O'Connor) meets the widowed Lillian's daughter (Ann Blyth), and eventually the former partners are reunited. The film concludes with the combined acts performing at a Liberty Bond rally in 1918.

1080 MILLION DOLLAR KID (Mono, Feb) Wallace Fox; *genre:* Comedy; *location:* United States; *coding:* Short, AF-AC, AF-W, AF-Free Fr?; *relevance:* 1.5.

The East Side Kids save a rich man from a mugging. In gratitude, he allows them to use the gymnasium in his home. His older son "won't be using it for some time now" because he is "overseas, flying for Uncle

Sam." The man's younger son does not go in for athletics—in fact, he is a member of the mugging gang. The news that his older brother was killed in action, and a well-intentioned thrashing by Muggs, combine to straighten out the young man, who joins the East Side Kids' club. In a sub-plot, the rich man's daughter is planning to marry Lt. Andre Dupree, apparently a Free French officer (the term "Free French" is never used, however). But the Kids learn Andre is actually a con man scheming to marry into the family fortune. He is exposed. There are a number of references to rationing and shortages, as well.

1081 MINISTRY OF FEAR (Para, Oct*) Fritz Lang; *genre:* War Drama; *location:* Britain; *coding:* Churchill, AF-Brit, Austria, Spy-Sab, Brit, Nazi, Short, Ref, Home Def, Collab?; *relevance:* 3.

Ray Milland wins a cake ("made with real eggs") at a bazaar held by the "Mothers of Free Nations." On the train back to London, a blind man hits him and steals the cake, but is then hit by a bomb and killed. Milland visits the headquarters of the organization, which he thinks may be the front for a Nazi spy ring. He meets Carla (Marjorie Reynolds) and her brother Willi. Milland finds a piece of microfilm near the spot where the blind man was blown up, proving his case. Carla realizes her brother is a Nazi spy, and kills him before he can kill Milland.

1082 THE MIRACLE OF MORGAN'S CREEK (Para, Jan*) Preston Sturges; *genre:* Comedy; *locations:* United States, Italy, Germany; *coding:* Jew, AF-Ger, AF-A, AF-W, Bonds, Hitler, Musso, FBI, WWI, Short, V, Jap, Russ, FDR, MacArthur; *relevance:* 2.5.

Trudy Kockenlocker (Betty Hutton) tells her father she is going to the movies with meek, 4-F Norval Jones (Eddie Bracken). Instead, she goes to a farewell dance for a group of soldiers, and comes home the next morning with no memory of what happened. Gradually, she recalls that she married one of the soldiers (using a false name), and when she learns she is pregnant, tries to marry Norval instead. After various complications, Norval is accused of bank robbery and arrested; Trudy has sextuplets on Christmas Eve (Hitler and Mussolini are outraged when they learn of this). The governor (Brian Donlevy, repeating his role from *The Great McGinty,* 1940) makes Norval an officer in the state militia, and declares that Trudy and Norval were married all the time. For many years, the word "pregnancy" and any depiction of a pregnant woman were taboo in Hollywood. *The Miracle of Morgan's Creek* manages to work around these handicaps (as well as indicating Trudy was actually *married* to the unknown sol-

dier, rather than being pregnant out of wedlock) in a very equivocal manner.

1083 MISTER SKEFFINGTON (WB, May*) Vincent Sherman; *genre:* War Drama; *location:* United States; *coding:* Atroc-Conc, Russ, Jew, Nazi, WWI, AF-A, AF-Fr, AF-Ger, Am Vol, Brit, Ger, Hist Am; *relevance:* 2.

1914: Fanny Trellis (Bette Davis) marries rich Jewish broker Job Skeffington (Claude Rains) for his money. During WWI, Fanny's irresponsible brother joins the Lafayette Escuadrille and is killed; Fanny blames her husband for this. Even the birth of her daughter does little to restrain Fanny's frivolous ways, and eventually Job takes his daughter to Europe to live. Years pass; when WWII breaks out, Fanny's daughter returns to the U.S. and is married. Job is reported to be in a Nazi concentration camp. One day, Fanny—now old and alone—learns Job has returned. She is ashamed to meet him, but when she does she finds he is blind, and thus will always see her as the beautiful young woman he married. Because of its excessive length (more than 2 hours), twenty minutes were deleted from this film after its New York premiere. A significant part of this deleted footage included a scene in which a WWI newsreel is screened for a private audience: comments about the goose-stepping German troops are made, and the Kaiser is hissed.

1084 MISTER WINKLE GOES TO WAR (Col, July*) Alfred E. Green; *genre:* Training/Combat; *locations:* United States, Pacific; *coding:* AF-MC, AF-Jap, AF-A, Draft, USO, Home Fr, Prod, Jap, AF-Blk, Short, Hist Am; *relevance:* 3.

In 1942: Wilbert Winkle (Edward G. Robinson) is a meek, middle-aged, henpecked bank clerk who is drafted at the age of 44. After passing the physical and going through basic training, he becomes a new man, even refusing to leave the Army when the draft age is lowered to 38. Winkle is sent to the South Pacific with his unit, and loses several of his friends in battle. He drives a bulldozer over an enemy foxhole, is wounded, decorated, and discharged with honors. Back home, he shows he is still a modest man. Interesting film dealing in part with the vagaries of the draft system, which would (at least in this film) take a married man of 44 during the first year of the war.

1085 MOONLIGHT AND CACTUS (Univ, Sept) Edward F. Cline; *genre:* Musical Comedy; *location:* United States; *coding:* AF-Mer, Fem Lab, Short?, Latin Am?; *relevance:* 2.

Merchant Marine officer Tom Seidel visits his ranch with some friends while on leave. He learns the ranch is now being operated by women, including the Andrews Sisters and Lou (Elyse Knox). Cattle are disappearing, but it is not rustlers: Tom's eccentric neighbor (Leo Carrillo) has been taking them for "safe-keeping" on his ranch (which is presumably staffed by men). Before his leave expires, Tom marries Lou. One of the songs in the film is "Send Me a Man, Amen," and another is entitled "Home" (possibly a reference to soldiers thinking of coming home).

1086 MURDER, MY SWEET (RKO, Dec*) Edward Dmytryk; *genre:* Crime; *location:* United States; *coding:* Short, Bonds; *relevance:* 1.

This film adaptation of Raymond Chandler's "Farewell, My Lovely" was completed in 1944 and actually released under the novel's title in December, but was withdrawn and re-titled (purportedly because some felt the original title, combined with Dick Powell's presence in the leading role, could mislead audiences into expecting a musical!) for its official release in early 1945. Private detective Philip Marlowe (Powell) is engaged by ex-con Moose Malloy to find a woman named Velma. He has no luck, but is later hired to help ransom some jewels stolen from Mrs. Grayle (Claire Trevor). The deal goes bad, and Marlowe's companion is murdered. He tries to locate the jewels and the murderer, then discovers Velma and Mrs. Grayle are one and the same. Malloy catches up with his faithless girlfriend, and they kill each other. There are a few minor topical references in this film, including a Bonds poster, and a gas ration sticker on a car.

1087 MUSIC IN MANHATTAN (RKO, July*) John H. Auer; *genre:* Musical Comedy; *location:* United States; *coding:* Latin Am, AF-A, AF-N, AF-W, AF-AC, Prod, Jap, Short; *relevance:* 2.5.

Anne Shirley is a musical comedy star who has to get to Washington to put on a show. In order to get a priority seat on an airplane, she poses as the wife of Philip Terry, an Army flyer who is to receive the Congressional Medal of Honor. However, the plan backfires and Anne must agree to pose as Terry's wife (in fact, they actually DO marry, intent on having the ceremony annulled later). But true love steps in and they decide to stay hitched.

1088 MY BEST GAL (Rep, Mar) Anthony Mann; *genre:* Musical; *location:* United States; *coding:* Draft, AF-A, USO, Bonds?; *relevance:* 2.

Kitty (Jane Withers) is from a long line of stage performers, but she and her grandfather Danny (Frank Craven) are now reduced to working in a drugstore near Broadway. Kitty meets Johnny (Jimmy Lydon), a young playwright who has written a musical about the young talent which congregates

at the drugstore, hoping for a break. Johnny tries to sell his show to producer Hodges, but withdraws when Hodges insists on using established talent instead of the youngsters themselves. Johnny changes his mind when he learns Danny needs expensive medical treatment; Kitty and the others are angry at first, but forgive Johnny (who has meanwhile been drafted into the Army) when they learn the truth. They convince Hodges to use them in the show by threatening to sue him, and the show is a big hit. When it goes on a Victory Tour, Johnny is in the audience at an Army camp performance, applauding his friends.

1089 MY BUDDY (Rep, Oct) Steve Sekely; *genre:* Crime; *locations:* United States, France; *coding:* AF-A, Postwar, WWI, Vet, AF-Ger, Ital, Blk, AF-N, AF-MC, AF-W; *relevance:* 2.

This film's title was taken from a popular song of 1922, which was revived in 1940 and then became a wartime hit. Father Donnelly (John Litel, with an Irish accent) tells the Post-War Planning Committee about Eddie (Don Barry), a WWI veteran: Eddie comes back from the war to find his mother living in poverty. He wants to get a job and marry his girlfriend, but no work is to be found. Finally, Eddie gets a job with bootlegger Oberta. Eddie is double-crossed by the gangster and sent to prison for 5 years. When he gets out, he forms his own gang and goes after Oberta's mob. Oberta is killed but Eddie is betrayed by a woman and shot down by the police. Litel warns the committee that they must plan for the post-WWII period to avoid creating more Eddies, and that every veteran must be guaranteed a job. A montage at the finale depicts marching men and women of the various armed services, while Senator Henry (Jonathan Hale) says "All of our gallant men and women in the armed forces can rest assured that the people of America ... will not let them down!" The plot of this film is somewhat reminiscent of *They Gave Him a Gun* ('37), which featured Franchot Tone as a WWI veteran turned criminal. Government plans to restore veterans to their pre-war occupational status resulted in the discharge of a number of women workers who had assumed the roles in wartime.

1090 MY PAL WOLF (RKO, Sept*) Alfred Werker; *genre:* War Drama; *location:* United States; *coding:* AF-A, Nor, Blk, Prod, Short; *relevance:* 2.5.

Gretchen Anstey's parents are too busy to care for her (her father is in war work, her mother runs a cosmetics firm), so the little girl lives on a farm in Virginia with stern governess Miss Munn. Gretchen finds Wolf, a German shepherd, in the woods near the

farm and befriends him. Miss Munn learns the dog has escaped from an Army training center, and has him picked up. The girl and some friends go to the center and Wolf escapes once more. Gretchen and Wolf travel to Washington, where she appeals to the Secretary of War in person. He tells her Wolf is needed for the war effort (the local children make a service star to hang out for him—during the war, banners hung on doors with blue stars indicated that a member of the household was in the service; a gold star showed that the family had lost a member in the war), but Gretchen gets a cute puppy to take his place (and Miss Munn gets fired). A previous exploration of this theme occurred in *War Dogs* (1942, q.v.).

1091 THE NAVY WAY (Para, Feb*) William Berke; *genre:* Training; *location:* United States; *coding:* AF-N, AF-W; *relevance:* 2.

This film details the training of a group of Navy recruits at the Great Lakes Naval Station. Among them: Johnny (Robert Lowery), an Italian-American boxer who is drafted just before he gets a shot at the title; Mal (Bill Henry), a rich young man; Frankie (Roscoe Karns), who enlists in anger after he sees his girlfriend kissing a soldier (it was really her cousin!); Steve, a cowboy whose son was recently killed in action; and Billy, a young man whose Naval officer father was killed in the First World War. Johnny's bad attitude causes friction in his unit, and he becomes Mal's romantic rival for the affections of pharmacist's mate Ellen (Jean Parker). After graduation from boot camp, Johnny—feeling betrayed by the news of Ellen's engagement to Mal—gets drunk and overstays his leave. Mal tries to bring him back to camp, but they are both arrested by the Shore Patrol. Johnny takes the blame so Mal is excused. It appears that Johnny will face a court martial and will not be able to join his pals when they ship out, but Mal's tearful contrition convinces the commanding officer to forgive the young man's irresponsible actions and poor record. Mal marches off with the others at the conclusion. This is an unusual film which not only shows Naval draftees (a rarity in Hollywood films), but also depicts Johnny as a *very* bitter and disgruntled "victim" of the draft. In contrast, another member of the unit is 56-year-old Lacey, who lied about his age so he could enlist (and who has six children, including sons in the Army and Navy). When Lacey proves physically incapable of carrying out his duties, he resigns rather than endanger his comrades by his weakness.

1092 NONE BUT THE LONELY HEART (RKO, Oct*) Clifford Odets; *genre:* Drama; *location:* Britain; *coding:* WWI?, Russ, Jew, Brit; *relevance:* 1.5.

This film is chiefly set in the period immediately prior to WWII, but in the final scenes there are oblique references made to the conflict. Cary Grant plays Ernie Mott, a shiftless young man from the slums of London. His mother (Ethel Barrymore) runs a second-hand merchandise store and cares about him, although the two rarely see each other. Grant takes up with a London gang, but soon quits. He discovers his mother is dying of cancer, and moves back home to help her. When Barrymore learns she is dying, she begins to traffic in stolen goods in order to lay away some money for her son. She is arrested and dies in the prison hospital, but not before she and Grant reconcile their differences. Grant tells drifter Barry Fitzgerald (whose son died in WWI) he is going off to "fight with the men who'll fight for a human way of life."

1093 NONE SHALL ESCAPE (Col, Feb*) Andre de Toth; *genre:* War Drama; *locations:* Germany, Poland; *coding:* Czech, Austria, AF-Pol, AF-Ger, Atroc-Conc, Atroc, Postwar, Hitler, Nazi, Pol, Jew, WWI, Blk, Russ, POW, Chi, Resist?, UN; *relevance:* 3.

Unusual but excellent film set in the postwar period which anticipates the war crimes trials held in Nuremberg and Japan: Nazi General Grimm (played by Alexander Knox, who also had the title role in *Wilson*, q.v.) goes before a war crimes tribunal. Grimm was a schoolteacher in the town of Litzbark, near the Polish border. After losing a leg in WWI, he comes home but his fiancee postpones their wedding. Grimm attacks a young girl and is driven out of his village, losing an eye in the process. He joins the Nazi party in Munich. When his brother protests, Grimm has him placed in a concentration camp. Later, Grimm returns to Litzbark as a general, with his nephew Willie as his aide. Willie is upset by his uncle's actions, which include deportation of the Jews, and the sentencing of Willie's girlfriend to work in the local "officer's club" (i.e., brothel). Grimm shoots his nephew (in the back, naturally) when Willie dares denounce the Nazis. The film ends with the trial judge warning that final victory will only be achieved if justice is served. As far as is known, this is the only Hollywood film made during the war which directly depicts the mass deportation of Jews to concentration camps. In one significant scene, Jews (wearing Star of David armbands) are urged by their rabbi to resist their forced deportation in railroad cars, and are instead shot down by Nazi guards. There is some evidence that Lester Cole—who wrote the film's screenplay—was influenced by an article written by Ben Hecht in early 1943 ("Remember Us"), which was then turned into a stage presentation entitled "We Will Never

Die" (it was produced in March 1943 in Madison Square Garden, and the following month in Constitution Hall, Washington, D.C.). The third episode of the program features three Nazis facing a postwar tribunal for their crimes, and the Jews they murdered help indict them.

1094 ONCE UPON A TIME (Col, Apr*) Alexander Hall; *genre:* Drama; *location:* United States; *coding:* AF-A, AF-N, Draft, AF-W, AF-Brit, Fem Lab, Prod?, Home Fr, Brit, Chi, FBI; *relevance:* 1.5.

This film begins with an opening title which refers to "a world that is so troubled today and where reality is so grim..." Cary Grant is a theatrical impresario who has fallen on hard times. He stumbles across a young boy (Ted Donaldson) who has a pet caterpillar, Pinky, that "dances" to the tune "Yes Sir, That's My Baby." Grant is greatly impressed and decides to capitalize on the amazing creature (he eventually makes a deal to sell it to Walt Disney to finance a new stage show). Eventually, Grant changes his mind and the caterpillar turns into a butterfly and flies away. Numerous servicemen and women appear in street scenes, and there are several overt references to the war. For example, in one scene a hard-boiled reporter (William Demarest) scoffs at the dancing caterpillar: "Let me know when Pinky puts on a uniform and bombs Tokyo—that's a story I can use." Later, a bomber crew adopts Pinky as their mascot and paints his picture on their airplane.

1095 ONE BODY TOO MANY (Para, Oct*) Frank McDonald; *genre:* Crime; *location:* United States; *coding:* Short; *relevance:* 1.

Jack Haley travels to an old house to sell life insurance to an eccentric millionaire. However, upon his arrival he learns the old man has just died. The heirs are gathered at the mansion for the reading of the will, and more murders occur before the killer is revealed. Bela Lugosi has a humorous supporting role as a butler whose poisoned coffee is repeatedly turned down by the guests. When Haley arrives at the house, the "B" and "A" gas ration stickers on his car are plainly visible (apparently one of these is an older, outdated sticker).

1096 ONE MYSTERIOUS NIGHT (Col, Oct*) Budd Boetticher; *genre:* Crime; *location:* United States; *coding:* UN, Home Fr, AF-W, AF-N, AF-A, Prod?, Short, Chi; *relevance:* 1.5.

Boston Blackie (Chester Morris) investigates the theft of the Blue Star of the Nile diamond, which was on display for the benefit of the Greater United Nations War Fund. Numerous uniformed personnel are seen attending the gem display. Blackie is first in-

troduced working for Manleder's Tool and Die Company, which was identified as a defense plant in the previous film in the series (*The Chance of a Lifetime*, 1943, q.v.). He is commissioned as a special police agent to solve the jewel robbery.

1097 PASSAGE TO MARSEILLES (WB, Feb*) Michael Curtiz; *genre:* War Drama; *locations:* Caribbean, Britain, France; *coding:* Blk, Austria, Vet?, V?, AF-Ger, AF-Raf, Munich, Vichy, Petain, Laval, War Corr, AF-Free Fr, De Gaulle, Hitler, Goebbels, Nazi, WWI, Fr, Collab; *relevance:* 3.

A complex series of interlocking flashbacks tells the story of Humphrey Bogart, a French journalist sent to a Caribbean penal colony for his opposition to the Fascists and the "Munich sellout" of 1938. Bogart and his companions escape and are picked up by a French freighter bound for Marseilles with a load of nickel. The Free French prevent the ship's cargo from falling into fascist hands, despite an attack by a Nazi plane, which is shot down. Bogart machineguns the surviving Nazi airmen on the plane's floating wing—this is not an "atrocity" since it is committed by one of the good guys (however, Warner Bros. had to delete this scene from foreign release prints in order to qualify for an export license from the OWI). The Vichy sympathizers on the ship—led by Sydney Greenstreet as Major Duval (perhaps meant to evoke the memory of Vichy premier Pierre Laval)—try to stop Bogart and his men, but fail. Bogart joins the Free French air force, dropping messages to his wife and child (living on a French farm) as he flies missions over the occupied continent. After Bogart is killed on a mission, American war correspondent John Loder (to whom the story has been told, and who is identified as a U.S. flying ace of the First World War) is assured by the French commander that Bogart's final letter to his son will be delivered.

1098 PASSPORT TO DESTINY (RKO, Jan*) Ray McCarey; *genre:* Adventure; *locations:* Britain, Germany, France; *coding:* Austria?, Hitler, AF-Raf, Goebbels, Atroc-Conc, Home Def, AF-Mer, Resist, Ger, Collab, Brit, AF-Brit, Nazi, Hess, Himmler, AF-Ger; *relevance:* 3.

A British charwoman (Elsa Lanchester), the widow of a British soldier (Charles Laughton, seen only in a photograph), decides to travel to Germany and kill Hitler. She takes a "magic charm" left to her by her late husband, which will protect her from all harm. Getting a job as a charlady in the Berlin Chancellery, Lanchester meets Goebbels, Lord Haw Haw, and Himmler, but does not get the chance to shoot the Fuehrer. During an Allied air raid, she escapes to England in a Luftwaffe plane along with two members of the anti–Nazi resistance. At one point, the Nazis tell Lanchester that her character name—Ella Muggins—sounds "funny." "Not half as funny as Schickelgruber!" Ella replies. This film is also known as *Passport to Adventure*.

1099 PIN UP GIRL (TCF, Apr*) H. Bruce Humberstone; *genre:* Musical Comedy; *location:* United States; *coding:* Home Fr?, AF-N, AF-A, AF-MC, Blk, Latin Am, Short, V, Jap, Prod-Farm, USO; *relevance:* 2.5.

Betty Grable and a friend are on their way from Missouri to become secretaries in wartime Washington. They stop in New York, and Grable gets a crush on a war hero (John Harvey—for a change, a Navy man instead of a pilot). She tells him she is a big musical comedy star, and has to adopt a second identity (as a mousy stenographer) in order to keep her secret. Eventually, everything is worked out and she becomes the favorite "pin up girl" of the armed forces. The film ends with an extended, non-musical sequence of Grable (in a sky-blue uniform) directing close-order drill, the manual of arms, and precision marching of a group of uniformed women. In Technicolor. One number ("Yankee Doodle Hayride"—sung by Martha Raye) promotes civilian assistance with farm work (a frequent Hollywood topic): "There ain't gonna be no hoedown, until we knock the foe down ... a pair of overalls is a uniform, too." There is also a reference to the OWI (Office of War Information), which oversaw Hollywood productions during the war. The famous photo of Grable in a bathing suit (an artist's rendering is shown behind the credits, and the photo itself appears several times in the film) was allegedly the servicemen's favorite pinup during WWII, and this film plays on her fame in this area (another popular pinup shot was Rita Hayworth, kneeling on a bed in a negligee).

1100 PRACTICALLY YOURS (Para, Dec*) Mitchell Leisen; *genre:* Romantic Comedy; *locations:* United States, Pacific; *coding:* Jap, AF-N, Home Fr, Prod, AF-Jap, Fem Lab; *relevance:* 2.

Dan Bellamy (Fred MacMurray) crashes his plane into a Japanese carrier, sinking it at the cost of his own life. His last words (heard on the radio) are relayed to the U.S.—he would like to return to his job in a typewriter factory, and he would like to kiss Peggy (Claudette Colbert). These sentiments make a posthumous hero of Dan, and Peggy (who still works in the factory, now converted to defense work) becomes the nation's sweetheart. However, it turns out that Dan *survived* the crash, and he returns to the States on furlough (in an amusing scene, Dan watches a newsreel about his "heroic" actions, and is assaulted by indignant theatre patrons

when he makes a wisecrack about the film!). Dan does not have the heart to tell everyone he REALLY said he wanted to kiss "Piggy," his dog! However, Dan and Peggy fall in love and are married on national radio at a ship-launching ceremony.

1101 THE PRINCESS AND THE PIRATE (RKO, Oct*) David Butler; *genre:* Comedy; *location:* Caribbean; *coding:* Jap, Russ, Latin Am, Prod?, AF-Brit; *relevance:* 1.

Bob Hope is Sylvester Crosby (a double joke: Hope's vaudeville name was "Lester," and "Crosby" obviously refers to Bing Crosby, who makes a cameo appearance in the film), an 18th-century ham actor who helps Margaret (Virginia Mayo) escape from a pirate attack, only to land on an island ruled by a ruthless governor (Walter Slezak—frequently cast as a Nazi during this period, as in *Lifeboat*, q.v.). As usual with Hope, there are a number of topical jokes, albeit anachronistic ones this time. For instance, "The Hook" (a pirate leader, played by Victor McLaglen) has a hook that is "made in Japan." There are plenty of cheesecake shots of Virginia Mayo (in anachronistic, revealing costumes) in this Technicolor film. This was Bob Hope's only 1944 film—by this time, he was famous for his overseas troop shows and his regular radio broadcasts from Army bases in the continental U.S. Among his regular troupe were singer Frances Langford and comedian Jerry Colonna. In 1943 alone, Hope's show appeared in England, Tunis, Algeria, Sicily, and on Tarawa in the South Pacific (among other stops).

1102 THE PURPLE HEART (TCF, Feb*) Lewis Milestone; *genre:* War Drama; *locations:* Japan, China; *coding:* AF-Brit, Ger, AF-AC, AF-N, War Corr, Sp, Port, Jap-Am Reloc, Hist Am, AF-Jap, Collab, Hirohito, Jap, Atroc, Jew, MacArthur, Chi, POW, Russ, Latin Am, Ital; *relevance:* 3.

A group of American flyers is captured after their plane (the "Mrs. Murphy") crashes in China (although the film never specifically uses Doolittle's name, this obviously refers to the Doolittle Raid on Tokyo in early 1942). The men are betrayed to the Japanese by a Chinese collaborator (who, after testifying in their trial, is killed in the courtroom by his own son—Benson Fong—an "honorary member" of the Americans' squadron). They are sent to Japan to be tried for war crimes, the Japanese claiming the plane bombed civilian targets in Japan. The U.S. airmen are a typical Hollywood ethnic mixture, including Jewish Lt. Greenbaum (Sam Levene), Italian-American Lt. Canelli (Richard Conte), Polish (or Czech?)-American Lt. Jan Skvoznik (Kevin O'Shea), and various WASPs (among them Dana Andrews and

Farley Granger). Their trial is witnessed by journalists from Axis countries as well as "neutral" nations such as Russia and Portugal. Despite torture and other pressure, the Americans refuse to reveal where their mission originated—although the Japanese say their lives will be spared if they do—and are all sentenced to death. While relatively little torture is shown (it takes place off-screen), the Japanese are portrayed in an extremely negative fashion. For example, when news of the fall of Corregidor reaches the courtroom, the "dignified" Japanese judges and officers go into a screaming frenzy of delight (a scene which the *New York Times* said is a "reminder of the sub-human quality of the enemy"). The film also depicts inter-service rivalry between the Japanese Navy and Army, with each branch attempting to place blame for the raid on the other. Since the Americans will not reveal how their heavily laden bombers managed to reach Japan (taking off from the aircraft carrier *Hornet*), they are sentenced to die, rather than being imprisoned in a POW camp. The men march to their death with dignity, and Dana Andrews warns the Japanese: "It won't be finished until your dirty little empire is wiped off the face of the earth!"

1103 THE RACKET MAN (Col, Jan) D. Ross Lederman; *genre:* Crime; *location:* United States; *coding:* Draft, Ital, Blk, Hist Am, Tojo, Hitler, Short, Blk Mkt, AF-A, FBI; *relevance:* 2.5.

Gangster Matt Benson (Tom Neal) is drafted. His attitude is very poor, and he does not get along with his Italian-American sergeant (Matt refers to him as a "foreign-born monkey"). After the two men have a fight, the sergeant loses his stripes and is sent overseas. When Matt learns his former instructor has been killed in action, the young man becomes a model GI: "Even mopping up the floor is like taking a swing at Hitler and Tojo." Matt is assigned to work undercover in an attempt to break up black market gangs, and is given a false discharge. Matt infiltrates a gang and saves a policeman friend by stepping in front of a bullet, thus dying for his country even though he never went overseas.

1104 RAINBOW ISLAND (Para, Sept*) Ralph Murphy; *genre:* Musical Comedy; *location:* Pacific; *coding:* Jap, AF-Mer, AF-N, AF-Jap; *relevance:* 2.

Three Merchant Marine sailors (Eddie Bracken, Gil Lamb, and Barry Sullivan) are marooned on a Pacific island when their ship is sunk. They commandeer a Japanese plane which lands on the island, but are fired on by U.S. Navy ships who think they are the enemy. The sailors land on Rainbow Island, inhabited by natives and Lona (Dorothy

Lamour), the daughter of an American ship-wrecked years before. The queen of the island and the high priest think Bracken is the reincarnation of their god. Eventually, the sailors, Lona and her father all escape in the Japanese plane. In Technicolor.

1105 RATIONING (MGM, Jan*) Willis Goldbeck; *genre:* Comedy; *location:* United States; *coding:* AF-N, AF-W, Chi, AF-MC, AF-A, AF-CG, WWI, USO, Short, Blk Mkt, Draft, Home Fr, Jap, Prod, Fem Lab; *relevance:* 2.5.

Wallace Beery runs a general store in a small mid-Western town; his nemesis is post-mistress Marjorie Main, who is also head of the local Rationing Board. She runs her one-woman office in a very bureaucratic manner, handing out page after page of forms for the smallest request. Fed up, Beery travels to Washington, where he asks his senator (his WWI commanding officer) to get him back in the Army. The senator instead makes Beery a member of the Rationing Board, under Main's supervision. In order to give his adopted son (now in the Army) a stake so the young man can marry Main's daughter, Beery sells a half-interest in his business to a shifty gas station proprietor, who gets involved in a black market beef ring. Beery manages to uncover the ring and all ends well. Scenes of Beery and others wrestling with government red tape and annoying regulations alternate with patriotic speeches about the necessity of rationing, and the result is a very ambivalent attitude towards the whole rationing system.

1106 RECKLESS AGE (Univ, Nov) Felix E. Feist; *genre:* Musical; *location:* United States; *coding:* AF-W, Blk; *relevance:* 1.

Gloria Jean chafes under the strict supervision of her rich grandfather, so she runs away. She gets a job working as a clerk in one of the stores in a dime store chain owned by her grandfather. The cast list of this film indicates that a "WAC" and a "WAVE" appear in one scene.

1107 ROGER TOUHY—GANGSTER (TCF, May*) Robert Florey; *genre:* Crime; *location:* United States; *coding:* Short, Draft, FBI, Draft Avoid?; *relevance:* 1.

Roger Touhy escaped from prison in October 1942, and was free for more than two months before being recaptured. Fox began shooting their version of his story less than a month later, but lawsuits (Touhy claimed the film would be an invasion of his privacy) and opposition by the Hays Office (which frowned on films about "real" gangsters) delayed the film's release until 1944. One topical point: Touhy's lack of a draft card is one factor leading to his arrest. Preston Foster was cast as the titular character.

1108 ROSIE THE RIVETER (Rep, Apr*)

Joseph Santley; *genre:* Musical Comedy; *location:* United States; *coding:* AF-AC, Prod, Fem Lab, AF-MC, AF-A, V, Latin Am, Bonds, Short, Hist Am, MacArthur, FBI, Spy-Sab; *relevance:* 3.

Housing is so scarce in the town near the Campbell Aircraft Plant that four people have to share one room: Rosie (Jane Frazee) and Vera (Vera Vague), who work the day shift, and Charlie (Frank Albertson) and Kelly (Frank Jenks), who work at night. Rosie's boyfriend is personnel manager at the defense plant, but he breaks up with her when he sees a picture of Rosie kissing Charlie. At the climax, a party is thrown to celebrate the plant's "E" pennant (given for excellence in production of war materials), and Charlie reveals his new job: as a U.S. Marine. At the OWI's request, the personnel manager's opposition to women working was removed from the script (although he *personally* does not like Rosie working). However, the government agency was not entirely satisfied with the final result: "The film deals chiefly with the personal lives of war workers and does not go deeply into their roles on the production front."

1109 SADDLE LEATHER LAW (Col, Dec) Benjamin Kline; *genre:* Western; *location:* United States; *coding:* Prod; *relevance:* 1.

Charles Starrett is a mineralogist searching for quartz, an important component of radio parts. He runs into a gang of crooks who want to take over a ranch and turn it into a gambling house.

1110 SAILOR'S HOLIDAY (Col, Mar*) William Berke; *genre:* Comedy; *location:* United States; *coding:* USO?, AF-Mer; *relevance:* 1.

Three Merchant Marine sailors (Arthur Lake, Bob Haymes, Lewis Wilson) on leave in Hollywood visit the movie studios (specifically Columbia, which produced the film). Lake's sailor is determined to kiss Rita Hayworth! They also meet two girls (Shelley Winters and Jane Lawrence), who wind up marrying two of the three sailors, all on a two-day pass!

1111 SAN DIEGO, I LOVE YOU (Univ, Sept) Reginald LeBorg; *genre:* Comedy; *location:* United States; *coding:* Blk?, Short, Prod, Brit?, AF-A, AF-N; *relevance:* 1.5.

Edward Everett Horton is a widowed schoolteacher who has invented a collapsible life raft. His five children encourage him to take his invention to San Diego so the Navy can see it. His eldest daughter (Louise Albritton) falls in love with wealthy industrialist Jon Hall. The life raft is a bust, but Horton's new explosive is a great contribution to the war effort.

1112 THE SCARLET CLAW (Univ, May) Roy William Neill; *genre:* Crime; *location:*

Canada; *coding:* Churchill, Brit, Can; *relevance:* 1.

Sherlock Holmes and Dr. Watson, visiting Canada, receive a letter from Lady Penrose asking for help. By the time they arrive at her village, the woman has been murdered. A "phantom" has been killing sheep and wandering through the marshes. Holmes discovers the phantom is actually a man wearing a phosphorescent costume; he also discovers that Lady Penrose was a witness in a murder trial years before. The killer was actor Alastair Ramson. Ramson kills the trial judge and the daughter of a former prison guard, before Holmes exposes him. The murderer is killed by the girl's father. The only war relevant point of this film came at the conclusion, when Holmes quotes a speech by Winston Churchill. There are some plot similarities between this picture and *The Hound of the Baskervilles*.

1113 SECRET COMMAND (Col, May*) Eddie Sutherland; *genre:* Spy; *location:* United States; *coding:* FBI, Spy-Sab, Nazi, Prod, War Corr, Ref?, AF-N, AF-A?, Intell Serv; *relevance:* 3.

Government agent Pat O'Brien gets a job in the shipyard run by his brother (Chester Morris), so he can crack a sabotage ring run by Gestapo Colonel Von Braun. The enemy agents' targets include a newly completed aircraft carrier. O'Brien is given a fake "wife" (Carole Landis) and children as part of his cover. After the Nazis are caught, O'Brien leaves to join Combat Intelligence for the duration, but he promises to return and make Landis his wife for real. Yet another example of a civilian with an important home front job going into the service so he can "really" make a contribution to the war effort (as if smashing a sabotage ring was not important). This film, based on a magazine serial also published as a novel, was produced by Pat O'Brien's independent company for Columbia release.

1114 SECRETS OF SCOTLAND YARD (Rep, June) George Blair; *genre:* Spy*; *locations:* Britain, Switzerland, Germany; *coding:* Hitler, Chamberlain, AF-Brit, Brit, WWI, Nazi, AF-Raf?, Pol, Russ, Jap, Ref, Spy-Sab; *relevance:* 3.

At the end of WWI, the Germans realize that the operations of the British Cipher Bureau helped the Allies win the war. For the *next* war, the Germans will be better prepared, and they plant an agent in England well ahead of time. In 1939, war breaks out again, and the Cipher office (headed by C. Aubrey Smith) is again an important part of the war effort. However, the German spy in the department murders John Usher (Edgar Barrier), just as Usher cracks a new Nazi code. John's twin brother Robert (also

Barrier) takes his place and helps expose the Nazi agent.

1115 SEE HERE, PRIVATE HAR-GROVE (MGM, Feb*) Wesley Ruggles; *genre:* Comedy/Training; *location:* United States; *coding:* AF-A, Draft, Nazi, Atroc-Conc, WWI, Blk, Vet, AF-AC, FDR; *relevance:* 2.5.

A 1942 bestseller by Marion Hargrove was turned into a film comedy starring Robert Walker as the absent-minded young newspaper reporter turned soldier. Also in the cast are Donna Reed (as love interest mostly absent in the original book), Keenan Wynn (as a fellow soldier), and Chill Wills (as a sergeant perpetually exasperated by Hargrove's ineptitude). The film is mostly a training-camp comedy, but with less slapstick than in similar efforts starring Abbott and Costello, Brown and Carney, and others. The *Film Daily* pointed out that "underlying the comedy theme is a more serious one … the transformation of Hargrove into a fighting man fully aware of his responsibilities as a defender of America's cause against the forces of tyranny." In one scene, Hargrove asks a fellow soldier why he hates the Nazis so much; the man replies, "I just get steamed up when I read how they push people around. Then I say to myself, it's time somebody pushed them around until their mean skulls rattle." A sequel, *What Next, Corporal Hargrove?* (MGM, 1945), took Hargrove to France.

1116 SENSATIONS OF 1945 (UA, June*) Andrew Stone; *genre:* Musical Comedy; *location:* United States; *coding:* AF-A, Short, AF-N, Latin Am, Blk, Russ, Ital, Brit; *relevance:* 1.5.

This film was released in 1944, despite the title (it was later re-released as just *Sensations*). Eleanor Powell is a dancer who takes over Eugene Pallette's press agent business, much to the dismay of Pallette's son Dennis O'Keefe. However, Powell's schemes to get publicity for her clients often cause trouble, and she finally returns to performing. O'Keefe, who has been discharged from the service due to an injury, re-enlists in the Army at the end, but he and Powell plan to get together romantically after the war. There are a few topical references in this film, which features a number of guest stars, including W.C. Fields, Sophie Tucker, and the bands of Cab Calloway and Woody Herman.

1117 SERGEANT MIKE (Col, Nov) Henry Levin; *genre:* Training/Combat; *locations:* United States, Pacific; *coding:* AF-N, AF-Jap, Hist Am, AF-A, Jap; *relevance:* 3.

Allen (Larry Parks) is assigned to the K-9 Corps after a stint in a machine gun squad. His canine partner is "Sgt. Mike," donated by a young boy whose father was killed in action. Allen and Sgt. Mike, along with another K-9 handler and his dog Pearl, are sent to the Pacific theater of war. During an assault on a Japanese-held island, Mike sniffs out two Japanese machine gun nests which are then eliminated, and Pearl saves her wounded handler from drowning by holding his head above water. Later, Pearl is killed by a sniper while carrying a message through enemy lines. Sgt. Mike makes it through, and U.S. troops arrive in time to wipe out the Japanese. The dog and his handler are decorated for their bravery. Note: during WWII, the Army unsuccessfully attempted to train some of its "four-footed GIs" to recognize Japanese soldiers by their smell. This was eventually discarded as unworkable.

1118 SEVEN DAYS ASHORE (RKO, Apr*) John H. Auer; *genre:* Musical Comedy; *locations:* United States, Pacific; *coding:* AF-Jap, Austral, AF-A, AF-N, AF-Mer, AF-MC, USO, Fr, Fem Lab, Jap, Blk, Latin Am, Home Def, Short, Bonds; *relevance:* 2.5.

After his ship rams a Japanese submarine, a Merchant Marine sailor (actually a rich young man "doing his bit" for the war effort) gets leave in San Francisco while repairs are being made. He tries to juggle three different girlfriends, and pays fellow sailors Wally Brown and Alan Carney to help him out. He picks the right woman in the end.

1119 SEVEN DOORS TO DEATH (PRC, Aug) Elmer Clifton; *genre:* Crime; *location:* United States; *coding:* —; *relevance:* 1.

Architect Chick Chandler helps solve a murder. There is one war-relevant dialogue remark in this otherwise irrelevant film: "I don't want to clean up again after your blitz."

1120 THE SEVENTH CROSS (MGM, Sept) Fred Zinnemann; *genre:* Resistance; *location:* Germany; *coding:* AF-Ger, Hitler, Ger, Jew, Nazi, Resist, Atroc-Conc, Neth; *relevance:* 3.

Based on a best-selling novel by German refugee Anna Seghers, this film is set in 1936 Germany. Seven prisoners escape from a Nazi concentration camp. One by one they are recaptured, then killed and hung on crosses outside the camp. George Heisler (Spencer Tracy) is the final escapee. He loses his faith in humanity when he runs into Germans who are either Nazi sympathizers or are too afraid to oppose the Hitler regime. Finally, he meets members of the resistance, and others who are willing to risk their lives to save him: Roeder (Hume Cronyn), an old friend employed in a munitions factory, Sauer (George Macready), an architect shamed by his wife into helping Heisler, and Toni (Signe Hasso), a waitress in a waterfront dive. Heisler boards a Dutch ship and is taken to freedom.

1121 SHADOWS IN THE NIGHT (Col, Oct) Eugene J. Forde; *genre:* Crime; *location:* United States; *coding:* Short, Prod?; *relevance:* 1.

In this Crime Doctor entry, Dr. Ordway (Warner Baxter) visits a mysterious house on the sea coast at the request of a young woman (Nina Foch). Someone is using a hypnotic gas to try and get her to commit suicide or, failing that, have her certified insane. Ordway exposes the culprit. Ordway's car has an "A" ration sticker on its windshield. Also, the young woman's scientist-uncle (George Zucco) shows Ordway a new synthetic fabric he has invented. "It should make you rich in times like these," Ordway remarks.

1122 SHE'S A SOLDIER TOO (Col, Sept*) William Castle; *genre:* War Drama; *location:* United States; *coding:* AF-A, Prod, Fem Lab; *relevance:* 2.

A soldier tries to locate his long-lost son, and is assisted by a female cabdriver (Nina Foch) in his quest. Beulah Bondi and Ida Moore are two elderly women who own a mansion that becomes a boarding house for war workers.

1123 SHE'S A SWEETHEART (Col, Dec) Del Lord; *genre:* Comedy/Drama; *location:* United States; *coding:* AF-A, USO, AF-N?; *relevance:* 2.5.

Mom (Jane Darwell) runs a canteen for servicemen on leave. Maxine (Jane Frazee) comes to work in the canteen, but sings and flirts with the boys, hoping to further her singing career. Rocky (Larry Parks) falls in love with Maxine and wants to marry her before he ships out, but they break up when he learns of her true motives for working with Mom. When Rocky is reported missing in action, Maxine changes her tune and becomes a valuable member of the canteen staff, volunteering for the dirtiest jobs. The War Department throws a party to honor Mom's contributions to the war effort, and Rocky appears and reconciles with Maxine. There are some similarities between this film and *Two Girls and a Sailor, Three Little Sisters,* and *Something for the Boys* (all q.v.), where homes are converted into unofficial servicemen's canteens (as opposed to "official" canteens such as the Stage Door Canteen in New York, or the Hollywood Canteen). Maxine's story is lifted almost directly from *Stage Door Canteen,* q.v.—in that film, it was Eileen (Cheryl Walker) who was using the canteen to further her show business ambitions.

1124 SHOW BUSINESS (RKO, Apr*) Edwin L. Marin; *genre:* Musical; *locations:* United States, France; *coding:* Blk, USO?, WWI, Vet, Fr, Ital?, AF-A; *relevance:* 1.5.

Although producer Eddie Cantor gave himself top billing, he and Joan Davis are really comic relief in support of George Murphy and Constance Moore. The film follows the show business careers of four troupers from the years prior to WWI, up until their success in Ziegfeld's *Whoopee* in 1929 (a Broadway musical that Cantor had actually appeared in). Murphy and Moore have the usual romantic and professional disagreements, but finally reconcile. There is a brief WWI sequence: Cantor, turned down by the Army, travels to France to entertain the troops. While singing at a military hospital, he suddenly hears Murphy join in on the song. Murphy had joined the Army and was wounded at Chateau-Thierry (but later recovers with no visible disabilities).

1125 THE SIGN OF THE CROSS *(added footage) (Para, Aug*) Cecil B. De-Mille; *genre:* Historical Drama; *location:* Italy; *coding:* Ital, AF-AC, Hitler, Nazi; *relevance:* 2.

This re-release of the 1932 DeMille film begins with newly shot footage. An American bomber flies over present-day Rome, dropping propaganda leaflets (in July 1943, Allied planes did drop leaflets on Italy, addressed to the "Italian people" from FDR and Churchill: "The time has come for you to decide whether Italians shall die for Mussolini and Hitler or live for Italy and for civilization"). Both a Protestant minister and a Catholic priest (Arthur Shields) are on board, and the priest tells the crew about the persecution of early Christians in pagan Rome. They also mention that the "Germans" had been in Rome before (specifically, Attila and his Huns), and draw parallels between the two eras: "Nero ... cared no more for the lives of others than Hitler does ... he burned this very Rome." The clouds below them part, and the 1932 film begins. Despite the new material, the 1944 version is about 20 minutes shorter than the original release version. The Germans had occupied Italy after Mussolini was deposed, and the Italians signed a separate armistice (September 1943), thus changing their status from a co-belligerent to an occupied country. Rome was liberated by the Allies in June 1944.

1126 SINCE YOU WENT AWAY (UA, July) John Cromwell; *genre:* War Drama; *location:* United States; *coding:* Juv, AF-Blk, Blk, Jew, Jap, Ital, Ger, Fem Lab, Bonds, Short, Ref, AF-Mer, AF-W, AF-MC, AF-A, AF-AC, AF-N, Home Fr, Prod, Blk Mkt, USO, Mil Exer, Mil School, Vet, Postwar?, Russ, Czech, Draft, FDR; *relevance:* 3.

Nearly three hours long, this film details "the story of an unconquerable fortress ... the American home." Claudette Colbert's husband joined the armed forces up despite

being a middle-aged father of two (Jennifer Jones and Shirley Temple). The departure of the breadwinner causes some financial hardships in this middle-class home: their black maid (Hattie McDaniel) has to be let go (she later returns, saying she disliked working for an "uptown" family). They decide to take in a boarder, so crusty retired military man Monty Woolley moves in. Robert Walker is Woolley's soldier grandson, who becomes Jones' boyfriend; Joseph Cotten is a Naval officer who is a friend of the family, but who would perhaps like to be something more to Colbert. The film depicts various events in the daily lives of this extended family: Tony is shipped out; Colbert gets a chance to visit her husband, but her train is side-tracked for a higher priority troop-train, and she misses seeing him; Jones gets a job as a nurses' aide, postponing her college career; there is a dance at a nearby military base. Then, a telegram arrives: Colbert's husband is missing in action in the Pacific. Walker is shipped out, and is later reported killed at Salerno. Cotten returns, having won the Navy Cross; Colbert gets a job as a welder in a shipyard. The film ends at Christmas, which is a bittersweet time for the whole family—until news arrives that Colbert's husband has been located, is well and is coming home.

1127 SING A JINGLE (Univ, Jan*) Edward C. Lilley; *genre:* Musical Comedy; *location:* United States; *coding:* AF-A, Short, Bonds, AF-N, Prod, Fem Lab; *relevance:* 2.

Allan Jones is a famous singer who gives a farewell concert before going in the Army, only to learn he has been rejected by the service. Using his real name, Jones gets a job in a defense plant as an engineer. He falls in love with the plant owner's daughter (June Vincent), and they plan a bond rally to raise money for a Navy ship to be named after the city (see also *Carolina Blues*, q.v.). Despite the machinations of a jealous rival, Jones wins the girl and the show is a big success. There are some similarities between this film and *Good Luck Mr. Yates*, q.v.

1128 SOMETHING FOR THE BOYS (TCF, Nov) Lewis Seiler; *genre:* Musical Comedy; *location:* United States; *coding:* AF-A, Jap, AF-Russ, Prod, Fem Lab, Short, Mil Exer, Latin Am; *relevance:* 3.

Three cousins (Michael O'Shea, Carmen Miranda, Vivian Blaine) inherit a southern mansion. To avoid losing their inheritance for unpaid taxes, the trio turns the plantation into a home for Army wives. They put on a show to raise money for renovations, and the plantation also becomes the command post in Army war games. There is a brief scene set in a munitions plant. Based on a stage musical with songs by Cole Porter. Judy Holliday appears in a small role. In Technicolor.

1129 SONG OF THE OPEN ROAD (UA, May*) S. Sylvan Simon; *genre:* Musical; *location:* United States; *coding:* Juv, USO, Prod-Farm; *relevance:* 2.

Teenage singer Jane Powell appears as a young film star who runs away from her tedious movie-making duties and joins the "U.S. Crops Corps," a group of young people who travel around helping harvest crops. When an emergency threatens the orange crop, Jane gets her Hollywood friends (including W.C. Fields and Edgar Bergen) to appear in person at the groves, attracting enough pickers to save the harvest.

1130 THE SPIDER WOMAN (Univ, Jan*) Roy William Neill; *genre:* Crime; *location:* Britain; *coding:* Blk?, Dipl?, Hitler, Musso; *relevance:* 1.

Sherlock Holmes (Basil Rathbone) solves the case of a woman (Gale Sondergaard) who uses spider venom to kill her victims. At the climax, Holmes tracks her to a London carnival, where he is trapped behind a shooting gallery target of Hitler (there is also one of Mussolini), while Dr. Watson unwittingly shoots at the bullseye (Hitler's heart)!

1131 STANDING ROOM ONLY (Para, Jan*) Sidney Lanfield; *genre:* Comedy; *location:* United States; *coding:* Prod, Short, AF-A, AF-N; *relevance:* 2.

Fred MacMurray wants to convert his toy factory to defense work, but needs permission from a Washington bureaucrat. Paulette Goddard travels with him to Washington to make their case, but they cannot find rooms and are forced to pose as servants in Roland Young's house while MacMurray tries to get his "priorities." Eventually MacMurray, Goddard, and their chief competitor are all hired as servants in the home of the bureaucrat, and MacMurray finally gets his plans approved. The "servant problem" was also the subject of *My Kingdom for a Cook* (1943), and *Make Your Own Bed* (1944), both q.v.

1132 STARS ON PARADE (Col, May) Lew Landers; *genre:* Musical Comedy; *location:* United States; *coding:* Short, Blk; *relevance:* 1.

Larry Parks and Lynn Merrick want to break in to the movies, but cannot get "discovered." They decide to put on a show featuring only new talent, and rent a vacant automobile showroom for their headquarters (new cars were not produced during the war—car dealers either rationed the last shipment of 1942 cars they received, dealt in used cars, or closed up "for the duration"). The show is a success and they get the desired movie contracts.

1133 STEP LIVELY (RKO, June*) Tim Whelan; *genre:* Musical Comedy; *location:* United States; *coding:* Draft, Fem Lab?; *relevance:* 1.

A semi-remake of *Room Service* (RKO, 1938), with Frank Sinatra and George Murphy. There are several references to the draft, and in one scene a woman cabdriver is shown. The latter was just one example of casting women in (pre-war) male-dominated professions (messengers were another frequent profession which "went female," at least in Hollywood).

1134 STORM OVER LISBON (Rep, Aug*) George Sherman; *genre:* War Drama; *location:* Portuguese; *coding:* Dipl?, Jap, Nazi, Spy-Sab, Ref, Czech, War Corr, AF-A, AF-N, POW, AF-MC, Jap-Ger Coop; *relevance:* 3.

Like Warners' *The Conspirators*, q.v., this was an attempt to make neutral Lisbon into the intrigue capital of the world (while Portugal was ruled by dictator Antonio Salazar, it was not allied with the Axis; in fact, Portugal allowed the Azores islands to be used by the Allies as a critical Atlantic base). Deresco (Erich von Stroheim) is a nightclub owner and Axis agent. Maritza (Vera Ralston) is spying on him for the Portugese police. John Craig (Richard Arlen) arrives in the city from the Far East, where he escaped from a Japanese POW camp with vital information on microfilm. Deresco tries to capture the film, but Craig manages to escape on the Clipper to America with Maritza's aid. The three principals also appeared in *The Lady and the Monster*, q.v., for Republic in 1944.

1135 THE STORY OF DR. WASSELL (Para, Apr*) Cecil B. DeMille; *genre:* War Drama; *locations:* United States, China, Java, Australia; *coding:* AF-W, Ref, AF-Austral, AF-Jap, AF-N, AF-MC, AF-Brit, AF-Neth, Austral, Brit, Chi, Neth, Jap, AF-AC, FDR; *relevance:* 3.

In early 1942, Navy doctor Wassell (Gary Cooper) is sent to Java to care for wounded sailors from two Navy ships. As the Japanese approach, Wassell manages to evacuate all but ten of his patients. He takes charge of these ten men personally, escaping from the island on the last ship out. After an arduous voyage, they arrive in Australia (Wassell loses only one patient), the doctor meets his nurse-girlfriend (Laraine Day), and Wassell is awarded the Navy Cross for his efforts. Based on a true story, with scenes shot in Mexico, this lavish Technicolor effort features one of the real-life sailors saved by Wassell, playing himself (Melvin Francis). The heroic story of Dr. Wassell (who in real life was nearly 60 years of age at the time of his adventure) was discussed in one of President Roosevelt's broadcast "Fireside Chats," on April 28, 1942. The OWI asked that the opening narration of the film omit a reference to the Japanese as a "dwarfish horde of island men."

The government agency also felt "while our British, Dutch, and Chinese allies are favorably portrayed, most of the Americans … are … preoccupied with slapstick humor and obsessed with the desire to get back to the U.S., to the complete exclusion of all other war aims."

1136 STRANGE AFFAIR (Col, Oct) Alfred E. Green; *genre:* Crime; *location:* United States; *coding:* Ger, Spy-Sab; *relevance:* 1.5.

Cartoonist Bill Harrison (Allyn Joslyn—another example of a character actor promoted to leading man status in wartime; see also Jerome Cowan in *Crime by Night*, q.v.) is also an amateur detective who becomes involved in a murder committed by members of a gang planning the escape of Nazis from an internment camp.

1137 STRANGERS IN THE NIGHT (Rep, Nov*) Anthony Mann; *genre:* Crime; *location:* United States; *coding:* AF-MC; *relevance:* 1.5.

Johnny Meadows (Bill Terry) returns to the U.S. after being wounded in action in the Pacific. During his convalescence, his will to live was supported by letters from Rosemary Blake, a young woman he had never met. Johnny arrives in Rosemary's hometown and is told by her mother that Rosemary is away on a trip. With the aid of the town's new doctor (Virginia Grey), Johnny eventually discovers Rosemary does not exist—she is a fictitious character created by the demented Mrs. Blake. Mrs. Blake tries to murder Johnny and the doctor, but is killed when a portrait of the imaginary Rosemary falls on her.

1138 THE SULLIVANS [aka **THE FIGHTING SULLIVANS**] (TCF, Feb*) Lloyd Bacon; *genre:* Biographical Drama; *locations:* United States, Pacific; *coding:* Tojo, Jap, Pearl Harb, AF-Jap, AF-MC, FDR, AF-N, AF-W, AF-Ital; *relevance:* 2.5.

This film's title was changed to *The Fighting Sullivans* after it had been in release for a short time. The film tells the true story of the Sullivan family of Waterloo, Iowa. Mr. Sullivan (Thomas Mitchell) works for the railroad; his wife (Selena Royle) supervises the five young brothers, who grow up an inseparable team (the family motto is "We stick together"). When they are young men, one of the brothers (Edward Ryan) gets married (to Anne Baxter). The family plans of the other four are disrupted by the Japanese attack on Pearl Harbor. The four single brothers decide to enlist in the Navy; Ryan decides (with his wife's agreement) to join them. The brothers, at their insistence, are all assigned to the same ship (the *Juneau*), and when the ship is sunk off Guadalcanal, all five perish, as four of the brothers sacrifice their lives trying to save the fifth, trapped

below decks. (earlier in the film, this is foreshadowed when the boys make a boat and it sinks). Despite the tragic conclusion, the film promotes family values and small-town Americanism, and the sacrifice of the Sullivans is not in vain. The film begins with a montage of the christening of the five boys, and concludes with Mrs. Sullivan "christening" the ship named after her sons.

1139 THE SULTAN'S DAUGHTER (Mono, Jan*) Arthur Dreifuss; *genre:* Adventure; *location:* Africa; *coding:* Arab, Hist Am, Ger, Blk, Collab; *relevance:* 3.

Stripper Ann Corio appears in the title role of this film. Nazi-types want to buy oil leases from her father (Charles Butterworth), but the stranded U.S. vaudeville team of Tim and Irene Ryan, and Edward Norris step in to save the day for the Allies.

1140 SUNDAY DINNER FOR A SOLDIER (TCF, Dec) Lloyd Bacon; *genre:* Comedy/Drama; *location:* United States; *coding:* Juv, Blk, USO, Jap, AF-AC, Vet, Hist Am; *relevance:* 2.

Despite their poverty, a poor family (three children, one young woman—Anne Baxter—and their grandfather, played by Charles Winninger) invite a B-17 waist-gunner (John Hodiak) from a nearby Army base for Sunday dinner on their dilapidated Florida houseboat. Grandfather is a Spanish-American War veteran who lost his leg in that conflict. In one sequence, the family goes to an amusement park with Hodiak and the children visit a shooting gallery featuring "Shoot a Jap" (see also *The Spider Woman*, q.v.). A poignant scene, illustrative of wartime separation and longing, features Baxter dancing alone in the ruined ballroom of an unfinished seaside resort. A repeated motif in this film shows the family waving in a friendly fashion to every military airplane that flies over their home.

1141 SUNDOWN VALLEY (Col, Mar) Benjamin Kline; *genre:* Western; *location:* United States; *coding:* Prod, AF-A, AF-N; *relevance:* 2.

One of the few 1944 Westerns to directly address the war. Gunsight Hawkins has, true to his name, developed a new gunsight, and his granddaughter (Jeanne Bates) wants to set up a factory to produce it for the government. Steve Denton (Charles Starrett) agrees to help, and convinces the local ranchers to work in the factory and run their ranches with skeleton crews. Gamblers Adams and Baxter fleece the workers at a sleazy roadhouse. An accident cuts back production at a crucial moment, but eventually the plant succeeds, the gamblers are beaten, and the roadhouse is turned into a recreation center for defense workers.

1142 SWEET AND LOWDOWN (TCF,

Sept) Archie Mayo; *genre:* Musical; *location:* United States; *coding:* Juv, AF-AC?, Mil School, AF-A, AF-N, AF-W, MacArthur, Latin Am, Blk, Hitler, Home Fr, Short; *relevance:* 1.5.

Benny Goodman, playing himself, visits the Chicago settlement house where he was raised. He gives James Cardwell a job with his band, but success goes to the younger man's head. At film's end, Cardwell goes back to his factory job (which is NOT specifically identified as a defense plant). There are several topical dialogue references in this musical drama. In one scene, the band is duped into playing at a military prep school.

1143 SWEETHEARTS OF THE U.S.A. (Mono, Mar) Lew Collins; *genre:* Comedy; *location:* United States; *coding:* Prod, Fem Lab, AF-W, Draft; *relevance:* 2.

Patsy (Una Merkel) works in a defense plant. Her roommate Helen joins the WACS. Helen and Patsy meet private detective Parkyakarkus, and singer Don Clark (Donald Novis). They form a 4-F band and turn an old "haunted house" into an entertainment center for war workers. Patsy also discovers a new manufacturing process.

1144 SWINGTIME JOHNNY (Univ, Jan*) Edward F. Cline; *genre:* Musical Comedy; *location:* United States; *coding:* AF-A?, Prod, Fem Lab; *relevance:* 2.5.

Jonathan (Peter Cookson) runs the Chadwick Pipe Organ Company, which is being changed over to defense work. It will soon produce shell casings, under the supervision of Slick Sparks. The Andrews Sisters (who do "Boogie Woogie Bugle Boy" *again*) and members of the Mitchell Ayres Orchestra sign up to work in the plant. However, Sparks has the first run of casings declared unfit, and Jonathan is nearly forced to sell the factory. Linda (Harriet Hilliard), Jonathan's girlfriend, romances Sparks and learns he is behind the plot to force the sale. The plant is saved.

1145 TAKE IT OR LEAVE IT (TCF, Aug) Benjamin Stoloff; *genre:* Comedy; *location:* United States; *coding:* AF-A, AF-N; *relevance:* 1.5.

Unknown leading players (ever hear of Eddie Ryan or Marjorie Massow?) were combined with footage from old Fox films and a current radio show ("Take It or Leave It," with Phil Baker). Ryan is a sailor who returns to New York; Massow is his pregnant wife. Her regular doctor is in the Army, so she wants her baby delivered by the eminent Dr. Preston. But Eddie cannot afford Preston's fee, so he goes on Baker's show and nearly wins enough money, but Marjorie goes into labor before Eddie can try for the jackpot. In the end, everything comes out all right. Interesting point: Ryan is apparently

discharged from the Navy well before the end of the war, without the usual Hollywood excuse of an injury.

1146 TAMPICO (TCF, Mar*) Lothar Mendes; *genre:* War Drama/Spy; *location:* Caribbean, Mexico; *coding:* Latin Am, Spy-Sab, AF-Mer, Nazi, AF-Mex, US-Mex Coop, Collab, Short, Ger, AF-Ger, AF-A, Intell Serv; *relevance:* 3.

Edward G. Robinson and Victor McLaglen are Captain and first mate of an oil tanker in the Gulf of Mexico. They pick up some survivors—including showgirl Kathie (Lynn Bari)—of a ship torpedoed by a Nazi sub. When the tanker docks in Mexico, Kathie is in danger of being deported since her passport went down with the ship. Robinson defends her and, shortly thereafter, marries her. Robinson's ship is ordered to sail once more, and—against McLaglen's advice—he tries to outrun a Nazi sub that suddenly appears. The tanker is torpedoed, but manages to ram the sub when it surfaces to finish them off. Robinson's ship sinks and his pal McLaglen is reported missing. Back in Tampico, the Mexican Navy commander suspects Kathie is a Nazi spy. Robinson argues with his wife, loses his commission, and gets drunk. He is approached by a Nazi spy who wants information on the sailing of other tankers. By pretending to cooperate, Robinson learns Kathie is innocent; McLaglen is the real spy, coerced into working with the Nazi agents. After a struggle, McLaglen is killed, and the other spies are apprehended by government agents. Robinson reconciles with Kathie.

1147 TEEN AGE (Ind, June*) Dick L'Estrange; *genre:* Drama; *location:* United States; *coding:* Juv, Prod, Prod-Farm, Fem Lab, Short; *relevance:* 2.

This independent production (from J.D. Kendis's "Continental Pictures") is an early "juvenile delinquency" film. It was produced in 1943, but since it was distributed independently on the exploitation circuit, there was no official national release date. The misadventures of a number of wayward teenagers are depicted, including a gang of "car-strippers" which steals and re-sells tires and accessories, girls who hang around unsavory roadhouses, and so on. Dan Murray (Johnny Duncan) belongs to the car-stripping gang, but eventually reforms just before he is killed. His father (Wheeler Oakman), an ex-convict, goes to work in a shipyard. Some of the other teens are sent to work on a farm "to help with the crops" since "farmer uniforms are mighty important right now." One of the girls goes to business college and then gets a job at the shipyard. A significant amount of the footage in this film was apparently culled from earlier films produced by Kendis in the 1930s.

1148 THEY LIVE IN FEAR (Col, Oct*) Josef Berne; *genre:* War Drama; *locations:* Germany, United States; *coding:* Ger, Hitler, Nazi, Czech, Fre Fr, Ref, Resist, Atroc, Atroc-Conc, Home Fr, Bonds, AF-A, AF-W, Prod-Farm, Prod?, Ital, Russ, Hist Am, V, FDR; *relevance:* 3.

This film opens in a Hitler Youth classroom, where the Nazi instructor shouts out his criticism of America, another foolish democracy foolish enough to "threaten" Nazi Germany. One of the students' mothers is brought into the room—she says she has lost three sons, one in Russia, one in Italy, and "him" (her own son turned her in for anti–Nazi sentiments!). Another student is Paul Graffen, who goes home and tells his family that he cannot go on pretending to be a good Nazi. If their anti–Nazi feelings are revealed, his father warns him, it could lead to death for them all. Paul and his fellow Hitler Youth are taken to Dachau, and are ordered to execute a group of prisoners (with shovels, since the prisoners are not worthy of a Nazi bullet). Paul manages to spare his assigned victim, Dr. Bauer, who gives the teenager a letter of introduction to a friend in America. Paul escapes to the United States and goes to see the principal of Ashland High School, who had studied with Bauer in Heidelberg before the war. Gradually, the German boy learns about American values such as freedom and democracy. He also finds an American girlfriend. However, this brings him in conflict with football player John, who constantly heckles the refugee, calling him "Mr. Master Race" and "Gestapo."

Paul is asked to make a speech at an assembly; however, a Czech immigrant tells him that his brother, a member of the Czech underground, once made a radio broadcast that endangered his family. An anonymous phone call (from John, of course) further unnerves Paul, who loses his composure during the speech, shouts "Heil Hitler!" and runs away in the face of the audience's displeasure. However, a letter from Paul to his mother reveals his true feelings about America, and even John feels bad. Paul goes back and makes his "real" speech, attacking the Nazis. The film ends as Paul graduates from high school and indicates that he will soon be joining the armed forces of his adopted country. This film has a number of inconsistencies and abrupt transitions, indicating some major last-minute changes in the script (the Columbia press synopsis is extremely different than the finished film). The *Motion Picture Herald* review was not too kind: "Nazi Turns Jitterbug" was their judgement. Otto Kruger is practically the only known performer in the cast.

1149 THIS IS THE LIFE (Univ, May*) Felix Feist; *genre:* Romantic Comedy; *location:* United States; *coding:* AF-A, USO?; *relevance:* 1.5.

Angela (Susanna Foster) travels to New York in pursuit of a singing career, leaving behind her friend Jimmy (Donald O'Connor). Angela has a crush on middle-aged Army surgeon Patric Knowles. A jealous Jimmy follows Angela to the city, and manages to set up Knowles with famous photographer Louise Albritton. Angela realizes Knowles was too old for her, and Jimmy enlists in the Army himself.

1150 THOUSANDS CHEER (MGM, Jan) George Sidney; *genre:* Musical; *location:* United States; *coding:* Ital, Musso, Fr, Hirohito?, AF-A, AF-W, AF-N, Hitler, Chi, Russ, Latin Am, V, USO, UN, Blk; *relevance:* 3.

Young concert singer Kathryn Grayson puts her career on hold to join her father, an Army colonel (John Boles); he is separated from her mother (Mary Astor). She falls in love with former circus acrobat Gene Kelly, now a disgruntled private who wants to join the Air Corps, although his attitude improves by the end of the film. Grayson helps organize entertainment for the troops, and the bulk of the film consists of guest appearances by MGM stars and musical performers, in staged and actual footage of camp shows. In one sequence, Mickey Rooney does impersonations, and mentions that Captain Clark Gable's whereabouts are a "military secret." The Technicolor film ends with the "United Nations Hymn," sung and played before a backdrop of flags of the Allied nations and "V" for Victory columns.

1151 THREE IS A FAMILY (UA, Nov) Edward Ludwig; *genre:* Comedy; *location:* United States; *coding:* Blk, AF-A, AF-N, Prod; *relevance:* 2.

Kitty (Marjorie Reynolds) moves into her parents' apartment with her 9-month-old twins after her Naval officer husband is transferred to Norfolk. Kitty goes to visit her husband, leaving the babies in the care of Sam (Charlie Ruggles), who would rather go to work in the defense plant in which he has invested $2500. Meanwhile, neighbors Hazel and Archie are expecting a child, but are on the verge of eviction because their landlord does not like children. Archie is inducted into the service—which means Hazel cannot legally be evicted—and Kitty and the twins decide to move in with her for the duration.

1152 THREE LITTLE SISTERS (Rep, July*) Joseph Santley; *genre:* Comedy; *location:* United States; *coding:* Nazi, AF-A, AF-W, AF-MC, AF-N, Hitler, Tojo, Blk, Home Def, USO; *relevance:* 2.5.

Soldier Bob Mason (William Terry) visits Lily, the Vermont girl who has been corresponding with him. Lily (Cheryl Walker) is one of three sisters; although she told Bob in her letters of her rich and glamorous life, in reality she is confined to a wheelchair, and her sisters have to take in washing to make ends meet. Learning of Bob's imminent arrival, teenage sister Sue (Mary Lee) borrows the keys to the vacant Manor House from her boyfriend so the girls can pretend to live there. Lily changes identities with sister Hallie (Ruth Terry), so Bob will not learn his penpal is an invalid. But Bob proves he is a good guy by falling in love with the real Lily. When the girls tell him they are going to turn "their" house into a serviceman's canteen, Bob tells his commanding officer, who lends his official assistance. Despite many mixups, all ends well—and Lily even has the prospect of being able to walk again.

1153 THREE MEN IN WHITE (MGM, May*) Willis Goldbeck; *genre:* Drama; *location:* United States; *coding:* Postwar?, Jap, Bonds, Short, Chi, AF-Chi, AF-A; *relevance:* 1.5.

Doctor Kildare (Lew Ayres) is away at war (in reality, conscientious objector Ayres was serving as a medic), so Dr. Gillespie (Lionel Barrymore) is given a number of young doctors to assist him. In this film—which contains a few topical references—the medicos are Keye Luke (as Dr. Lee from Brooklyn) and Van Johnson. In one scene, Dr. Lee tells Gillespie: "I'm so anxious to be your assistant, I'd pretty near give a blood transfusion to a Jap."

1154 THREE OF A KIND (Mono, July) D. Ross Lederman; *genre:* Comedy; *location:* United States; *coding:* Latin Am, Short, Prod?, Jap; *relevance:* 1.

Shemp Howard and Billy Gilbert are former vaudevillians who have to find work to support the orphaned son of a former stage colleague. They crash a radio show and are a big hit with the sponsor, but are thrown out by security before he can learn who they are. Eventually they become successful. Despite his billing as the third member of the comedy "team," Maxie Rosenbloom has a rather minor role in this entry. There are several minor topical dialogue references.

1155 THREE RUSSIAN GIRLS (UA, Jan*) F. Ozep, H. Kesler; *genre:* Combat; *location:* Russia; *coding:* Am Vol, Postwar?, US-Russ Coop, AF-Ger, Russ, AF-Russ, AF-W, AF-AC?, Nazi; *relevance:* 3.

As Nazis advance into Russia, a call goes out in Leningrad for volunteer nurses. A group of twenty young women report for duty, among them Natasha (Anna Sten), who is engaged to a Russian soldier. After an extended training sequence, the nurses are sent to a field hospital, where they care for Russian wounded in close proximity to the front lines. A Russian plane, attacked by German fighters, crashes. John Hill (Kent Smith), an American who was testing the plane with a Russian flyer, is rescued from the wreck, but his legs are paralyzed. Natasha helps care for him. When the Nazis approach, the hospital has to be evacuated. John and Natasha fall in love, and he regains the use of his legs. Natasha learns her fiance has been killed in action; she returns to the front, but is wounded and sent back to Leningrad, where she reunites with John just before he departs for America. They agree to meet when victory is won. This film was a remake of (and used footage from) a 1941 Russian film, *The Girl From Leningrad*. However, the "John Hill" character was a Hollywood addition: while Hollywood was willing to make films about our Russian allies, the Soviets were careful never to acknowledge American aid in any form, fictional story or otherwise. The film makes good use of patriotic Soviet songs in its score.

1156 TILL WE MEET AGAIN (Para, Aug*) Frank Borzage; *genre:* Resistance; *location:* France; *coding:* AF-Ger, Resist, AF-AC, AF-Fr, AF-Brit, Nazi, Hitler, Collab, Atroc; *relevance:* 3.

American flier John (Ray Milland) is shot down over France. The underground takes him to a convent to hide until he can escape to England. However, the Nazi officer in command of the area, along with Vitrey (Walter Slezak, once again a villain), the collaborationist mayor of the village, are beginning to suspect the nuns of Resistance activities. The Mother Superior is shot by an over-zealous Nazi, and the French girl who was to help John escape is arrested. Instead, young novice Clotilde (Barbara Britton) dresses in civilian garb and helps the airman reach the coast with valuable information about coastal fortifications, to be used in planning for the upcoming invasion of France. John and Clotilde become close in their journey—although she plans to become a nun and he is a happily married man—but she sacrifices herself so he can escape in the British submarine that arrives to pick him up. After Milland is gone, Clotilde is caught by Vitrey and the Nazis. The Nazi commander plans to send the young woman to the military brothels in Poland, but Vitrey regains his sense of honor and attacks the officer. In the struggle, Clotilde is shot and killed, but is spared dishonor. There are some similarities between the plot of this film and 1942's *Joan of Paris*, q.v.

1157 TIMBER QUEEN (Para, Jan*) Frank McDonald; *genre:* Adventure; *location:* United States; *coding:* Jew?, AF-AC, Jap, Prod, Draft, Bonds, Home Def; *relevance:* 2.

Russ Evans (Richard Arlen) is invalided out of the Air Corps after seeing action in the Pacific. While visiting Elaine (Mary Beth Hughes), the widow of a fellow pilot, Russ learns she is heir to timber leases in Alaska. However, these are mortgaged to Talbot, who plans to foreclose soon. Russ, Elaine and some friends go to Alaska in an attempt to cut enough timber to pay off Talbot. With the aid of some fugitive gangsters, Talbot's sinister plans are foiled, and the mortgage is paid off. A fair number of topical references in this film.

1158 TOMORROW, THE WORLD

(UA, Dec) Leslie Fenton; *genre:* War Drama; *location:* United States; *coding:* Juv, Jew, Ref, Postwar, Hitler, Nazi, Chi, Ger-Am?, Prod?, Atroc-Conc, Jap, Ger-Jap Coop; *relevance:* 3.

In the typical American small town where they live, widowed Professor Michael Frame (Fredric March) and his family await the arrival of 12-year-old Emil (Skippy Homeier), Frame's German nephew. Emil's late father was a great German liberal leader, but Emil himself is a Hitler Youth member who takes an instant dislike to Frame's Jewish girlfriend (Betty Field). Emil manages to break up the romance between his uncle and the young woman, but his pro–Nazi stance and sneaky ways soon turn the whole town against him (in one scene, Emil befriends a Chinese boy, believing him to be Japanese!). Emil tries to steal valuable War Department documents entrusted to Frame, and clubs the professor's daughter with a poker when she catches him. Frame tracks down his nephew, planning to turn him over to the police, but his daughter and (ex-)fiancee both suggest that Emil has been changed by his ordeal, and recommend mercy: "If we cannot solve the problem of one Nazi child now, heaven help the 12 million of them after the war." Homeier, who played the role of Emil in the stage version of this story, came to Hollywood to repeat it. The screen version was co-written by Ring Lardner, Jr.

1159 THE TOWN WENT WILD

(PRC, Dec) Ralph Murphy; *genre:* Comedy; *location:* United States; *coding:* Juv, Short?, Hist Am, V?; *relevance:* 1.

Edward Everett Horton and Tom Tully are two feuding small-town neighbors. The son of one family is in love with the daughter of the other, but their parents come to believe that a hospital mixup occurred, and the two young people might actually be brother and sister! It all turns out well in the end. Minor topical references in this film: one dialogue reference to "sabotage" of a rose garden, and several references which could refer to war work (a government "engineer in Alaska"). One car in the film may have a ration sticker in the windshield.

1160 TWILIGHT ON THE PRAIRIE

(Univ, Aug*) Jean Yarbrough; *genre:* Comedy; *location:* United States; *coding:* Prod-Farm, Prod; *relevance:* 1.5.

En route to Hollywood, an airplane carrying the Western band known as the "Buckaroos" is forced down in Little Lip, Texas. The war has reopened the local mines, so no rooms can be found in any of the town's hotels. Bucky (Johnny Downs) and the other band members sign on as ranch hands for the Bar-B Ranch (in order to get a place to sleep), planning to sneak out of town the next day. However, Bucky falls for the young and attractive ranch owner, Sally (Vivian Blaine). Furthermore, the band gets such good publicity for their "patriotic" act of working on the ranch, that it is impossible for them to leave. Bucky arranges to have their film shot on location at the Bar-B, and everyone is happy.

1161 TWO GIRLS AND A SAILOR

(MGM, Apr*) Richard Thorpe; *genre:* Musical Comedy; *location:* United States; *coding:* Jap, Latin Am, Brit, Russ, USO, AF-A, AF-N, AF-MC, Blk, V, Short?, Postwar; *relevance:* 3.

Long (two hours-plus) musical comedy with June Allyson and Gloria DeHaven as two small-time entertainers who set up an unofficial "servicemen's canteen" in their apartment. Van Johnson plays a rich Navy man who makes an anonymous contribution, allowing them to move the canteen into a nearby vacant warehouse. It might be noted that these "parties" are portrayed as entirely wholesome, innocent affairs, with no alcoholic beverages or "fooling around." Both women fall in love with Johnson: Allyson gets him in the end, and DeHaven has to settle for a soldier. Jimmy Durante and a number of musical performers appear, including Jose Iturbi, Lena Horne, Xavier Cugat, and Harry James.

1162 U-BOAT PRISONER (Col, Aug*)

Lew Landers; *genre:* Spy/Adventure; *locations:* Atlantic, United States; *coding:* Hitler, Brit, AF-Ger, Nazi, Goebbels, Goering, Spy-Sab, AF-N, AF-Mer, Latin Am, Neth, Pol, Fr, Hist Am, Un, Ger-Am, Collab, Atroc-Conc, Resist; *relevance:* 3.

This far-fetched film opens with a shot of its literary source, *U-Boat Prisoner (The Life Story of a Texas Sailor)* by Archie Gibbs. A German U-boat, carrying four kidnapped scientists (British, French, Dutch, and Polish) back to Germany to work on a secret weapons project, receives a message to pick up a German agent from an American freighter. The spy leaves the ship on a raft, but is spotted by sailor Archie Gibbs (Bruce Bennett). The freighter is attacked and sunk by the sub, but Gibbs swims to the raft, kills the traitor, and assumes his identity when the U-boat rescues him. On its way back to Germany, the German sub is depth-charged by an American destroyer. In an attempt to fool the Navy into thinking the sub has been sunk, the German captain puts a sick German sailor in one of the torpedo tubes and shoots him to the surface! However, his ruthlessness backfires: the sailor is picked up by a convoy straggler (the *Bolivar*, a Latin American historical reference), and lives long enough to reveal the existence of the U-boat. A cat and mouse game between the merchant ship, its destroyer escort, and the U-boat, results in the German submarine being damaged by its own magnetic mines! Gibbs, the scientists (one of whom, the Frenchman has turned traitor, informing the captain that Gibbs is *not* a Nazi, and that he and the Dutch scientist have been using the sub's radio to contact the Navy—they tap out "The Star Spangled Banner" to identify themselves), the U-boat captain and a few of his crew are trapped in the torpedo room of the doomed sub. They draw lots to see who shall escape via the torpedo tubes (one person has to remain behind to "fire" the tubes). Gibbs loses the draw. Although he is fatally shot by the U-boat captain, the French scientist summons enough strength to help Gibbs escape, then kills the German officer and dies. An epilogue shows the nonchalant Gibbs, back in the United States, accepting a berth on a new ship. Although there are some serious inconsistencies and fantastic plot developments (the script was revised at least four times after OWI reviews), this film does portray the Merchant Marine as an active partner in the war effort, cooperating with the Navy in the destruction of the U-boat.

1163 UNCERTAIN GLORY (WB, Apr*)

Raoul Walsh; *genre:* War Drama; *location:* France; *coding:* Nazi, Collab, AF-Fr, AF-Ger, FR, AF-Free Fr, AF-Raf, Resist, Atroc; *relevance:* 3.

French criminal Jean Picard (Errol Flynn) is saved from the guillotine when Allied bombs—intended for a Renault plant nearby—strike the prison compound (see *The Impostor*, q.v., for a similar lucky air raid). He escapes, but is recaptured by Inspector Bonet (Paul Lukas), who intends to return him to prison to await execution. They learn that French Resistance saboteurs blew up a railroad bridge while a German troop train was passing over it. The Nazis have taken 100 Frenchmen as hostages, and will shoot the innocent civilians unless the saboteurs surrender (these hostages are never shown in the film, but their families and friends are depicted). Picard and Bonet hatch a plan to have Picard give himself up as the saboteur, since he is condemned to die anyway. They get details of the explosion from one of the actual saboteurs, a Free French officer. Before escaping to England in a British plane, the man tells Picard and Bonet enough information to convince the Gestapo that Picard is the man they are seeking. Just before he is to turn himself in, Picard disappears, and Bonet fears the criminal has escaped. However, at the last moment Picard surrenders to the Gestapo to face certain death. Marianne, a young French woman who had fallen in love with Picard during their brief acquaintance, asks Bonet what Picard was like "deep in his heart." "He was a Frenchman," Bonet replies, and the film ends with the music of the "Marseillaise." The first major Nazi reprisals in occupied France occurred in October 1941, when 50 hostages were taken after the assassination of a German officer.

1164 THE UNWRITTEN CODE (Col, Oct) Herman Rotsten; *genre:* War Drama; *locations:* Atlantic, United States; *coding:* Hitler?, AF-Ger, AF-Brit, POW, AF-A, Nazi, Ger-Am; *relevance:* 3.

Two Germans survive the sinking of their POW ship en route to America. Karl Richter (Roland Varno) takes the place of a wounded British officer, whom he throws in the ocean. In America, Sgt. Terry Hunter (Tom Neal) is a guard at the POW camp. His girlfriend Mary (Ann Savage) is a nurse at a nearby hospital, and Karl—under his assumed name— is one of her patients. Karl goes to Mary's house to convalesce, and learns his fellow shipwreck survivor is a prisoner at the nearby camp. He plans to arm the prisoners and help them escape. However, Terry obtains a photo of the real British officer and exposes Karl, who is killed trying to escape. Historical note: almost 5,000 U.S. prisoners of war were killed when the unmarked Japanese transports they were sailing on were sunk by Allied submarines.

1165 UP IN ARMS (RKO, Feb*) Elliott Nugent; *genre:* Musical Comedy; *locations:* Pacific, United States; *coding:* Jap, Postwar, FDR, Latin Am, FDR, Short, Blk?, WWI, Atroc?, AF-Jap, Draft, Draft Avoid, Tojo, AF-N, AF-MC, AF-A, AF-W, POW, Ger, Spy-Sab, FBI; *relevance:* 2.5.

Hypochondriac Daniel Weems (Danny Kaye) is classified 1-A and drafted over his protests (he breaks into a song about the ordeal). Mary, his WAC girlfriend, accidentally winds up on the troop ship carrying him to the Pacific. Landing on a supposedly deserted island, Daniel runs into Japanese troops, but disguises himself as a Japanese officer and leads them into a trap. He returns to camp with the captured soldiers in tow, a la *Sergeant York.* Although he is now a hero, Daniel loses Mary to a fellow soldier

(Dana Andrews), but gets Dinah Shore as a consolation prize. In Technicolor.

1166 UP IN MABEL'S ROOM (UA, Mar*) Allan Dwan; *genre:* Comedy; *location:* United States; *coding:* Home Def, Prod, Russ; *relevance:* 1.5.

Gary Ainsworth (Dennis O'Keefe) is a designer at an aircraft plant. Although recently married to Geraldine (Marjorie Reynolds), he had been involved with Mabel (Gail Patrick), and once gave her a piece of lingerie with an inscription on it. The plot revolves around Gary's attempts to retrieve the incriminating piece of silk before his jealous wife finds out. There are numerous topical references in the dialogue of this film.

1167 THE VERY THOUGHT OF YOU (WB, Nov) Delmer Daves; *genre:* War Drama; *location:* United States; *coding:* Draft, Jew, AF-A, AF-W, AF-N, Tojo, Jap, Draft Avoid, Prod, Fem Lab, Home Fr, Short, Blk Mkt, Blk, Nazi, Jew, Pearl Harb; *relevance:* 3.

Sgt. Dave Stewart (Dennis Morgan) and his pal Fixit (Dane Clark) return to California from the Aleutians. They meet Janet (Eleanor Parker) and Cora (Faye Emerson), two women who work in a parachute factory. Dave and Janet pair off, as do Fixit and Cora. Despite their brief acquaintance, Dave and Janet get married, and he is sent to San Diego for special training. Janet's mother and older sister try to break up the marriage, but Dave and Janet reconcile before he is shipped out. Janet moves in with Cora. Some time later, Dave and Fixit come back to the U.S. after being wounded in action, and Dave gets to meet his new baby son. A sub-plot concerns Janet's obnoxious brother Cal, a 4-F who complains about women taking men's jobs, and asks how soldiers feel about their women dating other men while they (the soldiers) are away (Dave tells him a story about a soldier who deliberately ran in front of Japanese guns on Attu after receiving a "Dear John" letter). At the end of the film, Cal is reclassified 1-A.

1168 VOICE IN THE WIND (UA, Mar) Arthur Ripley; *genre:* War Drama; *locations:* Czechoslovakia, Portugal, Caribbean; *coding:* Czech, Ger, Nazi, Ref, Atroc, Atroc-Conc, Ital; *relevance:* 2.5.

"El Hombre" (Francis Lederer) joins the refugee community on the island of Guadalupe. Lederer is actually Jan Volny, a famous Czech pianist who had defied the Nazi occupation forces and played a patriotic piece at a concert. For this he was arrested, tortured, and sent to a concentration camp. Escaping while en route to the camp, Jan fled to Guadalupe via Lisbon, but the ordeal unhinged his mind, and he has amnesia. He goes to work for Angelo, a smuggler. Meanwhile, Jan's sweetheart Marya (Sigrid Gurie)

—who had also fled Czechoslovakia—winds up on the island, where she is wasting away from sorrow. Jan sinks Angelo's boat, ruining the smuggling business, and is mortally wounded by the gang. He makes it to Marya's bedside, where he sees her lifeless body, then dies.

1169 WATERFRONT (PRC, May) Steve Sekely; *genre:* Spy; *location:* United States; *coding:* AF-N, Ger-Am, Spy-Sab, Nazi, Atroc-Conc, FBI, Blk; *relevance:* 3.

A printed title at the opening of this film states: "While Nazi spy activities existed in some American ports prior to 1941, the counter-espionage activities of our Federal Bureau of Investigation have eliminated the espionage on American waterfronts." This seems to indicate this film is supposed to be taking place *prior* to Pearl Harbor, but some other clues in the film suggest otherwise. John Carradine is a German agent who contacts J. Carrol Naish, the Nazi's undercover representative in an American port city. Naish poses as an optometrist, and he tells Carradine his code book—which includes the names of all Nazi agents on the West Coast—has been stolen. The book was stolen by Zimmermann, who is in the employ of German-American insurance man Kramer. Kramer wants to use the book to help members of his family trapped in Germany, but Zimmermann double-crosses him and offers to sell the book back to Naish. Instead, Carradine murders the thief and retrieves the code book. He later kills Kramer, who was planning to confess to the FBI. Naish loses his nerve, and is also murdered by Carradine, but at the finale the Nazi agent is killed while trying to elude the police.

1170 A WAVE, A WAC, AND A MARINE (Mono, Nov) Phil Karlstein; *genre:* Comedy; *location:* United States; *coding:* AF-N, AF-A, AF-W, AF-MC; *relevance:* 1.5.

Henny Youngman is an agent who accidentally signs up the understudies instead of two Broadway stars. Margaret Ames (Sally Eilers) fires him for his mistake, since the real stars have been signed up by Margaret's ex-husband, a rival agent. Henny has *his* two girls perform in a nightclub, where they attract the attention of a big producer. However, one of the girls joins the WAVES, and the other enlists in the WACS. Margaret's ex-husband joins the Marines, but reconciles with his wife before he leaves. The producer decides to make a film with the two girls before they enter the service, and everyone is happy. Monogram advertised this film with the line: "No battle scenes, no message, just barrels of fun and jive to make you happy you're alive."

1171 WEEKEND PASS (Univ, Feb*) Jean Yarbrough; *genre:* Romantic Comedy;

location: United States; *coding:* Blk, AF-A, AF-N, AF-W, Mil School, Prod; *relevance:* 2.

Shipyard worker Johnny Adams (Noah Beery Jr.) has perfect attendance on the job for 18 months and wins $100 and a weekend pass, which he plans to spend quietly in a country inn. Instead, he meets Babs (Martha O'Donnell), who is running away because her grandfather wants her to join the WAVES (*she* wants to join the WACS). After various adventures, Johnny manages to return Babs to her grandfather, and she agrees to join the WAVES. Johnny just makes it back to work on time after his "peaceful" weekend. This is one of a very few films in which the defense worker-protagonist does not leave his industrial job for the armed forces. Ironically, his girlfriend *does* join the service!

1172 WHEN STRANGERS MARRY [aka BETRAYED] (Mono, Sept*) William Castle; *genre:* Drama; *location:* United States; *coding:* Fem Lab?, Home Fr, Blk, AF-N, AF-W, Short; *relevance:* 1.5.

A man attending a convention is murdered in his hotel room. A short time later, Millie (Kim Hunter) arrives at the hotel to meet Paul (Dean Jagger), her new husband. She accidentally bumps into Fred (Robert Mitchum), a former boyfriend who, when he hears she is married, wishes her the best of luck. Paul does not show up, and later calls Millie to meet him secretly. She fears he is mixed up in the crime; Paul admits he met the murdered man, but says he is innocent of the crime. It turns out Fred is the killer (he strangled the man with a pair of silk stockings Paul had bought as a present for Millie). There are a number of minor topical references in the film, including a fair number of uniformed extras in street and crowd scenes. This film was later re-released (with Mitchum given star billing) as *Betrayed*.

1173 WHEN THE LIGHTS GO ON AGAIN (PRC, Sept) William K. Howard; *genre:* War Drama; *location:* United States; *coding:* AF-A?, AF-MC, Draft?, Pearl Harb, Prod; *relevance:* 2.

Marine Ted Benson (James Lydon) receives a 30-day furlough to recover from wounds and battle fatigue. On his way home, he is in an accident and contracts amnesia. He is discovered by a reporter (Regis Toomey), and they head for Ted's home. On the way, Ted's story unfolds. He was the son of the town's richest citizen; his father wanted him to marry the daughter of the town banker, but Ted loved Arline. Quitting college, Ted went to work for Arline's father's newspaper, and eloped with his sweetheart. One day later, Pearl Harbor happened! Ted joined the Marines, reconciled with his father, and

left for action. Arriving in town, Ted finally regains his memory with the aid of his wife, Arline.

1174 WHERE ARE YOUR CHILDREN? (Mono, Jan) William Nigh; *genre:* Crime/Drama; *location:* United States; *coding:* Fem Lab, Prod, Short, AF-N, Juv; *relevance:* 3.

Judy (Gale Storm) lives with her brother and his wife in a shabby section of town. Originally from the East, they moved to California to work in the shipyards. Judy goes out with Danny (Jackie Cooper), but she is tricked into getting drunk and they are picked up by the juvenile probation officer. Danny joins the Navy, and Judy goes to visit him in San Diego, riding with some of Danny's friends. However, she learns they are in a stolen car, and when the others get in a fight at a gas station over ration coupons, Judy gets out. She makes it to San Diego in time to see Danny ship out. She is arrested as an accesory to the gas station crime (the attendant died of injuries), but is acquitted due to Danny's testimony. While waiting for him to return from the war, Judy promises to make herself useful by working in a day-care center for the children of defense workers.

1175 THE WHISTLER (Col, May*) William Castle; *genre:* Crime; *location:* United States; *coding:* Jap; *relevance:* 1.5.

Earl Conrad (Richard Dix—who appeared in a different role in each "Whistler" film), a plastics manufacturer, is depressed because he was unable to save his wife when the ship they were sailing on sank. He makes arrangements, through a third party, to be murdered. However, he receives a telegram from the Red Cross: his wife was rescued, and is alive in a Japanese internment camp! Conrad tries to cancel the "contract" on his life, but is unable to do so. Finally, he tries to sneak aboard a neutral ship carrying Japanese prisoners to be exchanged for American internees, and the killer makes his move. The police intervene in time to save Conrad, who then learns his wife had died, after all. First in a series based on a CBS radio anthology program narrated by a mysterious host (who is shown only as a shadow in the films). The series ran from 1942 to 1945—its trademark was the haunting 13-note "Whistler" theme.

1176 THE WHITE CLIFFS OF DOVER (MGM, Mar*) Clarence Brown; *genre:* War Drama; *locations:* Britain, France; *coding:* Hist Am, Ger, AF-W, Am Vol?, AF-Brit, AF-Fr, AF-Can, US-Brit Coop, Postwar, WWI, AF-A, Brit; *relevance:* 3.

Sentimental film inspired by a poem by Alice Duer Miller: the story begins in a British hospital in 1942. Sue (Irene Dunne) is a nurse, waiting for the expected casual-

ties from a British raid into France (the Dieppe raid of August 1942), since her son (Peter Lawford) is one of the British soldiers in action. She remembers how she came to England on vacation in 1914 (a flashback then begins). Sue was a young American woman who, after a whirlwind courtship, married Sir John Ashwood (Alan Marshal), a British nobleman. But their honeymoon cruise was interrupted by the outbreak of war, and Sir John was sent to the front with his regiment. Sue gives birth to a son, but her happiness is shattered when Sir John is killed in action just before the Armistice. Sue swears to raise her son John to "run and hide when the drums start rolling," but the young man joins his father's regiment when the next war begins. The flashback ends—John is brought to the hospital with other wounded men from the raid. He tells his mother he was in a shell hole with a Canadian and an American; the American said the Allies would have to create a "new world" and insure a real peace that "would stick." As John lies dying, American troops march by the hospital, and his mother says: "Your people and mine ... how well they march together ... they'll help bring peace again, a peace that *will* stick." In one scene—when young John is a boy (played by Roddy McDowall)—he plays host to two young German boys, who say Germany was not beaten in WWI, and that it will win "next time." They also admire the broad British country house lawn that "would make an excellent landing field" (cultural exchanges between British prep schools and German schools—who contributed members of the Hitler Youth—continued until 1938). The film also contains some clever parallels: Sue and Sir John—on leave—spend a weekend in Dieppe during WWI, and it is suggested that this is the time when their son is conceived. Their son is later mortally wounded in the Dieppe raid, and the gazebo that figured prominently in his parents' idyll is blown up! Also in the cast: Van Johnson, C. Aubrey Smith, and Dame May Whitty.

1177 WILSON (TCF, Aug*) Henry King; *genre:* Biography; *location:* United States; *coding:* Blk, AF-A, AF-N, UN?, Ger, Isolat, Pacifist, Latin Am, Ital, Spy-Sab, Fr, Brit, Belg, Russ, Dipl, Draft, Fem Lab, Postwar, Hist Am, Bonds, WWI; *relevance:* 2.5.

Although this film was not given general release until the summer of 1945, it was released as a special attraction nearly a year earlier. Over two hours long, this Technicolor biography of President Woodrow Wilson (Alexander Knox) concentrates chiefly on the First World War and its aftermath. One scene had particular relevance to contemporary audiences: Wilson berates the German ambassador, Count Bernstorff, for German militarism—"Won't you Germans ever be civilized? Won't you ever learn to keep your word? [Your mistreatment of others as] inferiors [has] discredited German Kultur and race superiority … [the Kaiser's actions] have made it … a fight for freedom and democracy against the most evil autocratic power this world has ever seen!" These statements were a little strong when applied to Kaiser Wilhelm and WWI, but they were very aptly applied to Hitler and Nazi Germany, as the filmmakers undoubtedly realized. The film is meticulously made but excessively talky and staid. For example, Wilson's speech to Congress asking for a declaration of war against Germany is recreated almost in its entirety.

1178 WING AND A PRAYER (TCF, Aug) Henry Hathaway; *genre:* Combat; *locations:* United States, Pacific; *coding:* Jap, Fil, Atroc, AF-N, AF-Jap, Jew?, Hist Am, Tojo, Pearl Harb; *relevance:* 3.

In the period just after Pearl Harbor, a Navy aircraft carrier (code-named "Carrier X") is ordered to fool the Japanese by appearing in various Pacific locations, making it seem that the U.S. fleet is widely scattered, thus luring the enemy into another assault on Hawaii (in reality, the Navy did make a number of hit and run carrier raids against Japanese island bases in February 1942, to keep the enemy off balance and "show the flag"). The ship is ordered to avoid combat, but the crew finally gets to engage the Japanese in the battle of Midway (June 4-6, 1942). Featured in this virtually all-male combat film are Don Ameche, Dana Andrews, and Charles Bickford. During the period when the ship is avoiding combat, a Navy plane is shot down and the pilot—in a life raft—is strafed by Japanese planes. See *Passage to Marseilles,* q.v., for a similar scene, but with the tables turned. Most of this film was shot at the Fox studios backlot, but some background footage was filmed on the USS *Yorktown.*

1179 WINGED VICTORY (TCF, Dec) George Cukor; *genre:* War Drama/Training; *locations:* United States, Pacific; *coding:* AF-W, Latin Am, AF-Jap, Russ, Chi, FDR, Churchill, Free Fr, Nazi, Postwar, Grk, AF-AC, UN; *relevance:* 3.

Film adaptation of a stage play about the Army Air Corps by Moss Hart. The film follows the training of various airmen, including Lon McAllister, and ends with their graduation and deployment to the South Pacific. Before graduation, when the airmen are waiting to get their assignments, a Chinese-American cadet is shown; during the graduation ceremony, Soviet and Free French visitors are shown in the audience. Most of the actors are AAF personnel on temporary detached duty, including Edmond O'Brien, Mark Daniels, Don Taylor, Alan Baxter, Kevin McCarthy, Red Buttons, Lee J. Cobb, Peter Lind Hayes, Barry Nelson, Gary Merrill, George Reeves, Karl Malden, and Martin Ritt. In one scene, the wives and girlfriends of the cadets (including Jeanne Crain, Judy Holliday, and Jo-Carroll Dennison) talk about "what we're fighting for"—they want to lead peaceful lives, live happily, and "have babies." In another scene, the airmen put on an all-male skit on the Pacific island where they are stationed, and one of the performers is a Carmen Miranda impersonator.

1180 WOMEN IN BONDAGE (Mono, Jan) Steve Sekely; *genre:* War Drama; *location:* Germany; *coding:* AF-Ger, Nazi, Russ, AF-AC, Hitler, Ger, Atroc?; *relevance:* 3.

Margot Bracken (Gail Patrick) returns to Germany after several years abroad. Her husband is serving with the German Army on the Russian front. Margot becomes section leader of a group of young women in her neighborhood. One of the women, Toni, loves a soldier but the Nazis will not let them marry because she's near-sighted. She becomes hysterical, is declared insane, and is shot. Margot's husband, mortally wounded, returns from Russia to spend his last days with his wife. Margot's Nazi supervisor tries to force her to bear another man's child, and Margot's husband commits suicide. As the film ends, Margot directs Allied bombers to a nearby munitions plant, and is killed when bombs destroy her home. An unusual film dealing with life under the Nazi regime, with no spies or "downed airmen" or other Allied characters; the allusions to the Nazi policy of selective breeding (eugenics) and euthanasia are also interesting.

1181 YOU CAN'T RATION LOVE (Para, Feb*) Lester Fuller; *genre:* Comedy; *location:* United States; *coding:* Draft?, Short, Home Def?; *relevance:* 2.

There are not enough college boys at Adams College due to the war. The girls all want to date handsome athlete Pete (Bill Edwards), but he is going steady with Betty (Betty Rhodes), so Marian (Marjorie Weaver) invents a "date rationing" plan, and Pete is rated at 30 points (a high total). In retaliation, Betty takes a 2-point nerd (Johnnie Johnston) and builds him up into the star of the varsity show. The rationing plan is vetoed by the faculty, but eventually all of the romantic complications are resolved.

1182 YOUTH RUNS WILD (RKO, June*) Mark Robson; *genre:* Crime; *location:* United States; *coding:* Juv, Prod, Home Fr, AF, Russ, Fem Lab, FDR; *relevance:* 1.5.

This was one of a handful of films dealing directly with juvenile delinquency in wartime. Teenagers Frankie and Sarah are next-door neighbors and are sweet on each other. Frankie wants to quit school and become a worker in a defense plant—his brother-in-law Danny (Kent Smith) is in the service, and both of his parents are in war work, so he feels left out. Sarah's parents are also war workers, and when they come home after a hard day at work, they rely on Sarah to serve their meals and take care of her younger sisters. Frankie falls in with a bad crowd, and goes to the defense plant to steal automobile tires from cars in the parking lot (since defense workers have priorities on getting replacements). They see a young child crying in the back seat of a parked car: his parents have no place to leave him while they are at work. The robbery is discovered and the teenagers are arrested, but are released in the custody of Danny, who has come home (he was wounded in action). Danny helps set up a recreation center for the children of defense workers: "after all, they are what we're fighting for." Meanwhile, Sarah has an argument with her parents and moves in with Toddy (top-billed Bonita Granville), an older girl who has her own place. Toddy gets Sarah a job at a roadhouse ("Rocky's"). Frankie sees Sarah there with a serviceman, and a fight breaks out. Toddy is fatally injured in the brawl. Frankie is sent to a "forestry camp" by the juvenile authorities; Sarah, sobered by the experience, promises to wait for him.

1945

1183 ADVENTURES OF KITTY O'DAY (Mono, Jan) William Beaudine; *genre:* Crime; *location:* United States; *coding:* Short, Blk; *relevance:* 1.

Sequel to *Detective Kitty O'Day* (1944, q.v.), again featuring Jean Parker as the meddlesome Kitty, this time investigating murders in the hotel where she works as a switchboard operator. Early in the film, the hotel manager admits Kitty is a far-from-perfect employee (she reads detective magazines on duty and listens in on private phone conversations), but "On account of the manpower shortage we must take what we can get." The "manpower shortage" phrase is repeated several more times in the film, but there are no other topical references.

1184 THE AFFAIRS OF SUSAN (Para, May*) William A. Seiter; *genre:* Romantic Comedy; *location:* United States; *coding:* AF-A, USO, Prod, Postwar; *relevance:* 2.

Broadway star Susan (Joan Fontaine)

returns from entertaining troops overseas. She accepts the marriage proposal of Richard (Walter Abel), an airplane manufacturer recently appointed to an important post-war planning position in Washington, where he will be in charge of reconverting aircraft plants to civilian use. However, Richard meets three other men Susan had once loved: Roger (George Brent), her ex-husband; poet Bill (Dennis O'Keefe); and lumber tycoon Mike (Don Defore). Each man tells his story about Susan. They all want to marry her, but Susan eventually decides to re-marry Roger.

1185 ANCHORS AWEIGH (MGM, Aug*) George Sidney; *genre:* Musical; *location:* United States; *coding:* AF-W, AF-MC, Ital?, AF-N, Latin Am, Bonds, Atroc, Chi, Jap; *relevance:* 2.

This films begins with an awards ceremony on the deck of an aircraft carrier, where sailors Frank Sinatra and Gene Kelly are given Silver Stars. They then go on a four-day leave in Hollywood. Wise-guy Kelly ("the best wolf in the whole Navy") meets aspiring singer Kathryn Grayson. He promises to get her an audition with pianist Jose Iturbi, but fails. Kelly then tries to foist Grayson on his innocent sidekick Sinatra, but Frankie is in love with Brooklyn girl Pamela Britton. At the end, Grayson gets the contract with Iturbi and gets Kelly, too. This Technicolor film reunites Grayson, Kelly and Iturbi from the previous year's *Thousands Cheer* q.v., this time putting Kelly in the Navy rather than the Army.

1186 APOLOGY FOR MURDER (PRC, Sept) Sam Newfield; *genre:* Crime; *location:* United States; *coding:* Short?; *relevance:* 1.

A reporter (Hugh Beaumont) becomes involved in a plot to murder the rich husband (Russell Hicks) of a beautiful woman (Ann Savage). Beaumont tells Savage, "You were always my first priority." Later, one character suggests that some blood he has discovered "could tie in with the murder of [Hicks]." Police Lt. Edwards replies, "It *could* tie in with the war, but I don't think it does."

1187 ARMY WIVES (Mono, Jan) Phil Rosen; *genre:* Romance; *location:* United States; *coding:* Blk?, USO, AF-A, Short?; *relevance:* 2.

Debutante Jerry (Elyse Knox) falls in love with soldier Barney (Rick Vallin) at a USO dance. They want to get married but cannot because Jerry's family does not approve, and she is a few days short of legal age. Jerry follows Barney to camp in Kentucky, but circumstances conspire to keep them apart. Finally, with the aid of a general's wife, Jerry and Barney are married in a taxi in Chicago, and manage to spend one night together before he is shipped overseas.

1188 BACK TO BATAAN (RKO, May*) Edward Dmytryk; *genre:* Resistance/Combat; *locations:* Philippines, Australia; *coding:* Juv, Jap, FDR, AF-A, AF-N, AF-W?, AF-AC, AF-Jap, Collab, Hirohito, Atroc, Fil, AF-Fil, Jew, MacArthur, POW, AF-MC, AF-CG, Resist; *relevance:* 3.

Colonel Joseph Madden (John Wayne) is ordered to continue resistance against the Japanese in the Philippines, even though the main U.S. forces have been defeated. He organizes American stragglers and Filipino Scouts into a guerrilla force. Among those in Madden's group are Scout officer Andres Bonifacio (Anthony Quinn—Quinn's character is named after a historical figure, a rebel Filipino who was executed by the Spanish rulers of the islands), an American schoolteacher (Beulah Bondi), and Maximo, a Filipino boy (Ducky Louie). Bonifacio, however, is despondent because his girlfriend Dalisay has become a propaganda broadcaster for the Japanese; he also criticizes the United States for failing to send aid to the Philippines. But, learning Dalisay is actually an Allied agent who is sending out military information in her "treasonous" broadcasts, Bonifacio agrees to continue the fight. Madden's forces attack the Japanese, hanging a Japanese officer who had hung the principal of Bondi's school for failing to lower the U.S. flag. They also massacre Japanese officers at a ceremony honoring the "independence" of the Philippines. [Japan actually declared the Philippines an "independent" nation in 1943. The United States, which had assumed control of the Philippines after the Spanish-American War, had promised to grant the islands independence after 10 years of "commonwealth" status, which began in 1935. Actual independence was achieved in 1946, after Japan had been defeated.] The Japanese capture and torture Maximo, hoping to learn the whereabouts of Madden's camp, but Maximo forces their truck over a steep cliff, and all perish. Two years later, Allied forces land on Leyte and the guerrillas help them in the reconquest of the Philippines. Ample screen time is given to Japanese atrocities in this film, which recreates the fall of Corregidor and the Bataan Death March. Wayne's character is not given any love interest in the course of the film, with the primary female roles going to schoolteacher Bondi, and Fely Franquelli as Quinn's girlfriend (Franquelli had previously played the Filipino volunteer nurse in *Cry "Havoc,"* q.v.).

1189 BEDSIDE MANNER (UA, June*) Andrew Stone; *genre:* Romantic Comedy; *location:* United States; *coding:* AF-MC, AF-W, AF-Russ, Russ, Short, Prod, Fem Lab, US-Russ Coop, MacArthur; *relevance:* 2.5.

Dr. Hedy Fredericks (Ruth Hussey) stops off in her hometown on the way to her new medical practice in Chicago. The town has grown enormously during wartime due to the influx of workers at the local aircraft plant. Hedy's uncle, the town doctor, is unable to cope with his expanded family medical practice duties. He wants Hedy to stay and help him out, but she is not interested. However, Hedy falls in love with airplane engineer Morgan Hale (John Carroll), and at the end decides to stay.

1190 A BELL FOR ADANO (TCF, Aug*) Henry King; *genre:* War Drama; *location:* Italy; *coding:* Mil School?, Dunkirk, Ger, Ital, AF-Ital, Brit, Musso, Ital, Eisenhower, Hitler, AF-A, AF-N; *relevance:* 3.

This film is based on a novel by John Hersey. John Hodiak is the U.S. military commander of a liberated Italian town. He tries to mix compassion with anti–Fascist activities, and falls in love with Italian girl Gene Tierney. The townspeople like his fair-minded ways (they replace Mussolini's portrait with one of Hodiak). He also helps the town replace its stolen church bell, which rings when he leaves for a new assignment. The administration of Italian territory after the fall of Mussolini and the retreat of the Nazi forces was a dry run for the eventual occupation of Germany and Japan, but was less extensive and relatively short-lived (Italian civil government had almost entirely replaced the Allied Military Government by December 1945). In part this may be attributed to the belief that the Italian people—and the civil service—were less dedicated to fascism than their German or Japanese counterparts. In this film, there is some criticism (by the Italian people) of a former fascist official, and there are scenes of returning Italian soldiers, but on the whole Italy and the Italian people are treated as a "liberated" nation rather than a conquered enemy.

1191 BETRAYAL FROM THE EAST (RKO, Mar*) William Berke; *genre:* Spy/Drama; *locations:* Japan, Panama, United States; *coding:* Atroc, Dipl, Nazi, AF-A, AF-N, War Corr, AF-Jap, Blk, Latin Am, FDR, Tojo, Hirohito, Jap, Spy-Sab, Jap-Ger Coop, Intell Serv, Collab?; *relevance:* 3.

Journalist Drew Pearson introduces this film, adapted from a novel, although he says it is "a true story—nobody could have made it up." The film begins in 1941. A U.S. reporter leaves Japan with information about a Japanese sabotage ring in the States, but is murdered before he can deliver the facts to Army Intelligence. Japanese agents hire Eddie (Lee Tracy), a former soldier, to obtain defense plans of the Panama Canal from a former comrade-in-arms. Eddie becomes romantically involved with Peggy (Nancy Kelly), actually an agent of G-2 (Military Intelligence). Peggy is murdered by the Japanese spies and their Nazi cohorts in Panama. Eddie exposes a Japanese naval officer, posing as a college student at Stanford, as the head of the spy ring, but is himself killed in a final shootout. Pearson says Eddie died in "an undeclared war ... [that] will end when the price of complacency has been paid.... It can't happen here again!" This film bears some similarity to *Blood on the Sun*, q.v., although it is set primarily in the United States. Some fairly graphic scenes of Japanese torture are included in the film.

1192 BETWEEN TWO WOMEN (MGM, Mar*) Willis Goldbeck; *genre:* Comedy/Drama; *location:* United States; *coding:* Jap, Bonds, Hirohito, Chi; *relevance:* 1.5.

Dr. Kildare was still away, so Van Johnson was cast in support of Lionel Barrymore's Dr. Gillespie. Johnson loves Marilyn Maxwell, but he also has to deal with Gloria DeHaven, a nightclub singer who has a mental problem. In one sequence, Maxwell offers to buy $100,000 worth of war bonds at a rally if Johnson kisses her. Keenan Wynn calls Johnson "Hirohito in disguise" if he does not do it, so Johnson makes the sacrifice and kisses the attractive blonde!

1193 BLONDE FROM BROOKLYN (Col, June) Del Lord; *genre:* Romantic Comedy; *location:* United States; *coding:* AF-A; *relevance:* 1.

An ex-soldier (Robert Stanton) teams up with a juke box operator (Lynn Merrick; for a brief period of time, "telephone juke boxes" were in vogue—customers would request songs from female operators) to form a musical act. They pretend to be Southerners and get a job promoting Dixie brand coffee. However, the young woman is confused with a missing heiress, and to avoid complications, the couple decides to drop their pose and become a legitimate singing team.

1194 BLOOD ON THE SUN (UA, June*) Frank Lloyd; *genre:* Drama; *location:* Japan; *coding:* Dipl, Atroc?, AF-Jap, Hirohito, Tojo, Jap, Russ, Chi, War Corr, Hitler, Hist Am, Spy-Sab, Collab; *relevance:* 2.5.

Produced by James Cagney's own company for United Artists release, this film is set in 1928 Japan. Cagney, writing for the English-language "Tokyo Chronicle," publishes an investigative report about a secret Japanese plan to conquer the Far East. The "Tanaka Plan" is denounced as a myth by Japanese officials (as it was in real life—the actual Tanaka Memorial was a document spelling out Japanese plans for the economic domination of Manchuria, not a blueprint for widespread military conquest), but Cagney obtains a copy of the document from

Eurasian spy Sylvia Sidney, who is in the employ of China. The plan is authenticated by a peace-loving Japanese nobleman, and Cagney gives it to Sidney to smuggle out of Japan, then reaches the American Embassy, despite attempts to kill him. The film overlooks one obvious point: IF Cagney delivered the plan, it obviously did not do much good, since WWII started anyway! [The original script had a different conclusion: Cagney escapes and delivers the document to the League of Nations, sparking a Japanese walkout.] This film personalizes Tojo (Robert Armstrong) as the chief villain, one of the relatively few Hollywood films in which Tojo or Hirohito was impersonated by an actor in a significant role (unlike the numerous Hitler characterizations). Ironically, during the period in which the film is set, Tojo was actually not a major political or military leader; he came to power later in the 1930s (and was deposed as Prime Minister in 1944). At the suggestion of the OWI, the producers deleted portions of a speech by Prince Tatsugi referring to "the white man's burden," and "colored races versus white races."

1195 BREWSTER'S MILLIONS (UA, Apr*) Allan Dwan; *genre:* Comedy; *location:* United States; *coding:* Vet, Prod, Blk, Postwar, Russ?, AF-W?, Home Fr, Fem Lab?, Jap, AF-A, AF-N, Nazi, Bonds, Short; *relevance:* 1.5.

Oft-filmed novel and play about Monty (Dennis O'Keefe), who must spend a $1 million inheritance in two months in order to inherit a much larger amount of money. This version begins as Monty returns from service in the Army. Some of the money can be given to charity, some spent on war bonds, but it all has to be spent before his 30th birthday, leaving him with no tangible assets—and he cannot even tell his friends about the codicil. A number of topical remarks are included in this comedy, including references to the War Labor Board, which refuses to approve a pay raise Monty wants to give his employees (as one more way of using up the million dollars).

1196 THE BRIGHTON STRANGLER (RKO, May*) Max Nosseck; *genre:* Horror; *location:* Britain; *coding:* Home Def, Brit, AF-W, AF-AC, AF-Raf, Nazi, Goering; *relevance:* 2.

Thriller with an interesting wartime ambiance. John Loder is an actor who plays "The Brighton Strangler" in a long-running London play. When German bombs hit the theatre (actual footage of the London Blitz is included here), Loder is hit on the head and gets amnesia. He makes the acquaintance of June Duprez, a young British servicewoman (her exact duties are never specified), who is secretly married to U.S. Army

flyer Michael St. Angel. They both travel to Brighton for the holidays, and Loder reenacts two murders from the play, strangling the mayor and chief inspector of police. He returns to London with Duprez and is about to carry out the play's final murder (hers), when the police, St. Angel, and Loder's fiancee (who wrote the play) spot them struggling on a hotel rooftop and begin to applaud! Loder stops strangling Duprez and takes a bow; unfortunately for him, he then falls off the roof and dies, just after returning to normal. In addition to Duprez and St. Angel, a considerable number of military extras appear in crowd scenes; a number of male civilians are shown carrying what appear to be large ladies' purses, but which were actually pouches for gas masks. There are also references to rationing and shortages, and a number of posters with war relevance. British actor Loder starred in two other war-oriented thrillers, *The Gorilla Man* (WB, 1942), and *The Mysterious Doctor* (WB, 1943), both q.v.

1197 BRING ON THE GIRLS (Para, Feb*) Sidney Lanfield; *genre:* Musical Comedy; *location:* United States; *coding:* AF-N, AF-W, AF-A, AF-MC, Blk, USO, Prod, Fem Lab, Home Fr, Short, Nazi; *relevance:* 2.

Millionaire Jay Bates (Eddie Bracken) joins the Navy to get away from people—especially women—who are only interested in him for his money. Phil Norris (Sonny Tufts) joins up to keep an eye on him as a favor to the law firm handling Jay's fortune. Jay falls in love with gold-digging cigarette girl Teddy (Veronica Lake), Phil's former fiancee. In the end, Phil and Teddy are reunited and Jay finds true happiness with singer Sue Thomas (Marjorie Reynolds). The Navy training of Jay and his pals is depicted in one VERY brief montage sequence; otherwise, they spend their time living it up in Miami (in real life, both Atlantic City and Miami hotels played host to a large number of servicemen in training). In Technicolor.

1198 CAPTAIN EDDIE (TCF, Sept*) Lloyd Bacon; *genre:* Biography; *locations:* France, Pacific, United States; *coding:* Ger-Am?, AF-Ger, AF-AC, AF-N, WWI, AF-Fr, Hist Am; *relevance:* 2.

The life story of Eddie Rickenbacker (Fred MacMurray) is told in flashback as he and several other men await rescue while adrift on a life raft in the Pacific during WWII. Rickenbacker's youth and his flying service in France during the First World War are detailed. Rickenbacker actually did survive a plane crash during WWII (October 1942), and was rescued from a life raft after 24 days. The film includes a re-creation of the well-known photograph of Rickenbacker standing next to his fighter which displays the "Hat in the Ring" insignia and painted crosses for the German planes he destroyed.

1199 THE CHICAGO KID (Rep, June) Frank McDonald; *genre:* Crime; *location:* United States; *coding:* Short, Blk Mkt; *relevance:* 1.5.

Warehouse worker Joe (Don Barry) borrows money from shifty Mike Thurber (Tom Powers). Thurber suggests Joe could pay off his debt with information about the "government-frozen commodities" in the warehouse where he works. Joe turns him down, but changes his mind when his unjustly convicted father dies in prison. Joe joins Thurber's gang, robbing warehouses and selling the goods on the black market. At the end, however, he sees the error of his ways and has a showdown with the gangsters, killing them although he is mortally wounded in the process.

1200 CHINA SKY (RKO, May*) Ray Enright; *genre:* War Drama; *location:* China; *coding:* Juv, AF-Jap, AF-Chi, Collab, Chi, Kor, Jap, Resist, POW, Atroc; *relevance:* 3.

The Chinese village of Wan-Li is a frequent target of Japanese air raids because it controls a vital mountain pass. Guerrilla leader Chen Ta (Anthony Quinn) comes to the village with wounded Japanese officer Yasuda (Richard Loo)—Chen Ta wants Yasuda to recover so he can be tried for war crimes. The village clinic is run by Dr. Gray Thompson (Randolph Scott) and Sara Durand (Ruth Warrick). Thompson has recently returned from the U.S. with his wife, socialite Louise (Ellen Drew). During the next air raid, Louise panics and loses the villagers' respect. Korean Dr. Kim (Philip Ahn), who is (unknown to the others) half-Japanese, is jealous of Thompson and of Chen Ta. Yasuda convinces Kim to help him escape. Kim dupes Louise into sending a message (she thinks it will bring a plane so she can go back to the U.S.). Meanwhile, Thompson and Sara treat Chen Ta's soldiers in the guerillas' moutain camp, and realize they are in love with each other. Japanese paratroopers attack the village; Thompson is wounded and Kim is killed by Yasuda, who escapes to lead his men in the assault. In the defense of the village, Louise loses her nerve again and is machine-gunned to death. Chen Ta and his men arrive at last, wiping out the Japanese and recapturing the wily Yasuda. Thompson and Sara make plans to rebuild their hospital. Although based on another Pearl S. Buck novel, *China Sky* was not produced on the same level as *The Good Earth* or *Dragon Seed* (1944, q.v.), but there are some similarities between the films (including the pejorative "devil dwarves," applied to the Japanese by the Chinese Chen Ta). One point of interest: the two primary *sympa-*

thetic Asian roles (Chen Ta and a Chinese nurse) are given to Caucasians Quinn and Carol Thurston, while the two *villainous* Asians are played by Richard Loo and Philip Ahn.

1201 CHINA'S LITTLE DEVILS (Mono, May) Monta Bell; *genre:* War Drama/Resist; *location:* China; *coding:* Juv, AF-FT, Chi, AF-Jap, Jap?, Resist, Sino-Jap War, Pearl Harb, Atroc; *relevance:* 3.

Youthful Chinese actor "Ducky" Louie, had the lead in this feature, after playing a plucky Filipino boy in *Back to Bataan*, q.v., and a plucky Chinese boy in *China Sky*, q.v. In this film, he is a plucky Chinese orphan adopted by a group of Flying Tigers, including Big Butch (Paul Kelly), and missionary Dr. Temple (Harry Carey). Nicknamed Little Butch, he organizes a group of refugee children who harass the Japanese. After Pearl Harbor and the subsequent entry of the U.S. into the war, the children rescue Dr. Temple from the Japanese, and also save the crew of a downed American bomber, including Big Butch. However, Little Butch is executed by the Japanese, and the film ends with Big Butch bombing Tokyo in his memory. This film is somewhat reminiscent of *The Boy from Stalingrad*, q.v.

1202 CHRISTMAS IN CONNECTICUT (WB, Aug*) Peter Godfrey; *genre:* Romantic Comedy; *location:* United States; *coding:* Hist Am?, Short, FBI, AF-Ger, Postwar, Bonds, Blk, Nazi, AF-A, AF-N, AF-W, Prod, Fem Lab; *relevance:* 2.

Barbara Stanwyck writes articles on homemaking for Sydney Greenstreet's magazine. As a publicity stunt, she is chosen to host Navy hero Dennis Morgan (named "Jefferson Jones," an example of the frequent linkage in wartime films between historical American figures and contemporary characters) for the holidays. However, Stanwyck is not only NOT an expert home-maker, she is not even married, does not own a house, and cannot cook! She convinces a friend to pose as her husband, borrows an old house in Connecticut, and hires S.Z. Sakall to do the cooking. The situation is complicated by the arrival of Greenstreet, who wants to observe the festivities firsthand (even he does not know Stanwyck is a fraud). Despite many pratfalls, Stanwyck manages to keep her job, falling in love with Morgan (and vice versa) in the process. The OWI was displeased by the "graphic and appetizing treatment of food throughout the film," since this display of conspicuous consumption "does not give a very favorable picture of the American home front during wartime."

1203 THE CLOCK (MGM, May*) Vincent Minelli; *genre:* Romance; *location:* United States; *coding:* AF-A, AF-W, AF-N,

Blk, Chi, Ital, USO, Bonds, Postwar, AF-Blk; *relevance:* 2.

Young soldier Robert Walker has a two-day leave in New York City. He meets Judy Garland under the clock in Penn Station. They spend the whole day and evening together, falling in love, but are accidentally separated on the subway. One of the most poignant scenes occurs in a department store, where the two young people look at furniture and speculate about a normal married life in the postwar period. They meet again under the clock, and get married just before Walker has to return to duty. The street scenes in this film are liberally populated with servicemen and women of all types; in the final scene, Walker and Garland are just one of numerous couples who have to part because one is in the service, including a black soldier who is seen with his wife.

1204 CONFLICT (WB, June) Curtis Bernhardt; *genre:* Crime; *location:* United States; *coding:* Short, V; *relevance:* 1.

Humphrey Bogart murders his wife because he has fallen in love with her younger sister (Alexis Smith). Sydney Greenstreet, a psychiatrist friend of the family, suspects Bogart of the crime. He plays on Bogart's guilty conscience with various tricks suggesting that the murdered woman is still alive, and at the end Bogart is exposed as the killer. Ration stickers are visible on automobiles, and a "V" stamp (a 3-cent "Win the War" issue) appears on a letter Bogart reads, but the war is not mentioned and no servicemen appear in the numerous crowd scenes. This film was made in the summer of 1943, but was not released until two years later. *The Big Sleep* (completed in January 1945, released 1946) and *Nobody Lives Forever* (completed November 1944, released 1946) are two other Warners films containing war-relevant material—both were released after the war.

1205 CORPUS CHRISTIE BANDITS (Rep, Apr*) Wallace A. Grissell; *genre:* Western; *location:* United States; *coding:* AF-AC, Postwar, Vet, Hist Am?; *relevance:* 1.5.

Captain Jim Christie (Allan Lane), a bomber pilot who saw action over Germany, returns to his home in Texas. His father tells him the story of their ancestor, Corpus Christie Jim (also Lane), a returning Civil War veteran who found his home state in ruins. The rest of the film is in flashback: Jim shoots the carpetbagger commissioner in self-defense, then turns outlaw, but eventually reforms and becomes a good citizen.

1206 COUNTER-ATTACK (Col, Apr*) Zoltan Korda; *genre:* War/Drama; *location:* Russia; *coding:* Blk, AF-W, Fr, Jew, Postwar, Rommel, AF-Ger, Ger, AF-Russ, Russ, Hitler, Nazi; *relevance:* 3.

A Russian sailor turned paratrooper (Paul Muni) is trapped behind German lines in the basement of a ruined building; also entombed alive with him are a Russian partisan (Marguerite Chapman), and a squad of German soldiers. Muni wants to discover where the Nazis have concentrated their forces; the Germans want to know where and how the Russians intend to cross a vital river. A game of wits and endurance ensues. Although Chapman is wounded, one German soldier (who was a miner—i.e., *a worker*—in civilian life) finally rebels against the Nazis and joins forces with Muni. Russian troops arrive in time to make use of the information Muni has obtained. This film was based on a Broadway play, which was in turn based on a Russian play (the film "opens up" the play by cutting between scenes in the cellar and scenes in which Larry Parks, one of Muni's cohorts, tries to get back to the Russian lines with information; he does not make it, but Muni's *dog* does—and winds up saving the day!). The film presents a somewhat less-romanticized view of the Russians (compared to *The North Star*, q.v., for example), although there is nothing particularly Russian about the characters or settings. The script was written by future Hollywood Ten member John Howard Lawson. OWI information indicates that the script was heavily revised a number of times to incorporate government suggestions, but the final film still fell short of their expectations: "changes [were made] that erase some of the material this office considered valuable ... the emphasis now being on action, not ideology." The OWI also did not appreciate the portrayal of a "good German," which could be construed as a point in favor of a "soft peace."

1207 CRIME DOCTOR'S COURAGE (Col, Feb) George Sherman; *genre:* Crime; *location:* United States; *coding:* Short, Latin Am; *relevance:* 1.

A man who has had several wives mysteriously die on their honeymoons with him is murdered just after marrying a new woman. The Crime Doctor (Warner Baxter) takes on the case. Two nightclub performers posing as "vampires" are also involved. An "A" gas rationing sticker is visible on the car used by the murder victim in the opening scene.

1208 THE CRIME DOCTOR'S WARNING (Col, Sept*) William Castle; *genre:* Crime; *location:* United States; *coding:* Draft?, Fr, Ital; *relevance:* 1.

Dr. Robert Ordway (Warner Baxter) investigates the murder of several young women, who all modeled for a particular painting. One of the suspects is neurotic artist Clive Lake. Lake tells Ordway he is not in the armed forces because "I was rejected." The real killer is exposed as an art dealer.

1209 DIVORCE (Mono, Aug) William Nigh; *genre:* Drama; *location:* United States; *coding:* AF-A?, Blk; *relevance:* 1.

Dianne Carter (Kay Francis) has been married and divorced four times. She pays a visit to her hometown, and is invited to the anniversary celebration of Bob and Martha Phillips (Bruce Cabot and Helen Mack). Bob, a recently discharged veteran, was Dianne's childhood sweetheart. She schemes to take him away from Martha; Bob wavers, but eventually comes back to his family.

1210 DOCKS OF NEW YORK (Mono, Mar*) Wallace Fox; *genre:* Comedy/Drama; *location:* United States; *coding:* Ref, Nazi, V?, Blk?, AF-Mer; *relevance:* 1.5.

The East Side Kids become involved with conspirators who plot to place their candidate on the throne of "Toscania" when the war is over. Sandra, the princess of Toscania, a "refugee" in the United States, is helped by the Kids, as well as Merchant Marine sailor Marty. Although the film deals with refugees from a fictional nation, there are references to the war, to the Gestapo, and to the "people [of Toscania] in bondage."

1211 DON JUAN QUILLIGAN (TCF, June) Frank Tuttle; *genre:* Comedy*; *location:* United States; *coding:* AF-A, AF-N, Draft; *relevance:* 1.5.

Tugboat captain William Bendix has a split personality—as "Pat" and "Mike," he has one wife in Brooklyn, and another in Utica. One personality gets drafted into the Army, and the other into the Navy. Bendix tries to kill off one of his personalities, but is then accused of murder! Everything is finally straightened out, and Bendix opts for the Navy as the service of his choice, dropping *both* wives!

1212 DUFFY'S TAVERN (Para, Sept*) Hal Walker; *genre:* Comedy; *location:* United States; *coding:* Vet, AF-?, Postwar?; *relevance:* 1.

Based on a popular radio program ("Duffy" was never heard on the show—the series' star was his bartender, Archie, played on radio and in the film by Ed Gardner). Victor Moore needs money to re-open his factory, which will employ a large number of ex-servicemen. Duffy arranges to hold a "block party," and all of the Paramount movie stars appear to help out. Among the guest stars: Bing Crosby, Betty Hutton, Alan Ladd, Eddie Bracken, and Dorothy Lamour. Good example of the way Hollywood jumped the gun on the end of the war, with a postwar theme going into production although hostilities were still going on.

1213 EADIE WAS A LADY (Col, Jan) Arthur Dreifuss; *genre:* Musical Comedy; *location:* United States; *coding:* V, AF-A, AF-N, AF-AC; *relevance:* 1.5.

Ann Miller is a debutante at an exclusive prep school who moonlights as a burlesque queen (under an assumed name), and falls in love with the owner of the theater she works in. Servicemen appear in the audience during the "Till You Came Along" number.

1214 THE ENCHANTED COTTAGE (RKO, Feb*) John Cromwell; *genre:* Romantic Fantasy; *location:* United States; *coding:* AF-AC, Pearl Harb, WWI, AF-MC, AF-A?, AF-N, USO, V; *relevance:* 1.5

Modernized version of a play by Sir Arthur Wing Pinero, first filmed in 1924. Robert Young rents a cottage from a WWI widow, then goes off to fight in WWII. Dorothy McGuire is the widow's dowdy housekeeper-companion. Young returns to the States after being shot down over Java, his face disfigured and one hand useless. Young's fiancee rejects him; however, he and McGuire fall in love, and as long as they are together in the cottage, their deformities and scars disappear.

1215 ESCAPE IN THE DESERT (WB, May*) Edward A. Blatt; *genre:* War Drama; *location:* United States; *coding:* Neth, Nazi, Jap, FBI, Short, Prod, Bonds, Spy-Sab, POW, AF-AC, AF-A, AF-N, AF-W, AF-Pol, AF-Free Fr, AF-Neth; *relevance:* 2.5.

Remake of *The Petrified Forest* (WB, 1936). Dutch pilot Philip Artveld (Philip Dorn), after victory in Europe, crosses the U.S. to report for duty in the Pacific. He is hitchhiking across Arizona when he is mistaken for one of four escaped Nazi POWs by Gramp (Samuel S. Hinds), proprietor of the ramshackle Last Chance Motel. Also at the motel are Gramp's grandson Danny, granddaughter Jane, and handyman Hank. The four REAL Nazis (led by Helmut Dantine) arrive at the Last Chance and hold everyone hostage, including a dentist (Alan Hale) and his wife who stop for gas. Philip and the others manage to overcome the Nazis at the finale. The film begins with an interesting scene in an airport in which military men of various nations appear. It was perhaps fortunate for the morale of Allied soldiers that the period between cessation of hostilities in Europe (May) and the end of the war in the Pacific (September) was relatively brief—wholesale transfers of troops from one theater to another would have obviously been extremely unpopular with men who felt that they had done their share already (although Dorn's character *volunteers* to help finish the job against the Axis).

1216 ESCAPE IN THE FOG (Col, Apr*) Budd Boetticher; *genre:* War Drama; *location:* United States; *coding:* Spy-Sab, AF-W, AF-N, Nazi, Chi; *relevance:* 2.5.

Nina Foch is a shell-shocked Navy nurse who has a recurring dream in which two men try to kill a third. She meets the third man in real life (William Wright). He is an agent of the Office of Psychological Warfare, and will soon be leaving for the Philippines with an important message. Nazi agents want that message. The climax of the film has Wright and Foch locked in a room which is filling with gas. Wright uses a magnifying glass and cigarette lighter to project the words "Hail Japan" on the glass door. The door is angrily smashed by patriotic Chinese passersby, thus saving the protagonists.

1217 THE FALCON IN SAN FRANCISCO (RKO, July) Joseph H. Lewis; *genre:* Crime*; *location:* United States; *coding:* Short, AF-?, AF-Mer, Chi?; *relevance:* 1.

The Falcon (Tom Conway) and his sidekick Goldie travel to San Francisco for a vacation. However, they become involved in a series of murders committed by rival smugglers competing for a shipment of raw silk which is arriving on a merchant ship disguised as hemp fibers. There are no overt war references in this film, but a few uniformed men are shown in one scene, and silk was war-oriented contraband (silk was not only hard to get during the war—since much of it is produced in the Far East—but it was also used to produce parachutes, so civilians had to do without).

1218 FIRST YANK INTO TOKYO (RKO, Sept*) Gordon Douglas; *genre:* War Drama; *locations:* Japan, United States; *coding:* AF-Chi, Pearl Harb, Fil, Kor, Resist, Jew, AF-Brit, AF-AC, AF-W, AF-A, AF-Jap, Atroc-Conc, Atroc, POW, Hirohito, Jap; *relevance:* 3.

Air Corps Major Steve Ross (Tom Neal) undergoes plastic surgery in order to penetrate the Japanese mainland on a secret mission. Ross lived in Japan with his family until 1937, and knows "every kink in their corkscrew psychology." Aided by the Korean underground, he impersonates a wounded Japanese soldier and gets a job at the Kamuri concentration camp, where an Allied scientist is being held prisoner (the Japanese do not know how valuable he is, but the man holds the secret to the completion of a secret weapon). Ross helps the scientist (and imprisoned American nurse Abby Drake—played by Barbara Hale) escape in a British sub, at the cost of his own life. The film ends with newsreel shots of the atomic bomb. Script changes were made at the last minute to link the imprisoned scientist with the atomic bomb, a ploy that made this film highly topical. This film also contains one of only two overt wartime references to the Bataan Death March (the other was in *Back to Bataan*, q.v.). In real life, there were around 175 POW camps in Japan, and some prisoners did work in Japanese war production

plants due to the manpower shortage there.

1219 FOREVER YOURS (Mono, Jan) William Nigh; *genre:* Drama; *location:* United States; *coding:* AF-A; *relevance:* 1.5.

One of Monogram's prestige releases of the season. Gale Storm is a young woman who spends part of her free time singing in a nightclub, donating her salary to help disabled veterans and children. Johnny Mack Brown, temporarily furloughed from Westerns, is an Army doctor called in when Storm is stricken with infantile paralysis (polio), and threatens to "will herself to die." Brown's treatments—he has been working with soldiers who have nerve damage—help cure her.

1220 GEORGE WHITE'S SCANDALS (RKO, Aug*) Felix E. Feist; *genre:* Musical Comedy; *location:* United States; *coding:* Blk, Latin Am, Short, Bonds, Brit, Dipl; *relevance:* 1.

Numerous musical production numbers take up a good deal of the running time of this film. There are two sub-plots as well: Joan Davis loves her co-star in the "Scandals," Jack Haley, but his spinster sister (Margaret Hamilton) stands between them; and director Philip Terry falls in love with the grown daughter (Martha Holliday) of a former "Scandals" chorus girl and a British nobleman. There are only a few minor topical references in this film: a "Buy War Bonds" poster is prominently displayed on a theatre wall, and there are two jokes about shortages.

1221 G.I. HONEYMOON (Mono, Apr) Phil Karlstein; *genre:* Comedy; *location:* United States; *coding:* AF-A; *relevance:* 2.

Gale Storm marries Army Lt. Peter Cookson, but he is ordered to report for duty immediately after the ceremony. Storm manages to get on the same train as her husband, but before they can consummate the marriage, he is ordered to report to the troop car. When they arrive at their destination, Storm rents an apartment, but various comedic events prevent the husband and wife from getting together. Finally, Cookson gets a 48-hour pass, and Storm puts on her wedding-night negligee, but word comes over the radio that all leaves are canceled. The film ends as Storm faints.

1222 GOD IS MY CO-PILOT (WB, Apr*) Robert Florey; *genre:* Biography/Combat; *locations:* China, United States, Burma, India; *coding:* AF-AC, Jap, Hist Am, AF-Brit, Blk, AF-Blk, Resist, V, AF-Jap, AF-Chi, AF-Ft, AF-Raf, AF-A, AF-N, FDR, MacArthur, Chi, Chiang, AF-Can, Pearl Harb, Hirohito, POW, Postwar?, Mil School, Short, Prod?; *relevance:* 3.

Adaptation of a popular book by Col. Robert Lee Scott: Scott (Dennis Morgan) grows up obsessed with the idea of flight, and joins the Army Air Corps after gradu-

ating from West Point in 1932. He is sent to the Far East after war begins, and joins the re-organized "Flying Tigers," now under Army Air Force auspices (General Chennault is played by Raymond Massey). Scott makes friends with Irish missionary Big Mike (Alan Hale), who "sound[s] more like a soldier than a missionary." "We both fight the forces of evil," Mike replies. Scott flies with the former Tigers—who are later replaced by fresh pilots from the States—against the Japanese, led by "Tokyo Joe" (Richard Loo), an ace known for taunting the Allied pilots (in English) over the radio. After numerous air battles, Scotty finally defeats the enemy pilot. There are numerous cutaways to Scott's hometown in Georgia, as his friends and neighbors follow his career in the service. Almost a sequel to Republic's 1942 *Flying Tigers*, this film contains a good deal of anti–Japanese invective. Col. Scott, hired as technical advisor for the film, also did some of the stunt flying on location. Five men were killed in a mid-air collision during the filming of the aerial sequences in Arizona. Note: there are a number of shots of the Tigers' insignia, a cartoon tiger (contributed by the Disney organization) leaping through the letter "V"—this insignia does not appear in *Flying Tigers*.

1223 GUEST WIFE (UA, July*) Sam Wood; *genre:* Comedy; *location:* United States; *coding:* War Corr, Chi, Short, Blk, Latin Am?; *relevance:* 1.

Don Ameche is a newspaper correspondent who gets a 10-day leave from his editor by claiming he has a wife (which he does not). So he "borrows" Claudette Colbert, who is really the wife of Dick Foran, and the predictable problems arise. There are a few minor references to shortages and rationing, and Ameche is portrayed as a foreign correspondent who reported from China and India, among other foreign locales.

1224 A GUY, A GAL AND A PAL (Col, Mar*) Oscar Boetticher Jr.; *genre:* Drama; *location:* United States; *coding:* AF-MC, Blk, FDR?, Short?; *relevance:* 2.

Helen (Lynn Merrick) and her nephew are traveling from Los Angeles to Washington, where she is to marry a government official. However, Helen cannot get a space on a train, so she pretends to be the wife of Marine hero Jimmy (Ross Hunter), on his way to receive the Congressional Medal of Honor. The couple has various adventures as they try to cross the country via train, plane and automobile. Finally, Jimmy and Helen arrive in the capital, and Helen decides to dump her fiance and really marry Jimmy. Once again, Hollywood reinforced the belief that home front work—while valuable—was inherently less manly than actually serving in the armed forces.

1225 THE HIDDEN EYE (MGM, Sept*) Richard Whorf; *genre:* Crime; *location:* United States; *coding:* AF-A, Blk; *relevance:* 1.

Long-delayed sequel to *Eyes in the Night* (MGM, 1942), q.v., with Edward Arnold as blind detective Duncan McLain. While the previous film dealt with spies involved in a murder, this entry contains only a minor topical reference (the character played by Paul Langton, Arnold's assistant, is described as a wounded veteran, who has been out of the Army for two months).

1226 THE HORN BLOWS AT MID-NIGHT (WB, Apr*) Raoul Walsh; *genre:* Fantasy/Comedy; *location:* United States; *coding:* AF, Short, Prod, Blk Mkt; *relevance:* 1.

Fantasy film whose alleged financial failure became the subject of running jokes on Jack Benny's radio show for a long time afterwards. Benny dreams he is an angel, sent to Earth to blow the signal to destroy the sinful world. Alexis Smith is his angelic girlfriend who comes to help him when a couple of fallen angels conspire to foil his mission. There are dialogue references to the black market, swing shift, etc., and a number of extras appear in military uniform.

1227 HOTEL BERLIN (WB, Mar*) Peter Godfrey; *genre:* War Drama; *location:* Germany; *coding:* AF-AC, WWI, Jew, FDR, Churchill, Collab, Dipl, AF-Ger, Fr, Pol?, Nor, Ger, Hitler, Nazi, Himmler, Goering, Russ, Stalin, Jap, Jew, Resist, Atroc-Conc; *relevance:* 3.

Vicki Baum was a German novelist best-known for *Grand Hotel*, which had been filmed by MGM in 1932. She moved to the United States in the 1930s and wrote a number of other books, including the derivative *Hotel Berlin*. Set in Nazi Germany during the final months of the war, the film version of the novel follows a diverse group of people in a large Berlin hotel: a film actress (Andrea King), a German general known as the "Butcher of Kharkov" (Raymond Massey) who hates the Nazis but is still a proud soldier (perhaps based on Field Marshal Erwin Rommel; like Rommel, Massey's character is forced to commit suicide by his Nazi superiors for plotting against Hitler), a hunted Resistance member (Helmut Dantine), a disillusioned scientist (Peter Lorre), a Gestapo official (Henry Daniell), and so on. Most of the film involves the various characters plotting to escape from Germany and thus avoid final retribution for their association with the Nazis. The OWI disliked the general thrust of the film: "Altogether *Hotel Berlin* portrays the Germans as a rather likeable lot...." The government reviewers disliked the film's references to a "widespread underground organization within Germany," and

felt that the film might "give the impression [the German people] hate Nazism and the whole system and that they have never been 'guilty.'"

1228 I LOVE A BANDLEADER (Col, Sept*) Del Lord; *genre:* Comedy; *location:* United States; *coding:* AF-A, Short, AF-N, Blk; *relevance:* 1.

Phil Harris is a house painter who loves music. When he is hit on the head and contracts amnesia, a press agent builds him up as "John Doe," a mystery bandleader who soon becomes an idol of the bobby-soxers. There are a few topically relevant remarks, some military uniforms seen in public, but the plot of the film has little or nothing to do with the war. In one scene, Harris's partner Eddie "Rochester" Anderson has the musician's female fans line up: "Girls with double-A priorities get the first autographs."

1229 IDENTITY UNKNOWN (Rep, Apr*) Walter Colmes; *genre:* Drama; *locations:* United States, France?; *coding:* AF-AC, AF-A, AF-Ger?, Postwar, Vet; *relevance:* 2.

Richard Arlen is a soldier who returns to the U.S. with amnesia. He was found in the ruins of a French farmhouse which had been bombed by the Germans, the only survivor of four soldiers. Adopting the name "Johnny March" (after the song "When Johnny Comes Marching Home"), Arlen visits the families of each of the four men, hoping to find out which man he really is. As it turns out, Arlen is really NONE of the four men—he is a pilot who crashed while trying to drop supplies to the trapped soldiers. However, during his travels Arlen manages to solve various family problems, and even falls in love with the widow of one of the dead men. The *Variety* review felt the happy ending (Arlen's romantic liaison with the widow) represented "an embodiment of the hopes of the war generation for a world that will feel the sacrifice was worthwhile."

1230 I'LL BE SEEING YOU (UA, Jan) William Dieterle; *genre:* War Drama; *location:* United States; *coding:* WWI, Short, Prod, FDR, Hist Am, Jap, Blk?, AF-Mer, AF-A, AF-N, AF-W, Postwar; *relevance:* 2.

Soldier Joseph Cotten returns to the United States to recover from a bayonet wound he suffered in the Pacific. Physically he is almost well, but the war has also caused psychological damage, and he needs friendly surroundings to overcome the trauma of battle. Cotten meets Ginger Rogers on a train. Rogers is going home on a Christmas furlough from prison (she accidentally killed her former boss, who was molesting her). Rogers brings Cotten back to the small town where her aunt and uncle live. Naturally, Rogers and Cotten fall in love. When Rogers' teenage cousin (Shirley Temple) lets the secret slip,

things look tough for a while. But Cotten promises to wait for Rogers to complete her sentence. Note: the title of this film comes from a popular song of the period which, while not overtly war-oriented, evokes feelings of separation, longing, and expectant waiting which certainly reflects the wartime ambiance.

1231 IT'S IN THE BAG! (UA, Apr*) Richard Wallace; *genre:* Comedy; *location:* United States; *coding:* Jew, Short, Home Fr; *relevance:* 1.

This film, starring radio comedian Fred Allen, was an uncredited version of the story "The Twelve Chairs." There are many cameo and guest appearances by stars like Jack Benny, Don Ameche, William Bendix, Victor Moore, and Robert Benchley. The topical references are restricted to a few isolated jokes and comments. For instance, Jack Benny (Allen's alleged "enemy") tries to tell a joke but never gets to finish it: "First I say, 'My uncle was drowned in his Victory Garden—'"

1232 THE JADE MASK (Mono, Jan) Phil Rosen; *genre:* Crime; *location:* United States; *coding:* Chi, Blk, Spy-Sab, Prod; *relevance:* 1.5.

Charlie Chan (Sidney Toler)—in U.S. government employ—solves the murder of a scientist who was developing a formula that makes wood as hard as steel. The killer was trying to obtain the secret for the enemy, and wore a rubber mask to disguise himself as one of the other suspects. Chan is assisted by his black chauffeur (Mantan Moreland), and yet another Chan son, Edwin Luke.

1233 JEALOUSY (Rep, July*) Gustav Machaty; *genre:* Drama; *location:* United States; *coding:* Fem Lab, Ref; *relevance:* 1.5.

Based on a story by Dalton Trumbo, this film stars Nils Asther as a refugee writer who cannot keep a job in the United States, and turns into a surly drunk. Jane Randolph, his wife, gets a job as a cab driver (a favorite Hollywood wartime profession for women—see also *Two O'Clock Courage*, and *She's a Soldier Too*, q.v.) to earn money for food and lodging. One of Randolph's passengers is a doctor (John Loder) who becomes romantically interested in her, but when Asther is murdered, Loder is a prime suspect. European refugees—generally fleeing Nazism—had been coming to Hollywood since the mid 1930s; they made the adjustment with varying degrees of success. Director Machaty was a Czech emigre, perhaps best known for directing Hedy Lamarr in *Ecstasy* (1933).

1234 KEEP YOUR POWDER DRY (MGM, Mar*) Edward Buzzell; *genre:* Training; *location:* United States; *coding:* Blk, AF-AC?, AF-A, AF-W, AF-N, Short; *relevance:* 3.

Lana Turner, Laraine Day, and Susan Peters are three young women who join the WACs. Turner is a rich young woman with an attitude problem: she has been living wastefully, and must now prove herself responsible enough to manage the money left to her by her grandfather. So, she decides to join the WACs. Once there, she clashes with Laraine Day, an Army brat who does not feel Turner has the proper attitude to make a good woman soldier. Their clashes are mediated by Peters, who is married to a soldier (he is later reported killed) and who joined up to do her bit. Agnes Moorehead is their commanding officer. Eventually, Turner shapes up, and she and Day are commissioned as WAC officers at the finale. The title song points out the purpose of the Women's Army Corps: "We can drive a truck, take our place in the mess [hall] ... we'll replace you men, while you fight at the front, for the WAC is a soldier too." Although this could be considered a film of especial interest to women, male audiences were undoubtedly entertained by the image of Lana Turner in tight overalls, bending over while tuning up a truck.

1235 LEAVE IT TO BLONDIE (Col, Feb*) Abby Berlin; *genre:* Comedy; *location:* United States; *coding:* Bonds; *relevance:* 1.

Blondie and Dagwood each contribute $100 to the Children's Camp Fund, but this breaks the household budget (money has also been set aside for war bonds). Son Alexander (formerly Baby Dumpling) enters a song in a contest, claiming it was written by Dagwood. However, the song was really written ten years before by Dagwood's uncle. Various mixups occur.

1236 LET'S GO STEADY (Col, Jan) Del Lord; *genre:* Musical Comedy; *location:* United States; *coding:* AF-A?, USO; *relevance:* 1.5.

A shifty New York music publisher takes $50 from a group of small-town young people (including Pat Parrish, Jackie Moran, and Mel Torme), but fails to publish their songs. They decide to promote their music by hiring a bandleader (Skinnay Ennis) and his band to play in Army camps, thus gaining national exposure.

1237 MAIN STREET AFTER DARK (MGM, Jan*) Edward Cahn; *genre:* Crime; *location:* United States; *coding:* AF-A, AF-N, AF-MC, Jap, Short, Blk Mkt, Latin Am; *relevance:* 2.5.

An atypical MGM B-picture, running under an hour in length, but still boasting the presence of Edward Arnold in the lead. Arnold is a police inspector out to catch a criminal family, led by a woman (obviously inspired by the story of "Ma" Barker; in this case the matriarch is "Ma" Gibson, played

by Selena Royle). The family makes its living "paddy-rolling" (stealing valuables from drunks, here almost exclusively drunken servicemen on leave). Ma's son Lefty comes home from prison (she told people he was in the Seabees in Alaska), and thinks about getting involved in the black market. Eventually the crooks are apprehended. The film was produced by Jerry Bresler, who had previously supervised the "Crime Does Not Pay" short subject series.

1238 THE MAN WHO WALKED ALONE (PRC, Mar*) Christy Cabanne; *genre:* Comedy; *location:* United States; *coding:* AF-A, Short, Jap, AF-Jap, WWI, Draft, MacArthur; *relevance:* 2.

Interesting attempt at a PRC "screwball" romantic comedy: Dave O'Brien is a recently discharged soldier (a war hero, of course, who served in the Pacific), who visits his "adopted" hometown of Plainfield (as in *The Human Comedy*, q.v., it was actually the hometown of a dead service pal that he heard a lot about and wanted to see). He meets society girl Kay Aldridge and they fall in love, despite Aldridge's rich boyfriend and her offbeat family.

1239 A MEDAL FOR BENNY (Para, June*) Irving Pichel; *genre:* War Drama; *location:* United States; *coding:* AF-A, Jap, Bonds, Latin Am; *relevance:* 1.5.

Benny Martin was run out of the California town of Pantera when he was a wild teenager. He left his girlfriend Lolita (Dorothy Lamour), father Charlie (J. Carrol Naish), and friend Joe Morales (Mexican star Arturo de Cordova) behind. While Benny is gone, Joe makes time with Lolita and takes advantage of Charlie. However, when the news arrives that Benny has been posthumously awarded the Medal of Honor for his actions in the Pacific, Joe and Lolita have to hide their relationship. To impress the military and political figures who are coming to town to present the medal to Charlie, the town fathers install the old man in a fancy house. But Charlie and Joe learn that this is only temporary window-dressing, and they move back to the old neighborhood. The ceremony takes place there, where Benny grew up. Based on a story co-written by John Steinbeck. Three-fourths of the nearly 400 Medals of Honor awarded during WWII went to members of the U.S. Army ground forces.

1240 MUSIC FOR MILLIONS (MGM, Feb*) Henry Koster; *genre:* War Drama; *location:* United States; *coding:* AF-A, AF-N, AF-W, AF-MC, Latin Am, Fem Lab, Draft, Jap, V, FDR?, Stalin?, Churchill?; *relevance:* 2.5.

Glossy MGM tearjerker. June Allyson, Marie Wilson, and Marsha Hunt are members of Jose Iturbi's orchestra, taking the place

of male musicians serving in the armed forces. Margaret O'Brien plays Allyson's protective little sister, and Jimmy Durante is Iturbi's assistant who helps out the young women with their problems. For example: Allyson's husband is overseas in the service, and she is pregnant. Word comes that her husband is missing in action, but the others decide not to tell her, since Allyson is ready to have her baby. Good news at the end, Allyson has a boy and her husband turns up alive. The film was produced and reviewed in 1944, and contains a good deal more topical material than many other 1945 releases—there are many uniformed extras in crowd scenes, ration stickers are visible on cars, war-oriented posters and signs appear in the background, and so on.

1241 NOTHING BUT TROUBLE (MGM, Mar) Sam Taylor; *genre:* Comedy; *locations:* United States, Pacific, Europe; *coding:* Hist Am, Ital, Short, Bonds, Fr, Nazi, Prod, Fem Lab, USO, Jap; *relevance:* 2.

This film begins in 1932, "when jobs were as hard to find as a girdle on a welder." Incompetent butler and cook Stan Laurel and Oliver Hardy lose their jobs after a colossal blunder, and decide to try their luck in some other country. In 1944—"when jobs were as easy to find as a girdle on a welder"—the boys return to the U.S. after being held prisoner by the Japanese. They go to work for the wealthy Mrs. Hawkley, who is so desperate for servants that *she* waits on *them!* In one sequence, the duo is given a ration book and sent out to buy a steak for Mrs. Hawkley's dinner party. They spend all of their money on other food and have to steal a steak from a lion's cage in the zoo (they do not know it is *horse* meat), but leave a page from their ration book in the cage in exchange. Stan and Ollie befriend young King Christopher of Orlandria, who is ruling his government-in-exile in the United States. The boy king (who loves Notre Dame football) is threatened with assassination by unscrupulous political rivals, but Laurel and Hardy help save him.

1242 OBJECTIVE BURMA! (WB, Feb*) Raoul Walsh; *genre:* Combat; *locations:* Burma, India; *coding:* Jap, AF-AC, AF-N, AF-A, AF-Jap, Hitler, Jew, Atroc, Bonds, AF-Chi, AF-Brit, Ital, India, War Corr; *relevance:* 3.

Major Nelson (Errol Flynn) and a troop of U.S. soldiers (along with a war correspondent, played by Henry Hull) are parachuted into Japanese-held territory in Burma to destroy a Japanese radar station. They then have to march through 150 miles of jungle to escape, since plans to pick them up by airplane go awry. They are beset on all sides by Japanese troops (who torture and kill some of the Allied soldiers). Only a few men survive, but their sacrifice makes possible the Allied invasion of Burma. There are several interesting sidelights to this long (142 minute), all-male combat film, which bears a certain resemblance to MGM's colonial adventure film *Northwest Passage* (1940). Between December 1944 and March 1945, British, Chinese, and U.S. troops undertook a major offensive in Burma which effectively broke the back of the Japanese forces. This film consequently appeared at a time when the Burmese theatre of war was in the news, and British audiences (and government officials) were outraged that little or no mention was made of British contributions in Burma theater of war (although in fact the British had been reluctant to undertake large-scale offensive action in Burma throughout 1943 and into 1944). The film was withdrawn from exhibition in England after only a week (it was re-released in 1952 with an apologetic prologue lauding the British military actions). However, in the film the U.S. soldiers *are* aided by both Chinese and Indian (Ghurka) soldiers in their mission. Real-life General "Vinegar Joe" Stilwell appears as a character in the film, impersonated by actor Erville Alderson.

1243 OUT OF THIS WORLD (Para, July) Hal Walker; *genre:* Musical Comedy; *location:* United States; *coding:* Fem Lab, AF-N?, Russ, Chi, Latin Am, India, Arab, Blk; *relevance:* 2.

Eddie Bracken is a nondescript messenger boy who is pressed into singing a number with Diana Lynn's all-girl orchestra at a small-town benefit show. He astounds everyone by singing just like Bing Crosby (Crosby dubbed Bracken's singing voice)!

Knowing a good thing when she hears one, Lynn signs Bracken up; but in order to get enough money to take the band to New York, Lynn has to sell shares in the enterprise. She accidentally sells 125%, a slight miscalculation which causes trouble later. Eventually, the whole thing is straightened out. One of the musical numbers (sung by Cass Daley), is "Sailor with an 8-Day Pass." Veronica Lake appears as a booking agent, and Bing Crosby's four sons make a cameo appearance as themselves.

1244 OVER 21 (Col, Aug*) Charles Vidor; *genre:* Training/Comedy; *location:* United States; *coding:* AF-A, Short, Postwar, Jew, Chi, Hitler, Stalin, Eisenhower, Churchill, AF-AC, Jap, Ger; *relevance:* 2.5.

Newspaper editor Alexander Knox enrolls in Officer Candidate School despite his age (39), so he can accurately understand the issues at stake in the war, and to understand the postwar world. His wife (Irene Dunne), a successful screenwriter, joins him during training and has to put up with the overcrowded housing situation near the Air Corps base in Florida. Added to this are the efforts of Knox's publisher (Charles Coburn) to get him discharged from the Army so Knox can take charge of the newspaper once more. This film contains a significant emphasis on military training, particularly the amount of material a potential officer must learn (Knox is hard-pressed to keep up with the younger men, but does graduate). Dunne secretly ghost-writes Knox's editorials while he is studying, but after he graduates she is offered his old position by Coburn in recognition of the quality of her work, a "home front" job. Based on a 1944 stage play by Ruth Gordon, this film has some points in common with *Pillow to Post*, q.v.

1245 PAN-AMERICANA (RKO, Feb*) John H. Auer; *genre:* Musical Comedy; *locations:* United States, Latin America; *coding:* Latin Am, Jap, AF-A, Fem Lab, War Corr; *relevance:* 1.

Philip Terry is a famous photographer, recently returned from covering the war in the Pacific, who is assigned by magazine publisher Robert Benchley to produce a series on the women of Latin America. Terry, Benchley, editor Eve Arden, and staff writer Audrey Long travel through Mexico, Cuba, and Brazil (with stops implied in other Latin countries), choosing beauties from each nation. Long is engaged to someone else, but she and Terry eventually fall in love with each other.

1246 THE PHANTOM OF 42ND STREET (PRC, May) Albert Herman; *genre:* Crime; *location:* United States; *coding:* Short; *relevance:* 1.

This murder mystery set in the New York theatrical district stars Dave O'Brien and Kay Aldridge (who were also teamed in *The Man Who Walked Alone*, q.v.). There is only one minor, oblique reference to shortages: in a cafe, the waitress says they can have their coffee "without cream or without milk."

1247 THE PHANTOM SPEAKS (Rep, May) John English; *genre:* Horror; *location:* United States; *coding:* Short, UN?; *relevance:* 1.

A psychic researcher (Stanley Ridges) is possessed by the vengeful spirit of an executed murderer, and goes on to kill the dead man's unfaithful wife, lawyer, and an unfriendly witness. The researcher is finally captured and sent to the electric chair, but the murderer's spirit vows "I'm not through yet!" Ration stickers are visible on several cars, and a newspaper headline reads "Senators Oppose League of Nations."

1248 PILLOW TO POST (WB, June*) Vincent Sherman; *genre:* Comedy; *location:* United States; *coding:* AF-A, AF-N, AF-MC, AF-W, AF-AC, Prod, Fem Lab, USO, Short, Jap, Blk, AF-Blk, Draft; *relevance:* 2.5.

Jean Howard (Ida Lupino) becomes a salesperson for her father's oil well supply company because the men salesmen are either in the service or in defense work. She wants to land a big order in Clayfield, but cannot get a hotel room due to the oil boom and a nearby Army base. She finally gets a room in an auto court by posing as the wife of Lt. Mallory (William Prince). Circumstances force Mallory to spend the night (platonically, of course) in the room with Jean. Naturally, they fall in love and plan to get married for real. Louis Armstrong and his orchestra appear in one sequence.

1249 POWER OF THE WHISTLER (Col, Apr*) Lew Landers; *genre:* Crime; *location:* United States; *coding:* Short, Russ, Blk; *relevance:* 1.

Richard Dix is a man who has amnesia after being hit by a car. He meets Janis Carter, who tries to help him discover his true identity. However, when Dix remembers who he is, it is bad news for all concerned: he is an escaped lunatic, who plans to murder the head of the asylum and the judge who sent him there! A ration sticker on a car windshield is virtually the only topical point of interest.

1250 PRIDE OF THE MARINES (WB, Sept) Delmer Daves; *genre:* Biography/Combat; *locations:* United States, Pacific; *coding:* AF-Jap, Blk, AF-W, Prod, Chi, Latin Am, AF-MC, AF-N, AF-A, Hitler, Hitohito, Tojo, Postwar, Vet, Pearl Harb, Jap, Jew, FDR, Hist Am, Draft, Short; *relevance:* 3.

This film was based on the life of Al Schmid, a decorated Marine hero whose story was featured in *Life* magazine in 1943. Factory worker Schmid (John Garfield) meets and falls in love with Ruth (Eleanor Parker) in the period before Pearl Harbor. When war begins, he joins the Marines and becomes engaged to Ruth just before he ships out for the Pacific. Al's unit is sent to Guadalcanal. One night, during a Japanese "banzai" attack across a river, Al is blinded by an enemy grenade. Sent back to San Diego for treatment, Al undergoes a series of operations but does not regain his eyesight. He becomes bitter, and does not want to travel to Philadelphia to receive the Navy Cross he has been awarded. Back home, his friends—and Ruth—try to encourage Al to begin adjusting to his condition, but he remains bitter and withdrawn. Finally, however, he regains his self-esteem and accepts the decoration in the name of his comrades in arms (there is also some intimation that his eyesight may be partially restored).

1251 RADIO STARS ON PARADE (RKO, Aug*) Leslie Goodwins; *genre:* Musical Comedy; *location:* United States; *cod-*

ing: AF-A, AF-N, AF-W, Blk, Short, USO; *relevance:* 1.5.

Wally Brown and Alan Carney are mistaken for talent agents. They try to find jobs for their clients, including singer Frances Langford. She gets a job with the Skinnay Ennis Band, which plays USO shows at Army camps (although this is not shown). Also a few minor topical references. Not really many radio "stars" in this film, aside from Ralph Edwards of "Truth or Consequences," and announcer Don Wilson (best known as Jack Benny's foil).

1252 ROUGH, TOUGH AND READY (Col, Mar*) Del Lord; *genre:* Adventure/ Comedy; *locations:* United States, Pacific; *coding:* AF-A, AF-W, AF-N; *relevance:* 2.5.

Obviously inspired by the earlier Edmund Lowe-Victor McLaglen "buddy" films (for example, *Call Out the Marines*, 1942, q.v.), this feature teamed McLaglen with Chester Morris. Jean Rogers and Morris are partners in a salvage business. Morris and McLaglen are friends and roommates, but rivals for Rogers' hand. Morris and his crew are employed by the Army Port Service, while Rogers joins the WACs. Although the two buddies have an argument, Morris risks his life to save McLaglen during a salvage dive in the Pacific, and they become friends once more.

1253 ROUGHLY SPEAKING (WB, Mar*) Michael Curtiz; *genre:* Drama; *location:* United States; *coding:* Home Fr, Can?, AF-A, AF-N, AF-W, Blk, WWI, Bonds, Pearl Harb, Fem Lab, Prod, Hitler, Jap, Ital, Pol; *relevance:* 1.5.

Two-hour tale of a family held together by the mother (Rosalind Russell). The film begins in the early years of the century, spans World War One, the Roaring Twenties, the Depression, and winds up in the contemporary period. Russell's second husband (Jack Carson), the scion of a rich family, flew with the Canadians in WWI, but at home he is overshadowed by his father. The ambitious Russell directs him into the burgeoning aircraft industry, but they are wiped out when the stock market crashes. As time passes, things finally begin to turn around, but Russell is not secure: "Every time I get my ship on an even keel, something goes bang" (there is a cut to newsreel footage of the attack on Pearl Harbor). Russell and Carson both get jobs in defense work, and their three sons all go into the service.

1254 SALOME, WHERE SHE DANCED (Univ, Apr*) Charles Lamont; *genre:* Historical Drama; *locations:* United States, Germany; *coding:* Ger, Austria, War Corr, Russ, Chi, Ref, Latin Am; *relevance:* 1.

Semi-Western in color set in the post-Civil War period. Yvonne DeCarlo is a dancer who discovers a plot by Prussia to invade Austria. She flees to the U.S. with correspondent Rod Cameron in order to evade the Prussian agents (including Albert Dekker) who want to silence her. Walter Slezak appears as a Russian. In addition to the obvious parallels between Prussia and Nazi Germany (the Prussians are referred to as "Huns," a standard WWI derogatory term for Germans, but also applied to the Nazis during WWII, albeit to a lesser degree), DeCarlo is referred to as a political "refugee." The German statesman Bismarck is portrayed in the film.

1255 SAMURAI (Cavalcade Pictures, Aug*) Raymond Cannon; *genre:* Spy; *locations:* United States, Europe, Japan, China; *coding:* War Corr, Jap, Chi, Spy-Sab, AF-Jap, Atroc, Fr, Ger, Ital, Brit, Hirohito, Tojo, AF-A; *relevance:* 3.

This independent film was copyrighted in 1944, but received only sporadic, exploitation-style release. Using large amounts of voiceover narration and stock footage to tell its story, the film begins in Tokyo after the devastating earthquake of 1923. An American "medical missionary" couple adopts a Japanese orphan, taking him back to the U.S. with them. The boy falls under the spell of a Japanese "priest" of the cult of "Bushido" in California, and grows up to become Ken Morrey (Paul Fung). After receiving his education in Germany, Italy, France, and England, Ken returns to the United States and begins to work as a spy for Japan. He travels to Japan and is later sent to China. Morrey is appointed future "governor of California" and sent back to America to spearhead Japanese spying and sabotage prior to Pearl Harbor. However, his adopted American brother exposes Ken's perfidy. After murdering his adoptive parents, Ken flees to the Japanese temple ("innocent-looking temples like these veil human monstrosities of deception," the narrator says) with the police in hot pursuit. After assisting in the ritual suicide of the priest, Ken is shot while trying to escape.

1256 THE SCARLET CLUE (Mono, May) Phil Rosen; *genre:* Crime; *location:* United States; *coding:* Blk, Spy-Sab?, Chi; *relevance:* 1.

Charlie Chan (Sidney Toler) is back, investigating a series of murders involving a plot to steal submarine radar plans. A scientist is murdered, and other murders occur in a radio-TV station whose manager is involved in the plot. Axis agents are not clearly specified as the organization behind the plot to steal the plans—it is possible that the criminals wanted to *sell* the plans to the Nazis, rather than being Nazis themselves.

Chan, once again in government service, is assisted by "son" Benson Fong, and Mantan Moreland.

1257 SCOTLAND YARD INVESTIGATOR (Rep, Sept*) George Blair; *genre:* Crime; *location:* Britain; *coding:* Fr, Brit, Postwar; *relevance:* 1.

This film takes place after the liberation of Paris. During the Nazi occupation of France, the British government had stored various valuable works of art in a secure vault. One of these was the "Mona Lisa," but now the French government wants it back. Chief of detectives of Scotland Yard Sir Aubrey Smith is embarassed to learn that Erich von Stroheim (von Stroheim's character name is "Carl Hoffmeyer," but he is apparently NOT supposed to be German) arranged to steal the painting and substitute another in its place. However, the switch is reversed and the French never find out that they nearly lost a great national treasure.

1258 THE SHANGHAI COBRA (Mono, Sept) Phil Karlson; *genre:* Crime; *location:* United States; *coding:* AF-Jap, Brit, Chi, Blk; *relevance:* 1.5.

Employees of a bank containing government radium deposits are murdered with cobra venom, injected via a needle planted in a juke box. The radium is destined for use in "hospitals, laboratories, factories" but is not specifically identified as a war material. Government agent Charlie Chan is called in because the same type of murders were committed in Shanghai in 1937. In a brief flashback scene, Chan describes how the killer was arrested, but it was the "first day Japanese bombers [flew] over Shanghai" (some documentary footage of planes and bombing follows). The killer was injured in the bombing and had bandages on his face (so no one knows what he looks like); he escaped from British custody then, but Chan catches up with him in 1945.

1259 SON OF LASSIE (MGM, June*) S. Sylvan Simon; *genre:* War Drama; *locations:* Norway, Britain; *coding:* AF-W, AF-Brit, AF-Ger, AF-Raf, Hitler, Nazi, Can, Brit, Nor, Resist, Intell Serv; *relevance:* 3.

RAF crewman Peter Lawford, son of Lassie's owner Donald Crisp, takes Lassie's son Laddie along with him on a recon flight over Norway. Their plane is shot down and Laddie and Lawford are separated. The Nazis use the dog to identify Lawford—who is being assisted by the Norwegian resistance in his effort to escape to England—but both man and dog eventually get home. This film includes yet another sequence featuring the training of "war dogs," a concept Hollywood found fascinating and featured in a number of films. Laddie runs away from a trainer firing a gun and is washed out of the program, but when a Nazi soldier later threatens Lawford with a pistol, Laddie leaps to his master's defense. The mountainous locations of this film were particularly well suited to Technicolor photography. As a point of information, Norway was never "liberated" by Allied forces during WWII: the German forces were withdrawn after the general surrender of May 1945. Trivia notes: Lawford's love interest in this film is June Lockhart, later to star in the *Lassie* television series. Also, Lassie herself was cast as a shell-shocked veteran war dog in *Courage of Lassie* (1946).

1260 A SONG TO REMEMBER (Col, Mar*) Charles Vidor; *genre:* Biography; *locations:* Poland, France; *coding:* Pol, Russ, Ger, Fr; *relevance:* 1.

Technicolor biography of Polish composer Frederic Chopin (Cornel Wilde). The film (which was a big box-office success) draws some parallels with contemporary events, although it plays fast and loose with historical facts. At the age of ten, Chopin is already recognized as a piano prodigy by his German teacher, Joseph Elsner (Paul Muni). However, Chopin is also politically precocious, and stares in outrage as he watches "Polish prisoners [being taken] to Siberia" by the Tsar's soldiers. When he reaches manhood, Chopin is invited to play at a dinner party for a local nobleman. He is late, because a Russian revolutionary has arrived to speak to the secret society of Polish patriots: "Life, liberty and the pursuit of happiness ... we have that one hope in common. Yet they tell us that the Polish people and the Russian people are enemies...Tyrants must have something in common, too." At the dinner party, Chopin refuses to perform before the new Russian governor-general: "I do not play before Tsarist butchers." He is forced to flee, and travels to Paris with Elsner. Chopin learns some of his friends were executed for helping him escape, and begins work on the patriotic "Polonaise." However, Chopin falls in love with George Sand (Merle Oberon), who convinces Chopin to devote himself to composing rather than performing, and disparages the "Polonaise." But when Konstantia (Nina Foch) arrives from Poland and tells him about the plight of the Polish freedom fighters, Chopin begins a concert tour of Europe in order to raise funds for the resistance forces. The strain of the tour exacerbates Chopin's tuberculosis, and after his final concert in Paris, he collapses and dies. This film was originally to be made in 1937 by Frank Capra with Francis Lederer as Chopin (interestingly enough, Muni was envisioned as Elsner even at this point), but the project was shelved after a legal dispute between Capra and Columbia over other matters. It is interesting that the villains in

this film are Russians (albeit pre–Soviet Tsarists) and the two most prominent German characters (Elsner and Franz Liszt) are presented in a positive light!

1261 A SPORTING CHANCE (Rep, June*) George Blair; *genre:* Comedy; *location:* United States; *coding:* Latin Am, Fem Lab, Prod; *relevance:* 1.

In this lightweight comedy, when a shipbuilding magnate dies, his society daughter (Jane Randolph) learns she can only inherit his wealth if she can get and hold down a job at his shipyard (incognito) for one year.

1262 THE STORY OF G.I. JOE (UA, July) William A. Wellman; *genre:* Combat; *locations:* North Africa, Italy; *coding:* Ital, AF-Ger, Arab?, AF-A, AF-AC, AF-W, War Corr, Latin Am?, Postwar, POW, Eisenhower; *relevance:* 3.

War correspondent Ernie Pyle (Burgess Meredith) joins an American Army unit in North Africa. Although he is middle-aged (born in 1900), Pyle is like one of the soldiers, eating and sleeping with them as the campaign goes on. Their convoy is strafed by a German Stuka, and one of the young soldiers, "Gawky," is killed. The unit adopts his pet puppy as their mascot. The men listen to the sultry voice of Nazi broadcaster Axis Sally, and think wistfully of their homes when "Lili Marlene" is played. The unit is exposed to the harsh realities of war when they observe a straggling line of American troops retreating in the rain. Later, a battle-hardened and cohesive fighting group, they fight their way across Italy. In one sequence, Brooklyn native Dondaro ducks into a ruined cafe during an artillery barrage and has a fleeting encounter with a voluptuous Italian girl, whose English is limited to "Okay." Sgt. Warnicki desperately seeks a working phonograph so he can play a recording of the voice of the son he has never seen. After a nasty encounter with German snipers in a bomb-damaged church, the village of San Vittorio is secured. The GIs feed the surviving Italian civilians, and a chaplain is found to marry a young soldier and an Army nurse. As the casualties mount during the grueling campaign to capture Monte Cassino during the winter of 1944, the few remaining original men in the unit seek solace in liquor and thoughts of home. General Eisenhower orders the mountaintop monastery bombed in an attempt to drive out the German defenders, but the enemy merely creates new positions in the rubble (newsreel footage and scenes from John Huston's 1945 documentary *The Battle of San Pietro* are incorporated in these scenes). Warnicki goes mad. The Allies finally win the battle, but the unit's beloved Captain Walker (Robert Mitchum; this was Mitchum's final film be-

fore the actor went into the Army; he served a short enlistment, receiving a hardship discharge as the "sole support" of his family) is killed—his body is carried down from the mountain on the back of a mule, and the soldiers bid him farewell (this incident was based on a real occurrence, covered in one of Pyle's columns). On the road to Rome, Pyle's voiceover narration concludes the film: "Surely, something good must come out of this ... I hope we can rejoice in our [ultimate] victory, but humbly.... As for those beneath the wooden crosses, we can only murmur, thanks pal, thanks." This film largely eschews the standard Hollywood war film heroics for a more realistic portrayal of war, but United Artists ironically considered it "a woman's picture" resembling "an hour-an-a-half visit with the boys on the battlefront." Pyle himself was later killed covering the invasion of Okinawa in April 1945.

1263 TEN CENTS A DANCE (Col, June*) Will Jason; *genre:* Comedy; *location:* United States; *coding:* AF-A; *relevance:* 1.

Two young women (Jane Frazee and Joan Woodbury) work in a dance hall and run con games on the side. They try to swindle two soldiers (Jimmy Lloyd and Robert Scott), but fall in love with them instead. Minor Columbia musical also featuring John Calvert as a confidence man.

1264 THE THIN MAN GOES HOME (MGM, Jan) Richard Thorpe; *genre:* Crime; *location:* United States; *coding:* Blk, Prod, Short, AF-A, AF-N, Jap, Spy-Sab?; *relevance:* 2.

Nick and Nora Charles (William Powell and Myrna Loy) travel to Nick's hometown for a visit with his parents (they go via train, which is very crowded and filled with men and women in uniform, a realistic reflection of wartime conditions). Nora buys a painting at a local gallery for Nick's birthday, and various murders and mysterious occurrences begin. It turns out that all of the paintings by a certain artist contain (under the paint) drawings from the local defense plant of airplane parts that would interest "foreign powers." Several murders are committed with a Japanese sniper's rifle, brought home from the Pacific by a returning veteran. There are also a few minor topical remarks.

1265 THIRTY SECONDS OVER TOKYO (MGM, Jan) Mervyn LeRoy; *genre:* Biography/Combat/Training; *locations:* Pacific, China, United States; *coding:* AF-AC, AF-Jap, Atroc, Jap, Pearl Harb, Resist, Nazi?, AF-N, AF-MC?, Bonds, Prod, Fem Lab, Chi, Chiang, AF-Chi, Hist Am, Blk?, Brit, Postwar, FBI; *relevance:* 3.

This film recreates—in semi-fictional form—the April 1942 air raid on Tokyo by U.S. bombers under the command of Lt.

Col. James Doolittle. While regular bombing of the Japanese homeland was not carried out for several more years, the initial raid was a morale-builder for the Allies, and sent a significant message to the Japanese people. Although Col. Doolittle appears in the film (portrayed by Spencer Tracy), the story revolves around Ted Lawson (played by Van Johnson—Capt. Ted Lawson was the author of the book upon which this film was based) and the crews of the planes participating in the mission (among the other airmen are Robert Walker, Robert Mitchum, and Don DeFore). The special training for the mission is detailed, then the mission is reconstructed (including some documentary footage of the aircraft carrier *Hornet*, from which the bombers were launched). Ted's plane crash-lands in China. The crew is rescued by Chinese partisans, but Ted's leg has to be amputated. The film ends as Ted returns to the United States, where he is reunited with his pregnant wife, Ellen (Phyllis Thaxter). The aftermath of the Doolittle raid was fictionalized in *The Purple Heart*, q.v.—in real life, eight American flyers were tried for "war crimes" and three of these were executed by their Japanese captors.

1266 THIS MAN'S NAVY (MGM, Feb*) William A. Wellman; *genre:* Training/Combat; *location:* United States, India; *coding:* AF-AC, AF-N, AF-Ger, Brit, Jap, India, Home Fr, AF-Jap, Chiang; *relevance:* 3.

Wallace Beery essays a typical Beery role in this film about U.S. Navy blimps during wartime. Beery, a blustering blowhard (with a heart of gold) "adopts" the disabled Jeff (Tom Drake), finds him a girlfriend, and gets a Navy doctor to help him walk again. Jeff joins the Navy, but while on anti-submarine patrol in Beery's blimp, the young man loses his nerve. Beery, disobeying orders, flies the blimp and destroys a German submarine. Embarassed, Jeff transfers to another branch of the Navy. Beery and his sidekick James Gleason are transferred to India; who should show up, now an airplane pilot for Naval Air Transport, but Jeff. Jeff volunteers to fly a British dignitary to Chungking, but their plane is shot down. Beery and Gleason pilot a blimp to rescue the survivors, but on the way back the gasbag is attacked by Japanese fighters. To "lighten the load," Beery and Gleason bail out. The others make it back safely, but are worried about the two men until the old salts are carried into town in rickshaws. The Navy had experimented with blimps for several decades, and in April 1942 put them on anti-submarine patrol in the Atlantic. The lighter-than-air ships could cruise long distances at fairly low speeds, the better to spot submarines preying on Allied convoys.

1267 THOSE ENDEARING YOUNG CHARMS (RKO, Apr*) Lewis Allen; *genre:* Romantic Comedy; *location:* United States; *coding:* V, AF-AC, AF-N, AF-W, AF-A, Home Fr, WWI?, Chi, Russ, Brit, Short, Blk; *relevance:* 2.5.

Jerry (Bill Williams), an Army private stationed in New Jersey, is in love with Helen (Laraine Day), who works in the perfume department of a New York department store. Jerry runs into an acquaintance, Hank (Robert Young), a bomber pilot temporarily stationed near the city. Hank moves in on Helen, to the dismay of Jerry (who knows Hank is a ladies' man) and Helen's mother. Although Helen is cautious at first, Hank's campaign to win her affection succeeds. However, he backs out at the last moment when he discovers he *really* cares for her. They quarrel, but reconcile on the runway just before Hank's squadron departs (presumably for the Pacific theatre of war). There are a number of references to shortages and rationing, and Helen's mother is depicted as an active member of the "Women's Uptown 84th Street Auxiliary War Relief Association," a typical humorous Hollywood gibe at various home front and home defense activities. This film is also notable for the large number of uniformed servicemen and women appearing in crowd scenes.

1268 THE THRILL OF A ROMANCE (MGM, July*) Richard Thorpe; *genre:* Romantic Comedy; *location:* United States; *coding:* Prod?, AF-AC?, Latin Am, Jap; *relevance:* 2.

Tommy (Van Johnson) is a much-decorated war hero (a fighter ace from the Pacific—this was very much the glamour "profession" of the war years) who comes home on convalescent leave. At a resort hotel, he meets and falls in love with Cynthia (Esther Williams), even though she has just been married. However, Cynthia's husband Bob (Carleton Young) is an industrialist who left for a big meeting in Washington right after their wedding. Tommy and Cynthia realize nothing can come of their romance, but when Bob gets back, he has bad news for his (presumably virginal) wife: his divorce from his previous wife is not final, so his marriage to Cynthia has to be annulled! This leaves the door wide open for Tommy. Yet another example of Hollywood giving preference to military heroes over men who "stayed at home," with rich businessman Bob losing his wife to the handsome hero Tommy. In Technicolor.

1269 THUNDERHEAD, SON OF FLICKA (TCF, Mar) Louis King; *genre:* Drama; *location:* United States; *coding:* AF-A, AF-N, AF-W, Short, Mil School; *relevance:* 1.

Most of the original cast of *My Friend Flicka* (TCF, 1943), q.v., return for this sequel, with Roddy McDowall as the horse-loving boy and Preston Foster as his father. Once again, the war-relevance in the film is minor: gasoline-rationing stickers on automobiles, and uniformed extras in the crowd at a racetrack. Horse-racing became very popular during the war as a source of entertainment; the legalized betting was also an enticement. But it became almost too popular for its own good—in early 1945, the War Production Board ordered racetracks closed for the duration, since the horseplayers were wasting gasoline and rubber to visit the hippodromes. In Technicolor.

1270 TO HAVE AND HAVE NOT (WB, Jan) Howard Hawks; *genre:* War Drama; *location:* Caribbean; *coding:* AF-Fr, Resist, Ger?, Blk, Free Fr, DeGaulle, AF-Ger, Vichy, Petain, Nazi; *relevance:* 2.5.

Ernest Hemingway's story about a down-on-his-luck fisherman coerced into smuggling in order to save his boat was heavily revised for topicality and crafted into a pseudo-*Casablanca* (more faithful adaptations were *The Breaking Point*, WB, 1950, and *The Gun Runners*, UA, 1958). On the Caribbean island of Martinique in the summer of 1940, the island's administration is controlled by Vichy partisans. American Harry Morgan (Humphrey Bogart) is approached by Free French supporters who want to charter his boat. He refuses, even though his most recent charter-fishing client has not yet paid his bill, and money is tight. Harry's politics are "minding my own business," and furthermore he knows that Vichy controls the French Navy, which has the power to confiscate his boat and send him to Devil's Island if he breaks their laws. Eventually, of course, Harry changes his mind, spurred on by Slim (Lauren Bacall), and by the brutal treatment dealt his loony sidekick (Walter Brennan—"Was you ever bit by a dead bee?"). This was Bacall's first film, and contains the famous "If you want anything just whistle" scene.

1271 TONIGHT AND EVERY NIGHT (Col, Feb*) Victor Saville; *genre:* War Drama; *location:* Britain; *coding:* Latin Am, AF-W, AF-Brit, AF-Raf, Brit, US-Brit Coop, AF-Russ, Hitler, AF-A, AF-N, Free Fr, Short, V; *relevance:* 3.

A *LIFE* magazine spread on London's Music Box theatre—which continued to function even during the Blitz—is the frame for the flashback story of Rosalind (Rita Hayworth), an American performer who has been with the show since the pre-war years. After war breaks out, an air raid disrupts a show, sending the cast and audience into the theatre cellar. While in the cellar, Rosalind meets RAF pilot Paul Lundy (Lee Bowman). At first Paul's wolfish actions turn Rosalind off, but eventually they fall in love. Rosalind's friend and co-worker Judy (Janet Blair) is killed by a German bomb on the night before Paul and Rosalind are to be married. Rosalind decides to stay in London to carry on with the show while Paul is shipped out to India. They plan to reunite after the war is over. Fairly lavish Technicolor musical drama produced and directed by Victor Saville, a British filmmaker. In one humorous scene, a dancer gets a job in the show by doing an "interpretive dance" to a speech by Adolf Hitler!

1272 TWICE BLESSED (MGM, July*) Harry Beaumont; *genre:* Comedy; *location:* United States; *coding:* Blk, Juv, Short, Fem Lab, Latin Am, Home Fr; *relevance:* 1.5.

Preston Foster and Gail Patrick got divorced because they did not agree on the way to raise children: they each got custody of one child (twins Lee and Lynn Wilde). Patrick's daughter is now a refined "egghead," while Foster's charge is a jiving bobby-soxer. The two girls meet and decide to change places, reuniting their parents as well. While the plot is not topical, there are a fair number of war and topical references in the dialogue such as "It's taken a war to teach us the slack [i.e., women] is as mighty as the trouser." There are also some signs, posters, etc., referring to the war (a sign on the wall of a soda fountain reads "NO CIGARETTES").

1273 TWO O'CLOCK COURAGE (RKO, Apr*) Anthony Mann; *genre:* Crime; *location:* United States; *coding:* Fem Lab, Brit; *relevance:* 1.

A remake of *Two in the Dark* (RKO, 1936): Tom Conway has amnesia, and is a murder suspect, to boot. Ann Rutherford, a female cabbie, lends him a helping hand so he can prove his innocence. A bullet graze brings Conway's memory back, and he is cleared. In the earlier version, the female lead (played by Margot Grahame) was an actress, not a cab driver; in this film, Rutherford says she *used* to be an actress but now drives a cab. However, there are no overt war references, no ration stickers, and in one scene Conway walks into a tailor shop and buys a new suit, with no mention of clothing ration coupons.

1274 UTAH (Rep, Mar) John English; *genre:* Western; *location:* United States; *coding:* Blk, Short; *relevance:* 1.

Chicago showgirl Dale Evans wants to sell the Utah ranch she inherited and invest the money in a musical show. Roy Rogers and Gabby Hayes, who work on the ranch, try to get her to change her mind so the ranch will not fall into the hands of sheepmen. Unscrupulous real estate man Grant Withers schemes to cheat Dale out of the land. Roy's

point of view prevails, but Dale puts on her show—a Western review—anyway. Although this is a contemporary film, there are no references to the war except for a "T" gas ration sticker on a station wagon ("T" stickers were for commercial vehicles).

1275 THE WAY AHEAD (TCF, June*) Carol Reed; *genre:* Training/Combat; *locations:* Britain, North Africa; *coding:* AF-Brit, AF-Ger, Ital, Brit, Churchill, Arab, FR, Russ, Jap, Hitler, Musso, Prod, Prod-Farm, Juv, Dunkirk, Rommel, WWI, AF-Raf, AF-Mer, AF-W, Home Def, Home Fr, Pacifist, AF-A; *relevance:* 3.

This film was produced in England and released there in 1944. In 1945, Twentieth Century–Fox imported the film, cut it by about 20 minutes, and added an on-screen prologue and concluding voiceover narration by noted American war correspondent Quentin Reynolds. In his opening remarks, Reynolds compares the British citizen-soldiers with the Minute Men of the American Revolution; at the conclusion, he says the story of the British "Tommies" is also the story "of our G.I. Joes, too ... a story that will never die." The film follows the training of a diverse group of British civilians—among them a reserve officer (David Niven), a stuffy department store clerk, a Scots farmer, and a building maintenance man (Stanley Holloway)—who have been inducted into the British Army. At first the men rebel against "meaningless" military discipline and training, but soon realize the value of the Army way of doing things, and form a cohesive fighting unit. Their troopship is sunk by a German sub in the Mediterranean on the way to the war zone; later, they engage in combat with the Germans in North Africa. This film, co-written by Eric Ambler and Peter Ustinov (who has a supporting role), was re-released after the war as *The Immortal Battalion*.

1276 WHAT A BLONDE (RKO, Jan*) Leslie Goodwins; *genre:* Comedy; *location:* United States; *coding:* Short, Ital; *relevance:* 2.5.

Leon Errol is a lingerie manufacturer whose business is declared non-essential, so he cannot get enough gas coupons for his car. He hires two riders for his car-pool, including Veda Ann Borg, a blonde who causes Errol trouble with his wife. Errol also needs silk (in short supply) for his products, and throughout the film an inventor keeps trying to sell him a formula for synthetic silk.

1277 WHERE DO WE GO FROM HERE? (TCF, June*) Gregory Ratoff; *genre:* Fantasy/Comedy; *location:* United States; *coding:* USO, Draft, AF-A, AF-W, AF-MC, Home Fr, Hist Am, Ger, Pol, Ital; *relevance:* 2.5.

Car dealer Fred MacMurray's franchise is closed for the duration (civilian automobiles were not manufactured during the war). MacMurray loves June Haver, an entertainer at the Servicemen's Canteen, but she will not go out with him because he is 4-F. Joan Leslie is in love with MacMurray, but he cannot see her for Haver. Rubbing a lamp he found in a scrap drive, MacMurray conjures up a genie (Gene Sheldon), who grants MacMurray his wish to be "in the Army." But MacMurray is transported to the days of the American Revolution, with *George Washington*'s army at Valley Forge! He spies on the Hessians, and makes a mock speech to them, referring to their conquest of Poland, and adding "Sieg Heil!" After helping George Washington cross the Delaware River, MacMurray is transported to various other historical locales by the genie, including Columbus's ship. Returning to the present, the genie helps MacMurray into the service: the WACs! Finally, everything is straightened out, and even the genie joins up. In Technicolor.

1278 WITHIN THESE WALLS (TCF, July) H. Bruce Humberstone; *genre:* Drama; *location:* United States; *coding:* AF-MC, AF-N; *relevance:* 1.

In 1943, Judge Howland (Thomas Mitchell) is appointed warden of a troubled prison. The stern judge tells the inmates to stop making trouble: "Fine young men and boys are out fighting, giving up their lives for you." Meanwhile, Howland's son tries to join the Marines, but the recruiting office spots him as underage. In order to prevent the boy from trying again—perhaps this time with the Navy—Howland brings the boy along to the prison with him. However, the young man rebels against his father and falls into bad company. 1945: the son is now an inmate at the very prison his father manages. During a jailbreak, he saves Warden Howland's life but is shot and killed. Howland changes his authoritarian ways and begins to treat the convicts as human beings.

1279 WITHOUT LOVE (MGM, May*) Harold S. Bucquet; *genre:* Romantic Comedy; *location:* United States; *coding:* AF-W, AF-N, AF-A, AF-AC, Blk, Latin Am, Free Fr, Ref, Prod, Short, Brit, Russ; *relevance:* 1.5.

Inventor Spencer Tracy is looking for a house in wartime Washington where he can work on a new oxygen helmet for pilots. He rents the home of recent widow Katherine Hepburn. She suggests that they get married (purely platonically, of course), so she can legitimately live with him and serve as his assistant. They do, but of course they fall in love for real, and the helmet is also a success. Keenan Wynn plays Hepburn's dejected, hard-drinking cousin who, after previous rejections, finally gets to join the Navy at the film's end.

1280 THE WOMAN IN GREEN (Univ, July) Roy William Neill; *genre:* Crime; *location:* Britain; *coding:* AF-Brit, Brit; *relevance:* 1.

Sherlock Holmes is called in to investigate the "Finger Murders," in which a series of young women have been killed, and their fingers cut off. The murders are actually part of a blackmail plot hatched by Professor Moriarity (Henry Daniell). Moriarity sends the hypnotized Corporal Williams, a British Army sniper recently given a medical discharge (for malaria he contracted while serving in the Far East), to kill Holmes. The detective escapes harm and eventually foils Moriarity's plans. Although this film is set in contemporary London, there are no other signs of the war.

1281 WONDER MAN (RKO, Apr*) Bruce Humberstone; *genre:* Musical Comedy; *location:* United States; *coding:* AF-A, AF-N, AF-W, Ital, Ger-Am, Russ?, Hist Am; *relevance:* 1.

Danny Kaye plays a nightclub entertainer murdered by gangsters to keep him from testifying against them. Kaye's ghost contacts his twin brother (also Kaye), a mild-mannered scholar, asking him to avenge his death. Various complications ensue as the live Kaye is periodically possessed by his wacky, frenetic brother's spirit. Vera-Ellen and Virginia Mayo are the romantic interests of Kaye #1 and Kaye #2. The topical relevance of this film is restricted to one scene with a sailor (Huntz Hall), a few Army officers in and around a nightclub, and a "Join the WACs" poster inside a bus. In Technicolor.

1282 YOU CAME ALONG (Para, Sept*) John Farrow; *genre:* Romance; *location:* United States; *coding:* AF-AC, AF-N, AF-A, AF-Raf?, AF-MC, AF-W, Bonds, Home Fr, Draft, Nazi, Blk, Brit?, Fem Lab, V, Prod?, Postwar, Eisenhower, US-Brit Coop; *relevance:* 2.5.

Three Air Corps heroes—Bob (Robert Cummings), "Shakespeare" (a former college professor, played by Don DeFore), and "Handsome" (Charles Drake; his character lost a leg in combat)—return to the U.S. from Europe for a Treasury Department bond tour. Ivy (Lizabeth Scott) is assigned as their escort. Bob and Ivy are attracted to each other, but agree not to get serious. Ivy learns that Bob has a fatal blood disease (apparently leukemia, but not specifically named) and is living on borrowed time. While in California, the flyers and Ivy attend the wedding of Ivy's sister to a Navy lieutenant. The bride tells Ivy she would marry her husband even if she knew he would not be coming back from the war. This convinces Bob and Ivy to tie the knot. They have a short and happy time together before Bob is ordered to report to Walter Reed Medical Center, and his disease finally catches up with him. Ivy is at his graveside for Bob's military funeral, and Handsome and Shakespeare fly their planes overhead in tribute.

Filmographic Appendices

Appendix A:
Feature Length Films Named As Pro-War Propaganda by Gerald Nye and Other Noninterventionists

After Mein Kampf? (British)
(A 1940 "semi-factual, semi-documentary" film largely comprised of reconstructed scenes. It was produced by British Crystal Pictures, Inc. See *Lib. Cong.*, LP9981; *FD*, Vol. 78, No. 58, September 20, 1940, p. 5)

Convoy (British)

Escape

Flight Command

Foreign Correspondent

The Great Dictator

The Man I Married (I Married a Nazi)

Man Hunt

The Mortal Storm

Mystery Sea Raider

Night Train (Night Train to Munich) (British)

The Ramparts We Watched

Sergeant York

That Hamilton Woman (Lady Hamilton)

They Dare Not Love

Victory in the West (Sieg im Weston) (German)
(Directed by Fritz Hippler, this 1941 release was a classic example of Nazi scare propaganda. It depicted their spring 1940 Blitzkrieig in the west that resulted in the defeat of France. See David Stewart Hull, *Film in the Third Reich* [New York: Simon and Schuster, 1973], p. 172)

The World in Flames (Paramount document, 1939)

Appendix B:
American Feature Films Reflecting an Awareness of International Issues, 1932–1936

1932	Director	Genre	Coding
Forgotten Commandments (Paramount)	L. Gasnier/W. Schorr	Drama	Soviet Union/Stalin
Shanghai Express (Paramount)	Josef von Sternberg	Adventure	Chinese Communist
Three on a Match (1st Nat)	Mervyn Le Roy	Drama	Contraband Message Manchurian Incident Musso
War Correspondent (Columbia)	Paul Sloane	War Drama	Chinese Communist
Washington Merry-Go-Round (Columbia)	James Cruze	Drama	Contraband Message Musso/Stalin
1933			
The Bitter Tea of General Yen (Columbia)	Frank Capra	Drama	Sino-Japanese Incident

1933	Director	Genre	Coding
Central Airport (1st Nat)	William A. Wellman	Adventure	World Rev
Clear All Wires (MGM)	George Hill	Drama	Soviet Union
			Stalin
Dancing Lady (MGM)	Robert E. Leonard	Drama	Contraband Message/Hitler
Design for Living (Paramount)	Ernst Lubitsch	Comedy	Contraband Message
			Disarmament Con
Diplomaniacs (RKO)	William A. Seiter	Comedy	World Peace Organization
Gabriel Over the White House (MGM)	Gregory LaCava	Drama	Disarmament Con
Men Must Fight (MGM)	Edgar Selwyn	Drama	World Peace Organization
			World War
The Nuisance (MGM)	Jack Conway	Drama	Contraband Message/Hitler
Shanghai Madness (Fox)	John Blystone	Adventure	Chinese Communist
Son of a Sailor (1st Nat)	Lloyd Bacon	Comedy-Drama	Contraband Message/Musso
State Fair (Fox)	Henry King	Drama	Contraband Message
			Disarmament Con/Musso
This Day and Age (Paramount)	Cecil B. DeMille	Drama	Fascist
The Wandering Jew (JAFA)	George Roland	Drama	Nazi German

1934			
Are We Civilized? (Raspin)	Edwin Carewe	Drama	Nazi German
Charlie Chan in London (Fox)	Eugene Forde	Mystery	Spy-Sab
Little Man, What Now? (Universal)	Frank Borzage	Drama	Fascist
Marie Galante (Fox)	Henry King	Mystery	Spy-Sab
The President Vanishes (Paramount)	William A. Wellman	Drama	Fascist/World War
Twenty Million Sweethearts (Warner Bros.)	Ray Enright	Musical	Contraband Message/Musso
Victims of Persecution (Bud Pollard Prods.)	Bud Pollard	Drama	Fascist
The World Moves On (Fox)	John Ford	War Drama	Contraband Message/Hitler
			Musso/Stalin

1935			
Broadway Gondolier (Warner Bros.)	Lloyd Bacon	Musical	Contraband Message/Musso
Chinatown Squad (Universal)	Murray Roth	Mystery	Chinese Communist
Death Flies East (Columbia)	Phil Rosen	Mystery	Spy-Sab
Murder in the Fleet (MGM)	Edward Sedgwick	Mystery	Spy-Sab
Oil for the Lamps of China (Warner Bros.)	Mervyn Le Roy	Drama	Chinese Communist
Storm Over the Andes (Universal)	W. Christy Cabanne	War Drama	Chaco War
Sweet Surrender (Universal)	Monte Brice	Musical Comedy	Contraband Message
			Peace Organization
Thanks a Million (Twentieth Century–Fox)	Roy Del Ruth	Musical Comedy	Contraband Message/Hitler
			Fascist

1936			
Big Brown Eyes (Paramount)	Raoul Walsh	Comedy	Contraband Message
			Italo-Ethiopian War
The General Died at Dawn (Paramount)	Lewis Milestone	Adventure	Fascist
Great Guy (Grand National Pictures)	John G. Blystone	Drama	Contraband Message
			SCW

1936	Director	Genre	Coding
Happy Go Lucky (Republic)	Aubrey Scotto	Musical Comedy	Spy-Sab
The House of a Thousand Candles (Republic)	Arthur Lubin	Spy	Spy-Sab
I Was a Captive of Nazi Germany (Malvina Picts)		Drama	Nazi German
Love on the Run (MGM)	W.S. Van Dyke	Comedy Drama	Spy-Sab
			Contraband Message
			World Peace Organization
Navy Wife (Twentieth Century–Fox)	Allan Dwan	Comedy Drama	Spy-Sab
Soak the Rich (Paramount)	Ben Hecht & Charles MacArthur	Comedy	Soviet Union
			Contraband Message/Hitler
			Stalin
These Three (MGM)	William Wyler	Drama	Contraband Message
			Italo-Ethiopian War

Appendix C:
American Film Serials Reflecting an Awareness of the World Crisis, 1937–1945[1]

"Feature versions" of serials—edited down and released theatrically—are not included in this list.

1937	*SOS Coast Guard*	(Republic)		*Don Winslow of the Navy*	(Universal)
1938	*Fighting Devil Dogs*	(Republic)		*Junior G-Men of the Air*	(Universal)
	Red Barry	(Universal)		*King of the Mounties*	(Republic)
				The Secret Code	(Columbia)
1939	*Dick Tracy's G-Men*	(Republic)		*Spy Smasher*	(Republic)
	Flying G-Men	(Columbia)		*The Valley of Vanishing Men*	(Columbia)
	The Phantom Creeps	(Universal)	1943	*Adventures of the Flying Cadets*	(Universal)
1940	*Drums of Fu Manchu*	(Republic)		*Adventures of Smilin' Jack*	(Universal)
	Junior G-Men	(Universal)		*Batman*	(Columbia)
	King of the Royal Mounted	(Republic)		*G-Men vs. the Black Dragon*	(Republic)
1941	*Dick Tracy vs Crime, Inc.*	(Republic)		*The Masked Marvel*	(Republic)
	Don Winslow of the Navy[2]	(Universal)		*Secret Service in Darkest Africa*	(Republic)
	King of the Texas Rangers	(Republic)	1944	*The Great Alaskan Mystery*	(Universal)
	Sea Raiders	(Universal)	1945	*Jungle Queen*	(Universal)
	Sky Raiders	(Universal)		*The Master Key*	(Universal)
	The Spider Returns	(Columbia)		*The Monster and the Ape*	(Columbia)
1942	*Captain Midnight*	(Republic)		*Secret Agent X-9*	(Universal)

Appendix D
Selected American Fictional Short Subjects Reflecting an Awareness of the World Crisis, 1937–1945

1937		Director
Servant of the People: The Story of the Constitution of the U.S.	(MGM)	Edward Cahn
1938		
Nostradamus (An Historical Mystery) [MGM Miniature]	(MGM)	David Miller

1939   Director
The Giant of Norway (The Man Who Couldn't Say No)
  [John Nesbitt's Passing Parade]   (MGM)   Edward Cahn
Sons of Liberty [Historical Featurette]   (Warner Bros.)   Michael Curtiz
The Story of Alfred Nobel (Am I to Blame) [John Nesbitt's Passing Parade] (MGM) Joe Newman
Three Little Sew and Sews [Three Stooges]   (Columbia)   Del Lord
While America Sleeps [Crime Does Not Pay]   (MGM)   Fred Zinnemann
Yankee Doodle Goes to Town [John Nesbitt's Passing Parade] (MGM)   Jacques Tourneur

1940
Boobs in Arms [Three Stooges]   (Columbia)   Jules White
Drafted in the Depot [Edgar Kennedy]   (RKO)   Lloyd French
The Flag Speaks   (MGM)   David Miller
March on Marines [Technicolor Special]   (Warner Bros.)   B. Reeves Eason
Our Monroe Doctrine   (Academic Films) G.A. Durlam
Service with the Colors [Technicolor Special]   (Warner Bros.)   B. Reeves Eason
Teddy, the Rough Rider [Historical Featurette]   (Warner Bros.)   Ray Enright
A Way in the Wilderness   (MGM)   Fred Zinnemann
You Nazty Spy [Three Stooges]   (Columbia)   Jules White

1941
Aeronutics [Pete Smith Specialties]   (MGM)   Francis Corby and
                                                                            S.B. Harrison
All the World's a Stooge [Three Stooges]   (Columbia)   Del Lord
Baby Blues [Our Gang]   (MGM)   Edward Cahn
The Blitz Kiss [El Brendel]   (Columbia)   Del Lord
Fightin' Fools [Our Gang]   (MGM)   Edward Cahn
Forbidden Passage [Crime Does Not Pay]   (MGM)   Fred Zinnemann
General Nuisance [Buster Keaton]   (Columbia)   Jules White
Helping Hands [Our Gang]   (MGM)   Edward Cahn
Here Comes the Cavalry [Technicolor Special]   (Warner Bros.)   D. Ross Lederman
I'll Never Heil Again [Three Stooges]   (Columbia)   Jules White
Meet the Fleet   (Warner Bros.)   B. Reeves Eason
More About Nostradamus [MGM Miniature]   (MGM)   David Miller
Our Declaration of Independence   (Academic Film) G.A. Durlam
Out of Darkness (Voice of Liberty) [John Nesbitt's Passing Parade] (MGM) Sammy Lee
A Quiet Fourth [Edgar Kennedy]   (RKO)   Harry D'Arcy
The Tanks Are Coming [Technicolor Special]   (Warner Bros.)   B. Reeves Eason
Wings of Steel [Technicolor Special]   (Warner Bros.)   B. Reeves Eason
Yankee Doodle Andy [Andy Clyde]   (Columbia)   Jules White

1942
Doin' Their Bit [Our Gang]   (MGM)   Herbert Glazer
Don't Talk [MGM Special]   (MGM)   Joe Newman
Duck Soup [Edgar Kennedy]   (RKO)   Ben Holmes
Even As I.O.U. [Three Stooges]   (Columbia)   Del Lord
For the Common Defense! [Crime Does Not Pay]   (MGM)   Allen R. Kenward
Further Prophecies of Nostradamus [MGM Miniature]   (MGM)   David Miller
The Great Glovers [Glove Slingers]   (Columbia)   Jules White
The Greenie [MGM Miniature]   (MGM)   H. Alexander
Hold 'Em Jail [Leon Errol]   (RKO)   Lloyd French
Keep 'Em Sailing [Crime Does Not Pay]   (MGM)   Basil Wrangell
Keeping in Shape [Robert Benchley]   (Paramount)   Leslie Roush
The Last Lesson   (MGM)   Allen Kenward
A Letter from Bataan   (Paramount)   William H. Pine
Mail Trouble [Leon Errol]   (RKO)   Lloyd French
Mighty Lak a Goat [Our Gang]   (MGM)   Herbert Glazer
Sock-a-Bye Baby [Three Stooges]   (Columbia)   Jules White
Three Smart Saps [Three Stooges]   (Columbia)   Jules White
Unexpected Riches [Our Gang]   (MGM)   Herbert Glazer
We Refuse to Die   (Paramount)   William H. Pine
Wedded Blitz [Leon Errol]   (RKO)   Henry James

1943

		Director
The Aldrich Family Gets In the Scrap	(Paramount)	Frank McDonald
Back from the Front [Three Stooges]	(Columbia)	Jules White
Benjamin Franklin, Jr. [Our Gang]	(MGM)	Herbert Glazer
A Blitz on the Fritz [Harry Langdon]	(Columbia)	Jules White
Blonde and Groom [Harry Langdon]	(Columbia)	Harry Edwards
Boobs in the Night [El Brendel]	(Columbia)	Del Lord
Calling All Kids [Our Gang]	(MGM)	Sam Baerwitz
Dizzy Detectives [Three Stooges]	(Columbia)	Jules White
Dizzy Pilots [Three Stooges]	(Columbia)	Jules White
Farmer for a Day [Andy Clyde]	(Columbia)	Jules White
Here at Home [MGM Miniature]	(MGM)	Walter Hart
Higher Than a Kite [Three Stooges]	(Columbia)	Del Lord
His Girl's Worst Friend	(Columbia)	Jules White
His Wedding Scare [El Brendel]	(Columbia)	Del Lord
I Can Hardly Wait [Three Stooges]	(Columbia)	Jules White
I Spied for You [El Brendel]	(Columbia)	Jules White
Indian Signs [Edgar Kennedy]	(RKO)	Charles Roberts
Kiss and Wake Up	(Columbia)	Jules White
A Maid Made Mad [Andy Clyde]	(Columbia)	Del Lord
Mr. Smug	(Columbia)	William Castle
My Tomato [Robert Benchley]	(MGM)	Will Jason
Pitchin' In the Kitchen	(Columbia)	Jules White
Plan for Destruction [Crime Does Not Pay]	(MGM)	Edward Cahn
Shoe Shine Boy	(MGM)	Walter Hart
Shot in the Escape [Billy Gilbert & Cliff Nazarro]	(Columbia)	Jules White
Spook Louder [Three Stooges]	(Columbia)	Del Lord
They Stooge to Conga [Three Stooges]	(Columbia)	Del Lord
Three Smart Guys [Our Gang]	(MGM)	Edward Cahn
Two Saplings [George Givot & Cliff Nazarro]	(Columbia)	Henry Edwards
What We Are Fighting For [America Speaks]	(Universal)	Erle C. Kenton
Wolf in Thief's Clothing [Andy Clyde]	(Columbia)	Jules White

1944

Feather Your Nest [Edgar Kennedy]	(RKO)	Hal Yates
Gents Without Cents [Three Stooges]	(Columbia)	Jules White
Love Your Landlord [Edgar Kennedy]	(RKO)	Charles E. Roberts
No Dough, Boys [Three Stooges]	(Columbia)	Jules White
The Yoke's On Me [Three Stooges]	(Columbia)	Jules White
A Tale of a Dog [Our Gang]	(MGM)	Cyril Endfield

1945

Booby Dupes [Three Stooges]	(Columbia)	Del Lord
The House I Live In [honorary Academy Award; with Frank Sinatra]	(RKO)	Mervyn LeRoy
I Am an American	(WB)	Crane Wilbur
It Happened in Springfield	(Warner Bros.)	Crane Wilbur
Phantom, Inc. [Crime Does Not Pay]	(MGM)	Harold Young
She Snoops to Conquer [Vera Vague]	(Columbia)	Jules White
What, No Cigarettes? [Edgar Kennedy]	(RKO)	Hal Yates

Appendix E:
British Features with References to the World Crisis
Released Through American Studios, 1937–1945[1]

This list includes war-relevant British films released in the U.S. by the major Hollywood companies between January 1, 1942, and September 30, 1945. Two British films released with added American footage (*Next of Kin* and *The Way Ahead*) are included in the main filmography.

A British film is defined as a motion picture produced in Great Britain; thus, while a number of the above-mentioned films were actually produced by British affiliates of Hollywood studios, or had American money invested in them, they are considered foreign films for our purposes.

More information about these films—including the extent of war-relevance of each—may be found in other reference works. We have listed them here to give an idea of the number of British films given general commercial release in the U.S. during the war. A few other foreign films saw release in the United States during this period, but most were restricted to "art" theaters or were shown only in foreign-language theaters in their original language versions.

1937

BULLDOG DRUMMOND AT BAY
(Republic, July) Norman Lee; *genre:* Mystery.

In this adventure the Bulldog (John Lodge) clashes with an international arms dealer named Kalinsky who uses a world peace organization, The Key Club, as a front. The action centers around the kidnapping of the inventor of a new plane in order to force him to relinquish its plans so they can be sold to an unspecified foreign power. The usual perils are overcome by our hero and his girl before the East European-like heavies are finally overcome.

DARK JOURNEY (United Artists, July)
Victor Saville; *genre:* Spy Drama.

Although the women's clothes are all the latest 1930's fashions, this motion picture, which stars Conrad Veidt and Vivien Leigh, takes place in the spring of 1918. The locale of this spy melodrama is neutral Sweden and the North Sea. Despite the love affair that evolves between the two antagonists, the film's dialogue reveals some distinctly anti–German biases that probably reflected changing British attitudes. For instance, in a discussion between two shop girls the following interchange takes place: "Is it a crime to be German? / Worse, it's a vulgarity." And at the film's conclusion, following the sinking of a U-boat, the Captain of the British ship smugly responds to a query viz. the captured German officer's future: "We don't shoot our POW's."

VICTORIA THE GREAT (RKO, Nov)
Herbert Wilcox; *genre:* Biography.

This is a film paen not only to the lady Queen (Anna Neagle) but to the people whom she represented and the Empire that she came to symbolize. A somewhat comic scene of the German-born Prince Albert suffering while crossing the English Channel in a storm would also appear to be meant to emphasize his lack of touch with British culture. A considerable portion of the film's plot is devoted to Victoria's relations with other world leaders, including Abraham Lincoln. The concluding scenes are in Technicolor.

WINGS OF THE MORNING (20th Century–Fox, Feb) Harold D. Schuster; *genre:* Drama.

Wings of the Morning was Britain's first Technicolor production. Spanning three generations the story centers around gypsies, romance and horse racing. Most of the action takes place in modern Ireland though. What is relevant here is that the Spanish branch of the aristocratic family has escaped from the Civil War. It is stated that they fled the "revolution," implying they eluded largely communist inspired excesses that swept through Republican Spain following the Franco led insurrection. References are made to the burning of churches and to escaping through Portugal. Considering his, in more recent years, highly touted lead role in *Blockade* (1938), q.v., it is interesting to note that Henry Fonda also starred in this work, which could be interpreted as sympathetic to the Fascist cause.

1938

I MARRIED A SPY (British title: SECRET LIVES, 1937) (Grand National) Edmond T. Greville; *genre:* Spy Drama.

German actress Brigitte Horney plays a young German-born woman who becomes a pawn of the French and German secret services during the First World War. Neil Hamilton is the French officer who marries her as part of his duty to the cause, but eventually they fall in love with each other. The *Variety* review remarked: "no special case is made for the espionage bureaus of either the German or the French side [but the] latter comes off with slight edge."

THE LADY VANISHES (20th Century–Fox, Nov) Alfred Hitchcock; *genre:* Spy Drama.

This thriller classic largely takes place on a train that is heading west from the Balkans. A young lady named Iris (Margaret Lockwood) meets a kindly old governess, Miss Froy, in the dining car. Soon afterwards, the latter mysteriously disappears. Iris tries to enlist the interest of her fellow passengers, but they remain indifferent. Assorted suspicious characters surface, including an alleged brain specialist played by Paul Lukas and a Cockney nun who is revealed to be wearing high heels beneath her habit. With the aid of a skeptical musicologist (Michael Redgrave) the nun's bandaged "patient" is unwrapped, thus freeing Miss Froy from captivity. She confides to the young couple that she is a British secret agent who has committed to memory via a coded folk tune the secret clause of a treaty that should squelch a potential threat to European peace. The climax occurs during a shoot out with sinister Teutonic types when the train makes an unscheduled stop in a forest near an unidentified border.

STORM IN A TEACUP (United Artists, Feb) Victor Saville; *genre:* Comedy/Drama.

In this British rewrite of a German play, a cocky young English newspaper man locks horns with the fascistic Provost (Mayor) Gow of a small Scottish town. Gow, who is running for Parliament, is the "Nordic" leader of the Caledonian League, a new party that espouses "Scotland for the Scottish." Gow's posturing while delivering speeches is very much in the style of Mussolini.

1939

GOODBYE MR. CHIPS (MGM, May)
Sam Wood; *genre:* Romantic Drama.

Based on a popular novel by James Hilton, this sentimental romance traces the life of a shy English schoolmaster (Robert Donat) between 1870 and 1933. A lengthy section in the latter part of the film, which is distinctly pacifistic, deals with the tragic impact of the first World War upon the teacher and his beloved mens' boarding school.

Q PLANES (Columbia, June) Tim Whelan; *genre:* Spy Drama.

A Scotland Yard Major and a test pilot, played by Lawrence Olivier, team up to track down spies attempting to procure the new type super-charger in Britain's latest bomber. Using a ray on board a camouflaged salvage vessel off the English coast the spies are able to capture several prototypes of the plane before being overcome by the bomber's captured pilots and the timely intervention of the Royal Navy.

SHIPYARD SALLY (20th Century–Fox, Oct) Monty Banks; *genre:* Comedy.

Gracie Fields plays the working class spokesperson for unemployed shipyard workers attempting to get government support for a revitalization of the industry. Released in Britain in the summer of 1939 this film's ultra patriotic shipbuilding/singing finale has an unmistakable national preparedness message. The scene concludes with a double exposure of the Union Jack and Gracie as she sings "Land of Hope and Glory."

TORPEDOED! (OUR FIGHTING NAVY) (Film Alliance of the U.S., Sept?) Norman Walker; *genre:* War Drama.

With a part-American cast (H.B. Warner, Noah Beery), this motion picture was released in the States immediately following the outbreak of European hostilities. It features the British Navy being sent to some small, vaguely South American, republic to help quell a rebellion.

U-BOAT 29 (A SPY IN BLACK) (Columbia, Oct) Michael Powell; *genre:* Spy Drama.

Produced before September, but not released in America until after the war began, the film takes place in a vaguely World War I setting. Only the uniforms and references to the German "Grand Fleet" give any clues to that effect. The story, itself, evolves around a German espionage attempt to arrange for a surprise massed submarine attack upon elements of the British fleet leaving Scapa Flow and the foiling of those efforts by a pair of British counterspies. Conrad Veidt again stars.

WE ARE NOT ALONE (Warner Bros., Nov) Edmund Goulding; *genre:* Drama.

In 1914 a small town English doctor (played by Paul Muni) persuades his wife to hire a young Austrian girl named Leni to be their timid son's governess. After his wife accidentally poisons herself on the day war is declared, he and the girl (an enemy alien using a forged passport) are hastily condemned for murder and sentenced to death. News bulletins of their trail are juxtaposed with those on the early battles of the first world war. Because the Austrian girl is suspected of being a spy, authorities allow the two to meet on the eve of their execution. With the room secretly wired, a military intelligence officer hopes that Leni will reveal her true mission. Instead, they learn only that the two have discovered their love for each other. Delivering an impassioned pacifistic speech, the kind doctor reassures a

frightened Leni: "We are not alone, [when] ... every minute, every second [martial drum rolling begins on the sound track] out there—thousands ... [are] sent to die, who have done no wrong.... Surely all their stupidity and suffering couldn't be the end of things.... It's just a bad beginning."

1940

AMONG HUMAN WOLVES (Film Alliance, Nov?) John Baxter; *genre:* Spy Drama.

A German spy who has stolen a newly developed cartridge in Paris is pursued to the Third Reich by Allied agents. The cartridge is retrieved before Nazi scientists can uncover its secrets. A dramatic escape is made across the German border.

BLACKOUT (CONTRABAND) (United Artists, Nov) Michael Powell; *genre:* Spy Drama.

This film deals with spies and counterspies during the early days of the war. A Danish freighter in the English Channel is escorted by a British patrol boat to a contraband port where its cargo is approved and clearance passes issued. But then the passes are stolen by German agents. The ship's captain and a female British agent (Valerie Hobson) relentlessly pursue the enemy, finally retrieving the passes in a blacked out London.

DANGEROUS CARGO (HELL'S CARGO) (Film Alliance, Sept?) Harold Huth; *genre:* Drama.

In a pre-war Mediterranean port ship commanders of the British, French and Soviet navies meet. When a drunken doctor from a tramp steamer is mysteriously murdered at a dockside dive mutual suspicions arise. However, it turns out that he was killed by the ship's owner who is transporting a cargo of contraband chemicals. The three naval officers pursue the ship in a destroyer under joint command. When the steamer is overtaken the half mad owner dumps the illegal cargo which forms a lethal gas cloud. The co-operating naval officers then must maneuver their destroyer through the cloud in order to rescue the people aboard a threatened passenger liner. The story is based on the 1939 award winning French film, *SOS Mediterranean*, that features a German naval officer instead of the Russian one.

THE LION HAS WINGS (United Artists, Jan) Michael Powell; Hurst; Brunell; *genre:* War Drama.

This was a highly propagandistic work that received wide distribution overseas. It opens by contrasting a pre-war peaceful England with an aggressive militaristic Nazi Germany. It then goes into the war where it reconstructs an RAF raid on the German naval base at Keil. The other part of this episodic film deals with Britain's fighter air defense against a German night bombing attack. Documentary footage is liberally integrated into the film. For the American version the original narrator, E.V.H. Emmett, has been replaced by Lowell Thomas.

MAD MEN OF EUROPE (AN ENGLISHMAN'S HOME) (Columbia, June) Albert de Courville; *genre:* War Drama.

Its original British title is the title of a 1909 pro-preparedness stage play upon which the film is based. Updated, it features the planned invasion of Britain by bombers and parachute troops as assisted by radio beams sent by a spy from the attic of an English family's home. The spy has completely fooled the pretty young girl, but not her more suspicious father and older brother. Thus her virtue and Britain's sacred soil are saved. The motion picture was made during the early months of the war and avoided directly condemning Nazi Germany. But by the time the film was released in America France was falling and a direct threat to Britain was far more likely. The provocative American title is most revelatory re American attitudes.

NIGHT TRAIN (GESTAPO; retitled **NIGHT TRAIN TO MUNICH)** (20th Century–Fox, Oct) Carol Reed; *genre:* Spy Drama.

The same screenwriters that penned Hitchcock's 1938 classic, *The Lady Vanishes*, were responsible for this witty spy melodrama. When Czechoslovakia is invaded, an elderly inventor of a new armor plate is spirited out of Prague to England. But his daughter is captured and placed in a concentration camp. The Gestapo then engineers her escape so that they may follow her to England and find her father. No sooner does she rejoin the old man than the Nazis kidnap the both of them to Germany. Rex Harrison, as a British Secret Service agent, then proceeds to Berlin, impersonates a German officer and bluffs his way to the Czech couple. The three escape aboard a night train to Munich and in the climax shoot it out with the Gestapo on an Alpine cable railway at the Swiss frontier.

PASTOR HALL (United Artists, Sept) Roy Boulting; *genre:* Drama.

This is an adaptation of the Ernst Toller play which was based on the experiences of Pastor Niemuller (here named Pastor Hall and played by Wilfrid Lawson) while in the hands of the Nazis. The story takes place in a German village in 1934 with the arrival of the Nazis. The Pastor's refusal to cooperate with the Brownshirts, such as in supplying the names of Jews, ultimately leads to his being sent to a concentration camp. He survives ruthless beatings as well as numerous other degradations before his escape can finally be arranged by a sympathetic camp officer. Although his daughter wants him to flee to America, he valiantly returns to his pulpit and delivers a final anti–Nazi sermon to his parishioners. Storm troopers gather outside and wait to shoot him down when he leaves the church (the act takes place off screen). This was the first British feature film to directly address the Germany people's loss of freedom to the Hitler regime. *Pastor Hall* encountered censorship problems in the United States. For instance, due to the violence portrayed in the concentration camp sequence and out of fear of inflaming the city's German population, the film was cut before being released in Chicago.

QUEEN OF DESTINY (SIXTY GLORIOUS YEARS: THE LIFE AND REIGN OF QUEEN VICTORIA) (RKO, Aug?) Herbert Wilcox; *genre:* Biography.

This is a Technicolor sequel to Wilcox's earlier work on the Queen's life that begins with her announcement to Parliament in 1840 of her engagement to Prince Albert. In this episodic work the Empire is portrayed at its best. National preparedness speeches are inserted.

THE SECRET "4" (FOUR JUST MEN) (Monogram, Jan) Walter Forde; *genre:* Drama.

The secret "4" are known to the world as a determined group who right wrongs. They discover that classified information is being leaked from the Foreign Office. Amid murder and intrigue an oriental agent is revealed to be involved in a plot to block the Suez Canal. The head of the conspiracy in Britain turns out to be none other than a self proclaimed pacifist Member of Parliament. In order to prevent his delivering a damaging speech in Parliament they kill him and dramatically warn the nation of the imminent threat to the Empire.

SPIES IN THE AIR (SPIES OF THE AIR) (Film Alliance, July) David MacDonald; *genre:* Spy Drama.

At a secret aerodrome in England a new fighter plane is receiving its preliminary tri-als. The test pilot is after both the plane and the head engineer's wife. The secret service becomes aware of the plot though and as a result the spy is killed in the plane while attempting to escape.

TORPEDO RAIDER (original American title: **BORN FOR GLORY; BROWN ON RESOLUTION; RETITLED FOREVER ENGLAND**) (Monogram, Feb) *genre:* War Drama.

This 1935 production was updated with inserted montage/newsreel sequences. The story centers around a British naval squadron that engages a "Nordic" flotilla in South American waters and the sacrifice of the long forgotten son of the English commander in order to assure the Royal Navy's victory. This film was probably re-released in America as a result of the dramatic encounter between the Royal Navy and the Graf Spee near Montevideo in December 1939.

TORSO MURDER MYSTERY (TRAITOR SPY) (Rialto-Pathe, Oct) Walter Summers; *genre:* Spy Drama.

The American actor Bruce Cabot plays the part of the traitor spy. He is an English citizen who makes a deal with enemy agents to sell them some secret plans, but then jacks up his price by 300 percent. They react negatively to this. To throw them off his trail he then murders a man who has a similar build to his. However, both the foreign agents and the British police discover his ruse. In a climactic encounter he and his beautiful lady choose a fiery death rather than face capture.

1941

CONVOY (RKO, Jan) Pen Tennyson; *genre:* War Drama.

This is a documentary style war drama in which the romantic background story is strictly secondary. It centers around the captain (Clive Brook) of the British convoy escort squadron leader, the cruiser Apollo, who fights a delaying action in the North Sea against a German pocket battleship Deutschland in order to give the merchant ships of the convoy a chance to escape to the safety of a home port.

MAIL TRAIN (INSPECTOR HORNLEIGH GOES TO IT) (20th Century–Fox, April) Walter Forde; *genre:* Comedy/Drama/Spy.

This detective comedy espionage thriller features the team of Gordon Harker and Alistair Sim. In the successful Inspector Hornleigh series (begun in 1939) the former plays a Cockney inspector and the latter his dumb Scots sergeant. In this motion picture the two are sent to the army to break up some petty pilfering but, instead, stumble upon a gang of "fifth columnists" and spies. The action climaxes on a mail train where the head spy, who has been posing as a dentist, is captured.

MISSING TEN DAYS (TEN DAYS IN PARIS) (Columbia, Feb) Tim Whelan; *genre:* Spy Drama.

Rex Harrison plays the victim of a nightclub shooting, who upon awakening in a Paris hospital finds he has a total lapse of memory for the past ten days. When he leaves the hospital he is approached by a man who mistakes him for a fellow spy. Our amnesiac good naturedly goes along with the role and winds up involved in murder and espionage. The spies have stolen plans of France's Maginot Line and have sabotaged a munitions train scheduled to enter the strategic fortifications. With the help of a beautiful girl Harrison is able to prevent disaster and see that the spies are apprehended.

THE SAINT'S VACATION (RKO, May) Leslie Fenton; *genre:* Spy Drama.

This was one of the studio films produced with funds frozen in England. And it is a Britisher, Hugh Sinclair, who plays the debonaire sleuth Simon Templar. On vacation in the Swiss Alps, the Saint becomes embroiled in international espionage centering around the possession of a harmless looking music box. In fact, it contains the key to a diagram of the circuitry of a new sound detection device.

THIS ENGLAND (World Pictures, Nov) David MacDonald; *genre:* War Drama.

The title invokes the famous nationalistic passage from Shakespeare's *Richard III:* "This blessed plot, this earth, this realm, this England." This highly propagandistic work catered to the stateside audience by featuring a female American journalist on assignment in wartime Britain. The film is an episodic recounting of English resistance to external threats as seen through the lives of five generations of a village family named Rockby. The most recent John Rockby, who relates the story, is prepared for battle against the Nazis. The American girl, played by Constance Cummings, pops up in each episode as some character.

THREE COCKEYED SAILORS (SAILORS THREE) (United Artists, July) Walter Forde; *genre:* War Drama.

Three happy-go-lucky tars are crew mates aboard the British battleship, H.M.S. *Ferocious*, which is searching for the German pocket battleship, *Ludendorff*. At a neutral South American port they get drunk and wind up on board the *Ludendorff*. After being imprisoned, a pro–British Austrian crew member helps them escape and miraculously take control of the ship. While taking their prize to England they come upon another Nazi raider and are forced to take on passengers from a captured British liner. The climax centers around a revolt of the German crew and an encounter with the *Ferocious*. The Germans are no match for the defenders of the White Ensign.

A VOICE IN THE NIGHT (FREEDOM RADIO) (Columbia, May?) Anthony Asquith; *genre:* War Drama.

Like the 1941 American release, *Underground*, q.v., this motion picture centers around a German resistance group that broadcasts against the regime over an illegal radio transmitter. The resistance leaders are the distinguished Viennese specialist Dr. Karl Roder (Clive Brook) and a young radio mechanic named Hans. The doctor's wife, a pro–Nazi actress named Irene (Diana Wynyard), is appointed "Director of Pageantry." The broadcasts over the "Freedom Radio" begin following Hans' fiancee being raped by a Storm Trooper and then being sent to a concentration camp. The mobile radio station is assiduously stalked by the Gestapo. After Karl announces over the air the Fuhrer's intentions to invade Poland, the ambulance from which he is broadcasting is surrounded and machine-gunned by the Nazis. Just as the Gestapo chief is about to report his triumph to his superiors, Hans comes on the air over a second transmitter. Irene, who is probably meant to resemble Leni Riefenstahl, redeems herself by dying with Karl.

1942

THE AVENGERS (British title: **THE DAY WILL DAWN**) (Paramount, Nov?) Harold French; *genre:* War Drama.

Just after the invasion of Poland, British reporter (Hugh Williams) discovers a secret U-boat base being built in Norway by the Germans. He also becomes fond of a young Norwegian woman (Deborah Kerr), but is detected by Nazi agents and barely escapes to England with his life. After the Nazi con-

quest of Norway, Williams is sent back to the country to pinpoint the submarine base for RAF bombers. Although the base is destroyed, Williams, Kerr, and seven Norwegians are sentenced to be shot by the Germans. However, a British commando raid saves most of them.

FLYING FORTRESS (Warner Bros., July) Walter Forde; *genre:* Combat.

Sky Kelly loses his commercial pilot's license due to a drunken escapade involving Jim Spence (Richard Greene), although Spence has too much influence to be penalized himself. Both Spence and Kelly hire on to ferry Flying Fortresses from the U.S. to England, and they take their feud with them. In England, the American decide to sign on with the RAF. On a bombing raid over Berlin, Spence heroically extinguishes a burning motor, and is in turn rescued by Kelly. The plane makes it back to England, and the two men are reconciled. Similar to *A Yank in the R.A.F.* and other Hollywood films—irresponsible playboy redeemed by a brave act.

FORTY-EIGHT HOURS (British title: **WENT THE DAY WELL?**) (United Artists, ?) Cavalcanti; *genre:* War Drama.

As part of a plan to pave the way for an imminent invasion of England, German soldiers, disguised as British troops, occupy a British village. They are assisted by the local squire, who is actually a German fifth columnist. The villagers rebel, and eventually all of the invaders are killed. Loosely based on a story by Graham Greene, the film is presented as a flashback from after the war. *Forty-Eight Hours* was apparently released in the U.S. in 1942 by United Artists, and then again in 1944 by AFE.

THE INVADERS (British title: **49TH PARALLEL**) (Columbia, Feb) Michael Powell; *genre:* Adventure.

Six survivors of a U-boat crew try to make it across Canada to the (then-neutral) United States (the British title refers to the border between these nations). The Germans are all captured or killed, until only a fanatic Nazi (Eric Portman) is left. He makes it across the border on a freight train but a Canadian soldier—on the same train—convinces the American border officials to send them both back. All-star film (Laurence Olivier, Raymond Massey, Leslie Howard) serves to illustrate the ethnic diversity of Canadians (who are nonetheless loyal to the British Crown). Partially financed by the Ministry of Information, Britain's propaganda office.

MAXWELL ARCHER, DETECTIVE (British title: **MEET MAXWELL ARCHER**) (Monogram, Jan) John Paddy Carstairs; *genre:* Crime.

John Loder plays an amateur detective who helps out an RAF pilot wrongfully accused of murdering the member of a spy ring. Loder clears the pilot and helps break up the gang (the OWI reviewer wrote: "The spy-ring might be any gang of racketeers—none of them makes any war-related cracks."

MISTER V (British title: **PIMPERNEL SMITH**) (United Artists, Feb) Leslie Howard; *genre:* Adventure/War Drama.

Leslie Howard plays a mild-mannered Cambridge professor who helps people escape from Nazi Germany (in 1939, before the invasion of Poland). The film chiefly concerns his expedition—with a small group of students (including one American)—to Germany to free a Polish newspaper editor who has been arrested by the Nazis. As the film ends, Howard escapes over the border to Switzerland but shouts "We'll be back." An updated version of *The Scarlet Pimpernel* (Howard had stared in the 1935 film version of that novel), directed and produced by the star.

ONE OF OUR AIRCRAFT IS MISSING (United Artists, Apr) Michael Powell, Emric Pressburger; *genre:* Adventure/Resistance.

An RAF plane crashes in occupied Holland, and the surviving crew members (including Eric Portman in a sympathetic role for once) are rescued by the Dutch resistance.

SHIPS WITH WINGS (United Artists, Jan) Sergei Nolbandov; *genre:* War Drama.

John Clements plays a cashiered RAF pilot who gets a job running a one-plane airline in the Greek islands before the outbreak of hostilities. He discovers that German agents are laying mines, intending to destroy the British aircraft carrier *Ark Royal* (an actual warship). Clements saves the ship, and returns to the service in time to lose his life in a bombing attack on a strategic dam. Over two hours long, in its original version.

SUICIDE SQUADRON (British title: **DANGEROUS MOONLIGHT**) (RKO/Republic, Apr) Brian Desmond Hurst; *genre:* War Drama/Combat.

A famous Polish pianist and member of the Polish Air Force (Anton Walbrook) is ordered to fly his plane to a neutral country before the Nazis capture Warsaw. He does not know that this was a deliberate plan on the part of his comrades to save his life. Walbrook goes to the U.S. and performs concerts for Polish Relief, eventually marrying an American newspaper reporter. However, he decides to go to England and join the Polish Squadron of the RAF, against his wife's wishes. She tells him that his life was spared so he could contribute to Poland's freedom through his artistry, but Walbrook refuses to change his mind. After his best friend is killed in aerial combat, Walbrook shoots down as many German planes as possible, then rams his craft into another. The crash leaves him with amnesia, but as the film ends, he begins to play the "Warsaw Concerto," and reconciles with his wife. The musical score for this film by Richard Addinsell is quite famous.

THIS WAS PARIS (Warner Bros., Feb) John Harlow; *genre:* Spy.

This film, set in 1940 Paris, begins with a series of cartoon drawings relating to the theme "Careless Talk Costs Lives," and a shot of a poster reading "The Enemy Is Always Listening." A hard-drinking American correspondent named Butch (Ben Lyon, an expatriate American actor who became a popular British film and radio personality, and who served in the RAF during WWII) is discouraged by censorship of his articles exposing Fifth Column activities. He becomes friends with Captain Bill Hamilton of British Intelligence. Bill is in love with Anne (Anne Dvorak), who is suspected of working with Axis agents operating out of a fashionable dress shop. When Germany invades France, Anne is working as a volunteer ambulance driver at the front. She unwittingly carries a message which allows German soldiers—disguised in French uniforms—to seize a strategic bridge. They do so, despite Bill's efforts to prevent this. Burch joins the refugees fleeing France, while Bill and Anne return to Paris, intent on settling scores at the dress shop. The film ends with a close-up of German jackboots and the title: "This Was Paris—But France Will Live Again."

TOWER OF TERROR (Monogram, Apr) Lawrence Huntington; *genre:* War Drama/Spy.

Michael Rennie plays a British agent who takes a post helping Wilfrid Lawson, a crazed lighthouse keeper (the "tower" of the title), hoping to thereby escape to England with vital information. He also helps a French girl (Movita) elude her Nazi pursuers.

UNPUBLISHED STORY (Columbia, Apr) Harold French; *genre:* Spy.

Set in 1940, Richard Greene plays a reporter who uncovers a Nazi sabotage ring working under the guise of a pacifist organization.

WINGS AND THE WOMAN (British title: **THEY FLEW ALONE**) (RKO, Aug) Herbert Wilcox; *genre:* Drama.

Anna Neagle plays aviation pioneer Amy Johnson (known as "Lady Lindbergh"), who marries then divorces pilot Jim Mollison. When war comes, she and her ex-husband hire on to ferry warplanes from the factory to their final destinations, and is later killed in a crash.

THE YOUNG MR. PITT (20th Century–Fox, July) Carol Reed; *genre:* Hist Biography.

In the latter years of the 18th century, William Pitt (Robert Donat) enters British politics and eventually becomes Prime Minister. Deliberately intended as a patriotic gesture, the film makes positive references to the American Revolution, and draws negative parallels between Revolutionary France and Germany, and Napoleon and Hitler.

1943

ADVENTURES OF TARTU (MGM, Aug) Harold S. Bucquet; *genre:* Spy.

Robert Donat plays a British chemist who was born in Romania and spent several years in Berlin. He is working for the bomb disposal squad during the Blitz when British Intelligence asks him to go to Czechoslovakia and destroy a Nazi poison-gas factory. He is parachuted into Romania, where he assumes the identity of "Tartu," a member of the "Iron Guard" (the local fascists). Eventually, he makes his way to Prague and is hired on at the gas plant. With the aid of the resistance (including Valerie Hobson), he manages to accomplish his mission and escape.

THE BELLS GO DOWN (United Artists, May) Basil Dearden; *genre:* Adventure.

Tommy Trinder and James Mason play two Auxiliary Fire Service fire-fighters in London during the 1940 Blitz. This topic was also addressed in a famous British documentary, *Fires Were Started*.

IN WHICH WE SERVE (United Artists, ?) Noel Coward; *genre:* Combat.

In the Mediterranean off Crete in 1941, a British destroyer is attacked and sunk. The survivors wait for rescue, and their individual stories unfold in flashback. Based on the true story of Lord Louis Mountbatten and

his ship the HMS *Kelly*, this film stars Noel Coward as the ship's captain, and features John Mills, Richard Attenborough, and Celia Johnson.

SOMEWHERE IN FRANCE (British title: **THE FOREMAN WENT TO FRANCE**) (United Artists, Feb) Charles Frend; *genre:* Adventure.

As France falls to the Nazis in 1940, a Welsh factory worker (Clifford Evans) and some British soldiers try to recover aircraft-plant valuable machinery before it falls into enemy hands. Their escape from embattled France is aided by American Constance Cummings. Based on a true story.

SPITFIRE (British title: **THE FIRST OF THE FEW**) (RKO, Apr) Leslie Howard; *genre:* Biog.

Leslie Howard and David Niven star in this film about R.J. Mitchell, the aeronautical engineer who designed the famous Spitfire fighter plane. The film covers his career from the late 1920s until the outbreak of war.

SQUADRON LEADER X (RKO, Jan) Lance Comfort; *genre:* Spy.

Eric Portman is a Nazi flying ace who impersonates a British airman in order to spread propaganda in Belgium. However, Portman is "rescued" by the resistance and sent "back" to England! He contacts Ann Dvorak, a former girlfriend (of German descent), and blackmails her into helping him. She manages to finally expose Portman as an imposter, and he is shot down by his own countrymen when he tries to escape in a stolen Spitfire.

TERROR HOUSE (British title: **THE NIGHT HAS EYES**) (Producers' Releasing Corporation, June) Leslie Arliss; *genre:* Crime.

James Mason is suspected of murder, and his experiences in the Spanish Civil War have made him just odd enough to be a likely candidate. However, it turns out he was framed.

WE'LL MEET AGAIN (Columbia, ?) Phil Brandon; *genre:* Musical.

Vera Lynn, whose recording of the title song became a wartime hit in England (and can be heard as late as *Dr. Strangelove*), plays a radio singer with a Scots soldier boyfriend.

1944

BELL-BOTTOM GEORGE (Columbia, ?) Marcel Varnel; *genre:* Spy Comedy.

Lancashire comedian George Formby (the top British boxoffice star from 1939 to 1943) is rejected by the service, but is picked up by the Shore Patrol while wearing a borrowed sailor's uniform; he helps break up a spy ring. Very popular in England, Formby is all but unknown in the United States.

ESCAPE TO DANGER (RKO, Feb) Lance Comfort and Mutz Greenbaum; *genre:* Spy.

Ann Dvorak plays a schoolteacher who pretends to be a Danish collaborator. She is sent to England on a spy mission for the Nazis, but is actually working for Allies. She teams up with Eric Portman to send disinformation to the Nazis, leading to a great British victory. However, Dvorak is finally shot by another Nazi agent, and Portman has to carry on the battle alone. From the same production team as *Squadron Leader X.*

GET CRACKING (Columbia, ?) Marcel Varnel; *genre:* Comedy.

Another George Formby comedy, this time featuring the comic as a member of the Home Guard.

MEN OF THE SEA (British title: **THE MAN AT THE GATE**) (Producers' Releasing Corporation, Apr) Norman Walker; *genre:* War Drama.

Wilfrid Lawson and Mary Jerrold play a Cornish couple who have lost one son to the sea (they are from a long line of fishermen), and convince their youngest son George to seek out another line of work. However, when war breaks out he joins the Royal Navy. This distresses the mother, and she is even more distraught when George's ship is sunk and he is reported missing. The family's remaining son Henry volunteers for the Navy, but the mother regains her faith in God and country and gives him her blessing. After she does, news comes that George has survived.

RHYTHM SERENADE (Columbia, ?) Gordon Wellesley; *genre:* Musical.

Another Vera Lynn vehicle; this time she is a factory worker who helps a former sailor recover his nerve, and also starts a nursery for the children of war plant workers.

UNCENSORED (20th Century–Fox, Jan) Anthony Asquith; *genre:* Resistance.

Eric Portman is a cabaret performer in occupied Belgium who is really working for the resistance. The Belgian underground publishes an anti–Nazi newspaper (hence the title of the film) with his aid. Portman is betrayed to the Nazis by his cabaret partner (because Portman was going to break up the act), but manages to escape and free the newspaper's staff as well.

UNDERGROUND GUERRILLAS (British title: **UNDERCOVER**) (Columbia, Sept) Sergei Nolbandov; *genre:* Resistance.

Loosely based on the Chetnik resistance movement in Yugoslavia, this film stars John Clements as "Milosh Petrovitch," who helps oppose the Nazi occupation of his country. Milosh is a Yugoslavian army officer who leads the active resistance, while his brother—a doctor—works undercover to assist the guerrillas. At the film's climax, Milosh and his forces are embroiled in a pitched battle with Nazi troops; his brother and father blow up a German munitions train (at the cost of their own lives), blocking a tunnel and thus preventing reinforcements from reaching the Germans.

YELLOW CANARY (RKO, Nov) Herbert Wilcox; *genre:* Spy.

Anna Neagle plays a British socialite who is suspected of Nazi sympathies but who reveals her true patriotism by infiltrating a Nazi spy ring in Canada and foiling an attempt to sabotage Halifax harbor.

1945

ADVENTURE FOR TWO (British title: **THE DEMI-PARADISE**) (Universal, ?) Anthony Asquith; *genre:* Comedy.

In 1939, a Russian inventor (Laurence Olivier) visits England to demonstrate his ice-breaking propeller, and is bemused by the "average Englishman." Eventually, through his experiences with the British people—particularly members of a ship-building family—he comes to appreciate the country and its personality, especially when he returns to England in 1941 (at which time England and Russia were allies against the Nazis).

COLONEL BLIMP (British title: **THE LIFE AND DEATH OF COLONEL BLIMP**) (United Artists, March) Michael Powell and Emric Pressburger; *genre:* Drama.

The life of a somewhat bumbling British officer (Roger Livesey) is traced from 1902 through 1943. Deborah Kerr has three roles as various women in his life, and Anton Walbrook portrays a German who is at first Livesey's enemy, but winds up as an anti–Nazi refugee during WWII.

MR. EMMANUEL (United Artists, Jan) Harold French; *genre:* Drama.

Felix Aylmer plays the title character, an old Jewish man who agrees to help out with a group of "refugee" boys from Germany (the film takes place several years before the outbreak of war). One of the boys is worried about his mother back in Germany (his father was killed in a concentration camp). Mr. Emmanuel agrees to go to Germany to find the boy's mother, who has stopped writing to him. In Berlin, Mr. Emmanuel is accused of murdering a Nazi official and arrested by the Gestapo, but is freed through the intervention of Elsie Silver, the daughter of an old friend who is now the mistress of a high-ranking Nazi. Before he leaves Germany, Mr. Emmanuel meets the woman he set out to find: but the boy's mother is now married to a Nazi, and wants nothing to do with news of her son. Back in England, Mr. Emmanuel lies and tells the young boy that his mother died nobly.

THE SILVER FLEET (Producers' Releasing Corporation, July) Vernon Sewell and Gordon Wellesley; *genre:* Resistance.

Ralph Richardson was cast as a Dutch shipping magnate who pretends to collaborate with the Nazis, but is really scheming to destroy a newly designed U-boat.

VACATION FROM MARRIAGE (British title: **PERFECT STRANGERS**) (MGM, Sept) Alexander Korda; *genre:* War Drama/Romance.

Robert Donat and Deborah Kerr play a colorless married couple whose lives are actually improved by the rigors and excitement of military service during the war. An Alexander Korda production which was released almost simultaneously in Great Britain and the United States (September 1945).

Appendix F: Possibly Relevant Films

This list includes either films that were not screened by the authors but which may contain war-relevant material, or films that were screened whose content was not sufficiently and overtly linked to the war to merit inclusion in the main list.

1937

CONQUEST (Metro-Goldwyn-Mayer): Shortly after the Walewska estate is ravaged by Russian invaders, Napoleon's armies come to the rescue of Poland. The French emperor then wins the heart of the Countess Walewska (Greta Garbo). The former "corporal" who "plans to conquer the world" could be construed as a veiled reference to Adolf Hitler. The presentation of Napoleon (Charles Boyer) as the savior of Poland from Russia would have resonated with a contemporary audience re: the 1934 "friendship" pact between Germany and Poland that was intended primarily as a guarantee against possible Soviet aggression. The generally sympathetic portrayal of Napoleon in defeat during the latter third of the film has pacifist undertones.

OUTLAWS OF THE ORIENT (Columbia): In this August release, American Chet Eaton (Jack Holt) is employed by General Cheng Kai Ling (as in Chiang Kai-shek?) to operate an oil drilling concession in northwest China. Problems arise when a Tatar "warlord" named Ho Fang attempts to seize the oil fields. Chet disperses Fang's men with dynamite bombs dropped from a company plane. Before and during 1937 the Nationalist Chinese government under Chiang continued to be challenged by assorted warlords and communist rebels. And, in July of 1937, the Sino-Japanese War had erupted.

RANGE DEFENDERS (Republic): One of Republic's popular "Three Mesquiteers" series, this film centers around the attempts of a vicious sheep rancher to dominate a rural area through the use of strong-arm tactics. Bernard F. Dick claims in *The Star Spangled Screen* (1987; pp. 47–48) that the rancher's blackshirted armpatch-wearing gang, who try to intimidate voters during an election for sheriff, are fascist surrogates. However, *no* fascist rhetoric is ever employed, nor are any connections made with a national or international right-wing political movement. Similar plots appear in *The Night Riders* (Republic, 1939) and other Westerns of the era, but few were clearly intended to be allegories.

THANK YOU, MR. MOTO (20th Century–Fox): In this second film of the Mr. Moto series, released in November, the famed Japanese-American detective played by Peter Lorre becomes involved in a deadly competition centering around the acquisition of seven ancient scrolls, alleged to together reveal the whereabouts of the buried treasures of Ghengis Khan. An international cast of crooks, including a White Russian (?) and a German, will commit any crime necessary to gain possession of the scrolls. With Chinese troops assisting, the climax takes place aboard a junk at the *Marco Polo Bridge*. On July 3, 1937, just outside of Peiping at the Marco Polo Bridge, an armed clash occurred between Chinese regulars and troops of the Imperial Japanese Army, which instigated an undeclared war between the two countries.

THIN ICE (20th Century–Fox): An Alpine resort hosts an international conference to sign a three-power "pact." Young Prince Rudolph (Tyrone Power) arrives in disguise, reluctantly assuming the role of power broker for his country. But as "Rudy Miller," he prefers developing relations with the local skating star, played by Sonja Heinie. The two other unnamed nations involved are represented by the Count and the Baron. The latter diplomat, fearing the failure of his mission, comments: "I'll never be able to face The Chancellor." Although the participating countries are never specifically identified, the official title of Germany's Fuehrer, Adolf Hitler, was Chancellor. Furthermore, reporters from several of the major powers are in attendance, periodically making frantic calls to Berlin, Tokyo, Rome and London.

1938

SERGEANT MURPHY (Warner Bros.): Sergeant Murphy is the name of a U.S. cavalry horse who is made skittish by the sound of artillery fire. His devoted keeper, Pvt. Dennis Reilly (Ronald Reagan), trains the horse to be a jumper and, after many trials, enters the retired Sgt. Murphy in Britain's Grand National. The film provides a sympathetic portrait of interwar barracks life in the U.S. Army. The final sequence in England reinforces cultural links with the former mother country while also indirectly suggesting closer military ties between the two nations.

WESTERN JAMBOREE (Republic): The plot of this late 1938 Gene Autry release deals with the attempts of a group of outlaws to find a helium gas floe on a ranch. They want to sell the helium to an unspecified foreign power "avidly seeking" the gas for use in its dirigibles. As pointed out in the film, the U.S. government has banned the export of helium. What is not mentioned, however, is that Nazi Germany was the only foreign power with a significant interest in airships. Note: In May 1937, the German Zeppelin *Hindenburg*, filled with highly combustible hydrogen gas, burst into flames during docking procedures at Lakehurst, New Jersey.

1939

BLONDIE BRINGS UP BABY (Columbia): The European war situation appears to be alluded to during an early scene in this November release. J.C. Dithers, who has left his construction company under Dagwood Bumstead's charge while he took a vacation, is glad to be back in the United States. Before Dithers is informed about a client reneging on a major contract, he tells Dagwood (Arthur Lake) how good it was to be greeted in New York harbor by the Statue of Liberty and tugboats flying the American flag. Dithers adds he told his wife: "Here's where we get a real cup of coffee"—presumably a reference to wartime rationing overseas.

HOTEL IMPERIAL (Paramount): The film's action takes place in December 1916, during World War I, at a small Galician hotel on the front between the Austro-Hungarian and Russian armies. A Russian spy played by J. Carroll Naish, is the primary heavy. The hero is a handsome Hungarian cavalry officer, played by popular leading man Ray Milland. With the exception of the 1939 re-release version of *All Quiet on the Western Front* (Universal), this is the only American produced film released between 1937 and 1941 to positively portray Austrian/German military forces. Since during the period of this film's release, in early 1939, the Soviets were pressuring the Balkan states for territorial concessions, the negative depiction of the Russian military in *Hotel Imperial* could be construed as an indirect attack upon the Soviet Union.

NAUGHTY BUT NICE (Warner Bros.): A young professor (Dick Powell) at a small college, has composed a classical symphony. While visiting New York City, he encounters a lady lyricist who, unbeknownst to him, converts the symphony's leitmotif into a popular swing melody. In the opening scene of this July release the professor states during a lecture that classical music is a palliative "in a world gone mad on many fronts." The anti-fascist Italian expatriate composer, Arturo Toscanini, is mentioned favorably.

TAIL SPIN (20th Century–Fox): The Women's Trans-Continental Air Race from Los Angeles to Cleveland is featured in this early 1939 release. Although this is primarily a ladies' film, one of the male leads is a naval officer who is a member of a group of carrier pilots from the USS *Ranger* attending the race. Between romantic activities, he helps the aviatrix (Alice Faye) repair her airplane. What is interesting re: the historical context of this civilian aviation film is the insertion of a military subtext—possibly reflecting increasing concerns over international tensions and the ongoing build-up of the U.S. Navy.

WALL STREET COWBOY (Republic): A crooked banker learns about a molybdenum deposit on the Circle R ranch owned by Roy Rogers and decides to foreclose on the cattleman's mortgage. Although not specifically pointed out in this August release, as fears of a European war increased the importance of this strategic material used in aircraft production gained exponentially in importance.

1940

ADVENTURE IN DIAMONDS (Paramount): Captain Stephen Dennett (George Brent), a Royal Air Force flier, becomes involved with international jewel thieves on board a liner bound for South Africa. He will later be seconded to the secret service in order to prevent the smuggling of the diamonds out of the country. Dennett's military rank and the strategic importance of diamonds create a linkage with World War II.

BLACK FRIDAY (Universal): Boris Karloff plays Dr. Ernest Sovac, who transplants part of a gangster's brain to save the life of meek college professor Kingsley. Karloff's role was originally written for Bela Lugosi, who was specifically identified as a "refugee scientist"—in the released film, this is only obliquely referred to.

CHARTER PILOT (20th Century–Fox): Hotshot American commercial pilot King Morgan (Lloyd Nolan) is sent to Honduras to straighten out problems surrounding his airline's contract with a mining outfit. Trouble is being generated by their main competitor, an airline company owned by an evil German named Faber (Henry Victor—regularly appearing as a Nazi villain in such wartime films as *To Be or Not to Be* and *Desperate Journey*). Even before the outbreak of World War II there had been increasing concerns in the United States related to the Third Reich's political and economic penetration of Latin America. While avoiding direct attacks upon Hitler's Germany, this December release nonetheless reflected the exacerbation of these fears following the Nazi defeat of France in June.

GIVE US WINGS (Monogram): A group of teenaged urban toughs learns aeronautical mechanics in a National Youth Administration Work Program plant. They pool their savings to pay for flying lessons, but are ineligible for pilot's licenses because none of them have graduated from high school. This leads to their entanglement with an unscrupulous owner of a crop dusting company. Though military preparedness is never mentioned, this December release would appear to reflect an increased determination in America to create a large pool of trained pilots.

HOLD THAT WOMAN (Producers' Releasing Corporation): People who repossess cars, known as "skip tracers," are featured in this film. At one point, the cocky male lead, played by James Dunn, makes an oblique topical comment by telling his girlfriend: "My job's as safe as democracy."

LITTLE OLD NEW YORK (20th Century–Fox): Among other obstacles to Englishman Robert Fulton (Richard Greene) completing his revolutionary steamboat in early 19th century America is a trade embargo imposed by President Jefferson. Fulton perseveres and eventually succeeds in circumventing the embargo. Designed to prevent the United States from becoming involved in the Napoleonic Wars, the highlighting of Jefferson's embargo in the film could be viewed as intentionally creating parallels with the contemporary debate in 1940 America over supplying war materials to belligerents.

YOUNG BILL HICKOK (Republic): A European agent named Nicholas Tower (John Miljan) is sent to America during the Civil War to organize a "Fifth Column" and seize western territory with their aid. "Wild" Bill Hickok, played by Roy Rogers, thwarts these subversive activities. The anachronistic use of the term "fifth column" would appear to be a deliberate attempt to create for the audience contemporary associative linkages. This film also reflected a growing wartime era trend in Hollywood films to invoke legendary American heroes.

1941

THE BRIDE CAME C.O.D. (Warner Bros.): A charter pilot played by James Cagney accepts a contract from a millionaire to kidnap his temperamental daughter. The comedic action really gets rolling after the heiress (Bette Davis) and the pilot crash land in the desert and find refuge in an abandoned mining town. An oblique reference to America's massive military build-up in 1941 occurs when a large formation of Army aircraft is observed passing overhead. A mild slap at the Dies Committee occurs with the local sheriff's response to the revelation by a reclusive old miner that he has never seen a movie: "Sounds un–American to me."

I WAS A PRISONER OF DEVIL'S ISLAND (Columbia): Joel Grant (Donald Woods), the American first officer on a French tramp steamer, has a fight with his captain over wages. The latter dies during the scuffle and Jeff is sentenced to three years on Devil's Island. The venality and brutality of prison officials exacerbate conditions for the prisoner's during an outbreak of jungle fever. A tough French Foreign Legion war veteran, placed on the island by the governor to secretly report upon the situation, helps Joel survive and terminate the corrupt rule of the Commandant. Despite a modus vivendi reached between the Vichy and U.S. governments in October 1940 regarding the status of French Caribbean possessions, this film would appear to reflect a continuing ambivalence in America toward the Vichy regime.

ROAD TO HAPPINESS (Monogram): Jeff Carter (John Boles) returns to America after four years in Europe studying voice. Having meanwhile been divorced by his wife, Jeff learns that his son was placed in a military school. Jeff retrieves his son and struggles in New York City to launch an operative career. One of three songs he sings is the patriotic "My Country Tis of Thee." Because the melody for this piece is identical to that of England's "God Save Our King," this performance could also be construed as a subtle pro–British gesture.

SECRET OF THE WASTELANDS (Paramount): "Hopalong" Cassidy (William Boyd) and his pals are hired by a party of archeologists to guide them to the ruins of an ancient walled city in the desert. Difficulties arise because a group of hard-working Chinese have diligently created a Utopian settlement in a hidden nearby valley whose gold mine is coveted by others. The "brains" of the Chinese community is a beautiful woman named May Soong. Madame Chiang Kai-shek, nee Mayling Soong, was well known in America as the wife of the Generalissimo of Nationalist China. Her older brother, T. V. Soong, was a western trained financial expert who was in the United States throughout most of 1941 as Chiang's personal representative negotiating military aid for China.

SWEETHEART OF THE CAMPUS (Columbia): This campus musical features Ruby Keeler in her final starring role. Under financial difficulties, the college converts its gym into a nightclub. One of the numerous songs performed is "Zig Me Baby with a Gentle Zag"—presumably inspired by the naval tactic of ships sailing in a zig zag pattern to avoid being torpedoed by submarines.

1942

ARE HUSBANDS NECESSARY? (Paramount): Ray Milland and Betty Field are a married couple who constantly tell little white lies to make their life easier, but one day their stories snowball and disrupt their lives. The studio pressbook synopsis for this romantic comedy describes a fancy car owned by a millionaire acquaintance of Milland as: "a brand new super-duper 'land yacht'—with five new tires." However, it is not known if there are specific references to the tire shortage in the film itself. Not screened.

BALL OF FIRE (RKO Radio Pictures): Release dates on this film vary, but the *Motion Picture Herald* lists January 1942 so it is included in this section. There is a verbal reference to the "Gestanko" (i.e., Gestapo), as well as "blitz," and "gas mask" references. However, there are no overt war references.

CADETS ON PARADE (Columbia): Freddie Bartholomew is expelled from military school and runs away. He becomes friends with newsboy Jimmy Lydon. It is difficult to imagine a film which begins in a military school not containing some war-relevant reference, but we have been unable to find clear confirmation of this. Not screened.

THE FALCON TAKES OVER (RKO Radio Pictures): This film was based on Raymond Chandler's novel "Farewell, My Lovely," with the Falcon (George Sanders) taking the place of Philip Marlowe. In one scene, would-be reporter Lynn Bari gives the Falcon a ride in her old car, which backfires repeatedly. "It's just practicing to be a tank," she says.

FOOTLIGHT SERENADE (20th Century–Fox): This musical comedy contains several peripheral references but no overt topical remarks. The finale is a number entitled "I'll Be Marching to a Love Song," with lyrics like "I'll be marching to a love song, while you're waiting for me..." but does not specifically mention the war or even military service.

THE GREAT MAN'S LADY (Paramount): Elderly Hannah Hoyt (Barbara Stanwyck) tells the story of her life with her late, famous husband to a young woman reporter. There is a prologue which states that "Not only behind great men, but behind the ordinary guy you will meet a Hannah Hoyt ... helping, pointing the road ahead, encouraging her man to reach his own pinnacle of success." This could be construed as an indirect reference to "home front" support of America's fighting men in the war.

MANTRAP (Republic): A retired Scotland Yard inspector living in the United States becomes involved in a murder case, to the chagrin of the local police. There is a *very* oblique reference to the war in the dialogue. Not screened.

OBLIGING YOUNG LADY (RKO Radio Pictures): A young girl is "kidnapped" by a secretary in an effort to reunite the girl's divorced parents. One of the characters in this film is a reporter (Edmond O'Brien) who has just returned from the Far East—he spent three years in China (presumably covering the war). There is also a dialogue reference to "sabotage."

PARDON MY SARONG (Universal): This Abbott and Costello vehicle is clearly NOT set during wartime, since the plot revolves around a yacht race in the Pacific! However, one of the cars in the opening section of the film *may* have a ration sticker on its windshield. A U.S. Navy ship later appears in one scene.

PIERRE OF THE PLAINS (Metro-Goldwyn-Mayer): This was the third film version of a 1907 play. This remake is set in the contemporary period; a French-Canadian trapper confronts a group of traders who are cheating Indian trappers. The leader of the villainous crew is called "Jap" Durkin.

RANDOM HARVEST (Metro-Goldwyn-Mayer): This film, set in England, was based on a novel by James Hilton. Ronald Colman loses his memory due to an injury in WWI. He meets Greer Garson on Armistice Day. They fall in love and are married, but several years later Colman is in an accident and promptly forgets about Garson, returning to his pre-war life. Garson has to track him down and try to win him back.

SEVEN SWEETHEARTS (Metro-Goldwyn-Mayer): Van Heflin is a reporter who travels to a Dutch community in Michigan to cover the tulip festival and falls in love with the oldest of seven unmarried daughters. Positive depiction of the Dutch. Not screened.

1943

THE DESPERADOES (Columbia): This is a period Western, set in 1863 Utah. Part of the film involves selling horses to the Army. In one scene, Edgar Buchanan says a bank safe is "built like a battleship." This is a rather anachronistic comment, since the term "battleship" was not in general use in 1863 (and most warships of the period were wooden, anyway).

FLESH AND FANTASY (Universal): This is a multi-story fantasy film. The first story is set in New Orleans during Mardi Gras. Michael (Robert Cummings) makes a vaguely topical remark, saying "the whole world [is] dark on both sides and disaster in the wind," indicating perhaps this was intended to take place prior to 1939.

FOLLOW THE BAND (Universal): The "Army Air Corps" song is played in this musical, but the context is not known; there is also a musical group called the "Bombardiers," but the Office of War Information reviewer did not find any overt war references. Not screened.

GALS, INC. (Universal): Leon Errol is a rich man who bankrolls a nightclub called "Gals, Incorporated." Aside from Glen Gray and the Casa Loma Orchestra, all of the talent and employees of the club are women, including the president of the corporation. Not screened.

HAPPY GO LUCKY (Paramount): This film is obviously not set during wartime, as it concerns rich people on vacation on a Caribbean island (some arrive in private yachts, others on a cruise ship). Mary Martin is a gold-digger out to snare a rich husband; Dick Powell is a broke beachcomber who agrees to help her, but of course they fall for each other, instead. There are several anachronistic remarks which could be construed as topical. In one scene, Eddie Bracken explains to Betty Hutton that he missed their wedding because he had measles: "the worse kind—*German* measles." Later, Powell describes millionaire Rudy Vallee to Martin as "the type that holds a flashlight while his mother puts on a spare tire—*if* she has one." (Emphasis added—in the original this is a throwaway line.)

HENRY ALDRICH HAUNTS A HOUSE (Paramount): Henry Aldrich runs into spooky goings-on at a haunted house. The ghostly happenings are caused by a gang which is counterfeiting bonds—in the dialogue they are simply called "bonds," and do not appear to be War Bonds. Not screened by the authors, but the bonds reference was checked for us by video collector Stark Maynard.

HIS BUTLER'S SISTER (Universal): Deanna Durbin leaves her hometown and travels to New York to try to make her way as a singer. She winds up impersonating a maid in the same household where her brother is a butler. There is a heavy "Russian" presence in this film—some scenes take place in a Russian restaurant, and Durbin sings in Russian. It is possible this is meant as a pro–Russian (i.e., Russia as an Allied nation) statement. One source states this is set in the "pre-war" period, although it is a more or less contemporary film. Not screened.

MADAME CURIE (Metro-Goldwyn-Mayer): Period biography of the scientist-wife (Greer Garson) of Pierre Curie (Walter Pidgeon) who carried on his work after her husband's death. Marie Curie is Polish, although she marries a Frenchman and spends most of her life in France (pro–Polish, pro–French overtones). At the end of the film she makes a speech condemning war.

THE MAN FROM THUNDER RIVER (Republic): This is a period Bill Elliott Western. Gabby Hayes plays his sidekick, but Eddie Lee has a significant, positive role as Wong, a Chinese ranch cook. This is rather unusual for the period, and may be a subtle comment on China as an Allied nation.

ONE DANGEROUS NIGHT (Columbia): In this Lone Wolf series' entry, there is a comment which *could* be construed as an oblique reference to the wartime speed limit of 35 miles per hour. Urged to drive faster, Jamison (Eric Blore) says "We're doing 30 now."

THE OX-BOW INCIDENT (20th Century–Fox): This is a period Western about a trio of cowboys who are accused of a crime and lynched, only to have their innocence proven afterwards. There are some generalized dialogue references to justice, the rule of law, civilization, and other "pro-democracy" ideals.

TORNADO (Paramount): The female lead character in this film is named "Victory" Kane. It is not known if there are other topical references in the film, although the plot is not overtly war-relevant. Not screened.

UNKNOWN GUEST (Monogram): The Monogram synopsis for this film credits "Cpl. Maurice King, U.S.M.C." as the producer; it is not known if this is the on-screen credit or not. The plot is non-topical. Not screened.

WHITE SAVAGE (Universal): This is a Maria Montez tropical film with no overt war references, although the villain, called "Sam Miller," is identified as being of German descent.

1944

BABES ON SWING STREET (Universal): This youth-oriented musical features a song entitled "Youth on the March," which may have topical lyrics, as well as a Russian musical number. However, the plot is not overtly topical. Not screened.

BLACK MAGIC (Monogram): This film is also known as *Meeting at Midnight.* Charlie Chan investigates murders at a house run by a medium. His sidekick Birmingham Brown (Mantan Moreland) makes a "gremlins" reference. Gremlins were fictional creatures blamed by pilots for trouble with their airplanes, and were generally a WWII invention, but the reference here is non-topical.

BRAZIL (Republic): Virginia Bruce is a writer who goes to Brazil for research purposes. She meets Tito Guizar, a popular singer and composer, who poses as his own twin brother so he can be her guide. Edward Everett Horton is Guizar's friend. The Republic synopsis says Horton runs a travel agency which is "closed for the duration," but it is not known if this is stated in the film itself. Strong Latin American theme. Not screened.

THE CONTENDER (Producers' Distributing Corporation): Buster Crabbe is a truck driver whose son is a military school student. In order to pay the steep school fees, Crabbe turns to boxing, but alcohol and a blonde nearly do him in. At the end, Crabbe's pals— "Gunner" and "Bomber," among others—set him straight. Not screened.

THE COWBOY AND THE SENORITA (Republic): Roy Rogers helps foil a plot to swindle teenager Mary Lee out of a gold mine she inherited. The villain tries to buy the allegedly worthless mine under the pretense of mining "manganese" (possibly a mineral useful for the war effort) rather than gold (he is lying, however). Dale Evans is the "senorita," who has a Hispanic surname and dark hair, but otherwise appears entirely Anglicized. Rogers and Guinn Williams are unemployed, roving cowboys (as in *Hands Across the Border*, q.v.), which would tend to divorce this contemporary film from the realities of the period (when every able-bodied man was expected to be in the service or in a war-related occupation).

DELINQUENT DAUGHTERS (Producers' Distributing Corporation): The PRC synopsis comments that juvenile delinquency occurs more frequently in wartime than at other times; one of the teenage characters is identified as the son of a woman factory worker who spends too little time with him. It is not known if she is a *defense* plant worker or not. Not screened.

HENRY ALDRICH PLAYS CUPID (Paramount): A cast listing for this film indicates a "Western Union girl" appears in one scene. However, it is not known if she is a messenger (which would qualify as Female Labor) or a clerk. The film's plot is non-topical. Not screened.

HOME IN INDIANA (20th Century–Fox): In one scene of this rural film, money for a horserace wager is raised via War Bonds (presumably by selling them prematurely). This is according to one print source; the script does not contain a clear indication of this.

KNICKERBOCKER HOLIDAY (United Artists): This is a period film about colonial New York (New Amsterdam, then) under Dutch rule. Peter Stuyvesant (Walter Huston) is portrayed as the dictatorial leader of the colony, opposed by the democratically inclined young hero.

THE MASK OF DIMITRIOS (Warner Bros.): Leyden (Peter Lorre), a mystery writer, begins to research the life of the international criminal Dimitrios (Zachary Scott), recently reported dead. Leyden learns Dimitrios faked his death so he could live on his ill-gotten gains; in the end, Dimitrios and a former associate (now trying to blackmail him) kill each other. This film is not set during wartime; however, Dimitrios's exploits include espionage and other political crimes, and the general aid of international intrigue is somewhat relevant. In addition, some critics feel Lorre's character—a Dutch national—is meant as a tribute to the Netherlands' contribution to the Allied cause (in the original novel, the protagonist is a British university professor turned novelist).

THE MONSTER MAKER (Producers' Distributing Corporation): A mad scientist infects a concert pianist with acromegaly in a plot to marry the pianist's daughter. The scientist (J. Carrol Naish) admits he is not the real Dr. Markoff, but that killing the doctor and stealing his identity "made it possible for me to escape from Europe."

NIGHT OF ADVENTURE (RKO Radio Pictures): Tom Conway plays a lawyer who is always getting involved in tough cases, to his wife's chagrin. At one point, he asks her if she is "being convoyed by any[one in] particular?" Not screened.

OKLAHOMA RAIDERS (Universal): In this Tex Ritter Western, outlaws try to drive ranchers out of a valley containing wild horses. The ranchers have a contract to sell these horses to the U.S. Army. This may be a period film. Not screened.

OUR HEARTS WERE YOUNG AND GAY (Paramount): This is a period film set in 1923. Cornelia Otis Skinner (Gail Russell) and Emily Kimbrough (Diana Lynn), two recent high school graduates, travel to Europe on their own. Before leaving they visit the steamship line office and see travel posters for Norway, Naples (Italy), Germany, and Japan. In France, they visit the Arch of Triumph and pay their respects at the eternal flame marking the tomb of the Unknown Soldier (while the "Marseillaise" plays in the background). An old French coachman thanks them "in the name of France." As the two girls set sail for home, Cornelia says "Goodbye, Europe...it'll never be the same again."

THAT'S MY BABY (Republic): A comic book publisher has not smiled in decades. His daughter and an artist (Richard Arlen) try to make him laugh, for his own good. This film has a number of "near" references, including comments about the manpower shortage ("If you want any help you better take what's available"), female labor (nearly all of the publisher's comic book artists are women), a dialogue reference to Eleanor Roosevelt, and one character who says "You know, the way things are now..." But no OVERT references to the war (and why is Richard Arlen not in the service—comic book artist is not exactly an essential occupation!).

1945

BOSTON BLACKIE'S RENDEZVOUS (Columbia): Steve Cochran is a mental patient who escapes from an asylum to meet a young woman (Nina Foch) whose picture he saw in a newspaper. He strangles a number of other women. Boston Blackie has to track him down before he kills his fantasy girl. There are three oblique war references in this film. At the beginning, the Runt refers to Blackie being "away in Washington" for four months. Later, hatcheck girl Iris Adrian says "Wappinger Falls? Is that something we captured?" Finally, Blackie jokes to Inspector Farraday: "I'm leaving for Murmansk." Murmansk was the Russian port through which much U.S. aid to the Soviets passed during the war.

CIRCUMSTANTIAL EVIDENCE (20th Century–Fox): Michael O'Shea is sentenced to death for murder due to the faulty evidence of three eyewitnesses. His friend Lloyd Nolan, a fellow WWI veteran who was decorated for bravery in combat, helps clear him. While this film appears contemporary, neither O'Shea nor Nolan looks old enough to have served in WWI, and there is no overt mention of WWII (one newspaper headline refers to a "Red Cross Drive" but this is not explicitly war-oriented).

THE CORN IS GREEN (Warner Bros.): Although this is a period film set in late 19th-century Wales, it demonstrates a fairly strong pro–British orientation. Bette Davis is a British schoolteacher who takes it upon herself to open a school for the inhabitants of a poor mining town.

HIGH-POWERED (Paramount): This film is about electrical linemen, but the advertising refers to their work on wires near a gasoline-manufacturing plant that makes gas to send "our B-29s to Tokyo!" Not screened.

JOHNNY ANGEL (RKO Radio Pictures): The exact release date of this film is unclear; it was reviewed in August, but some sources give December as the official release date. George Raft is a Merchant Marine captain who finds his father, also a ship's captain, murdered on his abandoned ship. The only witness to the crime is stowaway Paulette (Signe Hasso), described in some sources as a French "refugee."

MAMA LOVES PAPA (RKO Radio Pictures): This domestic comedy stars Leon Errol and Elisabeth Risdon (earlier teamed in the "Mexican Spitfire" series). The film opens as a delivery boy brings a box of groceries into Risdon's kitchen. She reads the list: "coffee, 10 pounds of sugar, one pound of butter, a six-pound roast— $1.04!" [There is a close-up of the roast] The boy says "Good beef is 17 cents a pound these days." "17 cents a pound—it's outrageous!" Risdon says. The camera shows a wall calendar, and the year is revealed to be 1905. This opening gag is obviously a commentary on WWII food rationing, since all of the items mentioned were rationed and/or somewhat scarce.

MOLLY AND ME (20th Century–Fox): This film stars Gracie Fields and Monty Woolley; the opening title sets it in "London 1937," conveniently sidestepping any topical intrusions. Fields is an actress who accepts the job as housekeeper for Woolley.

She learns that the rest of the staff is methodically swindling her employer—a particular point is made of the French chef, who orders large amounts of *meat* and *butter*, items which would have been of no particular interest in 1937 London, but were rationed during the war.

PENTHOUSE RHYTHM (Universal): There is one song in this musical which may be topical—"Let's Go, Americans." Not screened.

ROCKIN' IN THE ROCKIES (Columbia): The Three Stooges and the Hoosier Hotshots go prospecting. Moe Howard says "The government's cryin' for minerals," but there are no overt war references.

TELL IT TO A STAR (Republic): An all-girl band is formed to play in a hotel. However, whether this is specifically identified as a war-related development is not known. The plot is otherwise non-relevant. Not screened.

Appendix G: Films Released in October–December 1945 Containing War-Relevant Material

ADVENTURE (MGM): Clark Gable's first film after his discharge from the armed forces. He plays a Merchant Marine sailor who visits San Francisco after his ship was sunk by a "Jap sub" (he spent some time drifting on a life raft in the Pacific). Gable falls in love with a librarian, played by Greer Garson.

ALLOTMENT WIVES (Monogram): One of three Kay Francis vehicles released through Monogram, this film deals with a bigamy racket: unscrupulous women are marrying servicemen in order to collect the portion of the men's pay "allotted" to wives by the government. Paul Kelly is an Army investigator who exposes the racket.

CAPTAIN TUGBOAT ANNIE (Republic): Tugboat Annie (Jane Darwell) resumes her pre-war career as captain of a tugboat, after the tugboat fleet is de-commissioned by the government. Annie hires only ex-servicemen, including one disabled man, and a black (Mantan Moreland). Her friendly rival is the irascible Edgar Kennedy.

COLONEL EFFINGHAM'S RAID (20th Century–Fox): Set in the immediate pre-WWII period—Charles Coburn is an Army officer who retires and goes back to his hometown in Georgia to live. Upset at the apathy of the citizenry to the crooked politicians who want to change the sleepy character of the town, Coburn tries to stir up civic pride by writing editorials for the town newspaper. At the conclusion of the film, a group of National Guardsmen from the town are being sent off to war (WWII has just begun); they demand that the crooked

politicians be removed from office before they come back from combat.

CONFIDENTIAL AGENT (Warner Bros.): This film is set during the Spanish Civil War. Charles Boyer is a Spanish Republican agent who is sent to Great Britain to buy coal in order to keep it out of the hands of the Fascists (Franco's Nationalist forces are unable to obtain coal in Spain itself, because the miners refuse to work for fascists). Lauren Bacall is a British aristocrat who helps him out.

CORNERED (RKO): Dick Powell plays a former Canadian POW who travels across Europe and then to Argentina in search of the Vichy official who caused the death of Powell's French wife. Powell meets a group dedicated to tracking down Nazi war criminals. In the end, he catches the man he is tracking and kills him. Before he dies, the cornered Nazi contemptuously says: "Anglo-Saxons are not good fanatics … you attack evil—we understand it."

DANGER SIGNAL (Warner Bros.): Zachary Scott is a swindler who preys on lonely women. Posing as a wounded veteran, he rents a room in a house owned by Faye Emerson and her younger sister, Mona Freeman. Scott plays up to Emerson but switches his attentions to Freeman when he learns she will inherit a fortune. However, he is eventually killed by the husband of one of his earlier victims.

DANGEROUS PARTNERS (MGM): Signe Hasso and her husband survive an airplane

crash; they steal four wills, each worth one million dollars, from an unconscious passenger (Edmund Gwenn). Hasso enlists shady lawyer James Craig to help her collect the money, but when they learn Gwenn is part of a Nazi spy ring, Hasso and Craig demonstrate their innate goodness and patriotism.

DOLLFACE (20th Century–Fox): One of the songs (performed by Perry Como) in this musical refers to the fact that it was "mighty smoky over Tokyo" after the Allied bombings of that city.

FOLLOW THAT WOMAN (Paramount): Former "Ellery Queen" William Gargan plays a detective who joins the Army, but has to clear his wife of a murder charge while on leave.

A GAME OF DEATH (RKO Radio): This was a remake of *The Most Dangerous Game* (RKO, 1932), with the location shifted to an island in the Caribbean. The villain, "Count Zaroff" in the original (played by Leslie Banks), becomes a German in this version (Edgar Barrier).

HIT THE HAY (Columbia): Judy Canova is a hillbilly singer who is hired to perform by an opera company. Many uniformed servicemen appear in the crowd scenes, and there are several rationing/shortages jokes—her employer (a grocer) tries to keep her, offering her "a pound of butter every week," and then "two pounds of bacon." The opera impresario counters with "You'll make thousands of friends," but Judy says "With two pounds of bacon I could make *millions* of friends."

THE HOUSE ON 92ND ST (20th Century–Fox): Lloyd Nolan is an FBI agent who enlists the aid of a German-American (William Eythe) in breaking up a Nazi spy ring in New York which is trying to steal atomic bomb secrets. The gang is headed by Signe Hasso (who poses as a man for much of the film). The film was produced by Louis de Rochemont, formerly of "The March of Time," and directed by Henry Hathaway in a semi-documentary style.

KISS AND TELL (Columbia): Shirley Temple is a teenager who pretends to be pregnant in order to help her brother, a soldier who got secretly married while on a 72-hour furlough. Based on a Broadway play.

A LETTER FOR EVIE (MGM): Factory worker Marsha Hunt writes a letter to "any GI" and puts it in the pocket of a newly sewn uniform shirt. The shirt is issued to lecherous soldier John Carroll, who ignores it. Carroll's buddy Hume Cronyn replies, using Carroll's name and photo, and when they return to New York the two men get into a rivalry for Hunt.

LOVE LETTERS (Paramount): Joseph Cotten is an invalided British serviceman who pays a visit to the girlfriend (Jennifer Jones) of a wartime friend who was killed in action. Jones has amnesia; even worse, the beautiful love letters she received from her beloved were *really* written by Cotten.

PARDON MY PAST (Columbia): Fred MacMurray plays a discharged soldier who wants to start a mink farm in Wisconsin. However, he is mistaken for a rich playboy by gambler Akim Tamiroff, who wants to collect the money owed him.

PARIS UNDERGROUND (United Artists): British star Gracie Fields plays an Englishwoman who, along with American Constance Bennett, helps downed Allied fliers escape from occupied France. They are caught by the Nazis but are rescued just in time by the liberation of France by the Allies. Based on a 1943 book by Etta Shiber.

PRISON SHIP (Columbia): A Japanese tanker carrying Allied prisoners from a Pacific Island to Tokyo is used as a decoy to lure American submarines to destruction. An unsuccessful revolt by the captives leads the Japanese captain (Richard Loo) to order the shooting of dozens of women and children in retaliation. Nina Foch, a British newspaperwoman, and Robert Lowery are able to contact an American sub which surfaces to attack their ship, and the surviving prisoners are rescued. During the fall of 1944, several thousand Allied POWs died when the unmarked Japanese prison ship they were on was sunk by U.S. submarines.

THE SAILOR TAKES A WIFE (MGM): June Allyson falls for Navy man Robert Walker, and they are married. However, the marriage loses some of its luster when Walker is discharged; Walker is pursued by vamp Audrey Totter, and Allyson's boss is still after *her*. In the end, it all works out.

SHADOW OF TERROR (PRC): This was a spy film about a scientist whose secret explosive is sought by spies. At the last minute, newsreel footage of atomic bomb explosions was spliced in with the explanation (given in voice-over narration) that this was the "secret" the spies were after.

SING YOUR WAY HOME (RKO): Jack Haley plays a pompous war correspondent who wants to get back to the United States as quickly as possible, so he can cash in on his celebrity (he wrote a popular book on the war) with a lecture tour. In order to secure passage on a ship sailing from France, Haley agrees to chaperone a group of young entertainers on their way back home.

SNAFU (Columbia): Conrad Janis portrays an under-age boy who joins the service and sees action in the South Pacific before being detected (in a newsreel) by his parents and brought home. The 15-year-old veteran's stories of his war experiences, his readjustment to civilian life (and adolescence, after playing an adult role in the war), and the impact on his parents (Robert Benchley and Vera Vague) form the basis for this comedy. In one scene, Janis gives his mother a bloodstained Japanese battle flag for a souvenir; the visit of the pregnant Australian wife of one of his comrades also causes consternation among the family.

SPELLBOUND (United Artists): Gregory Peck has developed amnesia after bailing out of a medical transport plane during the war. Now he is impersonating the director of a mental hospital. Psychiatrist Ingrid Bergman uncovers Peck's deception, but also cures him of his guilt complex. Directed by Alfred Hitchcock.

THE STORK CLUB (Paramount): Betty Hutton saves a bum from drowning; however, the bum (Barry Fitzgerald) turns out to be a millionaire, and he proves to be very grateful. Hutton's boyfriend, Don DeFore, returns from combat service in the Pacific and thinks she has been unfaithful to him.

THEY WERE EXPENDABLE (MGM): John Ford directed this classic combat film about the men who served in PT boats during the Japanese invasion of the Philippines. It stars real-life Navy officer Robert Montgomery, and John Wayne. An Army nurse (Donna Reed) is the romantic interest.

TOKYO ROSE (Paramount): Osa Massen plays the notorious propaganda broadcaster for Japan (actually, several women played the part of "Tokyo Rose"). Some American POWs who have been tortured into making propaganda statements before neutral journalists escape during an air raid. The Chinese resistance helps them to a submarine, and they escape. The film ends with an announcement of the bombing of Hiroshima, and Russia's declaration of war on Japan.

TOO YOUNG TO KNOW (Warner Bros.): Robert Hutton is discharged from the service. He comes home and learns his ex-wife (desirous of starting a career) has given away their young child!

WALK IN THE SUN (United Artists): Dana Andrews and Richard Conte head the all-male cast in this Lewis Milestone film about an infantry unit which lands in Italy and takes "a walk in the sun." The climax of the film is an assault on a farmhouse occupied by German troops.

WEEKEND AT THE WALDORF (MGM): Remake of *Grand Hotel* (1932), set in New York's Waldorf-Astoria Hotel. Lana Turner has the Joan Crawford role as the hotel stenographer, and Van Johnson plays yet another handsome young officer.

WHAT NEXT, CORPORAL HARGROVE? (MGM): This sequel to *See Here, Private Hargrove*, q.v., follows the adventures of Hargrove (Robert Walker) as he and his artillery unit participate in the liberation of France. On one rainy day at the front, Hargrove complains about "trying to dig his way to Berlin." He survives capture by a German patrol and complications with a French village girl, but finally makes it to Paris.

Notes to the Introduction, Numbered Chapters, and Appendices

Introduction

1. Francis E. Merrill, *Social Problems on the Home Front* (New York: Harper & Bros., 1948), 1.

2. Siegfried Kracauer, *From Caligari to Hitler* (Princeton: Princeton University Press, 1947), 5.

3. In 1980, for instance, the attendance total was down to approximately 19.6 million weekly. Cobbett Steinberg, *Reel Facts* (New York: Vintage Books, 1982), 46.

4. To a certain extent we have also employed it, individually, in our respective doctoral dissertations.

5. Appendix F includes both films screened and not screened, but whose war-relevance was unconfirmed or marginal. Undoubtedly, there are a number of films not on this list which contain minor war references—particularly Universal, Columbia, and Monogram musicals which were very difficult to see, and for which little detailed print information was available.

6. Garth Jowett and James M. Linton, *Movies as Mass Communication* (New Park, CA: Sage, 1989), 116.

7. Readers unfamiliar with film scholarship may not realize that there is no single archive which owns "every film ever made." The authors had access to the huge copyright collection of the Library of Congress, but even this archive holds only *representatie* films, not *every* film. Commercial film and video rental outlets were utilized, and even the vast underground network of film/video collectors was tapped, but some films simply eluded our best efforts.

8. PRC musicals fall into the same category, but scripts for at least some of these films were available. Universal and Columbia generally did not deposit scripts for copyright purposes, and the brief studio-prepared synopses are not very detailed (and at times are actually *incorrect*!).

9. *The Story of Dr. Wassell* (Paramount, 1944) proved very difficult to see, although it was eventually obtained. This Technicolor production, directed by Cecil B. DeMille and starring Gary Cooper, is almost never shown on television for some unexplained reason. *The Hitler Gang* (Paramound, 1944) is another film which is rarely shown today. A number of films were obtained on videotape in the large "gray market" of video collectors. Ironically, such collectors are probably doing more to preserve America's film heritage (and make it *available* for viewing) than many official repositories.

Chapter 1

1. Refer to Alan Brinkley, *Voices of Protest: Huey Long, Father Coughlin and The Great Depression* (New York: Random House, 1982).

2. Refer to Harvey Klehr, *The Heyday of American Communism: The Depression Decade* (New York: Basic Book, 1984).

3. Refer to Page Smith, *Redeeming the Time: A People's History of the 1920s and the New Deal* (New York: McGraw-Hill, 1987).

4. Refer to Eileen Eagan, *Class, Culture and the Classroom: The Student Peace Movement of the 1930's* (Philadelphia: Temple University Press, 1981).

5. A good overview of politically conscious films produced in America during the Thirties is contained in Peter Roffman and Jim Purdy's, *The Hollywood Social Problem Film: Madness, Despair, and Politics from the Depression to the Fifties* (Bloomington: Indiana University Press, 1981).

6. Roger Daniels, *The Bonus March: An Episode in the Great Depression* (Westport, CT: Greenwood Press, 1971).

7. *The Wandering Jew*—*MPH* October 23, 1933: 59; *Var* October 24, 1933: 22; *Are We Civilized?*—*LC* LP4648; *FD* June 14, 1934, 6.

8. One could make the case, though, that at least three films from 1935 indirectly espouse pacifism or Christian brotherhood: *The Crusades* (Par.); *The Last Days of Pompeii* (RKO); *So Red the Rose* (Par.).

9. *LC*, LP5338; *MPH* March 9, 1935, 49.

10. *LC*, LP5540; *MPH* June 8, 1935, 73.

11. Robert J. Goldstein, *Political Repression in Modern America: From 1870 to the Present* (Boston: G. K. Hall, 1978), pp. 213–217. Ellen W. Schrecker, *No Ivory Tower: McCarthyism & the Universities* (New York: Oxford University Press, 1986), 63–83.

12. James Dugan and Laurence Lafore, *Days of Emperor and Clown: The Italo-Ethiopian War, 1935–1936* (Garden City, NY: Doubleday, 1973).

13. Mussolini was not an unpopular figure in the United States prior to the Italo-Ethiopian conflict. He was actually admired by many Americans, as evidenced in an amazing American film released in early 1924, just over a year after Mussolini's triumphal "March on Rome," entitled *The Eternal City* (1st Nat.). In the film Mussolini and his fascist Blackshirts save Italy from an aspiring dictator (played by Lionel Barrymore), who was conspiring with the "Reds" to overthrow the government. *LC*, LP19782; *MPH*, December 1, 1923, 55. Between 1929 and 1936 Mussolini is referred to in over a dozen feature length fictional films produced in America: *Chasing Through Europe* (Fox; 1929); *The Medicine Man* (Tiffany; 1930); *Ambassador Bill* (Fox; 1931); *A Connecticut Yankee* (Fox; 1931); *Front Page* (UA; 1931); *Street Scene* (UA; 1931); *Mr. Robinson Crusoe* (UA; 1932); *Three on a Match* (WB; 1932); *Washington Merry-Go-Round* (Col.; 1932); *Son of a Sailor* (1st Nat.); *State Fair* (Fox; 1933); *Twenty Million Sweethearts* (WB; 1934); *The World Moves On* (Fox; 1934); *Broadway Sweethearts* (WB; 1935); *Next Time We Love* (Un.; 1936).

14. *MPH* October 19, 1935: 86.

15. Dorothy Borg, *The United States and the Far Eastern Crisis of 1933–1938: From the Manchurian Incident through the Initial Stage of the Undeclared Sino-Japanese War* (Cambridge: Harvard University Press, 1964), 73–74, 459.

16. *NYT*, August 3, 1936, 11.

Chapter 2

1. Joanna Mensel Meskill, *Hitler and Japan: The Hollow Alliance* (New York: Atherton Press, 1966), 4–10.

2. Selig Adler, *The Isolationist Impulse: Its Twentieth Century Reaction* (New York: Free Press, 1957), 242–244.

3. Saul Friedlander, *Prelude to Downfall: Hitler and the United States, 1939–41* (London: Chatto and Windus, 1967), 3.

4. Robert Dallek, *Franklin D. Roosevelt and American Foreign Policy, 1932–1945* (New York: Oxford University Press, 1979), 205–206.

5. *Ibid.*, 202–205.

6. In a one-reel film released by the Republican National Committee in the fall of 1940, *The Truth About Taxes*, the argument is made that the working man has paid out tremendous taxes for wasteful and largely unsuccessful New Deal programs, while national defense has been neglected and is therefore "woefully inadequate." At the film's conclusion, the narration solicits the listener: "War!—it must not happen here.... Let us rid ourselves of our New Deal failure. We must elect Wendell Wilkie president and speedily become so strong no foe would dare attack us..."

7. James MacGregor Burns, *Roosevelt: The Lion and the Fox* (New York: Harcourt, Brace & World, 1956), 449.

8. *Ibid.*, 442–451.

9. Blum, et al., *The National Experience* 676, 692–3, 721–3.

10. *Ibid.*, 725.

11. Dallek, *Franklin D. Roosevelt and American Foreign Policy, 1932–1945*, 252–261.

12. Blum, et al., *The National Experience*, 726.

13. *Ibid.*, 728.

14. Eugene Franklin Wong, *On Visual Media Racism: Asians in the American Motion Pictures* (New York: Arno Press, 1978), 113–115, 222–123.

15. Jack Alicoate, ed., *The Film Daily Yearbook of Motion Pictures, 1969* (New York: Film Daily Inc., 1970), 98; Jowett, *Film, the Democratic Art* 483.

16. Alicoate, 98.

17. Refer to the Predominant Discernable Bias chart in the filmography for Part One.

18. Jane H. D. Schwar, "Interventionist Propaganda and Pressure Groups in the United States, 1937–1941," (unpublished doctoral dissertation, Ohio State University, 1973), 62. The Hollywood Anti-Nazi League became the Hollywood League for Democratic Action after the signing of the Nazi-Soviet Pact in 1939.

19. Larry Ceplair and Steven Englund, *The Inquisition in Hollywood: Politics in the Film Community, 1930–1960* (Garden City, NY: Anchor Press/Doubleday, 1980), 114.

20. For more detailed information on these films refer to the filmography. A British film released through 20th Century–Fox in 1937, *Wings of the Morning*, also referred to the Spanish Civil War. (Appendix E)

21. Ceplair and Englund, 109–110.

22. The so-called "Nuremberg Laws." See Hajo Holborn, *A History of Modern Germany, 1840–1945* (New York: Knopf, 1969), 759–760.

23. This atrocity, known as "Crystal Night," resulted in the recall of America's ambassador to Germany. See Friedlander, 8.

24. Combining Anti–Japanese, Anti–Soviet, Anti–German, Anti–Nazi, and Anti–Fascist films. See the coding statistics chart in the filmography for Part One.

25. Immediately following the outbreak of hostilities in Europe, the U.S. government requested that the release dates of two features with pro-military themes be moved up: *20,000 Men a Year* (TCF) and *Thunder Afloat* (MGM). *Variety* September 6, 1939, 6.

26. Mark L. Chadwin, *The Hawks of World War II* (Chapel Hill: University of North Carolina Press, 1968), 64–65.

27. *LC* LP 9933; *MPH* August 3, 1940, 39, 42. For a synopsis of *Pastor Hall*, see Appendix F.

28. The Editors of *Look* magazine, *Movie Lot to Beachhead: The Motion Picture Goes to War and Prepares for the Future* (New York: Arno Press, 1980), 64.

29. Wayne S. Cole, *Charles A. Lindbergh and the Battle Against American Intervention* (New York: Harcourt, Brace and Jovanovich, 1974), 167.

30. Edward Charles Wagenknecht, *The Films of D.W. Griffith* (New York: Crown, 1975), 95.

31. Wayne S. Cole, *Roosevelt and the Isolationists* (Lincoln: University of Nebraska Press, 1983), 474.

32. Schwar, 251.

33. Chadwin, 216.

34. *NYT* July 3, 1933, 14.

35. Refer to the Predominant Discernible Bias chart in the filmography for Part One.

36. Refer to the comments in Chapter One.

37. Refer to Appendix A.

38. Refer to the Predominant Discernible Bias chart in the filmography for Part One.

Chapter 3

1. David Culbert, ed., *Film and Propaganda in America: A Documentary History, Volume II, World War II, Part I* (Westport, CT: Greenwood Press, 1990), 5.

2. *Film and Propaganda in America*, pp. 8 & 9.

3. Culbert, *Film and Propaganda in America*, pp. 14 & 15.

4. A major article in a leading trade journal, *The Motion Picture Herald*, by George Spires, was entitled "189 FILMS ON WAR, PATRIOTISM AND PREPAREDNESS IN YEAR OF CONFLICT," and was subtitled "129 Features and 60 Shorts Influenced by Conflict Were Released from Hollywood, London, and Paris." The article proceeds to list each film project (some of which were later abandoned) by name, with a one-line description. *MPH* September 7, 1940: 47–48.

5. Culbert, *Film and Propaganda in America*, p. 17.

6. *Ibid*, p. 23.

7. William R. Klingaman, *1941: Our Lives in a World on the Edge* (New York: Harper & Row, 1988), p. 373.

8. Bernard Dick, *The Star-Spangled Screen: The American World War II Film* (Lexington: The University Press of Kentucky, 1985), p. 90.

Chapter 4

1. David White and Richard Averson, *The Celluloid Weapon: Social Comment in the American Film* (Boston: Beacon Press, 1972), p. 25.

2. Though *not* classified in this study under the CM heading, films containing allegorical messages also occur. They usually appear in historical or social dramas and are most often categorized as Pro-American and/or Pro-Democracy films. Examples of such films would include *The Grapes of Wrath* (TCF; 1940) and *Santa Fe Trail* (WB; 1940).

3. *Too Hot to Handle* is listed in the Filmography with a primary bias of Anti-Japanese. But the reference within the film to the Italo-Ethiopian War conforms to the CM profile.

4 Ceplair and Englund, *The Hollywood Inquisition*, p. 179.

5. Alistaire Horne, *The Price of Glory: Verdun, 1916* (New York: MacFadden Books, 1962), pp. 228–229.

6. Dan R. Richardson, *Comintern Army: The International Brigades and the Spanish Civil War* (Lexington: The University Press of Kentucky, 1982), p. 192.

7. Ulam, *Expansion and Coexistance*, pp. 229–233.

8. Richardson, *Comintern Army*, pp. 3–10.

Chapter 5

1. See Charles Chatfield, *For Peace and Justice: Pacifism in America, 1914–1941* (Boston: Beacon Press, 1971), pp. 277–286.

2. See Robert Harris and Jeremy Paxman, *A Higher Form of Killing: The Secret Story of Chemical and Biological Warfare* (New York: Hill and Wang, 1982), pp. 53–54.

3. Hugh Thomas, *The Spanish Civil War*, pp. 117–198.

4. The term would be used in only three other films from the period, all released 1941: *That Night in Rio* (TCF); *That Uncertain Feeling* (UA); *The Wild Man of Borneo* (MGM). Its usage in *That Uncertain Feeling* was unambiguously pejorative.

5. See John Mason Brown, *The Worlds of Robert E. Sherwood: Mirror to His Times, 1896–1939* (New York: Harper & Row, 1965), pp. 329–345.

6. See Richard Grunberger, *The 12-Year Reich: A Social History of Nazi Germany, 1933–1945* (New York: Holt, Rinehart and Winston, 1971), pp. 411–413.

7. *NYT*, February 4, 1939: 13.

Chapter 6

1. Edward O. Guerrant, *Roosevelt's Good Neighbor Policy* (Albuquerque: University of New Mexico Press, 1950) 119.

2. Guerrant 1.

3. Guerrant 117.

4. Guerrant 118.

5. Similarly, *Man of Conquest* (Republic, 1939) depicted the war of Texas secession from the Anglo side, with Santa Anna as the Mexican dictator/villain.

6. *Juárez* may also have been a hit prescient in its portrayal of French "aggression" in the New World—after the German invasion of France, American attention focused on the sizeable French naval forces located in the Caribbean, which were under the control of Vichy France. Although these ships never took any action against the Allies, their presence was unsettling. See Robert O. Paxton, *Vichy France: Old Guard and New Order, 1940–1944* (New York: Knopf, 1972) 103–1, and Patrick Abbazia, *Mr. Roosevelt's Navy* (Annapolis: Naval Institute Press, 1975) 113–117, 167–168.

7. John Storm Roberts, *The Latin Tinge* (New York: Oxford University Press, 1979) 105.

8. There were German spy rings operating in Mexico, Brazil,

Chile, and Argentina. They had varying degrees of success, but never posed a serious threat to the security of the hemisphere. See Leslie B. Rout, Jr., and John F. Bratzel, *The Shadow War* (Frederick, MD: University Publications of America, 1986).

Chapter 7

1. Mark Lincoln Chadwin, *The Warhawks: American Interventionists Before Pearl Harbor* (New York: Norton, 1970) 3–4.

2. The Spanish Civil War was a bit more problematic. Today, the "rightness" of the Republican side is often taken for granted, but Franco's forces—although supported by "bad guys" Hitler and Mussolini—were seen by many at the time (particularly the Catholic Church) as defenders of Western values against "godless Communists."

3. In fact the concept of "Pan Americanism" was closely linked to "Americanism" in this period: Hollywood promoted hemispheric solidarity and emphasized the "democratic ideals" of the New World. Not exactly a true picture of the political realities of the hemisphere, but good propaganda.

4. The "freedom of the human mind" remark might also have referred to the various scientists and intellectual refugees from Nazi Germany and other European locations, including Albert Einstein, who were making their homes in the United States at this time.

5. Senator Gerald Nye's committee accused Hollywood of promoting intervention through the production of films with these themes. See Chapter 3.

Chapter 8

1. *Variety* January 18, 1939: 12.

2. Starting in 1938 the importance of air power became a major theme. The rise of the Luftwaffe and the devastating effect of the Condor Legion in Spain and the Japanese air force in China were largely responsible for this. Motion pictures featuring American air power *not* listed as pro-military films include *Men with Wings* (1938) and *20,000 Men a Year* (1939).

3. The repercussions of Munich had a direct bearing on American policy on hemisphere defense. By the summer of 1938 Latin American students were receiving presidential permission to attend U.S. military service academies and young officers were being sent in increasing numbers for advanced training, such as flying. See Irwin F. Gellman, *Good Neighbor Diplomacy: United States Policies in Latin America, 1933–1945* (Baltimore: The Johns Hopkins University Press, 1979), pp. 129–130.

4. In 1926 Warner Brothers released *Private Izzy Murphy*, directed by Lloyd Bacon, which featured George Jessel as a Jewish boy who joins the Fighting 69th to impress an Irish girl (*LC*, LP23177). In a 1918 Edison film dealing with American Marines in France, *The Unbeliever*, a rabbi comforts a dying Roman Catholic.

Chapter 9

1. During the height of the Cold War, for instance, Hollywood saw Communist spies behind every nefarious occurrence (perhaps what J. Edgar Hoover called "The Crime of the Century"—the theft of the atomic bomb plans—had some bearing on this). In the 1960s, the success of the James Bond series brought about a rash of

imitators, some even more cartoonish (*A Man Called Dagger*, 1967), some relatively serious (*The Spy Who Came In from the Cold*, 1965).

2. See William Breuer, *Hitler's Undercover War: The Nazi Espionage Invasion of the U.S.A.* (New York: St. Martin's Press, 1989). For information on Japan's pre-war spying in the U.S. and elsewhere, see Richard Deacon, *Kempei Tai: A History of the Japanese Secret Service* (New York: Beaufort Books, 1983).

3. *Happy Go Lucky* (1936), mentioned earlier, included characters named "Matzdorf" and "Porozzi" in its spy ring, but this may have been mere coincidence, as this was rather early to link Germans and Italians in nefarious activities. *Calling Philo Vance* (Warner Bros., 1940) linked German, and Italian *and* Japanese spies (the spy for Japan was actually Chinese, but in Japan's employ).

4. An interesting account of German sabotage in America prior to the U.S. entry into WWI may be found in Jules Witcover, *Sabotage at Black Tom* (Chapel Hill, NC: Algonquin Books, 1989).

5. The term "fifth column" originated during the Spanish Civil War, but was popularized following the Nazi conquest of Norway. norway's chief Nazi sympathizer, Vikdun Quisling, had his name made synonymous with "traitor," although in retrospect it appears the Germans simply caught Norway unprepared and that there was no massive campaign of sabotage by a "fifth column." Harold Lavine, *Fifth Column in America* (New York: Doubleday, 1940) 1–10.

Chapter 10

1. See Geoffrey S. Smith, *To Save a Nation: American Counter-Subversives, The New Deal and the Coming of World War II* (New York: Basic Books, 1973), pp. 62–63.

2. Ladislas Farago, *The Game of the Foxes: The Untold Story of German Espionage in the United States and Great Britain During World War II* (New York: David McKay, 1971), pp. 56–65.

3. This includes one piece of footage of a huge swastika rising above a map of Germany, casting a shadow over the rest of Europe and eventually spreading over the United States. It is an obvious precursor of the graphics style later frequently used in Frank Capra's famous wartime series produced for the government, *Why We Fight*.

4. Similar comments are made in at least two other films: *You Can't Take It with You* (Columbia; 1938) and *Our Leading Citizen* (Paramount; 1939).

5. American Legionnaires break-up a Communist Party rally in *Public Deb No. 1* (TCF; 1940).

6. Stephen Louis Karpf, *The Gangster Film, 1930–1940* (New York: Arno Press, 1974), p. 232. The 1938 release, *Sinners in Paradise*, makes an oblique reference to the "dictator" in Europe. In fact, with the exception of Chaplin's merciless lampooning of Hitler as Adenoid Hynkel in *The Great Dictator*, there is no developed caricature or impersonation of Hitler in an American film prior to 1942.

7. *LC*, LP 8823, *Confessions of a Nazi Spy* Pressbook: 13.

8. Leonard Rubenstein, *The Great Spy Films* (Secaucus, NJ: The Citadel Press, 1979), p. 114.

9. This is a rather odd joke since the term Central Powers referred to the German, Austro-Hungarian, Ottoman Empire alliance of World War I.

10. In a never explained or commented upon gesture of set designing Thomas submachine guns and bombs are used as decorations above the coach windows and naval destroyer models and paintings of military planes adorn the dining car.

11. In a speech given by the Propaganda Minister in *Nazi Spry* (1939) Italy is mentioned as being "with us" (the Rome-Berlin Axis was signed in October 1936) and Japan is referred to as "our Ally"

(referring to the Anti–Comintern Pact of November 1936). By the time of the release of *World Premiere*, in August of 1941, the three Axis nations were formally aligned by the Tripartite Pact of September 1940.

12. Probably a takeoff on the Basque port of Bilbao that was, in fact, under blockade for several months until it was broken in the spring of 1937. See Roskill, *Naval Policy Between the Wars, II, 1930–1939*, pp. 372–373 and 377–381.

13. Starting in 1938, the aerial bombing of civilians began to frequently appear and/or be referred to in American films. Other examples from that year include: *International Settlement, Shadows Over Shanghai, Thanks for Everything, Too Hot to Handle.*

14. This was a common motif that carried on into World War II films. Examples would include: *Cairo* (MGM; 1942), *Chetniks* (TCF; 1943) and *Five Graves to Cairo* (Paramount; 1943).

15. There are distinct similarities in portrayal between Pallini and the Italian character in *Sahara* (Columbia; 1943).

16. No references to organized resistance *in* Germany involving radio transmissions have been found. The British did set up a "secret" resistance radio, manned by German POWs. See Peter Hoffmann, *The History of the German Resistance, 1933–1945* (Cambridge: MIT Press, 1977) and Gordon Wright, *The Ordeal of Total War, 1939–1945* (New York: Harper and Row, 1968) 75.

17. Hess had in fact secretly and apparently without authorization flown to Britain on May 10, 1941. He allegedly went with peace officers. The English were unimpressed and kept him under close arrest for the remainder of the war. This incident is still debated by historians. See Lord James Douglas-Hamilton, *Motive for a Mission: The Story Behind Hess' Flight to Britain* (London: Macmillan, 1971).

18. See James E. McSherry, *Stalin, Hitler and Europe, Vol. 2: The Imbalance of Power, 1939–1941* (Cleveland, OH: World, 1970), pp. 92–93.

19. It was not uncommon for lead characters in this period to be named after famous Americans. James Cagney, for instance, is Thomas Jefferson O'Toole in *Devil Dogs of the Air* (a 1941 reissue of the 1935 WB film). And in Paramount's *One Night in Lisbon* (1941) the American pilot is also named Huston.

20. During July of 1940 Japan pressured the British into temporarily closing the Burma Road into China and occupied areas of Kwangtung province that were contiguous to the New Territories of Hong Kong in a direct attempt to shut off supplies to the Nationalist Chinese government in Chungking. See John Hunter Boyle, *China and Japan at War, 1937–1945: The Politics of Collaboration* (Stanford, CA: Stanford University Press, 1972), pp. 299–305.

21. This is intriquing. It indicates either ignorance on the part of the prop department, budgetary restraints imposed by the studio, or a deliberate attempt to link the German and the Japanese armies in the mind of the public.

22. Wearing glasses, leering menacingly and shouting gutteral orders, he personifies the negative caricature of Japanese military officers that prevailed throughout World War II and for many years after in most relevant American combat films.

Chapter 11

1. This was the only pre-1942 American feature film to acknowledge that American volunteers had fought for Republican Spain again the rebel nationalists. During 1943 two American films would deal with the subject: *The Fallen Sparrow* (RKO) and *For Whom the Bell Tolls* (Paramount). The last American volunteers held prisoner

by Franco's fascist regime were not released until March 1940. See Carl Geiser, *Prisoners of the Good Fight: The Spanish Civil War, 1936–1939: Americans Against Franco Fascism* (Westport, CT: Lawrence Hill, 1986).

2. This scene was reused by Paramount in *World Premiere*, q.v. From a balcony above, the Italian spy Scaletti witnesses the fate of his incompetent predecessor.

3. Another example of tying fictional characters to specific historical events. This was the first British vessel sunk by a U-boat, and on the day (September 3rd) British declared war on Germany. See Geoffrey Perrett, *Days of Sadness, Years of Triumph*, p. 18.

4. Russell E. Shain, *An Analysis of Motion Pictures About War Released by the American Film Industry, 1930–1970* (New York: Arno, 1976), p. 135.

Chapter 12

1. One of the more notorious incidents had been the Royal Navy's seizure of the German supply ship *Altmarck* in neutral Norwegian waters in the winter of 1940. See Winston S. Churchill, *The Second World War: The Gathering Storm* (Boston: Houghton Mifflin, 1948), pp. 561–564.

2. Refer to Alistair Horne, *To Lose a Battle: France 1940* (Boston: Little, Brown, 1969).

3. See Liddell Hart, *History of the Second World War* (New York: G. P. Putnam's Sons, 1970), pp. 121–127.

4. A similar Italian prisoner is portrayed in the WWII classic, *Sahara* (Columbia; 1943).

5. The Italians had supplied munitions to Yemen beginning in 1923. See Denis Mack Smith, *Mussolini's Roman Empire* (New York: The Viking Press, 1976), pp. 33–34.

6. There is a similar conclusion to MGM's 1942 classic, *Mrs. Miniver*.

Chapter 13

1. Garry J. Clifford and Samuel R. Spencer, *The First Peacetime Draft* (Lawrence: University Press of Kansas, 1986); Ross Gregory, *America 1941: A Nation at the Crossroads* (New York: The Free Press, 1988), pp. 27–33.

2. Refer to Wiley Lee Umphlett, *The Movies Go to College: Hollywood and the World of College Life* (Rutherford, N.J.: Fairleigh Dickinson University Press, 1984).

3. Nearly forty percent of the first million men selected for the draft were rejected—over a third of them for reasons that could be directly attributed to nutritional deficiencies. James MacGregor Burns, *Roosevelt: The Soldier of Freedom, 1940–1945* (New York: Harcourt Brace Jovanovich, 1970), p. 54.

4. Craig W. Campbell, *Reel America and World War I* (Jefferson, N.C.: McFarland, 1985); Michael T. Isenberg, *War on Film: The American Cinema and World War I, 1914–1941* (Rutherford, N.J.: Fairleigh Dickinson University Press, 1981), pp. 177–78.

5. The House of Representatives passed the draft extension bill by a single vote. Burns, *Roosevelt: The Soldier of Freedom*, p. 120; Gregory, *America 1941*, pp. 43; 290.

6. Paramount was preparing a film to be titled "Absent Without Leave" in late 1941, but dropped plans to produce the film when the Japanese attacked Pearl Harbor. *New York Times* 14 December 1941.

Chapter 14

1. Raymond Fielding, *The March of Time, 1935–1961* (New York: Oxford University Press, 1978). In the 1980s the BBC produced an excellent multi-part series on the *MOT*. Refer also to Fielding, *The American Newsreel, 1911–1967* (Norman: University of Oklahoma Press, 1973).

2. *The Film Daily*, January 3, 1939: 6.

3. Mussolini had been stirring up trouble over Abyssnia for over a year prior to the Italian invasion in October 1935. The *MOT* newsreel ("Ethiopia," Vol. 1, No. 6) was released in the United States more than two weeks before Mussolini's fascist legions were unleashed in Africa. See George W. Baer, *The Coming of the Italian-Ethiopian War* (Cambridge, MA: Harvard University Press, 1967).

4. Fielding, *The March of Time* 199.

5. Sam Kula, "Newsactings," *American Film* 3 (APril 1978): 73.

6. *Motion Picture Herald* April 15, 1933: 28. Also see *Film Daily* April 8, 1933: 7.

7. *Motion Picture Herald* March 18, 1933: 34. The pressbook for this film, contained in the Library of Congress copyright files, is very interesting (*LC*, MP4061). The Library of Congress also has a print of this film (FEA 4816-4822).

8. *FD* March 11, 1933: 4.

9. *FD* December 10, 1934: 7.

10. M. C. Engelbrecht and Frank C. Hanighen, *Merchants of Death* (New York: Dodd, Mead, 1934).

11. *FD* November 30, 1934: 15. The *AFI Catalog* indicates that this film contains footage from a British anti-war feature, and possibly footage from American silent films!

12. *MPH* June 16, 1934: 83.

13. *MPH* October 26, 1935: 73.

14. *LC* MP 7075; *FD* January 20, 1937: 12. See Dallek, *Franklin D. Roosevelt and American Foreign Policy, 1933–1945* 132–4.

15. Isenberg, *War on Film* 79.

16. *FD* April 19, 1938: 6.

17. *LC* LP 8895.

18. *Variety* October 11, 1939: 18.

19. *LC* MP 10605; *FD* October 14, 1940: 7. The National Archives Film Division in Washington, DC has a print of this film (200.150).

20. *This Is England* was part of the "Cinescope" series, and was originally titled "Heart of Britain." *FD* April 9, 1941: 9.

21. *FD* October 8, 1941: 6.

22. This is an entry in the *Pete Smith's Speciality* series. *LC* LP 10789; *FD* November 12, 1941: 6.

23. Part of the *Magic Carpet* series. *FD* April 17, 1941: 7.

24. See *No Greater Sin* in the filmography for a fictional treatment of this theme. *FD* April 9, 1941: 7.

25. *FD* May 16, 1941: 11

26. *FD* May 16, 1941: 11.

27. Ken Weiss and Ed Goodgold, *To Be Continued* (NY: Crown, 1972) 115–192; Jack Mathis, *Valley of the Cliffhangers* (Northbrook, IL: Jack Mathis Advertising, 1975). Most of the serials released between 1937 and 1941 are available on commercial videotape.

28. Ulam, *Expansion and Coexistence* 247–250.

29. In 1942, a feature version of this serial was released under the title *Yukon Patrol*.

30. Douglas W. Churchill, "Hollywood Pledges Allegiance to America," *The New York Times Encyclopedia of Film* Volume 3 (New York: Times Books, 1984). It was originally published in the January 15, 1939 issue of the newspaper.

31. Many of the Warners and MGM fictional shorts are in the

MGM/UA collection owned by Turner Broadcasting. The Library of Congress has a print of *Sons of Liberty* (VBF 5067).

32. *LC* LP 8702.

33. *LC* LP 9086.

34. *LC* LP 8911.

35. *Film Daily* June 14, 1940: 6.

36. *Film Daily* November 26, 1940: 11.

37. The name of the country in this short may have been inspired by the 1937 Federal Theatre Project's vaudeville review, "Ready, Aim, Fire." In it, a fascist dictatorship in the country of "Moronia" was spoofed. John O'Connor and Lorraine Brown, editors, *Free, Adult, Uncensored: The Living History of the Federal Theatre Project* (Washington: New Republic Books, 1978) 137, 148.

38. Turkey, an ally of Germany during WWI, maintained a vaguely-defined neutrality throughout most of WWII. During 1941, Turkey's "neutrality" favored the Axis. Frank G. Weber, *The Evasive Neutral* (Columbia: University of Missouri Press, 1979).

39. *LC* LP 10382.

40. *LC* LP 10824; *Motion Picture Herald* October 25, 1941: 333.

41. *LC* LP 10836.

42. Even the 16mm "Soundies," musical shorts shown only on special juke boxes, contained topical references at times. *Take the "A" Train*, released in the fall, begins with the Delta Rhythm Boys performing in a subway station in which an Army recruiting poster can be prominently seen in the background. Doris Day sings "Is It Love or Is It Conscription?" in an April 1941 Soundie.

43. For a book-length analysis of war-relevant cartoons, see Michael S. Shull and David Wilt, *Doing Their Bit: Wartime American Animated Short Films, 1939–1945* (Jefferson, NC: McFarland, 1987).

44. *LC* MP 12803; *Motion Picture Herald* September 27, 1941: 290.

45. *LC* MP 118565; *Motion Picture Herald* December 13, 1941: 411.

Chapter 15

1. Clayton Koppes and Gregory D. Black, *Hollywood Goes to War* (New York: Free Press, 1987), 64.

2. Lawrence W. Levine, "The Folklore of Industrial Society" *American Historical Review* 97 (December 1992): 1372, 1398.

3. See Peter Paret, et al., *Persuasive Images* (Princeton: Princeton University Press, 1992), and George H. Roeder Jr., *The Censored War* (New Haven: Yale University Press, 1993), for examples of wartime posters and photographs that were published (or suppressed).

4. Flagg painted 46 posters during WWI, including an entire series of "Uncle Sam" posters of which the "I Want You" was the most popular. He returned to the propaganda poster field in WWII. Paret 70, 196.

5. Ian Jarvie, "The Burma Campaign on Film," *Historical Journal of Film Radio and Television* 8/1 (1988): 55–73.

6. Office of War Information files, Record Group 208; E-567, National Archives.

7. See Anthony Aldgate and Jeffrey Richards, *Britain Can Take It: The British Cinema in the Second World War* (Oxford: Basil Blackwell, 1986).

8. Ironically, the Indian-head emblem of the Lafayette Escadrille—the famed American flying squadron of World War One—features a swastika on the warrior's headdress! Major Charles J. Biddle, *The Way of the Eagle* (New York: Scribner's, 1919), 144.

9. For an even more graphic use of the swastika, see various wartime cartoons, including *Russian Rhapsody* (WB, 1944), in which an electrified Hitler contorts his body into a swastika! Michael Shull and David Wilt, *Doing Their Bit: Wartime American Animated Shorts* (Jefferson, NC: McFarland, 1987).

10. Winston S. Churchill, *The Second World War: Vol.2—Their Finest Hour* (Cambridge: Houghton-Mifflin, 1948), 25-26.

11. Advertising often stressed the "V" in a manufacturer's name or product name. Sometimes, when no "V" was present, one had to be invented: for instance, Kayser dubbed its new synthetic stockings "Victoray" (for rayon) (*Life* 30 November 1942).

12. Karal Ann Marling and John Wetenhall, *Iwo Jima: Monuments, Memories, and the American Hero* (Cambridge: Harvard University Press, 1991), 76.

13. See the chapter on images of the Enemy for a discussion of film depictions of fascist persecution of organized religion.

14. Colin Shindler, *Hollywood Goes to War* (London: Routledge & Kegan Paul, 1979), 37.

15. The first thousand-plane raid was carried out by the RAF at the end of May 1942, on Cologne, Germany. Depictions of the German "blitz" of England, while not frequent, still outnumbered portrayals of effects of Allied bombing on Germany.

16. Both *Bombardier* and *Behind the Rising Sun* were a little premature in their depiction of Allied bombing of the Japanese home islands. After the Doolittle raid in 1942, there were no major aerial bombing raids on Japan itself until late 1944, when the systematic bombing by B-29s began in earnest. These raids caused massive damage to Japan's major cities, since by this time Japan had little or no air defense capabilities.

17. Interestingly enough, a "Soundie" (a short musical film made to be shown on a special type of jukebox) released in January 1945 was entitled "U.S.A. by Day and the R.A.F. by Night"!

18. Over a million were left homeless; this single raid caused more damage than the later atomic bombing of Hiroshima! Russell Spurr, *A Glorious Way to Die* (New York: Newmarket Press, 1981), 82.

Chapter 16

1. John Morton Blum, *V Was for Victory* (New York: Harcourt Brace Jovanovich, 1976), 58.

2. Some remember John Wayne battling the forces of Imperial Japan while periodically delivering chauvinistic homilies. Actually, during the course of the war, Wayne appeared in nearly as many Westerns as war films (*In Old California, Tall in the Saddle*, et al). Many people—including some scholars—confuse the cinematic "reality" of combat in World War II with mid 1960s-early 1970s Combat films, like Beach Red (1967), *The Dirty Dozen* (1967), *The Bridge at Remagen* (1968), *Hell in the Pacific* (1969), *Catch 22* (1970), *M.A.S.H.* (1970), and so on. But, these films certainly owe as much or more to the Korean conflict and the Vietnam war as they do to any historical realities of WWII.

3. Some of these books tend to round up the usual suspects and then pontificate at length upon them—*Wake Island, Bataan, Destination Tokyo, Guadalcanal Diary, Objective Burma!* There is also a proclivity in these works to devote considerable attention to pre- or post-WWII (released before January 1942 and after September 1945) releases. See for example, Lawrence Suid, *Guts & Glory* (Reading, MA: Addison-Wesley, 1978), and Jeanine Basinger, *The World War II Combat Film* (New York: Columbia University Press, 1986).

4. Edward M. Kirby and Jack W. Harris, *Star-Spangled Radio* (Chicago: Ziff-Davis, 1948), 246.

5. This probably elicited ribald hoots from servicemen sta-

tioned overseas—many of whom may have similarly waited in line, on occasion, but for a brief encounter with one of the local professional ladies. For an interesting discussion of prostitution in wartime Honolulu, see Beth Bailey and David Farber, The First Strange Place (New York: Free Press, 1992), 95-132.

6. He is officially "missing in action," although his actual fate is not clear.

7. Reluctance to show American soldiers romancing foreign women was not extended to the various films depicting downed pilots in occupied Europe: relationships between American men and foreign (French, Belgian, even German) women develop in virtually all of these films. Of course, any of the romances in the European theatre at least had the advantage that the women were white, so that the taboo concept of miscegenation did not arise.

8. Some of these films include service wives who are pregnant with so-called "goodbye babies" (although this term is never used in a wartime film): In the Meantime Darling (a false alarm), and Thirty Seconds Over Tokyo, for instance.

9. See Part One.

10. In Parachute Nurse, a depressed trainee commits suicide by deliberately failing to pull the ripcord on her parachute, plunging to earth—in a rather graphic scene for the period—in front of her horrified fellow nurses!

11. Robert Bruce Sligh, The National Guard and National Defense (New York: Praeger, 1992), xv.

12. George Q. Flynn, The Draft 1940-1973 (Lawrence, KS: University Press of Kansas, 1993), 9-10.

13. This is a clear example of how Hollywood went to great lengths to avoid having men in combat situations say they were drafted; why would a conscientious objector "enlist"?! But this is explicitly stated in the film, along with his (draft) status: "1-A-O."

14. Sligh 119. However, the Guard was only authorized by Congress to serve in the United States and in U.S. possessions, and the mobilization was limited to one year. The following year, an extension was passed by Congress, and by the time that was up, the United States was at war.

15. Of course, some of these draftees went into the Navy, but the Army was still very heavily skewed towards draftees. Flynn 62, 85.

16. For readers unfamiliar with the Selective Service system of the time, "Class 1-A referred to men immediately available for service; class 2 contained men with some deferment ... Class 3 contained men deferred because of dependency or hardship; Class 4 designated men unqualified for service because of age, health, or some other factor." Flynn 58. Most jokes in films revolve around "1-A" and "4-F," the "top" and "bottom" classifications, respectively.

17. Flynn 47.

18. Howard Zinn, A People's History (New York: Harpers, 1980), 409.

19. If this sounds a little like Buck Privates, that is probably what RKO was hoping for. Brown and Carney were teamed up by the movie studio in a blatant attempt to garner some of Abbott and Costello's popularity, but any Abbott and Costello film is better than the best Brown-Carney outing.

20. The OWI disliked this film series (as did the Army, presumably), and there were no further Brown and Carney military adventures, unless one counts their foray into the Merchant Marine, in Seven Days Ashore (RKO, 1944). Although they play the same imbecilic roles as before, at least the characters' names were changed for this outing.

21. Flynn 21, 49. The induction age was lowered to 20 shortly after Pearl Harbor (Flynn 55), although the upper limit for registration was raised to 44 years of age; in June 1942 the age span became 18 to 45 (Flynn 62).

22. In December of 1942 a presidential order excused men over 38 from the draft. Flynn 56.

23. Over 21 (Columbia, 1945) also deals with an older man in the service. In this case, however, Alexander Knox plays a 39-year-old who enlists. As a newspaper editor, he rationalizes that he has to earn the right to editorialize to the 10 million men in the service. The film deals with the psychological stress of "making the team" (he attends Officer Candidate School). There are scenes of Knox reading manuals while shaving, after Taps (under his bed with a flashlight), on back of the man marching in front of him during field drill. In two scenes he literally sweats while taking his exams and explaining a problem to an instructor, but finally graduates as an officer.

24. Allen Berube, Coming Out Under Fire (New York: Free Press, 1990), 8, 21.

25. Although the government at times urged men to "wait until you are called," especially those in defense industry jobs.

26. Ironically, since most young men were in the service, the supply of young male actors in Hollywood was quite low. This explains in part why Van Johnson and Robert Walker (who were youthful-looking, although Johnson—born in 1916—and Walker—born in 1914—were both a bit older than the average GI) made so many films during the war years, and why "mature" actors claim most of the leading roles in war films.

27. Russell Buhite and David W. Levy, eds., FDR's Fireside Chats (Norman: University ofOklahoma Press, 1992), 243.

28. The only significant wartime Muslim character (at least, the only positive character so identified) is the Sudanese soldier played by Rex Ingram in Sahara (Columbia, 1943). Presumably there are Buddhists and Hindus among the Chinese and Indians appearing in various films, although no particular point is ever made of this. In Objective Burma!, dog tags of dead soldiers are collected: some are marked "P" (for Protestant) and "C" (for Catholic), but Jacobs' tag does not have a "J" (for Jewish).

29. This occurs in a stateside hospital in a discussion among wounded men; in combat action on Guadalcanal, Jews and Christians work smoothly as a team.

30. Major Caton (Wake Island) and Col. Madden (Back to Bataan) are special cases: in the first film, because the trapped Marine garrison is so small; in the latter, because Madden heads a mixed American/Filipino guerrilla force behind enemy lines.

31. Dana Polan, Power & Paranoia (New York: Columbia University Press, 1986), 72.

32. Robert Barrat plays MacArthur in They Were Expendable (MGM), which was released in late 1945.

33. These guidelines were actually for radio entertainers, as quoted in a November 18, 1942 Variety article, but Hollywood certainly received similar instructions. It is interesting to note that the two examples given are films (both in the "Flagg and Quirt" series) from 1926 and 1929, respectively. Kirby and Harris 14.

34. It is interesting to note that Nobody Lives Forever (WB), in which John Garfield plays a discharged soldier, contains a large number of scenes set in bars, nightclubs, etc. The film was completed in November 1944 but was not released until November 1946—could the film's release have been delayed due to the unflattering emphasis on alcohol consumption and crime indulged in by a veteran?

35. Beer was sold on military bases, although it was "3.2 beer," a low-alcohol version. The Office of Price Administration did not ration alcoholic beverages, but it did crack down on black market sales of alcohol and place strict price ceilings "in this important field where supplies are notoriously short." Office of Price Administration, Eighth Quarterly Report for the Period Ended December 31, 1943 (Washington: U.S. Government Printing Office, 1944), 64. Domestic distilleries resumed production of hard liquor for public consumption in 1944.

36. Ironically, Ira Hayes, one of the Marines credited with raising the flag on Iwo Jima, was dispatched to the United States on a bond tour but was ordered to rejoin his unit in the Pacific after only two weeks because of repeated drunkenness. Karal Ann Marling and John Wetenhall, *Iwo Jima: Monuments, Memories, and the American Hero* (Cambridge: Harvard University Press, 1991), 119-121.

37. Nearly 450 Japanese planes were shot down, largely due to the inexperienced pilots the Japanese were throwing into combat, and to the superiority of American planes, both in design and in sheer numbers. Russell Spurr, *A Glorious Way to Die* (New York: Newmarket Press, 1981), 67.

38. John W. Dower, *War Without Mercy* (New York: Pantheon, 1986), 64-66; this compares with the crazed Roger's Ranger who carries the severed head of a dead Indian around in a satchel in *Northwest Passage* (MGM, 1940). In "Battle of Buna," a *Life* photo-essay (15 February 1943), a photograph shows "An American and the Jap he killed," with the GI posing like a proud hunter with a trophy buck (to top it off, the soldier relates the story of his encounter with the enemy, adding it was "just like in the movies").

39. One of the more famous is *Man Hunt* (TCF, 1941). Based on a novel by Geoffrey Household, this film features Walter Pidgeon as a world-famous hunter who "stalks" Hitler (never intending to really kill him), but is then discovered and pursued by the Nazis.

40. See George H. Roeder, Jr., *The Censored War* (New Haven: Yale University Press, 1993) for examples of suppressed photos. Scenes such as the gory end result of a plane crash—burnt and mutilated flesh wrapped in twisted metal—are included in the Soviet-made "March of Time" episode *One Day of War—Russia* (1943), but were rarely if ever seen in American documentaries and newsreels of the period, let alone "entertainment" features.

41. This story seems to have been without factual foundation. But even when depicting "true" stories, Hollywood re-wrote the facts. The death of the five brothers in *The Sullivans* is portrayed as occurring when four of the five men go below to sick bay to retrieve their fifth and oldest brother, after the suicide crash of a crippled Japanese plane into their ship. In reality, after a series of surface naval engagements, the damaged cruiser *USS Juneau* was fatally hit by a torpedo from a Japanese sub; as a result of the devastating explosion, only 100 of the 700 crewmen were left alive. George Sullivan, one of the brothers, was among them. However, a communications breakdown resulted in news of the sinking not reaching shore: the survivors spent nine days in shark-infested water, and Sullivan was not one of the ten men finally rescued.

42. John Hersey, "Kamikaze," *Life* (30 July 1945), 75.

43. Burial and identification of the dead was usually the duty of the Graves Registration unit. However, Hollywood films occasionally include some token bits of verisimilitude: during the preinvasion preparation on board a transport ship in *Guadalcanal Diary*, an officer is shown dictating an order about the proper identification of bodies. Other films contain scenes where the personal effects of the deceased are collected, for shipment to their families: *Flying Tigers*, *Wing and a Prayer*, *Destination Tokyo*, *Cry Havoc*, *The Navy Comes Through*, and *Action in the North Atlantic*. It is interesting to note that personal effects were also checked in order to eliminate articles considered potentially upsetting to the loved ones of the deceased, such as pornography! Letters from unit commanders—such as Walker writes in *The Story of G.I. Joe*, were actually sent home with the personal effects; these were deliberately delayed 90 days to insure that the family had first received official notification.

44. Lee Kennett, *There's a War On* (New York: Scribners, 1987), 72.

45. Blum 76.

46. The "Command Performance" radio show brought servicemen entertainment (GIs wrote in and requested stars, songs, skits, etc.) but it also fulfilled their requests for sounds from home, including a soldier's baby crying, a dog barking, fog horns in San Francisco Bay, the slot machines in Las Vegas, and so on. Kirby and Harris 44-45.

47. Happy Land (TCF, 1943) has a very similar ending.

48. "Dear John" letters are downplayed, for obvious reasons. A serviceman who has returned from the front tells a story of such a letter that had fatal consequences (the soldier went berserk and charged straight into Japanese fire) in *The Very Thought of You*, and in *Christmas Holiday*, one character receives *his* "Dear John" upon graduation from Anti-Aircraft Artillery School. For the most part, however, hints that the girlfriend or wife back home was dissatisfied or unfaithful were rigidly suppressed.

49. Similar emotional responses are evoked in the "Have Yourself A Merry Little Christmas" number, from *Meet Me in St. Louis* (MGM, 1944). The snow reference in "White Christmas" itself must have aroused strong feelings in many servicemen, suffering from the heat in the seemingly seasonless Pacific or the North African desert. Even "Sunny Italy" had been converted by the technology of modern warfare into six months of heat and choking dust amid vast destruction, and six months of bitter cold and mud amidst even greater destruction and human misery.

50. *A Book of Facts About the WAC* (Washington, D.C.: Womens' Army Corps, 1944), 3.

51. Red Cross nurses were portrayed "over there" in several World War I films, including *Revelation* (Metro, 1918) and *We Can't Have Everything* (Artcraft, 1918). During the 5-year period preceding the United States' entry into World War II one American motion picture, *Yellow Jack* (MGM, 1938), featured Army nurses helping win the battle against yellow fever.

52. In England, however, adults of *both* sexes who were not in the armed forces or engaged in essential war work *were* liable for a "draft" into national service.

53. This film never clearly states that the "Aerial Nurse Corps of America" is part of the *Army*, in fact it goes out of its way to obscure any such relationship (probably due to the fictitious nature of the film).

54. Ironically, there were at least *five* feature films (plus cartoons and short subjects) about "war dogs"! Apparently a lot of people in Hollywood, at various studios, thought this was a neat concept.

55. This is based an incident that occurred in June 1942 on Long Island. See Geoffrey Perrett, *Days of Sadness, Years of Triumph* (New York: Coward, McCann & Geohegan, 1973), 212.

56. Particularly since, until the summer of 1942, coastal blackouts and convoying were not fully instituted. This tragically resulted in an unnecessarily large number of U-boat sinkings in the early months of 1942 along America's seaboard from the Gulf of Mexico to Maine. See Michael Gannon, *Operation Drumbeat* (New York: Harper & Row, 1990).

57. There were a few post-war films about the Coast Guard, including *Tars and Spars* (Columbia, 1946).

58. Well, not entirely. In *Salute to the Marines*, Marine Wallace Beery gets into a (pre-Pearl Harbor) brawl in a Philippines dive with some merchant seamen.

Chapter 17

1. Geoffrey Perrett, *Days of Sadness, Years of Triumph* (New York: Coward, McCann & Geohegan, 1973), 323.

2. Perrett 310.

3. Henry T. Sampson, *Blacks in Black and White* (Metuchen, NJ: Scarecrow Press, 1977), 173-5.

4. According to one source, even these bits and extra roles were not extensive enough: Dalton Trumbo, speaking at the 1943 Writers' Congress held in Los Angeles, "criticized the film industry for its failure to use blacks in crowd scenes and shots of war production lines..." Neil A. Wynn, *The Afro-American and the Second World War* (London: Paul Elek, 1976), 80.

5. Perrett 312-314.

6. Less impressed with Moreland's performances were many black critics, who felt he was yet another "comic black" stereotype. Moreland himself, in later years, apologized for his earlier roles, although the authors of this volume feel he often rose above his parts. See Sampson 241.

7. Blacks can be seen socializing with whites in the "Shanghai Lil" production number from *Footlight Parade* (WB, 1934). In *This Is the Army*, soldier Joe Louis appears, seated at a table, in one of the numbers set in the "Stage Door Canteen." Neither of these scenes, however, occurs in a "real" setting (within the context of the film). Several black couples are among those dancing in *Stage Door Canteen* (UA, 1943), although the black female hostesses and their black military partners are not highlighted (one black soldier *is* singled out in another scene, as the recipient of the Distinguished Service Cross).

8. Perrett 153.

9. Clayton R. Koppes and Gregory D. Black, *Hollywood Goes to War* (New York: Free Press, 1987), 181.

10. At least one source points out other ways Lee's character is subtly depicted as inferior to the whites: he is given less camera time, is called "Charcoal," is identified as a (reformed) pickpocket, and he displays "a simplistic religious faith." Koppes and Black 181.

11. Koppes and Black 312-3.

12. This scene takes on a bit of added meaning when one recalls that the Nazis openly criticized jazz as one more example of the "decadence" of America. Black entertainer Josephine Baker lived in France during the Nazi occupation and was active in Resistance activities.

13. Actually, the Army did not want blacks taken by the draft in large numbers, since existing black units could not handle such an influx (the Army was segregated at the time and blacks could only serve in these units or in newly created all-black units). George Q. Flynn, The Draft 1940-1973 (Lawrence: University Press of Kansas, 1993), 43.

14. Perrett 152.

15. Wynn 29.

16. Perrett 317. The first WAAC training class, numbering 440 women, included 40 black women—a carefully calculated quota matching the percentage of blacks in the overall U.S. population. See Martha S. Putney, *When the Nation Was in Need: Blacks in the Women's Army Corps During World War II* (Metuchen, NJ: Scarecrow Press, 1992), 1.

17. Perrett 318. One of the heroes of Pearl Harbor was Dorie Miller, a black Navy mess attendant who seized a machine gun and shot down a Japanese plane during the attack. Miller won the Navy Cross for his bravery; he was later killed in the Battle of the Coral Sea. Sampson 175.

18. Louis "spent most of his time [in the Army] touring Army bases and camps, giving talks and exhibition bouts," and was promoted to sergeant and awarded the Legion of Merit in 1945. Wynn 31.

19. In *Star Spangled Rhythm*, Eddie "Rochester" Anderson appears as a zoot-suited Lothario whose girlfriend (dancer Katherine Dunham) drops him for a black soldier; Rochester joins the Army so *he* can attract women!

20. When WWI began, there were only 4,000 black soldiers in the Army (less than 2% of the total); this had risen to 400,000 by 1918, or about 10% of the Army's wartime manpower. Perrett 37, 152.

21. The authors of this study cannot think of a single film featuring USO or other "camp show" entertainments with an *integrated* audience. Many shows feature black artists performing on the stage, but the servicemen and women watching them are all white.

22. *Mr. Winkle Goes to War* (Columbia, 1944) contains some footage of black soldiers training, but it is not clear if these troops are at the same camp as white draftee Winkle (Edward G. Robinson), or if it is a nearby installation.

23. A 1942 black production, *Take My Life* (Toddy) apparently features a group of black youngsters who enlist in the Army, but details of this film are extremely sketchy.

24. Peter Noble, *The Negro in Films* (Port Washington, NY: Kennikat Press, 1969), 152.

25. Noble 198.

26. Noble 198.

27. Spencer did not have a significant career in Hollywood after this film; indeed, until Sidney Poitier, no black male managed to sustain himself with leading roles in Hollywood films. Spencer did, however, appear in a 1950s German film of some interest. *Mein Bruder Josua* featured Spencer as an American GI serving with the American occupation troops in Germany.

28. Spencer reminds one somewhat of Paul Robeson—not too surprising, given that he understudied Robeson in the 1939 Broadway musical "John Henry." Noble 169. Later in the film, he sings "The St. Louis Blues."

29. Noble 199.

30. Jones is shown using a submachine gun during this raid, lending credence to the story that the character was based on black Pearl Harbor hero Dorie Miller.

31. Warner Brothers removed a black mess attendant role from *Action in the North Atlantic* (1943) at the request of the OWI; the government agency pointed out that this character was a reminder of segregation in the armed forces (although the film actually deals with the mostly *integrated* Merchant Marine). Koppes and Black 179-180. A black cook on a Navy submarine appears in *Gung Ho!* (Universal, 1943); a black sailor (again, presumably a cook) is seen on a ship in *Guadalcanal Diary* (TCF, 1943), although this character is shown wearing a helmet and a lifevest and is virtually indistinguishable from the (white) Marines with whom he converses (in a knowledgeable fashion) about the convoy they are sailing with.

32. J. Lee Ready, *The Forgotten Allies Volume I* (Jefferson, NC: McFarland, 1985), 152. Many of these countries severed relations with the Axis or actually declared war shortly after the attack on Pearl Harbor.

33. R.A. Humphreys, *Latin America and the Second World War Volume Two 1942-1945* (London: Athlone, 1982), 54.

34. Ready, *Forgotten Allies Vol. II* 153.

35. Ready, *Forgotten Allies Vol. I* 152-3.

36. Ready, *Forgotten Allies Vol. I* 367.

37. Mexico's film industry, on the other hand, made a number of war-oriented films about its contribution to the cause of democracy. These include the previously mentioned *Soy Puro Mexicano* [*I'm Pure Mexican*], *Cadetes de la Naval* [*Naval Cadets*, 1944], *Tres Hermanos* [*Three Brothers*, 1943], and *Escuadrón 201* [*Squadron 201*, 1945], the latter three covering the Mexican Navy, the U.S. Army (three Mexican-American brothers from Texas), and the Mexican Air Force.

38. George Murphy's character deliberately crashes his airplane, loaded with dynamite, into a bridge, but he has already been mortally wounded by a Japanese attack.

39. Clayton R. Koppes and Gregory D. Black, *Hollywood Goes to War* (New York: Free Press, 1987), 259.

40. *A Medal for Benny* (Paramount, 1945) concerns a Mexican-American winner of the Medal of Honor (although he is never seen, having been killed in action). *Bad Day at Black Rock* (MGM, 1954) and *Giant* (WB, 1956) also make reference to Latin war heroes.

41. Lewis, a Spaniard whose real name was Jorge Luis Montero, had been in Hollywood since the early days of sound. He frequently played Hispanic characters, but was equally at ease with Anglo roles.

42. Francis M. Nevins, *The Films of Hopalong Cassidy* (Waynesville, NC: The World of Yesterday, 1988), 189.

43. Contrary to conventional wisdom, positive Latino figures appear with some frequency in most sound Westerns, at the very least in equal numbers to significant appearances of *negative* Latino stereotypes. Duncan Renaldo, for instance, was one of the Three Mesquiteers for the 1939-40 season, and other Western films feature Hispanic secondary heroes on an occasional basis. Most are stereotyped to some degree, but are not negatively portrayed.

44. Interestingly, Hispanic performers Margo and Arturo de Córdova were not always stereotyped as Latin Americans or Spaniards; de Córdova, for instance, played a French pirate in *Frenchman's Creek* (TCF, 1944), and Margo was a French refugee in *Gangway for Tomorrow* (RKO, 1943), apparently on the theory that one foreigner was pretty much the same as another to American audiences.

45. John Storm Roberts, *The Latin Tinge* (New York: Oxford University Press, 1979), 105, 108.

Chapter 18

1. Among them the United States, Great Britain, the USSR, and China, as well as occupied countries such as Czechoslovakia, Yugoslavia, Belgium, and Norway, and even some non-combatants such as Cuba, Haiti, and Costa Rica. France, notably, was *not* included. The "provisional" government of liberated France finally signed in January 1945. Sigrid Arne, *United Nations Primer* (New York: Rinehart, 1945), 15.

2. Arne 15. The separate peace clause was probably included after the experience of World War One, when Russia prematurely concluded hostilities with Germany.

3. Lupe Velez and a male partner; actually, they are only referred to as "Mexican" once—for the rest of the film people keep referring to them as "Spanish" dancers! The dances they perform are non-specific "Latin" in nature.

4. Geoffrey Perrett, *Days of Sadness, Years of Triumph* (New York: Coward, McGann & Geoghegan, 1973), 65.

5. The "China" reference is skewed slightly upwards, since any Chinese character—including Chinese-Americans—was coded as Chinese.

6. See Part One, Chapter 12 for a discussion of the pro-British films of 1937-41.

7. All branches *except* the Royal Air Force, which was coded separately due to the frequency of references.

8. Coincidentally, Reagan had essayed a similar role in *International Squadron* (WB, 1941), and Stack played a Free Polish RAF pilot in *To Be or Not to Be* (UA, 1942). Bob Cummings mentions that he served in the Eagle Squadron before the U.S. entered the war in *You Came Along* (Paramount, 1945).

9. For information on the British campaign in Norway, see David Fraser, *And We Shall Shock Them* (London: Hodder and Stoughton, 1983), 31-53. Some of the Commando raids are detailed in Ian Dear, *Ten Commando* (New York: St. Martin's Press, 1987), 51-58.

10. Dear 21-25.

11. Bernard F. Dick, *The Star-Spangled Screen* (Lexington: University Press of Kentucky, 1985), 182-3.

12. David Reynolds, *The Creation of the Anglo-American Alliance 1937-41* (Chapel Hill: University of North Carolina Press, 1982), 23.

13. Ironically, the only other American characters in the film are portrayed as flashy and somewhat eccentric: two black dancers in zoot suits (The Hot Spots), and a group of jive-talking GIs who roar into a sleepy English village in jeeps. In contrast, the comic relief Britons (J. Pat O'Malley and Elsa Lanchester) seem positively restrained.

14. William Vincent, "Rita Hayworth at Columbia, 1941-1945," *Columbia Pictures: Portrait of a Studio* (Lexington: University Press of Kentucky, 1992), 126.

15. After Japan entered the war in late 1941, Australia (as a Commonwealth nation) requested that its troops on duty in Europe and Africa be returned to Australia to defend their country against Japanese invasion.

16. J. Lee Ready, *Forgotten Allies Vol.II* (Jefferson, NC: McFarland, 1985), 204.

17. Perrett, *Days of Sadness, Years of Triumph*, p. 421-422

18. Refer to Part One.

19. Refer to Part One.

20. *New York Times Encyclopedia of Film* (New York: New York Times Books, 1983), October 20, 1941 A. Interestingly, for the release of *Comrade X* in England a year later the original opening title attacking Russia as the "never, never land" was replaced by one that opens: "Please don't take the film seriously—it is just good-natured fun."

21. Although the Russian armed forces are referred to in at least twenty-three films and the fighting on the Russian front is mentioned in an equal number of films, the Red Army is portrayed in a sustained combat situation in only two films, *Three Russian Girls* and *Counter-Attack*. As discussed in more detail in the chapter on resistance, most films associated with action on the Russian front deal with the partisan struggle against the Nazi invaders.

22. The cinematic self-image of Americans at the time centered around the idyllicized mythic American small town (the "Andy Hardy" and "Henry Aldrich" series, for example) and 1930s historical films (*Juarez*, WB, 1938; *Drums Along the Mohawk*, 20th Fox, 1939; *Young Mr. Lincoln*, 20th Fox, 1939, for instance). The main facets of this image are noble, simplistic idealism, love of peace, individualism (but a willingness to work or fight collectively for the greater good), the sanctity of womanhood, a sense of fair play, innocence and altruism.

23. Melvin Small, "Buffoons and Brave Hearts: Hollywood Portrays the Russians," *California Historical Quarterly* 52/4 (Winter 1973): 332.

24. As if symbolic of the still very tenuous nature of the Soviet-American relationship in early 1942, there are no love scenes between "Miss V" (Lola Lane) and the American soldier until the final scene of the film, when the two are pictured in a romantic shot on the back of a wagon headed for safety across the border into neutral Switzerland. The other films mentioned, however, feature full-blown Russian/American love scenes.

25. The American public was fascinated by Russian women soldiers—in addition to the well-known Russian woman sniper, there was at least one Russian female fighter pilot who became a noted "ace," Lydia Litvak, who had 12 confirmed "kills" before lost in action against the Germans in 1943.

26. The cover of *Time* magazine for December 27, 1943 featured a portrait of the Patriarch of the Russian Orthodox Church. After spending a number of years in jail, the religious leader suddenly found his church "restored" by Stalin in the midst of the war. This may have been a plot by the Soviets to (a) win friends in the U.S. by refuting the "godless communist" charge, and/or (b) an attempt to revive the flagging spirits of a war-weary Russian people.

27. A short Soviet film featuring the Moscow Dance Festival was re-released by WB in 1942. Entitled *The Nation Dances*, the American commentary for the film included the revealing statement: "You can judge a nation by its dancing."

28. This is particularly evident in a documentary like the "Why We Fight" series film *Battle in Russia* (1943).

29. The authors are aware of only two articles that specifically address this topic: Robert Fyne, "From Hollywood to Moscow." *Literature/Film Quarterly*, Vol. 13, No. 3 (1985), pp. 194-199; and the previously-cited Small, "Buffoons and Brave Hearts: Hollywood Portrays the Russians, 1939-1944."

30. There was a little Red scare on American campuses following the Nazi-Soviet Pact. Refer to Ellen W. Schrecker, *No Ivory Tower: McCarthyism and the Universities* (New York: Oxford University Press), 1986, pp. 73-83.

31. A rare example of a direct reference to the Red Army is found in *Something for the Boys* (20th Fox; 1944). Interestingly, the original title of *Song of Russia* was "Songs of the Red Army." *NYTEF*, July 5, 1942 B.

32. In the film dealing with an American freighter on the Murmansk run, *Action in the North Atlantic* (WB, 1943), Soviet planes (referred to as "ours") escort the freighter, damaged by repeated German assaults, into port, but only *after* all the military action has taken place.

33. The Allies, particularly the Americans, were simultaneously uneasy at being unable at this time to take the military pressure off Russia by opening a Second Front in the west, while agonizing over a growing admiration of current Soviet military efforts and the persistent residual fear of the potential military/political/ideological power of the Red Army once the Germans had been defeated. Refer to Mark A. Stoler, "The 'Second' Front and American Fear of Soviet Expansionism, 1941-1943," *Military Affairs* 39/3 (1975), 136-141.

34. Some early examples of "yellow peril" films would include: *Foreign Invasion* (Imperial; 1912); *MPW*, July 13, 1912 p. 182 and *Shadows of the West* (Cinema Craft Motion Picture Company; 1921); Kenneth W. Munden, ed. *The American Film Institute Catalogue, 1921-1930* (New York: R.R. Bowker Company, 1971), p. 702 (F2.4948).

35. Refer to George A. Lensen, *The Strange Neutrality: Soviet-Japanese Relations During the Second World War, 1941-1945* (Tallahassee, FL: The Diplomatic Press), 1972. The Russo-Japanese Neutrality Pact is alluded to in *Behind the Rising Sun* (RKO, 1943) and *Purple Heart* (TCF, 1944).

36. The period during which *Jack London* was released provided another fortuitous linkage. In January 1944 the first details were publicly released in the U.S. with regards to the notorious Death March on Bataan. United Artists probably had this information in mind when it placed a series of sensational ads for *Jack London* in the February issues of the motion picture trade journals. It is interesting to note that despite the fact that considerable footage in the film is devoted to London's early life and career, his strong socialist beliefs are never mentioned.

37. Melvin Small, "How We Learned To Love The Russians," *The Historian* 36/3 (May 1974), 468.

38. It is interesting to realize that one institution—present in nearly every American small town and certainly visible in Hollywood's films about other Allied and occupied nations—is significantly missing from *The North Star*. The village has no church.

39. Ironically, Copland was viewed as a very "American" composer, particularly due to the use of folk motifs in his music.

40. This was almost certainly based on the well-publicized feat of a Soviet Captain Gastello, who actually *did* crash his plane into a column of Nazi tanks in the first week of the invasion. Alexander Werth, *Russia at War 1941-1945* (New York: Avon, 1964), 250.

41. The fact that no U.S. or British troops were involved in these battles could explain the relative lack of public interest in the Russian Front. Additionally, most Americans were unfamiliar with the names and places and the overall importance of this aspect of the war was also never popularly understood.

42. This section heading is a paraphrase of the title of a recent and interesting book on the United States and China during WWII: Wesley M. Bagby, *The Eagle-Dragon Alliance* (Newark: University of Delaware Press, 1992).

43. Christopher Thorne, *Allies of a Kind* (New York: Oxford University Press, 1978), 173.

44. Linton Wells, *Salute to Valor* (Freeport, NY: Books for Libraries Press, 1942), 256.

45. Thorne 181.

46. Communist Chinese forces were not ignored by the America media—although they were generally overlooked by Hollywood, a verbal reference in *Gung Ho!* (Universal, 1943) to the contrary (Randolph Scott makes a reference to the "Long March," which was actually made by Mao Tse-tung and his army, who were escaping from the Nationalist forces!). But for most Americans (including Franklin D. Roosevelt), Chiang *was* China.

47. Thorne 563.

48. The U.S. government, while supportive of Nationalist China, was also reluctant to wholeheartedly embrace the Chinese as brothers: the ban on Chinese immigration into the United States was still in force until the end of 1943, at which time it was lifted and the Chinese immigration quota was set—at 105 persons per year! Thorne 183, 325.

49. The film deals with a German-Japanese plot to steal the "Anglo-Chinese" plans for military action; in reality, the British distrusted Chiang Kai-shek and would certainly have had little reason to plan concerted military action with his forces prior to Pearl Harbor (the setting of the film).

50. Bagby 31, 35. The Burma Road also figures in the plot of *A Yank on the Burma Road* (MGM, 1942), and *Halfway to Shanghai* (Universal, 1942) as well as the pre-Pearl Harbor *Burma Convoy* (Universal, 1941). Axis agents are after plans for the new "air transport system" for supplying China—taking the place of the severed ground route—in *Night Plane from Chungking* (Paramount, 1943), which has a plot very similar to *Bombs Over Burma*.

51. The title of this film may have brought Madame Chiang Kai-shek to the minds of American audiences: Chungking was the Nationalist Chinese capital, and the U.S.-educated Madame Chiang was a fairly well-known public figure (in fact, she paid an extended visit to the United States in 1942, lobbying for additional aid to China).

52. Sessue Hayakawa had starred in a number of silent American films; in 1941, Keye Luke had the lead in *Phantom of Chinatown*, a Monogram film which wrapped up the "Mr. Wong" series (the first five had starred British actor Boris Karloff as the Chinese detective). Not until the brief career of Bruce Lee in the 1970s would American audiences be exposed to an Asian leading man as more than a one-shot novelty.

53. Clayton R. Koppes and Gregory D. Black, *Hollywood Goes to War* (New York: Free Press, 1987) 242.

54. Additionally, the doctor who amputates Ted Lawson's leg is American, as if to imply that the elderly Chinese doctor was not capable of performing the operation. Koppes and Black make several errors in referring to this film—they indicate that Lawson has *both* legs amputated, and that this is done by a Chinese doctor who speaks English (267). Actually, Lawson loses only one leg, an American doctor performs the operation, and the Chinese doctor speaks NO English (his son translates for him).

55. Ironically, the most blatant stereotype in these films was the black character played by Mantan Moreland. However, Moreland constantly rose above the stereotyping by virtue of his undeniable comic talent, although the Chan films do not always show him to best advantage.

56. Koppes and Black 239.

57. A large number of French troops were evacuated at Dunkirk; in fact, for at least part of the operation orders were given to remove *equal* numbers of French and British soldiers, for political reasons. However, the bulk of France's armed forces were trapped in the country when it capitulated.

58. Viorst 172.

59. Milton Viorst, *Hostile Allies* (New York: MacMillan, 1965), 36,41.

60. Viorst 50.

61. There is also a Free French member of the multi-national group in *Sahara* (1943), set in North Africa.

62. This is one of the rare wartime films to acknowledge the shift of troops from the European theatre of war to the Far East in preparation for the planned invasion of Japan. Japan's capitulation in August 1945 (after two atomic bombings) made massive transfers from Europe to Asia unnecessary.

Chapter 19

1. Eugene Franklin Wong, *On Visual Media Racism: Asians in the American motion pictures* (New York: Arno Press, 1978), 155-6.

2. Jeanne Basinger, *The World War II Combat Film* (New York: Columbia University Press, 1986), 28.

3. Refer to Part One.

4. Paul Fussell, *Wartime* (New York: Oxford University Press, 1989), 120.

5. Clayton Koppes and Gregory D. Black, *Hollywood Goes to War* (New York: Free Press, 1987), 282.

6. For example, the fat, drug-addicted Goering, club-footed womanizing Goebbels, etc., and the neurotic, Austrian-born Hitler were hardly "blonde Aryan supermen." See Joachim Fest, *The Face of the Third Reich* (New York: Pantheon, 1970).

7. Russell Earl Shain, *An Analysis of Motion Pictures About War Released by the American Film Industry, 1930-1970.* (New York: Arno Press, 1976), 219.

8. A film like *Mademoiselle Fifi* (RKO, 1944) goes back even further, drawing parallels between the Franco-Prussian War of 1870 and World War II; *Salome, Where She Danced* (Universal, 1945) also depicts militaristic Prussian villains in a 19th-century setting.

9. The dark and gaunt Carradine, sporting a thin mustache, did not resemble the real-life Heydrich, who was one of the few Nazi leaders to physically represent the Ayran ideal (tall and blonde).

10. It is possible this film was meant to be an allegorical re-telling of the rise and fall of Hitler himself.

11. Koppes and Black, *Hollywood Goes to War* 283.

12. There were also a number of pre-1942 films in this category: *Hitler—Beast of Berlin* (PDC, 1939), *Four Sons* (TCF, 1940) and *The Mortal Storm* (MGM, 1940), for instance.

13. They hijack a German military plane and force the pilot to fly them to freedom. However, Andrews accidentally drops his pistol. The pilot hands it back to him. "You *want* to leave Germany?" Andrews asks. "Confidentially, it would be a pleasure!" the man replies.

14. See Part One.

15. Alexander Poliakov, *Russians Don't Surrender* (New York: Dutton, 1942), 190-91.

16. Bernard F. Dick, *The Star Spangled Screen* (Lexington: University Press of Kentucky, 1985), 102.

17. Perhaps the quintessential "good German" was kindly, old Ludwig "Papa" Stossel.

18. The mere word "Gestapo" (a contraction of the German words for "Secret State Police") had become such a loaded signifier in the United States by *1941* that it was used as a negative adjective (inferring underhandedness and/or nastiness) by American film characters in numerous 1941 and 1942 Hollywood releases. *Confessions of Boston Blackie* (Columbia, 1941), *Man at Large* (TCF, 1941), *Affairs of Martha* (MGM, 1942) and *Alias Boston Blackie* (Columbia, 1942).

19. This could be compared with the lighter treatment of the theme in *The Great Dictator*, where Chaplin's "Hynkel" plays with a balloon globe.

20. Gregor Strasser was one of the early Nazi Party luminaries—played by Fritz Kortner in *The Hitler Gang*—who was eliminated in the "Night of the Long Knives" purge.

21. To reinforce the maniacal aspects of the sadistic acts wartime Nazis were prone to commit on film, Hollywood frequently directly linked Nazis in general with madness. For instance, Nazi spy ring headquarters are located in insane asylums in at least three motion pictures, *Dangerously They Live* (WB, 1942), *Fly by Night* (Paramount, 1942) and *The Gorilla Man* (WB, 1943). Captured Allies in these institutions are guaranteed to receive rough treatment.

The very name of the primary Nazi in *None Shall Escape*, Grimm, creates allegorical associations with the crazy and dangerous world of Grimm fairy tales.

22. Actually he had painted water color postcards in Vienna. Joachim Fest, *Hitler* (New York: Harcourt, 1974).

23. Fest, *Hitler*.

24. There were also some references to "Schicklegruber" in 1940-41 films, especially in *The Man I Married* (TCF, 1940).

25. While there are many fewer films in this vein dealing with the Japanese, *Back to Bataan* does contain the notorious scene where a Filipino school principal is hung by Japanese troops for refusing to lower the American flag.

26. This fear is made very explicit in the February 15, 1943 issue of *Life* magazine. A full-page ad sponsored by American Locomotive entitled "A High Honor for Your Daughter," shows three young women being ogled in a lineup by a Nazi official. The text refers to women from occupied countries being used for "selective breeding" by the Nazis, and warns Americans that any complacency or slackening of the war effort could bring this to pass for American girls!

27. "Der Fuehrer's Face" by Oliver Wallace.

28. One of Rumann's best-known Nazi roles came after the war, as Sgt. Schulz in *Stalag 17* (Paramount, 1953).

29. *MPH* 25 April, 1942: "Product Digest Section" 621.

30. The villainous Nazi character played by Walter Slezak in *The Fallen Sparrow* (RKO, 1943) has a very obvious club foot. Although this is taken from the source novel (1942), it is still possible that the original author (Dorothy B. Hughes) had this trait of Goebbels in mind.

31. Goering was a World War One flying ace, but this was conveniently overlooked by Allied propagandists, who chose to concentrate on his more recent—and visible—foibles.

32. Paul Fussell, *Wartime*, p. 138

33. After the entry of the United States into the war, the Allies agreed to concentrate their resources on defeating Hitler and Mussolini in Europe, then to turn and face Japan. This decision was a victory for Churchill and Stalin (the USSR, in fact, was not even

at war with Japan) whose forces were being hard-pressed by the Nazis. It was not necessarily popular with the American people, who were anxious to avenge the attack on Pearl Harbor.

34. H.H. Husted, *Thumb-Nail History of World War II* (Boston: Bruce Humphries, 1948), 132.

35. *Behind the Rising Sun* and *Bombardier*, for example, make a point of mentioning U.S. relief supplies which had been sent to Japan after a devastating earthquake in 1923. The obvious implication is that the Japanese were an ungrateful bunch.

36. A number of films contain examples of so-called Japanese "jitter tactics," what one would now consider "psychological warfare," but that during WWII was just another example of the "uncivilized" Japanese way of war. In the final combat scene in *Objective Burma!*, the Japanese soldiers are shown crawling about like snakes and calling out to "Joe," while in *Pride of the Marines* they shout, "Marinee —tonight you die!" Tokyo Joe's taunts over the radio in *God Is My Co-Pilot* are designed to unnerve American soldiers (it rarely works, however, and merely makes the Japanese seem inhuman).

37. This motif is reversed in *Sahara* (WB, 1943): an Italian soldier tries to ingratiate himself with his Allied captors by referring to a relative in the United States, who—he suggests hopefully—might have made the steel used to construct their tank!

38. Open or thinly veiled dissension between members of the Berlin-Tokyo Axis appears in a number of wartime films, including *The Devil with Hitler, That Nazty Nuisance, Destination Unknown, Invisible Agent, Lure of the Islands*, and *Black Dragons*. See the Espionage chapter for details of multi-national spy teams fighting among themselves.

39. Reinforcing the Japanese/animal analogy are films in which American *dogs* are linked in various ways with the Japanese enemy. Civilians in an Alaskan village actually set their dogs upon a Japanese raiding party near the conclusion of *Headin' for God's Country* (Monogram, 1942)—a fitting end for godless non-Christians invading the sacred soil of America. In *Sergeant Mike* (Columbia, 1944) a pair of Army dogs bravely participates in the conquest of a Japanese-held island, and the female dog heroically dies in the struggle.

40. John W. Dower, *War Without Mercy* (New York: Pantheon, 1986), 90, 111.

41. Perhaps the only other wartime film with a positive Japanese-American character is *Betrayal from the East*. Benson Fong plays "Oyama," who poses as a houseboy-gardener but is in the employ of Army Intelligence. Caught by the Japanese spy ring, he is tortured with a red-hot poker, and dies. Oyama is *presumably* a Japanese-American, but his character appears so briefly that this is never made clear (he could, for instance, be Chinese *posing* as Japanese).

42. There were few Japanese or Japanese-American actors in Hollywood. Sessue Hayakawa was a star in silent films (ironically, he later portrayed Japanese POW camp commandants in *Three Came Home*, 1951 and *The Bridge on the River Kwai*, 1957), but he was virtually unique in U.S. films (there were undoubtedly some bit players or performers who appeared in one or two films, but the next Japanese actor to become internationally known was Toshiro Mifune). Also, most actors of Japanese descent would have been barred from work in WWII Hollywood—and would most likely have been interned!

43. This is similar to a black jazz musician's paraphrase of the same song in *Reunion in France*: "I'll be glad when you're dead, you rascal, you—and Adolf, too!"

44. An argument could even be made that the character shown in *Star Spangled Rhythm* could be considered a generic Japanese caricature rather than a specific portrayal of Hirohito.

45. Films featuring isolated Japanese agents in the United States were somewhat less likely to feature atrocities, although there are certainly examples to be found even in these pictures.

46. Dower, *War Without Mercy* 9.

47. Dick 233.

48. This shot deliberately evokes the well-known 1937 United Press photo of a crying Chinese child in the ruins of Shanghai. Clark Gable, playing a newsreel photographer, fakes a similar shot in *Too Hot to Handle* (MGM, 1938).

49. *Back to Bataan* begins and ends with footage of actual survivors of Japanese POW camps in the Philippines, including a war-film archetype come to life, a real-life "Max Greenberg of Brooklyn, New York!"

50. In *The Purple Heart*, the prosecutor (Richard Loo) tells the American prisoners that Japan is united in its hate of "all foreigners," but the racial implications are still clear.

51. The German people were not entirely free of blame—a number of films make at least passing reference to the "military" nature of Germans, particularly Prussians, and to what would now be called the "military-industrial complex." *The Hitler Gang* (Paramount, 1944) and *The Master Race* (Columbia, 1944) are two pointed examples of this.

52. Japanese prisoners are seldom taken, probably because they invariably turn around and murder (or attempt to murder) their captors/rescuers. Perhaps the best example occurs in *Destination Tokyo*, where a downed Japanese flyer is rescued by the American submarine, but immediately stabs one of the sailors (in the back, no less)! *Guadalcanal Diary, Gung Ho!*, and *China Sky* (RKO, 1945) also contain good examples of this type of treachery.

53. The Pacific campaign was characterized by its viciousness and great loss of life. The battle for Tarawa (November 1943) lasted just three days, and resulted in nearly 5,000 Japanese and 1,000 Marine dead. 21,000 Japanese soldiers were killed on Iwo Jima. These numbers not only reflect the intensity of the fighting, but also the reluctance of the Japanese to surrender.

54. See John P. Diggins, *Mussolini and Fascism, The View from America* (Princeton, N.J.: Princeton University Press, 1972).

55. Although, in fact, Mussolini was a major political figure in Italy in 1922, well before Hitler rose to power.

56. Conte played another Italian-American G.I. in *A Walk in the Sun* (UA, 1945); Wally Cassell is "Pvt. Dondaro" in *The Story of G.I. Joe* (UA, 1945). Both of these films dealt with Allied ground combat in Italy, but with the occupying *Germans* as the primary protagonists.

57. Unlike the ubiquitous swastika, the symbol of Italian fascism—the *fasces* (a bundle of rods with a protruding axe-head)—is rarely shown. In *The Devil with Hitler*, it appears on Mussolini's pajamas!

58. The military alliance signed between Germany and Italy in May, 1939. Refer to Mario Toscano, *The Origins of the Pact of Steel* (Baltimore: The Johns Hopkins University Press, 1967).

59. The Italian Air Force and Navy were ignored in American films, with this single exception. No military action in which the Italian Navy is shown appears in a wartime Hollywood feature release (despite a significant Italian submarine contribution to the Axis war effort).

60. Refer to Walter R. Roberts, *Tito, Mihailovic and the Allies, 1941-1945* (New Brunswick, N.J.: Rutgers University Press, 1973).

61. Mussolini sent two Italian armies to fight beside the Germans in Russia. They were engaged in combat from late September 1941 until February 1943. Philip V. Cannistraro, ed., *Historical Dictionary of Fascist Italy* (Westport, CT: Greenwood Press, 1982).

62. Bill Mauldin, *Up Front* (New York: Holt, 1945), 64.

63. Italy's diplomatic corps is also disparaged in *Mission to Moscow* (WB, 1943). Soviet Foreign Minister Molotov slights the Italian

ambassador to Russia at a reception, offering him *Spanish* olives (the Italians and Soviets supported opposing sides in the Spanish Civil War). In *Casablanca* (WB, 1943), Vichy official Claude Rains says it would be a major Italian "victory" if the Italian military attache could get a word in edgewise with his German counterpart.

Chapter 20

1. David Schoenbrun, *Soldiers of the Night: The Story of the French Resistance* (New York: Dutton, 1980), 479.

2. "Fireside Chat" of President Franklin D. Roosevelt, 4/28/42. Russell D. Buhite and David W. Levy, eds., *FDR's Fireside Chats* (Norman: University of Oklahoma Press, 1992), 221.

3. "There is pre-Stalingard and post-Stalingrad resistance … Before 1943, realism was not on the side of those who opposed Hitler…. In the spring of 1943, however, the hope of ending Nazism finally became real." Jacques Semelin, *Unarmed Against Hitler* (Westport, CT: Praeger, 1993), 33.

4. Clayton Koppes and Gregory D. Black, *Hollywood Goes to War* (New York: Free Press, 1987), 295-7.

5. Though the public enthusiastically encouraged the Red Army's killing of tens of thousands of German soldiers, the underlying support for the communist Soviet Union was tenuous. The Nazi-Soviet non-aggression pact had revived anti-communist feelings in the United States in 1939-40, and even at the height of the U.S.-Russian "alliance," there were many who did not trust Russia.

6. These statements link him to the pre-Hitler militant communist Rote Fahne (Red Flag), and the communist-dominated Thaelmann and Garibaldi Battalions of the International Brigades; the anti-communist backlash in 1940 America aroused by the 1938 Nazi-Soviet Pact is ignored in this film, based on a play by leftist Lillian Hellman.

7. Among the Allies and occupied nations there were a number of monarchies: Great Britain, the Netherlands, Belgium, Norway, Denmark, and Yugoslavia, for example. However, very little mention is made in any wartime films of the crowned heads of these nations.

8. This film was heavily revised at the request of the OWI. In the Columbia press material, the country is referred to as "Starslava," but this name is never used in the film itself.

9. Sweden remained neutral during the war; Denmark was occupied by the Germans, but was not the scene of active fighting or serious, combative resistance.

10. *FDR's Fireside Chats* 221.

11. See Edward Homz, *Foreign Labor in Nazi Germany* (Princeton: Princeton University Press, 1967).

12. The Germans were also portrayed attempting to impress Belgian orphans into slave labor in the WWI-era *Till I Come Back to You* (Par-Art, 1918), directed by C.B. DeMille.

13. Although the American-led guerrillas later capture and hand the perpetrator on the same flagpole, scenes of fascist hangings and lynchings were calculated to outrage film audiences, particularly people who associated lynching with extremist racists or unruly mobs.

14. This is very strong for the period: the killing of children in Hollywood films of the time was practically unheard of.

15. 1.8 million French soldiers were taken prisoner by the Germans in 1940, and most were initially imprisoned in Germany itself. After a time, many of the wounded and ill were repatriated to France, where they would not be a burden on Germany. Constantin Joffé, *We Were Free* (New York: Smith & Durrell, 1943), 105, 211-2.

16. This film was an April 1944 release—in September and October of 1943, the Germans had actually burned the prestigious University of Naples before leaving the city. This was one of the worst examples of deliberate, senseless German vandalism during the war.

17. Czech universities had actually closed for the duration of the war in November 1939 (after patriotic demostrations by students in October, on National Day) as part of the Nazis' gradual anti-intellectual campaign. However, this cannot be blamed on Heydrich personally, since he was not appointed Reichsfuehrer until September 1941.

18. The name "France" is not used in this film, despite the overwhelming indicators that it is taking place there, probably because the filmmakers wanted to "internationalize" the plight of the occupied nations. However, given the references in the film, this merely seems odd (unlike *The Black Parachute*, which is set in a completely fictional nation with generic foreign names, etc.).

19. Despite the obvious connection between "Polandria" and "Poland," the country in *Tarzan Triumphs* is a fictional African kingdom, ruled by (white) Frances Gifford and populated by swarthy Caucasians (not African blacks).

20. Although all of the major "Chinese" characters are played by Anglos.

21. Allied assistance is portrayed in various European resistance films, but this is mostly limited to supplying arms to the citizens of the occupied nations or minor raids. *The Black Parachute* originally drew OWI criticism because the Larry Parks' character (an American journalist) took too large a role in the escape of King Stephen; the script was changed to beef up the role of the indigenous resistance movement.

22. This is also in the case in non–Resistance genre films about the Philippines: *Salute to the Marines* (MGM, 1943), *Cry Havoc* (MGM, 1944), *So Proudly We Hail!* (Paramount, 1943), *Bataan* (MGM, 1942), and so on.

23. Quinn's character is named "Andres Bonifacio," after an actual Filipino guerrilla who led an insurrection against the Spanish in 1896, but was later executed. The name of Jose Rizal is also mentioned in this film: Rizal, another early Filipino nationalist, also took up arms against Spain and paid for it with his life, in 1896.

24. In *Mission to Moscow*, Russian traitors do appear and are tried for treason; however, this highly biased version of the pre-war Purge trials depicts these people as political opportunists rather than anti–Soviet ideologues.

25. See *Hollywood's Undeclared War*.

26. A French fascist/royalist character, The Prince, appears in *The Fallen Sparrow* (RKO, 1943). The OWI was impressed by this characterization: "The portrayal of the fascistic French royalist who lives for the 'honor' of monarchical emblems, and who brands the democratic people who fought tyranny in the time of Napoleon as 'revolutionists,' is particularly effective because it differentiates between the people of France and French fascists." National Archives 785067; 11/10/44.

27. Alfred Hitchcock made two short films (*Bon Voyage* and *Madagascar Landing*) about the conflict between Vichy France and Free France during the war, for the British Ministry of Information. However, the British government never released them, apparently unwilling to involve itself in such a touchy subject.

28. In actuality, Groupes Mobiles de Reserve were created from the Vichy "Garde Mobile" to combat "terrorists" in April 1943. After November 1942, all of France was directly occupied by the Germans.

29. *The Moon Is Down*.

Chapter 21

1. Blayney F. Matthews, *The Specter of Sabotage* (Los Angeles: Lymanhouse, 1941), 15. Matthews, Director of Plant Protection at Warner Bros. studio and a former FBI agent, dedicated his book (published in December 1941) to Harry, Jack and Albert Warner, "courageous and far-seeing Americans, who were among the first ... to recognize the menace of the Fifth Column...."

2. Although spies and saboteurs (in real life) are generally two separate classes of agent, WWII films usually treat them as one and the same: "spies" are often involved in not only the theft of secret plans, but also in murder, destruction of government or private property vital to the war effort, propaganda, and whatever other generalized mischief they can think of. Additionally, our coding terms refer only to *enemy* agents as spy/saboteurs, although spy genre films may involve Allied espionage (such as *Invisible Agent*, Universal, 1942).

3. German agents had been operating in the United States since the early 1930s. Ladislas Farago, *The Game of Foxes* (New York: David McKay, 1971), 38–49.

4. Farago 433.

5. In *Redhead from Manhattan* (Columbia, 1943), the protagonists stumble across a cache of money and weapons buried on a Long Island beach by saboteurs, another reference to this case, and in *Junior Army* (Columbia, 1942) there is a brief reference to a German saboteur having been "landed from a submarine."

6. Will Irwin and Thomas M. Johnson, *What You Should Know About Spies and Saboteurs* (New York: Norton, 1943), 168.

7. Farago 445. Farago cites only two suspicious cases *after* Pearl Harbor, but he states that "considerable mischief was in progress and the United States was substantially damaged" by German sabotage before entering the war (432).

8. See Part One.

9. *I Dood It* (MGM, 1943) also seems like a pre-war product. Late in the film, an Axis scheme to destroy stored Lend-Lease supplies is rather awkwardly shoe-horned into the plot.

10. The film asserts that Japanese espionage in the U.S. is largely directed by the Black Dragon society (as does *Black Dragons*, Monogram 1942). This is mostly fiction.

11. A news broadcast heard in the film about the attack on Pearl Harbor says Japanese planes bombed business and residential areas of Honolulu "indiscriminately," a charge intended to portray the Japanese *military* as ruthless; we already know the *spies* are cruel and inhuman, based on their actions up to this point in the film.

12. Clayton R. Koppes and Gregory D. Black, *Hollywood Goes to War* (New York: Free Press, 1987), 72–77.

13. Italian-Americans are portrayed in several ways. Some are traditional Hollywood gangsters, and occasionally these are in league with the Axis. Just as often, however, there are Italian-Americans who are patriotic, often violently anti-fascist, and often prove their loyalty to the United States by joining the Army. See *The Racket Man* (Columbia, 1943) and *My Son, the Hero* (PRC, 1943), for two good examples.

14. There were 138 films with "Collaborator" coding references in the 1942-45 period of this study. However, these also include collaborators in occupied countries, considered in Chapter 7.

15. Actually, the *Normandie* fire (February 1942) was accidental. Perrett 208.

16. Beginning after WWI, many large police departments, had such squads—also known at times as "Red Squads"—which handled political crimes.

17. This is somewhat similar to Sanders' first Hollywood role, as the British officer who impersonates a captured German soldier-aristocrat in the WWI spy thriller *Lancer Spy* (TCF, 1937).

18. Magnesium was a vital war material—the Range Busters (deputized for the occasion) save a magnesium mine from destruction by saboteurs in *Cowboy Commandos* (Monogram, 1943).

19. The guard is the father of the young protagonist of this film. Coincidentally, PRC's *The Under Dog* (1943) also features a boy whose father works in a defense plant, but in this film it is the boy and his dog who spoil the saboteurs' plans!

20. Farago 38-50, 459.

21. Particularly compared with later films such as *Five Fingers* (TCF, 1952), which depicts espionage as a tedious, nerve-wracking job.

22. Of course, the U.S. was far enough removed from the theaters of war to take some of the immediacy out of espionage. Spies, at least in Hollywood films, wisely concentrate on stealing plans for secret weapons—conceivably of some use to the Axis war machine—rather than details of troop movements and deployments, or the location of fortifications and factories.

23. Egypt was occupied by British troops and served as a battleground, but the Egyptian government and armed forces were not actively involved in the war.

24. *The Devil with Hitler* (UA, 1942) and *That Nazty Nuisance* (UA, 1943) also follow this theme, with Hitler, Mussolini and the Japanese envoy "Suki-Yaki" scheming to outwit each other at all costs.

Chapter 22

1. Geoffrey Perrett, *Days of Sadness, Years of Triumph* (New York: Coward, McCann & Geohegan, 1973), 233.

2. Bonds were generally sold in banks and post offices, or at special bond rallies; Stamps, priced much lower (from .10 to $5.00), could be purchased in schools, stories, and other local outlets. Perrett 261.

3. Perrett 394.

4. One of the few films to cast any sort of critical eye on War Bonds is *Hi, Buddy* (Universal, 1943); in this film, a clubhouse for slum children is threatened by a sudden drop in donations—it seems that potential donors are buying Bonds instead!

5. Clayton R. Koppes and Gregory D. Black, *Hollywood Goes to War* (New York: Free Press, 1987), 154.

6. Koppes and Black 160.

7. Perrett 71, 86.

8. Perrett 261.

9. Perrett 299.

10. Perrett 299.

11. George Houston also plugs Bonds in song in *The Lone Rider in Cheyenne* (PRC, 1942). Bugs Bunny had beaten Autry to the screen with his version of Berlin's tune in an animated cartoon short entitled *Any Bonds Today?* (released in December 1941). There was also a "Soundies" version of this song. Michael Shull and David Wilt, *Doing Their Bit* (Jefferson, NC: McFarland, 1987), 75.

12. For several years during the war, PRC Pictures featured the "Minuteman" symbol and a Bonds plug after the end titles of their feature films. This was not coded as a reference for each individual film, since it does not come within the film itself (just as RKO Radio's Morse code "V," beamed from its corporate logo at the beginning of each film, was not considered a separate war reference). MGM films displayed a plug for Defense/War Bonds after the end credits on many of their films in the early months of 1942; 20th Century–Fox also carried an end-credit bonds endorsement, beginning in the summer of 1942.

13. Paul D. Casdorph, *Let the Good Times Roll* (New York: Paragon House, 1989), 82.

14. Casdorph 82.

15. Perrett 234.

16. In fact, some scrap could be sold to junk dealers; waste fats, turned in at the local butcher shop (the fat could be used in the manufacture of explosives), earned the housewife points towards her meat ration.

17. Perrett 194.

18. Perrett writes: "Among adults much of the earlier zeal was gone. In most months of 1944 the paper scrap drive fell short of its quota…" (394).

19. One of the most ironic uses of the Red Cross logo occurs in *Little Tokyo, USA* (TCF, 1942). A German-American spy smuggles a camera into the defense plant where he works, by hiding it in a Red Cross donation canister! Turning the camera over to his superiors, the spy says he will use the coins that were dropped in the can to "buy Defense Stamps."

20. Perrett 233.

21. Koppes and Black 93. Even WWII cartoons followed this trend, as evidenced in *A Jolly Good Furlough* (Paramount, 1943), among others. In this animated short, Popeye comes home on leave and his nephews seize the opportunity to show off their skills. Michael Shull and David Wilt, *Doing Their Bit* (McFarland, 1987), 121.

Chapter 23

1. Doris Weatherford, *American Women and World War II* (New York: Facts on File, 1990): 116.

2. Geoffrey Perrett, *Days of Sadness, Years of Triumph* (New York: Coward, McCann & Geohegan, 1973), 301.

3. Perrett 339. For example, there were approximately 17,000 military amputees in WWII; during the same period, 100,000 people lost a limb in industrial accidents. On the other hand, it should be noted that this statistic applies to *all* those in the armed forces, the majority of whom never saw combat. The risk of death or injury among *combat* personnel was, of course, much higher.

4. See George Q. Flynn, *The Mess in Washington* (Westport, CT: Greenwood Press, 1979). Officially, there were no blanket "occupational deferments." Local draft boards were free to make their own decisions, except for certain classes of labor (such as farmers) who were protected by Congressional action.

5. This is virtually the only film to depict a fatal industrial accident; there were instances of sabotage causing deaths (*Saboteur*, Universal 1942), and occasional crashes of airplanes in the testing stage, but defense plant accidents are rarely shown (*Swing Shift Maisie*, MGM 1943 contains a non-fatal accident).

6. This actually was similar to programs existing in several states; by 1943 "some 30,000 inmates of prisons worked part-time" in defense work, although most of the work was done at the prisons themselves. Flynn 56.

7. Perrett 308.

8. In *The Fighting Seabees* (Republic, 1944), the construction workers under contract to the armed forces want to get in the fight. They dislike being unarmed noncombatants who are exposed to danger but cannot fight back. The Navy solves this problem by creating the "Seabees," construction *battalions* (the British also had their "Pioneer" units, which provided the same sort of services).

9. In a way, this may have been more accurate than humorous: in an effort to promote greater flexibility in the workforce, some factories tried to simplify production tasks as much as possible, thus avoiding the slowdowns which could occur when a highly skilled worker was absent.

10. Flynn 172.

11. The "defense plant" production numbers in Rosie the Riveter (Republic, 1944) and *Star Spangled Rhythm* (Paramount, 1942), featuring scantily-clad chorus girls "working" in a aircraft plant, are hardly serious portrayals of women's contributions to the war effort!

12. Flynn 136. *The Hour Before the Dawn* (Paramount, 1944) is set in England; Franchot Tone appears as a conscientious objector who is *assigned* to farm work in lieu of military service. As far as is known, this was not tried in the United States, although there were instances of Axis prisoners of war working on private farms (and in the pulp and timber industries, over the objections of organized labor). Flynn 117.

13. Flynn 61.

Chapter 24

1. Films released January 1, 1945 through September 30, 1945 only.

2. U.S. Office of Price Administration, *First Quarterly Report for the Period Ended April 30, 1942* (Washington: U.S. Government Printing Office, 1942): 57. Tire rationing boards were established shortly after the attack on Pearl Harbor and rationing went into effect early in January 1942. Films mentioning the production of rubber include *Girl Trouble* (TCF, 1942), *White Cargo* (MGM, 1942), and *Tiger Fangs* (PRC, 1943). *Malaya* (MGM, 1949) deals with an attempt to get crude rubber out of the Far East before the Japanese can consolidate their hold on the area.

3. The original ration plan for private automobiles did not contain a "C" sticker; instead, an "X" ration was proposed for unrestricted gasoline purchases for doctors and other individuals considered "essential" drivers. Later, various special stickers were issued for commercial vehicles, farm vehicles, and so on, so that "D," "S," "T," "E," and "R" stickers may also be seen in some films of the period.

4. "The Hollywood Scene," *Motion Picture Herald* 28 August 1943: 34.

5. U.S. Office of Price Administration, *Sixth Quarterly Report* (Washington: U.S. Government Printing Office, 1943), 39.

6. No new civilian automobiles were produced after 1942. Stocks on hand, totaling just over 500,000 cars, were rationed to dealers, but by the end of 1944 less than 15,000 "new" cars remained in dealers' inventories for sale. U.S. Office of Price Administration, *Twelfth Quarterly Report for the Period ended December 31, 1944* (Washington: U.S. Government Printing Office, 1945), 60.

7. U.S. Office of Price Administration, *Fifth Quarterly Report for the Period Ended April 30 1943* (Washington: U.S. Government Printing Office, 1943): 18.

8. One exception occurs in *Footlight Glamour* (Columbia, 1943): informed by Dagwood that the Bumstead family is going to have a houseguest for an indefinite period, Blondie complains "You know how scarce food is." However, later in the film a running gag involving Dagwood's enormous sandwiches and an impoverished playwright's ravenous appetite make a mockery of this statement.

9. Beth Bailey and David Farber, *The First Strange Place: The Alchemy of Race and Sex in World War II Hawaii* (New York: Free Press, 1992), 171.

10. There were a few films in which these formerly downtrodden employees entered the armed forces, often—as in *Buck Privates* (Universal, 1941)—finding themselves in the same unit as their former employers (occasionally even becoming their military superiors; *The Best Years of Our Lives* hints at this class "leveling" indirectly, as

soda jerk Dana Andrews returns from the war as a commissioned officer, while banker Fredric March was a mere non-com).

11. Marshall B. Clinard, *The Black Market* (Montclair, NJ: Patterson Smith, 1969): 93.

12. Black market references numbered 8 in 1942, peaked at 12 in 1943, dropped back to 7 in 1944, and totaled only 3 in the 1945 period. Pejorative and/or humorous references to hoarding were not separately coded, but they were also more prevalent in 1942-43, when rationing was more of a novelty.

13. The OPA was the Office of Price Administration, created in April 1941 by President Roosevelt "to prevent price spiralling, rising cost of living, profiteering, and inflation…" U.S. Office of Price Administration, "First Quarterly Report for the Period ended April 30, 1942," 7.

Chapter 25

1. Films released through September 30, 1945 only.

2. Depictions of British "home defense" measures were also included in this category; Britain, of course, actually did suffer from German bombing and was under the threat of land invasion, so the images of civilians carrying gas mask pouches and the like were more immediately relevant to the realities of war.

3. Geoffrey Perrett, *Days of Sadness, Years of Triumph* (New York: Coward, McCann & Geoghegan, 1973), 231. La Guardia resigned after Pearl Harbor, realizing the job required full-time attention.

4. Great Britain's air raid wardens, civil defense workers, and Home Guard were, on the other hand, treated with considerable respect in Hollywood productions, perhaps because England was actually undergoing severe bombing. Even as late as *The Brighton Strangler* (RKO, 1945), a dedicated British air raid warden (Olaf Hytten, cast as John Loder's valet) makes an appearance.

5. The animated cartoon *Old Blackout Joe* (Columbia, 1942), beat Republic to the screen by several months with its depiction of a black air raid warden.

6. Clayton R. Koppes and Gregory D. Black, *Hollywood Goes to War* (New York: Free Press, 1987), 93.

7. The neon signs of Times Square in New York were turned off "for the duration" in April 1942. Perrett 232.

8. Michael Gannon, *Operation Drumbeat* (New York: Harper & Row, 1990), 185.

9. Gannon 344-345.

Chapter 26

1. Geoffrey Perrett, *Days of Sadness, Years of Triumph* (New York: Coward, McCann & Geohegan, 1973), 368.

2. Francis E. Merrill, *Social Problems on the Home Front* (New York: Harper, 1948), 145.

3. Monogram even released a series called "The Teen-Agers" beginning in 1946.

4. A postwar Errol Flynn film repeats this situation: *Never Say Goodbye* (WB, 1946), and *Dear Ruth* (Paramount, 1947) also used the same plot premise.

5. Perrett 348.

6. In *Star Spangled Rhythm* (Paramount, 1942), Hutton's major solo number is entitled "I'm Doin' It for Defense," and the lyrics leave little room for doubt about what "it" is. Preston Sturges has a cameo role (as himself) in this film, and allegedly cast Bracken and Hutton

in *The Miracle of Morgan's Creek* on the basis of their co-starring roles here.

7. Children are also executed in *Paris After Dark* (TCF, 1942).

8. The book was also the basis for a Walt Disney cartoon, *Education for Death* (1943).

9. Perrett 348.

10. *Delinquent Daughters* is included in our "ambiguous list," since the studio-supplied synopsis makes war-relevant comments, but the film itself has not been screened. *Reckless Age* (Universal, 1944) was a vehicle for Gloria Jean, hardly a candidate for juvenile delinquency; however, the title was suggestive of "rebellious youth," and the young star *did* run away from home in the film. This film *is* included in the filmography, for other reasons.

11. "Children of Mars" was part of RKO's "This is America" series, created to fill the gap after "The March of Time" left RKO for Twentieth Century–Fox distribution in mid-1942. These documentary shorts were shot silent and released with voiceover narration. Leonard Maltin, *The Great Movie Shorts* (New York: Bonanza Books, 1972), 210 and Mark Thomas McGee and R. J. Robertson, *The J.D. Films* (Jefferson, NC: McFarland, 1982), 11-13.

12. Koppes and Black list an additional title, *Look to Your Children*, as the "final" release title, but this is not correct (178). According to one source, among the deleted footage was a sub-plot in which an abused teenager kills his own father. The concluding montage—stock shots of the Boy Scouts, 4-H clubs, and other "wholesome" youth activities—was a studio addition. Joel Siegel, *Val Lewton: The Reality of Terror* (New York: Viking, 1973), 42, 143-4.

13. Perrett 349.

14. Some of the individual stories are footage lifted from 1930s exploitation films by J.D. Kendis, the producer of *Teen Age*.

Chapter 27

1. "Stop Making War Films, Showmen Tell Studios." *Motion Picture Herald* 25 September 1943: 23-24.

2. Red Kann, "What Hollywood Thinks About Production Trends," *Motion Picture Herald* 30 September 1944: 13-14.

3. "Stop Making War Films, Showmen Tell Studios."

4. Weaver, William R. "Studios Cut War Themes to 25% of Product." *Motion Picture Herald* 6 February 1943: 15.

5. "Soldiers Do Not Like War Films, Says Hubbell." *Motion Picture Herald* 28 August 1943: 21.

6. Allen L. Woll, *The Hollywood Musical Goes to War* (Chicago: Nelson-Hall, 1983), 161. Woll cites "almost four hundred" musicals released during wartime—combined with our figures, this means *at least* 25% of "escapist" musicals were actually war-relevant to one degree or another.

7. Woll, *The Hollywood Musical Goes To War* 92.

8. This is a bit reminiscent of the Abbott and Costello vehicle *In the Navy* (Universal, 1941), in which Dick Powell plays a crooner who joins up. *Here Come the Waves* has a similar premise—popular singer in the Navy—but in this film, the star (Bing Crosby) makes it clear *he* joined up for patriotic, not personal, reasons.

9. Servicemen watching this film in places like the South Pacific, the Aleutians, and Italy must have gotten a good laugh at this.

10. Like *This Is the Army*, *Hey Rookie* was actually based on a stage show, in this case one which ran for nine months on the West Coast. Clive Hirschhorn, *The Hollywood Musical* (New York: Crown 1981), 239.

11. Ann Sheridan allegedly turned down the Joan Leslie role in *Hollywood Canteen*, fearing servicemen who saw the film would

all expect to meet and fall in love with actresses at the canteen! James Robert Parish and Don E. Stanke, *The Forties Gals* (Westport, CT: Arlington House, 1980), 288-9.

12. In *Babes on Broadway* (MGM, 1942), Judy Garland makes her contribution to Anglo-American unity, singing "Chin Up, Cheerio, Carry On," to a group of British children.

13. "From Here On In," by Jule Styne and Sammy Cahn.

14. See Part One.

15. "Bring On the Girls" by Harold Adamson and Jimmy McHugh.

16. Cobbett Steinberg, *Reel Facts* (New York: Vintage, 1982), 58-9. During this period no other woman made the list more than five years in a row (Greer Garson, from 1942-46).

17. Actually, "Gay Nineties" films were made at Fox and other studios even during the 1930s and early 1940s — *Alexander's Ragtime Band* (TCF, 1938) and *The Strawberry Blonde* (WB, 1941) for instance — but *My Gal Sal* was one of the first wartime examples.

18. Clive Hirschhorn, *The Hollywood Musicaa* (New York: Crown, 1981), 263.

19. It should be noted that Woll in *The Hollywood Musical Goes to War* disagrees with this conclusion. His reading of the "nostalgia" films of the period is much darker (although he singles out only four such films for analysis).

20. Gessner, Robert. "Need Bitter War Films." *Variety* 11 March 1942: 1, 16.

21. Marion Hargrove's book was a collection of his newspaper columns detailing his humorous adventures as a draftee in the *pre-war* Army, and concludes with news of the attack on Pearl Harbor. Marion Hargrove, *See Here, Private Hargrove* (New York: Henry Holt, 1942). The movie sequel, *What Next, Cpl. Hargrove?* (MGM, 1945) *does* take Hargrove and his unit into combat (in France), but was released after the cessation of hostilities.

22. Bendix had a similar role in *Wake Island* (Paramount, 1942). Other character actors who brought a degree of levity to war films included Alan Hale (*Desperate Journey, Destination Tokyo*) and George Tobias (*Air Force, Objective Burma!*).

23. This film also includes a tough Marine (Barton MacLane) who is constantly searching for a "dead Jap" or a live GI with big feet — so he can replace his own worn-out shoes!

Chapter 28

1. Geoffrey Perrett, *Days of Sadness, Years of Triumph* (New York: Coward, McCann & Geohegan, 1973), 408.

2. Such planning, of course, was far less certain in England, and in occupied countries such as France even the form of postwar government was uncertain (assuming, of course, the Nazis would be defeated).

3. Galloway 109.

4. Sigrid Arne, *United Nations Primer* (New York: Rinehart, 1945), 10.

5. Perrett 421. The Moscow Pact, released on November 1, 1943, further clarified the Allies' attitudes towards war criminals (the USSR had not agreed to take part in the earlier commission).

6. Arne 20, 25.

7. Arne 53.

8. Herman Miles Somers, *Presidential Agency OWMR* (Cambridge: Harvard University Press, 1950), 1.

9. Perrett 301, 340.

10. H.H. Husted, *Thumb-Nail History of World War II* (Boston: Bruce Humphries, 1948), 361-2.

11. Husted 390, 393.

12. Husted 307.

13. Perrett 426.

14. See Arnold C. Brackman, *The Other Nuremberg: The Untold Story of the Tokyo War Crimes Trials* (New York: Morrow, 1987) and Philip R. Piccigallo, *The Japanese on Trial: Allied War Crimes Operations in the East, 1945-1951* (Austin: University of Texas Press, 1979).

15. Perrett 407.

16. E. Jay Howenstine, Jr., *The Economics of Demobilization* (Washington: Public Affairs Press, 1944), 17.

17. *Wilson* (TCF, 1944) also implicitly blames the "botched" peace of WWI (and the failure of the League of Nations concept) for the onset of World War Two.

18. Perrett 339, 341.

19. As soon as hostilities ceased in 1945, the government gave in to massive public pressure and began to demobilize servicemen as quickly as possible. Between October 1945 and February 1946, over 3/4 of a million men per *month* were released from the service; by June 1946, the process was virtually complete.

20. Similarly, protagonists turned down for military service were generally rejected for non-crippling flaws or illnesses: hay fever (Eddie Bracken in *Hail the Conquering Hero*, Paramount, 1944), a bum knee (George Raft in *Follow the Boys*, Universal, 1944), and "spots before my eyes" (*The Miracle of Morgan's Creek*, Paramount, 1944).

21. *The Best Years of Our Lives*, of course, features actual veteran Harold Russell, who had lost both hands. *The Men* (UA, 1950) depicts paraplegic veterans; Spencer Tracy is a one-armed veteran in *Bad Day at Black Rock* (MGM, 1954); Arthur Kennedy is a blind veteran in *Bright Victory* (Universal, 1951); William Bendix has a metal plate in his head in *The Blue Dahlia* (Paramount, 1946); and Lassie is a shell-shocked veteran war dog in *Courage of Lassie* (MGM, 1946)!

22. John Costello, *Virtue Under Fire* (Boston: Little, Brown and Co., 1985), 197.

Filmographic Appendix C

1. Weiss and Goodgold, *To Be Continued*, pp. 106–193; Jack Mathis, *Valley of the Cliff Hangers* (Northbrook, IL: Jack Mathis Advertising, 1975).

2. Although exhibition of the entire serial was not completed until the winter of 1942, its first episode was released in the fall of 1941. See *FD*, October 28, 1941, p. 7; *Lib. Cong.*, LP10798 (Chpt. 1).

Filmographic Appendix E

1. The lead title is that under which the film was released in the U.S. Titles within parentheses, unless otherwise specified, are the original British titles.

Several relevant British films were picked up by American studios for release in the United States, reviewed in American trade journals, but then apparently left in the can. They include: *Sons of the Sea* (1939; Grand Nat.): *The Briggs Family* (1940; WB); *Spy for a Day* (1940; Par.); *Atlantic Ferry* (1941; WB). Confirmation of the U.S. commercial release of some of Columbia's pick-ups (such as the George Formby films) has similarly been elusive.

Bibliography

Documents

Catalogue of Copyright Entries, Cumulative Series Motion Pictures, 1912–1939, Library of Congress, Washington, DC, 1951.
Catalogue of Copyright Entries, Cumulative Series Motion Pictures, 1940–1949, Library of Congress, Washington, DC: 1953.
OWI 208 Series. National Archives, Suitland, Maryland.
U.S. Office of Price Administration. *Quarterly Report.* 1942–1944. Washington, DC: U.S. Government Printing Office, 1942–45.
U.S. Office of War Information Files, Feature Length Films. Washington, DC: Library of Congress, Film Division.

Periodicals

The Christian Science Monitor, January 1942–December 1945.
The Film Daily Jan. 1932–Dec. 1945.
Life, 1942–1945.
Motion Picture Herald Dec. 1931–Dec. 1945.
New York Times Jan. 1932–Jan. 1942
The New York Times, Film Reviews, Jan. 1942–Dec. 1945.
Variety Jan. 1932–Jan. 1942
Variety, Jan. 1942–Dec. 1945.

Books and Articles

Abbazia, Patrick. *Mr. Roosevelt's Navy: The Private War of the U.S. Atlantic Fleet, 1939–1942.* Annapolis, MD: Naval Institute Press, 1975.
Abrams, Ray H., ed. *The American Family in World War II.* New York: Arno Press, 1972.
Adler, Les K. and Paterson, Thomas G. "Red Fascism: The Merger of Nazi Germany and Soviet Russia in the American Image of Totalitarianism, 1930's–1950's." *American Historical Review,* Vol. LXXV, No. 4 (April 1970): 1046–1064.
Alexander, Charles C. *Nationalism in American Thought, 1930–1945.* Chicago: Rand McNally & Co., 1969.
Alicoate, Jack, ed. *The Film Daily Year Book of Motion Pictures: 1937.* New York: Film Daily, 1938.
_____. *The Film Daily Year Book of Motion Pictures: 1938,* New York: Film Daily, 1939.
_____. *The Film Daily Year Book of Motion Pictures: 1939,* New York: Film Daily, 1940.
_____. *The Film Daily Year Book of Motion Pictures: 1940,* New York: Film Daily, 1941.
_____. *The Film Daily Year Book of Motion Pictures: 1941,* New York: Film Daily, 1942.

Altman, Charles F. "Towards a Historiography of American Film." *Cinema Journal,* Vol. XVI, No. 2 (Spring 1977): 1–25.
The American Film Institute Catalog: Feature Films, 1931–1940, 3 Vols. Berkeley: University of California Press, 1993.
Anderegg, Michael. "Home Front America and the Denial of Death in MGM's *The Human Comedy*" *Cinema Journal,* Vol. 34, No. 1 (1994), pp. 3–17.
Anderson, Karen. *Wartime Women: Sex Roles, Family Relations and the Status of Women During World War II.* Westport, CT: Greenwood Press, 1981.
Arne, Sigrid. *United Nations Primer.* New York: Rinehart, 1945.
Avisar, Ilvan. *Screening the Holocaust: Cinema's Images of the Unimaginable.* Bloomington: Indiana University Press, 1988.
Bagby, Wesley M. *The Eagle-Dragon Alliance.* Newark: University of Delaware Press, 1992.
Bailey, Beth and David Farber. *The First Strange Place: The Alchemy of Race and Sex in World War II Hawaii.* New York: The Free Press, 1992.
Baker, Joyce M. *Images of Women in Film: The War Years, 1941–1945.* Ann Arbor, MI: UMI Research Press, 1980.
Barnett, Robert W. *China—America's Ally.* New York: American Council Institute of Pacific Relations, 1942.
Barros, Alex. *Stop the Presses: The Newspaper Man in American Films.* Cranbury, NJ: A.S. Barnes, 1976.
Basinger, Jeanine. *The World War II Combat Film: Anatomy of a Genre.* New York: Columbia University Press, 1986.
"Battle of Buna." *Life* 15 February 1943: 17–29.
Baxter, John. *Hollywood in the Thirties.* New York: A. S. Barnes and Co., 1973.
Belton, John. *The Hollywood Professionals: Vol. 3, Howard Hawks, Frank Borzage and Edgar Ulmer.* New York: Tantivity Press, 1974.
Bennett, Edward M. *Franklin D. Roosevelt and the Search for Victory: American-Soviet Relations, 1939–1945.* Wilmington, DE: Scholarly Resources, 1990.
Bergan, Ronald. *The United Artists Story.* New York: Crown, 1986.
Bergman, Andrew. *We're in the Money: Depression America and Its Films.* New York: New York University Press, 1971.
Berube, Allen. *Coming Out Under Fire.* New York: Free Press, 1990.
Biddle, Major Charles J. *The Way of the Eagle.* New York: Charles Scribner's Sons, 1919.
Black, Gregory D. *Hollywood Censored.* New York: Cambridge UP, 1994.
Blum, John Morton. *V Was for Victory: Politics and American Culture During World War II.* New York: Harcourt Brace Jovanovich, 1976.
A Book of Facts About the WAC. Washington, DC: Women's Army Corps, 1944.
Brackman, Arnold C. *The Other Nuremberg: The Untold Story of the Tokyo War Crimes Trials.* New York: Morrow, 1987.

Breuer, William. *Hitler's Undercover War: The Nazi Espionage Invasion of the U.S.A.* New York: St. Martin's Press, 1989.

Braverman, Jordan. *To Hasten the Homecoming: How Americans Fought WWII Through the Media.* University Press of America, 1995.

Brinkley, David. *Washington Goes to War.* New York: Knopf, 1988.

Buhite, Russell D. and David W. Levy, eds. *FDR's Fireside Chats.* Norman: University of Oklahoma Press, 1992.

Burton, Jack. *The Blue Book of Hollywood Musicals.* Watkins Glen, NY: Century House, 1953.

Buscombe, Edward. "America on Screen? Hollywood Feature Films as Social and Political Evidence." *Politics and the Media: Film and Television for the Political Scientist and Historian.* Edited by M. S. Clark. Elmsford, NY: Pergamon Press, 1979.

Butler, Ivan. *The War Film.* New York: A. S. Barnes and Co., 1974.

Cameron, Craig M. *American Samurai: Myth, Imagination, and the Conduct of Battle in the First Marine Division, 1941–1951.* Cambridge University Press, 1994.

Campbell, D'Ann Mae. *Women at War with America: Private Lives in a Patriotic Era.* Cambridge, MA: Harvard University Press, 1984.

Canham, Kingsley. *The Hollywood Professionals Vol. 1: Michael Curtiz, Raoul Walsh, Henry Hathaway.* New York: Tantivity Press, 1973.

Cannistraro, Philip V., ed. *Historical Dictionary of Fascist Italy.* Westport, CT: Greenwood Press, 1982.

Cantril, Hadley and Mildred Strunk, eds. *Public Opinion, 1935–1946.* Princeton, NJ: Princeton University Press, 1951.

Capra, Frank. *Frank Capra: The Name Above the Title.* New York: Macmillan, 1971.

Carringer, Robert and Barry Sabath. *Ernst Lubitsch: A Guide to References and Resources.* Boston: G. K. Hall and Co., 1979.

Carson, Julia M.H. *Home Away from Home: The Story of the USO.* New York: Harper, 1946.

Casdorph, Paul D. *Let the Good Times Roll: Life at Home in America During World War II.* New York: Paragon House, 1989.

Ceplair, Larry and Steven Englund. *The Inquisition in Hollywood: Politics in the Film Community, 1930–1960.* Garden City, NY: Anchor Press/Doubleday, 1980.

Cervi, Mario. *The Hollow Legions: Mussolini's Blunder in Greece, 1940–41.* New York: Doubleday, 1971.

Chadwin, Mark L. *The Hawks of World War II: American Interventionists Before Pearl Harbor.* Chapel Hill, NC: University of North Carolina Press, 1968.

Chatfield, Charles. *For Peace and Justice: Pacifism in America, 1914–1941.* Knoxville: University of Tennessee Press, 1971.

Churchill, Winston S. *The Second World War: Vol. 2—Their Finest Hour.* Cambridge: Houghton-Mifflin, 1948.

Clifford, J. Garry and Samuel R. Spencer, Jr. *The First Peacetime Draft.* Lawrence: University Press of Kansas, 1986.

Clinard, Marshall B. *The Black Market.* Montclair, NJ: Patterson Smith, 1969.

Coates, K.S. and W.R. Morrison. *The Alaska Highway in World War II.* Norman: University of Oklahoma Press, 1992.

Cogley, John. *Report on Blacklisting, Vol. 1, Movies.* New York: The Fund for the Republic, 1956.

Cole, Jean Hascall. *Women Pilots of World War II.* Salt Lake City: University of Utah Press, 1992.

Cole, Wayne S. *America First: The Battle Against Intervention, 1940–1941.* Madison: University of Wisconsin Press, 1953.

_____. *Roosevelt and the Isolationists, 1932–1942.* Lincoln: University of Nebraska Press, 1983.

Costello, John. *Virtue Under Fire: How World War II Changed Our Social and Sexual Attitudes.* Boston: Little, Brown, 1985.

Cripps, Thomas. *Making Movies Black: The Hollywood Message Movie from World War II to the Civil Rights Era.* New York: Oxford University Press, 1993.

_____. "Movies, Race and World War II: *Tennessee Johnson* as an Anticipation of the Strategies of the Civil Rights Movement." *Prologue* 14 (Summer 1982): 48–67.

Culbert, David, ed. *Film and Propaganda in America: A Documentary History,* Vol. 2, World War II, Part I. Westport, CT: Greenwood Press, 1990.

_____. *Mission to Moscow* [screenplay]. Madison: University of Wisconsin Press, 1980.

Cull, Nicholas J. *Selling War: The British Propaganda Campaign Against Ameriacn Neutrality in World War II.* New York: Oxford University Press, 1995.

Dallek, Robert. *Franklin D. Roosevelt and American Foreign Policy, 1932–1945.* New York: Oxford University Press, 1979.

Dardis, Tom. *Some Time in the Sun.* New York: Scribner's, 1976.

Davis, Dave and Neal Goldberg. "Organizing the Screen Writers Guild—An Interview with John Howard Lawson." *Cineaste,* Vol. VIII, No. 2 (Fall 1977): 4–11; 58.

Dear, Ian. *Ten Commando.* New York: St. Martin's Press, 1987.

deJong, Louis. *The German Fifth Column in the Second World War.* Chicago: The University of Chicago Press, 1956.

Denton, Clive and Kingsley Canham. *The Hollywood Professionals: Vol. 5, King Vidor, John Cromwell and Mervyn LeRoy.* New York: Tantivity Press, 1976.

Diamond, Sander A. *The Nazi Movement in the United States, 1924–1941.* Ithaca, NY: Cornell University Press, 1974.

Dick, Bernard F. *The Star Spangled Screen: The American World War II Film.* Lexington: The University Press of Kentucky, 1985.

Diggins, John P. *Mussolini and Facism, The View from America.* Princeton, NJ: Princeton University Press, 1972.

Doherty, Thomas. Projections of War: *Hollywood, American Culture, and World War II.* New York: Columbia UP, 1993.

Dower, John W. *War Without Mercy: Race and Power in the Pacific War.* New York: Pantheon, 1986.

Drummond, Donald F. *The Passing of American Neutrality, 1937–1941.* New York: Greenwood Press, Publishers, 1968.

Dymytrk, Edward. *It's a Hell of a Life, But Not a Bad Living.* New York: The New York Times Book Co., 1978.

Eames, John D. *The MGM Story.* New York: Crown, 1975.

_____. *The Paramount Story.* New York: Crown, 1985.

Ebert, Jane and Marie-Beth Hall. *Crossed Currents: Navy Women from WWI to Tailhook.* New York: Brassey's, 1993.

Editors of *Look. Movie Lot to Beachhead: The Motion Picture Goes to War and Prepares for the Future.* Garden City, NY: Doubleday, Doran, 1945.

Ellul, Jacques. *Propaganda: The Formation of Men's Attitudes.* New York: Random House, 1965.

Elsaesser, Thomas. "Film History as Social History: The Dieterle Warner Brothers Bio-Pic." *Wide Angle* Vol. 8, No. 2 (1986): 15–31.

"Emphasize Comedy, Music in New Product Trend." *Motion Picture Herald* 16 January 1943: 13.

Estrin, Allen. *The Hollywood Professionals, Vol. 6: Frank Capra, Clarence Brown and George Cukor.* Cranberry, NJ: Tantivity Press, 1980.

"Exhibitors Protest at Flood of War Film, Ask Entertainment." *Motion Picture Herald* 8 May 1943: 12–14.

Fairbanks, Douglas, Jr. *The Salad Days.* New York: Doubleday, 1988.

Farago, Ladislas. *The Game of the Foxes: The Untold Story of German Espionage in the United States and Great Britain During World War II.* New York: David McKay Company, 1971.

Fest, Joachim. *The Face of the Third Reich*. New York: Pantheon, 1970.

_____. *Hitler*. New York: Harcourt Brace Jovanovich, 1974.

Fielding, Raymond. *The American Newsreel, 1911–1967*. Norman: University of Oklahoma Press, 1973.

_____. *The March of Time, 1935–1951*. New York: Oxford University Press, 1978.

Fitzgerald, Michael G. *Universal Pictures*. New Rochelle, NY: Arlington House, 1977.

Flynn, George Q. *The Draft, 1940–1973*. Lawrence: University Press of Kansas, 1993.

_____. *The Mess in Washington*. Westport, CT: Greenwood Press, 1979.

Ford, Daniel. *Flying Tigers*. Washington: Smithsonian Press, 1991.

"40% of Features in Work Have War as Theme." *Motion Picture Herald* 20 June 1942: 12.

Frakes, Margaret. "Why the Movie Investigation?" *The Christian Century*, (Sept. 24, 1941): 1172–74.

Fraser, David. *And We Shall Shock Them*. London: Hodder and Stoughton, 1983.

Friedlander, Saul. *Prelude to Downfall: Hitler and the United States, 1939–1941*. New York: Alfred A. Knopf, Inc., 1967.

Furhammer, Leif and Fulke Isakson. *Politics and Film*. New York: Praeger, 1971.

Fussell, Paul. *Wartime: Understanding and Behavior in the Second World War*. New York: Oxford University Press, 1989.

Fyne, Robert. "From Hollywood to Moscow." *Literature/Film Quarterly* 13/3 (1985): 194–199.

_____. *The Hollywood Propaganda of WWII*. Metuchen, NJ: Scarecrow Press, 1994.

Galloway, George B. *Postwar Planning in the United States*. New York: The Twentieth Century Fund, 1942.

Gannon, Michael. *Operation Drumbeat*. New York: Harper & Row, 1990.

Gellman, Irwin F. *Good Neighbor Diplomacy: United States Policies in Latin America, 1933–1945*. Baltimore: The Johns Hopkins University Press, 1979.

Gessner, Robert. "Need Bitter War Films." *Variety* 11 March 1942: 1, 16.

Glatzer, Richard and John Raeborn, eds. *Frank Capra: The Man and His Films*. Ann Arbor: The University of Michigan Press, 1975.

Goodman, Jack, ed. *While You Were Gone: A Report on Wartime Life in the United States*. New York: Simon and Schuster, 1946.

Graebner, William. *The Age of Doubt: American Thought and Culture in the 1940s*. Boston: G. K. Hall/Twayne, 1990.

Gregory, Ross. *America 1941: A Nation at the Crossroads*. New York: The Free Press, 1988.

Grunberger, Richard. *The Twelve Year Reich: A Social History of Nazi Germany, 1933–1945*. New York: Holt, Rinehart and Winston, 1971.

Guttmann, Allen. *The Wound in the Heart, America and the Spanish Civil War*. New York: Free Press of Glencoe, 1962.

Hargrove, Marion. *See Here, Private Hargrove*. New York: Henry Holt, 1942.

Harley, John Eugene. *World-Wide Influences of the Cinema: A Study of Official Censorship and the International Cultural Aspects of Motion Pictures*. Los Angeles: The University of Southern California Press, 1940.

Harries, Meirion and Susie. *Soldiers of the Sun: The Rise and Fall of the Imperial Japanese Army*. New York: Random House, 1991.

Hartmann, Susan M. *The Home Front and Beyond: American Women in the 1940s*. Boston: G. K. Hall, 1982.

Haugland, Vern. *The Eagle Squadron: Yanks in the RAF, 1940–1942*. London: David and Charles, 1979.

Heilbut, Anthony. *Exiled in Paradise: German Refugee Artists and Intellectuals in America, from the 1930's to the Present*. New York: The Viking Press, 1983.

Hersey, John. "Kamikaze." *Life* 30 July 1945: 68–75.

Higham, Charles. *Warner Brothers*. New York: Charles Scribner's Sons, 1975.

Hirschhorn, Clive. *The Hollywood Musical*. New York: Crown, 1981.

_____. *The Universal Story*. New York: Crown, 1983.

_____. *The Warner Brothers Story*. New York: Crown, 1979.

Hoffman, Peter. *The HIstory of the German Resistance 1933–45*. Boston: MIT Press, 1977.

Homz, Edward. *Foreign Labor in Nazi Germany*. Princeton: Princeton University Press, 1967.

Honey, Maureen. *Creating Rosie the Riveter: Class, Gender, and Propaganda During World War II*. Amherst: University of Massachusettes Press, 1984.

Hoopes, Roy. *Americans Remember the Home Front*. New York: Hawthorn, 1977.

Horak, Jan-Christopher. "The Palm Trees Were Gently Swaying: German Refugees from Hitler in Hollywood." *Image*, 25, Nos. 3–4 (Sept.-Dec. 1982): 29–37.

Howenstine, Jr., E. Jay. *The Economics of Demobilization*. Washington: Public Affairs Press, 1944.

Hoyt, Edwin P. *Hirohito: The Emperor and the Man*. New York: Praeger, 1992.

Humphreys, R. A. *Latin America and the Second World War*. 2 vols. London: Athlone, 1982.

Hurst, Richard Maurice. *Republic Studios: Between Poverty Row and the Majors*. Metuchen, NJ: The Scarecrow Press, 1979.

Hurstfield, Julian G. *America and the French Nation, 1939–1945*. Chapel Hill: The University of North Carolina Press, 1986.

Husted, H. H. *Thumb-Nail History of World War II*. Boston: Bruce Humphries, 1948.

Ienaga, Saburo. *The Pacific War, 1931–1945: A Critical Perspective on Japan's Role in World War II*. New York: Pantheon Books, 1978.

Iriye, Akira. *Across the Pacific: An Inner History of American-East Asian Relations*. New York: Harcourt, Brace and World, 1967.

_____. *Power and Culture: The Japanese-American War, 1941–1945*. Cambridge, MA: Harvard University Press, 1981.

Irwin, Will and Thomas M. Johnson. *What You Should Know About Spies and Saboteurs*. New York: Norton, 1943.

Isenberg, Michael T. *War on Film, The American Cinema and World War I, 1914–1941*. East Brunswick, NJ: Associated University Presses, 1981.

Jacobs, Helen Hall. *"By Your Leave, Sir": The Story of a WAVE*. New York: Dodd, 1943.

Jacobs, Lewis. *The Rise of the American Film*. Reprint edition 1940. New York: Teachers College Press, 1968.

_____. "World War II and the American Film." *Cinema Journal* 7/1 (Winter 1967-68): 1–21.

Jarvie, Ian. "The Burma Campaign on Film," *Historical Journal of Film, Radio, and Television* 8/1 (1988) 55–73.

Jewell, Richard B., with Vernon Harbin. *The RKO Story*. Westport, CT: Arlington House Publishers, 1982.

Joffé, Constantin. *We Were Free*. New York: Smith & Durrell, 1943.

Johnston, Winifred. *Memo on the Movies: War Propaganda, 1914–1939*. Norman, OK: Cooperative Books, 1939 (pamphlet).

Jones, Alfred Haworth. *Roosevelt's Image Brokers: Poets, Playwrights, and the Use of the Lincoln Symbol*. Port Washington, NY: Kennikat Press, 1974.

Jones, Dorothy B. "The Hollywood War Film: 1942–1944." *Hollywood Quarterly* 1/1 (October 1945): 1–19.

Jones, Ken D. and Arthur F. McClure. *Hollywood at War The American Motion Picture and WWII.* Cranbury, NJ: A. S. Barnes and Co., 1973.

Jowett, Garth. *Film: The Democratic Art.* Boston: Little Brown, 1976.

_____, and James M. Linton, *Movies as Mass Communication.* Newbury Park, CA: Sage, 1989.

Kagan, Norman. *The War Film.* New York: Pyramid Publishers, 1974.

Kane, Kathryn. *Visions of War: Hollywood Combat Films of World War II.* Ann Arbor, MI: UMI Research Press, 1982.

Kann, Red. "On the March." *Motion Picture Herald* 16 October 1943: 18.

Kaplan, E. Ann. *Fritz Lang: A Guide to References and Resources.* Boston: G. K. Hall and Company, 1981.

Karpf, Stephen Louis. *The Gangster Film, 1930–1940.* New York: Arno Press, 1974.

Kennett, Lee. *For the Duration: The United States Goes to War, Pearl Harbor—1942.* New York: Charles Scribners Sons, 1985.

_____. *G. I.: The American Soldier in World War II.* New York: Scribners, 1987.

Ketchum, Richard M. *The Borrowed Years, 1938–1941: America on the Way to War.* New York: Random House, 1989.

Kirby, Edward M. and Jack W. Harris, *Star-Spangled Radio.* Chicago: Ziff-Davis, 1948.

Klingaman, William K. *1941: Our Lives in a World on the Edge.* New York: Harper & Row, 1988.

Koppes, Clayton R. and Gregory D. Black. *Hollywood Goes to War: How Politics, Profits and Propaganda Shaped World War II Movies.* New York: Free Press/Macmillan, 1987.

_____. "What to Show the World: The Office of War Information and Hollywood, 1942–1945." *Journal of American History* 64/1 (1977): 87–105.

Kracauer, Siegfried. *From Caligari to Hitler.* Princeton: Princeton University Press, 1947.

_____. "National Types as Hollywood Presents Them." *Mass Culture, The Popular Arts in America.* Edited by Bernard Rosenberg and David M. White. Glencoe, IL: Free Press, 1957: 257–77.

Lamster, Frederick. *Souls Made Great Through Love and Adversity: The Film Work of Frank Borzage.* Metuchen, NJ: The Scarecrow Press, 1981.

Langer, William L. and S. Everett Gleason. *The Challenge to Isolationism, 1937–1940.* New York: Harper and Brothers, 1952.

_____. *The Undeclared War, 1940–1941,* New York: Harper and Brothers, 1953.

Langman, Larry and Ed Borg. *Encyclopedia of American War Films.* Garland, 1989.

Lavine, Harold. *Fifth Column in America.* New York: Doubleday, 1940.

_____, and James Wechsler. *War, Propaganda and the United States.* Reprint edition. New York: Garland Publishing, 1972 (originally published in 1940).

Lawson, John Howard. *Film in the Battle of Ideas.* New York: Masses and Mainstream, 1953.

Leigh, Michael. *Mobilizing Consent: Public Opinion and American Foreign Policy, 1937–1947.* Westport, CT: Greenwood Press, 1976.

Lensen, George A. *The Strange Neutrality: Soviet-Japanese Relations During the Second World War, 1941–1945.* Tallahassee, FL: The Diplomatic Press, 1972.

Levering, Ralph B. *American Opinion and the Russian Alliance, 1939–1945.* Chapel Hill: University of North Carolina Press, 1976.

Levine, Lawrence W. "The Folklore of Industrial Society," *American Historical Review* 97 (December 1992): 1369–1399.

Lingeman, Richard R. *Don't You Know There's a War On? The American Home Front, 1941–1945.* New York: G. P. Putnam's Sons, 1970.

Littlejohn, David. *The Patriotic Traitors.* New York: Doubleday, 1972.

Longmate, Norman. *How We Lived Then: A History of Everyday Life During the Second World War.* London: Arrow, 1973.

McBride, Joseph. *Frank Capra: The Catastrophe of Success.* New York: Simon and Schuster, 1992.

McCarthy, Todd and Charles Flynn, ed. *Kings of the B's: Working Within the Hollywood System.* New York: E. P. Dutton and Co., 1975.

McClelland, Doug. *The Golden Age of B Movies.* New York: Bonanza Books, 1978.

McClure, Arthur F. "Hollywood at War: The American Motion Picture and World War II, 1939–1945." *Journal of Popular Film,* Vol. I, No. 2 (Spring 1972): 123–135.

MacDonnell, Francis. *Insidious Foes: The Axis Fifth Column and the American Home Front.* New York: Oxford University Press, 1995.

McGee, Mark Thomas and R. J. Robertson. *The J. D. Films.* Jefferson, NC: McFarland, 1982.

Maddox, Thomas R. *Years of Estrangement: American Relations with the Soviet Union, 1933–1941.* Tallahassee: University Presses of Florida, 1980.

Maland, Charles J. *Chaplin and American Culture: The Evolution of a Star Image.* Princeton, NJ: Princeton University Press, 1989.

Maltin, Leonard. *The Great Movie Shorts,* New York: Crown, 1972.

Manning, Thomas G. *The Office of Price Administration: A World War II Agency of Control.* New York: Henry Holt, 1960.

Manvell, Roger. *Films and the Second World War.* New York: Dell Publishing Co., 1974.

Marling, Karal Ann and John W. Hall. *Iwo Jima: Monuments, Memories and the American Hero.* Cambridge: Harvard University Press, 1991.

Martin, James J. *American Liberalism and World Politics, 1931–1941: Liberalism's Press and Spokesmen on the Road Back to War Between Mukden and Pearl Harbor* (2 vols.). New York: The Devin-Adair Company, 1964.

Mast, Gerald. *The Comic Mind: Comedy and the Movies.* New York: The Bobbs-Merrill Co., 1973.

Mathews, Basil. *United We Stand.* Boston: Little, Brown & Co., 1944.

Mathis, Jack. *Valley of the Cliffhangers.* Northbrook, IL: Jack Mathis Advertising, 1975.

Matthews, Blayney F. *The Specter of Sabotage.* Los Angeles: Lymanhouse, 1941.

Maudlin, Bill. *Back Home.* New York: William Sloane, 1947.

_____. *Up Front.* New York: Holt, 1945.

Maynard, Richard A. *Propaganda on Film, A Nation at War.* Rochelle Park, NJ: Hayden Buck Company, 1975.

Meerse, David E. "To Reassure a Nation: Hollywood Presents World War II." *Film and History* 6/4 (Dec. 1976): 79–91.

Merrill, Francis E. *Social Problems on the Home Front: A Study of Wartime Influences.* New York: Harper and Brothers, 1948.

Michel, Henri. *The Shadow War: European Resistance 1939–45.* New York: Harper, 1972.

"The Military Touch." *Variety* 14 January 1942: 1.

Miller, Don. *"B" Movies: An Informal Survey of the American Low-Budget Film, 1933–1945.* New York: Curtis Books, 1973.

_____. *Hollywood Corral.* New York: Popular Library, 1976.

Miller, Randall M., ed. *Ethnic Images in American Film and Television.* Philadelphia: The Balch Institute, 1978.

Milward, Alan S. *War, Economy and Society, 1939–1945.* Los Angeles: University of California Press, 1977.

Missiaen, Jean-Claude and Jacques Siclier. *Jean Gabin*. Paris: Henri Veyrier, 1983.

Morrison, Denis. "Russian Characters in Yank Films Now Are Dignified and Gallant." *Variety*.

Mosse, George L. *Nazi Culture: Intellectual, Cultural and Social Life in the Third Reich*. New York: Grosset & Dunlap, 1966.

Nash, Gerald D. *The American West Transformed: The Impact of the Second World War*. Bloomington: Indiana University Press, 1985.

Nash, Jay Robert, ed. *The Motion Picture Guide*. Chicago: Cinebooks, 1985.

Nevins, Francis M. *The Films of Hopalong Cassidy*. Waynesville, NC: World of Yesterday, 1988.

The New York Times Encyclopedia of Film. New York: New York Times Books, 1983.

New York Times Film Reviews, 1913–1968. Vols. 2 and 3. New York: The New York Times and Arno Press, 1970.

Noble, Peter. *The Negro in Films*. Port Washington, NY: Kennikat Press, 1969.

O'Connor, John E. and Martin A. Jackson, eds. *American History/American Film: Interpreting the Hollywood Image*. New York: Frederick Ungar Publishing Co., 1979.

Oehling, Richard A. "Germans in Hollywood Films, Part II: The Changing Image, The Early Years, 1939–1942." *Film and History* 4/2 (May 1974): 8–10.

Okuda, Ted. *The Columbia Comedy Shorts: Two-Reel Hollywood Film Comedies, 1933–1958*. Jefferson, NC: McFarland, 1985.

_____. *Grand National, Producers Releasing Corporation, and Screen Guild Lippert: Complete Filmographies and Studio Histories*. Jefferson, NC: McFarland, 1989.

_____. *The Monogram Checklist: The Films of Monogram Pictures Corporation, 1931–1952*. Jefferson, NC: McFarland, 1987.

O'Neill, William. *A Democracy at War: America's Fight at Home and Abroad in WWII*. New York: Free Press, 1993.

Orriss, Bruce W. *When Hollywood Ruled the Skies*. Hawthorne, CA: Aero Associates, 1984.

Paret, Peter, Beth Irwin Lewis, and Paul Paret. *Persuasive Images*. Princeton: Princeton University Press, 1992.

Parish, James Robert and Don E. Stanke. *The Forties Gals*. Westport, CT: Arlington House, 1980.

_____, and Michael R. Pitts. *The Great Spy Pictures*. Metuchen, NJ: The Scarecrow Press, 1974.

_____, and Michael R. Pitts. *The Great Spy Pictures, II*. Metuchen, NJ: The Scarecrow Press, 1986.

Pells, Richard H. *Radical Visions and American Dreams*. New York: Harper and Row, 1973.

Pendo, Stephen. *Aviation in the Cinema*. Metuchen, NJ: The Scarecrow Press, 1985.

Perrett, Geoffrey. *Days of Sadness, Years of Triumph: The American People 1939–1945*. New York: Coward, McCann and Geoghegan, 1973.

_____. *There's a War to Be Won: The United States Army in World War II*. New York: Random House, 1991.

Piccigallo, Philip R. *The Japanese on Trial: Allied War Crimes Operations in the East, 1945–1951*. Austin: University of Texas Press, 1979.

Pitts, Michael R. *Famous Movie Detectives*. Metuchen, NJ: The Scarecrow Press, 1979.

_____. *Hollywood and American History: A Filmography of Over 250 Motion Pictures Depicting U.S. History*. Jefferson, NC: McFarland, 1984.

Polan, Dana. *Power and Paranoia: History, Narrative, and the American Cinema, 1940–1950*. New York: Columbia University Press, 1986.

Polenberg, Richard, ed. *America at War: The Home Front, 1941–1945.*

Englewood Cliffs, NJ: Prentice-Hall, 1968.

Poliakov, Alexander. *Russians Don't Surrender*. New York: Dutton, 1942.

Pronay, Nicholas and D. W. Spring, eds. *Propaganda, Politics and Film, 1918–45*. London: The Macmillan Press, 1982.

Putney, Martha S. *When the Nation Was In Need: Blacks in the Women's Army Corps During World War II*. Metuchen, NJ: Scarecrow Press, 1992.

Quick, Paddy. "Rosie the Riveter: Myths and Realities." *Radical America* 9, No. 4-5 (1975) 115–132.

Ramsaye, Terry, ed. *International Motion Picture Almanac: 1939–1940*, New York: Quigley Publishers, 1941.

Ready, J. Lee. *The Forgotten Allies*. 2 vols. Jefferson, NC: McFarland, 1985.

Rempel, Gerhard. *Hitler's Children: The Hitler Youth and the SS>* Chapel Hill: University of North Carolina Press, 1989.

Renov, Michael. *Hollywood's Wartime Woman: Representation and Ideology*. Ann Arbor, MI: UMI Research Press, 1988.

Reynolds, David. *The Creation of the Anglo-American Alliance, 1937–41: A Study in Competitive Co-operation*. Chapel Hill: The University of North Carolina Press, 1982.

Rhode, Eric. *A History of Cinema*. New York: Hill and Wang, 1976.

Richards, Jeffrey. *Visions of Yesterday*. London: Routledge and Kegan Paul, 1973.

Riesenberg, Felix. *Sea War: The Story of the U.S. Mechant Marine in World War II*. Westport, CT: Greenwood Press, 1974.

Roberts, John Storm. *The Latin Tinge*. New York: Oxford University Press, 1979.

Roberts, Walter R. *Tito, Mihailovic and the Allies, 1941–1945*. New Brunswick, NJ: Rutgers University Press, 1973.

Roeder, George H., Jr. *The Censored War*. New Haven: Yale University Press, 1993.

Roffman, Peter and Jim Purdy. *The Hollywood Social Problem Film: Madness, Despair and Politics from the Depression to the Fifties*. Bloomington: Indiana University Press, 1981.

Rogers, Donald. *Since You Went Away: From Rosie the Riveter to Bond Drives, World War II at Home*. New Rochelle, NY: Arlington House, 1973.

Rosten, Leo C. *Hollywood: The Movie Colony, The Movie Makers*. New York: Harcourt, Brace and Company, 1941.

Rout, Leslie B., Jr. and John F. Bratzel. *The Shadow War*. Frederick, MD: University Publications of America, 1986.

Russell, Judith and Renee Fantin. *Studies in Food Rationing*. Washington, DC: Office of Price Administration, 1947.

Sampson, Henry T. *Blacks in Black and White*. Metuchen, NJ: Scarecrow Press, 1977.

Sandeen, Eric J. "Anti-Nazi Sentiment in Film: Confessions of a Nazi Spy and the German-American Bond." *American Studies* Vol. 20, No. 2 (1979): 69–81.

Satterfield, Archie. *The Home Front: An Oral History of the War Years in America, 1941–1945*. New York: Playboy Press, 1981.

Schoenbrun, David. *Soldiers of the Night: The Story of the French Resistance*. New York: Dutton, 1980.

Schrecker, Ellen W. *No Ivory Tower: McCarthyism and the Universities*. New York: Oxford University Press, 1986.

Semelin, Jacques. *Unarmed Against Hitler: Civilian Resistance in Europe, 1939–1943*. Westport, CT: Praeger, 1993.

Sennett, Ted. *Hollywood Musicals*. New York: Abradale Press–H. N. Abrams, 1985.

Shain, Russell E. *An Analysis of Motion Pictures About War Released by the American Film Industry, 1930–1970*. New York: Arno Press, 1976.

Shindler, Colin. *Hollywood Goes to War: Films and American Society, 1939–1952*. London: Routledge and Kegan Paul, 1979.

Short, K. R. M., ed. *Feature Films as History.* Knoxville, TN: University of Tennessee Press, 1981.

Shull, Michael S. and David E. Wilt. *Doing Their Bit: Wartime American Animated Short Films, 1939–1945.* Jefferson, NC: McFarland, 1987.

Siegel, Joel. *Val Lewton: The Reality of Terror.* New York: Viking, 1973.

Simone, Sam P. *Hitchcock As Activist: Politics and the War Films.* Ann Arbor, MI: UMI Research Press, 1986.

Sklar, Robert. *Movie-Made America: A Cultural History of American Movies,* New York: Random House, 1975.

_____, and Charles Musser. *Resisting Images: Essays on Cinema and History.* Philadelphia: Temple University Press, 1990.

Sligh, Robert Bruce. *The National Guard and National Defense: the Mobilization of the Guard in World War II.* New York: Praeger, 1992.

Small, Melvin. "Buffoons and Brave Hearts: Hollywood Portrays the Russians, 1939–1944." *California Historical Quarterly* 52/4 (Winter 1973): 326–337.

_____. "How We Learned to Love the Russians: American Media and the Soviet Union During World War II." *The Historian* 36/3 (May 1974): 455–478.

Smith, Geoffrey S. "Isolationism, the Devil, and the Advent of the Second World War: Variations on a Theme." *International History Review,* Vol. 4 (Feb. 1982): 55–89.

_____. *To Save a Nation: American Countersubversives, the New Deal, and the Coming of World War II.* New York: Basic Books, 1973.

Smith, Paul, ed. *The Historian and Film.* New York: Cambridge University Press, 1976.

Soderbergh, Peter A. "The Grand Illusion: Hollywood and World War II, 1930–1945." *The University of Dayton Review* 5/3 (Winter 1968-1969): 13–21.

"Soldiers Do Not Like War Films, Says Hubbell." *Motion Picture Herald* 28 August 1943: 21.

Somers, Herman Miles. *Presidential Agency OWMR: The Office of War Mobilization and Reconversion.* Cambridge: Harvard University Press, 1950.

Spurr, Russell. *A Glorious Way to Die.* New York: Newmarket Press, 1981.

Stanley, Robert H. *The Celluloid Empire: A History of the American Movie Industry.* New York: Hastings House, 1978.

Steele, Richard W. "American Popular Opinion and the War Against Germany: The Issue of Negotiated Peace, 1942." *Journal of American History* 45 (Dec. 1978) 704-23.

_____. *Propaganda in an Open Society: The Roosevelt Administration and the Media, 1933–1941.* Westport, CT: Greenwood Press, 1985.

Steinberg, Cobbett. *Reel Facts.* New York: Vintage Books, 1982.

Stenehjem, Michele Flynn. *An American First: John T. Flynn and the America First Committee.* New Rochelle, NY: Arlington House Publishers, 1976.

Stoler, Mark A. "The Second Front and American Fear of Soviet Expansionism 1941–1943." *Military Affairs* 39/3 (1975): 136–141.

"Stop Making War Films, Showmen Tell Studios." *Motion Picture Herald* 25 September 1943: 23–24.

"Studios Avoid 'Peace Pix'." *Variety* 27 September 1944: 3.

Stveich, Birgit. "The Propaganda Business: The Roosevelt Administration and Hollywood." *Humboldt Journal of Social Relations* 16/1 (1990): 43–65.

Suid, Lawrence H. *Guts & Glory: Great American War Movies.* Reading, MA: Addison-Wesley, 1978.

Takaki, Ronald. *Strangers from a Different Shore: A History of Asian Americans.* Boston: Little, Brown, 1989.

Tannenbaum, Edward R. *The Fascist Experience: Italian Society and Culture, 1922–1945.* New York: Basic Books, 1972.

Taylor, John Russell. *Strangers in Paradise: The Hollywood Emigres, 1933–1950.* New York: Holt, Rinehart and Winston, 1983.

Taylor, Marjorie, comp. *The Language of World War II.* New York: H. W. Wilson, 1968.

Terkel, Studs. *"The Good War": An Oral History of World War Two.* New York: Pantheon, 1984.

Thomas, Tony and Aubrey Solomon. *The Films of 20th Century Fox.* Secaucus, NJ: The Citadel Press, 1979.

Thompson, Frank T. *William A. Wellman.* Metuchen, NJ: The Scarecrow Press, 1983.

Thorne, Christopher. *Allies of a Kind.* New York: Oxford University Press, 1978.

Thorpe, Margaret F. *America at the Movies.* New Haven, CT: Yale University Press, 1939.

Toscano, Mario. *The Origins of the Pact of Steel.* Baltimore: Johns Hopkins University Press, 1967.

Treadwell, Mattie E. *The Women's Army Corps.* United States Army in World War II. Special Studies. Washington, DC: Office of the Chief of Military History, Dept. of the Army, 1954.

Trommler, Frank and Joseph McTeigh, eds. *America and the Germans: An Assessment of a Three-Hundred Year History,* Vol. II: *The Relationship in the Twentieth Century.* Philadelphia: University of Pennsylvania Press, 1985.

Tuska, Jon. *The Detective in Hollywood.* New York: Doubleday and Co., 1978.

Tuttle, William M. *Daddy's Gone to War: The Second World War in the Lives of America's Children.* New York: Oxford University Press, 1993.

Twichell, Heath. *Northwest Epic: The Building of the Alaska Highway.* New York: St. Martin's Press, 1992.

Ugland, Richard M. "Education for Victory: The High School Victory Corps and Curriculum Adaptation During World War II." *History of Education Quarterly* (Winter 1979) 435–52.

Utley, Jonathan G. *Going to War with Japan, 1937–1941.* Knoxville: The University of Tennessee Press, 1985.

Vaeth, J. Gordon. *U.S. Navy Airships in the Battle of the Atlantic.* Annapolis, MD: Naval Institute Press, 1992.

Valenti, Peter L. "The Cultural Hero in the World War II Fantasy Film." *Journal of Popular Film & Television* 7/3 (1979): 310–21.

Valleau, Marjorie A. *The Spanish Civil War in American and European Films.* Ann Arbor, MI: UMI Research Press, 1982.

Vincent, William. "Rita Hayworth at Columbia, 1941–1945." *Columbia Pictures: Portrait of a Studio.* ed. Bernard F. Dick. Lexington: University Press of Kentucky, 1992.

Viorst, Milton. *Hostile Allies.* New York: Macmillan, 1965.

Walsh, Andrea S. *Women's Film and the Female Experience, 1940–1950.* New York: Praeger, 1984.

Walter, Willard. *War and the Family.* New York: Dryden Press, 1970.

Wanger, Walter. "120,000 American Ambassadors." *Foreign Affairs* Vol. 18, No. 1 (Oct. 1939): 45–59.

"War Themes Drop to 12% of Product for 1944–45." *Motion Picture Herald* 29 July 1944: 13.

Warner, Jack. *My First Hundred Years in Hollywood.* New York: Dover Publications, 1977.

Weatherford, Doris. *American Womanhood and World War II.* New York: Facts on File, 1990.

Weaver, William R. "Studios Cut War Themes to 25% of Product." *Motion Picture Herald* 6 February 1943: 15.

Weiss, Ken and Ed Goodgold. *To Be Continued.* New York: Crown, 1972.

Wells, Linton. *Salute to Valor.* Freeport, NY: Books for Libraries Press, 1942.

Werth, Alexander. *Russia at War 1941–45.* New York: Avon, 1964.

Westbrook, Brett. "Fighting for What's Good: Strategies of Propaganda in Lillian Hellman's 'Negro Picture' and *North Star.*" *Film History* 4/2 (1990): 165–78.

Westbrook, Robert. "I Want a Girl, Just Like the Girl That Married Harry James: American Women and the Problem of Political Obligation in World War II." *American Quarterly*, Vol. 42, No. 4 (December 1990), pp. 587–614.

White, David and Richard Averson. *The Celluloid Weapon: Social Comment in the American Film.* Boston: Beacon Press, 1972.

Wilcox, Walter W. *The Farmer in the Second World War.* Ames: The Iowa State press, 1947.

Wilkinson, Rupert. *American Tough: The Tough Guy Tradition and the American Character.* Westport, CT: Greenwood Press, 1984.

Willoughby, Malcolm F. *The U. S. Coast Guard in World War II.* Annapolis: Naval Institute Press, 1989.

Winkler, Allan M. *The Politics of Propaganda: The Office of War Information, 1942–1945.* New Haven, CT: Yale University Press, 1978.

Woll, Allen L. *The Hollywood Musical Goes to War.* Chicago: Nelson-Hall, 1983.

_____. *The Latin Image in American Film.* Los Angeles: University of California Press, 1977.

Wong, Eugene Franklin. *On Visual Media Racism: Asians in the American Motion Picture.* New York: Arno Press, 1978.

Wood, Michael. *America in the Movies or Santa Maria, It Had Slipped My Mind.* New York: Basic Books, 1975.

Wright, Gordon. *The Ordeal of Total War, 1939–1945.* New York: Harper & Row, 1968.

Wyman, David S. *The Abandonment of the Jews: America and the Holocaust, 1941–1945.* New York: Pantheon Books, 1984.

_____. *Paper Walls: America and the Refugee Crisis, 1938–1941.* Amherst: University of Massachusetts Press, 1968.

Wynn, Neil A. *The Afro-American and the Second World War.* London: Paul Elek, 1976.

Zeman, Zbynek. *Selling the War: Art and Propaganda in World War II.* New York: Exeter Books, 1982.

Unpublished Manuscripts

Arthur, Thomas Hahn. "The Political Career of an Actor: Melvyn Douglas and the New Deal." Ph.D. dissertation, Indiana University, 1973.

Colgan, Christine A. "Warner Brothers' Crusade Against the Third Reich: A Study in Anti-Nazi Activism and Film Production, 1933 to 1941." Ph.D. dissertation, University of Southern California, 1985.

Donald, Ralph R. "Hollywood and World War II: Enlisting Feature Films as Propaganda." Unpublished Ph.D. dissertation, 1987, University of Massachusetts.

Fyne, Robert J. "Hollywood Fights a War: A Comparison of the Images of the Fighting Man of World War II Combatants in Selected Hollywood Films Produced between September 1, !939 and December 7, 1941 with those Produced between December 8, 1941 and August 15, 1945." Ph.D. dissertation, New York University, 1976.

MacDonnell, Francis Michael. "Insidious Foes: The Axis Fifth Column and the American Home Front, 1938–1942." Ph.D. dissertation, Harvard University, 1991.

Muresianu, John M. "War of Ideas: American Intellectuals and the World Crisis, 1938–1943." Ph.D. dissertation, Harvard University, 1982.

Schwar, Jane H.D. "Interventionist Propaganda and Pressure Groups in the United States, 1937–1941." Ph.D. dissertation, Ohio State University, 1973.

Index to Page Numbers in the Text

Index to Entry Numbers
in the Filmographies

*References in **bold** are to the primary entry for that film.*